CASES AND MATERIALS
ON TORTS

ASPEN PUBLISHERS

CASES AND MATERIALS ON TORTS

Ninth Edition

Richard A. Epstein

*James Parker Hall
Distinguished Service Professor of Law
The University of Chicago*

*Peter and Kirsten Bedford Senior Fellow
The Hoover Institution
Stanford University*

Wolters Kluwer
Law & Business

AUSTIN   BOSTON   CHICAGO   NEW YORK   THE NETHERLANDS

ISBN 978-0-7355-6923-2

Library of Congress Cataloging-in-Publication Data

Epstein, Richard Allen, 1943-
  Cases and materials on torts / Richard A. Epstein. — 9th ed.
    p. cm.
  Includes index.
  ISBN 978-0-7355-6923-2
  1. Torts — United States — Cases. 2. Liability (Law) — United States — Cases. 3. Damages — United States — Cases. I. Title.

  KF1249.E67 2008
  346.7303 — dc22

                                              2008000950

About Wolters Kluwer Law & Business

Wolters Kluwer Law & Business is a leading provider of research information and workflow solutions in key specialty areas. The strengths of the individual brands of Aspen Publishers, CCH, Kluwer Law International and Loislaw are aligned within Wolters Kluwer Law & Business to provide comprehensive, in-depth solutions and expert-authored content for the legal, professional and education markets.

CCH was founded in 1913 and has served more than four generations of business professionals and their clients. The CCH products in the Wolters Kluwer Law & Business group are highly regarded electronic and print resources for legal, securities, antitrust and trade regulation, government contracting, banking, pension, payroll, employment and labor, and healthcare reimbursement and compliance professionals.

Aspen Publishers is a leading information provider for attorneys, business professionals and law students. Written by preeminent authorities, Aspen products offer analytical and practical information in a range of specialty practice areas from securities law and intellectual property to mergers and acquisitions and pension/benefits. Aspen's trusted legal education resources provide professors and students with high-quality, up-to-date and effective resources for successful instruction and study in all areas of the law.

Kluwer Law International supplies the global business community with comprehensive English-language international legal information. Legal practitioners, corporate counsel and business executives around the world rely on the Kluwer Law International journals, loose-leafs, books and electronic products for authoritative information in many areas of international legal practice.

Loislaw is a premier provider of digitized legal content to small law firm practitioners of various specializations. Loislaw provides attorneys with the ability to quickly and efficiently find the necessary legal information they need, when and where they need it, by facilitating access to primary law as well as state-specific law, records, forms and treatises.

Wolters Kluwer Law & Business, a unit of Wolters Kluwer, is headquartered in New York and Riverwoods, Illinois. Wolters Kluwer is a leading multinational publisher and information services company.

To the Memory of Bernard D. Meltzer (1914-2007)
Colleague, Wit, Gentleman, and Scholar

SUMMARY OF CONTENTS

PART ONE.   PHYSICAL AND MENTAL HARMS

PART TWO.   TORTS AGAINST NONPHYSICAL
INTERESTS

TABLE OF CONTENTS

PREFACE

This is now the ninth edition of this casebook, and the seventh one that I have prepared over the past 34 years. The origins of the casebook go back to the 1950s, when Charles O. Gregory and Harry Kalven, Jr., both exceptional and imaginative scholars, prepared the first edition, which was published in 1959. Their second edition followed some ten years later, and was in fact the book from which I first taught torts at the University of Southern California in 1969. In 1972 I joined the faculty of the University of Chicago Law School. In January 1974, with Gregory in retirement, my late colleague, Professor Kalven, asked me to collaborate with him on the third edition of Gregory and Kalven, Cases and Materials on Torts. Kalven's tragic death in October 1974 cut short our brief collaboration just as we were beginning our revision. Thereafter Professor Charles O. Gregory was kind enough to reenter the lists and to read and comment on the drafts I prepared of the third edition, which appeared in 1977. The work on the fourth edition of Epstein, Gregory and Kalven, which appeared in 1984, I did alone. Gregory died in April 1987, after a rich and full life. The fifth (1990), sixth (1995), seventh (2000), eighth (2004), and now ninth edition bear my name alone: the change of the guard between generations has now long been completed. Even so, much of case selection and organization of this book continue to owe much to Gregory and Kalven, who brought a pioneering spirit and rich imagination to the study of torts. I shall always be in their debt.

The ninth edition makes no major structural changes, but a few minor ones. Extensive treatments of tort liability in cyberspace now appear throughout the book, covering such topics as trespass to chattels, conversion and defamation. All of the materials on conversion have been moved from chapter 8, where they were located in the eighth edition, to chapter one, where they are conventionally grouped. Extensive references have been made to the key provisions of the Third Restatement of Torts: Liability for Physical Harm, which are now working their way to final approval at the American Law Institute. New material has been added on vaccine compensation programs, which have loomed large in recent years. At the same time the other major reforms of the eighth edition have been preserved, as I have kept the revisions that were made to the historical materials on the evolution of tort law, the expanded treatment of public nuisance law, the revisions in the modern defect cases in product liability law, and the heavier emphasis on American cases in areas of defamation and privacy.

Throughout, however, my intention has been to update the materials while seeking to preserve continuity with the earlier editions. In so doing, I have sought to keep one of the distinctive features of this casebook, which is to stress the alternative visions of tort law as they developed in the nineteenth (and now complete) twentieth centuries. Toward that end, I have retained those great older cases, both English and American, that have proved themselves time and again in the classroom, and which continue to exert great influence on the modern law. But by the same token, working through these revisions has made it clear to me that today neither the law of torts, nor this casebook, are shaped very heavily by the great transformation in tort law that took place between 1968 and 1980. Although those developments continue to remain important, they have in some instances been rejected. It is no longer likely that strict liability rules will exert greater sway in medical malpractice cases, nor that market share liability will expand beyond the original DES cases. At the same time, new and important developments on the liability of HMOs for refusing to authorize treatment, the application of the Supreme Court law on the use of expert witnesses in tort cases, and the potential exposure of tobacco companies to suit by health care organizations and unions have come on the scene in recent years. I have sought to keep pace with these new developments both through common law and, increasingly, through legislation.

Five Previous editions of this book were dedicated to the memory of Charles Gregory and Harry Kalven. Time has moved on. In 2004, I dedicated the eighth edition of the book to the memory of my contemporary, the late Gary Schwartz, who died in 2001, but who remains one of the most insightful, learned and fair-minded tort professors of any generation. For many years his kindness, generosity and insight helped improve the earlier editions of the case book. Time alas continues to move on. This past year my extraordinary colleague, Bernard D. Meltzer, himself a casebook author of great distinction, passed away at age 92. I dedicate the ninth edition of this book to him for all that he did to hone my own legal skills and to make the University of Chicago Law School the intense, vibrant and congenial place that I have called home for the past 36 years.

Time has also marched on in yet another sense. The ninth edition is the last that I shall do myself. I am delighted to announce that Professor Catherine M. Sharkey of New York University School of Law has agreed to join forces with me in a collaboration that will begin with the tenth edition.

Richard A. Epstein

Chicago
February 2008

ACKNOWLEDGMENTS

In preparing the ninth edition of this casebook I have been fortunate enough to draw on the comments of many teachers and students who have used the book. In preparing this edition, I have benefited from extensive comments on the earlier chapters by Stanton Krauss. In addition, I have received additional assistance and suggestions on various points of this volume from Jennifer Arlen, Michael Corrado, Thomas Miles, Paul Schwartz and Catherine Sharkey. This edition of the casebook also continues to benefit from comments that many people have made on previous editions, including Kenneth Abraham, Jennifer Arlen, Vincent Blasi, William Cohen, Michael Corrado, Richard Craswell, Theodore Eisenberg, Robert Ellickson, Stephen Gillers, James Henderson, Gail Heriot, Morton Horwitz, Jason Johnston, Spencer Kimball, Alvin Klevorick, Stanton Kraus, William Landes, Fred McChesney, Mark Miller, Cornelius Peck, Malla Pollock, Richard Posner, Glen Robinson, Howard Sacks, Gary Schwartz, Perry Sentell, Ken Simons, Geoffrey Stone, Alan Sykes, Aaron Twerski, Ernest Weinrib, and Jerry Wiley. I should also like to thank in addition all the unnamed casebook users who have filled in their forms to explain what they did and did not like about earlier editions of the book.

My largest debt, however, goes to the team of diligent research assistants who helped in the preption of this book. Chad Clamage, Uzair Kahani, Kayvan Noroozi, and Ramtin Teheri, did an enormous amount of work in preparing this edition. They were ably assisted by Corina Wilder Davis, Brad Grossman, Dan Fine, and Paul Laskow. Once again my secretary Katheryn Kepchar kept the paper flowing smoothly. I should also like to thank Carol McGeehan, Eric Holt, and Christine Hannan for seeing this project through at Aspen, and Patty Bergin for her diligent copyediting.

I should also like to thank the authors and copyright holders of the following works for permitting their inclusion in this book:

Abraham, Individual Action and Collective Responsibility: The Dilemma of Mass Tort Reform, 73 Va. L. Rev. 845, 860, 867-868 (1987). Reprinted with permission.

Abraham and Jeffries, Punitive Damages and the Rule of Law: The Role of Defendant's Wealth, 18 J. Legal Stud. 415, 417, 418 (1989). Reprinted with permission.

American Bar Association, Special Committee on Automobile Insurance Legislation, Automobile No-Fault Insurance (1978). Reprinted with permission.

American Law Institute, Restatement (Second) of the Law of Torts §§18, 46, 46(2), 315, 323, 324, 324A, 332, 339, 402A, 431, 478, 480, 494. Copyright © 1965 by the American Law Institute. Reprinted with permission of the American Law Institute.

American Law Institute, Restatement (Second) of the Law of Torts §§504, 519, 520, 520A, 522, 523, 524, 524A, 525, 538, 549, 559, 560(3), 575C, 577, 577A, 652B-E. Copyright © 1977 by the American Law Institute. Reprinted with permission of the American Law Institute.

American Law Institute, Restatement (Second) of the Law of Torts §826. Copyright © 1979 by the American Law Institute. Reprinted with permission of the American Law Institute.

Arnold, Accident, Mistake and Rules of Liability in the Fourteenth Century Law of Torts, 128 U. Pa. L. Rev. 361 (1979). Reprinted with permission.

Bender, A Lawyer's Primer on Feminist Theory and Tort, 38 J. Legal Education 34-35 (1988).

Bovbjerg, Sloan and Blumstein, Valuing Life and Limb in Tort: Scheduling "Pain and Suffering," 83 Nw. U.L. Rev. 908, 923-924 (1989).

Calabresi and Melamed, Property Rules, Liability Rules and Inalienability: One View of the Cathedral, 85 Harv. L. Rev. 1089 (1972). Copyright © 1972 by the Harvard Law Review Association. Reprinted with permission.

Epstein, Automobile No-Fault Plans: A Second Look at First Principles, 13 Creighton L. Rev. 769 (1980). Reprinted with permission.

Fletcher, Fairness and Utility in Tort Theory, 85 Harv. L. Rev. 537 (1972). Copyright © 1972 by the Harvard Law Review Association. Reprinted with permission.

Jaffe, Damages for Personal Injury: The Impact of Insurance, 18 Law & Contemp. Probs. 219 (1953). Reprinted with permission from a symposium on the Federal Employers' Liability Act appearing in Law and Contemporary Problems, Vol. 18, No. 2, published by the Duke University School of Law. Copyright © 1953 by Duke University.

James, The Qualities of the Reasonable Man in Negligence Cases, 16 Mo. L. Rev. 1 (1951). Copyright © 1951 by the Curators of the University of Missouri. Reprinted with permission.

Kronman, Mistake, Disclosure, Information and the Law of Contracts, 7 J. Legal Stud. 1 (1978). Copyright © 1978 by the University of Chicago Press. Reprinted with permission.

Posner, Economic Analysis of Law 192 (Aspen Law & Business, 5th ed. 1992). Copyright © 1992 by Richard A. Posner. Reprinted with permission.

Posner, Epstein's Tort Theory: A Critique, 8 J. Legal Stud. 457 (1979). Copyright © 1979 by the University of Chicago Press. Reprinted with permission.

Schuck, Rethinking Informed Consent, 103 Yale L.J. 899, 957-958 (1994).

Schwartz, Tort Law and the Economy in Nineteenth-Century America: A Reinterpretation, 90 Yale L.J. 1717 (1981). Reprinted with permission of the Yale Law Journal and Fred B. Rothman & Company from the Yale Law Journal, Vol. 90, pp. 1717, 1759-1762.

Seavey, Negligence — Subjective or Objective? 41 Harv. L. Rev. 1 (1927). Copyright © 1927 by the Harvard Law Review Association. Reprinted with permission.

Seavey, Reliance upon Gratuitous Promises or Other Conduct, 64 Harv. L. Rev. 913 (1951). Copyright © 1951 by the Harvard Law Review Association. Reprinted with permission.

Shavell, Suit, Settlement and Trial: A Theoretical Analysis under Alternative Methods for the Allocation of Legal Costs, 11 J. Legal Stud. 35, 58-60 (1981). Reprinted with permission.

Shukaitis, A Market in Personal Injury Tort Claims, 16 J. Legal Stud. 329, 329-330, 339-340 (1987). Reprinted with permission.

Sloan, Frank, Suing for Medical Malpractice 9-10 (1993).

Thomson, The Trolley Problem, 94 Yale L.J. 1395, 1395-1396 (1985).

Viscusi, Risk by Choice 43-44 (Harvard University Press, 1983). Reprinted with permission.

Weiler, Paul , The Case for No-Fault Medical Liability, 52 Md. L. Rev. 908, 919, 928-929, 931 (1993).

INTRODUCTION

The ninth edition of this casebook appears four years after the eighth edition, and some 49 years after Charles O. Gregory and Harry Kalven, Jr., published the first edition of this casebook in 1959. Those 49 years have been marked by both continuity and change in the law. From the late 1950s until the mid 1980s, these changes tended to move largely in one direction. With the exception of the law of defamation and privacy, tort liability expanded on almost all fronts. Today, however, the picture is far more clouded. In the traditional areas of physical injuries, tort liability appears to have reached its high water mark, and in some jurisdictions — California and New York — the tides have been receding. There are now many cases in which eyebrows should be raised because liability has been denied, not because it has been established.

In the midst of these ebbs and flows in tort liability, certain questions have remained with us in more or less the same form in which they were faced by the earliest of common law lawyers. The tension between the principles of negligence and strict liability in stranger cases surely falls into this class. The debates framed in the nineteenth-century cases have largely shaped the subsequent analysis in important areas of the law, such as those dealing with abnormally dangerous activities and with ordinary nuisances, both of which continue to take on additional importance in an age that shows greater preoccupation with environmental harms and toxic torts.

Yet in other areas we have witnessed major transformations, both in the types of cases brought to litigation, and in the choice of legal theories used to decide them. In 1959 — the year of the first edition — the paradigmatic tort action was still the automobile collision. When one thought of institutional tort defendants, the railroads came first to mind. The areas of products liability and medical malpractice cases were, when viewed with the benefit of hindsight, still in their early childhood, while mass torts and toxic torts (the two often go together) still lay a decade or more in the future.

The emergence of new types of litigation has taken its toll on traditional tort theory. The question of "proximate cause"—whether a remote consequence could properly be attributed to the wrongful conduct of the defendant—was the dominant issue of causation in 1959 and the major source of contention among academic writers. That is no longer true today. Increasingly, modern tort litigation concentrates on two other problems. The first involves the difficult questions of evidence and statistics necessary to establish the factual connection between, for example, the defendant's drug or waste discharge and the medical injuries of the plaintiff. The second involves the rules designed to deal with multiple causation when two or more parties are charged with responsibility for all or part of the same harms. Both of these shifts in emphasis have accelerated in the past generation, and are duly taken into account in this edition.

Notwithstanding the enormous substantive changes, the educational aims of this casebook are much the same as those of the previous eight editions. The primary goal remains one of giving to the student an accurate sense of both the legal evolution and the current legal position in tort law. In this context, that means incorporating into the book the output of the American Law Institute, which has now published multiple volumes of a Third Restatement dealing with Liability for Physical and Emotional Injury, Apportionment of Liability Among Multiple Defendants, and Products Liability. It also means taking into account the continuous set of legislative initiatives, which, not by coincidence alone, have taken place in the same areas that have generated the new Restatement output.

This casebook, however, would fail in its essential mission if it did not accomplish two other tasks. First, it should provide you an opportunity to examine the processes of legal method and legal reasoning, with an eye to understanding the evolution of legal rules, and the huge impact that these changes have had on our social institutions. Second, it should give students some sense of the different systematic and intellectual approaches that have been taken to the law of torts over the years.

The importance of understanding method and historical evolution cannot be underestimated in legal education. A casebook—certainly this casebook—is not a reference book, much less a treatise. Indeed with the rise of the online services, internal case and page references are cut back to a minimum, often without an explicit indication of omitted citations, in order to ease the flow of the text. The great problem of legal work today is not too little law, but too much. A click on a single principal case puts you on a trail that branches off in a thousand directions. Faced with this surfeit of information, the standard legal curriculum, by necessity, touches on only a small fraction of the huge and ever-growing body of judicial decisions, Restatement provisions and statutory material, much of which will change with time. The education of the lawyer of the future therefore rests on an ability to deal with a mass of legal materials, to identify the underlying assumptions, to determine possible implications for analogous cases, and, above all, to deal with the persistent uncertainty, ambiguity, and at times downright confusion in the law. To help with these tasks it is essential to trace the development of a legal principle over time, through a line of cases that illustrates its application and tests its limits. To that end this casebook contains many cases from the nineteenth century and before, even some that have long ceased to represent the current law. Much of the material in the ninth edition does not represent modern cases, but earlier decisions whose intellectual value has survived the passage of decades, or even centuries, including one short but insightful passage from the Lombard laws on comparative negligence that dates from 733 A.D! Likewise, in order to capture the nature of legal debate, in many principal cases I have reproduced not only the opinion of the court but those of concurring or dissenting judges. With *Fletcher v. Rylands, infra,* at 127 for example, five separate opinions from three different courts are reproduced, because each adds something to the total picture. These cases are often of exceptional value because their facts and variations in reasoning by the judges have made them focal points for subsequent analysis both in judicial opinions and in legal scholarship, where modern articles tend to gravitate to the discussion of the classic cases that have already been analyzed by previous generations of scholars.

A sound legal education requires more than attention to doctrinal and analytical skills. The law of torts in particular is one of the richest bodies of law, and it has been examined and explored from historical, philosophical, and institutional perspectives by judges and scholars alike. It is essential for all students to gain some sense of the diverse possible approaches to tort law, lest the constant probings of the Socratic method lead to an unhappy form of intellectual nihilism. The materials selected are designed, wherever possible, to allow torts to be confronted not only as a collection of discrete rules but also as a systematic intellectual discipline.

For the past four or five decades, judges and scholars have voiced fundamental disagreement about the proper orientation toward the tort law and about the proper choice of its key substantive rules. Speaking first to the question of general orientation, it is possible to identify three major positions. The traditional view—which had unspoken dominance at the time of the first two editions—looked upon the law of torts as a study in corrective justice, as an effort to develop a coherent set of principles to decide whether *this* plaintiff was entitled to compensation or other remedy from *this* defendant as a matter of fairness between the parties. Issues of public policy and social control were of course never absent from the judicial or academic discourse, but they did not dominate judicial or academic attitudes toward either particular cases or general theory. Fairness, justice, and equity, however elusive, were the dominant themes. Most laypeople, and many judges, instinctively approach most tort cases in just this fashion.

Over the past 40 or 50 years, the traditional approach has been under attack from two flanks. On the one hand there is renewed insistence, which today is often expressly articulated in the cases, that the compensation of injured parties is in itself a valid end of the tort law and that the doctrines of tort law that frustrate that objective must be hedged with limitations or totally eliminated unless strong justification is given for their retention. The older presumption that the plaintiff had to show "good cause" to hold a defendant liable (roughly speaking) has yielded in some quarters to a new presumption that the defendant who has demonstrably caused harm must show why liability should not be imposed. That shift in presumptions, which is today hotly contested, has two major implications. First, the risk of "inevitable accidents" were usually borne by the plaintiff under the dominant view from the late nineteenth to the mid-twentieth century, both for private and institutional defendants. But since that time institutional (but not individual) defendants have been much more likely to be required to respond in damages should the risks of these inevitable accident materials translate into physical or emotional harm. Institutional defendants charged with tort liability, it is said, can shift the loss to society at large, either by altering the nature and type of products sold and services provided, or by spreading the risk through liability insurance. Second, in suits against institutional defendants, defenses based on plaintiff's conduct—notably contributory negligence and assumption of risk— receive a narrower interpretation and no longer bar, but at most reduce, the plaintiff's recovery.

The second critique of the traditional approach comes from a different quarter, that of economic theory. Looking first at the tort law as a system of social control, advocates of the economic approach have generally argued that the proper function of the tort law is to lay down workable liability rules that create incentives for both individuals and firms to minimize (the sum of) the costs of accidents, the costs of their prevention, and the administrative costs of running the legal system. In this view of the subject, the compensation of individual parties is not an end in itself, but only a means to enlist private parties to help police the harmful activities of others. Tort law is thus understood as a part of a complex system that also contains criminal laws and legislative sanctions, not to mention contractual and customary limitations on proper conduct. Given its systematic orientation, this economic approach tends to downplay both the importance of corrective justice in the individual case and compensation for individual victims of accidents, treating the first as largely question-begging and the second as better achieved through voluntary first-party insurance arrangements, such as ordinary life, health or disability insurance. Until very recently its importance was largely academic, but today its influence in the decided cases is increasing. But it would be a mistake to state that in the decided cases it has overtaken the traditional intuitive reliance on fairness — except perhaps with the hardy band of law professors turned judges.

The diversity of opinions on the proper approach to the tort law carries over to disputes about the proper substantive basis of tort liability. From the earliest times until today courts have entertained three main theories — each subject to many variants — for recovery in tort. There is, first, recovery for harms intentionally inflicted by the defendant on the person or property of the plaintiff. Second, there is recovery for harms negligently inflicted, that is, through the want of reasonable or ordinary care. Last, there is recovery under a theory of strict liability, that is, for harms inflicted on the plaintiff by a defendant who acts without negligence and without any intention to harm.

In dealing with these three theories it is important to keep in mind several important themes that reassert themselves throughout the law of torts. One set of issues concerns the relationships between the general approach to the law of torts and the choice of specific theories of liability in particular cases. When does a concern for corrective justice require the use of a strict liability principle, a negligence principle, or an intentional tort principle? What about theories based on the need for individual compensation or on the use of the tort law as a device for minimizing accident costs by channeling scarce resources to their most efficient use? Conversely, it is important to ask which *limitations* on recovery are consistent with the basic theories of liability and with their basic orientation to the subject matter. In this connection it is important to ask the extent to which recovery should be denied because of (to use the standard classification) the plaintiff's own conduct — be it called contributory negligence or assumption of risk — the conduct of a third party, or an act of God when plaintiff has otherwise made out a good cause of action.

Finally, it is crucial to consider what might conveniently be termed the "boundary" questions in the law of torts. As stated, any of the three theories of liability — strict liability, negligence liability, or liability for intentional harms — could apply to any case involving harm. How do these different theories coexist across the full range of tort cases? To anticipate for a moment, does, for example, the commitment to a theory of strict liability in classical trespass cases — those involving the direct application of force on the person or property of another — require (or allow) the use of a similar theory in cases involving slips and falls on business or residential premises or for the harm caused by those engaged in ultrahazardous activities or the manufacture of dangerous products? Similarly, it must be asked whether the choice of a negligence theory in medical malpractice cases commits us to that theory for routine traffic accidents or whether a theory of intentional harms in assault cases commits us to that theory in defamation cases.

With our major conceptual dimensions identified, it is perhaps desirable to close this introduction with a word about the organization of this book. The subject matter of the law of torts can be approached from a large number of different perspectives, and the order of organization is by no means "neutral," since instructors with one outlook are apt to use certain materials in one order while those with a different outlook are apt to use somewhat different materials in yet another order. Here I have tried to adhere to traditional modes of presentation that can, it is hoped, be varied with minimum confusion to suit the tastes of different instructors.

Chapter 1 begins with an exploration of the principles of intentional harms that can be conveniently concluded before turning to the bulk of the materials, which deal with accidentally caused physical harm. The chapter covers first and foremost the cases of physical injuries to the person, to land and to chattels. In addition, it covers situations where the defendant takes or "converts" the plaintiff's property to his own uses, and then continues to address the various harm associated with wrongful imprisonment and the intentional infliction of emotional distress. It also contains an extensive discussion as to how the traditional principles of tort theory play out in cyberspace. Finally, these materials also consider the full range of justifications for such conduct, including consent, self-defense, and necessity. Chapter 2 introduces the recurrent tension between negligence and strict liability in the context of accidental physical injuries by examining the two alternatives in both their historical and analytical aspects. Chapter 3 then undertakes a detailed analysis of the negligence principle, which addresses the different interpretations that can be attached to the idea of unreasonable conduct, the role of custom and statute, and the issues of proof in both bench and jury trials. Chapter 4 turns to plaintiff's conduct, including contributory negligence, assumption of risk, and comparative negligence. Chapter 5 deals with the many difficult questions that arise when two or more parties may be held responsible for a single harm, in the context of first joint and several liability, in cases of multiple causation, and thereafter with vicarious liability, which covers cases where an employer is responsible for the wrongs of either an employee or, less frequently, an independent contractor. Chapter 6 then turns to two of the major issues of causation, cause-in-fact and proximate cause. Chapter 7 addresses affirmative duties to strangers and to persons with whom the defendant stands in some special relationship, which includes the full range of entrants onto land, and other persons over whom the defendant exercises some degree of control, including everyone from children, to students, to tenants and to psychiatric patients. Chapter 8 then deals with the traditional strict liability torts: animals, ultrahazardous activities, and nuisance. Chapter 9 examines the evolution of products liability from its nineteenth-century origins to its modern applications, and covers all the material that deals with defects in manufacturing, design and warning, as well as the ever more important question of when federal regulation displaces the common law development at the state level. Chapter 10 completes the exposition of the elements of the basic tort with an analysis of the rules for governing damages, both compensatory and punitive. Chapter 11 goes beyond the tort system narrowly defined and deals with the role of insurance in dealing with tort cases. It includes the major coverage disputes that have arisen in connection with such matters as pollution and asbestos, and concludes with a discussion of the conflicts of interest that arise between the insured and its insurers. Chapter 12 examines alternatives to the tort system, workers' compensation and the various forms of no-fault insurance for automobiles, products (especially vaccines), medical accidents, as well the special scheme of compensation put into place for the victims of the 9/11 disaster. It concludes with a short discussion of the comprehensive displacement of the tort law by New Zealand's comprehensive system of no-fault insurance.

The next four chapters of this book are concerned primarily with nonphysical injuries. Chapter 13 covers defamation from its common law origins to its constitutional complications. Chapter 14 then takes up the closely related issue of rights of privacy, both as they relate to the right of individuals to resist intrusions from the external world, and to control the use of their name and likeness, the so-called right of publicity. The next two chapters of the book deal with more traditional economic relationships: Chapter 15 is devoted to the law of misrepresentation (with a peek at modern securities law) and Chapter 16 is directed to the general subject of economic harms, here defined as those harms that do not flow from either bodily injury or property damage to the plaintiff. Chapter 17 rounds out the discussion by dealing with immunities from all sorts of torts for private persons and for public bodies and officials.

I have edited the materials with an eye toward smoother reading. Unless the context otherwise seems to require, I have followed a loose convention of using the female pronoun for plaintiffs and the male pronoun for defendants. Citations to cases (and to cases within cases), footnotes, and other quoted material have been eliminated or simplified without any special indication in order to remove clutter and preserve readability. The few footnotes that have been retained have their original numbering. The editor's footnotes are indicated by an asterisk.

References to W. Prosser and W. Keeton on Torts (5th ed. 1984) are simply to Prosser and Keeton on Torts. References to F. Harper, F. James, and O. Gray, The Law of Torts (3d ed. 2007) are simply to Harper, James

and Gray, Torts, unless an earlier edition is explicitly mentioned. I have
written my own treatise on the law of torts (Torts, Aspen Law & Business
1999), but have refrained from giving citations to it in this volume, lest
they appear with monotonous regularity. But I have included a List of
Chapters for that book, which indicates its coverage (see page xliii).
Virtually all of the issues that are covered in this casebook are also covered
in *Torts*.

TORTS

Richard A. Epstein
(Aspen Law & Business, 1999)

List of Chapters

TORTS

List of Abbreviations

Abbreviation	Full Citation
A.C.	Appeals Cases (to the House of Lords)
CFR	Code of Federal Regulations
ILCS	Illinois Compiled Statutes
K.B.	King's Bench
MPC	Model Penal Code
Q.B.	Queen's Bench
RT	Restatement of Torts
RST	Restatement (Second) of Torts
RTT: PH	Restatement (Third) of Torts: Liability for Physical Harm
RTT: PL	Restatement (Third) of Torts: Products Liability
RTUC	Restatement (Third) Unfair Competition
RSA	Restatement (Second) of Agency

CASES AND MATERIALS
ON TORTS

PART ONE
PHYSICAL AND MENTAL HARMS

1

INTENTIONALLY INFLICTED HARM: THE PRIMA FACIE CASE AND DEFENSES

SECTION A.   INTRODUCTION

It is best to begin our study of the law of torts with the rules governing liability for the intentional infliction of harm. At first blush, intentional torts are the easiest to comprehend — everyone, for example, understands a punch in the nose. But as these materials will reveal, punches in the nose come in all sizes and shapes. Intuitively, the need for legal redress is strongest for the deliberate injuries examined in this chapter. However, complications immediately arise. First, the law often distinguishes between the intent to commit an act that causes harm and the intent to cause the harm itself. Why and how is that distinction important? How does the tort conception of intention differ from the concept of mens rea (the guilty mind) found in the criminal law? Second, once the plaintiff has established her prima facie case for liability, what excuses and justifications are available to the defendant, and what qualifications surround them?

The intentional infliction of harm has traditionally covered a curious mix of situations. Most obviously, the law guards against physical harm to person or property. It also protects people against forcible dispossession of their land and against the taking, or conversion, of their personal property. Finally, it extends its protection against assaults, defined as threats to use force against the person, and (somewhat more haltingly) to affronts to personal dignity and emotional tranquility. The first part of the chapter discusses physical harms, which include the torts of battery (or trespass to the person) and trespass to real and personal property. Where on this continuum do trespasses in cyberspace fall? The conversion of Internet domain names? In addition, it examines the full range of defenses based on consent, insanity, defense of person and property, and necessity. The second half of the chapter examines the torts designed to protect dignitary or emotional interests: assault and offensive battery, false imprisonment, and the intentional infliction of emotional distress, as well as the interplay between the plaintiff's prima facie case and the available defenses.

SECTION B. PHYSICAL HARMS

1. *Trespass to Person, Land and Chattels*

Vosburg v. Putney
50 N.W. 403 (Wis. 1891)

The action was brought to recover damages for an assault and battery, alleged to have been committed by the defendant upon the plaintiff on February 20, 1889. The answer is a general denial. At the date of the alleged assault the plaintiff was a little more than fourteen years of age, and the defendant a little less than twelve years of age.

The injury complained of was caused by a kick inflicted by defendant upon the leg of the plaintiff, a little below the knee. The transaction occurred in a schoolroom in Waukesha, during school hours, both parties being pupils in the school. A former trial of the cause resulted in a verdict and judgment for the plaintiff for $2,800. The defendant appealed from such judgment to this court, and the same was reversed for error, and a new trial awarded.

[A more complete statement of the facts is found in the opinion by Orton, J., 47 N.W. 99, 99 (1890), on the initial appeal to the Wisconsin Supreme Court: "The plaintiff was about 14 years of age, and the defendant about 11 years of age. On the 20th day of February, 1889, they were sitting opposite to each other across an aisle in the high school of the village of Waukesha. The defendant reached across the aisle with his foot, and hit with his toe the shin of the right leg of the plaintiff. The touch was slight. The plaintiff did not feel it, either on account of its being so slight or of loss of sensation produced by the shock. In a few moments he felt a violent pain in that place, which caused him to cry out loudly. The next day he was sick, and had to be helped to school. On the fourth day he was vomiting, and Dr. Bacon was sent for, but could not come, and he sent medicine to stop the vomiting, and came to see him the next day, on the 25th. There was a slight discoloration of the skin entirely over the inner surface of the tibia an inch below the bend of the knee. The doctor applied fomentations, and gave him anodynes to quiet the pain. This treatment was continued, and the swelling so increased by the 5th day of March that counsel was called, and on the 8th of March an operation was performed on the limb by making an incision, and a moderate amount of pus escaped. A drainage tube was inserted, and an iodoform dressing put on. On the sixth day after this, another incision was made to the bone, and it was found that destruction was going on in the bone, and so it has continued exfoliating pieces of bone. He will never recover the use of his limb. There were black and blue spots on the shin bone, indicating that there had been a blow. On the 1st day of January before, the plaintiff received an injury just above the knee of the same leg by coasting, which appeared to be healing up and drying down at the time of the last injury. The theory of at least one of the medical witnesses was that the limb was in a diseased condition when this touch or kick was given, caused by microbes entering in through the wound above the knee, and which were revivified by the touch, and that the touch was the exciting or remote cause of the destruction of the bone, or of the plaintiff's injury. It does not appear that there was any visible mark made or left by this touch or kick of the defendant's foot, or any appearance of injury until the black and blue spots were discovered by the physician several days afterwards, and then there were more spots than one. There was no proof of any other hurt, and the medical testimony seems to have been agreed that this touch or kick was the exciting cause of the injury to the plaintiff. The jury rendered a verdict for the plaintiff of $2,800. The learned circuit judge said to the jury: 'It is a peculiar case, an unfortunate case, a case, I think I am at liberty to say that ought not to have come into court. The parents of these children ought, in some way, if possible, to have adjusted it between themselves.' We have much of the same feeling about the case."]

The case has been again tried in the circuit court, and the trial resulted in a verdict for plaintiff for $2,500. . . .

On the last trial the jury found a special verdict, as follows: "(1) Had the plaintiff during the month of January, 1889, received an injury just above the knee, which became inflamed, and produced pus? *Answer.* Yes. (2) Had such injury on the 20th day of February, 1889, nearly healed at the point of the injury? *A.* Yes. (3) Was the plaintiff, before said 20th of February, lame, as the result of such injury? *A.* No. (4) Had the tibia in the plaintiff's right leg become inflamed or diseased to some extent before he received the blow or kick from the defendant? *A.* No. (5) What was the exciting cause of the injury to the plaintiff's leg? *A.* Kick. (6) Did the defendant, in touching the plaintiff with his foot, intend to do him any harm? *A.* No. (7) At what sum do you assess the damages of the plaintiff? *A.* $2,500."

The defendant moved for judgment in his favor on the verdict, and also for a new trial. The plaintiff moved for judgment on the verdict in his favor. The motions of defendant were overruled, and that of the plaintiff granted. Thereupon judgment for plaintiff for $2,500 damages and costs of suit was duly entered. The defendant appeals from the judgment.

LYON, J. The jury having found that the defendant, in touching the plaintiff with his foot, did not intend to do him any harm, counsel for defendant maintain that the plaintiff has no cause of action, and that defendant's motion for judgment on the special verdict should have been granted. In support of this proposition counsel quote from 2 Greenl. Ev. §83, the rule that "the intention to do harm is of the essence of an assault." Such is the rule, no doubt, in actions or prosecutions for mere assaults. But this is an action to recover damages for an alleged assault and battery. In such case the rule is correctly stated, in many of the authorities cited by counsel, that plaintiff must show either that the intention was unlawful, or that the defendant is in fault. If the intended act is unlawful, the intention to commit it must necessarily be unlawful. Hence, as applied to this case, if the kicking of the plaintiff by the defendant was an unlawful act, the intention of defendant to kick him was also unlawful.

Had the parties been upon the play-grounds of the school, engaged in the usual boyish sports, the defendant being free from malice, wantonness, or negligence, and intending no harm to plaintiff in what he did, we should hesitate to hold the act of the defendant unlawful, or that he could be held liable in this action. Some consideration is due to the implied license of the play-grounds. But it appears that the injury was inflicted in the school, after it had been called to order by the teacher, and after the regular exercises of the school had commenced. Under these circumstances, no implied license to do the act complained of existed, and such act was a violation of the order and decorum of the school, and necessarily unlawful. Hence we are of the opinion that, under the evidence and verdict, the action may be sustained.

Certain questions were proposed on behalf of defendant to be submitted to the jury, founded upon the theory that only such damages could be recovered as the defendant might reasonably be supposed to have contemplated as likely to result from his kicking the plaintiff. The court refused to submit such questions to the jury. The ruling was correct. The rule of damages in actions for torts was held [in a prior case] to be that the wrong-doer is liable for all injuries resulting directly from the wrongful act, whether they could or could not have been foreseen by him. The chief justice and the writer of this opinion dissented from the judgment in that case, chiefly because we were of the opinion that the complaint stated a cause of action ex contractu [out of contract], and not ex delicto [out of tort], and hence that a different rule of damages — the rule here contended for — was applicable. We did not question that the rule in actions for tort was correctly stated. That case rules this on the question of damages.

[Judgment was reversed, and the case was remanded for a new trial because of error in a ruling on an objection to certain testimony.]

NOTES

1. *Centennial celebrity.* For well over 100 years, *Vosburg* has remained one of the most storied cases in American law. In *Vosburg v. Putney:* A Centennial Story, 1992 Wis. L. Rev. 877 (1992), Professor Zile probes every aspect of its social setting, legal proceedings, and aftermath. Zile relates the newspaper publicity, the spate of low-level criminal proceedings in justice court brought against the defendant, the possible medical malpractice action lurking in the background, and the political overtones under the incessant glare of newspaper publicity. The plaintiff, Andrew Vosburg, was a sickly boy from an ordinary farming background, whereas the defendant, George Putney, was the scion of a wealthy and prominent Wisconsin family whose ancestors arrived in Massachusetts in 1637. The Wisconsin volume also features shorter pieces by Henderson (at 853), Rabin (at 863), and Hurst (at 875).

2. *Defendant's intention and plaintiff's conduct.* Which, if any, of the jury's answers to the six questions may be incorrect in light of the medical evidence? Given the jury's response to the sixth question, can the defendant's act be treated as an intentional tort? Does it make a difference that the teacher had already called the class to order when the kick landed? If the pupils typically tapped each other on the leg under the desk to get each other's attention after the class had been called to order, should defendant's act be excused by the "implied license of the classroom"? Should a defendant's actual malice, wantonness, or negligence be treated in the same fashion for playground injuries? Should plaintiff have worn a shin guard to protect his leg from further injury? Should he have stayed home from school?

3. *Whither "unlawful" intent?* In Garratt v. Dailey, 279 P.2d 1091 (Wash. 1955), and 304 P.2d 681 (Wash. 1956), the plaintiff, an adult woman, brought a battery suit against Brian Dailey, a boy five years and nine months old, who caused her fractured hip when he was a guest in her backyard. Sharp factual disputes required two trials and two appellate decisions to resolve. The defendant claimed that he had tried to help the plaintiff by placing a chair under her as she was about to fall, but that he was too small to move it into place. His version was accepted by the trial judge at the first trial. However, the plaintiff's sister, who was present at the occasion, testified that the plaintiff, an "arthritic woman had begun the slow process of being seated when the defendant quickly removed the chair and seated himself upon it, and that he knew, with substantial certainty at the time, that she would attempt to sit in the place where the chair had been."

On appeal from the first judgment, 279 P.2d 1091, 1093-1094, the Washington Supreme Court addressed the issue of intent in the tort of battery:

It is urged that Brian's action in moving the chair constituted a battery. A definition (not all-inclusive but sufficient for our purpose) of a battery is the intentional infliction of a harmful bodily contact upon another. . . .

We have here the conceded volitional act of Brian, i.e., the moving of a chair. Had the plaintiff proved to the satisfaction of the trial court that Brian moved the chair while she was in the act of sitting down, Brian's action would patently have been for the purpose or with the intent of causing the plaintiff's bodily contact with the ground, and she would be entitled to a judgment against him for the resulting damages. Vosburg v. Putney. . . .

A battery would be established if, in addition to plaintiff's fall, it was proved that, when Brian moved the chair, he knew with substantial certainty that the plaintiff would attempt to sit down where the chair had been. . . .

The mere absence of any intent to injure the plaintiff or to play a prank on her or to embarrass her, or to commit an assault and battery on her would not absolve him from liability if in fact he had such knowledge. Without such knowledge, there would be nothing wrongful about Brian's act in moving the chair and, there being no wrongful act, there would be no liability.

On remand, the trial judge accepted the testimony of the plaintiff's sister, and awarded the plaintiff $11,000. That judgment was upheld on the second appeal. Is removing a chair tantamount to striking the plaintiff?

4. The Restatement account of battery intention. The common law of torts has been "codified" in the Restatement of Torts [RT]. The original version of this influential work was published in 1934 by the American Law Institute. It was prepared by a large and distinguished team of judges, practicing lawyers, and academics, with Professor Francis H. Bohlen as its chief reporter. The Restatement, as its name implies, emphasizes "restating" rather than "reforming" the law, but interstitial reform often occurs whenever the law is in flux or some conflict persists among the various states.

The Restatement (Second) of Torts [RST] appeared in four volumes, published between 1965 and 1979. The first 280 sections of the Second Restatement are devoted to every aspect of intentional torts. Its account of battery reads as follows:

§13. BATTERY: HARMFUL CONTACT
An actor is subject to liability to another for battery if
(a) he acts intending to cause a harmful or offensive contact with the person of the other or a third person, or an imminent apprehension of such a contact, and
(b) a harmful contact with the person of the other directly or indirectly results.

How does this definition square with the results in *Vosburg* and *Garratt?* The Second Restatement uses the term intention "to denote that the actor desires to cause consequences of his act, or that he believes that the consequences are substantially certain to result from it." RST §8A.

A piecemeal revision of the Restatement (Third) of Torts (RTT) has been in progress for the past dozen or so years. The Restatement (Third) of Torts: Liability for Physical Harm [RTT:LPH] covers both cases of knowledge and intention:

§1. INTENT
A person acts with the intent to produce a consequence if:
(a) the person acts with the purpose of producing that consequence; or
(b) the person acts knowing that the consequence is substantially certain to result.

How do these definitions apply to accidents on a large construction project where the general contractor knows that some unidentified worker will likely be killed or injured during the work? See W. Landes and R. Posner, The Economic Structure of Tort Law 149-150 (1987).

Note also that the Second Restatement approves of the result in *Vosburg*, which it describes as follows: "Intending an offensive contact, *A* lightly kicks *B* on the shin." §16, comment *a*, Illustration 1. Did the court in *Vosburg* treat the case as one of offensive battery?

Although the Restatement provisions are powerful authority, sometimes courts reject them. In White v. University of Idaho, 797 P.2d 108 (Idaho 1990), the defendant Neher, a music professor, was a social guest in the house of the plaintiff, one of his piano students. While she was writing, "Professor Neher walked up behind her and touched her back with both of his hands in a movement later described as one a pianist would make in striking and lifting the fingers from a keyboard." The plaintiff claimed she suffered a strong reaction, which necessitated the removal of a rib, and damage to her brachial plexus nerve that required the severing of her scalenus anterior muscles. The professor claimed he touched Mrs. White to show her the sensation of certain forms of playing, but meant no harm. She countered that the touching was nonconsensual. The Court held that she stated a valid claim for battery even though the defendant had not meant to either harm or offend her. The Court brushed aside any attempt to incorporate the requirement of offensive intent, noting curtly "we have not previously adopted the Restatement (Second) in Idaho and decline any invitation to do it now."

Another variation in the mental element in battery is found in Wagner v. Utah, 122 P.3d 599, 601-602 (Utah 2005). A mentally impaired man in the custody of state employees attacked the plaintiff without reason, while she was standing in the customer service line at K-Mart. The state would be immune from liability if the man's actions were treated as a battery, which in turn in raised the question of whether an insane person could have the requisite mental state. Wilkins, J., held that the battery had in fact been committed because the only required mental state was the intention to make contact with the plaintiff, not the intention to cause harm. "A person need not intend to cause harm or appreciate that his contact will cause harm so long as he intends to make a contact, and that contact is harmful."

5. *Transferred intent.* In Talmage v. Smith, 59 N.W. 656 (Mich. 1894), the plaintiff was struck in the eye by a stick that the defendant threw at two of the plaintiff's companions, when the three were trespassing upon the defendant's property. The defendant asserted that he did not see the plaintiff, much less intend to hurt him. The court held this claim immaterial: "The right of the plaintiff to recover was made to depend upon an intention on the part of the defendant to hit somebody, and to inflict an unwarranted injury upon someone. Under these circumstances, the fact that the injury resulted to another than was intended does not relieve the defendant from responsibility." Does it matter whether the injured plaintiff was trespassing on defendant's property?

See generally Prosser, Transferred Intent, 45 Tex. L. Rev. 650 (1967).

6. *Battery by smoke.* The question of intention in battery took a novel form in Shaw v. Brown & Williamson Tobacco Corp., 973 F. Supp. 539, 548 (D. Md. 1997). The plaintiff truck driver, a non-smoker, shared his cab with a heavy Raleigh smoker, and developed lung cancer as a result. His claim for battery for secondhand smoke against the tobacco company was rejected for its failure to allege sufficient intent:

> Williamson did not know with a substantial degree of certainty that second-hand smoke would touch any particular non-smoker. While it may have had knowledge that second-hand smoke would reach some non-smokers, the Court finds that such generalized knowledge is insufficient to satisfy the intent requirement for battery. Indeed, as defendant points out, a finding that Brown & Williamson has committed a battery by manufacturing cigarettes would be tantamount to holding manufacturers of handguns liable in battery for exposing third parties to gunfire. Such a finding would expose the courts to a flood of farfetched and nebulous litigation concerning the tort of battery. It is unsurprising that neither plaintiffs nor the Court have been able to unearth any case where a manufacturer of cigarettes or handguns was found to have committed a battery against those allegedly injured by its products.

Should plaintiff win on a theory of transferred intent? Should a case of battery be brought against the plaintiff's fellow truck driver?

Dougherty v. Stepp
18 N.C. 371 (1835)

This was an action of trespass quare clausum fregit [wherefore he broke the close], tried at Buncombe on the last Circuit, before his Honor Judge

MARTIN. The only proof introduced by the plaintiff to establish an act of trespass, was, that the defendant had entered on the unenclosed land of the plaintiff, with a surveyor and chain carriers, and actually surveyed a part of it, claiming it as his own, but without marking trees or cutting bushes. This, his Honor held not to be a trespass, and the jury, under his instructions, found a verdict for the defendant, and the plaintiff appealed.

RUFFIN, C.J. In the opinion of the Court, there is error in the instructions given to the jury. The amount of damages may depend on the acts done on the land, and the extent of injury to it therefrom. But it is an elementary principle, that every unauthorised, and therefore unlawful entry, into the close of another, is a trespass. From every such entry against the will of the possessor, the law infers some damage; if nothing more, the treading down the grass or the herbage or as here, the shrubbery. Had the locus in quo been under cultivation or enclosed, there would have been no doubt of the plaintiff's right to recover. Now our Courts have for a long time past held, that if there be no adverse possession, the title makes the land the owner's close. Making the survey and marking trees, or making it without marking, differ only in the degree, and not in the nature of the injury. It is the entry that constitutes the trespass. There is no statute, nor rule of reason, that will make a wilful entry into the land of another, upon an unfounded claim of right, innocent, which one, who sat up no title to the land, could not justify or excuse. On the contrary, the pretended ownership aggravates the wrong. Let the judgment be reversed, and a new trial granted.

Judgment reversed.

NOTES

1. Traditional forms of trespass to real property. Trespass quare clausum fregit (or trespass qcf) has long been granted to protect the plaintiff's interest in the exclusive possession of land and its improvements. It has been long settled that a trespass to real property takes place not only on the surface, but also with any intrusion above or below the surface of the land. In Smith v. Smith, 110 Mass. 302 (1872), the defendant was adjudged a trespasser when the eaves of his barn overhung the plaintiff's land. Further, in Neiswonger v. Goodyear Tire and Rubber Co., 35 F.2d 761 (N.D. Ohio 1929), airplane overflights within 500 feet of the ground, in violation of air traffic rules established by the Department of Commerce, were also treated as a common law trespass. The strict nature of the prima facie case should not exclude any justification for entry onto the land. Could the plaintiff in *Dougherty* have pleaded some necessity for entrance given his desire to determine whether he owned the land? Or should he have gotten a legal order for the survey to be made?

2. *Intention and damages in trespass to real property.* Owing to the passive and immovable nature of real property, the courts have generally adopted stringent standards of liability whenever the trespass results in actual harm. In Brown v. Dellinger, 355 S.W.2d 742, 747 (Tex. Civ. App. 1962), two children, aged seven and eight, were held liable for the loss of the plaintiff's $28,000 home. The court observed:

> The acts of the minor defendants in bringing matches onto the premises of [plaintiff] and igniting the fire in the charcoal burner in [plaintiff's] garage were all voluntary and purposeful and were acts which they even at their tender years had sufficient capacity to do, as evidenced by the fact that they did do such acts. Undoubtedly they did not intend for the fire to escape from the grill and spread to the curtain canvas and burn and damage the garage, house and contents thereof. However their acts of igniting an unauthorized fire on [plaintiff's] premises made them trespassers, and they must be held civilly liable for the consequences which directly flowed from their unauthorized acts of igniting the fire in question.

If the plaintiff's charcoal burner had been defective and the defendants had used it with all possible care, should the plaintiff still recover? If the defendants had been burned while using the defective burner, could they recover from the plaintiff for their personal injuries? If the defendants had started the fire on their own property, could the plaintiff recover under *Brown* if the fire had spread to his premises?

In Cleveland Park Club v. Perry, 165 A.2d 485 (D.C. 1960), the plaintiff operated a social club for the benefit of its members. One day while the defendant, a nine-year-old boy, was using the swimming pool, he dove down to a depth of seven feet, "and thinking there was no suction at the time," removed the drain cover and inserted a rubber ball. The ball was caught in a narrow portion of a pipe where it caused extensive damage, requiring the pool to be closed for repairs. The judgment for the defendant at trial was reversed on appeal, and a new trial ordered. The court stressed that in trespass cases "the intent controlling is the intent to complete the physical act and not the intent to cause injurious consequences." Did the defendant intend to place the ball in the mouth of the drain, or in the middle of the pipe? What weight should be given to his mistaken belief that there was no suction? Should it make a difference if the defendant was on the premises with the plaintiff's permission? Could the defendants in *Garratt*, *Brown*, and *Cleveland Park* be held liable on a negligence theory? See *infra* Chapter 3, Section A.

See generally Epstein, Intentional Harms, 4 J. Legal Stud. 391 (1975).

3. *Intangible trespasses.* In Public Service Co. of Colorado v. Van Wyk, 27 P.3d 377, 390 (Colo. 2001), the plaintiff sued in trespass for the harm attributable to the noise, radiation, and electromagnetic fields that

resulted from an upgrade in Public Service's utility system that had been approved by the state Public Utility Commission. Martinez, J., distinguished this case from physical trespasses in which particulate matter is deposited on plaintiff's land despite no visible intrusion, and held that, unlike claims for physical invasions,

> an intangible intrusion may give rise to a claim for trespass, but only if an aggrieved party is able to prove physical damage to the property caused by such intangible intrusion.
>
> Our holding here is consistent with the historical requirement of entry or use that interferes with possession for trespass liable to be established. The requirement that the intangible intrusion be intentional, and that a plaintiff prove physical damage caused by the intrusion safeguards against the concern that allowing trespass claims against intangible intrusions would produce too much liability. Moreover, a property owner forced to prove damage will be further limited to seeking redress in cases of serious or substantial invasions. The difficulty in proving a connection between minor damage and an intangible intrusion is too great to support litigiousness on the part of pestered property owners.

Martinez, J., also sustained plaintiff's nuisance claim that the defendant's actions depreciated the value of their property, caused mental distress and deprived them of the quiet use and enjoyment of their land. Why do those not count as consequential losses from the trespass? See Chapter 8 at 645.

4. Trespass to chattels at common law. In many respects the law of trespass to chattels parallels that of trespass to land, at least in cases of actual damages. One point of possible difference concerns the availability of damages or injunctions for the unauthorized use of chattels. The Restatement takes a position that resists the use of damage in these cases. RST §218, comment *e*, provides:

> The interest of a possessor of a chattel in its inviolability, unlike the similar interest of a possessor of land, is not given legal protection by an action for nominal damages for harmless intermeddlings with a chattel. In order that an actor who interferes with another's chattel may be liable, his conduct must affect some other and more important interest of the possessor. Therefore, one who intentionally intermeddles with another's chattel is subject to liability only if his intermeddling is harmful to the possessor's materially valuable interest in the physical condition, quality, or value of the chattel, or if the possessor is deprived of the use of the chattel for a substantial time, or some other legally protected interest of the possessor is affected as stated in Clause (c) [relating to the deprivation of use for a substantial time]. Sufficient legal protection . . . of his chattel is afforded by his privilege to use reasonable force to protect his protection against even harmless interference.

The Restatement's one illustration of nominal damages, RST §218, comment *e* illus. 2, reads in full:

> A child, climbs upon the back of *B*'s large dog and pulls its ears. No harm is done to the dog, or to any other legally protected interest of *B. A* is not liable to *B.*

With the Restatement's view compare, Blondell v. Consolidated Gas Co. 43 A. 817 (Md. 1908). A large group of gas company customers sought to attach governors to the company's gas meters. The meters measured the flow of gas. The governors regulated that flow. The plaintiff gas company urged that attaching governors to the meters could increase the danger of explosion. The defendants denied these allegations. The court sidestepped the question of whether the future damage might occur, by asking only whether the defendant had made unauthorized use of plaintiff's property:

> Now it seems to us that the large mass of testimony contained in the record showing, on the one hand, that the affixing of the governor was, and on the other hand that it was not injurious to the meter and its connections, is entirely beside the question. For whether the alleged acts were or were not productive of injury, they were in the eye of the law trespasses, if, as we have said, the meters are the plaintiff's property, and if the acts were unauthorized, there is a legal injury for which the plaintiff could recover, at least, nominal damages; and the continuation of which would be enjoined by a Court of Equity.

Should it make a difference whether the pipes are regarded as real or personal property?

Intel Corporation v. Hamidi
71 P.3d 296 (Cal. 2003)

WERDEGAR, J. Intel Corporation (Intel) maintains an electronic mail system, connected to the Internet, through which messages between employees and those outside the company can be sent and received, and permits its employees to make reasonable nonbusiness use of this system. On six occasions over almost two years, Kourosh Kenneth Hamidi, a former Intel employee, sent e-mails criticizing Intel's employment practices to numerous current employees [up to 35,000 in number per occasion] on Intel's electronic mail system. Hamidi breached no computer security barriers in order to communicate with Intel employees. He offered to, and did, remove from his mailing list any recipient who so wished. Hamidi's communications to individual Intel employees caused neither physical damage nor functional disruption to the company's computers, nor did they at any time deprive Intel of the use of its computers. The contents of the messages, however, caused discussion among employees and managers. [On several occasions, Intel sent notice to Hamidi by registered mail, asking him to cease and desist use of all its equipment.]

On these facts, Intel brought suit, claiming that by communicating with its employees over the company's e-mail system Hamidi committed the tort of trespass to chattels. The trial court granted Intel's motion for summary judgment and enjoined Hamidi from any further mailings. A divided Court of Appeal affirmed.

After reviewing the decisions analyzing unauthorized electronic contact with computer systems as potential trespasses to chattels, we conclude that under California law the tort does not encompass, and should not be extended to encompass, an electronic communication that neither damages the recipient computer system nor impairs its functioning. Such an electronic communication does not constitute an actionable trespass to personal property, i.e., the computer system, because it does not interfere with the possessor's use or possession of, or any other legally protected interest in, the personal property itself. The consequential economic damage Intel claims to have suffered, i.e., loss of productivity caused by employees reading and reacting to Hamidi's messages and company efforts to block the messages, is not an injury to the company's interest in its computers–which worked as intended and were unharmed by the communications–any more than the personal distress caused by reading an unpleasant letter would be an injury to the recipient's mailbox, or the loss of privacy caused by an intrusive telephone call would be an injury to the recipient's telephone equipment.

[Werdegar, J., then noted that the ruling did not block remedies for interference with contract or economic relations, intentional infliction of emotional distress, defamation, or publication of private facts.]

Nor does our holding affect the legal remedies of Internet service providers (ISP's) against senders of unsolicited commercial bulk e-mail (UCE), also known as "spam" [which overloads computer systems]. A series of federal district court decisions, beginning with CompuServe, Inc. v. Cyber Promotions, Inc. (S.D. Ohio 1997) 962 F. Supp. 1015, has approved the use of trespass to chattels as a theory of spammers' liability to ISP's, based upon evidence that the vast quantities of mail sent by spammers both overburdened the ISP's own computers and made the entire computer system harder to use for recipients, the ISP's customers.

DISCUSSION

I. CURRENT CALIFORNIA TORT LAW

Dubbed by Prosser the "little brother of conversion," the tort of trespass to chattels allows recovery for interferences with possession of personal property "not sufficiently important to be classed as conversion, and so to compel the defendant to pay the full value of the thing with which he has interfered."

Though not amounting to conversion, the defendant's interference must, to be actionable, have caused some injury to the chattel or to the plaintiff's rights in it. Under California law, trespass to chattels "lies where an intentional interference with the possession of personal property *has proximately caused injury.*" (Thrifty-Tel, Inc. v. Bezenek (1996) 46 Cal. App. 4th 1559, 1566, italics added.) . . .

The Restatement, too, makes clear that some actual injury must have occurred in order for a trespass to chattels to be actionable. Under Section 218 of the Restatement Second of Torts, dispossession alone, without further damages, is actionable, but other forms of interference require some additional harm to the personal property or the possessor's interests in it. [The court quotes the passage set out *supra* at 13.]

Intel suggests that the requirement of actual harm does not apply here because it sought only injunctive relief, as protection from future injuries. But as Justice Kolkey, dissenting below, observed, "[t]he fact the relief sought is injunctive does not excuse a showing of injury, whether actual or threatened." Indeed, in order to obtain injunctive relief the plaintiff must ordinarily show that the defendant's wrongful acts threaten to cause *irreparable* injuries, ones that cannot be adequately compensated in damages. . . . A fortiori, to issue an injunction without a showing of likely irreparable injury in an action for trespass to chattels, in which injury to the personal property or the possessor's interest in it *is* an element of the action, would make little legal sense.

[The court reiterated the absence of damage to the plaintiff's computer system itself, as happened in eBay v. Bidder's edge, see *infra* Note 2 and CompuServe, Inc. v. Cyber Promotions, Inc.]

In addition to impairment of system functionality, *CompuServe* and its progeny also refer to the ISP's loss of business reputation and customer goodwill, resulting from the inconvenience and cost that spam causes to its members, as harm to the ISP's legally protected interests in its personal property. Intel argues that its own interest in employee productivity, assertedly disrupted by Hamidi's messages, is a comparable protected interest in its computer system. We disagree. . . .

CompuServe's customers were annoyed because the system was inundated with unsolicited commercial messages, making its use for personal communication more difficult and costly. Their complaint, which allegedly led some to cancel their CompuServe service, was about *the functioning of CompuServe's electronic mail service.* Intel's workers, in contrast, were allegedly distracted from their work not because of the frequency or quantity of Hamidi's messages, but because of assertions and opinions the messages conveyed. Intel's complaint is thus about *the contents of the messages* rather than the functioning of the company's e-mail system. Even accepting *CompuServe*'s economic injury rationale, therefore, Intel's position represents a further extension of the trespass to chattels tort, fictionally recharacterizing the allegedly injurious effect of a communication's *contents* on recipients as an impairment to the device which transmitted the message.

This theory of "impairment by content" threatens to stretch trespass law to cover injuries far afield from the harms to possession the tort evolved to protect. . . .

Nor may Intel appropriately assert a *property* interest in its employees' time.

. . . We conclude, therefore, that Intel has not presented undisputed facts demonstrating an injury to its personal property, or to its legal interest in that property, that support, under California tort law, an action for trespass to chattels.

II. PROPOSED EXTENSION OF CALIFORNIA TORT LAW

We next consider whether California common law should be *extended* to cover, as a trespass to chattels, an otherwise harmless electronic communication whose contents are objectionable. We decline to so expand California law. . . .

Writing on behalf of several industry groups appearing as amici curiae, Professor Richard A. Epstein of the University of Chicago urges us to excuse the required showing of injury to personal property in cases of unauthorized electronic contact between computers, "extending the rules of trespass to real property to all interactive Web sites and servers." The court is thus urged to recognize, for owners of a particular species of personal property, computer servers, the same interest in inviolability as is generally accorded a possessor of land. In effect, Professor Epstein suggests that a company's server should be its castle, upon which any unauthorized intrusion, however harmless, is a trespass.

Epstein's argument derives, in part, from the familiar metaphor of the Internet as a physical space, reflected in much of the language that has been used to describe it: "cyberspace," "the information superhighway," e-mail "addresses," and the like. Of course, the Internet is also frequently called simply the "Net," a term, Hamidi points out, "evoking a fisherman's chattel." A major component of the Internet is the World Wide "Web," a descriptive term suggesting neither personal nor real property, and "cyberspace" itself has come to be known by the oxymoronic phrase "virtual reality," which would suggest that any real property "located" in "cyberspace" must be "virtually real" property. Metaphor is a two-edged sword.

Indeed, the metaphorical application of real property rules would not, by itself, transform a physically harmless electronic intrusion on a computer server into a trespass. That is because, under California law, intangible intrusions on land, including electromagnetic transmissions, are not actionable as trespasses (though they may be as nuisances) unless they cause physical damage to the real property. Since Intel does not claim Hamidi's electronically transmitted messages physically damaged its servers, it could not prove a trespass to land even were we to treat the computers as a type of real property. Some further extension of the conceit would be required, under which the electronic signals Hamidi sent would be recast as tangible intruders, perhaps as tiny messengers rushing through the "hallways" of Intel's computers and bursting out of employees' computers to read them Hamidi's missives. But such fictions promise more confusion than clarity in the law.

The plain fact is that computers, even those making up the Internet, are — like such older communications equipment as telephones and fax machines — personal property, not realty. Professor Epstein observes that "[a]lthough servers may be moved in real space, they cannot be moved in cyberspace," because an Internet server must, to be useful, be accessible at a known address. But the same is true of the telephone: to be useful for incoming communication, the telephone must remain constantly linked to the same number. . . . Does this suggest that an unwelcome message delivered through a telephone or fax machine should be viewed as a trespass to a type of real property? We think not. . . .

More substantively, Professor Epstein argues that a rule of computer server inviolability will, through the formation or extension of a market in computer-to-computer access, create "the right social result." In most circumstances, he predicts, companies with computers on the Internet will continue to authorize transmission of information through e-mail, Web site searching, and page linking because they benefit by that open access. When a Web site owner does deny access to a particular sending, searching, or linking computer, a system of "simple one-on-one negotiations" will arise to provide the necessary individual licenses.

Other scholars are less optimistic about such a complete propertization of the Internet. Professor Mark Lemley of the University of California, Berkeley, writing on behalf of an amici curiae group of professors of intellectual property and computer law, observes that under a property rule of server inviolability, "each of the hundreds of millions of [Internet] users must get permission in advance from anyone with whom they want to communicate and anyone who owns a server through which their message may travel." The consequence for e-mail could be a substantial reduction in the freedom of electronic communication, as the owner of each computer through which an electronic message passes could impose its own limitations on message content or source. . . . A leading scholar of Internet law and policy, Professor Lawrence Lessig of Stanford University, has criticized Professor Epstein's theory of the computer server as quasi-real property, previously put forward in the *eBay* case, on the ground that it ignores the costs to society in the loss of network benefits: "eBay benefits greatly from a network that is open and where access is free. It is this general feature of the Net that makes the Net so valuable to users and a source of great innovation. And to the extent that individual sites begin to impose their own rules of exclusion, the value of the network as a network declines. If machines must negotiate before entering any individual site, then the costs of using the network climb." (Lessig, The Future of Ideas: The Fate of the Commons in a Connected World (2001) p. 171; . . .)

We discuss this debate among the amici curiae and academic writers only to note its existence and contours, not to attempt its resolution. [The Court notes that legislative solutions are possible in both this situation and with spam.]

III. CONSTITUTIONAL CONSIDERATIONS

[The Court then declines to address the First Amendment claims that would arise if Intel had stated a claim for common law trespass. It then concluded:] Hamidi himself had no tangible presence on Intel property, instead speaking from his own home through his computer. He no more invaded Intel's property than does a protester holding a sign or shouting through a bullhorn outside corporate headquarters, posting a letter through the mail, or telephoning to complain of a corporate practice.

The judgment of the Court of Appeal is reversed.

KENNARD, J., concurring. Does a person commit the tort of trespass to chattels by making occasional personal calls to a mobile phone despite the stated objection of the person who owns the mobile phone and pays for the mobile phone service? Does it matter that the calls are not made to the mobile phone's owner, but to another person who ordinarily uses that phone? Does it matter that the person to whom the calls are made has not objected to them? Does it matter that the calls do not damage the mobile phone or reduce in any significant way its availability or usefulness? . . .

Intel has my sympathy. . . . [However,] [b]ecause plaintiff Intel has not shown that defendant Hamidi's occasional bulk e-mail messages to Intel's employees have damaged Intel's computer system or impaired its functioning in any significant way, Intel has not established the tort of trespass to chattels.

This is not to say that Intel is helpless either practically or legally. As a practical matter, Intel need only instruct its employees to delete messages from Hamidi without reading them and to notify Hamidi to remove their workplace e-mail addresses from his mailing lists. . . .

BROWN, J., dissenting. . . . Intel has invested millions of dollars to develop and maintain a computer system. It did this not to act as a public forum but to enhance the productivity of its employees. Kourosh Kenneth Hamidi sent as many as 200,000 e-mail messages to Intel employees. The time required to review and delete Hamidi's messages diverted employees from productive tasks and undermined the utility of the computer system. . . .

The majority repeatedly asserts that Intel objected to the hundreds of thousands of messages solely due to their content, and proposes that Intel seek relief by pleading content-based speech torts. This proposal misses the point that Intel's objection is directed not toward Hamidi's message but his use of Intel's property to display his message. Intel has not sought to prevent Hamidi from expressing his ideas on his Web site, through private mail (paper or electronic) to employees' homes, or through any other means like picketing or billboards. But as counsel for Intel explained during oral argument, the company objects to Hamidi's using Intel's property to advance his message.

Of course, Intel deserves an injunction even if its objections are based entirely on the e-mail's content. Intel is entitled, for example, to allow employees use of the Internet to check stock market tables or weather forecasts without incurring any concomitant obligation to allow access to pornographic Web sites. A private property owner may choose to exclude unwanted mail for any reason, including its content. Rowan v. U.S. Post Office Dept. 397 U.S. 728, 738 (1970).

MOSK, J., dissenting. . . . The majority fail to distinguish open communication in the public "commons" of the Internet from unauthorized intermeddling on a private, proprietary intranet. Hamidi is not communicating in the equivalent of a town square or of an unsolicited "junk" mailing through the United States Postal Service. His action, in crossing from the public Internet into a private intranet, is more like intruding into a private office mailroom, commandeering the mail cart, and dropping off unwanted broadsides on 30,000 desks. Because Intel's security measures have been circumvented by Hamidi, the majority leave Intel, which has exercised all reasonable self-help efforts, with no recourse unless he causes a malfunction or systems "crash."

NOTES

1. *Trespass in cyberspace*. How persuasive are the analogies between the telephone and the Internet? Do telemarketing phone calls made to persons who have enrolled on the National Do Not Call Registry, https://www.donotcall.gov/default.aspx, count as trespasses to chattels? If repeated, should they be enjoined? Is the plaintiff's suit a protest against the content of the emails or the unauthorized use of its servers? Would the result in *Hamidi* have been different if the defendant had, without disruption of service, used the plaintiff's servers to transfer information to third parties for profit? If the plaintiff is entitled to use self-help to keep the defendant off

its servers, why encourage a game of "cat-and-mouse" by denying the injunction? The injunction against *Hamidi* had been in effect for five years before the final decision of the California Supreme Court. Was there any evidence in the loss of connectivity on the net? Any reason to think that there might be?

The decision in *Hamidi* has generated an extensive cottage industry on the role of metaphor in organizing the relationship between trespasses in real space and cyberspace. What weight, if any, should be given to speaking of Internet sites as addresses located along an Internet highway? For an early warning against the use of trespass in cyberspace, see Burk, The Trouble with Trespass, 4 J. Small & Emerging Bus. L. 27 (2000). For an extensive criticism of the potential abuse in moving across contexts, see Hunter, Cyberspace as Place and the Tragedy of the Digital Anticommons, 91 Cal. L. Rev. 439 (2003), where the term "anticommons" refers to the destruction fragmentation of a unified space by the creation of arbitrary boundaries that impede communication. For a defense of the explicit translation of the notions of private and common property from real space to cyberspace, see Epstein, Intel v. Hamidi: The Role of Self-Help in Cyberspace?, 1 J.L. Econ. & Pol'y 147 (2005); McGowan, The Trespass Trouble and the Metaphor Muddle, 1 J.L. Econ. & Pol'y 109 (2005). For a prudential defense of *Hamidi*, see Lastowka, Decoding Cyberproperty, 40 Ind. L. Rev. 23 (2007), collecting all references.

2. Modern forms of trespass. Hamidi is only one of many cases that apply traditional common trespass rules to cyberspace. In eBay v. Bidder's Edge, Inc, 100 F. Supp. 2d 1058 (N.D. Cal. 2000), eBay sued Bidder's Edge (BE) for trespass to chattels. BE was an auction aggregator who enabled its customers the ability to compare bids for similar items sold on different online sites. To obtain the needed information, BE deployed Internet "spiders" to search eBay's online auction database thousands of times per hour, in order to post bidding updates on its own web site. Although eBay's database was publicly accessible, its stated policies forbade anyone from probing its space with spiders. When BE refused to discontinue its "spidering," the court granted eBay a preliminary injunction against BE's activities, finding that its repeated searches amounted to trespass to chattels, capable of impairing the operation of its site because the use of "BE's web crawlers exceeded the scope of any such consent when they began acting like robots by making repeated queries." Note that eBay had been prepared to issue BE site access under its standard licensing agreement, which would have generated payments to BE for any customers referred to its site. Should it matter that BE allowed customers to enter through a secondary portal where they would not see eBay's advertisements?

The post-*Hamidi* cases have generally followed the basic decision. Thus, in Sotelo v. DirectRevenue, LLC, 384 F. Supp. 2d 1219, 1229 (N.D. Ill. 2005), Gettleman, J., denied the defendant's motion to dismiss where the plaintiff pursued a trespass to chattels theory against the defendant who planted on plaintiff's computer "spyware," software capable of corrupting the plaintiff's data and tracking her Internet use. What if spyware did the latter but not the former? On the other hand, in In re Jetblue Airways Corp. Privacy Litigation, 379 F. Supp. 2d 299, 328-329 (E.D.N.Y. 2005) the court refused to apply a trespass to chattel theory to prevent the defendant from taking key passenger name records off Jetblue's computers, on the ground "even if their privacy interests were indeed infringed by the data transfer, such a harm does not amount to a diminishment of the quality or value of a materially valuable interest in their personal information." A similar effort to purloin data from plaintiff was subject to an injunction for the violation of trade secrets when the defendants stole information contained in plaintiff's bills of lading. Pestco, Inc. v. Associated Products, Inc., 880 A.2d 700 (Pa. Super. 2005).

2. *Conversion*

Poggi v. Scott
139 P. 815 (Cal. 1914)

HENSHAW, J. Plaintiff sued to recover from defendant the sum of two thousand dollars damages suffered by him by reason of the unlawful conversion by defendant of some two hundred barrels of plaintiff's wine. A nonsuit was granted upon the ground that plaintiff had failed to prove a sufficient case for the jury and from the judgment which followed he appeals.

[The plaintiff stored his wine barrels in a basement under lock and key in a room that he rented first from Judge Mouser and thereafter from his lessee, the Sanitary Laundry Company. Plaintiff visited his storeroom about twice a month. Mouser sold the building to the defendant, Scott, and testified that he had informed Scott of the plaintiff's lease with the Laundry Company. Mouser did not tell the plaintiff that the premises had been sold. Later the plaintiff discovered that his wine bottles had been carted off. It seems as though two men, Bernardini and Ricci knew that the wine was valuable. They called on Scott and told him that they wanted to buy some broken barrels stored in the basement. Scott went to the basement, located the barrels, tapped them to see if they were filled, and sold the allegedly empty barrels for $15.00 on condition that the men clean out the basement, which they did. Bernardini and Ricci were arrested for the theft of the wine, and Poggi brought this conversion action against Scott.]

In support of the nonsuit respondent argues that Scott thought he was disposing of so much junk or rubbish in the form of barrels, that, therefore, he cannot be held for the conversion of full barrels of wine or for the value of wine in barrels. Further it is said that it is fallacious to argue that the loss of the wine was the consequence of any act of Scott, or that any act of Scott produced it, or that there was any chain of connection, broken or unbroken, between Scott's act and the injury to Poggi, or that the loss to Poggi of his wine was the result, proximate or otherwise, of any act of Scott, or that Scott's act caused it in any sense at all.

If respondent's premises, as here stated, are correct, the conclusion of his nonliability is unassailable. But are they correct? The foundation for the action of conversion rests neither in the knowledge nor the intent of the defendant. It rests upon the unwarranted interference by defendant with the dominion over the property of the plaintiff from which injury to the latter results. Therefore, neither good nor bad faith, neither care nor negligence, neither knowledge nor ignorance, are of the gist of the action. "The plaintiff's right of redress no longer depends upon his showing, in any way, that the defendant did the act in question from wrongful motives, or generally speaking, even intentionally; and hence the want of such motives, or of intention, is no defense. Nor, indeed, is negligence any necessary part of the case. Here, then, is a class of cases in which the tort consists in the breach of what may be called an absolute duty; the act itself (in some cases it must have caused damage) is unlawful and redressible as a tort." (1 Bigelow on Torts, p.6.) And says Judge Cooley (Cubit v. O'Dett, 51 Mich. 347, [46 Atl. 679]): "Absence of bad faith can never excuse a trespass, though the existence of bad faith may sometimes aggravate it. Every one must be sure of his legal right when he invades the possession of another."

In consonance with the principles of law thus declared no question can arise of the defendant's responsibility under the evidence. Conceding all that may be argued as to the absence of improper motives on the part of the defendant, the all important fact yet remains, under his own testimony, that he sold barrels that did not belong to him and which did with their contents belong to the plaintiff. That he did not know that the barrels contained wine did not excuse his conduct. He had no legal right to sell the barrels whether or not they contained wine. He was exercising an unjustifiable and unwarranted dominion and control over the property of another and from his acts great loss resulted to that other. If he did not, in fact, know that the barrels contained wine, at least his suspicions were aroused that they were not empty as is evidenced by his statement to Bernardini that if the barrels were not empty and did contain something they would make a different bargain. . . .

[Reversed.]

NOTES

1. *The reach of conversion.* The intent requirement that caused such difficulty in *Vosburg* and *Perry* also presents problems in cases of conversion, whereby the defendant takes, or as in *Poggi*, sells, property belonging to

the plaintiff. Without question, the sale in question is deliberate in that the defendant claims ownership, or dominion, over the chattels that are taken or stolen. Yet as in cases of trespass to chattels or real property, the want of an intention to harm, or the existence of material mistake about the ownership or condition of the property does not excuse the conversion, which obliges the defendant to pay for the value of the goods taken, even if, as in *Poggi*, the defendant did not pocket the proceeds of that conversion or sale. In general, conversion can be committed by dealing with goods in the role of an owner, whether by buying, selling, using, altering, delivering the chattel, or, most critically, refusing to surrender the chattel to its proper owner. See RST §223, where comment *b* provides

> b. Necessity of intent. Conversion is always an intentional exercise of dominion or control over the chattel. Mere non-feasance or negligence, without such an intent, is not sufficient for conversion. (See §224.) If the actor has the intent to do the act exercising dominion or control, however, he is not relieved from liability by his mistaken belief that he has possession of the chattel or the right to possession, or that he is privileged to act. (See §244.)

Under the Restatement formulation, the chief difficulty lies in setting the boundaries between conversion and trespass to chattels under *Hamidi*. Trespass to chattels required the plaintiff to show that the defendant carried off goods which were in the plaintiff's *possession*. The Latin name for the wrong was *de bonis asportatis* (or trespass dba)—the asportation of chattels. Since the trespass is solely an offense to possession alone, the plaintiff could maintain the action even if some third party had a title paramount to either plaintiff's or defendant's. In contrast, conversion could be brought by any party who claimed either ownership rights in the thing or some right to its immediate possession.

Clearly, most cases of trespass to chattels are also conversions, and vice versa. But the overlap is not complete in either direction. Thus, conversion alone was held to lie for *A* against *C* when *C* had taken the property from *B*, who had previously taken it from *A*. Trespass was inappropriate because at the time of *C*'s wrong, *B* had possession of the goods. See J. B. Ames, Lectures in Legal History 60-61 (1913). Conversion, however, was proper because the plaintiff, as owner, had the immediate right to possession. See Gordon v. Harper, 101 Eng. Rep. 828 (K.B. 1796). For the complications created when chattels were bailed, mortgaged, leased, or subject to contract of sale, see The Winkfield, [1902] P. 42. See generally 1 Harper, James & Gray, Torts (3d ed.) §§2.16-2.25.

Conversely, only trespass would lie when the defendant had taken possession of the plaintiff's goods without claiming ownership of them. See, e.g., Fouldes v. Willoughby, 151 Eng. Rep. 1153 (Ex. 1841), in which the plaintiff passenger brought an action in conversion against the defendant ferryman, who removed plaintiff's horses from his ferry before setting sail. In dismissing the action, Lord Abinger, C.B., said that "a simple asportation of a chattel, without any intention of making any further use of it, although it may be a sufficient foundation for an action of trespass, is not sufficient to establish a conversion." The defendant in *Fouldes* offered to justify his conduct by saying that he removed the animals in order to induce the plaintiff, who was misbehaving, to leave the ferry. Should the success of that defense depend upon the choice of the original action? On trespass and conversion, see generally F. Pollock and R. Wright, Possession in the Common Law (1888); 1 Harper, James & Gray, Torts (3d ed.) §§2.14-2.15. On the earlier history of the various writs see F. W. Maitland, The Forms of Action at Common Law, Lectures V and VI (1936).

2. *Good and bad faith conversions.* Maye v. Tappan, 23 Cal. 306, 307-308 (1863), reconfirms the tough standard used in conversion cases. The defendant dug up gold-bearing earth from the plaintiffs' land, after the plaintiffs mistakenly, but sincerely, told the defendant that he owned the land. The court awarded the plaintiffs damages equal to the value of the gold, less the cost of its extraction and refinement, holding it "immaterial" "whether the defendants acted willfully and maliciously, or ignorantly and innocently, in digging up and taking away the gold-bearing earth."

Oliver Wendell Holmes defended that result in his classic book, The Common Law 97 (1881):

> Take first the case of trespass upon land attended by actual damage. When a man goes upon his neighbor's land, thinking it is his own, he intends the very act or consequence complained of. He means to intermeddle with a certain thing in a certain way, and it is just that intended intermeddling for which he is sued. It might be answered, to be sure, that it is not for intermeddling with property, but for intermeddling with the plaintiff's property, that a man is sued and that in the supposed cases the defendant is ignorant of one of the facts making up the total environment, and which must be present to make his action wrong. He is ignorant, that is to say, that the true owner either has or claims any interest in the property in question, and therefore he does not intend a wrongful act, because he does not mean to deal with his neighbor's property. But the answer to this is, that he does intend to do the damage complained of. One who diminishes the value of property by intentional damage knows it belongs to somebody. If he thinks it belongs to himself, he expects whatever harm he may do to come out of his own pocket. It would be odd if he were to get rid of the burden by discovering that it belonged to his neighbor. It is a very different thing to say he who intentionally does harm must bear the loss, from saying that one from whose acts harm follows accidentally, as a consequence which could not have been foreseen, must bear it.

Unlike determinations of liability, the measure of damages does depend on the defendant's mental state. Neither party in *Maye* thought the plaintiff intended to make a gift when he said that he thought that the defendant owned the gold deposit. Such mistakes are common in mining territory. Allowing the defendant to obtain a credit for the cost of extraction returns the situation to what it would have been if the mistake had not been made in the first place. The defendant need not make a gift of services to the plaintiff. But if he takes ore or cuts plaintiff's trees in bad faith (that is, with knowledge that they belong to another) he receives no offset for the labor expended, which discourages his conscious violation of the plaintiff's rights, for now he is left worse off than he would have been if he had not taken the gold at all.

3. *Trespass versus conversion: the measure of damage.* Notwithstanding the different theories for trespass and conversion, many wrongs fall within the scope of both. From the early 1600s, it was settled that the plaintiff could elect the more advantageous action when both were available. The choice often rested upon the type of relief the plaintiff wanted to secure. Originally, conversion proceeded on a theory of the "forced sale," under which the defendant, as the owner of the plaintiff's property, was now made to buy it at the full market price — even if the defendant was willing to return it. Today, that rule has been relaxed in most jurisdictions, and the innocent converter may generally return the property taken, at least if it has not suffered substantial damage, conditional upon payment for the loss of interim use or for repairs. RST §922.

Historically, the rule was otherwise with trespass to chattels, for the damages in question were limited to the reduction in value of the chattel. The defendant was therefore able to force the plaintiff to take the chattel back, so that the full price was awarded only in cases of complete destruction. For an exchange on the proper remedies for conversion, see Ayres, Protecting Property with Puts, 32 Val. U. L. Rev. 793, 813-818 (1998); Epstein, Protecting Property Rights with Legal Remedies: A Common Sense Reply to Professor Ayres, 32 Val. U. L. Rev. 833, 845-852 (1998).

Moore v. Regents of the University of California
793 P.2d 479 (Cal. 1990)

PANELLI, J. We granted review in this case to determine whether plaintiff has stated a cause of action against his physician and other defendants for using his cells in potentially lucrative medical research without his permission. Plaintiff alleges that his physician failed to disclose preexisting research and economic interests in the cells before obtaining consent to the medical procedures by which they were extracted. The superior court sustained all defendants' demurrers to the third amended complaint, and the Court of Appeal reversed. We hold that the complaint states a cause of action for breach of the physician's disclosure obligations, but not for conversion.

The plaintiff is John Moore (Moore), who underwent treatment for hairy-cell leukemia at the Medical Center of the University of California at Los Angeles (UCLA Medical Center). The five defendants are: (1) Dr. David W. Golde (Golde), a physician who attended Moore at UCLA Medical Center; (2) the Regents of the University of California (Regents), who own and operate the university; (3) Shirley G. Quan, a researcher employed by the Regents; (4) Genetics Institute, Inc. (Genetics Institute); and (5) Sandoz Pharmaceuticals Corporation and related entities (collectively Sandoz).

[Moore first visited UCLA Medical Center in 1976, shortly after he learned that he had hairy-cell leukemia. Dr. Golde confirmed the earlier diagnosis, and Moore's 14-pound plus spleen was removed, with his consent, in order to save his life. Even before the operation, Golde and Quan knew that Moore's blood products could have great commercial uses unrelated to his medical care. But neither Golde nor Quan informed Moore of their research plan or asked for his permission to use his spleen for medical research. Moore also flew in from Seattle to UCLA several times between 1976 and 1983, having been told falsely that these visits, which were designed to collect more research materials, were "necessary and required for his well-being." "On each of these visits Golde withdrew additional samples of 'blood, blood serum, skin, bone marrow aspirate, and sperm.'"

Sometime before August 1979, Golde established a cell line from Moore's T-lymphocytes, white blood cells that regulate the immune system. In 1981, the Regents applied for a patent on the cell line, listing Golde and Quan as inventors. "[B]y virtue of an established policy . . . , [the] Regents, Golde, and Quan would share in any royalties or profits . . . arising out of [the] patent." The patent issued in 1984, naming Golde and Quan as the inventors of the cell line and the Regents as the assignee of the patent.

With the Regents' assistance, Golde negotiated agreements for commercial development of the cell line and products to be derived from it. Under an agreement with Genetics Institute, Golde became a paid consultant with stock options, and Quan continued to work largely on the project. Sandoz joined the group in 1982.]

[Panelli, J., first concluded that nondisclosure of collateral research motives was a violation of the physicians' duties of disclosure.] Accordingly, we hold that a physician who is seeking a patient's consent for a medical procedure must, in order to satisfy his fiduciary duty and to obtain the patient's informed consent, disclose personal interests unrelated to the patient's health, whether research or economic, that may affect his medical judgment.

B. CONVERSION

Moore also attempts to characterize the invasion of his rights as a conversion—a tort that protects against interference with possessory and ownership interests in personal property. He theorizes that he continued to own his cells following their removal from his body, at least for the purpose of directing their use, and that he never consented to their use in potentially lucrative medical research. Thus, to complete Moore's argument, defendants' unauthorized use of his cells constitutes a conversion. As a result of the alleged conversion, Moore claims a proprietary interest in each of the products that any of the defendants might ever create from his cells or the patented cell line.

No court, however, has ever in a reported decision imposed conversion liability for the use of human cells in medical research. While that fact does not end our inquiry, it raises a flag of caution. In effect, what Moore is asking us to do is to impose a tort duty on scientists to investigate the consensual pedigree of each human cell sample used in research. To impose such a duty, which would affect medical research of importance to all of society, implicates policy concerns far removed from the traditional, two-party ownership disputes in which the law of conversion arose. Invoking a tort theory originally used to determine whether the loser or the finder of a horse had the better title, Moore claims ownership of the results of socially important medical research, including the genetic code for chemicals that regulate the functions of every human being's immune system.

. . . [W]e first consider whether the tort of conversion clearly gives Moore a cause of action under existing law. We do not believe it does. Because of the novelty of Moore's claim to own the biological materials at issue, to apply the theory of conversion in this context would frankly have to be recognized as an extension of the theory. Therefore, we consider next whether it is advisable to extend the tort to this context.

1. Moore's Claim Under Existing Law

"To establish a conversion, plaintiff must establish an actual interference with his *ownership* or *right of possession*. . . . Where plaintiff neither has title to the property alleged to have been converted, nor possession thereof, he cannot maintain an action for conversion."

Since Moore clearly did not expect to retain possession of his cells following their removal,[20] to sue for their conversion he must have retained an ownership interest in them. But there are several reasons to doubt that he did retain any such interest. First, no reported judicial decision supports Moore's claim, either directly or by close analogy. Second, California statutory law drastically limits any continuing interest of a patient in excised

---

20. In his complaint, Moore does not seek possession of his cells or claim the right to possess them. This is consistent with Health and Safety Code section 7054.4, which provides that "human tissues . . . following conclusion of scientific use shall be disposed of by interment, incineration, or any other method determined by the state department [of health services] to protect the public health and safety."

cells. Third, the subject matters of the Regents' patent—the patented cell line and the products derived from it—cannot be Moore's property.

Neither the Court of Appeal's opinion, the parties' briefs, nor our research discloses a case holding that a person retains a sufficient interest in excised cells to support a cause of action for conversion. We do not find this surprising, since the laws governing such things as human tissues, transplantable organs, blood, fetuses, pituitary glands, corneal tissue, and dead bodies deal with human biological materials as objects sui generis, regulating their disposition to achieve policy goals rather than abandoning them to the general law of personal property. It is these specialized statutes, not the law of conversion, to which courts ordinarily should and do look for guidance on the disposition of human biological materials. . . .

2. Should Conversion Liability Be Extended?

There are three reasons why it is inappropriate to impose liability for conversion based upon the allegations of Moore's complaint. First, a fair balancing of the relevant policy considerations counsels against extending the tort. Second, problems in this area are better suited to legislative resolution. Third, the tort of conversion is not necessary to protect patients' rights. For these reasons, we conclude that the use of excised human cells in medical research does not amount to a conversion.

Of the relevant policy considerations, two are of overriding importance. The first is protection of a competent patient's right to make autonomous medical decisions. That right, as already discussed, is grounded in well-recognized and long-standing principles of fiduciary duty and informed consent. This policy weighs in favor of providing a remedy to patients when physicians act with undisclosed motives that may affect their professional judgment. The second important policy consideration is that we not threaten with disabling civil liability innocent parties who are engaged in socially useful activities, such as researchers who have no reason to believe that their use of a particular cell sample is, or may be, against a donor's wishes.

To reach an appropriate balance of these policy considerations is extremely important. . . .

We need not, however, make an arbitrary choice between liability and nonliability. Instead, an examination of the relevant policy considerations suggests an appropriate balance: Liability based upon existing disclosure obligations, rather than an unprecedented extension of the conversion theory, protects patients' rights of privacy and autonomy without unnecessarily hindering research.

To be sure, the threat of liability for conversion might help to enforce patients' rights indirectly. This is because physicians might be able to avoid liability by obtaining patients' consent, in the broadest possible terms, to any conceivable subsequent research use of excised cells. Unfortunately, to extend the conversion theory would utterly sacrifice the other goal of protecting innocent parties. Since conversion is a strict liability tort, it would impose liability on all those into whose hands the cells come, whether or not the particular defendant participated in, or knew of, the inadequate disclosures that violated the patient's right to make an informed decision. In contrast to the conversion theory, the fiduciary-duty and informed-consent theories protect the patient directly, without punishing innocent parties or creating disincentives to the conduct of socially beneficial research.

To expand liability by extending conversion law into this area would have a broad impact. [The court then concludes that the creation of tort liability will dull the incentives for medical innovation.] If the use of cells in research is a conversion, then with every cell sample a researcher purchases a ticket in a litigation lottery. Because liability for conversion is predicated on a continuing ownership interest, "companies are unlikely to invest heavily in developing, manufacturing, or marketing a product when uncertainty about clear title exists."

If the scientific users of human cells are to be held liable for failing to investigate the consensual pedigree of their raw materials, we believe the Legislature should make that decision.

Finally, there is no pressing need to impose a judicially created rule of strict liability, since enforcement of physicians' disclosure obligations will protect patients against the very type of harm with which Moore was threatened. So long as a physician discloses research and economic interests that may affect his judgment, the patient is protected from conflicts of interest. Aware of any conflicts, the patient can make an informed decision to consent to treatment, or to withhold consent and look elsewhere for medical assistance. As already discussed, enforcement of physicians' disclosure obligations protects patients directly, without hindering the socially useful activities of innocent researchers.

For these reasons, we hold that the allegations of Moore's third amended complaint state a cause of action for breach of fiduciary duty or lack of informed consent, but not conversion.

LUCAS, C.J., and EAGLESON and KENNARD, JJ., concur.

[The concurring opinion of Arabian, J., is omitted.]

BROUSSARD, J., concurring and dissenting. . . .

II

. . . I dissent from the majority's conclusion that the facts alleged in this case do not state a cause of action for conversion.

If this were a typical case in which a patient consented to the use of his removed organ for general research purposes and the patient's doctor had no prior knowledge of the scientific or commercial value of the patient's organ or cells, I would agree that the patient could not maintain a conversion action. In that common scenario, the patient has abandoned any interest in the removed organ and is not entitled to demand compensation if it should later be discovered that the organ or cells have some unanticipated value. I cannot agree, however, with the majority that a patient may *never* maintain a conversion action for the unauthorized use of his excised organ or cells, even against a party who knew of the value of the organ or cells before they were removed and breached a duty to disclose that value to the patient. Because plaintiff alleges that defendants wrongfully interfered with his right to determine, prior to the removal of his body parts, how those parts would be used after removal, I conclude that the complaint states a cause of action under traditional, common law conversion principles. . . .

MOSK, J., dissenting.

[Mosk, J., first argues that an acceptance of legislative dominance does not require judicial passivity in applying traditional common law principles of conversion to "the recent explosive growth in the commercialization of biotechnology." Next, he argues that the current legislative schemes do not preclude the sale of human organs removed for medical reasons. He then turns to a comparison of conversion with the informed consent action. After noting the difficulties of proving causation in informed consent cases, he continues:]

The second reason why the nondisclosure cause of action is inadequate for the task that the majority assign to it is that it fails to solve half the problem before us: it gives the patient only the right to *refuse* consent, i.e., the right to prohibit the commercialization of his tissue; it does not give him the right to *grant* consent to that commercialization on the condition that he share in its proceeds. . . .

Reversing the words of the old song, the nondisclosure cause of action thus accentuates the negative and eliminates the positive: the patient can say no, but he cannot say yes and expect to share in the proceeds of his contribution. . . .

Third, the nondisclosure cause of action fails to reach a major class of potential defendants: all those who are outside the strict physician-patient relationship with the plaintiff. . . .

To the extent that a plaintiff such as Moore is unable to plead or prove a satisfactory theory of secondary liability, the nondisclosure cause of action will thus be inadequate to reach a number of parties to the commercial exploitation of his tissue. Such parties include, for example, any physician-researcher who is not personally treating the patient, any other researcher who is not a physician, any employer of the foregoing (or even of the treating physician), and any person or corporation thereafter participating in the commercial exploitation of the tissue. Yet some or all of those parties may well have participated more in, and profited more from, such exploitation than the particular physician with whom the plaintiff happened to have a formal doctor-patient relationship at the time.

NOTES

1. *Voluntary donation of blood samples for medical research.* What are the different consequences of the nondisclosure and conversion theories? This question in turn breaks down into two parts. The first looks back at this case: How much more in damages could Moore recover under the conversion theory than the nondisclosure theory? Under both theories what allowance should be made for the value added by the work of the research scientists? The second part of the question looks forward to future transactions. Once disclosures are made to patients, can they hold out for a royalty on future invention? Demand that the organ be destroyed? Go overseas to an establishment that will pay for the organ use? For the details of Moore's history, see Skloot, Taking the Least of You, N.Y. Times Magazine, Apr. 16, 2006, at 38. For an argument that contract principles should dominate these cases, with a weak default presumption against compensation, see Korobkin, "No Compensation" or "Pro Compensation": *Moore v. Regents* and Default Rules for Human Tissue Donations, 40 J. Health L. 1 (2007).

In Greenberg v. Miami Children's Hospital Research Institute, Inc., 264 F. Supp. 2d 1064 (S.D. Fla. 2003), the plaintiffs were parents of Ashkenazi Jewish children afflicted with Canavan's Disease, a fatal genetic affliction. In 1987, the plaintiff group approached Dr. Reuben Matalon, then in Chicago, with offers to provide him voluntarily with blood samples needed to isolate the gene for Canavan's disease. Matalon's research, first in Chicago and later in Miami, identified the key gene. Thereafter Matalon and his group patented the gene which enabled them to restrict research access of others to the gene. They also threatened suit against medical centers that offered Canavan testing. The plaintiffs claimed that they had collected the samples with the specific "understanding and expectations" that their use in research on the disease and the products of that research "would remain in the public domain." Their claim for a breach of the duty of informed consent was dismissed on the ground that all collection efforts took place outside any treatment relationship between physician and patient. Relying on *Moore*, Moreno, J., also rejected the count for conversion:

> First, Plaintiffs have no cognizable property interest in body tissue and genetic matter donated for research under a theory of conversion. . . .
>
> The Court finds that Florida statutory and common law do not provide a remedy for Plaintiffs' donations of body tissue and blood samples under a theory of conversion liability. Indeed, the Complaint does not allege that the

Defendants used the genetic material for any purpose but medical research. Plaintiffs claim that the *fruits* of the research, namely the patented material, was commercialized. This is an important distinction and another step in the chain of attenuation that renders conversion liability inapplicable to the facts as alleged. If adopted, the expansive theory championed by Plaintiffs would cripple medical research as it would bestow a continuing right for donors to possess the results of any research conducted by the hospital. At the core, these were donations to research without any contemporaneous expectations of return.

The Court did hold that the plaintiff's count for unjust enrichment survived summary judgment. How should the plaintiffs have proceeded at the outset in order to make sure that the results of their funded research remained in the public domain? And why should the gene itself be patentable, as opposed to the processes used for its isolation and detection? And if protected, should it be only with respect to its use in manufacturing, as opposed to its effect in situ?

2. *Statutory modifications.* Florida Statute §760.40 (West 2007) provides:

> (1) As used in this section, the term "DNA analysis" means the medical and biological examination and analysis of a person to identify the presence and composition of genes in that person's body. The term includes DNA typing and genetic testing.
>
> (2)(a) Except for [criminal prosecution and investigation], DNA analysis may be performed only with the informed consent of the person to be tested, and the results of such DNA analysis, whether held by a public or private entity, are the exclusive property of the person tested, are confidential, and may not be disclosed without the consent of the person tested. . . .
>
>> (b) A person who violates paragraph (a) is guilty of a misdemeanor of the first degree . . . .

3. *Conversion of intangible property.* In Kremen v. Cohen, 337 F.3d 1024, 1032-1034 (9th Cir. 2003), the plaintiff, Kremen, registered the domain name sex.com with the defendant, Internet domain registrar Network Solutions. Online Classifieds was listed as the owner of the domain name, with Kremen as the contact person. Shortly thereafter, Cohen, a long-time swindler, sent a letter to Network Solutions telling it that Online Solutions had dismissed Kremen, had decided to abandon the use of the domain name sex.com, and announced that it had no objection if Cohen used that name. Cohen promptly used the name to create "a lucrative online porn empire." Cohen's letter was a total fabrication, but Network Solutions never checked with Kremen to see if Cohen's claims were true. Once aware of the fraud, Kremen sued Cohen, who had fled to Mexico, and Network Solutions for conversion. Network Solutions first claimed that under the Restatement (Second) of Torts, §242, conversion for intangibles was

only available if the intangible had been "merged" into a document. Kozinski, J., rebuffed that claim: "On the contrary, courts routinely apply the tort to intangibles without inquiring whether they are merged in a document and, while it's often possible to dream up *some* document the intangible is connected to in some fashion, it's seldom one that represents the owner's property interest. . . . [The strict merger] rule cannot be squared with a jurisprudence that recognizes conversion of music recordings, radio shows, customer lists, regulatory filings, confidential information and even domain names." He then held that even if California law had such a requirement, it had been met because Kremen's name was stored in the defendant's Domain Name System, which counted as "a document (or perhaps more accurately a collection of documents). That it is stored in electronic form rather than on ink and paper is immaterial." Finally, he addressed the question of liability in ways reminiscent of *Rossi*:

> The [district] court was reluctant to apply the tort of conversion because of its strict liability nature. This concern rings somewhat hollow in this case because the district court effectively exempted Network Solutions from liability to Kremen altogether, whether or not it was negligent. Network Solutions made no effort to contact Kremen before giving away his domain name, despite receiving a facially suspect letter from a third party. A jury would be justified in finding it was unreasonably careless.
>
> We must, of course, take the broader view, but there is nothing unfair about holding a company responsible for giving away someone else's property even if it was not at fault. Cohen is obviously the guilty party here, and the one who should in all fairness pay for his theft. But he's skipped the country, and his money is stashed in some offshore bank account. Unless Kremen's luck with his bounty hunters improves, Cohen is out of the picture. The question becomes whether Network Solutions should be open to liability for its decision to hand over Kremen's domain name. Negligent or not, it was Network Solutions that gave away Kremen's property. Kremen never did anything. It would not be unfair to hold Network Solutions responsible and force *it* to try to recoup its losses by chasing down Cohen. This, at any rate, is the logic of the common law, and we do not lightly discard it.

Note that the scam in Kremen took place in 1994 just when the Web was getting started. The early standard contract contained none of the limitations against consequential damages (i.e., those damages that flow in consequence of the breach) for the misassignment of domain names that are now part of its standard agreement. Given that Network Solutions was uncompensated, why shouldn't its contractual standard of liability be that of acting in good faith? See Epstein, The Roman Law of Cyberconversion, 2005 Mich. St. L. Rev. 103 (2005). Note that courts continue to apply the tort of conversion to protect various forms of property. See, e.g., Thyroff v. Nationwide Mutual Insurance Co., 864 N.E.2d 1272, 1278 (N.Y. 2007), which held that "electronic records that were stored on a computer and were indistinguishable from printed documents—are subject to a claim of conversion in New York."

3. *Defenses to Intentional Torts*

a. **Consensual Defenses**

Mohr v. Williams
104 N.W. 12 (Minn. 1905)

BROWN, J. Defendant is a physician and surgeon of standing and character, making disorders of the ear a specialty, and having an extensive practice in the city of St. Paul. He was consulted by plaintiff, who complained to him of trouble with her right ear, and, at her request, made an examination of that organ for the purpose of ascertaining its condition. He also at the same time examined her left ear, but, owing to foreign substances therein, was unable to make a full and complete diagnosis at that time. The examination of her right ear disclosed a large perforation in the lower portion of the drum membrane, and a large polyp in the middle ear, which indicated that some of the small bones of the middle ear (ossicles) were probably diseased. He informed plaintiff of the result of his examination, and advised an operation for the purpose of removing the polyp and diseased ossicles. After consultation with her family physician, and one or two further consultations with defendant, plaintiff decided to submit to the proposed operation. She was not informed that her left ear was in any way diseased, and understood that the necessity for an operation applied to her right ear only. She repaired to the hospital, and was placed under the influence of anaesthetics; and, after being made unconscious, defendant made a thorough examination of her left ear, and found it in a more serious condition than her right one. A small perforation was discovered high up in the drum membrane, hooded, and with granulated edges, and the bone of the inner wall of the middle ear was diseased and dead. He called this discovery to the attention of Dr. Davis—plaintiff's family physician, who attended the operation at her request—who also examined the ear and confirmed defendant in his diagnosis. Defendant also further examined the right ear, and found its condition less serious than expected, and finally concluded that the left, instead of the right, should be operated upon; devoting to the right ear other treatment. He then performed the operation of ossiculectomy on plaintiff's left ear; removing a portion of the drum membrane, and scraping away the diseased portion of the inner wall of the ear. The operation was in every way successful and skillfully performed. It is claimed by plaintiff that the operation greatly impaired her hearing, seriously injured her person, and, not having been consented to by her, was wrongful and unlawful, constituting an assault and battery; and she brought this action to recover damages therefor.

The trial in the court below resulted in a verdict for plaintiff for $14,322.50. [The trial judge set aside the verdict as excessive and ordered a new trial. Both parties appealed from those orders. On appeal Brown, J., first refused to overturn the jury's finding of no emergency. He then held that plaintiff's consent to the operation could not be implied, and said in part:]

The last contention of defendant is that the act complained of did not amount to an assault and battery. This is based upon the theory that, as plaintiff's left ear was in fact diseased, in a condition dangerous and threatening to her health, the operation was necessary, and, having been skillfully performed at a time when plaintiff had requested a like operation on the other ear, the charge of assault and battery cannot be sustained; that, in view of these conditions, and the claim that there was no negligence on the part of defendant, and an entire absence of any evidence tending to show an evil intent, the court should say, as a matter of law, that no assault and battery was committed, even though she did not consent to the operation. In other words, that the absence of a showing that defendant was actuated by a wrongful intent, or guilty of negligence, relieves the act of defendant from the charge of an unlawful assault and battery.

We are unable to reach that conclusion, though the contention is not without merit. It would seem to follow from what has been said on the other features of the case that the act of defendant amounted at least to a technical assault and battery. If the operation was performed without plaintiff's consent, and the circumstances were not such as to justify its performance without, it was wrongful; and, if it was wrongful, it was unlawful. As remarked in 1 Jaggard, Torts, 437, every person has a right to complete immunity of his person from physical interference of others, except in so far as contact may be necessary under the general doctrine of privilege; and any unlawful or unauthorized touching of the person of another, except it be in the spirit of pleasantry, constitutes an assault and battery. In the case at bar, as we have already seen, the question whether defendant's act in performing the operation upon plaintiff was authorized was a question for the jury to determine. If it was unauthorized, then it was, within what we have said, unlawful. It was a violent assault, not a mere pleasantry; and, even though no negligence is shown, it was wrongful and unlawful. The case is unlike a criminal prosecution for assault and battery, for there an unlawful intent must be shown. But that rule does not apply to a civil action, to maintain which it is sufficient to show that the assault complained of was wrongful and unlawful or the result of negligence. . . . Vosburg v. Putney, 80 Wis. 523, 50 N.W. 403.

The amount of plaintiff's recovery, if she is entitled to recover at all, must depend upon the character and extent of the injury inflicted upon her, in determining which the nature of the malady intended to be healed and the beneficial nature of the operation should be taken into consideration, as well as the good faith of the defendant.

Orders affirmed.

NOTES

1. *Determining the scope of consent.* Did the physician in Mohr v. Williams violently attack or batter his patient solely because he did not obtain the requisite consent to perform the operation? Should Dr. Davis be treated as plaintiff's agent? Why did the trial judge conclude that the jury awarded excessive damages? (On remand, the jury awarded only nominal damages.) More modern cases take a less rigid view of the consent requirement. In Kennedy v. Parrott, 90 S.E.2d 754, 759 (N.C. 1956), the defendant surgeon, while performing the plaintiff's appendectomy, discovered several large cysts on the plaintiff's left ovary, which in his best medical judgment he intentionally punctured the cysts, without negligence. Unfortunately, the puncture cut one of plaintiff's blood vessels, from which she developed a painful phlebitis in her leg. The court denied her action for trespass even though she did not consent to the puncturing of the cysts, noting that in modern hospital settings surgeons could no longer turn to the guidance of family members. It concluded:

> In major internal operations, both the patient and the surgeon know that the exact condition of the patient cannot be finally and definitely diagnosed until after the patient is completely anesthetized and the incision has been made. In such case the consent—in the absence of proof to the contrary—will be construed as general in nature and the surgeon may extend the operation to remedy any abnormal or diseased condition in the area of the original incision whenever he, in the exercise of his sound professional judgment, determines that correct surgical procedure dictates and requires such an extension of the operation originally contemplated. This rule applies when the patient is at the time incapable of giving consent, and no one with authority to consent for him is immediately available.

Does *Kennedy* support the conventional view that "the absence of consent is a matter essential to the cause of action, and it is uniformly held that it must be proved by the plaintiff as a necessary part of his case." RST §13, comment *d*.

To avoid many of the factual issues in cases like *Mohr* and *Kennedy* physicians and hospitals often resort to a form similar to that found in

R. Morris and A. Moritz, *Doctor and Patient and the Law* (5th ed. 1971), including authorization for different procedures found in Clause 2. These forms are commonly modified in individual cases to prohibit from the outside certain kinds of procedures. In Hoofnel v. Segal, 199 S.W.3d 147, 151 (Ky. 2006), the plaintiff, a woman aged 56 and of limited education, came to the defendant physicians needing the removal of a lesion from her colon. The surgeon, Dr. Galandiuk, recommended that she be allowed to perform an operation to remove both plaintiff's uterus and ovaries. The plaintiff told her that she did not want "any of my female parts removed." Nonetheless, she later signed a consent form that authorized both procedures if necessary. During surgery Dr. Galandiuk consulted with Dr. Segal, and both agreed that the organs had to be removed because of their enlarged size and possible cancerous condition. Graves, J., held that the "clear and unambiguous words of the consent form" dominated the prior conversations.

> The essence of [appellant Hoofnel's] argument is that she did not actually intend for her signature to grant consent. Appellant testified that she told Dr. Galandiuk, during an initial consultation, that she did not want her ovaries or uterus removed. Even assuming this conversation to be accurate, her signature on the consent form directly authorized one of these procedures and thus superseded this previous intention. The additional surgical procedure to remove the uterus became medically necessary once the enlarged uterus was observed as it impaired and impeded Dr. Galandiuk's ability to resect the lesion in the colon. The existence of a signed consent form gives rise to a presumption that patients ordinarily read and take whatever other measures are necessary to understand the nature, terms and general meaning of consent. To hold otherwise would negate the legal significance to written consent forms signed by the patient and render the consent form completely unreliable.

Cooper, J., in dissent, protested the excessive reliance on the consent form relative to the entire "process" that proceeding and followed the signing. On the majority view, what overrides the "presumption" that attaches to the form? Why is this not a case of informed consent? On informed consent, see Chapter 3, Section D.

2. *Consent implied in fact.* Although consent is normally expressed in words, it may also be inferred from conduct. In O'Brien v. Cunard Steamship Co., 28 N.E. 266 (Mass. 1891), the plaintiff was an immigrant to the United States whose entry into this country required vaccination against smallpox. She stood in line with many other female passengers and held out her arm to the defendant's surgeon, who inspected it and noted the lack of the typical mark found after smallpox vaccinations. Thereafter he told her that she had to be vaccinated, and she replied that her previous vaccination had left no mark. The physician did not respond further, and

Consent to Operation, Anesthetics, and other Medical Services*

Date _____ Time _____ $\begin{array}{l}\text{A.M.}\\\text{P.M.}\end{array}$

1. I authorize the performance upon _____
   (myself or name of patient)
of the following operation _____, to be
   (state nature and extent of operation)
performed under the direction of Dr. _____.

2. I consent to the performance of operations and procedures in addition to or different from those now contemplated, whether or not arising from presently unforeseen conditions, which the above-named doctor or his associates or assistants may consider necessary or advisable in the course of the operation.

3. I consent to the administration of such anesthetics as may be considered necessary or advisable by the physician responsible for this service, with the exception of

_____.
   (state "none," "spinal anesthesia," etc.)

4. I consent to the photographing or televising of the operations or procedures to be performed, including appropriate portions of my body, for medical, scientific, or educational purposes, provided my identity is not revealed by the pictures or by descriptive texts accompanying them.

5. For the purpose of advancing medical education, I consent to the admittance of observers to the operating room.

6. I consent to the disposal by hospital authorities of any tissues or parts that may be removed.

7. I am aware that sterility may result from this operation. I know that a sterile person is incapable of becoming a parent.

8. The nature and purpose of the operation, possible alternative methods of treatment, the risks involved, and the possibility of complications have been fully explained to me. No guarantee or assurance has been given by anyone as to the results that may be obtained.

(cross out any paragraphs above which do not apply)

Signed _____
   (patient or person authorized to consent for patient)

Witness _____

---

*This is a general form of consent that will apply to various procedures by striking out the portions that are inapplicable.

plaintiff held up her arm and allowed the vaccination to take place, after which she received her entry ticket. The alternative to vaccination was detainment and quarantine. The court held that her consent barred her cause of action. "If the plaintiff's behavior was such as to indicate consent on her part, the surgeon was justified in his act, whatever her unexpressed feelings may have been. In determining whether she consented, he could be guided only by her overt acts and the manifestations of her feelings." Plaintiff "was one of a large number of women who were vaccinated on that occasion, without, so far as appears, a word of objection from any of them. They all indicated by their conduct that they desired to avail themselves of the provisions made for their benefit. There was nothing in the conduct of the plaintiff to indicate to the surgeon that she did not wish to obtain a card which would save her from detention at quarantine, and to be vaccinated, if necessary for that purpose." Would it have been rational for her to refuse treatment?

3. *Emergency rule.* Normally a patient has the right to accept or reject the proffered medical treatment, making an unauthorized operation a technical assault and battery even if no damage ensues. See Schloendorff v. Society of New York Hospital, 105 N.E. 92, 93 (N.Y. 1914). "Every human being of adult years and sound mind has a right to determine what shall be done with his own body; and a surgeon who performs an operation without his patient's consent, commits an assault, for which he is liable in damages. This is true except in cases of emergency where the patient is unconscious and where it is necessary to operate before consent can be obtained." Sometimes the emergency rule is cast in the language of implied consent. "Medical treatment also will be lawful under the doctrine of implied consent when a medical emergency requires immediate action to preserve the health or life of the patient." Allore v. Flower Hospital, 699 N.E.2d 560, 564 (Ohio App. 1997). This implied consent is a legal fiction, justified by the assumption that the plaintiff, as a rational agent, would have consented to the operation if she could have been asked. This rule thus protects otherwise helpless patients by encouraging others to assist them in time of need. Should the bystander whose quick intervention saves the plaintiff's life receive compensation? What about the surgeon who operates, even if unsuccessful? See Cotnam v. Wisdom, 104 S.W. 164 (Ark. 1907), allowing the action, but only for a successful outcome, while barring higher fees based on the physician's special knowledge of the decedent's wealth. Why are these two conditions attached to the compensation right?

4. *Minors, incompetents, and "substituted judgment."* How ought physicians treat minors and incompetents who are unable to give consent? The standard rule requires physicians to obtain, except in emergencies, the consent of a guardian. "[T]he general rule is that the consent of the parent is necessary for an operation on a child." Bonner v. Moran, 126 F.2d 121,

122 (D.C. Cir. 1941). Should the rule apply to teenagers? What if the parent consents to the operation but the child does not?

Substituted consent is also needed for adult incompetents who lack any capacity to make medical decisions on their own behalf. Generally, the law protects the guardian's good-faith decision from any judicial challenge or review. For example, in Brophy v. New England Sinai Hospital Inc., 497 N.E.2d 626 (Mass. 1986), the court allowed the wife and family of a man left in a permanent vegetative state to cut off all nutrition and hydration over the objections of his treating physicians, when everyone agreed that he would have requested termination if he had been competent. Does the autonomy principle compel the acceptance of the right to voluntary euthanasia? These issues often have constitutional overtones. In Cruzan v. Director, Missouri Department of Health, 487 U.S. 261 (1990), Missouri allowed a comatose patient to be disconnected from a life support system only on proof of "clear and convincing evidence" that she would have adopted that course of action if presented with the choice while still competent. The Court rebuffed the constitutional claim (brought under the due process clause). Rehnquist, C.J., noted that the sacredness of life under the law of homicide justified the use of "heightened evidentiary requirements" before cutting off life sustaining treatment. What if the state chose to criminalize the removal of life support in the face of an undisputed advance directive from the comatose person requiring the removal of life support?

5. *Substituted consent for the benefit of others.* Substituted judgment becomes more delicate when the proposed treatment or operation is for the benefit of another. In Lausier v. Pescinski, 226 N.W.2d 180 (Wis. 1975), the court held that it did not have the power to permit the removal of one of the incompetent's kidneys needed to save the life of his brother, even though the risk of harm to the incompetent was slight. The incompetent's guardian, his sister, opposed the operation because it "brought back memories of the Dachau concentration camp in Nazi Germany and of medical experiments on unwilling subjects." However, in Strunk v. Strunk, 445 S.W.2d 145 (Ky. App. 1969), the court applied the doctrine of substituted judgment to allow a kidney transplant in a similar case, when the application was supported by the incompetent's guardian. Finally, in Curran v. Bosze, 566 N.E.2d 1319, 1326 (Ill. 1990), the court upheld the right of a mother of two 3½-year-old twins to refuse to have her children tested to see if they could make bone marrow transplants to their 12-year-old half-brother who was dying of leukemia. The Court stated that "it is not possible to determine the intent of a 3½-year-old child with regard to consenting to a bone marrow harvesting procedure by examining the child's personal value system." Should the consent of the incompetent's guardian make a difference? How persuasive is the argument that the incompetent will benefit by the survival of his brother? Would the

incompetent have consented to the treatment if capable to do so? Is the result here consistent with that reached in the emergency cases?

6. *The constitutionalization of individual self-determination.* In Washington v. Glucksberg, 521 U.S. 702, 720 (1997), and Vacco v. Quill, 521 U.S. 793 (1997), the Supreme Court rejected the right of voluntary euthanasia in light of the state's strong interest that is reflected in an unbroken string of state criminal prohibitions. See, e.g., New York State's Task Force on Life and the Law (1994), which unanimously concluded that "[l]egalizing assisted suicide and euthanasia would pose profound risks to many individuals who are ill and vulnerable. . . . " The key element for the court was that the liberty interest to take one's own life was not one of "those fundamental rights and liberties which are, objectively, deeply rooted in this Nation's history and tradition and implicit in the concept of ordered liberty."

That narrow reading of the definition of liberty blocked plaintiff's claim in In Abigail Alliance for Better Access to Developmental Drugs v. von Eschenbach, 495 F.3d 695 (D.C. Cir. 2007). There, the plaintiffs sought to compel the FDA to give terminally ill cancer patients drugs the right of access to new therapies that had passed Phase I clinical trials — those which establish only that the drugs were not toxic in specified doses — even when the FDA had not licensed drug as "safe" and "effective" pursuant to its statutory powers. Griffith, J., in line with prior precedents that narrowly defined the liberty interest, denied the claim over the dissent of Rogers, J., who relied on *Schloendorff* to bolster her claim that the patient's right of self-determination was indeed a fundamental interest that could not be overturned without some powerful showing of a countervailing government interest, which she found lacking in circumstances where desperate patients had nowhere else to turn. The case has generated an enormous amount of controversy, for many in the medical profession saw in the position of the dissent a frontal assault on the entire structure of the modern regulatory state and a disregard for the sound medical information that only clinical trials could supply. Their equally vocal opponents saw this decision as evidence of the misguided excesses of the regulatory state. For a continuous update on the controversy, see, Wikipedia, Abigail's Alliance v. von Eschenbach, http://en.wikipedia.org/wiki/Abigail_Alliance_v._von_Eschenbach.

7. *Consent, nondisclosure, and the sexual transmission of diseases.* Consent also has a large role to play in nonmedical settings where once again it negates any claim of trespass to the person. Thus, even if consent were given, its effectiveness can be overridden if the consent was induced by fraud or even by nondisclosure of some material fact. That problem often arises with venereal diseases communicated by sexual intercourse. In McPherson v. McPherson, 712 A.2d 1043 (Me. 1998), the court held that the defendant's conduct was actionable if he intentionally misrepresented or failed to affirmatively disclose his diseased condition to his wife, in light

of their 31 years of marriage. Yet courts have generally refused to impose liability for simple negligence when a husband who has been involved in a clandestine extramarital affair does not "know or have reason to know" that he has a sexually communicable disease, as in *McPherson*. What weight should be attached to section 2307 of the New York Public Health Law, which provides that "[a]ny person who, knowing himself or herself to be infected with an infectious venereal disease, has sexual intercourse with another shall be guilty of a misdemeanor"? See generally Fischer, Fraudulently Induced Consent to Intentional Torts, 46 U. Cin. L. Rev. 71 (1977).

Canterbury v. Spence
464 F.2d 772 (D.C. Cir. 1972)

[The text of the opinion and notes thereto are found beginning on page 244.]

Hudson v. Craft
204 P.2d 1 (Cal. 1949)

CARTER, J. Plaintiffs appeal from a judgment of dismissal, because of their failure to amend their complaint, after a demurrer thereto was sustained with leave to amend.

Plaintiff (the reference herein will be to the one plaintiff, the other one being his father who makes a claim for hospital and medical expenses) alleges that he is 18 years of age; that defendants were conducting a carnival where one of the concessions, for which a separate admission fee was charged, consisted of boxing exhibitions; that such concession was conducted in violation of section 412 of the Penal Code, and the Business & Professions Code (chap. 2 of div. 8) in that prizes and prize money were given to contestants and no license to conduct the same had been obtained from the State Athletic Commission, and they were not conducted in accordance with the rules of the commission; that plaintiff, on the solicitation of defendants, and a promise of receiving $5.00, engaged in a boxing match and suffered personal injuries as the result of being struck by his opponent. Plaintiff's opponent in the match was also made a party defendant but was not served with process.

The basis and theory of liability, if any, in mutual combat cases has been the subject of considerable controversy. Proceeding from the premise that, as between the combatants, the tort involved is that of assault and battery, many courts have held that, inasmuch as each contestant has committed a battery on the other, each may hold the other liable for any injury inflicted although both consented to the contest. [The court cited many cases, including Teeters v. Frost, 292 P. 356 (Okla. 1930).] Being contrary to the maxim volenti non fit injuria [the willing suffer no injury], the courts have endeavored to rationalize the rule by reasoning that the state is a party where there is a breach of the peace, such as occurs in a combat, and that no one may consent to such breach. There are cases expressing a minority view and severe criticism has been leveled at the majority rule, such as, that it ignores the principle of pari delicto [equal wrong] and encourages rather than deters mutual combat. See Hart v. Geysel, 159 Wash. 632[, 294 P. 570]; Bohlen, Consent as Affecting Civil Liability for Breaches of the Peace, 24 Colum. L. Rev. 819 [1924]; . . . The Restatement adopts the minority view. An assent which satisfies the rules stated "prevents an invasion from being tortious and, therefore, actionable, although the invasion assented to constitutes a crime." (Rest., Torts, §60.) An example given thereunder is a boxing match where no license was had as required by law. The only case discovered involving the liability of a third-party promoter of the combat such as we have in the case at bar, is Teeters v. Frost, supra, where the court, following the majority position as to the liability of the participants as between themselves, was not confronted with any difficulty in deciding that the instigator was liable as an aider and abettor.

There is an exception to the rule stated in the Restatements, reading: "Where it is a crime to inflict a particular invasion of an interest of personality upon a particular class of persons, irrespective of their assent, and the policy of the law is primarily to protect the interests of such a class of persons from their inability to appreciate the consequences of such an invasion, and it is not solely to protect the interests of the public, the assent of such a person to such an invasion is not a consent thereto." (Rest., Torts, §61.) It is evident that the so-called exception and the foregoing discussion has to do only with consent as refuting liability, not with the basic tort upon which the liability is rested, assault and battery. Concerning the bearing of the factor of consent or assumption of risk on liability, the instant case, as will more fully appear from the later discussion herein, clearly falls within the exception stated in section 61 (supra) by reason of the declared public policy of the state.

If liability is predicated on the tort of battery, it might seem to follow that in order to hold the promoter liable, it would be necessary to impose responsibility upon the combatants as to each other on the theory that they are the principals while the instigator is only the aider and abettor. In view of the public policy of this state as expressed by initiative, legislation, rules of the Athletic Commission, and the Constitution, the promoter must be held liable as a principal regardless of what the rule may be as between the combatants.

From the beginning, this state has taken an uncompromising stand against uncontrolled prize fights and boxing matches.

[The court then reviewed the extensive history of boxing regulation in California from 1850 through 1942. When this fight took place, the law forbade any person under 18 from participating in a fight, required all fighters to undergo physical examinations before fighting, prescribed a maximum number of rounds and a minimum weight for gloves, required a physician to be in attendance at the fight, and required that a referee supervise the match and stop the fight if there were "too great a disparity between the boxers." The statute also authorized the boxing commission to adopt rules to set weight classes for fighters, define fouls in the ring, and provide for inspection and physical examination of the premises. Many, if not all, of these requirements were violated in the instant case.]

The foregoing declarations by the people, the Legislature, and the commission evince an unusually strong policy, obviously resting upon a detailed study of the problems relative to boxing matches. While there are other purposes underlying that policy, it is manifest that one of the chief goals is to provide safeguards for the protection of persons engaging in the activity. It may be that the actual participants, as well as the promoter, are liable criminally for a violation of the provisions, but insofar as the purpose is protection from physical harm, the chief offender would be the promoter — the activating force in procuring the occurrence of such exhibitions. It is from his uncontrolled conduct that the combatants are protected. Secondarily, the contestants are protected against their own ill-advised participation in an unregulated match. This is especially true in the case at bar where plaintiff is a lad of 18 years.

The foregoing policy compels the conclusion that the promoter is liable where he conducts boxing matches or prize fights without a license and in violation of the statutory provisions above discussed, regardless of the rights as between the contestants, and that the consent of the combatants does not relieve him of that liability. Manifestly the doctrine of pari delicto is not pertinent inasmuch as one of the main purposes of the statutes is to protect a class (combatants) of which plaintiff is a member. It may be observed that the basis of such liability finds some support in principle in the doctrine of negligence per se . . . , and strict liability arising from the nature of the conduct and its consequences . . . , the seriousness of which is here established by a statute with comprehensive regulatory features aimed at the goal of especial protection for a certain class. The end result is the same and the controlling factor is whether or not the expressed public policy is sufficiently urgent, explicit and comprehensive.

It is not necessary in the instant case to state a general rule inasmuch as each situation must have individual consideration. The nature and scope of the legislation here involved and above shown requires liability, especially when we consider that it calls for continuous and "on the spot" supervision of boxing matches. That feature alone is sufficient to distinguish it from such cases as a person operating a car without an operator's license and the like. Moreover, we have more here than the mere failure to obtain a license. While it could have been more accurately pleaded, it may be inferred that the defendants did not comply with the statutes from the allegation that they failed to so comply therewith in that they did not obtain a license and did not observe the rules and regulations of the Athletic Commission.

For the foregoing reasons, the judgment is reversed.

NOTES

1. *Minority view on consent to illegal acts.* Why is the fight promoter in *Hudson* responsible for blows inflicted by a third party if the other combatant is entitled to a defense of consent? Should violations of the legislative scheme be sufficient to impose liability per se on the promoter? See *infra* Chapter 3, Section E.

In Hart v. Geysel, 294 P. 570, 572 (Wash. 1930), the plaintiff's husband was killed by a blow struck in an illegal prizefight, in which he consented to participate. In adopting the minority and Restatement view, the court in *Hart*, over vigorous dissent, first noted that both fighters had violated the criminal statute, and therefore "it is not necessary to reward the one that got the worst of the encounter at the expense of his more fortunate opponent." The *Hart* court thus relied on two basic legal doctrines that the majority view implicitly rejected: (1) *volenti non fit injuria*, and (2) *ex turpi causa non oritur actio*, or no action shall arise out of an improper or immoral cause. Is the private action for damages a sensible aid to criminal enforcement? Does the denial of a private action encourage or discourage participation in illegal prizefights? Does the action against the promoter discourage prize fighting? Reduce the size of the purses? Both? For an excellent defense of the Restatement's adoption of the minority rule, see F. Bohlen, Consent as Affecting Civil Liability for Breaches of the Peace, 24 Colum. L. Rev. 819 (1924), reprinted in Studies in the Law of Torts at 577 (1926).

2. *Private rights of action for statutory rape.* In Barton v. Bee Line, Inc., 265 N.Y.S. 284 (App. Div. 1933), an underaged plaintiff, age 15-18 was the legal age of consent — brought an action for damages even though she had fully consented to sexual intercourse with the defendant's chauffeur for which he was guilty of statutory rape, a crime then punishable by up to ten years of imprisonment. The court refused to allow her to sue:

> Should a consenting female under the age of eighteen have a cause of action if she has full understanding of the nature of her act? It is one thing to say that society will protect itself by punishing those who consort with females under the age of consent; it is another to hold that knowing the nature of her act, such female shall be rewarded for her indiscretion. Surely public

policy — to serve which the statute was adopted — will not be vindicated by recompensing her for willing participation in that against which the law sought to protect her. The very object of the statute will be frustrated if by a material return for her fall we should unwarily put it in the power of the female sex to become seducers in their turn.

Distinguishable from the illegal boxing cases? Why does the RST take the alternative view and allow liability for statutory rape cases, but not for illegal boxing cases? See RST §892(A).

3. *Athletic injuries: formal settings.* The legal remedy for persons deliberately or recklessly injured in professional athletic contests has been the subject of frequent litigation. In most sports it is generally held that plaintiffs consent to injury from blows administered in accordance with the rules of the game, but not when the blows are deliberately illegal. In Hackbart v. Cincinnati Bengals, Inc., 601 F.2d 516, 520-521 (10th Cir. 1979), Dale Hackbart, a defensive back for the Denver Broncos, was injured by a blow struck by Charles "Booby" Clark, an offensive halfback for the Bengals. After the Broncos intercepted a pass, Clark, "acting out of anger and frustration, but without a specific intent to injure . . . stepped forward and struck a blow with his right forearm to the back of the kneeling plaintiff's head and neck with sufficient force to cause both players to fall forward to the ground." Although Hackbart suffered no immediate ill effects from the blow, he shortly thereafter experienced severe pains which, after two more brief game appearances, forced him to retire, ending a successful 13-year career. The trial court dismissed the action, chiefly on the ground that in the absence of legislation it was inappropriate to impose upon one professional football player a duty to care for the safety of another. The Tenth Circuit through Doyle, J., reversed:

> Contrary to the position of the court then, there are no principles of law which allow a court to rule out certain tortious conduct by reason of general roughness of the game or difficulty of administering it.
>
> Indeed, the evidence shows that there are rules of the game which prohibit the intentional striking of blows. Thus, Article 1, Item 1, Subsection C, provides that: "All players are prohibited from striking on the head, face or neck with the heel, back or side of the hand, wrist, forearm, elbow or clasped hands." Thus the very conduct which was present here is expressly prohibited by the rule which is quoted above. . . . Therefore, the notion is not correct that all reason has been abandoned, whereby the only possible remedy for the person who has been the victim of an unlawful blow is retaliation.

What result in the absence of a specific rule such as that referred to in the opinion? What if the owners of all teams agree that no tort actions should be brought for injuries suffered on the playing field? What about an agreement among the players to the same effect?

Courts have applied similar principles to high school and college athletic contests. In Nabozny v. Barnhill, 334 N.E.2d 258, 260-261 (Ill. App. 1975), the plaintiff goalie sustained severe and permanent injuries when kicked in the head inside the penalty area even though the defendant could have easily avoided any contact. The game was played under football association rules, under which any contact with the goalkeeper and any attempt to kick a ball in his possession while in the penalty area are infractions of the rules, even if such contact is unintentional. The court, while concerned about the negative impact of tort liability on legitimate athletic activities, held that "a player is liable for injury in a tort action if his conduct is such that it is either deliberate, wilful or with a reckless disregard for the safety of the other player so as to cause injury to that player, the same being a question of fact to be decided by a jury."

Hackbart and *Nabozny* received a narrow interpretation in Gauvin v. Clark, 537 N.E.2d 94, 97 (Mass. 1989), where the defendant "butt-ended" plaintiff (that is, hit him with the nonblade end of the hockey stick) in his midsection causing serious internal injuries. This deliberate blow had resulted in a major penalty and expulsion from the game under a rule enacted for the protection of the players. Nonetheless, the court denied recovery after the jury found, in a special verdict, that Clark had not acted "wilfully, wantonly or recklessly . . . Precluding the imposition of liability in case of negligence without reckless misconduct furthers the policy that '[r]igorous and active participation in sporting events should not be chilled by the threat of litigation.'" Why isn't this flagrant foul evidence of reckless misconduct notwithstanding the jury's finding?

More recently in Avila v. Citrus Community College District., 131 P.3d 383, 393 (Cal. 2006), the defendant's pitcher hit the plaintiff, a Rio Hondo CC varsity baseball player, in the head with a pitch, cracking his helmet and causing serious, unspecified injuries. The plaintiff alleged that "the pitch was an intentional 'beanball' thrown in retaliation for [a] previous hit batter or, at a minimum, was thrown negligently." Werdegar, J., showed no patience with either allegation. Citing neither *Hackbart* nor *Nabozny*, she held that the defendant school had a duty "to, at a minimum, not increase the risks inherent in the sport." Even so, the home team vowed not to control its own pitcher because intentional beanballs were an "inherent risk of the sport." "As Los Angeles Dodgers Hall of Fame pitcher Don Drysdale and New York Giants All Star pitcher Sal 'The Barber' Maglie have explained, intentionally throwing at batters can also be an integral part of pitching tactics, a tool to help get batters out by upsetting their frame of mind." Is throwing at batters the same as throwing beanballs? Is the pitcher personally liable if he is thrown out of the game? How does the purported justification for throwing beanballs tie in with the Third Restatement's definition of recklessness, which reads:

§2. RECKLESSNESS

A person acts recklessly in engaging in conduct if:

(a) the person knows of the risk of harm created by the conduct or knows facts that make the risk obvious to another in the person's situation, and

(b) the precaution that would eliminate or reduce the risk involves burdens that are so slight relative to the magnitude of the risk as to render the person's failure to adopt the precaution a demonstration of the person's indifference to the risk.

The comment then notes that "gross negligence carries a meaning that is less than recklessness." Comment *a*. Whatever its application to beanballs, this provision reflects the sturdy judicial distinction between recklessness and negligence. In Turcotte v. Fell, 502 N.E.2d 964, 969-970 (N.Y. 1986), the plaintiff, a professional jockey, sued *in negligence* when injured in a race by the defendant, who had violated track rules. The court refused to allow the action, contrasting this case with *Hackbart* and *Nabozny* as follows:

Although the foul riding rule is a safety measure, it is not by its terms absolute for it establishes a spectrum of conduct and penalties, depending on whether the violation is careless or willful and whether the contact was the result of mutual fault. As the rule recognizes, bumping and jostling are normal incidents of the sport. They are not, as were the blows in *Nabozny* and *Hackbart*, flagrant infractions unrelated to the normal method of playing the game and done without any competitive purpose. Plaintiff does not claim that Fell intentionally or recklessly bumped him; he claims only that as a result of carelessness, Fell failed to control his mount as the horses raced for the lead and a preferred position on the track. While a participant's "consent" to join in a sporting activity is not a waiver of all rules infractions, nonetheless a professional clearly understands the usual incidents of competition resulting from carelessness, particularly those which result from the customarily accepted method of playing the sport, and accepts them.

4. *Athletic injuries: informal settings.* In Marchetti v. Kalish, 559 N.E.2d 699 (Ohio 1990), plaintiff and defendant were playing a backyard game called "kick the can" in which players attempt to reach the home base, or can, before they are spotted by the player designated as "it." Once "it" sees another player, he places his foot on the can, and calls out the player's name, yelling "kick the can — one, two, three." (The rules of the game were sufficiently well articulated that the parties set them out in a joint appendix to the opinion.) On this occasion plaintiff, a 13-year-old girl, placed her foot on the ball, used in place of a can, and announced that the defendant, a 15-year-old boy, was "it." [Defendant], however, continued to run towards [plaintiff], colliding with her and kicking the ball out from under her foot. [Plaintiff] fell to the ground, and her right leg was broken in two places."

Plaintiff conceded that the injuries in question were not intentionally or recklessly inflicted. The Ohio Supreme Court entered a summary judgment for defendant, relying on both *Nabozny* and *Hackbart.* "[Plaintiff] argues that these cases from other jurisdictions are distinguishable from the present case because we are dealing with children involved in a simple neighborhood game rather than an organized contact sport." But the court held the distinction immaterial so long as the children "were engaging in some type of recreational or sports activity. Whether the activity is organized, unorganized, supervised or unsupervised, is immaterial to the standard of liability. . . . [B]efore a party may proceed with a cause of action involving injury resulted from a recreational or sports activity, reckless or intentional conduct must exist."

Marchetti was, if anything, extended by Gentry v. Craycraft, 802 N.E.2d 1116, 1118 (Ohio 2004), where the 4-year-old plaintiff was struck in the eye by a nail that the 11-year-old defendant was hammering into the board some two or three feet away, resulting in serious injuries. The Ohio Supreme Court sustained a summary judgment for the defendant, noting that the boys were engaged in a "recreational activity" for which liability depended on proof of recklessness. Sweeney, J., held that *Marchetti* was not limited "to active participants or to spectators old enough to appreciate the risks inherent with the sport or activity." "To hold otherwise would be to open the floodgates to a myriad of lawsuits involving the backyard games of children." Any liability for the parents for negligent supervision?

b. Insanity

McGuire v. Almy
8 N.E.2d 760 (Mass. 1937)

QUA, J. This is an action of tort for assault and battery. The only question of law reported is whether the judge should have directed a verdict for the defendant.

The following facts are established by the plaintiff's own evidence: In August, 1930, the plaintiff was employed to take care of the defendant. The plaintiff was a registered nurse and was a graduate of a training school for nurses. The defendant was an insane person. Before the plaintiff was hired she learned that the defendant was a "mental case and was in good physical condition," and that for some time two nurses had been taking care of her. The plaintiff was on "twenty-four hour duty." The plaintiff slept in the room next to the defendant's room. Except when the plaintiff was with the defendant, the plaintiff kept the defendant locked in the defendant's room. There was a wire grating over the outside of the window of that room. During the period of "fourteen months or so" while the plaintiff cared for the defendant, the defendant "had a few odd spells," when she showed some hostility to the plaintiff and said that "she would like to try and do something to her." The defendant had been violent at times and had broken dishes "and things like that," and on one or two occasions the plaintiff had to have help to subdue the defendant.

On April 19, 1932, the defendant, while locked in her room, had a violent attack. The plaintiff heard a crashing of furniture and then knew that the defendant was ugly, violent and dangerous. The defendant told the plaintiff and a Miss Maroney, "the maid," who was with the plaintiff in the adjoining room, that if they came into the defendant's room, she would kill them. The plaintiff and Miss Maroney looked into the defendant's room, "saw what the defendant had done," and "thought it best to take the broken stuff away before she did any harm to herself with it." They sent for one Emerton, the defendant's brother-in-law. When he arrived the defendant was in the middle of her room about ten feet from the door, holding upraised the leg of a low-boy as if she were going to strike. The plaintiff stepped into the room and walked toward the defendant, while Emerton and Miss Maroney remained in the doorway. As the plaintiff approached the defendant and tried to take hold of the defendant's hand which held the leg, the defendant struck the plaintiff's head with it, causing the injuries for which the action was brought. [After noting that the Massachusetts precedents had not settled the rules governing the liability of an insane person, the court continued:]

Turning to authorities elsewhere, we find that courts in this country almost invariably say in the broadest terms that an insane person is liable for his torts. As a rule no distinction is made between those torts which would ordinarily be classed as intentional and those which would ordinarily be classed as negligent, nor do the courts discuss the effect of different kinds of insanity or of varying degrees of capacity as bearing upon the ability of the defendant to understand the particular act in question or to make a reasoned decision with respect to it, although it is sometimes said that an insane person is not liable for torts requiring malice of which he is incapable. Defamation and malicious prosecution are the torts more commonly mentioned in this connection. A number of illustrative cases appear in the footnote. These decisions are rested more upon grounds of public policy and upon what might be called a popular view of the requirements of essential justice than upon any attempt to apply logically the underlying principles of civil liability to the special instance of the mentally deranged. Thus it is said that a rule imposing liability tends to make more watchful those persons who have charge of the defendant and who may be supposed to have some interest in preserving his property; that as an insane person must pay for his support, if he is financially able, so he ought also to pay for the damage which he does; that an insane person with abundant wealth ought not to continue in unimpaired enjoyment of the comfort which it brings while his victim bears the burden unaided; and there is also a suggestion that courts are loath to introduce into the great body of civil litigation the difficulties in determining mental capacity which it has been found impossible to avoid in the criminal field.

The rule established in these cases has been criticized severely by certain eminent text writers both in this country and in England, principally on the ground that it is an archaic survival of the rigid and formal medieval conception of liability for acts done, without regard to fault, as opposed to what is said to be the general modern theory that liability in tort should rest upon fault. Notwithstanding these criticisms, we think that as a practical matter there is strong force in the reasons underlying these decisions. They are consistent with the general statements found in the cases dealing with the liability of infants for torts. Fault is by no means at the present day a universal prerequisite to liability, and the theory that it should be such has been obliged very recently to yield at several points to what have been thought to be paramount considerations of public good. Finally, it would be difficult not to recognize the persuasive weight of so much authority so widely extended.

But the present occasion does not require us either to accept or to reject the prevailing doctrine in its entirety. For this case it is enough to say that where an insane person by his act does intentional damage to the person or property of another he is liable for that damage in the same circumstances in which a normal person would be liable. This means that in so far as a particular intent would be necessary in order to render a normal person liable, the insane person, in order to be liable, must have been capable of entertaining that same intent and must have entertained it in fact. But the law will not inquire further into his peculiar mental condition with a view to excusing him if it should appear that delusion or other consequence of his affliction has caused him to entertain that intent or that a normal person would not have entertained it.

We do not suggest that this is necessarily a logical stopping point. If public policy demands that a mentally affected person be subjected to the external standard for intentional wrongs, it may well be that public policy also demands that he should be subjected to the external standard for wrongs which are commonly classified as negligent, in accordance with what now seems to be the prevailing view. We stop here for the present, because we are not required to go further in order to decide this case, because of deference to the difficulty of the subject, because full and adequate discussion is lacking in most of the cases decided up to the present time, and because by far the greater number of those cases, however broad their statement of the principle, are in fact cases of intentional rather than of negligent injury.

Coming now to the application of the rule to the facts of this case, it is apparent that the jury could find that the defendant was capable of entertaining and that she did entertain an intent to strike and to injure the plaintiff and that she acted upon that intent. See Am. Law Inst. Restatement: Torts §§13, 14. We think this was enough. [The court then rejected the argument that the plaintiff had consented to or assumed the risk as a matter of law. In its view the risk became "plain and obvious" only after she entered the room, just before the assault, when an emergency sufficient to deny voluntary consent had already been created.]

Judgment for the plaintiff on the verdict.

NOTE

Intention and insanity. Under the insanity defense, what mental state must the defendant have toward her victim? What result if Almy had thought she was striking a creature from outer space? That her actions were in self-defense against an imagined assault by McGuire? Looking at the other side of the case, was the court right to reject defendant's assumption-of-risk defense in light of the elaborate preparations plaintiff took before entering defendant's room? In light of her role as a paid caretaker?

The vast majority of the decisions on the insanity defense have hewed to the uncompromising line set out in *McGuire*. For a justification of this position, see Gould v. American Family Mutual Insurance Co., 543 N.W.2d 282, 285 (Wis. 1996): "where a loss must be borne by one of two innocent persons, it shall be borne by him who occasioned it, and it has also been held that public policy requires the enforcement of the liability in order that those interested in the estate of the insane person, as relatives or otherwise, may be under inducement to restrain him and that tortfeasors may not simulate or pretend insanity to defend their wrongful acts causing damage to others."

The resistance to an insanity defense is equally powerful when the defendant's intention to cause harm is beyond dispute. In Polmatier v. Russ, 537 A.2d 468, 472 (Conn. 1988), the defendant Russ and his 2-year-old daughter visited his father-in-law's house. The defendant sat astride his father-in-law, beating him over the head with a beer bottle. He then searched two bedrooms in the house, found 30-30 ammunition and a Winchester rifle, and returned to the living room where he killed his father-in-law with two shots. The defendant was later found naked, sitting on a stump in a wooded area about two miles from the decedent's home, carrying his blood-soaked clothing and cradling his daughter in his arms. He was diagnosed as "suffering from a severe case of paranoid schizophrenia that involved delusions of persecution, grandeur, influence and reference, and also involved auditory hallucinations." The defendant was found unfit to stand for a criminal trial, but was held responsible for an intentional tort.

We note that we have not been referred to any evidence indicating that the defendant's acts were reflexive, convulsive or epileptic. Furthermore, under the Restatement (Second) of Torts §2, "act" is used "to denote an external manifestation of the actor's will and does not include any of its results, even the most direct, immediate, and intended." Comment b to this section provides in pertinent part: "A muscular reaction is always an act unless it is a purely reflexive reaction in which the mind and will have no share." Although the trial court found that the defendant could not form a rational choice, it did find that he could make a schizophrenic or crazy choice. Moreover, a rational choice is not required since "[a]n insane person may have an intent to invade the interests of another, even though his reasons and motives for forming that intention may be entirely irrational." Restatement (Second) of Torts §895J, comment c.

The court then rejected the further argument that the defendant must have been shown to have "acted for the *purpose* of causing," or with a "desire to cause the resulting injury."

What result in cases of automatism, where the sleepwalking defendant has done *no act* at all and thus cannot have committed any tort, intentional or otherwise? See generally Bohlen, Liability in Torts of Infants and Insane Persons, 23 Mich. L. Rev. 9 (1924), reprinted in his Studies in the Law of Torts at 543 (1926).

c. Self-defense

Courvoisier v. Raymond
47 P. 284 (Colo. 1896)

HAYT, C.J. It is admitted or proven beyond controversy that appellee received a gunshot wound at the hands of the appellant at the time and place designated in the complaint, and that as the result of such wound the appellee was seriously injured. It is further shown that the shooting occurred under the following circumstances:

That Mr. Courvoisier, on the night in question, was asleep in his bed in the second story of a brick building, situated at the corner of South Broadway and Dakota streets in South Denver; that he occupied a portion of the lower floor of this building as a jewelry store. He was aroused from his bed shortly after midnight by parties shaking or trying to open the door of the jewelry store. These parties, when asked by him as to what they wanted, insisted upon being admitted, and upon his refusal to comply with this request, they used profane and abusive epithets toward him. Being unable to gain admission, they broke some signs upon the front of the building, and then entered the building by another entrance, and passing upstairs commenced knocking upon the door of a room where defendant's sister was sleeping. Courvoisier partly dressed himself, and, taking his revolver, went upstairs and expelled the intruders from the building. In doing this he passed downstairs and out on the sidewalk as far as the entrance to his store, which was at the corner of the building. The parties expelled from the building, upon reaching the rear of the store, were joined by two or three others. In order to frighten these parties away, the defendant fired a shot in the air, but instead of retreating they passed around to the street in front, throwing stones and brickbats at the defendant, whereupon he fired a second and perhaps a third shot. The first shot fired attracted the attention of plaintiff Raymond and two deputy sheriffs, who were at the Tramway depot, across the street. These officers started toward Mr. Courvoisier, who still continued to shoot, but two of them stopped when they reached the men in the street, for the purpose of arresting them, Mr. Raymond alone proceeding towards the defendant, calling out to him that he was an officer and to stop shooting. Although the night was dark, the street was well lighted by electricity, and when the officer approached him defendant shaded his eyes, and, taking deliberate aim, fired, causing the injury complained of.

The plaintiff's theory of the case is that he was a duly authorized police officer, and in the discharge of his duties at the time that the defendant was committing a breach of the peace, and that the defendant, knowing him to be a police officer, recklessly fired the shot in question.

The defendant claims that the plaintiff was approaching him at the time in a threatening attitude, and that the surrounding circumstances were such as to cause a reasonable man to believe that his life was in danger, and that it was necessary to shoot in self-defense, and that defendant did so believe at the time of firing the shot. . . .

The next error assigned relates to the instructions given by the court to the jury and to those requested by the defendant and refused by the court. The second instruction given by the court was clearly erroneous. The instruction is as follows: "The court instructs you that if you believe from the evidence, that, at the time the defendant shot the plaintiff, the plaintiff was not assaulting the defendant, then your verdict should be for the plaintiff."

The vice of this instruction is that it excluded from the jury a full consideration of the justification claimed by the defendant. The evidence for the plaintiff tends to show that the shooting, if not malicious, was wanton and reckless, but the evidence for the defendant tends to show that the circumstances surrounding him at the time of the shooting were such as to lead a reasonable man to believe that his life was in danger, or that he was in danger of receiving great bodily harm at the hands of the plaintiff, and the defendant testified that he did so believe. [The court then reviewed the injured plaintiff's sworn version of the facts of the case and continued:]

. . . He then adds: "I saw a man come away from the bunch of men and come up towards me, and as I looked around I saw this man put his hand to his hip pocket. I didn't think I had time to jump aside, and therefore turned around and fired at him. I had no doubts but it was somebody that had come to rob me, because some weeks before Mr. Wilson's store was robbed. It is next door to mine."

By this evidence two phases of the transaction are presented for consideration: *First,* was the plaintiff assaulting the defendant at the time plaintiff was shot? *Second,* if not, was there sufficient evidence of justification for the consideration of the jury? The first question was properly submitted, but the second was excluded by the instruction under review. The defendant's justification did not rest entirely upon the proof of assault by the plaintiff. A riot was in progress, and the defendant swears that he was attacked with missiles, hit with stones, brickbats, etc.; that he shot plaintiff, supposing him to be one of the rioters. We must assume these facts as established in reviewing the instruction, as we cannot say what the jury might have found had this evidence been submitted to them under a proper charge.

By the second instruction the conduct of those who started the fracas was eliminated from the consideration of the jury. If the jury believed from the evidence that the defendant would have been justified in shooting one of the rioters had such person advanced towards him as did the plaintiff, then it became important to determine whether the defendant mistook plaintiff for one of the rioters, and if such a mistake was in fact made, was it excusable in the light of all the circumstances leading up to and surrounding the commission of the act? If these issues had been resolved by the jury in favor of the defendant, he would have been entitled to a judgment. Morris v. Platt, 32 Conn. 75.

[Judgment was reversed.]

NOTES

1. Mistake and self-defense. Note that court held that the defendant in *Courvoisier* could plead self-defense even if he mistakenly thought that he were under attack. In other cases of intentional harms, including cases of trespass and conversion, the risk of an innocent mistake usually falls on the party who makes it. What accounts for the different result in this case?

In Morris v. Platt, 32 Conn. 75 (1864), the court held that the accidental harming of an innocent bystander by force reasonably intended in self-defense to repel an attack by a third party is not actionable. The Restatement concurs, noting that the defendant is liable to the innocent third party "only if the actor realizes or should realize that his act creates an unreasonable risk of causing such harm." RST §75. Is that decision consistent with the trial judge's approach in *Courvoisier?* The appellate court's, given that the defendant in *Morris* had no intention to strike the plaintiff? Does the plaintiff in *Morris* have a cause of action against the defendant's assailant?

With *Morris*, contrast the Roman law approach. "Persons who do damage because they cannot otherwise defend themselves are innocent; for all statutes and legal systems allow one to repel force by force. But if in order to defend myself I throw a stone at my adversary, but hit, not him but a passer-by, I shall be liable under the Lex Aquilia [the general tort statute for wrongful damage]; for one is allowed to strike only the person who uses force, and then only when it is done for the purpose of protection and not revenge as well." Justinian's Digest 9.2.45.4.

Even though self-defense is universally recognized as a justification for intentionally inflicting harm, there is a persistent debate over the circumstances that limit its use. May a social outcast use force to protect himself from attack by a prominent businessman or scientist, temporarily gone mad, if both are trapped together in an elevator? If so, how does one measure the claims to personal integrity against those of social welfare? The Restatement (Second) §64, in a caveat, takes a discreet pass: "The Institute expresses no opinion as to whether there is a similar privilege of self-defense against conduct which the actor recognizes, or should recognize, to be entirely innocent." How ought the question be resolved?

2. Self-defense against actual attacks. The defense of self-defense is far more secure in those cases where the plaintiff has in fact attacked the defendant. But even here critical questions can arise: Who struck the first blow, and was the force excessive under the circumstances? In Boston v. Muncy, 233 P.2d 300, 301, 303 (Okla. 1951), the defendant encountered the plaintiff in a domino parlor after work and asked what had happened to an automobile heater — difficult to obtain because of post-World War II rationing — that he had promised to put aside for the defendant. The plaintiff denied having made such a promise. According to the plaintiff, the defendant then called plaintiff a liar and, without provocation, struck him over the right eye, causing serious damage. According to the defendant, "when he reminded plaintiff that he had promised to save a heater for him plaintiff called him a liar and made an attempt to hit him with his fist; that he then struck the plaintiff in self-defense." Plaintiff and defendant each had witnesses to support his version of the events. The defendant then asked for instructions that provided "the defendant had the right to exercise and use such reasonable force as may have reasonably appeared to him in good faith to be necessary to protect himself from bodily harm, even though he may not have been actually in danger." But the trial court, in instruction No. 8, said:

> . . . if at the time the defendant is alleged to have assaulted and struck the plaintiff the defendant in doing what he did was acting in an effort to protect his own person or life, and the circumstances then surrounding the defendant were such [that] the exercise of reasonable judgment would justify or induce in his mind an honest belief that he was in danger of receiving some

great bodily harm, judging from the standpoint of the defendant, then the defendant would be justified in doing what he did, and your verdict should be for the defendant.

The Oklahoma court held that the instruction 8 was prejudicial error because they "too narrowly" limited the right of self-defense. It remanded the case for a new trial, saying:

> The evidence is highly conflicting as to who was the aggressor. The jury might have found that plaintiff was the aggressor, but it also might have further found that defendant was not justified in apprehending or believing that plaintiff intended to inflict upon him some great bodily harm, and under the instruction it might have concluded that the defendant therefore had no right to stand his ground and defend himself against the attack and it was therefore its duty to render a verdict for plaintiff.

Does removing the word "great" from the trial judge's instructions entitle the defendant to use the minimum force necessary to protect himself, even from trivial harm? Should a squeamish and nervous person be held to a standard of "ordinary firmness and courage" that he could not meet in practice? If armed, could he have used a gun when an ordinary man could not have done so? See RST §63, comments *i* and *j*. For the complex rules governing self-defense, see RST §§63-76. For an excellent discussion of the problem see Fletcher, Proportionality and the Psychotic Aggressor: A Vignette in Comparative Criminal Theory, 8 Israel L. Rev. 367 (1973).

More recent cases also show the interaction between intention and negligence in self-defense cases. In Brown v. Robishaw, 922 A.2d 1086, 1093 (Conn. 2007), the plaintiff visited the home of his estranged wife to ask about their pending divorce proceedings, when he got into a nasty altercation with her current boyfriend, a codefendant, who was visiting her at the time. The boyfriend "pushed or threw" the plaintiff down the front steps of the house causing serious permanent injuries and deformities. The trial judge struck the defendants' plea of self-defense but allowed them to plead comparative negligence (see *infra* Chapter 4, Section E), after which the plaintiff recovered damages. Norcott, J., ordered a new trial, noting:

> The facts of this case involve the intersection between negligent and intentional torts. The plaintiff alleged that the defendant had handled him negligently. In reality, however, the plaintiff claims that the defendant committed the intentional tort of assault, and that the defendant's response to the plaintiff's behavior at Robishaw's door was unreasonable, and therefore, unjustified. It is undisputed that the defendant intentionally threw or pushed the plaintiff down the stairs of the house. . . . Thus, the self-defense analysis incorporates negligence principles, as the plaintiff correctly points out that a party who overreacts to a perceived threat may be held liable in

negligence if his actions are unreasonable in light of the circumstances. . . . In order to determine if the party unreasonably overreacted so that he may be held liable for negligence, however, the fact finder first would have to be presented with the party's claim of self-defense. The jury in the present case was not provided with the opportunity to accept or to reject that defense.

3. *Defense of third parties.* Under what circumstances may a person intervene in defense of a third party? What if he hurts the plaintiff in the mistaken, but reasonable, belief that a third party needs assistance? See RST §76, which notes that a person is privileged to defend a third party "under the same conditions and by the same means as those under and by which he is privileged to defend himself if the actor correctly or reasonably believes" that the third party is entitled to use force in self-defense and that his own intervention is necessary to protect that party. How should the issue be decided under *Courvoisier, Morris,* and Justinian's Digest 9.2.45.4?

d. Defense of Property

Bird v. Holbrook
130 Eng. Rep. 911 (C.P. 1825)

[The defendant had rented and occupied a walled garden in which they grew valuable tulips. The garden was located about a mile from his home, and it contained a single-room summer-house in which he and his wife had slept from time to time. Shortly before the present incident, the defendant's garden had been robbed of flowers and roots worth 20 pounds:] in consequence of which, for the protection of his property, with the assistance of another man, he placed in the garden a spring gun, the wires connected with which were made to pass from the door-way of the summer-house to some tulip beds, at the height of about fifteen inches from the ground, and across three or four of the garden paths, which wires were visible from all parts of the garden or the garden wall; but it was admitted by the Defendant, that the Plaintiff had not seen them, and that he had no notice of the spring gun and the wires being there. [The plaintiff, a 19-year-old youth, had gone into the garden between six and seven in the afternoon on March 21, 1825 for an innocent purpose—to get back a pea-fowl that had strayed—at the request of the female servant of its owner. The plaintiff had climbed on the wall at the back of the garden, and called out several times before jumping down into the garden. As he approached the summer-house, he triggered the spring gun, which discharged heavy shot that caused a severe wound above the knee.]

A witness to whom the Defendant mentioned the fact of his having been robbed, and of having set a spring gun, proved that he had asked the

Defendant if he had put up a notice of such gun being set, to which the Defendant answered, that "he did not conceive that there was any law to oblige him to do so," and the Defendant desired such person not to mention to any one that the gun was set, "lest the villain should not be detected." The Defendant stated to the same person that the garden was very secure, and that he and his wife were going to sleep in the summer-house in a few days. . . .

Merewether, Serjt. [i.e., highest order of counsel] for the defendant. . . . The main ground of the defence, however, is, that the Plaintiff cannot recover for an injury occasioned to him by his own wrongful act. Commodum ex injuria non oritur [an advantage cannot arise out of a wrongful act] and it is equally the principle of our law, that jus ex injuria non oritur [no right arises from a wrong]. If a man place broken glass on a wall, or spikes behind a carriage, one who wilfully encounters them, and is wounded, even though it were by night, when he could have no notice, has no claim for compensation. Volenti non fit injuria. [To a willing person, no injury is done.] The Defendant lawfully places a gun on his own property; he leaves the wires visible; he builds a high wall, expressly to keep off intruders; and if, under those circumstances, they are permitted to recover for an injury resulting from their scaling the wall, no man can protect his property at a distance.

Wilde in reply. . . . No illustration can be drawn from the use of spikes and broken glass on walls, & c. These are mere preventives, obvious to the sight, — unless the trespasser *chooses* a time of darkness, when no notice could be available, — mere preventives, injurious only to the persevering and determined trespasser, who can calculate at the moment of incurring the danger the amount of suffering he is about to endure, and who will, consequently, desist from his enterprise whenever the anticipated advantage is outweighed by the pain which he must endure to obtain it.

Best, C.J. I am of opinion that this action is maintainable. . . .

It has been argued that the law does not compel every line of conduct which humanity or religion may require; but there is no act which Christianity forbids, that the law will not reach: if it were otherwise, Christianity would not be, as it has always been held to be, part of the law of England. I am, therefore, clearly of opinion that he who sets spring guns, without giving notice, is guilty of an inhuman act, and that, if injurious consequences ensue, he is liable to yield redress to the sufferer. But this case stands on grounds distinct from any that have preceded it. In general, spring guns have been set for the purpose of deterring; the Defendant placed his for the express purpose of doing injury; for, when called on to give notice, he said, "If I give notice, I shall not catch him." He intended, therefore, that the gun should be discharged, and that the contents should be lodged in the body of his victim, for he could not be caught in any other way. On these principles the action is clearly maintainable, and particularly on the latter ground. The only thing which raised any doubt in my mind was the recent act of parliament; and if that had been purely prohibitory, there would be great weight in the argument which has been raised on it; because in a new prohibitory law we have the testimony of the legislature that there was no previous law against the thing prohibited. But the act is declaratory as to part, and prohibitory as to part; declaratory as to the setting of spring guns without notice, and the word "declared" is expressly introduced; prohibitory as to setting spring guns, even with notice, except in dwelling-houses by night. As to the case of Brock v. Copeland, Lord Kenyon proceeded on the ground that the Defendant had a right to keep a dog for the preservation of his house, and the Plaintiff, who was his foreman, knew where the dog was stationed. The case of the furious bull is altogether different; for if a man places such an animal where there is a public footpath, he interferes with the rights of the public. What would be the determination of the court if the bull were placed in a field where there is no footpath, we need not now decide; but it may be observed, that he must be placed somewhere, and is kept, not for mischief, but to renew his species; while the gun in the present case was placed purely for mischief. The case of the pit dug on a common has been distinguished, on the ground that the owner had a right to do what he pleased with his own land, and the Plaintiff could shew no right for the horse to be there.

. . . But we want no authority in a case like the present; we put it on the principle that it is inhuman to catch a man by means which may maim him or endanger his life, and, as far as human means can go, it is the object of English law to uphold humanity and the sanctions of religion. It would be, indeed, a subject of regret, if a party were not liable in damages, who, instead of giving notice of the employment of a destructive engine, or removing it, at least, during the day, expressed a resolution to withhold notice, lest, by affording it, he should fail to entrap his victim.

BURROUGH, J. The common understanding of mankind shews, that notice ought to be given when these means of protection are resorted to; and it was formerly the practice upon such occasions to give public notice in market towns. But the present case is of a worse complexion than those which have preceded it; for if the Defendant had proposed merely to protect his property from thieves, he would have set the spring guns only by night. The Plaintiff was only a trespasser: if the Defendant had been present, he would not have been authorised even in taking him into custody, and no man can do indirectly that which he is forbidden to do directly.

NOTES

1. The statutory response to the spring gun question. Spring guns were a constant source of tension in early nineteenth century England because of the systematic threat of armed bands of poachers, especially to large landowners. As noted in Bird v. Holbrook, the use of spring guns had been regulated by Parliamentary enactment shortly before the case was decided. The statute (7 & 8 Geo. 4, c. 18 §1-5 (1826)) was passed in response to the earlier decision of Ilott v. Wilkes, 106 Eng. Rep. 674 (K.B. 1820), where, in light of the risk of poaching, it was held: "A trespasser, having knowledge that there are spring-guns in a wood, although he may be ignorant of the particular spots where they are placed, cannot maintain an action for an injury received in consequence of his accidentally treading on the latent wire communicating with the gun, and thereby letting it off." The central provision of the statute stated:

> That from and after the passing of this Act, if any Person shall set or place or cause to be set or placed, any Spring Gun, Man Trap, or other Engine calculated to destroy human Life, or inflict grievous bodily Harm, with the Intent that the same or whereby the same may destroy or inflict grievous bodily Harm upon a Trespasser or other Person coming in contact therewith, the Person so setting or placing, or causing to be so set or placed, such Gun, Trap, or Engine as aforesaid, shall be guilty of a Misdemeanor. . . .

The Act exempted spring guns and similar devices set in dwelling houses between sunset and sunrise. It also "declared and enacted" that the Act did not apply to anything done prior to its passage. Suppose a person sets a spring gun in violation of the statute. If the gun is triggered by an individual against whom the application of direct force is warranted (e.g., a would-be assailant who enters a home during the day), does the statute override the homeowner's defense to the intruder's cause of action for personal injuries? Should it excuse the payment of the statutory fine? Note that the statute was repealed in its entirety, 24 & 25 Vict. c. 95 §1 (1861).

2. *An economic interpretation of* Bird v. Holbrook. Writing from an economic perspective, Judge Posner has analyzed *Bird* as follows:

> The issue in the case, as an economist would frame it, was the proper accommodation of two legitimate activities, growing tulips and raising peacocks. The defendant had a substantial investment in the tulip garden; he lived at a distance; and the wall had not proved effective against thieves. In an era of negligible police protection, a spring gun may have been the most cost-effective means of protection for the tulips. But since spring guns do not discriminate between the thief and the innocent trespasser, they deter owners of domestic animals from pursuing their animals onto other people's property and so increase the costs (enclosure costs or straying losses) of keeping animals. The court in *Bird* case implied an ingenious accommodation: One who sets a spring gun must post notices that he has done so. Then owners of animals will not be reluctant to pursue their animals onto property not so posted. A notice will be of no avail at night, but animals are

more likely to be secured then and in any event few owners would chase their straying animals after dark.

R. Posner, Economic Analysis of Law 205 (7th ed. 2007). For his more extensive analysis see Posner, Killing or Wounding to Protect a Property Interest, 14 J.L. & Econ. 201, 208-211 (1971).

What result if an injured child cannot read English? Is it ever proper to use spring guns on property that is not surrounded by a fence or protective wall? Should a landowner be entitled to set spring guns to protect a warehouse as well as a dwelling house? For an affirmative answer see Scheuermann v. Scharfenberg, 50 So. 335 (Ala. 1909).

3. *The malicious use of spring guns.* In Katko v. Briney, 183 N.W.2d 657, 659, 663 (Iowa 1971), the defendants owned an old, boarded-up house located several miles from their home, where they stored various old bottles, fruit jars and the like, which they considered to be antiques. Several times the windows in the house had been broken and the entire place "messed up." The defendants first posted "no trespass" signs, but the break-ins continued. Shortly before the injury to the plaintiff, the defendants placed a "shotgun trap" in one of the bedrooms. The gun was first positioned so as to hit an intruder in the stomach, but Mr. Briney, at his wife's insistence, lowered it to hit at the legs. He said that he set the gun "because I was mad and tired of being tormented," but insisted that he "did not intend to injure anyone." The plaintiff was shot in the legs and permanently injured when he entered the defendant's bedroom shortly after the gun was set. He had been to the place several times before, and had intended to steal some of the defendant's possessions. The plaintiff pleaded guilty to a charge of larceny and paid a fine of $50. He also sued the defendant for personal injuries and was awarded $20,000 in actual damages and $10,000 in punitive damages.

At trial the jury was instructed as follows:

Instruction 5 stated: "You are hereby instructed that one may use reasonable force in the protection of his property, but such right is subject to the qualification that one may not use such means of force as will take human life or inflict great bodily injury. Such is the rule even though the injured party is a trespasser and is in violation of the law himself."

Instruction 6 stated that the rule was not changed even if "the trespasser may be acting in violation of the law," except that "setting a 'spring gun' or a like dangerous device is justified would be when the trespasser was committing a felony of violence or a felony punishable by death, or where the trespasser was endangering human life by his act."

The Iowa Supreme Court approved these instructions on appeal and affirmed the judgment for the plaintiff below, without addressing the question of punitive damages, which had not been raised below. Larson, J., protested against awarding large "windfall" damages to a criminal defendant, noting that "where the evidence is sufficient to sustain a finding that the installation was intended only as a warning to ward off thieves and criminals, I can see no compelling reason why the use of such a device alone would create liability as a matter of law."

Katko stirred up great protest in Iowa and throughout the nation. Hundreds of strangers, including prison inmates, sent checks and cash over $10,000 to the Brineys. Briney remained unrepentant: "They used booby traps in Viet Nam, didn't they? Why can't we use them here to protect our property in this country?" Asked if he would do it again, Briney replied, "There's one thing I'd do different, though, I'd have aimed that gun a few feet higher." See a fuller account in the Chicago Tribune of April 25, 1975, at 1, col. 1.

4. *Wounding or killing in defense of property.* The Restatement (Second) of Torts takes a fairly permissive approach toward the use of force in defense of property.

> §85. USE OF MECHANICAL DEVICE THREATENING DEATH OR SERIOUS
>   BODILY INJURY
>
> The actor is so far privileged to use a device intended or likely to cause serious bodily harm or death for the purpose of protecting his land or chattels from intrusion that he is not liable for the serious bodily harm or death thereby caused to an intruder whose intrusion is, in fact, such that the actor, were he present, would be privileged to prevent or terminate it by the intentional infliction of such harm.

As RST §85 notes, issues surrounding the defense of property also arise when the defendant is present. In these cases should the privilege to use force be broader or narrower than in the spring gun case? In M'Ilovy v. Cockran, 2 A. K. Marsh 271 (Ky. 1820), the defendant, M'Ilovy, shot and severely wounded the plaintiff, Cockran, while the latter was attempting to tear down a fence on M'Ilovy's land. The court first held that the defendant did not have to request the plaintiff to leave when he was engaged in the active destruction of property, as would be the case for a simple entrance. However, it rejected the defendant's plea that this wounding was justified in defense of property, noting:

> in cases of *actual force,* as breaking open a gate or door, it is lawful to oppose force with force; and if one breaks down a gate, or comes into a close with force and arms, the possessor need not request him to depart, but may lay hands upon him immediately, for it is but returning violence with violence: so if one comes forcibly and takes away my goods, he may be opposed immediately, for there is no time to make a request: but, say the court, where one enters the close without actual force, although his entry will be construed a *force in law,* there must be a request to depart before the possessor can lay hands upon him and turn him out.

But although a wounding cannot be justified barely in defence of possession, yet if, in attempting to remove the intruder, or prevent his forcible entry, he should commit an assault upon the person of the possessor, or his family, and the owner should, in defence of himself or family, wound him, the wounding may, no doubt, be justified; but then, as the personal assault would form the grounds of justification, the plea should set out, specifically, the assault in justification.

e.   Recapture of Chattels

Kirby v. Foster
22 A. 1111 (R.I. 1891)

STINESS, J. The plaintiff was in the employ of the Providence Warehouse Co., of which the defendant, Samuel J. Foster, was the agent, and his son, the other defendant, an employee. A sum of fifty dollars belonging to the corporation had been lost, for which the plaintiff, a bookkeeper, was held responsible, and the amount was deducted from his pay. On January 20, 1888, Mr. Foster handed the plaintiff some money to pay the help. The plaintiff, acting under the advice of counsel, took from this money the amount due him at the time, including what had been deducted from his pay, put it into his pocket, and returned the balance to Mr. Foster, saying he had received his pay and was going to leave, and that he did this under advice of counsel. The defendants then seized the plaintiff and attempted to take the money from him. A struggle ensued, in which the plaintiff claims to have received injury, for which this suit is brought. The jury having returned a verdict for the plaintiff, the defendants petition for a new trial on exceptions to the rulings and refusals to rule of the presiding justice. It is unnecessary to repeat the several exceptions, since they involve substantially but one question, viz.: whether the defendants were justified in the use of force upon the plaintiff to retake the money from him. . . .

The defendants contend that the relation of master and servant subsisted between the plaintiff and Samuel J. Foster, the manager of the warehouse, whereby possession of money by the plaintiff was constructively possession by the manager, acting in behalf of the company and that the money having been delivered to the plaintiff for the specific purpose of paying the help, his conversion of it to his own use was a wrongful conversion amounting to embezzlement, which justified the defendants in using force in defence of the property under their charge. Unquestionably, if one takes another's property from his possession without right and against his will, the owner or person in charge may protect his possession, or retake the property, by the use of necessary force. He is not bound to stand by and submit to wrongful dispossession or larceny when he can stop it, and he is not guilty of assault in thus defending his right, by using force to prevent his property from being carried away. But this right of defence and recapture involves two things: first, possession by the owner, and, second, a purely wrongful taking or conversion, without a claim of right. If one has entrusted his property to another, who afterwards, honestly though erroneously, claims it as his own, the owner has no right to retake it by personal force. If he has, the actions of replevin and trover in many cases are of little use. The law does not permit parties to take the settlement of conflicting claims into their own hands. It gives the right of defence, but not of redress. The circumstances may be exasperating; the remedy at law may seem to be inadequate; but still the injured party cannot be arbiter of his own claim. Public order and the public peace are of greater consequence than a private right or an occasional hardship. Inadequacy of remedy is of frequent occurrence, but it cannot find its complement in personal violence. Upon these grounds the doctrine contended for by the defendants is limited to the defence of one's possession and the right of recapture as against a mere wrong-doer. It is therefore to be noted in this case that the money was in the actual possession of the plaintiff, to whom it had been entrusted for the purpose of paying help, who thereupon claimed the right to appropriate it to his own payment, supposing he might lawfully do so. Conceding that the advice was bad, nevertheless, upon such appropriation the plaintiff held the money adversely, as his own, and not as the servant or agent of the company. If his possession was the company's possession, then the company was not deprived of its property, and there could be neither occasion nor justification for violence. Possession by the company would be constructive merely, which would cease when the plaintiff exercised dominion and control on his own behalf under an honest claim of right. It is only in this way, in many cases, that conversion is established. Having thus appropriated the money to himself, it is urged that the act amounted to embezzlement, which justified the intervention of the defendants to prevent the consummation of the crime. We do not think this is so. The plaintiff stated what he had done, and the grounds upon which he claimed the right to do it, handing back the balance above what was due him. A controversy followed; he started to go out, but was stopped by the defendants, and then the assault took place. The sincerity of the plaintiff's belief that he had a right to retain the money is unquestionable. . . .

The defendants object to the charge of the court, that where a person has come into the peaceable possession of a chattel from another, the latter has no right to retake it by violence, whether the possession is lawful or unlawful, upon the ground that this rule would prevent the recapture of property obtained by trickery or fraud. The instruction must be considered not as an abstract proposition, but with reference to the case before the jury. Nothing appeared to show that the money has been procured by misrepresentation, trickery, or fraud. It was delivered to the plaintiff voluntarily, in the usual course of business. True, under the advice of a lawyer whom he had consulted, the plaintiff had previously determined to apply the money to his own payment when he should receive it; but this did not make the delivery itself fraudulent, nor did his intent to assert what he believed to be his right make that intent criminal. We think, therefore, with reference to the case as it stood, there was no error in the charge as given, nor in the refusals to charge as requested.

Exceptions overruled.

NOTES

1. Recapture of chattels. The self-help remedy of recapture is allowed when one person wrongfully obtained possession of the chattel by either force, fraud, or without claim of right. See RST §101. The privilege is broad, but not unlimited. Not only is forcible recapture denied after the voluntary transfer found in Kirby v. Foster, but it is also forbidden in a number of important commercial situations, most notably cases where the buyer or lessee of chattels has fallen behind in installment payments on property voluntarily delivered to him. Today, many of these transactions are governed by the Uniform Commercial Code, which permits a secured party to repossess collateral in the event of default without a judicial proceeding "if this can be done without breach of the peace." See U.C.C. §9-503.

Any privilege of recapture must be exercised promptly — the so-called hot pursuit requirement — or else it will be lost. As with restrictions on the use of force to defend real property, the constant tradeoff is between the benefits of self-help, which deters the initial unlawful taking, and the dangers of self-help, whose escalating violence may engulf bystanders.

2. "Recapture of land." Landlords have often been sued for assault and battery for using force to evict tenants who refuse to vacate the premises at the end of a lease. In many states, the landlord's statutory rights are modeled on the Forcible Entry Act, 1381, 5 Rich. 2, c.7, which makes it an indictable offense to enter upon land without a privilege; even with the privilege an owner may enter "not with a strong hand but in a peaceable and easy fashion." After years of uncertainty, the Court of Appeal in England finally held that although the violator may be indicted, the aggrieved tenant, being in the wrong, has no private right of action. See Hemmings v. Stoke Poges Golf Club, Ltd., 1 K.B. 720 (1920).

In the United States, the early common law cases generally followed the English approach and allowed a landlord to peaceably evict the tenant. Under this system, the tenant had a remedy only when entitled to remain on the premises, or when the eviction was forceful. See, e.g., Poppen v. Wadleigh, 51 N.W.2d 75 (Minn. 1952). With the rise of modern summary eviction statutes that expedite the landlord's ability to recover his premises by legal action, the judicial mood to landlords has stiffened. Thus, in Berg v. Wiley, 264 N.W.2d 145 (Minn. 1978), the court modified its earlier decisions by holding that the landlord committed a tort when he changed the locks on the restaurant leased by the plaintiff while she was away. The court refused to find the defendant's conduct "peaceable" under the common law rule, and concluded "the singular reason why actual violence did not erupt" when the locks were changed was the tenant's "absence and her subsequent self-restraint and resort to the judicial process." The *Berg* decision repudiates the older rule in the guise of applying it, for it rules out the possibility that any entry can ever be peaceable if not consented to by the tenant. Why force the landlord to resort to the judicial process rather than allowing the tenant a remedy (perhaps for treble or punitive damages) if the landlord's repossession falls outside the traditional common law justifications? See generally Comment, Landlord Eviction Remedies Act — Legislative Overreaction to Landlord Self-Help, 18 Wake Forest L. Rev. 25 (1982); Epstein, The Theory and Practice of Self-Help, 1 J.L. Econ. & Pol'y 1 (2005).

f. Necessity

Ploof v. Putnam
71 A. 188 (Vt. 1908)

MUNSON, J. It is alleged as the ground of recovery that on the 13th day of November, 1904, the defendant was the owner of a certain island in Lake Champlain, and of a certain dock attached thereto, which island and dock were then in charge of the defendant's servant; that the plaintiff was then possessed of and sailing upon said lake a certain loaded sloop, on which were the plaintiff and his wife and two minor children; that there then arose a sudden and violent tempest, whereby the sloop and the property and persons therein were placed in great danger of destruction; that to save these from destruction or injury the plaintiff was compelled to, and did, moor the sloop to defendant's dock; that the defendant by his servant unmoored the sloop, whereupon it was driven upon the shore by the tempest, without the plaintiff's fault; and that the sloop and its contents were thereby destroyed, and the plaintiff and his wife and children cast into the lake and upon the shore, receiving injuries.

This claim is set forth in two counts; one in trespass, charging that the defendant by his servant with force and arms wilfully and designedly unmoored the sloop; the other in case, alleging that it was the duty of the defendant by his servant to permit the plaintiff to moor his sloop to the dock, and to permit it to remain so moored during the continuance of the tempest, but that the defendant by his servant, in disregard of this duty, negligently, carelessly and wrongfully unmoored the sloop. Both counts are demurred to generally.

There are many cases in the books which hold that necessity, and an inability to control movements inaugurated in the proper exercise of a strict right, will justify entries upon land and interferences with personal property that would otherwise have been trespasses. A reference to a few of these will be sufficient to illustrate the doctrine. . . .

In trespass of cattle taken in *A*, defendant pleaded that he was seized of *C*, and found the cattle there damage feasant [causing damage], and chased them toward the pound, and that they escaped from him and went into *A*, and he presently retook them and this was held a good plea. 21 Edw. IV, 64 Vin. Ab. Trespass, H. a. 4 pl. 19. If one have a way over the land of another for his beasts to pass, and the beasts, being properly driven, feed the grass by morsels in passing, or run out of the way and are promptly pursued and brought back, trespass will not lie. See Vin. Ab. Trespass, K. a. pl. 1.

A traveller on a highway, who finds it obstructed from a sudden and temporary cause, may pass upon the adjoining land without becoming a trespasser, because of the necessity.

An entry upon land to save goods which are in danger of being lost or destroyed by water or fire is not a trespass. 21 Hen. VII, 27 Vin. Ab. Trespass, H. a. 4, pl. 24, K. a. pl. 3. In Proctor v. Adams, 113 Mass. 376 (1873), the defendant went upon the plaintiff's beach for the purpose of saving and restoring to the lawful owner a boat which had been driven ashore and was in danger of being carried off by the sea and it was held no trespass.

This doctrine of necessity applies with special force to the preservation of human life. One assaulted and in peril of his life may run through the close of another to escape from his assailant. 37 Hen. VII, pl. 26. One may sacrifice the personal property of another to save his life or the lives of his fellows. In Mouse's Case, 12 Co. 63, the defendant was sued for taking and carrying away the plaintiff's casket and its contents. It appeared that the ferryman of Gravesend took forty-seven passengers into his barge to pass to London, among whom were the plaintiff and defendant; and the barge being upon the water a great tempest happened, and a strong wind, so that the barge and all the passengers were in danger of being lost if certain ponderous things were not cast out, and the defendant thereupon cast out the plaintiff's casket. It was resolved that in case of necessity, to save the lives of the passengers, it was lawful for the defendant, being a passenger, to cast the plaintiff's casket out of the barge; that if the ferryman surcharge the barge the owner shall have his remedy upon the surcharge against the ferryman, but that if there be no surcharge, and the danger accrue only by the act of God, as by tempest, without fault of the ferryman, every one ought to bear this loss, to safeguard the life of a man.

It is clear that an entry upon the land of another may be justified by necessity, and that the declaration before us discloses a necessity for mooring the sloop. But the defendant questions the sufficiency of the counts because they do not negative the existence of natural objects to which the plaintiff could have moored with equal safety. The allegations are, in substance, that the stress of a sudden and violent tempest compelled the plaintiff to moor to defendant's dock to save his sloop and the people in it. The averment of necessity is complete, for it covers not only the necessity of mooring, but the necessity of mooring to the dock; and the details of the situation which created this necessity, whatever the legal requirements regarding them, are matters of proof and need not be alleged. It is certain that the rule suggested cannot be held applicable irrespective of circumstance, and the question must be left for adjudication upon proceedings had with reference to the evidence or the charge. . . .

Judgment affirmed and cause remanded.

NOTES

1. Necessity and self-help. While still at sea, were the plaintiffs entitled to use force to land on the dock if the defendant's servant had resisted them? To keep their boat moored to the dock? Note that under the general common law rules, the defendant's servants, while they may not resist plaintiff's entry to dock in conditions of necessity, are not obliged to lend a helping hand. See Chapter 7, Section B. Why the difference? Why should the master have to pay for his servant's torts? See Chapter 5, Section C.

2. General average contribution. Mouse's Case, 66 Eng. Rep. 1341 (K.B. 1609), discussed in cryptic form in *Ploof*, held "that in a case of necessity, for the saving of the lives of the passengers, it was lawful for the defendant, being a passenger, to cast the casket of the plaintiff out of the barge, with other things in it." Mouse's Case hints at the elaboration of the necessity principle in the law of admiralty under the rubric of general average contribution. Suppose a vessel is carrying cargo owned by a number of different parties when its master is confronted with a sudden emergency that jeopardizes the safety of the ship. Under the law of general average contribution, the master may jettison some of the cargo in order to save the ship and the remaining cargo. In order to prevent some property owners from being relatively disadvantaged by the loss of their cargo, they receive pro rata compensation from other parties, including the owner of the hull, so that the economic loss is prorated across all owners. In effect, in time of emergency all are treated as joint owners of all the property in question. This rule gives the master a desirable incentive to minimize the aggregate loss to all concerned. As each owner is placed, as it were, behind a veil of ignorance, he can do best by himself only if he does best by all owners of hull and cargo alike. On the complexities of the law of general average contribution see G. Gilmore and C. Black, The Law of Admiralty

§§5.1, 5.2 (2d ed. 1975). See also Landes and Posner, Salvors, Finders, Good Samaritans, and Other Rescuers: An Economic Study of Law and Altruism, 7 J. Legal Stud. 83, 106-108 (1978).

Vincent v. Lake Erie Transportation Co.
124 N.W. 221 (Minn. 1910)

O'BRIEN, J. The steamship Reynolds, owned by the defendant, was for the purpose of discharging her cargo on November 27, 1905, moored to plaintiff's dock in Duluth. While the unloading of the boat was taking place a storm from the northeast developed, which at about ten o'clock P.M., when the unloading was completed, had so grown in violence that the wind was then moving at fifty miles per hour and continued to increase during the night. There is some evidence that one, and perhaps two, boats were able to enter the harbor that night, but it is plain that navigation was practically suspended from the hour mentioned until the morning of the twenty-ninth, when the storm abated, and during that time no master would have been justified in attempting to navigate his vessel, if he could avoid doing so. After the discharge of the cargo the Reynolds signaled for a tug to tow her from the dock, but none could be obtained because of the severity of the storm. If the lines holding the ship to the dock had been cast off, she would doubtless have drifted away; but, instead, the lines were kept fast, and as soon as one parted or chafed it was replaced, sometimes with a larger one. The vessel lay upon the outside of the dock, her bow to the east, the wind and waves striking her starboard quarter with such force that she was constantly being lifted and thrown against the dock, resulting in its damage, as found by the jury, to the amount of $500.

We are satisfied that the character of this storm was such that it would have been highly imprudent for the master of the Reynolds to have attempted to leave the dock or to have permitted his vessel to drift away from it. One witness testified upon the trial that the vessel could have been warped into a slip, and that, if the attempt to bring the ship into the slip had failed, the worst that could have happened would be that the vessel would have been blown ashore upon a soft and muddy bank. The witness was not present in Duluth at the time of the storm, and, while he may have been right in his conclusions, those in charge of the dock and the vessel at the time of the storm were not required to use the highest human intelligence, nor were they required to resort to every possible experiment which could be suggested for the preservation of their property. Nothing more was demanded of them than ordinary prudence and care, and the record in this case fully sustains the contention of the appellant that, in holding the vessel fast to the dock, those in charge of her exercised good judgment and prudent seamanship.

It is claimed by the respondent that it was negligence to moor the boat at an exposed part of the wharf, and to continue in that position after it became apparent that the storm was to be more than usually severe. We do not agree with this position. The part of the wharf where the vessel was moored appears to have been commonly used for that purpose. It was situated within the harbor at Duluth, and must, we think, be considered a proper and safe place, and would undoubtedly have been such during what would be considered a very severe storm. The storm which made it unsafe was one which surpassed in violence any which might have reasonably been anticipated.

The appellant contends by ample assignments of error that, because its conduct during the storm was rendered necessary by prudence and good seamanship under conditions over which it had no control, it cannot be held liable for any injury resulting to the property of others, and claims that the jury should have been so instructed. An analysis of the charge given by the trial court is not necessary, as in our opinion the only question for the jury was the amount of damages which the plaintiffs were entitled to recover, and no complaint is made upon that score.

The situation was one in which the ordinary rules regulating property rights were suspended by forces beyond human control, and if, without the direct intervention of some act by the one sought to be held liable, the property of another was injured, such injury must be attributed to the act of God, and not to the wrongful act of the person sought to be charged. If during the storm the Reynolds had entered the harbor, and while there had become disabled and been thrown against the plaintiffs' dock, the plaintiffs could not have recovered. Again, if while attempting to hold fast to the dock the lines had parted, without any negligence, and the vessel carried against some other boat or dock in the harbor, there would be no liability upon her owner. But here those in charge of the vessel deliberately and by their direct efforts held her in such a position that the damage to the dock resulted, and, having thus preserved the ship at the expense of the dock, it seems to us that her owners are responsible to the dock owners to the extent of the injury inflicted.

In Depue v. Flatau, 111 N.W. 1 (Minn. 1907), this court held that where the plaintiff, while lawfully in the defendants' house, became so ill that he was incapable of traveling with safety, the defendants were responsible to him in damages for compelling him to leave the premises. If, however, the owner of the premises had furnished the traveler with proper accommodations and medical attendance, would he have been able to defeat an action brought against him for their reasonable worth?

In Ploof v. Putnam (Vt.) 71 Atl. 188, the Supreme Court of Vermont held that where, under stress of weather, a vessel was without permission moored to a private dock at an island in Lake Champlain owned by the defendant, the plaintiff was not guilty of trespass, and that the defendant was responsible in damages because his representative upon the island unmoored the vessel, permitting it to drift upon the shore, with resultant injuries to it. If, in that case, the vessel had been permitted to remain, and the dock had suffered an injury, we believe the shipowner would have been held liable for the injury done.

Theologians hold that a starving man may, without moral guilt, take what is necessary to sustain life but it could hardly be said that the obligation would not be upon such person to pay the value of the property so taken when he became able to do so. And so public necessity, in times of war or peace, may require the taking of private property for public purposes; but under our system of jurisprudence compensation must be made.

Let us imagine in this case that for the better mooring of the vessel those in charge of her had appropriated a valuable cable lying upon the dock. No matter how justifiable such appropriation might have been, it would not be claimed that, because of the overwhelming necessity of the situation, the owner of the cable could not recover its value.

This is not a case where life or property was menaced by any object or thing belonging to the plaintiffs, the destruction of which became necessary to prevent the threatened disaster. Nor is it a case where, because of the act of God, or unavoidable accident, the infliction of the injury was beyond the control of the defendant, but is one where the defendant prudently and advisedly availed itself of the plaintiffs' property for the purpose of preserving its own more valuable property, and the plaintiffs are entitled to compensation for the injury done.

Order affirmed.

LEWIS, J. I dissent. It was assumed on the trial before the lower court that appellant's liability depended on whether the master of the ship might, in the exercise of reasonable care, have sought a place of safety before the storm made it impossible to leave the dock. The majority opinion assumes that the evidence is conclusive that appellant moored its boat at respondents' dock pursuant to contract, and that the vessel was lawfully in position at the time the additional cables were fastened to the dock, and the reasoning of the opinion is that, because appellant made use of the stronger cables to hold the boat in position, it became liable under the rule that it had voluntarily made use of the property of another for the purpose of saving its own.

In my judgment, if the boat was lawfully in position at the time the storm broke, and the master could not, in the exercise of due care, have left that position without subjecting his vessel to the hazards of the storm, then the damage to the dock, caused by the pounding of the boat, was the result of an inevitable accident. If the master was in the exercise of due care, he was not at fault. The reasoning of the opinion admits that if the ropes, or cables, first attached to the dock had not parted, or if, in the first instance, the master had used the stronger cables, there would be no liability. If the master could not, in the exercise of reasonable care, have anticipated the severity of the storm and sought a place of safety before it became impossible, why should he be required to anticipate the severity of the storm, and, in the first instance, use the stronger cables?

I am of the opinion that one who constructs a dock to the navigable line of waters, and enters into contractual relations with the owner of a vessel to moor the same, takes the risk of damage to his dock by a boat caught there by a storm, which event could not have been avoided in the exercise of due care, and further, that the legal status of the parties in such a case is not changed by renewal of cables to keep the boat from being cast adrift at the mercy of the tempest.

JAGGARD, J. I concur with Lewis, J.

NOTES

1. Private necessity, assumption of risk, and unjust enrichment. Under traditional law, *Vincent* represents a case of "conditional" or "incomplete" privilege. The defendant may use or damage the plaintiff's dock, which he could not do in the absence of necessity, but, in contrast to self-defense, he must pay for the privilege with reasonable rental value or compensation for lost or damaged property, as the case may be. See RST §197. A case of incomplete privilege usually occurs between strangers, but it may also arise where a business invitee or social guest remains on an owner's property, after being asked to leave, to avoid facing the necessity. Does the majority opinion ever come to grips with the dissent's contention that the case turns on how the mooring contract allocated the risk of damages? How does one decide which risks the shipowner assumed when the contract does not expressly cover the problem? See generally Bohlen, Incomplete Privilege to Inflict Intentional Invasions of Interests of Property and Personalty, 39 Harv. L. Rev. 307 (1926), reprinted in his Studies in the Law of Torts at 614 (1926). See also Epstein, A Theory of Strict Liability, 2 J. Legal Stud. 151, 157-160 (1973); Weinrib, Causation and Wrongdoing, 63 Chi.-Kent L. Rev. 407, 425-429 (1987), Smith, Property and Property Rules, 79 N.Y.U. L. Rev. 1719 (2004).

Vincent may also be justified under a theory of "unjust enrichment," which requires the boat owner to compensate the dock owner for the benefit that he received from the use of the dock. How does that theory work if the shipowner's benefit is $10,000, and the harm to the dock $500? When the figures are reversed? When the ship is lost and the dock damaged? See generally, on unjust enrichment, Keeton, Conditional Fault in the Law of Torts, 72 Harv. L. Rev. 401, 410 (1959).

2. Necessity and bilateral monopoly. The private necessity issue also has an important contractual dimension. Suppose that a vessel in distress at sea seeks to dock where the normal mooring fee is $100. In a world in which prices are determined solely by private agreement, the dock owner may "hold out" for a larger fee, perhaps one approaching the value of the boat and cargo. If the boat owner complies with the demand, should he be held to the contractual price when the dock owner practiced neither fraud nor duress? The standard response, both in admiralty and at common law, is to void the contract and restrict the dock owner's recovery to a reasonable fee. The point has been made most forcefully with contracts for salvage, or rescue at sea by professional salvors:

> Courts of admiralty will enforce contracts made for salvage service and salvage compensation, where the salvor has not taken advantage of his power to make an unreasonable bargain; but they will not tolerate the doctrine that a salvor can take advantage of his situation, and avail himself of the calamities of others to drive a bargain; nor will they permit the performance of a public duty to be turned into a traffic of profit. The general interests of commerce will be much better promoted by requiring the salvor to trust for compensation to the liberal recompense usually awarded by the courts for such services.

Post v. Jones, 60 U.S. (19 How.) 150, 160 (1856). In practice, the holdout problem at sea is often averted by the common practice of referring salvage awards to arbitration, often through Lloyd's of London, where they are resolved in accordance with standard industry practice. Formerly, the salvor's award had been limited to the rescue of hull and cargo. Now that liability for pollution has become a major economic risk, salvage awards specifically include "liability salvage" for preventing spillage, notwithstanding the obvious measurement problems involved. See Brough, Liability Salvage — By Private Ordering, 19 J. Legal Stud. 95 (1990).

3. *Public necessity.* When are private or government agents privileged to destroy private property to protect the interests of the community at large? The problem has arisen chiefly in two contexts: first, where property is destroyed in order to prevent the destruction of a city by fire and, second, where it is destroyed to keep it from falling into enemy hands in time of war. In Mayor of New York v. Lord, 18 Wend. 126, 129 (N.Y. 1837), the court held that it was "well settled" that the privilege was absolute "in cases of actual necessity, to prevent the spreading of a fire, the ravages of a pestilence, the advance of a hostile army, or any other great public calamity, the private property of an individual may be lawfully taken and used or destroyed, for the relief, protection or safety of the many, without subjecting those, whose duty it is to protect the public interests, by or under whose direction such private property was taken or destroyed, to personal liability for the damage which the owner has thereby sustained." In the words of Bohlen, "since the benefit is solely social, there is no reason why one who acts as a champion of the public should be required to pay for

the privilege of so doing." Bohlen, Incomplete Privilege, 39 Harv. L. Rev. 307, 317-318 (1926); Studies in the Law of Torts at 627. Should the person whose property is converted to the public use be required against his will to become the champion of the public?

In many cases of public necessity, the property destroyed would have been lost anyway. The city fire would have consumed the homes demolished in order to prevent its spread; the industrial installations blown up would have been taken or destroyed by the enemy. In these cases, the plaintiff loses not because the privilege is complete, but because virtually all the loss is caused by a third party.

Sometimes, however, the property would *not* have been destroyed without the defendant's intervention. The fire died out before it reached the demolished homes; the enemy was unable to capture the installations. In these cases, the defendant must rest solely on the privilege. The Pennsylvania Supreme Court in Respublica v. Sparhawk, 1 U.S. 357, 362 (Pa. 1788) justified the complete privilege in this way: "We find, indeed, a memorable instance of folly recorded in the 3 Vol. of Clarendon's History, where it is mentioned, that the Lord Mayor of London, in 1666, when that city was on fire, would not give directions for, or consent to, the pulling down forty wooden houses, or to the removing the furniture, &c. belonging to the Lawyers of the Temple, then on the Circuit, for fear he should be answerable for a trespass; and in consequence of this conduct half that great city was burnt."

Sparhawk reveals the asymmetrical incentives found in all cases of public necessity. The public official who wrongly orders the destruction of property bears all the loss if his prediction proves false, but captures none of the gain if correct. Why then should he act at all? As the official cannot recoup his losses from the owners of the saved property, the only way to balance his incentives is to insulate him from liability, at least when he acts reasonably and in good faith. But this approach, taken alone, does not compensate the individual owners who suffer enormous private losses for the benefit of the community at large. Should an aggrieved landowner be allowed an action for restitution against the benefited landowners? From the government? If so, should it pay out of general revenues, or from special assessments levied against the parties benefited? On the general merits of personal and official immunity, see the symposium, Civil Liability for Government Officials: Property Rights and Official Accountability, 42 Law & Contemp. Probs. 8 (1978) and *infra* at Chapter 17, Section E.

4. Public necessity and just compensation. The complete privilege for public necessity is in constant tension with the basic constitutional principle that requires the government to compensate private owners whose property is taken for public use. For a vivid example that tests the line between the two doctrines during wartime, see United States v. Caltex, Inc., 344 U.S. 149 (1952), where the Court refused to order compensation for the demolition of an oil company's terminal facilities in Manila before the Japanese takeover, Black and Douglas, JJ., dissenting. Likewise, in National Board of Y.M.C.A.s v. United States, 395 U.S. 85 (1969), the Court found no compensable taking when United States army troops occupied the plaintiff's buildings located in the Panama Canal Zone after they had been placed under siege by rioting Panamanians who had already caused substantial damage to the structures. See Broeder, Torts and Just Compensation: Some Personal Reflections, 17 Hastings L.J. 217 (1965).

The issue of public necessity was obliquely raised in Scheuer v. Rhodes, 416 U.S. 232, 246-248 (1974), where several Kent State students were either killed or injured by the National Guardsmen sent to the campus by James Rhodes, then governor of Ohio. Chief Justice Burger addressed the relationship between official immunity and public necessity, noting that in times of civic disorder, the confusion and uncertainty created by fast moving events required the creation of some privilege. But he shrunk from making that privilege absolute, holding that

> [t]hese considerations suggest that, in varying scope, a qualified immunity is available to officers of the executive branch of government, the variation being dependent upon the scope of discretion and responsibilities of the office and all the circumstances as they reasonably appeared at the time of the action on which liability is sought to be based. It is the existence of reasonable grounds for the belief formed at the time and in light of all the circumstances, coupled with good-faith belief, that affords a basis for qualified immunity of executive officers for acts performed in the course of official conduct. Mr. Justice Holmes spoke of this, stating:
>
>> No doubt there are cases where the expert on the spot may be called upon to justify his conduct later in court, notwithstanding the fact that he had sole command at the time and acted to the best of his knowledge. That is the position of the captain of a ship. But even in that case great weight is given to his determination and the matter is to be judged on the facts as they appeared then and not merely in the light of the event. Moyer v. Peabody, 212 U.S. 78, 85 (1909).

At trial the jury verdict was for all defendants, including Rhodes. The case was later reversed on grounds of jury tampering, see Krause v. Rhodes, 570 F.2d 563 (6th Cir. 1977), and was settled thereafter.

Judith Jarvis Thomson, The Trolley Problem
94 Yale L.J. 1395 (1985)

Some years ago, Philippa Foot drew attention to an extraordinarily interesting problem. Suppose you are the driver of a trolley. The trolley rounds a bend, and there come into view ahead five track workmen, who have been repairing the track. The track goes through a bit of a valley at that point, and the sides are steep, so you must stop the trolley if you are to avoid running the five men down. You step on the brakes, but alas they don't work. Now you suddenly see a spur of track leading off to the right. You can turn the trolley onto it, and thus save the five men on the straight trace ahead. Unfortunately, Mrs. Foot has arranged that there is one track workman on that spur of track. He can no more get off the track in time than the five can, so you will kill him if you turn the trolley onto him. Is it morally permissible for you to turn the trolley?

Everybody to whom I have put this hypothetical case says, Yes, it is. Some people say something stronger than that it is morally *permissible* for you to turn the trolley: They say that morally speaking, you *must* turn it — that morality requires you to do so. Others do not agree that morality requires you to turn the trolley, and even feel a certain discomfort at the idea of turning it. But everybody says that it is true, at a minimum, that you *may* turn it — that it would not be morally wrong in you to do so.

Now consider a second hypothetical case. This time you are to imagine yourself to be a surgeon, a truly great surgeon. Among other things you do, you transplant organs, and you are such a great surgeon that the organs you transplant always take. At the moment you have five patients who need organs. Two need one lung each, two need a kidney each, and the fifth needs a heart. If they do not get those organs today, they will all die; if you find organs for them today you can transplant the organs and they will all live. But where to find the lungs, the kidneys, and the heart? The time is almost up when a report is brought to you that a young man who has just come into your clinic for his yearly check-up has exactly the right blood-type, and is in excellent health. Lo, you have your possible donor. All you need do is cut him up and distribute *his* parts among the five who need them. You ask, but he says, "Sorry. I deeply sympathize, but no." Would it be morally permissible for you to operate anyway? Everybody to whom I have put this second hypothetical says, No, it would not be morally permissible for you to proceed.

Here then is Mrs. Foot's problem: *Why* is it that the trolley driver may turn his trolley, though the surgeon may not remove the young man's lungs, kidneys, and heart? In both cases, one will die if the agent acts, but five will live who would otherwise die — net saving of four lives. What difference in the other facts of these cases explains the moral difference between them? I fancy that the theorists of tort and criminal law will find this problem as interesting as the moral theorist does.

NOTE

Moral and legal theories. Having restated Foot's problem, Professor Thomson then explores some possible responses. If, morally speaking, it is worse to kill than to let die, then the surgeon should not act while the trolley driver can turn the wheel because his only choice is between killing one and killing five. But suppose, as Thomson next suggests, a bystander is able to throw a switch that will divert the trolley from its original track, but can choose to do nothing, in which case the trolley will kill five? Is the bystander not justified in doing what the trolley driver may do?

Note also that one difference between the two cases rests on the observation that the crisis "suddenly" struck the driver, but not the surgeon. Accordingly, an alternative approach shifts attention to the long-term effects of adopting one rule or the other. So long as the trolley driver is held responsible whether he kills one or five, he faces two separate incentives: the first, which is the subject of the Thomson inquiry, is to minimize the number of deaths *once* the emergency occurs. The second is to check the brakes to prevent the emergency from arising in the first place — an incentive that remains in place so long as the liability rule remains fixed. But the effects on the famous surgeon in the prior period are quite different, for she will never be able to attract patients in the first place if she is intent on cutting them up to help others. Over the long haul, it might be possible to organize a voluntary market for the sale of organs either during life or after death, which has none of the downside of coerced transfers. Yet while organ donations are legal today, their sale is flatly prohibited by federal law. For a trenchant critique, see Cohen, Increasing the Supply of Transplant Organs: The Virtues of a Futures Market, 58 Geo. Wash. L. Rev. 1 (1989).

SECTION C.   EMOTIONAL AND DIGNITARY HARMS

1.   *Assault*

I. de S. and Wife v. W. de S.
At the Assizes, coram Thorpe, C.J., 1348 [or 1349] Year Book,
Liber Assisarum, folio 99, placitum 60

I. de S. & M. uxor ejus querunt de W. de S. de eo quod idem W. anno, & c., vi et armis, & c., apud S., in ipsam M. insultum fecit, et ipsam verberavit, & c. [I. de S. and his wife, M., sue W. de S. concerning that which in the year, etc., by force and arms, etc., at S. has made insults of the aforesaid M., and has beat her.] And W. pleaded not guilty. And it was found by verdict of the inquest that the said W. came in the night to the house of the said I., and would have bought some wine, but the door of the tavern was closed; and he struck on the door with a hatchet, which he had in his hand, and the woman plaintiff put her head out at a window and ordered him to stop; and he perceived her and struck with the hatchet, but did not touch the woman.

Whereupon the inquest said that it seemed to them that there was no trespass, since there was no harm done.

THORPE, C.J. There is harm, and a trespass for which they shall recover
damages, since he made an assault upon the woman, as it is found, although
he did no other harm. Wherefore tax his damages, & c. And they taxed the
damages at half a mark.

Thorpe, C.J., awarded that they should recover their damages, & c., and
that the other should be taken. Et sic nota, [And thus it was noted] that for
an assault one shall recover damages, & c.

Tuberville v. Savage
86 Eng. Rep. 684 (K.B. 1669)

Action of *assault, battery,* and *wounding.* The evidence to prove a provocation was, that the plaintiff put his hand upon his sword and said, "If *it were
not assize-time, I would not take such language from you.*" — The question was, If
that were an assault? — The Court agreed that it was not; for the declaration
of the plaintiff was, that he would not assault him, the Judges being in town;
and *the intention* as well as *the act* makes an assault. Therefore if one strike
another upon the hand, or arm, or breast in discourse, it is no assault, there
being no *intention* to assault; but if one intending to assault, strike *at* another
and miss him, this is an assault: so if he hold up his hand against another in
a threatening manner and say nothing, it is an assault. — In the principal
case the plaintiff had judgment.

W. Blackstone, Commentaries
Vol. 3, p. 120 (1765)

[A]ssault [is] an attempt to offer to beat another, without touching him: as
if one lifts up his cane, or his fist, in a threatening manner at another; or
strikes at him, but misses him; this is an assault, insultus, which Finch
describes to be "an unlawful setting upon one's person." This also is an
inchoate violence, amounting considerably higher than bare threats; and
therefore, though no actual suffering is proved, yet the party injured may
have redress by action of trespass vi et armis; wherein he shall recover
damages as compensation for the injury.

NOTES

1. *The social protection against assaults.* Does *I. de S.* give uniform
protection against mental distress from the threat of assault? Should the

defendant be liable for assault when he first struck the door with the hatchet if he knew that the plaintiff was inside? If he thought there was a good chance she was inside? Should it matter that the defendant struck the second blow — where? why? how? — only after he "perceived" the plaintiff?

The dangers to the social fabric from threats of force were forcefully stated in Allen v. Hannaford, 244 P. 700 (Wash. 1926). There the plaintiff had hired moving men to take her furniture from an apartment she had rented from the defendant. The defendant had claimed a lien on the plaintiff's furniture (that is, a right to seize the furniture, sell it, and apply the proceeds to unpaid back rent). When the defendant discovered that the furniture was being removed, she appeared with a pistol and threatened to shoot the moving men "full of holes" if they took a single piece of the plaintiff's furniture. Then "standing only a few feet from [plaintiff], she pointed the pistol at her face and threatened to shoot her." The court rejected the defendant's argument that she could not be guilty of an assault for brandishing an unloaded gun, saying "[w]hether there is an assault in a given case depends more upon the apprehensions created in the mind of the person assaulted than upon what may be the secret intentions of the person committing the assault." The court then affirmed the $750 verdict for the plaintiff, quoting the observations from Beach v. Hancock, 27 N.H. 223 (1853):

> One of the most important objects to be attained by the enactment of laws and the institutions of civilized society is, each of us shall feel secure against unlawful assaults. Without such security society loses most of its value. Peace and order and domestic happiness, inexpressibly more precious than mere forms of government, cannot be enjoyed without the sense of perfect security. We have a right to live in society without being put in fear of personal harm. But it must be a reasonable fear of which we complain. And it surely is not unreasonable for a person to entertain a fear of personal injury, when a pistol is pointed at him in a threatening manner, when, for aught he knows, it may be loaded, and may occasion his immediate death. The business of the world could not be carried on with comfort, if such things could be done with impunity.

If the gun was not pointed toward the plaintiff, did the defendant only make, to use Blackstone's distinction, a "mere threat" or did she commit an act of "inchoate violence"? Is there an assault if the plaintiff knows that the defendant is wielding an unloaded gun?

2. Mere words, conditional threats, and the use of force. The time-honored common law maxim — "mere words do not amount to an assault" — applies to strong words used during argument. It has been criticized as overlooking the subtle (and not-so-subtle) ways the voice alone can convey threats of the immediate or future use of force. Undoubtedly, this formula is meant to preclude liability in common situations in which intemperate or insulting speech injures feelings or arouses apprehension. In Tuberville v. Savage, why did the court assume that the plaintiff's words gave an accurate reading of his intention, instead of being a ruse to catch the defendant off guard? What result if it had not been "assize-time" (that is, if the judge were not in town), and the plaintiff had said, "If it were not for my generous nature, I would not take such language from you"?

The limits of the common law action for assault are also tested when the defendant makes a threat at a distance. In Brower v. Ackerly, 943 P.2d 1141 (Wash. App. 1997), the defendants ran a billboard advertising business. The plaintiff, who was active in civic affairs, reported to the Seattle City Council that many of the defendants' billboards were operated without permits and were kept off the tax rolls. When the City did not respond, the plaintiff filed a separate lawsuit against both it and the defendants. Two days later, an anonymous male caller began a campaign of telephone harassment against the plaintiff, which included calling him a "dick" and saying, "I'm going to find out where you live and I am going to kick your ass." After the calls were traced to one of the Ackerlys' sons, the action for assault ensued, in which the plaintiff argued that even though mere words do not constitute an assault, these "spoken threats became assaultive in view of the surrounding circumstances including the fact that the calls were made to his home, at night, creating the impression that the caller was stalking him." But the court denied the action, noting the absence of an immediate threat. Which matters more, the directness of the threat or the probability that it will be carried out?

3. The Second Restatement definition.

§21. ASSAULT
   (1) An actor is subject to liability to another for assault if
      (a) he acts intending to cause a harmful or offensive contact with the person of the other or a third person, or an imminent apprehension of such a contact, and
      (b) the other is thereby put in such imminent apprehension.

The Restatement (Second) of Torts then refines its use of the term "apprehension" in §24, comment b:

   b. *Distinction between apprehension and fright.* It is not necessary that the other believe that the act done by the actor will be effective in inflicting the intended contact upon him. It is enough that he believes that the act is capable of immediately inflicting the contact upon him unless something further occurs. Therefore, the mere fact that he can easily prevent the threatened contact by self-defensive measures which he feels amply capable of taking does not prevent the actor's attempt to inflict the contact upon him from being an actionable assault. So too, he may have every reason to believe that bystanders will interfere in time to prevent the blow threatened by the actor from taking effect and his belief may be justified by the event. Bystanders may intervene and prevent the actor from striking him. None the less, the actor's blow thus prevented from taking effect is an actionable assault. The apprehension which is sufficient to make the actor liable may have no relation to fear, which at least implies a doubt as to whether the actor's attempt is capable of certain frustration.

Ordinary English regards apprehension and fear as synonyms and not as distinct terms. The Restatement, therefore, consciously deviates from common usage to make the point that the plaintiff has suffered a compensable injury from a threat of attack that is easily warded off.

2. Offensive Battery

Alcorn v. Mitchell
63 Ill. 553 (1872)

SHELDON, J. The ground mainly relied on for the reversal of the judgment in this case is, that the damages are excessive, being $1000.

The case presented is this: There was a trial of an action of trespass between the parties, wherein the appellee was defendant, in the circuit court of Jasper county. At the close of the trial the court adjourned, and, immediately upon the adjournment, in the court room, in the presence of a large number of persons, the appellant deliberately spat in the face of the appellee.

So long as damages are allowable in any civil case, by way of punishment or for the sake of example, the present, of all cases, would seem to be a most fit one for the award of such damages.

The act in question was one of the greatest indignity, highly provocative of retaliation by force, and the law, as far as it may, should afford substantial protection against such outrages, in the way of liberal damages, that the public tranquillity may be preserved by saving the necessity of resort to personal violence as the only means of redress.

Suitors, in the assertion of their rights, should be allowed approach to the temple of justice without incurring there exposure to such disgraceful indignities, in the very presence of its ministers.

It is customary to instruct juries that they may give vindictive damages where there are circumstances of malice, wilfulness, wantonness, outrage and indignity attending the wrong complained of. The act in question was wholly made up of such qualities. It was one of pure malignity, done for the mere purpose of insult and indignity.

An exasperated suitor has indulged the gratification of his malignant feelings in this despicable mode. The act was the very refinement of malice.

The defendant appears to be a man of wealth; we can not say that he has been made to pay too dearly for the indulgence. . . .

The judgment must be affirmed.

NOTE

Basis of liability for offensive battery. What result in Alcorn v. Mitchell if the appellee spat at the appellant but missed? Does it make a difference whether the appellant knew that the appellee spat at him? That others in the courtroom knew?

The Restatement (Second) of Torts defines an offensive battery as follows:

> §18. BATTERY: OFFENSIVE CONTACT
>   (1) An actor is subject to liability to another for battery if
>   (a) he acts intending to cause a harmful or offensive contact with the person of the other or a third person, or an imminent apprehension of such a contact, and
>   (b) an offensive contact with the person of the other directly or indirectly results.
>   (2) An act which is not done with the intention stated in Subsection (1)(a) does not make the actor liable to the other for a mere offensive contact with the other's person although the act involves an unreasonable risk of inflicting it and, therefore, would be negligent or reckless if the risk threatened bodily harm.

There are many reported cases of nonharmful offensive batteries. In Respublica v. De Longchamps, 1 U.S. (1 Dall.) 111 (Pa. 1784), defendant struck the cane of the French ambassador and was prosecuted under the law of nations. The court remarked: "As to the assault, this is, perhaps, one of that kind, in which the insult is more to be considered than the actual damage; for, though no great bodily pain is suffered by a blow on the palm of the hand, or the skirt of the coat, yet these are clearly within the definition of assault and battery, and among gentlemen too often induce duelling and terminate in murder." The Restatement notes that knowledge that unpermitted conduct has taken place is not necessary to establish the battery. "*A* kisses *B* while asleep but does not waken or harm her. *A* is subject to liability to *B*." RST §18, comment *d*, illus. 2.

The protection afforded against offensive battery covers not only cases of direct contact with the plaintiff's person, but also contact with "anything so closely attached [to the plaintiff's person] that it is customarily regarded as a part thereof and which is offensive to a reasonable sense of personal dignity." RST §18, comment *c*. An example is the striking of the plaintiff's cane in the *Longchamps* case, *supra*; for other such acts see Clark v. Downing, 55 Vt. 259 (1882) (striking the horse that plaintiff was riding); Morgan v. Loyacomo, 1 So. 2d 510 (Miss. 1941) (seizing an object from plaintiff's hand); and Fisher v. Carrousel Motor Hotel, Inc., 424 S.W.2d 627 (Tex. 1967) (grabbing at plaintiff's plate); Leichtman v. WLW Jacor Communications Inc., 534 N.E.2d 697 (Ohio App. 1994) (blowing smoke in the face of an anti-smoking activist).

3. False Imprisonment

Bird v. Jones
115 Eng. Rep. 688 (K.B. 1845)

COLERIDGE, J. . . . This point is, whether certain facts, which may be taken as clear upon the evidence, amount to an imprisonment. . . .

A part of a public highway was inclosed, and appropriated for spectators of a boat race, paying a price for their seats. The plaintiff was desirous of entering this part, and was opposed by the defendant: but, after a struggle, during which no momentary detention of his person took place, he succeeded in climbing over the inclosure. Two policemen were then stationed by the defendant to prevent, and they did prevent, him from passing onwards in the direction in which he declared his wish to go: but he was allowed to remain unmolested where he was, and was at liberty to go, and was told that he was so, in the only other direction by which he could pass. This he refused for some time, and, during that time, remained where he had thus placed himself.

These are the facts: . . . that the plaintiff, being in a public highway and desirous of passing along it, in a particular direction, is prevented from doing so by the orders of the defendant, . . . But, although thus obstructed, the plaintiff was at liberty to move his person and go in any other direction, at his free will and pleasure: and no actual force or restraint on his person was used, unless the obstruction before mentioned amounts to so much. . . .

And I am of opinion that there was no imprisonment. To call it so appears to me to confound partial obstruction and disturbance with total obstruction and detention. A prison may have its boundary large or narrow, visible and tangible, or, though real, still in the conception only; it may itself be moveable or fixed: but a boundary it must have; and that boundary the party imprisoned must be prevented from passing; he must be prevented from leaving that place, within the ambit of which the party imprisoning would confine him, except by prison-breach. Some confusion seems to me to arise from confounding imprisonment of the body with mere loss of freedom: it is one part of the definition of freedom to be able to go whithersoever one pleases; but imprisonment is something more than the mere loss of this power; it includes the notion of restraint within some limits defined by a will or power exterior to our own.

. . . If it be said that to hold the present case to amount to an imprisonment would turn every obstruction of the exercise of a right of way into an imprisonment, the answer is, that there must be something like personal menace or force accompanying the act of obstruction, and that, with this, it will amount to imprisonment. I apprehend that is not so. If, in the course of a night, both ends of a street were walled up, and there was no egress from the house but into the street, I should have no difficulty in saying that the inhabitants were thereby imprisoned; but, if only one end were walled up, and an armed force stationed outside to prevent any scaling of the wall or passage that way, I should feel equally clear that there was no imprisonment. If there were, the street would obviously be the prison; and yet, as obviously, none would be confined to it.

[Defendant's request for a new trial was granted. The concurring opinion of Williams, J., is omitted.]

LORD DENMAN, C.J. [dissenting] . . . There is some difficulty perhaps in defining imprisonment in the abstract without reference to its illegality; nor is it necessary for me to do so, because I consider these acts as amounting to imprisonment. That word I understand to mean any restraint of the person by force. . . .

I had no idea that any person in these times supposed any particular boundary to be necessary to constitute imprisonment, or that the restraint of a man's person from doing what he desires ceases to be an imprisonment because he may find some means of escape.

It is said that the party here was at liberty to go in another direction. I am not sure that in fact he was, because the same unlawful power which prevented him from taking one course might, in case of acquiescence, have refused him any other. But this liberty to do something else does not appear to me to affect the question of imprisonment. As long as I am prevented from doing what I have a right to do, of what importance is it that I am permitted to do something else? How does the imposition of an unlawful condition show that I am not restrained? If I am locked in a room, am I not imprisoned because I might effect my escape through a window, or because I might find an exit dangerous or inconvenient to myself, as by wading through water or by taking a route so circuitous that my necessary affairs would suffer by delay?

It is said that, if any damage arises from such obstruction, a special action on the case may be brought. Must I then sue out a new writ stating that the defendant employed direct force to prevent my going where my business called me, whereby I sustained loss? And, if I do, is it certain that I shall not be told that I have misconceived my remedy, for all flows from the false imprisonment, and that should have been the subject of an action of trespass and assault? For the jury properly found that the whole of the defendant's conduct was continuous: it commenced in illegality; and the plaintiff did right to resist it as an outrageous violation of the liberty of the subject from the very first.

NOTES

1. *Three walls do not a prison make.* As Bird v. Jones illustrates, an action for false (i.e., wrongful) imprisonment depends on a showing of effective confinement, not a simple restriction on movement. In Whittaker v. Sandford, 85 A. 399, 402-403 (Me. 1912), a woman was given complete freedom of movement on defendant's palatial yacht, but when she occasionally allowed on shore, she was not given liberty to roam or to remain there. She was held to have been imprisoned while on the yacht so long as she was denied access to shore by a boat. But her damages were reduced from $1,100 to $500 because she was not kept in "close confinement." "She was afforded all the liberties of the yacht. She was taken on shore by her husband to do shopping and transact business at a bank. She visited neighboring islands with her husband and children, on one of which they enjoyed a family picnic. The case lacks the elements of humiliation and disgrace that frequently attend false imprisonment. She was respectfully treated as a guest in every way, except that she was restrained from quitting the yacht for good and all."

Section 36, comment *b,* of the Restatement (Second) of Torts reads: "The area within which another is completely confined may be large and need not be stationary. Whether the area from which the actor prevents the other from going is so large that it ceases to be a confinement within the area and becomes an exclusion from some other area may depend upon the circumstances of the particular case and be a matter for the judgment of the court and jury." Illustration 6 under this comment reads: "*A* by an invalid process restrains *B* within prison limits which are coterminous with the boundaries of a considerable town. *A* has confined *B*." The Restatement further suggests that wrongfully excluding the plaintiff from the United States would not amount to false imprisonment even though, in a sense, the plaintiff "may be said to be confined within the residue of the habitable world."

2. *Basis of liability for false imprisonment.* There is some confusion over the basis of liability for false imprisonment. Usually the defendant must intend to confine the plaintiff, with no liability for negligently caused imprisonments. See RST §35. That result seems appropriate for minor harms, in which the concern with dignity is paramount. Yet when the plaintiff suffers major physical harm from the defendant's imprisonment, ordinary negligence principles tend to take over. Thus, to use the Restatement illustration (§35, illus. 2), suppose that defendant mistakenly locked plaintiff

in a walk-in cold storage vault that he had permitted plaintiff to enter. If defendant discovers his mistake in time to release the plaintiff before serious injury results, the Restatement excuses him from the unpleasant consequences of the "momentary confinement." Where, however, the defendant discovers his mistake only hours later, the Restatement applies ordinary negligence principles if, for example, pneumonia occurs as a result of the confinement.

Coblyn v. Kennedy's, Inc.
268 N.E.2d 860 (Mass. 1971)

[The plaintiff, a 70-year-old man, five feet four inches tall, and dressed in a woolen shirt, topcoat, and hat, was shopping in defendant's store. Around his neck plaintiff wore an ascot he had previously purchased in Filene's, another department store. While trying on a sportscoat, the plaintiff took off his ascot and put it into his pocket. He purchased the coat, left it downstairs for alterations, and, as he was leaving the store, took the ascot out of his pocket and put it on again. At that moment the defendant Goss, an employee of Kennedy's, "loomed up" in front of the plaintiff and demanded that he stop and explain where he had gotten the ascot. As approximately eight to ten people looked on, the plaintiff agreed to return with Goss to the store. On the way up the stairs, the plaintiff experienced chest and back pains and had to stop several times. When they reached the second floor, the salesman who had sold plaintiff the sportscoat told Goss that the ascot was indeed the plaintiff's. The plaintiff was so upset by the incident that he required the attention of the store's nurse and was consequently hospitalized and treated for a "myocardial infarct." The jury awarded plaintiff $12,500 for false imprisonment. The defendant appealed.]

SPIEGEL, J. Initially, the defendants contend that as a matter of law the plaintiff was not falsely imprisoned. They argue that no unlawful restraint was imposed by either force or threat upon the plaintiff's freedom of movement. However, "[t]he law is well settled that '[a]ny general restraint is sufficient to constitute an imprisonment . . .' and '[a]ny demonstration of physical power which, to all appearances, can be avoided only by submission, operates as effectually to constitute an imprisonment, if submitted to, as if any amount of force had been exercised.' 'If a man is restrained of his personal liberty by fear of a personal difficulty, that amounts to a false imprisonment' within the legal meaning of such term."

We think it is clear that there was sufficient evidence of unlawful restraint to submit this question to the jury. Just as the plaintiff had stepped out of the door of the store, the defendant Goss stopped him, firmly grasped his arm and told him that he had "better go back and see the manager." There was another employee at his side. The plaintiff was an elderly man and there were other people standing around staring at him. Considering the plaintiff's age and his heart condition, it is hardly to be expected that with one employee in front of him firmly grasping his arm and another at his side the plaintiff could do other than comply with Goss's "request" that he go back and see the manager. . . .

The defendants next contend that the detention of the plaintiff was sanctioned by G. L. c. 231, §94B, inserted by St. 1958, c. 337. This statute provides as follows: "In an action for false arrest or false imprisonment brought by any person by reason of having been detained for questioning on or in the immediate vicinity of the premises of a merchant, if such person was detained in a reasonable manner and for not more than a reasonable length of time by a person authorized to make arrests or by the merchant or his agent or servant authorized for such purpose and if there were reasonable grounds to believe that the person so detained was committing or attempting to commit larceny of goods for sale on such premises, it shall be a defence to such action. If such goods had not been purchased and were concealed on or amongst the belongings of a person so detained it shall be presumed that there were reasonable grounds for such belief."

The defendants argue in accordance with the conditions imposed in the statute that the plaintiff was detained in a reasonable manner for a reasonable length of time and that Goss had reasonable grounds for believing that the plaintiff was attempting to commit larceny of goods held for sale.

It is conceded that the detention was for a reasonable length of time. We need not decide whether the detention was effected in a reasonable manner for we are of opinion that there were no reasonable grounds for believing that the plaintiff was committing larceny and, therefore, he should not have been detained at all. However, we observe that Goss's failure to identify himself as an employee of Kennedy's and to disclose the reasons for his inquiry and actions, coupled with the physical restraint in a public place imposed upon the plaintiff, an elderly man, who had exhibited no aggressive intention to depart, could be said to constitute an unreasonable method by which to effect detention. . . .

The defendants assert that the judge improperly instructed the jury in stating that "grounds are reasonable when there is a basis which would appear to the reasonably prudent, cautious, intelligent person." In their brief, they argue that the "prudent and cautious man rule" is an objective standard and requires a more rigorous and restrictive standard of conduct than is contemplated by G. L. c. 231, §94B. The defendants' requests for instructions, in effect, state that the proper test is a subjective one, viz., whether the defendant Goss had an honest and strong suspicion that the plaintiff was committing or attempting to commit larceny. . . .

If we adopt the subjective test as suggested by the defendants, the individual's right to liberty and freedom of movement would become subject to the "honest . . . suspicion" of a shopkeeper based on his own "inarticulate hunches" without regard to any discernible facts. In effect, the result would be to afford the merchant even greater authority than that given to a police officer. In view of the well established meaning of the words "reasonable grounds" we believe that the Legislature intended to give these words their traditional meaning. This seems to us a valid conclusion since the Legislature has permitted an individual to be detained for a "reasonable length of time."

We also note that an objective standard is the criterion for determining probable cause or reasonable grounds in malicious prosecution and false arrest cases. . . .

Exceptions overruled.

NOTES

1. Protection of person and property. In cases of false arrest, why should an innocent plaintiff bear the costs of the defendant's *reasonable* mistakes? These shoplifting cases continue to make their way into court with startling regularity, where the pattern is usually similar to that found in *Coblyn*. A customer returns to shop to exchange goods and is seen leaving without paying for the replacement goods, e.g., Forgie-Buccioni v. Hannaford Bros., Inc., 413 F.3d 175 (1st Cir. 2005); or, owing to a medical condition, engages in odd conduct that excites suspicion. See Dolgencorp, Inc. v. Pounders, 912 So.2d 523 (Ala. Civ. App. 2005). Yet the analytical framework is unchanged from *Coblyn*, where the shop owner's privilege, usually by statute, provides a defense in the event of reasonable mistake.

Nonetheless, other false imprisonment cases raise the more difficult question of whether the defendant's actions are justified as necessary to protect defendant's person and property. In Sindle v. New York City Transit Authority, 307 N.E.2d 245, 248 (N.Y. 1973), the defendant operated a school bus carrying between 65 and 70 junior high school students, including the plaintiff. Some of the other students became rowdy, committed acts of vandalism, and remained abusive even when warned by the driver. The driver abandoned his ordinary route, passed several stops, and drove to the police station. On the way, the plaintiff, who had not behaved improperly, jumped out of a side window, only to be run over by the bus's back wheels. The plaintiff abandoned his action for negligence (why?) and pitched the case solely on false imprisonment. The trial judge refused to allow the defendants to introduce any evidence that the imprisonment was reasonable, both in time and manner. The Court of Appeals reversed:

> In view of our determination, it would be well to outline some of the considerations relevant to the issue of justification. In this regard, we note that,

generally, restraint or detention, reasonable under the circumstances and in time and manner, imposed for the purpose of preventing another from inflicting personal injuries or interfering with or damaging real or personal property in one's lawful possession or custody is not unlawful. . . . Also, a parent, guardian or teacher entrusted with the care or supervision of a child may use physical force reasonably necessary to maintain discipline or promote the welfare of the child. (Penal Law, §35.10)

Similarly, a school bus driver, entrusted with the care of his student-passengers and the custody of public property, has the duty to take reasonable measures for the safety and protection of both — the passengers and the property. In this regard, the reasonableness of his actions — as bearing on the defense of justification — is to be determined from a consideration of all the circumstances. At a minimum, this would seem to import, a consideration of the need to protect the persons and property in his charge, the duty to aid the investigation and apprehension of those inflicting damage, the manner and place of the occurrence, and the feasibility and practicality of other alternative courses of action.

2. Consent. Consent is also a defense to an action for false imprisonment. Its scope may be difficult to determine, however, when the plaintiff seeks to retract the consent to confinement that was previously given. In Herd v. Weardale Steel, Coal & Coke Co., [1915] A.C. 67, plaintiff, a miner, entered defendant's mine for a shift that normally ended at 4:00 P.M. At 11:00 A.M. plaintiff, with 29 coworkers, asked to be taken to the surface, claiming that unsafe working conditions violated his employment contract and the applicable statutory provisions. An empty elevator was available to take the men up at 1:00 P.M., but was not offered to them until 1:30 P.M. The House of Lords found that the 30-minute delay did not constitute false imprisonment. Haldane, L.C., said: "The man chose to go to the bottom of the mine under these conditions, — conditions which he accepted. He had no right to call upon the employers to make use of special machinery put there at their cost, and involving cost in its working, to bring him to the surface just when he pleased." Was there a false imprisonment if the plaintiff had a legitimate safety grievance? What if the delay was not 30 minutes, but until the end of plaintiff's shift?

3. Deprogramming. As noted in *Sindle*, parental control and discipline is generally regarded as a defense in false imprisonment cases, just as in actions for assault and battery. The boundaries of this defense have been sorely tested when parents seize their children by force to counteract "cult" allegiances and control. In Peterson v. Sorlien, 299 N.W.2d 123, 129, 136 (Minn. 1980), the plaintiff, then a college student, fell under the influence of "The Way Ministry," a religious organization. Her schoolwork subsequently deteriorated, and she became "overly tired, unusually pale, distraught and irritable." After her junior year, her parents concluded that she had been a victim of "coercive persuasion" and took her to a "deprogrammer" who after several days of intensive treatment was able to restore her to her former sunny disposition. Plaintiff thereafter tried to persuade her fiancé to leave the cult, but he in turn urged her to return, which she did. She then sued her parents and her deprogrammer for false imprisonment and intentional infliction of emotional distress. The jury found for the parents and against the deprogrammer, and the Minnesota Supreme Court gave its cautious vindication of the parents' position: "We hold that when parents, or their agents, acting under the conviction that the judgmental capacity of their adult child is impaired, seek to extricate that child from what they reasonably believe to be a religious or pseudo-religious cult, and the child at some juncture assents to the actions in question, limitations upon the child's mobility do not constitute mean-ingful deprivations of personal liberty sufficient to support a judgment for false imprisonment. But owing to the threat that deprogramming poses to public order, we do not endorse self-help as a preferred alternative."

An uneasy dissent took the opposite view: "to hold that for seeking companionship and identity in a group whose proselytizing tactics may well be suspect, she must endure without a remedy the degrading and humili-ating treatment she received at the hands of her parents, is, in my opinion, totally at odds with the basic rights of young people to think unorthodox thoughts, join unorthodox groups, and proclaim unorthodox views. I would reverse the denial of recovery as to that cause of action."

What result if the plaintiff had been a minor when she first joined the cult, but over 18 when she returned? If plaintiff had stayed with her par-ents, could she have sued the cult for false imprisonment or intentional infliction of emotional distress?

4. *Modern false imprisonment cases.* Litigation in false imprisonment has increased in recent years as a common law addition to complex federal claims. For example, in Chellen v. John Pickle Co., 446 F. Supp. 2d 1247, 1276 (N.D. Okla. 2006), the plaintiffs, who were workers brought over from India to work for the defendant, sued for violations of the Fair Labor Standards Act (dealing with minimum wages of working conditions), and for violations of Title VII of the Civil Rights Act of 1964, which protects persons against discrimination on grounds of race, ethnicity or national origin. Appended to the case was a count for false imprisonment where the plaintiffs alleged that the defendants restricted their mobility away from the worksite. Eagan, J., allowed these actions saying:

> [D]efendants restricted the Chellen plaintiffs' movement, communications, privacy, worship, and access to health care. The evidence demonstrates that defendants kept the Chellen plaintiffs' travel documents. . . . [D]efendants unlawfully restrained the Chellen plaintiff's ability to move about as they wished. Although initially defendants permitted the Chellen plaintiffs some ability to leave the JPC plant for shopping, worship, visiting friends and

relatives on their own, or other activities, defendants discouraged the plaintiffs from leaving by telling them of unfounded dangers outside the gates. Later, defendants required the Chellen plaintiffs to obtain permission before leaving the premises, locked the main gates, employed an armed security guard to watch them, hired four "leadmen" from among the Chellen plaintiffs to report on the activities of the others, threatened the Chellen plaintiffs with arrest and deportation, and attempted to deport several of them back to India. Defendants assert no valid justification for these actions. . . . Defendants' actions constitute unlawful restraint, detention, or confinement.

What measure of damages?

4.   The Intentional Infliction of Emotional Distress: Extreme and Outrageous Conduct

Wilkinson v. Downton
[1897] 2 Q.B. 57

[The facts are set forth in the court's opinion. The jury gave a verdict of 1s. 10½ d. for transportation money given by plaintiff to friends to fetch her husband home and £100 for injuries caused by nervous shock. Defendant contended that no recovery should be allowed for the damage caused by nervous shock.]

WRIGHT, J. In this case the defendant, in the execution of what he seems to have regarded as a practical joke, represented to the plaintiff that he was charged by her husband with a message to her to the effect that her husband was smashed up in an accident, and was lying at The Elms at Leytonstone with both legs broken, and that she was to go at once in a cab with two pillows to fetch him home. All this was false. The effect of the statement on the plaintiff was a violent shock to her nervous system, producing vomiting and other more serious and permanent physical consequences at one time threatening her reason, and entailing weeks of suffering and incapacity to her as well as expense to her husband for medical attendance. These consequences were not in any way the result of previous ill-health or weakness of constitution; nor was there any evidence of predisposition to nervous shock or any other idiosyncrasy. . . .

[The court then stated that while the 1s. 10½ d. was recoverable in fraud and deceit, £100 for mental distress were not "parasitic" upon that action.]

I think, however, that the verdict may be supported upon another ground. The defendant has, as I assume for the moment, wilfully done an act calculated to cause physical harm to the plaintiff—that is to say, to infringe her legal right to personal safety, and has in fact thereby caused physical harm to her. That proposition without more appears to me to state a good cause of action, there being no justification alleged for the act. This wilful *injuria* is in law malicious, although no malicious purpose to cause the harm which was caused nor any motive of spite is imputed to the defendant.

It remains to consider whether the assumptions involved in the proposition are made out. One question is whether the defendant's act was so plainly calculated to produce some effect of the kind which was produced that an intention to produce it ought to be imputed to the defendant, regard being had to the fact that the effect was produced on a person proved to be in an ordinary state of health and mind. I think that it was. It is difficult to imagine that such a statement, made suddenly and with apparent seriousness, could fail to produce grave effects under the circumstances upon any but an exceptionally indifferent person, and therefore an intention to produce such an effect must be imputed, and it is no answer in law to say that more harm was done than was anticipated, for that is commonly the case with all wrongs. The other question is whether the effect was, to use the ordinary phrase, too remote to be in law regarded as a consequence for which the defendant is answerable. Apart from authority, I should give the same answer and on the same ground as the last question, and say that it was not too remote. . . .

[The court then discussed prior cases dealing mainly with emotional distress in negligence and slander.] That case [a slander case], however, appears to have been decided on the ground that in all the innumerable actions for slander there were no precedents for alleging illness to be sufficient special damage, and that it would be of evil consequence to treat it as sufficient, because such a rule might lead to an infinity of trumpery or groundless actions. Neither of these reasons is applicable to the present case. Nor could such a rule be adopted as of general application without results which it would be difficult or impossible to defend. Suppose that a person is in a precarious and dangerous condition, and another person tells him that his physician has said that he has but a day to live. In such a case, if death ensued from the shock caused by the false statement, I cannot doubt that at this day the case might be one of criminal homicide, or that if a serious aggravation of illness ensued damages might be recovered. I think, however, that it must be admitted that the present case is without precedent. . . .

There must be judgment for plaintiff for £100 1*s*. 10½ *d*.

NOTE

Parasitic damages. In Bouillon v. Laclede Gaslight Co., 129 S.W. 401, 402 (Mo. App. 1910), the defendant's meter reader tried to force his way in through the front door of the plaintiff's apartment while the plaintiff was pregnant and at risk for a miscarriage. He had several nasty exchanges with the plaintiff's nurse that the plaintiff overheard through the open front door, which also let in the cold air. That evening the plaintiff suffered chills, and the next day had a miscarriage that her physician attributed to the events of the prior day. Plaintiff was sick for an extended period of time after the incident, and suffered permanent impairments to her health. Nortoni, J., allowed plaintiff's cause of action.

> No one can doubt that the case fails to disclose an assault on plaintiff as the controversy was principally had with, and all the insulting language directed against, another, the nurse. However this may be, the facts reveal a valid ground of liability on the score of trespass, and this is true notwithstanding the damages laid are not for the commission of the initial act of trespass, but relate instead to its consequence alone. Although defendant's agent had a right to enter the basement beneath plaintiff's apartment for the purpose of reading the gas meter, it is entirely clear that he had no authority to enter or pass through plaintiff's flat for that purpose. She was not a consumer of gas and the gas meter was in no sense connected with her household. Plaintiff is assured peaceful repose of her home against unwarranted intrusion from others. A trespasser is liable to respond in damages for such injuries as may result naturally, necessarily, directly, and proximately in consequence of his wrong. This is true for the reason the original act involved in the trespass is unlawful. . . . The doctrine is that though a mere mental disturbance of itself may not be a cause of action in the first instance, fright and mental anguish are competent elements of damage if they arise out of a trespass upon the plaintiff's person or possession and may be included in a suit for the trespass if plaintiff chooses so to do, or, if a physical injury results from such fright, a cause of action accrues from the trespass for compensation as to the physical injury and its consequences alone, which may be pursued even though plaintiff seeks no compensation for the original wrong.

In both *Wilkinson* and *Bouillon*, the defendant committed independent torts, namely, deceit and trespass. Is there any need for a new independent tort when emotional damages are typically "parasitic" on an existing wrong? In 1 Street, Foundations of Legal Liability 466, 470 (1906), the author, in commenting on legal protection against mental distress observes that "[a] factor which is today recognized as parasitic will, forsooth, tomorrow be recognized as an independent basis of liability." Does *Boullion* shed any light on the question of damages in *Hamidi*?

American Law Institute, Restatement (Second) of Torts
(1966)

§46. OUTRAGEOUS CONDUCT CAUSING SEVERE EMOTIONAL DISTRESS

(1) One who by extreme and outrageous conduct intentionally or recklessly causes severe emotional distress to another is subject to liability for such emotional distress, and if bodily harm to the other results from it, for such bodily harm.

(2) Where such conduct is directed at a third person, the actor is subject to liability if he intentionally or recklessly causes severe emotional distress

(a) to a member of such person's immediate family who is present at the time, whether or not such distress results in bodily harm, or

(b) to any other person who is present at the time, if such distress results in bodily harm.

Caveat:

The Institute expresses no opinion as to whether there may not be other circumstances under which the actor may be subject to liability for the intentional or reckless infliction of emotional distress.

Comment . . .

d. Extreme and outrageous conduct. The cases thus far decided have found liability only where the defendant's conduct has been extreme and outrageous. It has not been enough that the defendant has acted with an intent which is tortious or even criminal, or that he has intended to inflict emotional distress, or even that his conduct has been characterized by "malice," or a degree of aggravation which would entitle the plaintiff to punitive damages for another tort. Liability has been found only where the conduct has been so outrageous in character, and so extreme in degree, as to go beyond all possible bounds of decency, and to be regarded as atrocious, and utterly intolerable in a civilized community. Generally, the case is one in which the recitation of the facts to an average member of the community would arouse his resentment against the actor, and lead him to exclaim, "Outrageous!"

The liability clearly does not extend to mere insults, indignities, threats, annoyances, petty oppressions, or other trivialities. The rough edges of our society are still in need of a good deal of filing down, and in the meantime plaintiffs must necessarily be expected and required to be hardened to a certain amount of rough language, and to occasional acts that are definitely inconsiderate and unkind. There is no occasion for the law to intervene in every case where someone's feelings are hurt. There must still be freedom to express an unflattering opinion, and some safety valve must be left through which irascible tempers may blow off relatively harmless steam. . . .

f. The extreme and outrageous character of the conduct may arise from the actor's knowledge that the other is peculiarly susceptible to emotional distress, by reason of some physical or mental condition or peculiarity. The conduct may become heartless, flagrant, and outrageous when the actor proceeds in the face of such knowledge, where it would not be so if he did not know. . . .

NOTES

1. Extreme and outrageous conduct. The Restatement formulation liability turns solely on the defendant's course of conduct, without proof of any other tort such as trespass or deceit. Modern cases place heavy reliance on the Restatement formulation in a wide number of different contexts.

(a) Strong arm tactics. In State Rubbish Collectors Association v. Siliznoff, 240 P.2d 282, 286 (Cal. 1952), the Acme Brewing company switched its account for the collection of garbage from Abramoff to Kosoff, who in turn assigned the account to Siliznoff. At a stormy meeting representatives of the State Rubbish Collectors Association threatened to beat up Siliznoff, destroy his property, and put him out of business unless he agreed to pay the association part of the proceeds from the Acme account. Siliznoff then promised to pay Abramoff $1,850 for the contract and gave the association a series of notes for that sum.

The association sued on the notes a year later. Siliznoff demanded that the notes be canceled because of duress and lack of consideration; he also filed a cross-complaint praying for "general and exemplary damages because of assaults made by plaintiff and its agents to compel him to join the association and pay Abramoff for the Acme account." Siliznoff recovered $1,250 general and special damages and $4,000 exemplary damages. On appeal the association contended that "the evidence does not establish an assault against defendant because the threats made all related to action that might take place in the future," and that there was no threat of "immediate physical harm." But the unanimous court, through Traynor, J., concluded that a cause of action was established "when it is shown that one, in the absence of any privilege, intentionally subjects another to mental suffering incident to serious threats to his physical well-being, whether or not the threats are made under such circumstances as to constitute a technical assault."

(b) Bill collection. In George v. Jordan Marsh Co., 268 N.E.2d 915, 921 (Mass. 1971), the plaintiff alleged that the defendant's bill collectors badgered her with phone calls during the late evening hours, sent her letters marked "account referred to law and collection department," wrote her that her credit was revoked and that she was liable for late charges, and engaged in other dunning tactics. The plaintiff further claimed that she did not owe the disputed sums because she had never guaranteed her son's unpaid debts. As a result of the calls, the plaintiff suffered a heart attack. Her attorney then protested defendant's "harassing" tactics, but the onslaught continued until the plaintiff suffered a second heart attack. After an exhaustive review of the earlier Massachusetts precedent, the court upheld the sufficiency of her claim for emotional distress under section 46 of the Restatement.

(c) Outrageous professional conduct. In Rockhill v. Pollard, 485 P.2d 28 (Or. 1971), the plaintiff, her mother-in-law, and her 10-month-old daughter, Marla, were all seriously injured in an automobile accident. Both women had serious cuts and bruises, and the daughter was apparently lifeless, with a ghostly pallor to her skin. A passing motorist took them to the office of the defendant physician, who, when summoned, did not examine either woman and gave Marla only a brief examination. When Marla starting vomiting, the defendant said it was a result of overeating. He then ordered the women to wait outside in the freezing rain until the plaintiff's husband arrived. The three were then taken to a hospital, where Marla was successfully operated on for a depressed skull fracture.

McAllister, J., found that the evidence supported a finding of conduct outrageous in the extreme, stressing the special duties that physicians owed their patients. "Certainly a physician who is consulted in an emergency has a duty to respect that interest, at least to the extent of making a good-faith attempt to provide adequate treatment or advice. We think a jury could infer from the evidence that defendant wilfully or recklessly failed to perform that duty."

Why does plaintiff have no action for medical malpractice or breach of contract?

(d) Dead bodies. In Estate of Trentadue v. United States, 397 F.3d 840, 855, 857-858 (10th Cir. 2005), the Bureau of Prisons (BOP) was responsible for returning the body of Kenneth Trentadue to his next of kin after he had been found dead in his cell, which it failed to do in a proper manner. Tymkovich, J., disposed of the plaintiffs' claim as follows:

> We agree with the district court that the government acted in deliberate disregard of a high probability that its actions would cause the Trentadues emotional distress. The Trentadues were a grieving family searching for answers in the wake of Kenneth Trentadue's untimely death. BOP's overall treatment of the Trentadue family, including its initial nondisclosure of the unusual circumstances of death, its obstinance concerning authorization for an autopsy, and its failure to inform the Trentadues of the body's battered condition amounted to outrageous conduct that "needlessly and recklessly" intensified the family's emotional distress. Thus the district court properly determined that plaintiffs proved the first, second, and third elements of the tort of emotional distress, intentional or reckless conduct, outrageousness, and causation.

However, because the district court did not make explicit findings as to the severity of each individual plaintiff's emotional distress, we are unable to determine from the district court's order whether . . . the emotional distress suffered by each plaintiff was severe under Oklahoma law.

He therefore remanded the case for further findings.

(e) *Collateral claims.* As with false imprisonment, frequently plaintiffs add counts for extreme and outrageous conduct to complaints that allege violations of complex regulatory contexts. One such claim was sustained in *Chellen*, along with its false imprisonment count. The issue has also arisen in cases of alleged forms of racial insults, see Patterson v. McLean Credit Union, 805 F.2d 1143 (4th Cir. 1986), where plaintiff alleged that her supervisor engaged in racially motivated harassment by "staring" at her for several minutes at a time, by assigning her too many tasks, by making her do sweeping and dusting jobs not assigned to whites, and by telling her that blacks were known to work "slower than" whites. Phillips, J., rejected the tort suit, noting that the allegations fell "far short" of the stringent requirements of North Carolina law. The plaintiff also raised civil rights law claims that were rebuffed by the Supreme Court which in Patterson v. McLean Credit Union, 491 U.S. 164 (1989) gave a relatively narrow construction of the scope of the protection afforded the plaintiff under 42 U.S.C. §1981. Plaintiffs have had more success in bypassing the stringent requirements of the tort by allowing claims for sexual harassment holding that "Title VII comes into play before the harassing conduct leads to a nervous breakdown. . . . So long as the environment would reasonably be perceived, and is perceived, as hostile or abusive, there is no need for it also to be psychologically injurious." Harris v. Forklift Systems, Inc., 510 U.S. 17, 22 (1993). These cases are typically judged by a "reasonable woman standard." See Ellison v. Brady, 924 F.2d 872, 879 (9th Cir. 1991).

2. *Constitutional overtones.* In other settings, the Supreme Court uses constitutional arguments to limit the scope of common law tort of intentional infliction of emotional distress in order to protect freedom of speech. Thus, in Hustler Magazine v. Falwell, 485 U.S. 46, 52 (1988), Hustler parodied Jerry Falwell by having him state in a mock "interview" that his "first time" was during a drunken incestuous rendezvous with his mother in an outhouse. In small print at the bottom of the page, the ad contains the disclaimer, "ad parody — not to be taken seriously." Rehnquist C.J., overturned a jury verdict for Falwell of $100,000 in actual damages and $50,000 in punitive damages against both Hustler and its publisher, Larry Flynt, on constitutional grounds. Stressing the press's need for "breathing room" under the First Amendment:

> Generally speaking the law does not regard the intent to inflict emotional distress as one which should receive much solicitude, and it is quite

understandable that most if not all jurisdictions have chosen to make it civilly culpable where the conduct in question is sufficiently "outrageous." But in the world of debate about public affairs, many things done with motives that are less than admirable are protected by the First Amendment. . . .

Were we to hold otherwise, there can be little doubt that political cartoonists and satirists would be subjected to damages awards without any showing that their work falsely defamed its subject. . . . The appeal of the political cartoon or caricature is often based on exploration of unfortunate physical traits or politically embarrassing events—an exploration often calculated to injure the feelings of the subject of the portrayal. The art of the cartoonist is often not reasoned or evenhanded, but slashing and one-sided. . . .

Rehnquist then noted that cartoonists such as Thomas Nast, who took on the Tweed Ring, which ran New York City in the late nineteenth century, would be at risk under the alternative rule. Is there a slippery slope from Nast to Flynt? Why no action for defamation?

2

STRICT LIABILITY AND NEGLIGENCE: HISTORIC AND ANALYTIC FOUNDATIONS

SECTION A. INTRODUCTION

We now turn to the central issue of tort theory: When is a defendant liable for the physical harm he accidentally or inadvertently causes? Historically, this apparently simple question has generated much debate but little consensus. One approach — traditional strict liability — holds the defendant prima facie liable for any harm that he causes to the plaintiff's person or property. The opposing negligence position allows the plaintiff to recover only if, intentional harms aside, the defendant acted with insufficient care. Both positions allow for affirmative defenses, especially those based on plaintiff's conduct.

The juxtaposition of these two approaches raises several thorny issues. Must one theory be accepted in total to the exclusion of the other, or is it possible to define appropriate areas for each? If the latter, has the law drawn the lines in the proper places? Note, too, that a causation requirement is a common bond between the two theories. But how should "causation" be interpreted? Does its meaning shift as we move from strict liability to negligence? And if so, how? Again, what is meant by "negligence"? Is it a technical term or one of ordinary language? Is it enough that the defendant was careless, or must he also owe the plaintiff some duty of care to make that carelessness not only morally blameworthy but also legally culpable? Finally, the opposition between the two theories regarding the prima facie case does not preclude some narrowing of the gap. For example, a court in a negligence case may impose the burden of proving due care on the defendant. How wide, then, is the gulf between the two systems?

Common law judges have examined these issues through a long historical dialogue. This chapter retraces much of that lengthy journey. Section B examines the tension between negligence and strict liability in the formative English cases. Section C traces the influence of the forms of action on the choice of liability rules. Section D follows the nineteenth-century debate over liability rules both in England and the United States after the abolition of the forms of action. Section E examines the same conflict in the twentieth century. The law in each period builds heavily on what has gone before, as previous precedents are followed, reshaped, expanded, or abandoned in litigation.

SECTION B.   THE FORMATIVE CASES

The Thorns Case (Hull v. Orange)
Y.B. Mich. 6 Ed. 4, f. 7, pl. 18 (1466)

A man brought a writ of Trespass quare vi et armis clausum fregit, etc. et herbam suam pedibus conculcando consumpsit, [Roughly: why by force and arms he broke into the plaintiff's close, and consumed his crops by trampling them with his feet] and alleged the trespass in 5 acres and the defendant said, as to the coming, etc. and as to the trespass in the 5 acres, not guilty and, as to the trespass in the 5 acres, that the plaintiff ought not to have an action for he says that he [the defendant] has an acre of land on which a thorn hedge grows, adjoining the said 5 acres, and that he [the defendant], at the time of the supposed trespass, came and cut the thorns, and that they, against his will, fell on the said acres of the plaintiff, and that he [the defendant] came freshly on to the said acres and took them, which is the same trespass for which he has conceived this action. And on this they demurred and it was well argued, and was adjourned.

And now Catesby says: Sir, it has been said that, if a man does some act, even if it be lawful, and by this act tort and damage are done to another against his will, yet, if he could by any means have eschewed the damage, he shall be punished for this act. Sir, it seems to me that the contrary is true, and, as I understand, if a man does a lawful act and thereby damage comes to another against his will, he shall not be punished. Thus, I put the case that I drive my cattle along the highway, and you have an acre of land lying next the highway, and my beasts enter your land and eat your grass, and I come freshly and chase them out of your land; now here, because the chasing out was lawful and the entry on the land was against my will, you shall not have an action against me. No more shall you have an action here, for the cutting was lawful and the falling on your land was against my will, and so the re-taking was good and lawful. And, Sir, I put the case that I cut my trees and the boughs fall on a man and kill him; in this case I shall not be attainted as of felony, for my cutting was lawful and the falling on the man was against my will. No more here, therefore, etc.

Fairfax: It seems to me that the contrary is true and I say that there is a difference where a man does a thing from which felony ensues and one from which trespass ensues; for in the case which Catesby puts there was no felony, since felony is of malice prepense and, as the act was against his will, it was not animo felonico. But if one cuts his trees and the boughs fall on a man and hurt him, in this case he shall have an action of Trespass. So, too, Sir, if a man shoots at the butts and his bow trembles in his hands and he kills a man ipso invito [against his will], this is no felony, as has been said. But if he wounds a man by his shooting, he shall have a good action of Trespass against him, and yet the shooting was lawful and the tort that the other had was against his will. And so here.

Pigot: To the same intent. I put the case that I have a mill and the water which comes to my mill runs past your land, and you have willows growing by the water, and you cut your willows and against your will they fall in the water and stop the water so that I have not sufficient water for my mill, in this case I shall have an action of Trespass, and yet the cutting was lawful and the falling was against my will. And so if a man has a fish-pond in his manor and he empties the water out of the pond to take the fishes and the water floods my land, I shall have a good action, and yet the act was lawful.

Yonge: The contrary seems to me to be true; and in such a case, where a man has dampnum absque injuria [harm without legal injury], he shall have no action, for if he has no tort he has no reason to recover damages. So in this case, when he came on to his close to take the thorns which had fallen on to it, this entry was not tortious, for when he cut them and they fell on his close ipso invito, the property in them was in him and thus it was lawful for him to take them out of his close; wherefore, notwithstanding that he has done damage, he has done no tort.

Brian: I think the contrary. To my intent, when any man does an act, he is bound to do it in such manner that by his act no prejudice or damage is done to others. Thus, in a case where I am building a house and, while the timber is being put up, a piece of it falls on my neighbour's house and damages it, he shall have a good action, and yet the building of the house was lawful and the timber fell me invito [against my will]. So, too, if a man makes an assault upon me and I cannot avoid him, and in my own defence I raise my stick to strike him, and a man is behind me and in raising my stick I wound him, in this case he shall have an action against me, and yet the raising of my stick to defend myself was lawful and I wounded him me invito. So in this case.

LITTLETON, J. To the same intent. If a man suffers damage, it is right that he be recompensed; and to my intent the case which Catesby has put is not law; for if your cattle come on to my land and eat my grass, notwithstanding you come freshly and drive them out, it is proper for you to make amends for what your cattle have done, be it more or less. . . . And, Sir, if it were law that he could enter and take the thorns, by the same reasoning, if he cut a great tree, he could come with his carts and horses to carry off the tree, which is not reason, for peradventure he has corn or other crops growing, etc. No more here may he do it, for the law is all one in great things and in small and so, according to the amount of the trespass, it is proper that he should make amends.

CHOKE, C.J. I think the same; for when the principal thing is not lawful, then the thing which depends upon it is not lawful. For when he cut the thorns and they fell on to my land, this falling was not lawful, and then his coming to take them away was not lawful. As to what has been said that they fell ipso invito, this is not a good plea; but he should have said that he could not do it in any other manner or that he did all that was in his power to keep them out; otherwise he shall pay damages. And, Sir, if the thorns or a great tree had fallen on his land by the blowing of the wind, in this case he might have come on to the land to take them, since the falling had then been not his act, but that of the wind.

NOTES

1. *Basis for liability in tort.* The *Thorns Case* is one of the earliest English cases to discuss in general terms the basis for liability in tort. Two judges, Littleton and Choke, offer their opinions after a spirited debate among five lawyers. Note that Catesby, for the defendant, tries to persuade the court that the defendant can commit a tort only if he has committed a crime. Does Fairfax, for the plaintiff, adequately respond to that contention? Give any explanation why it is in general false?

The major historical controversy over the *Thorns Case* is whether it adopts the theory of strict liability in tort. The case's connection to the negligence/strict liability debate seems attenuated at first glance given the defendant's deliberate entry onto the plaintiff's land. The sticking point in the case, however, is reminiscent of the dispute over the necessity defense in Chapter 1, *supra* at 68-79, for it concerns the scope of the defendant's privilege to retake his thorns from the defendant's property even if he causes damage thereby. Nonetheless, the language and the examples discussed in the case go far beyond this particular instance, for the judges and lawyers alike agree that the defendant has a privilege to enter and retake the thorns so long as the original cutting was not tortious. The choice between strict liability and negligence thus sets the appropriate boundaries for the privilege. What passages in the *Thorns Case* point to the strict liability rule? To some alternative rule? To negligence?

The historical basis of tort liability has been reviewed in Arnold, Accident, Mistake, and Rules of Liability in The Fourteenth Century Law of Torts, 128 U. Pa. L. Rev. 361, 374-375 (1979). Arnold concludes that "the inference to be drawn from all the available evidence is that in fourteenth-century tort actions civil liability was strict." He then identifies a number of grounds that allowed a defendant to escape liability. He points to "a familiar principle in the law of torts that no one was liable to make compensation for injuries that were attributable to some entirely providential cause," such as harms brought about by tempests, earthquakes, or fires of spontaneous origin, which are commonly grouped as Acts of God. Likewise, the plaintiff's own contributory negligence was also regarded a good defense because "it is the plaintiff, not the defendant, who is perceived as having 'done' the act resulting in injury." Within these settled principles, Arnold found only a few cases where the plaintiff alleged the defendant's negligence in his complaint, and fewer still where the defendant sought to raise his own lack of negligence as a defense. For Arnold, the clue to the substantive issue lies in the logic of pleading:

> The most telling difficulty is that the absence of pleas of this sort may simply be attributable not to any abstract liability rule but rather to a pleading rule that barred the defendant from asserting such facts purely as a technical matter. To simplify somewhat, a defendant in a writ of trespass was obligated to choose between two kinds of answer: He either had to deny the physical acts he was alleged to have done, or he had to admit them and assign a cause for them. In the case of an assault and battery, for instance, an acceptable "cause" would have been self-defense. Now if a defendant wanted to say that he had hit the plaintiff accidentally (that is, nonnegligently), his story would not technically have fit either of the two modes of responding to complaints. He had, in fact, hit the plaintiff, so a denial was obviously of no use; moreover, he had had no cause, no justification, for hitting him because "cause," as we have seen, was thought of in motivational terms. Here, the defendant's case was that he had had no motive at all in hitting the plaintiff, for the act of hitting him had been unintentional.

How do the justifications raised in the following cases fit into Arnold's theory?

2. *"Best efforts" as a means to avoid liability.* In Millen v. Fandrye, 79 Eng. Rep. 1259 (K.B. 1626), plaintiff sued for damage to his sheep when defendant's dog chased the sheep off defendant's land, where they had been trespassing. The dog, moreover, continued the chase even after the sheep had entered a neighbor's land. In giving judgment for the defendant on the plaintiff's demurrer to his plea, Crew, C.J., noted, "It seems to me that he might drive the sheep out with the dog, and he could not

withdraw his dog when he would in an instant. . . . [A] man cuts thorns and they fall into another man's land, and in trespass he justified for it; and the opinion was, that notwithstanding this justification trespass lies, because he did not plead that he did his best endeavour to hinder their falling there, yet this was a hard case; but this case is not like to [the instant case], for here it was lawful to chase them [the sheep] out of his own land, and he did his best endeavour to recall the dog, and therefore trespass does not lie."

Millen endorses Choke's view in the *Thorns Case,* but the result in *Millen* can also be reconciled with Littleton's purer version of strict liability. In *Millen,* the "best efforts" defense arose when the defendant was defending his property against the wrongful incursions of the plaintiff's sheep. The law in these cases tolerates the use of excessive force when the defendant tries in good faith to minimize the excess. The rule is a variation on the familiar theme that the aggressor takes his victim as he finds him. In contrast, the defendant's cutting in the *Thorns Case* was in no sense justified or excused by any prior wrong of the plaintiff, so that defendant did not have the latitude afforded by the self-defense issue. The hard case suggested by the facts in *Millen* arises when a third person sues after the defendant's dog drives the sheep onto the third person's property, even though the dog's owner tried to call him off. Should the landowner have a "best efforts" defense in that third party suit? See Morris v. Platt, *supra* Chapter 1, at 56.

3. *Justification in trespass.* In the *Tithe Case,* Y.B. Trin., 21 Hen. 7, f. 26, 27, 28, pl. 5 (1506), the plaintiff, a local parson, sued for the loss of corn tithed to him. The corn in question had been cut by a local farmer, who had placed it in a separate part of his field for the parson. The defendant removed the corn to plaintiff's barn, where it perished from causes not specified in the opinion. Defendant justified his conduct on the ground that plaintiff was in danger of losing the corn to beasts that were straying in the field. The courts disallowed the justification:

> KINGSMILL, J.: Where the goods of another are taken against his will, it must be justified either as a thing necessary for the Commonwealth or through a condition recognized by the law. First, as a thing concerning the Commonwealth, one may justify for goods taken out of a house when it is purely to safeguard the goods, or for breaking down a house to safeguard others; and so in time of war one may justify the entry into another's land to make a bulwark in defence of King and Country; and these things are justifiable and lawful for the maintenance of the Commonwealth. The other cause of justification is where one distrains [i.e., seizes to hold as security] my horse for his rent, and that is justifiable because the land was bound by such a condition of distress; and so in the case of other such conditions. Thus for these two reasons one may justify the taking of a thing against the will of its owner. But in this case here we are outside these reasons, for we are not within the cases of the Commonwealth nor in those of a condition; and, although it is

pleaded that this corn was in danger of being lost, yet it was not in such danger but that the party could have had his remedy. Thus, if I have beasts damage feasant, [causing damage] I shall not justify my entry to chase them out unless I first tender all amends. So here, when the defendant took the plaintiff's corn that it might not be destroyed, yet this is not justifiable. For if it had been destroyed, the plaintiff would have his remedy against those who destroyed it. And as for his having put it into the plaintiff's barn, yet he must keep it safe against any other mischance; and so no advantage thereby comes to the plaintiff. So this plea is not good.

REDE, C.J.: Although the defendant's intent here was good, yet the intent is not to be construed, though in felony it shall be; as where one shoots at the butts and kills a man, this is not felony, since he had no intent to kill him; and so of a tiler on a house where against his knowledge a stone kills a man, it is not felony. But where one shoots at the butts and wounds a man, although it be against his will, yet he shall be called a trespasser against his will. So it is necessary always to have a good case to justify; as in Trespass, a license is good justification. . . . But, to return to the case here, when he took the corn, although this was a good deed as regards the damage which cattle or a stranger might do to it, yet this is not a good deed and no manner of justification as regards the owner of the corn; for the latter would have his remedy by action against him who destroyed the corn, if it had been destroyed. Thus, if my beasts are damage feasant in another's land, I cannot enter to chase them out; and yet it would be a good deed to chase them out, to save them doing more damage. But it is otherwise where a stranger drives my horses into another's land, where they do damage; for here I may justify my entry to drive them out, since this tort has its beginning in the tort of another. But here, because the plaintiff could have his remedy if the corn had been destroyed, it was not lawful to take them; and it is not like the cases where things are in jeopardy of loss through water or fire and the like, for there the plaintiff has no remedy for the destruction against anyone. So the plea is not good.

The *Tithe Case* raises a variation on the necessity issue already encountered in *Vincent*. However, the defendant in *Vincent* acted to preserve his own property, whereas the defendant in the *Tithe Case* acted to preserve the plaintiff's property. Both Kingsmill and Rede allow the necessity defense when corn is moved to protect it against natural losses, but neither allow it when third parties threaten its destruction, on the unrealistic assumption that the owner faces no loss because he has a valid cause of action against the third party. With third party threats, therefore, the *Tithe Case* raises the same problem of asymmetrical incentives encountered in the public necessity cases, *supra* at 75. Why should anyone act to benefit a stranger if he must bear the risk of loss? One way to offset that risk is to allow the defendant to sue the plaintiff in restitution should he save the corn; but if that remedy is limited to a recovery of out-of-pocket expenses, then it will not cover for the extra risk of loss voluntarily assumed. Should the privilege cover the risk of loss from third parties as well as from natural events? Should a system of rewards be introduced? For discussion see Epstein, Holdouts, Externalities and the Single Owner: One More Salute to Ronald Coase, 36 J.L. & Econ. 553, 579-581 (1993).

Weaver v. Ward
80 Eng. Rep. 284 (K.B. 1616)

Weaver brought an action of trespass of assault and battery against Ward. The defendant pleaded, that he was amongst others by the commandment of the Lords of the Council a trained soldier in London, of the band of one Andrews captain; and so was the plaintiff, and that they were skirmishing with their musquets charged with powder for their exercise in re militari, [on military matters] against another captain and his band; and as they were so skirmishing, the defendant casualiter & per infortunium & contra voluntatem suam, [accidentally, and by misfortune, and against his own will] in discharging of his piece did hurt and wound the plaintiff. And upon demurrer by the plaintiff, judgment was given for him; for though it were agreed, that if men tilt or turney in the presence of the King, or if two masters of defence playing their prizes kill one another, that this shall be no felony; or if a lunatick kill a man, or the like, because felony must be done animo felonico [with felonious intent]: yet in trespass, which tends only to give damages according to hurt or loss, it is not so; and therefore if a lunatick hurt a man, he shall be answerable in trespass: and therefore no man shall be excused of a trespass (for this is the nature of an excuse, and not of a justification, prout ei bene licuit) [as it well appeared to him] except it may be judged utterly without his fault.

As if a man by force take my hand and strike you, or if here the defendant had said, that the plaintiff ran cross his piece when it was discharging, or had set forth the case with the circumstances, so as it had appeared to the Court that it had been inevitable, and that the defendant had committed no negligence to give occasion to the hurt.

NOTES

1. *Inevitable accident: conceptual difficulties.* In Weaver v. Ward, the court offers neither a definition of inevitable accident nor examples of its application. Many modern cases and commentators have tended to regard "inevitable accident" as a backhanded way of saying that the defendant acted neither negligently nor with intent to harm. See, e.g., Brown v. Kendall, *infra* at 123; Holmes, The Common Law, *infra* at 146. This argument is, however, inconsistent with the procedural posture of the

earlier cases, see *supra* at 105 at Note 1, and in any event seems odd on textual grounds because it renders the last clause (referring to antecedent negligence) wholly superfluous.

In order to reject this reading, however, it is necessary to propose an alternative. One possibility is that inevitable accident occupies a niche midway between strict liability and ordinary negligence. Gilles, Inevitable Accident in Classical English Tort Law, 43 Emory L.J. 575, 577 (1994) states the position as follows:

> The pre-nineteenth-century test for determining whether an accident was inevitable was typically described in terms such as "utterly without his fault," "did all that was in his power," "unavoidable necessity," and the like. To escape liability, defendants who had *prima facie* caused harm had to establish that they should not be viewed as responsible for the accident because some other cause had made it impossible, as a practical matter, to avoid injuring the plaintiff. Under this approach, the question was not whether the actors had behaved unreasonably — whether they *should* have avoided the accident — but whether they *could* have avoided it by greater practical care.

Yet another approach gives the term "inevitable accident" a literal reading that applies solely to those accidents that "had to happen," whether or not the defendant acted as he did. The defendant may have caused the harm, but the harm would have occurred from some other cause anyway. Within this narrower definition, the damage to the dock in *Vincent* is inevitable if it would have occurred whether or not the defendant made efforts to keep its ship fast to the dock during the storm.

Is there a case of inevitable accident in the *Thorns* case put by Choke, J., where the defendant enters the plaintiff's lands to recover a tree blown there by a great wind?

2. *Inevitable accident: historical treatment.* The full report of Smith v. Stone, 82 Eng. Rep. 533 (K.B. 1647), reads:

> Smith brought an action of trespasse against Stone pedibus ambulando [walking by his feet], the defendant pleads this speciall plea in justification, viz. that he was carryed upon the land of the plaintiff by force, and violence of others, and was not there voluntarily, which is the same trespasse, for which the plaintiff brings his action. The plaintiff demurs to this plea: in this case Roll Iustice said, that it is the trespasse of the party that carryed the defendant upon the land, and not the trespasse of the defendant: as he that drives my cattel into another mans land is the trespassor against him, and not I who am owner of the cattell.

Note that the defendant pleaded the compulsion of the third party specially because it was not a general denial as was the defense — it was not my act — in Weaver v. Ward.

With Smith v. Stone, contrast Gilbert v. Stone, 82 Eng. Rep. 539 (K.B. 1647):

> Gilbert brought an action of trespasse quare clausum fregit, and taking of a gelding, against Stone. The defendant pleads that he for fear of his life, and wounding of twelve armed men, who threatened to kill him if he did not [do the act] went into the house of the plaintiff, and took the gelding. The plaintiff demurred to this plea; Roll Iustice, This is no plea to justifie the defendant; for I may not do a trespasse to one for fear of threatnings of another, for by this means the party injured shall have no satisfaction, for he cannot have it of the party that threatned. Therefore let the plaintiff have his judgement.

Dickenson v. Watson, 84 Eng. Rep. 922 1218 (K.B. 1682) also gave a narrow construction to inevitable accident. The defendant, a tax-collector of "hearth-money," discharged his firearm when no one was in view, without intending to harm anyone. Nonetheless he shot the plaintiff while the plaintiff was walking along the road minding his own business. The court upheld a judgment for the plaintiff, "for in trespass the defendant shall not be excused without unavoidable necessity, which is not shewn here...."

In Gibbons v. Pepper, 91 Eng. Rep. 922 (K.B. 1695), the defendant was riding a horse on the highway. The horse, being frightened, bolted, carrying the defendant along until it struck and injured the plaintiff. The defendant also claimed that he called out to the plaintiff to take care, "but that notwithstanding the plaintiff did not go out of the way, but continued there." The defendant pleaded as his justification "that the accident was inevitable, and that the negligence of the defendant did not cause it." Again on demurrer, judgment was given for the plaintiff, "[o]f which opinion was the whole court. For if I ride upon a horse, and J. S. whips the horse so that he runs away with me and runs over any other person, he who whipped the horse is guilty of the battery, and not me. But if I by spurring was the cause of such accident, then I am guilty. In the same manner, if *A* takes the hand of *B* and with it strikes *C, A* is the trespasser and not *B*. And, per Curiam, the defendant might have given this justification in evidence upon the general issue pleaded. And therefore judgment was given for the plaintiff." Should the issue of plaintiff's conduct have been considered in light of Weaver v. Ward?

Gibbons rests on the assumption that the defendant's animal should be treated as the passive instrument of any third party who incites it to hurt the plaintiff or his property. Yet this equation between animal and inanimate object is far from evident, for it is evident that animals have wills of their own. Another approach is to hold the owner (vicariously) responsible for the harms caused by his animals, but to grant him an action over against

any third party who rode, spurred or otherwise caused the animal to do damage. In deciding between these two approaches, it is instructive to ask, who should bear the risk of insolvency of the third party, the owner of the animal or the victim? How should that question be answered if *A* picks *B*'s stick off the ground and uses it to strike *C*? For further elaboration of these examples, see Scott v. Shepherd, *infra* at 115, and Chapter 8, Section C.

3. *Inevitable accident: modern response.* Modern courts have rejected plaintiff's request for an inevitable accident instruction in the few cases where it has been requested. In Butigan v. Yellow Cab Co., 320 P.2d 500, 504 (Cal. 1958), the court repudiated its earlier flirtation with that defense in intersection collisions, noting that "an accident may be 'unavoidable or inevitable' where it is caused by a superior or irresistible force or by an absence of exceptional care which the law does not expect of the ordinary prudent man," and held that no defendant should be held to so high a standard of care: "In reality, the so-called defense of unavoidable accident has no legitimate place in our pleading. It appears to be an obsolete remnant from a time when damages for injuries to person or property directly caused by a voluntary act of the defendant could be recovered in an action of trespass and when strict liability would be imposed unless the defendant proved that the injury was caused through 'inevitable accident.'" In its place, ordinary negligence principles were held to govern so that "the defendant under a general denial may show any circumstance which militates against his negligence or its causal effect."

A similar view of the subject was taken in McWilliams v. Masterson, 112 S.W.3d 314 (Tex. App. 2003). The plaintiff was driving his car with his family at night at 65 miles per hour through a severe snowstorm on a four-lane highway when he attempted to pass an eighteen-wheeler in the right lane going about 50 miles per hour. Both drivers were within the speed limit. As the plaintiff attempted to move back to the right, he suddenly saw cattle ahead and struck one of the animals, which drove him back in front of the truck, resulting in the death of his wife and injuries to the other passengers. The defendant received an "unavoidable accident" instruction because of "the truism that some events or injuries may not be proximately caused by the negligence of anyone," but are best attributable to "fate." The defense was also held applicable to the two cattle owners, named Gabels, whose fence and gates were in good repair, on the ground that nothing could restrain their cattle in the face of the storm. According to a witness who testified about cattle's instincts: "Their 'instinct becomes very strong to . . . move away . . . until they come into an object and they'll keep pushing and pressing until they go through that object or over it or fall down and die . . .'" Thus, even though the court held the human and animal actions caused the various harms, the absence of all negligence was found to negate liability. Note that a rigorous system of strict liability protects the defendant Masterson who had the right of way at all times. But should it protect the

Gabels in light of their decision to keep cattle near the road? Under *Gibbons*? Under the rules for escaping animals announced in *Rylands, supra* at 130.

SECTION C.   THE FORMS OF ACTION

1.   *The Significance of the Forms*

These early historical materials show a close interplay between substantive and procedural issues. This section examines the early forms of action, which also exerted a strong, if unintended, influence upon the growth of the substantive tort law. In the well-known phrase of Henry Maine, "So great is the ascendancy of the Law of Actions in the infancy of Courts of Justice, that substantive law has at first the look of being gradually secreted in the interstices of procedure." H. Maine, Early Law and Custom 389 (1907). The most distinctive feature of the forms of action was their jurisdictional significance. Under the forms, the plaintiff could not simply state in his complaint the facts sufficient to get relief. See Federal Rules of Civil Procedure, Rule 8(a). He had to further show that his cause of action fell within one of the writs (royal orders used to commence civil actions) recognized at that time.

The choice of writs mattered. As Frederic W. Maitland observed in his masterly essay, The Forms of Action at Common Law 4-5 (1936 ed.):

> [T]o a very considerable degree the substantive law administered in a given form of action has grown up independently of the law administered in other forms. Each procedural pigeon-hole contains its own rules of substantive law, and it is with great caution that we may argue from what is found in one to what will probably be found in another; each has its own precedents. It is quite possible that a litigant will find that his case will fit some two or three of these pigeon-holes. If that be so he will have a choice, which will often be a choice between the old, cumbrous, costly, on the one hand, the modern, rapid, cheap, on the other. Or again he may make a bad choice, fail in his action, and take such comfort as he can from the hints of the judges that another form of action might have been more successful. The plaintiff's choice is irrevocable; he must play the rules of the game that he has chosen. Lastly he may find that, plausible as his case may seem, it just will not fit any one of the receptacles provided by the courts and he may take to himself the lesson that where there is no remedy there is no wrong.

2. *Trespass and Case*

Two writs — trespass and trespass on the case (or more simply "case") — covered most of the harms actionable at common law. By the final stages of the writ system, it was generally settled that trespass lay for the redress of harm caused by the defendant's direct and immediate application of force against the plaintiff's person or property. Case, on the other hand, covered all those "indirect" harms, not involving the use of force, actionable at common law. The classic illustration of the difference was given by Fortescue, J., in Reynolds v. Clarke: "[I]f a man throws a log into the highway, and in that act it hits me, I may maintain trespass, because it is an immediate wrong; but if as it lies there I tumble over it, and receive an injury, I must bring an action upon the case; because it is only prejudicial in consequence, for which originally I could have no action at all." 92 Eng. Rep. 410 (K.B. 1726). Is there an intelligible distinction between "slip and fall" cases and collision cases? If so, what is its significance?

The last sentence of Fortescue's opinion offers a view of the evolution of the substantive tort law. Under that view, royal recognition of the action of trespass came first because it offered vital protection against the direct use of force. Telltale signs of the original scope of the trespass writ are found in two of its Latin phrases: vi et armis, by force and arms, and contra pacem regis, against the peace of the king. According to the traditional view, the action on the case was a much later development, one that took place well after the Norman Conquest, toward the middle of the fourteenth century, when the royal courts completed a silent revolution by finally allowing tort actions to those plaintiffs who were not the victims of direct and immediate force. C.H.S. Fifoot, History and Sources of the Common Law, Tort and Contract, ch. 4 (1949).

Subsequently, however, Professor Milsom effectively, indeed decisively, challenged this view by demonstrating that the emergence of the action on the case as a distinct writ in the fourteenth century did not signal a transformation of the substantive law. S.F.C. Milsom, Historical Foundations of the Common Law ch. 11 (2d ed. 1981). Like the Latin "transgressio," trespass originally meant simply "wrong," and cases brought under that writ in royal courts covered not only wrongs involving the use of force, but all manner of other actionable harms as well. "If we identify trespass not with a narrow category of wrongs but with wrong generally, with the category of tort rather than a particular tort, we are a good deal closer to thinking fourteenth-century thoughts than we previously were." M. Arnold, Select Cases of Trespass from the King's Courts — 1307-1399, at ix (Selden Society, vol. 100 (1984)). Shades of that position are evident in the *Thorns*

Case, as when Pigot argued that cutting thorns that blocked water to the mill will give rise to an action for trespass, even in the absence of the direct use of force against the millowner.

The radical change in subsequent centuries, far from altering the underlying substantive principles, came about for procedural reasons. The courts no longer required the magic words, vi et armis and contra pacem regis, in situations in which their ordinary meanings did not apply. To support his thesis, Milsom collected from the old legal records a large number of writs framed in trespass in which the phrases vi et armis and contra pacem regis were included solely as legal fiction to secure the jurisdiction of the royal courts. The writ of trespass was, for example, broad enough to encompass suits brought by lower riparians who suffered flooding because upper riparians had not made the required repairs to their river walls. Similarly, early trespass actions were used to stop unfair competition by, for example, the owner of a fair against persons who had sold goods in violation of his exclusive franchise granted by the king. In neither case did the words vi et armis or contra pacem regis describe the event for which redress was sought.

Perhaps Milsom's most interesting case was an action for professional malpractice (to use the modern term) brought by the owner of a horse against a smith to whom he had entrusted the care of his animal. The plaintiff could not state his cause of action in simple and direct terms and still allege that the defendant's use of force and arms was in violation of the king's peace, necessary to attract royal jurisdiction. To speak of force and arms made the complaint internally inconsistent, for the plaintiff who entrusted the defendant with the care of his horse could not simultaneously attack the defendant's conduct as a breach of the king's peace. What could be done in order to escape this dilemma? Milsom explains:

> To excise the *vi et armis* and *contra pacem* left the perfectly good complaint from which the plaintiff had started: but it was not even technically a plea of the crown, and so was not within the jurisdiction of a royal court. To bring the matter to a royal court, therefore, he had to excise the other allegation, that which showed that the object was lawfully in the defendant's possession. Instead of complaining that the smith did his work so badly that the horse died, his writ would run something like this: why with force and arms the defendant killed the plaintiff's horse, to his damage and against the king's peace. The count would follow the writ, the defendant would plead Not Guilty, the jury would find him guilty or not guilty, and the record would look like that of an action for malicious injury by a stranger. Knowledge of what happened in later times might make us suspect that it was really a road accident or the like. But were it not for the chinks of a few unusual cases, there would be nothing to make us suspect the truth, except this: the defendants in many such actions for killing horses are named or described as

smiths. [S.F.C. Milsom, Historical Foundations of the Common Law 289 (2d ed. 1981).]

The royal judges eventually tired of these elaborate fictions, and in the Farrier's Case of 1372, they allowed the plaintiff to sue in royal court without pleading either vi et armis or contra pacem regis. The emergence of the action on the case was a triumph for judicial candor, but it did not expand the scope of the tort law in the royal courts. This development did, however, make it necessary to determine when each of the two distinct writs — trespass and case — were appropriate. Part of the impulse for clarifying the boundaries between the two writs was procedural. With trespass, the plaintiff could begin his suit with the stringent process of capias, whereby he could seize the defendant's personal property. With case, however, the plaintiff had to commence his action with the less coercive summons and complaint. That distinction was eliminated by statute in 1504. Yet by a statute of 1677 (16 & 17 Car. 2), a second procedural point separated the two writs. In the words of Lord Kenyon in Savignac v. Roome, 101 Eng. Rep. 470 (K.B. 1794): "if in an action of trespass the plaintiff recover less than 40 *s.,* he is entitled to no more costs than damages; whereas a verdict with nominal damages only in an action on the case carries all the costs."

The division in the writs between trespass and case raised substantive problems as well, as in the famous *Squib Case.*

Scott v. Shepherd
96 Eng. Rep. 525 (K.B. 1773)

Trespass and assault for throwing, casting, and tossing a lighted squib at and against the plaintiff, and striking him therewith on the face, and so burning one of his eyes, that he lost the sight of it, whereby, & c. On Not Guilty pleaded, the cause came on to be tried before Nares, J., last Summer Assizes, at Bridgwater, when the jury found a verdict for the plaintiff with £100 damages, subject to the opinion of the Court on this case: — On the evening of the fair-day at Milborne Port, 28th October, 1770, the defendant threw a *lighted squib,* made of gun powder, &c. from the street into the market-house, which is a covered building, supported by arches, and enclosed at one end, but open at the other and both the sides, where a large concourse of people were assembled; which lighted squib, so thrown by the defendant, fell upon the standing of one Yates, who sold gingerbread, & c. That one Willis instantly, and to prevent injury to himself and the said wares of the said Yates, took up the said lighted squib from off the said standing, and then threw it across the said market-house, when it fell upon another standing there of one Ryal, who sold the same sort of wares, who instantly, and to save his own goods from being injured, took up the said lighted squib from off the said standing, and then threw it to another part of the said market-house, and, in so throwing it, struck the plaintiff then in the said market-house in the face therewith, and the combustible matter then bursting, put out one of the plaintiff's eyes. *Qu.* If this action be maintainable? . . .

NARES, J., was of opinion, that trespass would well lie in the present case. That the natural and probable consequence of the act done by the defendant was injury to somebody, and therefore the act was illegal at common law. And the throwing of squibs has by statute W.3, been since made a nuisance. Being therefore unlawful, the defendant was liable to answer for the consequences, be the injury mediate or immediate. 21 Hen. 7, 28, is express that malus animus is not necessary to constitute a trespass. . . .

BLACKSTONE, J., was of opinion, that an action of trespass did not lie for Scott against Shepherd upon this case. He took the settled distinction to be, that where the injury is *immediate,* an action of trespass will lie; where it is only *consequential,* it must be an action on the case: Reynolds and Clarke, Lord Raym. 1401, Stra. 634; . . . The lawfulness or unlawfulness of the original act is not the criterion; though something of that sort is put into Lord Raymond's mouth in Stra. 635, . . . [L]awful or unlawful is quite out of the case; the solid distinction is between direct or immediate injuries on the one hand, and mediate or consequential on the other. And trespass never lay for the latter. If this be so, the only question will be, whether the injury which the plaintiff suffered was immediate, or consequential only; and I hold it to be the latter. The original act was, as against Yates, a trespass; not as against Ryal, or Scott. The tortious act was complete when the squib lay at rest upon Yates's stall. He, or any bystander, had, I allow, a right to protect themselves by removing the squib, but should have taken care to do it in such a manner as not to endamage others. But Shepherd, I think, is not answerable in an action of trespass and assault for the mischief done by the squib in the new motion impressed upon it, and the new direction given it, by either Willis or Ryal; who both were free agents, and acted upon their own judgment. This differs it from the cases put of turning loose a wild beast or a madman. They are only instruments in the hand of the first agent. Nor is it like diverting the course of an enraged ox, or of a stone thrown, or an arrow glancing against a tree; because there the original motion, the vis impressa, is continued, though diverted. Here the instrument of mischief was at rest, till a new impetus and a new direction are given it, not once only, but by two successive rational agents. But it is said that the act is not complete, nor the squib at rest, till after it is spent or exploded. It certainly has a power of doing fresh mischief, and so has a stone that has been thrown against my windows, and now lies still. Yet if any person gives that stone a new motion, and does farther mischief with it, trespass will not lie for that against the original thrower. No doubt but Yates may maintain trespass against Shepherd. And, according to the doctrine contended for, so may Ryal and Scott. Three actions for one single act! nay, it may be extended in infinitum. If a man tosses a football into the street, and, after being kicked about by one hundred people, it at last breaks a tradesman's windows; shall he have trespass against the man who first produced it? Surely only against the man who gave it that mischievous direction. But it is said, if Scott has no action against Shepherd, against whom must he seek his remedy? I give no opinion whether case would lie against Shepherd for the consequential damage; though, as at present advised, I think, upon the circumstances, it would. But I think, in strictness of law, trespass would lie against Ryal, the immediate actor in this unhappy business. Both he and Willis have exceeded the bounds of self-defence, and not used sufficient circumspection in removing the danger from themselves. The throwing it across the market-house, instead of brushing it down, or throwing [it] out of the open sides into the street, (if it was not meant to continue the sport, as it is called), was at least an unnecessary and incautious act. Not even menaces from others are sufficient to justify a trespass against a third person; much less a fear of danger to either his goods or his person — nothing but inevitable necessity; Weaver and Ward, Hob. 134; Gilbert and Stone, Al. 35, Styl. 72. . . . And I admit that the defendant is answerable in trespass for all the direct and inevitable effects caused by his own immediate act. — But what is his own immediate act? The throwing the squib to Yates's stall. Had Yates's goods been burnt, or his person injured, Shepherd must have been responsible in trespass. But he is not responsible for the acts of other men. The subsequent throwing across the market-house by Willis, is neither the act of Shepherd, nor the inevitable effect of it; much less the subsequent throwing by Ryal. . . . It is said by Lord Raymond, and very justly, in Reynolds and Clarke, "We must keep up the boundaries of actions, otherwise we shall introduce the utmost confusion." As I therefore think no immediate injury passed from the defendant to the plaintiff (and without such immediate injury no action of trespass can be maintained), I am of opinion, that in this action judgment ought to be for the defendant.

DE GREY, C.J. This case is one of those wherein the line drawn by the law between actions on the case and actions of trespass is very nice and delicate. Trespass is an injury accompanied with force, for which an action of trespass vi et armis lies against the person from whom it is received. The question here is, whether the injury received by the plaintiff arises from the force of the original act of the defendant, or from a new force by a third person. I agree with my Brother Blackstone as to the principles he has laid down, but not in his application of those principles to the present case. . . . [T]he true question is, whether the injury is the direct and immediate act of the defendant; and I am of opinion, that in this case it is. The throwing the squib was an act unlawful and tending to affright the bystanders. So far, mischief was originally intended; not any particular mischief, but mischief indiscriminate and wanton. Whatever mischief therefore follows, he is the author of it; — Egreditur personam, as the phrase is in criminal cases. And though criminal cases are no rule for civil ones, yet in trespass I think there is an analogy. Every one who does an unlawful act is considered as the doer of all that follows; if done with a deliberate intent, the consequence may amount to murder; if incautiously, to manslaughter. So too a person breaking a horse in Lincoln's Inn Fields hurt a man; held, that trespass lay: and that it need not be laid scienter. I look upon all that was done subsequent to the original throwing as a continuation of the first force and first act, which will continue till the squib was spent by bursting. And I think that any innocent person removing the danger from himself to another is justifiable; the blame lights upon the first thrower. The new direction and new force flow out of the first force, and are not a new trespass. . . . It has been urged, that the intervention of a free agent will make a difference: but I do not consider Willis ad Ryal as free agents in the present case, but acting under a compulsive necessity for their own safety and self-preservation. On these reasons I concur with Brothers Gould and Nares, that the present action is maintainable.

NOTE

Under which writ lies the cause of action? Scott proposes two complementary ways to determine the boundary line between trespass and case. One method held that trespass lay where the harm was direct, and case where it was consequential. The second method, championed by Nares, J., insisted that trespass also lies for all harm, direct or consequential, when the defendant's action is unlawful by statute, including one that declares the throwing of a lighted squib a public nuisance. In Reynolds v. Clarke, 92 Eng. Rep. 410 (K.B. 1726), moreover, the plaintiff's action for trespass was dismissed when the defendant fixed a spout in plaintiff's yard from which water leaked, thereby rotting the walls of plaintiff's house. Where the invasion is direct, and the harm is consequential, which action should prevail?

A similar dispute over the proper form of action arose in the celebrated case of Guille v. Swan, 19 Johns. (N.Y.) 381 (1822). There the defendant Guille flew in a balloon that landed in the garden of the plaintiff Swan. When the balloon landed it dragged for about 30 feet causing damage to Swan's potatoes and radishes. Given his perilous position, Guille called out to a workman in Swan's field for help in a voice that could be heard by the crowd assembled at the boundary line. About 200 people came tearing across plaintiff's land causing damage to his vegetables and flowers, for which Swan sued Guille in trespass. Guille sought to limit his liability to the damage that he had caused, not that of the crowd. But Spencer, C.J., upheld a jury verdict against Guille for the full $90 in damages.

> The *intent* with which an act is done, is by no means the test of liability of a party to an action of trespass. If the act causes the immediate injury, whether it was intentional or unintentional, trespass is the proper action to redress the wrong. [The court discusses Scott v. Shepherd among other cases, and continues.]
>
>   I will not say that ascending in a balloon is an unlawful act, for it is not so; but, it is certain, that the *Aeronaut* has no control over its motion horizontally; he is at the sport of the winds, and is to descend when and how he can; his reach[ing] the earth is a matter of hazard. He did descend on the premises of the plaintiff below, at a short distance from the place where he ascended. Now, if his descent, under such circumstances, would, ordinarily and naturally, draw a crowd of people about him, either from curiosity, or for the purpose of rescuing him from a perilous situation; all this he ought to have foreseen, and must be responsible for. Whether the crowd heard him call for help, or not, is immaterial; he had put himself in a situation to invite help, and they rushed forward, impelled, perhaps, by the double motive of rendering aid, and gratifying a curiosity which he had excited. Can it be doubted, that if the plaintiff in error [i.e. defendant-appellant] had beckoned to the crowd to come to his assistance, that he would be liable for their trespass in entering the enclosure? I think not. In that case, they would have been co-trespassers, and we must consider the situation in which he placed himself, voluntarily and designedly, as equivalent to a direct request to the crowd to follow him. In the present case, he did call for help and may have been heard by the crowd; he is, therefore, undoubtedly, liable for all the injury sustained.

In trespass?

3.   The Breakdown of the Forms

The lighted squib in Scott v. Shepherd and the descending balloon in Guille v. Swan posed novel challenges to the uncertain line between trespass and case. Yet their importance for judicial administration was small, for the English and American courts only rarely encountered lighted squibs or falling balloons. The division between the writs, however, was critical in cases involving accidents on the highway or the high seas that reached the courts in great numbers by the 1790s. In these cases, the courts were unable to make any firm or authoritative choice between trespass or case. The root problem was as much practical as theoretical. Even if courts could define conceptually the line between trespass and case, it need not be clear to the plaintiff in advance of trial whether her case fell on one side of the line or the other. If the plaintiff sued in trespass, the defendant could prevail by showing that his horse, which he had outfitted with too-weak reins, had bolted out of control. If the action were brought in case, the defendant might still prevail if he had indeed run right over the plaintiff. Collisions at sea were even more complicated. It was always a delicate judgment whether a captain had rammed his ship into another ship, or whether the wind or the sea (an act of God) had carried his disabled ship into the other craft. See, e.g., Ogle v. Barnes, 101 Eng. Reg. 1338 (K.B. 1799).

The situation was further complicated by the twin problems of vicarious liability and joinder of actions. If the plaintiff was run down by a carriage owned by the defendant, is trespass or case correct? If it turned out that the carriage was driven by the defendant's servant, it was settled that trespass against the master was not appropriate, no matter what action lay against the servant. McManus v. Crickett, 102 Eng. Rep. 580 (K.B. 1800); Sharrod v. London & N.W. Ry., 154 Eng. Rep. 1345 (Ex. 1849). The master did not apply direct and immediate force to the plaintiff; and even if trespass lay against the servant, it could not by any stretch of the imagination lie against the master, who was held accountable, if at all, on principles of vicarious liability. Yet, suppose the original action was brought in case, to cover the possibility that the coach had been driven by a servant in the defendant's employ. The plaintiff now ran the risk of nonsuit (that is, dismissal) if the defendant personally had driven the coach. Equally important, the rules governing the joinder of actions prohibited the plaintiff in an accident involving direct harm from suing both the owner and his servant-driver under the same writ: Trespass required one form of action and case required another. The limitations on two writs forced the plaintiffs and courts to play an uncertain shell game for the defendant's benefit, as several separate and expensive actions were needed to guard against all the unhappy possibilities that might emerge at trial.

How could the courts break the logjam? The most obvious proposal was to disregard tradition by allowing a plaintiff to include separate counts of trespass and case within a single writ. That result was achieved by statute by the middle of the nineteenth century by the Common Law Procedure Act 15 & 16 Vict., c. 76, §41 (1852), but the early nineteenth-century English judges were not prepared to introduce so bold a reform on their own initiative. A second possibility was to bend the rules by allowing the plaintiff to use trespass against the master when the servant caused immediate and direct harm, a proposal that would have eliminated the gamesmanship involved in the joinder of actions. Yet, here too, the writ tradition resisted judicial innovation.

In the end, the courts adopted a third solution. In the watershed case of Williams v. Holland, 131 Eng. Rep. 848 (C.P. 1833), the Court of Common Pleas held that the plaintiff could sue in case, no matter whether the harm was immediate or consequential, as long as the plaintiff could show that the harm occurred as a result of the defendant's negligence. The writ of trespass was still available for all immediate harms, whether willful or negligent, and only trespass would lie in cases of willful and immediate harm. Harms directly and negligently caused could under this rule be remedied in either trespass or case. Under the rule in Williams v. Holland, the plaintiff in virtually all running-down cases would prefer case to trespass because case allowed him, first, to avoid having to guess whether harm was immediate or consequential and, second, to join both master and servant in a single suit. Joinder of claims was unavailable under Williams v. Holland when the injury inflicted by the servant was both willful and direct, but that limitation hardly mattered since there were few road incidents of that sort. And when these cases did occur, the master was probably not liable. He could defend himself under an early version of the "frolic and detour" doctrine, an exception to the general rule of vicarious liability, applicable to cases of willful wrongs of servants committed outside the course of employment.

Williams v. Holland did more than usher in a procedural revolution; it also had a great bearing on the strict liability/negligence controversy. The earlier cases, such as Scott v. Shepherd, contained many hints that trespass would lie for direct harm caused by the defendant even in the absence of negligence or intent. The law invited actions under a causal theory of strict liability: you struck my wagon. After Williams v. Holland, the element of negligence assumed a more prominent role when it became essential for recovery in all highway accident cases for either direct or consequential damages. The English position was summed up by Bramwell, B., in Holmes v. Mather, L.R. 10 Ex. 261, 268–269 (1875), in giving judgment for the defendant:

> As to the cases cited, most of them are really decisions on the form of action, whether case or trespass. The result of them is this, and it is intelligible enough: if the act that does an injury is an act of direct force vi et armis, trespass is the proper remedy (if there is any remedy) where the act is wrongful, either as being wilful or as being the result of negligence. Where the act is not wrongful for either of these reasons, no action is maintainable, though trespass would be the proper form of action if it were wrongful.

Even after the English courts settled the substantive issue, some procedural consequences could still be traced to the writ system. In actions framed in trespass, the negligence issue originally came into the lawsuit through the back door with the defense of "inevitable accident." On the other hand, the plaintiff had to plead and prove negligence in actions on the case, even as defendant had to show himself free from fault in cases of direct harm. Stanley v. Powell, [1891] 1 Q.B. 86. Indeed, in England it took until 1959 for the law to require the plaintiff to both plead and prove negligence in all suits for unintended personal injury. Fowler v. Lanning, [1959] 1 Q.B. 426. The procedural problems created by the division between the two writs also carried over to other areas. To give but one example, it took until 1965 to hold that the same three-year statute of limitations applied to all personal injury actions, whether framed in trespass or negligence. Letang v. Cooper, [1965] 1 Q.B. 232.

The history of trespass and case in England is given here in much abbreviated form. For further materials see M. Arnold, Select Cases of Trespass from the King's Courts: 1307-1399 (Seldon Society, vol. 100, 1985); C.H.S. Fifoot, History and Sources of the Common Law, Tort and Contract ch. 9 (1949); A. Harari, The Place of Negligence in the Law of Torts ch. 11 and app. (1962); S.F.C. Milsom, Historical Foundations of the Common Law chs. 11, 13 (2d ed. 1981); M.J. Prichard, Trespass, Case and The Rule in Williams v. Holland, 22 Cambridge L.J. 234 (1964), an excellent article from which much of the account given here is drawn; Gregory, Trespass to Negligence to Absolute Liability, 37 Va. L. Rev. 359 (1951).

SECTION D. STRICT LIABILITY AND NEGLIGENCE IN THE LAST HALF OF THE NINETEENTH CENTURY

Toward the middle of the nineteenth century, the forms of action fell by the wayside in both England and the United States. Just before the English Common Law Procedure Acts of 1852 removed the last vestiges of the forms of action from English law, the widespread adoption of the so-called Field Codes — named after the reformer David Dudley Field, who championed the adoption of "code pleading" in New York — did the same thing in the United States. See First Report of Commissioners on Practice and Pleading (N.Y. 1848). The purpose of these reforms was simply to abolish the forms of action as procedural devices. "No rule of law, by which rights and wrongs are measured, will be touched, the object and effect of the change being only the removal of old obstructions, in the way of enforcing the rights, and redressing the wrongs." *Id.* at 146-147. Therefore, the legal precedents in tort, both in England and the United States survived the procedural reforms. With the removal of the forms, the choice between negligence and strict liability was thus inescapably presented in its most general form. See generally C. Clark, Code Pleading (2d ed. 1947).

The emergence of negligence as the dominant standard of civil liability in American tort law during the first half of the nineteenth century parallels the English experience. At the beginning of the nineteenth century, the writ system, with its distinction between trespass and case, raised the same problems throughout the United States that were encountered in England, as evidenced in *Guille, supra* at 118. Negligence was a shadowy concept, with a subordinate role in the tort law. In its primary sense, the negligence concept applied to the *nonfeasance* of individuals charged either by contract or statute with a duty of care. Smiths and surgeons were, for example, bound by contract to conduct their professions carefully, while jailors and those charged with the maintenance of the public highways were persons on whom statutes placed the duty of care. Negligence, in the sense of carelessness in the performance of some affirmative act that causes harm to a stranger, was not the prevalent conception.

Yet by 1830, the increase in collision cases slowly brought this second sense of negligence to the fore. For the case law of this period see Harvey v. Dunlop, (Hill & Denio) 193 (N.Y. 1843); Bridge Co. v. Lehigh Coal & Navigation Co., 4 Rawle 8 (Pa. 1833); Sullivan v. Murphy, 2 Miles 298, 2 Law Rep. 246 (1839). See generally for the account M. Horwitz, The Transformation of American Law: 1780 to 1860, 89-94 (1977).

Brown v. Kendall
60 Mass. 292 (1850)

It appeared in evidence, on the trial, which was before Wells, C.J., in the court of common pleas, that two dogs, belonging to the plaintiff and the defendant, respectively, were fighting in the presence of their masters; that the defendant took a stick about four feet long, and commenced beating the dogs in order to separate them; that the plaintiff was looking on, at the distance of about a rod [= 16.5 feet], and that he advanced a step or two towards the dogs. In their struggle, the dogs approached the place where the plaintiff was standing. The defendant retreated backwards from the dogs, striking them as he retreated; and as he approached the plaintiff, with his back towards him, in raising his stick over his shoulder, in order to strike the dogs, he accidentally hit the plaintiff in the eye, inflicting upon him a severe injury. . . .

SHAW, C.J. This is an action of trespass, vi et armis, brought by George Brown against George K. Kendall, for an assault and battery; and the original defendant having died pending the action, his executrix has been summoned in. The rule of the common law, by which this action would abate by the death of either party, is reversed in this commonwealth by statute, which provides that actions of trespass for assault and battery shall survive. Rev. Sts. c. 93, §7.

The facts set forth in the bill of exceptions preclude the supposition, that the blow, inflicted by the hand of the defendant upon the person of the plaintiff, was intentional. The whole case proceeds on the assumption, that the damage sustained by the plaintiff, from the stick held by the defendant, was inadvertent and unintentional; and the case involves the question how far, and under what qualifications, the party by whose unconscious act the damage was done is responsible for it. We use the term "unintentional" rather than involuntary, because in some of the cases, it is stated, that the act of holding and using a weapon or instrument, the movement of which is the immediate cause of hurt to another, is a voluntary act, although its particular effect in hitting and hurting another is not within the purpose or intention of the party doing the act.

It appears to us, that some of the confusion in the cases on this subject has grown out of the long-vexed question, under the rule of the common law, whether a party's remedy, where he has one, should be sought in an action of the case, or of trespass. This is very distinguishable from the question, whether in a given case, any action will lie. The result of these cases is, that if the damage complained of is the immediate effect of the act of the defendant, trespass vi et armis lies; if consequential only, and not immediate, case is the proper remedy. . . .

In these discussions, it is frequently stated by judges, that when one receives injury from the direct act of another, trespass will lie. But we think this is said in reference to the question, whether trespass and not case will lie, assuming that the facts are such, that some action will lie. These dicta are no authority, we think, for holding, that damage received by a direct act of force from another will be sufficient to maintain an action of trespass, whether the act was lawful or unlawful, and neither wilful, intentional, nor careless. . . .

We think, as the result of all the authorities, the rule is correctly stated by Mr. Greenleaf, that the plaintiff must come prepared with evidence to show either that the *intention* was unlawful, or that the defendant was *in fault;* for if the injury was unavoidable, and the conduct of the defendant was free from blame, he will not be liable. 2 Greenl. Ev. §§85 to 92. If, in the prosecution of a lawful act, a casualty purely accidental arises, no action can be supported for an injury arising therefrom. . . . In applying these rules to the present case, we can perceive no reason why the instructions asked for by the defendant ought not to have been given; to this effect, that if both plaintiff and defendant at the time of the blow were using ordinary care, or if at that time the defendant was using ordinary care, and the plaintiff was not, or if at that time, both the plaintiff and defendant were not using ordinary care, then the plaintiff could not recover.

In using this term, ordinary care, it may be proper to state, that what constitutes ordinary care will vary with the circumstances of cases. In general, it means that kind and degree of care, which prudent and cautious men would use, such as is required by the exigency of the case, and such as is necessary to guard against probable danger. A man, who should have occasion to discharge a gun, on an open and extensive marsh, or in a forest, would be required to use less circumspection and care, than if he were to do the same thing in an inhabited town, village, or city. To make an accident, or casualty, or as the law sometimes states it, inevitable accident, it must be such an accident as the defendant could not have avoided by the use of the kind and degree of care necessary to the exigency, and in the circumstances in which he was placed.

We are not aware of any circumstances in this case, requiring a distinction between acts which it was lawful and proper to do, and acts of legal duty. There are cases, undoubtedly, in which officers are bound to act under process, for the legality of which they are not responsible, and perhaps some others in which this distinction would be important. We can have no doubt that the act of the defendant in attempting to part the fighting dogs, one of which was his own, and for the injurious acts of which he might be responsible, was a lawful and proper act, which he might do by proper and safe means. If, then, in doing this act, using due care and all proper precautions necessary to the exigency of the case, to avoid hurt to others, in raising his stick for that purpose, he accidentally hit the plaintiff in his eye, and wounded him, this was the result of pure accident, or was involuntary and unavoidable, and therefore the action would not lie. Or if the defendant was chargeable with some negligence, and if the plaintiff was also chargeable with negligence, we think the plaintiff cannot recover without showing that the damage was caused wholly by the act of the defendant, and that the plaintiff's own negligence did not contribute as an efficient cause to produce it.

The court instructed the jury, that if it was not a necessary act, and the defendant was not in duty bound to part the dogs, but might with propriety interfere or not as he chose, the defendant was responsible for the consequences of the blow, unless it appeared that he was in the exercise of extraordinary care, so that the accident was inevitable, using the word not in a strict but a popular sense. This is to be taken in connection with the charge afterwards given, that if the jury believed, that the act of interference in the fight was unnecessary, (that is, as before explained, not a duty incumbent on the defendant,) then the burden of proving extraordinary care on the part of the defendant, or want of ordinary care on the part of plaintiff, was on the defendant.

The court is of opinion that these directions were not conformable to law. If the act of hitting the plaintiff was unintentional, on the part of the defendant, and done in the doing of a lawful act, then the defendant was not liable, unless it was done in the want of exercise of due care, adapted to the exigency of the case, and therefore such want of due care became part of the plaintiff's case, and the burden of proof was on the plaintiff to establish it. . . .

Perhaps the learned judge, by the use of the term extraordinary care, in the above charge, explained as it is by the context, may have intended nothing more than that increased degree of care and diligence, which the exigency of particular circumstances might require, and which men of ordinary care and prudence would use under like circumstances, to guard against danger. If such was the meaning of this part of the charge, then it does not differ from our views, as above explained. But we are of opinion, that the other part of the charge, that the burden of proof was on the defendant, was incorrect. Those facts which are essential to enable the plaintiff to recover, he takes the burden of proving. The evidence may be offered by the plaintiff or by the defendant; the question of due care, or want of care, may be essentially connected with the main facts, and arise from the same proof; but the effect of the rule, as to the burden of proof, is this, that when the proof is all in, and before the jury, from whatever side it comes, and whether directly proved, or inferred from circumstances, if it appears that the defendant was doing a lawful act, and unintentionally hit and hurt the plaintiff, then unless it also appears to the satisfaction of the jury, that the defendant is chargeable with some fault, negligence, carelessness, or want of prudence, the plaintiff fails to sustain the burden of proof, and is not entitled to recover.

New trial ordered.

NOTE

Negligence and economic growth. The rise of negligence in American tort law has been often viewed as a subsidy for the protection of infant industries. See, e.g., Gregory, Trespass, to Negligence, to Absolute Liability, 37 Va. L. Rev. 359 (1951). Subsequently, the thesis has been advanced by Professor Morton Horwitz in his influential work, The Transformation of American Law, 1780-1860, 99-101 (1977): "One of the most striking aspects of legal change during the antebellum period is the extent to which common law doctrines were transformed to create immunities from legal liability and thereby to provide substantial subsidies for those who undertook schemes of economic development." In his view the effort to obtain subsidies through common law rule instead of through the tax system was designed to "more easily disguise underlying political choices. Subsidy through the tax system, by contrast, inevitably involves greater danger of political conflict." In Horwitz's view, more empirical research is needed to compare the effects of taxation (typically low in the nineteenth century) with those attributable to changes in common law rules. "Nevertheless, it does seem fairly clear that the tendency of subsidy through legal change during this period was dramatically to throw the burden of economic development on the weakest and least active elements in the population."

The subsidy thesis itself has been challenged on several counts. First, it has been observed that "Brown [v. Kendall] itself, after all, did not involve industry; it involved private persons and a dog fight. Rather than simply promoting 'General Motors,' is it not more accurate to say that Chief Judge Shaw saw the change in moral terms as well, as a sound social policy not only for business but for every man?" Roberts, Negligence: Blackstone to Shaw to ?: An Intellectual Escapade in a Tory Vein, 50 Cornell L.Q. 191, 205 (1965). Is it a fair reply to say that Shaw well understood the implications of his decision upon the growth of industry and trade?

Gary Schwartz has also challenged the Horwitz thesis in his article Tort Law and the Economy in Nineteenth-Century America: A Reinterpretation, 90 Yale L.J. 1717 (1981). Schwartz's reading of the earlier English cases, and particularly the American cases around 1800, indicates that the negligence principle was then operative in many, if not most, instances. Thus, the widespread adoption of negligence toward the middle of the nineteenth century cannot be considered a legal transformation. In addition, Schwartz read and analyzed every nineteenth-century tort case decided in both California and New Hampshire, and found no support for the subsidy thesis and no effort by the courts to engage in the "dynamic, utilitarian" calculations that Horwitz attributes to them. Schwartz also noted that it was unlikely that the subsidy question could be kept underground in the face of explicit legislative debate over subsidies to both railroads and canals.

How should the subsidy question be evaluated from a theoretical perspective? Is it possible that some industries were hurt by the rule because they were unable to recover as plaintiffs for the harms inflicted upon them by firms in other industries? For the argument that manipulating general common law tort rules is a poor way to create interest group subsidies, see Epstein, The Social Consequences of Common Law Rules, 95 Harv. L. Rev. 1717 (1982). See also Schwartz, The Character of Early American Tort Law, 36 UCLA L. Rev. 641 (1989).

The same debate over negligence and strict liability also surfaced in the English cases shortly after *Brown*, with dramatically different results.

Fletcher v. Rylands
159 Eng. Rep. 737 (Ex. 1865)

[The following statement of facts is taken from the opinion of Blackburn, J., in the intermediate appellate court:

"It appears from the statement in the case, that the plaintiff was damaged by his property being flooded by water, which, without any fault on his part, broke out of a reservoir constructed on the defendants' land by the defendants' orders, and maintained by the defendants.

It appears from the statement in the case, that the coal under the defendants' land had, at some remote period, been worked out; but this was unknown at the time when the defendants gave directions to erect the reservoir, and the water in the reservoir would not have escaped from the defendants' land, and no mischief would have been done to the plaintiff, but for this latent defect in the defendants' subsoil. And it further appears, that the defendants selected competent engineers and contractors to make their reservoir, and themselves personally continued in total ignorance of what we have called the latent defect in the subsoil; but that these persons employed by them in the course of the work became aware of the existence of the ancient shafts filled up with soil, though they did not know or suspect that they were shafts communicating with old workings.

It is found that the defendants, personally, were free from all blame, but that in fact proper care and skill was not used by the persons employed by them, to provide for the sufficiency of the reservoir with reference to these shafts. The consequence was, that the reservoir when filled with water burst into the shafts, the water flowed down through them into the old workings, and thence into the plaintiff's mine, and there did the mischief."

The above statement of facts should be supplemented by a few additional facts drawn from Lord Cairns's opinion in the House of Lords. (1) the plaintiff had leased his coal mines from the Earl of Wilton; (2) the defendants had constructed their new reservoir upon other land of the Earl of Wilton, with his permission; (3) the reservoir in question was to be used to collect water for the defendants' mill; (4) the defendants had already placed, on their own nearby land, a small reservoir and a mill; (5) the plaintiff in the course of working his mines came across some abandoned shafts and mine passages of unknown origin; and (6) the reservoir burst when it was partially filled with water after one of the vertical shafts beneath it gave way.]

BRAMWELL, B. . . . Now, what is the plaintiff's right? He had the right to work his mines to their extent, leaving no boundary between himself and the next owner. By so doing he subjected himself to all consequences resulting from natural causes, among others, to the influx of all water naturally flowing in. But he had a right to be free from what has been called "foreign" water, that is, water artificially brought or sent to him directly, or indirectly by its being sent to where it would flow to him. The defendants had no right to pour or send water onto the plaintiff's works. Had they done so knowingly it is admitted an action would lie; and that it would if they did it again. That is also proved by the case of Hodgkinson v. Ennor[, 122 Eng. Rep. 446 (Ex. 1863)]. The plaintiff's right then has been infringed; the defendants in causing water to flow to the plaintiff have done that which they had no right to do; what difference in point of law does it make that they have done it unwittingly? I think none, and consequently that the action is maintainable. . . . As a rule the knowledge or ignorance of the damage done is immaterial. The burden of proof of this proposition is not on the plaintiff.

I proceed to deal with the arguments the other way. It is said there must be a trespass, a nuisance or negligence. I do not agree. . . . But why is this not a trespass? Wilfulness is not material. . . . Why is it not a nuisance? The nuisance is not in the reservoir, but in the water escaping. . . . [T]he act was lawful, the mischievous consequence is a wrong. Where two carriages come in collision, if there is no negligence in either it is as much the act of the one driver as of the other that they meet. The cases of carriers and innkeepers are really cases of contract, and, though exceptional, furnish no evidence that the general law in matters wholly independent of contract is not what I have stated. The old common law liability for fire, created a liability beyond what I contend for here. . . .

I think, therefore, on the plain ground that the defendants have caused water to flow into the plaintiff's mines which but for their, the defendants', act would not have gone there, this action is maintainable. I think that the defendants' innocence, whatever may be its moral bearing on the case, is immaterial in point of law. But I may as well add, that if the defendants did not know what would happen their agents knew that there were old shafts on their land — knew therefore that they must lead to old workings — knew that those old workings *might* extend in any direction, and consequently knew damage might happen. The defendants surely are as liable as their agents would be — why should not they and the defendants be held to act at their peril? But I own this seems to me rather to enforce the rule, that knowledge and wilfulness are not necessary to make the defendants liable, than to give the plaintiff a separate ground of action.

MARTIN, B. . . . First, I think there was no trespass. In the judgment of my brother Bramwell, to which I shall hereafter refer, he seems to think the act of the defendants was a trespass, but I cannot concur, and I own it seems to me that the cases cited by him, viz., Leame v. Bray[, 102 Eng. Rep. 724 (K. B. 1803)], and Gregory v. Piper, 9 B. & C. 591 (E.C.L.R. vol. 17)[, 109 Eng. Rep. 220 (K.B. 1829)], prove the contrary. I think the true criterion of trespass is laid down in the judgments in the former case, viz., that to constitute trespass the act doing the damage must be immediate, and that if the damage be mediate or consequential (which I think the present was) it is not a trespass. Secondly, I think there was no nuisance in the ordinary and generally understood meaning of that word, that is to say, something hurtful or injurious to the senses. The making a pond for holding water is a nuisance to no one. The digging a reservoir in a man's own land is a lawful act. It does not appear that there was any embankment, or that the water in the reservoir was ever above the level of the natural surface of the land, and the water escaped from the bottom of the reservoir, and in ordinary course would descend by gravitation into the defendants' own land, and they did not know of the existence of the old workings. To hold the defendants liable would therefore make them insurers against the consequence of a lawful act upon their own land when they had no reason to believe or suspect that any damage was likely to ensue.

No case was cited in which the question has arisen as to real property; but as to personal property the question arises every day, and there is no better established rule of law than that when damage is done to personal property, and even to the person, by collision either upon the road or at sea, there must be negligence in the party doing the damage to render him legally responsible, and if there be no negligence the party sustaining the damage must bear with it. The existence of this rule is proved by the exceptions to it, viz., the cases of the innkeeper and common carrier of goods for hire, who are quasi insurers. These cases are said to be by the custom of the realm, treating them as exceptions from the ordinary rule of law. In the absence of authority to the contrary, I can see no reason why damage to real property should be governed by a different rule or principle than damage to personal property. There is an instance also of damage to real property, when the party causing it was at common law liable upon the custom of the realm as a quasi insurer, viz., the master of a house if a fire had kindled there and consumed the house of another. In such case the master of the house was liable at common law without proof of negligence on his part. This seems to be an exception from the ordinary rule of law, and in my opinion affords an argument that in other cases such as the present there must be negligence to create a liability. For these reasons I think the first question ought to be answered in favour of the defendants. . . .

I have already referred to the judgment of my brother Bramwell, which I have carefully read and considered, but cannot concur in it. I entertain no doubt that if the defendants directly and by their immediate act cast water upon the plaintiff's land it would have been a trespass, and that they would be liable to an action for it. But this they did not do. What they did was this, they dug a reservoir in their own land and put water in it, which, by underground openings of which they were ignorant, escaped into the plaintiff's land. I think this a very different thing from a direct casting of water upon the land, and that the legal liabilities consequent upon it are governed by a different principle. . . .

I still retain the opinion I originally formed. I think . . . that to hold the defendant liable without negligence would be to constitute him an insurer, which, in my opinion, would be contrary to legal analogy and principle.

[Pollock, C.B., after stating that the issue was "one of great difficulty, and therefore of much doubt," wrote a brief opinion agreeing with Martin, B.]

Fletcher v. Rylands
L.R. 1 Ex. 265 (1866)

BLACKBURN, J. . . . The plaintiff, though free from all blame on his part, must bear the loss, unless he can establish that it was the consequence of some default for which the defendants are responsible. The question of law therefore arises, what is the obligation which the law casts on a person who, like the defendants, lawfully brings on his land something which, though harmless whilst it remains there, will naturally do mischief if it escape out of his land. It is agreed on all hands that he must take care to keep in that which he has brought on the land and keeps there, in order that it may not escape and damage his neighbours, but the question arises whether the duty which the law casts upon him, under such circumstances, is an absolute duty to keep it in at his peril, or is, as the majority of the Court of Exchequer have thought, merely a duty to take all reasonable and prudent precautions, in order to keep it in, but no more. If the first be the law, the person who has brought on his land and kept there something dangerous, and failed to keep it in, is responsible for all the natural consequences of its escape. If the second be the limit of his duty, he would not be answerable except on proof of negligence, and consequently would not be answerable for escape arising from any latent defect which ordinary prudence and skill could not detect.

Supposing the second to be the correct view of the law, a further question arises subsidiary to the first, viz., whether the defendants are not so far identified with the contractors whom they employed, as to be responsible for the consequences of their want of care and skill in making the reservoir in fact insufficient with reference to the old shafts, of the existence of which they were aware, though they had not ascertained where the shafts went to.

We think that the true rule of law is, that the person who for his own purposes brings on his lands and collects and keeps there anything likely to do mischief if it escapes, must keep it in at his peril, and, if he does not do so, is prima facie answerable for all the damage which is the natural consequence of its escape. He can excuse himself by shewing that the escape was owing to the plaintiff's default; or perhaps that the escape was the consequence of vis major, or the act of God; but as nothing of this sort exists here, it is unnecessary to inquire what excuse would be sufficient. The general rule, as above stated, seems on principle just. The person whose grass or corn is eaten down by the escaping cattle of his neighbour, or whose mine is flooded by the water from his neighbour's reservoir, or whose cellar is invaded by the filth of his neighbour's privy, or whose habitation is made unhealthy by the fumes and noisome vapours of his neighbour's alkali works, is damnified without any fault of his own; and it seems but reasonable and just that the neighbour, who has brought something on his own property which was not naturally there, harmless to others so long as it is confined to his own property, but which he knows to be mischievous if it gets on his neighbour's, should be obliged to make good the damage which ensues if he does not succeed in confining it to his own property. But for his act in bringing it there no mischief could have accrued, and it seems but just that he should at his peril keep it there so that no mischief may accrue, or answer for the natural and anticipated consequences. And upon authority, this we think is established to be the law whether the things so brought be beasts, or water, or filth, or stenches.

The case that has most commonly occurred, and which is most frequently to be found in the books, is as to the obligation of the owner of cattle which he has brought on his land, to prevent their escaping and doing mischief. The law as to them seems to be perfectly settled from early times; the owner must keep them in at his peril, or he will be answerable for the natural consequences of their escape; that is with regard to tame beasts, for the grass they eat and trample upon, though not for any injury to the person of others, for our ancestors have settled that it is not the general nature of horses to kick, or bulls to gore; but if the owner knows that the beast has a vicious propensity to attack man, he will be answerable for that too. [The opinion then exhaustively examines the earlier cases in support of the general proposition, and continues:]

. . . But it was further said by Martin, B., that when damage is done to personal property, or even to the person, by collision, either upon land or at sea, there must be negligence in the party doing the damage to render him legally responsible; and this is no doubt true, and as was pointed out by Mr. Mellish during his argument before us, this is not confined to cases of collision, for there are many cases in which proof of negligence is essential, as for instance, where an unruly horse gets on the footpath of a public street and kills a passenger . . . ; or where a person in a dock is struck by the falling of a bale of cotton which the defendant's servants are lowering . . . ; and many other similar cases may be found. But we think these cases distinguishable from the present. Traffic on the highways, whether by land or sea, cannot be conducted without exposing those whose persons or property are near it to some inevitable risk; and that being so, those who go on the highway, or have their property adjacent to it, may well be held to do so subject to their taking upon themselves the risk of injury from that inevitable danger; and persons who by the licence of the owner pass near the warehouses where goods are being raised or lowered, certainly do so subject to the inevitable risk of accident. In neither case, therefore, can they recover without proof of want of care or skill occasioning the accident; and it is believed that all the cases in which inevitable accident has been held an excuse for what prima facie was a trespass, can be explained on the same principle, viz., that the circumstances were such as to shew that the plaintiff had taken that risk upon himself. But there is no ground for saying that the plaintiff here took upon himself any risk arising from the uses to which the defendants should choose to apply their land. He neither knew what these might be, nor could he in any way control the defendants, or hinder their building what reservoirs they liked, and storing up in them what water they pleased, so long as the defendants succeeded in preventing the water which they there brought from interfering with the plaintiff's property.

The view which we take of the first point renders it unnecessary to consider whether the defendants would or would not be responsible for the want of care and skill in the persons employed by them, under the circumstances stated in the case.

Rylands v. Fletcher
L.R. 3 H.L. 330 (1868)

CAIRNS, L. C. . . . My Lords, the principles on which this case must be determined appear to me to be extremely simple. The Defendants, treating them as the owners or occupiers of the close on which the reservoir was constructed, might lawfully have used that close for any purpose for which it might in the ordinary course of the enjoyment of land be used, and if, in what I may term the natural use of that land, there had been any accumulation of water, either on the surface or underground, and if, by the operation of the laws of nature, that accumulation of water had passed off into the close occupied by the Plaintiff, the Plaintiff could not have complained that that result had taken place. If he had desired to guard himself against it, it would have lain upon him to have done so, by leaving, or by interposing, some barrier between his close and the close of the Defendants in order to have prevented the operation of the law of nature. . . .

On the other hand if the Defendants, not stopping at the natural use of their close, had desired to use it for any purpose which I may term a nonnatural use, for the purpose of introducing into the close that which in its natural condition was not in or upon it, for the purpose of introducing water either above or below ground in quantities and in a manner not the result of any work or operation on or under the land, — and if in consequence of their doing so, or in consequence of any imperfection in the mode of their doing so, the water came to escape and to pass off into the close of the Plaintiff, then it appears to me that that which the Defendants were doing they were doing at their own peril and, if in the course of their doing it, the evil arose to which I have referred, the evil, namely, of the escape of the water and its passing away to the close of the Plaintiff and injuring the Plaintiff, then for the consequence of that, in my opinion, the Defendants would be liable. . . .

LORD CRANWORTH. My Lords, I concur with my noble and learned friend in thinking that the rule of law was correctly stated by Mr. Justice Blackburn in delivering the opinion of the Exchequer Chamber. If a person brings, or accumulates, on his land anything which, if it should escape, may cause damage to his neighbour, he does so at his peril. If it does escape, and cause damage, he is responsible, however careful he may have been, and whatever precautions he may have taken to prevent the damage.

In considering whether a Defendant is liable to a Plaintiff for damage which the Plaintiff may have sustained, the question in general is not whether the Defendant has acted with due care and caution, but whether his acts have occasioned the damage. . . . And the doctrine is founded on good sense. For when one person, in managing his own affairs, causes, however innocently, damage to another, it is obviously only just that he should be the party to suffer. He is bound sic uti suo ut non laedat alienum. This is the principle of law applicable to cases like the present, and I do not discover in the authorities which were cited anything conflicting with it.

The doctrine appears to me to be well illustrated by the two modern cases in the Court of Common Pleas. . . . I allude to the two cases of Smith v. Kenrick[, 137 Eng. Rep. 205 (C.P. 1849)], and Baird v. Williamson[, 143 Eng. Rep. 831 (C.P. 1863)]. In the former the owner of a coal mine on the higher level worked out the whole of his coal, leaving no barrier between his mine and the mine on the lower level, so that the water percolating through the upper mine flowed into the lower mine, and obstructed the owner of it in getting his coal. It was held that the owner of the lower mine had no ground of complaint. The Defendant, the owner of the upper mine, had a right to remove all his coal. The damage sustained by the Plaintiff was occasioned by the natural flow or percolation of water from the upper strata. There was no obligation on the Defendant to protect the Plaintiff against this. It was his business to erect or leave a sufficient barrier to keep out the water, or to adopt proper means for so conducting the water as that it should not impede him in his workings. The water, in that case, was only left by the Defendant to flow in its natural course.

But in the later case of Baird v. Williamson the Defendant, the owner of the upper mine, did not merely suffer the water to flow through his mine without leaving a barrier between it and the mine below, but in order to work his own mine beneficially he pumped up quantities of water which passed into the Plaintiff's mine in addition to that which would have naturally reached it, and so occasioned him damage. Though this was done without negligence, and in the due working of his own mine, yet he was held to be responsible for the damage so occasioned. It was in consequence of his act, whether skilfully or unskilfully performed, that the Plaintiff had been damaged, and he was therefore held liable for the consequences. The damage in the former case may be treated as having arisen from the act of God; in the latter, from the act of the Defendant.

Applying the principle of these decisions to the case now before the House, I come without hesitation to the conclusion that the judgment of the Exchequer Chamber was right. . . . The Defendants, in order to effect an object of their own, brought on to their land, or on to land which for this purpose may be treated as being theirs, a large accumulated mass of water, and stored it up in a reservoir. The consequence of this was damage to the Plaintiff, and for that damage, however skilfully and carefully the accumulation was made, the Defendants, according to the principles and authorities to which I have adverted, were certainly responsible.

Judgment of the Court of Exchequer Chamber affirmed.

NOTES

1. Rylands v. Fletcher, the forms of action, and common law precedent. The initial debate between Martin and Bramwell harkens back to the forms of action by asking whether the harm was immediate or consequential. For them, the categorization of the loss was critical to deciding whether proof of negligence was required, as was necessary only with actions that formerly would have been on the case. On this question, does it make a difference that the reservoir was not in fact completely filled when its floor gave way? Blackburn, J., sidesteps the disagreement below, first by treating the harm as consequential, and then by applying a strict liability rule. Do the earlier precedents on cattle trespass, fire, nuisance, and filth escaping from privies support his decision, or were these all instances of "direct harm"?

The extent to which *Rylands* marks a departure from the earlier law has given rise to a spirited debate. Wigmore's view was that the case was soundly reasoned from its precedents: "Briefly, the [scattered classes of cases] wandered about, unhoused and unshepherded, except for casual attention, in the pathless fields of jurisprudence, until they were met, some thirty years ago, by the master-mind of Mr. Justice Blackburn, who guided them to the safe fold where they have since rested." Wigmore, Responsibility for Tortious Acts: Its History — III, 7 Harv. L. Rev. 441, 454 (1894). In contrast, the noted English torts scholar Frederick Pollock wrote of the decision that "carefully prepared as it evidently was, [it] hardly seems to make such grounds clear enough for universal acceptance." See Pollock, Torts 398-399 (1st ed. 1887). He concluded that "the policy of the law might not have been satisfied by requiring the defendant to insure diligence in proportion to the manifest risk." Pollock subsequently adopted the suggestion in Thayer, Liability Without Fault, 29 Harv. L. Rev. 801 (1916), that the principle of res ipsa loquitur (*infra* at Chapter 3, Section G.2) "which was hardly developed at the date of Rylands v. Fletcher, would suffice to cover the ground for all useful purposes in a simpler and more rational manner." See F. Pollock, Torts 507 (13th ed. 1929). Holmes, for his part, devoted relatively little attention to Rylands v. Fletcher, which he treated gingerly: "It may even be very much for the public good that the dangerous accumulation should be made (a consideration which might influence the decision in some instances, and differently in others): but as there is a limit to the nicety of an inquiry which is possible in a trial, it may be considered that the safest way to secure care is to throw the risk upon the person who decides what precautions shall be taken." Holmes, The Common Law, 117 (1881). Is this point universally true in all negligence cases?

2. *Scope of Rylands v. Fletcher?* Should *Rylands* apply to personal injury cases, or only property damages? See Transco plc v. Stockport Metropolitan Borough Council, [2003] U.K. H. L. 61, where Lord Bingham observed: "The rule in *Rylands v. Fletcher* is a sub-species of nuisance, which is itself a tort based on the interference by one occupier of the land with the right in or enjoyment of land by another occupier of land as such. From this simple proposition two consequences at once flow. First, as very clearly decided by the House in Read v. J. Lyons & Co., Ltd. [1947] A.C. 156, no claim in nuisance under the rule can arise if the events complained of take place wholly on the land of a single occupier. There must, in other words, be an escape from one tenement to another. Second, the claim cannot include a claim for death or personal injury, since such a claim does not relate to any right in or enjoyment of land." Would Blackburn, J. have denied recover if a workman had been killed by flooding? See, for a recent analysis of *Rylands,* Ripstein, Tort Law in a Liberal State, 1 J. Tort Law (Issue 2, Article 3), 27-30, treating *Rylands* as a fault-based case.

3. *Rylands v. Fletcher in historical context.* For an exhaustive account of the historical setting of *Rylands,* see Simpson, Legal Liability for Bursting Reservoirs, 13 J. Legal Stud. 209, 244 (1984). Simpson notes that during the nineteenth century dam failures were regarded as major disasters, perhaps as airplane crashes are today. *Rylands* itself followed several major dam failures in England, each of which had resulted in a massive loss of life and property and had prompted major campaigns of private relief to aid accident victims. Simpson also observed the following about nineteenth-century England: "Most large reservoirs (indeed, almost all) had been constructed under special statutory powers, conferred by private and local acts, and it would have been normal to turn to the legislation to determine what Parliament had laid down as to the legal liability of those responsible for them."

4. *"Non-natural use" and acts of third parties.* What importance should be attached to the qualification of "non-natural use" mentioned by Lord Cairns, but not by the other judges? One way to read the term "natural" is in opposition to "artificial" or "man-made." A second way is to read it in opposition to "unreasonable or inappropriate." The second reading appears to have been adopted in Rickards v. Lothian, [1913] A.C. 263, in which the defendant owned a business building with a lavatory on the fourth floor. One night, after the defendant's caretaker had made his usual tour of inspection, an unknown person entered the building, stuffed the lavatory with "various articles such as nails, penholders, string and soap," and turned the faucet on all the way. The next morning, the plaintiff discovered that his stock in trade had been damaged, and sued the defendant for his losses. The House of Lords held for the defendant, on the

ground that the case fell outside the scope of Rylands v. Fletcher because "the provision of a proper supply of water to the various parts of a house is not only reasonable, but has become, in accordance with modern sanitary views, an almost necessary feature of town life.... It would be unreasonable for the law to regard those who install and maintain such a system of supply as doing so at their own peril." Given the stable condition of the privy before the act of the third party, could the defendant have prevailed on causal grounds—the independent act of a third party—even if the lavatory, however common, was in Lord Cairns' sense a non-natural use? If water had leaked into the plaintiff's premises when the lavatory had been used in an ordinary manner, is the defendant liable under the rule of Rylands v. Fletcher? As interpreted in Rickards v. Lothian? What if the defendant had hired competent plumbers to repair the lavatory before the flooding took place?

The House of Lords reevaluated the phrase "non-natural use" in Cambridge Water Co. v. Eastern Counties Leather PLC, [1994] 2 A.C. 264, 309 in which toxic perchloroethenes (P.C.E.s) escaped from defendant E.C.L.'s tannery and slowly worked their way through an aquifer to plaintiff's borehole, located some 1.3 miles away in Sawton. Lord Goff rejected defendant's attempt to expand the definition of natural use to do away with the strict liability rule in *Rylands*.

> I am satisfied that the storage of chemicals in substantial quantities, and their use in the manner employed at E.C.L.'s premises, cannot fall within the exception [of natural and ordinary use]. For the purpose of testing the point, let it be assumed that E.C.L. was well aware of the possibility that P.C.E., if it escaped, could indeed cause damage, for example by contaminating any water with which it became mixed so as to render that water undrinkable by human beings. I cannot think that it would be right in such circumstances to exempt E.C.L. from liability under the rule of *Rylands v. Fletcher* on the ground that the use was natural or ordinary. The mere fact that the use is common in the tanning industry cannot, in my opinion, be enough to bring the use within the exception, nor the fact that Sawston contains a small industrial community which is worthy of encouragement or support. Indeed I feel bound to say that the storage of substantial quantities of chemicals on industrial premises should be regarded as an almost classic case of non-natural use; and I find it very difficult to think that it should be thought objectionable to impose strict liability for damage caused in the event of their escape.

Nonetheless the defendant prevailed on its appeal. The trial judge had found that "a reasonable supervisor at E.C.L. would not have foreseen, in or before 1976, that such repeated spillages of small quantities of solvent would lead to any environmental hazard or danger." Lord Goff then held that the rule in *Rylands* should not be exempt from the general test of reasonable foresight that in England applies in both nuisance and negligence cases. See *The Wagon Mound, infra* at Chapter 6. On a more functional level, he noted that the solution to the pressing environmental issues rested more on "informed and carefully structured legislation" instead of the revision of a common law rule. How would the foresight limitation apply the facts of *Rylands*?

For an excellent critique of the non-natural use requirement of Rylands v. Fletcher, see A. Harari, The Place of Negligence in the Law of Torts 157-167 (1962). For an evaluation of the recent developments, see Schwartz, Rylands v. Fletcher, Negligence, and Strict Liability, in The Law of Obligations 209 (Peter Cane and Jane Stapleton eds. 1998).

5. *Acts of God under Rylands v. Fletcher.* What distinguishes a mere "escape" from an act of God in *Rylands*? In Nichols v. Marsland, 2 Ex. D. 1 (1876), the plaintiff's land was flooded when the defendant's "ornamental pools" containing large amounts of water broke their banks during an extraordinary rainfall of unanticipated severity. Bramwell, B., found this storm to be an act of God, thus within the exception to Rylands v. Fletcher, and accordingly he affirmed a judgment for the defendant. The court also found no negligence in the construction or maintenance of the pools. Further, in Carstairs v. Taylor, L.R. 6 Ex. 217 (1871), the plaintiff, a tenant in the defendant's building, was unable to recover when rats ate through a box containing water that was collected by gutters from the roof of the building. Bramwell, B., noted that the box and gutters had been installed for the mutual benefit of both parties. Hence, the rule in Rylands v. Fletcher did not apply because the defendant did not bring the water into the structure for his purposes alone.

The act of God issue continues to play a powerful role in modern tort litigation. In In re Flood Litigation, 607 S.E.2d 863, 879 (W. Va. 2004), large numbers of property owners filed tort actions against a collection of defendant coal companies, railroads, landowners, and gas companies, claiming that their collective alteration of the landscape was responsible for the flooding damage under *Rylands*. Maynard, C.J., refused to apply *Rylands* on the ground that the defendants had not engaged in abnormally dangerous activities. In addressing the act of God defense, he first noted the difficulties in apportioning loss between natural forces and a defendant's activities, and continued:

> Accordingly, we hold that where a rainfall event of an unusual and unforeseeable nature combines with a defendant's actionable conduct to cause flood damage, and where it is shown that a discrete portion of the damage complained of was unforeseeable and solely the result of such event and in no way fairly attributable to the defendant's conduct, the defendant is liable only for the damages that are fairly attributable to the defendant's conduct. However, in such a case, a defendant has the burden to show by clear and

convincing evidence the character and measure of damages that are not the defendant's responsibility; and if the defendant cannot do so, then the defendant bears the entire liability.

Would this rule require liability in *Nichols* if any water in the ornamental pool escaped in the midst of the storm?

6. Default of plaintiff. What sorts of conduct might constitute "a default of the plaintiff" to which Blackburn, B. referred? Note that under Smith v. Kenrick, a plaintiff who removes all the coal up to the boundary of his mine is not in default under *Rylands*, even if the coal removed served as a barrier between plaintiff's and defendant's properties. In Holgate v. Bleazard, [1917] 1 K.B. 443, it was held that the plaintiff was not in default in a case of horse trespass when he had not repaired the fence around his own land as required by the covenant with his landlord. How would the case be decided if the covenant to fence had been made with the defendant?

Brown v. Collins
53 N.H. 442 (1873)

Trespass. . . . [The plaintiff owned a stone post with street lamp. The defendant was waiting by a railroad crossing on his wagon loaded with grain and drawn by two horses.] The horses became frightened by an engine on the railroad near the crossing, and by reason thereof became unmanageable, and ran, striking the post. . . . The shock produced by the collision with the post threw the defendant from his seat in the wagon, and he struck on the ground between horses, but suffered no injury except a slight concussion. The defendant was in the use of ordinary care and skill in managing his team, until they became frightened. . . .

DOE, J. . . . We take the case as one where, without actual fault in the defendant, his horses broke from his control, ran away with him, went upon the plaintiff's land, and did damage there, against the will, intent, and desire of the defendant. [The court then discusses the rule in Rylands v. Fletcher, continuing:]

. . . The rule of such cases is applied, by Blackburn, to everything which a man brings on his land, which will, if it escapes, naturally do damage. One result of such a doctrine is, that every one building a fire on his own hearth, for necessary purposes, with the utmost care, does so at the peril, not only of losing his own house, but of being irretrievably ruined if a spark from his chimney starts a conflagration which lays waste the neighborhood. "In conflict with the rule, as laid down in the English cases, is a class of cases in reference to damage from fire communicated from the adjoining premises. Fire, like water or steam, is likely to produce mischief if it escapes and goes beyond control; and yet it has never been held in this country that one building a fire upon his own premises can be made liable if it escapes upon his neighbor's premises, and does him damage without proof of negligence." Losee v. Buchanan, 51 N.Y. 476, 487 (1873).

Everything that a man can bring on his land is capable of escaping,—against his will, and without his fault, with or without assistance, in some form, solid, liquid, or gaseous, changed or unchanged by the transforming processes of nature or art,—and of doing damage after its escape. Moreover, if there is a legal principle that makes a man liable for the natural consequences of the escape of things which he brings on his land, the application of such a principle cannot be limited to those things: it must be applied to all his acts that disturb the original order of creation or, at least, to all things which he undertakes to possess or control anywhere, and which were not used and enjoyed in what is called the natural or primitive condition of mankind, whatever that may have been. This is going back a long way for a standard of legal rights, and adopting an arbitrary test of responsibility that confounds all degrees of danger, pays no heed to the essential elements of actual fault, puts a clog upon natural and reasonably necessary uses of matter, and tends to embarrass and obstruct much of the work which it seems to be man's duty carefully to do. The distinction made by Lord Cairns — Rylands v. Fletcher, L.R. 3 H.L. 330 — between a natural and non-natural use of land, if he meant anything more than the difference between a reasonable use and an unreasonable one, is not established in the law. Even if the arbitrary test were applied only to things which a man brings on his land, it would still recognize the peculiar rights of savage life in a wilderness, ignore the rights growing out of a civilized state of society, and make a distinction not warranted by the enlightened spirit of the common law: it would impose a penalty upon efforts, made in a reasonable, skillful, and careful manner, to rise above a condition of barbarism. It is impossible that legal principle can throw so serious an obstacle in the way of progress and improvement. Natural rights are, in general, legal rights; and the rights of civilization are, in a legal sense, as natural as any others. "Most of the rights of property, as well as of person, in the social state, are not absolute but relative" — Losee v. Buchanan, 51 N.Y. 485; and, if men ever were in any other than the social state, it is neither necessary nor expedient that they should now govern themselves on the theory that they ought to live in some other state. The common law does not usually establish tests of responsibility on any other basis than the propriety of their living in the social state, and the relative and qualified character of the rights incident to that state. . . .

It is not improbable that the rules of liability for damage done by brutes or by fire, found in the early English cases, were introduced, by sacerdotal influence, from what was supposed to be the Roman or the Hebrew law. 7 Am. L. Rev. 652, note; 1 Domat Civil Law (Strahan's translation, 2d ed.)

304, 305, 306, 312, 313; Exodus xxi:28-32, 36; xxii:5, 6, 9. It would not be singular if these rules should be spontaneously produced at a certain period in the life of any community. Where they first appeared is of little consequence in the present inquiry. They were certainly introduced in England at an immature stage of English jurisprudence, and an undeveloped state of agriculture, manufactures, and commerce, when the nation had not settled down to these modern, progressive, industrial pursuits which the spirit of the common law, adapted to all conditions of society, encourages and defends. They were introduced when the development of many of the rational rules now universally recognized as principles of the common law had not been demanded by the growth of intelligence, trade, and productive enterprise, — when the common law had not been set forth in the precedents, as a coherent and logical system on many subjects other than the tenures of real estate. At all events, whatever may be said of the origin of those rules, to extend them, as they were extended in Rylands v. Fletcher, seems to us contrary to the analogies and the general principles of the common law, as now established. To extend them to the present case would be contrary to American authority, as well as to our understanding of legal principles. . . .

Upon the facts stated, taken in the sense in which we understand them, the defendant is entitled to judgment.

NOTE

The reception of Rylands v. Fletcher into American common law. Initially *Rylands* received a frosty reception in the United States as it was explicitly repudiated not only in Brown v. Collins but also in Losee v. Buchanan, 51 N.Y. 483, 484-485 (1873). In *Losee,* the plaintiff sued for damages that resulted when the defendant's boiler, while being operated with all care and skill, exploded and "was projected and thrown onto the plaintiff's premises," causing damage to the buildings located thereon. The action was denied for the following reasons:

> By becoming a member of civilized society, I am compelled to give up many of my natural rights, but I receive more than a compensation from the surrender by every other man of the same rights, and the security, advantage and protection which the laws give me. So, too, the general rules that I may have the exclusive and undisturbed use and possession of my real estate, and that I must so use my real estate as not to injure my neighbor, are much modified by the exigencies of the social state. We must have factories, machinery, dams, canals and railroads. They are demanded by the manifold wants of mankind, and lay at the basis of all our civilization. If I have any of these upon my lands, and they are not a nuisance and are not so managed as

to become such, I am not responsible for any damage they accidentally and unavoidably do my neighbor. He receives his compensation for such damage by the general good, in which he shares, and the right which he has to place the same things upon his lands.

Why does the argument of implicit compensation work only in one direction? Does the greater security obtained under a uniform rule of strict liability supply the compensation to the defendant that justifies imposing liability in the instant case? For a further expansion of this theme of "reciprocity" see Fletcher, Fairness and Utility in Tort Law, 85 Harv. L. Rev. 537 (1972), at Chapter 8 *infra*. The test of reciprocity only shows a need for consistency of treatment between cases. How should one choose between the consistent use of the negligence and strict liability rules in disputes between neighbors? On the fate of *Losee* see Spano v. Perini, *infra* at 656.

In Turner v. Big Lake Oil Co., 96 S.W.2d 221, 226 (Tex. 1936), the court rejected Rylands v. Fletcher as inapplicable to Texas, where the storage of water in large cisterns was a "natural" use of the land:

> In Texas we have conditions very different from those which obtain in England. A large portion of Texas is an arid or semi-arid region. West of the 98th meridian of longitude, where the rainfall is approximately 30 inches, the rainfall decreases until finally, in the extreme western part of the State, it is only about 10 inches. This land of decreasing rainfall is the great ranch or livestock region of the state, water for which is stored in thousands of ponds, tanks, and lakes on the surface of the ground. The country is almost without streams and without the storage of water from rainfall in basins constructed for the purpose, or to hold waters pumped from the earth, the great live-stock industry of West Texas must perish. No such condition obtains in England. With us the storage of water is a natural or necessary and common use of the land, necessarily within the contemplation of the State and its grantees when grants were made, and obviously the rule announced in Rylands v. Fletcher, predicated upon different conditions, can have no application here.
>
> Again, in England there are no oil wells, no necessity for using surface storage facilities for impounding and evaporating salt waters therefrom. In Texas the situation is different. Texas has many great oil fields, tens of thousands of wells in almost every part of the State. Producing oil is one of our major industries. One of the by-products of oil production is salt water, which must be disposed of without injury to property or the pollution of streams. The construction of basins or ponds to hold this salt water is a necessary part of the oil business.

Does the need for water in Texas go to the issue of liability for the damage caused by water or to regulating its use by statute or a private

injunction? It would be disastrous to shut down the entire oil industry, but would the industry suffer any major dislocations if the use of water were allowed under a strict liability scheme, so long as the operators of oil rigs may store water as they please? See the discussion in Powell v. Fall, below.

In spite of the judicial concerns with the reach of *Rylands,* the case made substantial inroads in the first half of the twentieth century. As of 1984, Prosser and Keeton (Torts at 549) report that only 7 states reject the *Rylands* principle and 30 now accept it; that balance continues to swing in favor of the decision. Similar results are reported in 3 Harper, James & Gray §14.4. Representative of the modern trend is Clark-Aiken Co. v. Cromwell-Wright Co., 323 N.E.2d 876 (Mass. 1975), in which the Supreme Judicial Court of Massachusetts, after exhaustive discussion, unanimously applied *Rylands* when the plaintiff's land was flooded by waters that the defendant had stored behind an upstream dam that failed.

Powell v. Fall
5 Q.B. 597 (1880)

MELLOR, J. This was an action tried before me at Devizes without a jury. It was brought by the plaintiffs to recover a sum of £53 6s. 8d., in respect of injury done to a rick of hay upon a farm of the plaintiff, John Thomas Powell, adjoining a public highway, and which injury was caused by sparks escaping from the fire of a traction engine belonging to the defendant, which was then being propelled by steam power along the highway. The engine was constructed in conformity with the provisions of 24 & 25 Vict. c.70, and of 28 & 29 Vict. c.83, being the Acts then in force for regulating the use of locomotives on turnpike and other roads.

At the time when the injury was occasioned to the hay stack by the sparks of fire issuing from the defendant's engine, it was not travelling at a greater speed than that prescribed by the Acts referred to, nor was the injury occasioned by any negligence on the part of the defendant's servants conducting or managing the same. . . .

The 13th section of 24 & 25 Vict. c.70, is as follows: "Nothing in this Act contained shall authorize any person to use upon a highway a locomotive engine, which shall be so constructed or used as to cause a public or private nuisance, and every such person so using such engine shall notwithstanding this Act be liable to an indictment or action as the case may be, for such use where, but for the passing of this Act, such indictment or action could be maintained:" and by s.12 of 28 & 29 Vict. c.83, it is enacted that "Nothing in this Act contained shall authorize any person to use a locomotive which may be so constructed or used as to be a public nuisance at common law, and nothing herein contained shall affect the right of any person to recover damages in respect of any injury he may have sustained in consequence of the use of a locomotive." And it was further contended on the part of the plaintiffs that whilst the Acts entitled the defendant to use a locomotive properly constructed on the public highway, yet it never was intended by the legislature to exempt him from liability to damages in respect of any injury sustained by third persons in consequence of the use by him of a locomotive, and that it was wholly immaterial to the result that such injury arose from no want of care or negligence on the part of the defendant's servants in the management and use of the same. On the part of the defendant it was contended that the effect of the several statutes being to authorize the use of locomotives on public highways, if constructed and managed according to the provisions of such statutes, was to exempt the owners from liability to make good any injury arising from the use of locomotives, unless some improper construction of the engine, or some act of negligence in the use of it, could be imputed to such owners or their servants. I am of opinion that the contention on the part of the plaintiffs must prevail.

The principle which governs this case is that established by Fletcher v. Rylands, and affirmed in the House of Lords: Rylands v. Fletcher. . . .

The defendant appealed. . . .

BRAMWELL, L.J. I think that the judgment of Mellor, J., ought to be affirmed. The passing of the engine along the road is confessedly dangerous, inasmuch as sparks cannot be prevented from flying from it. It is conceded that at common law an action may be maintained for the injury suffered by the plaintiffs. The Locomotive Acts are relied upon as affording a defence, but instead of helping the defendant they shew not only that an action would have been maintainable at common law, but also that the right to sue for an injury is carefully preserved. It is just and reasonable that if a person uses a dangerous machine, he should pay for the damage which it occasions; if the reward which he gains for the use of the machine will not pay for the damage, it is mischievous to the public and ought to be suppressed, for the loss ought not to be borne by the community or the injured person. If the use of the machine is profitable, the owner ought to pay compensation for the damage. The plaintiffs are protected by the common law, and nothing adverse to their right to sue can be drawn from the statutes: the statutes do not make it lawful to damage property without paying for the injury. A great deal has been said about the liability of persons who have stored water which has subsequently escaped and done injury, and it has been urged that the emission of sparks from an engine is not so mischievous as the overflow of a large body of water. The arguments which we have heard are ingenious; but I need only say in reply to them that they have hardened my conviction that Rex v. Pease [168 Eng. Rep. 216 (K.B. 1832)] and Vaughan v. Taff Vale Ry. Co. (5 H. & N. 679 29 L. J. (Ex.) 247) were wrongly decided.

NOTES

1. The impact of statute on common law liability. In Vaughn v. Taff Vale Ry., 157 Eng. Rep. 1351, 1354 (Ex. 1860), disapproved by Bramwell, Cockburn, C.J., held that because the defendant operated the railroad under statutory authorization, plaintiff had to show negligence to hold it liable for damages:

> Although it may be true, that if a person keeps an animal of known dangerous propensities, or a dangerous instrument, he will be responsible to those who are thereby injured, independently of any negligence in the mode of dealing with the animal or using the instrument; yet when the legislature has sanctioned and authorized the use of a particular thing, and it is used for the purpose for which it was authorized, and every precaution has been observed to prevent injury, the sanction of the legislature carries with it this consequence, that if damage results from the use of such thing independently of negligence, the party using it is not responsible. . . . It is admitted that the defendants used fire for the purpose of propelling locomotive engines, and no doubt they were bound to take proper precaution to prevent injury to persons through whose lands they passed; but the mere use of fire in such engines does not make them liable for injury resulting from such use without any negligence on their part.

The effect of a statute upon a private cause of action was also raised in River Wear Commissioners v. Adamson, L.R. 2 App. Cas. 743, 767 (H.L. (E.) 1877), where the applicable statute provided that "the owner of every vessel . . . shall be answerable to the undertakers [plaintiffs] for any damage done by such vessel . . . and the master or person having charge of such vessel through whose wilful act or negligence any such damage is done, shall also be liable to make good the same." In *Adamson,* the defendant's boat was wrecked in a storm. After the crew abandoned it, it crashed into the plaintiff's dock. The owners of the ship were sued under the statute. Lord Blackburn, who wrote Rylands v. Fletcher, concurred in the judgment that the owners were not liable without proof of negligence:

> My Lords, the Common Law is, I think, as follows: — Property adjoining to a spot on which the public have a right to carry on traffic is liable to be injured by that traffic. In this respect there is no difference between a shop, the railings or windows of which may be broken by a carriage on the road, and a pier adjoining to a harbour or a navigable river or the sea, which is liable to be injured by a ship. In either case the owner of the injured property must bear his own loss, unless he can establish that some other person is in fault, and liable to make it good. And he does not establish this against a person merely by shewing that he is owner of the carriage or ship which did the mischief, for the owner incurs no liability merely because he is owner.

But he does establish such a liability against any person who either wilfully did the damage, or neglected that duty which the law casts upon those in charge of a carriage on land, and a ship or a float of timber on water, to take reasonable care and use reasonable skill to prevent it from doing injury, and that this wilfulness or neglect caused the damage.

Is the result consistent with the statute? At common law would the act of God exception under Rylands v. Fletcher apply?

2. *The subsequent history of Powell v. Fall.* "Over the next forty years, Powell v. Fall was repeatedly followed in cases involving traction-engines and steam-rollers which, though driven with due care, had scared horses, crushed water-mains, or started fires." Spencer, Motor-Cars and the Rule in Rylands v. Fletcher: A Chapter of Accidents in the History of Law and Motoring, [1983] Cambridge L.J. 65, 70. Spencer nonetheless reports that *Powell* could not exert enough influence to introduce strict liability back into the law of ordinary highway accidents, even though buses and cars were dangerous, with hard rubber tires and thin wheels prone to skidding. See Wing v. L.G.O.C., 25 Times L. Rep. 14 (1908), for skidding busses, and for ordinary cars, see Park v. L.G.O.C., 73 J.P. 283 (1909). Note that the early buses and autos were greeted with much public hostility. In part, the justification for these later cases was that cars (but not buses) are not run for profit within the rationale of *Powell. Id.* at 76-77.

Holmes, The Common Law
77-84, 88-96 (1881)

The object of the next two Lectures is to discover whether there is any common ground at the bottom of all liability in tort, and if so, what that ground is. Supposing the attempt to succeed, it will reveal the general principle of civil liability at common law. The liabilities incurred by way of contract are more or less expressly fixed by the agreement of the parties concerned, but those arising from a tort are independent of any previous consent of the wrong-doer to bear the loss occasioned by his act. If *A* fails to pay a certain sum on a certain day, or to deliver a lecture on a certain night, after having made a binding promise to do so, the damages which he has to pay are recovered in accordance with his consent that some or all of the harms which may be caused by his failure shall fall upon him. But when *A* assaults or slanders his neighbor, or converts his neighbor's property, he does a harm which he has never consented to bear, and if the law makes him pay for it, the reason for doing so must be found in some general view of the conduct which every one may fairly expect and demand from every other, whether that other has agreed to it or not.

Such a general view is very hard to find. The law did not begin with a theory. It has never worked one out. The point from which it started and that at which I shall try to show that it has arrived, are on different planes. In the progress from one to the other, it is to be expected that its course should not be straight and its direction not always visible. All that can be done is to point out a tendency, and to justify it. The tendency, which is our main concern, is a matter of fact to be gathered from the cases. But the difficulty of showing it is much enhanced by the circumstances that, until lately, the substantive law has been approached only through the categories of the forms of action. Discussions of legislative principle have been darkened by arguments on the limits between trespass and case, or on the scope of a general issue. In place of a theory of tort, we have a theory of trespass. And even within that narrower limit, precedents of the time of the assize and jurata have been applied without a thought of their connection with a long forgotten procedure.

Since the ancient forms of action have disappeared, a broader treatment of the subject ought to be possible. Ignorance is the best of law reformers. People are glad to discuss a question on general principles, when they have forgotten the special knowledge necessary for technical reasoning. But the present willingness to generalize is founded on more than merely negative grounds. The philosophical habit of the day, the frequency of legislation, and the ease with which the law may be changed to meet the opinions and wishes of the public, all make it natural and unavoidable that judges as well as others should openly discuss the legislative principles upon which their decisions must always rest in the end, and should base their judgments upon broad considerations of policy to which the traditions of the bench would hardly have tolerated a reference fifty years ago.

The business of the law of torts is to fix the dividing lines between those cases in which a man is liable for harm which he has done, and those in which he is not. But it cannot enable him to predict with certainty whether a given act under given circumstances will make him liable, because an act will rarely have that effect unless followed by damage, and for the most part, if not always, the consequences of an act are not known, but only guessed at as more or less probable. All the rules that the law can lay down beforehand are rules for determining the conduct which will be followed by liability if it is followed by harm, — that is, the conduct which a man pursues at his peril. The only guide for the future to be drawn from a decision against a defendant in an action of tort is that similar acts, under circumstances which cannot be distinguished except by the result from those of the defendant, are done at the peril of the actor; that if he escapes liability, it is simply because by good fortune no harm comes of his conduct in the particular event.

If, therefore, there is any common ground for all liability in tort, we shall best find it by eliminating the event as it actually turns out, and by considering only the principles on which the peril of his conduct is thrown upon the actor. We are to ask what are the elements, on the defendant's side, which must all be present before liability is possible, and the presence of which will commonly make him liable if damage follows.

The law of torts abounds in moral phraseology. It has much to say of wrongs, of malice, fraud, intent, and negligence. Hence it may naturally be supposed that the risk of a man's conduct is thrown upon him as the result of some moral shortcoming. But while this notion has been entertained, the extreme opposite will be found to have been a far more popular opinion — I mean the notion that a man is answerable for all the consequences of his acts, or, in other words, that he acts at his peril always, and wholly irrespective of the state of his consciousness upon the matter. . . .

As has just been hinted, there are two theories of the common-law liability for unintentional harm. Both of them seem to receive the implied assent of popular textbooks, and neither of them is wanting in plausibility and the semblance of authority.

The first is that of Austin, which is essentially the theory of a criminalist. According to him, the characteristic feature of law, properly so called, is a sanction or detriment threatened and imposed by the sovereign for disobedience to the sovereign's commands. As the greater part of the law only makes a man civilly answerable for breaking it, Austin is compelled to regard the liability to an action as a sanction, or, in other words, as a penalty for disobedience. It follows from this, according to the prevailing views of penal law, that such liability ought only to be based upon personal fault; and Austin accepts that conclusion, with its corollaries, one of which is that negligence means a state of the party's mind. These doctrines will be referred to later, so far as necessary.

The other theory is directly opposed to the foregoing. It seems to be adopted by some of the greatest common-law authorities, and requires serious discussion before it can be set aside in favor of any third opinion which may be maintained. According to this view, broadly stated, under the common law a man *acts* at his peril. It may be held as a sort of setoff, that he is never liable for omissions except in consequence of some duty voluntarily undertaken. But the whole and sufficient ground for such liabilities as he does incur outside the last class is supposed to be that he has voluntarily acted, and that damage has ensued. If the act was voluntary, it is totally immaterial that the detriment which followed from it was neither intended nor due to the negligence of the actor.

In order to do justice to this way of looking at the subject, we must remember that the abolition of the common-law forms of pleading has not changed the rules of substantive law. Hence, although pleaders now generally allege intent or negligence, anything which would formerly have been sufficient to charge a defendant in trespass is still sufficient, notwithstanding the fact that the ancient form of action and declaration has disappeared.

In the first place, it is said, consider generally the protection given by the law to property, both within and outside the limits of the last-named action. If a man crosses his neighbor's boundary by however innocent a mistake, or if his cattle escape into his neighbor's field, he is said to be liable in trespass quare clausum fregit. . . .

Now suppose that, instead of a dealing with the plaintiff's property, the case is that force has proceeded directly from the defendant's body to the plaintiff's body, it is urged that, as the law cannot be less careful of the persons than of the property of its subjects, the only defences possible are similar to those which would have been open to an alleged trespass on land. You may show that there was no trespass by showing that the defendant did no act; as where he was thrown from his horse upon the plaintiff, or where a third person took his hand and struck the plaintiff with it. In such cases the defendant's body is the passive instrument of an external force, and the bodily motion relied on by the plaintiff is not his act at all. So you may show a justification or excuse in the conduct of the plaintiff himself. But if no such excuse is shown, and the defendant has voluntarily acted, he must answer for the consequences, however little intended and however unforeseen. If, for instance, being assaulted by a third person, the defendant lifted his stick and accidentally hit the plaintiff, who was standing behind him, according to this view he is liable, irrespective of any negligence toward the party injured.

The arguments for the doctrine under consideration are, for the most part, drawn from precedent, but it is sometimes supposed to be defensible as theoretically sound. Every man, it is said, has an absolute right to his person, and so forth, free from detriment at the hands of his neighbors. In the cases put, the plaintiff has done nothing; the defendant, on the other hand, has chosen to act. As between the two, the party whose voluntary conduct has caused the damage should suffer, rather than one who has had no share in producing it. . . .

[Holmes then reviews the historical precedents set out in section A and continues.]

In spite, however, of all the arguments which may be urged for the rule that a man acts at his peril, it has been rejected by very eminent courts, even under the old forms of action. . . . But we may go further with profit, and inquire whether there are not strong grounds for thinking that the common law has never known such a rule, unless in that period of dry precedent which is so often to be found midway between a creative epoch and a period of solvent philosophical reaction. Conciliating the attention of those who, contrary to most modern practitioners, still adhere to the strict doctrine, by reminding them once more that there are weighty decisions to be cited adverse to it, and that, if they have involved an innovation, the fact that it has been made by such magistrates as Chief Justice Shaw goes far to prove that the change was politic, I think I may assert that a little reflection will show that it was required not only by policy, but by consistency. I will begin with the latter.

The same reasoning which would make a man answerable in trespass for all damage to another by force directly resulting from his own act, irrespective of negligence or intent, would make him answerable in case for the like damage similarly resulting from the act of his servant, in the course of the latter's employment. The discussions of the company's negligence in many railway cases would therefore be wholly out of place, for although, to be sure, there is a contract which would make the company liable for negligence, that contract cannot be taken to diminish any liability which would otherwise exist for a trespass on the part of its employees.

More than this, the same reasoning would make a defendant responsible for all damage, however remote, of which his act could be called the cause. So long, at least, as only physical or irresponsible agencies, however unforeseen, cooperated with the act complained of to produce the result, the argument which would resolve the case of accidentally striking the plaintiff, when lifting a stick in necessary self-defence, adversely to the defendant, would require a decision against him in every case where his act was a factor in the result complained of. The distinction between a direct application of force, and causing damage indirectly, or as a more remote consequence of one's act, although it may determine whether the form of action should be trespass or case, does not touch the theory of responsibility, if that theory be that a man acts at his peril. As was said at the outset, if the strict liability is to be maintained at all, it must be maintained throughout. A principle cannot be stated which would retain the strict liability in trespass while abandoning it in case. It cannot be said that trespass is for acts alone, and case for consequences of those acts. All actions of trespass are for consequences of acts, not for the acts themselves. And some actions of trespass are for consequences more remote from the defendant's act than in other instances where the remedy would be case.

An act is always a voluntary muscular contraction, and nothing else. The chain of physical sequences which it sets in motion or directs to the plaintiff's harm is no part of it, and very generally a long train of such sequences intervenes. An example or two will make this extremely clear.

When a man commits an assault and battery with a pistol, his only act is to contract the muscles of his arm and forefinger in a certain way, but it is the delight of elementary writers to point out what a vast series of physical changes must take place before the harm is done. Suppose that, instead of firing a pistol, he takes up a hose which is discharging water on the sidewalk, and directs it at the plaintiff, he does not even set in motion the physical causes which must cooperate with his act to make a battery. Not only natural causes, but a living being, may intervene between the act and its effect. Gibbons v. Pepper [91 Eng. Rep. 922 (K.B. 1695)], which decided that there was no battery when a man's horse was frightened by accident or a third person and ran away with him, and ran over the plaintiff, takes the distinction that, if the rider by spurring is the cause of the accident, then he is guilty. In Scott v. Shepherd[, 96 Eng. Rep. 525 (K.B. 1773)], already mentioned, trespass was maintained against one who had thrown a squib into a crowd, where it was tossed from hand to hand in self-defence until it burst and injured the plaintiff. Here even human agencies were a part of the chain between the defendant's act and the result, although they were treated as more or less nearly automatic, in order to arrive at the decision.

Now I repeat, that, if principle requires us to charge a man in trespass when his act has brought force to bear on another through a comparatively short train of intervening causes, in spite of his having used all possible care, it requires the same liability, however numerous and unexpected the events between the act and the result. If running a man down is a trespass when the accident can be referred to the rider's act of spurring, why is it not a tort in every case, as was argued in Vincent v. Stinehour [7 Vt. 62 (1835)], seeing that it can always be referred more remotely to his act of mounting and taking the horse out?

Why is a man not responsible for the consequences of an act innocent in its direct and obvious effects, when those consequences would not have followed but for the intervention of a series of extraordinary, although natural, events? The reason is, that, if the intervening events are of such a kind that no foresight could have been expected to look out for them, the defendant is not to blame for having failed to do so. . . .

But there is no difference in principle between the case where a natural cause or physical factor intervenes after the act in some way not to be foreseen, and turns what seemed innocent to harm, and the case where such a cause or factor intervenes, unknown, at the time; as for the matter of that, it did in the English cases cited. If a man is excused in the one case because he is not to blame, he must be in the other. The difference taken in Gibbons v. Pepper, cited above, is not between results which are and those which are not the consequences of the defendant's acts: it is between consequences which he was bound as a reasonable man to contemplate, and those which he was not. Hard spurring is just so much more likely to lead to harm than merely riding a horse in the street, that the court thought that the defendant would be bound to look out for the consequences of the one, while it would not hold him liable for those resulting merely from the other; because the possibility of being run away with when riding quietly, though familiar, is comparatively slight. If, however, the horse had been unruly, and had been taken into a frequented place for the purpose of being broken, the owner might have been liable, because "it was his fault to bring a wild horse into a place where mischief might probably be done."

To return to the example of the accidental blow with a stick lifted in self-defence, there is no difference between hitting a person standing in one's rear and hitting one who was pushed by a horse within range of the stick just as it was lifted, provided that it was not possible, under the circumstances, in the one case to have known, in the other to have anticipated, the proximity. In either case there is wanting the only element which distinguishes voluntary acts from spasmodic muscular contractions as a ground of liability. In neither of them, that is to say, has there been an opportunity of choice with reference to the consequence complained of, — a chance to guard against the result which has come to pass. A choice which entails a concealed consequence is as to that consequence no choice.

The general principle of our law is that loss from accident must lie where it falls, and this principle is not affected by the fact that a human being is the instrument of misfortune. But relatively to a given human being anything is accident which he could not fairly have been expected to contemplate as possible, and therefore to avoid. In the language of the late Chief Justice Nelson of New York: "No case or principle can be found, or if found can be maintained, subjecting an individual to liability for an act done without fault on his part. . . . All the cases concede that an injury arising from inevitable accident, or, which in law or reason is the same thing, from an act that ordinary human care and foresight are unable to guard against, is but the misfortune of the sufferer, and lays no foundation for legal responsibility." [Harvey v. Dunlop, Lalor 193 (N.Y. Sup. Ct. 1843).] If this were not so, any act would be sufficient, however remote, which set in motion or opened the door for a series of physical sequences ending in damage such as riding the horse, in the case of the runaway, or even coming to a place where one is seized with a fit and strikes the plaintiff in an unconscious spasm. Nay, why need the defendant have acted at all, and why is it not enough that his existence has been at the expense of the plaintiff? The requirement of an act is the requirement that the defendant should have made a choice. But the only possible purpose of introducing this moral element is to make the power of avoiding the evil complained of a condition of liability. There is no such power where the evil cannot be foreseen. . . .

A man need not, it is true, do this or that act, — the term *act* implies a choice, — but he must act somehow. Furthermore, the public generally profits by individual activity. As action cannot be avoided, and tends to the public good, there is obviously no policy in throwing the hazard of what is at once desirable and inevitable upon the actor.

The state might conceivably make itself a mutual insurance company against accidents, and distribute the burden of its citizens' mishaps among all its members. There might be a pension for paralytics, and state aid for those who suffered in person or estate from tempest or wild beasts. As between individuals it might adopt the mutual insurance principle *pro tanto,* and divide damages when both were in fault, as in the *rusticum judicium* of the admiralty, or it might throw all loss upon the actor irrespective of fault. The state does none of those things, however, and the prevailing view is that its cumbrous and expensive machinery ought not to be set in motion unless some clear benefit is to be derived from disturbing the status quo. State interference is an evil, where it cannot be shown to be a good. Universal insurance, if desired, can be better and more cheaply accomplished by private enterprise. The undertaking to redistribute losses simply on the ground that they resulted from the defendant's act would not only be open to these objections, but, as it is hoped the preceding discussion has shown, to the still graver one of offending the sense of justice. Unless my act is of a nature to threaten others, unless under the circumstances a prudent man would have foreseen the possibility of harm, it is no more justifiable to make me indemnify my neighbor against the consequences, than to make me do the same thing if I had fallen upon him in a fit, or to compel me to insure him against lightning.

NOTE

Liability Ex Ante or Ex Post. The Holmes excerpt above represents the most influential theoretical statement on behalf of a negligence rule tied to the principle of reasonable foresight. One key to his argument is that standards of conduct must be known in advance, which is not possible if liability is made to turn exclusively on the outcome of the event. Hence his emphasis on the reasonableness of the defendant's conduct, irrespective of the outcome. Yet why should that be so? The contrary argument for strict liability starts with the premise that no party can take comfort in a standard that speaks only of reasonable care under the circumstances. But any party is able to decide what precautions to take if instructed from the outset that he or she is responsible for the harms that are caused either by the direct application of force on the one hand or the creation of dangerous conditions (e.g., traps) on the other. Those rules could be extended to hold owners of animals strictly responsible for the damage their animals cause, wholly irrespective of the level of precautions taken. No longer is it necessary to distinguish between ordinary riding and hard spurring. This system, moreover, does not discourage taking precautions. To be sure, the defendant pays the full price for all harms caused. Yet by the same token, the defendant gets the benefit of the reduced level of accidents for which liability should be imposed. The defendant that knows the standard can then choose the appropriate level of care without having to guess in advance what rules of conduct the law might require. How does the choice between ex ante and ex post rules play out in the following case?

SECTION E. STRICT LIABILITY AND NEGLIGENCE IN MODERN TIMES

Stone v. Bolton
[1950] 1 K.B. 201 (C.A.)

[The plaintiff, Bessie Stone, lived on Beckenham Road, a side street next to a cricket ground. One day, as she had just walked through the gate in front of her house, she was struck on the head by a cricket ball that had been hit out of the grounds. The ball was hit by a visiting player, and by all accounts, was one of the longest balls — travelling about 100 yards before it struck the plaintiff — that had ever been hit at the grounds during the previous 40 years. The cricket ground was found at trial to be "quite large enough for all practical purposes," even after it was remodeled in 1910 or 1911 to allow for construction of Beckenham Road. The field itself was surrounded by a 12-foot-high fence or hoarding which, owing to a rise in the ground, was about 17 feet above the street on the Beckenham Road side. The southern wicket from which the ball was struck was about 78 yards from Beckenham Road fence. Witnesses testified that over a 30-year period about six to ten balls had been hit onto Beckenham Road, and that several others had landed in the garden of one Brownson, the nearest neighborhood house to the cricket grounds. The plaintiff did not sue the batsman or his club but she did sue the home cricket club and all of its members. She first alleged that the grounds constituted a public nuisance. She separately alleged common law negligence, claiming that the defendants had placed the cricket pitch too close to Beckenham Road, that they had failed to erect a fence of sufficient height to prevent balls from being hit onto the road, and that they had otherwise failed to insure that cricket balls would not be hit into the road. At trial, Oliver, J., gave judgment to the defendants on both the public nuisance and negligence counts. The Court of Appeal reversed the judgment on the negligence claim by a two-to-one vote.]

JENKINS, L.J. . . . The case as regards negligence, therefore, seems to me to resolve itself into the question whether, with the wickets sited as they were, and the fence at the Beckenham Road end as it was, on August 9, 1947, the hitting into Beckenham Road of the ball which struck and injured the plaintiff was the realization of a reasonably foreseeable risk, or was in the nature of an unprecedented occurrence which the defendants could not reasonably have foreseen.

On the evidence this question seems to me to admit of only one answer. Balls had been hit into Beckenham Road before. It is true this had happened only at rare intervals, perhaps no more than six times in thirty seasons. But it was known from practical experience to be an actual possibility in the conditions in which matches were customarily played on the ground from about 1910 onwards, that is to say, with the wickets sited substantially as they were, and the fence at the Beckenham Road end, I gather, exactly as it was as regards height and position on August 9, 1947. What had happened several times before could, as it seems to me, reasonably be expected to happen again sooner or later. It was not likely to happen often, but it was certainly likely to happen again in time. When or how often it would happen again no one could tell, as this would depend on the strength of the batsmen playing on the ground (including visitors about whose capacity the defendants might know nothing) and the efficiency or otherwise of the bowlers. In my opinion, therefore, the hitting out of the ground of the ball which struck and injured the plaintiff was a realization of a reasonably foreseeable risk, which because it could reasonably be foreseen, the defendants were under a duty to prevent.

The defendants had, in fact, done nothing since the rearrangement of the ground on the making of Beckenham Road in or about 1910, whether by heightening the fence (e.g., by means of a screen of wire netting on poles) or by altering the position of the pitch, to guard against the known possibility of balls being hit into Beckenham Road. It follows that, if I have rightly defined the extent of the defendants' duty in this matter, the hitting out of the ground of the ball which injured the plaintiff did involve a breach of that duty for the consequences of which the defendants must be held liable to the plaintiff in damages. . . .

It was also, I think, suggested that no possible precaution would have arrested the flight of this particular ball, so high did it pass over the fence. This seems to me an irrelevant consideration. If cricket cannot be played on a given ground without foreseeable risk of injury to persons outside it, then it is always possible in the last resort to stop using that ground for cricket. The plaintiff in this case might, I apprehend, quite possibly have been killed. I ask myself whether in that event the defendants would have claimed the right to go on as before, because such a thing was unlikely to happen again for several years, though it might happen again on any day on which one of the teams in the match included a strong hitter. No doubt as a practical matter the defendants might decide that the double chance of a ball being hit into the road and finding a human target there was so remote that, rather than go to expense in the way of a wire screen or the like, or worse still abandon the ground, they would run the risk of such an occurrence and meet any ensuing claim for damages if and when it arose. But I fail to see on what principle they can be entitled to require people in Beckenham Road to accept the risk, and, if hit by a ball, put up with the possibly very serious harm done to them as damnum sine injuria, unless able to identify, trace, and successfully sue the particular batsman who made the hit.

Bolton v. Stone
[1951] A.C. 850

[The defendants then appealed to the House of Lords, which unanimously ruled in their favor.]

LORD REID. . . . This case, therefore raises sharply the question what is the nature and extent of the duty of a person who promotes on his land operations which may cause damage to persons on an adjoining highway. Is it that he must not carry out or permit an operation which he knows or ought to know clearly can cause such damage, however improbable that result may be, or is it that he is only bound to take into account the possibility of such damage if such damage is a likely or probable consequence of what he does or permits, or if the risk of damage is such that a reasonable man, careful of the safety of his neighbor, would regard that risk as material? . . .

Counsel for the respondent in this case had to put his case so high as to say that, at least as soon as one ball had been driven into the road in the ordinary course of a match, the appellants could and should have realized that that might happen again and that, if it did, someone might be injured; and that that was enough to put on the appellants a duty to take steps to prevent such an occurrence. If the true test is foreseeability alone I think that must be so. Once a ball has been driven on to a road without there being anything extraordinary to account for the fact, there is clearly a risk that another will follow, and if it does there is clearly a chance, small though it may be, that someone may be injured. On the theory that it is foreseeability alone that matters it would be irrelevant to consider how often a ball might be expected to land in the road and it would not matter whether the road was the busiest street, or the quietest country lane; the only difference between these cases is in the degree of risk.

It would take a good deal to make me believe that the law has departed so far from the standards which guide ordinary careful people in ordinary life. In the crowded conditions of modern life even the most careful person cannot avoid creating some risks and accepting others. What a man must not do, and what I think a careful man tries not to do, is to create a risk which is substantial. Of course there are numerous cases where special circumstances require that a higher standard shall be observed and where that is recognized by the law. But I do not think that this case comes within any such special category. It was argued that this case comes within the principle in Rylands v. Fletcher, but I agree with your Lordships that there is no substance in this argument. In my judgment the test to be applied here is whether the risk of damage to a person on the road was so small that a reasonable man in the position of the appellants, considering the matter from the point of view of safety, would have thought it right to refrain from taking steps to prevent the danger.

In considering that matter I think that it would be right to take into account not only how remote is the chance that a person might be struck but also how serious the consequences are likely to be if a person is struck; but I do not think that it would be right to take into account the difficulty of remedial measures. If cricket cannot be played on a ground without creating a substantial risk, then it should not be played there *at all*. I think that this is in substance the test which Oliver, J., applied in this case. He considered whether the appellants' ground was large enough to be safe for all practical purposes and held that it was. This is a question not of law but of fact and degree. It is not an easy question and it is one on which opinions may well differ. I can only say that having given the whole matter repeated and anxious consideration I find myself unable to decide this question in favour of the respondent. But I think that this case is not far from the borderline. If this appeal is allowed, that does not in my judgment mean that in every case where cricket has been played on a ground for a number of years without accident or complaint those who organize matches there are safe to go on in reliance on past immunity. I would have reached a different conclusion if I had thought that the risk here had been other than extremely small, because I do not think that a reasonable man considering the matter from the point of view of safety would or should disregard any risk unless it is extremely small.

LORD RADCLIFFE. My Lords, I agree that this appeal must be allowed. I agree with regret, because I have much sympathy with the decision that commended itself to the majority of the members of the Court of Appeal. I can see nothing unfair in the appellants being required to compensate the respondent for the serious injury that she has received as a result of the sport that they have organized on their cricket ground at Cheetham Hill. But the law of negligence is concerned less with what is fair than with what is culpable, and I cannot persuade myself that the appellants have been guilty of any culpable act or omission in this case.

. . . [A] breach of duty has taken place if they show the appellants guilty of a failure to take reasonable care to prevent the accident. One may phrase it as "reasonable care" or "ordinary care" or "proper care"—all these phrases are to be found in decisions of authority—but the fact remains that, unless there has been something which a reasonable man would blame as falling beneath the standard of conduct that he would set for himself and require of his neighbour, there has been no breach of legal duty. And here, I think, the respondent's case breaks down. It seems to me that a reasonable man, taking account of the chances against an accident happening, would not have felt himself called upon either to abandon the use of the ground for cricket or to increase the height of his surrounding fences. He would have done what the appellants did: in other words, he would have done nothing. Whether, if the unlikely event of an accident did occur and his play turn to another's hurt, he would have thought it equally proper to offer no more consolation to his victim than the reflection that a social being is not immune from social risks, I do not say, for I do not think that that is a consideration which is relevant to legal liability.

NOTES

1. *Negligence, strict and vicarious liability in Bolton v. Stone.* The plaintiff in Bolton v. Stone might have sued any of three possible defendants: the batsman from the visiting team, the visiting team, or the owner of the home team. Should an action lie against the batsman on a theory of strict liability? If so, is the visiting team vicariously liable for the torts of its servant? See *infra* Chapter 5, Section C. Could vicarious liability also be imposed on the owners of the cricket field, or is it limited to employers? Note that at common law, the owner of property was held responsible for fires set on his land by his guests, but not those set by strangers. See the opinion of Markham, J., in Beaulieu v. Finglam, *infra* at 175.

Alternatively, how should the negligence action against the defendant be evaluated? What would be the relevance of the location of the cricket field? The shape of the pitch? The efforts of the home team to get the batsman out? The balls that landed in Brownson's garden? In dealing with the negligence issue, note that the dominant offensive strategy in cricket, a game in which, unlike baseball, runs are plentiful (a batsman hitting for a century is not uncommon) while outs (of which there are ten per inning) represent major setbacks for the batting team. The astute batsman there-fore will normally try to keep the ball on the ground, knowing that if it crosses the boundary at the edge of the field, he will get four runs. Hitting the ball out of the field on a fly is worth six runs, but carries with it a substantial risk of being caught. Hence the infrequency of long hits.

Bolton had an uneasy public reception. Professor Goodhart's note on the case, for example, was entitled "Is It Cricket?" 67 Law Q. Rev. 460 (1951). In order to soften the public criticism, the Cricket Clubs in England that supported the defendants' appeal to the House of Lords wrote to the editor of the Law Quarterly Review that they "have done everything that they can to see that Stone does not suffer financially. In fact, so far as they are concerned, she has been left in possession of the damages originally awarded." Note, 68 Law Q. Rev. 3 (1952). Defendants also waived costs of £3,000, to which they were entitled under the English winner-take-all system. Glanville Williams developed the notion of "ethical compensation" to defend this peculiar turn of events, The Aims of the Law of Tort, 4 Current Legal Probs. 137 (1951). Salmond on Torts 30 (13th ed. 1961) notes that "one who is under no legal liability for damage caused to another may yet think it right and proper to offer some measure of compensation." Is the principle of ethical compensation needed in a strict liability system?

Does it account for the divergence between the legal and the moral duty? For criticism of Bolton v. Stone, see A. Harari, The Place of Negligence in the Law of Torts 170-179 (1962).

2. *Cricket versus golf?* With *Bolton*, contrast Rinaldo v. McGovern, 587 N.E.2d 264, 267 (N.Y. 1991). There one of two defendants — it was not clear who — sliced a golf ball that "soared" off the course and shattered plaintiff's windshield as she "happened" to drive her car down a public street. In rejecting plaintiff's negligence claim, Titone, J., held that neither defendant could be held liable for "what amounted to no more than his poorly hit tee shot," and that the defendants had no duty to warn persons who were not in the intended line of flight and who, in any event, could not have responded to the warning even if they had heard it. The court also rejected any distinction between individuals who chose to live next to the fairway on golf course grounds and strangers who drove along the public street. Titone, J., then continued:

> Plaintiffs' cause of action based on the claimed negligence of the defendant golfer is similarly untenable. Although the object of the game of golf is to drive the ball as cleanly and directly as possible toward its ultimate intended goal (the hole), the possibility that the ball will fly off in another direction is a risk inherent in the game. Contrary to the view of the dissenters below, the presence of such a risk does not, by itself, import tort liability. The essence of tort liability is the failure to take reasonable steps, where possible, to minimize the chance of harm. Thus, to establish liability in tort, there must be both the existence of a recognizable risk and some basis for concluding that the harm flowing from the consummation of that risk was reasonably preventable.
>
> Since "even the best professional golfers cannot avoid an occasional 'hook' or 'slice,'" it cannot be said that the risk of a mishit golf ball is a fully preventable occurrence. To the contrary, even with the utmost concentration and the "tedious preparation" that often accompanies a golfer's shot, there is no guarantee that the ball will be lofted onto the correct path. For that reason, we have held that the mere fact that a golf ball did not travel in the intended direction does not establish a viable negligence claim. To provide an actionable theory of liability, a person injured by a mishit golf ball must affirmatively show that the golfer failed to exercise due care by adducing proof, for example, that the golfer "aimed so inaccurately as to unreasonably increase the risk of harm."

What result under *Bolton* in a suit against the golf club? What difference would it make if plaintiff were speeding toward the golf ball when her car was struck? Driving away from it?

3. *Corrective justice and Bolton v. Stone.* Bolton v. Stone raises important questions about the proper theoretical orientation to tort law. A *corrective*

justice approach sees the law as providing *rectification* or *redress* for an invasion of a legal right. This view presupposes that law, solely as a matter of fairness between the parties to a dispute, undoes the imbalance created by the violation of a preexisting right, most notably the right to exclusive control over one's body and property. Violations of these rights are usually (but not exclusively) understood in terms of physical invasions. Explicit concern with long-term incentive effects on either the wrongdoer or victim are not part of the basic equation, and are often thought extrinsic to the basic purpose of the law or, as is sometimes said, that corrective justice "provides the immanent critical standpoint informing the law's effort to work itself pure." Weinrib, Corrective Justice in a Nutshell, 52 U. Toronto L. J. 349, 356 (2002); See also Witt, Contingency, Immanence, and Inevitability in the Law of Accidents, 1 J. Tort L., Issue 2, Article 1, at 13 (2006).

In Bolton v. Stone, the prima facie causal case against the batsman is simply "he hit me." This causal paradigm has been defended in Epstein, A Theory of Strict Liability, 2 J. Legal Stud. 151, 168-169 (1973):

> Once this simple causal paradigm is accepted, its relationship to the question of responsibility for the harm so caused must be clarified. Briefly put, the argument is that proof of the proposition *A* hit *B* should be sufficient to establish a prima facie case of liability. I do not argue that proof of causation is equivalent to a conclusive demonstration of responsibility. Both the modern and classical systems of law are based upon the development of prima facie cases and defenses thereto. They differ not in their use of presumptions but in the elements needed to create the initial presumption in favor of the plaintiff. The doctrine of strict liability holds that proof that the defendant caused harm creates that presumption because proof of the non-reciprocal source of the harm is sufficient to upset the balance where one person must win and the other must lose. There is no room to consider, as part of the prima facie case, allegations that the defendant intended to harm the plaintiff, or could have avoided the harm he caused by the use of reasonable care. The choice is plaintiff or defendant, and the analysis of causation is the tool which, prima facie, fastens responsibility upon the defendant. Indeed for most persons, the difficult question is often not whether these causal assertions create the presumption, but whether there are in fact any means to distinguish between causation and responsibility, so close is the connection between what a man does and what he is answerable for.

The corrective justice principle has also been invoked on defense of a negligence rule on the ground that the defendant's standard of conduct should be set no higher than the standard the plaintiff could demand from herself. If, therefore, the plaintiff cannot identify any flaw in the defendant's conduct, she cannot characterize that conduct as *wrongful*. Thus, it is said that "corrective justice requires annulling a departure from the pre-existing distribution of money or honors in accordance with merit, but only when the departure is the result of *an act of injustice,* causing injury." Posner, The Concept of Corrective Justice in Recent Theories of Tort Law, 10 J. Legal Stud. 187, 200 (1981). The same idea is expressed by Glanville Williams in The Aims of the Law of Tort, 4 Current Legal Probs. 137, 151 (1951):

> Finally there is the compensatory or reparative theory, according to which one who has caused injury to another must make good the damage whether he was at fault or not. This is the same as the theory of ethical compensation except that it does not require culpability on the part of the defendant. If valid, it justifies strict liability, which the theory of ethical compensation does not. The difficulty is, however, to state it in such a form as to make it acceptable. If it is said that a person who has been damaged by another ought to be compensated, we readily assent, moved as we are by sympathy for the victim's loss. But what has to be shown is not merely that the sufferer ought to be compensated, but that he ought to be compensated by the defendant. In the absence of any moral blame of the defendant, how is this demonstration possible?

An alternative account of wrongful conduct ties into the system of pleadings outlined by Arnold, *supra* at 105, by stressing the difference between strict and absolute liability. For these purposes, absolute liability refers to a legal system that treats causation of plaintiff's harm by defendant's acts as the *only* question relevant to liability, leaving no room for any excuse or justification. Strict liability starts with the same prima facie case, and rules out all defenses based on the defendant's level of care. But it still allows other defenses based, for example, on plaintiff's misconduct or inevitable accident, narrowly construed. Absolute liability may offend the principle of corrective justice, but strict liability explicates the idea of wrongfulness, not in terms of negligence or intention, but in terms of these other substantive defenses.

4. *Economic efficiency as an alternative to corrective justice.* Not all accounts of modern tort law regard corrective justice as the touchstone of liability, and much of modern tort scholarship has sought to develop alternative economic accounts of the tort system. One early notable explication of an economic approach is contained in Calabresi and Melamed, Property Rules, Liability Rules and Inalienability: One View of the Cathedral, 85 Harv. L. Rev. 1089, 1093-1094 (1972):

> Perhaps the simplest reason for a particular entitlement is to minimize the administrative costs of enforcement. This was the reason Holmes gave for letting the costs lie where they fall in accidents unless some clear societal benefit is achieved by shifting them. By itself this reason will never justify any

result except that of letting the stronger win, for obviously that result minimizes enforcement costs. Nevertheless, administrative efficiency may be relevant to choosing entitlements when other reasons are taken into account. This may occur when the reasons accepted are indifferent between conflicting entitlements and one entitlement is cheaper to enforce than the others. It may also occur when the reasons are not indifferent but lead us only slightly to prefer one over another and the first is considerably more expensive to enforce than the second.

But administrative efficiency is just one aspect of the broader concept of economic efficiency. Economic efficiency asks that we choose the set of entitlements which would lead to that allocation of resources which could not be improved in the sense that a further change would not so improve the condition of those who gained by it that they could compensate those who lost from it and still be better off than before. This is often called Pareto optimality. To give two examples, economic efficiency asks for that combination of entitlements to engage in risky activities and to be free from harm from risky activities which will most likely lead to the lowest sum of accident costs and of costs of avoiding accidents. It asks for that form of property, private or communal, which leads to the highest product for the effort of producing.

Technically speaking, what Calabresi and Melamed called Pareto efficiency is known as Kaldor-Hicks efficiency. Pareto efficiency requires that the winners *actually* compensate the losers so that at least some one is better off and no one is worse off than before. Kaldor-Hicks efficiency is satisfied with a demonstration that hypothetical *compensation was possible*. Stated otherwise, it allows the move to go forward so long as the gains to the winner are sufficient to compensate the losers, even if such compensation is not made. The Pareto standard is less problematic but more demanding; the Kaldor-Hicks standard is the opposite. Note that both standards preclude social changes that yield systematic losses. Is there a fair distribution of the gains under the Pareto standard if one person gains huge amounts and everyone else is left indifferent? For a recent retrospective on the Calabresi/Melamed paper, see Symposium, Property Rules, Liability Rules, and Inalienability: A Twenty-Five Year Retrospective, 106 Yale L.J. 2081-2213 (1997), with articles by among others, Epstein, Krier and Schwab, Levmore, and Rose. See also Schwab, Property Rules and Liability Rules: The Cathedral in Another Light, 70 N.Y.U. L. Rev. 440 (1995).

Transaction costs, i.e., the costs involved in establishing and enforcing both property rights and contractual arrangements, are critical to the economic analysis. If these could be held to zero, the initial distribution of rights would be of little economic consequence, as private parties could, through repeated, costless, and instantaneous transactions, move all resources to their highest valued use. The end use of any resource would be the same regardless of its original owner. Thus, the decisions about property rights would only affect their initial distribution, but not their final allocation. See Coase, The Problem of Social Cost, 3 J.L. & Econ. 1 (1960), for the initial elaboration of what is today known as the Coase theorem. In all real world situations, however, transaction costs are positive, if not prohibitive. In contractual situations, the high costs of transacting can be reduced when either courts or legislatures announce standard "gap-filling" terms for matters on which the parties are silent. In tort cases between strangers, however, antecedent voluntary transactions are typically unattainable. The tort rule, therefore, cannot be displaced before harm occurs, and must govern liability afterwards. What factors should be considered in fashioning the ideal liability rule where there are high transaction costs? Drawing heavily on Calabresi's book, The Cost of Accidents, Calabresi and Melamed, *supra* at 1096-1097, tackled this problem as follows:

> (1) that economic efficiency standing alone would dictate that set of entitlements which favors knowledgeable choices between social benefits and the social costs of obtaining them, and between social costs and the social costs of avoiding them; (2) that this implies, in the absence of certainty as to whether a benefit is worth its costs to society, that the cost should be put on the party or activity best located to make such a cost-benefit analysis; (3) that in particular contexts like accidents or pollution this suggests putting costs on the party or activity which can most cheaply avoid them; (4) that in the absence of certainty as to who that party or activity is, the costs should be put on the party or activity which can with the lowest transaction costs act in the market to correct an error in entitlements by inducing the party who can avoid social costs most cheaply to do so; and (5) that since we are in an area where by hypothesis markets do not work perfectly — there are transaction costs — a decision will often have to be made on whether market transactions or collective fiat is most likely to bring us closer to the Pareto optimal result the "perfect" market would reach.

How does one determine which party is "best located to make a cost-benefit analysis" if the parties to the accident are neither identified, nor known to each other, before the accident occurs? What should be done if the defendant knows more about the probability of harm to another, but the plaintiff knows more about its likely extent? How does this analysis apply to Bolton v. Stone? For the other cases in this chapter?

Hammontree v. Jenner
97 Cal. Rptr. 739 (Cal. App. 1971)

LILLIE, J. Plaintiffs Maxine Hammontree and her husband sued defendant for personal injuries and property damage arising out of an automobile accident. The cause was tried to a jury. Plaintiffs appeal from judgment entered on a jury verdict returned against them and in favor of defendant.

The evidence shows that on the afternoon of April 25, 1967, defendant was driving his 1959 Chevrolet home from work; at the same time plaintiff Maxine Hammontree was working in a bicycle shop owned and operated by her and her husband; without warning defendant's car crashed through the wall of the shop, struck Maxine and caused personal injuries and damage to the shop.

Defendant claimed he became unconscious during an epileptic seizure, losing control of his car. He did not recall the accident, but his last recollection before it was leaving a stop light after his last stop, and his first recollection after the accident was being taken out of his car in plaintiffs' shop. Defendant testified he has a medical history of epilepsy and knows of no other reason for his loss of consciousness except an epileptic seizure. [The defendant first learned of his epileptic condition in 1952 and from that time until his accident, he was under the constant care of a neurologist who treated him first with dilantin and then with phelantin. The defendant's last seizure was in 1953, and thereafter he had no trouble at all. His physician testified that he had seen the defendant on a regular basis over the years and that at all times he was "doing normally." He further testified that he believed that it was "safe" for the defendant to drive with the medication, even though it was impossible for the defendant to drive during a seizure.]

In 1955 or 1956 the Department of Motor Vehicles was advised that defendant was an epileptic and placed him on probation under which every six months he had to report to the doctor who was required to advise it in writing of defendant's condition. In 1960 his probation was changed to a once-a-year report . . . .

[The plaintiffs withdrew their negligence count, but the trial judge instructed the jury on negligence and res ipsa loquitur. The jury found for the defendant. The plaintiff then appealed the refusal of the trial judge to grant summary judgment in their favor by failing to give an instruction on absolute liability.][1]

Under the present state of the law found in appellate authorities beginning with Waters v. Pacific Coast Dairy, Inc., [131 P.2d 588 (Cal. App. 1942)] (driver rendered unconscious from sharp pain in left arm and shoulder) through Ford v. Carew & English, [200 P.2d 828 (Cal. App. 1948)] (fainting spells from strained heart muscles), Zabunoff v. Walker,

---

1. "When the evidence shows that a driver of a motor vehicle on a public street or highway loses his ability to safely operate and control such vehicle because of some seizure or health failure, that driver is nevertheless legally liable for all injuries and property damage which an innocent person may suffer as a proximate result of the defendant's inability to so control or operate his motor vehicle.

"This is true even if you find the defendant driver had no warning of any such impending seizure or health failure."

[13 Cal. Rptr. 463 (Cal. App. 1961)] (sudden sneeze), and Tannyhill v. Pacific Motor Trans. Co., [38 Cal. Rptr. 774 (Cal. App. 1964)] (heart attack), the trial judge properly refused the instruction. The foregoing cases generally hold that liability of a driver, suddenly stricken by an illness rendering him unconscious, for injury resulting from an accident occurring during that time rests on principles of negligence. . . .

Appellants seek to have this court override the established law of this state which is dispositive of the issue before us as outmoded in today's social and economic structure, particularly in the light of the now recognized principles imposing liability upon the manufacturer, retailer and all distributive and vending elements and activities which bring a product to the consumer to his injury, on the basis of strict liability in tort expressed first in Justice Traynor's concurring opinion in Escola v. Coca Cola Bottling Co., [150 P.2d 436 (Cal. 1944)]; and then in Greenman v. Yuba Power Products, Inc., [377 P.2d 897 (Cal. 1963)]; Vandermark v. Ford Motor Co., [391 P.2d 168 (Cal. 1964)]; and Elmore v. American Motors Corp., [451 P.2d 84 (Cal. 1969)]. These authorities hold that "A manufacturer [or retailer] is strictly liable in tort when an article he places on the market, knowing that it is to be used without inspection for defects, proves to have a defect that causes injury to a human being." (*Greenman* supra.) Drawing a parallel with these products liability cases, appellants argue, with some degree of logic, that only the driver affected by a physical condition which could suddenly render him unconscious and who is aware of that condition can anticipate the hazards and foresee the dangers involved in his operation of a motor vehicle, and that the liability of those who by reason of seizure or heart failure or some other physical condition lose the ability to safely operate and control a motor vehicle resulting in injury to an innocent person should be predicated on strict liability.

We decline to superimpose the absolute liability of products liability cases upon drivers under the circumstances here. The theory on which those cases are predicated is that manufacturers, retailers and distributors of products are engaged in the business of distributing goods to the public and are an integral part of the over-all producing and marketing enterprise that should bear the cost of injuries from defective parts. . . . This policy hardly applies here and it is not enough to simply say, as do appellants, that the insurance carriers should be the ones to bear the cost of injuries to innocent victims on a strict liability basis. In Maloney v. Rath, [445 P.2d 513 (Cal. 1968)], followed by Clark v. Dziabas, [445 P.2d 517 (Cal. 1968)], appellant urged that defendant's violation of a safety provision (defective brakes) of the Vehicle Code makes the violator strictly liable for damages caused by the violation. While reversing the judgment for defendant upon another ground, the California Supreme Court refused to apply the doctrine of strict liability to automobile drivers. The situation involved two users of the highway but the problems of fixing responsibility under a system of strict liability are as complicated in the instant case as those in Maloney v. Rath, and could only create uncertainty in the area of its concern. As stated in *Maloney*, at page 446: "To invoke a rule of strict liability on users of the streets and highways, however, without also establishing in substantial detail how the new rule should operate would only contribute confusion to the automobile accident problem. Settlement and claims adjustment procedures would become chaotic until the new rules were worked out on a case-by-case basis, and the hardships of delayed compensation would be seriously intensified. Only the Legislature, if it deems it wise to do so, can avoid such difficulties by enacting a comprehensive plan for the compensation of automobile accident victims in place of or in addition to the law of negligence."

The instruction tendered by appellants was properly refused for still another reason. Even assuming the merit of appellants' position under the facts of this case in which defendant knew he had a history of epilepsy, previously had suffered seizures and at the time of the accident was attempting to control the condition by medication, the instruction does not except from its ambit the driver who suddenly is stricken by an illness or physical condition which he had no reason whatever to anticipate and of which he had no prior knowledge.

The judgment is affirmed.

WOOD, P.J., and THOMPSON, J., concurred.

Appellants' petition for a hearing by the Supreme Court was denied December 16, 1971.

NOTES

1. *Physician liability.* Should the treating physician of an epileptic driver be held responsible to an injured third party if he fails to warn his patients of the relevant risk and erroneously supplies favorable documentation to the Department of Transportation that allows her to obtain a driver's license? In Schmidt v. Mahoney, 659 N.W.2d 552, 555 (Iowa 2003), Carter, J., answered that question in the negative, noting:

> [I]t is highly likely that a consequence of recognizing liability to members of the general public . . . will be that physicians treating patients with seizure disorders will become reluctant to allow them to drive or engage in any other activity in which a seizure could possibly harm a third party. In order to curtail liability, physicians may become prone to make overly restrictive recommendations concerning the activities of their patients and will exercise their role as reporters to the department of transportation in an inflexible manner not in their patient's best interest.

Does the insulation of the physician from liability strengthen or weaken the case for strict liability against the driver?

2. *Why the choice between negligence and strict liability is so difficult.* For over 200 years courts have vacillated over the key choice between negligence and strict liability. It is useful to locate the source of this uneasiness and to explain why this tension is not likely resolve itself quickly. First, note that courts seek to identify some social gain to justify the manifest social costs of litigation. Compensation of the plaintiff, taken alone, fails to justify this expense as long as first-party insurance is available. That insurance allows each person to choose the type of coverage desired based upon an intimate knowledge of personal needs and circumstances that no tort defendant could ever obtain. What overcomes the initial bias for first-party coverage?

Since compensation alone does not supply the missing ingredient, the case for tort liability rests on the need to fashion incentives that reduce the costs of accidents and their prevention. Negligence liability thus seems unproblematic because the tort rule unambiguously provides incentives to avoid costs that exceed the benefits that they generate. To see why, think of the optimal level of care as the same amount of care that a single person would take if he himself were the only person at risk for property damage or bodily injury. That individual would prefer suffering the consequences of some accidents to bearing the greater costs of avoiding them.

A tort suit arises only because the victim and injurer are separate parties. At this point intuitions cut in two contrary directions. One impulse imposes liability to force the defendant-injurer to internalize the costs that his conduct would otherwise impose on others. The law makes the actor bear the same costs he would incur if he were the sole owner. The rival impulse is to dismiss the plaintiff's suit because the defendant acted just as the plaintiff would (and should) have acted under the same circumstances: He took the optimal level of precautions by treating the plaintiff's loss as if it were his own. There is no occasion for the law to intervene because the defendant has already taken the optimal level of precaution just like a sole owner. The strict liability theory makes a defendant bear the plaintiff's loss; the negligence theory imposes liability only when it spots a shortfall in the defendant's basic behavior. How then to choose between them?

One possible evaluation invokes the considerations of reciprocity encountered in *Losee, supra* at 141. Unfortunately, the norm of reciprocity is consistent with either general system, whether negligence or strict liability. The incentive effects of the two rules are the same when viewed from the "ex ante" perspective (that is, before the harm), and it is difficult to identify any systematic distributional consequences that flow from the choice of liability rules. This stalemate tends to make administrative costs the deciding factor in the debate. Yet again, the relevant considerations tug in both directions. The strict liability rule eliminates the need to make a nice determination of the standard of care; it also eliminates the need to ask whether the defendant complied with that standard. But the negligence rule cuts out some expensive lawsuits (since plaintiff must do more to win), although the ones that remain are of greater complexity. The tradeoff between these two effects rests on empirical judgments about their relative magnitude: do we worry more about the cost per suit, or the number of suits?

This inquiry takes us a long way from the principles of fundamental fairness or immanence traditionally and plausibly invoked on *both* sides of the controversy. Yet, if this tradeoff shapes the strict liability/negligence debate, it is easy to see why a consensus has been so slow in developing. While the choice of rule has an enormous impact in deciding specific cases, the overall social consequences are less dramatic than first meet the eye. Since both rules create the same basic incentives and have, roughly speaking, the same administrative costs, either can provide a workable foundation for tort law. Indeed, so great are similarities between them that the vast majority of cases come out the same way under either rule. It is only when these tort rules are contrasted with radical systemwide changes such as no-fault automobile insurance or workers' compensation that major differences can be detected. At this point, therefore, it is best to leave the grand question and turn to the more detailed operation of the dominant negligence system.

3

THE NEGLIGENCE ISSUE

Thayer, Public Wrong and Private Action
27 Harv. L. Rev. 317, 318 (1914)

In the law of negligence no doctrine is useful or appropriate which cannot be plainly and simply stated, and which, when so stated, does not respond to the test of common sense.

Leon Green, Judge and Jury
185 (1930)

In other words, we may have a process for passing judgment in negligence cases, but practically no "law of negligence" beyond the process itself.

SECTION A.   INTRODUCTION

The inconclusive debate between negligence and strict liability theories, which was the subject of the last chapter, only affirms the critical—many would say dominant—role of negligence in the law of unintentional harms. This chapter explores how that negligence principle, both in theory and practice, *limits* a defendant's liability for these accidental harms. In dealing with these issues, it is important to draw a preliminary distinction between negligence as a form of subpar conduct and negligence as a separate and distinct tort. The former is the second element (breach) of the tort of negligence, which in its modern elaboration contains four distinct elements: duty, breach, causation, and damage. A plaintiff must meet all four requirements to establish the prima facie case (which, in turn, is subject to the various defenses discussed *infra* in Chapter 4). These four elements are:

First, *duty*: did the defendant owe the plaintiff a duty to conform his conduct to a standard necessary to avoid an unreasonable risk of harm to others?

Second, *breach*: did the defendant's conduct, whether by way of act or omission, fall below the applicable standard of care?

Third, *causation*: was the defendant's failure to meet the applicable standard of care causally connected to the plaintiff's harm? Often this inquiry is divided into two parts: causation in fact and proximate causation.

Fourth, *damages*: did the plaintiff suffer harm?

This chapter concentrates on the second of these questions, so critical in ordinary tort litigation—whether the defendant was negligent, defined as engaging in "conduct which falls below the standard established by law for the protection of others against unreasonable risk of harm." RST §282. The issue of causation is addressed together in Chapter 6, and that of affirmative duties is the topic of Chapter 7. The discussion of damages is postponed until Chapter 10.

The question of negligence spans all of tort law. Its dictates apply not only to ordinary individuals, with the full range of human strengths and frailties, but also to small businesses, large corporations, government entities, unions, and nonprofit associations. This chapter is designed to give some sense of the reach and application of the negligence principle in its institutional settings. Accordingly, Section B develops the commonsense interpretation of negligence, and the efforts to breathe life into the abstract concept of the reasonable person. The key inquiry asks, what allowances, if any, the law should make for the weaknesses of those individuals who are not blessed with the knowledge, skill, or ability of that durable but hypothetical construct of negligence—the reasonable person.

Section C then traces the evolution of negligence as applied to all reasonable persons, by examining the "balancing of interests" needed to determine whether the risks taken by the defendant are justified by the ends sought. The Restatement simply states that "[c]onduct is negligent if its disadvantages outweigh its advantages, while conduct is not negligent if its advantages outweigh its disadvantages." RTT:LPH §3, comment *e*. At the abstract level, this inquiry delves into the uses and limitations of the various economic interpretations of the negligence principle, which are often couched in "risk-benefit" or "cost-benefit" terms, where risk stresses probability of harm, without regard to a severity element built into the cost formula. *Id.* Which measure is more accurate from an economic point of view? Concretely, the skillful lawyer typically supplements that basic approach by pointing to some specific "untaken precaution" that, if taken, could have prevented the accident that actually occurred. See Grady, Untaken Precautions, 18 J. Legal Stud. 139 (1989). At trial, the plaintiff tries to show that some inexpensive precaution (a railing, a warning, or an inspection) could have prevented some likely serious injury, while the defendant tries to show that the precaution was excessively costly, redundant, ineffective, or downright dangerous. In hotly contested cases, there is no shortcut for a complete mastery of a case's relevant social and technical facts. Of necessity, skilled negligence lawyers become experts on everything from printing presses to toxic chemicals, from product warnings to complex surgery. Indeed, within law firms, personal injury law is often broken down by subject matter, such as highway accidents, medical malpractice, machine tools, chemicals, athletic injuries, or hunting accidents, and not by abstract doctrinal category.

Sometimes, however, the law supplies guideposts in the featureless landscape created by the concept of an unreasonable risk. Our general analysis of negligence is accordingly supplemented in Section D by looking at the relationship between customary practice and negligence. Section E extends the same inquiry to the criminal statutes, and explores how safety regulations are used to determine whether the parties have acted negligently.

The last two sections of the chapter deal with the trial of a negligence case. Section F examines the allocation of responsibility between judge and jury and, in that connection, the success of judicial efforts to create uniform standards of conduct as a matter of law. Section G then examines the principles governing the proof of negligence at trial, especially the doctrine of res ipsa loquitur — the thing speaks for itself (but usually not as clearly as we would like).

SECTION B.   THE REASONABLE PERSON

It is sometimes said that the study of negligence is the study of the mistakes a reasonable man might make (Harry Kalven, Jr.).

Vaughan v. Menlove
132 Eng. Rep. 490 (C.P. 1837)

[The plaintiff owned two cottages in the County of Salop, which he rented out to two tenants. The defendant was a neighbor who had placed certain buildings and a hay stack, or rick, on his own property, near the plaintiff's two cottages.]

At the trial it appeared that the rick in question had been made by the Defendant near the boundary of his own premises; that the hay was in such a state when put together, as to give rise to discussions on the probability of fire: that though there were conflicting opinions on the subject, yet during a period of five weeks, the Defendant was repeatedly warned of his peril; that his stock was insured; and that upon one occasion, being advised to take the rick down to avoid all danger, he said "he would chance it." He made an aperture or chimney through the rick; but in spite, or perhaps in consequence of this precaution, the rick at length burst into flames from the spontaneous heating of its materials; the flames communicated to the Defendant's barn and stables, and thence to the Plaintiff's cottages, which were entirely destroyed.

PATTESON, J., before whom the cause was tried, told the jury that the question for them to consider, was, whether the fire had been occasioned by gross negligence on the part of the Defendant; adding, that he was bound to proceed with such reasonable caution as a prudent man would have exercised under such circumstances.

A verdict having been found for the Plaintiff, a rule nisi for a new trial was obtained [i.e., defendant appealed], on the ground that the jury should have been directed to consider, not, whether the Defendant had been guilty of gross negligence with reference to the standard of ordinary prudence, a standard too uncertain to afford any criterion; but whether he had acted bona fide to the best of his judgment; if he had, he ought not to be responsible for the misfortune of not possessing the highest order of intelligence. The action under such circumstances, was of the first impression. . . .

TALFOURD SERJT. and WHATELY, shewed cause [for plaintiff].

The pleas having expressly raised issues on the negligence of the Defendant, the learned Judge could not do otherwise than leave that question to the jury. . . . And the action, though new in specie, is founded on a principle fully established, that a man must so use his own property as not to injure that of others. On the same circuit a defendant was sued a few years ago, for burning weeds so near the extremity of his own land as to set fire to and destroy his neighbours' wood. The plaintiff recovered damages, and no motion was made to set aside the verdict. Then, there were no means of estimating the defendant's negligence, except by taking as a standard, the conduct of a man of ordinary prudence: that has been the rule always laid down, and there is no other that would not be open to much greater uncertainties.

R. V. RICHARDS, in support of the rule [for defendant].

First, there was no duty imposed on the Defendant, as there is on carriers or other bailees, under an implied contract, to be responsible for the exercise of any given degree of prudence: the Defendant had a right to place his stack as near to the extremity of his own land as he pleased . . . : under that right, and subject to no contract, he can only be called on to act bona fide to the best of his judgment: if he has done that, it is a contradiction in terms, to inquire whether or not he has been guilty of gross negligence. At all events what would have been gross negligence ought to be estimated by the faculties of the individual, and not by those of other men. The measure of prudence varies so with the varying faculties of men, that it is impossible to say what is gross negligence with reference to the standard of what is called ordinary prudence. . . .

TINDAL, C.J. I agree that this is a case primae impressionis [of first impression]; but I feel no difficulty in applying to it the principles of law as laid down in other cases of a similar kind. Undoubtedly this is not a case of contract, such as a bailment or the like where the bailee is responsible in consequence of the remuneration he is to receive: but there is a rule of law which says you must so enjoy your own property as not to injure that of another; and according to that rule the Defendant is liable for the consequence of his own neglect: and though the Defendant did not himself light the fire, yet mediately, he is as much the cause of it as if he had himself put a candle to the rick; for it is well known that hay will ferment and take fire if it be not carefully stacked. It has been decided that if an occupier burns weeds so near the boundary of his own land that damage ensues to the property of his neighbour, he is liable to an action for the amount of injury done, unless the accident were occasioned by a sudden blast which he could not foresee: Tuberville v. Stamp (1 Salk. 13 [1697]). But put the case of a chemist making experiments with ingredients, singly innocent, but when combined, liable to ignite if he leaves them together, and injury is thereby occasioned to the property of his neighbour, can any one doubt that an action on the case would lie?

It is contended, however, that the learned Judge was wrong in leaving this to the jury as a case of gross negligence, and that the question of negligence was so mixed up with reference to what would be the conduct of a man of ordinary prudence that the jury might have thought the latter the rule by which they were to decide; that such a rule would be too uncertain to act upon; and that the question ought to have been whether the Defendant had acted honestly and bona fide to the best of his own judgment. That, however, would leave so vague a line as to afford no rule at all, the degree of judgment belonging to each individual being infinitely various: and though it has been urged that the care which a prudent man would take, is not an intelligible proposition as a rule of law, yet such has always been the rule adopted in cases of bailment, as laid down in Coggs v. Bernard (2 Ld. Raym. 909 [1703]). Though in some cases a greater degree of care is exacted than in others, yet in "the second sort of bailment, viz. commodatum or lending gratis, the borrower is bound to the strictest care and diligence to keep the goods so as to restore them back again to the lender; because the bailee has a benefit by the use of them, so as if the bailee be guilty of the least neglect he will be answerable; as if a man should lend another a horse to go westward, or for a month; if the bailee put this horse in his stable, and he were stolen from thence, the bailee shall not be answerable for him: but if he or his servant leave the house or stable doors open, and the thieves take the opportunity of that, and steal the horse, he will be chargeable, because the neglect gave the thieves the occasion to steal the horse." The care taken by a prudent man has always been the rule laid down; and as to the supposed difficulty of applying it, a jury has always been able to say, whether, taking that rule as their guide, there has been negligence on the occasion in question.

Instead, therefore, of saying that the liability for negligence should be co-extensive with the judgment of each individual, which would be as variable as the length of the foot of each individual, we ought rather to adhere to the rule which requires in all cases a regard to caution such as a man of ordinary prudence would observe. That was in substance the criterion presented to the jury in this case, and therefore the present rule must be discharged.

PARK, J. I entirely concur in what has fallen from his lordship. Although the facts in this case are new in specie, they fall within a principle long established, that a man must so use his own property as not to injure that of others. [Park, J., then recited extensively from Tuberville v. Stamp, *infra* at 175 at note 1, and concluded:]

As to the direction of the learned judge, it was perfectly correct. Under the circumstances of the case it was proper to leave it to the jury whether with reference to the caution which would have been observed by a man of ordinary prudence, the Defendant had not been guilty of gross negligence. After he had been warned repeatedly during the five weeks as to the consequences likely to happen, there is no colour for altering the verdict, unless it were to increase the damages.

VAUGHAN, J. The principle on which this action proceeds, is by no means new. It has been urged that the Defendant in such a case takes no duty on himself; but I do not agree in that position: every one takes upon himself the duty of so dealing with his own property as not to injure the property of others. It was, if any thing, too favourable to the Defendant to leave it to the jury whether he had been guilty of gross negligence; for when the Defendant upon being warned as to the consequences likely to ensue from the condition of the rick, said, "he would chance it," it was manifest he adverted to his interest in the insurance office. The conduct of a prudent man has always been the criterion for the jury in such cases: but it is by no means confined to them. . . . Here, there was not a single witness whose testimony did not go to establish gross negligence in the Defendant. He had repeated warnings of what was likely to occur, and the whole calamity was occasioned by his procrastination.

Rule discharged. [Appeal denied.]

NOTES

1. Liability for fire at common law. Vaughn is scarcely the first common law decision addressing liability for fire at common law. However, the earlier decisions that dealt with the matter adopted a strict liability position, holding the owner responsible not only for the fires that he set on his property, but also for those set by his family or servants. See Beaulieu v. Finglam, Y.B. 2 Hen. 4, f. 18, pl. 6 (1401). These cases often presented hidden difficulties in that it was often unclear whether the plaintiff's claim rested on the defendant's setting of the fire, or his failure to watch it after it was properly set. In Tuberville v. Stamp, 91 Eng. Rep. 1072 ([K.B.] 1697), the court required a defendant to guard the fire in his field as well as in his house, subject to this caveat. "If he kindle it at a proper time and place, and the violence of the wind carry it into his neighbour's ground and prejudice him, this is fit to be given in evidence." Why don't *Beaulieu* and *Tuberville* require the use of the strict liability standard in *Vaughan*? Does the distinction between ordinary and gross negligence matter? See, in this regard, the famous bon mot of Baron Rolfe who described gross negligence as the same thing as ordinary negligence "with the addition of a vituperative epithet." Wilson v. Brett, 152 Eng. Rep. 737 (Ex. 1843).

2. The standard of care for bailments. The prospect of variable standards of care in fire cases led the judges to examine the traditional common law rules of liability for bailments (i.e., consensual arrangements under which goods are delivered to another with the intention that they be redelivered at some future time). In the leading case of Coggs v. Bernard, 92 Eng. Rep. 107 (Q.B. 1704), Holt, C.J., explicitly adopted the six types of bailments in Roman law, each with its distinct standard of care. He categorized them as: (1) gratuitous bailment for safekeeping (depositum); (2) bailment for the bailee's use (commodatum); (3) a simple pawn (vadium); (4) bailment for hire (locatio rei); (5) bailment whereby the bailee agrees for a fee to operate or manage the thing bailed (locatio operis faciendi); and (6) the bailment of a thing to be managed (not merely stored) by the bailee without compensation (mandatum). The underlying principle subjects the bailee to a standard of care varying in proportion to the benefit that he derives from the bailment. He is held liable for the "slightest negligence" where the loan is for his own benefit or use, but for only gross neglect when he undertakes safekeeping for the bailor. If both parties benefit, the usual standard is that of ordinary care. In all cases it is, of course, possible to vary the standard of care by private agreement. How successful is defendant's implicit argument that the law of bailment authorizes the use of a good faith standard in disputes between neighbors? If both the good-faith and reasonable care standards are used consensually, how can either be too uncertain to be serviceable? Which standard should be used when?

3. Guest statutes. At one time, the different levels of care required at common law for gratuitous and commercial bailments influenced the standard of care owed by automobile drivers to their guests. During the 1920s and 1930s, many states passed statutes providing that the driver of a car could be liable to a nonpaying guest, in somewhat varying formulations, only if willful misconduct, recklessness, or gross negligence were established. All these rules rested on the perception that passengers who do not pay for protection are entitled only to a lower level of care. Massaletti v. Fitzroy, 118 N.E. 168 (Mass. 1917); Note, The Common Law Basis of Automobile Guest Statutes, 43 U. Chi. L. Rev. 798 (1976).

In practice, guest statutes imposed a far heavier burden on plaintiffs than an ordinary negligence standard. But even eminent judges have disagreed whether plaintiffs have met the more exacting standard of liability. In Conway v. O'Brien, 111 F.2d 611 (2d Cir. 1940), the Vermont guest statute permitted a passenger to recover from his host only for "gross negligence." Judge Learned Hand kept the plaintiff from the jury when the defendant was driving at 15 miles per hour on the wrong side of a narrow highway while coming around a sharp curve. "Had he been driving twice as fast, or on a much travelled highway, we might think otherwise; but on that road and at that speed it seems to us that his fault was only a routine dereliction, not grave enough to fall within the statute. It is plain from the Vermont decisions that we cannot properly devolve the entire responsibility for a decision upon a jury." The Supreme Court reversed and remanded for trial, with Justice Reed concluding that the question should reach the jury under Vermont law: "[It] seems quite plain that a jury might find a driver of a car familiar with the locality grossly negligent, when with three guests and without a signal he rounds a blind, sharp curve at fifteen miles per hour on the wrong side into a narrow bridge entrance." Conway v. O'Brien, 312 U.S. 492, 494 (1941).

In the 1920s, the first round of guest statutes was sustained against the charge that they violated the equal protection clause of the Fourteenth Amendment. See Silver v. Silver, 280 U.S. 117 (1928), in which the Supreme Court held that the risk of collusive suits between passengers and drivers was sufficiently great to warrant the legislature's singling guest cases out for special attention. A second wave of constitutional challenges at the state level, beginning with Brown v. Merlo, 506 P.2d 212 (Cal. 1973), proved successful in overturning these statutes in about half the states that had them. In recent years, the constitutional debate has ebbed, as most state legislatures have repealed their guest statutes. Quite possibly, driving is now so common an activity that special dispensation for guest passengers does not square well with modern social expectations. For the current state-by-state tally, see 3 Harper, James & Gray, Torts §16.15 n.4.

Holmes, The Common Law
107-109 (1881)

Supposing it now to be conceded that the general notion upon which liability to an action is founded is fault or blameworthiness in some sense, the question arises, whether it is so in the sense of personal moral shortcoming, ... Suppose that a defendant were allowed to testify that, before acting, he considered carefully what would be the conduct of a prudent man under the circumstances, and, having formed the best judgment he could, acted accordingly. If the story was believed, it would be conclusive against the defendant's negligence judged by a moral standard which would take his personal characteristics into account. But supposing any such evidence to have got before the jury, it is very clear that the court would say, Gentlemen, the question is not whether the defendant thought his conduct was that of a prudent man, but whether you think it was.

Some middle point must be found between the horns of this dilemma.

The standards of the law are standards of general application. The law takes no account of the infinite varieties of temperament, intellect, and education which make the internal character of a given act so different in different men. It does not attempt to see men as God sees them, for more than one sufficient reason. In the first place, the impossibility of nicely measuring a man's powers and limitations is far clearer than that of ascertaining his knowledge of law, which has been thought to account for what is called the presumption that every man knows the law. But a more satisfactory explanation is, that, when men live in society, a certain average of conduct, a sacrifice of individual peculiarities going beyond a certain point, is necessary to the general welfare. If, for instance, a man is born hasty and awkward, is always having accidents and hurting himself or his neighbors, no doubt his congenital defects will be allowed for in the courts of Heaven, but his slips are no less troublesome to his neighbors than if they sprang from guilty neglect. His neighbors accordingly require him, at his proper peril, to come up to their standard, and the courts which they establish decline to take his personal equation into account.

The rule that the law does, in general, determine liability by blameworthiness, is subject to the limitation that minute differences of character are not allowed for. The law considers, in other words, what would be blameworthy in the average man, the man of ordinary intelligence and prudence, and determines liability by that. If we fall below the level in those gifts, it is our misfortune so much as that we must have at our peril, for the reasons just given. But he who is intelligent and prudent does not act at his peril, in theory of law. On the contrary, it is only when he fails to exercise the foresight of which he is capable, or exercises it with evil intent, that he is answerable for the consequences.

There are exceptions to the principle that every man is presumed to possess ordinary capacity to avoid harm to his neighbors, which illustrate the rule, and also the moral basis of liability in general. When a man has a distinct defect of such a nature that all can recognize it as making certain precautions impossible, he will not be held answerable for not taking them. A blind man is not required to see at his peril; and although he is, no doubt, bound to consider his infirmity in regulating his actions, yet if he properly finds himself in a certain situation, the neglect of precautions requiring eyesight would not prevent his recovering for an injury to himself, and, it may be presumed, would not make him liable for injuring another. So it is held that, in cases where he is the plaintiff, an infant of very tender years is only bound to take the precautions of which an infant is capable; the same principle may be cautiously applied where he is defendant. Insanity is a more difficult matter to deal with, and no general rule can be laid down about it. There is no doubt that in many cases a man may be insane, and yet perfectly capable of taking the precautions, and of being influenced by the motives, which the circumstances demand. But if insanity of a pronounced type exists, manifestly incapacitating the sufferer from complying with the rule which he has broken, good sense would require it to be admitted as an excuse.

Roberts v. Ring
173 N.W. 437 (Minn. 1919)

HALLAM, J. Plaintiff brings this action on behalf of his minor son, John B. Roberts, seven years old, to recover damages for injury from collision with defendant's automobile. The jury found for defendant. Plaintiff appeals. Plaintiff assigns as error certain portions of the charge. Defendant contends that the charge was without error and further contends that as a matter of law, defendant was without negligence and that the boy was negligent.

1. Defendant was driving south on a much traveled street in Owatonna. He was seventy-seven years old. His sight and hearing were defective. A buggy was approaching him from the south. There were other conveyances on the street. The travel was practically blocked. The boy ran from behind the buggy across the street to the west and in front of defendant's automobile. There is evidence that he had been riding on the rear of the buggy. He himself testified that he was crossing the street. As he passed in front of defendant's automobile he was struck and injured.

The question of defendant's negligence was a proper one to be submitted to the jury. Defendant was driving from four to five miles an hour, not a negligent rate of speed. If he was negligent, it was in failing to keep a proper lookout and in failing to promptly stop his car. He testified that he saw the boy when he was four or five feet from the automobile. It is a matter of common knowledge that an automobile traveling four or five miles an hour can be stopped within a very few feet, yet defendant knocked the boy down and his car passed clear over him. If defendant saw the boy, as he now claims, he was not alert in stopping his car. If he did not see him as he is alleged to have stated to others he was not keeping a sharp lookout in this crowded street. We are of the opinion that the evidence was such as to raise an issue of fact as to his negligence.

2. The question of the boy's negligence was likewise for the jury. Had a mature man acted as did this boy he might have been chargeable with negligence as a matter of law. But a boy of seven is not held to the same standard of care in self-protection. In considering his contributory negligence the standard is the degree of care commonly exercised by the ordinary boy of his age and maturity. It would be different if he had caused injury to another. In such a case he could not take advantage of his age or infirmities.

As to the negligence of defendant the court charged:

In determining whether the defendant was guilty of negligence you may take into consideration . . . the age of the defendant . . . and whether or not the defendant had any physical infirmities.

. . . As above indicated, defendant's infirmities did not tend to relieve him from the charge of negligence. On the contrary they weighed against him. Such infirmities, to the extent that they were proper to be considered at all, presented only a reason why defendant should refrain from operating an automobile on a crowded street where care was required to avoid injuring other travelers. When one, by his acts or omissions causes injury to others, his negligence is to be judged by the standard of care usually exercised by the ordinarily prudent normal man.

Order reversed.

NOTE

Beginners and experts. The law of negligence sometimes makes adjustments in setting a standard of care for various classes of persons. The Third Restatement on Liability for Physical Harm follows *Roberts* by refusing to take old age, as such, into account, although it takes into account such infirmities associated with old age by using the standard of a reasonably careful person with the same physical condition. RTT:LPH §11, comment *c*.

The question of variable standards of care also arises with different levels of performance that is expected from beginners and experts in certain endeavors. The use of a lower standard of care for beginners encourages them to undertake activities that they might not otherwise attempt, but it also exacts a subsidy from the people they unfortunately hurt, and not from the public at large. To avoid that risk, the general rule holds beginners to the standard of care expected of those who are reasonably skilled and practiced in the art. See, for example, Stevens v. Veenstra, 573 N.W.2d 341 (Mich. App. 1997). One critical exception covers cases in which the plaintiff has assumed the risk that the defendant will exercise a lower standard of care, as happens when an experienced driver agrees to teach a novice how to drive. Holland v. Pitocchelli, 13 N.E.2d 390 (Mass. 1938). See generally RST §299, comment *d,* basically endorsing a rule requiring a defendant to meet the objective standard of care. In the Third Restatement, below average skills and judgment are "generally ignored" in order to prevent the multiplication of separate standards and to forestall the risk of fraud. RTT: LPH §12, comment *b.* The inexperienced driver continues to get the benefit of the lower standard against his driving instructor, but not against an injured pedestrian who did not assume the risk. *Id.*

The converse problem arises when a defendant has greater skills than most people in a particular line of endeavor. The Second Restatement provides that the defendant is "required to exercise the skill and knowledge normally possessed by members of that profession or trade in good standing in similar communities," but that standard is subject to an important caveat — "unless he represents that he has greater or less skill" than the average. RST §299A. The Restatement (Third) on Liability for Physical Injury similarly holds that the case for the higher rule is strongest when the two parties have agreed to it, or when the defendant is engaged in dangerous activities. RTT:LPH §12. But it does not issue any categorical rule, noting that "skills or knowledge are circumstances to be taken into account in determining whether the actor has behaved as a reasonably careful person." It also expresses some doubt as to whether the skilled skier or skilled driver should be held to a higher standard if sued for a skiing accident or a highway collision, respectively. *Id.,* comment *a.* Is there any minimum standard of care that a defendant must exercise in order to remain a member of a profession in good standing?

Daniels v. Evans
224 A.2d 63 (N.H. 1966)

[Plaintiff's decedent, a 19-year-old youth, was killed when his motorcycle collided with defendant's automobile. A trial by jury resulted in a verdict for plaintiff, and the only alleged error argued on appeal was the trial court's charge pertaining to the standard of care required of the decedent.]

LAMPRON, J. As to the standard of care to be applied to the conduct of the decedent Robert E. Daniels, 19 years of age, the Trial Court charged the jury in part as follows:

"Now, he is considered a minor, being under the age of twenty-one, and a minor child must exercise the care of the average child of his or her age, experience and stage of mental development. In other words, he is not held to the same degree of care as an adult."

Concededly these instructions substantially reflect the rule by which the care of a minor has been judged heretofore in the courts of our State. Charbonneau v. MacRury [, 153 A. 457 (N.H. 1931)]. However an examination of the cases will reveal that in most the minors therein were engaged in activities appropriate to their age, experience and wisdom. These included being a pedestrian, riding a bicycle, riding a horse, [and] coasting.

We agree that minors are entitled to be judged by standards commensurate with their age, experience, and wisdom when engaged in activities appropriate to their age, experience, and wisdom. Hence when children are walking, running, playing with toys, throwing balls, operating bicycles, sliding or engaged in other childhood activities their conduct should be judged by the rule of what is reasonable conduct under the circumstances among which are the age, experience, and stage of mental development of the minor involved.

However, the question is raised by the defendant in this case whether the standard of care applied to minors in such cases should prevail when the minor is engaged in activities normally undertaken by adults. In other words, when a minor undertakes an adult activity which can result in grave danger to others and to the minor himself if the care used in the course of the activity drops below that care which the reasonable and prudent adult would use, the defendant maintains that the minor's conduct in that instance should meet the same standards as that of an adult.

Many recent cases have held that "when a minor assumes responsibility for the operation of so potentially dangerous an instrument as an automobile, he should . . . assume responsibility for its careful and safe operation in the light of adult standards." 2 Idaho L. Rev., 103, 111 (1965); Dellwo v. Pearson, 107 N.W.2d 859 (Minn. 1961). The rule has been recognized in Restatement (Second), Torts, §283A, comment *c*. . . . In an annotation in 97 A.L.R.2d 872 at page 875 it is said that recent decisions "hold that when a minor engages in such activities as the operation of an automobile or similar power driven device, he forfeits his rights to have the reasonableness of his conduct measured by a standard commensurate with his age and is thenceforth held to the same standard as all other persons."

One of the reasons for such a rule has been stated thusly in Dellwo v. Pearson, supra: "To give legal sanction to the operation of automobiles by teen-agers with less than ordinary care for the safety of others is impractical today, to say the least. We may take judicial notice of the hazards of automobile traffic, the frequency of accidents, the often catastrophic results of accidents, and the fact that immature individuals are no less prone to accidents than adults. . . . [I]t would be unfair to the public to permit a minor in the operation of a motor vehicle to observe any other standards of care and conduct than those expected of all others. A person observing children at play . . . may anticipate conduct that does not reach an adult standard of care or prudence. However, one cannot know whether the operator of an approaching automobile . . . is a minor or an adult, and usually cannot protect himself against youthful imprudence even if warned." . . .

RSA 262-A:2 which establishes rules of the road for the operation of motor vehicles on our highways reads as follows: "Required Obedience to Traffic Laws. It is unlawful and . . . a misdemeanor for *any person* to do any act forbidden or fail to perform any act required in this chapter." (Emphasis supplied.) This is some indication of an intent on the part of our Legislature that all drivers must, and have the right to expect that others using the highways, regardless of their age and experience, will, obey the traffic laws and thus exercise the adult standard of ordinary care. . . .

The rule charged by the Trial Court pertaining to the standard of care to be applied by the jury to the conduct of the minor plaintiff Robert E. Daniels in the operation of the motorcycle was proper in "the bygone days" when children were using relatively innocent contrivances. However in the circumstances of today's modern life, where vehicles moved by powerful motors are readily available and used by many minors, we question the propriety of a rule which would allow such vehicles to be operated to the hazard of the public, and to the driver himself, with less than the degree of care required of an adult.

We are of the opinion that to apply to minors a more lenient standard in the operation of motor vehicles, whether an automobile or a motorcycle, than that applied to adults is unrealistic, contrary to the expressed legislative policy, and inimical to public safety. Furthermore when a minor is operating a motor vehicle there is no reason for making a distinction based on whether he is charged with primary negligence, contributory negligence, or a causal violation of a statute and we so hold.

We hold therefore that a minor operating a motor vehicle, whether an automobile or a motorcycle, must be judged by the same standard of care as an adult and the defendant's objection to the Trial Court's charge applying a different standard to the conduct of plaintiff's intestate was valid. . . .

Exception sustained.

NOTES

1. Adult and child activities. In Charbonneau v. MacRury, 153 A. 457, 462-463 (N.H. 1931), overruled by Daniels v. Evans, the court justified its use of a variable standard of care for infants as follows:

Unless infants are to be denied the environment and association of their elders until they have acquired maturity, there must be a living relationship between them on terms which permit the child to act as a child in his stage of development. As well expect a boy to learn to swim without experience in the water as to expect him to learn to function as an adult without contact with his superiors. For the law to hold children to the exercise of the care of adults "would be to shut its eyes, ostrich-like to the facts of life and to burden unduly the child's growth to majority." [Shulman, The Standard of Care Required of Children, 37 Yale L.J. 618 (1928)]. During the period of his development he must participate in human activities on some basis of reason. Reason requires that indulgence be shown him commensurate with his want of development as indicated by his age and experience. Id. 621. Though strictly speaking it is the resultant qualities reasonably attributable to these factors that measure his capacity, it is sufficient, as a practical matter, to speak of age and experience as inclusive of these qualities. . . .

In Goss v. Allen, 360 A.2d 388 (N.J. 1976), the court affirmed a jury instruction that a 17-year-old beginning skier be held, not to the adult standard of care, but to a standard appropriate to youths of the same age. In distinguishing the case from other adult activities — driving a car or motorcycle or hunting — the court noted that youths did not need a license to ski. The unhappy dissent noted in a footnote: "No license is required for a motorized bike, but a ten-speed bike can be pedaled at 25 miles per hour on a flat road. The U.S. Consumer Product Safety Commission reports that there are 500 to 1000 fatalities and about 500,000 permanently crippled each year from bicycle mishaps," and insisted that the loss of an eye "resulting from a carelessly thrown dart, or stone, or firecracker, the death caused by a bicycle, or an individual seriously maimed due to an errant skier — all are indisputable proof of 'potentially hazardous' activity — even when the activity was not subject to government licensing."

In Dellwo v. Pearson, 107 N.W.2d 859 (Minn. 1961), a 12-year-old defendant was held to the adult standard of care in the operation of a speed boat, even though there was apparently no licensing statute for such boats. In Harrelson v. Whitehead, 365 S.W.2d 868 (Ark. 1963), a 15-year-old plaintiff operating a motorcycle was held to the adult standard of care on the issue of contributory negligence. Jackson v. McCuiston, 448 S.W.2d 33 (Ark. 1969), held that a 13-year-old farm boy should be judged by the adult standard of care in operating a tractor-propelled stalk cutter, a large piece of machinery with a dangerous cutting blade. In Purtle v. Shelton, 474 S.W.2d 123 (Ark. 1971), the Arkansas court cut back on *Jackson*, refusing to hold a 17-year-old boy to the adult standard of care in the use of dangerous firearms. It held that a lower standard for minors was appropriate because deer hunting was not exclusively an adult activity. One dissenting justice protested: "Because a bullet fired from the gun by a minor is just as deadly as a bullet fired by an adult, I'm at a loss to understand why one with 'buck fever' because of his minority is entitled to exercise any less care than any one else deer hunting. One killed by a bullet so fired would be just as dead in one instance as the other and without any more warning." Is hunting more or less of an adult activity than driving? Most recently, in Hudson-Connor v. Putney, 86 P.3d 106, 111 (Or. App. 2004), Brewer, J., held first that it was not an adult activity for a 14-year-old child to entrust a golf cart to an 11-year-old plaintiff, and further, that driving a golf cart on private property was not an adult activity: "To obtain a license to operate an automobile on the highways, a driver must demonstrate mastery of those skills by passing a knowledge test, a driving skills test, and, if the driver is under the age of 18, a safe driving practices test. No such license is required to operate a motorized golf cart on premises that are not open to the public. Significantly, there is no evidence in the record that the operation of golf carts on private premises and automobiles on premises open to the public requires similar driving skills beyond the most rudimentary level. In short, on the factual record before us, we conclude that the operation of a motorized golf cart on private premises does not require adult qualifications." Should the differential standard matter if, as here, the defendant crashed into the plaintiff when he stepped by mistake on the accelerator instead of the brake?

The Third Restatement adheres to the general rule, holding a child to the standard of "a reasonably careful person of the same age, intelligence, and experience." RTT:LPH §10. In addition to the exception for adult-like activities, it also provides that a child under five years of age is incapable of negligence. Does this confer additional duties on the child's guardian?

2. Reasonable plaintiff versus reasonable defendant. In Daniels v. Evans, the court held both child plaintiffs and child defendants to the same standard of care in highway accidents, a view that is widely followed today. See RTT: LPH §10, comment *e*. While the case law has moved toward the unitary standard of care for all youthful drivers, the case for a general dual standard was advanced in James, The Qualities of the Reasonable Man in Negligence Cases, 16 Mo. L. Rev. 1, 1-2 (1951):

> By and large the law has chosen external, objective standards of conduct. The reasonably prudent man is, to be sure, endowed with some of the qualities of the person whose conduct is being judged, especially where the latter has greater knowledge, skill, or the like, than people generally. But many of the actor's shortcomings such as awkwardness, faulty perception, or poor judgment, are not taken into account if they fall below the general level of the community. This means that individuals are often held guilty of legal fault for failing to live up to a standard which as a matter of fact they cannot meet. Such a result shocks people who believe in refining the fault principle so as to make legal liability correspond more closely to personal moral shortcoming. There has, therefore, been some pressure towards the adoption of a more subjective test. But if the standard of conduct is relaxed for *defendants* who cannot meet a normal standard, then the burden of accident loss resulting from the extra hazards created by society's most dangerous

groups (e.g. the young, the novice, the accident prone) will be thrown on the innocent victims of substandard behavior. Such a conclusion shocks people who believe that the compensation of accident victims is a more important objective of modern tort law than a further refinement of the tort principle, and that compensation should prevail when the two objectives conflict. The application of a relaxed subjective standard to the issue of *plaintiff's* contributory negligence, however, involves no such conflict. On this issue the forces of the two objectives combine to demand a subjective test: the refinement of the fault principle furthers the compensation of accident victims by cutting down a defense that would stand in its way. For this reason the writer has elsewhere developed the thesis that there should be an explicit double standard of conduct, namely, an external standard for a defendant's negligence, and a (relaxed) subjective standard for contributory negligence. Even if this thesis is rejected, the same result probably prevails anyhow, because the application of the legal standard is largely left to the jury, and juries, by and large, tend to resolve doubts on both issues in favor of plaintiffs.

Using separate standards for negligence and contributory negligence leaves the outcome unclear when both parties are children and both are injured. Should the result depend on whether either or both are insured? Note that the double standard necessarily increases the administrative costs of both settlement and litigation. James's early argument, moreover, is regarded as less persuasive under a comparative negligence regime, which reduces the impact of a finding of contributory negligence by allowing apportionment of loss between the parties. See generally Restatement (Third) of Torts: Apportionment of Liability [RTT:AL] §3 (abolishing special ameliorative doctrines for defining plaintiff's negligence); RST §283 ("Unless the actor is a child, the standard of conduct to which he must conform to avoid being negligent is that of a reasonable man under like circumstances."); RTT:LPH §10, comment *e* (regarding children). Note, however, some differences in standards may still be required in professional interactions between physicians and patients, given the fundamental difference in roles.

Breunig v. American Family Insurance Co.
173 N.W.2d 619 (Wis. 1970)

[Plaintiff brought this action for personal injuries sustained when his car was struck by a car driven by Erma Veith, an insured of the defendant. The accident occurred when Mrs. Veith's car veered across the center of the road into the lane in which plaintiff was traveling. Defendant argued that Mrs. Veith "was not negligent because just prior to the collision she suddenly and without warning was seized with a mental aberration or delusion which rendered her unable to operate the automobile with her conscious mind." The jury returned a verdict finding her causally negligent on the theory she "had knowledge or forewarning of her mental delusions or disability." From the award of $7,000 damages, the defendant insurance company appeals.]

HALLOWS, C.J. There is no question that Erma Veith was subject at the time of the accident to an insane delusion which directly affected her ability to operate her car in an ordinarily prudent manner and caused the accident. The specific question considered by the jury under the negligence inquiry was whether she had such foreknowledge of her susceptibility to such a mental aberration, delusion or hallucination as to make her negligent in driving a car at all under such conditions.

. . . The evidence established that Mrs. Veith, while returning home after taking her husband to work, saw a white light on the back of a car ahead of her. She followed this light for three or four blocks. Mrs. Veith did not remember anything else except landing in a field, lying in the side of the road and people talking. She recalled awaking in the hospital.

The psychiatrist testified Mrs. Veith told him she was driving on a road when she believed that God was taking ahold of the steering wheel and was directing her car. She saw the truck coming and stepped on the gas in order to become airborne because she knew she could fly because Batman does it. To her surprise she was not airborne before striking the truck but after the impact she was flying. . . .

The insurance company argues Erma Veith was not negligent as a matter of law because there is no evidence upon which the jury could find that she had knowledge or warning or should have reasonably foreseen that she might be subject to a mental delusion which would suddenly cause her to lose control of the car. Plaintiff argues there was such evidence of forewarning and also suggests Erma Veith should be liable because insanity should not be a defense in negligence cases.

The case was tried on the theory that some forms of insanity are a defense to and preclude liability for negligence under the doctrine of Theisen v. Milwaukee Automobile Mut. Ins. Co.[, 19 N.W.2d 393 (Wis. 1963)]. We agree. Not all types of insanity vitiate responsibility for a negligent tort. The question of liability in every case must depend upon the kind and nature of the insanity. The effect of the mental illness or mental hallucinations or disorder must be such as to affect the person's ability to understand and appreciate the duty which rests upon him to drive his car with ordinary care, or if the insanity does not affect such understanding and appreciation, it must affect his ability to control his car in an ordinarily prudent manner. And in addition, there must be an absence of notice or forewarning to the person that he may be suddenly subject to such a type of insanity or mental illness.

In *Theisen* we recognized one was not negligent if he was unable to conform his conduct through no fault of his own but held a sleeping driver negligent as a matter of law because one is always given conscious warnings of drowsiness and if a person does not heed such warnings and continues to drive his car, he is negligent for continuing to drive under such conditions. But we distinguished those exceptional cases of loss of consciousness resulting from injury inflicted by an outside force, or fainting, or heart attack, or epileptic seizure, or other illness which suddenly incapacitates the driver of an automobile when the occurrence of such disability is not attended with sufficient warning or should not have been reasonably foreseen. . . .

There are authorities which generally hold insanity is not a defense in tort cases except for intentional torts. Restatement, 2 Torts, 2d, p. 16, sec. 283 B, and appendix (1966) and cases cited therein. These cases rest on the historical view of strict liability without regard to the fault of the individual. Prosser, in his Law of Torts (3d ed.), p. 1028, states this view is a historical survival which originated in the dictum in Weaver v. Ward (1616), Hob. 134, 80 English Reports 284, when the action of trespass still rested upon strict liability. He points out that when the modern law developed to the point of holding the defendant liable for negligence, the dictum was repeated in some cases.

The policy basis of holding a permanently insane person liable for his tort is: (1) Where one of two innocent persons must suffer a loss it should be borne by the one who occasioned it; (2) to induce those interested in the estate of the insane person (if he has one) to restrain and control him and; (3) the fear an insanity defense would lead to false claims of insanity to avoid liability. . . .

We think the statement that insanity is no defense is too broad when it is applied to a negligence case where the driver is suddenly overcome without forewarning by a mental disability or disorder which incapacitates him from conforming his conduct to the standards of a reasonable man under like circumstances. These are rare cases indeed, but their rarity is no reason for overlooking their existence and the justification which is the basis of the whole doctrine of liability for negligence, i.e., that it is unjust to hold a man responsible for his conduct which he is incapable of avoiding and which incapability was unknown to him prior to the accident.

We need not reach the question of contributory negligence of an insane person or the question of comparative negligence as those problems are not now presented. All we hold is that a sudden mental incapacity equivalent in its effect to such physical causes as a sudden heart attack, epileptic seizure, stroke, or fainting should be treated alike and not under the general rule of insanity. . . .

The insurance company argues that since the psychiatrist was the only expert witness who testified concerning the mental disability of Mrs. Veith and the lack of forewarning that as a matter of law there was no forewarning and she could not be held negligent and the trial court should have so held.

While there was testimony of friends indicating she was normal for some months prior to the accident, the psychiatrist testified the origin of her mental illness appeared in August, 1965, prior to the accident. In that month Mrs. Veith visited the Necedah Shrine where she was told the Blessed Virgin had sent her to the shrine. She was told to pray for survival. Since that time she felt it had been revealed to her the end of the world was coming and that she was picked by God to survive. Later she had visions of God judging people and sentencing them to Heaven or Hell; she thought Batman was good and was trying to help save the world and her husband was possessed of the devil. Mrs. Veith told her daughter about her visions.

The question is whether she had warning or knowledge which would reasonably lead her to believe that hallucinations would occur and be such as to affect her driving an automobile. Even though the doctor's testimony is uncontradicted, it need not be accepted by the jury. It is an expert's opinion but it is not conclusive. It is for the jury to decide whether the facts underpinning an expert opinion are true. . . . The jury could find that a woman, who believed she had a special relationship to God and was the chosen one to survive the end of the world, could believe that God would take over the direction of her life to the extent of driving her car. Since these mental aberrations were not constant, the jury could infer she had knowledge of her condition and the likelihood of a hallucination just as one who has knowledge of a heart condition knows the possibility of an attack. While the evidence may not be strong upon which to base an inference, especially in view of the fact that two jurors dissented on this verdict and expressly stated they could find no evidence of forewarning, nevertheless, the evidence to sustain the verdict of the jury need not constitute the great weight and clear preponderance.

The insurance company claims the jury was perverse because the verdict is contrary both to the evidence and to the law. We think this argument is without merit.

NOTES

1. *Insanity in automobile cases.* In light of the difficulties of proof under the insanity system, why not make liability turn solely on conformity with the rules of the road? Note, however, that the *Breunig* approach to insanity still governs automobile accidents. In Ramey v. Knorr, 124 P.3d 314, 319-320 (Wash. App. 2005), the defendant Knorr turned her car around on I-405 and rammed headlong into the plaintiff in an attempt to commit suicide. Her defense of sudden mental incapacity was rejected because the record showed "that in 1994, Knorr had a mental breakdown and was hospitalized for ten days. During that period, Knorr believed the person she worked for was conspiring to steal her and her husband's assets, was going to kill them, and was poisoning her. She also had concerns about

her brother being a murderer. . . . Knorr was diagnosed with possible delusional disorder, was put on medication, and was advised to see a psychiatrist. . . . [B]eginning in March 2001, Knorr's delusional thoughts about her brother being a murderer came back. . . . [B]y November 2001, her thoughts escalated and Mr. Knorr tried to get her to agree to go to the hospital. Knorr wanted to wait until after the holidays to go to the hospital and had an appointment scheduled for two days after the accident."

2. *Institutionalized insane persons. Breunig*, however, has been narrowed in custodial settings. In Gould v. American Family Mutual Insurance, 543 N.W.2d 282 (Wis. 1996), the defendant, an institutionalized patient with Alzheimer's disease, injured his paid caregiver. The Court refused to apply *Breunig*.

> In sum, we agree with the Goulds that ordinarily a mentally disabled person is responsible for his or her torts. However, we conclude that this rule does not apply in this case because the circumstances totally negate the rationale [in *Breunig*] behind the rule and would place an unreasonable burden on the negligent institutionalized mentally disabled. When a mentally disabled person injures an employed caretaker, the injured party can reasonably foresee the danger and is not "innocent" of the risk involved. By placing a mentally disabled person in an institution or similar restrictive setting, "those interested in the estate" of that person are not likely to be in need of an inducement for greater restraint. It is incredible to assert that a tortfeasor would "simulate or pretend insanity" over a prolonged period of time and even be institutionalized in order to avoid being held liable for damages for some future civil act. Therefore, we hold that a person institutionalized, as here, with a mental disability, and who does not have the capacity to control or appreciate his or her conduct cannot be liable for injuries caused to caretakers who are employed for financial compensation.

Thereafter, in Jankee v. Clark County, 612 N.W.2d 297, 316 (Wis. 2000), the Wisconsin Supreme Court refused to impose liability on an institution that had not restrained the plaintiff, a mental health patient, who had injured himself while trying to escape by jumping through a window that he had pried open in the county psychiatric hospital. Following *Breunig*, Prosser, J., held the insane *plaintiff* to an objective standard of care, again to minimize the level of institutionalization required of insane people. Prosser, J., distinguished *Gould*, noting the perverse incentive on the psychiatric hospital "to intensify security considerations for the mentally disabled, not to protect the disabled but rather to protect themselves from liability," for example, by "restor[ing] bars to all windows in the facility." How do these cases square up with James' rationale for a lower standard for contributory negligence?

In Creasy v. Rusk, 730 N.E.2d 659, 667 (Ind. 2000), however, the court denied liability to a caregiver who was injured by an institutionalized patient. "Unlike the typical victim supporting the Restatement rationale, Creasy [the plaintiff] was not a member of the public at large, unable to anticipate or safeguard against the harm she encountered. Creasy knew of Rusk's violent history. She could have changed her course of action or requested additional assistance when she recognized Rusk's state of mind on the evening when she received the alleged injury." Similarly in Berberian v. Lynn, 845 A.2d 122, 129 (N.J. 2004), yet another Alzheimer's case, the court held that "a mentally disabled patient . . . does not owe his or her caregiver a duty of care." Why not resolve these cases (and *McGuire, supra* at 50) with assumption of risk, leaving the plaintiff with worker's compensation coverage? See generally Light, Rejecting the Logic of Confinement: Care Relationships and the Mentally Disabled Under Tort Law, 109 Yale L.J. 381 (1999).

Fletcher v. City of Aberdeen
338 P.2d 743 (Wash. 1959)

FOSTER, J. . . . For the purpose of placing electric wires underground, the city dug a ditch in the parking strip adjacent to the sidewalk at the intersection of Broadway and Fourth streets in the city of Aberdeen. Suitable barricades were erected to protect pedestrians from falling into the excavation, but, unfortunately, at the time of the mishap in question, one of the city's employees had removed the barriers to facilitate his work in the excavation. When he went elsewhere to work, he negligently failed to replace the barricades, which left the excavation unprotected. In approaching the intersection, the respondent husband, who had been blind since his eighth year, had his kit of piano-tuning tools in his left hand and his cane in his right. With the cane he was cautiously feeling his way. Because the protective barriers had been removed, the existence of the excavation was unknown to the respondent. By the use of the cane, the barriers would have protected the respondent if they had been in place. The jury was entitled to find that the city was negligent in removing the barriers without providing other warning.

. . . The city's argument is that it had discharged its duty by the erection of barricades. It may be assumed for present purposes, that the barriers originally erected were sufficient to discharge the city's duty of maintaining its streets and adjacent parking strips in a reasonably safe condition for pedestrian use. However, the city's argument completely ignores the undisputed evidence that its workman had removed the barricades and that the accident in question occurred during this interval. The duty of maintaining the sidewalks and adjacent parking strips is a continuing one. . . .

The city assigns error upon the giving of instruction No. 9.[1] The city contends that this instruction places a higher degree of care upon it with

---

1. "You are instructed that that portion of a city street lying between the sidewalk and the curb, commonly referred to as the parking strip, is as much a part of the public street as any other portion. It

reference to the parking strips than the degree of care required as to sidewalks. This argument overlooks instructions Nos. 7 and 7A in which the jury was told that the city was not an insurer and was required only to keep the streets and sidewalks in a reasonably safe condition, that this duty did not require a complete barricade but that only reasonable warning was required, and that it was a question of fact whether the city discharged this duty. . . .

The city assigns error upon the refusal to instruct as requested that "The fact that the plaintiff is blind does not impose on the City any higher degree of care." . . . The supreme court of Oregon recently commented:

" . . . Public thoroughfares are for the beggar on his crutches as well as the millionaire in his limousine. Neither is it the policy of the law to discriminate against those who suffer physical infirmity. The blind and the halt may use the streets without being guilty of negligence if, in so doing, they exercise that degree of care which an ordinarily prudent person similarly afflicted would exercise under the same circumstances. . . ." Weinstein v. Wheeler, 127 Or. 406 (1928). . . .

The city is charged with knowledge that its streets will be used by those who are physically infirm as well as those in perfect physical condition. . . . The obligations are correlative. The person under a physical disability is obliged to use the care which a reasonable person under the same or similar disability would exercise under the circumstances. The city, on the other hand, is obliged to afford that degree of protection which would bring to the notice of the person so afflicted the danger to be encountered. There was no error, therefore, in the denial of the appellant's requested instruction No. 13. . . .

The judgment is, therefore, affirmed.

WEAVER, C.J., and DONWORTH, OTT and HUNTER, JJ., concur.

NOTE

Legal blindness. The Third Restatement says that "the conduct of an actor with physical disability is negligent only if it does not conform to that of a reasonably careful person with the same disability." RTT:LPH §11(a). In Poyner v. Loftus, 694 A.2d 69 (D.C. 1997), a legally blind plaintiff, capable of seeing about six to eight feet in front of him, was injured as he walked up an incline to the defendant's cleaners about four feet above street level. A bush had been removed from the end of the incline, which plaintiff would have seen had he not been distracted by a call from down

---

is not unlawful for a person to step upon or walk across a parking strip. It is the duty of the municipality to keep its parking strips in a reasonably safe condition so that persons traveling thereon, exercising ordinary prudence and caution, may do so with safety."

the street. The court affirmed a summary judgment for defendant, noting that plaintiff's testimony conclusively showed his own negligence when "he turned his head, but continued to walk forward," for those with defective eyesight must take keener watchfulness in conducting their own affairs. Why not apply comparative negligence?

Robinson v. Pioche, Bayerque & Co.
5 Cal. 460 (1855)

Appeal from the Superior Court of the City of San Francisco

Action for damages sustained by the plaintiff in falling into an uncovered hole, dug in the sidewalk in front of defendants' premises. . . .

HEYDENFELDT, J.... If the defendants were at fault in leaving an uncovered hole in the sidewalk of a public street, the intoxication of the plaintiff cannot excuse such gross negligence. A drunken man is as much entitled to a safe street, as a sober one, and much more in need of it.

The judgment is reversed and the cause remanded.

Denver & Rio Grande R.R. v. Peterson
69 P. 578 (Colo. 1902)

CAMPBELL, C.J. The care required of a warehouseman is the same, whether he be rich or poor. For, if the fact that he is rich requires of him greater care than if he possessed only moderate means or is poor, then, if he were extremely poor, the care required might be such as practically to amount to nothing; and no one would claim that such an uncertain and sliding rule should be the measure of his liability. . . .

NOTE

The relevance of wealth to negligence liability. Peterson suggests that the level of care required of a defendant is constant regardless of its wealth. Professors Abraham and Jeffries in Punitive Damages and the Rule of Law: The Role of Defendant's Wealth, 18 J. Legal Stud. 415, 416-418 (1989), justified the rule as follows:

> The two major purposes for awarding compensatory tort damages are deterrence of socially undesirable conduct and compensation of the victims of such misconduct.
>
> First, and most importantly, the defendant's wealth is irrelevant to deterrence. Whether the defendant is rich or not simply has no logical

bearing on the inhibitory role of the threat of tort liability. Deterrence theory is based on the (usually and to one or another extent plausible) assumption that actors weigh the expected costs and benefits of their future actions. Specifically, a potentially liable defendant will compare the benefits it will derive from an action that risks tort liability against the discounted present expected value of the liability that will be imposed if the risk occurs. Whether a defendant is wealthy or poor, this cost-benefit calculation is the same. If, as is likely, a wealthy defendant derives no greater benefit from a given action than a poor defendant, then both will be equally deterred (or equally undeterred) by the threat of tort liability. A defendant's existing assets do not increase the expected value of a given future action. Therefore they do not require any adjustment in the level of sanction needed to offset that expected value. The defendant's wealth or lack of it is thus irrelevant to the deterrence of socially undesirable conduct, and evidence on the subject is inadmissible in the typical tort action claiming compensatory damages. . . .

Defendant's wealth is also irrelevant to the compensation aims of conventional tort liability. The successful tort plaintiff is entitled to recover in full for all losses proximately resulting from the action for which the defendant is held liable. The wealth available to the defendant to satisfy this obligation may be an important practical concern in settlement negotiations, but it is irrelevant to plaintiff's right of recovery. If evidence of the defendant's wealth were admissible, and if the jury took such considerations into account, the plaintiff's right to recover and the magnitude of the defendant's liability would depend on the identity of the defendant, rather than on the nature of the defendant's action and the extent of the plaintiff's loss. Although juries sometimes act as if they knew the extent of the defendant's wealth—to the point that commentators have coined the term "deep pocket" to explain the phenomenon—the law governing recovery of compensatory damages excludes such considerations as best it can.

The position of Abraham and Jeffries has been challenged in Arlen, Should Defendants' Wealth Matter?, 21 J. Legal Stud. 413, 422 (1992). Professor Arlen first notes that all individuals are risk averse (that is, they will pay a premium in order to avoid uncertainty) and then concludes that wealthier persons should be subjected to a higher standard of care. She writes: "If individuals are risk averse, then, all other things being equal, a wealthier potential defendant has a lower marginal utility of wealth than does a poorer potential defendant: he is, in other words, less adversely affected by a given expenditure on care than is a poorer person." The richer person thus sacrifices less utility for any given unit of wealth than does the poor person. This conclusion holds whether or not a defendant is able to purchase liability insurance. In principle, Arlen's argument calls not for a simple division of defendants into rich and poor persons, but for an infinite gradation of defendants by wealth. How is such a system to be administered? Does it matter how pronounced risk aversion proves in practice? What standard should be applied to corporate defendants with both rich and poor shareholders? Note that at present, proof of defendant's insurance or net worth is not admissible into evidence in most states and under the Federal Rules of Evidence, R. 411. It is, however, discoverable. See Fed. R. Civ. P. 26(b)(2).

A recent contribution to this debate by Kaplow & Shavell, Should Legal Rules Favor the Poor? Clarifying the Role of Legal Rules and the Income Tax in Redistributing Income, 20 J. Legal. Stud. 821, 823 (2000), rejects the proposition that any substantive legal rule should offer a special preference to the poor because:

> the income tax system possesses several clear advantages over legal rules as a means of redistribution. Notably, the income tax system affects the entire population and, by its nature treats individuals on the basis of their income. By contrast, the influence of legal rules often is confined to the small fraction of individuals who find themselves involved in legal disputes. Also, legal rules often are very imprecise tools for redistribution because there tends to be substantial income variation within groups of plaintiffs and defendants (so that much of the redistribution will be in the wrong direction). Additionally, many legal rules — such as those of contract, corporate, and commercial law — often leave the distribution of income essentially unchanged because price adjustments negate the distributive effects of the legal rules.

SECTION C. CALCULUS OF RISK

This section turns to the judicial efforts to fashion and apply a standard of reasonable care. Our discussion proceeds on two levels. The first deals with the commonsense, intuitive meaning of negligence as it applies to ordinary individuals and corporate or business entities. The second addresses the judicial effort to impart a more precise economic meaning to the term, adopting the language of costs and benefits — the "calculus" of risk. Both approaches have uneasily coexisted throughout the history of the common law.

Blyth v. Birmingham Water Works
156 Eng. Rep. 1047 (Ex. 1856)

[The defendants owned a nonprofit waterworks charged by statute with the laying of water mains and fire plugs in the city streets. The pipes were to be buried 18 inches under ground. The fireplug in the instant case was built "according to the best known system, and the materials of it were at the time of the accident sound and in good order."]

On the 24th of February, a large quantity of water, escaping from the neck of the main, forced its way through the ground into the plaintiff's house. The apparatus had been laid down 25 years, and had worked well during that time. The defendants' engineer stated, that the water might have forced its way through the brickwork round the neck of the main, and that the accident might have been caused by the frost, inasmuch as the expansion of the water would force up the plug out of the neck, and the stopper being encrusted with ice would not suffer the plug to ascend. One of the severest frosts on record set in on the 15th of January, 1855, and continued until after the accident in question. An incrustation of ice and snow had gathered about the stopper, and in the street all round, and also for some inches between the stopper and the plug. The ice had been observed on the surface of the ground for a considerable time before the accident. A short time after the accident, the company's turncock removed the ice from the stopper, took out the plug, and replaced it.

The judge left it to the jury to consider whether the company had used proper care to prevent the accident. He thought that, if the defendants had taken out the ice adhering to the plug, the accident would not have happened, and left it to the jury to say whether they ought to have removed the ice. The jury found a verdict for the plaintiff for the sum claimed. . . .

ALDERSON, B. I am of opinion that there was no evidence to be left to the jury. The case turns upon the question, whether the facts proved shew that the defendants were guilty of negligence. Negligence is the omission to do something which a reasonable man, guided upon those considerations which ordinarily regulate the conduct of human affairs, would do, or doing something which a prudent and reasonable man would not do. The defendants might have been liable for negligence, if, unintentionally, they omitted to do that which a reasonable person would have done, or did that which a person taking reasonable precautions would not have done. A reasonable man would act with reference to the average circumstances of the temperature in ordinary years. The defendants had provided against such frosts as experience would have led men, acting prudently, to provide against; and they are not guilty of negligence, because their precautions proved insufficient against the effects of the extreme severity of the frost of 1855, which penetrated to a greater depth than any which ordinarily occurs south of the polar regions. Such a state of circumstances constitutes a contingency against which no reasonable man can provide. The result was an accident, for which the defendants cannot be held liable.

BRAMWELL, B. The Act of Parliament directed the defendants to lay down pipes, with plugs in them, as safety-valves, to prevent the bursting of the pipes. The plugs were properly made, and of proper material; but there was an accumulation of ice about this plug, which prevented it from acting properly. The defendants were not bound to keep the plugs clear. It appears to me that the plaintiff was under quite as much obligation to remove the ice and snow which had accumulated, as the defendants. However that may be, it appears to me that it would be monstrous to hold the defendants responsible because they did not foresee and prevent an accident, the cause of which was so obscure, that it was not discovered until many months after the accident had happened.

Verdict to be entered for the defendants.

NOTE

The influence of Blyth. Baron Alderon's definition of negligence continues to exert enormous influence on modern tort litigation. Section 2:10 of the New York Pattern Jury Instructions — Civil (West 2006) reads:

> Negligence is lack of ordinary care. It is a failure to use that degree of care that a reasonably prudent person would have used under the same circumstances. Negligence may arise from doing an act that a reasonably prudent person would not have done under the circumstances, or, on the other hand, from failing to do an act that a reasonably prudent person would have done under the same circumstances.

In applying this formula in *Blyth*, should the focus be on the design of the original system or on the removal of the ice after the storm? If the former, is it sufficient if the pipes withstand the frost found in "ordinary years?" If the latter, does the formula indicate who has the duty to remove the ice, and why?

Eckert v. Long Island R.R.
43 N.Y. 502 (1871)

... The case, as made by the plaintiff, was, that the deceased received an injury from a locomotive engine of the defendant, which resulted in his death, on the 26th day of November, 1867, under the following circumstances:

He was standing in the afternoon of the day named, in conversation with another person about fifty feet from the defendant's track, in East New York, as a train of cars was coming in from Jamaica, at a rate of speed estimated by the plaintiff's witnesses of from twelve to twenty miles per hour. The plaintiff's witnesses heard no signal either from the whistle or the bell upon the engine. The engine was constructed to run either way without turning, and it was then running backward with the cow-catcher next [to] the train it was drawing, and nothing in front to remove obstacles from the track. The claim of the plaintiff was that the evidence authorized the jury to find that the speed of the train was improper and negligent in that particular place, it being a thickly populated neighborhood, and one of the stations of the road.

The evidence on the part of the plaintiff, also showed, that a child three or four years old, was sitting or standing upon the track of the defendant's road as the train of cars was approaching, and was liable to be run over, if not removed; and the deceased, seeing the danger of the child, ran to it, and seizing it, threw it clear of the track on the side opposite to that from which he came; but continuing across the track himself, was struck by the step or some part of the locomotive or tender, thrown down, and received injuries from which he died the same night.

The evidence on the part of defendant, tended to prove that the cars were being run at a very moderate speed, not over seven or eight miles per hour, that the signals required by law were given, and that the child was not on the track over which the cars were passing, but on a side track near the main track.

So far as there was any conflict of evidence or question of fact, the questions were submitted to the jury. At the close of the plaintiff's case, the counsel for the defendant moved for a nonsuit upon the ground that it appeared that the deceased's negligence contributed to the injury, and the motion was denied and an exception taken. After the evidence was all in, the judge was requested by the counsel for the defendant to charge the jury, in different forms, that if the deceased voluntarily placed himself in peril from which he received the injury, to save the child, whether the child was or was not in danger, the plaintiff could not recover, and all the requests were refused and exceptions taken, and the question whether the negligence of the intestate contributed to the accident was submitted to the jury. The jury found a verdict for the plaintiff, and the judgment entered thereon was affirmed, on appeal, by the Supreme Court, and from the latter judgment the defendant has appealed to this court.

GROVER, J. The important question in this case arises upon the exception taken by the defendant's counsel to the denial of his motion for a nonsuit, made upon the ground that the negligence of the plaintiff's intestate contributed to the injury that caused his death. The evidence showed that the train was approaching in plain view of the deceased, and had he for his own purposes attempted to cross the track, or with a view to save property placed himself voluntarily in a position where he might have received an injury from a collision with the train, his conduct would have been grossly negligent, and no recovery could have been had for such injury. But the evidence further showed that there was a small child upon the track who, if not rescued, must have been inevitably crushed by the rapidly approaching train. This the deceased saw, and he owed a duty of important obligation to this child to rescue it from its extreme peril, if he could do so without incurring great danger to himself. Negligence implies some act of commission or omission wrongful in itself. Under the circumstances in which the deceased was placed, it was not wrongful in him to make every effort in his power to rescue the child, compatible with a reasonable regard for his own safety. It was his duty to exercise his judgment as to whether he could probably save the child without serious injury to himself. If, from the appearances, he believed that he could, it was not negligence to make an attempt so to do, although believing that possibly he might fail and receive an injury himself. He had no time for deliberation. He must act instantly, if at all, as a moment's delay would have been fatal to the child. The law has so high a regard for human life that it will not impute negligence to an effort to preserve it, unless made under such circumstances as to constitute rashness in the judgment of prudent persons. For a person engaged in his ordinary affairs, or in the mere protection of property, knowingly and voluntarily to place himself in a position where he is liable to receive a serious injury, is negligence, which will preclude a recovery for an injury so received; but when the exposure is for the purpose of saving life, it is not wrongful, and therefore not negligent unless such as to be regarded either rash or reckless. The jury were warranted in finding the deceased free from negligence under the rule as above stated. . . .

ALLEN, J., dissenting. The plaintiff's intestate was not placed in the peril from which he received the injury resulting in his death, by any act or omission of duty of the defendants, its servants, or agents. He went upon the track of the defendant's road in front of an approaching train, voluntarily, in the exercise of his free will, and while in the full possession of all his faculties, and with capacity to judge of the danger. His action was the result of his own choice, and such choice not compulsory. He was not compelled, or apparently compelled, to take any action to avoid a peril, and harm to himself, from the negligent or wrongful act of the defendant, or the agents in charge of the train. The plaintiff's rights are the same as those of the intestate would have been, had he survived the injury and brought the action, and must be tested by the same rules; and to him and consequently to the plaintiff, the maxim volenti non fit injuria applies. It is a well established rule, that no one can maintain an action for a wrong, when he consents or contributes to the act which occasions his loss. One who with liberty of choice, and knowledge of the hazard of injury, places himself in a position of danger, does so at his own peril, and must take the consequences of his act.

Terry, Negligence
29 Harv. L. Rev. 40, 42-44 (1915)

To make conduct negligent the risk involved in it must be unreasonably great; some injurious consequences of it must be not only possible or in a sense probable, but unreasonably probable. It is quite impossible in the business of life to avoid taking risks of injury to one's self or others, and the law does not forbid doing so; what it requires is that the risk be not unreasonably great. The essence of negligence is unreasonableness; due care is simply reasonable conduct. There is no mathematical rule of percentage of probabilities to be followed here. A risk is not necessarily unreasonable because the harmful consequence is more likely than not to follow the conduct, nor reasonable because the chances are against that. A very large risk may be reasonable in some circumstances, and a small risk unreasonable in other circumstances. When due care consists in taking precautions against harm, only reasonable precautions need be taken, not every conceivable or possible precaution. And precautions need not be taken against every conceivable or foreseeable danger, but only against probable dangers. The books are full of cases where persons have been held not negligent for not guarding against a certain harmful event, on the ground that they need not reasonably have expected it to happen. . . .

The reasonableness of a given risk may depend upon the following five factors:

(1) The magnitude of the risk. A risk is more likely to be unreasonable the greater it is.

(2) The value or importance of that which is exposed to the risk, which is the object that the law desires to protect, and may be called the principal object. The reasonableness of a risk means its reasonableness with respect to the principal object.

(3) A person who takes a risk of injuring the principal object usually does so because he has some reason of his own for such conduct, — is pursuing some object of his own. This may be called the collateral object. In some cases, at least, the value or importance of the collateral object is properly to be considered in deciding upon the reasonableness of the risk.

(4) The probability that the collateral object will be attained by the conduct which involves risk to the principal; the utility of the risk.

(5) The probability that the collateral object would not have been attained without taking the risk; the necessity of the risk. The following case will serve as an illustration.

The plaintiff's intestate, seeing a child on a railroad track just in front of a rapidly approaching train, went upon the track to save him. He did save him, but was himself killed by the train. The jury were allowed to find that he had not been guilty of contributory negligence. The question was of course whether he had exposed himself to an unreasonably great risk. Here the above-mentioned elements of reasonableness were as follows:

(1) The magnitude of the risk was the probability that he would be killed or hurt. That was very great.

(2) The principal object was his own life, which was very valuable.

(3) The collateral object was the child's life, which was also very valuable.

(4) The utility of the risk was the probability that he could save the child. That must have been fairly great, since he in fact succeeded. Had there been no fair chance of saving the child, the conduct would have been unreasonable and negligent.

(5) The necessity of the risk was the probability that the child would not have saved himself by getting off the track in time.

Here, although the magnitude of the risk was very great and the principal object very valuable, yet the value of the collateral object and the great utility and necessity of the risk counterbalanced those considerations, and made the risk reasonable. The same risk would have been unreasonable, had the creature on the track been a kitten, because the value of the collateral object would have been small. There is no general rule that human life may not be put at risk in order to save property; but since life is more valuable than property, such a risk has often been held unreasonable in particular cases, which has given rise to dicta to the effect that it is always so. But in the circumstances of other cases a risk of that sort has been held reasonable.

Seavey, Negligence — Subjective or Objective?
41 Harv. L. Rev. 1, 8 n.7 (1927)

We must not assume that we can rely upon any formula in regard to "balancing interests" to solve negligence cases. The phrase is only a convenient one to indicate factors which may be considered and should not connote any mathematical correspondence. Thus I would assume that an actor is liable if, to save his own horse of equal value with the plaintiff's, he were to take a fifty per cent chance of killing the plaintiff's horse, while it would at least be more doubtful whether he might not take a fifty per cent chance of killing another to save his own life. In either event, if the plaintiff's and the defendant's interests are considered of equal value, the defendant would not be liable upon the theory of balancing interests. Upon the same theory one doing an unlawful act or an act in preparation for one, would be liable to any one injured as a consequence, since, by hypothesis, his act has no social value. In the field of negligence, interests are balanced only in the sense that the purposes of the actor, the nature of his act and the harm that may result from action or inaction are elements to be considered. Some of these elements are not considered when the actor knows or desires that his conduct will result in interference with the plaintiff or his property. Thus if, to save his life, *A* intentionally destroys ten cents worth of *B*'s property, *A* must pay; if, however, he takes a ten per cent chance of killing *B* in an effort to save his own life, his conduct might not be found to be wrongful, although obviously *B* would much prefer, antecedently, to lose ten cents worth of property than to submit to a ten per cent chance of being killed.

NOTE

An economic or moral calculus. It is perhaps useful to formalize the intuitions that are present in Terry and Seavey. The Terry calculus is as follows: The magnitude of the risk multiplied by the value of the exposed object equals the expected loss from the relevant conduct. The value of the desired, or principal, object multiplied by the *difference* between the probability of success *with* the risk and the probability of success *without* the risk is the expected gain. The action is negligent if the expected loss exceeds the expected gain. Does that formula capture the meaning of rashness in *Eckert*? Does it allow for errors brought on by the necessity of a hasty decision? Note too that the Seavey observations take a different view, treating the deliberate destruction of ten cents worth of property a compensable event, no matter how great the gain, but treating the 50 percent loss of another life as noncompensable, because the expected gain exceeds the expected loss. Why balance in the one case but not in the other?

Osborne v. Montgomery
234 N.W. 372 (Wis. 1931)

On August 30, 1928, the plaintiff Lester Osborne, then a boy of thirteen years of age, was employed by the Wisconsin State Journal in running errands. He was returning to his place of employment on a bicycle. Traveling westerly on East Washington avenue, he turned northerly on Pinckney street and as he proceeded north on Pinckney street he followed a car driven by the defendant. The defendant stopped his car for the purpose of leaving some clothing at a cleaner's. The defendant opened the door to his car intending to step from it on the left-hand side. The defendant's car at the time of the accident stood between a line of cars parked at the curb and the easterly rail of the street car tracks. As the defendant's car stopped and the door opened, and the plaintiff endeavored to pass, the right handle bar of his bicycle came in contact with the outside edge of the door, tipping the bicycle and throwing the plaintiff to the ground, causing the injuries complained of.

There was a jury trial, the jury found the defendant negligent as to lookout and the opening of his car door, but that he was not negligent in stopping his car where he did; that defendant's negligence was the cause of the injury; that the plaintiff was not guilty of contributory negligence; and assessed plaintiff's damages at $2,500. . . . [The instruction of the trial judge on the definition of negligence read as follows: "1. By ordinary care is meant that degree of care which the great mass of mankind, or the type of that mass, the ordinarily prudent man, exercises under like or similar circumstances. 2. Negligence is the want of ordinary care."]

ROSENBERRY, C.J. Manifestly, not every want of care results in liability. In order to measure care some standards must be adopted. Human beings must live in association with each other, as a consequence of which their rights, duties, and obligations are relative, not absolute. We apply the standards which guide the great mass of mankind in determining what is proper conduct of an individual under all the circumstances and say that he was or was not justified in doing the act in question. While it is true that the standard thus set up is varying and indefinite, it is nevertheless one which may be fairly and justly applied to human conduct. Such a standard is usually spoken of as ordinary care, being that degree of care which under the same or similar circumstances the great mass of mankind would ordinarily exercise.

In a consideration of this subject it is easy to get lost in a maze of metaphysical distinctions, or perhaps it may better be said it is difficult not to be so lost. The defect in the instruction is that it indicates no standard by which the conduct of the defendant is to be measured. In support of the instruction it is argued that the great mass of mankind do not indulge in conduct which results in harm to others; and therefore it must follow that if one does an act which results in injury to another, he departs from the standards which are followed by the great mass of mankind. The argument is based upon an inference not readily drawn, and, in addition to that, the premise is not sound. We are constantly doing acts which result in injury to others which are not negligent and do not result in liability. Many of the cases classified as those damnum absque injuria and cases where the damages are said to be consequential and remote are illustrations of this. While the acts result in injury to others, they are held to be not negligent because they are in conformity to what the great mass of mankind would do under the same or similar circumstances. The statement is true in all situations where liability exists, but it does not exclude situations where liability does not exist.

The fundamental idea of liability for wrongful acts is that upon a balancing of the social interests involved in each case, the law determines that under the circumstances of a particular case an actor should or should not become liable for the natural consequences of his conduct. One driving a car in a thickly populated district on a rainy day, slowly and in the most careful manner, may do injury to the person of another by throwing muddy or infected water upon that person. Society does not hold the actor responsible because the benefit of allowing people to travel under such circumstances so far outweighs the probable injury to bystanders that such conduct is not disapproved. Circumstances may require the driver of a fire truck to take his truck through a thickly populated district at a high rate of speed, but if he exercises that degree of care which such drivers ordinarily exercise under the same or similar circumstances, society, weighing the benefits against the probabilities of damage, in spite of the fact that as a reasonably prudent and intelligent man he should foresee that harm may result, justifies the risk and holds him not liable.

[Reversed and remanded on the question of damages only.]

Cooley v. Public Service Co.
10 A.2d 673 (N.H. 1940)

PAGE, J. On November 29, 1935, the telephone company maintained a cable on Taylor Street, Manchester, running north and south. This cable consisted of a lead sheath, inside which were carried a large number of wires connected with the service stations of its subscribers. The cable was supported by rings from a messenger wire strung on the telephone company poles. The construction conformed to standard practices, and the messenger wire was grounded every thousand feet. The sheath of the cable also was grounded. The telephone company further maintained at the station which the plaintiff was using when she received her injuries, two protective devices for grounding foreign currents in order to prevent their entrance to the house and to the subscriber's instrument. There is no evidence that these devices did not operate perfectly.

At a point about a mile distant from the plaintiff's house, the Public Service Company's lines, east and west along Valley Street, crossed the telephone cable at right angles and some eight or ten feet above it. These lines were not insulated.

Shortly after midnight, during a heavy storm, several of the Public Service wires over the intersection of Valley and Taylor Streets broke and fell to the ground. One of them came into contact with the telephone messenger. This particular wire of the defendant carried a voltage of about 2300. Consequently an arc was created, which burned through the messenger and nearly half through the cable before the current was shut off. . . .

When the contact of the wires occurred, the plaintiff was standing at the telephone, engaged in a long-distance conversation. The contact created a violent agitation in the diaphragm of the receiver and a loud explosive noise. The plaintiff fell to the floor. She has since suffered from what her physicians describe as traumatic neurosis, accompanied by loss of sensation on the left side.

[Plaintiff sued the power company and the telephone company. At the trial the jury found for the telephone company but against the power company. The power company appealed, and the judgment was reversed.]

Apparently there is no claim that the negligence of the defendant caused the wires to fall. The plaintiff's sole claim is that the defendant could have anticipated (1) that its wire might fall for a variety of reasons, which is true; (2) that a telephone subscriber in such case might hear a great noise, which also is true; (3) that as a result of fright thereby induced the user of the telephone would suffer physical injuries, which, as we have seen, is a rare contingency, though it may be anticipated. It is urged that the defendant's consequent duty was to maintain such devices at cross-overs as would prevent one of its falling wires from coming into contact with a telephone wire.

The devices suggested are two. The first is a wire-mesh basket suspended from the poles of the defendant at the point of cross-over, above the cable and below the defendant's wires. Two forms were suggested. One would be about six by eight feet. The other would be of an unassigned width and would stretch the full distance between defendant's poles. In either case the basket would be insulated. The theory is that falling wires, though alive, would remain harmless in the basket.

[The court, after detailed examination of these proposals, concluded that each of these suggested devices would have entailed a greater risk of electrocution to people passing on the street, even assuming that they might have reduced the risk of loud noises to those using the telephone. The court then continued, in part:]

There was evidence that baskets and similar devices were used by the telephone company, some years ago, for the protection of their wires at cross-overs. But the verdict establishes its lack of duty thus to protect its customers in this particular instance. There was no evidence that electric light companies ever erected baskets or insulated wires in such situations, and there was positive evidence that standard construction practices do not require either. The plaintiff cannot claim that the defendant maintained a system less carefully devised than one conforming to accepted practice. It is conceded, however, that due care might require some device better than the usual one. If the plaintiff and persons in her situation could be isolated, and duties to others ignored, due care might require the use of such devices as are here urged.

But the same reasoning that would establish a duty to do so raises another duty to the people in the street, not to lessen the protective effect of their circuit-breaking device. . . .

In the case before us, there was danger of electrocution in the street. As long as the telephone company's safety devices are properly installed and maintained, there is no danger of electrocution in the house. The only foreseeable danger to the telephone subscriber is from noise — fright and neuroses. Balancing the two, the danger to those such as the plaintiff is remote, that to those on the ground near the broken wires is obvious and immediate. The balance would not be improved by taking a chance to avoid traumatic neurosis of the plaintiff at the expense of greater risk to the lives of others. To the extent that the duty to use care depends upon relationship, the defendant's duty of care towards the plaintiff is obviously weaker than that towards the man in the street.

The defendant's duty cannot, in the circumstances, be to both. If that were so, performance of one duty would mean non-performance of the other. If it be negligent to save the life of the highway traveler at the expense of bodily injury resulting from the fright and neurosis of a telephone subscriber, it must be equally negligent to avoid the fright at the risk of another's life. The law could tolerate no such theory of "be liable if you do and liable if you don't." The law does not contemplate a shifting duty that requires care towards *A* and then discovers a duty to avoid injury incidentally suffered by *B* because there was due care with respect to *A*. Such a shifting is entirely inconsistent with the fundamental conception that the duty of due care requires precisely the measure of care that is reasonable under all the circumstances. 2 Restatement Torts, §§291-295. . . .

It is not doubted that due care might require the defendant to adopt some device that would afford protection against emotional disturbances in telephone-users without depriving the traveling public of reasonable protection from live wires immediately dangerous to life. Such a device, if it exists, is not disclosed by the record. The burden was upon the plaintiff to show its practicability. Since the burden was not sustained a verdict should have been directed for the defendant.

Other exceptions therefore require no consideration.

Judgment for the defendant. All concurred.

NOTE

Activity level versus care level. The plaintiff in *Cooley* tried to find fault with how the power company maintained its wires above ground. Accordingly, Page, J., never had to ask whether the power company made a sound decision to place the wires above ground in the first place. If that claim had been asserted, should courts and juries examine only the level of care once the defendant has decided to undertake a given activity, or should they also examine the type or level of the defendant's activity?

The theoretical point is raised in Shavell, Strict Liability Versus Negligence, 9 J. Legal Stud. 1, 2-3 (1980). There Shavell discusses the "unilateral case," "by which it is meant the actions of injurers but not of victims are assumed to affect the probability or severity of losses."

> By definition, under the negligence rule all that an injurer needs to do to avoid the possibility of liability is to make sure to exercise due care if he

engages in his activity. Consequently *he will not be motivated to consider the effect on accident losses of his choice of whether to engage in his activity or, more generally, of the level at which to engage in his activity;* he will choose his level of activity in accordance only with the personal benefits so derived. But surely any increase in his level of activity will typically raise expected accident losses (holding constant the level of care). Thus he will be led to choose too high a level of activity; the negligence rule is not "efficient."

Consider by way of illustration the problem of pedestrian-automobile accidents (and, as we are now discussing the unilateral case, let us imagine the behavior of pedestrians to be fixed). Suppose that drivers of automobiles find it in their interest to adhere to the standard of due care but that the possibility of accidents is not thereby eliminated. Then, in deciding how much to drive, they will contemplate only the enjoyment they get from doing so. Because (as they exercise due care) they will not be liable for harm suffered by pedestrians, drivers will not take into account that going more miles will mean a higher expected number of accidents. Hence, there will be too much driving; an individual will, for example, decide to go for a drive on a mere whim despite the imposition of a positive expected cost to pedestrians.

However, under a rule of strict liability, the situation is different. Because an injurer must pay for losses whenever he is involved in an accident, he will be induced to consider the effect on accident losses of both his level of care *and* his level of activity. His decisions will therefore be efficient. Because drivers will be liable for losses sustained by pedestrians, they will decide not only to exercise due care in driving but also to drive only when the utility gained from it outweighs expected liability payments to pedestrians.

Does it follow as a matter of definition that choices of activity level are outside judicial review under a negligence standard? Recall in this context the suggestion made in Bolton v. Stone, *supra* at 154, that it might have been negligent to play cricket *at all* if the field could not be made safe. Is a jury as competent in making decisions on activity levels as it is on care levels? Should it examine the pedestrian's care level?

United States v. Carroll Towing Co.
159 F.2d 169 (2d Cir. 1947)

L. HAND, J. These appeals concern the sinking of the barge, 'Anna C,' on January 4, 1944, off Pier 51, North River. [That sinking gave rise to two separate claims for damages. The first was brought by the United States against the Carroll Towing Company for the loss of a load of flour which it was shipping on the Barge Anna C, which was owned by the Conners Company. The second suit was brought by the Conners Company against Carroll Towing and the Grace Line, to whom it had chartered its tug, the "Carroll," for the loss of the barge, and to which the contributory negligence of the Conners Company was raised as a partial defense. The proceedings took place in admiralty, and the trial judge found that Carroll, but not the Grace Line, was responsible for one-half the loss of the damage to the Anna C and for the entire loss of the flour.

The record revealed that the Conners Company had chartered the Anna C to the Pennsylvania Railroad "at a stated hire per diem, by a charter of the kind usual in the Harbor, which included the services of a bargee, apparently limited to the hours 8 A.M. to 4 P.M." The accident arose when the tug Carroll attempted a tricky maneuver to move another barge that had been tied up in a tier of barges on the so-called Public Pier just to the north of Pier 52 where the Anna C was berthed. The first barge on the Public Pier was tied directly to it. Thereafter each of the other barges was tied in a separate line to the barge next in from it to the pier. The Anna C was the innermost barge in a tier of five on Pier 52. A line had been run from one of the barges on the Public Pier to one of the barges in the Anna C's tier. When the Carroll sought to untie this line in order to move that barge from the public pier, it dislodged all the barges from Pier 52. A strong current took the barges to the south where the Anna C sank after its hull was pierced below water by the propeller of a tanker berthed at Pier 51. Learned Hand, J., held first that the Grace Line had to share responsibility with Carroll Towing for the damage to the Anna C because its employee had assisted in the maneuvering of the Carroll. He then continued:]

We do not therefore attribute it as in any degree a fault of the "Anna C" that the flotilla broke adrift. Hence she may recover in full against the Carroll Company and the Grace Line for any injury she suffered from the contact with the tanker's propeller, which we shall speak of as the "collision damages." On the other hand, if the bargee had been on board, and had done his duty to his employer, he would have gone below at once, examined the injury, and called for help from the "Carroll" and the Grace Line tug. Moreover, it is clear that these tugs could have kept the barge afloat, until they had safely beached her, and saved her cargo. This would have avoided what we shall call the "sinking damages." Thus, if it was a failure in the Conner Company's proper care of its own barge, for the bargee to be absent, the company can recover only one third of the "sinking" damages from the Carroll Company and one third from the Grace Line [under an admiralty rule that divided damages equally among all three culpable parties.] For this reason the question arises whether a barge owner is slack in the care of his barge if the bargee is absent.

As to the consequences of a bargee's absence from his barge there have been a number of decisions; and we cannot agree that it is never ground for liability even to other vessels who may be injured. As early as 1843, Judge Sprague in Clapp v. Young, [Fed. Cas. No. 2786,] held a schooner liable which broke adrift from her moorings in a gale in Provincetown Harbor, and ran down another ship. The ground was that the owners of the offending ship had left no one on board, even though it was the custom in that harbor not to do so. [A review of other cases follows.]

It appears from the foregoing review that there is no general rule to determine when the absence of a bargee or other attendant will make the owner of the barge liable for injuries to other vessels if she breaks away from her moorings. However, in any cases where he would be so liable for injuries to others, obviously he must reduce his damages proportionately, if the injury is to his own barge. It becomes apparent why there can be no such general rule, when we consider the grounds for such a liability. Since there are occasions when every vessel will break from her moorings, and since, if she does, she becomes a menace to those about her; the owner's duty, as in other similar situations, to provide against resulting injuries is a function of three variables: (1) The probability that she will break away; (2) the gravity of the resulting injury, if she does; (3) the burden of adequate precautions. Possibly it serves to bring this notion into relief to state it in algebraic terms: if the probability be called P; the injury, L; and the burden, B; liability depends upon whether B is less than L multiplied by P: i.e., whether B is less than PL. Applied to the situation at bar, the likelihood that a barge will break from her fasts and the damage she will do, vary with the place and time; for example, if a storm threatens, the danger is greater; so it is, if she is in a crowded harbor where moored barges are constantly being shifted about. On the other hand, the barge must not be the bargee's prison, even though he lives aboard; he must go ashore at times. We need not say whether, even in such crowded waters as New York Harbor a bargee must be aboard at night at all; it may be that the custom is otherwise, as Ward, J., supposed in 'The Kathryn B. Guinan,' [176 F. 301 (2d Cir. 1910)]; and that, if so, the situation is one where custom should control. We leave that question open; but we hold that it is not in all cases a sufficient answer to a bargee's absence without excuse, during working hours, that he has properly made fast his barge to a pier, when he leaves her. In the case at bar the bargee left at five o'clock in the afternoon of January 3rd, and the flotilla broke away at about two o'clock in the afternoon of the following day, twenty-one hours afterwards. The bargee had been away all the time, and we hold that his fabricated story was affirmative evidence that he had no excuse for his absence. At the locus in quo — especially during the short January days and in the full tide of war activity — barges were being constantly "drilled" in and out. Certainly it was not beyond reasonable expectation that, with the inevitable haste and bustle, the work might not be done with adequate care. In such circumstances we hold — and it is all that we do hold — that it was a fair requirement that the Conners Company should have a bargee aboard (unless he had some excuse for his absence), during the working hours of daylight.

NOTES

1. *An economic interpretation of negligence?* One approach to the facts of *Carroll Towing* asks whether the charge of negligence against the Conners

Company has the same weight in its dual roles: As a defendant in the United States' suit for the lost flour and as a plaintiff in its own suit against Carroll Towing and Grace Line. In particular, could the United States claim to be a third-party beneficiary to the contract between Conners and the Pennsylvania Railroad? Does Conner owe any duty to the stranger that hits it? See Smith v. Kenrick, *supra* at 154.

Hand's use of the formula — whether PL is less than B — has spawned a burgeoning academic literature on the economic interpretation of negligence and, by implication, the entire tort law. Judge Posner, A Theory of Negligence, 1 J. Legal Stud. 29, 32-33 (1972), opened the debate by arguing that the Hand formula provides an operational definition of unreasonable risk under the negligence law:

> Hand was adumbrating, perhaps unwittingly, an economic meaning of negligence. Discounting (multiplying) the cost of an accident if it occurs by the probability of occurrence yields a measure of the economic benefit to be anticipated from incurring the costs necessary to prevent the accident. The cost of prevention is what Hand meant by the burden of taking precautions against the accident. It may be the cost of installing safety equipment or otherwise making the activity safer, or the benefit forgone by curtailing or eliminating the activity. If the cost of safety measures or of curtailment — whichever cost is lower — exceeds the benefit in accident avoidance to be gained by incurring that cost, society would be better off, in economic terms, to forgo accident prevention. A rule making the enterprise liable for the accidents that occur in such cases cannot be justified on the ground that it will induce the enterprise to increase the safety of its operations. When the cost of accidents is less than the cost of prevention, a rational profit-maximizing enterprise will pay tort judgments to the accident victims rather than incur the larger cost of avoiding liability. Furthermore, overall economic value or welfare would be diminished rather than increased by incurring a higher accident-prevention cost in order to avoid a lower accident cost. If, on the other hand, the benefits in accident avoidance exceed the costs of prevention, society is better off if those costs are incurred and the accident averted, and so in this case the enterprise is made liable, in the expectation that self-interest will lead it to adopt the precautions in order to avoid a greater cost in tort judgments.

The Third Restatement, RTT: LPH, takes the same "balancing approach" to negligence:

§3. NEGLIGENCE

A person acts negligently if the person does not exercise reasonable care under all the circumstances. Primary factors to consider in ascertaining whether the person's conduct lacks reasonable care are the foreseeable likelihood that the person's conduct will result in harm, the foreseeable severity of any harm that may ensue, and the burden of precautions to eliminate or reduce the risk of harm.

Does the Restatement's definition embody the Hand formula? Are the two uses of the term "foreseeable" redundant? If the three elements are only "primary factors," what other elements could be considered? What is the relationship between Hand formula and the customary account of "ordinary care" or the "reasonably prudent person"? The effort to reduce negligence to the three elements in the Hand formula has been subject to wholesale attacks. Thus, in Wright, Hand, Posner, and the Myth of the "Hand Formula," 4 Theoretical Inquiries in Law 145, 273 (2003), Professor Wright argues that the Hand formula, under which "legal liability for harms caused by such [negligent] conduct, depends on whether the aggregate risks (expected losses or costs) created by the conduct are greater than the aggregate utility (expected gains or benefits) of the conduct," does not reflect the basic commitment of the tort law. The article examines all of Hand's opinions on negligence, and concludes that only a small fraction of these cases make reference to or rely upon his cost benefit formula. He then concludes:

> If one then follows the legal realists' advice and looks carefully, in those cases in which the aggregate-risk-utility test is mentioned, at what the courts are actually doing rather than (merely) at what they are saying, one finds that the courts almost never attempt to apply the test; instead, the test is merely trotted out as *dicta* or boilerplate separate from the real analysis. The very few judges who actually try to apply the test either fail in the attempt to do so or end up using the test as window-dressing for results reached on other (justice-based) grounds.

A similar theme is developed in Kelley, The *Carroll Towing Company* Case and the Teaching of Tort Law, 45 St. Louis U. L.J. 731 (2001); Zipursky, Sleight of Hand, 48 Wm. & Mary L. Rev. 1999 (2007), which argue for justice-based accounts that stress the importance of personal integrity against the invasions of others. Why is that not an argument for strict liability? Within the negligence framework, could any system of justice afford to ignore the diminishing marginal value of additional precautions? How else might the negligence formula of reasonable care be framed? Whatever the general view of the matter, Judge Posner continues to promote the Hand formula in his judicial decisions. In Halek v. United States, 178 F.3d 481 (7th Cir. 1999), the plaintiff, an experienced elevator repairman, lost his balance, tripped, and got his hand caught at the nip point of a pulley system that was guarded by an immovable cage that the Navy had left open on one side. The plaintiff could have turned off the system before reaching for the bolt, but chose not to do so because of the anticipated short period of his exposure. Judge Posner applied the Hand formula noting: "Given the gravity of the injury that was likely to occur to anyone who fell into the machinery, the nontrivial probability of getting caught in unshielded machinery if one is working in close proximity to it, and the trivial expense of making the case easily removable and therefore safe, the district judge was justified in finding the defendant negligent." Could any reconfiguration of the cage make that workplace "safe"? What result if the removal of the cage could create some alternative hazard? Should this be regarded as a case of sequential performance in which the danger is treated as open and obvious? See Gyerman v. United States Line, *infra* at 333. What about contractual assumption of risk?

2. *Measurement problems under the Hand formula.* How does a court or jury find the information needed to apply the Hand formula? Hand himself was sensitive to the problem. In Moisan v. Loftus, 178 F.2d 148, 149 (2d Cir. 1949), he wrote:

> The difficulties are in applying the rule, . . . they arise from the necessity of applying a quantitative test to an incommensurable subject-matter and the same difficulties inhere in the concept of "ordinary" negligence. [Of the three factors, B, P, and L,] care is the only one ever susceptible of quantitative estimate, and often that is not. The injuries are always a variable within limits, which do not admit of even approximate ascertainment and, although probability might theoretically be estimated, if any statistics were available, they never are and, besides, probability varies with the severity of the injuries. It follows that all such attempts are illusory, and, if serviceable at all, are so only to center attention upon which one of the factors may be determinative in any given situation.

What should be done if the estimates of B, P, and L can each vary independently by a factor of 10? If human life (unlike property damage) has no estimable market value? Does the ordinary care formulation eliminate or conceal this problem?

3. *Marginal precautions and the Hand formula.* One conceptual problem under the Hand formula involves choosing the correct interval for assessing defendant's conduct. Suppose the defendant could take an extra $100 in precautions that would yield $150 in additional benefits. At first blush, the defendant should take these precautions given that *in aggregate* the expected benefits exceed the expected costs. Nonetheless, a closer analysis reveals that this action could lead to excessive care. The key point is that in economic terms additional precautions should be tested *at the margin* and only taken so long as an additional dollar of precautions reduces the expected costs of injury by at least a dollar. Thus, in the example above, suppose that the first $60 in precautions yield $120 in benefits, while the next $40 in precautions yield only $30 in benefits. In principle the lesser precaution is more desirable because it generates $60 in *net* benefits ($120 – $60), while the next $40 in precautions generates *minus* $10 in net benefits ($30 – $40). The lesser precaution therefore generates the greater

social benefit. On this analysis, therefore, the plaintiff does conclusively establish negligence by showing only a net social gain from taking the proposed precautions. In principle, the defendant should be allowed to show that some lower level of precaution would have generated a higher net social return. Assuming this issue can be litigated, how should the burdens of proof be distributed on the question of marginal precautions?

This analysis has important implications for applying the Hand formula in cases of self-risk. As a theoretical matter, the Hand formula is capacious enough to take into account any potential losses that a bargee has either as a potential plaintiff or potential defendant. Thus, if the expected loss of a bargee's conduct to some third party (such as the United States for its flour) were $100 and the additional "sinking" damages to the barge itself were $50, then the defendant should be regarded as negligent if the costs of its precautions were less than $150, not $100. Stated otherwise, the avoidance of harm to self reduces the incremental cost in preventing harms to others. See Cooter and Porat, Does Risk to Oneself Increase the Care Owed to Others? Law and Economics in Conflict, 29 J. Legal Stud. 19 (2000), concluding that "omitting the injurer's possible harm to himself causes courts to set the legal standard of care too low." Does this observation apply medical malpractice? To the failure to correct latent defects in premises of which the defendant has knowledge and the plaintiff does not?

4. *Risk neutrality.* On its face, the Hand formula treats all individuals as risk neutral. A risk-neutral actor responds to the expected gains or losses of a future uncertain event by simply multiplying the probability of its occurrence by its magnitude, as in the Hand formula itself. In practice, however, sometimes people prefer risk and sometimes they are averse to it. These tastes can vary across persons. In essence, people who prefer risk gain positive satisfaction from taking chances, while people who are averse to risk are prepared to pay to avoid confronting it. Thus, a person who prefers risk would prefer a 10 percent chance of losing $100 to a certainty of losing $10. Conversely, the risk-averse person prefers the certainty of losing $10 to a 10 percent chance of losing $100. Risk preference and risk aversion are both matters of degree; it is quite possible that some would pay only $11 to avoid the 10 percent chance of a $100 loss while others might pay as much as $20. For a defense of the risk neutrality assumption in the Hand formula see W. Landes and R. Posner, The Economic Structure of Tort Law 55-57 (1987). Should neutrality be presumed if most individuals and most corporations are risk averse? Note that some modern literature in the field of cognitive biases suggests that individuals may be risk preferrers in the domain of losses and risk averse in the domain of gains. See, e.g., S. Plous, The Psychology of Judgment and Decision Making 96 (1993). Why do people both gamble and buy liability insurance?

5. *Does efficiency require negligence?* Under the orthodox economic accounts of the tort law, the Hand formula is not the only road to social

efficiency. Strict liability with contributory negligence, or even a system of negligence without contributory negligence, should also induce (as a first approximation) optimal behavior by both parties. The proposition was demonstrated in Brown, Toward an Economic Theory of Liability, 2 J. Legal Stud. 323 (1973), and more complete expositions can be found in W. Landes and R. Posner, The Economic Structure of Tort Law ch. 3 (1987), and S. Shavell, Economic Analysis of Accident Law 26-46 (1987).

The basic intuition behind the position is as follows. Let us assume that each (rationally self-interested) party wishes to minimize the sum of its precaution and accident costs. When liability is predicated on proof of defendant's negligence alone, the defendant will take care, even *without* the defense of contributory negligence: the cost of precautions is below that of the anticipated liability. Once the plaintiff knows that the defendant will take care, the plaintiff also knows that all prospect of recovery is thereby precluded. The plaintiff therefore now has (wholly without regard to the contributory negligence defense) an incentive to take the optimal level of care as well. Both parties will behave optimally, even without the contributory negligence defense.

Similarly, under strict liability, the plaintiff will recover unless barred by contributory negligence. Yet so long as precautions are cheaper than expected accidents, the rational plaintiff will take care in order to preserve the right of action. Once the defendant knows that the plaintiff will not misbehave, even under strict liability, the defendant has an incentive to choose the optimal level of care to minimize the sum of his precaution and accident costs. Again both sides will take proper care, although only one party has a duty of care.

Brown's proofs generate a certain paradoxical result: Since all persons are rational, no one can ever be negligent. Yet negligence is commonplace, and so the question is, why? The most obvious explanation is that error pervades the behavior of both the judges and juries who operate the legal system, making every trial something of a rational gamble. Similar types of error are likely to influence private actors who are ignorant of the rules, and even those who struggle to comply with them. In addition, private actors may fail to comply with the law if they are broke, stressed, demoralized, bored, or fatigued. Moving in the opposite direction, highly sophisticated individuals might choose not to take care because they believe that other persons with whom they may interact will not take care. Each side thus behaves strategically in anticipation of the predicted error of the other side. Finally, the increased possibilities for good care may simply increase the ways to be negligent. The physician who could do nothing to help a patient in 1900 could be found negligent in a thousand ways in 2008 precisely because his increased ability to help patients casts suspicion on his conduct where intervention fails. See generally Grady, Why Are People Negligent? Technology, Nondurable Precautions, and the Medical Malpractice Explosion, 82 Nw. U. L. Rev. 293 (1988).

6. Discontinuities and the choice between negligence and strict liability. Theories of negligence and strict liability differ as well in one other important respect. Under strict liability, small errors in choosing the optimal level of care will typically generate only small consequences. The defendant is liable for all the accidents he causes, so that small shifts in care levels generate only small changes in either the frequency or severity of harm to other. But under negligence, the defendant who hovers close to the line could find that a small decrease in the level of care results in exposing him to liability for all accidents instead of none. In light of this pronounced discontinuity, one counterintuitive argument holds that the negligence standard induces a somewhat higher level of care than the strict liability rule, especially by defendants anxious to avoid falling off that liability cliff. See Grady, A New Positive Economic Theory of Negligence, 92 Yale L.J. 799 (1983). Grady's analysis of error has in turn been challenged in Calfee and Craswell, Some Effects of Uncertainty on Compliance with Legal Standards, 70 Va. L. Rev. 965, 982 (1984), who concluded that it is unclear whether a negligence standard will induce too much or too little care by defendants, and may under different circumstances do some of each. They posit that the defendant who takes too little care may not "get caught." The risk of falling off a cliff occurs in only some fraction of the cases while the savings from less care is obtained in all, making it difficult to determine the net effects of error on care levels.

7. The scope of the Hand formula. As stated, the Hand formula purports to be a uniform standard of liability that is sufficient to cover all cases. In practice, the question arises as to its reach in the full range of cases. The remaining materials in this section look at some situations involving highway accidents and common carriers in which the Hand formula is arguably only part of the story.

H. Laurence Ross, Settled Out of Court
The Social Process of Insurance Claims Adjustment 98-99 (2d ed. 1980)

The formal law of negligence liability, as stated in casebooks from the opinions of appellate courts, is not easily applied to the accident at Second and Main. It deals with the violation of a duty of care owed by the insured to the claimant and is based on a very complex and perplexing model of the "reasonable man," in this case the reasonable driver. . . . In their day-to-day work, the concern with liability is reduced to the question of whether either or both parties violated the rules of the road as expressed in common traffic laws. Taking the doctrine of negligence per se to an extreme doubtless unforeseen by the makers of the formal law, adjusters tend to define a claim as one of liability or of no liability depending only on whether a rule was violated, regardless of intention, knowledge, necessity, and other such qualifications that might receive sympathetic attention even from a traffic court judge. Such a determination is far easier than the task proposed in theory by the formal law of negligence.

To illustrate, if Car *A* strikes Car *B* from the rear, the driver of *A* is assumed to be liable and *B* is not. In the ordinary course of events, particularly where damages are routine, the adjuster is not concerned with *why A* struck *B*, or with whether *A* violated a duty of care to *B*, or with whether *A* was unreasonable or not. These questions are avoided, not only because they may be impossible to answer, but also because the fact that *A* struck *B* from the rear will satisfy all supervisory levels that a payment is in order, without further explanation. Likewise, in the routine case, the fact that *A* was emerging from a street governed by a stop sign will justify treating this as a case of liability, without concern for whether the sign was seen or not, whether there was adequate reason for not seeing the sign, etc. In short, in the ordinary case the physical facts of the accident are normally sufficient to allocate liability between the drivers. Inasmuch as the basic physical facts of the accident are easily known — and they are frequently ascertainable from the first notice — the issue of liability is usually relatively easy to dispose of.

Lyons v. Midnight Sun Transportation Services, Inc.
928 P.2d 1202 (Alaska 1996)

PER CURIAM.

I. FACTS AND PROCEEDINGS

Esther Hunter-Lyons was killed when her Volkswagen van was struck broadside by a truck driven by David Jette and owned by Midnight Sun Transportation Services, Inc. When the accident occurred, Jette was driving south in the right-hand lane of Arctic Boulevard in Anchorage. Hunter-Lyons pulled out of a parking lot in front of him. Jette braked and steered to the left, but Hunter-Lyons continued to pull out further into the traffic lane. Jette's truck collided with Hunter-Lyons's vehicle. David Lyons, the deceased's husband, filed suit, asserting that Jette had been speeding and driving negligently.

At trial, conflicting testimony was introduced regarding Jette's speed before the collision. Lyons's expert witness testified that Jette may have been driving as fast as 53 miles per hour. Midnight Sun's expert testified that Jette probably had been driving significantly slower and that the collision could have occurred even if Jette had been driving at the speed limit, 35 miles per hour. Lyons's expert later testified that if Jette had stayed in his own lane, and had not steered to the left, there would have been no collision. Midnight Sun's expert contended that steering to the left when a vehicle pulls out onto the roadway from the right is a normal response and is generally the safest course of action to follow.

Over Lyons's objection, the jury was given an instruction on the sudden emergency doctrine.[1] The jury found that Jette, in fact, had been negligent, but his negligence was not a legal cause of the accident. Lyons appeals, arguing that the court should not have given the jury the sudden emergency instruction.

II. ANALYSIS AND DISCUSSION

The sudden emergency doctrine is a rule of law which states that a person confronted with a sudden and unexpected peril, not resulting from that person's own negligence, is not expected to exercise the same judgment and prudence the law requires of a person in calmer and more deliberate moments. The person confronted with the imminent peril must, however, act as a reasonable person would under the same conditions.

[The Court first held that the use of the sudden emergency instruction count was harmless error since the jury decided in favor of defendant on the ground that his conduct was not the legal cause of plaintiff's injury.]

B. SUDDEN EMERGENCY INSTRUCTION DISAPPROVED

[W]e take this opportunity to disapprove of the instruction's further use. It adds nothing to the established law that the duty of care, which all must exercise, is to act reasonably under the circumstances. The instruction is potentially confusing. Although we cannot say that the instruction is never appropriate, we discourage its employment. In support of this admonition, we offer the following background.

The sudden emergency doctrine arose as a method of ameliorating the, sometimes harsh, "all or nothing" rule in contributory negligence systems. . . .

Although the doctrine came out of the contributory negligence regime, there is nothing about it which is inherently incompatible with a comparative fault system. Comparative negligence is a method of apportioning

---

1. Jury Instruction # 17 read [in part]:

> Midnight Sun claims that it is not liable for plaintiffs' harm because David Jette acted with reasonable care in an emergency situation.
>
> In an emergency, a person is not expected or required to use the same judgment and care that is required in calmer and more deliberate moments. If, in an emergency, a person acts as a reasonably careful person would act in a similar emergency, there is no negligence even though afterwards it might appear that a different course of action would have been better and safer.

liability for a particular accident among the various parties who have been deemed negligent. The sudden emergency doctrine, in turn, is an expression of the applicable standard of care against which particular actions are judged in order to determine whether they were negligent in character. The fault of one person, determined in the light of a sudden emergency instruction, can be compared to the fault of another person, whose negligence may have created the emergency, with no logical inconsistency. . . .

We believe that the sudden emergency instruction is a generally useless appendage to the law of negligence. With or without an emergency, the standard of care a person must exercise is still that of a reasonable person under the circumstances. With or without the instruction, parties are still entitled to present evidence at trial which will establish what the circumstances were, and are also entitled to argue to the jury that they acted as a reasonable person would have in light of those circumstances. Thus, barring circumstances that we cannot at the moment hypothesize, a sudden emergency instruction serves no positive function. Further, the instruction may cause confusion by appearing to imply that one party is less blameworthy than the other. Therefore, we hold that it should not be used unless a court finds that the particular and peculiar facts of a case warrant more explanation of the standard of care than is generally required. . . .

Affirmed.

NOTE

The emergency rule. The Third Restatement's emergency instruction reads as follows: "If an actor is confronted with an unexpected emergency requiring rapid response, this is a circumstance to be taken into account in determining whether the actor's resulting conduct is that of the reasonably careful person." RTT:LPH §9. Is the proper response under these circumstances to say that the party facing the emergency created by the other party is protected so long as he acts in good faith to minimize the loss? Did Jette face any conflict of interest in deciding what to once Hunter-Lyons entered Arctic Highway? What result if Jette had careened into a car driving north on the opposite side of the road?

Andrews v. United Airlines
24 F.3d 39 (9th Cir. 1994)

KOZINSKI, Circuit Judge.

We are called upon to determine whether United Airlines took adequate measures to deal with that elementary notion of physics—what goes up, must come down. For, while the skies are friendly enough, the ground can be a mighty dangerous place when heavy objects tumble from overhead compartments.

I

During the mad scramble that usually follows hard upon an airplane's arrival at the gate, a briefcase fell from an overhead compartment and seriously injured plaintiff Billie Jean Andrews. No one knows who opened the compartment or what caused the briefcase to fall, and Andrews doesn't claim that airline personnel were involved in stowing the object or opening the bin. Her claim, rather, is that the injury was foreseeable and the airline didn't prevent it.

The district court dismissed the suit on summary judgment, and we review de novo. This is a diversity action brought in California, whose tort law applies.

II

The parties agree that United Airlines is a common carrier and as such "owe[s] both a duty of utmost care and the vigilance of a very cautious person towards [its] passengers." Acosta v. Southern Cal. Rapid Transit Dist., 465 P.2d 72 (1970). Though United is "responsible for any, even the slightest, negligence and [is] required to do all that human care, vigilance, and foresight reasonably can do under all the circumstances," *Acosta*, 465 P.2d at 72, it is not an insurer of its passengers' safety, Lopez v. Southern Cal. Rapid Transit Dist., 710 P.2d 907 (1985). "[T]he degree of care and diligence which [it] must exercise is only such as can reasonably be exercised consistent with the character and mode of conveyance adopted and the practical operation of [its] business. . . . " Id.

To show that United did not satisfy its duty of care toward its passengers, Ms. Andrews presented the testimony of two witnesses. The first was Janice Northcott, United's Manager of Inflight Safety, who disclosed that in 1987 the airline had received 135 reports of items falling from overhead bins. As a result of these incidents, Ms. Northcott testified, United decided to add a warning to its arrival announcements, to wit, that items stored overhead might have shifted during flight and passengers should use caution in opening the bins. This announcement later became the industry standard.

Ms. Andrews's second witness was safety and human factors expert Dr. David Thompson, who testified that United's announcement was ineffective because passengers opening overhead bins couldn't see objects poised to fall until the bins were opened, by which time it was too late. Dr. Thompson also testified that United could have taken additional steps to prevent the hazard, such as retrofitting its overhead bins with baggage nets, as some airlines had already done, or by requiring passengers to store only lightweight items overhead.

United argues that Andrews presented too little proof to satisfy her burden [to withstand summary judgment] under Anderson v. Liberty Lobby, Inc., 477 U.S. 242 (1986). One hundred thirty-five reported incidents, United points out, are trivial when spread over the millions of passengers travelling on its 175,000 flights every year. Even that number overstates the problem, according to United, because it includes events where passengers merely observed items falling from overhead bins but no one was struck or injured. Indeed, United sees the low incidence of injuries as incontrovertible proof that the safety measures suggested by plaintiff's expert would not merit the additional cost and inconvenience to airline passengers.

III

It is a close question, but we conclude that plaintiff has made a sufficient case to overcome summary judgment. United is hard-pressed to dispute that its passengers are subject to a hazard from objects falling out of overhead bins, considering the warning its flight crews give hundreds of times each day. The case then turns on whether the hazard is serious enough to warrant more than a warning. Given the heightened duty of a common carrier, even a small risk of serious injury to passengers may form the basis of liability if that risk could be eliminated "consistent with the character and mode of [airline travel] and the practical operation of [that] business. . . ." *Lopez*, 710 P.2d at 907. United has demonstrated neither that retrofitting overhead bins with netting (or other means) would be prohibitively expensive, nor that such steps would grossly interfere with the convenience of its passengers. Thus, a jury could find United has failed to do "all that human care, vigilance, and foresight reasonably can do under all the circumstances." *Acosta*, 465 P.2d at 72.

The reality, with which airline passengers are only too familiar, is that airline travel has changed significantly in recent years. As harried travelers try to avoid the agonizing ritual of checked baggage, they hand-carry more and larger items — computers, musical instruments, an occasional deceased relative. The airlines have coped with this trend, but perhaps not well enough. Given its awareness of the hazard, United may not have done everything technology permits and prudence dictates to eliminate it. . . .

Jurors, many of whom will have been airline passengers, will be well equipped to decide whether United had a duty to do more than warn passengers about the possibility of falling baggage. A reasonable jury might conclude United should have done more; it might also find that United did enough. Either decision would be rational on the record presented to the district court which, of course, means summary judgment was not appropriate.

Reversed and remanded.

NOTE

Negligence and the common carrier. Is the utmost care standard in *Andrews* consistent with the Hand formula? How would *Andrews* come out on that test? The utmost care standard has had an uneven history in common carrier cases. In Kelly v. Manhattan Ry., 20 N.E. 383, 385 (N.Y. 1889), the plaintiff slipped on heavy snow that had accumulated during the night on the stairs leading to the train station. Peckham, J., rejected the utmost care standard for this situation, reserving it for those distinctive railroad operations in which the passenger had no control over the operation of the train, as when injury "occurs from a defect in the road-bed, machinery, or in the construction of the cars." He observed that the level of serious injury or death from those "compelled" to use the rails was far higher than those associated with ancillary facilities, such as "platforms, halls, stairways, and the like." In principle, the Hand formula could accommodate these differences, by insisting that greater peril requires greater precaution independent of the utmost care standard. In light of that observation, *Kelly* was overturned in Bethel v. New York City Transit Authority, 703 N.E.2d 1214, 1216-1217 (N.Y. 1998). The plaintiff was injured when a movable bus seat collapsed as she attempted to sit down. *Bethel* treated *Kelly* as a bygone response to "the advent of the age of steam railroads in 19th century America. Their primitive safety features resulted in a phenomenal growth in railroad accident injuries and with them, an explosion in personal injury litigation, significantly affecting the American tort system." Levine, J., observed that the earlier development represented a needless departure from the fundamental doctrine of negligence, which relies on a "sliding scale" that makes the level of care commensurate with the level of danger involved in a particular activity. In his view, contemporary negligence jurisprudence has undermined "both of the main policy justifications for exacting of common carriers a duty of extraordinary care. The two most often expressed rationales for duty of highest care were (1) the perceived ultrahazardous nature of the instrumentalities of public rapid transit, and (2) the status of passengers and their relationship to the carrier, notably their total dependency upon the latter for safety precautions." Why should a broken seat generate one consequence on a bus and another in the station? What is wrong with a strict duty to keep seats safe, subject to a defense of assumption of risk when passengers know of the defect before they sit down? How is *Andrews* decided under *Bethel*? Under *Kelly*?

SECTION D.   CUSTOM

The general principles of negligence law leave judges and juries a great deal of latitude in deciding cases. Sometimes that latitude is a sign of the strength of the system, for it supplies the flexibility necessary to apply traditional standards to new situations without having to fundamentally remake the substantive law. Unfortunately, the "featureless generality" of reasonable care also introduces a large element of uncertainty even into ostensibly routine cases. Using custom to set the standard of care is one way to reduce this uncertainty. Customs lack the generality of the basic reasonable care standard, but within their specific area of application they promise greater direction than any broader standard can provide.

This section deals with the role of custom in negligence cases. Should custom be given the same deference in actions between strangers as in actions arising out of consensual relationships (employer-employee, physician-patient)? Should custom carry the same weight when used as a shield (defendant argues that he is not negligent because his conduct conforms to custom), as it is given when used as a sword (plaintiff argues that defendant is negligent because his conduct fails to conform to custom)?

Titus v. Bradford, B. & K. R. Co.
20 A. 517 (Pa. 1890)

[The defendant railroad operated a narrow gauge railroad track between Bradford and Smethport. This line was connected with the standard-gauge tracks of major lines, and part of the defendant's business was to transfer over its tracks the loaded and unloaded freight cars of major carriers. The transfers were accomplished by means of a "hoist" which lifted car bodies from the standard trucks (bases) used on the major lines and set them down on the narrow trucks in use on the defendant's lines. Most of the car bodies from the major lines were designed with flat bottoms, which could be set down relatively easily on the flat trucks in use on the narrow-gauge rails. A substantial portion of the defendant's business, however, involved the transfer of cars from the New York, Pennsylvania and Ohio Railroad. These "Nypano" cars had slightly rounded bottoms, "shaped somewhat like the bottom of a common saucer," which fit into correspondingly shaped trucks when in use on the Nypano lines. When transferred to the defendant's tracks, however, this car body did not sit securely on its truck, since its bottom was about three inches higher at its edges than at its center. In order to prevent the car bodies from wobbling and toppling when the defendant's train was in motion, the defendant's employees routinely secured them with blocks of hard wood which were either bolted in place or tied in place with telegraph wire.

The decedent had worked on the defendant's railroad with the Nypano cars for nearly two years and was quite familiar with the methods used to secure them to the flat trucks. In the spring of 1888, he became a brakeman on the line. On June 7, 1888, in that capacity, he was riding atop a loaded Nypano freight car. Before setting off, the train's conductor had visually inspected the blocks and believed that they had been properly tied in place with telegraph wire. As the train rounded a curve at a speed of between 7 and 10 miles per hour, it started to sway from side to side. The decedent, who was sitting by the brake wheel on the top rear of the car, tried to run forward over the load to the car in front of him, but could not reach the safety of the next car before his car tipped over. He jumped off onto the track and was killed when struck by the car immediately behind him. A subsequent investigation showed that some of the wire fastening around the blocks of his car had come loose, which allowed the block to become dislodged and the car to wobble and tumble.

"The contention of the plaintiff in this case is, that the company was negligent in using on this narrow-gauge road these standard car bodies," this "on account of the ill-adoption of this car body to the truck." The jury returned a verdict for the plaintiff in the amount of $5,325, and the defendant appealed.]

MITCHELL, J. We have examined all the testimony carefully, and fail to find any evidence of defendant's negligence. The negligence declared upon is the placing of a broad-gauge car upon a narrow-gauge truck, and the use of "an unsafe, and not the best appliance, to wit, the flat centre plate"; or, as expressed by the learned judge in his charge, in using on the narrow-gauge road the standard car bodies, and particularly the New York, Pennsylvania & Ohio car body described by the witnesses. But the whole evidence, of plaintiff's witnesses as well as of defendant's, shows that the shifting of broad-gauge or standard car bodies on to narrow-gauge trucks for transportation, is a regular part of the business of narrow-gauge railroads, and the plaintiff's evidence makes no attempt to show that the way in which it was done here was either dangerous or unusual. . . . Cazely and Richmond say it was the custom to haul these broad-gauge cars on the narrow-gauge trucks, though most of the broad-gauge were Erie cars, of a somewhat different construction; and Morris says the car in question was put on a Hays truck, fitted for carrying standard-gauge cars on a narrow-gauge road, and that this particular kind of "Nypano" car was so hauled quite often. These are plaintiff's own witnesses, and none of them say the practice was dangerous. The nearest approach to such testimony is by Morris, who says he "had his doubts."

But, even if the practice had been shown to be dangerous, that would not show it to be negligent. Some employments are essentially hazardous, as said by our Brother Green, in North. C. Ry. Co. v. Husson, 101 Pa. 1 [(1882)], of coupling railway cars; and it by no means follows that an employer is liable "because a particular accident might have been prevented by some special device or precaution not in common use." All the cases agree that the master is not bound to use the newest and best appliances. He performs his duty when he furnishes those of ordinary character and reasonable safety, and the former is the test of the latter; for, in regard to the style of implement or nature of the mode of performance of any work, "reasonably safe" means safe according to the usages, habits, and ordinary risks of the business. Absolute safety is unattainable, and employers are not insurers. They are liable for the consequences, not of danger but of negligence; and the unbending test of negligence in methods, machinery, and appliances is the ordinary usage of the business. No man is held by law to a higher degree of skill than the fair average of his profession or trade, and the standard of due care is the conduct of the average prudent man. The test of negligence in employers is the same, and however strongly they may be convinced that there is a better or less dangerous way, no jury can be permitted to say that the usual and ordinary way, commonly adopted by those in the same business, is a negligent way for which liability shall be imposed. Juries must necessarily determine the responsibility of individual conduct, but they cannot be allowed to set up a standard which shall, in effect, dictate the customs or control the business of the community. . . .

It is also entirely clear that defendant's third point should have been affirmed. The deceased had been a brakeman on this train for five or six months, during which this mode of carrying broad-gauge cars had been used; cars similar to the one on which the accident occurred had been frequently carried, and that very car at least once, about ten days before. He not only thus had ample opportunity to know the risks of such trains, but he had his attention specially called to the alleged source of the accident, by having worked, just before becoming a brakeman, on the hoist by which the car bodies were transferred to the trucks. It was a perfectly plain case of acceptance of an employment, with full knowledge of the risks.

Judgment reversed.

Mayhew v. Sullivan Mining Co.
76 Me. 100 (1884)

[The plaintiff, an independent contractor, had been hired by the defendant to trace veins of new ore. During the course of his duties, the plaintiff worked on a platform in a mine shaft some 270 feet below ground. Near one corner of the platform was a "bucket-hole" which the plaintiff used in his work. The plaintiff alleged that on the day of the accident the defendant "carelessly and negligently caused a hole three feet in length by twenty-six inches in breadth to be cut for a ladder-hole in the platform near the centre of it directly back of the bucket-hole and twenty inches distant therefrom, without placing any rail or barrier about it, or any light or other warning there, and without giving plaintiff notice that any such dangerous change had been made in the platform; and that without any knowledge of its existence or fault on his part, the plaintiff, in the ordinary course of his business having occasion to go upon the platform fell through this new hole a distance of thirty-five feet, and received serious injury." The ladder-hole was made by one Stanley under the direction of the superintendent. The defendant sought to ask Stanley at trial whether he had "ever known ladder holes at a low level to be railed or fenced around," whether "as a miner" he thought it was "feasible" to use a ladder-hole with a railing around it, or whether he had "ever seen a ladder-hole in a mine, below the surface, with a railing around it." The court refused to allow the questions to be asked. Thereafter the jury found negligence and returned a verdict for the plaintiff of $2,500.]

BARROWS, J. Defendants' counsel claim that the favorable answers to these questions which they had a right to expect would have tended to show that there was no want of "average ordinary care" on the part of the defendants. We think the questions were properly excluded. The nature of the act in which the defendants' negligence was asserted to consist, with all the circumstances of time and place, whether of commission or omission, and its connection with the plaintiff's injury, presented a case as to which the jury were as well qualified to judge as any expert could be. It was not a case where the opinion of experts could be necessary or useful. . . . . If the defendants had proved that in every mining establishment that has existed since the days of Tubal-Cain, it has been the practice to cut ladder-holes in their platforms, situated as this was while in daily use for mining operations, without guarding or lighting them, and without notice to contractors or workmen, it would have no tendency to show that the act was consistent with ordinary prudence or a due regard for the safety of those who were using their premises by their invitation. The gross carelessness of the act appears conclusively upon its recital. Defendants' counsel argue that "if it should appear that they rarely had railings, then it tends to show no want of ordinary care in that respect," that "if one conforms to custom he is so far exercising average ordinary care." The argument proceeds upon an erroneous idea of what constitutes ordinary care. "Custom" and "average" have no proper place in its definition.

It would be no excuse for a want of ordinary care that carelessness was universal about the matter involved, or at the place of the accident, or in the business generally. . . .

The T.J. Hooper
53 F.2d 107 (S.D.N.Y. 1931)

[The operator of the tugboats *The T.J. Hooper* and the *Montrose* was sued under a towing contract when two barges and their cargo of coal were lost in a gale off the coast of New Jersey while in transit from Virginia to New York. The gist of the negligence claim was that neither tug was equipped with reliable radios that would have allowed them to receive the storm warnings broadcast in both the morning and the afternoon of March 8, 1928, by the naval station at Arlington. Four other tugs, the *Mars*, the *Menominee*, *The A.L. Walker*, and the *Waltham*, were on the same northbound route as *The T.J. Hooper*. They had received the messages and put safely into the Delaware breakwater.]

COXE, DISTRICT JUDGE: This raises the question whether the *Hooper* and *Montrose* were required to have effective radio sets to pick up weather reports broadcast along the coast. Concededly, there is no statutory law on the subject applicable to tugs of that type, the radio statute applying only to steamers "licensed to carry, or carrying, fifty or more persons"; and excepting by its terms "steamers plying between ports, or places, less than two hundred miles apart." U.S. Code Annotated, title 46, §484. The standard of seaworthiness is not, however, dependent on statutory enactment, or condemned to inertia or rigidity, but changes "with advancing knowledge, experience, and the changed appliances of navigation." It is particularly affected by new devices of demonstrated worth, which have become recognized as regular equipment by common usage.

Radio broadcasting was no new or untried thing in March, 1928. Everywhere, and in almost every field of activity, it was being utilized as an aid to communication, and for the dissemination of information. And that radio sets were in widespread use on vessels of all kinds is clearly indicated by the testimony in this case. Twice a day the government broadcast from Arlington weather reports forecasting weather conditions. Clearly this was important information which navigators could not afford to ignore.

Captain Powell, master of the *Menominee*, who was a witness for the tugs, testified that prior to March, 1928, his tug, and all other seagoing tugs of his company, were equipped by the owner with efficient radio sets, and that he regarded a radio as part "of the necessary equipment" of every reasonably well-equipped tug in the coastwise service. He further testified that 90 per cent of the coastwise tugs operating along the coast were so equipped. It is, of course, true that many of these radio sets were the personal property of the tug master, and not supplied by the owner. This was so with the *Mars, Waltham,* and *Menominee;* but, notwithstanding that fact, the use of the radio was shown to be so extensive as to amount almost to a universal practice in the navigation of coastwise tugs along the coast. I think therefore there was a duty on the part of the tug owner to supply effective receiving sets.

How have the tugs met this requirement? The *Hooper* had a radio set which belonged to her master, but was practically useless even before the tug left Hampton Roads, and was generally out of order. . . .

I hold therefore ... (2) that the tugs *T.J. Hooper* and *Montrose* were unseaworthy in failing to have effective radio sets, capable of receiving weather reports on March 8th, ... (3) that the claims of the cargo owners against the tugs should be allowed. ...

The T.J. Hooper
60 F.2d 737 (2d Cir. 1932)

[On appeal from the decision below. The court first noted that the evidence supported the claim that *The T.J. Hooper* would have taken shelter if its captain had received the naval broadcasts.]

L. HAND, J. They did not, because their private radio receiving sets, which were on board, were not in working order. These belonged to them personally, and were partly a toy, partly a part of the equipment, but neither furnished by the owner, nor supervised by it. It is not fair to say that there was a general custom among coastwise carriers so to equip their tugs. One line alone did it; as for the rest, they relied upon their crews, so far as they can be said to have relied at all. An adequate receiving set suitable for a coastwise tug can now be got at small cost and is reasonably reliable if kept up; obviously it is a source of great protection to their tows. Twice every day they can receive these predictions, based upon the widest possible information, available to every vessel within two or three hundred miles and more. Such a set is the ears of the tug to catch the spoken word, just as the master's binoculars are her eyes to see a storm signal ashore. Whatever may be said as to other vessels, tugs towing heavy coal laden barges, strung out for half a mile, have little power to manoeuvre, and do not, as this case proves, expose themselves to weather which would not turn back stauncher craft. They can have at hand protection against dangers of which they can learn in no other way.

Is it then a final answer that the business had not yet generally adopted receiving sets? There are, no doubt, cases where courts seem to make the general practice of the calling the standard of proper diligence; we have indeed given some currency to the notion ourselves. Indeed in most cases reasonable prudence is in fact common prudence; but strictly it is never its measure; a whole calling may have unduly lagged in the adoption of new and available devices. It never may set its own tests, however persuasive be its usages. Courts must in the end say what is required; there are precautions so imperative that even their universal disregard will not excuse their omission. But here there was no custom at all as to receiving sets; some had them, some did not; the most that can be urged is that they had not yet become general. Certainly in such a case we need not pause; when some have thought a device necessary, at least we may say that they were right, and the others too slack. The statute [46 U.S.C.A. §484] does not bear on this situation at all. It prescribes not a receiving, but a transmitting set, and for a very different purpose; to call for help, not to get news. We hold the tugs therefore because had they been properly equipped, they would have got the Arlington reports. The injury was a direct consequence of this unseaworthiness.

Decree affirmed.

NOTES

1. *The relationship between custom and negligence.* The four opinions in the three previous cases express different views on the relationship between custom and negligence. *Mayhew* has gained little following, either in its own time or today. *Titus* once enjoyed a considerable following, especially in the context of industrial accidents, although the balance of authority was probably against it even during the nineteenth century. See, e.g., Maynard v. Buck, 100 Mass. 40 (1868), and Wabash Railway v. McDaniels, 107 U.S. 454 (1883). The unrelenting attack on *Titus* often took a strong theoretical turn. Thus, Miller, The So-Called Unbending Test of Negligence, 3 Va. L. Rev. 537, 543 (1916), argued that the *Titus* rule would deter new innovations by firms that might otherwise be prepared to make them, because "the rule of the 'unbending test' constrains him to adopt the unsafe method in order to bring himself within the rule and escape the charge of negligence." Sound? Do firms in a competitive industry have an incentive to innovate in order to lower wage levels? In a monopolistic industry?

The *T.J. Hooper* did not therefore mark a radical break from tradition, although its allusion that "a whole calling may have unduly lagged in the adoption of new and available devices" has allowed wholesale attacks on standard industry policy, not only in admiralty cases but in such other areas as industrial accidents and product liability cases. Some sense of this approach is found in Bimberg v. Northern Pacific Ry., 14 N.W.2d 410, 413 (Minn. 1944), a wrongful death action brought under the Federal Employers' Liability Act. The defendant argued that designing a trestle was "an engineering problem for solution by the railroads and not by the courts," but the court took a different view of the subject:

> Local usage and general custom, either singly or in combination, will not justify or excuse negligence. They are merely foxholes in one of the battlefields of law, providing shelter, but not complete protection against charges of negligence. The generality of its plan of construction for trestles or bridges cannot excuse a railroad company from responsibility for negligence in its construction. Such plan of construction, commonly followed and "fortified," as defendant insists, "by many years of successful railroad operation," may be evidence of due care, but it cannot avail to establish as safe in law that which is dangerous in fact.

Even after these decisions, the precise relationship between custom and negligence remains controversial. Should compliance with custom establish a prima facie case of due care? Or should it only be evidence tending to show that the defendant did not take unreasonable risks of harm to others? On this question, the Third Restatement downgrades the role of custom, holding that compliance with the custom of the community "is evidence that the actor's conduct is not negligent, but does not preclude a finding of negligence," while a departure from custom "in a way that increases risk is evidence of the actor's negligence but does not require a finding of negligence." RTT:LPH §13(a)-(b). Comment *b*, on compliance, echoes *The T.J. Hooper*: "Possibly, the entire community or industry has lagged: all members of the group to which the actor belongs may have been inattentive to new developments or may have been pursuing self-interest in a way that has encouraged the neglect of a reasonable precaution." Conversely, the Restatement notes that departure from custom usually carries with it "significant weight. As a practical matter, the party who has departed from custom can counter the effect of this evidence by questioning the intelligence of the custom, by showing that its operation poses different or less serious risks than those occasioned by others engaging in seemingly similar activities, or by showing that it has adopted an alternative method for reducing or controlling risks that is at least as effective as the customary method." *Id.*, comment *c*.

  2. *Custom and cost-benefit analysis.* Hand's decision in *The T.J. Hooper* complements his analysis in *Carroll Towing, supra* at 206. Although *Carroll* articulates Hand's use of a cost-benefit formula, *The T.J. Hooper* denies any conclusive weight to custom — its major rival in setting the standard of care. Hand's view has received overwhelming acceptance in the courts and among the commentators. For a dissenting view on the subject, see Epstein, The Path to *The T.J. Hooper*: The Theory and History of Custom in the Law of Tort, 21 J. Legal Stud. 1, 4-5 (1992), which argues as follows:

> [G]iven the imperfections of the legal system, the conventional wisdom that places cost-benefit analysis first and custom second is incorrect in at least two ways. First, in cases that arise out of a consensual arrangement, negligence is often the appropriate standard for liability, and, where it is so, custom should be regarded as conclusive evidence of due care in the absence of any contractual stipulation to the contrary. It is quite possible in some consensual settings no custom will emerge, at which point the negligence inquiry will be inescapably ad hoc. But where consistent custom emerges, regardless of its origins, it should be followed. Second, in stranger cases — that is, those where the harm does not fall on a contracting party or someone with whom the defendant has a special relationship — negligence should normally not be the appropriate standard of care, so that reliance on custom is as irrelevant as the negligence issue to which custom alone is properly directed. But where negligence is adopted in these stranger cases, then custom is normally

not the appropriate standard because it registers the preferences of the parties to the custom, not those who are victimized by it. It should be taken into account, but given no dispositive weight. . . .

Note that *The T.J. Hooper* arose out of a consensual situation, like most of the litigation over custom. Accordingly, the choice between the customary and cost-benefit approaches lies at the heart of understanding the distribution of power between the market and the courts in setting the standards of conduct for defendants in all lines of business and endeavors. Here the Hand formula turns out in practice to be far more *interventionist* than any standard of care based on custom. These cost-benefit tests are used to challenge the rationality of markets, while formulas based on custom accept and rely on some level of implicit rationality in market behavior.

How do customs emerge? Should it make any difference whether we are dealing with customs in a closely knit industry or with those that reach a broad commercial market? Whether we are dealing with parties who have overlapping roles (that is, transactions between merchants in the same line of business) or with parties having specialized distinctive relationships (e.g., physician/patient or landlord/tenant)?

3. *Custom and private rules of conduct.* Can the plaintiff use the defendant's established rules that govern the conduct of his employees as evidence of negligence? In Fonda v. St. Paul City Ry., 74 N.W. 166, 169 (Minn. 1898), the plaintiff, an injured pedestrian, sued the defendant for the negligence of its servant in the operation of its train. The plaintiff was "a stranger to and not an employee of," the defendant, so that his "conduct could not have been in any way affected or influenced" by rules of which he had no knowledge. Mitchell, J., differentiated these internal house rules from statutes and municipal ordinances because of the perverse incentives created. "The effect of it is that, the more cautious and careful a man is in the adoption of rules in the management of his business in order to protect others, the worse he is off, and the higher the degree of care he is bound to exercise. A person may, out of abundant caution, adopt rules requiring of his employees a much higher degree of care than the law imposes. This is a practice that ought to be encouraged, and not discouraged. But, if the adoption of such a course is to be used against him as an admission, he would naturally find it to his interest not to adopt any rules at all." Is that the case if the proprietor can advertise his compliance with higher standards?

In any event, more recent cases have shown a willingness to allow the plaintiff to introduce the defendant's own internal rules on the standard of care question. In Lucy Webb Hayes National Training School v. Perotti, 419 F.2d 704, 710 (D.C. Cir. 1969), the plaintiff's decedent had been admitted into the defendant's psychiatric hospital as a mental patient for observation and treatment. Shortly after being admitted, the decedent slipped past the nurses' station that separated the secured portion of the floor, Ward 7-W, into the unsecured area on the same floor. While the defendant's attendant was leading the decedent back to Ward 7-W, he bolted away, jumped through a window, and plunged to his death. The plaintiff argued that the hospital fell short of its own internal standard by allowing the decedent to wander from the closed to the open ward.

> We think the jury could find negligence upon the part of the hospital from this evidence without the assistance of expert testimony. The jurors might not be able to determine the necessity for a closed ward for mental patients of the type admitted to Ward 7-W, nor to evaluate the need for restrictions upon the movement of patients into and out of the closed ward. But the hospital itself had made these decisions. It could, of course, have presented evidence that the limitations upon patient movement constituted more than due care, or were unrelated to patient safety. Indeed, witnesses did testify for the hospital that the open and closed wards were separated by a locked door chiefly, or only, to isolate the more disturbed patients from those not so acutely ill. On the basis of all the evidence, however, the jury could reasonably conclude that the hospital's failure to observe the standards it had itself established represented negligence.

For the modern equivocation on the question of private standards, see RT:LPH §13, comment *f*, which first notes "allowing the defendant's departure from its own standard to be used against the defendant might seem unfair, since it penalizes the defendant who has voluntarily provided an extra measure of safety." On the other hand, it continues, "the plaintiff may well have relied on the defendant's standard (or the defendant's general reputation for safety) in choosing to deal with the defendant; furthermore, the plaintiff may well be paying for at least the general costs of compliance which the standard imposes on the defendant." Should general reputation play the same role as an internal directive?

4. *Updating custom.* In Trimarco v. Klein, 436 N.E.2d 502 (N.Y. 1982), the plaintiff was injured in 1976 when he slipped in his bathroom and received serious lacerations from crashing against a shower door made of ordinary glass estimated to be between 1/16 and 1/4 of an inch thick. The shower door had been installed in the 1950s, when the use of ordinary glass was standard practice. Since the mid-1960s, the common practice in New York City had been to use safer tempered glass "whether to replace broken glass or to comply with the request of a tenant." The plaintiff in this instance did not know that ordinary glass was used in his shower door. Reversing a decision of the Appellate Division, the New York Court of Appeals allowed the plaintiff to reach the jury. The court first noted that evidence of custom was admissible because "it reflects the judgment and experience and conduct of many," and because "its relevancy and reliability comes too from the direct bearing it has on feasibility, for its

focusing is on the practicability of a precaution in actual operation and the readiness with which it can be employed." Nonetheless, the court refused to give the custom conclusive weight, noting "[a]fter all, customs and usages run the gamut of merit like anything else." The court then concluded that "it was also for the jury to decide whether, at the point in time when the accident occurred, the modest cost and ready availability of safety glass and the dynamics of the growing custom to use it for shower enclosures had transformed what once may have been considered a reasonably safe part of the apartment into one which, in light of later developments, no longer could be so regarded."

Must all old shower doors be replaced? Sprinklers and burglar alarms be retrofitted in old buildings?

Lama v. Borras
16 F.3d 473 (1st Cir. 1994)

STAHL, J. Defendants-appellants Dr. Pedro Borras and Asociacion Hospital del Maestro, Inc. (Hospital) appeal from a jury verdict finding them liable for medical malpractice to plaintiffs Roberto Romero Lama (Romero) and his wife, Norma. . . . Finding no error, we affirm.

I. BACKGROUND

Since the jury found defendants liable, we recount the facts in the light most favorable to plaintiffs, drawing all reasonable inferences in their favor; we do not evaluate the credibility of witnesses or the weight of the evidence. . . .

In 1985, Romero was suffering from back pain and searching for solutions. Dr. Nancy Alfonso, Romero's family physician, provided some treatment but then referred him to Dr. Borras, a neurosurgeon. Dr. Borras concluded that Romero had a herniated disc and scheduled surgery. Prior to surgery, Dr. Borras neither prescribed nor enforced a regime of absolute bed rest, nor did he offer other key components of "conservative treatment." Although Dr. Borras instructed Romero, a heavy smoker, to enter the hospital one week before surgery in order to "clean out" his lungs and strengthen his heart, Romero was still not subjected to standard conservative treatment.

While operating on April 9, 1986, Dr. Borras discovered that Romero had an "extruded" disc and attempted to remove the extruding material. Either because Dr. Borras failed to remove the offending material or because he operated at the wrong level, Romero's original symptoms returned in full force several days after the operation. Dr. Borras concluded that a second operation was necessary to remedy the "recurrence."

Dr. Borras operated again on May 15, 1986. Dr. Borras did not order pre- or post-operative antibiotics. It is unclear whether the second operation was successful in curing the herniated disc. In any event, as early as May 17, a nurse's note indicates that the bandage covering Romero's surgical wound was "very bloody," a symptom which, according to expert testimony, indicates the possibility of infection. On May 18, Romero was experiencing local pain at the site of the incision, another symptom consistent with an infection. On May 19, the bandage was "soiled again." A more complete account of Romero's evolving condition is not available because the Hospital instructed nurses to engage in "charting by exception," a system whereby nurses did not record qualitative observations for each of the day's three shifts, but instead made such notes only when necessary to chronicle important changes in a patient's condition.

On the night of May 20, Romero began to experience severe discomfort in his back. He passed the night screaming in pain. At some point on May 21, Dr. Edwin Lugo Piazza, an attending physician, diagnosed the problem as discitis — an infection of the space between discs — and responded by initiating antibiotic treatment. Discitis is extremely painful and, since it occurs in a location with little blood circulation, very slow to cure. Romero was hospitalized for several additional months while undergoing treatment for the infection.

After moving from Puerto Rico to Florida, the Romeros filed this diversity tort action in United States District Court for the District of Puerto Rico. Plaintiffs alleged that Dr. Borras was negligent in four general areas: (1) failure to provide proper conservative medical treatment; (2) premature and otherwise improper discharge after surgery; (3) negligent performance of surgery; and (4) failure to provide proper management for the infection. While plaintiffs did not claim that the Hospital was vicariously liable for any negligence on the part of Dr. Borras, they alleged that the Hospital was itself negligent in [its] failure to prepare, use, and monitor proper medical records. . . .

[At trial the jury awarded plaintiffs $600,000, and the district court rejected defendant's motion for a judgment as a matter of law under Fed. R. Civ. P. 50(b), as well as defendant's motion for a new trial under Fed. R. Civ. P. 59. The district court concluded that had Dr. Borras used conservative treatment, he might have obviated all the risks of a complex laminectomy, and that better record keeping could have allowed hospital personnel to detect the infection at an earlier stage, and finally that the hospital staff could have been negligent in handling the dressings and bandages.]

We find the reasoning of the district court to be substantially sound and therefore affirm the result.

III. DISCUSSION

A. MEDICAL MALPRACTICE UNDER PUERTO RICO LAW

We begin our analysis by laying out the substantive law of Puerto Rico governing this diversity suit. To establish a prima facie case of medical malpractice in Puerto Rico, a plaintiff must demonstrate: (1) the basic norms of knowledge and medical care applicable to general practitioners or specialists; (2) proof that the medical personnel failed to follow these basic norms in the treatment of the patient; and (3) a causal relation between the act or omission of the physician and the injury suffered by the patient.

The burden of a medical malpractice plaintiff in establishing the physician's duty is more complicated than that of an ordinary tort plaintiff. Instead of simply appealing to the jury's view of what is reasonable under the circumstances, a medical malpractice plaintiff must establish the relevant national standard of care....

Naturally, the trier of fact can rarely determine the applicable standard of care without the assistance of expert testimony. The predictable battle of the experts then creates a curious predicament for the fact-finder, because an error of judgment regarding diagnosis or treatment does not lead to liability when expert opinion suggests that the physician's conduct fell within a range of acceptable alternatives. While not allowed to speculate, the fact-finder is of course free to find some experts more credible than others.

Proof of causation is also more difficult in a medical malpractice case than in a routine tort case because a jury must often grapple with scientific processes that are unfamiliar and involve inherent uncertainty. A plaintiff must prove, by a preponderance of the evidence, that the physician's negligent conduct was the factor that "most probably" caused harm to the plaintiff. As in the case of duty, however, a jury normally cannot find causation based on mere speculation and conjecture; expert testimony is generally essential....

B. NEGLIGENCE OF DR. BORRAS

The Borras Defendants claim that plaintiffs failed to introduce any evidence sufficient to prove either (1) the relevant standards of acceptable medical practice or (2) the causal link between Dr. Borras' conduct and harm to the plaintiffs. While plaintiffs may not have been able to substantiate the broad attack outlined in their complaint, we focus here on only one allegation of negligence: Dr. Borras' failure to provide conservative treatment prior to the first operation.

Defendants argue that plaintiffs failed to prove a general medical standard governing the need for conservative treatment in a case like that of Romero. We disagree. Plaintiffs' chief expert witness, Dr. George Udvarhelyi, testified that, absent an indication of neurological impairment, the standard practice is for a neurosurgeon to postpone lumbar disc surgery while the patient undergoes conservative treatment, with a period of absolute bed rest as the prime ingredient. In these respects, the views of defendants' neurosurgery experts did not diverge from those of Dr. Udvarhelyi. For example, Dr. Luis Guzman Lopez testified that, in the absence of extraordinary factors, "all neurosurgeons go for [conservative treatment] before they finally decide on [an] operation." Indeed, when called by plaintiffs, Dr. Borras (who also testified as a neurosurgery expert) agreed on cross-examination with the statement that "bed rest is normally recommended before surgery is decided in a patient like Mr. Romero," and claimed that he *did* give conservative treatment to Romero.

In spite of Dr. Borras' testimony to the contrary, there was also sufficient evidence for the jury to find that Dr. Borras failed to provide the customary conservative treatment. Dr. Alfonso, Romero's family physician, testified that Dr. Borras, while aware that Romero had not followed a program of absolute bed rest, proceeded with surgery anyway. Although Romero was admitted to the hospital one week before surgery, there was evidence that Dr. Borras neither prescribed nor attempted to enforce a conservative treatment regime. In fact, there was evidence that Dr. Borras' main goal was simply to admit Romero for a week of smoke-free relaxation, not absolute bed rest, because Romero's heavy smoking and mild hypertension made him a high-risk surgery patient. In short, we agree with the district court that the jury could reasonably have concluded that Dr. Borras failed to institute and manage a proper conservative treatment plan.

The issue of causation is somewhat more problematic. There are two potential snags in the chain of causation. First, it is uncertain that premature surgery was the cause of Romero's infection. Second, it is uncertain whether conservative treatment would have made surgery unnecessary. With respect to the first problem, the Puerto Rico Supreme Court has suggested that, when a physician negligently exposes a patient to risk-prone surgery, the physician is liable for the harm associated with a foreseeable risk. In this case, it is undisputed that discitis was a foreseeable risk of lumbar disc surgery.

Turning to the second area of uncertainty, we observe that nearly all of the experts who testified on the subject for both plaintiffs and defendants were of the opinion that conservative treatment would eliminate the need for surgery in the overwhelming majority of cases. Nonetheless, defendants introduced expert testimony that, because Romero suffered from an "extruded" disc, conservative treatment would not have helped. Dr. Udvarhelyi testified, however, that an extruded disc is indeed amenable to conservative treatment. With competent expert testimony in the record, the jury was not left to conjure up its own theories of causation. And certainly, the jury was free to credit some witnesses more than others. The question is admittedly close, but the jury could have reasonably found that Dr. Borras' failure to administer conservative treatment was the "most probable cause" of the first operation.

We conclude that plaintiffs introduced legally sufficient evidence to support each element of at least one major allegation of negligence on the part of Dr. Borras. We therefore hold that the district court properly denied the Borras Defendants' Rule 50 and 59 motions.

C. NEGLIGENCE OF ASOCIACION HOSPITAL DEL MAESTRO

While plaintiffs made a number of allegations against the Hospital, we focus on the allegation that the failure of hospital nurses to report on each nursing shift was a negligent cause of the late detection of Romero's infection.

The Hospital cannot seriously dispute that plaintiffs introduced sufficient evidence on the elements of duty and breach. [The court then held that the jury could properly find that the nursing staff's failure to keep qualitative notes of each nursing shift, as required under regulation, could count as the proximate cause of the harm. It first noted that the sketchy notes could have delayed the diagnosis of plaintiff's excessive bleeding at the site of the wound, which in turn "could have prevented the infection from reaching the disc interspace in the critical period prior to May 20."]

Affirmed.

NOTES

1. *The standard of care in medical malpractice case.* Although *Lama* is decided under Puerto Rican law, its basic principles are indistinguishable from those applicable in virtually all common law jurisdictions. Today, the typical standards for medical malpractice actions require that "a doctor must use that degree of skill and learning which is normally possessed and used by doctors in good standing in a similar practice in similar communities and under like circumstances," approved in Kalsbeck v. Westview Clinic, P.A., 375 N.W.2d 861, 868 (Minn. App. 1985), or that "[a] physician who undertakes a mode or form of treatment which a reasonable and prudent member of the medical profession would undertake under the same or similar circumstances shall not be subject to liability for harm caused thereby to the patient." Hood v. Phillips, 554 S.W.2d 160, 165 (Tex. 1977).

Often, no single custom covers a given issue. In Jones v. Chidester, 610 A.2d 964, 965, 969 (Pa. 1992), the court set up the "two schools" problem as follows:

A medical practitioner has an absolute defense to a claim of negligence when it is determined that the prescribed treatment or procedure has been approved by one group of medical experts even though an alternate school of thought recommends another approach, or it is agreed among experts that alternative treatments and practices are acceptable. The doctrine is applicable only where there is more than one method of accepted treatment or procedure. In specific terms, however, we are called upon in this case to decide once again whether a school of thought qualifies as such when it is advocated by a "considerable number" of medical experts or when it commands acceptance by "respective, reputable and reasonable" practitioners. The former test calls for a quantitative analysis, while the latter is premised on qualitative grounds.

The court then noted that the precedents left the question unresolved, and continued:

It is incumbent upon us to settle this confusion. The "two schools of thought doctrine" provides a complete defense to malpractice. It is therefore insufficient to show that there exists a "small minority" of physicians who agree with the defendant's questioned practice. Thus, the Superior Court's "reputable and respected by reasonable medical experts" test is improper. Rather, there must be a considerable number of physicians, recognized and respected in their field, sufficient to create another "school of thought."

2. Error in judgment. One common refrain in medical malpractice cases is that adverse outcomes alone do not establish liability because the physician does not insure a patient against the adverse consequences of treatment. That rule would be unworkable, especially for patients in a distressed condition at the onset of treatment, who would be required to pay an additional insurance premium for the expanded scope of liability. The law of negligence must therefore develop rules that disentangle poor outcomes from poor treatment. At one time, it was common to say that physicians should not be held responsible for "mere errors in judgment" made in the course of treatment or diagnosis.

That form of instruction has fallen into disfavor today. In Hirahara v. Tanaka, 959 P.2d 830, 834 (Haw. 1998), the decedent was hospitalized for routine treatment of a rectal abscess. He was placed "in a jackknife position, with his head and feet below his raised buttocks." By mistake the anesthesiologist administered a hyperbaric anesthetic, whose specific gravity exceeded that of spinal fluid. In consequence, the anesthetic drained into the brain where it reduced the decedent's air supply. A warning bell rang, indicating low oxygen. The defendant surgeon then spoke to the decedent, who was still conscious and able to breathe. It was not clear whether the surgery had begun at that time. In any event, while the surgery was under way the alarm sounded again, and this time, the decedent was unresponsive. The defendant continued the surgery, after which the decedent died on the operating table of cardiac arrest. A suit against the anesthesiologist was dismissed with prejudice (indicating settlement). The defendant was granted an instruction that read, "A physician is not necessarily negligent because he errs in judgment or because his efforts prove unsuccessful." Plaintiff appealed a verdict for the defendant, and the case was reversed and remanded for a new trial:

> We perceive the source of confusion engendered by the use of "error in judgment" language as a failure to specify from which relative temporal vantage point the doctor's selection of a particular course of treatment was "error." It is not negligent for a physician, based on the knowledge that he reasonably possesses at the time, to select a particular course of treatment among acceptable medical alternatives. This is true even though, in hindsight, the choice was inappropriate. However, it is a breach of the duty of care for a physician to make an erroneous choice if, at the time he made the choice, he should have had knowledge that it was erroneous. This proposition is difficult to explain to a lay jury. Moreover, it is adequately covered by alternate instructions that a physician's liability cannot be premised solely on a harmful result if he or she conforms to the professional standard of care. Therefore, we hold that any jury instruction that states that a physician is not necessarily liable for an "error in judgment" is confusing and misleading and should not be given to the jury.

Should the surgeon be allowed to rely on the judgment of the anesthesiologist in deciding whether to continue with surgery?

3. *Setting the customary standard.* Expert testimony offers the most common way of determining the applicable standard of care. But other sources are also available. In Morlino v. Medical Center of Ocean County, 706 A.2d 721, 729-730 (N.J. 1998), the defendant emergency room physician, Dr. Dugenio, prescribed Ciprofloxacin to the plaintiff, then eight and one-half months pregnant, when she complained of a serious sore throat. Her fetus was dead the next day. Before prescribing the drug the defendant consulted the Physician's Desk Reference, "a compilation of information about prescription drugs that is published annually and distributed to the medical professional free of charge." The PDR contains a list of indications and contraindications for the use of various drugs, alone and in combination, for treating various conditions. It contained the following warning: CIPROFLOXACIN SHOULD NOT BE USED IN CHILDREN OR PREGNANT WOMEN, noting that animal studies indicated some fetal risk. Having read this warning, Dr. Dugenio nonetheless prescribed the

drug because he was concerned that an influenza bacteria, if untreated, could lead to greater patient illness, which in turn could jeopardize the fetus's own welfare. In affirming a jury verdict for the defendants, Pollock, J., had allowed evidence of PDR warnings to establish the applicable standard of care for prescribing medicine, but cautioned:

> Nevertheless, drug manufacturers do not design package insets and PDR entries to establish a standard of medical care. Manufacturers write drug package inserts and PDR warnings for many reasons including compliance with FDA requirements, advertisement, the provision of useful information to physicians, and an attempt to limit the manufacturer's liability. After a drug has been on the market for a sufficient period of time, moreover, physicians may rely more on their own experience and the professional publications of others than on a drug manufacturer's advertisements, inserts, or PDR entries. . . .
>
> Accordingly, we hold that the package inserts and PDR references alone do not establish the standard of care. It follows that a physician's failure to adhere to PDR warnings does not by itself constitute negligence. Reliance on the PDR alone to establish negligence would both obviate expert testimony on an issue where it is needed and could mislead the jury about the appropriate standard of care.

4. Rejection of the customary standard. The most notable break from the standard of customary care took place over a quarter of a century ago in *Helling v. Carey*, 519 P.2d 981 (Wash. 1974). The plaintiff first consulted the defendant from 1959 to 1968, largely to treat an eye irritation caused by contact lenses. By the end of 1968, when plaintiff was 32, defendant suspected that she had glaucoma — a disease of the eye caused by pressure on the optic nerve — after she complained of impaired peripheral vision. The defendant then administered a pressure test which confirmed the diagnosis. The plaintiff suffered a permanent impairment of her vision. The defendant introduced expert evidence that the applicable standard of professional care did not require pressure tests for patients under 40, given that glaucoma is rare for patients in that group. Finding this a "unique case," Hunter, J., relied on *The T.J. Hooper* to reject the medical custom. Reversing a directed verdict for the defendant below, he found the need for the test to be "so imperative" to hold that the test was required as a matter of law:

> The incidence of glaucoma in one out of 25,000 persons under the age of 40 may appear quite minimal. However, that one person, the plaintiff in this instance, is entitled to the same protection, as afforded persons over 40, essential for timely detection of the evidence of glaucoma where it can be arrested to avoid the grave and devastating result of this disease. The test is a simple pressure test, relatively inexpensive. There is no judgment factor

involved, and there is no doubt that by giving the test the evidence of glaucoma can be detected. The giving of the test is harmless if the physical condition of the eye permits. The testimony indicates that although the condition of the plaintiff's eyes might have at times prevented the defendants from administering the pressure test, there is an absence of evidence in the record that the test could not have been timely given.

In his concurrence, Utter, J., urged adoption of a virtual strict liability standard in order to avoid the placing of "stigma of moral blame" upon a physician that followed the community standard.

In applying strict liability there are many situations where it is imposed for conduct which can be defined with sufficient precision to insure that application of a strict liability principle will not produce miscarriages of justice in a substantial number of cases. If the activity involved is one which can be defined with sufficient precision, that definition can serve as an accounting unit to which the costs of the activity may be allocated with some certainty and precision. With this possible, strict liability serves a compensatory function in situations where the defendant is, through the use of insurance, the financially more responsible person. . . .

How does Hunter's argument fare under the Hand formula? What factors should be relevant to the cost-benefit analysis in *Helling*? Note that 96 percent of the patients diagnosed as potential glaucoma cases by the pressure tests do not have the disease. See Wiley, The Impact of Judicial Decisions on Professional Conduct: An Empirical Study, 55 S. Cal. L. Rev. 345, 388 n.143 (1982), which also argues that given these false positives, the test is not cost-justified even under the Hand formula, assuming that the previous damage awards were reliable measures of plaintiff's loss.

Helling provoked a swift statutory response. Washington Revised Code §4.24.290 (2007), for example, now provides that in actions for professional negligence against physicians and other health care providers, the plaintiff must "prove by a preponderance of the evidence that the defendant or defendants failed to exercise that degree of skill, care, and learning possessed at that time by other persons in the same profession, and that as a proximate result of such failure the plaintiff suffered damages, but in no event shall the provisions of this section apply to an action based on the failure to obtain the informed consent of a patient."

Helling was also given a narrow reading in Meeks v. Marx, 550 P.2d 1158 (Wash. App. 1976), where the court concluded that "[a] thorough analysis of that decision leads us to conclude the holding there was intended to be restricted solely to its own 'unique' facts, i.e., cases in which an ophthalmologist is alleged to have failed to test for glaucoma under the same or similar circumstances." The strict liability boomlet has died, and customary care standard has survived. But why reject *The T.J. Hooper* in medical malpractice cases? One influential explanation is offered in Morris, Custom and Negligence, 42 Colum. L. Rev. 1147, 1164-1165 (1942):

> Why should conformity to the practice protect a physician from liability? Drovers, railroads, merchants, etc., are not so protected. The doctor escapes liability even though he conforms only to the practice in his locality or the practice in similar localities. And treatment need not conform to a general usage, it need only be like that used by some reputable doctors. If all doctors reasonably developed and applied their skill and knowledge, the conformity test might be the equivalent of reasonable care under the circumstances. Doctors as a class may be more likely to exert their best efforts than drovers, railroads, and merchants but they are human and subject to the temptations of laziness and unthinking acceptance of traditions. The rationale is: no other standard is practical. Our judges and juries are usually not competent to judge whether or not a doctor has acted reasonably. The conformity test is probably the only workable test available. . . .
>
> The patient who has endured suffering is an appealing plaintiff. Juries are likely to favor him. And it is widely known that doctors usually carry liability insurance. But a doctor who loses a malpractice case stands to lose more than the amount of the judgment — he may also lose his professional reputation and his livelihood. These considerations heighten the need for a test of malpractice that will protect doctors against undeserved liability. The law may be academically deficient in countenancing an excuse that may occasionally be based on the negligence of the other doctors. But the grossly incompetent practitioner will find little comfort in the tests of malpractice. A few negligent doctors may escape, but the quack will not. The reasonably prudent man "test" would enable the ambulance chaser to make a law suit out of any protracted illness.

See also Epstein, Medical Malpractice: The Case for Contract, 1 Am. B. Found. Res. J. 87, 108-113 (1976). For a modern critique of Morris's position, see Steven Hetcher, Creating Safe Social Norms in a Dangerous World, 73 So. Cal. L. Rev. 1 (1999).

5. *The locality rule.* If the customary standard has survived, the locality rule, as defended by Morris, has taken a beating in the modern age of national medical standards and accreditation, complete with board-certified physicians. The key transitional decision is Brune v. Belinkoff, 235 N.E.2d 793 (Mass. 1968). There, the plaintiff claimed that the defendant anesthesiologist negligently administered a spinal anesthetic during the delivery of plaintiff's baby in October 1958. The defendant, practicing in New Bedford, Massachusetts, gave plaintiff an eight-milligram dosage of pontocaine. Eleven hours later plaintiff attempted to climb out of bed, but slipped and fell, suffering persistent injuries. Medical evidence established that her fall was due to an excessive dosage of pontocaine. Some medical evidence was introduced to show that good

medical practice required a dosage of less than five milligrams. Other evidence, including that of defendant, tended to show that the dosage given was customary in New Bedford, and that the smaller dosages given in New York and Boston were appropriate because of the different obstetrical procedures used in those two cities. "The New Bedford obstetricians use supra fundi pressure (pressure applied to the uterus during delivery) which 'requires a higher level of anesthesia.'"

The trial judge instructed the jury that the defendant's care "must measure up to the standard of professional care and skill ordinarily possessed by others in his profession in the community, which is New Bedford, and its environs, of course, where he practices, having regard to the current state of advance of the profession. If, in a given case, it were determined by a jury that the ability and skill of the physician in New Bedford were 50 percent inferior to that which existed in Boston, a defendant in New Bedford would be required to measure up to the standard of skill and competence and ability that is ordinarily found by physicians in New Bedford." Spaulding, J., upheld the plaintiff's exception to that charge, noting that the traditional locality rule announced in Small v. Howard, 128 Mass. 131 (1880), rightly protected a jack-of-all-trades general practitioner performing difficult surgery in a small country village. But for today's high-powered specialists he opted for a national standard:

> The time has come when the medical profession should no longer be Balkanized by the application of varying geographic standards in malpractice cases. Accordingly, Small v. Howard is hereby overruled. The present case affords a good illustration of the inappropriateness of the "locality" rule to existing conditions. The defendant was a specialist practising in New Bedford, a city of 100,000, which is slightly more than fifty miles from Boston, one of the medical centers of the nation, if not the world. This is a far cry from the country doctor in Small v. Howard, who ninety years ago was called upon to perform difficult surgery. Yet the trial judge told the jury that if the skill and ability of New Bedford physicians were "fifty percent inferior" to those obtaining in Boston the defendant should be judged by New Bedford standards, "having regard to the current state of advance of the profession." This may well be carrying the rule of Small v. Howard to its logical conclusion, but it is, we submit, a reductio ad absurdum of the rule.
>
> The proper standard is whether the physician, if a general practitioner, has exercised the degree of care and skill of the average qualified practitioner, taking into account the advances in the profession. In applying this standard it is permissible to consider the medical resources available to the physician as *one* circumstance in determining the skill and care required. Under this standard some allowance is thus made for the type of community in which the physician carries on his practice. . . .

Under the modern rule, should a rural clinic be required to have the same equipment as a state-of-the-art university hospital? See Morreim, Cost Containment and the Standard of Medical Care, 75 Cal. L. Rev. 1719 (1987).

6. *Expert witnesses in medical malpractice cases.* One important consequence of the passing of the locality rule is that experts from all parts of the country may testify against local physicians. That result is most common with board-certified physicians, where the general position today is that qualified experts may offer testimony that is not speculative. In some states the matter has been codified. Section 9-19-41 of Rhode Island General Laws (2007), for example, provides that in medical malpractice cases for professional negligence "only those persons who by knowledge, skill, experience, training, or education qualify as experts in the field of the alleged malpractice shall be permitted to give expert testimony as to the alleged malpractice." That rule still paves the way for extensive jousting, as the Rhode Island Supreme Court stated in Sheeley v. Memorial Hospital, 710 A.2d 161, 166 (R.I. 1998), in allowing the expert testimony of an inactive physician who kept up with his field against a second-year family practice resident:

> The resources available to a physician, his or her specific area of practice, or the length of time he or she has been practicing are all issues that should be considered by the trial justice in making his or her decision regarding the qualification of an expert. No one issue, however, should be determinative. Furthermore, except in extreme cases, a witness who has obtained board certification in a particular specialty related to the procedure in question, especially when that board certification reflects a national standard of training and qualification, should be presumptively qualified to render an opinion.

Should the defendant be allowed to introduce local experts to testify on the persistence of local differences in the standard of care? Similarly, a Connecticut statute (Conn. Gen. Stat. §52-184c(c) (2007)), for example, distinguishes between physicians who do, and do not, hold themselves out as board-certified specialists. Roughly speaking, its general scheme allows a board-certified specialist with five years' training to testify in any case within his sphere of competence, and allows non-board-certified physicians to testify only in suits brought against non-board-certified doctors, but not against board-certified doctors. There is no requirement that the physicians in either class be licensed in Connecticut.

7. *Variations of care levels within institutions.* At the other end of the system, some early cases adopted a lower standard of care for interns and residents who could only be expected to "possess such skill and use such care and diligence in handling of emergency cases as capable medical

college graduates serving hospitals as interns ordinarily possess under similar circumstances." Rush v. Akron General Hospital, 171 N.E.2d 378, 381 (Ohio App. 1957). Subsequent cases have pushed heavily toward a uniform standard of care. In Clark v. University Hospital-UMDNJ, 914 A.2d 838, 843 (N.J. Super. 2006), the two defendant residents were alleged to have improperly used a nasogastric tube to clear out the contents of the decedent's intestines after he had been severely injured in an automobile crash. Both doctors argued that they should be held to the standard of residents, not general physicians. Lefelt, J., rejected the argument in no uncertain terms:

> [R]educing the standard of care for licensed doctors in their residencies because of the limited nature of their training would set a problematic precedent. For example, should we reduce the standard for doctors who are inexperienced in a particular procedure that they negligently performed? Or should we also reduce the standard of care for doctors who graduated in the lower third of their medical school? Defendants held themselves out as doctors and should be held to the standard of care they claimed to profess. Anything less would not comport with the care William Clark expected and was entitled to receive.

8. *Contract for cure.* In Sullivan v. O'Connor, 296 N.E.2d 183, 186 (Mass. 1973), plaintiff, an entertainer by profession, alleged that defendant, a plastic surgeon, orally promised to improve the appearance of her nose but failed to achieve the desired result. Kaplan, J., expressed skepticism toward medical contracts for specific results.

> It is not hard to see why the courts should be unenthusiastic or skeptical about the contract theory. Considering the uncertainties of medical science and the variations in the physical and psychological conditions of individual patients, doctors can seldom in good faith promise specific results. Therefore it is unlikely that physicians of even average integrity will in fact make such promises. Statements of opinion by the physician with some optimistic coloring are a different thing, and may indeed have therapeutic value. But patients may transform such statements into firm promises in their own minds, especially when they have been disappointed in the event, and testify in that sense to sympathetic juries. If actions for breach of promise can be readily maintained, doctors, so it is said, will be frightened into practising "defensive medicine." On the other hand, if these actions were outlawed, leaving only the possibility of suits for malpractice, there is fear that the public might be exposed to the enticements of charlatans, and confidence in the profession might ultimately be shaken. The law has taken the middle of the road position of allowing actions based on alleged contract, but insisting on clear proof. Instructions to the jury may well stress this requirement and point to tests of truth, such as the complexity or difficulty of an operation as bearing on the probability that a given result was promised.

If the parties may contract for cure, why are they not allowed to contract for care in accordance with the physician's own best efforts?

Sullivan was followed in Clevenger v. Haling, 394 N.E.2d 1119 (Mass. 1979), in which a majority of the court refused to allow the plaintiff to reach the jury for the birth of an unwanted child after a tubal ligation, which her physician had described as "a permanent thing" adding "you are not going to have any more children after this operation."

Canterbury v. Spence
464 F.2d 772 (D.C. Cir. 1972)

[The plaintiff-appellant first consulted Dr. Spence, the defendant-appellee, after experiencing severe back pain in December 1958. After a preliminary examination, Dr. Spence had the appellant undergo a myelogram — a procedure in which dye is injected into the spinal column which is then examined for disease or other disorder — that revealed that the appellant suffered from a "filling defect" in the region of his fourth thoracic vertebra. Dr. Spence told the appellant that he needed a laminectomy — an operation on the posterior arch of the vertebra — to correct what he suspected was a ruptured disc. He did not tell the appellant the details of the proposed operation, nor did the appellant inquire about them. Next, Dr. Spence contacted the appellant's mother and told her, when asked, that the operation he proposed was a serious one, but "not any more than any other operation." The appellee performed the operation on February 11, 1959, only to discover that the appellant's spinal cord was swollen and in very poor condition. He did what he could to relieve the pressure on the cord and left the appellant in bed to recuperate.

For the first day or so, the appellant's recuperation proceeded normally. However, at least according to appellant's testimony, he was allowed, contrary to the appellee's original instructions, to void unattended. While doing so, he slipped off the side of the bed, there being no one there to assist and no side rail to break his fall. Several hours later the appellant had difficulty breathing and suffered near-complete paralysis from the waist down. The appellee performed another emergency operation that night, and the appellant's condition improved thereafter. "Despite extensive medical care, he [the appellant] has never been what he was before. Instead of the back pain, even years later, he hobbled about on crutches, a victim of paralysis of the bowels and urinary incontinence. In a very real sense this lawsuit is an understandable search for reasons."]

ROBINSON, J. Appellant filed suit in the District Court on March 7, 1963, four years after the laminectomy and approximately two years after he attained his majority. The complaint stated several causes of action against each defendant. Against Dr. Spence it alleged, among other things, negligence in the performance of the laminectomy and failure to inform him beforehand of the risk involved. Against the hospital the complaint charged negligent post-operative care in permitting appellant to remain unattended after the laminectomy, in failing to provide a nurse or orderly to assist him at the time of his fall, and in failing to maintain a side rail on his bed. The answers denied the allegations of negligence and defended on the ground that the suit was barred by the statute of limitations.

. . . Appellant introduced no evidence to show medical and hospital practices, if any, customarily pursued in regard to the critical aspects of the case, and only Dr. Spence, called as an adverse witness, testified on the issue of causality. Dr. Spence described the surgical procedures he utilized in the two operations and expressed his opinion that appellant's disabilities stemmed from his pre-operative condition as symptomized by the swollen, nonpulsating spinal cord. He stated, however, that neither he nor any of the other physicians with whom he consulted was certain as to what that condition was, and he admitted that trauma can be a cause of paralysis. Dr. Spence further testified that even without trauma paralysis can be anticipated "somewhere in the nature of one percent" of the laminectomies performed, a risk he termed "a very slight possibility." He felt that communication of that risk to the patient is not good medical practice because it might deter patients from undergoing needed surgery and might produce adverse psychological reactions which could preclude the success of the operation.

At the close of appellant's case in chief, each defendant moved for a directed verdict and the trial judge granted both motions. The basis of the ruling, he explained, was that appellant had failed to produce any medical evidence indicating negligence on Dr. Spence's part in diagnosing appellant's malady or in performing the laminectomy; that there was no proof that Dr. Spence's treatment was responsible for appellant's disabilities; and that notwithstanding some evidence to show negligent post-operative care, an absence of medical testimony to show causality precluded submission of the case against the hospital to the jury. The judge did not allude specifically to the alleged breach of duty by Dr. Spence to divulge the possible consequences of the laminectomy.

We reverse. The testimony of appellant and his mother that Dr. Spence did not reveal the risk of paralysis from the laminectomy made out a prima facie case of violation of the physician's duty to disclose which Dr. Spence's explanation did not negate as a matter of law. There was also testimony from which the jury could have found that the laminectomy was negligently performed by Dr. Spence, and that appellant's fall was the consequence of negligence on the part of the hospital. The record, moreover, contains evidence of sufficient quantity and quality to tender jury issues as to whether and to what extent any such negligence was causally related to appellant's post-laminectomy condition. These considerations entitled appellant to a new trial.

Suits charging failure by a physician adequately to disclose the risks and alternatives of proposed treatment are not innovations in American law. They date back a good half-century, and in the last decade they have multiplied rapidly. There is, nonetheless, disagreement among the courts and the commentators on many major questions, and there is no precedent of our own directly in point. For the tools enabling resolution of the issues on this appeal, we are forced to begin at first principles.

The root premise is the concept, fundamental in American jurisprudence, that "[e]very human being of adult years and sound mind has a right to determine what shall be done with his own body. . . . " Schloendorff v. Soc'y of N.Y. Hosp., 105 N.E. 92, 93 (N.Y. 1914). True consent to what happens to one's self is the informed exercise of a choice, and that entails an opportunity to evaluate knowledgeably the options available and the risks attendant upon each. The average patient has little or no understanding of the medical arts, and ordinarily has only his physician to whom he can look for enlightenment with which to reach an intelligent decision. From these almost axiomatic considerations springs the need, and in turn the requirement, of a reasonable divulgence by physician to patient to make such a decision possible[15] . . . .

A reasonable revelation in these respects is not only a necessity but, as we see it, is as much a matter of the physician's duty. It is a duty to warn of the dangers lurking in the proposed treatment, and that is surely a facet of due care. It is, too, a duty to impart information which the patient has every right to expect.[27] The patient's reliance upon the physician is a trust of the kind which traditionally has exacted obligations beyond those associated with arms-length transactions. His dependence upon the physician for information affecting his well-being, in terms of contemplated treatment, is well-nigh abject. . . .

15. In duty-to-disclose cases, the focus of attention is more properly upon the nature and content of the physician's divulgence than the patient's understanding or consent. Adequate disclosure and informed consent are, of course, two sides of the same coin — the former a sine qua non of the latter.

But the vital inquiry on duty to disclose relates to the physician's performance of an obligation, while one of the difficulties with analysis in terms of "informed consent" is its tendency to imply that what is decisive is the degree of the patient's comprehension. As we later emphasize, the physician discharges the duty when he makes a reasonable effort to convey sufficient information although the patient, without fault of the physician, may not fully grasp it.

27. Some doubt has been expressed as to ability of physicians to suitably communicate their evaluations of risks and the advantages of optional treatment, and as to the lay patient's ability to understand what the physician tells him. Karchmer, Informed Consent: A Plaintiff's Medical Malpractice "Wonder Drug," 31 Mo. L. Rev. 29, 41 (1966). We do not share these apprehensions. The discussion need not be a disquisition, and surely the physician is not compelled to give his patient a short medical education; the disclosure rule summons the physician only to a reasonable explanation. That means generally informing the patient in nontechnical terms as to what is at stake: the therapy alternatives open to him, the goals expectably to be achieved, and the risks that may ensue from particular treatment and no treatment. . . . So informing the patient hardly taxes the physician, and it must be the exceptional patient who cannot comprehend such an explanation at least in a rough way.

Thus the physician has long borne a duty, on pain of liability for unauthorized treatment, to make adequate disclosure to the patient.[36] The evolution of the obligation to communicate for the patient's benefit as well as the physician's protection has hardly involved an extraordinary restructuring of the law.

Duty to disclose has gained recognition in a large number of American jurisdictions, but more largely on a different rationale. The majority of courts dealing with the problem have made the duty depend on whether it was the custom of physicians practicing in the community to make the particular disclosure to the patient. If so, the physician may be held liable for an unreasonable and injurious failure to divulge, but there can be no recovery unless the omission forsakes a practice prevalent in the profession. We agree that the physician's noncompliance with a professional custom to reveal, like any other departure from prevailing medical practice, may give rise to liability to the patient. We do not agree that the patient's cause of action is dependent upon the existence and nonperformance of a relevant professional tradition.

There are, in our view, formidable obstacles to acceptance of the notion that the physician's obligation to disclose is either germinated or limited by medical practice. To begin with, the reality of any discernible custom reflecting a professional consensus on communication of option and risk information to patients is open to serious doubt. We sense the danger that what in fact is no custom at all may be taken as an affirmative custom to maintain silence, and that physician-witnesses to the so-called custom may state merely their personal opinions as to what they or others would do under given conditions. We cannot gloss over the inconsistency between reliance on a general practice respecting divulgence and, on the other hand, realization that the myriad of variables among patients makes each case so different that its omission can rationally be justified only by the effect of its individual circumstances. Nor can we ignore the fact that to bind the disclosure obligation to medical usage is to arrogate the decision on revelation to the physician alone. Respect for the patient's right of self-determination on particular therapy demands a standard set by law for physicians rather than one which physicians may or may not impose upon themselves. . . .

36. We discard the thought that the patient should ask for information before the physician is required to disclose. Caveat emptor is not the norm for the consumer of medical services. Duty to disclose is more than a call to speak merely on the patient's request, or merely to answer the patient's questions; it is a duty to volunteer, if necessary, the information the patient needs for intelligent decision. The patient may be ignorant, confused, overawed by the physician or frightened by the hospital, or even ashamed to inquire. . . . Perhaps relatively few patients could in any event identify the relevant questions in the absence of prior explanation by the physician. Physicians and hospitals have patients of widely divergent socio-economic backgrounds, and a rule which presumes a degree of sophistication which many members of society lack is likely to breed gross inequities.

The majority rule, moreover, is at war with our prior holdings that a showing of medical practice, however probative, does not fix the standard governing recovery for medical malpractice. Prevailing medical practice, we have maintained, has evidentiary value in determinations as to what the specific criteria measuring challenged professional conduct are and whether they have been met, but does not itself define the standard. That has been our position in treatment cases, where the physician's performance is ordinarily to be adjudicated by the special medical standard of due care. We see no logic in a different rule for nondisclosure cases, where the governing standard is much more largely divorced from professional considerations. And surely in non-disclosure cases the fact-finder is not invariably functioning in an area of such technical complexity that it must be bound to medical custom as an inexorable application of the community standard of reasonable care.

... We hold that the standard measuring performance of that duty [to disclose] by physicians, as by others, is conduct which is reasonable under the circumstances.

Once the circumstances give rise to a duty on the physician's part to inform his patient, the next inquiry is the scope of the disclosure the physician is legally obliged to make. The courts have frequently confronted this problem but no uniform standard defining the adequacy of the divulgence emerges from the decisions. Some have said "full" disclosure, a norm we are unwilling to adopt literally. It seems obviously prohibitive and unrealistic to expect physicians to discuss with their patients every risk of proposed treatment—no matter how small or remote and generally unnecessary from the patient's viewpoint as well. Indeed, the cases speaking in terms of "full" disclosure appear to envision something less than total disclosure, leaving unanswered the question of just how much.

The larger number of courts, as might be expected, have applied tests framed with reference to prevailing fashion within the medical profession. Some have measured the disclosure by "good medical practice," others by what a reasonable practitioner would have bared under the circumstances, and still others by what medical custom in the community would demand. We have explored this rather considerable body of law but are unprepared to follow it. ...

In our view, the patient's right of self-decision shapes the boundaries of the duty to reveal. That right can be effectively exercised only if the patient possesses enough information to enable an intelligent choice. The scope of the physician's communications to the patient, then, must be measured by the patient's need, and that need is the information material to the decision. Thus the test for determining whether a particular peril must be divulged is its materiality to the patient's decision: all risks potentially affecting the decision must be unmasked. And to safeguard the patient's interest in achieving his own determination on treatment, the law must itself set the standard for adequate disclosure.

Optimally for the patient, exposure of a risk would be mandatory whenever the patient would deem it significant to his decision, either singly or in combination with other risks. Such a requirement, however, would summon the physician to second-guess the patient, whose ideas on materiality could hardly be known to the physician. That would make an undue demand upon medical practitioners, whose conduct, like that of others, is to be measured in terms of reasonableness. Consonantly with orthodox negligence doctrine, the physician's liability for nondisclosure is to be determined on the basis of foresight, not hindsight; no less than any other aspect of negligence, the issue on nondisclosure must be approached from the viewpoint of the reasonableness of the physician's divulgence in terms of what he knows or should know to be the patient's informational needs. If, but only if, the fact-finder can say that the physician's communication was unreasonably inadequate is an imposition of liability legally or morally justified. . . .

From these considerations we derive the breadth of the disclosure of risks legally to be required. The scope of the standard is not subjective as to either the physician or the patient; it remains objective with due regard for the patient's informational needs and with suitable leeway for the physician's situation. In broad outline, we agree that "[a] risk is thus material when a reasonable person, in what the physician knows or should know to be the patient's position, would be likely to attach significance to the risk or cluster of risks in deciding whether or not to forego the proposed therapy."

The topics importantly demanding a communication of information are the inherent and potential hazards of the proposed treatment, the alternatives to that treatment, if any, and the results likely if the patient remains untreated. The factors contributing significance to the dangerousness of a medical technique are, of course, the incidence of injury and the degree of the harm threatened. A very small chance of death or serious disablement may well be significant; a potential disability which dramatically outweighs the potential benefit of the therapy or the detriments of the existing malady may summon discussion with the patient.[86]

There is no bright line separating the significant from the insignificant; the answer in any case must abide a rule of reason. Some dangers — infection, for example — are inherent in any operation; there is no obligation to communicate those of which persons of average sophistication are aware. Even more clearly, the physician bears no responsibility for discussion of hazards the patient has already discovered, or those having no

86. See Bowers v. Talmage, 159 So. 2d 888 (Fla. App. 1963) (3% chance of death, paralysis or other injury, disclosure required); Scott v. Wilson, 396 S.W.2d 532 (Tex. Civ. App. 1965), aff'd, 412 S.W.2d 299 (Tex. 1967) (1% chance of loss of hearing, disclosure required). Compare, where the physician was held not liable: Stottlemire v. Cawood, 213 F. Supp. 897 (D.D.C. 1963) (1/800,000 chance of aplastic anemia); Yeates v. Harms, 393 P.2d 982 (Kan. 1964) (1.5% chance of loss of eye); Starnes v. Taylor, 272 N.C. 386, 158 S.E.2d 339, 344 (1968) (1/250 to 1/500 chance of perforation of esophagus).

apparent materiality to patients' decision on therapy. The disclosure doctrine, like others marking lines between permissible and impermissible behavior in medical practice, is in essence a requirement of conduct prudent under the circumstances. Whenever nondisclosure of particular risk information is open to debate by reasonable-minded men, the issue is for the finder of the facts.

Two exceptions to the general rule of disclosure have been noted by the courts. Each is in the nature of a physician's privilege not to disclose, and the reasoning underlying them is appealing. . . . The first comes into play when the patient is unconscious or otherwise incapable of consenting, and harm from a failure to treat is imminent and outweighs any harm threatened by the proposed treatment. When a genuine emergency of that sort arises, it is settled that the impracticality of conferring with the patient dispenses with need for it. Even in situations of that character the physician should, as current law requires, attempt to secure a relative's consent if possible. But if time is too short to accommodate discussion, obviously the physician should proceed with the treatment.

The second exception obtains when risk-disclosure poses such a threat of detriment to the patient as to become unfeasible or contraindicated from a medical point of view. It is recognized that patients occasionally become so ill or emotionally distraught on disclosure as to foreclose a rational decision, or complicate or hinder the treatment, or perhaps even pose psychological damage to the patient. Where that is so, the cases have generally held that the physician is armed with a privilege to keep the information from the patient, and we think it clear that portents of that type may justify the physician in action he deems medically warranted. The critical inquiry is whether the physician responded to a sound medical judgment that communication of the risk information would present a threat to the patient's well-being.

The physician's privilege to withhold information for therapeutic reasons must be carefully circumscribed, however, for otherwise it might devour the disclosure rule itself. The privilege does not accept the paternalistic notion that the physician may remain silent simply because divulgence might prompt the patient to forego therapy the physician feels the patient really needs. That attitude presumes instability or perversity for even the normal patient, and runs counter to the foundation principle that the patient should and ordinarily can make the choice for himself.

No more than breach of any other legal duty does nonfulfillment of the physician's obligation to disclose alone establish liability to the patient. . . . [A]s in malpractice actions generally, there must be a causal relationship between the physician's failure to adequately divulge and damage to the patient.

A causal connection exists when, but only when, disclosure of significant risks incidental to treatment would have resulted in a decision against it.

The patient obviously has no complaint if he would have submitted to the therapy notwithstanding awareness that the risk was one of its perils. On the other hand, the very purpose of the disclosure rule is to protect the patient against consequences which, if known, he would have avoided by foregoing the treatment. The more difficult question is whether the factual issue on causality calls for an objective or a subjective determination.

It has been assumed that the issue is to be resolved according to whether the fact-finder believes the patient's testimony that he would not have agreed to the treatment if he had known of the danger which later ripened into injury. We think a technique which ties the factual conclusion on causation simply to the assessment of the patient's credibility is unsatisfactory. To be sure, the objective of risk-disclosure is preservation of the patient's interest in intelligent self-choice on proposed treatment, a matter the patient is free to decide for any reason that appeals to him. When, prior to commencement of therapy, the patient is sufficiently informed on risks and he exercises his choice, it may truly be said that he did exactly what he wanted to do. But when causality is explored at a post-injury trial with a professedly uninformed patient, the question whether he actually would have turned the treatment down if he had known the risks is purely hypothetical: "Viewed from the point at which he had to decide, would the patient have decided differently had he known something he did not know?" And the answer which the patient supplies hardly represents more than a guess, perhaps tinged by the circumstance that the uncommunicated hazard has in fact materialized.

In our view, this method of dealing with the issue on causation comes in second-best. It places the physician in jeopardy of the patient's hindsight and bitterness. It places the factfinder in the position of deciding whether a speculative answer to a hypothetical question is to be credited. It calls for a subjective determination solely on testimony of a patient-witness shadowed by the occurrence of the undisclosed risk.

Better it is, we believe, to resolve the causality issue on an objective basis: in terms of what a prudent person in the patient's position would have decided if suitably informed of all perils bearing significance. If adequate disclosure could reasonably be expected to have caused that person to decline the treatment because of the revelation of the kind of risk or danger that resulted in harm, causation is shown, but otherwise not. The patient's testimony is relevant on that score of course but it would not threaten to dominate the findings. . . .

We now delineate our view on the need for expert testimony in non-disclosure cases. [The court then held that "[l]ay witness testimony can competently establish a physician's failure to disclose particular risk information, the patient's lack of knowledge of the risk, and the adverse consequences following the treatment. Experts are unnecessary to a showing of the materiality of a risk to a patient's decision on treatment, or to the reasonably, expectable effect of risk disclosure on the decision."

The court then held that plaintiff's cause of action for breach of the duty to disclose was governed by the negligence statute with its three-year period of limitation, and consequently was not barred by the one-year battery statute.]

This brings us to the remaining question, common to all three causes of action: whether appellant's evidence was of such caliber as to require a submission to the jury.

[The court then ordered a new trial because: (1) the appellant testified that he was not told of the hazards of the operation; (2) his mother was told that the laminectomy was no more serious than any other operation; (3) Dr. Spence himself testified about the 1% risk of paralysis; and (4) there was no evidence that appellant's "emotional makeup was such that concealment of the risk of paralysis was medically sound.[138]"]

NOTES

1. *The case on remand.* What issues were left to be resolved in *Canterbury* on remand? If the risk of paralysis from falling out of bed is common knowledge, does it make a difference that the defendant did not disclose the risk of paralysis from the operation itself? How ought *Canterbury's* prior condition be taken into account in assessing damages? On retrial the jury found for the defendants. Its decision was affirmed on appeal, without opinion. 509 F.2d 537 (D.C. Cir. 1975).

2. *The expansion of informed consent.* The duty of informed consent, which started with ordinary physicians, is now routinely imposed on other health care providers. In Hannemann v. Boyson, 698 N.W.2d 714, 718, 730 (Wis. 2005), the defendant chiropractor was charged with both improper manipulation of the defendant's spinal cord and with the (admitted) failure to disclose that "chiropractic treatment carried a risk of [the patient suffering a] stroke or other neurovascular injuries." Wilcox, J., held:

> [A]lthough the practice of chiropractic and the practice of medicine are distinct health care professions, the obligation of the practitioners of both to disclose the risks of the treatment and care they provide should be the same. While the actual disclosures will inevitably vary between doctors and

---

138. Dr. Spence's opinion—that disclosure is medically unwise—was expressed as to patients generally, and not with reference to traits possessed by appellant. His explanation was:

> I think that I always explain to patients the operations are serious, and I feel that any operation is serious. I think that I would not tell patients that they might be paralyzed because of the small percentage, one per cent, that exists. There would be a tremendous percentage of people that would not have surgery and would not therefore be benefited by it, the tremendous percentage that get along very well, 99 per cent.

chiropractors, the nature of the duty and limitations thereon should be the same. A patient of chiropractic has the same right as a patient of medical practice to be informed of the material risks of the proposed treatment or procedure so that he may make an informed decision whether to consent to the procedure or treatment. As such, we hold that the scope of a chiropractor's duty to obtain informed consent is the same as that of a medical doctor.

He further held, in line with modern practice, that the informed consent count was separate from the improper manipulation count, and therefore required a separate submission to the jury.

Here, the verdict not only omitted the cause question on informed consent, it omitted the first two questions as well. Thus, the jury was never asked whether the risk of stroke was information that a reasonable patient would want to know in deciding whether to submit to chiropractic treatment. The jury was never asked whether a reasonable patient in Hannemann's position would have submitted to chiropractic treatment if presented with such information. Finally, the jury was never asked whether the failure to inform Hannemann of the risk of a stroke was the cause of his injuries.

3. *The British rejection of* Canterbury. The duty to disclose, now widely accepted in the United States, has run into strong hostility in England. In Sidaway v. Bethlem Royal Hospital, [1985] All Eng. Rep. 1018, 1030, 1031, the English Court of Appeal explicitly rejected *Canterbury* in a case in which the defendant surgeon did tell a patient undergoing an elective laminectomy of the 1 or 2 percent risk of minor nerve damage, but decided not to mention the under-one-percent risk of permanent damage to the spinal cord. The dismissal of the plaintiff's suit below was affirmed on appeal with Dunn, L.J., saying:

I confess that I reach this conclusion with no regret. The evidence in this case showed that a contrary result would be damaging to the relationship of trust and confidence between doctor and patient, and might well have an adverse effect on the practice of medicine. It is doubtful whether it would be of any significant benefit to patients, most of whom prefer to put themselves unreservedly in the hands of their doctors. This is not in my view 'paternalism', to repeat an evocative word used in argument. It is simply an acceptance of the doctor/patient relationship as it has developed in this country. The principal effect of accepting the proposition advanced by the plaintiff would be likely to be an increase in the number of claims for professional negligence against doctors. This would be likely to have an adverse effect on the general standard of medical care, since doctors would inevitably be concerned to safeguard themselves against such claims, rather than to concentrate on their primary duty of treating their patients.

British judges remain more skeptical of informed consent cases. In Pearce v. United Bristol Healthcare NHS Trust, 48 BMLR 118 (1998), Lord Woolf MR stated: "Obviously the doctor, in determining what to tell a patient, has to take into account all the relevant considerations, which include the ability of the patient to comprehend what he has to say to him or her and the state of the patient at the particular time, both from the physical point of view and an emotional point of view. There can often be situations where a course different from the normal has to be employed. However, where there is what can realistically be called a 'significant risk', then, in the ordinary event, as I have already indicated, the patient is entitled to be informed of that risk." The court went on to conclude that an increased risk of one to two in 1,000 that a child might be stillborn if not delivered was not "significant."

However, in Burke v. Leeds Health Authority EWCA Civ 51 (2001), a differently constituted Court of Appeal held that two oncologists had not been negligent in omitting to remind the parents of a child, who was about to undergo intense chemotherapy, that the start of treatment could be delayed. From a clinical perspective an immediate start to therapy was desirable, but a postponement would have been a viable option. The Court of Appeal held that what a doctor had to tell patients or their representatives and at what point, was a matter for the doctor and was a question of medical judgment.

4. Materiality of risk. What level of risk is needed to trigger the duty to disclose? In Kozup v. Georgetown University, 663 F. Supp. 1048, 1053-1054 (D.D.C. 1987), the parents of the decedent, Matthew Kozup, brought an informed consent claim against the defendant hospital, which in 1983 transfused Matthew at birth with blood contaminated with the AIDS virus, from which he died three years later. Flannery, J., dismissed the suit against the hospital, holding that the AIDS risk was not material in 1983. The court stressed that in January 1983, only a single case of possible transfusion-related AIDS had been diagnosed out of the 3.5 million annual blood donations. Moreover, its viral agent HTLV-III would only be identified 15 months later. It then addressed the causation question as follows:

> However, in addition to this flaw in plaintiffs' theory, a second equally fatal problem remains. Even if plaintiffs could show that the risk of AIDS would have been material to their decision regarding Matthew's transfusions, plaintiffs must also show that the hospital's failure to warn of that risk *caused* the injury involved. That is, plaintiffs must show that "disclosure of significant risks incidental to treatment would have resulted in a decision against it." *Canterbury.* No reasonable jury could conclude on the facts of this case that, had the Kozups been informed of a one in 3.5 million possibility of contracting AIDS, they would have declined to permit Georgetown's

physicians to transfuse blood into their son. Matthew was premature and his birth was accompanied by many complications including hypovolemia. The transfusions were absolutely necessary to save his life.

The case was remanded for a new trial on appeal, Kozup v. Georgetown University, 851 F.2d 437 (D.C. Cir. 1988). The court agreed that the informed consent count failed on materiality, but remanded the case for a new trial on an alternative battery count, noting that no parental consent had been obtained at all. It rejected, at least for summary judgment purposes, the hospital's theory that "there is no necessity to obtain parent consent for life-saving treatment." If the claim were valid, what are the damages?

In subsequent cases, expert evidence was able to establish that blood banks were negligent in failing to perceive material transfusion risks of AIDS in early 1983. See, e.g., United Blood Services v. Quintana, 827 P.2d 509 (Colo. 1992). Knowledge advanced so rapidly between January and May of 1983 that the focus of attention at the latter time was not with informed consent but developing effective institutional safeguards against the transmission of AIDS. Note that conformity with professional blood bank testing standards is not an absolute defense after *The T.J. Hooper*. What safeguards, if any, should be introduced to deal with the risk of 20/20 hindsight? For a sharp criticism of blood bank practices in the critical 1983 period, see Eckert, The AIDS Blood-Transfusion Cases: A Legal and Economic Analysis of Liability, 29 San Diego L. Rev. 203, 294 (1992), calling for a general regime of strict liability for blood banks to "encourage them to solicit donors in low-risk areas and to screen them more carefully."

5. *Communication breakdown. Canterbury* indicates that the physician has a duty to disclose, but no obligation to insure the patient's comprehension. That requirement was put to the test in Acuna v. Turkish, 894 A.2d 1208, 1213 (N.J. Super. 2006). There the plaintiff was having kidney problems during the sixth to seventh week of her fourth pregnancy. The defendant recommended that she have an abortion, and answered in the negative to the question "is the baby already there?" From the testimony, "the term 'baby' meant something different to Acuna and Turkish. For her, it meant an embryo or fetus; for the doctor, a human being following birth." The court therefore concluded "that summary judgment was inappropriate because a reasonable patient would not have received the information necessary to make an informed decision." What result if the plaintiff could not have survived the pregnancy?

6. *Particularity of disclosure.* Recently, courts have resisted demands for disclosure of the full range of treatment alternatives in complex cases. In Valles v. Albert Einstein Medical Center, 805 A.2d 1232, 1239-1240 (Pa. 2002), the decedent, Lope Valles, was admitted into the defendant medical center for treatment of a suspected abdominal aortic aneurysm — a

weakness in the wall of the aorta. The initial exploratory procedure to locate the aneurysm resulted in the deterioration of the decedent's kidney function. The written consent form did not disclose the risk of renal damage, but the treating physician claimed that he customarily disclosed that the dyes used could damage the kidneys. The renal complications required a postponement of the corrective surgery for the aneurysm, which was successfully concluded about one month later. Owing to the need for long-term dialysis, the treating physicians recommended the use of a "Permacath" device, suitable for prolonged dialysis. The surgical resident advised Vallas of certain risks associated with the insertion of Permacath, "including bleeding, infection, collapsing of a lung and death," but he did not discuss the relative advantages and disadvantages from different place-ments in veins in the neck, chest or groin. When the treating physician, Dr. Morros, tried inserting the Permacath in a chest vein, the decedent suffered adverse reactions, went into cardiac arrest and died. The trial court kept the informed consent case from the jury, but the Superior Court reversed, and allowed the case to go to the jury, saying that "informed consent applies to the method or manner of surgery and the risks associ-ated therewith." The Pennsylvania Supreme Court rebuffed this position:

> We recently reiterated . . . that "the doctrine of informed consent is a limited one." In light of this limited scope, we find that the manner or method in which the surgeon performs the proposed procedure is not encompassed within the purview of the informed consent doctrine. Although there were several methods of performing the particular surgery, there was only one surgery proposed: the insertion of a Permacath. Appellant does not dispute that Valles was adequately informed of the risks attending the surgery: bleeding, lung collapse, and death. That the subclavian vein [in the chest] may not have been the optimum site is not an issue of informed consent, but of negligence in the physician's decision to place the Permacath at that site.

The dissent argued that "where a physician believes that there is more than one viable site for performing a surgical procedure, the location for the procedure concerns alternative types of treatment available to the patient. Further, the plaintiff should be advised of those alternative types of treatment, i.e., the viable locations for the surgery, as well as the risks associated with each location." Who is right? Previously, the Pennsylvania Superior Court had held that a physician had a duty to inform a patient in need of a heart valve replacement of viable alternative types of valves and the risks associated with each. See Stover v. Association of Thoracic and Cardiovascular Surgeons, 635 A.2d 1047, 1051-1052 (Pa. Super. Ct. 1994). Distinguishable?

7. *On the edges of disclosure.* In Truman v. Thomas, 611 P.2d 902, 906 (Cal. 1980), the decedent died of cervical cancer at age 30. The plaintiff contended that the defendant physician was guilty of medical malpractice

because he did not inform the decedent of the risks of cervical cancer, which might have been detected by a Pap smear, a procedure which he had from time to time urged her to undergo. The court held that the jury could find that the defendant had breached his duty to disclose by failing to make clear the necessity for the Pap smear.

> If a patient indicates that he or she is going to *decline* the risk-free test or treatment, then the doctor has the additional duty of advising of all material risks of which a reasonable person would want to be informed before deciding not to undergo the procedure. On the other hand, if the recommended test or treatment is itself risky, then the physician should always explain the potential consequences of declining to follow the recommended course of action.

The dissent argued that extending informed consent to routine cases would "impose upon doctors the intolerable burden of having to explain diagnostic tests to healthy patients." In *Truman* the defendant treated the plaintiff for multiple ailments over the five-year period. Under the court's decision must a physician explain every routine test to every patient? At every visit?

8. *Expert testimony in informed consent cases.* In Bly v. Rhoads, 222 S.E.2d 783, 787-788 (Va. 1976), the plaintiff sued under an informed consent theory for the adverse consequences of a hysterectomy. The court followed *Canterbury* insofar as it allowed the plaintiff "to establish by lay evidence that his physician did not disclose particular risk information and that he, the patient, had no knowledge of the risk." It also agreed that lay evidence was sometimes admissible "to show the adverse consequences following treatment," and it left open the possibility that infrequently "the duty of disclosure is so obvious that expert testimony should not be required." But it broke with *Canterbury* in requiring expert evidence on the full range of complex issues raised by the disclosure question.

> We believe the better rule, which we now adopt, is to require a patient-plaintiff to show by qualified medical experts whether and to what extent information should be disclosed by the physician to his patient. This rule would not, contrary to what *Canterbury* suggests, impose an undue burden upon the patient-plaintiff. After all, in the usual case, the patient unquestionably will have obtained experts to establish the negligent treatment phase of his malpractice action.

Bly represents the majority view on expert evidence, which is often codified. See, e.g., Ark. Code Ann. §16-114-206(b) (2007), which was sustained against a constitutional challenge in Eady v. Lansford, 92 S.W.3d 57, 61 (Ark. 2002), in the absence of any showing "that the legislation is *not* rationally related to achieving any legitimate objective of the government. . . . "

Indeed, the court intimated that protecting the medical profession against vexatious litigation justified both requiring expert testimony and adopting the customary care standard rejected in *Canterbury*.

9. *Objective and subjective causation.* In Cobbs v. Grant, 502 P.2d 1 (Cal. 1972), the court adopted the objective causation standard of *Canterbury*, notwithstanding its tension with the autonomy principle, because it declined to place the "physician in jeopardy of the patient's bitterness and disillusionment" resulting from "20/20 hindsight." The opposite position was taken in Arena v. Gingrich, 748 P.2d 547 (Or. 1988), construing Oregon's informed consent statute (Or. Rev. Stat. §677.097 (2005)), which provided that informed consent could be obtained only if the physician explained "[i]n general terms the procedure or treatment to be under-taken," the "alternative procedures or methods of treatment, if any," and the "risks, if any, to the procedure or treatment." Thereafter, the physician had to ask the patient if he or she desired a fuller explanation. Linde, J., held that the statute precluded the objective standard: "The statute having defined the standard of disclosure without required reference to what a prudent patient reasonably would want to know, we shall not reintroduce that hypothetical prudent patient by the back door of 'causation.'"

10. *Legislative response to informed consent.* In the wake of Canterbury v. Spence, many legislatures codified the law of informed consent, often at the request of insurance companies and medical organizations. Consider the impact and worth of the New York legislation (New York Pub. Health Law §2805-d (McKinney 2007)).

> 1. Lack of informed consent means the failure of the person providing the professional treatment or diagnosis to disclose to the patient such alternatives thereto and the reasonably foreseeable risks and benefits involved as a reason-able medical . . . practitioner under similar circumstances would have disclosed, in a manner permitting the patient to make a knowledgeable evaluation.
>
> 2. The right of action to recover for medical . . . malpractice based on a lack of informed consent is limited to those cases involving either (a) non-emergency treatment, procedure or surgery, or (b) a diagnostic procedure which involved invasion or disruption of the integrity of the body.
>
> 3. For a cause of action therefor it must also be established that a rea-sonably prudent person in the patient's position would not have undergone the treatment or diagnosis if he had been fully informed and that the lack of informed consent is a proximate cause of the injury or condition for which recovery is sought.
>
> 4. It shall be a defense to any action for medical . . . malpractice based upon an alleged failure to obtain such an informed consent that:
>> (a) the risk not disclosed is too commonly known to warrant disclo-sure; or
>> (b) the patient assured the medical . . . practitioner he would undergo the treatment, procedure or diagnosis regardless of the risk involved, or

the patient assured the medical . . . practitioner that he did not want to be informed of the matters to which he would be entitled to be informed; or
　(c) consent by or on behalf of the patient was not reasonably possible; or
　(d) the medical . . . practitioner, after considering all of the attendant facts and circumstances, used reasonable discretion as to the manner and extent to which such alternatives or risks were disclosed to the patient because he reasonably believed that the manner and extent of such disclosure could reasonably be expected to adversely and substantially affect the patient's condition.

How does this statutory regime differ from Canterbury v. Spence? Is the statute preferable to a general good faith standard whereby doctors make whatever disclosures they regard as appropriate under the circumstances?

　11. *A contract solution to informed consent.* A more radical approach to the informed consent issue would allow physicians and patients to determine the proper scope of disclosure by private agreement. Arguments supporting that conclusion are found in Epstein, Medical Malpractice, The Case for Contract, 1 Am. B. Found. Res. J. 87, 119-128 (1976). A more bittersweet evaluation is found in Schuck, Rethinking Informed Consent, 103 Yale L.J. 899, 957-958 (1994), which notes the tension between the defense of autonomous choices and the use of the prudent patient standard for disclosure:

> Like the "reasonable person" standard and other objective standards in tort law, the existing uniform approach to informed consent has two virtues: it is cheaper to know and administer, and it seeks to protect patients against gross inequalities of bargaining power vis-à-vis providers. But a doctrine that treats all patients and physician-patient relationships as essentially homogenous when in fact they are not exacts a price. Specifically, the law requires a level of informed consent that is different from the level that many consumers or groups of consumers want and for which they would be willing to pay if the choice were presented to them. The existing doctrine, then suffers from an ironic, if endemic vice: it deprives patients of choice in the name of choice.

On informed consent, see generally Twerski & Cohen, The Second Revolution in Informed Consent: Comparing Physicians to Each Other, 94 Nw. U. L. Rev. 1 (1999); Grimm, Informed Consent For All! No Exceptions, 37 N.M. L. Rev. 39 (2007).

　12. *Overall assessment of the medical malpractice system.* At this point it is perhaps appropriate to take stock of the effectiveness of the malpractice system in preventing accidents and supplying compensation. One comprehensive book on the subject, P. Weiler, Medical Malpractice On Trial 14 (1991), reports that two major studies — one in California during the 1970s, and a New York study from the late 1980s — together reviewed the patient records of some 50,000 hospitalizations (some 20,000 in California

and 30,000 in New York). Both studies found that the instances of negligent treatment resulting in patient harm far exceeded the number of malpractice cases filed, and, by greater margins, the number of cases in which recovery occurred. The New York investigation (in which Weiler took part), for example, estimated that about one in one hundred patients suffered serious injury or death attributable to negligent medical treatment; yet suit was filed for only one of each eight valid claims, with compensation paid in only half those claims. Worse still, "a substantial proportion of the claims actually filed were for cases in which we had concluded on the basis of hospital records that no medical injury at all had occurred, much less one caused by medical negligence." It was not possible to determine whether the compensation actually paid was in the meritorious cases. Stated otherwise, these studies suggest that the liability system picks out the wrong cases for suit, and thus produces a higher error rate than if *no* suits had been filed at all.

For a more optimistic study see F. Sloan, Suing for Medical Malpractice 9-10 (1993), based on a detailed examination of the obstetrical and emergency room claims filed in Florida, one of the most active malpractice states, between 1986 and 1989.

> If the system of liability determination and compensation is indeed "broken," this should be most obvious in a state like Florida. . . . Yet in spite of some weaknesses, we find that the system works better than media accounts and frequent complaints from the health care community would lead one to expect. Overall, claimants appear to be satisfied with the process even when they do not receive compensation. Claimants, not their lawyers, tend to initiate the process. Injured parties find lawyers, not the reverse. Liability determination is not capricious. There is overall agreement between the independent evaluations of our study's physician panelists and the outcomes of the cases. Compensation was much more likely to have been paid when the panelists found evidence of physician liability than when they did not. On the whole, claimants did not even recover their total past and future economic losses, after when we accounted for funds they obtained from collateral sources, such as health and disability insurance.

Finally, a comprehensive review of all tort systems, Dewees & Trebilcock, The Efficacy of the Tort System and Its Alternatives: A Review of the Empirical Evidence, 30 Osgoode Hall L.J. 57 (1992), concluded that it is exceedingly difficult to find any empirical evidence of a strong deterrent effect of the system of medical malpractice liability. It cites work by the Weiler group which suggests that a 10 percent increase in malpractice claims should lead to a 4 percent reduction in the level of medical accidents, and then notes that Canadian doctors are only 20 percent as likely to be sued as U.S. doctors, and pay insurance premiums around 10 percent of those paid by U.S. doctors, yet "there appears to be no evidence that

Canadian physicians are more careless than their U.S. counterparts." Dewees and Trebilcock conclude that the medical malpractice system fares badly, both in absolute terms and in comparison with automobile insurance, in providing compensation to injured parties and in meeting the concerns of corrective justice. Physician dissatisfaction with the current system remains high, and recent studies show a real crunch in the insurance markets, especially for high-risk specialties such as obstetrics and surgeries. The current status quo has not been subject to any major nationwide change, even if the stated extent of medical malpractice liability has retreated somewhat from its highs of the 1970s and 1980s. At this point the sharp differences in opinion remain. Physicians continue to press for limits on liability in visible public ways. See, e.g., Parson, Illinois Doctors Press for a Malpractice Limit, Chi. Trib., July 9, 2004, §3, at 1. Yet on the other side, commentators continue to urge that the problem is not too much malpractice litigation but too much medical malpractice. See T. Baker, The Medical Malpractice Myth (2007), and Chessik, Medical Litigation Is Not the Problem, 26 N. Ill. U. L. Rev. 563 (2006) (debunking myths that plaintiffs file too many frivolous lawsuits and identifying the real problem as too much medical negligence).

SECTION E.   STATUTES AND REGULATIONS

This section explores the ways in which criminal statutes can add precision to the general negligence standard of reasonable care. The term "statute" is to be construed broadly, for it covers also all sorts of regulations and ordinances. RTT:LPH §1, comment *a*. Typically, a statute involved in a negligence case provides for the state to administer some penalty, usually a fine, but sometimes incarceration or, on occasion, injunctive relief. The traditional context for this inquiry was in connection with traffic accidents, where statutes still remain important. But modern litigation now frequently extends to the full range of health and safety statutes characteristic of the modern democratic state.

Analytically, the first question is how any statute comes to be a source of private rights. When the statute expressly creates a private remedy for one injured by its violation, a court merely has to follow the explicit statutory command. Frequently, however, statutes are silent on whether they create private rights of action, so that the first judicial task is to set some "default" rule for statutory construction: Where the statute is silent, when should the private right of action be inferred? Sometime courts assume that a private action is authorized by some "overriding" legislative intention. Yet that inference is contestable since the statutory silence is compatible with the opposite position that direct criminal penalties are the sole remedy for statutory violations. Given the wide variety of statutes on the books, it is doubtful that either extreme position (automatic creation or automatic denial of a private action) represents the best that the courts can do in the absence of more specific legislative guidance. The initial task is to develop a set of principles to help determine when courts should infer private rights of action. Next, it is necessary to see how the statutory cause of action folds into the standard elements of the tort of negligence and the potential defenses thereto.

Anon.
87 Eng. Rep. 791 (K.B. 1703)

HOLT, C.J. For wherever a statute enacts anything, or prohibits anything, for the advantage of any person, that person shall have remedy to recover the advantage given him, or to have satisfaction for the injury done him contrary to law by the same statute; for it would be a fine thing to make a law by which one has a right, but no remedy but in equity. . . .

Thayer, Public Wrong and Private Action
27 Harv. L. Rev. 317, 321-323 (1914), reprinted in Selected Essays on the Law of Torts 276, 280-281 (1924)

Before the ordinance the plaintiff, injured by the runaway horse, must have based his action on negligence. Whether the defendant was negligent in leaving the horse unhitched would have been for the jury to say, unless this was so clear one way or the other that the court must deal with it as a "question of law" (so-called); i.e., as a point on which fair minds could reach but one conclusion. In any situation less extreme the whole matter would have been within the jury's province. And the jury was bound in deciding it to use the test of the "ordinary prudent man." They could not acquit the defendant of negligence without saying that an ordinary prudent man would have left his horse unhitched under these circumstances; that with such a horse as this, and in such a place, the prudent man would have foreseen no danger to others — for the foresight of the prudent man in the defendant's position (in other words, the probability of danger from his standpoint) is the test of negligence. The jury was justified either in accepting or rejecting the theory that he was negligent, for the mere fact of submitting the issue of negligence to them means that a finding either way is warranted by the evidence. The reasonableness of the defendant's conduct was thus in the eye of the law an open question, depending on the circumstances and the inferences fairly to be drawn from them.

Suppose now the situation to be changed by the single circumstance of the ordinance, all other facts remaining the same. Can the issue of negligence any longer be left to the jury? Not unless they would be justified in finding for either party; and what must a finding for the defendant on this issue mean? That an ordinary prudent man, knowing the ordinance — for upon familiar principles he can claim no benefit from his ignorance of the law — would have chosen to break it, "reasonably" believing that damage would not result from his action. It must then, upon this view, be deemed consistent with ordinary prudence for an individual to set his own opinion against the judgment authoritatively pronounced by constituted public authority, for the ordinance has prohibited leaving *all* horses unhitched, without exception, and has done this in order to prevent just such consequences as have occurred. It has thus declared the danger to be so serious and constant that a less sweeping prohibition would be inadequate. And when eminent courts, using familiar phraseology, state that the breach of the ordinance is not "negligence per se," but only "evidence of negligence," and leave the question of negligence as a fact to the jury, they are doing nothing less than informing that body that it may properly stamp with approval, as reasonable conduct, the action of one who has assumed to place his own foresight above that of the legislature in respect of the very danger which it was legislating to prevent.

NOTES

1. Thayer in action. The power of statutory commands still retains the force that Thayer attributed to them nearly 100 years ago. In Schmitz v. Canadian Pac. Ry. Co., 454 F.3d 678, 684 (7th Cir. 2006), the plaintiff was an inspector who fell into a hole alongside the tracks when defendant had not cleared away the vegetation as required by federal regulation. The trial judge did not instruct the jury on the mandatory regulation, and his decision was reversed on appeal.

> There can be little doubt that the omission of an instruction on [the regulation] prejudiced Schmitz's case. Canadian Pacific argues that the jury still heard the essence of Schmitz's claim regarding the regulation — that Schmitz alleged the railroad was negligent because it did not keep the vegetation trimmed. But there is a world of difference between telling the jury that Schmitz alleged the railroad should have taken a particular precaution and telling the jury that federal law *required* the railroad to take that very precaution. By not instructing the jury on the federal regulation, the district judge left it up to the jury to decide whether the railroad had a duty to keep the vegetation trimmed. The regulation answers that question in the affirmative — the railroad was required under federal law to keep the vegetation trimmed. The jury should have been deciding only whether the

railroad violated the regulation and whether the violation was a cause of Schmitz's injury.

2. *Defective statutes as a source of duty.* Thayer relies on the common notion of legislative supremacy to justify the rule that noncompliance with a statute counts as negligence per se. One test of his thesis examines the role of statutory provisions not currently in force. Assume that an otherwise valid criminal safety statute is invalid because of a technical defect in the enacting procedure. On Thayer's view, could it set the standard of care in a negligence action? In Clinkscales v. Carver, 136 P.2d 777, 778-779 (Cal. 1943), Traynor, J., held that while the state could not criminally enforce its laws when it erected a stop sign pursuant to a defective statute, nonetheless for a highway user it "was negligence as a matter of law to disregard the stop sign."

> If a through artery has been posted with stop signs by the public authorities in the customary way and to all appearances by regular procedure, any reasonable man should know that the public naturally relies upon their observance. If a driver from a side street enters the ostensibly protected boulevard without stopping, in disregard of the posted safeguards, contrary to what drivers thereon could reasonably have expected him to do, he is guilty of negligence regardless of any irregularity attending the authorization of the signs.

3. *Subsequently enacted statutes.* In Hammond v. International Harvester Co., 691 F.2d 646, 651 (3d Cir. 1982), the defendant manufactured a skid load tractor that, at the option of the purchaser, was not equipped with a roll-over protective structure and side screens (ROPS) that could have prevented the driver from falling out of the operator's seat. To show that the tractor was defectively designed without the ROPS, the court allowed the plaintiff, an employee of the purchaser, to introduce into evidence OSHA regulations that took effect only after the manufacture of the vehicle, requiring a removable ROPS for tractors used both outdoors and inside farm buildings with low clearances. "We recognize that these OSHA regulations do not directly govern the instant case because the tractor in question was manufactured at least six months prior to the effective date of the regulations. Nevertheless, OSHA's very decision to promulgate these regulations provides strong support for the proposition that a loader tractor — even one which must frequently pass through a low door — does not possess every element necessary to make it safe for use unless it comes equipped with a ROPS." How should a manufacturer design its equipment when it has knowledge of pending regulations, some of which may not be adopted? May the defendant introduce evidence that the dangers in removing and reattaching the ROPS exceeded any benefits that it might provide? Could it do so if the regulation had been in effect at the time of the accident?

Osborne v. McMasters
41 N.W. 543 (Minn. 1889)

MITCHELL, J. Upon the record in this case it must be taken as the facts that defendant's clerk in his drug-store, in the course of his employment as such, sold to plaintiff's intestate a deadly poison without labelling it "Poison," as required by statute; that she, in ignorance of its deadly qualities, partook of the poison, which caused her death. Except for the ability of counsel and the earnestness with which they have argued the case, we would not have supposed that there could be any serious doubt of defendant's liability on this state of facts. It is immaterial for present purposes whether section 329 of the Penal Code or section 14, c. 147, Laws 1885, or both, are still in force, and constitute the law governing this case. The requirements of both statutes are substantially the same, and the sole object of both is to protect the public against the dangerous qualities of poison. It is now well settled, certainly in this state, that where a statute or municipal ordinance imposes upon any person a specific duty for the protection or benefit of others, if he neglects to perform that duty he is liable to those for whose protection or benefit it was imposed for any injuries of the character which the statute or ordinance was designed to prevent, and which were proximately produced by such neglect. . . .

Defendant contends that this is only true where a right of action for the alleged negligent act existed at common law; that no liability existed at common law for selling poison without labelling it, and therefore none exists under this statute, no right of civil action being given by it. Without stopping to consider the correctness of the assumption that selling poison without labelling it might not be actionable negligence at common law, it is sufficient to say that, in our opinion, defendant's contention proceeds upon an entire misapprehension of the nature and gist of a cause of action of this kind. The common law gives a right of action to every one sustaining injuries caused proximately by the negligence of another. The present is a common-law action, the gist of which is defendant's negligence, resulting in the death of plaintiff's intestate. Negligence is the breach of legal duty. It is immaterial whether the duty is one imposed by the rule of common law requiring the exercise of ordinary care not to injure another, or is imposed by a statute designed for the protection of others. In either case the failure to perform the duty constitutes negligence, and renders the party liable for injuries resulting from it. The only difference is that in the one case the measure of legal duty is to be determined upon common-law principles, while in the other the statute fixes it, so that the violation of the statute constitutes conclusive evidence of negligence, or, in other words, negligence per se. The action in the latter case is not a statutory one, nor does the statute give the right of action in any other sense except that it makes an act negligent which otherwise might not be such, or at least only evidence of negligence. All that the statute does is to establish a fixed standard by which the fact of negligence may be determined. The gist of the action is still negligence, or the non-performance of a legal duty to the person injured. Judgment affirmed.

Restatement (Second) of Torts

§286.   WHEN STANDARD OF CONDUCT DEFINED BY LEGISLATION OR REGULATION WILL BE ADOPTED

The court may adopt as the standard of conduct of a reasonable man the requirements of a legislative enactment or an administrative regulation whose purpose is found to be exclusively or in part
   (a) to protect a class of persons which includes the one whose interest is invaded, and
   (b) to protect the particular interest which is invaded, and
   (c) to protect that interest against the kind of harm which has resulted, and
   (d) to protect that interest against the particular hazard from which the harm results.

Restatement of The Law of Torts: Liability for Physical Harm

§14.   STATUTORY VIOLATIONS AS NEGLIGENCE PER SE

An actor is negligent if, without excuse, the actor violates a statute that is designed to protect against the type of accident the actor's conduct causes, and if the accident victim is within the class of persons the statute is designed to protect.

California Evidence Code §669(a)
(West 2003)

The failure of a person to exercise due care is presumed if:
   (1) He violated a statute, ordinance, or regulation of a public entity;
   (2) The violation proximately caused death or injury to person or property;
   (3) The death or injury resulted from an occurrence of the nature which the statute, ordinance, or regulation was designed to prevent; and

(4) The person suffering the death or the injury to his person or property was one of the class of persons for whose protection the statute, ordinance, or regulation was adopted.

NOTES

1. Who is protected? Even where the statute supports a negligence action, the plaintiff must show that she falls within the class of protected individuals, a result that is often achieved when a single statute is found to serve multiple purposes. In Stimpson v. Wellington Service Corp., 246 N.E.2d 801, 805 (Mass. 1969), the defendant drove a 137-ton rig over city streets without having obtained the needed statutory permit. The weight of defendant's truck dislocated and broke the pipes in plaintiff's building, flooding the premises. The court found that the statute had a dual purpose. "Undoubtedly the primary purpose of the statute was to protect the ways themselves from injury from overloaded vehicles. But the Cambridge authorities, in considering an application for a permit under the statute, should have weighed as well other possible effects of the proposal, particularly because of the prohibition of the city ordinance against moving over city streets vehicles so loaded as to be likely to injure property. Failure to apply for a permit meant that the appropriate authority did not have the opportunity to appraise the risks and probabilities and to refuse the permit or impose conditions."

Arguably, a narrower view of the scope of regulatory protection was taken in Burnett v. Imerys Marble, Inc., 116 P.3d 460, 463-464 (Wyo. 2005). The plaintiff, an employee of Thurel Mason Trucking, fell off the top of a flatbed truck as he sought to place tarps on top of a load of marble that he had earlier picked up from the defendant's facility. He argued that the truck was unsafe because it failed to comply with federal regulations promulgated pursuant to the Federal Mine Safety and Health Act of 1977 (30 U.S.C. §801 et seq.), whose "first priority" was the protection of the miner. Golden, J., dismissed for two reasons:

First, Burnett is not a miner because he is not an individual working in a mine. . . . Second, it is clear that the purpose of the Mine Act is to protect against the hazards associated with mining. As the district court recognized, the hazard that Burnett encountered was not a mining hazard but a hazard of his job as a commercial trucker. Indeed, Burnett acknowledged that tarping was a normal part of his job as a trucker. He tarped approximately ninety percent of his loads, many of which are in no way related to Imerys or other mining operations. Thus, Burnett's accident was not a product of the hazard the Mine Act was intended to protect against. Accordingly, we must conclude that the requirements of Restatement (Second) of Torts §286 are not met.

2. *Actions "for any injuries of the character which the statute or ordinance was designed to prevent."* In Gorris v. Scott, L.R. 9 Ex. 125, 129 (1874), the plaintiff had shipped a number of sheep with the defendant shipowner who failed to pen them in accordance with the requirement of the Contagious Disease (Animals) Act of 1869. The animals were washed overboard in a storm and "were lost by reason of the neglect to comply" with administrative orders issued pursuant to the statute. Notwithstanding this causal connection between plaintiff's harm and defendant's breach of statutory duty, Kelly, C.B., denied plaintiff's recovery:

> [I]f we could see that it was the object, or among the objects of this Act, that the owners of sheep and cattle coming from a foreign port should be protected by the means described against the danger of their property being washed overboard, or lost by the perils of the sea, the present action would be within the principle.
>
>   But, looking at the Act, it is perfectly clear that its provisions were all enacted with a totally different view; there was no purpose, direct or indirect, to protect against such damage; but, as is recited in the preamble, the Act is directed against the possibility of sheep or cattle being exposed to disease on their way to this country. . . . That being so, if by reason of the default in question the plaintiffs' sheep had been overcrowded, or had been caused unnecessary suffering, and so had arrived in this country in a state of disease, I do not say that they might not have maintained this action. But the damage complained of here is something totally apart from the object of the Act of Parliament, and it is in accordance with all the authorities to say that the action is not maintainable.

Could the plaintiff have maintained an action for breach of the contract of carriage? What about a common claim for negligence action in not having pens, irrespective of the statute?

The statutory purpose doctrine in *Gorris* received a cool reception from the United States Supreme Court in Kernan v. American Dredging Co., 355 U.S. 426 (1958), in which a seaman lost his life when an open-flame kerosene lamp on the deck of a scow ignited inflammable vapors lying above an accumulation of petroleum products that had collected on the surface of a river. A Coast Guard regulation required that such lamps be at a height of not less than eight feet, but the lamp in question was less than three feet above the water. If the lamp had been mounted at the required height, it would not have ignited the vapors. Even though it appeared that the regulation was aimed at the risk of collision and not of fire, the Court, in a five-to-four decision, permitted recovery on the ground that "many of the refined distinctions necessary in common law tort doctrine," including the statutory purpose limitation, did not apply in the special context of the Federal Employers' Liability Act and the Jones Act.

Thus, in Abrahams v. Young & Rubincam, Inc., 79 F.3d 234, 237 (2d Cir. 1996), Winter, J., stressed the difference between the two types of negligence cases: "At common law, so long as the plaintiff category is foreseeable, there is no requirement that the risk of injury to the plaintiff, and the risk of the harm that actually occurred, were what made the defendant's actions wrongful in the first place. With statutory claims, the issue is, instead, one of statutory intent: was the plaintiff (even though foreseeably injured) in the category the statute meant to protect, and was the harm that occurred (again, even if foreseeable), the 'mischief' the statute sought to avoid," but its reasoning was in turn questioned by Posner, J., in Shadday v. Omni Hotels Management Corp., 477 F.3d 511, 517-518 (7th Cir. 2007): "The violation of a statutory standard of care is negligence; so is a violation of a common law duty of care. In either case, the puzzle of the line of cases that descends from *Gorris* is why the defendant, having been negligent, should get off scot-free just because the harm that would have been averted had he been careful was not foreseeable. No doubt the framers of the Contagious Diseases (Animals) Act made no judgment that the cost of pens was less than the expected cost of a mass drowning of unpenned animals, but that seems irrelevant. Given that the ship-owner was under a legal duty to pen the sheep, why should he not be liable for a disaster that would have been averted if only he had complied with his duty?"

3. *Private rights of action under federal statutes.* In recent times, one vital question is whether plaintiffs may maintain tort actions for defendant's breach of a *federal* statute or regulation. Here all the usual difficulties are compounded because the right has to be tested under both federal and state law. At the federal level, the earlier tendency was to freely imply causes of action, as is done in state courts dealing with state statutes. Thus, in J. I. Case Co. v. Borak, 377 U.S. 426 (1964), the Supreme Court held that, in light of the "broad remedial purposes" of the Securities Exchange Act of 1934, a shareholder had an implied cause of action for damages against his corporation for misrepresentations in violation of section 14(a) of that statute, which prohibits the use of false or misleading information in proxy fights for corporate control. Subsequently, however, the Supreme Court has taken a much more restrictive view of the availability of federal relief. In the watershed case of Cort v. Ash, 422 U.S. 66, 78 (1975), the Court held that there was no private action for damages (as opposed to injunctive relief) in favor of a corporate shareholder against the corporate directors for violation of 18 U.S.C. §610, which as a criminal matter prohibits corporations from making "a contribution or expenditure in connection with any election at which Presidential and Vice Presidential electors . . . are to be voted for." It observed:

> In determining whether a private remedy is implicit in a statute not expressly providing one, several factors are relevant. First, is the plaintiff "one of the class for whose *especial* benefit the statute was enacted," . . . that is, does the statute create a federal right in favor of the plaintiff? Second, is there any indication of legislative intent, explicit or implicit, either to create such a remedy or to deny one? . . . Third, is it consistent with the underlying purposes of the legislative scheme to imply such a remedy for the plaintiff? . . . And finally, is the cause of action one traditionally relegated to state law, in an area basically the concern of the States, so that it would be inappropriate to infer a cause of action based solely on federal law?

Subsequent Supreme Court decisions only confirm the hostile attitude to implied private rights of action; *Cort* has applied in tort cases as well. For example, section 10 of the 1899 Rivers and Harbors Act, 33 U.S.C. §403, proscribed the "creation of any obstruction not affirmatively authorized by Congress, to the navigable . . . waters of the United States." In California v. Sierra Club, 451 U.S. 287 (1981), the Supreme Court, reversing the court of appeals below, held that the statute did not authorize a private right of action to persons harmed by the diversion of public waters on the ground that they did not suffer special damages under *Cort*. And in City of Milwaukee v. Illinois, 451 U.S. 304 (1981), the Court refused to allow a private federal cause of action for nuisance, which it regarded as inconsistent with the comprehensive scheme of control imposed by the federal water pollution acts. Is the decision sound if, at the time of passage, it had been common practice in both state and federal courts freely to imply private rights of action? See Stewart & Sunstein, Public Programs and Private Rights, 95 Harv. L. Rev. 1195 (1982), stressing the importance of historical background understandings.

In the event of no federal preemption, express or implied, is the state free to adopt or reject the federal standard as a basis for a private suit? In Lowe v. General Motors Corp., 624 F.2d 1373, 1379 (5th Cir. 1980), the court held that the plaintiff stated a valid state law cause of action when he alleged that the recall and notice practices of the defendant, General Motors, did not comply with the National Traffic and Motor Vehicle Safety Act, 15 U.S.C.A. §1402(a), on the ground that the tests of Cort v. Ash were inapplicable to a wrongful death action maintained under Alabama law. "This Court has often held that violation of a Federal law or regulation can be evidence of negligence, and even evidence of negligence per se."

Martin v. Herzog
126 N.E. 814 (N.Y. 1920)

[The decedent was killed in a collision between the buggy he was driving and defendant's automobile. The accident occurred after dark, and decedent was driving the buggy without any lights, in violation of a statute.

The defendant requested a ruling that the absence of a light on the plaintiff's vehicle was "prima facie evidence of contributory negligence." This request was refused, and the jury was instructed that it might consider the absence of lights as some evidence of negligence, but not conclusive evidence of negligence. The plaintiff next requested a charge that "the fact that the plaintiff's intestate was driving without a light is not negligence in itself," and to this the court acceded. The jury found the defendant liable and the decedent free from contributory negligence and the plaintiff had judgment. The appellate division reversed for error in the instructions. Affirmed.]

CARDOZO, J. We think the unexcused omission of the statutory signals is more than some evidence of negligence. It *is* negligence in itself. Lights are intended for the guidance and protection of other travelers on the highway (Highway Law, sec. 329a). By the very terms of the hypothesis, to omit, willfully or heedlessly, the safeguards prescribed by law for the benefit of another that he may be preserved in life or limb, is to fall short of the standard of diligence to which those who live in organized society are under a duty to conform. . . . In the case at hand, we have an instance of the admitted violation of a statute intended for the protection of travelers on the highway, of whom the defendant at the time was one. Yet the jurors were instructed in effect that they were at liberty in their discretion to treat the omission of lights either as innocent or as culpable. They were allowed to "consider the default as lightly or gravely" as they would (Thomas, J., in the court below). They might as well have been told that they could use a like discretion in holding a master at fault for the omission of a safety appliance prescribed by positive law for the protection of a workman. Jurors have no dispensing power by which they may relax the duty that one traveler on the highway owes under the statute to another. It is error to tell them that they have. The omission of these lights was a wrong, and being wholly unexcused was also a negligent wrong. No license should have been conceded to the triers of the facts to find it anything else.

We must be on our guard, however, against confusing the question of negligence with that of the causal connection between the negligence and the injury. A defendant who travels without lights is not to pay damages for his fault unless the absence of lights is the cause of the disaster. A plaintiff who travels without them is not to forfeit the right to damages unless the absence of lights is at least a contributing cause of the disaster. To say that conduct is negligence is not to say that it is always contributory negligence.

. . . A statute designed for the protection of human life is not to be brushed aside as a form of words, its commands reduced to the level of cautions, and the duty to obey attenuated into an option to conform.

NOTE

Negligence per se and excuses. Tedla v. Ellman, 19 N.E.2d 987, 989 (N.Y. 1939), offers an instructive contrast with *Martin*. Plaintiff and her brother, a deaf mute, were walking along a divided highway shortly after dark, pushing baby carriages filled with junk that they had collected for sale as part of their regular business. Instead of walking on the far left-hand side of the double highway, as required by statute so as to face oncoming traffic, they walked on the far right-hand side so that the traffic going in their direction approached them from behind. Defendant struck them with his car, hurting the plaintiff and killing her brother. The defendant's negligence was clearly established at trial and judgment was entered for plaintiff. The only issue on appeal was "whether, as matter of law, disregard of the statutory rule that pedestrians shall keep to the left of the center line of a highway constitutes contributory negligence which bars any recovery by the plaintiff." To answer that question, Judge Lehman noted that prior to the enactment of the statute, the common law custom usually required pedestrians to walk against traffic in order to be alert to dangers from oncoming traffic. The general customary rule, however, also contained a customary exception that required pedestrians to walk with the traffic when the traffic coming from behind was much lighter than the oncoming traffic. The case thus presented a knotty issue of statutory construction: Should the court read a customary exception to a statute that embodied the customary rule? If the statute had defined "specified safeguards against recognized dangers," Judge Lehman would have applied the rule in Martin v. Herzog. But since this statute was designed to "codify, supplement or even change common-law rules," themselves designed to prevent accidents, Lehman implied the exception to the statute for the plaintiff's benefit. In an argument that appears to turn on legislative intent, Lehman rebuffed the defendant as follows:

> Disregard of the statutory rule of the road and observance of a rule based on immemorial custom, it is said, is negligence which as matter of law is a proximate cause of the accident, though observance of the statutory rule might, under the circumstances of the particular case, expose a pedestrian to serious danger from which he would be free if he followed the rule that had been established by custom. If that be true, then the Legislature has decreed that pedestrians must observe the general rule of conduct which it has prescribed for their safety even under circumstances where observance would subject them to unusual risk; that pedestrians are to be charged with negligence as matter of law for acting as prudence dictates. It is unreasonable to ascribe to the Legislature an intention that the statute should have so extraordinary a result, and the courts may not give to a statute an effect not intended by the Legislature.

The one-sentence dissent argued that the plaintiff's action should have been dismissed on the authority of Martin v. Herzog.

The Second Restatement, §288A, comment *i*, illustration 6 endorses the court's position in *Tedla,* as does RTT:LPH §15(e), covering cases where "the actor's compliance with the statute would involve a greater risk of physical harm to the actor or to others than noncompliance." Both Restatements also provide that violations of a statute may be excused by necessity or emergency, or by reason of incapacity, as is the case with various forms of common law negligence. In addition, the Third Restatement states that statutory causes of action should be judged by negligence, and not strict liability standards, by providing that a statutory violation is excused when "the actor exercises reasonable care in attempting to comply with the statute." RTT:LPH §15(b). "Accordingly, the common law recognizes that the person can rebut negligence per se by showing that the person made a reasonable effort to comply with the statute," as with the driver who makes reasonable efforts to inspect or maintain brakes that fail. *Id.*, comment *c*.

Brown v. Shyne
151 N.E. 197 (N.Y. 1926)

LEHMAN, J. The plaintiff employed the defendant to give chiropractic treatment to her for a disease or physical condition. The defendant had no license to practice medicine, yet he held himself out as being able to diagnose and treat disease, and under the provisions of the Public Health Law (Cons. Laws, ch. 45) he was guilty of a misdemeanor. The plaintiff became paralyzed after she had received nine treatments by the defendant. She claims, and upon this appeal we must assume, that the paralysis was caused by the treatment she received. She has recovered judgment in the sum of $10,000 for the damages caused by said injury.

At the close of the plaintiff's case the plaintiff was permitted to amend the complaint to allege "that in so treating the plaintiff the defendant was engaged in the practice of medicine contrary to and in violation of the provisions of the Public Health Law of the State of New York in such case made and provided, he at the time of so treating plaintiff not being a duly licensed physician or surgeon of the State of New York." Thereafter the trial judge charged the jury that they might bring in a verdict in favor of the plaintiff if they found that the evidence established that the treatment given to the plaintiff was not in accordance with the standards of skill and care which prevail among those treating disease. He then continued: "This is a little different from the ordinary malpractice case, and I am going to allow you, if you think proper under the evidence in the case, to predicate negligence upon another theory. The public health laws of this State prescribe that no person shall practice medicine unless he is licensed so to do by the Board of Regents of this State and registered pursuant to statute. . . . This statute to which I have referred is a general police regulation. Its violation, and it has been violated by the defendant, is some evidence, more or less cogent, of negligence which you may consider for what it is worth, along with all the other evidence in the case. If the defendant attempted to treat the plaintiff and to adjust the vertebrae in her spine when he did not possess the requisite knowledge and skill as prescribed by the statute to know what was proper and necessary to do under the circumstances, or how to do it, even if he did know what to do, you can find him negligent." In so charging the jury that from the violation of the statute the jury might infer negligence which produced injury to the plaintiff, the trial justice in my opinion erred.

The provisions of the Public Health Law prohibiting the practice of medicine without a license granted upon proof of preliminary training and after examination intended to show adequate knowledge, are of course intended for the protection of the general public against injury which unskilled and unlearned practitioners might cause. If violation of the statute by the defendant was the proximate cause of the plaintiff's injury, then the plaintiff may recover upon proof of violation; if violation of the statute has no direct bearing on the injury, proof of the violation becomes irrelevant. For injury caused by neglect of duty imposed by the penal law there is civil remedy; but of course the injury must follow from the neglect.

Proper formulation of general standards of preliminary education and proper examination of the particular applicant should serve to raise the standards of skill and care generally possessed by members of the profession in this State; but the license to practice medicine confers no additional skill upon the practitioner; nor does it confer immunity from physical injury upon a patient if the practitioner fails to exercise care. Here, injury may have been caused by lack of skill or care; it would not have been obviated if the defendant had possessed a license yet failed to exercise the skill and care required of one practicing medicine. True, if the defendant had not practiced medicine in this State, he could not have injured the plaintiff, but the protection which the statute was intended to provide was against risk of injury by the unskilled or careless practitioner, and unless the plaintiff's injury was caused by carelessness or lack of skill, the defendant's failure to obtain a license was not connected with the injury. The plaintiff's cause of action is for negligence or malpractice. The defendant undertook to treat the plaintiff for a physical condition which seemed to require remedy. Under our law such treatment may be given only by a duly qualified practitioner who has obtained a license. . . .

No case has been cited where neglect of a statutory duty has given rise to private cause of action where it has not appeared that private injury has been caused by danger against which the statute was intended to afford protection, and which obedience to the statute would have obviated. . . .

It is said that the trial justice did not charge that plaintiff might recover for defendant's failure to obtain a license but only that failure to obtain a license might be considered "some evidence" of defendant's negligence. Argument is made that even if neglect of the statutory duty does not itself create liability, it tends to prove that injury was caused by lack of skill or care. That can be true only if logical inference may be drawn from defendant's failure to obtain or perhaps seek a license that he not only lacks the skill and learning which would enable him to diagnose and treat disease generally, but also that he lacks even the skill and learning necessary for the physical manipulation he gave to this plaintiff. Evidence of defendant's training, learning and skill and the method he used in giving the treatment was produced at the trial and upon such evidence the jury could base a finding either of care or negligence, but the absence of a license does not seem to strengthen inference that might be drawn from such evidence, and a fortiori would not alone be a basis for such inference. Breach or neglect of duty imposed by statute or ordinance may be evidence of negligence only if there is logical connection between the proven neglect of statutory duty and the alleged negligence.

CRANE, J., dissenting. . . . I think this rule all too liberal to the defendant. What he did was prohibited by law. He could not practice medicine without violating the law. The law did not recognize him as a physician. How can the courts treat him as such? Provided his act, in violation of the law, is the direct and proximate cause of injury, in my judgment he is liable, irrespective of negligence. It seems somewhat strange that the courts, one branch of the law, can hold up for such a man the standards of the licensed physician, while the Legislature, another branch of the law, declares that he cannot practice at all as a physician. The courts thus afford the protection which the Legislature denies.

What is the rule which is to guide us in determining whether a violation of a statute or ordinance is evidence of negligence? It is no answer to say that the statute provides a penalty, and, therefore, no other consequences can follow. Such is not the law. We are to determine it, as I read the authorities, from the purpose and object of the law, and also from the fact whether a violation of the law may be the direct and proximate cause of an injury to an individual. . . .

The prohibition against practicing medicine without a license was for the very purpose of protecting the public from just what happened in this case. The violation of this statute has been the direct and proximate cause of the injury. The courts will not determine in face of this statute whether a faith healer, a patent medicine man, a chiropractor, or any other class of practitioner acted according to the standards of his own school, or according to the standards of a duly licensed physician. The law, to insure against ignorance and carelessness, has laid down a rule to be followed, namely, examinations to test qualifications, and a license to practice. If a man, in violation of this statute, takes his chances in trying to cure disease, and his acts result directly in injury, he should not complain if the law, in a suit for damages, says that his violation of the statute is some evidence of his incapacity.

NOTES

1. Medical practice without a license. In cases like *Brown* the implicit premise of the plaintiff's argument is that she would have escaped all injury if the defendant had not treated her. Is that premise sustainable if the plaintiff would have had to face equal risk from a treatment by a licensed physician? Should the want of the license be evidence of any increased risk? RTT:LPH §14, comment *h* appears to endorse the outcome in *Brown*: "In light, then, of the combination of the statutory-purpose doctrine and ordinary principles of scope of liability, the lack of a license is not negligence per se on the part of the actor, nor is it evidence tending to show the actor's negligence." With this view compare Section 4504 of the New York Civil Practice Law and Rules (Consol. 2007):

> (d) Proof of negligence; unauthorized practice of medicine. In any action for damages for personal injuries or death against a person not authorized to practice medicine . . . for any act or acts constituting the practice of medicine, when such act or acts were a competent producing proximate or contributing cause of such injuries or death, the fact that such person practiced medicine without being so authorized shall be deemed prima facie evidence of negligence.

Does the statute overrule *Brown*? Adopt the position of the dissent?

2. Licenses and highway accidents. A similar analysis applies to unlicensed drivers involved in highway accidents, where the basic rule appears to be that "mere lack of an operator's license is not in itself evidence of negligence in the operation of a motor vehicle, in the absence of some causal connection between the injury and the failure to have the license." Mattero v. Silverman, 176 A.2d 270, 274 (N.J. Super. 1961). But due weight attaches to the word "mere." In Klanseck v. Anderson Sales & Service Co., 393 N.W.2d 356, 357 (Mich. 1986), the plaintiff, a new motorcyclist, was injured just after the purchase of a new Honda motorcycle. In passing on the plaintiff's conduct, the court held that "where evidence is presented which raises an issue regarding a driver's incompetence or inexperience as a causal factor in an accident, the jury may be instructed that it may draw an inference of negligence from the violation of the licensing statute." The Third Restatement takes the same view, distinguishing the case in which a driver does not have a license because he failed to file for renewal from one in which the defendant does not have a license because he has failed a driving test. RTT:LPH §14, comment *h*.

The question of licensing has still greater urgency in connection with medical devices subject to regulation by the Food and Drug Administration. In Talley v. Danek Med., Inc., 179 F.3d 154, 159-160 (4th Cir. 1999), a surgeon in back surgery used a Dyna-Lok internal fixation device manufactured by defendant, which failed when several of its screws came loose.

Plaintiff's claim rested in part on the ground that the FDA had not approved this device for general use thereby making the defendant for its violation of the Federal Food, Drug and Cosmetic Act. Niemeyer, J., rejected her claim:

> [W]here a particular statutory requirement does not itself articulate a standard of care but rather requires only regulatory approval, or a license, or a report for the administration of a more general underlying standard, violation of that administrative requirement itself is not a breach of a standard of care. This violation rather indicates only a failure to comply with an administrative requirement, not the breach of a tort duty. By analogy, such a violation also cannot be the proximate cause of the injury.

He then concluded:

> The administrative requirement that a given device be approved by the FDA before being marketed — as opposed to a specific substantive requirement that a device be safe and effective — is only a tool to facilitate administration of the underlying regulatory scheme. Because it lacks any independent substantive content, it does not impose a standard of care, the breach of which could form the basis of a negligence per se claim. Its breach is analogous to the failure to have a drivers license.

3. *Statutory duty and proximate cause.* The general principles of proximate cause allow a defendant to defeat recovery in some instances when the wrong of a third person "severs" causal connection between the defendant's negligence and the plaintiff's injury. This defense remains available in cases involving breach of statutory duty. In Ross v. Hartman, 139 F.2d 14, 15-16 (D.C. Cir. 1943), the defendant's agent left an unlocked car in a public alley with keys in the ignition. He intended for the car to be taken into an overnight garage, but did not notify anyone at the garage of his intention. Within two hours, a thief stole the car and negligently ran over the plaintiff. The defendant's conduct was in breach of an ordinance that made it illegal to allow an unlocked car "to stand or remain unattended on any street or in any public place." Edgerton, J., held that the deliberate intervention by the thief did not take the case outside the statutory prohibition:

> The particular ordinance involved here is one of a series which require, among other things, that motor vehicles be equipped with horns and lamps. Ordinary bicycles are required to have bells and lamps, but they are not required to be locked. The evident purpose of requiring motor vehicles to be locked is not to prevent theft for the sake of owners or the police, but to promote the safety of the public in the streets. An unlocked motor vehicle creates little more risk of theft than an unlocked bicycle, or for that matter an

unlocked house, but it creates much more risk that meddling by children, thieves, or others will result in injuries to the public. The ordinance is intended to prevent such consequences. Since it is a safety measure, its violation was negligence. This negligence created the hazard and thereby brought about the harm which the ordinance was intended to prevent. It was therefore a legal or "proximate" cause of the harm. Both negligence and causation are too clear in this case, we think, for submission to a jury.

There are practical as well as theoretical reasons for not excusing him. The rule we are adopting tends to make the streets safer by discouraging the hazardous conduct which the ordinance forbids. It puts the burden of the risk, as far as may be, upon those who create it. Appellee's agent created a risk which was both obvious and prohibited. Since appellee was responsible for the risk, it is fairer to hold him responsible for the harm than to deny a remedy to the innocent victim.

The opposite result was reached on similar facts in Richards v. Stanley, 271 P.2d 23, 26-27 (Cal. 1954), but there the San Francisco Municipal Code contained a proviso that barred the use of the ordinance in a private tort action. Traynor, J., also held that plaintiff had no action for common law negligence, noting that simply because an owner left a key in the ignition "does not assure that it will be driven, as he does when he lends it to another." Unless, therefore, he had some special reason to think that the car would be left in a dangerous locale, he was not subject to any general duty of care:

> In view of the fact that the risk of negligent driving she created was less than the risk she might intentionally have created without negligence by entrusting her car to another, and in the light of the rule that she owed no duty to protect plaintiff from harm resulting from the activities of third persons, we conclude that her duty to exercise reasonable care in the management of her automobile did not encompass a duty to protect plaintiff from the negligent driving of a thief.

The two dissenting would have left the plaintiff's common law claim to the jury. What if thieves are far more likely than guests to drive dangerously? If Justice Traynor's position is rejected, what result if the thief non-negligently struck the plaintiff?

4. *Dram shop statutes.* Causation issues also loom large in so-called dram shop litigation. When the basic statute makes it illegal to sell alcoholic beverages to a customer, the question arises whether the provider of the alcohol is responsible if the customer thereafter injures either a third person or himself while driving under the influence. The early common law rule treated the driver as the sole cause of the accident. "The rule was based on the obvious fact that one cannot be intoxicated by reason of liquor furnished him if he does not drink it." Nolan v. Morelli, 226 A.2d 383

(Conn. 1967). In Vesely v. Sager, 486 P.2d 151 (Cal. 1971), the court repudiated that rule. To establish the basic duty, it relied on Evidence Code §669(a), *supra* at 269, and Business and Professions Code §25602(a), which provides: "Every person who sells, furnishes, gives, or causes to be sold, furnished, or given away, any alcoholic beverage to any habitual or common drunkard or to any obviously intoxicated person is guilty of a misdemeanor." It then held that the plaintiff could recover from the provider of alcohol under a rule of proximate causation that holds "an actor may be liable if his negligence is a substantial factor in causing an injury, and he is not relieved of liability because of the intervening act of a third person if such act was reasonably foreseeable at the time of his negligent conduct."

Vesely was extended in Ewing v. Cloverleaf Bowl, 572 P.2d 1155 (Cal. 1978), when a bartender served the decedent, who had wanted to get drunk to celebrate his twenty-first birthday, ten shots of 151 proof rum. The willful misconduct of the bartender was held to overcome the contributory negligence of his patron. Shortly thereafter, in Coulter v. Superior Court (Schwartz & Reynolds & Co., RPI), 577 P.2d 669 (Cal. 1978), the California Supreme Court held that both the dram shop act and "modern" common law negligence principles allowed an action by an injured party against a noncommercial entity—here an apartment owner and manager—who supplied alcohol to an obviously intoxicated person when the provider knew that the person to whom the alcohol was provided intended to drive. Dram statute liability did not go down well with California voters, and these decisions were overruled by legislation. Cal. Bus. & Prof. Code §25602 (West 2003):

§25602. SALES TO DRUNKARD OR INTOXICATED PERSON; OFFENSE;
        CIVIL LIABILITY
   (a) Every person who sells, furnishes, gives, or causes to be sold, furnished, or given away, any alcoholic beverage to any habitual or common drunkard or to any obviously intoxicated person is guilty of a misdemeanor.
   (b) No person who sells, furnishes, gives, or causes to be sold, furnished, or given away, any alcoholic beverage pursuant to subdivision (a) of this section shall be civilly liable to any injured person or the estate of such person for injuries inflicted on that person as a result of intoxication by the consumer of such alcoholic beverage.
   (c) The Legislature hereby declares that this section shall be interpreted so that the holdings in cases such as Vesely v. Sager . . . and Coulter v. Superior Court . . . be abrogated in favor of prior judicial interpretation finding the consumption of alcoholic beverages rather than the serving of alcoholic beverages as the proximate cause of injuries inflicted upon another by an intoxicated person.

Why the explicit case citations in section (c)?

The statute was sustained against constitutional attacks, though with obvious misgivings, in Cory v. Shierloh, 629 P.2d 8, 12 (Cal. 1981), on the ground that the plaintiff driver bore the ultimate responsibility. The court refused to "speculate on the influences that might have prompted the Legislature to answer this acute and growing problem by narrowly *restricting* rather than *enlarging* civil liability." Do increased criminal sanctions count as an effective substitute for this private right of action?

The Pennsylvania Supreme Court expressly parted company with *Coulter* on the liability of the social host in Klein v. Raysinger, 470 A.2d 507 (Pa. 1983). It held that there was no common liability on the part of a social host who served alcoholic beverages to adults who later injured persons on the highway. The companion case of Congini v. Portersville Valve Co., 470 A.2d 515 (Pa. 1983), however, allowed an action against a social host who served liquor to a minor in violation of the local criminal code, which made it a summary criminal offense to serve liquor to anyone "less than 21 years of age." The line between commercial and social situations is not always clear. In Koehnen v. Dufour, 590 N.W.2d 107 (Minn. 1999), a 17-year-old who hosted a party for her friends at her father's house was treated as a social host even though she charged $2 to $4 for beer. A divided court found that "the Legislature intended to insulate social hosts from liability *regardless of the terms under which they provide their guests with liquor.*"

A similar resistance to the creation of liability for social hosts was expressed in Shea v. Matassa, 918 A.2d 1090, 1092 (Del. Super. Ct. 2007), where the court refused to create a common law action for dram shop liability against either a tavern owner or a social host, again for explicitly prudential reasons:

> We conclude that the General Assembly, not this Court, should decide whether to create a cause of action for dram shop liability or social host liability. The General Assembly heavily regulates the sale and use of alcohol and by so doing has clearly announced its intent to occupy exclusively the field of policy making in that subject area. Furthermore, the parties raise controversial and competing public policy questions which the General Assembly can more effectively debate, consider and resolve through the legislative process.

Local statutory variations in dram shop laws make it almost impossible to state the common law in this area. See generally 3 Harper, James & Gray, Torts §17.5 n.21.

Uhr v. East Greenbush Cent. Sch. Dist.
720 N.E.2d 886 (N.Y. 1999)

ROSENBLATT, J.

Education Law §905(1) requires school authorities in the State of New York to examine students between 8 and 16 years of age for scoliosis at least once in each school year. The principal issue on this appeal is whether the statute authorizes a private right of action.

[In the 1992-1993 school year the plaintiff, a pupil in the East Greenbush Central School District, was screened for scoliosis, but the tests were negative. In the following school year, she was not so checked. However, in 1995, as a ninth grader, an examination for scoliosis indicated that she suffered from the condition.] Her parents, who are also plaintiffs in this action, then had her examined by an orthopedic doctor who concluded that her scoliosis had progressed to the point that surgery was required instead of the braces that often can be utilized when the condition is diagnosed earlier. The infant [i.e., minor] plaintiff underwent surgery in July 1995. [The plaintiffs then sued both under Education Law §905 and for common law negligence. The lower courts rejected both claims.]

Education Law §905 (1) states that "[m]edical inspectors or principals and teachers in charge of schools in this state shall . . . examine all . . . pupils between eight and sixteen years of age for scoliosis, at least once in each school year." Education Law §905(2) provides that "[n]otwithstanding any other provisions of any general, special or local law, the school authorities charged with the duty of making such tests or examinations of pupils for the presence of scoliosis pursuant to this section shall not suffer any liability to any person as a result of making such test or examination, which liability would not have existed by any provision of law, statutory or otherwise, in the absence of this section." Finally, Education Law §911 charges the Commissioner of Education with the duty of enforcing the provisions of sections 901 through 910 of the Education Law and authorizes the Commissioner to "adopt rules and regulations" for such purpose.

THE TEST FOR THE AVAILABILITY OF A PRIVATE RIGHT OF ACTION

As plaintiffs point out, the District's obligation to examine for scoliosis is plain enough. A statutory command, however, does not necessarily carry with it a right of private enforcement by means of tort litigation.

The availability of a private right of action for the violation of a statutory duty — as opposed to one grounded in common-law negligence — is not a new concept. When a statute itself expressly authorizes a private right of action there is no need for further analysis. When a statute is silent, as it is here, courts have had to determine whether a private right of action may be fairly implied. . . . In making the determination, we ask:

> "(1) whether the plaintiff is one of the class for whose particular benefit the statute was enacted;

"(2) whether recognition of a private right of action would promote the legislative purpose; and

"(3) whether creation of such a right would be consistent with the legislative scheme."

[After concluding that the plaintiffs satisfied the first two parts, the court discussed the last requirement.] Plaintiffs argue that a private right of action is not only consistent with Education Law §905 (1) but also necessary for its operation. They assert that the statute offers no other practical means of enforcement and that a private right of action is imperative, in order to give it life. We disagree and conclude that a private right of action would not be consistent with the statutory scheme. To begin with, the statute carries its own potent official enforcement mechanism. The Legislature has expressly charged the Commissioner of Education with the duty to implement Education Law §905 (1) and has equipped the Commissioner with authority to adopt rules and regulations for such purpose. Moreover, the Legislature has vested the Commissioner with power to withhold public funding from noncompliant school districts. Thus, the Legislature clearly contemplated administrative enforcement of this statute. The question then becomes whether, in addition to administrative enforcement, an implied private right of action would be consistent with the legislative scheme.

It would not. The evolution of Education Law §905 (2) is compelling evidence of the Legislature's intent to immunize the school districts from any liability that might arise out of the scoliosis screening program. By the language of Education Law §905 (2) the Legislature deemed that the school district "shall not suffer any liability to any person as a result of *making* such test or examination" (emphasis added). Plaintiffs contend that by implication, the District is denied immunity for *failing* to perform the examination. In effect, plaintiffs would interpret the statute as conferring immunity for misfeasance but not nonfeasance. On the other hand, the District contends that it would be incongruous for the Legislature to accord immunity for one circumstance but not the other.

Plaintiffs' reading of the statute might have some appeal if we did not have persuasive evidence as to the Legislature's intent to immunize the school districts for both nonfeasance and misfeasance. . . . Revealingly, the Legislature evidently saw no need to amend Education Law §905 in any other way, although obviously aware of [two Appellate Division decisions that had refused to create a private right or action.] Its failure to otherwise amend the statute is strong evidence of the Legislature's conclusion that the Appellate Divisions had correctly interpreted the statute's immunity provision.

There is also the matter of cost to the school districts, as evidenced by the Legislature's expressed sensitivity in that regard. Orthopedists through the New York State Society of Orthopaedic Surgeons and other professionals from the Scoliosis Association, Inc. agreed to volunteer their time and expertise to train existing school personnel on the relatively simple examination procedure. In forecasting its cost, the Legislature anticipated that the program would have minimal financial impact on school districts. Allowing a private right of action against the government as opposed to a private entity has direct and obvious financial consequences to the public.

Given the Legislature's concern over the possible costs to the school districts — as evidenced by the statutory immunity provision and the other legislative statements reflecting those concerns — we conclude that the Legislature did not intend that the districts bear the potential liability for a program that benefits a far wider population. If we are to imply such a right, we must have clear evidence of the Legislature's willingness to expose the governmental entity to liability that it might not otherwise incur. The case before us reveals no such legislative intent.

In sum, we conclude that a private right of action to enforce Education Law §905 (1) is inconsistent with the statute's legislative scheme and therefore cannot be fairly implied

COMMON-LAW NEGLIGENCE

[The Court then held that the plaintiffs did not state a cause of action for common law negligence.]

Affirmed.

NOTES

1. *Statutory causes of action under complex administrative schemes. Uhr* represents the modern judicial reluctance to infer private rights of action from the breach of statutory duties created under complex administrative schemes. An early glimpse of this trend is found in Lucy Webb Hayes National Training School v. Perotti, 419 F.2d 704, 712 (D.C. Cir. 1969), which distinguished Ross v. Hartman, *supra* at 277. The decedent killed himself by jumping through a glass window shortly after he was committed to the defendant institution. The 1909 regulations for private hospitals prohibited them from keeping "any delirious or maniacal patient" in a room "not properly barred or closed." The court did not dwell on the question of proximate cause raised previously in *Ross.* Rather, it refused to create the private right of action at all:

The traffic ordinance in *Ross* was one directed straight to the motoring public, who were expected to know and heed its requirements. In this case, the regulation related to the licensing of private hospitals in the District of Columbia.

The Department of Public Health, which apparently is responsible for the enforcement of the regulation involved, approved the design of Sibley Memorial Hospital, . . . and recommended that the Commissioners of the District of Columbia license its operation, which they did. . . .

Regulations relating to a licensing process are often enacted with the reasonable expectation that the licensing authority will exercise some judgment in applying the general rule to the specific case. To invoke a doctrine of negligence per se in such circumstances robs the regulation of the flexibility that its draftsmen may well have envisioned for it. We conclude that in this case the instruction that violation of the regulation would be negligence per se was erroneous, and requires a new trial. The correct standard . . . is that the hospital's negligence should be "decided on all relevant evidence, including violation of any safety regulation found to be applicable, and consequently admissible in evidence, but including also facts tending to show due care" on the part of the hospital in the construction and operation of [its facilities].

A similar hostility was expressed in Elliot v. City of New York, 747 N.E.2d 760 (N.Y. 2001). Plaintiff fell out of a bleacher seat that was not protected by guard, as required by the city building code. The trial judge had held that the breach of the municipal building code amounted to negligence per se. The Court of Appeals reversed on the ground that a breach of rules of a "subordinate rule-making body" did not count as negligence per se because only the state had power to pass a statute:

[C]haracterizing the vast multitude of ordinances that have been adopted by New York City as State statutes would result in considerable fragmentation and uncertainty in the application of the common law of our State. Furthermore, since the City retains the authority to amend or repeal its Administrative Code provisions, including [that applicable here], without the need of State legislative action, we decline to transform the status of this provision from that of a local enactment to a State statute. In the absence of a violation of a statutorily imposed duty in this case, a negligence per se finding was unwarranted and defendants are entitled to a reversal and a new trial.

2. *Casting the net too wide?* An unwillingness to imply private rights of action is also found in Perry v. S.N., 973 S.W.2d 301, 309 (Tex. 1998). The plaintiff suffered child abuse at a school that was attended by the children of several of the defendants, who had witnessed these acts, but had failed to report them, in violation of Texas Family Code §261.109(a). This statute required *any person* who "has cause to believe that a child's physical or mental health or welfare has been or may be adversely affected by abuse" to file a report with the Police or with the Department of Protective

and Regulatory Services. Phillips, J., refused to allow a private right of action against these parents under a theory of negligence per se. "Because a decision to impose negligence per se could not be limited to cases charging serious misconduct like the one at bar, but rather would impose immense potential liability under an ill-defined standard on a broad class of individuals whose relationship to the abuse was extremely indirect, we hold that it is not appropriate to adopt Family Code section 261.109(a) as establishing a duty and standard of conduct in tort."

Posner, J., also refused to extend the net in Cuyler v. United States, 362 F.3d 949, 955 (7th Cir. 2004), an action under the Federal Tort Claims Act, where the defendant failed to report a child abuser who went on to inflict injuries on the decedent — an unrelated child for whom she baby sat some time later. "A 'homemaker' who not willfully but merely carelessly failed to report suspected abuse by a babysitter, perhaps fearing that the babysitter would sue her for defamation, . . . might on the plaintiff's view of the statute find herself sued years later because the babysitter had abused *another* child."

On the other hand, private rights of action have been allowed for breach of the standards of care applicable to nursing homes under both Medicare and Medicaid, for traditional reasons, as was explained in McLain v. Mariner Health Care, Inc., 631 S.E.2d 435, 438 (Ga. 2006):

> It is obvious that as a resident of the nursing home owned by Mariner, McLain's father belonged to the class of persons for whom these statutes and regulations were intended to protect, and that the injuries set forth in the complaint, and which we assume to have occurred for purposes of a motion to dismiss, were among those these same statutes and regulations were designed to prevent. Likewise, the complaint's allegations of violations of the same statutes and regulations would be competent evidence of Mariner's breach of duty under a traditional negligence action.

And so it is back to first principles.

SECTION F. JUDGE AND JURY

The law of negligence (indeed the entire law of tort) does more than articulate standards for liability. It also develops a wide range of legal institutions to apply its basic commands to individual cases. Our legal system divides the responsibility for deciding questions of fact between judge and jury. The purpose of this section is to examine how that division takes place. A divided system necessarily precludes the possibility that either judge or jury takes complete control over the individual case unless both parties to the dispute waive a jury trial. Yet, by the same token, the division of responsibility is not arbitrary, for the jury is not simply told: "You are to decide, on the basis of all you have heard and in terms of your sense of fairness, whether the defendant should pay for the damage sustained by the plaintiff in this case." That total delegation of responsibility has been rejected for two reasons. First, judges fear that the jury might abuse its unlimited power by deciding cases contrary to established principles of law. This fact is especially true when the jury is motivated by obvious passion and prejudice, or even by more subtle forms of class, social, or economic bias. Second, judges believe that unlimited jury discretion repudiates or at least undermines the central principle of distributive justice—that like cases should be treated alike, no matter what substantive principles apply.

One form of judicial control is found in the judge's instructions to the jury at the close of the case. These instructions embody the relevant principles of law. Substantive law is often made when the lawyers for either party challenge those instructions on appeal. Appellate courts set aside jury verdicts based on erroneous and prejudicial instructions precisely because they believe that juries should and do follow their instructions.

Sometimes mistakes seem quite minor. In Louisville & Nashville R.R. v. Gower, 3 S.W. 824, 827 (Tenn. 1887), the plaintiff, an employee of the defendant railroad, was hurt while attempting to couple two cars. Snodgrass, J., speaking for the court, reversed a judgment for the plaintiff and ordered a new trial:

> The charge was otherwise incorrect and misleading, particularly in defining the care necessary to have been exercised by Plaintiff Gower in order to entitle him to recovery. The Court, after telling the jury that "it was the duty of the plaintiff to exercise such a degree of care in making the coupling as a man of ordinary prudence" would have done, adds: "Just such care as one of you, similarly employed, would have exercised under such circumstances. If he exercised that degree of care, and was nevertheless injured, he is entitled to your verdict. If he failed to exercise that degree of care, he can not recover."
>
> The charge as to the exercise of such care as a man of ordinary prudence would have done was correct, but it was thought not full enough by the judge, who illustrated what he meant by reference to the care which each one of the jurymen would have exercised. His charge, so limited, was erroneous. It does not appear that all or any of the members of the jury were men of ordinary prudence, and yet the judge tells them that what he means by the "exercise of such care as a man of ordinary prudence would have exercised" is that it was the exercise of such care as one of them would have exercised if similarly situated. Under this instruction, if any member of the jury thought he would

have done what Gower did in the coupling, he would of course have determined that Gower acted with the care required, and was entitled to recover. This illustration, used to define what he meant by "the care of a man of ordinary prudence" and thereby becoming its definition, was erroneous. The care he was required to exercise was that of a man of ordinary prudence in that dangerous situation, and not "just such care as one of the jury similarly situated" would have done, be that much or little as each member might be very prudent or very imprudent.

A second form of judicial control lies in the court's power to keep certain questions of fact from the jury. In Metropolitan Railway v. Jackson, 3 A.C. 193, 197 (1877), the issue on appeal was, "Was there at the trial any evidence of negligence by the defendant that ought to have been left to a jury?" Chancellor Cairns remarked as follows:

> There was not, at your Lordships' bar, any serious controversy as to the principles applicable to a case of this description. The Judge has a certain duty to discharge, and the jurors have another and a different duty. The Judge has to say whether any facts have been established by evidence from which negligence *may be* reasonably inferred; the jurors have to say whether, from those facts, when submitted to them, negligence *ought to be* inferred. It is, in my opinion, of the greatest importance in the administration of justice that these separate functions should be maintained, and should be maintained distinct. It would be a serious inroad on the province of the jury, if, in a case where there are facts from which negligence may reasonably be inferred, the Judge were to withdraw the case from the jury upon the ground that, in his opinion, negligence ought not to be inferred; and it would, on the other hand, place in the hands of the jurors a power which might be exercised in the most arbitrary manner, if they were at liberty to hold that negligence might be inferred from any state of facts whatever.

As *Metropolitan Railway* suggests, the jury's traditional role is to find the "facts" to which it then applies the "law." Obviously, any finding of negligence fits uneasily into this sharp dichotomy between *law* and *fact*. Is it helpful to think of negligence as a "mixed issue of law and fact," as it is frequently called?

This section develops several themes: What is the role of the jury in law and in actual practice in setting the standard of care? What difference does it make who decides this issue? How does the court limit or control the jury's exercise of discretion? How does the presence of the jury affect the litigation strategy of the lawyers? Is there any way to assure uniformity of jury decisions in similar cases? Do juries ever nullify the legal rules articulated in appellate decisions? See generally James, Functions of Judge and Jury in Negligence Cases, 58 Yale L.J. 667 (1949).

Holmes, The Common Law
110-111, 120-124 (1881)

If, now, the ordinary liabilities in tort arise from failure to comply with fixed and uniform standards of external conduct, which every man is presumed and required to know, it is obvious that it ought to be possible, sooner or later, to formulate these standards at least to some extent, and that to do so must at last be the business of the court. It is equally clear that the featureless generality, that the defendant was bound to use such care as a prudent man would do under the circumstances, ought to be continually giving place to the specific one, that he was bound to use this or that precaution under these or those circumstances. The standard which the defendant was bound to come up to was a standard of specific acts or omissions, with reference to the specific circumstances in which he found himself. If in the whole department of unintentional wrongs the courts arrived at no further utterance than the question of negligence, and left every case, without rudder or compass, to the jury, they would simply confess their inability to state a very large part of the law which they required the defendant to know, and would assert, by implication, that nothing could be learned by experience. But neither courts nor legislatures have ever stopped at that point. . . .

The principles of substantive law which have been established by the courts are believed to have been somewhat obscured by having presented themselves oftenest in the form of rulings upon the sufficiency of evidence. When a judge rules that there is no evidence of negligence, he does something more than is embraced in an ordinary ruling that there is no evidence of a fact. He rules that the acts or omissions proved or in question do not constitute a ground of legal liability, and in this way the law is gradually enriching itself from daily life, as it should. Thus, in Crafter v. Metropolitan Railway Co.[, L.R. 1 C.P. 300 (1866)], the plaintiff slipped on the defendant's stairs and was severely hurt. The cause of his slipping was that the brass nosing of the stairs had been worn smooth by travel over it, and a builder testified that in his opinion the staircase was unsafe by reason of this circumstance and the absence of a hand-rail. There was nothing to contradict this except that great numbers of persons had passed over the stairs and that no accident had happened there, and the plaintiff had a verdict. The court set the verdict aside, and ordered a non-suit. The ruling was in form that there was no evidence of negligence to go to the jury; but this was obviously equivalent to saying, and did in fact mean, that the railroad company had done all that it was bound to do in maintaining such a staircase as was proved by the plaintiff. A hundred other equally concrete instances will be found in the text-books . . .

On the other hand, if the court should rule that certain acts or omissions coupled with damage were conclusive evidence of negligence unless explained, it would, in substance and in truth, rule that such acts or omissions were a ground of liability, or prevented a recovery, as the case might be. . . .

The cases which have raised difficulties needing explanation are those in which the court has ruled that there was prima facie evidence of negligence, or some evidence of negligence to go to the jury.

Many have noticed the confusion of thought implied in speaking of such cases as presenting mixed questions of law and fact. No doubt, as has been said above, the averment that the defendant has been guilty of negligence is a complex one: first, that he has done or omitted certain things; second, that his alleged conduct does not come up to the legal standard. And so long as the controversy is simply on the first half, the whole complex averment is plain matter for the jury without special instructions, just as a question of ownership would be where the only dispute was as to the fact upon which the legal conclusion was founded. But when a controversy arises on the second half, the question whether the court or the jury ought to judge of the defendant's conduct is wholly unaffected by the accident, whether there is or is not also a dispute as to what that conduct was. If there is such a dispute, it is entirely possible to give a series of hypothetical instructions adapted to every state of facts which it is open to the jury to find. If there is no such dispute, the court may still take their opinion as to the standard. The problem is to explain the relative functions of court and jury with regard to the latter.

When a case arises in which the standard of conduct, pure and simple, is submitted to the jury, the explanation is plain. It is that the court, not entertaining any clear views of public policy applicable to the matter, derives the rule to be applied from daily experience, as it has been agreed that the great body of the law of tort has been derived. But the court further feels that it is not itself possessed of sufficient practical experience to lay down the rule intelligently. It conceives that twelve men taken from the practical part of the community can aid its judgment. Therefore it aids its conscience by taking the opinion of the jury.

But supposing a state of facts often repeated in practice, is it to be imagined that the court is to go on leaving the standard to the jury forever? Is it not manifest, on the contrary, that if the jury is, on the whole, as fair a tribunal as it is represented to be, the lesson which can be got from that source will be learned? Either the court will find that the fair teaching of experience is that the conduct complained of usually is or is not blameworthy, and therefore, unless explained, is or is not a ground of liability; or it will find the jury oscillating to and fro, and will see the necessity of making up its mind for itself. There is no reason why any other such question should not be settled, as well as that of liability for stairs with smooth strips of brass upon their edges. The exceptions would mainly be found where the standard was rapidly changing, as, for instance, in some questions of medical treatment.

If this be the proper conclusion in plain cases, further consequences ensue. Facts do not often exactly repeat themselves in practice; but cases with comparatively small variations from each other do. A judge who has long sat at nisi prius ought gradually to acquire a fund of experience which enables him to represent the common sense of the community in ordinary instances far better than an average jury. He should be able to lead and to instruct them in detail, even where he thinks it desirable, on the whole, to take their opinion. Furthermore, the sphere in which he is able to rule without taking their opinion at all should be continually growing.

Baltimore and Ohio R.R. v. Goodman
275 U.S. 66 (1927)

HOLMES, J. This is a suit brought by the widow and administratrix of Nathan Goodman against the petitioner for causing his death by running him down at a grade crossing. The defence is that Goodman's own negligence caused the death. At the trial, the defendant asked the Court to direct a verdict for it, but the request, and others looking to the same direction, were refused, and the plaintiff got a verdict and a judgment which was affirmed by the Circuit Court of Appeals. 10 F.(2d) 58.

Goodman was driving an automobile truck in an easterly direction and was killed by a train running southwesterly across the road at a rate of not less than sixty miles an hour. The line was straight, but it is said by the respondent that Goodman "had no practical view" beyond a section house two hundred and forty-three feet north of the crossing until he was about twenty feet from the first rail, or, as the respondent argues, twelve feet from danger, and that then the engine was still obscured by the section house. He had been driving at the rate of ten or twelve miles an hour, but had cut down his rate to five or six miles at about forty feet from the crossing. It is thought that there was an emergency in which, so far as appears, Goodman did all that he could.

We do not go into further details as to Goodman's precise situation, beyond mentioning that it was daylight and that he was familiar with the crossing, for it appears to us plain that nothing is suggested by the evidence to relieve Goodman from responsibility for his own death. When a man goes upon a railroad track he knows that he goes to a place where he will be killed if a train comes upon him before he is clear of the track. He knows that he must stop for the train, not the train stop for him. In such circumstances it seems to us that if a driver cannot be sure otherwise whether a train is dangerously near he must stop and get out of his vehicle, although obviously he will not often be required to do more than to stop and look. It seems to us that if he relies upon not hearing the train or any signal and takes no further precaution he does so at his own risk. If at the last moment

Goodman found himself in an emergency it was his own fault that he did not reduce his speed earlier or come to a stop. It is true as said in Flannelly v. Delaware & Hudson Co., 225 U.S. 597 [1912], that the question of due care very generally is left to the jury. But we are dealing with a standard of conduct, and when the standard is clear it should be laid down once for all by the Courts. See Southern Pacific Co. v. Berkshire, 254 U.S. 415 [1921].

Judgment reversed.

Pokora v. Wabash Ry.
292 U.S. 98 (1934)

[The defendant operated four tracks at a level crossing. As plaintiff approached them, these included a switch track, a through track, and then two more switch tracks. Because of the boxcars on the first track, he could not see the main track. Plaintiff stopped, tried to look, and listened, but he heard no bell or whistle. He did not get out of his truck to obtain a better view, as the dictum in Baltimore & Ohio R.R. v. Goodman seemed to require under such circumstances. The trial court directed a verdict for defendant on its finding that plaintiff had been contributorily negligent and this judgment was affirmed below. Reversed and remanded.]

CARDOZO, J. Standards of prudent conduct are declared at times by courts, but they are taken over from the facts of life. To get out of a vehicle and reconnoitre is an uncommon precaution, as everyday experience informs us. Besides being uncommon, it is very likely to be futile, and sometimes even dangerous. If the driver leaves his vehicle when he nears a cut or curve, he will learn nothing by getting out about the perils that lurk beyond. By the time he regains his seat and sets his car in motion, the hidden train may be upon him. . . . Often the added safeguard will be dubious though the track happens to be straight, as it seems that this one was, at all events as far as the station, about five blocks to the north. A train traveling at a speed of thirty miles an hour will cover a quarter of a mile in the space of thirty seconds. It may thus emerge out of obscurity as the driver turns his back to regain the waiting car, and may then descend upon him suddenly when his car is on the track. Instead of helping himself by getting out, he might do better to press forward with all his faculties alert. So a train at a neighboring station, apparently at rest and harmless, may be transformed in a few seconds into an instrument of destruction. At times the course of safety may be different. One can figure to oneself a roadbed so level and unbroken that getting out will be a gain. Even then the balance of advantage depends on many circumstances and can be easily disturbed. Where was Pokora to leave his truck after getting out to reconnoitre? If he was to leave it on the switch, there was the possibility that the box cars would be shunted down upon him before he could regain his seat. The defendant did not show whether there was a locomotive at the forward end, or whether the cars were so few that a locomotive could be seen. If he was to leave his vehicle near the curb, there was even stronger reason to believe that the space to be covered in going back and forth would make his observations worthless. One must remember that while the traveler turns his eye in one direction, a train or a loose engine may be approaching from the other.

Illustrations such as these bear witness to the need for caution in framing standards of behavior that amount to rules of law. The need is the more urgent when there is no background of experience out of which the standards have emerged. They are then, not the natural flowerings of behavior in its customary forms, but rules artificially developed, and imposed from without. Extraordinary situations may not wisely or fairly be subjected to tests or regulations that are fitting for the common-place or normal. In default of the guide of customary conduct, what is suitable for the traveler caught in a mesh where the ordinary safeguards fail him is for the judgment of a jury. The opinion in Goodman's case has been a source of confusion in the federal courts to the extent that it imposes a standard for application by the judge, and has had only wavering support in the courts of the states. We limit it accordingly.

NOTES

1. *Stop, look, and listen.* Notwithstanding *Pokora*'s respectful disapproval of *Goodman*, since 1927 *Goodman* has been cited hundreds of times, often with approval. Most critically, plaintiffs today face a rough time in cases involving collisions with trains moving through open country on single tracks. For instance, the court in Ridgeway v. CSX Transportation, Inc., 723 So. 2d 600 (Ala. 1998), emphatically upheld a contributory negligence defense as a matter of law in a single track wrongful death case. It concluded that the statutory requirement to "stop, look, and listen" was "firmly rooted in our caselaw." The outcome was the same in Jewell v. CSX Transportation, Inc., 135 F.3d 361 (6th Cir. 1998), where three members of the Jewell family were travelling east across a railroad track on an elevated portion of the road, crossed the track, going southwest, at a 45 to 47 degree angle, while going about 60 miles per hour. The plaintiff-appellants argued that under the Kentucky law the intersection should be treated as "extrahazardous" so that there was, wholly apart from statute, an obligation "to have gates, lights, or other warnings." Bell, J. affirmed the trial judge's decision not to give the extrahazardous instruction in the absence of "any physical obstruction to Greg Jewell's [the driver] view of the train," holding

> The district court was correct in its determination that the test for an extra-hazardous crossing under Kentucky law is whether there is a real and

substantial obstruction to sight or hearing. The district court was also correct in its determination that this test requires an actual physical inability to see or hear, and not merely such human factors as a disinclination to look for a train due to the angle of the intersection, distractions or diversions.

In this case there was no structure or object that would have impaired Greg Jewell's view of the train. Appellants' expert, Dr. Harry Snyder, testified that if one stands in the road where the driver's eye would be, a train would be visible from the last 2,200 feet to the crossing. He testified that "[t]here is nothing in the way. There is nothing physically between the road and the train to get in the way except the vehicle that one might be driving in." Moreover, the road is straight for the last 1300 feet as it approaches the crossing and the train would have been visible for this entire distance. There was evidence that given the speeds of the truck and the train, Greg Jewell would have had ample time from his first opportunity to see the train to stop the truck. There is no question of fact that there was no physical obstruction at the crossing that prevented Greg Jewell from seeing the train. . . .

In contrast, plaintiffs enjoy their greatest success in cases like *Pokora* when it is no longer clear that the railroad has the right of way. In Toschi v. Christian, 149 P.2d 848, 851 (Cal. 1944), plaintiff was hurt when the truck he was driving was struck at a crossing by defendant's train. The crossing was located in the heart of the business district, and the defendant customarily employed flagmen whose job was to signal drivers that the tracks were *not* clear, so as to warn them that it was unsafe for any drivers to cross them. At the time of this particular accident, defendant's flagman was literally experimenting with mirrors, and without the flagman's guidance, plaintiff drove his truck across the tracks. "As he drove onto the first track . . . light from the mirror, with which the flagman was still playing, was flashed in his eyes, blinding him. He stopped, and immediately his truck was struck. . . ."

Schauer, J., noted:

> The "stop, look and listen" rule, urged by defendants, will not be applied to factual bases where its application would be unreasonable. In the circumstances of this case, which comprise a six-track railroad yard crossing, switching operations progressing almost constantly, the employment of two flagmen by the railroad, whose duties involve traffic control on the highway and to some extent on the railroad, and a practical necessity for travelers on the highway to rely on the flagmen's signals because ordinarily it would be impossible for such travelers after they had observed railroad traffic approaching to know whether it would cross or stop short of the highway, the "stop, look and listen" rule is not wholly appropriate and cannot operate to establish contributory negligence as a matter of law.

Pokora is followed in the Third Restatement, which rejects the idea that uniform rules can decide concrete cases: "what looks at first to be a constant or recurring issue of conduct in which many parties engage may reveal on closer inspection many variables that can best be considered on a case-by-case basis." RTT:LPH §8, comment *c*.

2. *Jury determinations in FELA cases.* Today juries are given broad discretion in suits for industrial accidents brought under the Federal Employers' Liability Act, 45 U.S.C. §51 et seq. (2000). This Act makes every interstate railroad liable in damages for injuries to its employees caused by the negligence of the railroad through any of its officers, agents, or employees, "or by reason of any defect or insufficiency" in any of its premises or equipment. FELA's 1939 amendments eliminated the defense of assumption of risk in all its forms and provided that contributory negligence should not bar an employee's action, but only that "the damages shall be diminished by the jury in proportion to the amount of negligence attributable to such employee."

In Wilkerson v. McCarthy, 336 U.S. 53, 62-64, (1949), the plaintiff was injured when he slipped on a board covered with oil and grease while taking a shortcut over a pit in the repair shop, even after the railroad had chained off the boardwalk to prevent employees from using it. The Utah Supreme Court overturned the jury verdict for the plaintiff, but a badly fractured Supreme Court reinstated its verdict. Justice Black upheld that jury verdict, writing:

> There are some who think that recent decisions of this Court which have required submission of negligence questions to a jury make, "for all practical purposes, a railroad an insurer of its employees." This assumption, that railroads are made insurers where the issue of negligence is left to the jury, is inadmissible. It rests on another assumption, this one unarticulated, that juries will invariably decide negligence questions against railroads. . . . Courts should not assume that in determining these questions of negligence juries will fall short of a fair performance of their constitutional function. . . .
>
> In reaching its conclusion as to negligence, a jury is frequently called upon to consider many separate strands of circumstances, and from these circumstances to draw its ultimate conclusion on the issue of negligence. Here there are many arguments that could have been presented to the jury in an effort to persuade it that the railroad's conduct was not negligent, and many counter arguments which might have persuaded the jury that the railroad was negligent. The same thing is true as to whether petitioner was guilty of contributory negligence. Many of such arguments were advanced by the Utah Supreme Court to support its finding that the petitioner was negligent and that the railroad was not. But the arguments made by the State Supreme Court are relevant and appropriate only for consideration by the jury, the tribunal selected to pass on the issues. For these reasons, the trial court should have submitted the case to the jury, and it was error for the Utah Supreme Court to affirm its action in taking the case from the jury.

Frankfurter, J., concluded that juries should be allowed to decide negligence issues that in the end involve nice questions of degree. But he took the occasion to launch a broader attack on the negligence system:

> The difficulties in these cases derive largely from the outmoded concept of "negligence" as a working principle for the adjustments of injuries inevitable under the technological circumstances of modern industry. This cruel and wasteful mode of dealing with industrial injuries has long been displaced in industry generally by the insurance principle that underlies workmen's compensation laws. For reasons that hardly reflect due regard for the interests of railroad employees, "negligence" remains the basis of liability for injuries to them. It is, of course, the duty of courts to enforce the Federal Employers' Liability Act, however outmoded and unjust in operation it may be. But so long as negligence rather than workmen's compensation is the basis of recovery, just so long will suits under the Federal Employers' Liability Act lead to conflicting opinions about "fault" and "proximate cause."

Chief Justice Vinson would have kept the case from the jury, saying in a brief dissent: "In my view of the record, there is no evidence, nor any inference which reasonably may be drawn from the evidence when viewed in the light most favorable to the petitioner, which could sustain a verdict for him." Justice Jackson then offered a fuller defense of the decision of Utah Supreme Court to take the case from the jury:

> This record shows that both the wheel pit into which plaintiff fell and the board on which he was trying to cross over the pit were blocked off by safety chains strung between posts. Plaintiff admits he knew the chains were there to keep him from crossing over the pit and to require him to go a few feet farther to walk around it. After the chains were put up, any person undertaking to use the board as a cross walk had to complete involved contortions and gymnastics, particularly when, as was the case with petitioner, a car was on the track 23½. A casual examination of the model filed as an exhibit in this Court shows how difficult was such a passage. Nevertheless, the Court holds that if employees succeeded in disregarding the chains and forced passage frequently enough to be considered "customary," and the railroad took no further action, its failure so to do was negligence. The same rule would no doubt apply if the railroad's precautions had consisted of a barricade, or an armed guard.

To this day, FELA still requires proof of negligence. As *Wilkerson* reveals, the quantum of evidence of negligence needed can be very thin, and subsequent cases have confirmed that so long as the employer's negligence has played "any part, even the slightest" in bringing about the injury, then recovery under the FELA is appropriate. See Rogers v. Missouri Pacific R.R., 352 U.S. 500 (1957).

3. *Should tort actions be left to the jury?* Why should any negligence case, or indeed any tort action, be tried by juries at all? The civil law countries of Western Europe do not use juries to assess either liability or damages, and even the English courts rely on juries only in exceptional cases. Ward v. James, [1966] 1 Q.B. 273, 295. "Whenever a man is on trial for serious crime, or when in a civil case a man's honour or integrity is at stake, or when one or other party must be deliberately lying, then the trial by jury has no equal. But in personal injury cases trial by jury has given place of late to trial by judge alone, the reason being simply this, that in these cases trial by a judge alone is more acceptable to the great majority of people."

The arguments for and against the use of juries are numerous and familiar. On the positive side, juries bring the sense of the community to the difficult estimations of reasonable care required under a negligence system. Juries also provide a check against the domination of the legal system by government officials and professional people. On the negative side, an expensive jury system only runs by taxing the unwilling individuals who are paid a fraction of their market wage for jury duty. Juries may be subject to passion and prejudice, and, even when fair-minded, find themselves overwhelmed with the complex technical issues raised by medical malpractice and products liability claims. In order to reduce the cost of jury trials, courts have been urged to impanel smaller juries of 6 or 8 instead of 12 jurors. Yet the price of reducing the direct costs of jury operation is to decrease the level of community participation, diversity, and reliability of jury efforts. For evaluations of these proposals, see Diamond and Zeisel, "Convincing Empirical Evidence" on the Six-Member Jury, 41 U. Chi. L. Rev. 281 (1974); Vidmar, The Performance of the American Civil Jury: An Empirical Perspective, 40 Ariz. L. Rev. 849 (1998); Saks, The Smaller the Jury, the Greater the Unpredictability, 79 Judicature 263 (1996); Robbennolt, Evaluating Juries by Comparison to Judges: A Benchmark for Judging?, 32 Fla. St. U. L. Rev. 469 (2005).

It has proved difficult to assemble hard empirical data on jury behavior, for it is generally considered unethical to monitor the deliberations of actual juries and too expensive to impanel enough mock juries to obtain a reliable data base. The Chicago jury study, undertaken in the 1960s, defended civil juries on the ground that they usually reach the same results as judges sitting as triers of facts, leaving judges themselves generally pleased with their behavior. See Kalven, The Dignity of the Civil Jury, 50 Va. L. Rev. 1055 (1964). If juries typically reach the same conclusions as judges, do they add anything more to the system than higher costs? More recently, Sentell, The Georgia Jury and Negligence: The View From the Trenches, 28 Ga. L. Rev. 1 (1993), relied on survey data of trial lawyers and found a significant (but far from unanimous) sentiment that today many judges are more pro-plaintiff than juries, at least on the issue of liability. On damages, however, judges were generally thought less likely to award "runaway verdicts" than a jury.

In addition, it appears that, with injuries held constant, the size of the plaintiff's recovery depends largely on the identity of the defendant. Thus one study found that juries ratcheted up awards against defendants with "deep pockets."

> Compared with individual defendants, our model predicts that corporate defendants pay 34 percent larger awards, after controlling for plaintiffs' injuries and type of legal case. If the plaintiff is permanently and severely injured, the deep-pocket effect is much stronger — a corporate defendant pays almost 4.5 times as much as an individual, on average. Similarly, government defendants are estimated to pay 50 percent more than individuals (averaged over all plaintiff injuries; there were too few cases of permanently and severely injured plaintiffs suing government defendants to analyze these separately). Finally, medical malpractice awards against doctors are almost 2.5 times as great as awards against other individuals in average case types, and awards against hospitals are 85 percent larger. . . .
>
> There are several plausible explanations for the observed jury behavior. First, jurors may balance the benefit of greater compensation for the plaintiff against the harm to the defendant. While a relatively modest award against an individual defendant might cause him great financial hardship, the same award against a corporation would impose only miniscule losses on each of its stockholders. In addition, it may be impossible for jurors to separate the insult implicit in a tort from the harm to the plaintiff. Thus jurors may require doctors to provide greater compensation to victims of malpractice, not only because doctors are usually heavily insured and are wealthier than other defendants, but also because of the special trust a patient places in his or her doctor.

Hammitt, Carroll, & Relles, Tort Standards and Jury Decisions, 14 J. Legal Stud. 751, 754-756 (1985).

Juries (and judges) may be subject to other biases as well. The psychological literature has established that individual judgments are often subject to so-called hindsight bias, wherein events that have actually occurred are thought to have been more likely than in fact they really were. The difficulties that bias poses for the administration of a negligence system is discussed in Rachlinski, A Positive Psychological Theory of Judging in Hindsight, 65 U. Chi. L. Rev. 571, 572, 574 (1998).

> The hindsight bias clearly has implications for the legal system. Consider, for example, the dilemma of a defendant who, despite taking reasonable care, has caused an accident and has been sued. The defendant's level of care will be reviewed by a judge or jury who already knows that it proved inadequate to avoid the plaintiff's injury. Consequently, the defendant's level of care will seem less reasonable in hindsight than it did in foresight. Reasonableness must be determined from the perspective of the defendant at

the time that the precautions were taken, but the hindsight bias ensures that subsequent events will influence that determination. The law relies on a process that assigns liability in a biased manner. . . .

Despite calls for reforms to eliminate the influence of the hindsight bias, courts have already done a remarkable job of adapting to the limitations of human judgment in hindsight. They have avoided adopting generic solutions that psychological research predicts would be unsuccessful. Instead, the courts have developed rules that take advantage of specific opportunities to avoid the bias. For example, when a reliable ex ante assessment of reasonable care is available, such as custom in medical malpractice, courts rely on it rather than their own independent assessment of reasonable care. Rules that avoid the more pernicious aspects of the bias have also developed: rules such as the inadmissibility of subsequent remedial measures as evidence of negligence.

Rachlinski notes that efforts to cope with the hindsight bias have moved the negligence standard closer to a strict liability rule. Should this tendency be of equal importance in medical malpractice and highway accident cases? Should we expect judges or juries to be more susceptible to this bias? Will the systematic bias make actors take excessive care to avoid large adverse judgments?

SECTION G.   PROOF OF NEGLIGENCE

1. *Problems of Proof*

Success in prosecuting or defending negligence actions hinges greatly on what the parties can prove at trial. Of course the parties must investigate, collect, and preserve many types of evidence in anticipation of the long delays between the occurrence of an accident and the final determination of a case. Much relevant evidence comes from lay witnesses and addresses questions such as, was the defendant driving the yellow car? Or, was the light green or red when the intersection collision took place? Most modern litigation, especially in medical malpractice and products liability cases, also requires expert evidence on matters such as the proper standard of care or causation. That expert testimony is always surrounded with ambiguity. Even though experts may not take contingent fees, they are chosen by the parties and, therefore, have some stake in the outcome of the case. Many experts are full-time professionals and thus repeat players, with allegiances to either plaintiff or defendant interests. The preparation and cross-examination of expert witnesses is a major component of modern tort litigation, although the practical and strategic issues fall outside the scope of this book.

In offering evidence on the question of negligence, Clarence Morris has observed that "the plaintiff has usually exhausted the possibilities of proof once he has shown: (1) what defendant did, (2) how dangerous it was, (3) defendant's opportunity to discern danger, (4) availability of safer alternatives, and (5) defendant's opportunity to know about safer alternatives." Morris, Proof of Negligence, 47 Nw. U. L. Rev. 817, 834 (1953).

This section, however, is not primarily concerned with these general matters of proof, which are properly taken up in courses on evidence, trial practice, or clinical education. One question of proof has, however, a long and close association with the law of tort. The doctrine of res ipsa loquitur — literally, Latin for "the thing speaks for itself" — has frequently been invoked when the plaintiff seeks to establish the defendant's negligence by circumstantial evidence. In some cases, the plaintiff seeks to reach and persuade a jury on the strength of the doctrine itself. Other times the plaintiff combines the doctrine with lay and expert testimony. This section traces the development and use of the doctrine, first with ordinary accident cases, and then in medical malpractice cases.

2. Res Ipsa Loquitur

Byrne v. Boadle
159 Eng. Rep. 299 (Ex. 1863)

[Plaintiff's complaint stated that he was passing along the highway in front of defendant's premises when he was struck and badly hurt by a barrel of flour that was apparently being lowered from a window above, which was on the premises of the defendant, a dealer in flour. Several witnesses testified that they saw the barrel fall and hit plaintiff. The defendant claimed "that there was no evidence of negligence for the jury." The trial court, agreeing, nonsuited plaintiff after the jury had assessed the damages at £50. On appeal in the Court of Exchequer, the plaintiff argued that the evidence was sufficient to support a verdict in his favor. In response, the defendant's lawyer argued that it was consistent with the evidence that the purchaser of the flour or some complete stranger was supervising the lowering of the barrel of flour and that its fall was not attributable in any way to defendant or his servants. Pollock, C.B.: "The presumption is that the defendant's servants were engaged in removing the defendant's flour. If they were not it was competent to the defendant to prove it." Defendant's attorney replied that "Surmise ought not to be substituted for strict proof when it is thought to fix a defendant with serious liability. The plaintiff should establish his case by affirmative evidence. . . . The plaintiff was bound to give affirmative proof of negligence. But there was not a scintilla of evidence, unless the occurrence is of itself evidence of negligence." Pollock, C.B.: "There are certain cases of which it may be said res ipsa loquitur and this seems one of them. In some cases the Court had held that the mere fact of the accident having occurred is evidence of negligence, as, for instance, in the case of railway collisions."] ·

POLLOCK, C.B. We are all of opinion that the rule must be absolute to enter the verdict for the plaintiff. The learned counsel was quite right in saying that there are many accidents from which no presumption of negligence can arise, but I think it would be wrong to lay down as a rule that in no case can presumption of negligence arise from the fact of an accident. Suppose in this case the barrel had rolled out of the warehouse and fallen on the plaintiff, how could he possibly ascertain from what cause it occurred? It is the duty of persons who keep barrels in a warehouse to take care that they do not roll out, and I think that such a case would, beyond all doubt, afford prima facie evidence of negligence. A barrel could not roll out of a warehouse without some negligence, and to say that a plaintiff who is injured by it must call witnesses from the warehouse to prove negligence seems to me preposterous. So in the building or repairing a house, or putting pots on the chimneys, if a person passing along the road is injured by something falling upon him, I think the accident alone would be prima facie evidence of negligence. Or if an article calculated to cause damage is put in a wrong place and does mischief, I think that those whose duty it was to put it in the right place are prima facie responsible, and if there is any state of facts to rebut the presumption of negligence, they must prove them. The present case upon the evidence comes to this, a man is passing in front of the premises of a dealer in flour, and there falls down upon him a barrel of flour. I think it apparent that the barrel was in the custody of the defendant who occupied the premises, and who is responsible for the acts of his servants who had the control of it; and in my opinion the fact of its falling is prima facie evidence of negligence, and the plaintiff who was injured by it is not bound to show that it could not fall without negligence, but if there are any facts inconsistent with negligence it is for the defendant to prove them. [Judgment affirmed.]

NOTES

1. *Res ipsa loquitur and circumstantial evidence.* Res ipsa loquitur aids the plaintiff by allowing proof of defendant's negligence by circumstantial evidence. In Byrne v. Boadle, was the critical difficulty in establishing negligence in how the barrel was handled, or in showing that the person who dropped the barrel was someone for whom the defendant was responsible? In this connection, what is the relationship between res ipsa loquitur and the law of vicarious liability for employees and independent

contractors? See Note 1, *supra* at 158, and Chapter 5. Could the plaintiff have recovered if a thief had dropped the barrel out of the window?

Chief Justice Erle supplied one standard account of res ipsa loquitur in Scott v. London & St. Katherine Docks Co., 159 Eng. Rep. 665 (Ex. 1865). "There must be reasonable evidence of negligence; but where the thing is shown to be under the management of the defendant or his servants, and the accident is such as in the ordinary course of things does not happen if those who have the management use proper care, it affords reasonable evidence, in the absence of explanation by the defendants, that the accident arose from want of care."

In Wakelin v. London & S.W. Ry., [1886] 12 A.C. 41, 45-46 (H.L.E.), plaintiff's deceased was struck and killed by one of defendant's trains. The view of the track was unobstructed at the time of the accident, and there was no specific evidence of any negligent act or omission by the defendant. The trial judge allowed the case to go to the jury, which returned a verdict for plaintiff. The House of Lords overturned the decision, with Lord Halsbury noting:

> In this case I am unable to see any evidence of how this unfortunate calamity occurred. One may surmise, and it is but surmise and not evidence, that the unfortunate man was knocked down by a passing train while on the level crossing; but assuming in the plaintiff's favour that fact to be established, is there anything to shew that the train ran over the man rather than that the man ran against the train? I understand the admission in the answer to the sixth interrogatory to be simply an admission that the death of the plaintiff's husband was caused by contact with the train. If there are two moving bodies which come in contact, whether ships, or carriages, or even persons, it is not uncommon to hear the person complaining of the injury describe it as having been caused by his ship, or his carriage, or himself having been run into, or run down, or run upon; but if a man ran across an approaching train so close that he was struck by it, is it more true to say that the engine ran down the man, or that the man ran against the engine? Neither man nor engine were intended to come in contact, but each advanced to such a point that contact was accomplished. . . .

Does res ipsa loquitur as formulated in *Scott* help the plaintiff in *Wakelin*? What about a doctrine of strict liability?

The English doctrine soon worked its way over to the United States, as summarized in Witt, Toward a New History of American Accident Law: Classical Tort Law and the Cooperative First Party Insurance Movement, 114 Harv. L. Rev. 690, 772 (2001):

> In the United States, the English res ipsa decisions led to a wave of burden-shifting cases. Landslides occurring in a railroad cut derailing a train; cinders and bolts falling from elevated railways; overhead telegraph wires

falling upon the road below; falling bricks, buildings, scaffolds, or elevators; collapsing gangway planks; exploding boilers; and suddenly starting machinery — all came at one time or another under the rule shifting the burden of proof to the defendant to disprove that it had been negligent.

Wigmore on Evidence §2509 (1st ed. 1905) in turn sets out the basic conditions for using res ipsa loquitur, which Prosser thereafter put into canonical form:

(1) The event must be of a kind which ordinarily does not occur in the absence of someone's negligence;

(2) It must be caused by an agency or instrumentality within the exclusive control of the defendant; and

(3) It must not have been due to any voluntary action or contribution on the part of the plaintiff. [Prosser and Keeton at 244.]

The Restatement (Second) of Torts takes a somewhat more expansive view of the doctrine.

§328D. RES IPSA LOQUITUR

(1) It may be inferred that harm suffered by the plaintiff is caused by negligence of the defendant when

(a) the event is of a kind which ordinarily does not occur in the absence of negligence;

(b) other responsible causes, including the conduct of plaintiff and third persons, are sufficiently eliminated by the evidence; and

(c) the indicated negligence is within the scope of the defendant's duty to the plaintiff.

(2) It is the function of the court to determine whether the inference may be reasonably drawn by the jury, or whether it must be necessarily drawn.

(3) It is the function of the jury to determine whether the inference is to be drawn in any case where different conclusions may be reasonably reached.

For its part, the RTT: LPH purports to simplify the doctrine as follows:

§17. RES IPSA LOQUITUR

The factfinder may infer that the defendant has been negligent when the accident causing the plaintiff's physical harm is a type of accident that ordinarily happens as a result of the negligence of a class of actors of which the defendant is the relevant member.

What changes if any do the new formulations make to prior case law?

2. *From the terrace, hotel, etc.* In Larson v. St. Francis Hotel, 188 P.2d 513, 515 (Cal. App. 1948), the plaintiff, while walking on the sidewalk next to the hotel, was hit by a chair apparently thrown out of one of the

hotel's windows as "the result of the effervescence and ebullition of San Franciscans in their exuberance of joy on V-J Day, August 14, 1945." The court refused to apply res ipsa loquitur:

> While, as pointed out by plaintiff, the rule of exclusive control "is not limited to the actual physical control but applies to the right of control of the instrumentality which causes the injury" it is not clear to us how this helps plaintiff's case. A hotel does not have exclusive control, either actual or potential, of its furniture. Guests have, at least, partial control. Moreover, it cannot be said that with the hotel using ordinary care "the accident was such that in the ordinary course of events . . . would not have happened." On the contrary, the mishap would quite as likely be due to the fault of a guest or other person as to that of defendants. The most logical inference from the circumstances shown is that the chair was thrown by some such person from a window. It thus appears that this occurrence is not such as ordinarily does not happen without the negligence of the party charged, but, rather, one in which the accident ordinarily might happen despite the fact that the defendants used reasonable care and were totally free from negligence. To keep guests and visitors from throwing furniture out windows would require a guard to be placed in every room in the hotel, and no one would contend that there is any rule of law requiring a hotel to do that.

In Connolly v. Nicollet Hotel, 95 N.W.2d 657, 669 (Minn. 1959), defendant's hotel was "taken over" by a Junior Chamber of Commerce national convention, whose antics gave the management ample notice of drinking, revelry, and hooliganism on the premises. Plaintiff was injured when struck by some unidentified falling object. The court distinguished *Larson* as a case with a surprise celebration. In an opinion that never used the words "res ipsa loquitur," the court reinstated the jury's $30,000 verdict for the plaintiff, and reversed the trial judge's judgment notwithstanding the verdict for defendant. "We have said many times that the law does not require every fact and circumstance which make up a case of negligence to be proved by direct and positive evidence or by the testimony of eyewitnesses, and the circumstantial evidence alone may authorize a finding of negligence. Negligence may be inferred from all the facts and surrounding circumstances, and where the evidence of such facts and circumstances is such as to take the case out of the realm of conjecture and into the field of legitimate inference from established facts, a prima facie case is made."

Should vicarious liability be extended to cover wrongs committed by guests on hotel premises? In ordinary apartments?

3. Res ipsa loquitur and guest statutes. In its conventional form, res ipsa loquitur governs only negligence cases, so the doctrine presents difficulties when the defendant's liability is predicated on grounds other than negligence. In Galbraith v. Busch, 196 N.E. 36, 38-39 (N.Y. 1935), the plaintiff was a guest in an automobile owned by her daughter and driven by the defendant Busch under the daughter's direction. The plaintiff was injured when the car suddenly swerved from the highway even though the road was in good condition, the weather was clear, and the traffic was light. The trial judge held that these circumstances were sufficient to raise a presumption of negligence, which shifted the burden of proof to the defendant, who in turn offered no evidence, which Judge Lehman in the Court of Appeals treated as a "suspicious form of conduct." Lehman, J., then noted that the burden of proof "perhaps, logically and properly" should be shifted to the defendant if "it owed a duty to the plaintiff to exercise reasonable care both in the operation and maintenance or repair of the automobile." Nonetheless he held that in this case the applicable substantive law precluded the use of res ipsa loquitur.

> Here the plaintiff was only a guest in the car. She assumed the risk of any defect in the automobile which was not known to the defendants. They assumed the duty to exercise reasonable care for her protection in the operation of the automobile. They were under no duty to exercise care to discover and repair defects not known to them. The evidence, though unexplained, cannot possibly lead to an inference that the accident was due to lack of care in the operation of the automobile, for the probability that it occurred from a break in its mechanism is at least equally great. All that the evidence shows is that the accident may have occurred from any one of many causes, including, perhaps, negligence in operation.

What result if driver error were a much more common cause of accidents than mechanical failure? Why did none of the three occupants of the car take the stand?

Galbraith was apparently overruled ("sapped of all practical application to the real world") in Pfaffenbach v. White Plains Express Corp., 216 N.E.2d 324, 325-326 (N.Y. 1966). There, plaintiff, a passenger in her friend's automobile, was injured when the car was struck by defendant's truck, which had skidded across the midline of the highway. Defendant gave no explanation of the accident. The court held that whenever a vehicle comes over to the wrong side of the road, a prima facie case of negligence is made, subject, of course, to explanation by defendant.

In his concurrence in *Pfaffenbach*, Burke, J., observed:

> Proof of "mere skidding" is prima facie evidence of negligence in this case where the plaintiff was *not* a passenger in defendant-respondent's car. There are obvious distinctions between a plaintiff who is a guest-passenger and one who is a stranger. The former not only assumes some risk in accepting gratuitous transportation but also is in the advantageous position of having the opportunity to observe whether the defendant exercised reasonable care in the operation of the vehicle. (Galbraith v. Busch.) On the other hand, the stranger who is injured by defendant's vehicle's skidding into the opposite

flowing lane of traffic or up onto a sidewalk, under conditions known to the defendant alone, is at a singular disadvantage. . . . In such a case[, moreover,] the plaintiff does not assume the same risk of unknown defects as would the owner of the vehicle or his guests.

4. *Acts of God and res ipsa loquitur.* How ought res ipsa loquitur apply when a ship or plane is lost without a trace? In Walston v. Lambersten, 349 F.2d 660 (9th Cir. 1965), defendant's boat disappeared at sea while crab fishing. The ship was in seaworthy condition when it left port and had been seen by other fishermen "going along just like a duck, easy." Plaintiffs suggested that the ship might have sunk because of a sudden redistribution of its weight after the catch had been taken aboard. The court of appeals affirmed the district court's refusal to apply res ipsa loquitur, noting that "the sea itself contains many hazards, and an inference of liability of the shipowner for the mysterious loss of his vessel should not be lightly drawn." One such hazard mentioned at trial was that of striking "deadheads," such as partially submerged logs.

Acts of God can enter into road cases in a more complex fashion. In Bauer v. J.H. Transport, Inc., 150 F.3d 759 (7th Cir. 1998), the decedent was driving her pick-up north on a windy and rainy day when it was crushed after being struck by the defendant's tractor trailer, going south at between 50 and 58 miles per hour, which had rolled over, also killing its driver. The road had been partially shielded from the west wind by a stand of trees. When this shield ended, the defendant contended that a powerful gust of wind had hit the tractor, causing it to roll over across the lanes. Initially, the defendant had requested a separate instruction for this Act of God defense, but withdrew that request. The defendant instead posited that the driver's negligence was not the proximate cause of the accident. Both the trial and the appellate court upheld the jury verdict for the defendant. Rovner, J., explained that the defendant, as "master of his own case" was not obliged to plead an Act of God as an affirmative defense, but could instead rely on the claim that the weather was "the sole proximate cause of the accident." She then continued:

> The fact that the collision in this case occurred on the decedent's side of the road does not alter the outcome of his analysis. Illinois law is replete with cases indicating that where an accident occurs because the defendant was driving on the wrong side of the road or left the roadway, a prima facie case of negligence has been established and the defendant is required to adduce evidence that some circumstance other than his own negligence was responsible for his vehicle straying from the right side of the road. . . .
>
> There can be no doubt that J.B. Hunt, in compliance with these precedents, adduced evidence tending to show that something other than the negligence of its driver — the weather — was responsible for its truck moving from the right side of the road an into the path of Pointer's vehicle. . . .

What result in this case under a system of strict liability? Is the speed of the tractor trailer relevant to the outcome? How far have we come from the rule that exonerates a defendant who sets a fire that spreads because of a sudden gust of wind?

5. *Directed verdicts with res ipsa loquitur.* In some cases, a plaintiff presents enough circumstantial evidence to obtain a directed verdict under res ipsa loquitur. In Newing v. Cheatham, 540 P.2d 33 (Cal. 1975), plaintiff's decedent was killed when a plane owned and piloted by defendant's decedent crashed in mountainous terrain about 13 miles east of Tijuana, Mexico. The plaintiff's evidence indicated that the only possible cause of the crash was the negligence of the defendant in running out of fuel while in flight. The defendant had been drinking beer for about an hour on the morning of the crash. When the wreckage of the plane was examined, the smell of alcohol was found on the pilot's breath, as well as on the breath of a second passenger. None was found on plaintiff's decedent's breath. Eight or nine empty beer cans were also uncovered. Visibility was excellent; the weather was calm; there was no evidence of a mid-air collision; the plane's clock indicated that the crash took place at a time when it could be reasonably expected for the plane's fuel supply to be exhausted; and after the crash the plane's fuel tanks did not contain sufficient fuel to feed the motor.

The evidence also pointed to the pilot's exclusive control over the plane. He owned the plane; he was the only licensed pilot on board the aircraft; he was at the controls when the crash took place; and the applicable federal air regulations imposed upon him ultimate responsibility while airborne. Finally no evidence suggested that the plaintiff's decedent's voluntary conduct could have contributed to the crash, since he did not know how to fly and at the time of the crash was seated in a rear seat out of reach of the controls. The California Supreme Court upheld the trial court's decision to take the case from the jury and to direct a verdict for the plaintiff.

The plaintiff did not fare so well in Morejon v. Rias Construction Co., 851 N.E.2d 1143, 1146-1147 (N.Y. 2006). There the decedent was a deliveryman who was first injured when building material owned by the defendant construction company fell from the roof of a house where it had done some work. The decedent's relatives stated at their depositions that they had accompanied the decedent to the site of the accident, but they could not identify the man who let them into the house. Nor did they report to him that there had been any accident. Further testimony indicated that the decedent did not seek medical care until two months after the accident. The defendant testified that his crews had ceased work at the alleged site of the accident three days before it occurred. Rosenblatt, J., reaffirmed "that only in the rarest of res ipsa loquitur cases may a plaintiff win summary judgment or a directed verdict. That would happen only when the plaintiff's circumstantial proof is so convincing and the defendant's response so weak that the inference of defendant's negligence is inescapable." Should the defendant get summary judgment in *Morejon*?

The Third Restatement notes that most states treat res ipsa loquitur as creating only a permissive inference that a jury is entitled to make, although a few states treat it as a rebuttable presumption, which requires the defendant to come forward with evidence or suffer a judgment as a matter of law. See RTT:LPH §17, comment *j*; see also Cox v. Paul, 828 N.E.2d 907, 912 (Ind. 2005), noting the difference. What defendant would remain silent even if res ipsa loquitur created only a permissive inference of negligence?

Colmenares Vivas v. Sun Alliance Insurance Co.
807 F.2d 1102 (1st Cir. 1986)

BOWNES, C.J. Appellants are plaintiffs in a diversity action to recover damages for injuries they suffered in an accident while riding an escalator. After the parties had presented their evidence, the defendants moved for and were granted a directed verdict. The court held that there was no evidence of negligence and that the doctrine of res ipsa loquitur, which would raise a presumption of negligence, did not apply. We reverse the directed verdict and remand the case to the district court because we hold that res ipsa loquitur does apply.

I. BACKGROUND

The relevant facts are not in dispute. On February 12, 1984, Jose Domingo Colmenares Vivas and his wife, Dilia Arreaza de Colmenares, arrived at the Luis Munoz Marin International Airport in Puerto Rico. They took an escalator on their way to the Immigration and Customs checkpoint on the second level. Mrs. Colmenares was riding the escalator on the right-hand side, holding the moving handrail, one step ahead of her husband. When the couple was about halfway up the escalator, the handrail stopped moving, but the steps continued the ascent, causing Mrs. Colmenares to lose her balance. Her husband grabbed her from behind with both hands and prevented her from falling, but in doing so, he lost his balance and tumbled down the stairs. Mr. and Mrs. Colmenares filed a direct action against the Sun Alliance Insurance Company (Sun Alliance), who is the liability insurance carrier for the airport's owner and operator, the Puerto Rico Ports Authority (Ports Authority). Sun Alliance brought a third-party contractual action against Westinghouse Electric Corporation (Westinghouse) based on a maintenance contract that required Westinghouse to inspect, maintain, adjust, repair, and replace parts as needed for the escalator and handrails, and to keep the escalator in a safe operating condition. . . .

The trial was conducted on January 30 and 31, 1986. Appellants called four witnesses. The Ports Authority's contract and maintenance supervisor testified about his daily weekday inspections of the escalator, about the maintenance contract with Westinghouse, about inspection and maintenance procedures, and about the accident report and subsequent repair and maintenance of the escalator. The Ports Authority's assistant chief of operations testified about the accident report. Appellants' testimony concerned the accident and their injuries.

. . . After hearing the parties' arguments, the court ruled that there was no evidence that the Ports Authority had been negligent, and that the case could not go to the jury based on res ipsa loquitur because at least one of the requirements for its application—that the injury-causing instrumentality was within the exclusive control of the defendant—was not met. . . .

II. RES IPSA LOQUITUR

Under Puerto Rico law, three requirements must be met for res ipsa loquitur ("the thing speaks for itself") to apply: "(1) the accident must be of a kind which ordinarily does not occur in the absence of someone's negligence; (2) it must be caused by an agency or instrumentality within the exclusive control of the defendant; [and] (3) it must not be due to any voluntary action on the part of the plaintiff." Community Partnership v. Presbyterian Hosp., 88 P.R.R. 379, 386 (1963). If all three requirements are met, the jury may infer that the defendant was negligent even though there is no direct evidence to that effect.

A. THE FIRST REQUIREMENT: INFERENCE OF NEGLIGENCE

The first requirement that must be met for res ipsa loquitur to apply is that "the accident must be such that in the light of ordinary experience it gives rise to an inference that someone has been negligent." It is not clear to us whether the district court decided that this requirement was met, although the court did suggest that it was giving the benefit of the doubt on this question to the appellants. We hold that this requirement was met because an escalator handrail probably would not stop suddenly while the escalator continues moving unless someone had been negligent.[2]

---

2. In some jurisdictions, the courts have taken the position that escalator operators are common carriers owing the highest degree of care to their passengers. . . . To our knowledge, the Puerto Rico courts have not equated escalators to common carriers, and such a determination is not properly made by this court in the first instance. For the purposes of this appeal, however, it would not matter if the stricter standard did apply, because we hold that an inference of negligence has been raised even under the lower reasonable care standard.

This requirement would not be met if appellants had shown nothing more than that they had been injured on the escalator, because based on this fact alone it would not be likely that someone other than the appellants had been negligent. See Conway v. Boston Elevated Ry. Co., 152 N.E. 94 (Mass. 1926) (negligence element not satisfied when all that had been shown was that a child's hand had been caught beneath the escalator handrail belt); Fuller v. Wurzburg Dry Goods Co., 158 N.W. 1026 (Mich. 1916) (negligence may not be inferred from a fall on an escalator because the plaintiff did not show that the escalator was improperly constructed or that it malfunctioned). Here, it was not disputed that the handrail malfunctioned and stopped suddenly, an event that foreseeably could cause riders to lose their balance and get injured. Thus, the evidence gave rise to an inference that someone probably had been negligent in operating or maintaining the escalator, and the first requirement for the application of res ipsa loquitur was met.

B. THE SECOND REQUIREMENT: EXCLUSIVE CONTROL

The second requirement for res ipsa loquitur to apply is that the injury-causing instrumentality — in this case, the escalator — must have been within the exclusive control of the defendant. The district court found that this requisite was not met, despite the parties' stipulation that "[t]he escalator in question is property of and is under the control of the Puerto Rico Ports Authority." We agree that this stipulation was not by itself enough to satisfy the res ipsa loquitur requirement. It did not exclude the possibility that someone else also had control over the escalator; indeed, the stipulation said that Westinghouse maintained the escalator. We hold, however, that the Ports Authority effectively had exclusive control over the escalator because the authority in control of a public area had a nondelegable duty to maintain its facilities in a safe condition.

Few courts have required that control literally be "exclusive." . . . The exclusive control requirement, then, should not be so narrowly construed as to take from the jury the ability to infer that a defendant was negligent when the defendant was responsible for the injury-causing instrumentality, even if someone else might also have been responsible. The purpose of the requirement is not to restrict the application of the res ipsa loquitur inference to cases in which there is only one actor who dealt with the instrumentality, but rather "to eliminate the possibility that the accident was caused by a *third party.*" It is not necessary, therefore, for the defendant to have had actual physical control; it is enough that the defendant, and not a third party, was ultimately responsible for the instrumentality. Thus, res ipsa loquitur applies even if the defendant shares responsibility with another, or if the defendant is responsible for the instrumentality even though someone else had physical control over it. It follows that a defendant charged with a nondelegable duty of care to maintain an instrumentality in a safe condition effectively has exclusive control over it for the purposes of applying res ipsa loquitur. Unless the duty is delegable, the res ipsa loquitur inference is not defeated if the defendant had shifted physical control to an agent or contracted with another to carry out its responsibilities.

We hold that the Ports Authority could not delegate its duty to maintain safe escalators. There are no set criteria for determining whether a duty is nondelegable; the critical question is whether the responsibility is so important to the community that it should not be transferred to another. The Ports Authority was charged with such a responsibility. It was created for a public purpose, which included the operation and management of the airport. A concomitant of this authority is the duty to keep the facilities it operates in a reasonably safe condition. The public is entitled to rely on the Ports Authority — not its agents or contractors — to see that this is done. The Ports Authority apparently recognized this responsibility, for its maintenance and contract supervisor conducted daily weekday inspections of the escalators despite the maintenance contract with Westinghouse.

Duties have been seen as nondelegable in several analogous situations. For example, a public authority may not delegate to an independent contractor its responsibility to see that work in a public place is done carefully. Also, a government may not delegate its responsibility to maintain safe roads and similar public places. Finally, an owner has a nondelegable duty to keep business premises safe for invitees. These examples demonstrate a general tort law policy not to allow an entity to shift by contract its responsibility for keeping an area used by the public in a safe condition. It would be contrary to this policy to allow the owner and operator of an airport terminal to delegate its duty to keep its facility safe. We hold, therefore, that the district court erred in ruling that the exclusive control requirement was not met.

C. THE THIRD REQUIREMENT: THE PLAINTIFF'S ACTIONS

The third requirement that must be met for res ipsa loquitur to apply is that the accident must not have been due to the plaintiff's voluntary actions. The district court found, and we agree, that there was no evidence that Mr. and Mrs. Colmenares caused the accident. Indeed, there is no indication that they did anything other than attempt to ride the escalator in the ordinary manner. Therefore, we hold that all three requirements were met and that the jury should have been allowed to consider whether the Ports Authority was liable based on the permissible inference of negligence raised by the application of res ipsa loquitur. . . .

TORRUELLA, C.J. I must regretfully dissent. . . .

In my view, *solely* because the handrail stopped and Mrs. Colmenares fell, without further evidence as to why or how the handrail malfunctioned, does not give rise to an inference of *negligence* by the Ports Authority. . . .

The malfunctioning of an escalator presents an even stronger argument against the raising of an inference of negligence without additional proof as to the cause of the malfunction. Although a court can take notice that an escalator is a complicated piece of machinery, it has no basis of common knowledge for inferring that its malfunction is the result of the operator's negligence. . . .

NOTES

1. *A difference of views?* What result in *Colmenares* if both the handrails and the steps had stopped simultaneously? With *Colmenares*, contrast Holzhauer v. Saks & Co., 697 A.2d 89, 93 (Md. 1997), where plaintiff was injured when he tumbled back down the steps after the escalator on which he was riding suddenly stopped. The court refused to allow the plaintiff to use res ipsa loquitur, saying:

> For safety reasons, the escalator in question was equipped with two emergency stop buttons, located at the top and bottom of the escalator, respectively. When either button is pushed, if the escalator is functioning as intended, the escalator will stop. The buttons are safety devices designed to stop the escalator quickly should a hand, foot, or article of clothing become caught; thus, ready accessibility to the buttons is only sensible. We cannot say that the escalator would not stop in the absence of Appellees' negligence because the escalator would also stop whenever any person pushed one of the emergency stop buttons.
>
> The record is silent as to whether anyone did, in fact, push one of the stop buttons, but this is of little concern. The facts need not show that a stop button definitely was pushed to preclude reliance on *res ipsa;* they need only show that something other than Appellees' negligence was just as likely to cause the escalator to stop. The fact that the escalator had never malfunctioned before the day in question, and has not malfunctioned since, makes it equally likely, if not slightly more likely, that the escalator did not malfunction on the day in question but, rather, that it stopped because somebody intentionally or unintentionally pushed an emergency stop button.

In addition, the court held that the plaintiff could not satisfy the exclusive control requirement of res ipsa loquitur, observing: "Hundreds of Saks & Co.'s customers have unlimited access to the emergency buttons each day." Is the case distinguishable from *Colmenares*, where the handrail stopped and the steps kept moving?

The problems with escalators also arise with automatic doors where there is a similar difference of opinion. In the leading case of Rose v. New York Port Authority, 293 A.2d 371, 375 (N.J. 1972), the plaintiff claimed damages when struck by an automatic glass door while moving about Kennedy Airport. "Here the occurrence bespeaks negligence. Members of the public passing through automatic doors, whether in an airport, office building or supermarket do so generally without sustaining injury. What happened to the plaintiff here is fortunately unusual and not commonplace. It strongly suggests a malfunction which in turn suggests negligence." But that inference was not drawn in Kmart v. Bassett, 769 So. 2d 282 (Ala. 2000), in which the plaintiff, an 83-year-old woman who used a cane, stepped on a rubber mat outside a Kmart to activate the automatic doors. As she progressed one third of the way, the door closed on her, resulting in a fall that led to a fractured hip. The jury awarded $289,000, and the trial judge denied the defendant's post verdict motion for a judgment in its favor. The Alabama Supreme Court reversed. It refused to find negligence in Kmart's decision not to have a regular maintenance contract and to wait for signs of trouble before calling for repairs, and it further rejected the argument that failures of this sort could not happen in the absence of negligence, noting that "a mere misfunction would be insufficient to invoke the doctrine of res ipsa loquitur under Alabama law." Should it make a difference if the door worked after the accident or not? Should the door be designed so as to avoid closing if someone is on the mat, no matter how slowly she moves?

2. *Exclusive control and the workers' compensation statutes.* In some instances, an injured party is prevented from suing his employer in tort because the exclusive remedy provisions of the workers' compensation statutes block the tort action. In these cases, the plaintiff attempts to show that some third-party defendant has "exclusive" control of the dangerous instrumentality to support the use of res ipsa. That strategy worked in Miles v. St. Regis Paper Co., 467 P.2d 307, 310 (Wash. 1970). The decedent was an employee of the "D" Street Rafting Company who was crushed to death by a load of logs that suddenly rolled off the defendant railroad's flatcar while he was releasing one of its binders. There was conflicting evidence as to whether the accident could have been caused by the movement of the train and indeed whether the train had moved at all. Even though the decedent's employer directed the loading operations, a divided court found that the railroad company, which responded to the orders of employees of the rafting company, had "exclusive control" over the movement of the train.

> The question of control poses a close and difficult problem. Appellant makes a strong argument that employees of "D" Street Rafting Company had exclusive control of not only the unloading of the logs involving the use of the

crane, but also other operations, including positioning of the cars and movement of the train. There is conflicting testimony, and the hand on the throttle of the switch engine was obviously the hand of the engineer or the fireman (employees of the railroad). Furthermore, any movement of the train ultimately was the responsibility and within the exclusive control of such employees. It is not denied that movement of the train and positioning of the railroad flatcars loaded with logs occurred in accordance with the unloading plans and desires of employees of "D" Street Rafting Company, communicated by hand signal or otherwise to the foreman of the railroad switching crew and relayed by him to the engine crew. We believe that the ultimate decision to move the train was made by employees of the railroad. Thus, in terms of the requisites for application of res ipsa loquitur in this case, we are convinced that at the time of the accident the train of flatcars loaded with logs was in the "exclusive control" of the railroad.

Does a finding of "exclusive control" in *Colmenares* require one here?

3. *Plaintiff's conduct and conduct of a third party.* In many negligence actions the dangerous instrumentality in question has passed through the hands of a third party, only to cause injury while being used by the plaintiff. In these cases, "the plaintiff's mere possession of a chattel which injures him does not prevent a res ipsa case where it is made clear that he has done nothing abnormal and *has used the thing only for the purpose for which it was intended.*" Prosser, Res Ipsa Loquitur in California, 37 Cal. L. Rev. 183, 201-202 (1949).

Similarly res ipsa loquitur was invoked in Benedict v. Eppley Hotel Co., 65 N.W.2d 224, 229 (Neb. 1954). The plaintiff-appellee was injured when a folding chair collapsed after she had been sitting on it for some 20 or 30 minutes while participating in a bingo game. After the accident it was discovered that the screws and bolts on one side of the chair were missing.

> [Plaintiff's] acts in reference to the chair were limited to transportation of it from where she first saw it in the hallway connecting the Embassy Room and the ballroom of the Rome Hotel to the table in the latter room where the game was in progress and sitting on it. She occupied the chair as an invitee of appellant. She had no right or duty to examine it for defects. She had a right to assume it was a safe instrumentality for the use she had been invited by appellant to make of it. Appellant had the ownership, possession, and control of the chair under the circumstances of this case and it was obligated to maintain it in a reasonably safe condition for the invited use made of it by the appellee. The fact that the chair when it was being properly used for the purpose for which it was made available gave way permits an inference that it was defective and unsafe and that appellant had not used due care in reference to it.

See also RTT:LPH §17, comment *h*, which notes that plaintiff's conduct only bears on the application of the doctrine when it is in the basic causal sequence that creates the original harm. Thus the plaintiff in *Colmenares* can only rely on the doctrine by excluding his own conduct as a source of the escalator malfunction. But the possible contributory negligence of the plaintiff in Byrne v. Boadle could not prevent the use of res ipsa loquitur since the plaintiff had no control whatsoever over the barrel of flour.

The same principles apply if the injured party is a stranger to the initial transaction. The Third Restatement takes a strong stand against the preservation of the exclusive control requirement, noting that it functions as a poor "proxy" for negligence. For example, an injured pedestrian should normally be able to rely on res ipsa loquitur in a suit against a driver if his car's brakes fail a day after purchase despite the driver's exclusive control of the car at the time of the accident. Instead, there is a high likelihood of the manufacturer's responsibility for a product defect. RTT:LPH §17, comment *b*.

4. Assessing the probabilities of negligence. Conceptually the most difficult part of the res ipsa loquitur test comes from attaching a precise meaning to the phrase "ordinarily does not occur in the absence of negligence." In most cases, courts intuit whether this test is satisfied. Thus, the court in McDougald v. Perry, 716 So. 2d 783, 786 (Fla. 1998), used res ipsa loquitur when the defendant's 130 pound spare tire came out from its angled cradle underneath defendant's tractor-trailer as it was being driven over some railroad tracks. It bounced in the air, and struck plaintiff's jeep. The incident "is the type of accident which, on the basis of common experience and as a matter of general knowledge, would not occur but for the failure to exercise reasonable care by the person who had control of the spare tire."

The Third Restatement shows sensitivity to this difficulty by requiring the plaintiff to negotiate special hurdles created by issues of compound probabilities. Thus, if a given accident of a certain class only occurs two-thirds of the time with negligence, and that negligence is attributable to the defendant only two-thirds of the time, the res ipsa loquitur should not apply. Even if the accident does not ordinarily happen without the occurrence of negligence, it ordinarily happens without the negligence of this defendant, since the evidence establishes that the defendant is likely to be the responsible party only four-ninths (two-thirds multiplied by two-thirds) of the time. RTT:LPH §17, comment *b*.

The phrase "ordinarily does not occur in the absence of negligence" is fraught with additional difficulties. Linguistically, the expression has generally been taken to signify either "(1) that the probability of the injury given the exercise of reasonable care is quite small, or (2) that the probability of the injury given reasonable care is smaller than the probability of the injury given negligence, or (3) that the probability of the injury given reasonable care is much smaller than the probability of the injury given negligence." Kaye, Probability Theory Meets Res Ipsa Loquitur, 77 Mich.

L. Rev. 1456, 1465 (1979). Yet, as Kaye points out, none of these three commonsense statements captures the ultimate issue, namely, whether the probability that the defendant was negligent, given the occurrence of the injury, is greater than 50 percent. The first expression only notes that the probability of accident is quite small when there is reasonable care, but if the defendant exercises reasonable care an overwhelming proportion of the time, it could still prove more likely than not that reasonable care was in fact exercised in the particular case.

Thus, suppose that it is established that a hand grenade has exploded prematurely because it contains a defective fuse. See, e.g., McGonigal v. Gearhart Industries, Inc., 788 F.2d 321 (5th Cir. 1986). Assume further liability turns solely on whether the defective fuse escaped detection because the manufacturer's employees negligently inspected it before shipment. To analyze this situation, consider two examples. First, suppose there is a one-in-a-thousand chance of a defective grenade slipping through a reasonable inspection and a one-in-two chance of a defective grenade slipping through a negligent inspection. If the defendant is careful 99.9 percent of the time, then for every one million units produced, 999,000 of them are properly inspected. Of these, we should expect to see 999 instances of failure, none of which are attributable to defendant's negligence. By the same token, we should expect to see an additional 500 failures (half of the 1,000 units that remain), all of which are attributable to negligence. To be sure, any negligently prepared unit is much more likely to be defective than a carefully manufactured one (as in Kaye's proposition (2)), for a 50 percent failure rate is 500 times a 0.1 percent failure rate. Yet — and the point is critical — by the same token it is more likely (by odds 999 to 500) that any defective unit comes from the group of carefully inspected grenades than from the group of negligently inspected grenades, and thus would not satisfy the "ordinarily does not occur in the absence of negligence" requirement.

That conclusion, however, is very sensitive to the choice of numbers. Suppose now that the defendant's inspections were careful only 99 percent of the time, and careless 1 percent of the time. If the probability of a bad grenade slipping through the careful inspection remains 0.1 percent, then 990 defective grenades would be produced when care was exercised (one one-thousandth of 990,000). In addition, however, 5,000 defective units (half of 10,000) would be produced with negligence, making it better than five-to-one odds that the grenade came from the badly inspected batch.

These two examples show the difficulties in linking the probability of negligence conditional on the occurrence of the accident, with the increase in the likelihood of an accident given the shift from care to negligence. Kaye's article contains a formal demonstration, invoking the use of Bayes' theorem, of why in general that jump should be made only in the third situation set out above, namely, the probability of injury when defendant takes due care is much smaller than the probability of injury when the defendant is negligent.

On the intricacies of statistical inference, see also Comment, Mathematics, Fuzzy Negligence and the Logic of Res Ipsa Loquitur, 75 Nw. U. L. Rev. 147 (1980). See also Guthrie, Rachlinski and Wistrich, Inside the Judicial Mind, 86 Cornell L. Rev. 777, 808-809 (2001), where the authors surveyed federal magistrate judges on a variation of this problem that assumed that a barrel (à la *Byrne*) breaks loose only 1 percent of the time if properly handled, but 90 percent of the time if improperly handled, and employees handle the barrels properly 99.9 percent of the time. The judges were asked to state the odds that the fall of the barrel was attributable to negligence. About 41 percent of the judges said that the barrel's fall attributable to negligence fell between 0 and 25 percent of the cases; 8.8 percent chose the interval between 25 and 50 percent; 10.1 percent chose the interval between 51 and 75 percent, and 40.3 percent chose 76 and 100 percent. The right answer is 8.3 percent. To calculate this, assume that there are 100,000 lifts. The 99,900 safe lifts result in breakage 999 times (99,900 multiplied by 0.01), while the 100 improper lifts result in breakage 90 times (100 multiplied by 0.9). The 90 breaks due to improper handling constitute roughly 8.3 percent of the 1089 total breaks (90 divided by (90 plus 999)). Note the size of the intervals makes it doubtful that the judges who picked the right answer correctly made the needed calculations. But query, if taught the basic insight about base rates first, could they have calculated the right answer?

Ybarra v. Spangard
154 P.2d 687 (Cal. 1944)

GIBSON, C.J. This is an action for damages for personal injuries alleged to have been inflicted on plaintiff by defendants during the course of a surgical operation. The trial court entered judgments of nonsuit as to all defendants and plaintiff appealed.

On October 28, 1939, plaintiff consulted defendant Dr. Tilley, who diagnosed his ailment as appendicitis, and made arrangements for an appendectomy to be performed by defendant Dr. Spangard at a hospital owned and managed by defendant Dr. Swift. Plaintiff entered the hospital, was given a hypodermic injection, slept, and later was awakened by Doctors Tilley and Spangard and wheeled into the operating room by a nurse whom he believed to be defendant Gisler, an employee of Dr. Swift. Defendant Dr. Reser, the anesthetist, also an employee of Dr. Swift, adjusted plaintiff for the operation, pulling his body to the head of the operating table and, according to plaintiff's testimony, laying him back against two hard objects at the top of his shoulders, about an inch below his neck. Dr. Reser then administered the anesthetic and plaintiff lost consciousness. When he awoke early the following morning he was in his hospital room attended by defendant Thompson, the special nurse, and another nurse who was not made a defendant.

Plaintiff testified that prior to the operation he had never had any pain in, or injury to, his right arm or shoulder, but that when he awakened he felt a sharp pain about half way between the neck and the point of the right shoulder. He complained to the nurse, and then to Dr. Tilley, who gave him diathermy treatments while he remained in the hospital. The pain did not cease, but spread down to the lower part of his arm, and after his release from the hospital the condition grew worse. He was unable to rotate or lift his arm, and developed paralysis and atrophy of the muscles around the shoulder. He received further treatments from Dr. Tilley until March, 1940, and then returned to work, wearing his arm in a splint on the advice of Dr. Spangard.

Plaintiff also consulted Dr. Wilfred Sterling Clark, who had X-ray pictures taken which showed an area of diminished sensation below the shoulder and atrophy and wasting away of the muscles around the shoulder. In the opinion of Dr. Clark, plaintiff's condition was due to trauma or injury by pressure or strain, applied between his right shoulder and neck.

Plaintiff was also examined by Dr. Fernando Garduno, who expressed the opinion that plaintiff's injury was a paralysis of traumatic origin, not arising from pathological causes, and not systemic, and that the injury resulted in atrophy, loss of use and restriction of motion of the right arm and shoulder.

Plaintiff's theory is that the foregoing evidence presents a proper case for the application of the doctrine of res ipsa loquitur, and that the inference of negligence arising therefrom makes the granting of a nonsuit improper. Defendants take the position that, assuming that plaintiff's condition was in fact the result of an injury, there is no showing that the act of any particular defendant, nor any particular instrumentality, was the cause thereof. They attack plaintiff's action as an attempt to fix liability "en masse" on various defendants, some of whom were not responsible for the acts of others; and they further point to the failure to show which defendants had control of the instrumentalities that may have been involved. Their main defense may be briefly stated in two propositions: (1) that where there are several defendants, and there is a division of responsibility in the use of an instrumentality causing the injury, and the injury might have resulted from the separate act of either one of two or more persons, the rule of res ipsa loquitur cannot be invoked against any one of them; and (2) that where there are several instrumentalities, and no showing is made as to which caused the injury or as to the particular defendant in control of it, the doctrine cannot apply. We are satisfied, however, that these objections are not well taken in the circumstances of this case.

The doctrine of res ipsa loquitur has three conditions: "(1) the accident must be of a kind which ordinarily does not occur in the absence of someone's negligence; (2) it must be caused by an agency or instrumentality within the exclusive control of the defendant; (3) it must not have been due to any voluntary action or contribution on the part of the plaintiff." (Prosser, Torts, p. 295.) It is applied in a wide variety of situations, including cases of medical or dental treatment and hospital care. . . .

There is, however, some uncertainty as to the extent to which res ipsa loquitur may be invoked in cases of injury from medical treatment. This is in part due to the tendency, in some decisions, to lay undue emphasis on the limitations of the doctrine, and to give too little attention to its basic underlying purpose. The result has been that a simple, understandable rule of circumstantial evidence, with a sound background of common sense and human experience, has occasionally been transformed into a rigid legal formula, which arbitrarily precludes its application in many cases where it is most important that it should be applied. If the doctrine is to continue to serve a useful purpose, we should not forget that "the particular force and justice of the rule, regarded as a presumption throwing upon the party charged the duty of producing evidence, consists in the circumstance that the chief evidence of the true cause, whether culpable or innocent, is practically accessible to him but inaccessible to the injured person." (9 Wigmore, Evidence [3d ed. 1940], §2509, p. 382.)

The present case is of a type which comes within the reason and spirit of the doctrine more fully perhaps than any other. The passenger sitting awake in a railroad car at the time of a collision, the pedestrian walking along the street and struck by a falling object or the debris of an explosion, are surely not more entitled to an explanation than the unconscious patient on the operating table. Viewed from this aspect, it is difficult to see how the doctrine can, with any justification, be so restricted in its statement as to become inapplicable to a patient who submits himself to the care and custody of doctors and nurses, is rendered unconscious, and receives some injury from instrumentalities used in his treatment. Without the aid of the doctrine a patient who received permanent injuries of a serious character, obviously the result of someone's negligence, would be entirely unable to recover unless the doctors and nurses in attendance voluntarily chose to disclose the identity of the negligent person and the facts of establishing liability. If this were the state of the law of negligence, the courts, to avoid gross injustice, would be forced to invoke the principles of absolute liability, irrespective of negligence, in actions by persons suffering injuries during the course of treatment under anesthesia. But we think this juncture has not yet been reached, and the doctrine of res ipsa loquitur is properly applicable to the case before us.

The condition that the injury must not have been due to the plaintiff's voluntary action is of course fully satisfied under the evidence produced herein; and the same is true of the condition that the accident must be one which ordinarily does not occur unless someone was negligent. We have here no problem of negligence in treatment, but of distinct injury to a healthy part of the body not the subject of treatment, nor within the area covered by the operation. The decisions in this state make it clear that such circumstances raise the inference of negligence, and call upon the defendant to explain the unusual result. . . .

The argument of defendants is simply that plaintiff has not shown an injury caused by an instrumentality under a defendant's control, because he has not shown which of the several instrumentalities that he came in contact with while in the hospital caused the injury; and he has not shown that any one defendant or his servants had exclusive control over any particular instrumentality. Defendants assert that some of them were not the employees of other defendants, that some did not stand in any permanent relationship from which liability in tort would follow, and that in view of the nature of the injury, the number of defendants and the different functions performed by each, they could not all be liable for the wrong, if any.

We have no doubt that in a modern hospital a patient is quite likely to come under the care of a number of persons in different types of contractual and other relationships with each other. For example, in the present case it appears that Doctors Smith, Spangard and Tilley were physicians or surgeons commonly placed in the legal category of independent contractors and Dr. Reser, the anesthetist, and defendant Thompson, the special nurse, were employees of Dr. Swift and not of the other doctors. But we do not believe that either the number or relationship of the defendants alone determines whether the doctrine of res ipsa loquitur applies. Every defendant in whose custody the plaintiff was placed for any period was bound to exercise ordinary care to see that no unnecessary harm came to him and each would be liable for failure in this regard. Any defendant who negligently injured him, and any defendant charged with his care who so neglected him as to allow injury to occur, would be liable. The defendant employers would be liable for the neglect of their employees and the doctor in charge of the operation would be liable for the negligence of those who became his temporary servants for the purpose of assisting in the operation.

In this connection, it should be noted that while the assisting physicians and nurses may be employed by the hospital, or engaged by the patient, they normally become the temporary servants or agents of the surgeon in charge while the operation is in progress, and liability may be imposed upon him for their negligent acts under the doctrine of respondeat superior. Thus a surgeon has been held liable for the negligence of an assisting nurse who leaves a sponge or other object inside a patient, and the fact that the duty of seeing that such mistakes do not occur is delegated to others does not absolve the doctor from responsibility for their negligence. . . .

It may appear at the trial that, consistent with the principles outlined above, one or more defendants will be found liable and others absolved, but this should not preclude the application of the rule of res ipsa loquitur. The control, at one time or another, of one or more of the various agencies or instrumentalities which might have harmed the plaintiff was in the hands of every defendant or of his employees or temporary servants. This, we think, places upon them the burden of initial explanation. Plaintiff was rendered unconscious for the purpose of undergoing surgical treatment by the defendants; it is manifestly unreasonable for them to insist that he identify any one of them as the person who did the alleged negligent act.

The other aspect of the case which defendants so strongly emphasize is that plaintiff has not identified the instrumentality any more than he has the particular guilty defendant. Here, again, there is a misconception which, if carried to the extreme for which defendants contend, would unreasonably limit the application of the res ipsa loquitur rule. It should be enough that the plaintiff can show an injury resulting from an external force applied while he lay unconscious in the hospital; this is as clear a case of identification of the instrumentality as the plaintiff may ever be able to make.

[The court then discusses a series of precedents.]

In the face of these examples of liberalization of the tests for res ipsa loquitur, there can be no justification for the rejection of the doctrine in the instant case. As pointed out above, if we accept the contention of defendants herein, there will rarely be any compensation for patients injured while unconscious. A hospital today conducts a highly integrated system of activities, with many persons contributing their efforts. There may be, e.g., preparation for surgery by nurses and interns who are employees of the hospital; administering of an anesthetic by a doctor who may be an employee of the hospital, an employee of the operating surgeon, or an independent contractor; performance of an operation by a surgeon and assistants who may be his employees, employees of the hospital, or independent contractors; and post surgical care by the surgeon, a hospital physician, and nurses. The number of those in whose care the patient is placed is not a good reason for denying him all reasonable opportunity to recover for negligent harm. It is rather a good reason for re-examination of the statement of legal theories which supposedly compel such a shocking result.

We do not at this time undertake to state the extent to which the reasoning of this case may be applied to other situations in which the doctrine of res ipsa loquitur is invoked. We merely hold that where a plaintiff receives unusual injuries while unconscious and in the course of medical treatment, all those defendants who had any control over his body or the instrumentalities which might have caused the injuries may properly be called upon to meet the inference of negligence by giving an explanation of their conduct.

The judgment is reversed.

NOTES

1. *Procedural complexities in res ipsa loquitur.* On retrial in *Ybarra* the defendants testified that to their knowledge nothing had gone wrong in the operation. The California Court of Appeals held that the trial judge could still find for the plaintiff on the strength of the circumstantial evidence in the case. Ybarra v. Spangard, 208 P.2d 445 (Cal. App. 1949). For criticism of Ybarra v. Spangard, see Seavey, Res Ipsa Loquitur: Tabula in Naufragio, 63 Harv. L. Rev. 643 (1950).

One early defense of the use of res ipsa loquitur in medical malpractice cases was as a tool to overcome the "conspiracy of silence" among physicians. "One may suspect that the courts are not reluctant to use res ipsa loquitur as a deliberate instrument of policy to even the balance against the professional conspiracy of silence; but with two exceptions the decisions give no hint of anything more than the obvious inference from the circumstantial evidence alone," Prosser, Selected Topics on the Law of Torts 346 (1954), citing Ybarra v. Spangard.

Today the rise of modern discovery devices and the active market in expert testimony have quieted these conspiratorial concerns, so much so that the Third Restatement holds that res ipsa loquitur should be regarded exclusively as a doctrine of circumstantial evidence unrelated to any differential of knowledge between the parties. "The plaintiff may invoke res ipsa even though the defendant is as ignorant of the facts of the accident as the plaintiff is." RTT:LPH §17, comment *i*.

Should *Ybarra* be treated as a pure res ipsa loquitur case given that Dr. Clark testified that believed that the source of the injury was pressure applied between the shoulder and neck? In fact, modern anesthesiologists guard against just such pressure, by cushioning that area, especially in long operations. What result if this risk were not fully understood when the operation took place? Note that the modern law is alert to the prospect that plaintiffs in medical malpractice cases often mount a doubled-edged attack, using both specific expert testimony of negligence on the one hand, while relying on res ipsa on the other. Most courts will allow this two-front attack to proceed, see RTT:LPH §17, comment *g*, but the strategy could easily backfire if the plaintiff prevails at trial only for an appellate court to reverse the judgment on the ground that the res ipsa loquitur instruction was improper. Note the Restatement (Third) takes the position that the "better rule, now accepted by most courts, is that expert testimony is admissible in a medical-malpractice res ipsa loquitur case, and indeed is frequently necessary in order to justify submitting the res ipsa claim to the jury." RTT: LPH §17, comment *c*.

2. *Common understanding and res ipsa loquitur.* Courts often require the plaintiff in medical malpractice cases to present expert testimony in order to reach the jury. One key exception to this rule arises when the jury has

"common knowledge" that the harm would not have occurred without defendant's negligence, as, for example, when a misapplied hot water bottle burns the plaintiff. However, the common knowledge exception rarely applies when complex medical judgments and procedures are in issue. In Farber v. Olkon, 254 P.2d 520 (Cal. 1953), the plaintiff, a mental incompetent, suffered broken bones after being subjected to electroshock therapy. The court explicitly distinguished *Ybarra* as a case where "plaintiff while unconscious on an operating table received injuries to a healthy part of his body, not subject to treatment or within the area covered by his operation." It then refused to apply the common knowledge test given the undisputed testimony by defendant's experts "that electroshock therapy is designed to have 'an effect upon the entire body'" in the hope that the convulsion will improve the patient's mental condition. Likewise, in Salgo v. Stanford University Board of Trustees, 317 P.2d 170 (Cal. App. 1957), the court held that progress in medical research might well be thwarted if jurors were allowed to find negligence on the basis of their common knowledge when new procedures were tried. Accordingly, it required expert evidence to establish negligence when paralysis had resulted from a translumbar aortogram, a procedure in which the aorta is injected with fluids in order to find blockages in the circulatory system.

Other cases, however, have upheld a finding of negligence on the basis of common knowledge alone. In Bardessono v. Michels, 478 P.2d 480, 486 (Cal. 1971), plaintiff received a series of injections of cortisone and local anesthetic for the treatment of tendonitis in his shoulder. All the injections caused plaintiff excruciating pain, and shortly after their completion he developed partial paralysis. The court held that the jury was properly instructed when told that "it could infer negligence from the happening of the accident alone." The court distinguished *Salgo* and said:

> In cases in which the physician or surgeon has injected a substance into the body, the courts have followed the test that if the routine medical procedure is relatively commonplace and simple, rather than special, unusual and complex, the jury may properly rely upon its common knowledge in determining whether the accident is of a kind that would ordinarily not have occurred in the absence of someone's negligence. Whether the case falls into the category of the commonplace or the unusual must necessarily turn upon a conglomerate of medical facts; only if the facts clearly show that the procedure is so unusual and complex that the jury could not rest their understanding of it upon their common knowledge should the court refuse a tendered res ipsa loquitur instruction, based on common knowledge.

If the needle damaged one of the plaintiff's nerves, does that establish negligence or only causation? In *Bardessono*, defendant testified that she had made the same sort of injection hundreds of times without adverse effects. How should the jury have weighed that evidence?

With *Bardessono*, contrast Greenberg v. Michael Reese Hospital, 396 N.E.2d 1088, 1094 (Ill. App. 1979), aff'd in part and rev'd in part, 415 N.E.2d 390, 397 (Ill. 1980). Plaintiff had been treated with radiation for enlarged tonsils and adenoids during the 1940s and 1950s, when such treatment was routine at Michael Reese Hospital. The treatment was discontinued when it was discovered that it could result in tumorous growths in or near the thyroid gland. The court rejected an analogy between these cases and radiation burn cases to which res ipsa loquitur applies:

> In the radiation burn cases, the reasoning takes two steps: first, that there is no medical reason to use radiation sufficient to cause extensive burns and, second, that the doctor in fact used excess radiation and therefore was negligent. Here, however, plaintiffs concede that irradiation of tonsils was a widely used therapeutic treatment, specifically chosen by the referring physician in the light of surgical dangers and poliomyelitic implications. The only possible inference which res ipsa loquitur could provide in the case at bar is that tumors, having resulted in some percentage of cases from either organic or external stimulus, are the result of negligent medical judgment. Res ipsa loquitur arises from a clearly negligent act (i.e., application of excessive doses of radiation) which leads to an almost certain outcome (radiation burns). Unlike these radiation burn cases, the original diagnostic decision to use tonsillar irradiation is at best debatably negligent. Whether or not a medical judgment to use an alternative form of therapy is legally negligent is properly contested at trial, and should not be subject to a presumption of negligence arising solely from the bad result.

The Illinois Supreme Court remanded on the res ipsa question, stating only that "we are unable to say that no set of facts can be proved which will entitle plaintiff to recover," without addressing the difference between excess radiation and tumor cases. Can res ipsa loquitur be used to establish whether the radiation caused the tumors?

Finally, even in medical malpractice cases, it is possible to find situations where courts will use res ipsa loquitur to give plaintiffs a judgment as a matter of law. In Quinby v. Plumsteadville Family Practice, Inc., 907 A.2d 1061, 1077 (Pa. 2006), the decedent, a quadriplegic for over 25 years, was placed on his right side for an operation to remove a small lesion from the left side of his head. When the operation was completed, the decedent, who had been left unattended, somehow fell off the bed, sustaining injuries that led to his death. The trial judge refused to instruct on res ipsa loquitur. Baer, J., held that the plaintiff was entitled to a directed verdict on defendant's negligence:

The only fact that was in dispute during trial was the positioning of Decedent on the table. This fact, however, is inconsequential to assessing Defendants' negligence. Even if Decedent was placed on his back in the center of the table as Defendants maintain, the fact remains that Decedent fell from the table to the floor, and Defendants have not offered any evidence explaining the cause of the fall. Pursuant to the above discussion, this is not the type of event that occurs without negligence; the evidence sufficiently eliminates other causes; and the negligence was within the scope of Defendants' duty to Decedent.

3. *Conditional res ipsa loquitur.* In many malpractice cases, the causation question gives rise to a two-step inquiry. First, was the patient's death or injury caused by the defendant's conduct or by a natural event? Second, if the former, was defendant was negligent? In dealing with these cases, res ipsa loquitur may be inapplicable for the first question, but relevant to second, under the doctrine of conditional res ipsa loquitur, which was explained in Allendorf v. Kaiserman Enterprises, 630 A.2d 402, 405 (N.J. Super. Ct. 1993) as follows:

> If the evidence presents a factual issue as to how an accident occurred, and the res ipsa loquitur doctrine would be applicable under only one version of the accident, the court should give a "conditional" res ipsa loquitur instruction, under which the jury is directed first to decide how the accident happened and to consider res ipsa loquitur only if it finds that the accident occurred in a manner which fits the doctrine.

For example, in Quin v. George Washington University, 407 A.2d 580 (D.C. 1979), the decedent died of massive internal bleeding after having his spleen removed. The dispute was whether the bleeding was triggered by a weakness in the wall of the splenic vein or was due to improper suturing of the end of the vein during surgery. Since the evidence was divided as to the location of the injury, the court affirmed the refusal of the judge below to give a conditional res ipsa loquitur instruction, noting that res ipsa loquitur would apply only if the source of the bleeding was located at the suture. Could special verdicts guard against the confusion of a conditional res ipsa loquitur instruction? If so, how might one have been framed in *Quin*?

4. *Res ipsa loquitur and multiple defendants. Ybarra* has also been extended in recent years to actions against multiple defendants sued under different substantive theories. In Anderson v. Somberg, 338 A.2d 1, 5, 9-10 (N.J. 1975), plaintiff suffered serious injuries when the tip of a surgical forceps (a rongeur) broke off in his spinal canal and remained lodged there despite the efforts of defendant physician to remove it. The plaintiff brought actions against four separate defendants: against the physician, for negligence in the operation; against the hospital, for negligently furnishing a defective instrument; against the medical distributor who supplied the

rongeur, on a warranty theory; and against the manufacturer of the rongeur, on a strict products liability theory. The jury returned a verdict in
favor of each of the four defendants against the plaintiff; the decision was
reversed by the appellate division, which held that the jury was obligated to
impose liability on at least one of the named defendants. The New Jersey
Supreme Court, by a four-to-three vote, applied res ipsa loquitur to this
case of multiple defendants, noting that this "development represents a
substantial deviation from earlier conceptions of res ipsa loquitur and has
more accurately been called 'akin to res ipsa loquitur,' or 'conditional res
ipsa loquitur.'" The dissent noted that other surgeons, perhaps numbering
20, could have created the defect but were not joined as defendants.

The New Jersey Court unanimously reaffirmed *Anderson* in Chin v.
St. Barnabas Medical Center, 734 A.2d 778, 783 (N.J. 1999). There the
decedent, a 45-year-old woman, died of a massive air embolism that
occurred during a routine "diagnostic hysteroscopy"—a procedure used to
determine abnormalities in the uterus. The procedure in question required
the cooperation of many physicians and nurses, and the evidence suggested
that a hysterscope had been misused by one of two nurses charged with
hooking it up to various devices, so that gas instead of fluid was pumped
into her uterus. Because the tubes had been disconnected before an investigation could be made, no one could determine which nurse had erred.
Handler, J., held that under *Anderson* the jury had to come back with a
verdict against at least one defendant. The jury then exonerated the
manufacturer, but on the basis of common knowledge, and without expert
testimony, divided responsibility between two nurses, the treating physician, and the hospital given that Chin "was unconscious, helpless, and
utterly blameless." "It is not contested that the air embolism could have
been caused only by negligent use of the hysteroscope. All the potential
defendants, that is, all those who participated in the chain of events leading
up to Ms. Chin's injury, were sued in this case."

With *Anderson* and *Chin*, contrast Darrah v. Bryan Memorial Hospital,
571 N.W.2d 783, 786 (Neb. 1998). The plaintiff suffered ulnar nerve
damage at the site where an intravenous line was inserted postoperatively.
The court refused the res ipsa loquitur instruction because "the district
court found that the damage to Darrah's ulnar nerve could have occurred
during or after surgery while he was hospitalized at BMH. . . . '[T]he requirement of exclusive control cannot be satisfied in view of the absence of
the operating surgeons and the anesthesiologist as party defendants. These
are parties who control the activities during surgery and they are neither
agents [n]or employees of the defendant hospital.'" The Third Restatement authorizes the use of res ipsa loquitur to "smoke out" the culpable
defendant, at least when all are simultaneously present in the operating
room, noting that one defendant can escape liability by pointing a finger at
another. RTT:LPH §17, comment *f*.

5. Statutory modification of res ipsa loquitur in medical malpractice cases. In one sense, res ipsa loquitur seems more useful today than ever before, for as medical knowledge increases, the fraction of unexplained accidents tends to diminish so that fewer cases can be chalked up to Acts of God. For a defense of the "counterintuitive idea" that the lower the costs of precautions, the more reliable it is to use res ipsa loquitur to establish negligence, see Grady, Res Ipsa Loquitur and Compliance Error, 142 U. Pa. L. Rev. 887 (1994). Nonetheless, res ipsa loquitur has led medical groups to fear that the doctrine will become (as it often is in stranger cases) the opening wedge to a doctrine of strict liability that functions poorly in medical malpractice contexts. In order to limit its scope, and that of the use of common knowledge, medical groups have obtained passage of statutes, such as the following:

NEV. REV. STAT. §41A.100 (2005)

1. Liability for personal injury or death is not imposed upon any provider of medical care based on alleged negligence in the performance of that care unless evidence consisting of expert medical testimony, material from recognized medical texts or treatises or the regulations of the licensed medical facility wherein the alleged negligence occurred is presented to demonstrate the alleged deviation from the accepted standard of care in the specific circumstances of the case and to prove causation of the alleged personal injury or death, except that such evidence is not required and a rebuttable presumption that the personal injury or death was caused by negligence arises where evidence is presented that the personal injury or death occurred in any one or more of the following circumstances:

(a) A foreign substance other than medication or a prosthetic device was unintentionally left within the body of a patient following surgery;

(b) An explosion or fire originating in a substance used in treatment occurred in the course of treatment;

(c) An unintended burn caused by heat, radiation or chemicals was suffered in the course of medical care;

(d) An injury was suffered during the course of treatment to a part of the body not directly involved in the treatment or proximate thereto; or

(e) A surgical procedure was performed on the wrong patient or the wrong organ, limb or part of a patient's body.

How does this statute apply to the cases discussed in this section?

4

PLAINTIFF'S CONDUCT

SECTION A. INTRODUCTION

This chapter examines the ways that the plaintiff's own conduct affects her right to recover damages for her harms. This inquiry becomes inescapable once the defendant claims that the plaintiff's harm was her own fault. As is often the case with legal principles, however, this commonsense objection resists any easy transformation into workable and clear rules. In one sense, the phrase "it was not my fault" does not implicate the issues discussed in this chapter. Thus, when the plaintiff is the only person involved in bringing about the accident, the defendant can simply deny his own responsibility and say truthfully that the plaintiff was the sole cause of her own harm. Because the plaintiff has failed to make out a prima facie case, her possible contributory negligence or assumption of risk need never be raised as independent affirmative defenses. The defendant's objection amounts to a general denial that the defendant had anything to do with the matter — a defense as valid in a strict liability system as it is in a negligence system.

The claim that the plaintiff should not recover because her injury was her own fault also arises when the defendant plainly has had involvement in bringing about the plaintiff's harm, as when the defendant negligently runs over the plaintiff who has darted into the street from between two parked cars. Notwithstanding the plaintiff's good prima facie case, does the plaintiff's own involvement in bringing about her injury *disentitle* her in whole or in part from recovering damages?

This chapter explores the two major versions of the "plaintiff's conduct" defense: contributory negligence and assumption of risk. Contributory negligence is established when the plaintiff has not taken reasonable care, and in consequence of her default has suffered injury. At common law the plaintiff's negligence, if established on the facts, generally barred her from any recovery in ordinary negligence cases, subject to a number of important exceptions regarding the defendant's "last clear chance" to avoid the harm, or to his willfulness in causing it.

The second key defense is assumption of risk. Unlike contributory negligence, it does not ask whether the plaintiff's conduct has inadvertently fallen below an acceptable standard of care; nor does it embody in any obvious causal component. Instead, it asks whether the plaintiff has deliberately and voluntarily encountered a known risk created by the defendant's negligence and, if she has, it holds that she should not be allowed to recover for the consequent harm. Notwithstanding its intuitive plausibility, the assumption of risk defense has generated protracted analysis and often bitter controversy. Its place in tort law has been passionately defended in the name of laissez-faire economics that affords pride of place to individual responsibility. With equal passion, it has also been denounced as an exploitive doctrine inconsistent with modern social norms of responsibility. Some scholars have even argued that, properly understood, assumption of risk has no place at all in a mature system of tort law. See, e.g., James, Assumption of Risk, 61 Yale L.J. 141 (1952).

With the contours of contributory negligence and assumption of risk thus established, we will investigate the pronounced movement, both by legislation and at common law, toward comparative negligence. That principle holds that the plaintiff's negligence should not typically bar her cause of action, but should only reduce the amount of damages recoverable. We will have to examine, therefore, how the various forms of the comparative negligence principle interact with both contributory negligence and assumption of risk, and how they mesh with a strict liability system.

SECTION B. CONTRIBUTORY NEGLIGENCE

1. *Basic Doctrine*

Butterfield v. Forrester
103 Eng. Rep. 926 (K.B. 1809)

This was an action on the case for obstructing a highway, by means of which obstruction the plaintiff, who was riding along the road, was thrown down with his horse, and injured, &c. At the trial before Bayley, J., at Derby, it appeared that the defendant, for the purpose of making some repairs to his house, which was close by the road side at one end of the town, had put up a pole across this part of the road, a free passage being left by another branch or street in the same direction. That the plaintiff left a public house not far distant from the place in question at 8 o'clock in the evening in August, when they were just beginning to light candles, but while there was light enough left to discern the obstruction at 100 yards distance: and the witness, who proved this, said that if the plaintiff had not been riding very hard he might have observed and avoided it: the plaintiff however, who was riding violently, did not observe it, but rode against it, and fell with his horse and was much hurt in consequence of the accident; and there was no evidence of his being intoxicated at the time. On this evidence Bayley, J., directed the jury, that if a person riding with reasonable and ordinary care could have seen and avoided the obstruction; and if they were satisfied that the plaintiff was riding along the street extremely hard, and without ordinary care, they should find a verdict for the defendant: which they accordingly did.

Vaughan Serjt. now objected to this direction, on moving for a new trial; and referred to Buller's Ni. Pri. 26, where the rule is laid down, that "if a man lay logs of wood across a highway though a person may with care ride safely by, yet if by means thereof my horse stumble and fling me, I may bring an action."

BAYLEY, J. The plaintiff was proved to be riding as fast as his horse could go, and this was through the streets of Derby. If he had used ordinary care he must have seen the obstruction so that the accident appeared to happen entirely from his own fault.

LORD ELLENBOROUGH, C.J. A party is not to cast himself upon an obstruction which has been made by the fault of another, and avail himself of it, if he do not himself use common and ordinary caution to be in the right. In cases of persons riding upon what is considered to be the wrong side of the road, that would not authorise another purposely to ride up against them. One person being in fault will not dispense with another's using ordinary care for himself. Two things must concur to support this action, an obstruction in the road by the fault of the defendant, and no want of ordinary care to avoid it on the part of the plaintiff.

Per Curiam. Rule refused.

Beems v. Chicago, Rock Island & Peoria R.R.
12 N.W. 222 (Iowa 1882)

BECK, J. . . . We will now consider the action of the court in overruling the [railroad's] motion for judgment non-obstante. The intestate met his death in making an attempt to uncouple the tender from a car. The special findings of the jury show that when he went between the cars to uncouple them they were moving at an improper and unusual rate of speed. Counsel for defendant insist that this finding establishes the fact of contributory negligence on the part of the intestate. The petition alleges that defendant's employees in charge of the engine were negligent, in failing to obey a direction given them by a signal made by the intestate to check the speed of the cars. The testimony tends to support this allegation. The jury were authorized to find from the testimony that deceased made two attempts to uncouple the cars while they were moving. After the first attempt he came out from between the cars, and signaled directions to check their speed; he immediately went again between the cars to make the second attempt to uncouple them. His signal was not obeyed. He was authorized to believe that the motion of the car would be checked, and he was not required to wait, before acting, to discover whether obedience would be given to his signal. The jury could have found that after the signal had been given, and after he had gone between the cars, if their speed had been checked, he would not have been exposed to danger. His act, therefore, in going between the cars after having made the signal to check their speed, was not necessarily contributory negligence. . . .

The court instructed the jury that if intestate's foot was caught between the rails and he "was thus held and run over, *without any negligence on the part of the other employees of defendant,* such as is charged in the petition, then the plaintiff cannot recover anything." The defendant asked an instruction, which was refused, to the effect that if the intestate's foot was caught between the rails the defendant is not liable, even though the jury should find the negligence charged in the petition. The instruction given is correct. If intestate was run over by reason of defendant's negligence, surely it cannot be claimed that defendant is not liable, because intestate's foot was caught between the rails. It would be a strange doctrine to hold that defendant could back its trains with unusual speed, without obeying signals to move more slowly, and thus negligently run over a brakesman, and would not be liable, for the reason that the unfortunate man was fastened to the spot by his foot being held between the rails. Whatever was the intestate's condition at the time of the accident, whether free to move, or fastened to the place, the defendant is liable if its cars were negligently driven over him.

Schwartz, Tort Law and the Economy in Nineteenth-Century America: A Reinterpretation
90 Yale L.J. 1717, 1759-1762 (1981)

Professor Friedman describes the tort defense of contributory negligence as a "cunning trap" set by courts for nineteenth-century accident victims;[310] Professor Malone argues that nineteenth-century courts frequently were aggressive in withdrawing the contributory negligence issue from the jury in order carefully to monitor industry liability.[311] These assessments are contradicted, however, by the nineteenth-century experience in New Hampshire and California.

Each state's Supreme Court from an early date accepted the traditional rule of contributory negligence as a complete defense. Both Courts were openly ambivalent about the rule, however. . . .

The California Court placed the contributory-negligence burden of proof on the defendant, and regarded a technical misassignment of the burden of proof as reversible error, even when the defendant was the Central Pacific. . . . When allocating decisionmaking between judge and jury, the New Hampshire Court specified that the contributory negligence issue could be taken away from the jury only in "extraordinary" circumstances; the California Court frequently used language almost as strong.

In administering tort appeals, the two states' Courts developed a variety of maxim-like ideas emphasizing the lenient and forgiving quality of the contributory negligence standard. Thus, a plaintiff was not required to exercise "great care" or to behave in a "very timid or cautious" way; contributory negligence was not proven by an "indiscretion" or a mere "error of judgment," let alone by a "misjudgment" in retrospect. If the plaintiff was "startled and alarmed," that was taken into account in evaluating the reasonableness of his conduct. Momentary distraction is a "most common occurrence" on city streets and "falls far short" of contributory negligence. If the plaintiff forgot what he knew about the particular danger, the Court could say that "people are liable to lapses of memory." Attenuating maxims like these were almost totally lacking in the Courts' opinions dealing with the possible negligence of tort defendants, who were frequently held to a standard of the "utmost care." Whatever, then, the symmetry in form of the doctrines of negligence and contributory negligence, they were administered under an emphatic, if implicit, double standard. . . .[333]

[Professor Schwartz then observes that a detailed analysis of the disposition of all contributory negligence cases in California and New Hampshire is consistent with the impression created by judicial language. Contributory

---

310. L. Friedman, A History of American Law (1973), at 411-412. According to Professor Levy, nineteenth-century plaintiffs making "a misstep, however slight, from the ideal standard of conduct," were routinely and unfairly denied recoveries. L. Levy, The Law of the Commonwealth and Chief Justice Shaw (1957) at 319. For acceptance of the doctrine of "slight" contributory negligence, see W. Prosser, Law of Torts 421 (4th ed. 1971).

311. Malone, The Formative Era of Contributory Negligence, at 151, 152, 182. Professors Levy and Ursin — supposedly writing about California law specifically — claim that "the nineteenth-century [contributory negligence] doctrine could fairly have been called the rule of railroad and industrial immunity." Levy & Ursin, Tort Law in California: At the Crossroads, 67 Calif. L. Rev. 497, 509 (1979).

333. That is, when the conduct of the defendant and the plaintiff combined to expose the plaintiff to a major risk, the Courts subjected the defendant to a stern negligence obligation even while defining the plaintiff's contributory negligence obligation in a mild and permissive way.

negligence is rarely found as a matter of law; jury verdicts for the plaintiff on the issue are both frequent and usually upheld; jury verdicts for defendants are often set aside, typically because of a defect in jury instructions.]

NOTE

The scope and function of contributory negligence. Professor Schwartz continues his attack on the proposition that American tort law gave special protection to industry and corporations in Schwartz, The Character of Early American Tort Law, 36 UCLA L. Rev. 641 (1989).

Apart from the history, there has been an extensive debate over whether any defense based upon plaintiff's misconduct is needed. In order to see what is at stake, it is useful to divide cases between stranger cases (including highway accidents) and consensual cases (including the employer/employee relation). *Butterfield* illustrates the first class of cases while *Beems* illustrates the latter class. In the first situation, the ability of each party to act prudently does not depend on cooperation with the other. In the second situation, coordination is the order of the day. With the first case, therefore, it becomes more likely that the standards of care imposed on plaintiffs and defendants will be the same, as was the case when infant plaintiffs were charged with contributory negligence measured by objective standards in highway cases.

What rules ought to govern these cases? One possibility is to eliminate the defense of contributory negligence altogether. See W. Landes and R. Posner, The Economic Structure of Tort Law 75-76 (1987). Under the Hand formula, the argument proceeds along the lines that the defendant can always escape liability by showing that he took cost-justified precautions against accidents. The "no-negligence" defense, therefore, provides the rational defendant with all the protection needed against unwarranted suits. Notwithstanding this argument, the defense is retained in practice because the defendant's negligence may be hotly contested in cases where the plaintiff's negligence is evident. The use of the contributory negligence defense, thus, offers a buffer against the uncertainties in the basic negligence calculation.

In stranger cases, a strict liability rule could also be adopted. Owing to the greater scope of potential liability, some affirmative defense based on plaintiff's conduct is now needed. Contributory negligence might play a more critical role, lest the plaintiff take great risks at the defendant's expense. But marrying strict liability with a contributory negligence system is oddly asymmetrical when both parties start from a position of initial parity. See, e.g., Brown, Toward an Economic Theory of Liability, 2 J. Legal Stud. 323, 351 (1973). Suppose two cars crash head-on when neither driver is negligent. Under strict liability with contributory negligence, each driver must compensate the other for his loss: The relative extent of the two sets of injuries, itself largely a matter of luck, is simply reversed by legal action. Note, however, that a comprehensive system of strict liability escapes this inelegance. The negligence of both parties is irrelevant but causation is not. If the prima facie case was that the defendant struck the plaintiff, then the causal defense is that the plaintiff blocked the defendant's right of way, as by entering an intersection when the light was red or by crossing the midline of the highway. The defendant need not show that plaintiff's violation of the rule of the road was brought about by her negligence or wrongful intention. See the excerpt from H. Laurence Ross, Settled Out of Court, *supra* Chapter 3 at 214. It is of course odd to speak of "strict liability defenses" because a person cannot be liable to himself. Yet, once it is recognized that causal principles operate on both sides, the rules of fairness require apportionment between the causal contributions of the two parties, based on the force at impact and the rights of ways of the two vehicles. For an account of joint causation under a thoroughgoing system of strict liability, see Epstein, Defenses and Subsequent Pleas in a System of Strict Liability, 3 J. Legal Stud. 165, 174-185 (1974).

This analysis need not carry over to consensual cases where the parties may have differential access to knowledge and a different ability to take care. In *Beems*, the court was clearly moved by the dependence that the hapless plaintiff below the cars had on the decisions made by the workers who were safely above. There was little need to create legal incentives for the plaintiff to do the right thing in light of his evident peril; more so, for the defendant's employees who occupied a position of relative safety. But in other cases, the plaintiff's capacity to avoid a known hazard may well be far greater. In these cases should the level of responsibility be raised to be commensurate with that degree of control?

Gyerman v. United States Lines Co.
498 P.2d 1043 (Cal. 1972)

[The plaintiff, a longshoreman employed by the Associated Banning Company, was injured while unloading fishmeal sacks that had just been brought into the warehouse of the defendant, United States Lines. Fishmeal, it seems, is a very difficult cargo to handle because it is packaged in sacks that have a tendency to rip and spill. In order to combat this danger, several common precautions are usually taken: only 18 to 22 sacks of fishmeal are placed on any one pallet and then only three or four layers high; the sacks are "bulkheaded," or tied together, in order to prevent them from falling; and, for maximum stability, they are aligned as are bricks in a wall, with no sack directly on top of another. The plaintiff had been assigned to "break down" the sacks into units that were only two pallets high. Before he began work, he noted that the sacks were not properly arranged. There were 30 sacks per pallet; the sacks were not bulkheaded; and they were not arrayed in brick-like fashion. He complained to Noel, the United States Lines chief marine clerk, that it was dangerous to proceed with the work in question, but was told that nothing could be done about it.

At no time, however, did the plaintiff speak to his own supervisor, even though the union contract with his employer provided first that "Longshoremen shall not be required to work when in good faith they believe that to do so is to immediately endanger health and safety" and established a grievance procedure "to determine whether a condition is safe or unsafe," and, second, that a joint labor-management committee should be immediately convened to resolve any outstanding safety issue. During the first three days of his work an unusually large number of sacks fell off the forklift, but no harm resulted. On the afternoon of the fourth day, about 12 sacks simultaneously fell off a load that he was moving and one of them, after bumping into the others, came toward him. Although the exact physical sequence of events was never established, the plaintiff did sustain injuries to his back and legs as a result of the incident. The trial judge, sitting without a jury, found that the defendant, United States Lines, was negligent in its failure to stack the fishmeal sacks in a safe way, conduct that was also a violation of the statutory duty to furnish every employee a "safe" place of employment. He found further that the defendant's negligence was a proximate cause of the plaintiff's harm. But he also found that the plaintiff's negligence in failing to stop work in the face of a known danger barred his cause of action. After disposing of two preliminary procedural points, the California Supreme Court considered the effect of plaintiff's contributory negligence upon his cause of action.]

SULLIVAN, J. . . .

3. CONTRIBUTORY NEGLIGENCE. . . .

"Contributory negligence is conduct on the part of the plaintiff which falls below the standard to which he should conform for his own protection, and which is a legally contributing cause co-operating with the negligence of the defendant in bringing about the plaintiff's harm." (Rest. 2d Torts (1965) §463). The question of contributory negligence is ordinarily one of fact for the determination of the trier of fact.

"A plaintiff is required to exercise only that amount of care which would be exercised by a person of ordinary prudence in the same circumstances." Where a person must work under possibly unsafe or dangerous conditions, the amount of care he must exercise for his own safety may well be less than would otherwise be required by reason of the necessity of his giving attention to his work. The burden of proving that the plaintiff was negligent and that such negligence was a proximate cause of the accident is on the defendant.

In the instant case, absent evidence of the contract governing plaintiff's employment and of the custom and practice affecting stevedoring, we doubt that the record would provide evidentiary support for the finding that plaintiff violated a standard of due care for his own safety. Considered in the light of the realities of his working life, the laborer's duty may become considerably restricted in scope. In some instances he may find himself powerless to abandon the task at hand with impunity whenever he senses a possible danger; in others, he may be uncertain as to which person has supervision of the job or control of the place of employment, and therefore unsure as to whom he should direct his complaint; in still others, having been encouraged to continue working under conditions where danger lurks but has not materialized, he may be baffled in making an on-the-spot decision as to the imminence of harm. All of these factors enter into a determination whether his conduct falls below a standard of due care.

In the case before us the standard of due care required of laborers in general is explicated by evidence of duty imposed by contract and by custom upon the particular type of laborer involved. Custom alone, of course, does not create the standard of proper diligence. "Indeed in most cases reasonable prudence is in fact common prudence but strictly it is never its measure. . . ." (The T. J. Hooper). Nevertheless, although custom does not fix the standard of care, evidence of custom is ordinarily admissible for its bearing upon contributory negligence.

[The court then reviewed the facts of the case and concluded that the evidence supported the finding that the plaintiff failed to use ordinary care for his own protection.]

We must now inquire whether defendant sustained its burden of establishing that plaintiff's failure to report the unsafe condition was a "legally contributing cause . . . in bringing about the plaintiff's harm." (Rest. 2d Torts, §463.) As previously noted, the trial court appears to have determined that plaintiff's failure was a proximate cause of his injuries because if plaintiff had reported the condition it would have been corrected.

On this issue the positions of the parties may be summarized thusly: Plaintiff argues that the burden was on defendant to prove that if plaintiff *had* reported the condition to his own supervisor instead of to defendant's supervisor, the condition would have been corrected or made safer. Defendant asserts that it was not incumbent upon it to prove that the condition complained of was correctable and that in any event there is evidence supporting the trial court's finding.

The burden of proof rests on each party to a civil action as to each fact essential to his claim or defense. A party claiming a person failed to exercise due care has the burden of proof on that issue. The burden of proving all aspects of the affirmative defense of contributory negligence, including causation, rests on the defendant, unless the elements of the defense may be inferred from the plaintiff's evidence. The burden must be met by more than conjecture or speculation. Merely because plaintiff asserts that his own negligence, if any, could not have caused his injury, does not shift to him the burden of proof on the issue. Otherwise denial of any essential element of the defense case would shift the burden of proof on that issue to the plaintiff.

[The Court then quotes from Restatement (Second) of Torts, §465, set out *infra* at 340, Note 4.]

We turn now to the facts of the case before us. It is obvious, of course, from what we have said that plaintiff did not create or maintain the dangerous and unsafe conditions of storage. The trial court found upon substantial evidence that defendant negligently maintained and operated its warehouse under those conditions. It was defendant who had control of the cargo and directed its disposition and high stacking throughout the warehouse. Defendant alone created this risk of harm which materialized in the toppling of the stacks.

Nor did the trial court find that plaintiff was negligent in his operation of the forklift or in his "breaking down" the particular stack of fishmeal whose sacks fell from the top of the load and injured him. In short there is no finding that any negligent conduct of plaintiff, operating with defendant's negligence, brought about the shifting and eventual dislodging of the sacks. According to the trial court's findings, plaintiff's negligence consisted solely in *his failure to report* the dangerous condition to his own supervisor. Our task then is to find in the record evidence showing, or from which it can be reasonably inferred, that this omission was a substantial factor in bringing about plaintiff's harm.

Defendant's theory of causation is that if plaintiff had reported the dangerous condition to his Associated Banning supervisor, that firm would have made the condition safer. An examination of the record, however, discloses no evidence establishing this theory. Indeed, although defendant vigorously asserts that the record supports a finding of proximate cause, it points to only one page of the extensive record for such evidence. At this part of the record, defendant's witness Hargett [manager of labor relations for Associated Banning, whose "duties were to represent not only Associated Banning but the industry as a whole in negotiations and disputes pertaining to contracts between the longshoremen and the various employers belonging to the Pacific Maritime Association"] responded on direct examination to a question about what a longshoreman should do upon encountering an unsafe condition. Hargett replied that he would have to get another lot to work on or "have supervision called, . . . and we would have sent men there to take care of the situation, if he was in such a condition he couldn't operate."

In our view this testimony does not show that the stacks would have been made safer. Although it indicates that the problem would have received immediate attention, it provides no clue as to what, if anything, could have been done to break down the stacks of fishmeal more safely than by the use of forklifts. Indeed, other than the vague statement as to sending "men there to take care of the situation" no evidence at all was offered as to specific measures that would be taken. Nor does evidence as to the existence of a grievance procedure, formalized in the ILWU-PMA contract constitute proof that in the particular situation culminating in plaintiff's injury, steps would have been taken to make the situation safer. Finally the trial court's suggestions made in its memorandum of decision that the offending bags could have been removed by using ladders or having other forklift drivers remove them one at a time are not based upon evidence in the record and therefore do not support the finding. Indeed such suggestions only point up the complete lack of defense evidence in the record on this critical issue. The record does not establish that plaintiff's failure to report the dangerous condition was a substantial factor in bringing about the fall of the sacks.

In view of the foregoing we conclude that defendant did not meet its burden of proving that plaintiff's contributory negligence was a proximate cause of his injuries.

[The court then remanded the case for a retrial on the questions of the plaintiff's contributory negligence and its causal connection to the plaintiff's own harm. It noted that though the plaintiff's negligence had been sufficiently established by evidence below, the court was "not satisfied" that in the instant case the two issues were so "separate and distinct" that the issue of proximate cause could not be tried alone "without such confusion or uncertainty as would amount to a denial of a fair trial."]

The issue of defendant's negligence has been properly determined and we see no reason why it should be relitigated. Retrial should be had on the issue of plaintiff's contributory negligence (including the issue of whether such negligence, if any, was the proximate cause of the accident) and, if such issue is resolved favorably to plaintiff, on the issue of damages.

The judgment is reversed and the cause is remanded with directions for a new trial limited to the issues of plaintiff's contributory negligence and of damages. Each party shall bear his or its own costs on appeal.

WRIGHT, C.J., MCCOMB, PETERS, TOBRINER, and BURKE, JJ., concurred.

NOTES

1. Contributory negligence and breach of statutory duty. In *Gyerman*, do the particulars of how best to deal with the stacking of the fishmeal stacks matter if the plaintiff could have refused to work on them? Should the defense of contributory negligence be excluded because the improper stacking of the fishmeal sacks violated the defendant's statutory duty to provide a safe place to work? In Koenig v. Patrick Construction Corp., 83 N.E.2d 133, 135 (N.Y. 1948), the court refused to allow the defenses of either contributory negligence of assumption of risk when the plaintiff was a member of the class of persons for whose benefit a particular statute the state Scaffold Law, §240(1), was enacted:

> Workmen such as the present plaintiff, who ply their livelihoods on ladders and scaffolds, are scarcely in a position to protect themselves from accident. They usually have no choice but to work with the equipment at hand, though danger looms large. The legislature recognized this and to guard against the known hazards of the occupation required the employer to safeguard the workers from injury caused by faulty or inadequate equipment. If the employer could avoid this duty by pointing to the concurrent negligence of the injured worker in using the equipment, the beneficial purpose of the statute might well be frustrated and nullified.

Why can't workers decline risky employment? Receive additional compensation for dangerous work? Are individual employees powerless when represented by a union able to bargain with the employer over safety issues? The rigor of *Koenig* has been subsequently tempered. In Weininger v. Hagedorn & Co., 695 N.E.2d 709 (N.Y. 1998), the court cryptically held that liability could not be established under the scaffolding statute if the plaintiff was the "sole cause" of the accident.

2. Contributory negligence in medical malpractice actions. In Dunphy v. Kaiser Foundation Health Plan of Mid-Atlantic States, 698 A.2d 459, 465 (D.C. 1997), the plaintiff suffered an amputation of his right foot subsequent to the defendant's failure to diagnose his osteomyelitis or bone infection. In overturning a lower court holding that the plaintiff had been guilty of contributory negligence as a matter of law, Wagner, C.J., wrote: "In the context of a medical negligence case, the physician's superior knowledge and expertise in the subject area and the generally limited knowledge of the patient concerning the dangers associated with the illness and treatment may negate the critical elements of contributory negligence, specifically the knowledge and appreciation of the risks and dangers associated with certain medical treatments." The asserted negligence of the plaintiff was his refusal to wear a cast to treat an unrelated ulcer, which the trail judge found to be a substantial factor contributing to the amputation. Plaintiff's evidence that the failure to make an earlier diagnosis and treatment brought about the amputation was held sufficient to take the contributory negligence question to the jury. Wholly apart from the causation question, should the patient's inferior knowledge matter in the face of a sufficient warning to follow certain stipulated procedures?

3. *Contributory negligence and custodial care.* What level of care should be required of people who, by virtue of being in custodial care, have demonstrated their inability to act reasonably on their own behalf? In Padula v. State, 398 N.E.2d 548, 551 (N.Y. 1979), the two plaintiffs, inmates at the Iroquois Narcotic Rehabilitation Center, and several of their friends were able, through the negligence of the center's guards, to gain access to the center's printing room. There they found some ditto fluid, rich in methyl alcohol, which they drank after mixing it "with an orange preparation called Tang." One plaintiff died and the second became blind. The court of appeals held that their suit was not barred. Relying heavily upon its earlier decision in Fuller v. Preis, *infra* at 512, it first held that actions done under an irresistible impulse, even without specific proof of a mental disease, do not sever causal connection. It continued:

> [W]hatever the contributory or comparative negligence rule may ultimately be held to be as to a person under the influence of drugs in a noncustodial situation as to which we express no opinion, we think that in relation to persons in the custody of the State for treatment of a drug problem, contributory (or comparative) negligence should turn not on whether the drug problem or its effects be categorized as a mental disease nor on whether the injured person understood what he was doing, but on whether based upon the entire testimony presented (including objective behavioral evidence, claimant's subjective testimony and the opinions of experts) the trier of fact concludes that the injured person was able to control his actions.

The court was particularly impressed by the clear testimony that "not only Padula and Modaferi [the blind claimant] but six other residents drank the Ditto-Tang concoction notwithstanding that the warning [which spoke of death or blindness] had been read to them." Any action against the supplier of the methyl alcohol? Is there any analogy to the position of the plaintiff in *Beem*? In *Gyerman*?

4. *Contributory negligence and private necessity.* Should the defense of contributory negligence be available against a plaintiff who runs into the path of a negligently speeding car on the public highway to escape from a gang attack? In Raimondo v. Harding, 341 N.Y.S.2d 679 (App. Div. 1973), the court reversed the decision below, noting that a "person faced with an emergency and who acts, without opportunity for deliberation, to avoid an accident may not be charged with contributory negligence if he acts as a reasonably prudent person would act under the same emergency circumstances, even though it appears afterwards that he did not take the

safest course or exercise the best judgment." The Third Restatement adopts this basic position, noting, for plaintiffs and defendants alike, that the law of negligence takes into account "an unexpected emergency requiring rapid response." RTT:LPH §9. The standard caveat to this position is that no party can rely on an emergency created by his prior negligence. *Id.*, comment *d*. Is *Raimondo* consistent with Vincent v. Lake Erie, *supra* at 71?

5. *Causation and contributory negligence.* The Restatement (Second) of Torts provides:

§465. CAUSAL RELATION BETWEEN HARM AND PLAINTIFF'S NEGLIGENCE

(1) The plaintiff's negligence is a legally contributing cause of his harm if, but only if, it is a substantial factor in bringing about his harm and there is no rule restricting his responsibility for it.

(2) The rules which determine the causal relation between the plaintiff's negligent conduct and the harm resulting to him are the same as those determining the causal relation between the defendant's negligent conduct and resulting harm to others.

The causal complications with contributory negligence are well illustrated by two famous Connecticut cases. In Smithwick v. Hall & Upson Co., 21 A. 924 (Conn. 1890), plaintiff was working on a narrow platform erected in front of defendant's icehouse, about 15 feet above the ground. The defendant's foreman warned plaintiff to stay away from the east side of the platform which had no railing because he feared that the plaintiff could slip on the ice. Plaintiff disregarded that instruction, but was hurt when the east portion of the ice house buckled. The defendant's negligence in maintaining the icehouse was conceded, but the plaintiff's contributory negligence was not treated as causally relevant because the resulting harm was "not within the risk," that is, the class of events that made it dangerous for the plaintiff to venture to the east side in the first place. See discussion of *Wagon Mound, infra* at 536, Chapter 6. What was the risk of plaintiff working on the east side of the platform? Would the plaintiff still have been injured if he had followed orders?

In the companion case of Mahoney v. Beatman, 147 A. 762, 768 (Conn. 1929), plaintiff was driving a Rolls Royce at about 60 miles per hour, while it was still daylight, on a gravel-shouldered, two-lane concrete turnpike, with a clear view in both directions. Defendant was approaching in a Nash from the other direction. He turned to speak to somebody in the back seat and permitted the Nash to cross over the middle of the highway into plaintiff's lane. Plaintiff, in order to avoid a head-on collision, pulled the Rolls Royce partly off onto the shoulder, leaving only his left wheels on the pavement. The Nash hit and grazed the Rolls Royce's left-hand front hub cap and spare tire, causing an estimated $200 worth of damage. The Rolls

Royce proceeded for about 125 feet along the road then suddenly turned across the highway, climbed a small bank, and hit a tree and a stone wall, sustaining about $5,650 in additional damage.

The trial court, sitting without a jury, found that defendant's Nash was on the wrong side of the road, that the speed of the Rolls Royce was "unreasonable but it did not contribute to the collision which was due entirely to the negligence of the defendant," but that the speed of the Rolls Royce did "materially hamper plaintiff's chauffeur in controlling the car after the collision and owing to it he completely lost control of it." Thereupon the trial court awarded "nominal damages" of $200 to the plaintiff. On appeal, plaintiff was given judgment for $5,850 for damage to his car. The Supreme Court of Connecticut treated the defendant's negligence as *the* proximate cause of plaintiff's entire damage. The case illustrates the distinction between causation and coincidence. To be sure, the plaintiff's speeding did not contribute to the collision, which could have happened had he been driving at 45 miles per hour while at that same location. Yet the speeding did cause the plaintiff to lose control thereafter and thus contribute to the balance of the damage to the Rolls Royce. What result under comparative negligence? See generally Green, *Mahoney v. Beatman: A Study in Proximate Cause*, 39 Yale L.J. 532 (1930), reprinted in Green, Judge and Jury 226 (1930); Epstein, Defenses and Subsequent Pleas in a System of Strict Liability, 3 J. Legal Stud. 165, 181-184 (1974).

6. *Burden of proof on contributory negligence. Gyerman* follows the universal modern rule that the defendant bears the burden of proof on the issues of contributory negligence and its causal relationship to plaintiff's harm. Nevertheless, a significant minority of states once required the plaintiff to establish her freedom from contributory negligence as a part of the basic cause of action. The rule probably arose when the intervening negligence of another actor, including the plaintiff, severed the causal connection between the defendant's negligence and the plaintiff's harm. See the discussion of the last clear chance rule *infra* at 357, Note 2. Because the plaintiff bore the burden of proof on proximate cause, it was but a small step to say that she bore the burden of proof on contributory negligence. That rule in turn created genuine difficulties in wrongful death actions when the decedent could not defend her own conduct. Initially, the courts shifted the burden back to the defendant in death cases, and over time the exception expanded into the current rule. Today death cases are often governed by a rule that holds "in the absence of any evidence as to the conduct of a person who died of injuries received in an accident, there is the presumption that he, acting on the instinct of self-preservation, was in the exercise of ordinary care," and is thus in a stronger position that an injured plaintiff. Thompson v. Mehlhaff, 698 N.W.2d 512, 526 (S.D. 2005).

LeRoy Fibre Co. v. Chicago, Milwaukee & St. Paul Ry.
232 U.S. 340 (1914)

[As part of its business of making flax, plaintiff stored about 700 tons of straw in 230 stacks on its own land. The stacks were lined up in two rows. The defendant's right of way ran about 70 feet from the first row and 85 feet from the second. One day a high wind carried sparks from a passing train to one of the stacks of flax located in the row further from the tracks. That fire eventually consumed all the flax. The jury found, first, that the defendant's servants had negligently operated its locomotive by allowing it to emit large quantities of sparks and live cinders and, second, that this act of negligence was a cause of the plaintiff's harm. Consistent with its instructions, the jury also found the plaintiff guilty of contributory negligence by placing the exposed stacks within one hundred feet of the railroad's right of way. The Supreme Court was asked to decide whether there was any question of contributory negligence to leave to the jury at all.]

MCKENNA, J. . . . It will be observed, the [plaintiff's] use of the land was of itself a proper use — it did not interfere with nor embarrass the rightful operation of the railroad. It is manifest, therefore, the questions certified . . . are but phases of the broader one, whether one is limited in the use of one's property by its proximity to a railroad or, to limit the proposition to the case under review, whether one is subject in its use to the careless as well as to the careful operation of the road. We might not doubt that an immediate answer in the negative should be given if it were not for the hesitation of the Circuit Court of Appeals evinced by its questions, and the decisions of some courts in the affirmative. That one's uses of his property may be subject to the servitude of the wrongful use by another of his property seems an anomaly. It upsets the presumptions of law and takes from him the assumption and the freedom which comes from the assumption, that the other will obey the law, not violate it. It casts upon him the duty of not only using his own property so as not to injure another, but so to use his own property that it may not be injured by the wrongs of another. How far can this subjection be carried? Or, confining the question to railroads, what limits shall be put upon their immunity from the result of their wrongful operation? In the case at bar, the property destroyed is described as inflammable, but there are degrees of that quality; and how wrongful must be the operation? In this case, large quantities of sparks and "live cinders" were emitted from the passing engine. Houses may be said to be inflammable, and may be, as they have been, set on fire by sparks and cinders from defective or carelessly handled locomotives. Are they to be subject as well as stacks of flax straw, to such lawless operation? And is the use of farms also, the cultivation of which the building of the railroad has preceded? Or is that a use which the railroad must have anticipated and to which it hence owes a duty, which it does not owe to other uses? And why? The question is especially pertinent and immediately shows that the rights of one man in the use of his property cannot be limited by the wrongs of another. The doctrine of contributory negligence is entirely out of place. Depart from the simple requirement of the law, that every one must use his property so as not to injure others, and you pass to refinements and confusing considerations. There is no embarrassment in the principle even to the operation of a railroad. Such operation is a legitimate use of property; other property in its vicinity may suffer inconveniences and be subject to risks by it, but a risk from wrongful operation is not one of them.

HOLMES, J., partially concurring. . . . If a man stacked his flax so near to a railroad that it obviously was likely to be set fire to by a well-managed train, I should say that he could not throw the loss upon the road by the oscillating result of an inquiry by the jury whether the road had used due care. I should say that although of course he had a right to put his flax where he liked upon his own land, the liability of the railroad for a fire was absolutely conditioned upon the stacks being at a reasonably safe distance from the train. . . .

If I am right so far, a very important element in determining the right to recover is whether the plaintiff's flax was so near to the track as to be in danger from even a prudently managed engine. Here certainly, except in a clear case, we should call in the jury. I do not suppose that anyone would call it prudent to stack flax within five feet of the engines or imprudent to do it at a distance of half a mile, and it would not be absurd if the law ultimately should formulate an exact measure, as it has tended to in other instances; but at present I take it that if the question I suggest be material we should let the jury decide whether seventy feet was too near by the criterion that I have proposed. . . .

I do not think we need trouble ourselves with the thought that my view depends upon differences of degree. The whole law does so as soon as it is civilized. Negligence is all degree — that of the defendant here degree of the nicest sort; and between the variations according to distance that I suppose to exist and the simple universality of the rules in the Twelve Tables or the Leges Barbarorum, there lies the culture of two thousand years.

I am authorized to say that the Chief Justice concurs in the opinion that I express.

NOTE

Reciprocal causation. LeRoy Fibre illustrates the close connection between property rights and causation. Thus, unlike the joint causation cases discussed earlier, this case does not involve a collision caused by two moving parties, or by any action of the plaintiff that blocked or hindered the operation of the railroad. In the Court's view, therefore, the issue of contributory negligence cannot arise because the plaintiff (even by stacking his flax close to the tracks) has done nothing to invade physically the railroad's right of way. The case is similar to Smith v. Kenrick, *supra* Chapter 2 at 134, which held that a mine owner was under no duty to erect a barrier to keep "foreign" water discharged by the defendant from flooding his mine. Thus, it differs sharply from cases of joint causation that arise, say, in intersection collisions, see *supra* Note at 332.

On the other side, the majority position is vulnerable because it gives no incentives for victims to reduce their storage activities to appropriate levels. See Meese, The Externality of Victim Care, 68 U. Chi. L. Rev. 1201, 1218 (2001). That position is hinted at in Holmes's dissenting opinion that stresses less the absence of physical invasion (here by plaintiff of defendant's property) and more the cheaper precautions that the plaintiff could have taken to prevent the fire. His position had in fact received a fair bit of support in some of the earlier nineteenth-century cases that imposed duties on farmers to minimize their losses from fires set by passing locomotives, even at distances that Holmes thought were within the safe zone. Thus, in Kansas Pacific Ry. v. Brady, 17 Kan. 380, 386 (1877), the defendant railroad set fire to plaintiff's hay, which was stacked between one and one-half and two miles away from the tracks. The court first found that there was evidence of defendant's negligence in the operation of the train, and turned to the question of contributory negligence:

> If the defendant was negligent at all as against the plaintiffs, it was really as much because said hay was stacked in a dangerous place, and because dry grass was allowed to intervene all the way from the stack to the railway track, as because said fire was permitted to escape. Now as the burning of said hay was the result of the acts and omissions of both the plaintiffs and the defendant, it would seem that the acts and omissions of both parties should have been submitted to the jury. Both parties may have been negligent, and the acts and omissions of both should have been subject to the scrutiny of the jury. But it is claimed that the plaintiffs could not under any circumstances be considered negligent. It is claimed that they had a right to stack their hay as they did stack it, in a dangerous place, with dry grass all around it, and without taking any precautions for its protection. And this is claimed upon the theory that every man has a right to use his own property as he pleases without reference to the great inconvenience he may thereby impose upon others. Is this theory, or rather the plaintiffs' application thereof, correct? . . . Why should any person be allowed to invite the destruction of his own property by his own negligence, so that he might by recovering for the loss thereof lessen the estate of another to that extent? Why should any person be allowed to so use his own property that in the natural course of things he would most likely injure the estate of another to the extent of the value of such property? Or, why should he have it within his power to so use his own property as to make it so hazardous for others to use theirs that such others must necessarily abandon the use of theirs?

In Svea Insurance Co. v. Vicksburg, S. & P. Ry., 153 F. 774 (W.D. La. 1907), the court noted that fire cases required the jury to take into account the "reciprocal duties" of both parties. This theme of reciprocity has received its most famous elaboration in Coase, The Problem of Social Cost, 3 J.L. & Econ. 1, 2 (1960).

> The question is commonly thought of as one in which *A* inflicts harm on *B* and what has to be decided is: how should we restrain *A*? But this is wrong. We are dealing with a problem of a reciprocal nature. To avoid the harm to *B* would inflict harm on *A*. The real question that has to be decided is: should *A* be allowed to harm *B* or should *B* be allowed to harm *A*? The problem is to avoid the more serious harm. I instanced . . . the case of a confectioner the noise and vibrations from whose machinery disturbed a doctor in his work. To avoid harming the doctor would inflict harm on the confectioner. The problem posed by this case was essentially whether it was worth while, as a result of restricting the methods of production which could be used by the confectioner, to secure more doctoring at the cost of a reduced supply of confectionery products. Another example is afforded by the problem of straying cattle which destroy crops on neighbouring land. If it is inevitable that some cattle will stray, an increase in the supply of meat can only be obtained at the expense of a decrease in the supply of crops. The nature of the choice is clear: meat or crops. What answer should be given is, of course, not clear unless we know the value of what is obtained as well as the value of what is sacrificed to obtain it. To give another example, Professor George J. Stigler instances the contamination of a stream. If we assume that the harmful effect of the pollution is that it kills the fish, the question to be decided is: is the value of the fish lost greater or less than the value of the product which the contamination of the stream makes possible.

For a general discussion of these fire cases see Grady, Common Law Control of Strategic Behavior: Railroad Sparks and the Farmer, 17 J. Legal Stud. 15 (1988), attacking the rigid property rights logic of McKenna, J., in *LeRoy Fibre.*

Derheim v. N. Fiorito Co.
492 P.2d 1030 (Wash. 1972)

[The plaintiff's car collided with defendant's truck when defendant made a left turn in violation of the rules of the road. The plaintiff was not wearing a seat belt at the time of the accident. The defendant sought to introduce expert evidence at trial to establish that the plaintiff's conduct was a form of contributory negligence, which in any event should be taken into account to reduce damages under the doctrine of avoidable consequences. The trial judge, however, refused to allow the defendant to raise the seat belt defense in its amended answer. He also refused to allow the defendant's expert to testify that if the plaintiff had worn his seat belt at the time of the accident, he would not have suffered the injuries for which the suit was brought. After a verdict and judgment for the plaintiff, the case was certified for immediate hearing by the Washington Supreme Court.]

HUNTER, J. . . . We are thus called upon to determine the rule in this state with respect to the so-called "seat belt defense." No subject in the field of automobile accident litigation, with the possible exception of no-fault insurance, has received more attention in recent years than has the seat or lap belt defense. The question being one of first impression in this state, we have reviewed the published material extensively, concluding that while the research and statistical studies indicate a far greater likelihood of serious injuries in the event of nonuse, nevertheless the courts have been inconsistent in their handling of the defense. This inconsistency seems to result from the fact that the defense does not fit conveniently into the familiar time-honored doctrines traditionally used by the courts in deciding tort cases. Thus, the conduct in question (failure to buckle up) occurs *before* defendant's negligence, as opposed to contributory negligence which customarily is thought of in terms of conduct contributing to the accident itself. While more precisely, contributory negligence is conduct contributing, with the negligence of the defendant in bringing about the plaintiff's harm, it is a rare case indeed where the distinction need be made. Furthermore, while states with comparative negligence do not have the problem to the same extent, contributory negligence in many states (such as Washington) is a complete bar to any recovery by a plaintiff — an obvious unjust result to apply in seat belt cases. The same result would be reached if the defense were presented in terms of assumption of risk, that is, that one who ventures upon the highway without buckling up is voluntarily assuming the risk of more serious injuries resulting from a possible accident proximately caused by the negligence of another.

The doctrine of avoidable consequences has been suggested as a possible solution to this conceptual dilemma, but here again, the problem is one of appearing to stretch the doctrine to fit an unusual fact pattern. As a legal theory, avoidable consequences is closely akin to mitigation of damages, and customarily is applied when plaintiff's conduct *after* the occurrence fails to meet the standards of due care. Moreover, courts have traditionally said that a defendant whose negligence proximately causes an injury to plaintiff, "takes the plaintiff as he finds him."

The practical implications of allowing seat belt evidence has also given the courts pause. For example, most automobiles are now manufactured with shoulder straps in addition to seat belts, and medical evidence could be anticipated in certain cases that particular injuries would not have resulted if both shoulder belts and seat belts had been used. Additionally, many automobiles are now equipped with headrests which are designed to protect one from the so-called whiplash type of injury. But to be effective, its height must be adjusted by the occupant. Should the injured victim of a defendant's negligence be penalized in ascertainment of damages for failure to adjust his headrest? Furthermore, the courts are aware that other protective devices and measures are undergoing testing in governmental and private laboratories, or are on the drawing boards. The concern is, of course, that if the seat belt defense is allowed, would not the same analysis require the use of all safety devices with which one's automobile is equipped? A further problem bothers the courts, and that is the effect of injecting the seat belt issue into the trial of automobile personal injury cases. The courts are concerned about unduly lengthening trials and if each automobile accident trial is to provide an arena for a battle of safety experts, as well as medical experts, time and expense of litigation might well be increased.

These problems, legal and practical, are found in reviewing the most recent cases decided by other jurisdictions confronting the issue.

[The court then reviewed a series of then recent cases in other jurisdictions, some accepting and some rejecting the "seat belt defense," and continued:]

We believe the cases in those jurisdictions rejecting the "seat belt defense" are the better reasoned cases. It seems extremely unfair to mitigate the damages of one who sustains those damages in an accident for which he was in no way responsible, particularly when, as in this jurisdiction, there is no statutory duty to wear seat belts.

For the reasons heretofore stated, we believe the trial court was correct in refusing admission of evidence on the "seat belt defense."

The judgment of the trial court is affirmed.

NOTES

1. *The seat belt defense.* Should the result in *Derheim* flip over if seat belt use were mandated by statute? Contrast *Derheim* with the following observations of Gabrielli, J., in Spier v. Barker, 323 N.E.2d 164, 167-168 (N.Y. 1974):

> We today hold that nonuse of an available [i.e, already installed] seat belt, and expert testimony in regard thereto, is a factor which the jury may consider, in light of all the other facts received in evidence, in arriving at its determination as to whether the plaintiff has exercised due care, not only to avoid injury to himself, but to mitigate any injury he would likely sustain. However, as the trial court observed in its charge, the plaintiff's nonuse of an available seat belt should be strictly limited to the jury's determination of the plaintiff's damages and should not be considered by the triers of fact in resolving the issue of liability. Moreover, the burden of pleading and proving that nonuse thereof by the plaintiff resulted in increasing the

extent of his injuries and damages, rests upon the defendant. That is to say, the issue should not be submitted to the jury unless the defendant can demonstrate, by competent evidence, a causal connection between the plaintiff's nonuse of an available seat belt and the injuries and damages sustained. . . .

Since section 383 of the Vehicle and Traffic Law does not require occupants of a passenger car to make use of available seat belts, we hold that a plaintiff's failure to do so does not constitute negligence per se. . . . Likewise, we do not subscribe to the holdings of those cases in which the plaintiff's failure to fasten his seat belt may be determined by the jury to constitute contributory negligence as a matter of common law. In our view, the doctrine of contributory negligence is applicable only if the plaintiff's failure to exercise due care causes, in whole or in part, *the accident,* rather than when it merely exacerbates or enhances the severity of his injuries. That being the case, holding a nonuser contributorily negligent would be improper since it would impose liability upon the plaintiff for all his injuries though use of a seat belt might have prevented none or only a portion of them.

. . . We concede that the opportunity to mitigate damages prior to the occurrence of an accident does not ordinarily arise, and that the chronological distinction, on which the concept of mitigation damages rest, is justified in most cases. However, in our opinion, the seat belt affords the automobile occupant an unusual and ordinarily unavailable means by which he or she may minimize his or her damages *prior* to the accident. Highway safety has become a national concern; we are told to drive defensively and to "watch out for the other driver." When an automobile occupant may readily protect himself, at least partially, from the consequences of a collision, we think that the burden of buckling an available seat belt may, under the facts of the particular case, be found by the jury to be less than the likelihood of injury when multiplied by its accompanying severity.

Another objection frequently raised is that the jury will be unable to segregate the injuries caused by the initial impact from the injuries caused by the plaintiff's failure to fasten his seat belt. In addition to underestimating the abilities of those trained in the field of accident reconstruction, this argument fails to consider other instances in which the jury is permitted to apportion damages (i.e., as between an original tort-feasor and a physician who negligently treats the original injury).

2. *Statutory response to the seat belt defense.* The availability of the seat belt defense in tort litigation is today heavily regulated by statute, as almost 40 states have adopted different regimes, most of which sharply restrict the availability of defense. For a tally, see V. Schwartz, Comparative Negligence 106-110 (4th ed. 2002). For a good analysis, see Comment, The Seatbelt Defense: A Doctrine Based in Common Sense, 38 Tulsa L. Rev. 405, 416 n.121, 421 n.156 (2002), which reports that of the 39 statutes that deal with the question, 24 decline to allow the defense. The remainder allow it only in limited form.

Washington and New York have both joined the list of states that have legislated on the issue, and each has followed the path set out in its earlier common law decisions. Washington Revised Code §46.61.688(6), enacted in 1986, and recently amended to cover electric vehicles, provides categorically that failure to use a seat belt as required by statute "does not constitute negligence, nor may failure to wear a safety belt assembly be admissible as evidence of negligence in any civil action." A similar rule of inadmissibility applies to the failure to use a separate "child restraint system" device for children under six years old. Wash. Rev. Code Ann. §46.61.687(3) (2007). The 1984 New York statute for its part provides that noncompliance with its seat belt law "shall not be admissible as evidence in any civil action in a court of law in regard to the issue of liability but may be introduced into evidence in mitigation of damages provided the party introducing said evidence has pleaded such non-compliance as an affirmative defense." N.Y. Veh. & Traf. Law §1229-c(8) (Consol. 2007). Illinois follows the Washington rule on the nonadmissibility of contributory negligence, but regards any violation of the statute as a "petty offense and subject to a fine not to exceed $25." 625 Ill. Comp. Stat. 5/12-603.1 (West 2007). Louisiana shows a similar vacillation. Before 1988 it allowed seat belt evidence in the damage phase of the trial but limited any reduction in awards to 2 percent. La. Rev. Stat. Ann. §32:295.1 (West 1988). Between 1988 and 1997, it allowed seat belt users a 10 percent discount on any fine for a moving violation. LSA-RS 32: 295 (I) (1994 Supp.). Since 1997, Louisiana treats failure to wear a seat belt as inadmissible in a civil action. La. Rev. Stat. Ann. §32:295.1 (West 2007). Why should a statute call for a small fine, or a forgiveness on other fines, but bar its use in private litigation? Would it have been preferable for a statute to provide that failure to use a seat belt reduces tort damages by 25 percent, regardless of the particular circumstances of the accident?

3. *The helmet defense.* Closely allied to the seat belt defense is the helmet defense for motorcyclists and their passengers. As with seat belts, the helmet defense has both a legislative and a common law dimension. In Dare v. Sobule, 674 P.2d 960, 963 (Colo. 1984), the court excluded the helmet defense to bar or diminish damages after the legislature repealed its law requiring helmets in 1977. Echoing *Derheim*, it argued:

> First, a defendant should not diminish the consequences of his negligence by the failure of the injured party to anticipate defendant's negligence in causing the accident itself. Second, a defense premised on an injured party's failure to wear a protective helmet would result in a windfall to tortfeasors who pay only partially for the harm their negligence caused. Third, allowing the defense would lead to a veritable battle of experts as to what injuries would have or have not been avoided had the plaintiff been wearing a helmet.

The opposite attitude was taken more recently in Stehlik v. Rhoads, 645 N.W.2d 889 (Wis. 2002), in which the plaintiff, who had been drinking, suffered serious head injuries when the all-terrain vehicle he was driving toppled. The court started from the assumption that helmets, like seatbelts, save lives. See Helmkamp, A Comparison of State-Specific All-Terrain Vehicle Related Death Rates, 1990-1999, 91 Am. J. Pub. Health 1792 (2001). It concluded that the jury could take the plaintiff's misconduct into account separate and apart from any negligence of the plaintiff in bringing about the accident in the first place.

The rise and fall of helmet statutes has been influenced by federal intervention. In 1966 the federal government tied the distribution of funds for highway construction to states' willingness to pass motorcycle helmet laws. These were adopted in 47 states by 1975, and the number of motorcycle fatalities fell by half, from about 12 per 10,000 riders to about 6 per 10,000 riders. In 1976 Congress repealed its 1966 statute; 27 states then proceeded to repeal or modify their helmet laws, so that by 1978 the fatality rate climbed to about 9 per 10,000, where it has remained roughly constant until today. The recent trend has been for states to reinstitute or tighten the helmet laws, in part to reduce medical costs, which in California have totaled between $60 and $100 million in public funds alone. See generally Hakim, Traffic Safety Officials See Sharp Rise in Motorcycle Fatalities, N.Y. Times, April 21, 2002, at A16.

2. Last Clear Chance

Fuller v. Illinois Central R.R.
56 So. 783 (Miss. 1911)

[Decedent, a man of over 70, was riding his one-horse wagon on a north-south dirt road that crossed a straight stretch of railroad track that ran perpendicular to it. The decedent had his head down; he did not stop, look, or listen, and did not observe defendant's oncoming train. This train, a light one, came down the tracks one-half hour late, at around 40 miles per hour, faster than usual or appropriate. The decedent was in plain view on the track some 660 feet from the crossing, and the uncontradicted evidence was that the defendant's engineer could have stopped the light train within 200 feet. The record was silent as to what the engineer of the train did or thought when the decedent came into plain view on the tracks, but he did not slow the train down. The only signal he gave was a routine whistle-blast some 20 seconds before the train crashed into the wagon. The decedent was instantly killed. In response to contributory negligence, the plaintiff alleged that the defendant's servant had the last clear chance to avoid injury either by braking or promptly sounding a warning whistle. At trial judgment was given for the defendant.]

McLAIN, J. . . . The rule is settled beyond controversy or doubt, first, that all that is required of the railroad company as against a trespasser is the abstention from wanton or willful injury, or that conduct which is characterized as gross negligence; second, although the injured party may be guilty of contributory negligence, yet this is no defense if the injury were willfully, wantonly, or recklessly done or the party inflicting the injury was guilty of such conduct as to characterize it as gross; and, third, that the contributory negligence of the party injured will not defeat the action if it is shown that the defendant might by the exercise of reasonable care and prudence have avoided the consequence of the injured party's negligence. This last principle is known as the doctrine of the "last clear chance." The origin of this doctrine is found in the celebrated case of Davies v. Mann, 10 Mees & W. 545, [152 Eng. Rep. 588 (Ex. 1842)]. The plaintiff in that case fettered the front feet of his donkey, and turned him into the public highway to graze. The defendant's wagon, coming down a slight descent at a "smartish" pace, ran against the donkey, and knocked it down, the wheels of the wagon passing over it, and the donkey was killed. In that case Lord Abinger, C.B., says: "The defendant has not denied that the ass was lawfully in the highway, and therefore we must assume it to have been lawfully there. But, even were it otherwise, it would have made no difference, for, as the defendant might by proper care have avoided injuring the animal and did not, he is liable for the consequences of his negligence, though the animal might have been improperly there." While Park, B., says: "Although the ass might have been wrongfully there, still the defendant was bound to go along the road at such a pace as would be likely to prevent mischief. Were this not so, a man might justify the driving over goods left on the public highway or even a man lying asleep there, or probably running against the carriage going on the wrong side of the road." It is impossible to follow this case through its numerous citations in nearly every jurisdiction subject to Anglo-American jurisprudence. For the present it will be sufficient to say that the principle therein announced has met with practically almost universal favor. It has been severely criticized by some textwriters. The groans, ineffably and mournfully sad, of Davies' dying donkey, have resounded around the earth. The last lingering gaze from the soft, mild eyes of this docile animal, like the last parting sunbeams of the softest day in spring, has appealed to and touched the hearts of men. There has girdled the globe a band of sympathy for Davies' immortal "critter." Its ghost, like Banquo's ghost, will not down at the behest of the people who are charged with inflicting injuries, nor can its groanings be silenced by the rantings and excoriations of carping critics. The law as enunciated in that case has come to stay. The principle has been clearly and accurately stated in 2 Quarterly Law Review, p. 207, as follows: "The party who last has a clear opportunity of avoiding the accident, notwithstanding the negligence of his opponent, is considered solely responsible for it." . . .

. . . The facts in the instant case show that for a distance of six hundred and sixty feet west of the crossing where Mr. Fuller was run over and injured the track was perfectly straight; that there were no obstructions; that there was nothing to prevent those in charge of the train from seeing the perilous position of the plaintiff, and it may be that, if the engineer and fireman were on the lookout, they saw, or by the exercise of reasonable care and diligence might have seen, the perilous position of the plaintiff. No alarm was given. Nothing was done to warn the deceased of the approaching train. He evidently was unconscious of its approach.

The only warning that was given him was too late to be of any benefit whatever, as the train was upon him at the time the two short blasts of the whistle were given. . . . Even if the engineer had not made an effort to stop or check his train, but had contented himself with giving the alarm at the point when he did see, or could have seen by the exercise of reasonable care on his part, the catastrophe in all probability could have been averted.

It must be observed that this is not the case of a pedestrian who approaches or who is on the track. In such cases the engineer has the right ordinarily to act upon the assumption that the party will get out of danger. Mr. Fuller was in a wagon, and the engineer could have seen that he was going to cross the track, and could only with difficulty extricate himself from his perilous position. . . .

Reversed and remanded.

American Law Institute, Restatement (Second) of Torts
(1966)

§479. LAST CLEAR CHANCE: HELPLESS PLAINTIFF

A plaintiff who has negligently subjected himself to a risk of harm from the defendant's subsequent negligence may recover for harm caused thereby if, immediately preceding the harm,

(a) the plaintiff is unable to avoid it by the exercise of reasonable vigilance and care, and

(b) the defendant is negligent in failing to utilize with reasonable care and competence his then existing opportunity to avoid the harm, when he

(i) knows of the plaintiff's situation and realizes or has reason to realize the peril involved in it or

(ii) would discover the situation and thus have reason to realize the peril, if he were to exercise the vigilance which it is then his duty to the plaintiff to exercise.

§480. LAST CLEAR CHANCE: INATTENTIVE PLAINTIFF

A plaintiff who, by the exercise of reasonable vigilance, could discover the danger created by the defendant's negligence in time to avoid the harm to him, can recover if, but only if, the defendant

(a) knows of the plaintiff's situation, and

(b) realizes or has reason to realize that the plaintiff is inattentive and therefore unlikely to discover his peril in time to avoid the harm, and

(c) thereafter is negligent in failing to utilize with reasonable care and competence his then existing opportunity to avoid the harm.

NOTES

1. *Sequential conduct.* The doctrine of last clear chance addresses the problem of sequential conduct, that is, situations in which the action of one party takes place after the other person has completed his conduct or has irrevocably committed himself to a given course of conduct, as in *Fuller*. The basic insight in this area is that once the defendant becomes aware of the plaintiff's peril, then he becomes obligated to react to that danger by taking steps to avoid it. The conduct that was optimal without knowledge of the peril is no longer so. The problem is in a sense reciprocal to the one in *Gyerman*, where the victim had the last clear chance to avoid the harm. In these sequential cases, should one regard the last party as the cheaper cost avoider, and thus the party best able to bear the loss? The attractiveness of that position has made the doctrine something of a favorite of law and economics scholars, even though many lawyers regard last clear chance as a transitional doctrine on the road to a comparative negligence regime. See James, Last Clear Chance—Transitional Doctrine, 47 Yale L.J. 704 (1938).

The potential use of the doctrine is conveniently illustrated by Davies v. Mann, 152 Eng. Rep. 588 (Ex. 1842), so poignantly retold in *Fuller*, in which the plaintiff first left his donkey in plain view on the highway, only to have it run over by the defendant's wagon. Making contributory negligence an absolute bar reduces the likelihood that the plaintiff will leave his donkey in the road in the first place. Necessarily, however, the contributory negligence defense reduces the defendant's incentive to avoid killing the donkey, even when the defendant knows or has reason to know of the danger. Yet the defendant cannot take advantage of that position once he knows or has reason to know of the danger. The last clear chance exception applies only in a small fraction of cases, so the plaintiff can hardly count on it to protect her interests when deciding where to leave her donkey. Thus, the exception to the contributory negligence rule only bites where it is likely to be most effective.

For general discussions of this problem see Shavell, Torts in Which Victim and Injurer Act Sequentially, 26 J.L. & Econ. 589 (1983); Wittman, Optimal Pricing of Sequential Inputs: Last Clear Chance, Mitigation of Damages, and Related Doctrines in the Law, 10 J. Legal Stud. 65 (1981).

2. Scope of the doctrine. To make good her case on last clear chance, the plaintiff usually had to show that the defendant was guilty of something more than ordinary negligence, which, as the Restatement implied, presupposes either knowledge that the plaintiff is in peril, or "negligence so reckless as to betoken indifference to knowledge." Woloszynowski v. New York Central R.R., 172 N.E. 471, 472 (N.Y. 1930). The plaintiff met that burden in the grisly case of Kumkumian v. City of New York, 111 N.E.2d 865, 868 (N.Y 1953), a wrongful death action in which the City's subway train ran over the decedent who was lying on the track some 1400 feet before the station. The train had halted three times after its tripping device came in contact with something on the tracks. After the first two stops, the brakeman inspected the tracks but found nothing. Only after the third time did the brakeman and engineer discover the decedent's mangled corpse, "actually steaming" on the track. There was some evidence that the fatal injuries were incurred only when the decedent was struck by the tripcocks of the third and fourth cars. Froessel, J., held that the trial judge properly left the case to the jury on a theory of last clear chance:

> Surely we cannot say, as a matter of law, under the last clear chance doctrine, that the motorman and conductor were not negligent in *twice* disregarding the emergency equipment, which is not placed in service to be ignored, and were merely chargeable with an error of judgment. At least it became a question of fact as to whether such conduct constitutes "negligence so reckless as to betoken indifference to knowledge" and whether they "ignored the warning" while there was still opportunity to avoid the accident. It matters not that they received the warning through a faultless mechanical instrumentality rather than a human agency, so long as they had "the requisite knowledge upon which a reasonably prudent man would act." The jury was entitled to find that lack of knowledge on the part of defendant's employees as to decedent's position of danger did not come about through mere lack of vigilance in observing the tracks, but rather as the result of their own willful indifference to the emergency called to their attention by the automatic equipment, to which clear warning they paid no heed. When they did belatedly carry out their plain duty to investigate, they found decedent, and it may be inferred that they would have seen him had they carried out that duty after the second stop — still belatedly, yet in time to have saved his life. We are of the opinion that plaintiff made out at least a prima facie case under the doctrine of last clear chance.

Judge Fuld wrote a brief dissent denying the applicability of last clear chance. "Certainly, neither the motorman nor the conductor knew that any person was in peril in time to have prevented his death, and the evidence is insufficient to support the inference that they *should* have known."

3. *Reckless plaintiff versus reckless defendant.* In Washington Metropolitan Area Authority v. Johnson, 726 A.2d 172, 175-176, 178 (D.C. Ct. App. 1999), the decedent flung herself onto the tracks of an oncoming train only to be killed when the defendant's intoxicated conductor ran over her. Even though the defendant was a common carrier, the court refused to apply last clear chance to a plaintiff who had "voluntarily . . . invited the particular harm that occurred," no matter how deficient the conduct of the defendant's servant.

> Plaintiff argues that this analysis wrongly emphasizes the conduct of Ms. Johnson to the exclusion of the behavior of the train operator, whom the jury found to have been reckless both in his primary negligence and in failing to take the last clear chance. However, there is widespread authority for the principle that when the plaintiff and the defendant are equally at fault, "the law leaves both parties where it finds them. Griffin v. Shively, 315 S.E.2d 210-213 (Va. 1984). Thus, the Restatement (Second) of Torts §503(3) (1965) provides:
>
> > A plaintiff whose conduct is in reckless disregard of [her] own safety is barred from recovery against a defendant whose reckless disregard of the plaintiff's safety is a legal cause of the plaintiff's harm.

The dissent argued two points:

> First, the majority's analysis, which focuses exclusively on the suicide's conduct, undermines the policies which result in imposition of liability in those situations where the defendant has the last clear chance to avoid injury by exercising reasonable. Second, the premise for the majority's analysis, that Ms. Johnson, a suicide, acted with the requisite voluntariness and knowledge, is inconsistent with society's condemnation of suicide and is not supported by the record . . . which shows that Ms. Johnson had a history of serious mental illness requiring numerous hospitalizations.

SECTION C.   IMPUTED CONTRIBUTORY NEGLIGENCE

Mills v. Armstrong (*The Bernina*)
13 App. Cas. 1 (H.L.E. 1888)

[Plaintiffs' decedents were employees on the SS *Bushire* when that ship collided with the SS *Bernina*, due to the mutual negligence of those in charge of and operating each ship. The trial court imputed the contributory negligence of those in charge of their ship to the decedents so as to bar their recovery. The court of appeals reversed the decision of the trial judge, and its decision was affirmed in the House of Lords.]

LORD HERSCHELL. . . . The question arises whether, under these circumstances, the appellants are liable. The appellants having, as they admit, been guilty of negligence from which the respondents have suffered loss, a prima facie case of liability is made out against them. How do they defend themselves? They do not allege that those whom the respondents represent were personally guilty of negligence which contributed to the accident. Nor, again, do they allege that there was contributory negligence on the part of any third person standing in such a legal relation towards the deceased men as to cause the acts of that third person, on principles well settled in our law, to be regarded as their acts, as, e.g., the relation of master and servant, or employer and agent acting within the scope of his authority. But they rest their defence solely upon the ground that those who were navigating the vessel in which the deceased men were being carried were guilty of negligence, without which the disaster would not have occurred. In support of the proposition that this establishes a defence they rely upon the case of Thorogood v. Bryan[, 137 Eng. Rep 452 (1849),] which undoubtedly does support their contention. . . . That action was one brought under Lord Campbell's Act against the owner of an omnibus by which the deceased man was run over and killed. The omnibus in which he had been carried had set him down in the middle of the road instead of drawing up to the kerb, and before he could get out of the way he was run over by the defendant's omnibus, which was coming along at too rapid a pace to be able to pull up. The learned judge directed the jury that "if they were of opinion that want of care on the part of the driver of Barber's omnibus in not drawing up to the kerb to put the deceased down, or any want of care on the part of the deceased himself, had been conducive to the injury, in either of those cases — notwithstanding the defendant, by her servant, had been guilty of negligence — their verdict must be for the defendant." The jury gave a verdict for the defendant, and the question was then raised, on a rule for a new trial on the ground of misdirection, whether the ruling of the learned judge was right. The Court held that it was.

It is necessary to examine carefully the reasoning by which this conclusion was arrived at. Coltman, J., said: "It appears to me that, having trusted the party by selecting the particular conveyance, the plaintiff has so far identified himself with the owner and her servants, that if any injury results from their negligence, he must be considered a party to it. In other words, the passenger is so far identified with the carriage in which he is travelling, that want of care of the driver will be a defence of the driver of the carriage which directly caused the injury." [The other two judges agreed, for the same reasons.]

With the utmost respect for these eminent judges, I must say that I am unable to comprehend this doctrine of identification upon which they lay so much stress. In what sense is the passenger by a public stagecoach, because he avails himself of the accommodation afforded by it, identified with the driver? The learned judges manifestly do not mean to suggest (though some of the language used would seem to bear that construction) that the passenger is so far identified with the driver that the negligence of the latter would render the former liable to third persons injured by it. I presume that they did not even mean that the identification is so complete as to prevent the passenger from recovering against the driver's master: though if "negligence of the owner's servants is to be considered negligence of the passenger," or if he "must be considered a party" to their negligence, it is not easy to see why it should not be a bar to such an action. In short, as far as I can see, the identification appears to be effective only to the extent of enabling another person whose servants have been guilty of negligence to defend himself by the allegation of contributory negligence on the part of the person injured. But the very question that had to be determined was, whether the contributory negligence of the driver of the vehicle was a defence as against the passenger when suing another wrongdoer. To say that it is a defence because the passenger is identified with the driver, appears to me to beg the question, when it is not suggested that this identification results from any recognised principles of law, or has any other effect than to furnish that defence, the validity of which was the very point in issue. Two persons may no doubt be so bound together by the legal relation in which they stand to each other, that the acts of one may be regarded by the law as the acts of the other. But the relation between the passenger in a public vehicle, and the driver of it, certainly is not such as to fall within any of the recognized categories in which the act of one man is treated in law as the act of another.

I pass now to the other reasons given for the judgment in Thorogood v. Bryan. Maule, J., says: "On the part of the plaintiff it is suggested that a passenger in a public conveyance has no control over the driver. But I think that cannot with propriety be said. He selects the conveyance. He enters into a contract with the owner, whom by his servant, the driver, he employs to drive him. If he is dissatisfied with the mode of conveyance he is not obliged to avail himself of it. . . . But, as regards the present plaintiff, he is not altogether without fault; he chose his own conveyance, and must take the consequences of any default on the part of the driver whom he thought fit to trust."

I confess I cannot concur in this reasoning. I do not think it well founded either in law or in fact. What kind of control has the passenger over the driver which would make it reasonable to hold the former affected by the negligence of the latter? And is it any more reasonable to hold him so affected because he chose the mode of conveyance, that is to say, drove in an omnibus rather than walked, or took the first omnibus that passed him instead of waiting for another? And when it is attempted to apply this reasoning to passengers travelling in steamships or on railways, the unreasonableness of such a doctrine is even more glaring.

The only other reason given is contained in the judgment of Cresswell, J., in these words: "If the driver of the omnibus the deceased was in had by his negligence or want of due care and skill contributed to an injury from a collision, his master clearly could maintain no action. And I must confess I see no reason why a passenger who employs the driver to convey him stands in any better position." Surely, with deference, the reason for the difference lies on the very surface. If the master in such a case could maintain no action, it is because there existed between him and the driver the relation of master and servant. It is clear that if his driver's negligence alone had caused the collision, he would have been liable to an action for the injury resulting from it to third parties. The learned judge would, I imagine, in that case have seen a reason why a passenger in the omnibus stood in a better position than the master of the driver. I have now dealt with all the reasons on which the judgment in Thorogood v. Bryan was founded, and I entirely agree with the learned judges in the Court below in thinking them inconclusive and unsatisfactory.

NOTES

1. *Joint enterprise and the "both ways test."* Initially, American courts embraced Thorogood v. Bryan. As the years passed, however, the rule was repudiated in state after state for reasons much like those articulated in Mills v. Armstrong. Uniformly today, the negligence of the driver will not be imputed to the passenger in the usual collision case.

Mills v. Armstrong is generally subject to one critical exception. When the defendant can establish that the passenger and the driver have entered into some relationship that makes the passenger vicariously liable for the driver's torts, the courts may impute the negligence of the driver to the passenger. Although such joint enterprise could conceivably arise from the simple driver-passenger relationship, the courts have tended to require more, sometimes dwelling on the "community of interest" that such an enterprise presupposes. See RST §491, comments *b* & *g*.

The hostile attitude toward the joint enterprise rule is well illustrated by Dashiell v. Keauhou-Kona Co., 487 F.2d 957, 959-961 (9th Cir. 1973). Mr. Dashiell was injured, jointly through the negligence of his wife, who was driving a golf cart in which he was a passenger, and the negligence of the defendant. By a vote of two to one, the court reversed the judgment given to the defendant below, holding the joint enterprise defense inapplicable as a matter of law:

We find that on the facts of this case, at no time did the relationship of joint enterprise or joint venture exist between Mr. and Mrs. Dashiell within the meaning of imputed negligence. This is not a typical case of a business venture of a character similar to a partnership where two or more parties undertake, for some pecuniary purpose, a contractual obligation resulting in the liability of each for the negligence of the other. . . .

Additionally, applying the concept of imputed contributory negligence to the facts of this case would needlessly frustrate some basic policies of tort law. Mr. Dashiell was found by the jury to be blameless, and since negligence law is based on personal fault, it would be both illogical and inequitable to deny him recovery unless he were under a duty to control the actions of Mrs. Dashiell as she drove the golf cart. The record reflects no basis on which to find any duty of control. The original purpose of defining the joint enterprise relationship was vicarious liability, in order to increase the number of those liable to provide a financially responsible person to injured third parties. That purpose is absent when related to the Dashiells; in fact, application of the imputed contributory negligence rule would have the opposite effect of freeing from liability another party who is at fault even though the person denied recovery is blameless.

Dashiell reflects the modern dissatisfaction with the once fashionable "both ways test," which provided that if *A* could be held vicariously liable for the torts of *B*, then the contributory negligence of *B* should be imputed to *A*, barring *A*'s recovery. Should Mr. Dashiell be vicariously liable if Mrs. Dashiell had injured the defendant? What result in *The Bernina* under the both ways test?

2. Imputed negligence in parent-child cases. In Hartfield v. Roper, 21 Wend. 615, 618-619 (N.Y. 1839), the court barred the action of a two- or three-year-old infant because of his parents' negligence in allowing him to wander into a roadway, where he was struck and injured by a sleigh driven by the defendants Roper and Newall. The court insisted that it was both "folly and gross neglect" for the child's parents to allow him to wander into the road. While conceding that such parental foolishness could not excuse or justify either any deliberate injury or gross neglect of the defendants, the court nonetheless denied that plaintiff's recovery:

An infant is not *sui juris*. He belongs to another, to whom discretion in the care of his person is exclusively confided. That person is keeper and agent for this purpose; and in respect to third persons, his act must be deemed that of the infant; his neglect, the infant's neglect. Suppose a hopeless lunatic suffered to stray by his committee, lying in the road like a log, shall the traveller, whose sleigh unfortunately strikes him, be made amenable in damages? The neglect of the committee to whom his custody is confided shall be imputed to him. It is a mistake to suppose that because the party injured is incapable of personal discretion, he is, therefore, above all law. An infant or lunatic is liable personally for wrongs which he commits against the person and property of others. And when he complains of wrongs to himself, the defendant has a right to insist that he should not have been the heedless instrument of his own injury. He cannot, more than any other, make a profit of his own wrong. *Volenti non fit injuria.* If his proper agent and guardian has suffered him to incur mischief, it is much more fit that he should look for redress to that guardian, than that the latter should negligently allow his ward to be in the way of travellers, and then harass them in courts of justice, recovering heavy verdicts for his own misconduct.

Hartfield has been repudiated by either common law decision or statute in virtually all jurisdictions. New York, for example, overturned the rule by statute in 1935. N.Y. Dom. Rel. Law §73, now N.Y. Gen. Oblig. Law §3-111 (McKinney 2007). See generally Gregory, Vicarious Responsibility and Contributory Negligence, 41 Yale L.J. 831 (1932); 2 Harper, James & Gray, Torts ch. 23. Does the rule make more sense in a regime of comparative negligence?

SECTION D.   ASSUMPTION OF RISK

Lamson v. American Axe & Tool Co.
58 N.E. 585 (Mass. 1900)

Tort, under the employers' liability act, St. 1887, c. 270, for personal injuries occasioned to the plaintiff while in the defendant's employ. Trial in the Superior Court, before Lawton, J., who directed the jury to return a verdict for the defendant; and the plaintiff alleged exceptions, which appear in the opinion.

HOLMES, C.J. This is an action for personal injuries caused by the fall of a hatchet from a rack in front of which it was the plaintiff's business to work at painting hatchets, and upon which the hatchets were to be placed to dry when painted. The plaintiff had been in the defendant's employment for many years. About a year before the accident new racks had been substituted for those previously in use, and it may be assumed that they were less safe and were not proper, but were dangerous on account of the liability of the hatchets to fall from the pegs upon the plaintiff when the racks were jarred by the motion of machinery near by. The plaintiff complained to the superintendent that the hatchets were more likely to drop off than when the old racks were in use, and that now they might fall upon him, which they could not have done from the old racks. He was answered in substance that he would have to use the racks or leave. The accident which he feared happened, and he brought this suit.

The plaintiff, on his own evidence, appreciated the danger more than any one else. He perfectly understood what was likely to happen. That likelihood did not depend upon the doing of some negligent act by people in another branch of employment, but solely on the permanent conditions of the racks and their surroundings and the plaintiff's continuing to work where he did. He complained, and was notified that he could go if he would not face the chance. He stayed and took the risk. . . . He did so none the less that the fear of losing his place was one of his motives.

Exceptions overruled.

NOTES

1. The fellow servant rule. Lamson represents only one manifestation of the assumption of risk defense in the area of its birth, the law of industrial accidents. The original version of the assumption of risk defense was embodied in the common employment (or fellow servant) rule that Chief Justice Shaw (following the English decision of Priestley v. Fowler, 150 Eng. Rep. 1030 (Ex. 1837)) had endorsed nearly 60 years before in Farwell v. Boston & Worcester R.R. Corp., 45 Mass. 49, 58-59 (1842). In *Farwell*, the defendant employed the plaintiff as an engineer. While engaged in his work, the plaintiff lost his right hand when another of the defendant's servants carelessly threw the wrong switch down the line. The employer had not been negligent in the selection and supervision of the "trusty" switchman. The court had to decide whether the railroad could be charged with the negligence of its employee in an action brought by that employee's fellow servant. Shaw conceded that a *stranger* could hold the railroad vicariously liable for the wrongs of its servant. But he denied that the principle could benefit the plaintiff, who in his view had assumed the risk: "the implied contract of the master does not extend to indemnify the servant against the negligence of anyone but himself." Shaw then contrasted the position of an employee with that of a passenger:

> The liability of passenger carriers is founded on similar considerations. They are held to the strictest responsibility for care, vigilance and skill, on the part of themselves and all persons employed by them, and they are paid accordingly. The rule is founded on the expediency of throwing the risk upon those who can best guard against it. Story on Bailments, §590 et seq.

Shaw then concluded as follows:

> In applying these principles to the present case, it appears that the plaintiff was employed by the defendants as an engineer, at the rate of wages usually paid in that employment, being a higher rate than the plaintiff had before received as a machinist. It was a voluntary undertaking on his part, with a

full knowledge of the risks incident to the employment; and the loss was sustained by means of an ordinary casualty, caused by the negligence of another servant of the company. Under these circumstances, the loss must be deemed to be the result of a pure accident, like those to which all men, in all employments, and at all times, are more or less exposed; and like similar losses from accidental causes, it must rest where it first fell, unless the plaintiff has a remedy against the person actually in default; of which we give no opinion.

The fellow servant rule was, if anything, far more uncompromising than the assumption of risk rule in *Lamson.* In *Farwell,* for example, the risk was assumed by status alone, since the plaintiff was in total ignorance of the dangerous condition that could cause harm. In an unavailing effort to escape the fellow servant rule, plaintiff's counsel in *Farwell* sought to confine it to the conditions applicable in Priestley v. Fowler, where the two servants (jointly loading a butcher's wagon) were in face-to-face contact, and not under the immediate supervision of their common employer. But Shaw resisted any such compromise by extending the rule to employees who worked in "different departments" of the same business, however defined.

The common employment rule did not long retain its pristine simplicity in *Farwell.* Perhaps its most important refinement was the "vice-principal" exception, whereby certain duties of the employer discharged by supervisory personnel were regarded as nondelegable: the duty to supply the proper equipment, to furnish a safe work place, and the like. For a comparison to the duties of common carriers, see Kelly v. Manhattan Ry., *supra* Chapter 3 at 220. The precise delineation of this exception generated many inconsistent judicial decisions, collected in C. Labatt, Master and Servant §§1433-1553 (2d ed. 1913). Indeed Lord Cairns repudiated the whole vice-principal exception in England in the celebrated (or infamous) case of Wilson v. Merry, 1 L.R.-S. & D. App. 326 (H.L.E. 1868), which reaffirmed *Priestley* in its original rigor.

Mere compromises in the basic principle did not, however, satisfy the critics of the fellow servant rule. In 1 T.G. Shearman and A.A. Redfield, Negligence vi, vii (5th ed. 1898), the authors denounced the rule in these words:

> A small number of able judges, devoted, from varying motives, to the supposed interests of the wealthy classes, and caring little for any others, boldly invented an exception to the general rule of masters' liability, by which servants were deprived of its protection. Very appropriately, this exception was first announced in South Carolina, then the citadel of human slavery. It was eagerly adopted in Massachusetts, then the centre of the factory system, where some decisions were then made in favor of great corporations, so preposterous that they have been disregarded in every other State, without

even the compliment of refutation. It was promptly followed in England, which was then governed exclusively by landlords and capitalists. . . .

As the courts, while asserting unlimited power to create new and bad law, denied their power to correct their own errors, the legislature intervened, and to a large extent the whole defence of "common employment" has been taken away in Great Britain. And now, not a single voice is raised in Great Britain in justification of the doctrine once enforced by the unanimous opinions of the English courts. The infallible Chief Justice Shaw and Chancellor Cairns have fallen so low, on *this* point at least, that "there are none so poor as to do them reverence. . . ."

That same view has been voiced by twentieth-century writers as well. See L. Friedman, A History of American Law 413, 414 (1973); see also Schwartz, Tort Law and the Economy in Nineteenth-Century America: A Reinterpretation, 90 Yale L.J. 1717, 1768-1775 (1981). For a defense of the rule on the contractual grounds originally advanced by Shaw, see Posner, A Theory of Negligence, 1 J. Legal Stud. 29, 67-71 (1972); for an exhaustive account of its origins in Priestley v. Fowler, see Stein, *Priestley v. Fowler* (1837) and the Emerging Tort of Negligence, 44 B. C. L. Rev. 689 (2003), disputing *Priestley*'s role in the origin of common employment.

2. *Employer liability acts.* Lamson was brought not at common law, but under the Massachusetts Employers' Liability Act. Based on an English statute of the same name (43 Vict. c. 42 (1880)), that act, among other things, held employers to a general rule of negligence liability and abolished the fellow servant rule. See generally Epstein, The Historical Origins and Economic Structure of Workers' Compensation Law, 16 Ga. L. Rev. 775, 778 (1982). Rejection of the fellow servant rule, however, did not by itself remove the common law version of assumption of risk into the ELA, as defined in *Lamson*, or in the parallel in English decisions; see, e.g., Thomas v. Quartermaine, 18 Q.B.D. 685 (1887); Smith v. Baker, [1891] A.C. 325.

The newer version of assumption of risk, however, depended critically on the employee's continued willingness to work in the face of known risks, often after complaints had been voiced and rejected. In St. Louis Cordage Co. v. Miller, 126 F. 495 (8th Cir. 1903), Sanborn, J., defended assumption of risk as a manifestation of freedom of contract. Lord Bramwell took a similar stance in Smith v. Baker & Sons, [1891] A.C. 325, 344, in which the plaintiff, while engaged in his employment, was injured when a stone that was being lifted over his head fell and hit him. The House of Lords accepted the plaintiff's contention that he did not assume the risk because he had no specific knowledge that he was about to be struck, but Bramwell, that staunch and unreconstructed defender of laissez-faire, dissented, putting his case in the language of the bargain.

It is a rule of good sense that if a man voluntarily undertakes a risk for a reward which is adequate to induce him, he shall not, if he suffers from the risk, have a compensation for which he did not stipulate. He can, if he chooses, say, "I will undertake the risk for so much, and if hurt, you must give me so much more, or an equivalent for the hurt." But drop the maxim. Treat it as a question of bargain. The plaintiff here thought the pay worth the risk, and did not bargain for a compensation if hurt: in effect, he undertook the work, with its risks, for his wages and no more. He says so. Suppose he had said, "If I am to run this risk, you must give me 6s. a day and not 5s.," and the master agreed, would he in reason have a claim if he got hurt? Clearly not. What difference is there if the master says, "No I will only give you 5s."? None. I am ashamed to argue it.

How does Bramwell know that this workplace bargain precluded compensation for injury? How could he, or the majority of the House of Lords, find out whether it did? In one sense, the larger issue in *Smith* was not whether this plaintiff had assumed this risk, but whether as a matter of law he, or any other employee, could assume it by contract. The legal willingness to ban or limit the assumption of risk defense in industrial accident cases advanced by degrees, and culminated in its abolition by a 1939 amendment to the Federal Employers' Liability Act (45 U.S.C. §54). The defense is also eliminated under the standard workers' compensation statutes adopted in most states shortly after World War I. But the defense continues to operate in actions brought against third parties not covered by these statutes. See, e.g., Dullard v. Berkeley Associates Co., 606 F.2d 890 (2nd Cir. 1979) (general contractors). For the early developments, see Bohlen, Voluntary Assumption of Risk, 20 Harv. L. Rev. 14, 17-18 (1906).

3. *Risk premium.* Both Shaw in *Farwell* and Bramwell in *Smith* alluded to the possibility that higher wages compensate for risky employment. Much modern research holds that workers in dangerous employments receive a "risk premium" to cover their added risk before any loss occurs. Measuring the risk premium today is a chancy business at best. Some of the most careful empirical work on this question has been done by W. Kip Viscusi, Risk by Choice 43-44 (1983), who reports as follows:

> In my study of workers' subjective risk perceptions, I found that workers who believed that they were exposed to dangerous or unhealthy conditions received over $900 annually (1980 prices) in hazard pay. It is especially noteworthy that an almost identical figure was obtained when I used an objective industry injury risk measure as the risk variable. The similarity of the findings using subjective and objective measures of risk lends strong empirical support to the validity of the risk premium analysis.
>
> Unfortunately, these results do not enable us to conclude that markets work perfectly. Is the premium less or more than would prevail if workers

and employers were fully cognizant of the risks? The size of the premium only implies that compensating differentials are one element of market behavior. A more meaningful index is the wage premium per unit of risk. If it is very likely that a worker will be killed or injured, a $900 risk premium can be seen as a signal that the compensating differential process is deficient. The average blue-collar worker, however, faces an annual occupational death risk of only about 1/10,000 and a less than 1/25 risk of an injury severe enough to cause him to miss a day or more of work. Consequently, the observed premium per unit of risk is quite substantial, with the implicit value of life being on the order of $2 million or more for many workers.

The safety incentives created by market mechanisms are much stronger than those created by OSHA standards; a conservative estimate of the total job risk premiums for the entire private sector is $69 billion, or almost 3,000 times the total annual penalties now levied by OSHA. Whereas OSHA penalties are only 34 cents per worker, market risk premiums per worker are $925 annually. This figure would be even higher if we added in the premiums that are displaced by the workers' compensation system, which provides an additional $11.8 billion in compensation to workers.

What happens to the risk premium when the OSHA protections are increased along with workers' compensation benefits? In Lott & Manning, Have Changing Liability Rules Compensated Workers Twice for Occupational Hazards? Earnings Premiums and Cancer Risks, 29 J. Legal Stud. 99 (2000), the authors note that in the early years workers received a risk premium when the possibility of receiving workers' compensation benefits (which often excluded illnesses) was low, but suffered a reduction in risk premium of between 43 and 108 percent when workers' compensation benefits were made available. In effect, the size of the premium is reduced when ex post compensation is made available. See Viscusi & Aldy, The Value of a Statistical Life: A Critical Review of Market Estimates Throughout the World, AEI-Brookings Joint Center For Regulatory Studies, Related Publication 03-2 (2003), available at http://www.aei-brookings.org/admin/authorpdfs/page.php?id=239.

Murphy v. Steeplechase Amusement Co.
166 N.E. 173 (N.Y. 1929)

CARDOZO, C.J. The defendant, Steeplechase Amusement Company, maintains an amusement park at Coney Island, New York. One of the supposed attractions is known as "The Flopper." It is a moving belt, running upward on an inclined plane, on which passengers sit or stand. Many of them are unable to keep their feet because of the movement of the belt, and are thrown backward or aside. The belt runs in a groove, with padded walls on either side to a height of four feet, and with padded flooring beyond the walls at the same angle as the belt. An electric motor, driven by current furnished by the Brooklyn Edison Company, supplies the needed power.

Plaintiff, a vigorous young man, visited the park with friends. One of them, a young woman, now his wife, stepped upon the moving belt. Plaintiff followed and stepped behind her. As he did so, he felt what he describes as a sudden jerk, and was thrown to the floor. His wife in front and also friends behind him were thrown at the same time. Something more was here, as every one understood, than the slowly-moving escalator that is common in shops and public places. A fall was foreseen as one of the risks of the adventure. There would have been no point to the whole thing, no adventure about it, if the risk had not been there. The very name above the gate, the Flopper, was warning to the timid. If the name was not enough, there was warning more distinct in the experience of others. We are told by the plaintiff's wife that the members of her party stood looking at the sport before joining in it themselves. Some aboard the belt were able, as she viewed them, to sit down with decorum or even to stand and keep their footing; others jumped or fell. The tumbling bodies and the screams and laughter supplied the merriment and fun. "I took a chance," she said when asked whether she thought that a fall might be expected.

Plaintiff took the chance with her, but, less lucky than his companions, suffered a fracture of a knee cap. He states in his complaint that the belt was dangerous to life and limb in that it stopped and started violently and suddenly and was not properly equipped to prevent injuries to persons who were using it without knowledge of its dangers, and in a bill of particulars he adds that it was operated at a fast and dangerous rate of speed and was not supplied with a proper railing, guard or other device to prevent a fall therefrom. No other negligence is charged.

We see no adequate basis for a finding that the belt was out of order. It was already in motion when the plaintiff put his foot on it. He cannot help himself to a verdict in such circumstances by the addition of the facile comment that it threw him with a jerk. One who steps upon a moving belt and finds his heels above his head is in no position to discriminate with nicety between the successive stages of the shock, between the jerk which is a cause and the jerk, accompanying the fall, as an instantaneous effect. There is evidence for the defendant that power was transmitted smoothly, and could not be transmitted otherwise. If the movement was spasmodic, it was an unexplained and, it seems, an inexplicable departure from the normal workings of the mechanism. An aberration so extraordinary, if it is to lay the basis for a verdict, should rest on something firmer than a mere descriptive epithet, a summary of the sensations of a tense and crowded moment. But the jerk, if it were established, would add little to the case. Whether the movement of the belt was uniform or irregular, the risk at greatest was a fall. This was the very hazard that was invited and foreseen.

Volenti non fit injuria. One who takes part in such a sport accepts the dangers that inhere in it so far as they are obvious and necessary, just as a fencer accepts the risk of a thrust by his antagonist or a spectator at a ball game the chance of contact with the ball. The antics of the clown are not the paces of the cloistered cleric. The rough and boisterous joke, the horseplay of the crowd, evokes its own guffaws, but they are not the pleasures of tranquillity. The plaintiff was not seeking a retreat for meditation. Visitors were tumbling about the belt to the merriment of onlookers when he made his choice to join them. He took the chance of a like fate, with whatever damage to his body might ensue from such a fall. The timorous may stay at home.

A different case would be here if the dangers inherent in the sport were obscure or unobserved, or so serious as to justify the belief that precautions of some kind must have been taken to avert them. Nothing happened to the plaintiff except what common experience tells us may happen at any time as the consequence of a sudden fall. Many a skater or a horseman can rehearse a tale of equal woe. A different case there would also be if the accidents had been so many as to show that the game in its inherent nature was too dangerous to be continued without change. The president of the amusement company says that there had never been such an accident before. A nurse employed at an emergency hospital maintained in connection with the park contradicts him to some extent. She says that on other occasions she had attended patrons of the park who had been injured at the Flopper, how many she could not say. None, however, had been badly injured or had suffered broken bones. Such testimony is not enough to show that the game was a trap for the unwary, too perilous to be endured. According to the defendant's estimate, two hundred and fifty thousand visitors were at the Flopper in a year. Some quota of accidents was to be looked for in so great a mass. One might as well say that a skating rink should be abandoned because skaters sometimes fall.

There is testimony by the plaintiff that he fell upon wood, and not upon a canvas padding. He is strongly contradicted by the photographs and by the witnesses for the defendant, and is without corroboration in the testimony of his companions who were witnesses on his behalf. If his observation was correct, there was a defect in the equipment, and one not obvious or known. The padding should have been kept in repair to break the force of any fall. The case did not go to the jury, however, upon any such theory of the defendant's liability, nor is the defect fairly suggested by the plaintiff's bill of particulars, which limits his complaint. The case went to the jury upon the theory that negligence was dependent upon a sharp and sudden jerk.

The judgment of the Appellate Division and that of the Trial Term [for the plaintiff] should be reversed, and a new trial granted, with costs to abide the event.

POUND, CRANE, LEHMAN, KELLOGG and HUBBS, JJ., concur; O'BRIEN, J., dissents.

NOTES

1. Historical criticisms of Murphy. For a strong "dissenting" opinion, see Simon, *Murphy v. Steeplechase Amusement Co.*: While the Timorous Stay at Home, the Adventurous Ride the Flopper, in Tort Stories 179 (Rabin & Sugarman, eds. 2003). The article argues that the flopper was more dangerous than Cardozo suggested. It was only 16 inches wide, and had to be entered while moving at a speed of 7 miles per hour, in contrast to the 1 to 1.5 miles per hour of the standard escalator, and the evidence of the sudden jerk was more persuasive than Cardozo acknowledged. But at the same time, it may have been safer than other rides (e.g., the Whirlpool, or Human Roulette Wheel), in standard use at Coney Island, then the amusement capital of the world.

2. Assumption of risk and the duty to warn. One important issue in these amusement park cases is the extent to which assumption of risk can survive the recent expansion of the duty to warn. In Russo v. The Range, Inc., 395 N.E.2d 10, 13-14 (Ill. App. 1979), the plaintiff was injured while riding down the "giant slide" owned and operated by the defendant. Before entering the amusement park, he purchased a ticket that on the reverse side read: "the person using this ticket so assumes all risk of personal injury." At the top of the slide defendant placed a warning and instructions for its proper use. The plaintiff also admitted that he had taken several similar rides at the amusement park before the accident, but claimed that he had "no knowledge that the slide would cause his body to fly in the air as he rode it—the event which he says caused his injury." The court allowed plaintiff's case to reach the jury. "From these same facts the Range relies on it is possible to infer that Russo's ride down the slide was an abnormal occurrence caused by some danger unknown to him and a risk he did not assume. It is the presence of this possibility which precludes summary judgment."

Modern providers of rides routinely take aggressive steps to deal with the risks, often using bold signs to that effect. See Desai v. Silver Dollar City, Inc., 493 S.E.2d 540, 545 (Ga. App. 1997), where the conspicuous warning, "CAUTION: DO NOT EXIT RAFT UNTIL ATTENDANT INSTRUCTS YOU TO. . . . FAILURE TO ABIDE BY THESE RULES MAY RESULT IN INJURY TO YOUR SELF OR OTHERS," gave the defendant a summary judgment against a plaintiff who disregarded instructions by trying to help her 65-year-old mother out of a "wobbly" raft before it stopped.

The precautions taken with rides are not just confined to warnings. One recent incident, not reported in judicial opinions, involves the Disney

World Resorts Mission:SPACE full-throttle ride. That ride itself purports to simulate the rigorous training that is needed for astronauts undertaking a 2036 mission to Mars in an imaginary X-2 Deep Space Shuttle. The riders are put into teams of four and loaded into a spinning centrifuge that exposes them to forces twice that of gravity, where each member of the team has specific tasks to discharge, including lift-off and a slingshot ride around the moon. The rides are accompanied by warnings of nausea, headache, dizziness,s and disorientation. Several million people each year take the ride. Over a one-year period, paramedics at the park treated 194 guests, most of whom were over 55 years of age, for a variety of ailments, including dizziness, nausea, vomiting, chest pains, and irregular heart-beats. Two persons with preexisting conditions died — one a 4-year-old boy with an undiagnosed heart condition, and the other a 49-year-old woman from a brain bleed due to high pressure. In response, Disney World in-troduced in 2006 a "half-throttle" ride without the centripetal effects and large gravitational forces. The lines for the original full throttle line are far longer. Should the known availability of a half-throttle ride insulate Disney from all risk of injuries from the normal operation of the full-throttle ride? Is there any exposure if the warnings on the full-throttle ride are not more severe than those of the half-throttle ride? Should all persons over 55 years be excluded from the full-throttle ride? For continuous updates, see http://en.wikipedia.org/wiki/Mission:_Space#Motion_sickness_and_injuries.

3. Spectator sports and assumption of risk. A large body of cases relies on the assumption of risk defense to deny recovery to spectators injured at sporting events. The defense proceeds at two levels. First, at the wholesale level, courts hold that all spectators share the common knowledge of injury from attending these events. Second, at the retail level, particularized evidence tends to confirm that any individual plaintiff has this knowledge, such as the risk of being hit by a hockey puck, Moulas v. PBC Productions, Inc. 570 N.W.2d 739 (Wis. App. 1997), affirmed by an equally divided court, 576 N.W.2d 929 (Wis. 1998), or a baseball.

The chinks in the armor of this defense arise in special settings where spectators are said to be induced into letting down their guard. Thus, in Maisonave v. The Newark Bears, Gourmet Services, 852 A.2d 233, 236 (N.J. Super. Ct. App. Div. 2004), the plaintiff spectator was struck in the face by a foul ball as he stood before a vending cart operated by the de-fendant Gourmet Dining Service, which had a concession contract from the team. The carts were needed because the concession areas were still under construction. By agreement between the defendants, they were positioned close to the field so that customers could continue to watch the game. The plaintiff, himself an experienced baseball player and long-time fan, was hit while reaching into his wallet to pay for his purchase. Building on pre-cedents that require operators of sports facilities to screen high risk places,

Coleman, J., held that the plaintiff was entitled to a jury trial on the question of whether the defendants had breached their duty:

> While watching the game, either seated or standing in an unprotected viewing area, spectators reasonably may be expected to pay attention and to look out for their own safety; but the activities and ambiance of a concession area predictably draw the attention of even the most experienced and the most wary fan from the action on the field of play. It is not only foreseeable, but inevitable, that in the process of placing orders or reaching for money or accepting the purchases or striking up conversations with others on line, spectators will be distracted from the action on the field and the risk of injury from flying objects will be increased significantly. The defendants are engaged in a commercial venture which by its nature induces spectators to let down their guard. They have a concomitant duty to exercise reasonable care to protect them during such times of heightened vulnerability. The imposition of a duty under these circumstances, particularly where it involves a temporary arrangement, is not only fair but reasonable.

What result if a fan sitting in the stands is injured while reaching for his wallet to buy a hot dog from a roving vendor?

4. *Assumption of risk in professional sports.* In Maddox v. City of New York, 487 N.E.2d 553, 556-557 (N.Y. 1985), the plaintiff was an outfielder for the New York Yankees whose professional career was effectively ended after he sustained severe damage to his knee when he slipped in the "wet and muddy" outfield while chasing after a fly ball. He sued the Yankees as his employer, the Mets as lessees of Shea Stadium, and New York City as the stadium's owner. The plaintiff knew about the general condition of the field, and the court held that "[h]is continued participation in the game in light of that awareness constituted assumption of risk as a matter of law, entitling defendants to a summary judgment." The court reasoned as follows:

> There is no question that the doctrine requires not only knowledge of the injury-causing defect but also appreciation of the resultant risk, but awareness of the risk is not to be determined in a vacuum. It is, rather, to be assessed against the background of the skill and experience of the particular plaintiff, and in that assessment a higher degree of awareness will be imputed to a professional than to one with less than professional experience in the particular sport. In that context plaintiff's effort to separate the wetness of the field, which he testified was above the grassline, from the mud beneath it in which his foot became lodged must be rejected for not only was he aware that there was "some mud" in the centerfield area, but also it is a matter of common experience that water of sufficient depth to cover grass may result in the earth beneath being turned to mud. We do not deal here . . . with a hole in the playing field hidden by grass, but with water, indicative of the presence of mud, the danger of which plaintiff was sufficiently aware to

complain to the grounds keepers. It is not necessary to the application of assumption of risk that the injured plaintiff have foreseen the exact manner in which his or her injury occurred, so long as he or she is aware of the potential for injury of the mechanism from which the injury results.

5. *Primary and secondary assumption of risk.* In Meistrich v. Casino Arena Attractions, Inc., 155 A.2d 90 (N.J. 1959), the plaintiff fell while skating on defendant's rink. Plaintiff's evidence showed that "defendant departed from the usual procedure in preparing the ice, with the result that it became too hard and hence too slippery for the patron of average ability using skates sharpened for the usual surface." Weintraub, C.J., speaking for a unanimous court, held that a jury could infer that the defendant's negligence was a proximate cause of the accident. It also held that a "jury could permissibly find [the plaintiff] carelessly contributed to his injury when, with that knowledge, he remained on the ice and skated cross-hand with another." He nonetheless ordered a new trial because of what he regarded as a faulty instruction below on assumption of risk, namely the trial court's instruction: "that assumption of risk may be found if plaintiff knew or reasonably should have known of the risk, notwithstanding that a reasonably prudent man would have continued in the face of the risk."

Weintraub, C.J., critically reviewed the history of assumption of risk in industrial accidents, and in the course of his opinion articulated the distinction between primary and secondary assumption of risk as follows:

> We here speak solely of the area in which injury or damage was neither intended nor expressly contracted to be non-actionable. In this area, assumption of risk has two distinct meanings. In one sense (sometimes called its "primary" sense), it is an alternative expression for the proposition that defendant was not negligent, i.e., either owed no duty or did not breach the duty owed. In its other sense (sometimes called "secondary"), assumption of risk is an affirmative defense to an established breach of duty. In its primary sense, it is accurate to say plaintiff assumed the risk whether or not he was "at fault," for the truth thereby expressed in alternate terminology is that defendant was not negligent. But in its secondary sense, i.e., as an affirmative defense to an established breach of defendant's duty, it is incorrect to say plaintiff assumed the risk whether or not he was at fault. . . .
>
> In applying assumption of risk in its secondary sense in areas other than that of master and servant, our cases have consistently recognized the ultimate question to be whether a reasonably prudent man would have moved in the face of a known risk, dealing with the issue as one of law or leaving it to the jury upon the same standard which controls the handling of the issue of contributory negligence. . . .

One consequence of this definition is that the cases from Chapter 1, *supra* at 47, Note 3, that hold that the plaintiff must show intentional or reckless behavior in the defendant to recover from the defendant are all cases of assumption of risk in its primary sense, as there is no ordinary duty of care. *Meistrich* differs from these cases because the action is brought not against a competitor or participant but the owner or occupier of established premises who generally owes a duty of care. In its secondary sense, assumption of risk is only an aspect of contributory negligence. Unlike the situation in *Lamson* or *Murphy*, the plaintiff in *Meistrich* knew that the defendant was in breach of its obligation to provide a safe skating surface before he fell. Why then is he not under an obligation to leave the ice? If he does, can he get his money back? Is *Murphy* a case of primary or secondary assumption of risk?

6. *Assumption of risk and abandonment of rights.* Many cases address assumption of risk in its secondary sense when the defendant has negligently or unlawfully created a dangerous condition which the plaintiff must endure in the exercise of her ordinary rights. In Marshall v. Ranne, 511 S.W.2d 255, 260 (Tex. 1974), the defendant's vicious boar bit the plaintiff while the plaintiff was walking from his house to his car. The plaintiff had often complained about the boar's vicious condition to the defendant. An expert marksman, he also had passed up several good opportunities to shoot the boar, not wanting to do such an "unneighborly thing." At trial the jury denied plaintiff's recovery, first because he had been contributorily negligent in not shooting the boar when he had the chance, and second because he voluntarily assumed the risk of harm. The supreme court, reversing the decision below, held that contributory negligence was not a defense in a case of strict liability. It then addressed the role of voluntary assumption of risk:

> We hold that there was no proof that plaintiff had a free and voluntary choice, because he did not have a free choice of alternatives. He had, instead, only a choice of evils, both of which were wrongfully imposed upon him by the defendant. He could remain a prisoner inside his own house or he could take the risk of reaching his car before defendant's hog attacked him. Plaintiff could have remained inside his house, but in doing so, he would have surrendered his legal right to proceed over his own property to his car so he could return to his home in Dallas. The latter alternative was forced upon him against his will and was a choice he was not legally required to accept. . . . The dilemma which defendant forced upon plaintiff was that of facing the danger or surrendering his rights with respect to his own real property, and that was not, as a matter of law the voluntary choice to which the law entitled him.

See RST §496E.

What is the appropriate measure of damages, given that the plaintiff may take insufficient care if full tort recovery is allowed? Professor Rose-Ackerman, Dikes, Dams, and Vicious Harms: Entitlement and Efficiency in Tort Law, 18 J. Legal Stud. 25, 26 (1989), proposes the following rule: "victims should be paid for the level of preventive activity that would be efficient *plus* the consequential damage that would have resulted if these precautions had been taken. The payment would be made to all victims *whether or not they actually have taken care.* Since the level of damages is independent of their behavior, victims would have an incentive to act efficiently." Should the rule apply even if there is only a 1 percent chance that a rabid animal will bite its owner's neighbor? Or if the precautions when taken only reduce, but do not eliminate, the chance of being attacked?

The problem of implicit coercion in secondary assumption of risk cases surfaced in ADM Partnership v. Martin, 702 A.2d 730 (Md. 1997), when the plaintiff Martin was injured when she fell on a walkway covered with snow and ice while making a delivery to the defendant's premises. The court held that the plaintiff had, as a matter of law, known, appreciated, and voluntarily confronted the risk in question even though she had claimed that she used the walkway "as a result of being coerced by the economic necessity of securing a service contract for her employer and for her continued employment." The court rejected that proposition as a matter of law when the plaintiff could produce no objective evidence that she had ever been threatened with a loss of her job. The court then quoted its earlier decision in Gibson v. Beaver, 226 A.2d 273, 276 (Md. 1967)

> The plaintiff takes a risk voluntarily . . . where the defendant has a right to face him with the dilemma of "take it or leave" — in other words, where [the] defendant is under no duty to make the conditions of their association any safer than they appear to be. In such a case it does not matter that the plaintiff is coerced to assume the risk by some force not emanating from defendant, such as poverty, dearth of living quarters, or a sense of moral responsibility.

Suppose she braved the snow because she was under an employer ultimatum, what then?

7. *Assumption of risk: the fireman's rule.* One context in which the defense of assumption of risk refuses to die involves the so-called fireman's rule, which covers police officers and other public officials charged with the maintenance of public order. When a public officer responds to a fire alarm or a request for police assistance brought about by the negligent or indeed criminal conduct of the defendant, recovery is barred for injuries thereby incurred. The fireman's rule is based squarely on the doctrine of assumption of risk: "one who has knowingly and voluntarily confronted a hazard cannot recover for injuries sustained thereby." Walters v. Sloan, 571 P.2d 609, 612 (Cal. 1979). The public policy reasons behind the principle were well set out by Weintraub, C.J., shortly after his opinion in *Meistrich*, in Krauth v. Geller, 157 A.2d 129, 130-131 (N.J. 1960):

> [I]t is the fireman's business to deal with that very hazard [the fire] and hence, perhaps by analogy to the contractor engaged as an expert to remedy dangerous situations, he cannot complain of negligence in the creation of

the very occasion for his engagement. In terms of duty, it may be said there is none owed the fireman to exercise care so as not to require the special services for which he is trained and paid. Probably most fires are attributable to negligence, and in the final analysis the policy decision is that it would be too burdensome to charge all who carelessly cause or fail to prevent fires with the injuries suffered by the expert retained with public funds to deal with those inevitable, although negligently created, occurrences. Hence, for that risk, the fireman should receive appropriate compensation from the public he serves both in pay which reflects the hazard and in workmen's compensation benefits for the consequences of the inherent risks of the calling.

Nonetheless, the firefighter's rule has been eroded by statute. In Guiffrida v. Citibank Corp., 790 N.E.2d 772, 779 (N.Y. 2003), the plaintiff firefighter suffered serious burns when his oxygen tank went empty while fighting a blaze in a doughnut shop at a building held in trust by Citibank. New York law held that a defendant who fails to make proper building inspections is liable in damages for harms "directly or indirectly" caused by a fire on the premises. Rosenblatt, J., held that the plaintiff was entitled to a jury trial: "DiCicco's [a fellow firefighter] statement that he did not observe a functioning fire extinguishing system, combined with the violation orders which, at the very least, show that the fire suppression system had been altered and required testing, raise a factual question as to whether defendant's violations resulted in a malfunctioning fire control system that directly or indirectly caused plaintiff's injuries by failing to prevent the fire or by exacerbating it."

For an analysis of the arguments behind the recent erosion of the fireman's rule, see Heidt, When Plaintiffs Are Premium Planners for Their Injuries: A Fresh Look at the Fireman's Rule, 82 Ind. L.J. 745 (2007).

Dalury v. S-K-I Ltd.
670 A.2d 795 (Vt. 1995)

JOHNSON, J: We reverse the trial court's grant of summary judgment for defendants S-K-I, Ltd. and Killington, Ltd. in a case involving an injury to a skier at a resort operated by defendants. We hold that the exculpatory agreements which defendants require skiers to sign, releasing defendants from all liability resulting from negligence, are void as contrary to public policy.

While skiing at Killington Ski Area, plaintiff Robert Dalury sustained serious injuries when he collided with a metal pole that formed part of the control maze for a ski lift line. Before the season started, Dalury had purchased a midweek season pass and signed a form releasing the ski area from liability. The relevant portion reads:

RELEASE FROM LIABILITY AND CONDITIONS OF USE

1. I accept and understand that Alpine Skiing is a hazardous sport with many dangers and risks and that injuries are a common and ordinary occurrence of the sport. As a condition of being permitted to use the ski area premises, I freely accept and voluntarily assume the risks of injury or property damage and release Killington Ltd., its employees and agents from any and all liability for personal injury or property damage resulting from negligence, conditions of the premises, operations of the ski area, actions or omissions of employees or agents of the ski area or from my participation in skiing at the area, accepting myself the full responsibility for any and all such damage or injury of any kind which may result.

Plaintiff also signed a photo identification card that contained this same language.

Dalury and his wife filed a complaint against defendants, alleging negligent design, construction, and replacement of the maze pole. Defendants moved for summary judgment, arguing that the release of liability barred the negligence action. The trial court, without specifically addressing plaintiffs' contention that the release was contrary to public policy, found that the language of the release clearly absolved defendants of liability for their own negligence. . . .

[W]e hold the agreement is unenforceable. . . .

I.

This is a case of first impression in Vermont. While we have recognized the existence of a public policy exception to the validity of exculpatory agreements, in most of our cases, enforceability has turned on whether the language of the agreement was sufficiently clear to reflect the parties' intent . . .

Even well-drafted exculpatory agreements, however, may be void because they violate public policy. . . .

The leading judicial formula for determining whether an exculpatory agreement violates public policy was set forth by Justice Tobriner of the California Supreme Court. Tunkl v. Regents of Univ. of Cal., 383 P.2d 441, 445-46, (Cal. 1963). An agreement is invalid if it exhibits some or all of the following characteristics:

> [1.] It concerns a business of a type generally thought suitable for public regulation. [2.] The party seeking exculpation is engaged in performing a service of great importance to the public, which is often a matter of practical necessity for some members of the public. [3.] The party holds itself out as willing to perform this service for any member of the public who seeks it, or at least for any member coming within certain established standards. [4.] As a result of the essential nature of the service, in the economic setting of the transaction, the party invoking exculpation possesses a decisive advantage of

bargaining strength against any member of the public who seeks [the party's] services. [5.] In exercising a superior bargaining power the party confronts the public with a standardized adhesion contract of exculpation, and makes no provision whereby a purchaser may pay additional reasonable fees and obtain protection against negligence. [6.] Finally, as a result of the transaction, the person or property of the purchaser is placed under the control of the seller, subject to the risk of carelessness by the seller or [the seller's] agents.

Applying these factors, the court concluded that a release from liability for future negligence imposed as a condition for admission to a charitable research hospital was invalid. Numerous courts have adopted and applied the *Tunkl* factors. . . .

Other courts have incorporated the *Tunkl* factors into their decisions. . . . In Jones [v. Dressel, 623 P.2d 370, 376 (Colo. 1981)], the court concluded, based on the *Tunkl* factors, that no duty to the public was involved in air service for a parachute jump, because that sort of service does not affect the public interest. Using a similar formula, the Wyoming Supreme Court concluded that a ski resort's sponsorship of an Ironman Decathlon competition did not invoke the public interest. Milligan v. Big Valley Corp., 754 P.2d 1063, 1066-67 (Wyo. 1988).

On the other hand, the Virginia Supreme Court recently concluded, in the context of a "Teflon Man Triathlon" competition, that a preinjury release from liability for negligence is void as against public policy because it is simply wrong to put one party to a contract at the mercy of the other's negligence. Hiett v. Lake Barcroft Community Ass'n, 418 S.E.2d 894, 897 (Va. 1992). . . .

Having reviewed these various formulations of the public policy exception . . . we recognize that no single formula will reach the relevant public policy issues in every factual context. . . .

II.

Defendants urge us to uphold the exculpatory agreement on the ground that ski resorts do not provide an essential public service. They argue that they owe no duty to plaintiff to permit him to use their private lands for skiing, and that the terms and conditions of entry ought to be left entirely within their control. Because skiing, like other recreational sports, is not a necessity of life, defendants contend that the sale of a lift ticket is a purely private matter, implicating no public interest. We disagree.

Whether or not defendants provide an essential public service does not resolve the public policy question in the recreational sports context. The defendants' area is a facility open to the public. They advertise and invite skiers and nonskiers of every level of skiing ability to their premises for the price of a ticket. At oral argument, defendants conceded that thousands of people buy lift tickets every day throughout the season. Thousands of people ride lifts, buy services, and ski the trails. Each ticket sale may be, for some purposes, a purely private transaction. But when a substantial number of such sales take place as a result of the seller's general invitation to the public to utilize the facilities and services in question, a legitimate public interest arises.

The major public policy implications are those underlying the law of premises liability. In Vermont, a business owner has a duty "of active care to make sure that its premises are in safe and suitable condition for its customers." . . . We have already held that a ski area owes its customers the same duty as any other business — to keep its premises reasonably safe.

The policy rationale is to place responsibility for maintenance of the land on those who own or control it, with the ultimate goal of keeping accidents to the minimum level possible. Defendants, not recreational skiers, have the expertise and opportunity to foresee and control hazards, and to guard against the negligence of their agents and employees. They alone can properly maintain and inspect their premises, and train their employees in risk management. They alone can insure against risks and effectively spread the cost of insurance among their thousands of customers. Skiers, on the other hand, are not in a position to discover and correct risks of harm, and they cannot insure against the ski area's negligence.

If defendants were permitted to obtain broad waivers of their liability, an important incentive for ski areas to manage risk would be removed, with the public bearing the cost of the resulting injuries. It is illogical, in these circumstances, to undermine the public policy underlying business invitee law and allow skiers to bear risks they have no ability or right to control. . . .

Defendants argue that the public policy of the state, as expressed in the "Acceptance of inherent risks" statute, 12 V.S.A. 1037[2], indicates a willingness on the part of the Legislature to limit ski area liability. Therefore, they contend that public policy favors the use of express releases such as the one signed by plaintiff. On the contrary, defendants' allocation of responsibility for skiers' injuries is at odds with the statute. The statute places responsibility for the "inherent risks" of any sport on the participant, insofar as such risks are obvious and necessary. A ski area's own negligence, however, is neither an inherent risk nor an obvious and necessary one in the sport of skiing. Thus, a skier's assumption of the inherent risks of skiing does not abrogate the ski area's duty "to warn of or correct dangers which in the exercise of reasonable prudence in the circumstances could have been foreseen and corrected."

Reversed and remanded.

2. "Notwithstanding the provisions of section 1036 of this title, a person who takes part in any sport accepts as a matter of law the dangers that inhere therein insofar as they are obvious and necessary." 12 V.S.A. §1037.

NOTES

1. *Assumption of risk by contract: other contexts.* The basic framework set out
in Tunkl v. Regents of University of California, 383 P.2d 441, 445-446
(Cal. 1963), has been frequently invoked by courts passing on the validity
of contractual waivers. Wagenblast v. Odessa School District No. 105-157-
166J, 758 P.2d 968 (Wash. 1988), invoked *Tunkl's* six criteria to strike
down an agreement whereby parents released the school district from all
liability in negligence related to their children's participation in inter-
scholastic athletics, preferring to examine liability on a case by case basis.
In contrast, in Zivich v. Mentor Soccer Club, Inc., 696 N.E.2d 201, 205
(Ohio 1998), the court upheld a similar exemption clause when plaintiff
was hurt while swinging from an unanchored soccer goal shortly after
winning an intrasquad contest. The court wanted to spare the huge
number of volunteer members in such organizations as the Little League
and the American Youth Soccer Organization "the risks and overwhelming
costs of litigation." Should different rules apply to schools and nonprofit
leagues? See generally Developments in the Law—Nonprofit Corporations, 105 Harv. L. Rev. 1578 (1992).

Tunkl received a frostier reception in Seigneur v. National Fitness Institute, 752 A.2d 631, 639 (Md. App. 2000), in which the plaintiff, who had
been injured while working with weights, sought to bypass an exculpation
clause that said she participated in the program "at her sole risk." The court
found that this clause "unambiguously excused" the defendants, and then
held it was valid as a matter of public policy, because furnishing gyms was
not "an activity of great public importance nor of a practical necessity." It
concluded that even though they were "a good idea . . . ultimately, they are
not essential to the state or its citizens. And any analogy to schools, hospitals, housing (public or private) and public utilities therefore fails." Why
not a per se rule of legality?

2. *Procedural obstacles to assumption of risk.* Even in those cases where a
waiver of liability is not contrary to public policy, courts scrutinize the
procedures to see if they are fairly obtained. In Obstetrics & Gynecologists
Ltd. v. Pepper, 693 P.2d 1259, 1260 (Nev. 1985), the plaintiff signed an
arbitration agreement under which both parties explicitly waived their
right to jury trial. The defendant clinic had a standard rule that it would
refuse service to all women who refused to sign that form. The plaintiff
signed that agreement when she went to the clinic for an oral contraceptive, but had no recollection of having done so or having its terms
explained to her. After she suffered a stroke that left her partially paralyzed, she sued the defendant for negligently prescribing the drug. The
district court denied defendant's motion to stay pending arbitration and to
direct arbitration, and its decision was affirmed on appeal, noting that the

defendant bore the burden of showing that a binding agreement had been formed:

> The district court could certainly have found that the arbitration agreement was an adhesion contract. An adhesion contract has been defined as a standardized contract form offered to consumers of goods and services essentially on a "take it or leave it" basis, without affording the consumer a realistic opportunity to bargain, and under such conditions that the consumer cannot obtain the desired product or service except by acquiescing to the form of the contract. . . . The arbitration agreement before us clearly falls into this category. It was prepared by appellant medical clinic and presented to respondent as a condition of treatment. Respondent had no opportunity to modify any of its terms; her choices were to sign the agreement as it stood or to forego treatment at the clinic.
>
> An adhesion contract need not be unenforceable if it falls within the reasonable expectations of the weaker or "adhering" party and is not unduly oppressive. However, courts will not enforce against an adhering party a provision limiting the duties or liabilities of the stronger party absent plain and clear notification of the terms and an understanding consent.
>
> . . . . Respondent stated [by affidavit] that she did not remember receiving any information regarding the terms of the arbitration agreement. Appellant's receptionist stated [by affidavit] that the general policy of the clinic was to inform the patient that any questions he or she might have would be answered. The contents of both affidavits are perfectly consistent with the conclusion that the agreement was never explained to respondent. On these facts the district court may well have found that respondent did not give an informed consent to the agreement and that no meeting of the minds occurred . . .

With evident uneasiness, courts have continued to refuse to enforce arbitration clauses in particular cases. In Sosa v. Paulos, 924 P.2d 357 (Utah 1996), the court first announced that arbitration agreements are "favored" in Utah, but refused to enforce a written arbitration agreement presented to the plaintiff "less than one hour prior to surgery, after Ms. Sosa was undressed and in her surgical clothing." The court refused to strike the agreement on grounds of "substantive unconscionability" because it found no evidence that the arbitration panel, which would consist solely of neutrally selected orthopedic surgeons, "will be biased in favor of malpractice defendants." But it found the agreement procedurally unconscionable because the short time allowed meant the plaintiff "felt 'rushed and hurried' to sign the documents and did not read them." Which form of unconscionability poses the greater threat to the widespread use of arbitration agreements?

3. Institutional arbitration. With *Pepper* contrast Madden v. Kaiser Foundation Hospitals, 552 P.2d 1178, 1185 (Cal. 1976), upholding an arbitration clause contained in a contract between a state employee and the defendant foundation. An appropriate state board negotiated the contract behalf of individual employees, which permitted the plaintiff to select her own health maintenance organization from a list of available groups, some of which offered the plaintiff the right to a jury trial. The defendant's plan required arbitration of all medical disputes on a take-it-or-leave-it basis. The court held the plaintiff was subject to the arbitration clause, even though she claimed to be unaware that it was part of the agreement.

> In the characteristic adhesion contract case, the stronger party drafts the contract, and the weaker has no opportunity, either personally or through an agent, to negotiate concerning its terms. The Kaiser plan, on the other hand, represents the product of negotiation between two parties, Kaiser and the board, possessing parity of bargaining strength. Although plaintiff did not engage in the personal negotiation of the contract's terms, she and other public employees benefitted from representation by a board, composed in part of persons elected by the affected employees, which exerted its bargaining strength to secure medical protection for employees on more favorable terms than any employee could individually obtain.

Should ordinary individuals not represented by third party group agents be deprived of the option of relinquishing their right to a jury trial?

Arbitration received a chillier reception in Engalla v. Permanente Medical Group, Inc., 938 P.2d 903, 909, 911, 912-913 (Cal. 1997). Mosk, J., ordered a trial on whether to set Kaiser's medical malpractice arbitration plan aside on grounds of fraud. The plaintiff challenged both the impartiality and timeliness of the Kaiser plan. The agreement called for each side to name one arbitrator, with the two designated arbitrators naming a third, or neutral, arbitrator, but in fact, unbeknownst to plaintiff "in reality the selection is made by defense counsel after consultation with the Kaiser medical-legal department." Mosk, J., also noted that the appointment of a neutral arbitrator was a tedious process with delays in 99 percent of the cases. Fewer than 3 percent of the arbitrators were appointed within 180 days, with an average period until appointment of 863 days. He therefore remanded the case for further factual findings on whether Kaiser had engaged in fraudulent conduct that would justify setting aside the arbitration provision.

An interesting twist on the arbitration clauses is found in Woodside Homes of California, Inc. v. Superior Court, 132 Cal. Rptr. 2d 35, 45 (Cal. App. 2003), which sustained a provision in a home purchase contract that required the seller and buyer of the home to submit any lawsuit "relating to the condition, design or construction of any portion of the [purchased home]" to "judicial reference"—which requires the dispute to be submitted to a "referee," "a retired judge or attorney with substantial experience in real estate matters." The reference proceeding allowed for discovery, required a stenographic record, and called on the referee to make findings of fact and law, which are appealable through the court system. Hollenhorst, Acting P.J., held this system, which he distinguished from a conventional arbitration case, should nonetheless be governed by similar principles. He further held that this agreement was neither substantively nor procedurally unconscionable and then observed more generally:

> Why have provisions for arbitration or similar methods of dispute resolution outside the courtroom become so popular in contracts drawn up by the party who is overwhelmingly likely to be the defendant if a dispute arises? There are several possible reasons, some of which are perfectly neutral and operate evenhandedly; some may be stated more than one way, depending on one's philosophical bent. The "defendant in waiting" may believe that juries are unpredictable. It may believe that juries cannot be trusted with complicated cases, or that jurors may lose interest in a long case and return an ill-informed or arbitrary verdict. It may believe that juries are biased against "business." It may believe that a trained neutral trier of fact will make a fairer decision.

Do any of these rationales redound to the benefit of the plaintiff in the long run?

4. *Contracting out of medical malpractice liability generally.* Arbitration clauses represent only the tip of the iceberg in the larger dispute over whether the parties can contract out of the tort rules that now govern medical malpractice litigation. Professor Robinson puts the case for market freedom on all issues of liability forcefully:

> In terms of utilitarian efficiency, contractual arrangements allow parties to achieve the most efficient combination of efforts to manage risk in accordance with their respective comparative advantages and their respective risk preferences. The moral argument proceeds along similar lines but emphasizes the fact that contractual allocation promotes individual freedom of choice, constrained only by the need to accommodate the divergent interests of the contracting parties. To justify private ordering one need not suppose that it always yields "good" or "fair" results. It is enough that, in general, private parties are likely to achieve results that are at least as good and fair for themselves as would be achieved by paternalistic intervention.

Robinson, Rethinking the Allocation of Medical Malpractice Risks between Patients and Providers, 49 Law & Contemp. Probs. 172, 189 (1986). Robinson's article (as well as others by Danzon, Epstein, and Havighurst) provoked the following response from the English scholar P.S. Atiyah in Atiyah, Medical Malpractice and the Contract/Tort Boundary 49 Law & Contemp. Probs. 287, 296 (1986):

> The real market enthusiasts appear to envisage a situation in which a competitive market offers a range of benefit and risk packages suitable to the

individual desires, risk-averseness, and wallets of various patients. If all the bargaining is in practice to be done collectively (by employers and unions whose interests of course are not always identical with those of employees), however, the reality is that the rules which will govern the physician/patient relationship will not be tailored to the individual patient's needs at all. They will be fixed by third parties, just as much as the tort rules are. There may, it is true, be more choice available in the market, but this argument takes us back to our starting point about information, risk evaluation, and bargaining power. If the patient does not understand the differences in the packages offered to him, choice by itself means little, and the presumption of efficiency in outcome is rebutted.

See generally Symposium, Medical Malpractice: Can the Private Sector Find Relief?, 49 Law & Contemp. Probs. 1-348 (Spring, 1986). See also P. Danzon, Medical Malpractice: Theory, Evidence, and Public Policy 208-217 (1985), for a qualified endorsement of the contract solution, and P. Weiler, Medical Malpractice On Trial 113 (1991), for a "highly dubious [view] of the brave new world of no-liability," which Weiler thinks will emerge from any contractual regime. See also Arlen & MacLeod, Malpractice Liability for Physicians and Managed Care Organizations, 78 N.Y. U. L. Rev. 1929 (2003), arguing against the contract solution for being unable to regulate the myriad of physician actions that could in principle be subject to negligence liability.

SECTION E. COMPARATIVE NEGLIGENCE

1. At Common Law

Lombard Laws, King Luitprand
Law 136.VII. (A.D. 733)

It has likewise been made known to us that a certain man has a well in his courtyard and, according to custom, it has a prop and lift for raising the water. Another man who came along stood under that lift and, when yet another man came to draw water from the well and incautiously released the lift, the weight came down on the man who stood under it, and he was killed. The question then arose over who should pay composition for this death, and it has been referred to us. It seems right to us and to our judges that the man who was killed, since he was not an animal but had the power of reason like other men, should have noticed where he stood or what weight was above his head. Therefore, two-thirds of the amount of his composition shall be assessed to him [the dead man], and one-third of the amount at which he was valued according to law shall be paid as composition by the man who incautiously drew the water. He shall pay the composition to the children or to the near relatives who are the heirs of the dead man, and the case shall be ended without any feud or grievance since it was done unintentionally. Moreover, no blame should be placed on the man who owns the well because if we placed the blame on him, no one hereafter would permit other men to raise water from their wells, and since all men cannot have a well, those who are poor would die and those who are traveling through would also suffer need.

Beach, Contributory Negligence
12-13 (2d ed. 1892)

The reasons of the rule which denies relief to a plaintiff guilty of contributory negligence have been previously stated. The common law refuses to apportion damages which arise from negligence. This it does upon considerations of public convenience and public policy, and upon this principle, it is said, depends also the rule which makes the contributory negligence of a plaintiff a complete defense. For the same reason, when there is an action in tort, where injury results from the negligence of two or more persons, the sufferer has a full remedy against any one of them, and no contribution can be enforced between the tort feasors. The policy of the law in this respect is founded upon the inability of human tribunals to mete out exact justice. A perfect code would render each man responsible for the unmixed consequences of his own default; but the common law, in view of the impossibility of assigning all effects to their respective causes, refuses to interfere in those cases where negligence is the issue, at the instance of one whose hands are not free from the stain of contributory fault, and where accordingly the impossibility of apportioning the damage between the parties does not exist, the rule is held not to apply.

Prosser, Comparative Negligence
41 Cal. L. Rev. 1, 3-4 (1953)

There has been much speculation as to why the rule thus declared found such ready acceptance in later decisions, both in England and in the United States. The explanations given by the courts themselves never have carried much conviction. Most of the decisions have talked about "proximate cause," saying that the plaintiff's negligence is an intervening, insulating cause between the defendant's negligence and the injury. But this cannot be supported unless a meaning is assigned to proximate cause which is found nowhere else. If two automobiles collide and injure a bystander, the negligence of one driver is not held to be a superseding cause which relieves the other of liability; and there is no visible reason for any different conclusion when the action is by one driver against the other. It has been said that the defense has a penal basis, and is intended to punish the plaintiff for his own misconduct; or that the court will not aid one who is himself at fault, and he must come into court with clean hands. But this is no explanation of the many cases, particularly those of the last clear chance, in which a plaintiff clearly at fault is permitted to recover. It has been said that the rule is intended to discourage accidents, by denying recovery to those who fail to use proper care for their own safety; but the assumption that the speeding motorist is, or should be, meditating on the possible failure of a lawsuit for his possible injuries lacks all reality, and it is quite as reasonable to say that the rule promotes accidents by encouraging the negligent defendant. Probably the true explanation lies merely in the highly individualistic attitude of the common law of the early nineteenth century. The period of development of contributory negligence was that of the industrial revolution, and there is reason to think that the courts found in this defense, along with the concepts of duty and proximate cause, a convenient instrument of control over the jury, by which the liabilities of rapidly growing industry were curbed and kept within bounds.

Li v. Yellow Cab Co. of California
532 P.2d 1226 (Cal. 1975)

[The accident in question resulted from the negligence of both parties. The plaintiff had attempted to cross three lanes of oncoming traffic in order to enter a service station; the defendant's driver was traveling at an excessive speed when he ran a yellow light just before striking the plaintiff's car. The trial court held that the plaintiff was barred from recovery by her own contributory negligence.]

SULLIVAN, J. In this case we address the grave and recurrent question whether we should judicially declare no longer applicable in California courts the doctrine of contributory negligence, which bars all recovery when the plaintiff's negligent conduct has contributed as a legal cause in any degree to the harm suffered by him, and hold that it must give way to a system of comparative negligence, which assesses liability in direct proportion to fault. As we explain in detail infra, we conclude that we should. In the course of reaching our ultimate decision we conclude that: (1) The doctrine of comparative negligence is preferable to the "all-or-nothing" doctrine of contributory negligence from the point of view of logic, practical experience, and fundamental justice; (2) judicial action in this area is not precluded by the presence of section 1714 of the Civil Code, which has been said to "codify" the "all-or-nothing" rule and to render it immune from attack in the courts except on constitutional grounds; (3) given the possibility of judicial action, certain practical difficulties attendant upon the adoption of comparative negligence should not dissuade us from charting a new course — leaving the resolution of some of these problems to future judicial or legislative action; (4) the doctrine of comparative negligence should be applied in this state in its so-called "pure" form under which the assessment of liability in proportion to fault proceeds in spite of the fact that the plaintiff is equally at fault as or more at fault than the defendant and finally; (5) this new rule should be given a limited retrospective application.

I

[The court then notes the once dominant common law rule treated contributory negligence as an absolute defense subject to a limited last clear chance exception.]

It is unnecessary for us to catalogue the enormous amount of critical comment that has been directed over the years against the "all-or-nothing" approach of the doctrine of contributory negligence. The essence of that criticism has been constant and clear: the doctrine is inequitable in its operation because it fails to distribute responsibility in proportion to fault. Against this have been raised several arguments in justification, but none have proved even remotely adequate to the task [quoting Prosser's 1953 article]. The basic objection to the doctrine — grounded in the primal concept that in a system in which liability is based on fault, the extent of fault should govern the extent of liability — remains irresistible to reason and all intelligent notions of fairness.

Furthermore, practical experience with the application by juries of the doctrine of contributory negligence has added its weight to analyses of its inherent shortcomings: "Every trial lawyer is well aware that juries often do in fact allow recovery in cases of contributory negligence, and that the compromise in the jury room does result in some diminution of the damages because of the plaintiff's fault. But the process is at best a haphazard and most unsatisfactory one." (Prosser, Comparative Negligence.) . . . It is manifest that this state of affairs, viewed from the standpoint of the health and vitality of the legal process, can only detract from public confidence in the ability of law and legal institutions to assign liability on a just and consistent basis. . . .

It is in view of these theoretical and practical considerations that to this date 25 states, have abrogated the "all-or-nothing" rule of contributory negligence and have enacted in its place general apportionment *statutes* calculated in one manner or another to assess liability in proportion to fault. In 1973 these states were joined by Florida, which effected the same result by *judicial* decision. (Hoffman v. Jones (Fla. 1973) 280 So. 2d 431.) We are likewise persuaded that logic, practical experience, and fundamental justice counsel against the retention of the doctrine rendering contributory negligence a complete bar to recovery — and that it should be replaced in this state by a system under which liability for damage will be borne by those whose negligence caused it in direct proportion to their respective fault. . . . [6a]

II

It is urged that any change in the law of contributory negligence must be made by the Legislature, not by this court. Although the doctrine of contributory negligence is of judicial origin — its genesis being traditionally attributed to the opinion of Lord Ellenborough in Butterfield v. Forrester (K.B. 1809) 103 Eng. Rep. 926 — the enactment of section 1714 of the Civil Code in 1872 codified the doctrine as it stood at that date and, the argument continues, rendered it invulnerable to attack in the courts except on constitutional grounds.

[The court then exhaustively examined section 1714 of the California Civil Code, which provides that "Everyone is responsible, not only for the result of his willful acts, but also for an injury occasioned to another by his want of ordinary care or skill in the management of his property or person, except so far as the latter has, willfully or by want of ordinary care, brought the injury upon himself. The extent of liability in such cases is defined by the Title on Compensatory Relief." The court concluded that "it was not the intention of the Legislature in enacting section 1714 of the Civil Code, as well as other sections of that code declarative of the common law, to insulate the matters therein expressed from further judicial development; rather it was the intention of the Legislature to announce and formulate existing common law principles and definitions for purposes of orderly and concise presentation and with a distinct view toward continuing judicial evolution."]

III

We are thus brought to the second group of arguments which have been advanced by defendants and the amici curiae supporting their position. Generally speaking, such arguments expose considerations of a practical

---

6a. In employing the generic term "fault" throughout this opinion we follow a usage common to the literature on the subject of comparative negligence. In all cases, however, we intend the term to import nothing more than "negligence" in the accepted legal sense. [In the original advance sheets, the court stated a comparative negligence test that would allocate liability "in direct proportion to the extent of the parties' causal responsibility." 119 Cal. Rptr. 858 (1975), advance sheets only. Footnote 6a did not appear. — ED.]

nature which, it is urged, counsel against the adoption of a rule of comparative negligence in this state even if such adoption is possible by judicial means.

The most serious of these considerations are those attendant upon the administration of a rule of comparative negligence in cases involving multiple parties. One such problem may arise when all responsible parties are not brought before the court: it may be difficult for the jury to evaluate relative negligence in such circumstances, and to compound this difficulty; such an evaluation would not be res judicata in a subsequent suit against the absent wrongdoer. Problems of contribution and indemnity among joint tortfeasors lurk in the background.

A second and related major area of concern involves the administration of the actual process of fact-finding in a comparative negligence system. The assigning of a specific percentage factor to the amount of negligence attributable to a particular party, while in theory a matter of little difficulty, can become a matter of perplexity in the face of hard facts.

The temptation for the jury to resort to a quotient verdict in such circumstances can be great. These inherent difficulties are not, however, insurmountable. Guidelines might be provided the jury which will assist it in keeping focussed upon the true inquiry and the utilization of special verdicts or jury interrogatories can be of invaluable assistance in assuring that the jury has approached its sensitive and often complex task with proper standards and appropriate reverence.

The third area of concern, the status of the doctrines of last clear chance and assumption of risk, involves less the practical problems of administering a particular form of comparative negligence than it does a definition of the theoretical outline of the specific form to be adopted. Although several states which apply comparative negligence concepts retain the last clear chance doctrine, the better reasoned position seems to be that when true comparative negligence is adopted, the need for last clear chance as a palliative of the hardships of the "all-or-nothing" rule disappears and its retention results only in a windfall to the plaintiff in direct contravention of the principle of liability in proportion to fault. As for assumption of risk, we have recognized in this state that this defense overlaps that of contributory negligence to some extent and in fact is made up of at least two distinct defenses. "To simplify greatly, it has been observed . . . that in one kind of situation, to wit, where a plaintiff *unreasonably* undertakes to encounter a specific known risk imposed by a defendant's negligence, plaintiff's conduct, although he may encounter that risk in a prudent manner, is in reality a form of contributory negligence. . . . Other kinds of situations within the doctrine of assumption of risk are those, for example, where plaintiff is held to agree to relieve defendant of an obligation of reasonable conduct toward him. Such a situation would not involve contributory negligence but rather a reduction of defendant's duty of care." We think it clear that the adoption of a system of comparative negligence should entail the merger of the defense of assumption of risk into the general scheme of assessment of liability in proportion to fault in those particular cases in which the form of assumption of risk involved is no more than a variant of contributory negligence.

Finally there is the problem of the treatment of willful misconduct under a system of comparative negligence. In jurisdictions following the "all-or-nothing" rule, contributory negligence is no defense to an action based upon a claim of willful misconduct (see Rest. 2d Torts, §503), and this is the present rule in California.[19] As Dean Prosser has observed, "[this] is in reality a rule of comparative fault which is being applied, and the court is refusing to set up the lesser fault against the greater." (Prosser, Torts, *supra* 426, at §65.) The thought is that the difference between willful and wanton misconduct and ordinary negligence is one of kind rather than degree in that the former involves conduct of an entirely different order,[20] and under this conception it might well be urged that comparative negligence concepts should have no application when one of the parties has been guilty of willful and wanton misconduct. It has been persuasively argued, however, that the loss of deterrent effect that would occur upon application of comparative fault concepts to willful and wanton misconduct as well as ordinary negligence would be slight, and that a comprehensive system of comparative negligence should allow for the apportionment of damages in all cases involving misconduct which falls short of being intentional. The law of punitive damages remains a separate consideration. . . .

The existence of the foregoing areas of difficulty and uncertainty has not diminished our conviction that the time for a revision of the means for dealing with contributory fault in this state is long past due and that it lies within the province of this court to initiate the needed change by our decision in this case. Two of the indicated areas (i.e., multiple parties and willful misconduct) are not involved in the case before us, and we consider it neither necessary nor wise to address ourselves to specific problems of this nature which might be expected to arise. . . .

Our decision in this case is to be viewed as a first step in what we deem to be a proper and just direction, not as a compendium containing the

---

19. BAJI No. 3.52 (1971 re-revision) currently provides: "Contributory negligence of a plaintiff is not a bar to his recovery for an injury caused by the wilful or wanton misconduct of a defendant. (¶) Wilful or wanton misconduct is intentional wrongful conduct, done either with knowledge, express or implied, that serious injury to another will probably result, or with a wanton and reckless disregard of the possible results. An intent to injure is not a necessary element of wilful or wanton misconduct. (¶) To prove such misconduct it is not necessary to establish that defendant himself recognized his conduct as dangerous. It is sufficient if it be established that a reasonable man under the same or similar circumstances would be aware of the dangerous character of such conduct."

20. "Disallowing the contributory negligence defense in this context is different from last clear chance; the defense is denied not because defendant had the last opportunity to avoid the accident but rather because defendant's conduct was so culpable it was different in 'kind' from the plaintiff's. The basis is culpability rather than causation." (Schwartz, supra, §5.1, p. 100; fn. omitted.)

answers to all questions that may be expected to arise. Pending future judicial or legislative developments, we are content for the present to assume the position taken by the Florida court in this matter: "We feel the trial judges of this State are capable of applying [a] comparative negligence rule without our setting guidelines in anticipation of expected problems. The problems are more appropriately resolved at the trial level in a practical manner instead of a theoretical solution at the appellate level. The trial judges are granted broad discretion in adopting such procedures as may accomplish the objectives and purposes expressed in this opinion." (280 So. 2d at pp. 439-440.)

It remains to identify the precise form of comparative negligence which we now adopt for application in this state. Although there are many variants, only the two basic forms need be considered here. The first of these, the so-called "pure" form of comparative negligence, apportions liability in direct proportion to fault in all cases. This was the form adopted by the Supreme Court of Florida in Hoffman v. Jones, supra, and it applies by statute in Mississippi, Rhode Island, and Washington. Moreover it is the form favored by most scholars and commentators. The second basic form of comparative negligence, of which there are several variants, applies apportionment based on fault *up to the point* at which the plaintiff's negligence is equal to or greater than that of the defendant—when that point is reached, plaintiff is barred from recovery. Nineteen states have adopted this form or one of its variants by statute. The principal argument advanced in its favor is moral in nature: that it is not morally right to permit one more at fault in an accident to recover from one less at fault. Other arguments assert the probability of increased insurance, administrative, and judicial costs if a "pure" rather than a "50 percent" system is adopted, but this has been seriously questioned.

We have concluded that the "pure" form of comparative negligence is that which should be adopted in this state. In our view the "50 percent" system simply shifts the lottery aspect of the contributory negligence rule to a different ground. As Dean Prosser has noted, under such a system "[i]t is obvious that a slight difference in the proportionate fault may permit a recovery and there has been much justified criticism of a rule under which a plaintiff who is charged with 49 percent of the total negligence recovers 51 percent of his damages, while one who is charged with 50 percent recovers nothing at all."[22] (Prosser, Comparative Negligence) In effect "such a rule distorts the very principle it recognizes, i.e., that persons are responsible for their acts to the extent their

---

22. This problem is compounded when the injurious result is produced by the combined negligence of several parties. For example in a three-car collision a plaintiff whose negligence amounts to one-third or more recovers nothing; in a four-car collision the plaintiff is barred if his negligence is only one-quarter of the total. [The original 1931 Wisconsin comparative negligence statute contained the words "not as great as" instead of the current words "not greater than."—ED.]

fault contributes to an injurious result. The partial rule simply lowers, but does not eliminate, the bar of contributory negligence."

We also consider significant the experience of the State of Wisconsin, which until recently was considered the leading exponent of the "50 percent" system. There that system led to numerous appeals on the narrow but crucial issue whether plaintiff's negligence was equal to defendant's. Numerous reversals have resulted on this point, leading to the development of arcane classifications of negligence according to quality and category. (See cases cited in Vincent v. Pabst Brewing Co., 177 N.W.2d 513, at 513 [(Wis. 1970)] (dissenting opn.).) . . .

[The court then held its rule should apply in all cases in which the trial had not yet begun. It noted that there was some unfairness in denying the benefits of the comparative negligence rule to other plaintiffs who had sought to raise the issue on appeal while granting them to Nga Li, but justified its result for creating a good incentive in future cases for parties to "raise issues involving renovation of unsound or outmoded legal doctrines." The judgment was reversed. Mosk, J., concurring and dissenting, took exception to that portion of the opinion that held the rule of comparative negligence should apply to all cases in which the trial had not yet begun. Clark, J., (with McComb, J., concurring) dissented on the ground that section 1714 of the Civil Code codified the common law rule on contributory negligence, which could only be displaced by other legislation.]

NOTES

1. Historical origins of the comparative negligence system. Although comparative negligence has met with widespread favor only in recent years, Georgia enacted a comparative negligence statute as early as 1855; Mississippi adopted pure comparative negligence in 1919; and Wisconsin introduced comparative negligence by legislation in 1931. From its humble roots, comparative negligence has become a veritable giant. As recently as 1968, only five states had adopted some form of comparative negligence by statute. Then the dam broke. Between 1969 and 1973, 19 additional states adopted some form of comparative negligence by legislation so that by the time Hoffman v. Jones and *Li* were decided, the common law rule had been abandoned in about half the states. Today virtually all states have some form of comparative negligence, usually by legislation and occasionally by judicial decision. Indeed, the only jurisdictions not to have some form of the doctrine are Alabama, District of Columbia, Maryland, North Carolina, and Virginia. For detailed tallies see V. Schwartz, Comparative Negligence, Appendix A, 513-518 (4th ed.

2002); H. Woods and B. Deere, Comparative Fault, Appendix (3d ed. 1996 & Supp. 2002).

For a comment on *Li,* see Fleming, Foreword: Comparative Negligence At Last — by Judicial Choice, 64 Cal. L. Rev. 239 (1976).

2. Comparative negligence in admiralty. Traditionally, courts of admiralty apportioned damages under a rule of "divided damages," whereby an equal division of property damage was required whenever two ships were guilty of negligence, no matter what their relative degrees of fault. See The Schooner Catharine v. Dickinson, 58 U.S. 170 (1854). In United States v. Reliable Transfer Co., 421 U.S. 397, 405, 411 (1975), the plaintiff's tanker, the *Mary A. Whalen,* crashed into the rocks after her captain attempted dangerous turning maneuvers that failed in part because the Coast Guard had failed to maintain its breakwater lights. "The District Court found that the vessel's grounding was caused 25% by the failure of the Coast Guard to maintain the breakwater light and 75% by the fault of the *Whalen,*" but owing to the admiralty rules divided damages equally. A unanimous Supreme Court jettisoned the rule of divided damages in favor of the pure form of comparative negligence less than two months before Li v. Yellow Cab. The old rule of divided damages survived "only when the parties are equally at fault or when it is not possible fairly to measure the comparative degree of their fault." Justice Stewart wrote:

> An equal division of damages is a reasonably satisfactory result only where each vessel's fault is approximately equal and each vessel thus assumes a share of the collision damages in proportion to its share of the blame, or where proportionate degrees of fault cannot be measured and determined on a rational basis. The rule produces palpably unfair results in every other case. For example, where one ship's fault in causing a collision is relatively slight and her damages small, and where the second ship is grossly negligent and suffers extensive damage, the first ship must still make a substantial payment to the second. "This result hardly commends itself to the sense of justice any more appealingly than does the common law doctrine of contributory negligence. . . . " G. Gilmore & C. Black, The Law of Admiralty 528 (2d ed. 1975). . . .

Reliable Transfer brought the admiralty rules in United States courts into conformity with those applied by all other leading maritime nations. See the Maritime Conventions Act, 1 & 2 Geo. V., c. 57 (1911), and the comparative negligence rules applicable in personal injury actions under the Jones Act, 46 U.S.C. app. §688 (2000).

3. "Impure" comparative negligence by judicial legislation. In Bradley v. Appalachian Power Co., 256 S.E.2d 879, 885 (W.Va. 1979), the West Virginia Supreme Court adopted comparative negligence by judicial action but declined to follow *Li* in its choice of the pure form.

We do not accept the major premise of pure comparative negligence that a party should recover his damages regardless of his fault, so long as his fault is not 100 percent. Without embarking on an extended philosophical discussion of the nature and purpose of our legal system, we do state that in the field of tort law we are not willing to abandon the concept that where a party substantially contributes to his own damages, he should not be permitted to recover for any part of them. We do recognize that the present rule that prohibits recovery to the plaintiff if he is at fault in the slightest degree is manifestly unfair, and in effect rewards the substantially negligent defendant by permitting him to escape any responsibility for his negligence.

Our present judicial rule of contributory negligence is therefore modified to provide that a party is not barred from recovering damages in a tort action so long as his negligence or fault does not equal or exceed the combined negligence or fault of the other parties involved in the accident.

Does the *Bradley* rule encourage the plaintiff to join as many parties to the suit as possible? What should be done if, for example, a landlord and tenant are joined in a suit arising out of a single incident on common property?

4. *Economic analysis of comparative negligence.* The efficiency analysis of comparative negligence has been, on balance, somewhat more tentative than the fairness arguments made in its favor. Once again, the issue is how to coordinate the behavior of two parties, each of whom will vary the level of care provided as a function of the level of care provided by the other side. At one level, therefore, the familiar paradox of the Hand formula reasserts itself in this context. Where the parties and the court both possess full information, neither will behave negligently. Suppose that the expected loss is $100 and the optimal levels of joint precautions are $30 by the plaintiff and $40 by the defendant. If comparative negligence were to leave the plaintiff with 20 percent of the expected loss, it might appear that she might not take the precaution because her cost of avoidance ($30) is greater than her residual loss ($20). Nonetheless, this analysis is incomplete because it ignores the response of the defendant who will prefer to spend $40 on precaution in order to avoid $80 worth of loss. Yet once that step is taken, the plaintiff will now prefer to take precautions as well, for the $30 spent could avoid a $100 loss that might otherwise occur.

This stylized account is highly sensitive to its initial assumptions. If the defendant thought he would have to spend $50 in order to avoid a 40 percent chance of a $100 loss, he would not take precautions and thus would be held negligent. But if the plaintiff knew or had reason to believe that the defendant would make this blunder, then her informed decision would not be to take care because the $30 precaution is now more expensive than the $20 in unrecoverable losses.

See R. Posner, Economic Analysis of Law 172-177 (6th ed. 2003). See also S. Shavell, An Economic Analysis of Accident Law 15-16 (1987); Haddock and Curran, An Economic Theory of Comparative Negligence, 14 J. Legal Stud. 49 (1985); Cooter and Ulen, An Economic Case for Comparative Negligence, 61 N.Y.U. L. Rev. 1067 (1986).

The analysis, however, is still more rarified because neither party knows whether both parties will be at fault if an accident occurs when they are deciding on acting. Both also face the possibility of injuring only themselves, or being involved in accidents in which only one party is negligent. Nor do the parties have any reliable information on the relation between the dollar cost of precautions and expected damages when making their initial decisions. Worse still, virtually no one knows what legal regime applies in any state. (The differential incentive effects of the various rules are virtually impossible to plot out, in light of practical concerns, such as (a) the risk that the defendant will be insolvent, (b) the possibility of jury error, (c) the payment of contingent fees and other expenses of suit, (d) the lower standard for contributory negligence, and (e) the internal difficulties of the Hand formula.) See generally Schwartz, Contributory and Comparative Negligence: A Reappraisal, 87 Yale L.J. 697 (1978).

How would the analysis be altered under the old admiralty rule of even division? Under the 50 percent negligence threshold, as in Wisconsin and West Virginia?

5. *Doctrinal complications — revisited.* The rise of comparative negligence has forced courts to revisit many of the legal issues that arose when contributory negligence and assumption of risks were absolute defenses. What follows is a sampler of reactions to those problems.

a. Last clear chance. An overwhelming majority of cases have followed *Li*'s lead in jettisoning the separate last clear chance doctrine. In Spahn v. Town of Port Royal, 499 S.E.2d 205, 208 (S.C. 1998), the South Carolina Supreme Court, an early holdout, joined the parade, finding that the critical "authorities are persuasive that the rationalization for last clear chance as a matter of proximate cause is simply unnecessary where the jury may compare the parties' negligence." See generally Calabresi and Cooper, New Directions in Tort Law, 30 Val. U. L. Rev. 859, 872 (1996) ("The doctrine of last clear chance, which ameliorated the harshness of the all-or-nothing contributory negligence rule, typically disappears under comparative negligence."). In apportioning damages, should the jury be instructed to attach greater weight to defendant's conduct when he has had the last clear chance?

b. Assumption of risk. The traditional distinction, endorsed in *Li*, between primary and secondary assumption of risk has held fast. In Knight v. Jewett, 834 P.2d 696 (Cal. 1992), the plaintiff broke her little finger in a casual coed game of touch football, after she had cautioned the defendant "not to play so rough," and threatened to quit the game. On the next play the defendant leaped to intercept a pass; he touched the ball, came down on plaintiff's back, and fell on plaintiff's hand breaking her little finger. The trial judge granted defendant's motion for summary judgment on the ground that "reasonable implied assumption of risk" continues to operate after *Li*. In upholding that ruling, George, J., treated this case as one of primary assumption of risk because the defendant owed the plaintiff only a duty to avoid reckless misbehavior, but was at most guilty of ordinary negligence, effectively cutting out plaintiff's cause of action.

Kennard, J., dissented on the ground that the categorical rule should not apply. In her view, it is important to determine assumption of risk on an individual basis. "To establish the defense a defendant must prove that the plaintiff voluntarily accepted a risk with knowledge and appreciation of that risk." One possible way to reconcile the two decisions is to hold that the recklessness rule constitutes the basic default position, but can be displaced if a defendant agreed to observe some higher standard of care in the individual case. Could that displacement of the basic norm be made here?

c. Strict liability and sudden emergencies. In Bohan v. Rizzo, 679 A.2d 597 (N.H. 1996), the plaintiff suffered serious injuries when he fell off a bicycle after being threatened by the defendant's dog, for which he claimed damages under a New Hampshire statute that held dog owners strictly liable. N.H. RSA 466:19. The New Hampshire comparative negligence statute, RSA 507:7-d applied to "any action . . . to recover damages in tort for death, personal injury or property damage, if such [contributory] fault was not greater than the fault of the defendant." The court applied this statute to plaintiff's strict liability action with this qualification.

> Accordingly, we hold that RSA 507:7-d applies to cases brought under RSA 466:19. We interpret "comparative fault" slightly differently, however, in the context of a strict liability case than in a negligence case. Prior to the enactment of RSA 507:7-d, we noted that, by definition, strict liability and "comparative negligence" are incompatible concepts, because strict liability imposes liability on defendants without regard to their fault. We avoid construing statutes in a manner that would produce such "seemingly illogical results." Instead, courts should look to "comparative causation" in evaluating damages in strict liability cases.

The court then held that the failure to allow the comparative fault defense was harmless error:

> The record below, however, is devoid of evidence that the plaintiff knowingly put himself into a dangerous situation or provoked the dog, thereby creating or exacerbating his risk of harm. On the contrary, the defendants merely allege that the plaintiff did not act properly in *reacting* to the attack by the defendants' dog, *i.e.*, that he did not respond appropriately to the surprise situation in which he found himself and for which he cannot be held responsible. There is no evidence tending to show that the plaintiff had time to think about what alternative evasive action he might take, such as might rise to the level of "plaintiff's misconduct."

d. Intentional torts. In Morgan v. Johnson, 976 P.2d 619 (Wash. 1999), the plaintiff and defendant, never married, had had a child some years before and resumed a stormy and complex relationship after their daughter, who had lived with her mother, became curious about her biological father. One evening, both plaintiff and defendant left a bar together while drunk. It appeared that the defendant had threatened plaintiff with a knife, dragged her to the car, and beat her with the interior rearview mirror. The court rejected the defendant's argument that the plaintiff's intoxication should be a defense to an intentional tort, noting that the term "fault" under Washington RCW 4.22.015 covered all acts or omissions that were negligent or reckless, or which were the subject of a strict liability or product liability claim. "The statute does not mention intentional torts. Our prior cases interpreting the statute confirm this omission was intentional. . . . The definition is intended to encompass all degrees of fault in tort actions short of intentionally caused harm."

In Blazovic v. Andrich, 590 A.2d 222, 231 (N.J. 1991), a case arising out of a barroom brawl, the court deviated from the majority view, stating:

> [W]e reject the concept that intentional conduct is "different in kind" from both negligence and wanton and willful conduct, and consequently cannot be compared with them. Instead, we view intentional wrongdoing as "different in degree" from either negligence or wanton and willful conduct. To act intentionally involves knowingly or purposefully engaging in conduct "substantially certain" to result in injury to another. In contrast, wanton and willful conduct poses a highly unreasonable risk of harm likely to result in injury. Neither that difference nor the divergence between intentional conduct and negligence precludes comparison by a jury. The different levels of culpability inherent in each type of conduct will merely be reflected in the jury's apportionment of fault. By viewing the various types of tortious conduct in that way, we adhere most closely to the guiding principle of comparative fault — to distribute the loss in proportion to the respective faults of the parties causing that loss.

The court then reduced plaintiff's recovery against the owner of a bar to reflect the intentional wrongs of its patrons who had previously settled with the plaintiff.

e. Violation of safety act. In Hardy v. Monsanto Enviro-Chem Systems, Inc., 323 N.W.2d 270, 273, 274 (Mich. 1982), the court relied on the advent of Michigan's comparative negligence scheme to reject its earlier view, in Funk v. General Motors Corp., 220 N.W.2d 641 (Mich. 1974), that refused to treat the plaintiff's violation of a safety act as a form of contributory negligence. *Hardy* held:

> Since the defense of comparative negligence serves not to undermine but to enhance safety in the workplace, we are of the view that comparative neg-

ligence is available in those cases where *Funk* . . . formerly prohibited the application of the contributory negligence defense. . . .

[A]t some point a worker must be charged with *some* responsibility for his own safety-related behavior. If a worker continues to work under extremely unsafe conditions when a reasonable worker under all the facts and circumstances would "take a walk," the trier of fact might appropriately reduce the plaintiff's recovery under comparative negligence. Comparative negligence enhances the goal of safety in the workplace under these conditions since it gives the worker some financial incentive to act in a reasonable and prudent fashion.

With *Hardy* contrast Roy Crook & Sons, Inc. v. Allen, 778 F.2d 1037 (5th Cir. 1985), in which the court refused to reduce the recovery in a wrongful death case under FELA and the Jones Act by the wrongful conduct of the decedent when the decedent was in violation of a safety statute passed for his protection. The decision rested on the explicit language of FELA, which contained both a comparative negligence provision and an exception for safety statutes, *infra* at 398.

f. Seat belt defense. In Amend v. Bell, 570 P.2d 138 (Wash. 1977), the Washington Supreme Court held that Derheim v. Fiorito, *supra* at page 346, rejecting the seat belt defense, remained good law even under the state's pure comparative negligence rule. In the absence of a statutory requirement, the court did not want to enmesh itself in "a veritable battle of experts" over the nature and effects of the seat belt defense. That result was codified by statute, *supra* at 346.

The integration of the seat belt defense with comparative negligence was addressed in Iowa Code §321.449, which allowed for a reduction "by an amount not to exceed five percent of the damages awarded after any reductions for comparative fault."

g. Imputed negligence. In LaBier v. Pelletier, 665 A.2d 1013 (Me. 1995), a four-year-old child was struck by a car while his mother talked to a neighbor. The trial court instructed the jury to return a verdict for the plaintiffs only if the combined causative negligence of the child and his mother was less than that of the defendant. The Maine Supreme Court, finding these instructions erroneous, set aside the jury's verdict in favor of the defendant, and remanded for a new trial. The court adopted the Restatement (Second) of Torts §488, which provides that "[a] child who suffers physical harm is not barred from recovery by the negligence of his parent, either in the parent's custody of the child or otherwise."

Other states have rejected imputed parental (and spousal) negligence by statute. Wash. Rev. Code §4.22.020 (2007) provides:

The contributory fault of one spouse shall not be imputed to the other spouse or the minor child of the spouse to diminish recovery in an action by the other spouse or the minor child of the spouse, or his or her legal representative, to recover damages caused by fault resulting in death or in injury to the person or property, whether separate or community, of the spouse. In an action brought for wrongful death or loss of consortium, the contributory fault of the decedent or injured person shall be imputed to the claimant in that action.

h. Limited capacity. In Maunz v. Perales, 76 P.3d 1027, 1032 (Kan. 2003), the court held that comparative negligence could be a defense in a medical malpractice case involving the suicide of a patient in a noncustodial setting, upholding a verdict that allocated 79 percent of the fault to the decedent, and 21 percent to the defendant psychiatrist.

> First, our state legislature has statutorily established a policy of comparing the negligence of all persons involved in a civil wrong, in one trial, and awarding damages in tort based on comparative fault. In adopting comparative negligence our legislature, like others, has made it clear that people generally have a duty to exercise ordinary care for their own safety. In view of our legislature's clear determination, this court . . . should resist granting a judicial exemption from our legislature's mandate.
>
> Second, the cases cited by plaintiffs are of dubious value because all but one involve a patient injured while in the physical custody of the defendant medical care provider. These cases are in consensus that where a known, actively suicidal patient is hospitalized, the hospital and health care providers assume the patient's duty of self-care.

2. By Legislation

As the decision of the California Supreme Court in Li v. Yellow Cab points out, there has been a massive legislative move towards comparative negligence since 1970. A representative sample of the possible forms of comparative negligence legislation is given below. For a full collection of the statutes see V. Schwartz, Comparative Negligence, Appendix B (4th ed. 2002). H. Woods and B. Deere, Comparative Fault, Appendix (3d ed. 1996 & Supp. 2002). A sampler follows.

Federal Employers' Liability Act
35 Stat. 66 (1908), 45 U.S.C. §53 (2000)

§53. That in all actions hereafter brought against any such common carrier or railroad under or by virtue of any of the provisions of this Act to recover damages for personal injuries to an employee, or where such injuries have resulted in his death, the fact that the employee may have been guilty of contributory negligence shall not bar a recovery, but the damages shall be diminished by the jury in proportion to the amount of negligence attributable to such employee: *Provided,* that no such employee who may be injured or killed shall be held to have been guilty of contributory negligence in any case where the violation by such common carrier of any statute enacted for the safety of employees contributed to the injury or death of such employee.

New York
N.Y. Civil Practice Law and Rules §§1411-1412 (McKinney 1997)

§1411. In any action to recover damages for personal injury, injury to property, or wrongful death, the culpable conduct attributable to the claimant or to the decedent, including contributory negligence or assumption of risk, shall not bar recovery, but the amount of damages otherwise recoverable shall be diminished in the proportion which the culpable conduct attributable to the claimant or decedent bears to the culpable conduct which caused the damages.

§1412. Culpable conduct claimed in diminution of damages, in accordance with section fourteen hundred eleven, shall be an affirmative defense to be pleaded and proved by the party asserting the defense.

Pennsylvania
42 Pa. Cons. Stat. Ann. §7102 (Purdon 1998)

(a) General rule. In all actions brought to recover damages for negligence resulting in death or injury to person or property, the fact that the plaintiff may have been guilty of contributory negligence shall not bar a recovery by the plaintiff or his legal representative where such negligence was not greater than the causal negligence of the defendant or defendants against whom recovery is sought, but any damages sustained by the plaintiff shall be diminished in proportion to the amount of negligence attributed to the plaintiff.

(b) Recovery against joint defendant; contribution. Where recovery is allowed against more than one defendant, each defendant shall be liable for that proportion of the total dollar amount awarded as damages in the ratio of the amount of his causal negligence to the amount of causal negligence attributed to all defendants against whom recovery is allowed. The plaintiff may recover the full amount of the allowed recovery from any defendant against whom the plaintiff is not barred from recovery. Any defendant who is so compelled to pay more than his percentage share may seek contribution.

(c) Downhill skiing.

(1) The General Assembly finds that the sport of downhill skiing is practiced by a large number of citizens of this Commonwealth and also

attracts to this Commonwealth large numbers of nonresidents significantly contributing to the economy of this Commonwealth. It is recognized that as in some other sports, there are inherent risks in the sport of downhill skiing.

(2) The doctrine of voluntary assumption of risk as it applies to downhill skiing injuries and damages is not modified by subsections (a) and (b).

Wisconsin
Wis. Stat. Ann. §895.045 (West 1997)

§895.045. Contributory negligence shall not bar recovery in an action by any person or his legal representative to recover damages for negligence resulting in death or in injury to person or property, if that negligence was not greater than the negligence of the person against whom recovery is sought, but any damages allowed shall be diminished in the proportion to the amount of negligence attributable to the person recovering.*

Restatement (Third) of Torts — Apportionment of Liability
(2007)

§7. EFFECT OF PLAINTIFF'S NEGLIGENCE WHEN PLAINTIFF SUFFERS
AN INDIVISIBLE INJURY

Plaintiff's negligence (or the negligence of another person for whose negligence the plaintiff is responsible) that is a legal cause of an indivisible injury to the plaintiff reduces the plaintiff's recovery in proportion to the share of responsibility the factfinder assigns to the plaintiff (or other person for whose negligence the plaintiff is responsible).

NOTES

1. Computational exercises. In examining the respective merits of the principal comparative negligence systems, see how they apply to the following hypothetical seven situations assuming that the negligence of each of the parties contributed causally to the total damage sustained. Does a comparison of the particular numerical results suggest any reason to prefer one system over another?

---

* The original 1931 Wisconsin comparative negligence statute contained the words "not as great as" instead of the current words "not greater than." — ED.

    I. *A*, who is 10 percent negligent, suffers $10,000 damages; *B*, who is 90 percent negligent, suffers no damage.

   II. *A*, who is 60 percent negligent, suffers $10,000 damages; *B*, who is 40 percent negligent, suffers no damage.

  III. *A*, who is 30 percent negligent, suffers $2,000 damages; *B*, who is 70 percent negligent, suffers $8,000 damages.

  IV. *A*, who is approximately 50 percent negligent, suffers $2,000 damages; *B*, who is approximately 50 percent negligent, suffers $8,000 damages.

   V. *A* and *B* are equally negligent; *A* suffers $10,000 damages, while *B* suffers no damage.

For further complications, see Chapter 5, *infra* at 447, Note 3.

2. Comparative negligence and the control of juries. Special verdicts play an important role in administering a comparative negligence system given that the plaintiff's final damage award is dependent upon both the extent of her total damages and her degree of negligence. A verdict that states only a dollar figure for the plaintiff's award becomes difficult to interpret after trial. An award of $60,000 to a plaintiff who has suffered $150,000 damages could be attacked as inadequate if a finding of contributory negligence totally bars the plaintiff's recovery since the jury has no valid reason for awarding only partial compensation. Under pure comparative negligence, however, that verdict is consistent with a finding that the plaintiff was 60 percent negligent. General verdicts conceal a jury's thought processes from both the trial judge and the appellate court. Special verdicts promise greater control.

Should courts require special verdicts on both the degree of negligence of each party and on the total amount of the plaintiff's? Or should special verdicts be ordered only at the request of either party or otherwise be left to the discretion of the court? Note that an Idaho statute allows any party to request the court to "direct the jury to find separate special verdicts determining the amount of damages and the percentage of negligence or comparative responsibility attributable to each party," after which the court makes the appropriate reduction in damages for the successful plaintiff. Idaho Code §6-802 (2007). The Idaho statute only allows recovery when the plaintiff's negligence "was not as great as the negligence, gross negligence or comparative responsibility of the person against whom recovery is sought." Idaho Code §6-801 (2007). Is there a greater need for the special verdict here or under pure comparative negligence?

3. Insurance complications. One collateral complication under comparative negligence concerns the amount of damages that can be recovered when, as so often happens in routine collision cases, each party is a tortfeasor as well as an accident victim. When contributory negligence was an absolute bar, it was difficult, if not impossible, for both parties to obtain judgment because if both were at fault typically neither could recover. Accident cases, therefore, resulted in a single judgment against one defendant that was then discharged by the insurance carrier up to its policy limits. Today, comparative negligence makes it possible for each party to recover from the other. Thus, assume that *A* has $100,000 in damages and was 25 percent responsible for her loss, while *B* has $200,000 in damages and was 75 percent responsible for his loss. If *A* alone were injured, she should recover $75,000 in damages from *B*. Likewise, if *B* alone were injured, he should be able to recover $50,000 in damages from *A*. In Jess v. Herrmann, 604 P.2d 208, 212 (Cal. 1979), the question before the California Supreme Court was whether, as the statute seemed to require, the two damage awards should be set off against each other, so that the insurer of *B* pays *A* $25,000, or whether, in the alternative, *A*'s insurer should pay *B* $50,000 *and* *B*'s insurer should pay *A* $75,000.

The court held that the statutory set-off was available only when the parties in question were not covered by insurance. In its view, the insurance function would not be well served if the application of the mandatory set-off rule were allowed to produce "the anomalous situation in which a liability insurer's responsibility under its policy depends as much on the extent of injury suffered by its own insured as on the amount of damages sustained by the person its insured has negligently injured." The dissent argued that the court misconstrued the applicable statutory language, and that it did not explain the way in which the rule was to operate in situations in which either or both parties had limited insurance coverage.

5

MULTIPLE DEFENDANTS: JOINT, SEVERAL, AND VICARIOUS LIABILITY

SECTION A. INTRODUCTION

One of the most salient features of modern tort law is the increased frequency of lawsuits in which the plaintiff seeks recovery from multiple defendants. The expansion of tort liability, for example, allows suits for medical injuries to be brought simultaneously against all the physicians who provided professional services, against the hospital and its staff, and against the various suppliers of the equipment and medicines used during the course of treatment. A similar trend allows an injured party to sue not only the other driver in an automobile collision case, but also the car's manufacturer or dealer, and the public and private parties responsible for designing or running the traffic system. Toxic torts litigation often allows injured parties literally to join as defendants hundreds of firms whose release of small quantities of hazardous materials contributes to some substantial injury.

This chapter groups together two problems raised in multiple party litigation. The first section discusses joint and several liability among various codefendants. At the outset a bit of clarification is needed to understand these three separate relationships. Joint liability refers to the situation where each of several obligors — any person who bears an obligation — can be responsible for the entire loss if the others are unable to pay. But a determination of joint liability says nothing about the relationship among the obligors once the obligee has been paid. Several liability refers to a situation where each person has an obligation parallel to that of the others. Unlike the rule for joint liability, the share of any final judgment against one party is not increased by the default of another. Third, joint-and-several liability refers to any situation where the obligors are joint to the obligee, but bear several liability amongst themselves, at least if all are available to pay. In many ways, the apportionment of liability between codefendants picks up on the apportionment questions between a single plaintiff and defendant under the comparative negligence regimes discussed in the last chapter.

The second section deals with vicarious liability, which examines the principles that determine the liability of employers for the wrongs of their servants and their independent contractors. The liability of one person — the employer — is said to be "vicarious" because he bears responsibility solely for what another party — the employee — has done. Vicarious liability cases do *not* involve two independent causal agents, each responsible for the harm either in whole or in part. Matters can become quite complex when multiple wrongdoers working for multiple employers are all involved in the same incident, as typically happens today in environmental litigation.

SECTION B. JOINT AND SEVERAL LIABILITY

The first common law case to endorse joint and several liability was Merryweather v. Nixan, 101 Eng. Rep. 1337 (K.B. 1799). The plaintiff sued two defendants for conversion of machinery belonging to the plaintiff's mill. The headnote announced: "If A recover in tort against two defendants, and levy the whole damages on one, that one cannot recover a moiety against the other for his contribution; aliter, in assumpsit [contract]." *Merryweather* offers no explanation for why one defendant has an action against the other in contract cases at the same time there is a no-contribution rule in tort cases. The usual explanation for the difference is that the law of partnership and voluntary guarantees routinely provided for the pro rata division of responsibility among defendants, an objective easily achieved for monetizable obligations. Tort claims, however, did not offer that easy mode of division, so that the hostility toward apportionment in contributory negligence cases carried over to disputes between codefendants. The common rationale was that a wrongdoer could not bring suit against another party whose wrong was no greater than its own. The plaintiff in tort actions could decide which of two solvent defendants had to bear the entirety of the loss: If A recovered $100 from B, B in turn could not recover $50 from his codefendant, even if the two were equally to blame. As a matter of initial expectations, both defendants might be equally at risk. But in practice, the plaintiff could extract her full pound of flesh from either defendant to the exclusion of the other. In addition, if one defendant made only partial payment, the plaintiff could then sue the second defendant for the remainder. In *Merryweather*, this rule only applied to what appears to have been an intentional conversion. But in time the no-contribution rule was extended to ordinary negligence actions as well.

One occasional safety valve for the unhappy defendant saddled with full liability was to seek indemnity, as opposed to contribution, from his co-defendant for the full amount of the loss. Such indemnities have long been and are still allowed by contract, see Restatement (Third) of Torts: Apportionment of Liability [RTT:AL] §22. Should indemnification also be allowed in the absence of an agreement?

Union Stock Yards Co. of Omaha v. Chicago, Burlington, & Quincy R.R.
196 U.S. 217 (1905)

[The plaintiff terminal company was responsible for moving the switching cars for the defendant railroad in its yard. One of the cars under its control had a defective nut, which either the terminal company or the railroad could have discovered by reasonable inspection. Both parties were found negligent in failing to carry out that inspection, injuring the plaintiff's employee in consequence. Plaintiff then paid its employee damages, which it sought to recover from the defendant.]

MR. JUSTICE DAY. . . .

Coming to the very question to be determined here, the general principle of law is well settled that one of several wrongdoers cannot recover against another wrongdoer, although he may have been compelled to pay all the damages for the wrong done. In many instances, however, cases have been taken out of this general rule, and it has been held inoperative in order that the ultimate loss may be visited upon the principal wrongdoer, who is made to respond for all the damages, where one less culpable, although legally liable to third persons, may escape the payment of damages assessed against him by putting the ultimate loss upon the one principally responsible for the injury done. These cases have, perhaps, their principal illustration in that class wherein municipalities have been held responsible for injuries to persons lawfully using the streets in a city, because of defects in the streets or sidewalks caused by the negligence or active fault of a property owner. In such cases, where the municipality has been called upon to respond because of its legal duty to keep public highways open and free from nuisances, a recovery over has been permitted for indemnity against the property owner, the principal wrongdoer, whose negligence was the real cause of the injury. . . .

In a case cited and much relied upon at the bar, Gray v. Boston Gas Light Co., 114 Mass. 149 (1873), a telegraph wire was fastened to the plaintiff's chimney without his consent, and, the weight of the wire having pulled the chimney over into the street, to the injury of a passing traveler, an action was brought against the property owner for damages, and notice was duly given to the gas company, which refused to defend. Having settled the damages at a figure which the court thought reasonable, the property owner brought suit against the gas company, and it was held liable. In the opinion the court said:

> When two parties, acting together, commit an illegal or wrongful act the party who is held responsible for the act cannot have indemnity or contribution from the other, because both are equally culpable or *particeps criminis*, and the damage results from their joint offense. This rule does not apply when one does the act or creates the nuisance, and the other does not join therein, but is thereby exposed to liability and suffers damage. He may recover from the party whose wrongful act has thus exposed him. In such cases the parties are not in *pari delicto* as to each other, though, as to third persons, either may be held liable. . . .

Other cases might be cited, which are applications of the exception engrafted upon the general rule of non-contribution among wrongdoers, holding that the law will inquire into the facts of a case of the character shown with a view to fastening the ultimate liability upon the one whose wrong has been primarily responsible for the injury sustained. . . .

The case then stands in this wise: The railroad company and the terminal company have been guilty of a like neglect of duty in failing to properly inspect the car before putting it in use by those who might be injured thereby. We do not perceive that, because the duty of inspection was first required from the railroad company, the case is thereby brought within the class which holds the one primarily responsible, as the real cause of the injury, liable to another less culpable, who may have been held to respond for damages for the injury inflicted. It is not like the case of the one who creates a nuisance in the public streets; or who furnishes a defective dock; or the case of the gas company, where it created the condition of unsafety by its own wrongful act; or the case of the defective boiler, which blew out because it would not stand the pressure warranted by the manufacturer. In all these cases the wrongful act of the one held finally liable created the unsafe or dangerous condition from which the injury resulted. The principal and moving cause, resulting in the injury sustained, was the act of the first wrongdoer, and the other has been held liable to third persons for failing to discover or correct the defect caused by the positive act of the other.

In the present case the negligence of the parties has been of the same character. Both the railroad company and the terminal company failed by proper inspection to discover the defective brake. The terminal company, because of its fault, has been held liable to one sustaining an injury thereby.

We do not think the case comes within that exceptional class which permits one wrongdoer who has been mulcted in damages to recover indemnity or contribution from another.

[Judgment for defendant affirmed.]

NOTES

1. Contribution versus indemnity. In *Union Stock Yards* should an action for contribution or indemnity be allowed if the cost of inspection was low to the railroad and high to the stockyard? How does *Union Stockyards* come out under a rule that allows the passive party to obtain contribution or indemnity from the active one? Under a rule that allows the party secondarily responsible to obtain contribution or indemnity from the party primarily responsible?

2. Release of joint tortfeasors. What effect should a release given by the plaintiff to one defendant have on the cause of action that he might have maintained against the others? For all joint tortfeasors, including those who did not act in concert, the traditional common law rule treated the release of one as a release of all, regardless of the amount of consideration received in exchange, unless the plaintiff obtained an express reservation of rights from the settling defendant. The joint tortfeasors were said to be but one person in the law, and they owed a single indivisible obligation to the plaintiff. The rule gave a "free ride" to the other defendants whenever the plaintiff's lawyer did not appreciate the legal consequences of the release. Recent cases have tended to reject the automatic release rule, at least for independent tortfeasors. In Hess v. Ford Motor Co., 41 P.3d 46, 49 (Cal. 2002), the plaintiff was left a paraplegic when the Ford pick-up truck in which he was riding rolled over. The plaintiff's settlement with the truck's driver's insurer contained, by mistake, a release that discharged "all other persons, firms, corporations, associations or partnerships." The plaintiff also sued Ford under multiple theories. Ford attempted to use this unambiguous settlement language to limit its liability. However, Brown, J., allowed the introduction of extrinsic evidence to correct a mutual mistake of the settling parties, and to show that the release was only intended to exonerate the driver and his insurer. By the same token, when a plaintiff executes a comprehensive release with a tortfeasor's insurance company that covers "all other persons, firms or corporations who are or might be liable from any and all claims" that arise out of the accident, his release bars a suit against the tortfeasor even though the tortfeasor was not specifically named in the release. White v. Laidlaw Transit, Inc., 796 N.Y.S.2d 466 (N.Y. App. Div. 2005). Note that the Third Restatement also provides that releases should be interpreted by standard contract principles. "If there is a dispute over whether a particular individual is released, the burden of pleading and proving that the settlement releases the individual is on the party claiming release." RTT:AL §24, comment *g*. Normally a release of "all persons" will be insufficient to overcome that presumption unless the settling defendant has some affiliation or connection with the other parties to the lawsuit. *Id*.

California Civil Procedure Code
§§875-877.5 (West 2007)

SECTION 875. JUDGMENT AGAINST TWO OR MORE DEFENDANTS; CONTRIBUTION; SUBROGATION BY INSURER; RIGHT OF INDEMNITY; SATISFACTION OF JUDGMENT IN FULL.

(a) Where a money judgment has been rendered jointly against two or more defendants in a tort action there shall be a right of contribution among them as hereinafter provided.

(b) Such right of contribution shall be administered in accordance with the principles of equity.

(c) Such right of contribution may be enforced only after one tortfeasor has, by payment, discharged the joint judgment or has paid more than his pro rata share thereof. It shall be limited to the excess so paid over the pro rata share of the person so paying and in no event shall any tortfeasor be compelled to make contribution beyond his own pro rata share of the entire judgment.

(d) There shall be no right of contribution in favor of any tortfeasor who has intentionally injured the injured person.

(e) A liability insurer who by payment has discharged the liability of a tortfeasor judgment debtor shall be subrogated to his right of contribution.

(f) This title shall not impair any right of indemnity under existing law, and where one tortfeasor judgment debtor is entitled to indemnity from another there shall be no right of contribution between them.

(g) This title shall not impair the right of a plaintiff to satisfy a judgment in full as against any tortfeasor judgment debtor.

SECTION 876. DETERMINATION OF PRO RATA SHARE.

(a) The pro rata share of each tortfeasor judgment debtor shall be determined by dividing the entire judgment equally among all of them.

(b) Where one or more persons are held liable solely for the tort of one of them or of another, as in the case of the liability of a master for the tort of his servant, they shall contribute a single pro rata share, as to which there may be indemnity between them.

SECTION 877. RELEASE OF ONE OR MORE JOINT TORTFEASORS OR
CO-OBLIGORS; EFFECT UPON LIABILITY OF OTHERS.

[The section provides inter alia that a release shall not discharge any
third party "unless its terms so provide."]

SECTION 877.5. SLIDING SCALE RECOVERY AGREEMENT; DISCLOSURE
TO COURT AND JURY; SERVICE OF NOTICE OF INTENT
TO ENTER.

[This section requires prompt disclosure to the court of any agreement
whereby the liability of a party will be reduced if it testifies as a witness for
the plaintiff. The court shall disclose to the jury the "existence and content"
of that agreement, unless disclosure will cause unfair prejudice or mislead
the jury. Unless the judge rules otherwise for good cause, the agreement is
only effective if other parties receive notice of an intent to enter an
agreement at least 72 hours prior to entering that agreement.]

NOTE

Statutory repudiation of the joint and several liability rule. In contrast to
the stark all-or-nothing allocations of the common law, the California
statute adopted a regime of pro rata liability that allowed each defendant
to recover from his codefendants any amount above his own share. Thus,
if one defendant paid the full $100, he could recoup $50 in a separate
action from the second defendant, so long as judgment had been
entered against both. Statutory contribution was not available for intentional
harms, nor did it displace any available indemnity actions. Other rules
governed cases of vicarious liability. The California statute was initially
passed in 1957 before the adoption of pure comparative negligence in *Li.*
Does it make sense to have a regime of pure comparative negligence between plaintiffs and defendants and a regime of pro rata apportionment
among defendants?

American Motorcycle Association v. Superior Court
578 P.2d 899 (Cal. 1978)

[In this case the California Supreme Court addressed the proper
apportionment of liability in suits against multiple defendants. At the
outset, the court stated its conclusions as follows:

(1) That the doctrine subjecting multiple defendants to "joint and several liability" to a single plaintiff was neither abolished nor limited by the decision in *Li*.

(2) That a doctrine of partial equitable indemnity should be adopted at common law to permit apportionment of loss among codefendants on pure comparative principles.

(3) That the California contribution statutes do not "preclude" the development of a common law doctrine of comparative indemnity, and

(4) That under this system of equitable contribution, any defendant may maintain an action against any other party, whether or not joined in the original suit, but that the trial judge may postpone trial of the indemnity action in order "to avoid unduly complicating the plaintiff's suit."]

TOBRINER, J. . . . In light of these determinations, we conclude that a writ of mandate should issue, directing the trial court to permit petitioner-defendant to file a cross-complaint for partial indemnity against previously unjoined alleged concurrent tortfeasors.

1. THE FACTS

[The plaintiff, Glen Gregos, was injured in a novice motorcycle race that he claimed was negligently organized and run by two defendants, the American Motorcycle Association (AMA) and the Viking Motorcycle Club (Viking). Thereafter the AMA sought leave of the court to file a cross-complaint against Gregos's parents, alleging their negligence and improper supervision of their minor son. It also asked declaratory relief that its portion of the judgment be reduced by the amount of the "allocable negligence" of the parents.]

2. THE ADOPTION OF COMPARATIVE NEGLIGENCE IN *LI* DOES NOT
   WARRANT THE ABOLITION OF JOINT AND SEVERAL LIABILITY OF
   CONCURRENT TORTFEASORS . . .

In the instant case AMA argues that the *Li* decision, by repudiating the all-or-nothing contributory negligence rule and replacing it by a rule which simply diminishes an injured party's recovery on the basis of his comparative fault, in effect undermined the fundamental rationale of the entire joint and several liability doctrine as applied to concurrent tortfeasors. . . .

AMA argues that after *Li* (1) there *is* a basis for dividing damages, namely on a comparative negligence basis, and (2) a plaintiff is no longer necessarily "innocent," for *Li* permits a negligent plaintiff to recover damages. AMA maintains that in light of these two factors it is logically inconsistent to retain joint and several liability of concurrent tortfeasors after *Li*. As we explain, for a number of reasons we cannot accept AMA's argument.

First, the simple feasibility of apportioning fault on a comparative negligence basis does not render an indivisible injury "divisible" for purposes of the joint and several liability rule. [A] concurrent tortfeasor is liable for the whole of an indivisible injury whenever his negligence is a proximate cause of that injury. In many instances, the negligence of each of several concurrent tortfeasors may be sufficient, in itself, to cause the entire injury; in other instances, it is simply impossible to determine whether or not a particular concurrent tortfeasor's negligence, acting alone, would have caused the same injury. Under such circumstances, a defendant has no equitable claim vis-à-vis an injured plaintiff to be relieved of liability for damage which he has proximately caused simply because some other tortfeasor's negligence may also have caused the same harm. In other words, the mere fact that it may be possible to assign some percentage figure to the relative culpability of one negligent defendant as compared to another does not in any way suggest that each defendant's negligence is not a proximate cause of the entire indivisible injury.

Second, abandonment of the joint and several liability rule is not warranted by AMA's claim that, after *Li*, a plaintiff is no longer "innocent." Initially, of course, it is by no means invariably true that after *Li* injured plaintiffs will be guilty of negligence. In many instances a plaintiff will be completely free of all responsibility for the accident, and yet, under the proposed abolition of joint and several liability, such a completely faultless plaintiff, rather than a wrongdoing defendant, would be forced to bear a portion of the loss if any one of the concurrent tortfeasors should prove financially unable to satisfy his proportioned share of the damages.

Moreover, even when a plaintiff is partially at fault for his own injury, a plaintiff's culpability is not equivalent to that of a defendant. In this setting, a plaintiff's negligence relates only to a failure to use due care for his own protection, while a defendant's negligence relates to a lack of due care for the safety of others. Although we recognized in *Li* that a plaintiff's self-directed negligence would justify reducing his recovery in proportion to his degree of fault for the accident,[2] the fact remains that insofar as the

2. A question has arisen as to whether our *Li* opinion, in mandating that a plaintiff's recovery be diminished in proportion to the plaintiff's negligence, intended that the plaintiff's conduct be compared with each individual tortfeasor's negligence, with the cumulative negligence of all named defendants or with all other negligent conduct that contributed to the injury. The California BAJI Committee, which specifically addressed this issue after *Li*, concluded that "the contributory negligence of the plaintiff must be proportioned to the combined negligence of plaintiff and of all the tortfeasors, whether or not joined as parties . . . whose negligence proximately caused or contributed to plaintiff's injury."

We agree with this conclusion, which finds support in decisions from other comparative negligence jurisdictions. In determining to what degree the injury was due to the fault of the plaintiff, it is logically essential that the plaintiff's negligence be weighed against the combined total of all other causative

plaintiff's conduct creates only a risk of self-injury, such conduct, unlike that of a negligent defendant, is not tortious.

Finally, from a realistic standpoint, we think that AMA's suggested abandonment of the joint and several liability rule would work a serious and unwarranted deleterious effect on the practical ability of negligently injured persons to receive adequate compensation for their injuries. One of the principal by-products of the joint and several liability rule is that it frequently permits an injured person to obtain full recovery for his injuries even when one or more of the responsible parties do not have the financial resources to cover their liability. In such a case the rule recognizes that fairness dictates that the "wronged party should not be deprived of his right to redress," but that "[t]he wrongdoers should be left to work out between themselves any apportionment." (Summers v. Tice 199 P.2d 1, 5 (1948).) The *Li* decision does not detract in the slightest from this pragmatic policy determination.

[The court then noted that the overwhelming weight of judicial and academic opinion supports its conclusion.]

3. UPON REEXAMINATION OF THE COMMON LAW EQUITABLE INDEMNITY DOCTRINE IN LIGHT OF THE PRINCIPLES UNDERLYING *LI*, WE CONCLUDE THAT THE DOCTRINE SHOULD BE MODIFIED TO PERMIT PARTIAL INDEMNITY AMONG CONCURRENT TORTFEASORS ON A COMPARATIVE FAULT BASIS . . .

In California, as in most other American jurisdictions, the allocation of damages among multiple tortfeasors has historically been analyzed in terms of two, ostensibly mutually exclusive, doctrines: contribution and indemnification. In traditional terms, the apportionment of loss between multiple tortfeasors has been thought to present a question of contribution; indemnity, by contrast, has traditionally been viewed as concerned solely with whether a loss should be entirely shifted from one tortfeasor to another, rather than whether the loss should be shared between the two. As we shall explain, however, the dichotomy between the two concepts is more formalistic than substantive, and the common goal of both doctrines, the equitable distribution of loss among multiple tortfeasors, suggests a need for a reexamination of the relationship of these twin concepts.

---

negligence; moreover, inasmuch as a plaintiff's actual damages do not vary by virtue of the particular defendants who happen to be before the court, we do not think that the damages which a plaintiff may recover against defendants who are joint and severally liable should fluctuate in such a manner.

Early California decisions, relying on the ancient law that "the law will not aid a wrongdoer," embraced the then ascendant common law rule denying a tortfeasor any right to contribution whatsoever. [The Court then reviewed the 1957 legislation set out above.]

[T]he equitable indemnity doctrine originated in the common sense proposition that when two individuals are responsible for a loss, but one of the two is more culpable than the other, it is only fair that the more culpable party should bear a greater share of the loss. Of course, at the time the doctrine developed, common law precepts precluded any attempt to ascertain comparative fault; as a consequence, equitable indemnity, like the contributory negligence doctrine, developed as an all-or-nothing proposition.

Because of the all-or-nothing nature of the equitable indemnity rule, courts were, from the beginning, understandably reluctant to shift the entire loss to a party who was simply slightly more culpable than another. As a consequence, throughout the long history of the equitable indemnity doctrine courts have struggled to find some linguistic formulation that would provide an appropriate test for determining when the relative culpability of the parties is sufficiently disparate to warrant placing the entire loss on one party and completely absolving the other.

A review of the numerous California cases in this area reveals that the struggle has largely been a futile one. . . .

Indeed, some courts, as well as some prominent commentators, after reviewing the welter of inconsistent standards utilized in the equitable indemnity realm, have candidly eschewed any pretense of an objectively definable equitable indemnity test. . . .

If the fundamental problem with the equitable indemnity doctrine as it has developed in this state were simply a matter of an unduly vague or imprecise linguistic standard, the remedy would be simply to attempt to devise a more definite verbal formulation. In our view, however, the principal difficulty with the current equitable indemnity doctrine rests not simply on a question of terminology, but lies instead in the all-or-nothing nature of the doctrine itself. . . .

In order to attain such a system in which liability for an indivisible injury caused by concurrent tortfeasors will be borne by each individual tortfeasor "in direct proportion to [his] respective fault," we conclude that the current equitable indemnity rule should be modified to permit a concurrent tortfeasor to obtain partial indemnity from other concurrent tortfeasors on a comparative fault basis. In reaching this conclusion, we point out that in recent years a great number of courts, particularly in jurisdictions which follow the comparative negligence rule, have for similar reasons adopted, as a matter of common law, comparable rules providing for comparative contribution or comparative indemnity.

4. CALIFORNIA'S CONTRIBUTION STATUTES DO NOT PRECLUDE
THIS COURT FROM ADOPTING COMPARATIVE PARTIAL INDEMNITY AS A
MODIFICATION OF THE COMMON LAW EQUITABLE INDEMNITY
DOCTRINE

[The court held that the express preservation of indemnity actions in section 875(f) justified its current decision, and that the legislature in 1957, before *Li*, "had no intention of completely withdrawing the allocation of loss issue from judicial review." The court then addressed the question of settlements.]

[Section 877's policy of encouraging settlements] can, and should, be preserved as an integral part of the partial indemnity doctrine that we adopt today. Thus, while we recognize that section 877, by its terms, releases a settling tortfeasor only from liability for contribution and not partial indemnity, we conclude from a realistic perspective the legislative policy underlying the provision dictates that a tortfeasor who has entered into a "good faith settlement" with the plaintiff must also be discharged from any claim for partial or comparative indemnity that may be pressed by a concurrent tortfeasor. . . . Moreover, to preserve the incentive to settle which section 877 provides to injured plaintiffs, we conclude that a plaintiff's recovery from nonsettling tortfeasors should be diminished only by the amount that the plaintiff has actually recovered in a good faith settlement, rather than by an amount measured by the settling tortfeasor's proportionate responsibility for the injury.

Accordingly, . . . we hold that under the common law of this state a concurrent tortfeasor may seek partial indemnity from another concurrent tortfeasor on a comparative fault basis. . . .

Let a peremptory writ of mandate issue directing the trial court (1) to vacate its order denying AMA leave to file its proposed cross-complaint, and (2) to proceed in accordance with the views expressed in this opinion. Each party shall bear its own costs.

CLARK, J., dissenting. . . . The majority reject the *Li* principle in two ways. First, they reject it by adopting joint and several liability holding that each defendant — including the marginally negligent one — will be responsible for the loss attributable to his codefendant's negligence. To illustrate, if we assume that the plaintiff is found 30 percent at fault, the first defendant 60 percent, and a second defendant 10 percent, the plaintiff under the majority's decision is entitled to a judgment for 70 percent of the loss against each defendant, and the defendant found only 10 percent at fault may have to pay 70 percent of the loss if his codefendant is unable to respond in damages.

The second way in which the majority reject *Li*'s irresistible principle is by its settlement rules. Under the majority opinion, a good faith settlement releases the settling tortfeasor from further liability, and the "plaintiff's recovery from nonsettling tortfeasors should be diminished only by the amount that the plaintiff has actually recovered in a good faith settlement, rather than by an amount measured by the settling tortfeasor's proportionate responsibility for the injury." The settlement rules announced today may turn *Li*'s principle upside down — the extent of dollar liability may end up in inverse relation to fault.

[Clark, J., then noted that the inversion takes place under the credit rule when a central defendant settles for a small sum. Thus, if *P* is 30 percent responsible, *D₁* is 10 percent responsible, and *D₂* 60 percent responsible, if *D₂* settles for 20 percent, *D₁* could be held responsible for 50 percent of the loss, notwithstanding his 10 percent share of responsibility. Under the carve out rule *P* could pursue *D₁* only for 10 percent of the loss no matter how much she obtained from *D₂*. Clark, J., also argued that if *D₂* was insolvent, *P* could recover only 25 percent of the loss — 10 percent from *P* compared to 30 percent from *D₁*].

I do not suggest return to the old contributory negligence system. The true criticism of that system remains valid: one party should not be required to bear a loss which by definition two have caused. However, in departing from the old system of contributory negligence numerous approaches are open, but the Legislature rather than this court is the proper institution in a democratic society to choose the course. . . .

NOTES

1. *Dole v. Dow: joint tortfeasors and workers' compensation.* The first important modern case to repudiate the general "no contribution" rule was Dole v. Dow Chemical Co., 282 N.E.2d 288, 292 (N.Y. 1972). Defendant Dow Chemical supplied the George Urban Milling Company with a poison, methyl bromide, used to control insects and pests. Urban fumigated its storage bin with the methyl bromide, but did not allow sufficient time for it to dissipate before allowing its employee, Dole, to enter the bin, where he subsequently died. The plaintiff sued Dow for not giving the decedent a direct warning about the dangerous properties of the methyl bromide. Dow denied its own negligence, and brought a suit against Urban, claiming that Urban itself was negligent in failing to comply with Dow's detailed instructions for using methyl bromide. The court held that "where a third party is found to have been responsible for a part, but not all, of the negligence for which a defendant is cast in damages, the responsibility for that party is recoverable by the prime defendant against the third party. To reach that end there must necessarily be an apportionment of responsibility in negligence between those parties."

Dole thus routinely permitted a flank attack by a plaintiff against an employer otherwise protected against direct suit for damages by the exclusive remedy provision of the workers' compensation statutes. That gap in the employer's armor was closed in part in 1996 by N.Y. Workers' Comp. §11, which provided that an employer should "not be liable for contribution or indemnity to any third person . . . unless such third person proves through competent medical evidence that such employee has sustained a 'grave injury' . . . ." Grave injury was defined to include major loss of limb, paraplegia or quadriplegia, total or permanent blindness or deafness, and loss of multiple fingers or toes. In Castro v. United Container Machinery Group, 761 N.E.2d 1014 (N.Y. 2001), the court held that the loss of five fingertips did not constitute a "grave injury." It quoted with approval the governor's justification for the Act: "In making this change, the bill restores the basis of the bargain between business and labor — that workers obtain necessary medical care benefits and compensation for workplace injuries regardless of fault while employers obtain a degree of economic protection from devastating lawsuits." Why not make the ban against third party suits total? For more on exclusive remedies, see Chapter 13, Section D.

2. *Contribution: strict liability and negligence.* American Motorcycle only addressed the problem of apportionment when both defendants were sued for negligence. Apportionment between plaintiff and defendant has, however, been allowed when plaintiff sues on a strict liability theory, see Bohan v. Ritzo, Chapter 4, *supra* at 395. In Safeway Stores, Inc. v. Nest-Kart, 579 P.2d 441, 446 (Cal. 1978), the California Supreme Court adopted the same rule in suits between codefendants. The plaintiff was injured when a supermarket cart collapsed. The plaintiff sued Safeway, the supermarket owner, in negligence, and Nest-Kart, the cart manufacturer, in strict liability. The jury found Safeway 80 percent responsible and Nest-Kart 20 percent responsible.

Safeway's motion to apportion losses evenly between the defendants was granted, and Nest-Kart's appeal followed. On appeal, the court rejected Safeway's contention that the principles of apportionment could not operate with negligence and strict liability theories in light of the ease in which the jury made the 80/20 apportionment. It continued:

> Finally, we note that a contrary conclusion, which confined the operation of the comparative indemnity doctrine to cases involving solely negligent defendants, would lead to bizarre, and indeed irrational, consequences. Thus, if we were to hold that the comparative indemnity doctrine could only be invoked by a negligent defendant but not a strictly liable defendant, a manufacturer who was actually negligent in producing a product would frequently be placed in a better position than a manufacturer who was free from negligence but who happened to produce a defective product, for the negligent manufacturer would be permitted to shift the bulk of liability to more negligent cotortfeasors, while the strictly liable defendant would be denied the benefit of such apportionment.

Does *Safeway* bear on whether contributory negligence should be allowed as a defense in products liability cases? See Daly v. General Motors, reprinted *infra* at 832.

3. *Insolvent defendants in joint tortfeasor cases.* Further complications arise with the insolvency of one or more multiple defendants. *American Motorcycle* seems to hold that the remaining defendants bear *all* of the risk of an insolvent codefendant, but Evangelatos v. Superior Court (Van Waters & Rogers, Inc., RPI), 753 P.2d 585, 590 (Cal. 1988), seemed to apply a different rule. "[M]ore recent decisions also make clear that if one or more tortfeasors prove to be insolvent and are not able to bear their fair share of the loss, the shortfall created by such insolvency should be apportioned equitably among the remaining culpable parties—both defendants and plaintiffs."

To revert to Justice Clark's 30/60/10 hypothetical, if the 60 percent defendant is insolvent, *American Motorcycle* placed 70 percent of the loss on the 10 percent defendant. It appears that *Evangelatos* splits that 60 percent loss between plaintiff and defendant in accordance with their responsibility, so that the plaintiff can recover only 25 percent of her loss from the solvent defendant, representing his own 10 percent responsibility plus one quarter (10 divided by 40) of the remaining 60 percent of the loss, or 15 percent. The Third Restatement adopts a similar rule: "if a defendant establishes that a judgment for contribution cannot be collected fully from another defendant, the court reallocates the uncollectible portion of the damages to all other parties, including the plaintiff, in proportion to the percentages of comparative responsibility assigned to the other parties." RTT:AL §21. The exceptions to this rule cover intentional tortfeasors (*id.* §12), persons acting in concert (*id.* §15), vicarious liability (*id.* §13), and persons who fail to protect plaintiff from the specific risk of an intentional tort (*id.* §14).

The mechanics of these questions are often troublesome. In the two examples that follow assume that all injured parties sue all other parties to the dispute. Under the various scenarios, how much can each injured party recover from the others?

   I. *A*, 40 percent negligent, suffers $12,000 damages; *B*, 30 percent negligent, suffers $8,000 damages; *C*, 30 percent negligent, suffers no damage at all.
   II. *A*, 20 percent negligent, suffers $20,000 in damages; *B*, who is 40 percent negligent, suffers $10,000 in damages. *C*, who is 10 percent negligent, suffers no damage; *D*, who is approximately 30 percent negligent, also suffers no damage.

4. *Several liability for multiple defendants?* The Restatement's approach of partial reapportionment was not applied in Brown v. Keill, 580 P.2d 867, 873-874 (Kan. 1978). In that case, the court held that the Kansas

comparative negligence statute (Kan. Stat. Ann. §60-258a (2007)), allowing recovery if plaintiff's negligence "was less than" defendant's causal negligence, abrogated the traditional rule of joint and several liability, and created several liability only. Thus, subsection (d) provides:

> Where the comparative negligence of the parties in any action is an issue and recovery is allowed against more than one party, each such party shall be liable for that portion of the total dollar amount awarded as damages to any claimant in the proportion that the amount of such party's causal negligence bears to the amount of the causal negligence attributed to all parties against whom such recovery is allowed.

The court first held that the plain language of the statute compelled the result. It then argued that a limitation of losses for defendants was not inconsistent with sound social policy:

> The perceived purpose in adopting K.S.A. 60-258a is fairly clear. The legislature intended to equate recovery and duty to pay to degree of fault. Of necessity, this involved a change of both the doctrine of contributory negligence and of joint and several liability. There is nothing inherently fair about a defendant who is 10% at fault paying 100% of the loss, and there is no social policy that should compel defendants to pay more than their fair share of the loss. Plaintiffs now take the parties as they find them. . . . Previously, when the plaintiff had to be totally without negligence to recover and the defendants had to be merely negligent to incur an obligation to pay, an argument could be made which justified putting the burden of seeking contribution on the defendants. Such an argument is no longer compelling because of the purpose and intent behind the adoption of the comparative negligence statute.

To revert to Clark's, J., hypothetical, in the event of the insolvency of the 60 percent defendant, the 10 percent defendant continues to bear 10 percent of the loss, with the rest being borne by the plaintiff.

More recently, the traditional rule of joint and several liability has held firm in asbestos cases brought against railroads under the FELA. In Norfolk & Western Railway Co. v. Ayres, 538 U.S. 135, 160 (2003), Ginsburg, J., held that the statutory language of the FELA, 45 U.S.C. §51, meant exactly what it said, no more, no less. It provides that every railroad "shall be liable in damages" to any employee "in whole or in part from the negligence of . . . such carrier." Ginsburg, J., stated that "[n]othing in the statutory text instructs that the amount of damages payable by a liable employer bears reduction when the negligence of a third party also contributed in part to the injury-in-suit." She then noted that the statute contained explicit provisions dealing with comparative negligence (*id.* §53), and refused to import into the statute a new apportionment scheme without explicit textual warrant. Accordingly, the railroad could be held liable in full if its negligence, however slightly, contributed to the plaintiff's harm. Does joint and several liability make as much sense with 100 defendants in a cumulative trauma case as with two in an accident case?

5. *Statutory modifications of joint and several liability.* The common law rule of joint and several liability has proved to be a hot item for legislative reform. One chief concern has been the marginal defendant whose tiny fraction of responsibility has required it to bear the full damages attributable to more culpable, but wholly or largely insolvent, defendants. One possible response to this problem is to abolish the rule outright, as was done by statute in Colorado, Utah, and Wyoming. See Colo. Rev. Stat. §13-21-111.5 (2007); Utah Code Ann. §78-27-38 (2007); Wyo. Stat. §1-1-109 (2007). A second response is to relieve the plight of marginal defendants with ad hoc fixes. Thus, Iowa abolished joint liability for defendants found to be 50 percent or less at fault. Iowa Code 668.4 (2007). New Jersey set a 60 percent threshold for joint and several liability for both economic and non-economic damages. New Jersey Stat. 2A:15-5.2 (2007). Finally, New Hampshire allows a judgment for the full amount of damages to be entered against a co-defendant found 50 or more percent at fault, but allows only for several liability against a co-defendant found less than 50 percent at fault. N.H. Rev. Stat. Ann. §507:7-e (2007).

In 1986, New York amended its basic code (N.Y. CPLR 1601(1)) to provide that a joint tortfeasor whose culpability is less than 50 percent is not jointly liable for all of plaintiff's non-economic damages, but only for its proportionate share. This code also states that the culpability of third parties shall be ignored — thereby imposing a greater liability on the defendants in court — "if the claimant proves that with due diligence he or she was unable to obtain jurisdiction over such person in said action . . . ." The proviso clearly allows the plaintiff to attribute to the defendants in the suit jointly the shares of parties who went insolvent before the suit, but there has been a split of opinion whether the plaintiff was "unable to obtain jurisdiction" over a defendant who went into bankruptcy only after the initial suit was brought, such that all actions against it were "stayed." The court in In re Brooklyn Navy Yard Asbestos Litigation, 971 F.2d 831 (2nd Cir. 1992), reallocated the shares of the bankrupt defendants to the nonsettling defendants in the case. Thereafter in Kharmah v. Metropolitan Chiropractic Center, 733 N.Y.S.2d 165 (N.Y. App. Div. 2001), the New York court, whose decision prevails on questions of state law, held that "if the [defendants]' culpability is 50% or less, their exposure for non-economic damages should be limited proportionately to their share of fault," which now represents the accepted view in federal and state court. See also Bifaro v. Rockwell Automation, 269 F. Supp. 2d 143 (W.D.N.Y. 2003); In re New York City Asbestos Litigation, 750 N.Y.S.2d 469 (N.Y. Sup. Ct. 2002).

In 1986, by popular referendum, California modified its own joint and several liability rule to counteract what the referendum identified as "the deep pocket rule." The current provision reads as follows:

CAL. CIV. CODE §1431.2 (WEST 2007). SEVERAL LIABILITY FOR NONECONOMIC DAMAGES

(a) In any action for personal injury, property damage, or wrongful death, based upon principles of comparative fault, the liability of each defendant for non-economic damages shall be several only and shall not be joint. Each defendant shall be liable only for the amount of non-economic damages allocated to that defendant in direct proportion to that defendant's percentage of fault, and a separate judgment shall be rendered against that defendant for that amount.

For a state near you, see the compilation in the Third Restatement. RTT:AL §17. By the most recent tally, 15 jurisdictions have pure joint and several liability; 15 states have several liability only; 7 states allow for reallocation of losses from insolvent to solvent defendants; and 10 states have complex regimes that typically allow for only several liability of noneconomic damages and joint and several liability of economic damages. Also, see http://www.namic.org/reports/tortReform/JointAndSeveralLiability.asp. One issue that remains is the effect of settlement on nonsettling defendants.

McDermott, Inc. v. AmClyde and River Don Castings, Ltd.
511 U.S. 202 (1994).

STEVENS, J. A construction accident in the Gulf of Mexico gave rise to this admiralty case. In advance of trial, petitioner, the plaintiff, settled with three of the defendants for $1 million. Respondents, however, did not settle, and the case went to trial. A jury assessed petitioner's loss at $2.1 million and allocated 32% of the damages to respondent AmClyde and 38% to respondent River Don Castings, Ltd. (River Don). The question presented is whether the liability of the nonsettling defendants should be calculated with reference to the jury's allocation of proportionate responsibility, or by giving the nonsettling defendants a credit for the dollar amount of the settlement. We hold that the proportionate approach is the correct one . . . .

II

[Stevens, J., first notes the abolition of the equal share rule United States v. Reliable Transfer Co., 421 U.S. 397 (1975), *supra* Chapter 4, Section E, in favor of a rule] requiring that damages be assessed on the basis of proportionate fault when such an allocation can reasonably be made. . . .

Our decision in *Reliable Transfer* was supported by a consensus among the world's maritime nations and the views of respected scholars and judges. No comparable consensus has developed with respect to the issue in the case before us today. It is generally agreed that when a plaintiff settles with one of several joint tortfeasors, the nonsettling defendants are entitled to a credit for that settlement. There is, however, a divergence among respected scholars and judges about how that credit should be determined. Indeed, the American Law Institute (ALI) has identified three principal alternatives and, after noting that "each has its drawbacks and no one is satisfactory," decided not to take a position on the issue. Restatement (Second) of Torts § 886A, pp. 343-344 (1977). The ALI describes the three alternatives as follows:

> (1) The money paid extinguishes any claim that the injured party has against the party released and the amount of his remaining claim against the other tortfeasor is reached by crediting the amount received; but the transaction does not affect a claim for contribution by another tortfeasor who has paid more than his equitable share of the obligation.
>
> (2) The money paid extinguishes both any claims on the part of the injured party and any claim for contribution by another tortfeasor who has paid more than his equitable share of the obligation and seeks contribution. Ibid. (As in alternative (1), the amount of the injured party's claim against the other tortfeasors is by subtracting the amount of the settlement from the plaintiff's damages.)
>
> (3) The money paid extinguishes any claim that the injured party has against the released tortfeasor and also diminishes the claim that the injured party has against the other tortfeasors by the amount of the equitable share of the obligation of the released tortfeasor.

The first two alternatives involve the kind of "*pro tanto*" credit that respondents urge us to adopt. The difference between the two versions of the *pro tanto* approach is the recognition of a right of contribution against a settling defendant in the first but not the second. The third alternative, supported by petitioner, involves a credit for the settling defendants' "proportionate share" of responsibility for the total obligation. Under this approach, no suits for contribution from the settling defendants are permitted, nor are they necessary, because the nonsettling defendants pay no more than their share of the judgment.

The proportionate share approach [ALI Option 3] would make River Don responsible for precisely its share of the damages, $798,000 (38% of $2.1 million). A simple application of the pro tanto approach would allocate River Don $1.1 million in damages ($2.1 million total damages minus the $1 million settlement). [The Court then considered some other adjustments to damages not relevant to the setoff questions raised in this case.]

III

In choosing among the ALI's three alternatives, three considerations are paramount: consistency with the proportionate fault approach of *Reliable Transfer*, promotion of settlement, and judicial economy. ALI Option 1, *pro tanto* setoff with right of contribution against the settling defendant, is clearly inferior to the other two, because it discourages settlement and leads to unnecessary ancillary litigation. It discourages settlement, because settlement can only disadvantage the settling defendant. If a defendant makes a favorable settlement, in which it pays less than the amount a court later determines is its share of liability, the other defendant (or defendants) can sue the settling defendant for contribution. The settling defendant thereby loses the benefit of its favorable settlement. In addition, the claim for contribution burdens the courts with additional litigation. The plaintiff can mitigate the adverse effect on settlement by promising to indemnify the settling defendant against contribution, as McDermott did here. This indemnity, while removing the disincentive to settlement, adds yet another potential burden on the courts, an indemnity action between the settling defendant and plaintiff.

The choice between ALI Options 2 and 3, between the *pro tanto* rule without contribution against the settling tortfeasor and the proportionate share approach, is less clear. The proportionate share rule is more consistent with *Reliable Transfer*, because a litigating defendant ordinarily pays only its proportionate share of the judgment. Under the *pro tanto* approach, however, a litigating defendant's liability will frequently differ from its equitable share, because a settlement with one defendant for less than its equitable share requires the nonsettling defendant to pay more than its share.[14] Such deviations from the equitable apportionment of damages will be common, because settlements seldom reflect an entirely accurate prediction of the outcome of a trial. Moreover, the settlement figure is likely to be significantly less than the settling defendant's equitable share of the loss, because settlement reflects the uncertainty of trial and provides the plaintiff with a "war chest" with which to finance the litigation against the remaining

---

14. Suppose, for example, that a plaintiff sues two defendants, each equally responsible, and settles with one for $250,000. At trial, the non-settling defendant is found liable, and plaintiff's damages are assessed at $1 million. Under the *pro tanto* rule, the nonsettling defendant would be liable for 75% of the damages ($750,000, which is $1 million minus $250,000). The litigating defendant is thus responsible for far more than its proportionate share of the damages. It is also possible for the *pro tanto* rule to result in the nonsettlor paying less than its apportioned share, if, as in this case, the settlement is greater than the amount later determined by the court to be the settlors' equitable share.

defendants. Courts and legislatures have recognized this potential for unfairness and have required "good-faith hearings" as a remedy. When such hearings are required, the settling defendant is protected against contribution actions only if it shows that the settlement is a fair forecast of its equitable share of the judgment. Nevertheless, good-faith hearings cannot fully remove the potential for inequitable allocation of liability. First, to serve their protective function effectively, such hearings would have to be minitrials on the merits, but in practice they are often quite cursory. More fundamentally, even if the judge at a good-faith hearing were able to make a perfect forecast of the allocation of liability at trial, there might still be substantial unfairness when the plaintiff's success at trial is uncertain.[19] In sum, the *pro tanto* approach, even when supplemented with good-faith hearings, is likely to lead to inequitable apportionments of liability, contrary to *Reliable Transfer*.

The effect of the two rules on settlements is more ambiguous. Sometimes the *pro tanto* approach will better promote settlement. This beneficial effect, however, is a consequence of the inequity discussed above. The rule encourages settlements by giving the defendant that settles first an opportunity to pay less than its fair share of the damages, thereby threatening the nonsettling defendant with the prospect of paying more than its fair share of the loss. By disadvantaging the party that spurns settlement offers, the *pro tanto* rule puts pressure on all defendants to settle. While public policy wisely encourages settlements, such additional pressure to settle is unnecessary. The parties' desire to avoid litigation costs, to reduce uncertainty, and to maintain ongoing commercial relationships is sufficient to ensure nontrial dispositions in the vast majority of cases. Under the proportionate share approach, such factors should ensure a similarly high settlement rate. The additional incentive to settlement provided by the *pro tanto* rule comes at too high a price in unfairness. Furthermore, any conclusion that the *pro tanto* rule generally encourages more settlements requires many simplifying assumptions, such as low litigation costs. Recognition of the reality that a host of practical considerations may be

---

19. Suppose again, as in footnote 14, that plaintiff sues two equally culpable defendants for $1 million and settles with one for $250,000. At the good-faith hearing, the settling defendant persuasively demonstrates that the settlement is in good faith, because it shows that its share of liability is 50% and that plaintiff has only a 50% chance of prevailing at trial. The settlement thus reflects exactly the settling defendant's expected liability. If plaintiff prevails at trial, the nonsettling defendant will again be liable for 75% of the judgment even though its equitable share is only 50%. The only way to avoid this inequity is for the judge at the good-faith hearing to disallow any settlement for less than $500,000, that is, any settlement which takes into account the uncertainty of recovery at trial. Such a policy, however, carries a grave cost. It would make settlement extraordinarily difficult, if not impossible, in most cases. As a result, every jurisdiction that conducts a good-faith inquiry into the amount of the settlement takes into account the uncertainty of recovery at trial.

more significant than stark hypotheticals persuades us that the *pro tanto* rule has no clear advantage in promoting settlements.[24]

The effect of the two rules on judicial economy is also ambiguous. The *pro tanto* rule, if adopted without the requirement of a good-faith hearing, would be easier to administer, because the relative fault of the settling defendant would not have to be adjudicated either at a preliminary hearing or at trial. Nevertheless, because of the large potential for unfairness, no party or amicus in this suit advocates the *pro tanto* rule untamed by good-faith hearings. Once the *pro tanto* rule is coupled with a good-faith hearing, however, it is difficult to determine whether the *pro tanto* or proportionate share approach best promotes judicial economy. Under either approach, the relative fault of the parties will have to be determined. Under the *pro tanto* approach, the settling defendant's share of responsibility will have to be ascertained at a separate, pretrial hearing. Under the proportionate share approach, the allocation will take place at trial. The *pro tanto* approach will, therefore, save judicial time only if the good-faith hearing is quicker than the allocation of fault at trial. Given the cursory nature of most good-faith hearings, this may well be true. On the other hand, there is reason to believe that reserving the apportionment of liability for trial may save more time. First, the remaining defendant (or defendants) may settle before trial, thus making any determination of relative culpability unnecessary. In addition, the apportionment of damages required by the proportionate share rule may require little or no additional trial time. The parties will often need to describe the settling defendant's role in order to provide context for the dispute. Furthermore, a defendant will often argue the "empty chair" in the hope of convincing the jury that the settling party was exclusively responsible for the damage. The *pro tanto* rule thus has no clear advantage with respect to judicial economy.

In sum, although the arguments for the two approaches are closely matched, we are persuaded that the proportionate share approach is superior, especially in its consistency with *Reliable Transfer*.

IV

[The Court then rejected the defendant's argument that the proportionate share approach was improper because it could result in the plaintiff recovering more than his total loss.]

... It seems to us that a plaintiff's good fortune in striking a favorable bargain with one defendant gives other defendants no claim to pay less

---

24. An excellent discussion of the effect of the various rules on settlement is Kornhauser & Revesz, Settlement Under Joint and Several Liability, 68 N.Y.U. L. Rev. 427 (1993) [, discussed in Note 2 at page 426].

than their proportionate share of the total loss. In fact, one of the virtues of the proportionate share rule is that, unlike the *pro tanto* rule, it does not make a litigating defendant's liability dependent on the amount of a settlement negotiated by others without regard to its interests.

V

The judgment of the Court of Appeals is reversed, and the case is remanded for further proceedings consistent with this opinion.

NOTES

1. *Settlement of multiple party actions.* In essence, Stevens, J., adopts the approach of the Clark dissent in *AMA*, which has been generally followed. In Murphy v. Florida Keys Electric Cooperative Association, 329 F.3d 1311, 1313, 1315 (11th Cir. 2003), three people were in a small boat piloted by a member of the Ashman family, which collided with an "electrical pole abutment support structure" owned by defendant Florida Keys Electric Co-op Association, Inc. The injured passenger and the family of the decedent, the other passenger, sued and settled their claim with Florida Keys on a proportionate share basis under *McDermott.* Florida Keys then promptly sued the Ashmans, whom the plaintiffs had declined to sue, for indemnity and contribution in a third party complaint. Carnes, J., first noted that the law on the status of the third party claim "[has] lurched back and forth like a drunken sailor." He held "that a settling defendant cannot bring a suit for contribution against a nonsettling defendant who was not released from liability to the plaintiff by the settlement agreement." He explained the situation as follows:

> There are two ways to look at what Florida Keys is seeking to do, and both are telling. One way is that Florida Keys is seeking to escape the bargain it struck with the Murphys about the extent of its liability, trying to litigate with the Ashmans the issue of how much it should have paid the Murphys and then recover from the Ashmans any excess it did pay. That will not do, because the Ashmans are not responsible for the bargain Florida Keys struck with the Murphys. The other way to look at Florida Keys' position is that it is seeking to recover from the Ashmans the amount of the settlement it paid to the Murphys that is attributable to the Ashmans' liability. That will not do either, because none of the settlement is attributable to the Ashmans' liability, which was not released in whole or part. We hold Florida Keys to its bargain: it paid for a discharge of its liability to the Murphys, and that is all it got.

The proportionate share rule has gained ground in nonadmiralty contexts. To be sure, the Restatement equivocated on the matter before opting for the proportionate share rule, which it terms the "comparative share credit," defined as "the percentage of comparative responsibility assigned to the settling tortfeasor multiplied by the total damages of the plaintiff." RTT:AL §16 and comment *c*.

2. Bargaining toward settlement. Suppose that a plaintiff has a claim for $100 against two defendants, and settles against the first defendant for $20. As should be clear after *Murphy*, under the proportionate share approach, the $20 settlement cuts out 50 percent of the claim against the remaining defendant, whose proportionate liability is $50. Accordingly, the plaintiff can never recoup from the second defendant the $30 forgone in the first settlement. And, most emphatically, the second defendant has no need for any recourse against the settling defendant since the two claims are treated as wholly independent. Similarly, if the first settlement for some reason gives an excess award of $70, the apportionment rule still lets the plaintiff recover $50 from the nonsettling defendant. Independence is thus preserved both ways, not solely for the advantage of the defendant. See Austin v. Raymark Industries, Inc., 841 F.2d 1184 (1st Cir. 1988). The proportionate share rule means the defendants do not have to engage in any form of strategic behavior, because their exposure to liability is the same whether they settle first or second, regardless of how the case is resolved.

Matters are quite different under the pro tanto rule, where the initial settlement of $20 leaves the plaintiff with the opportunity to recover $80 against the second defendant. The increased exposure for the second defendant makes strategic negotiations paramount. In Kornhauser & Revesz, Settlements Under Joint and Several Liability, 68 N.Y.U. L. Rev. 427 (1993), relied on by the Supreme Court, the authors explain how the settlement strategies under the pro tanto method depend on the correlation in the success rates on the two claims. One extreme possibility is that the risks of liability for the two defendants are *independent*, that is, the success against one defendant "does not depend upon whether the plaintiff prevails against, loses to, or settles with the other defendant." The other extreme occurs when the two risks are perfectly *correlated*, that is, success or failure against one defendant implies the same result against the other.

Consider first the "independent" situation if administrative costs are treated as zero, and both defendants are fully solvent. Suppose a plaintiff with $100 in damages has a separate cause of action against each defendant, each of which cause carries an independent 50 percent chance of winning a full recovery. In total, her expected recovery from litigation is $75. She will recover the full $100 if both defendants are found liable, or if either is; that is, in 75 percent of the cases. But she will recover nothing in the 25 percent of cases in which neither is found liable. Here, settlement is not possible. Note that each defendant expects to pay nothing in half the cases. In 25 percent of the cases, each defendant will be liable alone for the full damages, and in 25 percent of the cases, each defendant will bear half the total liability of $100. Taking these last two possibilities together, the expected liability for each defendant is $(0.25)(\$100) + (0.25)(\$50) = \$37.50$. So if plaintiff offers to take $37.50 from each defendant (the maximum either would pay), then at most one defendant would accept that offer. Once the first defendant takes the offer, it is no longer in the interest of the second defendant to settle, for it faces liability only for the 50 percent of the time that it loses, in which event it can set off the $37.50 the plaintiff has recovered from the other defendant. In the end therefore its expected liability from continuing with litigation after the other defendant has settled is $(0.50)(\$100 - \$37.50) = \$31.25$, so it will not settle for more than that amount. It follows therefore that the plaintiff's total anticipated recovery, given its initial settlement is equal to $\$37.50 + \$31.25 = \$68.75$, which is lower than her expected $75 recovery from suing both defendants. So the settlement cannot work. Indeed Revesz and Kornhauser show that no pair of offers to both defendants can leave all three parties better off from settlement than from suit.

If the probabilities of success or failure are perfectly correlated, however, settlement is possible, for now the plaintiff's expected success from litigation is reduced to only $50, since whenever she loses against one party she loses against the other. Hence her expected recovery from suit equals $50, $25 from each party. Under these circumstances an offer of (say) $10 to one defendant will be accepted, since it will leave both parties better off: the plaintiff has an anticipated recovery of $10 + (0.50)($90) for $55, while the settling defendant reduces its exposure from $25 to $10. Indeed settlement with both parties is possible, for if plaintiff offers to take $25 from one defendant, that offer will be accepted, and thereafter the second defendant is better off taking any offer up to $37.50 given that its residual liability is equal to $(0.50)(\$75)$. When the claims are correlated, the plaintiff gives up nothing by settling with one plaintiff, whereas she must give up something when the claims against the two defendants are independent. Settlement is therefore easier when claims correlate than when they are independent.

These illustrations rest on restrictive assumptions. In most cases, positive litigation costs would tend to drive parties to settlement. Likewise a plaintiff is often worried about the solvency of some defendants. In addition, most cases will involve intermediate states with rough independence on some issues (say liability) and rough correlation on other issues (say damages). The mindboggling complications that follow are, to say the least, not well understood. Recall that none of these strategic complications arises under the proportionate share rule given the total independence of the two claims.

3. Mary Carter *agreements*. In Booth v. Mary Carter Paint Co, 202 So.2d 8 (Fla. App. 1967), the court approved an agreement whereby a "settling" defendant remained in a case with his codefendants even after signing a secret agreement with the plaintiff that allowed him to reduce his share of the total damage award as the damage awards levied against his codefendants increased. These *Mary Carter* agreements came under constant attack, and in Ward v. Ochoa, 284 So.2d 385 (Fla. 1973), the court held that their terms had to be disclosed to the opposing side during discovery and to the jury at the request of other codefendants. The disclosure remedy, however, did not prevent the settling defendant from participating in all phases of litigation, including the use of preemptory challenges and cross-examination. In Dosdourian v. Carsten, 624 So.2d 241, 245, 246 (Fla. 1993), a unanimous court prospectively held that all such agreements were void as against public policy and outlawed their use. Grimes, J., wrote:

> The main argument in favor of Mary Carter agreements is that they promote settlement. However, while it is true that a Mary Carter agreement accomplishes a settlement with one of the defendants, the intent of the agreement is to proceed with the trial against the other. Some agreements even give the settling defendant veto authority over a prospective settlement with the other defendant. Therefore, the existence of Mary Carter agreements may result in an increased number of trials, and they certainly increase the likelihood of post trial attacks on verdicts alleged to have been unfairly obtained as a result of such agreements. Of course, if the existence of the agreement is known, it is possible that the other defendant may feel compelled to also reach a settlement. However, in that event the remaining defendant may have been unfairly coerced into settling for more than his fair share of liability. . . .

Attitudes toward Mary Carter agreements remain ambivalent. In Hashem v. Les Stanford Oldsmobile, Inc., 697 N.W.2d 558, 572 (Mich. App. 2005), the court said both that "wise judicial policy must favor disclosure of such agreements," only to backtrack from a fixed rule because of the interests "in encouraging settlements and avoiding prejudice to the parties." Its bottom line left the matter within the discretion of the trial court. Why not use a uniform rule? See generally Bernstein and Klerman, An Economic Analysis of Mary Carter Settlement Agreements, 83 Geo. L.J. 2215 (1995); Comment, Quality Not Quantity: An Analysis of Confidential Settlements and Litigants' Economic Incentives, 154 U. Pa. L. Rev. 433 (2005).

SECTION C. VICARIOUS LIABILITY

Ira S. Bushey & Sons, Inc. v. United States
398 F.2d 167 (2d Cir. 1968)

FRIENDLY, J. While the United States Coast Guard vessel *Tamaroa* was being overhauled in a floating drydock located in Brooklyn's Gowanus Canal, a seaman [named Lane] returning from shore leave late at night, in the condition for which seamen are famed, turned some wheels on the drydock wall. He thus opened valves that controlled the flooding of the tanks on one side of the drydock. Soon the ship listed, slid off the blocks and fell against the wall. Parts of the drydock sank, and the ship partially did — fortunately without loss of life or personal injury. The drydock owner [Bushey] sought and was granted compensation by the District Court for the Eastern District of New York in an amount to be determined, 276 F. Supp. 518; the United States appeals. . . .

The Government attacks imposition of liability on the ground that Lane's acts were not within the scope of his employment. It relies heavily on section 228(1) of the Restatement of Agency 2d which says that "conduct of a servant is within the scope of employment if, but only if: . . . (c) it is actuated, at least in part by a purpose to serve the master." Courts have gone to considerable lengths to find such a purpose, as witness a well-known opinion in which Judge Learned Hand concluded that a drunken boatswain who routed the plaintiff out of his bunk with a blow, saying "Get up, you big son of a bitch, and turn to," and then continued to fight, might have thought he was acting in the interest of the ship. Nelson v. American-West African Line, 86 F.2d 730 (2d Cir. 1936). It would be going too far to find such a purpose here; while Lane's return to the *Tamaroa* was to serve his employer, no one has suggested how he could have thought turning the wheels to be, even if — which is by no means clear — he was unaware of the consequences.

In light of the highly artificial way in which the motive test has been applied, the district judge believed himself obliged to test the doctrine's continuing vitality by referring to the larger purposes respondeat superior is supposed to serve. He concluded that the old formulation failed this test. We do not find his analysis so compelling, however, as to constitute a sufficient basis in itself for discarding the old doctrine. It is not at all clear, as the court below suggested, that expansion of liability in the manner here suggested will lead to a more efficient allocation of resources. As the most astute exponent of this theory has emphasized, a more efficient allocation can only be expected if there is some reason to believe that imposing a particular cost on the enterprise will lead it to consider whether steps should be taken to prevent a recurrence of the accident. Calabresi, The Decision for Accidents: An Approach to Non-Fault Allocation of Costs, 78 Harv. L. Rev. 713, 725-34 (1965). And the suggestion that imposition of liability here will lead to more intensive screening of employees rests on highly questionable premises.[5] The unsatisfactory quality of the allocation of resource rationale is especially striking on the facts of this case. It could well be that application of the traditional rule might induce drydock owners, prodded by their insurance companies, to install locks on their valves to avoid similar incidents in the future, while placing the burden on shipowners is much less likely to lead to accident prevention.[7] It is true, of course, that in many cases the plaintiff will not be in a position to insure, and so expansion of liability will, at the very least, serve respondeat superior's loss spreading function. But the fact that the defendant is better able to afford damages is not alone sufficient to justify legal responsibility, see Blum & Kalven, Public Law Perspectives on a Private Law Problem (1965), and this overarching principle must be taken into account in deciding whether to expand the reach of respondeat superior.

A policy analysis thus is not sufficient to justify this proposed expansion of vicarious liability. This is not surprising since respondeat superior, even within its traditional limits, rests not so much on policy grounds consistent with the governing principles of tort law as in a deeply rooted sentiment that a business enterprise cannot justly disclaim responsibility for accidents which may fairly be said to be characteristic of its activities. It is in this light that the inadequacy of the motive test becomes apparent. Whatever may have been the case in the past, a doctrine that would create such drastically different consequences for the actions of the drunken boatswain in *Nelson* and those of the drunken seaman here reflects a wholly unrealistic attitude toward the risks characteristically attendant upon the operation of a ship. We concur in the statement of Mr. Justice Rutledge in a case involving violence injuring a fellow-worker, in this instance in the context of workmen's compensation:

"Men do not discard their personal qualities when they go to work. Into the job they carry their intelligence, skill, habits of care and rectitude. Just as inevitably they take along also their tendencies to carelessness and camaraderie, as well as emotional make-up. In bringing men together, work brings these qualities together, causes frictions between them, creates occasions for lapses into carelessness, and for fun-making and emotional flare-up .... These expressions of human nature are incidents inseparable

---

5. We are not here speaking of cases in which the enterprise has negligently hired an employee whose undesirable propensities are known or should have been. See Koehler v. Presque-Isle Transp. Co., 141 F.2d 490 (2d Cir. 1943).

7. Although it is theoretically possible that shipowners would demand that drydock owners take appropriate action, see Coase, The Problem of Social Cost, 3 J.L. & Economics 1 (1960), this would seem unlikely to occur in real life.

from working together. They involve risks of injury and these risks are inherent in the working environment." Hartford Accident & Indemnity Co. v. Cardillo, 112 F.2d 11, 15 (D.C. Cir. 1940) . . . .

Put another way, Lane's conduct was not so "unforeseeable" as to make it unfair to charge the Government with responsibility . . . . Here it was foreseeable that crew members crossing the drydock might do damage, negligently or even intentionally, such as pushing a Bushey employee or kicking property into the water. Moreover, the proclivity of seamen to find solace for solitude by copious resort to the bottle while ashore has been noted in opinions too numerous to warrant citation. Once all this is granted, it is immaterial that Lane's precise action was not to be foreseen . . . . Consequently, we can no longer accept our past decisions that have refused to move beyond the *Nelson* rule, since they do not accord with modern understanding as to when it is fair for an enterprise to disclaim the actions of its employees.

One can readily think of cases that fall on the other side of the line. If Lane had set fire to the bar where he had been imbibing or had caused an accident on the street while returning to the drydock, the Government would not be liable; the activities of the "enterprise" do not reach into areas where the servant does not create risks different from those attendant on the activities of the community in general. We agree with the district judge that if the seaman "upon returning to the drydock, recognized the Bushey security guard as his wife's lover and shot him," 276 F. Supp. at 530, vicarious liability would not follow; the incident would have related to the seaman's domestic life, not to his seafaring activity, and it would have been the most unlikely happenstance that the confrontation with the paramour occurred on a drydock rather than at the traditional spot. Here Lane had come within the closed-off area where his ship lay, to occupy a berth to which the Government insisted he have access, and while his act is not readily explicable, at least it was not shown to be due entirely to facets of his personal life. The risk that seamen going and coming from the *Tamaroa* might cause damage to the drydock is enough to make it fair that the enterprise bear the loss. It is not a fatal objection that the rule we lay down lacks sharp contours in the end, as Judge Andrews said in a related context, "it is all a question [of expediency,] . . . of fair judgment, always keeping in mind the fact that we endeavor to make a rule in each case that will be practical and in keeping with the general understanding of mankind." Palsgraf v. Long Island R.R. Co., 162 N.E. 99, 104 (N.Y. 1928) (dissenting opinion) . . . .

[Affirmed.]

NOTES

1. *Respondeat superior: history.* Vicarious liability refers generally to cases where one person is held responsible for the wrongful acts of another by

virtue of some status connection between them. This principle, which often goes under the Latin label respondeat superior ("let the superior answer"), enjoys an unquestioned acceptance in all common law jurisdictions. Its universal adoption makes the undercurrent of academic dissatisfaction with the rule somewhat surprising, stemming in large measure from an inability to identify and defend its precise rationale. Thus, Holmes, in his famous articles on Agency, [4 Harv. L. Rev. 345 (1891), 5 Harv. L. Rev. 1 (1891),] treated respondeat superior as an anomaly that "must be explained by some cause not manifest to common sense alone." His doubt stemmed from his nineteenth-century view that treated individual conduct as the sole basis for legal responsibility. In this vein, he wrote: "I assume that common-sense is opposed to making one man pay for another man's wrong, unless he has actually brought the wrong to pass. . . . I therefore assume that common-sense is opposed to the fundamental theory of agency . . . ."

For a sustained attack on vicarious liability as a doctrine that "has attained its luxuriant growth through carelessness and false analogy" see T. Baty, Vicarious Liability (1916). What made the doctrine of respondeat superior so remarkable to early commentators was that it was a bastion of strict liability that withstood the late nineteenth-century onslaught of negligence liability. Thus, while typically respondeat superior could apply only if the servant negligently discharged his duties, the defendant employer did not have to be similarly negligent in selecting or supervising the employee. To the contrary, an unbroken line of cases invoked vicarious liability even when the employer had expressly, indeed emphatically, forbidden the very conduct that constituted employee negligence. See Limpus v. London General Omnibus Co., 158 Eng. Rep. 993 (Ex. 1862). Notwithstanding some early hesitation, from 1700 on, vicarious liability turned on the tort arising out of the servant's employment, not on the negligence of the employer in selection or supervision, and certainly not on the narrow theory that the employer had authorized, expressly or impliedly, the commission of the very tort for which he was vicariously charged. Hern v. Nichols, 91 Eng. Rep. 256 (Ex. 1708). Thus Blackstone writes: "If a servant, lastly, by his negligence does any damage to a stranger, the master shall answer for his neglect; if a smith's servant lames a horse while shoeing him, an action lies against the master, and not against the servant. But in these cases, the damage must be done, while his actually employed in the master's service; otherwise the servant shall answer for his own misbehaviour." 1 Bl. Comm. 418-419 (1765).

The law today holds both master and servant liable for torts that arise out of and in the course of employment. One explanation for that dual system of liability involves the deep pocket of the master. In River Wear Commissioners v. Adamson, 2 A.C. 743 (H.L.(E.) 1876), Lord Blackburn was explicit: "In the great majority of cases the servant actually guilty of the negligence is poor, and unable to make good the damage, especially if it is considerable, and the master is at least comparatively rich, and consequently it is generally better to fix the master with liability; but there is also concurrent liability in the servant, who is not discharged from liability because his master also is liable."

A similar conclusion is reached in Smith, Frolic and Detour, 23 Colum. L. Rev. 444, 455-456 (1923). There Young B. Smith, following Baty's work on vicarious liability, listed the nine traditional rationales for vicarious liability: control; profit; revenge; carefulness and choice; identification; evidence; indulgence; danger; and satisfaction. Having concluded that none of these could fully account for the doctrine, he offered his own explanation: "A reason which occurs to the writer is that which has been offered in justification of workmen's compensation statutes. In substance it is the belief that it is socially more expedient to spread or distribute among a large group of the community the losses which experience has taught are inevitable in the carrying on of industry, than to cast the loss upon a few." Why isn't loss-spreading more cheaply accomplished through first-party insurance?

2. *Efficiency arguments.* In more modern scholarship, vicarious liability has been defended on efficiency grounds by placing greater stress on loss prevention. See Sykes, The Economics of Vicarious Liability, 93 Yale L.J. 1231 (1984). Sykes explicitly compares two possible legal regimes. In the first, that of pure personal liability, the injured third party has recourse only against the employee, who in turn can seek an indemnity against the employer. In the second, that of vicarious liability, the employer (along with the employee) is directly liable, and in turn enjoys possible rights of indemnity against the erring employee. As between the employer and the employee, Sykes observes that the employer is usually the superior riskbearer because of the greater access to insurance markets, especially when the employer is a public corporation whose shareholders are able to diversify their individual portfolios by investing in many different firms. The direct action against the employer tends to place the loss initially on the superior riskbearer. Vicarious liability also reduces the risk that the insolvency of a particular employee will impose an uncompensated risk on a third party. In addition, the doctrine reduces the need to have an extensive network of voluntary contracts between employees and employers to make the employer the ultimate riskbearer when the employee is, in fact, solvent. Finally, vicarious liability protects third parties who know that some firm employee is responsible for the loss, but cannot determine which one is responsible.

3. *Frolic and detour: traditional applications.* Under vicarious liability, it is still necessary to determine which acts fall within the scope of employment. Employees do not always act as employees when they are supposed to be on the job. Difficulties on this score frequently arise when the employee deviates from the route set by his employer for personal reasons. The

general rule today is, roughly, that respondeat superior covers small deviations, but not large ones. See, for example, Riley v. Standard Oil Co., 132 N.E. 97 (N.Y. 1921), in which the court recognized that "[n]o hard and fast rule on the subject either in space or time can be applied," and then held that driving four blocks out of the way on a personal errand did not take the employee out of his master's employment. More recently, in Broadway v. Kelly Brothers Contractors, 803 So.2d 1155, 1157 (Miss. 2000), the employee killed a three-year-old boy while driving his employer's truck to church from which he had planned to visit a worksite. The court held that it was for the jury to decide whether the employee "had the authority to determine his own itinerary such that he was within the scope and course of his employment at the time of the accident."

In principle, it is unclear whether the frolic and detour rule will tend to increase or reduce the number of overall accidents. On the one hand, imposing vicarious liability creates a strong incentive for the employer to monitor the behavior of the employee. If the deviation is effectively curtailed, the employee might undertake the same mission outside of work, having to travel a greater distance and probably creating a higher accident rate. Alternatively, the errand may become so burdensome that the employee will not undertake it at all. In the first case, using an expansive vicarious liability rule will tend to increase the number of accidents. In the second case, the expansive rule will reduce the accident level. Often it is not clear which effect will dominate. It is, therefore, not surprising that no hard and fast rule covers these cases. See generally Sykes, The Boundaries of Vicarious Liability: An Economic Analysis of the Scope of Employment Rule and Related Legal Doctrines, 101 Harv. L. Rev. 563 (1988).

4. Intentional torts. The limits of vicarious liability are also tested in the area of intentional torts. As is evident from *Bushey*, the intentional tort of an employee may be within the course of employment if intended to serve the employer's interest. But clearly in many cases that test is rejected. In Lisa M. v. Henry Mayo Newhall Memorial Hospital, 907 P.2d 358, 364 (Cal. 1995), the defendant's technician, Tripoli, committed sexual assault on the plaintiff when alone with her in an examining room during the course of an ultrasound examination on the pregnant plaintiff. Werdegar, J., rejected a theory of "positional causation" and held that the hospital was not vicariously liable for the wrong.

> As with these nonsexual assaults, a sexual tort will not be considered engendered by the employment unless its motivating emotions were fairly attributable to work-related events or conditions. Here the opposite was true: a technician simply took advantage of solitude with a naive patient to commit an assault for reasons unrelated to his work. Tripoli's job was to perform a diagnostic examination and record the results. The task provided no occasion for a work-related dispute or any other work-related emotional

involvement with the patient. The technician's decision to engage in conscious exploitation of the patient did not arise out of the performance of the examination, although the circumstances of the examination made it possible

Lisa M. was followed in Kephart v. Genuity, Inc, 38 Cal. Rptr. 3d 845, 855 (Cal. App. 2006), when the defendant's employee Graham, in a prolonged fit of road rage, forced the plaintiff's car off the highway, where it overturned, leaving her a quadriplegic. Scotland, P.J., explained why that action was outside the scope of employment.

> [W]hen he got onto Interstate 205, Graham was on the same route that he would have taken had he been going straight to the airport. In this sense, the place in which the incident occurred was consistent with his being on a special errand business trip.
>
> On the other hand, the jury reasonably could find that Graham left his home at least five hours earlier than was required by his business trip and that, as he testified, he did so entirely for personal reasons. Indeed, evidence showed that Genuity scheduled training sessions to begin on Tuesday so as not to interfere with employees' personal time on weekends. And Graham scheduled his flight for early Monday morning so as not to impose on his personal weekend time. Consequently, the time of the incident was well removed from any requirement of Graham's employment.

What result if the road rage occurred after dinner and on the way to the airport?

5. *Negligent hiring.* Sometimes employers may be held responsible for negligent hiring or supervision, even for intentional wrongs that fall outside the employee's scope of employment. In Schechter v. Merchants Home Delivery, Inc., 892 A.2d 415, 432 (D.C. 2006), two workers hired by the defendant MHD robbed Ms. Schechter, an 80-year-old widow, while installing a new washing machine in her house. Schwelb, J., held that the actions necessarily fell outside the course of employment, but nonetheless allowed the plaintiff to reach a jury on the theory of negligent hiring, on the issue whether "[MHD] utterly failed in its duty to supervise, train and maintain . . . its delivery personnel." In *Schechter*, one of the employees had a criminal record for burglary. Is that sufficient to grant plaintiff a summary judgment on the negligent hiring issue?

6. *Vicarious liability in the modern regulatory state.* In recent years, the Supreme Court has grappled with the extent to which the common law principles of vicarious liability survive in the modern regulatory state. In Meritor Savings Bank v. Vinson, 477 U.S. 57 (1986), the Supreme Court refused to hold definitively that the common law rules of vicarious liability applied to sexual harassment cases brought under Title VII of the Civil Rights Act of 1964, searching instead for a middle position between two extremes. On the

one side, it refused an employer "automatically" liable for the wrongs of its supervisory employee, whether or not it had notice of those wrongs. On the other, it held that the bank could be found liable even if the employee had not first pursued available remedies against the employer under the applicable grievance provisions. Thereafter in Burlington Industries v. Ellerth, 524 U.S. 742 (1998), the Court first announced "the general rule is that sexual harassment by a supervisor is not conduct within the scope of employment," but held further that employers were vicariously liable when a supervisor with immediate or successively higher authority over the employee created a hostile environment, subject to two affirmative defenses. First, the liability does not attach to an employer who exercised reasonable care to promptly prevent and correct any sexually harassing behavior. Secondly, liability could not be imposed for the benefit of employees who unreasonably "failed to take advantage of any preventive or corrective opportunities provided by the employer to avoid harm otherwise," which operates as a form of contributory negligence. In dissent, Thomas, J., argued for a uniform standard of employer liability. Is there any reason to deviate from the common law rules developed above?

7. *The "borrowed servant."* When a given person works for two employers, which should be held vicariously liable? The problem of divided authority arises in the construction industry, for example, when a general contractor hires a crane operator from a crane company for specialized work. The crane company retains the general power to hire and fire and to impose safety regulations, work rules, and the like; the construction company designates the operator's particular tasks on the job. Which firm is responsible for the wrongful acts of the servant? Cardozo, J., gave this answer: "The rule now is that, as long as the employee is furthering the business of his general employer by the service rendered to another, there will be no inference of a new relation unless command has been surrendered, and no inference of its surrender from the mere fact of its division." Charles v. Barrett, 135 N.E. 199, 200 (N.Y. 1922).

Recent cases have tended to hold both employers responsible for the torts of the borrowed servant. In Morgan v. ABC Manufacturer, 710 So.2d 1077, 1081 (La. 1998), the court rejected any effort to partition responsibility between the general and special employer, holding both jointly liable for the employee's tort: "Since liability is based on the *right* of control, rather than actual control of the employee at the time of the accident, it is unreasonable to choose between the two employers when each shares the *right* to control the employee's actions."

See generally Note, Borrowed Servants and the Theory of Enterprise Liability, 76 Yale L.J. 807, 820 (1967).

8. *Employer's indemnification.* May an employer, as the passive and innocent party, recoup his losses against the individual employee whose active negligence caused the original accident and, therefore, the employer's

loss? That right of indemnification has been nearly universally adopted in all American courts, see, e.g., Fireman's Fund American Insurance Co. v. Turner, 488 P.2d 429 (Or. 1971); and in England, see Lister v. Romford Ice & Cold Storage, [1957] A.C. 555. But often the employee is unable to answer for the loss, or the employer has taken out insurance to cover both parties, so that actions for indemnification are rare, and unpopular. See, e.g., James, Indemnity, Subrogation, and Contribution and the Efficient Distribution of Accident Losses, 21 NACCA L.J. 360 (1958).

9. *Beyond vicarious liability: owner-consent statutes.* Even when the defendant does not employ the actual wrongdoer, he may be liable under so-called owner-consent statutes that entitled the victim of a tort to sue both the driver of a vehicle and its owner even if the driver is not engaged in the owner's business. For example, New York Vehicle and Traffic Law §388(1) (McKinney 2007) provides:

> Every owner of a vehicle used or operated in this state shall be liable and responsible for death or injuries to person or property resulting from negligence in the use or operation of such vehicle, in the business of such owner or otherwise, by any person using or operating the same with the permission, express or implied, of such owner. . . .

The effect of that statute is likely preempted in part by the "Graves Amendment" found in the Safe, Accountable, Flexible, Efficient Transportation Equity Act, 49 U.S.C. §30106(a) (2007), enacted in 2005, which provides:

> (a) In general. — An owner of a motor vehicle that rents or leases the vehicle to a person (or an affiliate of the owner) shall not be liable under the law of any State or political subdivision thereof, by reason of being the owner of the vehicle (or an affiliate of the owner), for harm to persons or property that results or arises out of the use, operation, or possession of the vehicle during the period of the rental or lease, if—
> (1) the owner (or an affiliate of the owner) is engaged in the trade or business of renting or leasing motor vehicles; and
> (2) there is no negligence or criminal wrongdoing on the part of the owner (or an affiliate of the owner).

The Graves Act was in turn held unconstitutional by at least one lower New York State court in Graham v. Dunkley, 827 N.Y.S.2d 513 (N.Y. Sup. Ct. 2006). "This court cannot conclude that §388 has a "substantial effect" on interstate commerce unless it agrees with the proposition that every civil lawsuit that results in a monetary judgment, and involves an insured, has a substantial effect on interstate commerce. . . . [Section 388] does not concern a commodity or instrumentality of interstate commerce, . . . but rather, it is simply a statute in derogation of common law which codifies one aspect of New York State's substantive tort doctrine of imputed liability: vicarious liability attributable to motor vehicle owners." Can any act regulating transportation be beyond the scope of the federal government? Stay tuned.

10. Joint enterprise. A principle of vicarious liability also holds each partner to a joint enterprise vicariously liable for the wrongs of his partner. Ordinary commercial partnerships fall within the rule. But beyond those cases its use has been circumscribed by the courts. In Heick v. Bacon, 561 N.W.2d 45 (Iowa 1997), the court refused to treat a passenger and driver as a joint enterprise while on a pleasure trip that took them from bar to bar to drink and join in certain games. The court rejected the minority rule that "the mere association of the driver and the passenger in the use of the vehicle for any purpose in which they have a common interest of any kind" constituted a joint enterprise. The injured party could not sue the passenger because she did not have a "mutual 'right of control' over the operation of the vehicle." In some courts the joint enterprise doctrine is restricted to those joint enterprises in which the two parties share a common pecuniary purpose. Do the usual rationales for vicarious liability carry over to the joint enterprise cases?

11. Independent contractors. One issue in *Schechter*, *supra* at 435, Note 5, was whether the delivery men who stole from Ms. Schechter should be classified as employees or independent contractors. That issue makes no difference when, as in *Schechter*, the work in question falls outside the scope of employment. But it would make an enormous difference if MHD had been sued by a pedestrian for injuries sustained when hit by the deliverymen in the ordinary course of their business. If independent contractors, MHD would not be liable for their wrongs. If employees, MHD would be liable. The line between employees and independent contractors is often vague, and could turn on such matters as whether the asserted employees work for multiple firms, wear uniforms, or get paid a regular salary. The uncertainties in this area are of long standing. In Sanford v. Goodridge, 13 N.W.2d 40, 43 (Iowa 1944), the court articulated the key distinction as follows:

> The principles governing the determination of the question as to whether a contract is independent upon the part of the contractor or one of employment is easy of statement but sometimes difficult of application. An independent contractor is one who, by virtue of his contract, possesses independence in the manner and method of performing the work he has contracted to perform for the other party to the contract. This other party to the contract must relinquish the right of control ordinarily enjoyed by an employer of labor and reserve only control as to the results of the contract before the independent-contractor relationship is created. Whether the party for whom the work was to be performed had the right to dictate and control the manner, means, and details of performing the service is the test to be applied. If he did have such rights, then, under the doctrine of respondeat superior, he is liable for the workman's tort. If he did not have such rights, then the workman did not have a master who could be required to respond in damages to the person injured by the workman.

The court then held that a route driver for the defendant newspaper, who injured the plaintiff in a traffic accident, was not an independent contractor, since the employer retained effective control over his day-to-day operations, notwithstanding contract language that described the route operator as an independent contractor. "It will not do for an employer to make a contract which in many clauses loudly proclaims the independence of his contracting workman and in other clauses circumvents this granted freedom by retaining in himself all the control that employers ordinarily possess over their employees."

12. *Employer liability for independent contractors.* One important exception to the no-vicarious liability rule for independent contractors arises when the independent contractor does work on the employer's premises. "When the injury is a direct result of the work contracted for, it is generally held that if the owner of a lot employs a contractor to make an excavation on it which removes the lateral support of a building of an adjoining owner the doctrine of respondeat superior is applicable, and the liability of the owner of the lot is to be determined as though he actually made the excavation himself." Law v. Phillips, 68 S.E.2d 452, 459 (W.Va. 1952). The same principle applies to damage from blasting or the cutting of electrical conduits, water pipes, or gasoline lines located below the ground.

The Restatement (Second) of Torts states the applicable principle as follows:

> §427. NEGLIGENCE AS TO DANGER INHERENT IN THE WORK
> One who employs an independent contractor to do work involving a special danger to others which the employer knows or has reason to know to be inherent in or normal to the work, or which he contemplates or has reason to contemplate when making the contract, is subject to liability for physical harm caused to such others by the contractor's failure to take reasonable precautions against such danger.

13. *Critique of the independent contractor rules.* The widely accepted limitations on an employer's liability for independent contractors has been subject to a withering critique in Arlen & McLeod, Beyond Master-Servant: A Critique of Vicarious Liability, in Exploring Tort Law 111, 114-115 (M. S. Madden ed., 2005), who start with the premise that individual liability will not efficiently deter accidents for "wealth-constrained agents."

> Vicarious liability also is inefficient because it distorts independent contractor relations by providing organizations which hire independent contracts with excessive incentives to employ thinly capitalized independent contractors, . . . notwithstanding that [they] are more likely to take excessive risks because they face little risk of tort liability for any harms caused. . . .
> [In addition], vicarious liability fails to provide organizations with efficient incentives to use other tools available to them, such as financial incentives, to

induce wealth-constrained independent contractors to take efficient care to prevent harm to others. Organizations bear the full cost of care, but they do not obtain the full benefit of preventing accidents, when their independent contractors cannot pay for the harms they cause.

Are the exceptions noted above sufficient to account for this externalization risk? If not, how far should the liability for independent contractors extend? Should any buyer of a dangerous product be liable for the torts committed by independent suppliers with whom it stands in an arm's length relationship?

Perhaps in response to concerns similar to those raised by Arlen and McLeod, courts have refined the operation of the independent contractor rule in connection with hospitals, many of which contract out their emergency room operations to separate organizations, often without clear external differentiation of control. Although the general rule says that these entities may not be held liable for the negligence of physicians employed by these organizations, courts will find liability for the wrongs of independent contractors under a theory of "ostensible" or "apparent" agency. See Solich v. Wheeling, 543 F. Supp. 576 (W.D. Pa. 1982). More recently, the question has arisen whether these principles could be invoked to hold various health care plans responsible for the alleged wrongs of the physicians who participate (to use a neutral word) in cooperative ventures with these health care systems.

Petrovich v. Share Health Plan of Illinois, Inc.
719 N.E.2d 756 (Ill. 1999)

BILANDIC, J. The plaintiff brought this medical malpractice action against a physician and others for their alleged negligence in failing to diagnose her oral cancer in a timely manner. The plaintiff also named her health maintenance organization (HMO) as a defendant. The central issue here is whether the plaintiff's HMO may be held vicariously liable for the negligence of its independent-contractor physicians under agency law. . . .

We hold that the plaintiff has presented sufficient evidence to entitle her to a trial on whether Share is vicariously liable under the doctrines of apparent and implied authority.

[The plaintiff (who died during suit) alleged that her treating physician, Dr. Kowalski, and her HMO, Share, were responsible for the negligent and tardy diagnosis of her tongue cancer. Share did not employ Dr. Kowalski, but operated as "a financing entity that arranges and pays for health care by contracting with independent medical groups and practitioners." Physicians in Share's network "are required to complete an application procedure and meet with Share's approval." Share operated under a "capitation" system, which compensated physicians on a per patient basis, and maintained its own "quality assurance program." All Share members receive a handbook that states the Share will provide for "all your healthcare needs" and "comprehensive high quality services," and describes Share as a "good partner in sickness and in health." But the handbook does not mention that Share physicians are independent contractors who are not its employees, but instead refers to them as "your Share physician."]

Share's primary care physicians, under their agreements with Share, are required to approve patients' medical requests and make referrals to specialists. These physicians use Share's standard referral forms to indicate their approval of the referral. Dr. Kowalski testified at an evidence deposition that she did not feel constrained by Share in making medical decisions regarding her patients, including whether to order tests or make referrals to specialists. . . .

Plaintiff was not aware of the type of relationship that her physicians had with Share. At the time she received treatment, plaintiff believed that her physicians were employees of Share.

ANALYSIS

This appeal comes before us amidst great changes to the relationships among physicians, patients and those entities paying for medical care.

Traditionally, physicians treated patients on demand, while insurers merely paid the physicians their fee for the services provided. Today, managed care organizations (MCOs) have stepped into the insurer's shoes, and often attempt to reduce the price and quantity of health care services provided to patients through a system of health care cost containment. MCOs may, for example, use prearranged fee structures for compensating physicians. MCOs may also use utilization-review procedures, which are procedures designed to determine whether the use and volume of particular health care services are appropriate. MCOs have developed in response to rapid increases in health care costs.

HMOs, i.e., health maintenance organizations, are a type of MCO. HMOs are subject to both state and federal laws . . .

This court has never addressed a question of whether an HMO may be held liable for medical malpractice. Share asserts that holding HMOs liable for medical malpractice will cause health care costs to increase and make health care inaccessible to large numbers of people. Share suggests that, with this consideration in mind, this court should impose only narrow, or limited, forms of liability on HMOs. We disagree with Share that the cost-containment role of HMOs entitles them to special consideration. The principle that organizations are accountable for their tortious actions and those of their agents is fundamental to our justice system. There is no exception to this principle for HMOs. Moreover, HMO accountability is essential to counterbalance the HMO goal of cost-containment. To the extent that HMOs are profit-making entities, accountability is also needed to counterbalance the inherent drive to achieve a large and ever-increasing profit margin. Market forces alone "are insufficient to cure the deleterious [e]ffects of managed care on the health care industry." Herdrich v. Pegram, 154 F.3d 362, 374-75 (7th Cir. 1998), [reversed 530 U.S. 211 (2000) — Ed.]. Courts, therefore, should not be hesitant to apply well-settled legal theories of liability to HMOs where the facts so warrant and where justice so requires. . . .

As a general rule, no vicarious liability exists for the actions of independent contractors. Vicarious liability may nevertheless be imposed for the actions of independent contractors where an agency relationship is established under either the doctrine of apparent authority, or the doctrine of implied authority

I. APPARENT AUTHORITY

Apparent authority, also known as ostensible authority, has been a part of Illinois jurisprudence for more than 140 years. Under the doctrine, a principal will be bound not only by the authority that it actually gives to another, but also by the authority that it appears to give. The doctrine functions like an estoppel. Where the principal creates the appearance of authority, a court will not hear the principal's denials of agency to the prejudice of an innocent third party, who has been led to reasonably rely upon the agency and is harmed as a result.

This court first applied the apparent authority doctrine in a medical malpractice context in Gilbert v. Sycamore Municipal Hospital, 622 N.E.2d 788 (Ill. 1993). In *Gilbert*, a patient suffered a heart attack after being treated and released by a physician at a hospital emergency room. The patient brought an action against the hospital, charging that the hospital was vicariously liable for the physician's negligence in failing to diagnose the patient's heart problem. The trial court awarded summary judgment to the hospital, holding that the hospital could not be held vicariously liable because the emergency room physician was an independent contractor. This court reversed. We held that a genuine issue of material fact existed as to whether the physician was acting as the hospital's apparent agent.

The *Gilbert* decision was grounded in "two realities of modern hospital care." First, hospitals, in essence, have become "big business." Hospitals increasingly hold themselves out to the public as the providers of health care, particularly in their marketing. Hospitals also benefit financially from the health care delivered in their emergency rooms. Second, the reasonable expectations of the public have changed. Patients have come to rely on the reputation of the hospital in seeking out emergency care. These patients would naturally assume that the physicians attending the emergency room are employees of the hospital, unless put on notice otherwise. Consequently, *Gilbert* held that, unless the patient knows or should have known that the physician providing treatment is an independent contractor, vicarious liability can attach to a hospital for the medical malpractice of its physicians under the apparent authority doctrine.

Gilbert sets forth and explains the elements necessary to prove apparent agency against a hospital. These elements are a "holding out" by the hospital and "justifiable reliance" by the plaintiff. . . .

We now hold that the apparent authority doctrine may also be used to impose vicarious liability on HMOs.

To establish apparent authority against an HMO for physician malpractice, the patient must prove (1) that the HMO held itself out as the provider of health care, without informing the patient that the care is given by independent contractors, and (2) that the patient justifiably relied upon the conduct of the HMO by looking to the HMO to provide health care services, rather than to a specific physician. Apparent agency is a question of fact.

A. HOLDING OUT

[The court then held that holding out could be established because the "record contains no indication that plaintiff knew or should have known of these private contractual agreements between Share and its physicians," given that she did not receive clear notice that her care was supplied by independent contractors.]

B. JUSTIFIABLE RELIANCE

. . . The element of justifiable reliance is met where the plaintiff relies upon the HMO to provide health care services, and does not rely upon a specific physician. This element is not met if the plaintiff selects his or her own personal physician and merely looks to the HMO as a conduit through which the plaintiff receives medical care. . . . A person who seeks care from the HMO itself accepts that care in reliance upon the HMO's holding itself out as the provider of care.

Share maintains that plaintiff cannot establish the justifiable reliance element because she did not select Share. . . .

We reject Share's argument. It is true that, where a person selects the HMO and does not rely upon a specific physician, then that person is relying upon the HMO to provide health care. . . . Equally true, however, is that where a person has no choice but to enroll with a single HMO and does not rely upon a specific physician, then that person is likewise relying upon the HMO to provide health care. In the present case, the record discloses that plaintiff did not select Share. Plaintiff's employer selected Share for her. Plaintiff had no choice of health plans whatsoever. Once Share became plaintiff's health plan, Share required plaintiff to obtain her primary medical care from one of its primary care physicians. If plaintiff did not do so, Share did not cover plaintiff's medical costs. In accordance with Share's requirement, plaintiff selected Dr. Kowalski from a list of physicians that Share provided to her. Plaintiff had no prior relationship with Dr. Kowalski. As to Dr. Kowalski's selection of Dr. Friedman [the cancer specialist] for plaintiff, Share required Dr. Kowalski to make referrals only to physicians approved by Share. Plaintiff had no prior relationship with Dr. Friedman. We hold that these facts are sufficient to raise the reasonable inference that plaintiff relied upon Share to provide her health care services.

II. IMPLIED AUTHORITY

. . . The cardinal consideration for determining the existence of implied authority is whether the alleged agent retains the right to control the manner of doing the work. Where a person's status as an independent contractor is negated, liability may result under the doctrine of *respondeat superior*. Plaintiff contends that the facts and circumstances of this case show that Share exerted sufficient control over Drs. Kowalski and Friedman so as to negate their status as independent contractors. Share responds that the act of providing medical care is peculiarly within a physician's domain because it requires the exercise of independent medical judgment. Share thus maintains that, because it cannot control a physician's exercise of medical judgment, it cannot be subject to vicarious liability under the doctrine of implied authority.

Amicus Illinois State Medical Society (Society), the physicians group, supports imposing vicarious liability upon HMOs for the medical malpractice of their physicians under the doctrine of implied authority. [The Society stressed two elements of control:] (1) the right to make prospective decisions of medical necessity and (2) the right to refuse to pay for health care that the HMO perceives to be inappropriate or outside the scope of its policy. These contracts may even bar a physician from providing medical care to a patient without obtaining advance approval from the HMO. Second, the Society points to HMO cost-containment practices. . . . Third, the Society notes the HMO use of utilization-review processes. According to the Society, where HMOs retain the right to make decisions about what health care is "medically necessary" or "medically appropriate," physicians are no longer in control of treatment. The Society asserts that prospective utilization-review procedures are the most harmful form of interference perpetrated by HMOs. In a typical scenario, the physician recommends that certain care be provided to the patient, but the HMO denies to provide the care finding that it is not necessary or appropriate. Lastly, the Society warns that HMO control is not always easy to discern. It explains that the complex relationships involved "raise incredibly intricate fact patterns which limit like the walls in a maze the ability of physicians or patients to freely make decisions based upon their best judgment."

We now address whether the implied authority doctrine may be used against HMOs to negate a physician's status as an independent contractor.... We reject Share's claim that, for purposes of the implied authority doctrine, the exercise of medical judgment by physicians can never be subject to control by an HMO. Physicians, of course, should not allow the exercise of their medical judgment to be corrupted or controlled.

Physicians have professional ethical, moral and legal obligations to provide appropriate medical care to their patients. These obligations on physicians, however, will not act to relieve an HMO of its own legal responsibilities. Where an HMO effectively controls a physician's exercise of medical judgment, and that judgment is exercised negligently, the HMO cannot be allowed to claim that the physician is solely responsible for the harm that results. In such a circumstance, both the physician and the HMO are liable for the harm that results. We therefore hold that the implied authority doctrine may be used against an HMO to negate a physician's status as an independent contractor....

[The court then reviews Share's capitation system of compensation, its system of quality assurance review, and its control over referrals as means whereby the HMO controls the behavior of participating physicians.

The court then accepted plaintiff's contention that Share's "quality assurance review," when conducted on both a concurrent and retrospective basis counts as another incident of employer control.]

We conclude that plaintiff has presented adequate evidence to entitle her to a trial on the issue of implied authority. All the facts and circumstances before us, if proven at trial, raise the reasonable inference that Share exerted such sufficient control over Drs. Kowalski and Friedman so as to negate their status as independent contractors. As discussed above, plaintiff presents relevant evidence of Share's capitation method of compensation, Share's "quality assurance review," Share's referral system and Share's requirement that its primary care physicians act as gatekeepers for Share. These facts support plaintiff's argument that Share subjected its physicians to control over the manner in which they did their work....

From all the above facts and circumstances, a trier of fact could reasonably infer that Share promulgated such a system of control over its physicians that Share effectively negated the exercise of their independent medical judgment, to plaintiff's detriment. We note that Dr. Kowalski testified at an evidence deposition that she did not feel constrained by Share in making medical decisions regarding her patients, including whether to order tests or make referrals to specialists. This testimony is not controlling at the summary judgment stage. The trier of fact is entitled to weigh all the conflicting evidence above against Dr. Kowalski's testimony.

CONCLUSION

An HMO may be held vicariously liable for the negligence of its independent-contractor physicians under both the doctrines of apparent authority and implied authority. Plaintiff here is entitled to a trial on both doctrines. . . . Affirmed.

NOTES

1. Emergency rooms versus HMOs. To what extent could Share have avoided liability by clearly disclosing in its individual subscriber contracts its full business arrangements with its physicians, and then disclaiming all liability for their wrongs? Would a theory of vicarious liability be necessary if Share had actually limited the tests that Dr. Kowalski could have ordered for the plaintiff? Why would a patient want to sue the HMO if the physician is insured? Are the emergency room cases like *Gilbert* an adequate precedent for imposing vicarious liability on HMOs for their cost-control and gate-keeping functions? For an argument against the switch, see Epstein & Sykes, The Assault of Managed Care: Vicarious Liability, ERISA Preemption, and Class Actions, 30 J. Legal Stud. 625, 638 (2001):

> When physicians establish independent practices and carry substantial malpractice insurance on their own, . . . the case for vicarious liability [of Managed Care Oganizations] is much weaker. The physicians' personal assets, including malpractice coverage, become considerable, and the problem of potential insolvency greatly diminishes. Further, the ability of hospitals or MCOs to monitor these independent physicians is extremely limited, as there is no one with greater medical expertise in the hierarchy regularly overseeing their work. We thus doubt that vicarious liability for independent physicians with their own malpractice coverage will accomplish much beyond adding a party to litigation, which is of course costly in itself and opens the prospect of side deals between plaintiffs and physician defendants.

2. Legislative reform and ERISA preemption. The current scene is further complicated by the enormous role played by the Employment Retirement and Income Security Act of 1974, 29 U.S.C. §§1001-1461, commonly known as ERISA. Section 1144(a) of ERISA contains a broad preemption provision, which, subject to exception, "shall supersede any and all State laws insofar as they may now or hereafter relate to any employee benefit plan described in section 1003(a)." The scope of the "relate to" language, subject to extensive litigation, has received a broad construction insofar as it relates to ordinary tort actions against parties involved in the administration of employee benefit plans.

The Supreme Court has discussed ERISA preemption in two recent cases. In Pegram v. Herdrich, 530 U.S. 211, 221 (2000), a patient was required by her husband's HMO to wait eight days for an ultrasound test, only to suffer a ruptured appendix in the interim. The plaintiff sought to use ERISA as a sword. She alleged that the HMO's capitation plan, by "rewarding its physician owners for limiting medical care, entailed an inherent or anticipatory breach of an ERISA fiduciary duty, since these terms created an incentive to make decisions in the physicians' self-interest rather than the exclusive interests of plan participants." Souter, J., rejected that view:

> Since inducement to ration care goes to the very point of any HMO scheme, and rationing necessarily raises some risks while reducing others (ruptured appendixes are more likely; unnecessary appendectomies are less so), any legal principle purporting to draw a line between good and bad HMOs would embody, in effect, a judgment about socially acceptable medical risk. A valid conclusion of this sort would, however, necessarily turn on facts to which courts would probably not have ready access; correlations between malpractice rates and various HMO models, similar correlations involving fee-for-services models, and so on. . . . But such complicated factfinding and such a debatable social judgment are not wisely required of courts unless for some reason resort cannot be had to the legislative process, with its preferable form for comprehensive investigations and judgments of social value such as optimum treatment levels and health care expenditure.

The court therefore declined to "federalize malpractice litigation in the name of fiduciary duty. . . . " Finally, it also noted the imposition of the new fiduciary duty would necessarily preempt all state tort law in the area, which was inconsistent with the basic principle that "there is no ERISA preemption without clear manifestation of congressional purpose."

The preemption issue arose yet again in Aetna Health Inc. v. Davila, 542 U.S. 200, 218-219 (2004), when patients of two health care plans sued for personal injuries, claiming their health care plans denied them benefits to which they were entitled under the Texas Health Care Liability Act (THCLA), which imposes the following duty of ordinary care on health care various actors for health care organizations.

Texas Civil Practice and Remedies Code Annotated §88.001 (Vernon 2007). Definitions in this chapter:

> . . .
>
> (10) "Ordinary care" means, in the case of a health insurance carrier, health maintenance organization, or managed care entity, that degree of care that a health insurance carrier, health maintenance organization, or managed care entity of ordinary prudence would use under the same or similar

circumstances. In the case of a person who is an employee, agent, ostensible agent, or representative of a health insurance carrier, health maintenance organization, or managed care entity, "ordinary care" means that degree of care that a person of ordinary prudence in the same profession, specialty, or area of practice as such person would use in the same or similar circumstances.

These actions were for the personal injuries sustained by the denial of care, not for the cost of the benefits denied, for which ERISA makes statutory provision. The Fifth Circuit had found that these damage actions survived preemption under *Pegram* because the suit sought damages for "mixed eligibility and treatment decisions that were not fiduciary in nature." Thomas, J., writing for a unanimous Supreme Court, steamrolled over this effort to limit the scope of ERISA preemption, which he held should be construed broadly.

> A benefit determination under ERISA, though, is generally a fiduciary act. . . . Hence, a benefit determination is part and parcel of the ordinary fiduciary responsibilities connected to the administration of a plan. . . . *Pegram*, in highlighting its conclusion that "mixed eligibility decisions" were not fiduciary in nature, contrasted the operation of "[t]raditional trustees administer[ing] a medical trust" and "physicians through whom HMOs act." A traditional medical trust is administered by "paying out money to buy medical care, whereas physicians making mixed eligibility decisions consume the money as well." And, significantly, the Court stated that "[p]rivate trustees do not make treatment judgments." But a trustee managing a medical trust undoubtedly must make administrative decisions that require the exercise of medical judgment. Petitioners are not the employers of respondents' treating physicians and are therefore in a somewhat analogous position to that of a trustee for a traditional medical trust.

Thomas, J., next noted the full range of sanctions that ERISA has available to constrain the behavior of its regulated parties, including extensive procedures for the review of claim denials. He then concluded: "These regulations, on their face, apply equally to health benefit plans and other plans, and do not draw distinctions between medical and nonmedical benefits determinations." He accordingly reversed the decisions below. On remand, both plaintiffs dismissed their cases with prejudice. After *Davila*, the state law tort developments in *Petrovich* only apply to health plans not covered by ERISA. The topic of vicarious liability has spread far from its common law roots.

6

CAUSATION

SECTION A. INTRODUCTION

This chapter examines the topic of causation, which, in one guise or another, is an indispensable element in every tort case, no matter what its underlying theory of liability. Once the plaintiff has established that the defendant has engaged in some wrongful conduct, she must link that conduct to her harm. In practice that requirement of causal linkage generally raises two distinct issues, which shall be considered in turn: cause in fact and proximate cause. For the distinction, see RTT:LPH §26, comment *a*.

Under the "cause in fact" rubric, we address the empirical substrate of causal connection that need to be resolved in any tort suit. In the ordinary highway case, for example, the defendant will triumph on the cause in fact question if he can show that the plaintiff's injury existed prior to the collision. The defendant did not cause (in fact) any harm that occurred before his wrongful conduct; nor is the defendant responsible for any harm that was caused by some independent event. The same type of analysis carries over to far more complicated causal connections, including those involving the covert operation of drugs and chemicals that through ingestion or exposure may be responsible for the plaintiff's disease or disability. In the modern setting, moreover, issues of cause in fact are no longer limited to situations in which the plaintiff searches for a discrete cause of a known and certain harm. Especially thorny issues arise when the plaintiff claims that the defendant's conduct has caused not an injury itself, but only an increased risk or hazard of injury—the so-called lost chance—that is itself compensable. These puzzles over causation become more intractable because of the deep intellectual tension built into the standard definitions.

The Restatement Third offers this definition of factual cause:

§26 FACTUAL CAUSE

> Tortious conduct must be a factual cause of physical harm for liability to be imposed. Conduct is a factual cause of harm when the harm would not have occurred absent the conduct . . . .

The comments make clear that this account implies that a factual cause must be "a necessary condition for the outcome," RTT:LPH §26, comment *b*, and go on to note that in the many cases of joint causation an "actor's tortious conduct need be only *a* [as opposed to *the*] factual cause of the other's harm." Working out the implications of these positions is hard work and often depends on the underlying contours of the plaintiff's basic theory of relief.

The extensive discussion of factual causation sets up the second inquiry into causation: the distinct issue of whether the cause was "proximate" to the harm. The Second Restatement substituted the bland term "legal cause" for proximate cause, but that innovation was never widely accepted, so the term "proximate cause" has been retained, RTT:LPH §26, comment *a*, although with evident reluctance. Chapter 6 of the Third Restatement is entitled "Scope of Liability (Proximate Cause)," with this notable caveat: "The Institute fervently hopes that the Restatement Fourth of Torts will not find the parenthetical necessary." Whatever one's views on the engrained legal terminology, an initial note of caution is needed because a literal reading of "proximate" as "nearest" misstates the role of the doctrine, which is to see whether more distant acts or events, in either time or space, can create a prima facie case for liability. Here the issues are not factual but conceptual: Once the facts are laid out, what are the harms attributable to the defendant whose own actions are combined with those of other persons and natural events? This issue of proximate cause presupposes that some harmful consequence suffered by the plaintiff was caused in fact by the defendant. Often the chain of events and actions that link the plaintiff's injury to the defendant's conduct is long and tortuous.

Under the traditional account of proximate cause the key question is whether the defendant's conduct could be regarded as a "substantial factor" in bringing about plaintiff's harm. But that terminology too is disfavored in the Third Restatement. See RTT:LPH §26, comment *j*, which dismisses the phrase as "obscure" and sticks with the but-for or necessary condition accounts of causation. The phrase continues to be deployed nonetheless. See, e.g., Boone v. William w. Backus Hosp., 864 A.2d 1, 17 (Conn. 2005). No matter what the rubric, the much-engrained substantial factor test often leads to an inquiry that asks whether any of the intervening or concurrent human actions or natural events that occur after defendant's conduct but before the plaintiff's harm sever the causal connection between them. The analysis is typically conducted in connection with negligence theories, but must also be adapted to deal with the more important areas of strict liability that remain in the law. The same issues of causation also arise with all the various no-fault systems considered in Chapter 12, *infra.*

Analytically, the problem of proximate cause can be addressed in two distinct ways. The forward-looking approach asks whether the chain of events that in fact occurred was sufficiently "foreseeable," "natural" or "probable" at the outset for the defendant to be held liable for the ultimate harm. That judgment is made from the standpoint of the defendant at the time the tortious act was committed, and denies recovery for those harms that are not "within the risk." The approach has an obvious connection with the negligence standard of liability which finds reasons to excuse a defendant for liability for improbable or unforeseeable acts. The second approach starts with the injury and works back toward the wrongful action of the defendant, seeking to determine whether any act of a third party or the plaintiff, or any natural event, has severed the causal connection between the harm and the defendant's wrongful conduct. Here the question is only whether, when all the evidence is in, it is permissible to say that the defendant "did it," that is, brought about the plaintiff's harm. This approach dominated both Roman law and the early common law, and is commonly associated as much with strict liability as negligence systems. The interaction between the "foresight" and "directness" perspectives, as they are respectively called, is the subject of Section C of this chapter. The materials are organized in historical sequence to trace the evolution and permutation of the basic doctrine from its nineteenth-century origins to its more contemporary applications. The first part of this section deals with physical injuries; the second with the negligent infliction of emotional distress.

As a rough generalization, the cause in fact issues appear to have gained in importance relative to the proximate-cause issues in the past generation. Why might this be so?

SECTION B.   CAUSE IN FACT

New York Central R.R. v. Grimstad
264 F. 334 (2d Cir. 1920)

Action of Elfrieda Grimstad, administratrix of the estate of Angell Grimstad, deceased, against the New York Central Railroad Company. Judgment for plaintiff, and defendant brings error. Reversed.

WARD, C.J. This is an action under the Federal Employers' Liability Act (Comp. St. Sec. 8657-8665) to recover damages for the death of Angell

Grimstad, captain of the covered barge *Grayton,* owned by the defendant railroad company. The charge of negligence is failure to equip the barge with proper life-preservers and other necessary and proper appliances, for want of which the decedent, having fallen into the water, was drowned.

The barge was lying on the port side of the steamer *Santa Clara,* on the north side of Pier 2, Erie Basin, Brooklyn, loaded with sugar in transit from Havana to St. John, N.B. The tug *Mary M,* entering the slip between Piers 1 and 2, bumped against the barge. The decedent's wife, feeling the shock, came out from the cabin, looked on one side of the barge, and saw nothing, and then went across the deck to the other side of the barge, and discovered her husband in the water about 10 feet from the barge holding up his hands out of the water. He did not know how to swim. She immediately ran back into the cabin for a small line, and when she returned with it he had disappeared.

It is admitted that the decedent at the time was engaged in interstate commerce. The court left it to the jury to say whether the defendant was negligent in not equipping the barge with life-preservers and whether, if there had been a life-preserver on board, Grimstad would have been saved from drowning.

The jury found as a fact that the defendant was negligent in not equipping the barge with life-preservers. Life-preservers and life belts are intended to be put on the body of a person before getting into the water, and would have been of no use at all to the decedent. On the other hand, life buoys are intended to be thrown to a person when in the water, and we will treat the charge in the complaint as covering life buoys.

Obviously the proximate cause of the decedent's death was his falling into the water, and in the absence of any testimony whatever on the point, we will assume that this happened without negligence on his part or on the part of the defendant. On the second question, whether a life buoy would have saved the decedent from drowning, we think the jury were left to pure conjecture and speculation. A jury might well conclude that a light near an open hatch or rail on the side of a vessel's deck would have prevented a person's falling into the hatch or into the water, in the dark. But there is nothing whatever to show that the decedent was not drowned because he did not know how to swim, nor anything to show that, if there had been a life buoy on board, the decedent's wife would have got it in time, that is, sooner than she got the small line, or, if she had, that she would have thrown it so that her husband could have seized it, or, if she did, that he would have seized it, or that, if he did, it would have prevented him from drowning.

The court erred in denying the defendant's motion to dismiss the complaint at the end of the case.

Judgment reversed.

NOTES

1. The life you save.... In Ford v. Trident Fisheries Co., 122 N.E. 389, 390 (Mass. 1919), the decedent fell overboard from his shipping vessel and drowned. The negligence alleged by the plaintiff was that the rescue boat was "lashed to the deck instead of being suspended from davits" from which it could be easily lowered. The court held that even if the defendant was negligent, "there is nothing to show they in any way contributed to Ford's death. He disappeared when he fell from the trawler, and it does not appear that if the boat had been suspended from davits and a different method of propelling it had been used he could have been rescued."

What is the precedential value of *Grimstad*? In Kirincich v. Standard Dredging Co., 112 F.2d 163, 164 (3d Cir. 1940), "the deceased fell off a dredge close to shore and was carried away by the falling tide while shipmates tried to save him with inadequate life-saving equipment, such inadequacy of equipment being the negligence alleged." The trial judge had dismissed plaintiff's cause of action, but the Third Circuit reversed and remanded for trial. Clark, C.J., observed in part:

> In the light, then, of this logic and these examples, would Kirincich have drowned even if a larger and more buoyant object than the inch heaving line had been thrown within two feet of him? If he could swim, even badly, there would be no doubt. Assuming he could not, we think he might (the appropriate grammatical mood) have saved himself through the help of something which he could more easily grasp. We can take judicial notice of the instinct of self-preservation that at first compensates for lack of skill. A drowning man comes to the surface and clutches at what he finds there — hence the significance of size and buoyancy in life saving apparatus. In other words, we prefer the doctrine of Judge Learned Hand in the case of Zinnel v. United States Shipping Board Emergency Fleet Corp., 10 F.2d 47, 49 [(2d Cir. 1925)]: "There of course remains the question whether they might have also said that the fault caused the loss. About that we agree no certain conclusion was possible. Nobody could, in the nature of things, be sure that the intestate would have seized the rope, or, if he had not, that it would have stopped his body. But we are not dealing with a criminal case, nor are we justified, where certainty is impossible, in insisting upon it.... we think it a question about which reasonable men might at least differ whether the intestate would not have been saved, had it been there," to that of his colleague, Judge Hough, dissenting in that case, and concurring in the earlier case of New York Central R. Co. v. Grimstad, 2 Cir., 264 F. 334, 335.

More modern cases explicitly confer upon the jury broad powers of decision in cases of rescue at sea. In Reyes v. Vantage Steamship Co., 609 F.2d 140, 144 (5th Cir. 1980), the decedent, while drunk, jumped off his boat and tried to swim to a mooring buoy some several hundred feet away.

Immediately after striking the water members of the crew saw that he was in mortal danger. The decedent struggled against a strong current only to drown, his energy spent, some 20 feet from the buoy. Since the ship was under a duty of maritime rescue, liability depended on the causal connection between the failed rescue and the decedent's drowning. Coast Guard regulations required a ship to have a rocket-powered line-throwing appliance capable of throwing at least 1,500 feet of line. The district court first denied relief. On appeal the court initially entered a judgment for the plaintiff, but on rehearing reversed and remanded for a finding on causation. "The District Court on remand must be prepared to determine whether there was time for a crew member to go to the hypothetical storage location, obtain the hypothetical line-throwing appliance, move it to the appropriate firing location, and fire the appliance—all before Reyes went limp in the water." The court also noted that it was necessary to take into account "some possibility that a line or lines fired over or near Reyes might have harmed him or perhaps impeded his labored swimming," as well as the likelihood that the line would have reached Reyes and whether he "would have obeyed an order" to take it. The court then refused to place "the difficult burden of proving causation on the widow of the deceased seaman." On remand, the district court entered a judgment for the plaintiff, finding that defendant's negligence was 15 percent of the cause of death. Note that the Third Restatement endorses the hypothetical, or counterfactual approach, noting the factual difficulties in marginal cases where the defendant's deviation from the accepted standard of care is slight. RTT: LPH §26, comment *e*.

2. *Switching the burden of proof on causation.* In Haft v. Lone Palm Hotel, 478 P.2d 465, 474-475 (Cal. 1970), the plaintiffs brought wrongful death actions when a father and son drowned in the pool at the defendant's Palm Springs motel. The applicable statute provided that "lifeguard service shall be provided or signs shall be erected clearly indicating that such service is not provided." The defendant neither provided the lifeguard service nor posted the signs, and no evidence explained how the deaths actually took place. The court, through Tobriner, J., first observed that "to hold that a pool owner, who has failed to satisfy either of the section's alternative requirements, may limit his liability to that resulting from his 'lesser' failure to erect a sign, would of course effectively read out of the section the primary requirement of providing lifeguard service." (Sound?) He then addressed the burden of proof on causation as follows:

> The troublesome problems concerning the causation issue in the instant case of course arise out of the total lack of direct evidence as to the precise manner in which the drownings occurred. Although the paucity of evidence on causation is normally one of the burdens that must be shouldered by a

plaintiff in proving his case, the evidentiary void in the instant action results primarily from defendants' failure to provide a lifeguard to observe occurrences within the pool area. The main purpose of the lifeguard requirement is undoubtedly to aid those in danger, but an attentive guard does serve the subsidiary function of witnessing those accidents that do occur. The absence of such a lifeguard in the instant case thus not only stripped decedents of a significant degree of protection to which they were entitled, but also deprived the present plaintiffs of a means of definitively establishing the facts leading to the drownings.

Clearly, the failure to provide a lifeguard greatly enhanced the chances of the occurrence of the instant drownings. In proving (1) that defendants were negligent in this respect, and (2) that the available facts, at the very least, strongly suggest that a competent lifeguard, exercising reasonable care, would have prevented the deaths, plaintiffs have gone as far as they possibly can under the circumstances in proving the requisite causal link between defendants' negligence and the accidents. To require plaintiffs to establish "proximate causation" to a greater certainty than they have in the instant case, would permit defendants to gain the advantage of the lack of proof inherent in the lifeguardless situation which they have created. Under these circumstances the burden of proof on the issue of causation should be shifted to defendants to absolve themselves if they can.

This burden shifting rationale was rejected in Schwabe v. Custer's Inn Associates, LPP, 15 P.3d 903 (Mont. 2000), in which the decedent drowned in a pool that did have a no lifeguard sign, but which lacked the on-site personnel, required by statute when no lifeguard was present, capable of performing cardio pulmonary respiration (CPR). Owing to the length of time that the decedent was underwater, the court concluded that no intervention would have saved the decedent.

Zuchowicz v. United States
140 F.3d 381 (2nd Cir. 1998)

CALABRESI, J. The defendant, the United States of America, appeals from a judgment of the United States District Court for the District of Connecticut (Warren W. Eginton, Judge). This suit under the Federal Tort Claims Act, 28 U.S.C. §§1346(b), 2671-2680, was originally filed by Patricia Zuchowicz, who claimed to have developed primary pulmonary hypertension, a fatal lung condition, as a result of the defendant's negligence in prescribing an overdose of the drug Danocrine. Following Mrs. Zuchowicz's death in 1991, her husband, Steven, continued the case on behalf of his wife's estate, claiming that the defendant was responsible for her death. After a bench trial, the district court awarded the plaintiff $1,034,236.02 in damages. . . .

I. BACKGROUND

A. DRUG, ILLNESS, AND DEATH

1. *The Overdose*

The facts, as determined by the district court, are as follows. On February 18, 1989, Mrs. Zuchowicz filled a prescription for the drug Danocrine at the Naval Hospital pharmacy in Groton, Connecticut. The prescription erroneously instructed her to take 1600 milligrams of Danocrine per day, or twice the maximum recommended dosage. The defendant has stipulated that its doctors and/or pharmacists were negligent and violated the prevailing standard of medical care by prescribing this wrong dosage.

Mrs. Zuchowicz took the 1600 milligrams of Danocrine each day for the next month. Thereafter, from March 24 until May 30, she took 800 milligrams per day. While taking Danocrine she experienced abnormal weight gain, bloating, edema, hot flashes, night sweats, a racing heart, chest pains, dizziness, headaches, acne, and fatigue. On May 30, she was examined by an obstetrician/gynecologist in private practice who told her to stop taking the Danocrine. During the summer, she continued to experience severe fatigue and chest tightness and pain, and began having shortness of breath. In October 1989, she was diagnosed with primary pulmonary hypertension ("PPH"), a rare and fatal disease in which increased pressure in an individual's pulmonary artery causes severe strain on the right side of the heart. At the time she was diagnosed with the disease, the median life expectancy for PPH sufferers was 2.5 years. Treatments included calcium channel blockers and heart and lung transplantation.

Mrs. Zuchowicz was on the waiting list for a lung transplant when she became pregnant. Pregnant women are not eligible for transplants, and pregnancy exacerbates PPH. Mrs. Zuchowicz gave birth to a son on November 21, 1991. She died one month later, on December 31, 1991. . . .

B. THE EXPERT TESTIMONY . . .

[Plaintiff's expert] Dr. Matthay testified that he was confident to a reasonable medical certainty that the Danocrine caused Mrs. Zuchowicz's PPH. When pressed, he added that he believed the *overdose* of Danocrine to have been responsible for the disease. His conclusion was based on the temporal relationship between the overdose and the start of the disease and the differential etiology method of excluding other possible causes. While Dr. Matthay did not rule out *all* other possible causes of pulmonary hypertension, he did exclude all the causes of secondary pulmonary hypertension. On the basis of Mrs. Zuchowicz's history, he also ruled out all previously known drug-related causes of primary pulmonary hypertension.

Dr. Matthay further testified that the progression and timing of Mrs. Zuchowicz's disease in relation to her overdose supported a finding of drug-induced PPH. Dr. Matthay emphasized that, prior to the overdose, Mrs. Zuchowicz was a healthy, active young woman with no history of cardiovascular problems, and that, shortly after the overdose, she began experiencing symptoms of PPH such as weight gain, swelling of hands and feet, fatigue, and shortness of breath. He described the similarities between the course of Mrs. Zuchowicz's illness and that of accepted cases of drug-induced PPH, and he went on to discuss cases involving classes of drugs that are known to cause other pulmonary diseases (mainly anti-cancer drugs). He noted that the onset of these diseases, which are recognized to be caused by the particular drugs, was very similar in timing and course to the development of Mrs. Zuchowicz's illness. . . .

II

B. WERE THE DISTRICT COURT'S FACTUAL FINDINGS WITH RESPECT TO CAUSATION CLEARLY ERRONEOUS? . . .

4. *Was Danocrine a But For Cause of Mrs. Zuchowicz's Illness and Death?* . . .

We hold that, on the basis of Dr. Matthay's testimony alone, the finder of fact could have concluded — under Connecticut law — that Mrs. Zuchowicz's PPH was, more likely than not, caused by Danocrine. While it was not possible to eliminate all other possible causes of pulmonary hypertension, the evidence presented showed that the experts had not only excluded all causes of secondary pulmonary hypertension, but had also ruled out all the previously known drug-related causes of PPH. In addition, Dr. Matthay testified, based on his expertise in pulmonary diseases, that the progression and timing of Mrs. Zuchowicz's illness in relationship to the timing of her overdose supported a finding of *drug-induced* PPH to a reasonable medical certainty. In this respect, we note that in the case before us, unlike many toxic torts situations, there was not a long latency period between the onset of symptoms and the patient's exposure to the drug that was alleged to have caused the illness. Rather, as Dr. Matthay testified, the plaintiff began exhibiting symptoms typical of drug-induced PPH shortly after she started taking the Danocrine. Under the circumstances, we cannot say that the fact finder was clearly erroneous in determining that, more probably than not, the Danocrine caused Mrs. Zuchowicz's illness.

5. *Was the Overdose a But For Cause of Mrs. Zuchowicz's Illness and Death?*

To say that Danocrine caused Mrs. Zuchowicz's injuries is only half the story, however. In order for the causation requirement to be met, a trier of fact must be able to determine, by a preponderance of the evidence, that the defendant's *negligence* was responsible for the injury. In this case, defendant's negligence consisted in prescribing an overdose of Danocrine to Mrs. Zuchowicz. For liability to exist, therefore, it is necessary that the fact finder be able to conclude, more probably than not, that the *overdose* was the cause of Mrs. Zuchowicz's illness and ultimate death. The mere fact that the exposure to Danocrine was likely responsible for the disease does not suffice.

The problem of linking defendant's negligence to the harm that occurred is one that many courts have addressed in the past. A car is speeding and an accident occurs. That the car was involved and was a cause of the crash is readily shown. The accident, moreover, is of the sort that rules prohibiting speeding are designed to prevent. But is this enough to support a finding of fact, in the individual case, that *speeding* was, in fact, more probably than not, the cause of the accident? The same question can be asked when a car that was driving in violation of a minimum speed requirement on a super-highway is rear-ended. Again, it is clear that the car and its driver were causes of the accident. And the accident is of the sort that minimum speeding rules are designed to prevent. But can a fact finder conclude, without more, that the driver's negligence in *driving too slowly* led to the crash? To put it more precisely — the defendant's negligence was strongly causally linked to the accident, and the defendant was undoubtedly a *but for* cause of the harm, but does this suffice to allow a fact finder to say that the defendant's *negligence* was a *but for* cause?

At one time, courts were reluctant to say in such circumstances that the wrong could be deemed to be the cause. They emphasized the logical fallacy of *post hoc, ergo propter hoc,* and demanded some direct evidence connecting the defendant's wrongdoing to the harm. . . .

All that has changed, however. And, as is so frequently the case in tort law, Chief Judge Cardozo in New York and Chief Justice Traynor in California led the way. In various opinions, they stated that: if (a) a negligent act was deemed wrongful *because* that act increased the chances that a particular type of accident would occur, and (b) a mishap of that very sort did happen, this was enough to support a finding by the trier of fact that the negligent behavior caused the harm. Where such a strong causal link exists, it is up to the negligent party to bring in evidence denying *but for* cause and suggesting that in the actual case the wrongful conduct had not been a substantial factor.

Thus, in a case involving a nighttime collision between vehicles, one of which did not have the required lights, Judge Cardozo stated that lights were mandated precisely to reduce the risk of such accidents occurring and that this fact sufficed to show causation unless the negligent party demonstrated, for example, that in the particular instance the presence of very bright street lights or of a full moon rendered the lack of lights on the vehicle an unlikely cause. See Martin v. Herzog. . . .

The case before us is a good example of the above-mentioned principles in their classic form. The reason the FDA does not approve the prescription of new drugs at above the dosages as to which extensive tests have been performed is because all drugs involve risks of untoward side effects in those who take them. Moreover, it is often true that the higher the dosage the greater is the likelihood of such negative effects. At the approved dosages, the benefits of the particular drug have presumably been deemed worth the risks it entails. At greater than approved dosages, not only do the risks of tragic side effects (known and unknown) increase, but there is no basis on the testing that has been performed for supposing that the drug's benefits outweigh these increased risks. . . . It follows that when a negative side effect is demonstrated to be the result of a drug, and the drug was wrongly prescribed in an unapproved and excessive dosage (*i.e.* a strong causal link has been shown), the plaintiff who is injured has generally shown enough to permit the finder of fact to conclude that the excessive dosage was a substantial factor in producing the harm.

In fact, plaintiff's showing in the case before us, while relying on the above stated principles, is stronger. For plaintiff introduced some direct evidence of causation as well. On the basis of his long experience with drug-induced pulmonary diseases, one of plaintiff's experts, Dr. Matthay, testified that the timing of Mrs. Zuchowicz's illness led him to conclude that the overdose (and not merely Danocrine) was responsible for her catastrophic reaction.

Under the circumstances, we hold that defendant's attack on the district court's finding of causation is meritless. . . .

Affirmed.

NOTES

1. *Substantive theory and causal connections.* Forging the causal links in plaintiff's case resists easy universalization under the Restatement Third's test of factual causation, for in every case the precise account of causation is heavily dependent on the underlying substantive theory of liability. In ordinary stranger cases decided under a theory of strict liability, for example, it is usually necessary to show some push/pull type of causal connection between what the defendant did and what happened to the plaintiff. Thus, the plaintiff can recover, for example, by showing that the weight of the defendant's truck on a public highway was sufficient to place downward pressure on the highway that broke the pipe located below it. But if the substantive offense (be it under strict liability or under a negligence per se rule) requires that the truck be above some permitted weight, then the causal question requires her to show that the *excess* weight made the difference. See Stimpson v. Wellington Service Corp., 246 N.E.2d 801

(Mass. 1969). Similarly, in the *Grimstad* line of cases, the pertinent question is whether the rescue could have been accomplished if the vessel had been outfitted with the proper equipment. In medical malpractice cases, strict liability theories are not viable, making the causal issues more complex. In *Zuchowicz* is it relevant that the current labels list the maximum permissible daily dosage at 400 mgs for some conditions and 200 mgs for others, with a strict warning against double dosing in the event that one dose was missed? More concretely, how did Calabresi, J., decide that the excess dosage of Danocrine made the difference? Suppose that the incremental dosage supplied only a 5 percent benefit, but increased the risk of death from 10 to 11 percent, and that no one thinks that this extra benefit is worth the extra risk. Has the case for causation been made out? Could the plaintiff get to the jury on this undisputed evidence? For a recognition of the problems with "incremental risk" in overdose cases, see RTT:LPH §26, comment *f*, and illustrations 1 & 2.

2. *Slip-and-fall cases.* Another group of cases that raises difficult questions of cause in fact are the so-called slip-and-fall cases. In Reynolds v. Texas & Pacific Ry., 37 La. Ann. 694, 698 (1885), plaintiff, a 250-pound woman, after hurrying out of a lighted waiting room, fell down the unlighted steps leading to the train platform. The defendant argued that "she might well have made the mis-step and fallen even had it been broad daylight," but the court affirmed judgment for plaintiff, noting:

> We concede that this is possible, and recognize the distinction between post hoc and propter hoc. But where the negligence of the defendant greatly multiplies the chances of accident to the plaintiff, and is of a character naturally leading to its occurrence, the mere possibility that it might have happened without the negligence is not sufficient to break the chain of cause and effect between the negligence and the injury. Courts, in such matters, consider the natural and ordinary course of events, and do not indulge in fanciful suppositions. The whole tendency of the evidence connects the accident with the negligence.

3. *Cause in fact in products liability cases.* In Engberg v. Ford Motor Co., 205 N.W.2d 104, 106 (S.D. 1973), plaintiff's husband was killed when he drove his station wagon, purchased two weeks earlier from the defendant, off the highway into a ditch. No other cars were involved in the accident and the parties were unable to establish the precise sequence of events leading up to the decedent's death. The plaintiff supported her claim that defendant's seat belt was of insufficient strength to withstand the impact of a crash by introducing evidence that the belt was found "buckled but broken" after the fatal crash, and that no blood was found inside the car. Her expert witnesses further testified that:

> the seat belt severed in this case because the boot and belt were rubbing on the frame of the seat causing them to give way under the pressure of less

than expectable force. He also stated that in his opinion, the design of the assembly and the installation of the belt was improper to prevent the rubbing that caused the severance. He further testified, over the defendant's objection, that the absence of internal damage to the vehicle indicated that the fatal injury occurred outside of the car and that had the seat belt remained intact and the decedent remained inside the car, the amount of injury would have been minor.

[The defendant's expert witness in turn] testified that the boot and seat belt could not in any way come into contact with the frame of the seat. [He] also testified that based upon the type and location of the cut, it was his opinion that the seat belt had been severed by the metal capsule that ties together the wires of the seat and that the capsule had been moved from where it was originally installed by the manufacturer.

There was additional evidence in the case that the decedent did not properly adjust his seat belt before the crash and that there was ample room for him to slip out under the belt when the crash took place.

The court held that the case was properly left for the jury because defendant could not show that plaintiff's version of the case was "contradicted by its undisputed physical facts," and it further rejected the defendant's contention that it was pure "speculation" to conclude that the decedent would have survived if the seat belt had remained intact. What additional facts need to be established in order for the defendant to be entitled to a directed verdict? For the plaintiff to be entitled to a directed verdict?

Finally, in Sanchez v. Hillerich & Bradsby, 128 Cal. Rptr. 2d 529 (Cal. App. 2002), the plaintiff pitcher, for California State University, Northridge, was struck by a line drive hit by Correa, a University of Southern California batter, using an aluminum Air Attack 2 bat. The bat was manufactured by the defendant, and contained "a pressurized air bladder which, according to its designer, substantially increases the speed at which the ball leaves the surface of the bat." The trial judge dismissed the case on that ground that "because the speed of the ball leaving the bat was never established, no causation attributed to the increased risk of use of the [bat] could be established." On appeal, the court held that once the increased speed was established, the plaintiff should reach the jury: "absent other factors (none are suggested) it follows that the ball must have reached the appellant sooner than if Correa had used a bat other than the Air Attack 2. Dr. Kent [plaintiff's expert] opined that the ball which hit Correa was traveling at a speed of up to 107.8 miles per hour, given appellant a reaction time of .32 and .37 seconds, below the acceptable minimum time recognized by the NCAA." Must it also be shown that the plaintiff could have reacted in time to avoid the injury had the batter been using another bat?

"Proximate cause is a rule of physics and not a criterion of negligence." Collier v. Citizens Coach Co., 330 S.W.2d 74, 76 (Ark. 1959). Is that true or

false in light of the cases thus far considered? Reconsider the answer in both
normative and positive terms at the end of this chapter.

General Electric Co. v. Joiner
522 U.S. 136 (1997)

CHIEF JUSTICE REHNQUIST delivered the opinion of the Court.

We granted certiorari in this case to determine what standard an
appellate court should apply in reviewing a trial court's decision to admit or
exclude expert testimony under Daubert v. Merrell Dow Pharmaceuticals,
Inc., 509 U.S. 579 (1993). We hold that abuse of discretion is the appropriate standard. We apply this standard and conclude that the District
Court in this case did not abuse its discretion when it excluded certain
proffered expert testimony.

I

Respondent Robert Joiner began work as an electrician in the Water &
Light Department of Thomasville, Georgia (City) in 1973. This job
required him to work with and around the City's electrical transformers,
which used a mineral-based dielectric fluid as a coolant. Joiner often had to
stick his hands and arms into the fluid to make repairs. The fluid would
sometimes splash onto him, occasionally getting into his eyes and mouth.
In 1983 the City discovered that the fluid in some of the transformers was
contaminated with polychlorinated biphenyls (PCB's). PCB's are widely
considered to be hazardous to human health. Congress, with limited
exceptions, banned the production and sale of PCB's in 1978.

Joiner was diagnosed with small cell lung cancer in 1991. He sued
petitioners in Georgia state court the following year. Petitioner Monsanto
manufactured PCB's from 1935 to 1977; petitioners General Electric and
Westinghouse Electric manufactured transformers and dielectric fluid. In
his complaint Joiner linked his development of cancer to his exposure to
PCB's and their derivatives, polychlorinated dibenzofurans (furans) and
polychlorinated dibenzodioxins (dioxins). Joiner had been a smoker for
approximately eight years, his parents had both been smokers, and there
was a history of lung cancer in his family. He was thus perhaps already at a
heightened risk of developing lung cancer eventually. The suit alleged
that his exposure to PCB's "promoted" his cancer; had it not been for his
exposure to these substances, his cancer would not have developed for
many years, if at all.

Petitioners removed the case to federal court. Once there, they moved
for summary judgment. They contended that (1) there was no evidence that

Joiner suffered significant exposure to PCB's, furans, or dioxins, and (2) there was no admissible scientific evidence that PCB's promoted Joiner's cancer. . . .

The District Court ruled that there was a genuine issue of material fact as to whether Joiner had been exposed to PCB's. But it nevertheless granted summary judgment for petitioners because (1) there was no genuine issue as to whether Joiner had been exposed to furans and dioxins, and (2) the testimony of Joiner's experts had failed to show that there was a link between exposure to PCB's and small-cell lung cancer. The court believed that the testimony of respondent's experts to the contrary did not rise above "subjective belief or unsupported speculation." 864 F. Supp. 1310, 1326 (N.D. Ga. 1994). Their testimony was therefore inadmissible.

The Court of Appeals for the Eleventh Circuit reversed. 78 F.3d 524 (1996). It held that "[b]ecause the Federal Rules of Evidence governing expert testimony display a preference for admissibility, we apply a particularly stringent standard of review to the trial judge's exclusion of expert testimony." Id. at 529. Applying that standard, the Court of Appeals held that the District Court had erred in excluding the testimony of Joiner's expert witnesses. . . .

We granted petitioners' petition for a writ of certiorari, and we now reverse. . . .

II

. . . We have held that abuse of discretion is the proper standard of review of a district court's evidentiary rulings. . . . The Court of Appeals suggested that *Daubert* somehow altered this general rule in the context of a district court's decision to exclude scientific evidence. But *Daubert* did not address the standard of appellate review for evidentiary rulings at all. It did hold that the "austere" *Frye* standard of "general acceptance" had not been carried over into the Federal Rules of Evidence. But the opinion also said:

> That the *Frye* test was displaced by the Rules of Evidence does not mean, however, that the Rules themselves place no limits on the admissibility of purportedly scientific evidence. Nor is the trial judge disabled from screening such evidence. To the contrary, under the Rules the trial judge must ensure that any and all scientific testimony or evidence admitted is not only relevant, but reliable.

Thus, while the Federal Rules of Evidence allow district courts to admit a somewhat broader range of scientific testimony than would have been admissible under *Frye*, they leave in place the "gatekeeper" role of the trial judge in screening such evidence. A court of appeals applying "abuse-of-discretion" review to such rulings may not categorically distinguish between rulings allowing expert testimony and rulings disallowing it. We likewise reject respondent's argument that because the granting of summary judgment in this case was "outcome determinative," it should have been subjected to a more searching standard of review. On a motion for summary judgment, disputed issues of fact are resolved against the moving party — here, petitioners. But the question of admissibility of expert testimony is not such an issue of fact, and is reviewable under the abuse-of-discretion standard....

III

We believe that a proper application of the correct standard of review here indicates that the District Court did not abuse its discretion. Joiner's theory of liability was that his exposure to PCB's and their derivatives "promoted" his development of small-cell lung cancer. In support of that theory he proffered the deposition testimony of expert witnesses....

The District Court agreed with petitioners that the animal studies on which respondent's experts relied did not support his contention that exposure to PCB's had contributed to his cancer. The studies involved infant mice that had developed cancer after being exposed to PCB's. The infant mice in the studies had had massive doses of PCB's injected directly into their peritoneums or stomachs. Joiner was an adult human being whose alleged exposure to PCB's was far less than the exposure in the animal studies. The PCB's were injected into the mice in a highly concentrated form. The fluid with which Joiner had come into contact generally had a much smaller PCB concentration of between 0-500 parts per million. The cancer that these mice developed was alveologenic adenomas; Joiner had developed small-cell carcinomas. No study demonstrated that adult mice developed cancer after being exposed to PCB's. One of the experts admitted that no study had demonstrated that PCB's lead to cancer in any other species.

Respondent failed to reply to this criticism. Rather than explaining how and why the experts could have extrapolated their opinions from these seemingly far-removed animal studies, respondent chose "to proceed as if the only issue [was] whether animal studies can ever be a proper foundation for an expert's opinion." *Joiner,* 864 F. Supp. at 1324. Of course, whether animal studies can ever be a proper foundation for an expert's opinion was not the issue. The issue was whether *these* experts' opinions were sufficiently supported by the animal studies on which they purported to rely. The studies were so dissimilar to the facts presented in this litigation that it was not an abuse of discretion for the District Court to have rejected the experts' reliance on them.

The District Court also concluded that the four epidemiological studies on which respondent relied were not a sufficient basis for the experts' opinions. The first such study involved workers at an Italian capacitor plant who had been exposed to PCB's. The authors noted that lung cancer deaths among ex-employees at the plant were higher than might have been expected, but concluded that "there were apparently no grounds for associating lung cancer deaths (although increased above expectations) and exposure in the plant." Id. at 172. Given that [the authors] were unwilling to say that PCB exposure had caused cancer among the workers they examined, their study did not support the experts' conclusion that Joiner's exposure to PCB's caused his cancer. [The Court then conducted similar reviews of three other studies.]

[Respondent] claims that because the District Court's disagreement was with the conclusion that the experts drew from the studies, the District Court committed legal error and was properly reversed by the Court of Appeals. But conclusions and methodology are not entirely distinct from one another. Trained experts commonly extrapolate from existing data. But nothing in either *Daubert* or the Federal Rules of Evidence requires a district court to admit opinion evidence that is connected to existing data only by the *ipse dixit* of the expert. A court may conclude that there is simply too great an analytical gap between the data and the opinion proffered. That is what the District Court did here, and we hold that it did not abuse its discretion in so doing.

[The Court then remanded for a determination of "whether Joiner was exposed to furans and dioxins, and whether if there was such exposure, the opinions of Joiner's experts would then be admissible. . . . "]

JUSTICE BREYER, concurring.

. . . [M]odern life, including good health as well as economic well-being, depends upon the use of artificial or manufactured substances, such as chemicals. And it may, therefore, prove particularly important to see that judges fulfill their *Daubert* gatekeeping function, so that they help assure that the powerful engine of tort liability, which can generate strong financial incentives to reduce, or to eliminate, production, points toward the right substances and does not destroy the wrong ones. [Justice Breyer then endorses a suggestion from the *amici* brief of the New England Journal of Medicine that judges "be strongly encouraged to make use of their inherent authority . . . to appoint experts."]

JUSTICE STEVENS, concurring in part and dissenting in part.

. . . Unlike the District Court, the Court of Appeals expressly decided that a "weight of the evidence" methodology was scientifically acceptable. To this extent, the Court of Appeals' opinion is persuasive. It is not intrinsically "unscientific" for experienced professionals to arrive at a conclusion by weighing all available scientific evidence — this is not the sort of "junk science" with which *Daubert* was concerned. After all, as Joiner points out, the Environmental Protection Agency (EPA) uses the same methodology to assess risks, albeit using a somewhat different threshold than that required in a trial. Petitioners' own experts used the same scientific approach as well. And using this methodology, it would seem that an expert could reasonably have concluded that the study of workers at an Italian capacitor plant, coupled with data from Monsanto's study and other studies, raises an inference that PCB's promote lung cancer. . . .

In any event, it bears emphasis that the Court has not held that it would have been an abuse of discretion to admit the expert testimony. . . .

NOTES

1. Beyond Daubert. In Kumho Tire Co. v. Carmichael, 526 U.S. 137, 148 (1999), the Supreme Court held that a district court's gatekeeper function under *Daubert* extended to technical as well as scientific evidence, in this case the engineering testimony about the possible causes of a tire blowout. Justice Breyer noted that:

> it would prove difficult, if not impossible, for judges to administer evidentiary rules under which a gatekeeping obligation depended upon a distinction between "scientific" knowledge and "technical" or "other specialized" knowledge. There is no clear line that divides the one from the others. Disciplines such as engineering rest upon scientific knowledge. Pure scientific theory itself may depend for its development upon observation and properly engineered machinery.

More recently, in Weisgram v. Marley Co. 528 U.S. 440, 455-456 (2000), the plaintiff prevailed at trial on the question of product defect solely on the strength of expert evidence that the district court had ruled admissible. The Court of Appeal disqualified that expert testimony as speculative under *Daubert*, and then entered a judgment as a matter of law for the defendant. The Supreme Court rejected plaintiff's contention that he was entitled to an "automatic remand" in order to refurbish his case with additional evidence, noting that it "is implausible to suggest, post-*Daubert*, that parties will initially present less than their best expert evidence in the expectation of a second chance should their first try fail."

2. The Bendectin saga. In *Daubert*, the defendant obtained summary judgment on the causation issue after the plaintiff's team of eight recognized experts were prepared to testify that Bendectin, a drug once commonly used to control nausea during pregnancy, could cause birth defects, largely by reinterpreting the data contained in peer review studies that had denied the causal association between Bendectin and birth defects. *Daubert* rejected the traditional test of Frye v. United States, 293 F. 1013,

1014 (D.C. Cir. 1923), which had allowed as admissible only expert testimony that had been "generally accepted" as reliable by the scientific community. It then remanded the case for further consideration, noting that both lower courts erroneously "focused almost exclusively on 'general acceptance,' as gauged by publication and the decision of other courts," not taking into account sufficiently other measures of reliability and relevance, including the tightness of "fit" between the evidence presented and the charge to be proved.

In a bruising opinion on remand, Kozinski, J., broke with earlier decisions that had freely allowed plaintiff's expert to testify on the relationship between Bendectin and birth defects, see, e.g., Oxendine v. Merrell Dow Pharmaceuticals, Inc., 506 A.2d 1100, 1110 (D.C. 1986), and upheld summary judgment under the revised standard, noting that none of plaintiff's experts "are proposing to testify about matters growing naturally and directly out of research they have conducted independent of the litigation," and far from publishing their results in peer-reviewed journals, "the only place their theories and studies have been published is in the pages of federal and state reporters." See Daubert v. Merrell Dow Pharmaceuticals, Inc., 43 F.3d 1311, 1317, 1318 (9th Cir. 1995). In one sense his decision came too late because Richardson-Merrell had already pulled Bendectin from the market because of its fear of continued lawsuits. "[W]hile Bendectin usage declined from 1 million new therapy starts in 1979 to zero in 1984, there has been no change in the incidence of birth defects." Lynch v. Merrell-National Laboratories, Inc., 830 F.2d 1190, 1194 (1st Cir. 1987).

3. *The thimerosal litigation.* Kozinski's J.'s decision in *Daubert* proved highly influential in Doe v. Ortho-Clinical Diagnostics, 440 F. Supp. 2d 465, 474 (M.D.N.C. 2006), where the plaintiff, an autistic child, sued Ortho-Clinical for negligence, breach of warranty, and negligent and intentional misrepresentation. Each claim rested on the assertion that thimerosal, a component RhoGAM, the defendant's biologic — that is, a complex, large, living molecule often found in blood or vaccines — administered to the plaintiff's mother during pregnancy, caused the plaintiff's autism. That claim depended on showing, first, general causation — namely, that defendant's product was of the type that could have caused the injuries in question — and, second, specific causation — namely, making out that causal connection in the instant case. The court's exhaustive review of the qualifications and proferred testimony of the plaintiff's expert physicians reads, as is typical in these cases, like summary judgment for the defendant on both causal issues. For example, Beaty, J., observed that Dr. Geier did not have the formal qualifications as a pediatric neurologist to testify on the relevant causal issues. As did Kozinski, J., in *Daubert,* Beaty, J., also conducted his own extensive review "of a motley assortment of diverse literature" that Dr. Geier presented. He noted that "Dr. Geier could not point to a single study,

including his own writing, that conclusively determined that the amount of thimerosal in RhoGAM when given not to the fetus but to the mother, as in this case, could cause autism . . . .Moreover, Dr. Geier's conclusion that the peer-reviewed literature he has relied upon supports his theory that autism can be caused by thimerosal is flatly contradicted by all of the epidemiological studies available at this time." The link between thimerosal and autism also arises in litigation under the National Childhood Vaccine Injury Compensation Act, considered, *infra* Chapter 12, Section C.

4. State court response. Post-*Daubert*, state courts have had to wrestle with the question of whether to keep the somewhat higher *Frye* standard or to move toward the *Daubert* rule. In Goeb v. Tharaldson, 615 N.W.2d 800, 812-816 (Minn. 2000), the plaintiffs alleged that they were injured by harmful exposure to Dow Chemical's insecticide Dursban. The Minnesota court opted to keep to the more restrictive *Frye* standard it had adopted in State v. Mack, 292 N.W.2d 764 (Minn. 1980). Blatz, C.J., first recognized that:

> critics of the *Frye* general acceptance standard claim that it may at times exclude cutting-edge but otherwise demonstrably reliable, probative evidence, and thus represents a more conservative approach to the admissibility of scientific evidence. For example, the *Frye* standard might exclude a new, but reliable, methodology or test because of the inherent time lag between the development of a new scientific technique and its general acceptance in the field. . . .
>
> By comparison, because *Daubert* stresses a more liberal and flexible approach to the admission of scientific testimony, it has been viewed as relaxing the barriers to the admissibility of expert evidence. *See, e.g., Joiner.* . . .
>
> The *Frye* general acceptance standard has been criticized for other reasons, most notably that it improperly defers to scientists the legal question of admissibility of scientific evidence. . . . However, in repossessing the power to determine admissibility for the courts, *Daubert* takes from scientists and confers upon judges uneducated in science the authority to determine what is scientific. This approach which necessitates that trial judges be "amateur scientists," has also been frequently criticized. . . . By comparison, the *Frye* general acceptance standard ensures that the persons most qualified to assess scientific validity of a technique have the determinative voice.

Blatz, C.J., then opted for the *Frye* standard even though rule 702 of the Minnesota code was identical to the federal standard.

Just how great is the practical difference between *Daubert* and *Frye*, both of which are far stricter than the more permissive standard used in *Oxendine*? For the claim that *Daubert* has markedly increased the number of challenges to statistical data, see Kaye, The Dynamics of *Daubert*, 87 Va. L. Rev. 1933, 1936-1937 (2001), who cautions that the "'intellectual rigor' standard of *Kumho* . . . must be applied with some caution lest it become a subterfuge for excluding expert testimony that is less than ideal but still within the range of reasonable scientific debate." For a study, see Cheng & Yoon, Does *Frye* or *Daubert* Matter?: A Study of Scientific Admissibility Standards, 91 Va. L. Rev. 471, 475 (2005), noting that, as of 2005 the scorecard reads: 24 states have adopted *Daubert*, 14 states have adopted *Frye*, and 12 states have adopted some other standard. The paper then concludes that a detailed examination offers strong support for the theory "that the choice between a *Frye* and *Daubert* standard does not make any practical difference." See also Bernstein & Jackson, The *Daubert* Trilogy in the States, 44 Jurimetrics 351 (2004).

5. *The Agent Orange litigation.* Proving causation in fact was also the central issue in suits brought mainly by servicemen and their offspring who claimed that Agent Orange (or more specifically dioxin, a deadly by-product of its production) caused a large class of serious but undifferentiated illnesses and birth defects. The individual suits were consolidated into a class before Weinstein, J., with individual plaintiffs having the right to opt out of the class. The main class settled for $180,000,000, with the moneys placed in a trust fund for distribution to the victims. In a subsequent action, Weinstein, J., anticipated *Joiner* and dismissed the suits of the opt-out plaintiffs because the evidence (including animal and epidemiological studies) did not support proof of causal connection. See In re "Agent Orange" Product Liability Litigation, 611 F. Supp. 1223, 1241 (E.D.N.Y. 1985). Why should the settlement have provided for any award given the summary judgment that followed? On Agent Orange generally, see P. Schuck, Agent Orange on Trial: Mass Toxic Disasters in the Courts (1986).

The Agent Orange cases illustrate the three levels of causation relevant in toxic torts cases. These are summarized by Professor Abraham in Individual Action and Collective Responsibility: The Dilemma of Mass Tort Reform, 73 Va. L. Rev. 845, 860, 867-868 (1987), as follows:

> To meet traditional burdens of proof in a regime that emphasizes individual responsibility, the plaintiff must show what I shall call *substance, source,* and *exposure* causation. That is, he must prove that the substance for which the defendant is responsible can cause his injury or disease, that the defendant and not someone else was the source of the substance, and that he was in fact exposed to the substance in a way that has caused his disease. In many cases, proof of some of these elements is simple; in some cases, proof of one automatically proves another. For example, when a particular disease is caused almost exclusively by a particular substance, the occurrence of the disease is the substance's "signature." Proof that the plaintiff has the disease, therefore, is also proof of both exposure and substance causation. In many cases, however, meeting the traditional burden of proof as to each of these elements is no minor accomplishment.

Abraham then expressed his doubt that the traditional tort models could work in cases like Agent Orange where no signature disease is found. How does Abraham's framework apply to asbestosis? To the other cases in this section?

6. *The Third Restatement on proof of factual causation.* The Third Restatement offers an extended exegesis on proof of causation in toxic substance and disease cases that deliberately skirts the *Daubert* issue. RTT:LPH §28, comment *c.* After noting how judicial dissatisfaction with jury performance in both the Agent Orange and Bendectin litigation led to greater judicial scrutiny of expert testimony, it criticizes as "incorrect" the current tendency to require full scientific proof such that medical injury and toxic tort claims cannot go forward "without statistically significant epidemiologic evidence." In its view it is mistaken to think that "science" presents an "objective" method of establishing evidence, when the chief function of the court is to identify "the minimum amount of evidence" needed to draw a permissive inference of causation without undue speculation.

Herskovits v. Group Health Cooperative
664 P.2d 474 (Wash. 1983)

DORE, J. This appeal raises the issue of whether an estate can maintain an action for professional negligence as a result of failure to timely diagnose lung cancer, where the estate can show probable reduction in statistical chance for survival but cannot show and/or prove that with timely diagnosis and treatment, decedent probably would have lived to normal life expectancy.

Both counsel advised that for the purpose of this appeal we are to *assume* that the respondent Group Health Cooperative of Puget Sound and its personnel negligently failed to diagnose Herskovits' cancer on his first visit to the hospital and *proximately* caused a 14 percent reduction in his chances of survival. It is undisputed that Herskovits had less than a 50 percent chance of survival at all times herein.

The main issue we will address in this opinion is whether a patient, with less than a 50 percent chance of survival, has a cause of action against the hospital and its employees if they are negligent in diagnosing a lung cancer which reduces his chances of survival by 14 percent. . . . [The trial judge granted defendant's motion for summary judgment.]

I

. . . Dr. Ostrow [plaintiff's expert] testified that if the tumor was a "stage 1" tumor in December 1974, Herskovits' chance of a 5-year survival would have been 39 percent. In June 1975, his chances of survival were 25 percent assuming the tumor had progressed to "stage 2." Thus, the delay in diagnosis may have reduced the chance of a 5-year survival by 14 percent. . . .

Plaintiff contends that medical testimony of a reduction of chance of survival from 39 percent to 25 percent is sufficient evidence to allow the proximate cause issue to go to the jury. Defendant Group Health argues conversely that Washington law does not permit such testimony on the issue of medical causation and requires that medical testimony must be at least sufficiently definite to establish that the act complained of "probably" or "more likely than not" caused the subsequent disability. It is Group Health's contention that plaintiff must prove that Herskovits "probably" would have survived had the defendant not been allegedly negligent; that is, the plaintiff must prove there was at least a 51 percent chance of survival. . . .

II

This court has held that a person who negligently renders aid and consequently increases the risk of harm to those he is trying to assist is liable for any physical damages he causes. Brown v. MacPherson's, Inc., 545 P.2d 13 (Wash. 1975). In *Brown*, the court cited Restatement (Second) of Torts §323 (1965), which reads:

> One who undertakes . . . to render services to another which he should recognize as necessary for the protection of the other's person or things, is subject to liability to the other for physical harm resulting from his failure to exercise reasonable care to perform his undertaking, if
> (a) his failure to exercise such care increases the risk of such harm, . . .

This court heretofore has not faced the issue of whether, under section 323(a), proof that the defendant's conduct increased the risk of death by decreasing the chances of survival is sufficient to take the issue of proximate cause to the jury. Some courts in other jurisdictions have allowed the proximate cause issue to go to the jury on this type of proof. These courts emphasized the fact that defendants' conduct deprived the decedents of a "significant" chance to survive or recover, rather than requiring proof that with absolute certainty the defendants' conduct caused the physical injury. The underlying reason is that it is not for the wrongdoer, who put the possibility of recovery beyond realization, to say afterward that the result was inevitable.

Other jurisdictions have rejected this approach, generally holding that unless the plaintiff is able to show that it was *more likely than not* that the harm was caused by the defendant's negligence, proof of a decreased chance of survival is not enough to take the proximate cause question to the jury. Cooper v. Sisters of Charity, Inc., 272 N.E.2d 97 (Ohio 1971). These courts have concluded that the defendant should not be liable where the decedent more than likely would have died anyway.

The ultimate question raised here is whether the relationship between the increased risk of harm and Herskovits' death is sufficient to hold Group Health responsible. Is a 36 percent (from 39 percent to 25 percent) reduction in the decedent's chance for survival sufficient evidence of causation to allow the jury to consider the possibility that the physician's failure to timely diagnose the illness was the proximate cause of his death? We answer in the affirmative. To decide otherwise would be a blanket release from liability for doctors and hospitals any time there was less than a 50 percent chance of survival, regardless of how flagrant the negligence.

Conclusion

. . . We reject Group Health's argument that plaintiffs *must show* that Herskovits "probably" would have had a 51 percent chance of survival if the hospital had not been negligent. We hold that medical testimony of a reduction of chance of survival from 39 percent to 25 percent is sufficient evidence to allow the proximate cause issue to go to the jury.

Causing reduction of the opportunity to recover (loss of chance) by one's negligence, however, does not necessitate a total recovery against the negligent party for all damages caused by the victim's death. Damages should be awarded to the injured party or his family based only on damages caused directly by premature death, such as lost earnings and additional medical expenses, etc.

We reverse the trial court and reinstate the cause of action.

Pearson, J. (concurring) I agree with the majority that the trial court erred in granting defendant's motion for summary judgment. I cannot, however, agree with the majority's reasoning in reaching this decision.

[Pearson, J., then conducted an exhaustive review of the cases and explicitly adopted the position in King, Causation, Valuation, and Chance in Personal Injury Torts Involving Preexisting Conditions and Future Consequences, 90 Yale L.J. 1353 (1981).]

King's basic thesis is explained in the following passage, which is particularly pertinent to the case before us.

> Causation has for the most part been treated as an all-or-nothing proposition. Either a loss was caused by the defendant or it was not. . . . A plaintiff ordinarily should be required to prove by the applicable standard of proof that the defendant caused the loss in question. *What* caused a loss, however, should be a separate question from what the *nature and extent* of the loss are. This distinction seems to have eluded the courts, with the result that lost chances in many respects are compensated either as certainties or not at all.

To illustrate, consider the case in which a doctor negligently fails to diagnose a patient's cancerous condition until it has become inoperable. Assume further that even with a timely diagnosis the patient would have had only a 30% chance of recovering from the disease and surviving over the long term. There are two ways of handling such a case. Under the traditional approach, this loss of a not-better-than-even chance of recovering from the cancer would not be compensable because it did not appear more likely [than] not that the patient would have survived with proper care. Recoverable damages, if any, would depend on the extent to which it appeared that cancer killed the patient sooner than it would have with timely diagnosis and treatment, and on the extent to which the delay in diagnosis aggravated the patient's condition, such as by causing additional pain. A more rational approach, however, would allow recovery for the loss of the chance of cure even though the chance was not better than even. The probability of long-term survival would be reflected in the amount of damages awarded for the loss of the chance. While the plaintiff here could not prove by a preponderance of the evidence that he was denied a cure by the defendant's negligence, he could show by a preponderance that he was deprived of a 30% chance of a cure. [90 Yale L.J. at 1363-1364.]

Under the all-or-nothing approach typified by Cooper v. Sisters of Charity, Inc., a plaintiff who establishes that but for the defendant's negligence the decedent had a 51-percent chance of survival may maintain an action for that death. The defendant will be liable for all damages arising from the death, even though there was a 49-percent chance it would have occurred despite his negligence. On the other hand, a plaintiff who establishes that but for the defendant's negligence the decedent had a 49-percent chance of survival recovers nothing.

[The dissent of Brachtenberg, J., is omitted.]

DOLLIVER, J. (dissenting) . . . I favor the opposing view and believe the reasoning in Cooper v. Sisters of Charity, Inc., also cited by the majority, is more persuasive. In discussing the rule to be adopted the Ohio Supreme Court stated:

> . . . Traditional proximate cause standards require that the trier of the facts, at a minimum, must be provided with evidence that a result was more likely than not to have been caused by an act, in the absence of any intervening cause.
>
> Lesser standards of proof are understandably attractive in malpractice cases where physical well being, and life itself, are the subject of litigation. The strong intuitive sense of humanity tends to emotionally direct us toward a conclusion that in an action for wrongful death an injured person should be compensated for the loss of any chance for survival, regardless of its remoteness. However, we have trepidations that such a rule would be so loose that it would produce more injustice than justice. Even though there exists authority for a rule allowing recovery based upon proof of causation by evidence not meeting the standard of probability, we are not persuaded by their logic. . . .

We consider the better rule to be that in order to comport with the standard of proof of proximate cause, plaintiff in a malpractice case must prove that defendant's negligence, *in probability,* proximately caused the death.

(Citations omitted.) *Cooper,* at 251-252.

NOTES

1. Judicial response to the lost chance doctrine. What is the relevance of the 36 percent "reduction in survival" figure to Dore, J.'s analysis? How does the case come out if we posit that the missed diagnosis increased the risk of death from 61 percent to 75 percent? What result if the lost chance reduced the five-year survival rate from 5 percent to zero? Or increased the chance of death from 95 percent to 100 percent?

The lost chance doctrine received an apparent endorsement in Restatement (Third) Physical Harm (Basic Principles) §26, comment *n,* in line with recent cases that have invoked the lost chance doctrine to cover situations of missed diagnosis, on the one hand, or inappropriate or tardy treatment, on the other. In Holton v. Memorial Hospital, 679 N.E.2d 1202, 1213 (Ill. 1997), the court embraced the lost chance doctrine, in part out of its concerns with incentives. "Disallowing tort recovery in medical malpractice actions on the theory that a patient was already too ill to survive or recover may operate as a disincentive on the part of health care providers to administer quality medical care to critically ill or injured patients." In most cases, the measure of damages is computed simply by looking at the percentage reduction in the value of life or limb involved in the individual case, allowing for a 14 percent recovery (39 percent minus 25 percent) in *Herskovits.*

Some cancer cases present far more complex factual scenarios. In Verdicchio v. Ricca, 843 A.2d 1042, 1062 (N.J. 2004), the defendant physician was found negligent in failing to discover a cancer tumor in the decedent teenager's left leg. But the evidence was unclear whether at that time the cancer had metastasized to the plaintiff's lungs where it could prove fatal. The jury held the defendant responsible for 55 percent of the $8 million loss, and awarded the plaintiffs $4.4 million. The plaintiff's expert testified that the decedent had about an 85 percent five-year survival rate if the tumor had been diagnosed in timely fashion before it metastasized to the lung, but only a 20 to 30 percent chance for a five-year survival metastasizing. The trial judge set the verdict aside because the plaintiffs had not established that the tumor spread only after the diagnosis was missed. Long, J., reinstated the award for the full $8 million because "the increased risk to which Dr. Ricca exposed Stephen was a substantial factor in bringing about the harm that ultimately befell him":

Although the Verdicchios' expert was unable to render an opinion whether the cancer had metastasized by January 1994, his testimony was clear that, as a matter of medical probability, Dr. Ricca's delay increased the risk that Stephen would lose the opportunity for effective treatment of the cancer. . . .

The Verdicchios' case did not depend on proof that Stephen's cancer had not metastasized in January. Nor were they required to establish statistical probabilities of survival. . . .

LaVecchia, J., dissented on the ground that "Dr. Morrow's testimony failed to establish an increased-risk of harm that satisfied [New Jersey's] 'causal connection' requirement." With *Verdicchio*, contrast Alberts v. Schultz, 975 P.2d 1279 (N.M. 1999), where the defendant's delayed diagnosis of plaintiff's potential gangrene was not held to create a lost chance because the plaintiff could not demonstrate that he was in good enough physical condition to allow the needed surgery to take place even if a timely referral had been made.

2. *The incentive effects of the lost chance doctrine.* A minority of states still reject the doctrine out of a concern as to how it fits into the larger system of damage compensation. See Fennell v. Southern Maryland Hospital Center, Inc., 580 A.2d 206, 209 nn.1-3 (Md. 1990), in which the court wrote:

> If loss of chance damages are to be recognized, amendments to the wrongful death statute should also be considered. As a class, medical malpractice plaintiffs benefit from the fact that they are entitled to recover 100% of their damages from a defendant whose negligence caused only 51% of their loss because it is more probable than not that the defendant's negligence caused the loss. Reciprocally, a defendant whose negligence caused less than 50% of a plaintiff's loss pays nothing because it is [more] probable that the negligence did not cause the loss. If a plaintiff whose decedent had a 49% chance of survival, which was lost through negligent treatment, is permitted to recover 49% of the value of the decedent's life, then a plaintiff whose decedent had a 51% chance of survival, which was lost through negligent treatment, perhaps ought to have recovery limited to 51% of the value of the life lost. The latter result would require a change in our current wrongful death statute.

Was there overcompensation in *Verdicchio*? For a statutory endorsement of the no lost chance position, see Mich. Comp. Laws. Ann. §600.2912a(2)(b)(2) (2007): "In an action alleging medical malpractice . . . the plaintiff cannot recover for loss of an opportunity to achieve a better result unless the opportunity was greater than 50%." What about other kinds of torts actions? *Fennell*'s concern can be recast as an inquiry into the optimal level of deterrence in the tort system. Under the lost chance doctrine, errors in individual cases will not "cancel out" in the long run, so that defendants may be systematically overtaxed for harms that they did *not* cause. Consider a group of 100 cases. Defendant has a 25 percent chance of causing the death in 50 of them and a 75 percent chance of causing the death in the other 50. On balance, the defendant has caused half the deaths [$(0.25 \times 50) + (0.75 \times 50) = 50$]. Yet under the *Herskovits* rule, the defendant will be charged for 62.5 deaths [$(0.25 \times 50) + (1 \times 50) = 62.5$], which leads to overdeterrence. The *Fennell* rule tends to yield better results because, even though the defendants are undercharged when the chance of loss is less than 50 percent, they are overcharged when it is more. The two errors balance each other out, at least if the losses are evenly distributed about a mean of 50 percent probability, in which case the all-or-nothing rule reduces the level of error below what it would be with a proportionate share rule. See Kaye, The Limits of the Preponderance of the Evidence Standard: Justifiably Naked Statistical Evidence and Multiple Causation, 1982 Am. B. Found. Res. J. 487.

Kaye's conclusion does not hold, however, when the defendant undertakes a large number of similar actions, each of which is less than 50 percent likely to cause harm. The refusal to allow any plaintiff to recover now results in systematic underdeterrence, because a defendant who is, say, 40 percent responsible for loss in each of 100 cases pays nothing at all. See S. Shavell, Economic Analysis of Accident Law 117 (1987), which criticizes the 50 percent threshold on the ground that it "will result in injurers' never being liable for the losses they cause; it may thus provide grossly inadequate incentives to reduce risk." What should be done if the percentage reduction in life chances is uncertain?

3. *Compensation for future tortious risk only.* The probabilistic tests of causation can also be pressed into service to calculate current awards for tortious risk that has not ripened into actual injury. Suppose a release of radioactive materials increases by 10 percent the expected number of cancers in a community over the next 30 years, from 100 to 110. The 50 percent cutoff denies recovery in all cases, and thus leads to the underdeterrence noted by Shavell. Yet holding the defendant liable in all 110 cancer cases would force the defendant to pay for 100 cancers that he did not cause, thereby inducing him to take excessive precautions.

One way to get the incentives aligned is to require the defendant to compensate the "tortious risk" today, without the occurrence of actual injury. Professor Robinson so argues in Probabilistic Causation and Compensation for Tortious Risk, 14 J. Legal Stud. 779 (1985). Should, for example, a 10 percent increase in risk trigger 110 actions today each for about 9 percent of present discounted value, necessarily barring all future claims when they arise? Most courts have avoided this huge administrative hassle when no one can determine either the increased rate of risk or which individuals fall into the exposed class. One variation on this theme was allowed in Jackson v. Johns-Manville Sales Corp., 781 F.2d 394, 413, 414 (5th Cir. 1986) where a plaintiff, who had already contracted asbestosis, was awarded a recovery for "probable future consequences" in light of the 50 percent chance of contracting cancer thereafter.

4. Enhanced risk of injury and medical monitoring. The enhanced risk of future injury has led to many class actions to recover the costs of medical monitoring of potential future diseases. That position was stoutly rejected in Henry v. Dow Chemical Co., 701 N.W.2d 684, 690-691 (Mich. 2005), where the plaintiff sought to recover medical monitoring expenses for their exposure to the dioxin component of Agent Orange that Dow manufactured. Noting that a physical injury has long been a part of the negligence claim, Corrigan, J., continued:

> The requirement of a present physical injury to person or property serves a number of important ends for the legal system. First, such a requirement defines more clearly who actually possesses a cause of action. In allowing recovery only to those who have actually suffered a present physical injury, the fact-finder need not engage in speculations about the extent to which a plaintiff possesses a cognizable legal claim. Second, such a requirement reduces the risks of fraud, by setting a clear minimum threshold — a present physical injury — before a plaintiff can proceed on a claim.
>
> Finally, [in] the absence of such a requirement, it will be inevitable that judges, as in the instant case, will be required to answer questions that are more appropriate for a legislative than a judicial body: How far from the Tittibawassee River must a plaintiff live in order to have a cognizable claim? What evidence of exposure to dioxin will be required to support such a claim? What level of medical research is sufficient to support a claim that exposure to dioxin, in contrast to exposure to another chemical, will give rise to a cause of action?

In In re Marine Asbestos Cases, 265 F.3d 861, 867 (9th Cir. 2001), the court was prepared in principle to allow a medical monitoring claim that it then rejected on more limited grounds: "Here, the plaintiffs have not shown that a treatment exists for asbestos-related diseases, or that there is clinical value to administering any such treatment before the onset of symptoms of these diseases. Plaintiffs maintain that all they seek is a single baseline medical examination. Yet they have submitted no evidence that a single examination would yield any clinical benefit." See generally Guzelian, Hillner, & Guzelian, A Quantitative Methodology for Determining the Need for Exposure-Prompted Medical Monitoring, 79 Ind. L.J. 57 (2004); Mark Geistfeld, The Analytics of Duty: Medical Monitoring and Related Forms of Economic Loss, 88 Va. L. Rev. 1921 (2002).

Kingston v. Chicago & N.W. Ry.
211 N.W. 913 (Wis. 1927)

OWEN, J. . . . We therefore have this situation: The northeast fire was set by sparks emitted from defendant's locomotive. This fire, according to the finding of the jury, constituted a proximate cause of the destruction of plaintiff's property. This finding we find to be well supported by the evidence. We have the northwest fire, of unknown origin. This fire, according to the finding of the jury, also constituted a proximate cause of the destruction of the plaintiff's property. This finding we also find to be well supported by the evidence. We have a union of these two fires 940 feet north of plaintiff's property, from which point the united fire bore down upon and destroyed the property. We therefore have two separate, independent, and distinct agencies, each of which constituted the proximate cause of plaintiff's damage, and either of which, in the absence of the other, would have accomplished such result.

It is settled in the law of negligence that any one of two or more joint tortfeasors, or one of two or more wrongdoers whose concurring acts of negligence result in injury, are each individually responsible for the entire damage resulting from their joint or concurrent acts of negligence. This rule also obtains "where two causes, each attributable to the negligence of a responsible person, concur in producing an injury to another, either of which causes would produce it regardless of the other, . . . because, whether the concurrence be intentional, actual, or constructive, each wrongdoer, in effect, adopts the conduct of his co-actor, and for the further reason that it is impossible to apportion the damage or to say that either perpetrated any distinct injury that can be separated from the whole. The whole loss must necessarily be considered and treated as an entirety." Cook v. M., St. P. & S.S.M.R. Co., 74 N.W. 561, 566 (1898). That case presented a situation very similar to this. One fire, originating by sparks emitted from a locomotive, united with another fire of unknown origin and consumed plaintiff's property. There was nothing to indicate that the fire of unknown origin was not set by some human agency. The evidence in the case merely failed to identify the agency. In that case it was held that the railroad company which set one fire was not responsible for the damage committed by the united fires because the origin of the other fire was not identified [and could well have been of natural, not human origins]. . . .

From our present consideration of the subject we are not disposed to criticise the doctrine which exempts from liability a wrongdoer who sets a fire which unites with a fire originating from natural causes, such as lightning, not attributable to any human agency, resulting in damage. It is also conceivable that a fire so set might unite with a fire of so much greater proportions, such as a raging forest fire, as to be enveloped or swallowed up by the greater holocaust, and its identity destroyed, so that the greater fire could be said to be an intervening or superseding cause. But we have no such situation here. These fires were of comparatively equal rank. If there was any difference in their magnitude or threatening aspect, the record indicates that the northeast fire was the larger fire and was really regarded as the menacing agency. At any rate there is no intimation or suggestion that the northeast fire was enveloped and swallowed up by the northwest fire. We will err on the side of the defendant if we regard the two fires as of equal rank.

According to well settled principles of negligence, it is undoubted that if the proof disclosed the origin of the northwest fire, even though its origin be attributed to a third person, the railroad company, as the originator of the northeast fire, would be liable for the entire damage. There is no reason to believe that the northwest fire originated from any other than human agency. It was a small fire. It had traveled over a limited area. It had been in existence but for a day. For a time it was thought to have been extinguished. It was not in the nature of a raging forest fire. The record discloses nothing of natural phenomena which could have given rise to the fire. It is morally certain that it was set by some human agency.

Now the question is whether the railroad company, which is found to have been responsible for the origin of the northeast fire, escapes liability because the origin of the northwest fire is not identified, although there is no reason to believe that it had any other than human origin. An affirmative answer to that question would certainly make a wrongdoer a favorite of the law at the expense of an innocent sufferer. The injustice of such a doctrine sufficiently impeaches the logic upon which it is founded. Where one who has suffered damage by fire proves the origin of a fire and the course of that fire up to the point of the destruction of his property, one has certainly established liability on the part of the originator of the fire. Granting that the union of that fire with another of natural origin, or with another of much greater proportions, is available as a defense, the burden is on the defendant to show that by reason of such union with a fire of such character the fire set by him was not the proximate cause of the damage. No principle of justice requires that the plaintiff be placed under the burden of specifically identifying the origin of both fires in order to recover the damages for which either or both fires are responsible. . . .

While under some circumstances a wrongdoer is not responsible for damage which would have occurred in the absence of his wrongful act, even though such wrongful act was a proximate cause of the accident, that doctrine does not obtain "where two causes, each attributable to the negligence of a responsible person, concur in producing an injury to another, either of which causes would produce it regardless of the other." This is because "it is impossible to apportion the damage or to say that either perpetrated any distinct injury that can be separated from the whole," and to permit each of two wrongdoers to plead the wrong of the other as a defense to his own wrongdoing would permit both wrongdoers to escape and penalize the innocent party who has been damaged by their wrongful acts.

The fact that the northeast fire was set by the railroad company, which fire was a proximate cause of plaintiff's damage, is sufficient to affirm the judgment. This conclusion renders it unnecessary to consider other grounds of liability stressed in respondent's brief.

By the Court. — Judgment affirmed.

NOTES

1. *Fires: human and natural.* Kingston addresses two situations: one in which both fires are set by human causes, and a second where only one such fire is set. Is it wise to adopt a rule of joint and several liability when both fires are set by human origin and a rule of no liability when only one fire is so set? Why not a rule of several liability that holds the named defendant responsible for one-half the damage regardless of how the other fire was set? Which rule gives the railroad the proper incentives to take the optimal level of care?

What weight should be attached when the two fires arrive at slightly different times? In particular, how should the following cases be treated? Case 1: Fire A, of natural origin, burns plaintiff's premises. Minutes later, fire B, set by defendant, reaches plaintiff's property. Fire B would have destroyed plaintiff's property if fire A had not destroyed it first. Case 2: Same sequence of events, only fire A is of human origin and B is of natural origin. Should the twice-blessed plaintiff be better off in the second case than he is in the first? Case 3: Same as above, only both fires are of human origin.

2. *Restatement views on the joint causation cases.* The Third Restatement strongly endorses the view that all joint tortfeasors are fully responsible for the undivided consequences of their own actions. Thus, RTT:LPH §27 reads:

> If multiple acts exist, each of which alone would have been a factual cause under §26 of the physical harm at the same time, each act is regarded as a factual cause of the harm.

The Third Restatement then holds that joint liability is proper whether two or more causes act synergistically so that the combined effect is greater than the sum of the parts, as when neither of two fires alone is sufficient to destroy the plaintiff's property. *Id.* at comment *a*. The rule also covers cases of over-determined harm. Thus, if three men combine to push a car over a cliff, then all are liable even if the force applied by any two would have been sufficient. *Id.* at comment *f*, illustration 3. That same rule applies to the release of toxic substances, subject only to a de minimis exception that rests not on factual causation, but on public policy. *Id.* at comment *g*. Finally if each of two chemicals is singly harmless, but deadly in combination, both may be held jointly responsible if the other conditions of liability are satisfied. *Id.* at comment *c*, illustration 1.

3. Apportionment of damages. In the cases mentioned above, no portion of the harm was uniquely attributable to any particular defendant. But what if some causal segregation is possible? On that question the Second Restatement has proved hugely influential.

§433A. APPORTIONMENT OF HARM TO CAUSES

(1) Damages for harm are to be apportioned among two or more causes where

(a) there are distinct harms, or

(b) there is a reasonable basis for determining the contribution of each cause to a single harm.

(2) Damages for any other harm cannot be apportioned among two or more causes.

Comment . . .

d. Divisible harm. . . . [W]here the cattle of two or more owners trespass upon the plaintiff's land and destroy his crop, the aggregate harm is a lost crop, but it may nevertheless be apportioned among the owners of the cattle, on the basis of the number owned by each, and the reasonable assumption that the respective harm done is proportionate to that number. . . .

Such an apportionment is commonly made in cases of private nuisance, where the pollution of a stream, or flood, or smoke, or dust, or noise, from different sources, has interfered with the plaintiff's use or enjoyment of his land. Thus where two or more factories independently pollute a stream the interference with the plaintiff's use of the water may be treated as divisible in terms of degree, and may be apportioned among the owners of the factories, on the basis of evidence of the respective quantities of pollution discharged into the stream.

The Third Restatement also endorses apportionment when there is a "reasonable basis for the factfinder to determine . . . the amount of damages separately caused" by each party. RTT:AL §26(b).

The cases that address these apportionment problems are legion. In Smith v. J.C. Penney Co., Inc., 525 P.2d 1299, 1305-1306 (Or. 1974), the plaintiff was wearing a coat purchased from J.C. Penney made of flammable material supplied, as the jury found, by defendant Bunker-Ramo. The coat was set ablaze by a fire started through the negligence of the defendant service station employees. Bunker-Ramo contended that since "there is no way to segregate the damages as between the various defendants," plaintiff should not recover from any of them. The court, however, thought otherwise:

There was evidence in this case that as a practical matter plaintiff's injuries were indivisible; that is, the jury could not make any reasonable determination that certain injuries were caused by the gasoline fire and other injuries were caused by the coat.

An employee of the Enco Service Station had gasoline sprayed on his trousers and was engulfed in the same fire as plaintiff, yet suffered only minor burns to his legs. The jury could infer from this that plaintiff would not have incurred severe burns to her lower extremities if she had not been wearing the coat. There was evidence that burning material dripped from the coat, although there was no direct evidence that such dripping material landed on plaintiff's legs or feet. There was evidence that the burning coat radiated such heat that the jury could find it burned plaintiff's lower extremities. There also was testimony that the fierce burning of the coat and the emission of gases in the process would have impeded a wearer from rapidly escaping a fire.

Most important is that there is evidence that the greatest injury to plaintiff arises out of the totality of her condition. There is testimony that she is physically and psychologically permanently disabled and unable to lead a normal life. This cannot be attributed to a burn on her foot, her head, or her body but only to her entire condition.

Should the gasoline station be held liable for the full extent of the damage, given that its employee suffered only minor burns from the same fire?

Similar problems arise in connection with persons who receive successive injuries in unrelated incidents. In Piner v. Superior Court (Jones RPI), 962 P.2d 909 (Ariz. 1998), the plaintiff was hit twice in rear-end collisions on the same day. He had experienced some discomfort in his back, neck, arms, and head after the first accident and felt similar symptoms after the second encounter. The court carried over its statutory system of several liability under the Uniform Contribution Among Tortfeasors Act, Ariz. Rev. Stat. §§12-2501 to 12-2509, to cases in which "successive acts of negligence resulted in two injuries yielding an indivisible result," in order to avoid the "unfair regime" that let both parties escaped liability for indivisible injuries.

Similarly in Browning v. Ringel, 995 P.2d 351, 358 (Idaho 2000), the court held that the "trial court did not err in apportioning damages for [plaintiff's] right shoulder and neck injuries between injuries caused by the accident and any preexisting degenerative condition, even though she may not have been symptomatic prior to the accident." How should damages be apportioned if, in the absence of the precipitating accident, the plaintiff could have expected five pain-free years?

4. *Apportionment under CERCLA.* The Second Restatement's apportionment rules have helped courts fill the gaps in CERCLA (Comprehensive Environmental Response, Compensation and Liability Act) (aka Superfund) that imposes strict and joint liability for defendants who discharge or release pollution. In Matter of Bell Petroleum Services, Inc., 3 F.3d 889, 903-904 (5th Cir. 1993), three successive operators — Leigh, Bell, and Sequa — ran chrome-plating operations on an industrial site from 1967 to 1977. The United States sued all three parties for chromium contamination of the

ground water. The United States settled with Bell for $1,000,000 and with Leigh for $100,000, and then sought to hold Sequa responsible for $1,866,000 for past damages, and to keep it jointly and severally liable (with other defendants) for all future costs needed to maintain the groundwater system. Jolly, J., accepted Sequa's contention that the costs of chromium contamination should be apportioned among the defendants, explicitly relying on the illustrations from RST §433A, comment *d* to identify reasonable grounds for apportionment provided with, not "absolute certainty," but "a reasonable and rational approximation of each defendant's individual contribution to the contamination."

> In response to the EPA's motion for summary judgment [against apportionment], Sequa introduced evidence regarding chrome flake purchases during each operator's tenure. It also introduced evidence with respect to the value of the chrome-plating done by each, as well as summaries of sales. Given the number of years that had passed since the activities were conducted, the records of these activities were not complete. However, there was testimony from various witnesses regarding the rinsing and wastewater disposal practices of each defendant, and the amount of chrome-plating activity conducted by each.
>
> During [the hearing on joint responsibility], Sequa introduced expert testimony regarding a volumetric approach to apportionment. The first expert, Henderson, calculated the total amount of chromium that had been introduced into the environment by Leigh, Bell, and Sequa, collectively and individually. The second expert, Mooney, calculated the amount of chromium that would have been introduced into the environment by each operator on the basis of electrical usage records.

Bell Petroleum was sharply distinguished in United States v. Burlington Northern & Santa Fe Ry., 479 F.3d 1113, 1134, 1135, 1137 (9th Cir. 2007). "A now-defunct company, Brown & Bryant, Inc. (B&B), owned and operated a facility [in Arvin, California] at which toxic chemicals were stored and distributed. Part of the land on which the chemical operation was located was owned by two railroad companies (the Railroads), and some of the chemicals used by B&B were supplied and delivered to the facility by Shell Oil Company." The EPA and California's Department of Toxic Substances Control spent large sums in clean up operations. With B&B out of business, the EPA and the California DTSC could sue only the railroads and Shell. The district court used a formulaic approach to charge the railroads with 9 percent of the harm. They owned 19.1 percent of the total site, which they leased out to B&B for 45 percent of the time of its operations, and were responsible for only 66 percent of the hazardous wastes at the locations it used. Multiplying these three figures, the district court calculated a 6 percent share of liability, which it increased by 5 percent to offset any calculation errors. Berzon, J., rejected this method of apportionment by applying RST

§433A to clean-up costs. Unlike the parallel activities of the three defendants in *Bell Petroleum* "each party had a different role in the contamination process." Berzon, J., then attacked the calculations below:

> [First], the operations on the site were dynamic, with fertilizer rigs stored on the Railroad parcel and filled up on the B&B parcel. Empty pesticide cans were stored on the Railroad parcel before they were crushed and disposed of. . . . A simple calculation of land ownership does not capture any data that reflect this dynamic, unitary operation of the single Arvin facility.
>
> [Second], its simple fraction based on the time that the Railroads owned the land cannot be a basis for apportionment. The fraction it chose assumes constant leakage on the facility as a whole or constant contamination traceable to the facility as a whole for each time period; no evidence suggests that to be the case. Again, if adequate information were available, it would make sense to eliminate the Railroads' liability for the period before B&B leased the Railroad parcel. The evidentiary vacuum concerning the amount of contamination traceable to the pre-lease period, however, precludes any such calculation here . . .
>
> [Third], the district court assumed equal contamination and cleanup cost from all the chemicals' leakage. This methodology entirely failed to account for the possibility that leakage of one chemical might contribute to more contamination than leakage of another, because of their specific physical properties. Similarly, the cost of cleanup depends upon which contaminants are present; some contaminants are more expensive than others to extract from the soil . . .

Berzon, J., also rejected Shell's request for apportionment because its evidence was insufficient to make out any "rough approximation of [Shell's] contamination," whether measured by the proportion of pollution contributed or the cost of its remediation. Should the numerical uncertainties matter to the railroads' apportionment if they were as likely to reduce its contribution as to increase it?

Apportionment disputes also crop up between codefendants. In Boeing Co. v. Cascade Corp., 207 F.3d 1177, 1185 (9th Cir. 2000), Boeing had to clean up its site, which had been contaminated by its own pollution and that from Cascade's nearby plant. Cascade claimed that its pollution, which accounted for 70 percent of the waste material, imposed no extra obligation on Boeing. Kleinfeld, J., held that CERCLA should not deviate from the common law rules on apportionment, given the substantial risk of strategic behavior. "A party that had discharged into a mixed plume could wait for another discharger to incur the costs of investigation, and have a fair chance of leaving the other polluter stuck with the entire bill. . . . To leave one party shouldering the entire cost of investigation and remediation while another rides for free frustrates this goal [of fair appointment among defendants], rather than ensuring that those who caused the contamination pay their fair share of the costs associated with clean-up." Should the same standards for apportionment apply to government and contribution claims? LeVerrier, Are Some Polluters More Equal than Others? A Critique of Caselaw Establishing Preferential Treatment of Federal Potentially Responsible Parties (PRPS) Under CERCLA, 17 Touro L. Rev. 503 (2001). Note, however, that in all cases the right of contribution rests only with those persons who have brought suit "during or following any civil action," which the Supreme Court has read to deny the right of contribution — in this instance by the buyer of a polluted site against its seller — who has undertaken a "purely voluntary" clean up. See Cooper Industries, Inc. v. Aviall Services Inc., 543 U.S. 157 (2004). How ought the current site holder proceed after *Cooper Industries*?

5. *Theoretical allocation of damages between joint tortfeasors.* How should apportionment be made whenever the action of each defendant is not sufficient in itself to cause the harm? For concreteness, assume that the probability of harm given *A*'s actions alone is 20 percent, and that the probability of harm given *B*'s act alone is 40 percent. Both acts occur and the harm follows. Rizzo & Arnold, Causal Apportionment in the Law of Torts: An Economic Theory, 80 Colum. L. Rev. 1399 (1980), proposed to allocate the loss according to the parties' "probabilistic marginal product." More simply stated, each party bears a fraction of the loss whose numerator is equal to the probability that his act alone would cause harm and whose denominator is the possibility that either act taken independently would cause harm. In the example given above, *A*'s portion of the harm is 0.2/(0.2 + 0.4), or one-third, while *B*'s portion of the harm is 0.4/(0.2 + 0.4), or two-thirds.

This formula presupposes, of course, some reasonably precise way to measure the independent probabilities of both *A* and *B*'s actions, which might prove difficult unless they are recurrent events for which probability estimates are easily available. The formula also fails to provide an obvious answer for the common case in which the probability of harm, given the wrongful conduct of *A* or *B*, with either acting alone, is zero. See Kruskal, Terms of Reference: Singular Confusion about Multiple Causation, 15 J. Legal Stud. 427 (1986). For other ins and outs of the debate, see Kaye and Aicken, A Comment on Causal Apportionment, 13 J. Legal Stud. 191 (1984), and Rizzo & Arnold, Causal Apportionment: Reply to the Critics, 15 J. Legal Stud. 219 (1986). What is wrong with a simple solution that divides the liability by the number of codefendants?

Summers v. Tice
199 P.2d 1 (Cal. 1948)

CARTER, J. Each of the two defendants appeals from a judgment against them in an action for personal injuries. Pursuant to stipulation the appeals have been consolidated.

Plaintiff's action was against both defendants for an injury to his right eye and face as the result of being struck by bird shot discharged from a shotgun. The case was tried by the court without a jury and the court found that on November 20, 1945, plaintiff and the two defendants were hunting quail on the open range. Each of the defendants was armed with a 12 gauge shotgun loaded with shells containing 7-1/2 size shot. Prior to going hunting plaintiff discussed the hunting procedure with defendants, indicating that they were to exercise care when shooting and to "keep in line." In the course of hunting plaintiff proceeded up a hill, thus placing the hunters at the points of a triangle. The view of defendants with reference to plaintiff was unobstructed and they knew his location. Defendant Tice flushed a quail which rose in flight to a 10-foot elevation and flew between plaintiff and defendants. Both defendants shot at the quail, shooting in plaintiff's direction. At that time defendants were 75 yards from plaintiff. One shot struck plaintiff in his eye and another in his upper lip. Finally it was found by the court that as the direct result of the shooting by defendants the shots struck plaintiff as above mentioned and that defendants were negligent in so shooting and plaintiff was not contributorily negligent.

[The court upheld the findings below on defendants' negligence and plaintiff's lack of contributory negligence and assumption of risk.]

The problem presented in this case is whether the judgment against both defendants may stand. It is argued by defendants that they are not joint tort feasors, and thus jointly and severally liable, as they were not acting in concert, and that there is not sufficient evidence to show which defendant was guilty of the negligence which caused the injuries — the shooting by Tice or that by Simonson. Tice argues that there is evidence to show that the shot which struck plaintiff came from Simonson's gun because of admissions allegedly made by him to third persons and no evidence that they came from his gun. Further in connection with the latter contention, the court failed to find on plaintiff's allegation in his complaint that he did not know which one was at fault — did not find which defendant was guilty of the negligence which caused the injuries to plaintiff.

Considering the last argument first, we believe it is clear that the court sufficiently found on the issue that defendants were jointly liable and that thus the negligence of both was the cause of the injury or to that legal effect. It found that both defendants were negligent and "That as a direct and proximate result of the shots fired by *defendants, and each of them,* a birdshot pellet was caused to and did lodge in plaintiff's right eye and that another birdshot pellet was caused to and did lodge in plaintiff's upper lip." In so doing the court evidently did not give credence to the admissions of Simonson to third persons that he fired the shots, which it was justified in doing. It thus determined that the negligence of both defendants was the legal cause of injury — or that both were responsible. Implicit in such finding is the assumption that the court was unable to ascertain whether the shots were from the gun of one defendant or the other or one shot from each of them. The one shot that entered plaintiff's eye was the major factor in assessing damages and that shot could not have come from the gun of both defendants. It was from one or the other only.

It has been held that where a group of persons are on a hunting party, or otherwise engaged in the use of firearms, and two of them are negligent in firing in the direction of a third person who is injured thereby, both of those so firing are liable for the injury suffered by the third person, although the negligence of only one of them could have caused the injury. (Moore v. Foster, 182 Miss. 15 [(1938)]; Oliver v. Miles, 144 Miss. 852 [(1926)].) These cases speak of the action of defendants as being in concert as the ground of decision, yet it would seem they are straining that concept and the more reasonable basis appears in Oliver v. Miles, supra. There two persons were hunting together. Both shot at some partridges and in so doing shot across the highway injuring plaintiff who was travelling on it. The court stated they were acting in concert and thus both were liable. The court then stated: "We think that . . . each is liable for the resulting injury to the boy, although no one can say definitely who actually shot him. *To hold otherwise would be to exonerate both from liability, although each was negligent, and the injury resulted from such negligence.*" [Emphasis added.]

When we consider the relative position of the parties and the results that would flow if plaintiff was required to pin the injury on one of the defendants only, a requirement that the burden of proof on that subject be shifted to defendants becomes manifest. They are both wrongdoers — both negligent toward plaintiff. They brought about a situation where the negligence of one of them injured the plaintiff, hence it should rest with them each to absolve himself if he can. The injured party has been placed by defendants in the unfair position of pointing to which defendant caused the harm. If one can escape, the other may also and plaintiff is remediless. Ordinarily defendants are in a far better position to offer evidence to determine which one caused the injury. . . .

Cases are cited for the proposition that where two or more tort feasors acting independently of each other cause an injury to plaintiff, they are not joint tort feasors and plaintiff must establish the portion of the damage caused by each, even though it is impossible to prove the portion of the injury caused by each. In view of the foregoing discussion it is apparent that defendants in cases like the present one may be treated as liable on the same basis as joint tort feasors, and hence the last-cited cases are distinguishable inasmuch as they involve independent tort feasors.

In addition to that, however, it should be pointed out that the same reasons of policy and justice shift the burden to each of defendants to absolve himself if he can — relieving the wronged person of the duty of apportioning the injury to a particular defendant, apply here where we are concerned with whether plaintiff is required to supply evidence for the apportionment of damages. If defendants are independent tort feasors and thus each liable for the damage caused by him alone, and, at least, where the matter of apportionment is incapable of proof, the innocent wronged party should not be deprived of his right to redress. The wrongdoers should be left to work out between themselves any apportionment. Some of the cited cases refer to the difficulty of apportioning the burden of damages between the independent tort feasors, and say that where factually a correct division cannot be made, the trier of fact may make it the best it can, which would be more or less a guess, stressing the factor that the wrongdoers are not in a position to complain of uncertainty. . . .

The judgment is affirmed.

NOTE

Alternative liability. Prior to *Summers*, some courts were more reluctant to indulge in the fancy footwork needed to apportion harm. In Adams v. Hall, 2 Vt. 9, 11 (1829), the plaintiff's sheep were killed by two dogs, each owned by two separate defendants. Once the evidence showed that the two dogs did not have a common owner, the court refused to allow the plaintiff to recover against either. "Hall was under no obligation to keep the other defendant's dog from killing sheep; nor *vice versa*. Then, shall each become liable for the injury done by the other's dog, merely because the dogs, without the knowledge or consent of the owners did the mischief in company? We think not." Hutchinson, J., then analogized the case to one where two servants of different owners combined to destroy property without the knowledge and consent of their masters, and concluded that there too neither master would be liable.

Summers differs from *Kingston,* in which *both A and B* are causally responsible, because in *Summers either A or B, but not both* is causally responsible for the plaintiff's harm. Is a regime of joint and several liability equally appropriate for both situations? A regime whereby each defendant is liable only for 50 percent of the harm? On the court's reasoning in *Summers,* what result if ten persons were in the hunting party? One hundred? How would the decision look if both defendants were covered by liability insurance issued by the same carrier?

Summers v. Tice has been approved of in RST §433B(3), and RTT:LPH §28(b), comment *g*, so long as both defendants acted "tortiously." *Id.* at comment *h*.

Skipworth v. Lead Industries Association
690 A.2d 169 (Pa. 1997)

CAPPY, J. This is an appeal by allowance from the order of the Superior Court, affirming the entry of summary judgment by the Court of Common Pleas of Philadelphia County. For the reasons that follow, we now affirm.

Dominique Skipworth ("Skipworth") was born on September 18, 1988. Between September 10, 1990 and May 8, 1991, she was hospitalized for lead poisoning on three separate occasions. She also received outpatient therapy for lead poisoning in August 1991, and again in June 1992. During this time, she resided at only one home, located at 2840 West Stiles Street in Philadelphia. This residence, which had been rented by Skipworth's guardian, Pandora Williams ("Williams"), was estimated to have been built circa 1870. Testing of Skipworth's residence revealed the presence of lead-based paint at various locations throughout the home.

On March 17, 1992, Skipworth filed an action through her legal guardian, Williams, and her co-legal guardian and mother, Ernestine Richardson (collectively referred to as "Appellants") against several manufacturers of lead pigment ("the pigment manufacturers") and their alleged successors as well as a trade association, Lead Industries Association, Inc. ("LIA"). Appellants alleged that Skipworth suffered physical and neuropsychological injuries as a result of lead poisoning from the lead paint in her home. Appellants stipulated that they could not identify the manufacturer of the lead pigment which Skipworth ingested, and admitted that they could not identify when such pigment was made, sold, or applied to her home. Appellants, however, alleged that they had identified and joined in this action substantially all of the manufacturers of lead pigment used in residential house paint from 1870 until production of lead pigment ceased in 1977. Appellants thus proceeded against the pigment manufacturers and LIA (collectively referred to as "Appellees") by invoking theories of collective liability, namely market share liability, alternate liability, conspiracy, and concert of action.

Appellees filed a motion for summary judgment. The trial court granted Appellees' motion for summary judgment as to all counts of Appellants' complaint.

[The Superior Court affirmed on all counts, holding that "such an extensive policy shift as adopting market share liability was not for an intermediate appellate court to make."] We now affirm. . . .

The first question presented in this appeal is whether this court should adopt the market share liability theory in the context of lead poisoning cases. The market share liability theory provides an exception to the general rule that a plaintiff must establish that the defendant proximately caused his or her injury. A sharply divided California Supreme Court was the first court to adopt this theory of liability. See *Sindell v. Abbott Laboratories*, 607 P.2d 924 (Cal. 1980). The *Sindell* case involved a plaintiff who developed cancer as a result of her mother's ingestion during pregnancy of diethylstilbestrol ("DES"), a drug with an identical formula manufactured by several different companies. Because of the inability to trace the source of the DES due to its fungible nature and the long time lapse between its sale and the development of health problems, the plaintiff was unable to identify, through no fault of her own, the manufacturer of the DES ingested by her mother.

The *Sindell* court concluded that the plaintiff need not identify which particular manufacturer made the DES ingested by her mother, and held that the manufacturers of the product identical to the one which harmed plaintiff were liable in shares proportional to their share of the market at the time plaintiff's mother ingested the drug, regardless of actual causation. The *Sindell* court stated that market share liability is appropriate where the following factors are present: all the named defendants are potential tort-feasors; the allegedly harmful products are identical and share the same defective qualities (or were "fungible"); the plaintiff is unable to identify which defendant caused her injury through no fault of her own; and, substantially all of the manufacturers which created the defective products during the relevant time are named as defendants. The rationale for adopting this theory was that "each manufacturer's liability would approximate its responsibility for the injuries caused by its own products."

Pennsylvania, on the other hand, follows the general rule that a plaintiff, in order to recover, must establish that a particular defendant's negligence was the proximate cause of her injuries. Adoption of the market share liability theory would result in a significant departure from this rule. Although we realize that there may arise a situation which would compel us to depart from our time-tested general rule, such a situation is not presented by the matter *sub judice*. Application of market share liability to lead paint cases such as this one would lead to a distortion of liability which would be so gross as to make determinations of culpability arbitrary and unfair.

The extent to which liability would be contorted in a lead pigment case were market share liability to be applied is brought into sharp focus when the facts presented by this case are compared with the situation presented by a typical DES case, which is the type of case for which this theory was created. Such a comparison has revealed to us two major factors which compel us to conclude that adoption of market share liability in the context of a lead pigment case would unacceptably distort liability. First, the relevant time period in question is far more extensive than the relevant time period in a DES case. In this case, Appellants cannot identify any particular application, or applications, of lead paint which have caused Skipworth's health problems. Thus, they "pinpoint" a more than one hundred year period from the date the house was built until the lead paint ceased being sold for residential purposes as the relevant time period. In contrast, the relevant time period in a DES case is necessarily limited to the nine months that the patient ingesting the product was pregnant.

The difficulty in applying market share liability where such an expansive relevant time period as one hundred years is at issue is that entities who could not have been the producers of the lead paint which injured Skipworth would almost assuredly be held liable. Over the one hundred year period at issue, several of the pigment manufacturers entered and left the lead paint market. Thus, application of the market share theory to this situation would virtually ensure that certain pigment manufacturers would be held liable where they could not possibly have been a potential tortfeasor; therefore, the first prong of the *Sindell* test would not be met.

The second factor which persuades us that adoption of market share liability here would be inappropriate is that lead paint, as opposed to DES, is not a fungible product. All DES used for treatment of pregnant women was manufactured according to an identical formula and presented an identical risk of harm. *Sindell*, 607 P.2d at 936. In contrast, it is undisputed that lead pigments had different chemical formulations, contained different amounts of lead, and differed in potential toxicity.

Appellants contend that "whether all of the lead pigment [the pigment manufacturers] manufactured was exactly the same, in every respect, [is] irrelevant...." We do not see this problem being so easily dismissed. Uncontested evidence shows that differing formulae of lead paint result in differing levels of bioavailability[5] of the lead. Because of differences in bioavailability, a child who ingests dust or chips of lead paint containing equal amounts of lead "derived from two lead paints will *not* generally develop equal elevation in internal lead level from the two paints. Rather, more highly bioavailable lead has a greater impact than lead in less bioavailable form." R.R. at 314a-315a (emphasis in the original). Thus, differing formulae of lead paint has a direct bearing on how much damage a lead paint manufacturer's product would cause.

Contrary to Appellants' bald assertion that this is an irrelevant consideration, it is actually fatal to their claim that application of market share liability to these defendants would be appropriate. Market share liability is grounded on the premise that it ensures that "each manufacturer's liability would approximate its responsibility for the injuries caused by its own products." *Sindell*, 607 P.2d at 937. Yet, in this case, apportioning liability based upon a manufacturer defendant's share of the market (even if it were possible to obtain an accurate statistic considering the lengthy relevant time period at question) would not serve to approximate that defendant's responsibility for injuries caused by its lead paint. For example, a manufacturer whose lead product had a lower bioavailability than average would have caused less damage than its market share would indicate. Thus, application of market share liability to such a manufacturer would impose on it a disproportionately high share of the damages awarded.

---

5. The term "bioavailability" refers to "the extent to which the lead is in a form which is easily internalized by the body, *i.e.*, the extent to which it is in a form which can be physiologically transported through the lungs, gastrointestinal tract, skin, etc. and absorbed into the bloodstream...." R.R. at 313a-314a.

As we find that application of market share liability to lead paint cases would grotesquely distort liability, we decline to apply it in this case.

The next question concerns whether the trial court correctly entered summary judgment in favor of Appellees on Appellants' alternative liability count. Section 433B(3) of the Restatement (Second) of Torts, which sets forth the alternative liability theory, states that:

> [w]here the conduct of two or more actors is tortious, and it is proved that harm has been caused to the plaintiff only by one of them, but there is uncertainty as to which one has caused it, the burden is upon each such actor to prove that he has not caused the harm. The theory of alternative liability dictates that tortfeasors who act in concert will be held jointly and severally liable for the plaintiff's injury unless the tortfeasors are able to prove that they have not caused the harm.

The leading case on this doctrine was Summers v. Tice, 199 P.2d 1 (Cal. 1948). [The court then summarized the decision.]

We adopted this theory of liability in Snoparsky v. Baer, 266 A.2d 707 (Pa. 1970). In *Snoparsky*, several stones were thrown at plaintiff by the defendants. Only one stone, however, struck and injured the plaintiff. The plaintiff in *Snoparsky* was allowed to proceed under alternative liability because the tortious conduct of defendant was simultaneous and identical, and the plaintiff joined all potential tortfeasors as defendants.

The trial court correctly concluded that alternate liability theory is inapplicable to the matter *sub judice*. First, Appellees did not act simultaneously in producing the lead paint. Over the one hundred year period at issue, several of the named Appellees entered and left the lead paint market. Second, it is uncontroverted that Appellants have failed to join all entities which manufactured lead paint over the one hundred year period, and therefore have failed to join all potential tortfeasors. . . .

[Third appellants] have failed to introduce evidence which would support their cause of action for civil conspiracy. First, Appellants have failed to introduce evidence that Appellees were acting in concert. Second, Appellants have also failed to demonstrate malice on the part of Appellees.

The final question for this court to review is whether the trial court properly entered summary judgment in favor of Appellees on Appellants' concert of action claim. This theory provides in pertinent part that "[f]or harm resulting to a third person from the tortious conduct of another, one is subject to liability if he (a) does a tortious act in concert with the other or pursuant to a common design with him. . . . " Restatement (Second) of Torts, §876.

[The Court then expressly held] that a claim of concerted action cannot be established if the plaintiff is unable to identify the wrongdoer or the person who acted in concert with the wrongdoer. . . .

We find that Appellants failed to establish that they had a cause of action for concert of action as they are unable to identify the manufacturer of any of the lead pigment found at Skipworth's residence that was ingested by her and allegedly caused her injuries.

[Affirmed].

NOTES

1. Market share in DES cases. Sindell v. Abbott Laboratories, 607 P.2d 924, 936, 937, 939 (Cal. 1980), relied on, Comment, DES and a Proposed Theory of Enterprise Liability, 46 Fordham L. Rev. 963 (1978), when it introduced the theory of market share liability for DES. In 1938 the British research team that first synthesized the drug placed it in the public domain after which it was manufactured by national, regional, and local producers — perhaps 300 in total. Its fungible nature led Mosk, J., to defend the market share rule as an extension of *Summers.*

> Where, as here, all defendants produced a drug from an identical formula and the manufacturer of the DES which caused plaintiff's injuries cannot be identified through no fault of plaintiff, a modification of the rule of *Summers* is warranted. . . .
>
> [W]e hold it to be reasonable in the present context to measure the likelihood that any of the defendants supplied the product which allegedly injured plaintiff by the percentage which the DES sold by each of them for the purpose of preventing miscarriage bears to the entire production of the drug sold by all for that purpose. Plaintiff asserts in her briefs that Eli Lilly and Company and 5 or 6 other companies produced 90 percent of the DES marketed. If at trial this is established to be the fact, then there is a corresponding likelihood that this comparative handful of producers manufactured the DES which caused plaintiff's injuries, and only a 10 percent likelihood that the offending producer would escape liability.
>
> If plaintiff joins in the action the manufacturers of a substantial share of the DES which her mother might have taken, the injustice of shifting the burden of proof to defendants to demonstrate that they could not have made the substance which injured plaintiff is significantly diminished. . . .
>
> The presence in the action of a substantial share of the appropriate market also provides a ready means to apportion damages among the defendants. Each defendant will be held liable for the proportion of the judgment represented by its share of that market unless it demonstrates that it could not have made the product which caused plaintiff's injuries. . . . Once plaintiff has met her burden of joining the required defendants, they in turn may cross-complaint against other DES manufacturers, not joined in the action, which they can allege might have supplied the injury-causing product.

The dissent of Richardson, J., objected: "In adopting the foregoing rationale the majority rejects over 100 years of tort law which required that before tort liability was imposed a 'matching' of defendant's conduct and plaintiff's injury was absolutely essential."

2. *Calculating market shares.* Making market share calculations has proved difficult because DES was sold for many different uses in many different tablet sizes, making gross sales a poor indicator of a firm's percentage of the DES market directed to pregnant women. In addition, the plaintiffs were born in different years where the markets were differently constituted. Half were also born outside California. *Sindell* settled in September 1983, before discovery was taken on any of these factual issues. The partial information on market shares led the court in McCormack v. Abbott Laboratories, 617 F. Supp. 1521, 1527 (D. Mass. 1985), to proceed as follows: First, let each defendant establish its (small) share and then divide the remainder equally among the remaining defendants. "Assume hypothetically, five prima facie defendants, of whom one shows an actual share of 12%. The four remaining defendants will each be potentially liable for 22%." This system of allocation prevents any plaintiff from charging any defendant the share attributable to absent third parties. "Assume hypothetically, five prima facie defendants who show that their actual shares are, respectively, 5%, 10%, 15%, 20% and 25%. Plaintiff could recover a maximum of 75% of her damages."

Sindell originally held that each defendant could be held liable for the shares of absent or insolvent defendants no matter how small its share of the market. The California Supreme Court stepped back from that implication in two stages. In Murphy v. E.R. Squibb & Sons, Inc., 710 P.2d 247, 255 (Cal. 1985), it held that the "substantial share" requirement of *Sindell* was not met when the plaintiff sued only one manufacturer, Squibb, with a 10 percent market share. Subsequently, in Brown v. Superior Court (Abbott Laboratories, RPI), 751 P.2d 470 (Cal. 1988), Mosk, J., held that defendant was responsible only for its proportionate share of the loss, so that the entire loss could not be thrown on a defendant with an "insignificant" market share.

Shortly thereafter in Hymowitz v. Eli Lilly & Co., 539 N.E.2d 1069, 1078 (N.Y. 1989), the New York Court of Appeals held that *Sindell* based the proportionate liability of each defendant pharmaceutical company on its sales in the "national market" for DES used in pregnancy. *Hymowitz* then concluded that since liability was based "on the overall risk produced" no exculpation evidence could be allowed in individual cases. While defendant's exculpation evidence allows it to escape liability in a given case, that evidence will not reduce its overall burden, for its *increased* share of liability for the remaining cases in the pool exactly offset its saving in the individual case. Thus, if four defendants have equal 25 percent market shares, and a fifth defendant can establish that it was not involved in 5 of 100 cases, then the pool must be readjusted to hold each of the other four responsible for

25/95ths of the remaining judgments. So if each case is worth $100,000, its liability will remain at $2.5 million whether it pays $25,000 for each of 100 cases, or pays 25/95ths of $100,000, or, roughly $26,316 for each of 95 cases. Since gains and losses net out, it is cheaper administratively in the long run if *no one* can exonerate himself in the individual case.

Sindell has spawned an enormous amount of academic literature. See, e.g., Robinson, Multiple Causation in Tort Law: Reflections on the DES Cases, 68 Va. L. Rev. 713 (1982); Bernstein, Hymowitz v. Eli Lilly and Co., Tort Stories 151 (2003) for an informative account of the frustrations and tribulations of the DES litigation.

3. Market share liability in lead cases. The suits against the manufacturers of lead pigment, rebuffed in *Skipworth,* received a much warmer reception in Thomas v. Mallett, 701 N.W.2d 523, 562, 563 (Wis. 2005), where Butler, J., allowed a infant plaintiff injured by lead poisoning to sue, in addition to the family landlord, the lead pigment manufacturers under a risk-contribution theory — a variation on *Sindell's* market-share liability. Butler, J., first held that lead carbonate, the active agent in the defendants' pigment, was a fungible product, as lead pigments differed only in "degree, not function," because "white lead carbonates were produced utilizing 'virtually identical chemical formulas' such that all white lead carbonates were 'identically defective.'" He then addressed the defendants' other objections to the risk-contribution theory:

> [The] Pigment Manufacturers contend that the risk-contribution theory should not be extended because Thomas's lead poisoning could have been caused from many different sources. We agree that the record indicates that lead poisoning can stem from the ambient air, many foods, drinking water, soil, and dust.
>
> Further, the Pigment Manufacturers argue that the risk-contribution theory should not be extended because lead poisoning does not produce a "signature injury." As alternate explanations for Thomas's cognitive deficits, the Pigment Manufacturers have brought forth evidence that genetics, birth complications causing damage to the central nervous system, severe environmental deprivation, inadequate parenting, parental emotional disorders, and child abuse could all, in varying ways, cause such impairments.
>
> These arguments have no bearing on whether the risk-contribution theory should be extended to white lead carbonate claims. Harm is harm, whether it be "signature" or otherwise. Even under the risk-contribution theory, the plaintiff still retains a burden of establishing causation . . .
>
> [In addition,] the record is replete with evidence that shows the Pigment Manufacturers actually magnified the risk through their aggressive promotion of white lead carbonate, even despite the awareness of the toxicity of lead.

The bottom line was that the considerations that proved decisive in *Skipworth* became jury questions in *Thomas*. Wilcox, J., dissented:

> It is often said that bad facts make bad law. Today's decision epitomizes that ancient legal axiom. The end result of the majority opinion is that the defendants, lead pigment manufacturers, can be held liable for a product they may or may not have produced, which may or may not have caused the plaintiff's injuries, based on conduct that may have occurred over 100 years ago when some of the defendants were not even part of the relevant market.

For the academic inspiration in *Thomas*, see Rostron, Beyond Market Share Liability: A Theory of Proportional Share Liability for Nonfungible Products, 52 U.C.L.A. L. Rev. 151 (2004).

4. Market share: beyond DES. In other cases, the courts have taken their cue from *Skipworth*, by refusing to extend *Sindell* beyond fungible products like DES. Thus, in Shackil v. Lederle Laboratories, 561 A.2d 511, 523 (N.J. 1989), the New Jersey Supreme Court held the market share doctrine did not apply to the diphtheria-pertussis-tetanus (DPT) vaccine, whose pertussis component caused the infant plaintiff to have a seizure disorder resulting in serious and permanent brain damage. Not all DPT vaccines were prepared in the same way so they did not necessarily hold out the same level of risk. The courts have overwhelmingly rejected the theory in asbestos cases, in light of the nonfungible natures of the exposures. The court in Black v. Abex Corp., 603 N.W.2d 182 (N.D. 1999) did not relax the fungibility restriction when plaintiff sought to confine liability to four manufacturers of "friction products" used in brake linings that contained between 7 and 75 percent asbestos fibers. The court noted that "[i]t seems obvious that a product which contains seventy-five percent asbestos would create a greater risk of harm than one which contains only seven percent." Thus, there is no longer a "singular risk factor" that makes it appropriate to use the *Sindell* theory. Also, in Spencer v. Baxter International, Inc., 163 F. Supp. 2d 74 (D. Mass. 2001), the court refused to apply a market share theory on behalf of a hemophiliac who died of AIDS related illnesses. Finally, in Hamilton v. Beretta, 750 N.E. 2d 1055 (NY 2001), the New York Court of Appeals refused to extend *Hymowitz* to cases of manufacturer's potential gun liability noting that "guns are not identical, fungible products. . . . [G]iven the negligent marketing theory on which plaintiffs tried this case — plaintiffs have never asserted that the manufacturers' marketing techniques were uniform. . . . Defendants engaged in widely-varied conduct creating varied risks." For a defense of a system of proportionate liability that recognizes that some gun injuries would have been caused in the absence of negligent marketing, see Twerski & Sebok, Liability Without Cause? Further Ruminations on Cause-in-Fact as Applied to Handgun Liability, 32 Conn. L. Rev. 1379 (2000).

SECTION C.   PROXIMATE CAUSE (HEREIN OF DUTY)

1.   *Physical Injury*

Bacon, The Elements of the Common Lawes of England
(1630)

Reg. I. In jure non remota causa sed proxima spectatur. [In law, not the remote, but the proximate cause is to be looked at.] It were infinite for the law to judge the causes, and their impulsions one of another; therefore it contenteth it selfe with the immediate cause, and judgeth of acts by that, without looking to any further degree.

Street, Foundations of Legal Liability
Vol. I, p. 110 (1906)

The terms "proximate" and "remote" are thus respectively applied to recoverable and non-recoverable damages.... It is unfortunate that no definite principle can be laid down by which to determine this question. It is always to be determined on the facts of each case upon mixed considerations of logic, common sense, justice, policy and precedent.... The best use that can be made of the authorities on proximate cause is merely to furnish illustrations of situations which judicious men upon careful consideration have adjudged to be on one side of the line or the other.

Ryan v. New York Central R.R.
35 N.Y. 210 (1866)

On the 15th July 1854, in the city of Syracuse, the defendants, by the careless management, or through the insufficient condition, of one of their engines, set fire to their woodshed, and a large quantity of wood therein. The plaintiff's house, situated at a distance of one hundred and thirty feet from the shed, soon took fire from the heat and sparks, and was entirely consumed, notwithstanding diligent efforts were made to save it. A number of other houses were also burned by the spreading of the fire.

These facts having been proved on the part of the plaintiff, the defendants' counsel moved for a nonsuit, which was granted, and an exception taken. And the judgment having been affirmed at general term, the plaintiff appealed to this court.

HUNT, J. [after stating the facts]. The question may be thus stated: A house in a populous city takes fire, through the negligence of the owner or his servant; the flames extend to and destroy an adjacent building: Is the owner of the first building liable to the second owner for the damage sustained by such burning?

It is a general principle, that every person is liable for the consequences of his own acts; he is thus liable in damages for the proximate results of his own acts, but not for remote damages. It is not easy, at all times, to determine what are proximate and what are remote damages. . . .

[After discussing cases of direct ignition of plaintiff's property by defendants' negligence, the court continued:] Thus far the law is settled, and the principle is apparent. If, however, the fire communicates from the house of *A.* to that of *B.*, and that is destroyed, is the negligent party liable for his loss? And if it spreads thence to the house of *C.*, and thence to the house of *D.*, and thence consecutively through the other houses, until it reaches and consumes the house of *Z.*, is the party liable to pay the damages sustained by these twenty-four sufferers? The counsel for the plaintiff does not distinctly claim this, and I think it would not be seriously insisted, that the sufferers could recover in such case. Where, then, is the principle upon which *A.* recovers and *Z.* fails?

It has been suggested, that an important element exists in the difference between an intentional firing and a negligent firing merely; that when a party designedly fires his own house or his own fallow-land, not intending, however, to do any injury to his neighbor, but a damage actually results, that he may be liable for more extended damages than where the fire originated in accident or negligence. It is true, that the most of the cases where the liability was held to exist, were cases of an intentional firing. The case, however, of Vaughan v. Menlove (3 Bing. N.C. 468) was that of a spontaneous combustion of a hay-rick; the rick was burned, the owner's buildings were destroyed, and thence the fire spread to the plaintiff's cottage, which was also consumed; the defendant was held liable.

Without deciding upon the importance of this distinction, I prefer to place my opinion upon the ground, that, in the one case, to wit, the destruction of the building upon which the sparks were thrown by the negligent act of the party sought to be charged, the result was to have been anticipated, the moment the fire was communicated to the building; that its destruction was the ordinary and natural result of its being fired. In the second, third or twenty-fourth case, as supposed, the destruction of the building was not a natural and expected result of the first firing. That a building upon which sparks and cinders fall should be destroyed or seriously injured, must be expected, but that the fire should spread and other buildings be consumed, is not a necessary or a usual result. That it is possible, and that it is not unfrequent, cannot be denied. The result, however, depends, not upon any necessity of a further communication of the fire, but upon a concurrence of accidental circumstances, such as the degree of the heat, the state of the atmosphere, the condition and materials of the adjoining structures and the direction of the wind. These are accidental and varying circumstances; the party has no control over them, and is not responsible for their effects.

My opinion, therefore, is, that this action cannot be sustained, for the reason that the damages incurred are not the immediate but the remote result of the negligence of the defendants. The immediate result was the destruction of their own wood and sheds beyond that, it was remote. . . .

To sustain such a claim as the present, and to follow the same to its legitimate consequences, would subject to a liability against which no prudence could guard, and to meet which no private fortune would be adequate. Nearly all fires are caused by negligence, in its extended sense. In a country where wood, coal, gas and oils are universally used, where men are crowded into cities and villages, where servants are employed, and where children find their home in all houses, it is impossible, that the most vigilant prudence should guard against the occurrence of accidental or negligent fires. A man may insure his own house, or his own furniture, but he cannot insure his neighbor's building or furniture, for the reason that he has no interest in them. To hold that the owner must not only meet his own loss by fire, but that he must guaranty the security of his neighbors on both sides, and to an unlimited extent, would be to create a liability which would be the destruction of all civilized society. No community could long exist, under the operation of such a principle. In a commercial country, each man, to some extent, runs the hazard of his neighbor's conduct, and each, by insurance against such hazards, is enabled to obtain a reasonable security against loss. To neglect such precaution, and to call upon his neighbor, on whose premises a fire originated, to indemnify him instead, would be to award a punishment quite beyond the offence committed. It is to be considered, also, that if the negligent party is liable to the owner of a remote building thus consumed, he would also be liable to the insurance companies who should pay losses to such remote owners. The principle of subrogation would entitle the companies to the benefit of every claim held by the party to whom a loss should be paid.

. . . The remoteness of the damage, in my judgment, forms the true rule on which the question should be decided, and which prohibits a recovery by the plaintiff in this case. Judgment should be affirmed.

NOTES

1. *Fire!* The earlier common law cases took a much harder line toward the spread of fire. In Beaulieu v. Finglam, Y.B. 2 Hen. 4, f. 18, pl. 6 (1401), Chapter 3 at 175, Markham, J., made it clear that the liability extended to the actions not only of the owner but also of all his guests. He was

protected against liability only for fires set by strangers. The following dialogue then ensured: Hornby [the defendant's lawyer]: "The defendant will be undone and impoverished all his days if this action is to be maintained against him; for then twenty other such suits will be brought against him." Thirning, C.J.: "What is that to us? It is better that he should be undone than that the law be changed for him." Why this shift in view in *Ryan*, when the defendant is a railroad, not an individual landowner?

For a contemporary English contrast to *Ryan*, see Smith v. London & South Western Ry., 6 C.P. 14 (1870). A spark from defendant's engine started a fire in some heaps of the railway's cut grass. Fanned by a high wind, the flames spread through a stubble field not owned by the railroad until it consumed plaintiff's cottage. Kelly, C.B., allowed recovery noting that "there was negligence in the defendants in not removing these trimmings, and that they thus become responsible for all the consequences of their conduct, and that the mere fact of the distance of this cottage from the point where the fire broke out does not affect their liability."

Speaking of *Ryan* and the similar case of Kerr v. Pennsylvania R.R., 62 Pa. 353 (1870), the Supreme Court, in Milwaukee & St. Paul Ry. v. Kellogg, 94 U.S. 469 (1876), said: "Those cases have been the subject of much criticism since they were decided; and it may, perhaps, be doubted whether they have always been quite understood. If they were intended to assert the doctrine that when a building has been set on fire through the negligence of a party, and a second building has been fired from the first, it is a conclusion of law that the owner of the second has no recourse to the negligent wrong-doer, they have not been accepted as authority for such a doctrine, even in the States where the decisions were made." See generally Schwartz, Tort Law and the Economy in Nineteenth-Century America: A Reinterpretation, 90 Yale L.J. 1717, 1746-1747 (1981). See also note to *Leroy Fibre, supra* at 342.

2. *"Ordinary and natural result of defendant's negligence."* *Ryan* placed a narrow construction on the phrase "ordinary and natural result" of the defendant's negligence. That phrase must be construed not only with intervening natural events, but also with intervening human conduct. Thus, in *City of Lincoln*, 15 P.D. 15, 18 (1889), the plaintiff's vessel, the *Albatross*, was totally disabled in a collision with the *City of Lincoln* wholly through the fault of the latter vessel. The *Albatross* lost its compass, log, log glass, and charts, and the captain was unsuccessful in his efforts to bring the ship to port. The court first noted that the "only inquiry in all these cases is whether the damage complained of is the natural and reasonable result of the defendant's act," and found the test satisfied if the damage was "such a consequence as in the ordinary course of things would flow from the act." Lindley, L.J., continued:

> We have then to consider what is the meaning of "the ordinary course of things." Sir Walter Phillimore has asked us to exclude from it all human conduct.

I can do nothing of the kind. I take it that reasonable human conduct is part of the ordinary course of things. So far as I can see my way to any definite proposition I should say that the ordinary course of things does not exclude all human conduct, but includes at least the reasonable conduct of those who have sustained the damage, and who are seeking to save further loss. That principle was acted on in Jones v. Boyce, which I have always regarded as sound law. Let us see, then, what occurred in the present case, and what was the real cause of the loss of this vessel. It was the fact that the captain was, by the collision, deprived of the means of ascertaining his position and of properly navigating his ship. He was deprived of his compass, his log-line, and his charts. His ship was not utterly unmanageable but she was in a very bad state, and the necessary consequence of all this was that this captain lost his vessel without any negligence on his part. Under these circumstances the case falls within the rule I have laid down as to the term "ordinary course of things." Therefore, I am of opinion that the owners of the *City of Lincoln* must pay for the loss of the *Albatross*.

3. Plaintiff's response to emergencies. The problem of intervening actions also arises whenever a sudden emergency requires the plaintiff's immediate action. In Jones v. Boyce, 171 Eng. Rep. 540, 541 (K.B. 1816), cited in *City of Lincoln,* plaintiff jumped from defendant's coach after it had gotten out of control and broke his leg. It was established both that defendant was negligent and that plaintiff would not have been hurt if he had remained in his place. In instructing the jury, Lord Ellenborough stated:

> To enable the plaintiff to sustain the action, it is not necessary that he should have been thrown off the coach; it is sufficient if he was placed by the misconduct of the defendant in such a situation as obliged him to adopt the alternative of a dangerous leap, or to remain at certain peril; if that position was occasioned by the default of the defendant, the action may be supported. On the other hand, if the plaintiff's act resulted from a rash apprehension of danger, which did not exist, and the injury which he sustained is to be attributed to rashness and imprudence, he is not entitled to recover.

The jury found for the plaintiff.

The same result was reached in Tuttle v. Atlantic City R.R., 49 A. 450, 451 (N.J. 1901). One of defendant's trains jumped the tracks while being moved around a freight yard in "a flying drill" and headed toward the plaintiff. "Acting under the impulse of fear," she ran for safety and hurt her knee. If she had stayed put, she would not have been struck. The court affirmed the judgment of the jury, noting that it would be truly "extraordinary" for the plaintiff not to try to escape. "The true rule governing cases of this character may be stated as follows: That if a defendant, by negligence, puts the plaintiff under a reasonable apprehension of personal physical injury, and plaintiff, in a reasonable effort to escape, sustains physical injury, a right of action arises to recover for the physical injury and the mental disorder naturally incident to its occurrence."

One simple principle that links together all three of these cases is this: If the plaintiff acts in good faith to minimize the risk of loss from a dangerous situation of the defendant's making, then those actions do not sever causal connection. In some instances, now generally disfavored courts have invoked a foresight limitation to bar recovery in these emergency cases, even when the plaintiff has undertaken a good faith action. Thus, in Mauney v. Gulf Refining Co., 9 So. 2d 780, 782 (Miss. 1942), the plaintiff, carrying her two-year-old child in her arms, tripped over a chair in her husband's cafe while trying to flee after being warned by neighbors that defendant's delivery truck was on fire and likely to explode. The court denied recovery on the ground that if the plaintiff "didn't see a chair in her own place of business, it would impose an inadmissible burden upon the defendants to say that they should have foreseen from across the street and through the walls of a building on another corner what appellant didn't see right at her feet. . . . " What degree of precision is required in working a foreseeability test? See, e.g., Williams, The Risk Principle, 77 L. Q. Rev. 179, 183 (1961): "The test of foreseeability does not require all the details of what happens to be foreseeable; it is enough if it is foreseeable in general outline." Is there any difficulty in holding the defendant liable under a directness standard?

Berry v. Sugar Notch Borough
43 A. 240 (Pa. 1899)

. . . Trespass for personal injuries. Before Woodward, P.J. . . .

Verdict and judgment for plaintiff for $3,162.50. Defendant appealed. . . .

FELL, J. The plaintiff was a motorman in the employ of the Wilkes-Barre and Wyoming Valley Traction Company on its line running from Wilkes-Barre to the borough of Sugar Notch. The ordinance by virtue of which the company was permitted to lay its track and operate its cars in the borough of Sugar Notch contained a provision that the speed of the cars while on the streets of the borough should not exceed eight miles an hour. On the line of the road, and within the borough limits, there was a large chestnut tree, as to the condition of which there was some dispute at the trial. The question of the negligence of the borough in permitting it to remain must, however, be considered as set at rest by the verdict. On the day of the accident the plaintiff was running his car on the borough street in a violent windstorm, and as he passed under the tree it was blown down, crushing the roof of the car and causing the plaintiff's injury. There is some conflict of testimony as to the speed at which the car was running, but it seems to be fairly well established that it was considerably in excess of the rate permitted by the borough ordinance.

We do not think that the fact that the plaintiff was running his car at a higher rate of speed than eight miles an hour affects his right to recover. It may be that in doing so he violated the ordinance by virtue of which the company was permitted to operate its cars in the streets of the borough, but he certainly was not for that reason without rights upon the streets. Nor can it be said that the speed was the cause of the accident, or contributed to it. It might have been otherwise if the tree had fallen before the car reached it; for in that case a high rate of speed might have rendered it impossible for the plaintiff to avoid a collision which he either foresaw or should have foreseen. Even in that case the ground for denying him the right to recover would be that he had been guilty of contributory negligence, and not that he had violated a borough ordinance. The testimony however shows that the tree fell upon the car as it passed beneath. With this phase of the case in view, it was urged on behalf of the appellant that the speed was the immediate cause of the plaintiff's injury, inasmuch as it was the particular speed at which he was running which brought the car to the place of the accident at the moment when the tree blew down. This argument, while we cannot deny its ingenuity, strikes us, to say the least, as being somewhat sophistical. That his speed brought him to the place of the accident at the moment of the accident was the merest chance, and a thing which no foresight could have predicted. The same thing might as readily have happened to a car running slowly, or it might have been that a high speed alone would have carried him beyond the tree to a place of safety. It was also argued by the appellant's counsel that, even if the speed was not the sole efficient cause of the accident, it at least contributed to its severity, and materially increased the damage. It may be that it did. But what basis could a jury have for finding such to be the case and, should they so find, what guide could be given them for differentiating between the injury done this man and the injury which would have been done a man in a similar accident on a car running at a speed of eight miles an hour or less?

The judgment is affirmed.

NOTES

1. *Coincidence and causation.* In *Berry,* the plaintiff's breach of a safety statute was not causally connected with his injuries because it did not increase the risk or hazard of his being struck. Is it relevant that the increased speed reduced the time that the plaintiff was exposed to potential injury? Increased the possibility of damage in the event of a collision with a fallen log? With *Berry,* compare Mahoney v. Beatman, *supra* at 341. Note that the Third Restatement endorses the outcome in *Berry.* RTT:LPH §30, comment *a,* illustration 1. Any contributory negligence for driving too slowly?

The problem of coincidence arose in a somewhat different form in Central of Georgia Ry. v. Price, 32 S.E. 77, 77-78 (Ga. 1898). Through its negligence the railroad did not drop the plaintiff off at her station. She spent the night at a hotel to which she had been escorted by the railroad's conductor. At the hotel, she was given a furnished room outfitted with a kerosene lamp, which exploded and set fire to the mosquito netting covering the bed. In her efforts to put out the fire, the plaintiff severely burnt her hands. The court first rejected her argument that the railroad should be liable because the hotel proprietor was its agent. It then held that the plaintiff's harm was too remote from the railroad's negligence:

> The negligence of the company consisted in passing the station where the passenger desired to alight, without giving her an opportunity to get off. Taking her version of the manner in which she was injured, the injury was occasioned by the negligence of the proprietor of the hotel or his servants in giving her a defective lamp. The negligence of the company in passing her station was therefore not the natural and proximate cause of her injury. There was the interposition of a separate, independent agency,—the negligence of the proprietor of the hotel, over whom, as we have shown, the railway company neither had nor exercised any control. The injuries to the plaintiff were not the natural and proximate consequences of carrying her beyond her station, but were unusual, and could not have been foreseen or provided against by the highest practicable care. The plaintiff was not entitled to recover for such injuries, and the court erred in overruling the motion for new trial.

The plaintiff was exposed, however, to an increased risk, in Hines v. Garrett, 108 S.E. 690, 695 (Va. 1921). A railroad conductor negligently carried the 19-year-old plaintiff almost a mile past her stop at night, forcing her to walk back this distance through an unsettled area. During her walk back she was raped once by a soldier and once by a hobo, both unidentified. Allowing her to recover against the railroad, the court said, in part: "We do not wish to be understood as questioning the general proposition that no responsibility for a wrong attaches whenever an independent act of a third person intervenes between the negligence complained of and the injury. But . . . this proposition does not apply where the very negligence alleged consists of exposing the injured party to the act causing the injury. It is perfectly well settled and will not be seriously denied that whenever a carrier has reason to anticipate the danger of an assault upon one of its passengers, it rests under the duty of protecting such passenger against the same."

2. *Independent and dependent causes.* Still another variation on the causal theme arises when each of two successive acts is sufficient to harm the plaintiff, but the plaintiff is exposed to the second cause only because of the prior negligence of the first. In these situations, the second act is said

to be "dependent" on the first, so that the second defendant is normally responsible only for the incremental damages, if any, brought about by his action. In Dillon v. Twin State Gas & Electric Co., 163 A. 111, 115 (N.H. 1932), plaintiff's decedent, a boy of 14, lost his balance while trespassing on the superstructure of a bridge and grabbed defendant's high-voltage wires as he fell. The current killed him and the shock apparently threw his body back onto the girder. The defendant power company was not found responsible for the boy's fall given his trespass, but it was found responsible for the boy's exposure to the uncovered charged wires. The defendant's motion for a directed verdict on the issue of liability was denied, and that decision was affirmed on appeal. Allen, J., wrote:

> In leaning over from the girder and losing his balance he was entitled to no protection from the defendant to keep from falling. Its only liability was in exposing him to the danger of the charged wires. If but for the current in the wires he would have fallen down on the floor of the bridge or into the river, he would without doubt have been either killed or seriously injured. Although he died from electrocution, yet, if by reason of his preceding loss of balance he was bound to fall except for the intervention of the current, he either did not have long to live or was to be maimed. In such an outcome of his loss of balance, the defendant deprived him not of a life of normal expectancy, but of one too short to be given pecuniary allowance, in one alternative, and not of normal but of limited, earning capacity, in the other. . . .

3. An apparent condition of safety. Problems of causal intervention also arise when dangerous objects are passed from hand to hand. In Pittsburg Reduction Co. v. Horton, 113 S.W. 647, 648-649 (Ark. 1908), the defendant discarded a dynamite cap on its unenclosed plant premises near a public school. The cap was picked up by Charlie Copple, age ten, who placed it in a tin box with other caps, and played with it on several occasions in his house. His mother, who later testified that she did not know what they were, would pick the caps up when Charlie was done playing. About a week after he found the cap, Charlie traded it to Jack Horton, age 13, for some writing paper. Horton thought that "the cap was the shell of a .22 cartridge that had been shot." He was picking the dirt out of the cap with a match when the cap exploded, so injuring his hand that it had to be amputated. Charlie's father, a miner, denied knowing that the cap was in the house until after the accident. Horton brought suit against the defendant company and its foreman, but his claim was denied.

> In the present case the facts are practically undisputed. Charlie Copple's father was an employee of a company engaged in a similar business to that of appellant company. Naturally, his avocation and the proximity of his residence to the mines made both himself and his wife familiar with the nature of explosives. True, Mrs. Copple says that she did not know what the shells

contained, but she did know that they were shells for some kind of explosives, that her son brought them home, and that he played with them. She admits that when he would leave them on the floor she would pick them up and lay them away for him. This continued for a week, and then, with her knowledge, he carried them to school. Her course of conduct broke the causal connection between the original negligent act of appellant and the subsequent injury of the plaintiff. It established a new agency, and the possession of Charlie Copple of the caps or shells was thereafter referable to the permission of his parents, and not to the original taking. Charlie Copple's parents having permitted him to retain possession of the caps, his further acts in regard to them must be attributable to their permission, and were wholly independent of the original negligence of appellants.

Horton and similar cases were analyzed in great detail in Beale, The Proximate Consequences of An Act, 33 Harv. L. Rev. 633, 650, 651, 656 (1920), which offered the following two generalizations:

> If the defendant's active force has come to rest, but in a dangerous position, creating a new or increasing an existing risk of loss, and the foreseen danger comes to pass, operating harmfully on the condition created by defendant and causing the risked loss, we say that the injury thereby created is a proximate consequence of the defendant's act. . . .
>
> On the other hand, where defendant's active force has come to rest in a position of apparent safety, the court will follow it no longer; if some new force later combines with this condition to create harm, the result is remote from the defendant's act.

With reference to cases like *Horton*, Beale concluded that "if the explosive gets into the hands of an adult the defendant's force has ceased to be an active danger; if the explosive thereafter gets into the hands of a child, defendant is not the proximate cause of anything this child may do with it." Should the result be the same even if the adult did not know that the cap was dangerous? The outcome in *Horton* has also been defended in Grady, Proximate Cause and the Law of Negligence, 69 Iowa L. Rev. 363, 420 (1984): "In situations when the last wrongdoer would feel especially disposed to remain at a low level of precaution because of an expectation that the original wrongdoer would be held liable for a lion's share of the expected harm that would result from their joint omissions, the direct-consequences doctrine cuts off the liability of the original wrongdoer and makes the last wrongdoer solely responsible for the damage. This was the result in the *Horton* case." Why not allow the first wrongdoer an action of indemnity against the intermediate wrongdoer instead of cutting off all relief? What likelihood is there that Horton will sue the Copples? Note that there is no proximate cause question once the cap is disabled.

Brower v. New York Central & H.R.R.
103 A. 166 (N.J. 1918)

SWAYZE, J. This is a case of a grade-crossing collision. We are clear that the questions of negligence and contributory negligence were for the jury. If there were nothing else, the testimony of the plaintiff as to signals of the flagman would carry the case to the jury. The only question that has caused us difficulty is that of the extent of the defendant's liability. The complaint avers that the horse was killed, the wagon and harness, and the cider and barrels with which the wagon was loaded, were destroyed. What happened was that as a result of the collision, aside from the death of the horse and the destruction of the wagon, the contents of the wagon, consisting of empty barrels and a keg of cider, were scattered and probably stolen by people at the scene of the accident. The driver, who was alone in charge for the plaintiff, was so stunned that one of the railroad detectives found him immediately after the collision in a fit. There were two railroad detectives on the freight train to protect the property it was carrying against thieves, but they did nothing to protect the plaintiff's property. The controversy on the question of damages is as to the right of the plaintiff to recover the value of the barrels, cider and blanket. . . . It is now argued that the defendant's negligence was not in any event the proximate cause of the loss of this property since the act of the thieves intervened. The rule of law which exempts the one guilty of the original negligence from damage due to an intervening cause is well settled. The difficulty lies in the application. Like the question of proximate cause, this is ordinarily a jury question. . . .

We think these authorities justified the trial judge in his rulings as to the recovery of the value of the barrels, cider and blanket. The negligence which caused the collision resulted immediately in such a condition of the driver of the wagon that he was no longer able to protect his employer's property; the natural and probable result of his enforced abandonment of it in the street of a large city was its disappearance and the wrongdoer cannot escape making reparation for the loss caused by depriving the plaintiff of the protection which the presence of the driver in his right senses would have afforded. "The act of a third person," said the Supreme Judicial Court of Massachusetts, "intervening and contributing a condition necessary to the injurious effect of the original negligence, will not excuse the first wrongdoer, if such act ought to have been foreseen." Lane v. Atlantic Works, 111 Mass. 136 [(1872)]. A railroad company which found it necessary or desirable to have its freight train guarded by two detectives against thieves is surely chargeable with knowledge that portable property left without a guard was likely to be made off with. Again, strictly speaking, the act of the thieves did not intervene between defendant's negligence and the plaintiff's loss; the two causes were to all practical intent simultaneous and concurrent; it is rather a case of a joint tort than an intervening cause. . . . An illustration will perhaps clarify the case. Suppose a fruit vendor at his stand along the street is rendered unconscious by the negligence of the defendant, who disappears, and boys in the street appropriate the unfortunate vendor's stock in trade; could the defendant escape liability for their value? We can hardly imagine a court answering in the affirmative. Yet the case is but little more extreme than the jury might have found the present case. . . .

GARRISON, J., dissenting. The collision afforded an opportunity for theft of which a thief took advantage, but I cannot agree that the collision was therefore the proximate cause of loss of the stolen articles. Proximate cause imports unbroken continuity between cause and effect, which, both in law and in logic, is broken by the active intervention of an independent criminal actor. This established rule of law is defeated if proximate cause be confounded with mere opportunity for crime. A maladjusted switch may be the proximate cause of the death of a passenger who was killed by the derailment of the train, or by the fire or collision that ensued, but it is not the proximate cause of the death of a passenger who was murdered by a bandit who boarded the train because of the opportunity afforded by its derailment. This clear distinction is not met by saying that criminal intervention should be foreseen, for this implies that crime is to be presumed and the law is directly otherwise.

NOTES

1. *Deliberate intervention by third parties.* The position taken in the *Brower* dissent was endorsed in Watson v. Kentucky & Indiana Bridge & R.R., 126 S.W. 146, 151 (Ky. 1910), in which a tank car containing gasoline derailed through defendant's negligence. As the gas leaked out, a man named Duerr threw a match on it, starting a large fire. The defendant introduced evidence that Duerr had just been discharged by the defendant, had intended to commit arson, and had been indicted for the crime. The plaintiff's evidence suggested that Duerr was lighting a cigar when he carelessly threw the match on the gasoline. The court held that the jury should decide whether Duerr had acted maliciously or negligently, but that if his actions were malicious, the defendant was entitled to a directed verdict on proximate cause grounds.

> [If] the act of Duerr was malicious, we quite agree with the trial court that it was one which the appellees could not reasonably have anticipated or guarded against, and in such case the act of Duerr, and not the primary negligence of the appellee Bridge & Railroad Company, in any of the particulars charged, was the efficient or proximate cause of appellant's injuries. The mere fact that the concurrent cause or intervening act was unforeseen

will not relieve the defendant guilty of the primary negligence from liability, but if the intervening agency is something so unexpected or extraordinary as that he could not or ought not to have anticipated it, he will not be liable and certainly he is not bound to anticipate the criminal acts of others by which damage is inflicted, and hence is not liable therefor.

Why relieve the defendant of liability if the proper precautions against negligence would have prevented the malicious harm?

2. *The last wrongdoer and beyond.* Cases like *Brower* and *Watson* call into question the proper test of causation. Under the earliest tests of proximate causation, the defendant was held liable only when he was the "last wrong-doer" whose conduct contributed to the loss: criminal conduct obviously severed causal connection on this view. More generally, the last actor need not be the last wrongdoer, for his actions could be blameless or even praiseworthy. The efforts of the captain to save his ship in *City of Lincoln* did not sever causal connection; nor did plaintiff's efforts to escape a moving train in *Tuttle*. Likewise, the actions of infants and incompetents would not break the chain of causation, at least in those cases where the law does not regard their actions as tortious. Nevertheless, the test is highly restrictive for it blocks causal recovery not only when the deliberate wrong of a third party intervenes but also when the negligence of a third party intervenes.

Although this "last wrongdoer" test had some early champions (see T. Beven, Negligence in Law 45 (3d ed. 1908)), it was necessarily breached whenever the negligence of one defendant did not sever causal connection to a prior actor. Thus, in Atherton v. Devine, 602 P.2d 634, 636-637 (Okla. 1979), the plaintiff was injured in a road accident attributable to the defendant's negligence. The ambulance that took the plaintiff to the hospital was involved in another collision, aggravating the original injuries. The Oklahoma Supreme Court, reversing the decision below, held that the first collision was a "substantial factor" in causing the subsequent injury, so the harm was not too remote:

> It has long been the rule in Oklahoma that an original wrongdoer, negligently causing injury to another is liable for the negligence of a physician who treats the injured person where the negligent treatment results in the aggravation of injuries, so long as the injured person exercises good faith in the choice of his physician. . . .
>
> As a matter of principle, there would seem to be no material distinction between medical treatment required because of the tortious act, and transportation required to reach an institution where medical treatment is available. The use of an ambulance, like the use of a surgeon's scalpel, is necessitated by the tortfeasor's wrong, and either may be used negligently.

Even after the negligence barrier was overcome, many causal theorists continued to believe that deliberate and malicious acts should in general negate causal connection. Thus, Hart and Honoré offer this general test of causation: "The general principle of the traditional doctrine is that *the free, deliberate and informed act or omission of a human being, intended to exploit the situation created by the defendant, negatives any causal connection.*" Causation in the Law 136 (2d ed. 1985) (italics in original). The commonsense defense of this position rests on the observation that the original actor did not constrain the conduct of the malicious intervenor, but only facilitated his mischief. Yet it was just the creation of additional opportunities for harm that allowed the plaintiff to recover against the railroad in Hines v. Garrett (*supra* at 504) or indeed in *Brower* itself, so this test too is generally regarded as too restrictive on recovery.

3. *The Second Restatement approach.* The role of deliberate third party intervention, under the Second Restatement's "substantial factor" test, is taken up in two critical provisions:

§448.   INTENTIONALLY TORTIOUS OR CRIMINAL ACTS DONE UNDER
OPPORTUNITY AFFORDED BY ACTOR'S NEGLIGENCE

The act of a third person in committing an intentional tort or crime is a superseding cause of harm to another resulting therefrom, although the actor's negligent conduct created a situation which afforded an opportunity to the third person to commit such a tort or crime, unless the actor at the time of his negligent conduct realized or should have realized the likelihood that such a situation might be created, and that a third person might avail himself of the opportunity to commit such a tort or crime.

§449.   TORTIOUS OR CRIMINAL ACTS THE PROBABILITY OF WHICH MAKES
ACTOR'S CONDUCT NEGLIGENT

If the likelihood that a third person may act in a particular manner is the hazard or one of the hazards which makes the actor negligent, such an act whether innocent, negligent, intentionally tortious, or criminal does not prevent the actor from being liable for harm caused thereby.

The Restatement's position is that the defendant should be liable precisely because the third party *did* exploit the dangerous condition created by the defendant. Thus, *Watson,* for example, should result in no liability if Duerr had independently laid plans to set off an explosion near the railroad's cars, a most unlikely supposition on the facts of the case. In addition both *Brower* and *Watson* tacitly acknowledge distinct limits to causal responsibility, wholly without reference to foreseeability, even if the malicious acts of a third party do not sever causal connection. In *Brower* the consequences of defendant's action cease once the railroad gathers up the barrels and places them under a competent guard. In *Watson* the liability ends once the spilled gasoline is collected and removed to a position of safety.

Generally, the cases uniformly follow the Second Restatement. In Bigbee v. Pacific Telephone and Telegraph Co., 665 P.2d 947 (Cal. 1983), the plaintiff was trapped in a telephone booth located in a parking lot 15 feet from a major thoroughfare. The plaintiff saw an oncoming car careening out of control. He was struck by Leona Roberts, a drunk driver, when he was unable to wrestle the door open in time to escape. After holding that the phone company could be found negligent both in its placement and its maintenance of the booth, Bird, C.J., brushed aside the defendant's proximate cause argument, noting that it "is of no consequence that the harm to the plaintiff came about through the negligent or reckless acts of Roberts," citing Restatement (Second) Torts §449.

Watson in turn was repudiated in Britton v. Wooten, 817 S.W.2d 443 (Ky. 1991). Possible third-party arson destroyed a grocery store in which the defendant had negligently stacked excessive amounts of flammable trash. Plaintiff had leased the building to defendant. Relying on the Second Restatement, the court concluded, "we reject any all-inclusive general rule that, as respondent contends, 'criminal acts of third parties . . . relieve the original negligent party from liability.'" Likewise in Bell v. Board of Education, 687 N.E.2d 1325 (N.Y. 1998), the defendant school board left the plaintiff behind at a sixth grade drug awareness fair near her school. On her way back she was accosted by three boys, and taken to the house of one where she was raped and sodomized. The court affirmed a jury verdict for the plaintiff, holding that "we cannot say that the intervening act of rape was unforeseeable as a matter of law." Does *Bell* present the same increased risk or hazard as *Hines, supra* at 504?

4. *The Third Restatement approach.* The conceptual terminology of the Second Restatement gets a rude reception in the Third Restatement whose key provision on intervening causes states only that "[w]hen a force of nature or an independent act is also a factual cause of physical harm, an actor's liability is limited to those harms that result from the risks that made the actor's conduct tortious." RTT:LPH §34. Its comments keep up the drumbeat: "Despite the continuing influence of the Second Restatement of Torts, much of the formalism of its treatment of superseding causes has been supplanted in the latter part of the 20th century with the recognition that there are always multiple causes of an outcome and that the existence of intervening causes does not ordinarily elide a prior actor's liability." *Id.* at comment *a.* Typically, the results in particular cases show no difference between the two Restatements, leaving it unclear whether the Third Restatement's preferred language will displace the ingrained usage of the Second.

5. *Plaintiff's suicide as an intervening cause.* The principles of proximate causation are tested whenever the plaintiff's decedent, having been hurt by the wrongful conduct of the defendant, commits suicide while suffering from nervous shock or mental depression brought about by the accident. The early common law cases treated suicide as an intervening cause.

Scheffer v. Railroad Co., 105 U.S. 249 (1881), held as a matter of law that neither the decedent's insanity nor suicide was the natural and probable consequence of the defendant's negligence.

Modern cases usually allow the question to go to the jury. In Fuller v. Preis, 322 N.E.2d 263, 266, 269 (N.Y. 1974), the decedent, a medical doctor, walked away from an automobile accident in the belief that he was uninjured. About seven months after the accident he executed his will and two days later took his life. In the period between the accident and his death, the decedent experienced recurrent seizures that required him to abandon his medical practice. In addition, his wife, partially paralyzed by polio, suffered "nervous exhaustion" and his mother became ill with cancer. Breitel, C.J., held that it was a jury question whether the cause of the decedent's death was the automobile accident or the illnesses of his wife and mother. Breitel, C.J., continued: "When the suicide is preceded by a history of trauma, brain damage, epileptic seizures, aberrational conduct, depression and despair, it is at the very least a fair issue of fact whether the suicide was the rational act of a sound mind or the irrational act or irresistible impulse of a deranged mind evidenced by a physically damaged brain." How do we deal with the joint causation issues?

In Johnson v. United States, 263 F.3d 753, 756-757 (7th Cir. 2001), the decedent hung himself in his cell where he had been held for six months awaiting trial for extortion. His initial psychological screening revealed no particular disorder, but his condition deteriorated markedly, and eventually the decedent picked and scratched at himself until he bled "copiously." His cellmate urged that he be given psychiatric counseling, but decedent's sick-call form was ignored by the physician's assistant who had neglected to read the request, but told him to make an appointment to see the jail psychologist. He hanged himself 12 hours later. The government conceded negligence, but defended the case on causation. At the bench trial below, Kocaras, J. awarded the plaintiffs $1.8 million in damages, which was reversed on appeal by Posner, J., who held that the decedent's "underlying unhappiness" because of his personal situation, and not the immediate sores, should be regarded as the cause of death. He further held that "[i]t is sheer conjecture that an interview with the jail psychologist would have produced sufficient information to have enabled the psychologist to infer that Johnson was a suicide risk and place him on suicide watch. . . ." If the cellmate could detect the deterioration in condition, then why not the jail psychologist?

Wagner v. International Ry.
133 N.E. 437 (N.Y. 1921)

CARDOZO, J. [after a brief statement of preliminary facts about the electric railway's trestle:] Plaintiff and his cousin Herbert boarded a car at a station near the bottom of one of the trestles. Other passengers, entering at the same time, filled the platform, and blocked admission to the aisle. The platform was provided with doors, but the conductor did not close them. Moving at from six to eight miles an hour, the car, without slackening, turned the curve. There was a violent lurch, and Herbert Wagner was thrown out, near the point where the trestle changes to a bridge. The cry was raised, "Man overboard." The car went on across the bridge, and stopped near the foot of the incline. Night and darkness had come on. Plaintiff walked along the trestle, a distance of four hundred and forty-five feet, until he arrived at the bridge, where he thought to find his cousin's body. He says that he was asked to go there by the conductor. He says, too, that the conductor followed with a lantern. Both these statements the conductor denies. Several other persons, instead of ascending the trestle, went beneath it, and discovered under the bridge the body they were seeking. As they stood there, the plaintiff's body struck the ground beside them. Reaching the bridge, he had found upon a beam his cousin's hat, but nothing else. About him, there was darkness. He missed his footing, and fell.

The trial judge held that negligence toward Herbert Wagner would not charge the defendant with liability for injuries suffered by the plaintiff unless two other facts were found: First, that the plaintiff had been invited by the conductor to go upon the bridge; and second, that the conductor had followed with a light. Thus limited, the jury found in favor of the defendant. Whether the limitation may be upheld, is the question to be answered.

Danger invites rescue. The cry of distress is the summons to relief. The law does not ignore these reactions of the mind in tracing conduct to its consequences. It recognizes them as normal. It places their effects within the range of the natural and probable. The wrong that imperils life is a wrong to the imperiled victim; it is a wrong also to his rescuer. The state that leaves an opening in a bridge is liable to the child that falls into the stream, but liable also to the parent who plunges to its aid. . . . The railroad company whose train approaches without signal is a wrongdoer toward the traveler surprised between the rails, but a wrongdoer also to the bystander who drags him from the path (Eckert v. L.I.R.R. Co., 43 N.Y. 502). . . . The rule is the same in other jurisdictions. . . . The risk of rescue, if only it be not wanton, is born of the occasion. The emergency begets the man. The wrongdoer may not have foreseen the coming of a deliverer. He is accountable as if he had. . . .

The defendant says that we must stop, in following the chain of causes, when action ceases to be "instinctive." By this, is meant, it seems, that rescue is at the peril of the rescuer, unless spontaneous and immediate. If there has been time to deliberate, if impulse has given way to judgment, one cause, it is said, has spent its force, and another has intervened. In this case, the plaintiff walked more than four hundred feet in going to Herbert's aid. He had time to reflect and weigh; impulse had been followed by choice; and choice, in the defendant's view, intercepts and breaks the sequence. We find no warrant for thus shortening the chain of jural causes. We may assume, though we are not required to decide, that peril and rescue must be in substance one transaction; that the sight of the one must have aroused the impulse to the other; in short, that there must be unbroken continuity between the commission of the wrong and the effort to avert its consequences. If all this be assumed, the defendant is not aided. Continuity in such circumstances is not broken by the exercise of volition. . . . So sweeping an exception, if recognized, would leave little of the rule. "The human mind," as we have said (People v. Majone, 91 N.Y. 211, 212), "acts with celerity which it is sometimes impossible to measure." The law does not discriminate between the rescuer oblivious of peril and the one who counts the cost. It is enough that the act, whether impulsive or deliberate, is the child of the occasion.

The defendant finds another obstacle, however, in the futility of the plaintiff's sacrifice. [The court then discussed whether or not plaintiff was contributorily negligent and concluded that under the emergency conditions he was not.]

Whether Herbert Wagner's fall was due to the defendant's negligence, and whether plaintiff in going to the rescue, as he did, was foolhardy or reasonable in the light of the emergency confronting him, were questions for the jury.

NOTE

Danger invites rescue? Is the decision in *Wagner* a fair extension of *City of Lincoln* or of *Tuttle*? Should the plaintiff's recovery be barred if the conductor had mounted adequate rescue efforts without the plaintiff's assistance? If he had told the plaintiff to stay in the train? If Herbert were thought to be dead? Whatever its soundness, the "rescue doctrine" is well established today. See RTT:LPH §32, noting that any unreasonable rescue efforts by plaintiff should be covered by comparative negligence and not the doctrine of superseding cause. *Id.* at comment *a*. Elsewhere the functions of the rescue doctrine were described in McCoy v. American Suzuki Motor Corp., 961 P.2d 952, 956 (Wash. 1998) as follows:

> First, it informs a tortfeasor it is foreseeable a rescuer will come to the aid of a person imperiled by the tortfeasor's actions, and, therefore, the tortfeasor owes the rescuer a duty similar to the duty he owes the person he imperils. Second, the rescue doctrine negates the presumption that the rescuer assumed the risk of injury when he knowingly undertook the dangerous rescue, so long as he does not act rashly or recklessly.

To achieve rescuer status one must demonstrate: (1) the defendant was negligent to the person rescued and such negligence caused the peril or appearance of peril to the person rescued; (2) the peril or appearance of peril was imminent; (3) a reasonably prudent person would have concluded such peril or appearance of peril existed; and (4) the rescuer acted with reasonable care in effectuating the rescue.

In re Polemis & Furness, Withy & Co.
[1921] 3 K.B. 560

BANKES, L.J. By a time charterparty dated February 21, 1917, the respondents chartered their vessel to the appellants. Clause 21 of the charterparty was in these terms.

["The act of God, the King's enemies, loss or damage from fire on board in hulk or craft, or on shore, arrest and/or restraint of princes, rulers, and people, collision, an act, neglect, or default whatsoever of pilot, master, or crew in the management or navigation of the ship, and all and every of the dangers and accidents of the seas, canals, and rivers, and of navigation of whatever nature or kind always mutually excepted." This charterparty was the agreement whereby the shipowner leased the ship to the "charterers" — the appellants in this case. The "mutually excepted" language meant on its face that each side had to bear its own losses from the stated contingencies. The court first held that the language of clause 21 did not release the charterers from the consequences of their negligence.]

The vessel was employed by the charterers to carry a cargo to Casablanca in Morocco. The cargo included a quantity of benzine or petrol in cases. While discharging at Casablanca a heavy plank fell into the hold in which the petrol was stowed, and caused an explosion, which set fire to the vessel and completely destroyed her. The owners claimed the value of the vessel from the charterers, alleging that the loss of the vessel was due to the negligence of the charterers' servants. The charterers contended that they were protected by the exception of fire contained in clause 21 of the charterparty, and they also contended that the damages claimed were too remote. The claim was referred to arbitration, and the arbitrators stated a special case for the opinion of the Court. Their findings of fact are as follows.

(*a*)   That the ship was lost by fire.
(*b*)   That the fire arose from a spark igniting petrol vapour in the hold.
(*c*)   That the spark was caused by the falling board coming into contact with some substance in the hold.

(d)   That the fall of the board was caused by the negligence of the Arabs (other than the winchman) engaged in the work of discharging.

(e)   That the said Arabs were employed by the charterers or their agents the Cie. Transatlantique on behalf of the charterers, and that the said Arabs were the servants of the charterers.

(f)   That the causing of the spark could not reasonably have been anticipated from the falling of the board, though some damage to the ship might reasonably have been anticipated.

(g)   There was no evidence before us that the Arabs chosen were known or likely to be negligent.

Then they state the damages, £196,165 1s. 11d. These findings are no doubt intended to raise the question whether the view taken, or said to have been taken, by Pollock, C.B., in Rigby v. Hewitt[, 155 Eng. Rep. 103 (Ex. 1850), and Greenland v. Chaplin (5 [Ex.] 243, 155 [Eng. Rep.] 104, [1850]), or the view taken by Channell, B., and Blackburn, J., in Smith v. London & South Western Ry. Co. (3 L. R. 6 C.P. 21 [(1870)]), is the correct one. . . .

Assuming the Chief Baron to have been correctly reported in the Exchequer Reports, the difference between the two views is this: According to the one view, the consequences which may reasonably be expected to result from a particular act are material only in reference to the question whether the act is or is not a negligent act; according to the other view, those consequences are the test whether the damages resulting from the act, assuming it to be negligent, are or are not too remote to be recoverable. [Bankes, L.J., then quoted from H.M.S. London, [1914] P. 72, in part, as follows:] ". . . In Smith v. London and South Western Ry. Co., Channell, B., said: 'Where there is no direct evidence of negligence, the question what a reasonable man might foresee is of importance in considering the question whether there is evidence for the jury of negligence or not . . . but when it has been once determined that there is evidence of negligence, the person guilty of it is equally liable for its consequences, whether he could have foreseen them or not.' And Blackburn, J., in the same case said: 'What the defendants might reasonably anticipate is only material with reference to the question, whether the defendants were negligent or not, and cannot alter their liability if they were guilty of negligence.' " . . .

In the present case the arbitrators have found as a fact that the falling of the plank was due to the negligence of the defendants' servants. The fire appears to me to have been directly caused by the falling of the plank. Under these circumstances I consider that it is immaterial that the causing of the spark by the falling of the plank could not have been reasonably anticipated. The appellants' junior counsel sought to draw a distinction between the anticipation of the extent of damage resulting from a negligent act, and the anticipation of the type of damage resulting from such an act. He admitted that it could not lie in the mouth of a person whose negligent act had caused damage to say that he could not reasonably have foreseen the extent of the damage, but he contended that the negligent person was entitled to rely upon the fact that he could not reasonably have anticipated the type of damage which resulted from his negligent act. I do not think that the distinction can be admitted. Given the breach of duty which constitutes the negligence, and given the damage as a direct result of that negligence, the anticipations of the person whose negligent act has produced the damage appear to me to be irrelevant. I consider that the damages claimed are not too remote.

WARRINGTON, L.J. [referring to a discussion by Beven on Negligence, observed:] . . . The result may be summarised as follows: The presence or absence of reasonable anticipation of damage determines the legal quality of the act as negligent or innocent. If it be thus determined to be negligent, then the question whether particular damages are recoverable depends only on the answer to the question whether they are the direct consequence of the act. Sufficient authority for the proposition is afforded by Smith v. London and South Western Ry. Co., in the Exchequer Chamber, and particularly by the judgments of Channell, B., and Blackburn, J. . . . In the present case it is clear that the act causing the plank to fall was in law a negligent act, because some damage to the ship might reasonably be anticipated. If this is so then the appellants are liable for the actual loss, that being on the findings of the arbitrators the direct result of the falling board. . . .

SCRUTTON, L.J. . . . . The second defence is that the damage is too remote from the negligence, as it could not be reasonably foreseen as a consequence. On this head we were referred to a number of well known cases in which vague language, which I cannot think to be really helpful, has been used in an attempt to define the point at which damage becomes too remote from, or not sufficiently directly caused by, the breach of duty, which is the original cause of action, to be recoverable. For instance, I cannot think it useful to say the damage must be the natural and probable result. This suggests that there are results which are natural but not probable, and other results which are probable but not natural. I am not sure what either adjective means in this connection; if they mean the same thing, two need not be used; if they mean different things, the difference between them should be defined. And as to many cases of fact in which the distinction has been drawn, it is difficult to see why one case should be decided one way and one another. . . . To determine whether an act is negligent, it is relevant to determine whether any reasonable person would foresee that the act would cause damage; if he would not, the act is not negligent. But if the act would or might probably cause damage, the fact that the damage it in fact causes is not the exact kind of damage one would expect is immaterial, so long as the damage is in fact directly traceable to the negligent act, and not due to the operation of independent causes having no connection with the negligent act, except that they could not avoid its results. Once the act is negligent, the fact that its exact operation was not foreseen is immaterial. . . . In the present case it was negligent in discharging cargo to knock down the planks of the temporary staging, for they might easily cause some damage either to workmen, or cargo, or the ship. The fact that they did directly produce an unexpected result, a spark in an atmosphere of petrol vapour which caused a fire, does not relieve the person who was negligent from the damage which his negligent act so directly caused.

NOTE

Culpability versus compensation. The judges in *Polemis* relied on *Smith,* *supra* at 500, which was a stranger case. In a famous bon mot, Professor Seavey said, "Prima facie at least, the reasons for creating liability should limit it." Seavey, Mr. Justice Cardozo and the Law of Torts, 39 Colum. L. Rev. 20, 34; 52 Harv. L. Rev. 372, 386; 48 Yale L.J. 390, 404 (1939). How does Seavey's argument apply under a regime of strict liability? In light of the contractual exclusion of clause 21, *Polemis* presented a case of an incomplete contract between the owner and charterer because it did not specify the allocation of loss in the event of negligence by either party. What result if the contract had provided explicitly that all unforeseeable risks of the charterer's negligence were to be borne by the shipowner? Is that likely to have been the ex ante arrangement between the parties?

Whatever its merits, the *Polemis* rule has long been followed in many American jurisdictions. In Christianson v. Chicago, St. P., M. and O. Ry., 69 N.W. 640, 641 (Minn. 1896), the plaintiff was riding on the rear of a railroad's hand car, moving west. His hand car was being overtaken by a second car, driven by his foreman, going at a faster rate in the same direction. The plaintiff lost his balance and fell off the car, only to be struck and severely injured by the second hand car. Mitchell, J., upheld jury determinations that exonerated the plaintiff from charges of contributory negligence and found the defendant negligent. He continued:

> The main contention, however, of defendant's counsel, is that, conceding that those on the rear car were negligent, yet plaintiff's injuries were not the proximate result of such negligence; or, perhaps to state his position more accurately, that it is not enough to entitle plaintiff to recover that his injuries were the natural consequence of this negligence, but that it must also appear that, under all the circumstances, it might have been reasonably anticipated that such injury would result. With this legal premise assumed, counsel argues that those on the rear car could not have reasonably anticipated that plaintiff would fall from the car. . . .
>
> The doctrine contended for by counsel would establish practically the same rule of damages resulting from tort as is applied to damages resulting from breach of contract, under the familiar doctrine of Hadley v. Baxendale,

9 Exch. 341. This mode of stating the law is misleading, if not positively inaccurate. It confounds and mixes the definition of "negligence" with that of "proximate cause."

What a man may reasonably anticipate is important, and may be decisive, in determining whether an act is negligent, but is not at all decisive in determining whether that act is the proximate cause of an injury which ensues. . . . Consequences which follow in unbroken sequence, without an intervening efficient cause, from the original negligent act, are natural and proximate and for such consequences the original wrongdoer is responsible, even though he could not have foreseen the particular results which did follow. Smith v. Railway Co., L. R. 6 C. P. 14.

Tested by this rule, we think that it is clear that the negligence of those on the rear car was the proximate cause of plaintiff's injuries; at least, that the evidence justified the jury in so finding. Counsel admitted on the argument that if, by derailment or other accident, the front car had been suddenly stopped, and a collision and consequent injuries to plaintiff had resulted, the negligence of those on the rear car would have been the proximate cause. But we can see no difference in principle between the case supposed and the present case. The causal connection between the negligent act and the resulting injury would be the same in both cases. The only possible difference is that it might be anticipated that the sudden stoppage of the car was more likely to happen than the falling of one of its occupants upon the track.

What result under a modern foreseeability test?

Palsgraf v. Long Island R.R.
162 N.E. 99 (N.Y. 1928)

Appeal from a judgment of the Appellate Division of the Supreme Court in the second judicial department, entered December 16, 1927, affirming a judgment in favor of plaintiff entered upon a verdict.

[The following excerpts are from the majority opinion of Seeger, J., in the Appellate Division, 222 App. Div. 166 (1927):]

The defendant contends that the accident was not caused by the negligence of the defendant.

The sole question of defendant's negligence submitted to the jury was whether the defendant's employees were "careless and negligent in the way they handled this particular passenger after he came upon the platform and while he was boarding the train." This question of negligence was submitted to the jury by a fair and impartial charge and the verdict was supported by the evidence. The jury might well find that the act of the passenger in undertaking to board a moving train was negligent, and that the acts of the defendant's employees in assisting him while engaged in that negligent act were also negligent. Instead of aiding or assisting the passenger engaged in such an act, they might better have discouraged and warned him not to board the moving train. It is quite probable that without their assistance the passenger might have succeeded in boarding the train and no accident would have happened, or without the assistance of these employees the passenger might have desisted in his efforts to board the train. In any event, the acts of defendant's employees, which the jury found to be negligent, caused the bundle to be thrown under the train and to explode. It is no answer or defense to these negligent acts to say that the defendant's employees were not chargeable with notice that the passenger's bundle contained an explosive. . . .

It must be remembered that the plaintiff was a passenger of the defendant and entitled to have the defendant exercise the highest degree of care required of common carriers.

[The dissenting opinion of Lazansky, P.J., in the appellate division reads as follows:]

The facts may have warranted the jury in finding the defendant's agents were negligent in assisting a passenger in boarding a moving train in view of the fact that a door of the train should have been closed before the train started, which would have prevented the passenger making the attempt. There was also warrant for a finding by the jury that as a result of the negligence of the defendant a package was thrown between the platform and train, exploded, causing injury to plaintiff, who was on the station platform. In my opinion, the negligence of defendant was not a proximate cause of the injuries to plaintiff. Between the negligence of defendant and the injuries, there intervened the negligence of the passenger carrying the package containing an explosive. This was an independent, and not a concurring act of negligence. The explosion was not reasonably probable as a result of defendant's act of negligence. The negligence of defendant was not a likely or natural cause of the explosion, since the latter was such an unusual occurrence. Defendant's negligence was a cause of plaintiff's injury, but too remote.

[The appellate division split three to two for plaintiff. The Court of Appeals reversed by a four to three vote.]

CARDOZO, C.J. Plaintiff was standing on a platform of defendant's railroad after buying a ticket to go to Rockaway Beach. A train stopped at the station, bound for another place. Two men ran forward to catch it. One of the men reached the platform of the car without mishap, though the train was already moving. The other man, carrying a package, jumped aboard the car, but seemed unsteady as if about to fall. A guard on the car, who had held the door open, reached forward to help him in, and another guard on the platform pushed him from behind. In this act, the package was dislodged, and fell upon the rails. It was a package of small size, about fifteen inches long, and was covered by a newspaper. In fact it contained fireworks, but there was nothing in its appearance to give notice of its contents. The fireworks when they fell exploded. The shock of the explosion threw down some scales at the other end of the platform, many feet away. The scales struck the plaintiff, causing injuries for which she sues.

The conduct of the defendant's guard, if a wrong in its relation to the holder of the package, was not a wrong in its relation to the plaintiff, standing far away. Relatively to her it was not negligence at all. Nothing in the situation gave notice that the falling package had in it the potency of peril to persons thus removed. Negligence is not actionable unless it involves the invasion of a legally protected interest, the violation of a right. "Proof of negligence in the air, so to speak, will not do" (Pollock, Torts, p. 455 [11th ed.]). The plaintiff as she stood upon the platform of the station might claim to be protected against intentional invasion of her bodily security. Such invasion is not charged. She might claim to be protected against unintentional invasion by conduct involving in the thought of reasonable men an unreasonable hazard that such invasion would ensue. These, from the point of view of the law, were the bounds of her immunity, with perhaps some rare exceptions, survivals for the most part of ancient forms of liability, where conduct is held to be at the peril of the actor. If no hazard was apparent to the eye of ordinary vigilance, an act innocent and harmless, at least to outward seeming, with reference to her, did not take to itself the quality of a tort because it happened to be a wrong, though apparently not one involving the risk of bodily insecurity, with reference to someone else. . . . The plaintiff sues in her own right for a wrong personal to her, and not as the vicarious beneficiary of a breach of duty to another.

A different conclusion will involve us, and swiftly too, in a maze of contradictions. A guard stumbles over a package which has been left upon a platform. It seems to be a bundle of newspapers. It turns out to be a can of dynamite. To the eye of ordinary vigilance, the bundle is abandoned waste, which may be kicked or trod on with impunity. Is a passenger at the other end of the platform protected by the law against the unsuspected hazard concealed beneath the waste? If not, is the result to be any different, so far as the distant passenger is concerned, when the guard stumbles over a valise which a truckman or a porter has left upon the walk? The passenger far away, if the victim of a wrong at all, has a cause of action, not derivative, but original and primary. His claim to be protected against invasion of his bodily security is neither greater nor less because the act resulting in the invasion is a wrong to another far removed. In this case, the rights that are said to have been violated, the interests said to have been invaded, are not even of the same order. The man was not injured in his person nor even put in danger. The purpose of the act, as well as its effect, was to make his person safe. If there was a wrong to him at all, which may very well be doubted, it was a wrong to a property interest only, the safety of his package. Out of this wrong to property, which threatened injury to nothing else, there has passed, we are told, to the plaintiff by derivation or succession a right of action for the invasion of an interest of another order, the right to bodily security. The diversity of interests emphasizes the futility of the effort to build the plaintiff's right upon the basis of a wrong to some one else. The gain is one of emphasis, for a like result would follow if the interests were the same. Even then, the orbit of the danger as disclosed to the eye of reasonable vigilance would be the orbit of the duty. One who jostles one's neighbor in a crowd does not invade the rights of others standing at the outer fringe when the unintended contact casts a bomb upon the ground. The wrongdoer as to them is the man who carries the bomb, not the one who explodes it without suspicion of the danger. Life will have to be made over, and human nature transformed, before prevision so extravagant can be accepted as the norm of conduct, the customary standard to which behavior must conform.

The argument for the plaintiff is built upon the shifting meanings of such words as "wrong" and "wrongful," and shares their instability. What the plaintiff must show is "a wrong" to herself, i.e. a violation of her own right, and not merely a wrong to someone else, nor conduct "wrongful" because unsocial, but not "a wrong" to any one. We are told that one who drives at reckless speed through a crowded city street is guilty of a negligent act and, therefore, of a wrongful one irrespective of the consequences. Negligent the act is, and wrongful in the sense that it is unsocial, but wrongful and unsocial in relation to other travelers, only because the eye of vigilance perceives the risk of damage. If the same act were to be committed on a speedway or a race course, it would lose its wrongful quality. The risk reasonably to be perceived defines the duty to be obeyed, and risk imports relation; it is risk to another or to others within the range of apprehension (Seavey, Negligence, Subjective or Objective, 41 H.L. Rv. 6). This does not mean, of course, that one who launches a destructive force is always relieved of liability if the force, though known to be destructive, pursues an unexpected path. "It was not necessary that the defendant should have had notice of the particular method in which an accident would occur, if the possibility of an accident was clear to the ordinarily prudent eye" (Munsey v. Webb, 231 U.S. 150, 156 [(1913)]). Some acts, such as shooting, are so imminently dangerous to any one who may come within reach of the missile, however unexpectedly, as to impose a duty of prevision not far from that of an insurer. Even today, and much oftener in earlier stages of the law, one acts sometimes at one's peril (Jeremiah Smith, Tort and Absolute Liability, 30 H.L. Rv. 328; Street, Foundations of Legal Liability, vol. 1, pp. 77, 78). Under this head, it may be, fall certain cases of what is known as transferred intent, an act willfully dangerous to *A* resulting by misadventure in injury to *B* (Talmage v. Smith, 101 Mich. 370, 374). These cases aside, wrong is defined in terms of the natural or probable, at least when unintentional (Parrot v. Wells-Fargo Co. [The Nitro-Glycerine Case], [82 U.S.] 15 Wall. [524 (1872)]). The range of reasonable apprehension is at times a question for the court, and at times, if varying inferences are possible, a question for the jury. Here, by concession, there was nothing in the situation to suggest to the most cautious mind that the parcel wrapped in newspaper would spread wreckage through the station. If the guard had thrown it down knowingly and willfully, he would not have threatened the plaintiff's safety, so far as appearances could warn him. His conduct would not have involved, even then, an unreasonable probability of invasion of her bodily security. Liability can be no greater where the act is inadvertent.

Negligence, like risk, is thus a term of relation. Negligence in the abstract, apart from things related, is surely not a tort, if indeed it is understandable at all. . . .

The law of causation, remote or proximate, is thus foreign to the case before us. The question of liability is always anterior to the question of the measure of the consequences that go with liability. If there is no tort to be redressed, there is no occasion to consider what damage might be recovered if there were a finding of a tort. We may assume, without deciding, that negligence, not at large or in the abstract, but in relation to the plaintiff, would entail liability for any and all consequences, however novel or extraordinary. There is room for argument that a distinction is to be drawn according to the diversity of interests invaded by the act, as where conduct negligent in that it threatens an insignificant invasion of an interest in property results in an unforeseeable invasion of an interest of another order, as e.g., one of bodily security. Perhaps other distinctions may be necessary. We do not go into the question now. The consequences to be followed must first be rooted in a wrong.

[Reversed].

ANDREWS, J., dissenting. Assisting a passenger to board a train, the defendant's servant negligently knocked a package from his arms. It fell between the platform and the cars. Of its contents the servant knew and could know nothing. A violent explosion followed. The concussion broke some scales standing a considerable distance away. In falling they injured the plaintiff, an intending passenger.

Upon these facts may she recover the damages she has suffered in an action brought against the master? The result we shall reach depends upon our theory as to the nature of negligence. Is it a relative concept — the breach of some duty owing to a particular person or to particular persons? Or where there is an act which unreasonably threatens the safety of others, is the doer liable for all its proximate consequences, even where they result in injury to one who would generally be thought to be outside the radius of danger? This is not a mere dispute as to words. We might not believe that to the average mind the dropping of the bundle would seem to involve the probability of harm to the plaintiff standing many feet away whatever might be the case as to the owner or to one so near as to be likely to be struck by its fall. If, however, we adopt the second hypothesis we have to inquire only as to the relation between cause and effect. We deal in terms of proximate cause, not of negligence.

Negligence may be defined roughly as an act or omission which unreasonably does or may affect the rights of others, or which unreasonably fails to protect oneself from the dangers resulting from such acts. Here I confine myself to the first branch of the definition. Nor do I comment on the word "unreasonable." For present purposes it sufficiently describes that average of conduct that society requires of its members. . . .

But we are told that "there is no negligence unless there is in the particular case a legal duty to take care, and this duty must be one which is owed to the plaintiff himself and not merely to others." (Salmond, Torts, 24 [6th ed.].) This, I think too narrow a conception. Where there is the unreasonable act, and some right that may be affected there is negligence whether damage does or does not result. That is immaterial. Should we drive down Broadway at a reckless speed, we are negligent whether we strike an approaching car or miss it by an inch. The act itself is wrongful. It is a wrong not only to those who happen to be within the radius of danger but to all who might have been there—a wrong to the public at large. Such is the language of the street. Such is the language of the courts when speaking of contributory negligence. Such is again and again their language in speaking of the duty of some defendant and discussing proximate cause in cases where such a discussion is wholly irrelevant on any other theory. . . . Due care is a duty imposed on each one of us to protect society from unnecessary danger, not to protect A, B or C alone.

It may well be that there is no such thing as negligence in the abstract. "Proof of negligence in the air, so to speak, will not do." In an empty world negligence would not exist. It does involve a relationship between man and his fellows. But not merely a relationship between man and those whom he might reasonably expect his act would injure. Rather, a relationship between him and those whom he does in fact injure. If his act has a tendency to harm some one, it harms him a mile away as surely as it does those on the scene. We now permit children to recover for the negligent killing of the father. It was never prevented on the theory that no duty was owing to them. A husband may be compensated for the loss of his wife's services. To say that the wrongdoer was negligent as to the husband as well as to the wife is merely an attempt to fit facts to theory. An insurance company paying a fire loss recovers its payment of the negligent incendiary. We speak of subrogation—of suing in the right of the insured. Behind the cloud of words is the fact they hide, that the act, wrongful as to the insured, has also injured the company. Even if it be true that the fault of father, wife or insured will prevent recovery, it is because we consider the original negligence not the proximate cause of the injury. (Pollock, Torts, 463 [12th ed.].)

In the well-known Polemis Case, Scrutton, L.J., said that the dropping of a plank was negligent for it might injure "workman or cargo or ship." Because of either possibility the owner of the vessel was to be made good for his loss. The act being wrongful the doer was liable for its proximate results. Criticized and explained as this statement may have been, I think it states the law as it should be and as it is.

The proposition is this. Every one owes to the world at large the duty of refraining from those acts that may unreasonably threaten the safety of others. Such an act occurs. Not only is he wronged to whom harm might reasonably be expected to result, but he also who is in fact injured, even if he be outside what would generally be thought the danger zone. There needs be duty due the one complaining but this is not a duty to a particular individual because as to him harm might be expected. Harm to some one being the natural result of the act, not only that one alone, but all those in fact injured may complain. . . . Unreasonable risk being taken, its consequences are not confined to those who might probably be hurt.

If this be so, we do not have a plaintiff suing by "derivation or succession." Her action is original and primary. Her claim is for a breach of duty to herself—not that she is subrogated to any right of action of the owner of the parcel or of a passenger standing at the scene of the explosion.

The right to recover damages rests on additional considerations. The plaintiff's rights must be injured, and this injury must be caused by the negligence. We build a dam, but are negligent as to its foundations. Breaking, it injures property down stream. We are not liable if all this happened because of some reason other than the insecure foundation. But when injuries do result from our unlawful act we are liable for the consequences. It does not matter that they are unusual, unexpected, unforeseen and unforeseeable. But there is one limitation. The damages must be so connected with the negligence that the latter may be said to be the proximate cause of the former.

These two words have never been given an inclusive definition. What is a cause in a legal sense, still more what is a proximate cause, depend in each case upon many considerations, as does the existence of negligence itself. Any philosophical doctrine of causation does not help us. A boy throws a stone into a pond. The ripples spread. The water level rises. The history of that pond is altered to all eternity. It will be altered by other causes also. Yet it will be forever the resultant of all causes combined. Each one will have an influence. How great only omniscience can say. You may speak of a chain, or if you please, a net. An analogy is of little aid. Each cause brings about future events. Without each the future would not be the same. Each is proximate in the sense it is essential. But that is not what we mean by the word. Nor on the other hand do we mean sole cause. There is no such thing.

Should analogy be thought helpful, however, I prefer that of a stream. The spring, starting on its journey, is joined by tributary after tributary. The river, reaching the ocean, comes from a hundred sources. No man may say whence any drop of water is derived. Yet for a time distinction may be possible. Into the clear creek, brown swamp water flows from the left. Later, from the right comes water stained by its clay bed. The three may remain for a space, sharply divided. But at last, inevitably no trace of separation remains. They are so commingled that all distinction is lost.

As we have said, we cannot trace the effect of an act to the end, if end there is. Again, however, we may trace it part of the way. A murder at Serajevo may be the necessary antecedent to an assassination in London twenty years hence. An overturned lantern may burn all Chicago. We may follow the fire from the shed to the last building. We rightly say the fire started by the lantern caused its destruction.

A cause, but not the proximate cause. What we do mean by the word "proximate" is, that because of convenience, of public policy, of a rough sense of justice, the law arbitrarily declines to trace a series of events beyond a certain point. This is not logic. It is practical politics. Take our rule as to fires. Sparks from my burning haystack set on fire my house and my neighbor's. I may recover from a negligent railroad. He may not. Yet the wrongful act as directly harmed the one as the other. We may regret that the line was drawn just where it was, but drawn somewhere it had to be. We said the act of the railroad was not the proximate cause of our neighbor's fire. Cause it surely was. The words we used were simply indicative of our notions of public policy. Other courts think differently. But somewhere they reach the point where they cannot say the stream comes from any one source. . . .

It is all a question of expediency. There are no fixed rules to govern our judgment. There are simply matters of which we may take account. We have in a somewhat different connection spoken of "the stream of events." We have asked whether that stream was deflected — whether it was forced into new and unexpected channels. This is rather rhetoric than law. There is in truth little to guide us other than common sense.

There are some hints that may help us. The proximate cause, involved as it may be with many other causes, must be, at the least, something without which the event would not happen. The court must ask itself whether there was a natural and continuous sequence between cause and effect. Was the one a substantial factor in producing the other? Was there a direct connection between them, without too many intervening causes? Is the effect of cause on result not too attenuated? Is the cause likely, in the usual judgment of mankind, to produce the result? Or by the exercise of prudent foresight could the result be foreseen? Is the result too remote from the cause, and here we consider remoteness in time and space. . . . Clearly we must so consider, for the greater the distance either in time or space, the more surely do other causes intervene to affect the result. When a lantern is overturned the firing of a shed is a fairly direct consequence. Many things contribute to the spread of the conflagration — the force of the wind, the direction and width of streets, the character of intervening structures, other factors. We draw an uncertain and wavering line, but draw it we must as best we can.

Once again, it is all a question of fair judgment, always keeping in mind the fact that we endeavor to make a rule in each case that will be practical and in keeping with the general understanding of mankind. . . .

This last suggestion is the factor which must determine the case before us. The act upon which defendant's liability rests is knocking an apparently harmless package onto the platform. The act was negligent. For its proximate consequences the defendant is liable. If its contents were broken, to the owner; if it fell upon and crushed a passenger's foot, then to him. If it exploded and injured one in the immediate vicinity, to him also . . . Mrs. Palsgraf was standing some distance away. How far cannot be told from the record — apparently twenty-five or thirty feet. Perhaps less. Except for the explosion, she would not have been injured. We are told by the appellant in his brief "it cannot be denied that the explosion was the direct cause of the plaintiff's injuries." So it was a substantial factor in producing the result — there was here a natural and continuous sequence — direct connection. The only intervening cause was that instead of blowing her to the ground the concussion smashed the weighing machine which in turn fell upon her. There was no remoteness in time, little in space. And surely, given such an explosion as here it needed no great foresight to predict that the natural result would be to injure one on the platform at no greater distance from its scene than was the plaintiff. Just how no one might be able to predict. Whether by flying fragments, by broken glass, by wreckage of machines or structures no one could say. But injury in some form was most probable.

Under these circumstances I cannot say as a matter of law that the plaintiff's injuries were not the proximate result of the negligence. That is all we have before us. The court refused to so charge. No request was made to submit the matter to the jury as a question of fact, even would that have been proper upon the record before us.

The judgment appealed from should be affirmed, with costs.

NOTES

1. *The secret history of Palsgraf v. Long Island R.R. Palsgraf* has inspired extensive detective work to uncover its facts. Judge Noonan, Persons and Masks of the Law ch. 4 (1976), notes, among other things, that the "plaintiff was a Brooklyn janitress and ex-housewife, 43 years of age" who earned $416 per year. She was accompanied on the trip by her two daughters. Noonan suggests that the "scales must have been toppled *not by the explosion* of the fireworks but by the crowd running in panic on the platform" and that although the plaintiff "had been hit by the scales on the arm, hip and thigh" the chief source of her complaint was "a stammer and stutter" that appeared about one week after the accident, and which may have been intensified by the litigation itself.

Not to be outdone, Judge Posner disputes Noonan's explanation of the source of injury. In Cardozo: A Study in Reputation 38-39 (1990), he relies on a front page New York Times report of the accident, "Bomb Blast Injures 13 in Station Crowd," (August 25, 1924, p.1) that stated the explosion was not only loud enough to cause a stampede but violent enough to cause extensive damage to the train station, and to send several of the 13 people it injured to the hospital with minor injuries. For more on *Palsgraf,* see Prosser, *Palsgraf* Revisited, 52 Mich. L. Rev. 1, 4-5 (1953), reprinted in Selected Topics on the Law of Torts 191, 195-196 (1954). Why didn't the defendant owe the plaintiff the highest duty of care since it was a common carrier and she was her passenger? Would the conductor have been negligent if he had knocked the package out of the passenger's arm while trying to prevent him from boarding the train while it was in motion? Should Palsgraf have recovered if she stood next to the passenger carrying the package given that the railroad conductor had no notice of its contents? Should a total stranger injured by the blast be able to recover from the railroad if its conductors had innocently set off the bomb? Could the railroad, if held liable, sue the passenger for indemnification if he were solvent?

With *Palsgraf,* compare The Nitroglycerine Case, Parrot v. Wells-Fargo Co., 82 U.S. 524 (1872), in which an unmarked package containing nitroglycerine was delivered to defendant's place of business, which was located in its landlord's building. When the defendant's servants tried to open the package, it exploded, killing them and damaging the building. The Supreme Court noted that different outcomes were required for the servants' wrongful death actions and the landlord's property damage claim. For property damage the landlord could recover without proof of negligence, basing its case on a covenant in its lease with the defendant. For the death actions the lease was, however, inapplicable, and the cause of action failed for want of proof of negligence, given that the parcel gave no notice of its dangerous contents. For the suggestion that *Palsgraf* should be understood on those "notice" grounds only, see the opinion of Judge Friendly in Petition of Kinsman Transit Co., 338 F.2d 708 (2d Cir. 1964), from which excerpts are reprinted *infra* at 543.

2. *Harm within the risk.* Note that the Second Restatement §281 appears to follow Cardozo on the duty requirement:

> c. *Risk to class of which plaintiff is member.* If the actor's conduct creates a recognizable risk of harm only to a particular class of persons, the fact that it causes harm to a person of a different class, to whom the actor could not reasonably have anticipated injury, does not render the actor liable to the persons so injured.

How does one decide which class a particular person belongs to? In examining this question, Professor Seavey poses a case in which the defendant leaves a ten-pound can of nitroglycerin on a table from which it is knocked off by a child. It hurts the child's foot but, miraculously, does not explode. If defendant had left a can of water of similar size on the table, he could not be held negligent: Since the risk that materialized was unrelated to the explosive power of the nitroglycerin, the plaintiff could not recover. See Seavey, Mr. Justice Cardozo and the Law of Torts, 39 Colum. L. Rev. 20, 35; 52 Harv. L. Rev. 372, 385; 48 Yale L.J. 390, 405 (1939); compare RST §281, illustration 2.

A second case is put forth in R. Keeton, Legal Cause in the Law of Torts, 77 Harv. L. Rev. 595 (1963-1964). The defendant "negligently" places unlabeled rat poison on a shelf full of food. The shelf happens to be near a stove that gives off heat, and the heat causes the poison to explode, injuring the plaintiff. Keeton argues that this plaintiff should be denied recovery on grounds that the negligent *aspect* of the defendant's conduct is not the cause of the plaintiff's harm? Williams, The Risk Principle, 77 Law Q. Rev. 179, 185-190 (1961).

The Third Restatement of Torts states its general test for the scope of liability (avoiding the term proximate cause) as follows:

§29.   LIMITATIONS ON LIABILITY FOR TORTIOUS CONDUCT
An actor's liability is limited to those physical harms that result from the risks that made the actor's conduct tortious.

Does this test support the position of Cardozo or Andrews in *Palsgraf*? Whatever that answer, the Restatement Third accepts the efforts of both Seavey and Keeton to isolate particular harms that fall outside the risk. Thus, it holds as a matter of law that a defendant hunter who carelessly entrusts his loaded gun to a child is not liable if she drops it on her toe, breaking it. RTT:LPH §29, comment *d*, illustration 3. Note the common thread in all these cases: It turns out after the fact that the aspect of the defendant's behavior that increased the risk of harm to the plaintiff never materialized. The nitroglycerin did not explode; the poison was not consumed; the gun did not go off. Are all these cases distinguishable from *Palsgraf*, which involves the materialization of a risk from a dangerous but unknown condition? What about a solution that holds the railroad liable for triggering the bomb, with an action over against the person who carried it? For a sustained attack on the harm within the risk test for resulting in too many cases of undercompensation, see Hurd & Moore, Negligence in the Air, 3 Theoretical Inq. L. 333 (2002), calling for its abandonment "root and branch."

3. *The "substantial factor" test.* For all of Cardozo's eloquence, one of the most memorable phrases in *Palsgraf* comes from Andrews's query of whether the defendant's conduct was a "substantial factor" in producing the harm. That phrase has been adopted as the test of legal, or proximate, cause under the Restatement (Second) of Torts.

§431. WHAT CONSTITUTES LEGAL CAUSE

The actor's negligent conduct is a legal cause of harm to another if
    (a) his conduct is a substantial factor in bringing about the harm, and
    (b) there is no rule of law relieving the actor from liability because of the
manner in which his negligence has resulted in the harm.

*Comment a: Distinction between substantial cause and cause in the philosophical
sense.* In order to be a legal cause of another's harm, it is not enough that the
harm would have not occurred had the actor not been negligent. Except as
stated in §432(2) [dealing with joint causation], this is necessary, but it is not
itself sufficient. The negligence must also be a substantial factor in bringing
about the plaintiff's harm. The word "substantial" is used to denote the fact
that the defendant's conduct has such an effect in producing the harm as to
lead reasonable men to regard it as a cause, using that word in the popular
sense, in which there always lurks the idea of responsibility, rather than in
the so-called "philosophic sense," which includes everyone of the great
number of events without which any happening would not have occurred.
Each of these events is a cause in the so-called "philosophical sense," yet the
effect of many of them is so insignificant that no ordinary mind would think
of them as causes.

4. Jury instructions on proximate causation. The role of the Second Restatement's substantial factor test was examined in Mitchell v. Gonzales, 819 P.2d
872, 877-878 (Cal. 1991). The decedent, 12-year-old Damechie Mitchell,
drowned while vacationing with the defendants and their 14-year-old son
Luis. Damechie did not know how to swim, but with the Gonzales's permission he went out on a raft with Luis and his sister Yoshi only to drown
when the boys engaged in horseplay on the raft while Luis's father slept on
the beach. The decedent's parents charged Luis with negligence for his
conduct on the raft and Luis's parents with negligent supervision. The jury
found that the defendants were negligent, but that their negligence was not
the proximate cause of the death.

At trial the judge gave the defendants' requested instruction (BAJI 3.75)
a "but-for" test of cause in fact, which provides: "A proximate cause of injury
is a cause which, in natural and continuous sequence, produces the injury
and without which the injury would not have occurred." The test gets its
name from the "without which" clause, and also adopts the precise language of the *Andrews* dissent. The rival "substantial factor" instruction
(BAJI 3.76) requested by the plaintiff reads: "A legal cause of injury is a
cause which is a substantial factor in bringing about the injury."

By a divided vote, the court treated the "but-for" instruction as always
prejudicial to the plaintiffs. The court also noted its dislike for the term
"proximate cause," and adopted Prosser's view that the term was just an
unfortunate "legacy of Sir Francis Bacon." It also pointed to experimental
studies which indicated subjects interpreted the term to "'approximate
cause,' 'estimated cause,' or some fabrication." The court then adopted the

"substantial factor" test because it was largely free of these confusions, was generally intelligible to juries, and helped to clarify issues in joint causation. Accordingly, any but-for instruction was prejudicial error because it "overemphasized the condition temporally closest to the death" (Damechie's inability to swim) and downplayed how the negligent supervision of Mr. and Mrs. Gonzales contributed to the loss. Kennard, J., dissented on the ground that the court should not displace a standard instruction without developing a better alternative, noting that the substantial factor test fails to supply "meaningful guidance" on the proximate cause issue. What is wrong with asking whether the parents could have to a reasonable certainty prevented Damechie's death if they had properly watched the children at play? Forbidden them to go out on the raft?

The Second Restatement's terminology also received a mixed reception over the use of the Second Restatement's term "superseding cause" to talk about events after the defendant's negligence that break causal connection. See RST §442. In Kahn v. East Side Union High School District, 75 P.3d 30, 47 (Cal. 2003), the plaintiff was a member of her high school's junior varsity team who broke her neck while executing a shallow dive in a racing pool while warming up at a competitive school meet. The court held that a directed verdict for the school district on supervening cause grounds was improper so long as there was some issue whether her coaching, training and preparation contributed to her injury. "The question whether plaintiff's voluntary decision to practice the shallow-water dive without supervision constituted a *supervening* cause of her injury depends on whether her conduct 'was within the scope of the reasons imposing the duty upon the actor to refrain from negligent conduct.'"

In Barry v. Quality Steel Products, 820 A.2d 258, 266 (Conn. 2006), the court rejected any superseding cause instructions based on the Second Restatement because they only "serve to complicate what is fundamentally a proximate cause analysis." Accordingly, it reversed a directed verdict for the defendant manufacturer and seller of defective brackets, which had failed in part because the plaintiff's employer had improperly installed the roof brackets and failed to provide the needed scaffolding to protect the plaintiffs from a fall. In the court's view, apportionment under a comparative negligence regime was the proper way to deal with multiple sources of negligence. "The test of proximate cause is whether the defendant's conduct is a substantial factor in bringing about the plaintiff's injuries." What result if sound brackets would have certainly failed given the employer's improper installation?

The Third Restatement rejects all permutations of the substantial factor, intervening cause and supervening cause language. See RTT:LPH §26, comment *j*, and §34, comment *b*, dismissing both the phrases "intervening acts" and "superseding causes" as "conclusory labels." Can any single verbal account for causation work for all stranger (including explosion), rescue, malpractice, and supervision cases? If not, how should the causal element of each type of case be addressed? Which set of instructions would be appropriate in *Berry*? *Palsgraf*? The following case?

Marshall v. Nugent
222 F.2d 604 (1st Cir. 1955)

[A truck owned by the defendant oil company cut the corner as it headed north around a sharp curve on an icy New Hampshire highway, forcing off the road a southbound car driven by the plaintiff's son-in-law, Harriman. Prince, the driver of the truck, offered to help pull Harriman's car back onto the highway and suggested that the plaintiff go around the curve to the south in order to warn oncoming cars of the unexpected danger. As the plaintiff was getting into position on the west side of the highway, the defendant, Nugent, who was driving northbound, suddenly saw his way blocked by the oil truck on one side of the road and Prince and Harriman on the other. In an effort to avoid a collision with them, he pulled the car over to the left where it went into a skid, hit a plank guard fence on the west side of the highway, and glanced off it into the plaintiff, severely hurting him.

The jury returned a verdict for Nugent (sound?) and another for Marshall against the oil company. The second contention of the oil company on appeal was that the wrongful conduct of its driver was not the proximate cause of the plaintiff's injury.]

MAGRUDER, C.J. . . . Coming then to contention (2) above mentioned, this has to do with the doctrine of proximate causation, a doctrine which appellant's arguments tend to make out to be more complex and esoteric than it really is. To say that the situation created by the defendant's culpable acts constituted "merely a condition," not a cause of plaintiff's harm, is to indulge in mere verbiage, which does not solve the question at issue, but is simply a way of stating the conclusions, arrived at from other considerations, that the casual relation between the defendant's act and the plaintiff's injury is not strong enough to warrant holding the defendant legally responsible for the injury.

The adjective "proximate," as commonly used in this connection, is perhaps misleading, since to establish liability it is not necessarily true that the defendant's culpable act must be shown to have been the next or immediate cause of the plaintiff's injury. In many familiar instances, the defendant's act may be more remote in the chain of events and the plaintiff's injury may more immediately have been caused by an intervening force of nature, or an intervening act of a third person whether culpable or not, or even an act by the plaintiff bringing himself in contact with the dangerous situation resulting from the defendant's negligence. Therefore, perhaps, the phrase "legal cause," as used in Am. L. Inst., Rest. of Torts §431, is preferable to "proximate cause"; but the courts continue generally to use "proximate cause," and it is pretty well understood what is meant.

Back of the requirement that the defendant's culpable act must have been a proximate cause of the plaintiff's harm is no doubt the widespread conviction that it would be disproportionately burdensome to hold a culpable actor potentially liable for all the injurious consequences that may flow from his act, i.e., that would not have been inflicted "but for" the occurrence of the act. This is especially so where the injurious consequence was the result of negligence merely. And so, speaking in general terms, the effort of the courts has been, in the development of this doctrine of proximate causation, to confine the liability of a negligent actor to those harmful consequences which result from the operation of the risk, or of a risk, the foreseeability of which rendered the defendant's conduct negligent.

Of course, putting the inquiry in these terms does not furnish a formula which automatically decides each of an infinite variety of cases. Flexibility is still preserved by the further need of defining the risk, or risks, either narrowly, or more broadly, as seems appropriate and just in the special type of case.

Regarding motor vehicle accidents in particular, one should contemplate a variety of risks which are created by negligent driving. There may be injuries resulting from a direct collision between the carelessly driven car and another vehicle. But such direct collision may be avoided, yet the plaintiff may fall and injure himself in frantically racing out of the way of the errant car. Or the plaintiff may be knocked down and injured by a human stampede as the car rushes toward a crowded safety zone. Or the plaintiff may faint from intense excitement stimulated by the near collision, and in falling sustain a fractured skull. Or the plaintiff may suffer a miscarriage or other physical illness as a result of intense nervous shock incident to a hair-raising escape. This bundle of risks could be enlarged indefinitely with a little imagination. In a traffic mix-up due to negligence, before the disturbed waters have become placid and normal again, the unfolding of events between the culpable act and the plaintiff's eventual injury may be bizarre indeed; yet the defendant may be liable for the result. In such a situation, it would be impossible for a person in the defendant's position to predict in advance just how his negligent act would work out to another's injury. Yet this in itself is no bar to recovery.

[Magruder J. then notes that close cases on proximate cause are normally left to the jury.]

Exercising [our] judgment on the facts in the case at bar, we have to conclude that the district court committed no error in refusing to direct a verdict for the defendant Socony on the issue of proximate cause. . . .

Plaintiff Marshall was a passenger in the oncoming Chevrolet car, and thus was one of the persons whose bodily safety was primarily endangered by the negligence of Prince, as might have been found by the jury, in "cutting the corner" with the Socony truck in the circumstances above related. In that view, Prince's negligence constituted an irretrievable breach of duty to the plaintiff. Though this particular act of negligence was over and done with when the truck pulled up alongside of the stalled Chevrolet without having actually collided with it, still the consequences of such past negligence were in the bosom of time, as yet unrevealed. If the Chevrolet had been pulled back onto the highway, and Harriman and Marshall, having got in it again, had resumed their journey and had had a collision with another car five miles down the road, in which Marshall suffered bodily injuries, it could truly be said that such subsequent injury to Marshall was a consequence in fact of the earlier delay caused by the defendant's negligence, in the sense that but for such delay the Chevrolet car would not have been at the fatal intersection at the moment the other car ran into it. But on such assumed state of facts, the courts would no doubt conclude, "as a matter of law," that Prince's earlier negligence in cutting the corner was not the "proximate cause" of this later injury received by the plaintiff. That would be because the extra risks to which such negligence by Prince had subjected the passengers in the Chevrolet car were obviously entirely over; the situation had been stabilized and become normal, and, so far as one could foresee, whatever subsequent risks the Chevrolet might have to encounter in its resumed journey were simply the inseparable risks, no more and no less, that were incident to the Chevrolet's being out on the highway at all. But in the case at bar, the circumstances under which Marshall received the personal injuries complained of presented no such clear-cut situation.

As we have indicated, the extra risks created by Prince's negligence were not all over at the moment the primary risk of collision between the truck and the Chevrolet was successfully surmounted. Many cases have held a defendant, whose negligence caused a traffic tie-up, legally liable for subsequent property damage or personal injuries more immediately caused by an oncoming motorist. This would particularly be so where, as in the present case, the negligent traffic tie-up and delay occurred in a dangerous blind spot, and where the occupants of the stalled Chevrolet, having got out onto the highway to assist in the operation of getting the Chevrolet going again, were necessarily subject to risks of injury from cars in the stream of northbound traffic coming over the crest of the hill. It is true, the Chevrolet car was not owned by the plaintiff Marshall, and no doubt, without violating any legal duty to Harriman, Marshall could have crawled up onto the snowbank at the side of the road out of harm's way and awaited there, passive and inert, until his journey was resumed. But the plaintiff, who as a passenger in this Chevrolet car had already been subjected to a collision risk by the negligent operation of the Socony truck, could reasonably be expected to get out onto the highway and lend a hand to his host in getting the Chevrolet started again, especially as Marshall himself had an interest in facilitating the resumption of the journey in order to keep his business appointment in North Stratford. Marshall was therefore certainly not an "officious intermeddler," and whether or not he was barred by contributory negligence in what he did was a question for the jury, as we have already held. The injury Marshall received by being struck by the Nugent car was not remote, either in time or place, from the negligent conduct of defendant Socony's servant, and it occurred while the traffic mix-up occasioned by defendant's negligence was still persisting, not after the traffic flow had become normal again. In the circumstances presented we conclude that the district court committed no error in leaving the issue of proximate cause to the jury for determination.

NOTE

A resumption of normal conditions. Why shouldn't the plaintiff get a directed verdict on the admitted facts of *Marshall*? Note Magruder's decision stresses that causation has run its course with the dissipation of the extra risks created by defendant's negligence. In Union Pipe Co. v. Allbritton, 898 S.W.2d 773 (Tex. 1995), a pump manufactured by the defendant caught fire in a Texaco Chemical plant in which the plaintiff worked as a trainee employee. The plaintiff assisted her supervisor in putting out the fire and, after it was extinguished, she followed him over an aboveground pipe rack, some two and one-half feet high in order to make repairs on a broken valve. Once the valve was fixed, she followed him back over the pipe rack where she fell and injured herself. Her supervisor said that his "bad habits" led him to walk over the pipe instead of taking the safer alternative around it. The plaintiff argued that the defective pump was a cause of her injuries. "But for the pump fire, she asserts, she would never have walked over the pipe rack, which was wet with water or firefighting foam." Owen, J., rejected her argument:

> Even if the pump fire were in some sense a "philosophic" or "but for" cause of Allbritton's injuries, the forces generated by the fire had come to rest when she fell off the pipe rack. The fire had been extinguished, and Allbritton was walking away from the scene. Viewing the evidence in the light most favorable to Allbritton, the pump fire did no more than create the condition that made Allbritton's injuries possible. We conclude that the circumstances surrounding her injuries are too remotely connected with Union Pump's conduct or pump to constitute a legal cause of her injuries.

Spector, J., argued in dissent:

> The record reflects that at the time Sue Albritton's injury occurred, the forces generated by the fire in question had *not* come to rest. Rather, the

emergency situation was continuing. The whole area of the fire was covered in water and foam; in at least some places, the water was almost knee-deep. Allbritton was still wearing hip boots and other gear, as required to fight the fire. Viewing all the evidence in the light most favorable to Allbritton, . . . the pump defect was both a "but-for" cause and a substantial factor in bringing about Allbritton's injury, and was therefore a cause in fact.

What is the factual dispute in *Union Pump*? Do the conceptual arguments go beyond those advanced by Beale? Should they?

Overseas Tankship (U.K.) Ltd. v. Morts Dock & Engineering Co., Ltd. *(Wagon Mound (No. 1))*
[1961] A.C. 388 (P.C. Aust.)

[The appellants, defendants in the original cause of action, had carelessly discharged oil from their ship while it was berthed in Sydney harbor. After their ship set sail, the oil was carried by the wind and tide to the plaintiff's wharf, which was used for repair work on other ships in the harbor. Plaintiff's supervisor was concerned about the spread of the oil and he ordered his workmen to do no welding or burning in the area until further orders. He made some inquiries with the manager of the CalTex Oil Company where the *Wagon Mound* was berthed, which, coupled with his own knowledge, satisfied him that the oil was not flammable. He accordingly instructed his men to resume their welding operations and directed them as well to take care that no flammable material should fall off the wharf into the oil.

About two and one-half days later, the plaintiff's wharf was destroyed when the oil caught fire. "The outbreak of fire was due, as the trial judge found, to the fact that there was floating in the oil underneath the wharf a piece of debris on which lay some smouldering cotton waste or rag which had been set on fire by molten metal falling from the wharf: that the cotton waste or rag burst into flames: that the flames from the cotton waste set the floating oil afire either directly or by first setting fire to a wooden pile coated with oil, and that after the floating oil became ignited; the flames spread rapidly over the surface of the oil and quickly developed into a conflagration which severely damaged the wharf." "The trial judge also made the all-important finding, which must be set out in his own words: 'The *raison d'être* of furnace oil is, of course, that it shall burn, but I find the defendant did not know and could not reasonably be expected to have known that it was capable of being set afire when spread on water.'" The trial judge also found that the oil had caused, apart from the conflagration, some slight damage when it mucked up the plaintiff's wharf.]

VISCOUNT SIMONDS. . . . There can be no doubt that the decision of the Court of Appeal in *Polemis* plainly asserts that, if the defendant is guilty of negligence, he is responsible for all the consequences whether reasonably foreseeable or not. The generality of the proposition is perhaps qualified by the fact that each of the Lords Justices refers to the outbreak of fire as the direct result of the negligent act. There is thus introduced the conception that the negligent actor is not responsible for consequences which are not "direct," whatever that may mean. It has to be asked, then, why this conclusion should have been reached. The answer appears to be that it was reached upon a consideration of certain authorities, comparatively few in number, that were cited to the court. Of these, three are generally regarded as having influenced the decision. [The Court then reviewed Smith v. London & South Western Railway Co. ((1870) L.R. 6 C.P. 14), *supra* at 500]. It would perhaps not be improper to say that the law of negligence as an independent tort was then of recent growth and that its implications had not been fully examined.

[The Privy Council then considered the H.M.S. London [1914] P. 72 and Weld Blundell v. Stephens [1970] A.C. 956, and concluded with a famous passage from the latter case by Lord Sumner:] "What a defendant ought to have anticipated as a reasonable man is material when the question is whether or not he was guilty of negligence, that is, of want of due care according to the circumstances. This, however, goes to culpability, not to compensation." [After discussion of some other English precedents, the opinion continues:]

The impression that may well be left on the reader of the scores of cases in which liability for negligence has been discussed is that the courts were feeling their way to a coherent body of doctrine and were at times in grave danger of being led astray by scholastic theories of causation and their ugly and barely intelligible jargon. . . .

Enough has been said to show that the authority of *Polemis* has been severely shaken though lip service has from time to time been paid to it. In their Lordships' opinion it should no longer be regarded as good law. It is not probable that many cases will for that reason have a different result, though it is hoped that the law will be thereby simplified, and that in some cases, at least, palpable injustice will be avoided. For it does not seem consonant with current ideas of justice or morality that for an act of negligence, however slight or venial, which results in some trivial foreseeable damage the actor should be liable for all consequences however unforeseeable and however grave, so long as they can be said to be "direct." It is a principle of civil liability, subject only to qualifications which have no present relevance, that a man must be considered to be responsible for the probable consequences of his act. To demand more of him is too harsh a rule, to demand less is to ignore that civilized order requires the observance of a minimum standard of behaviour.

This concept applied to the slowly developing law of negligence has led to a great variety of expressions which can, as it appears to their Lordships, be harmonized with little difficulty with the single exception of the so-called rule in *Polemis*. For, if it is asked why a man should be responsible for the natural or necessary or probable consequences of his act (or any other similar description of them) the answer is that it is not because they are natural or necessary or probable, but because, since they have this quality, it is judged by the standard of the reasonable man that he ought to have foreseen them. Thus it is that over and over again it has happened that in different judgments in the same case, and sometimes in a single judgment, liability for a consequence has been imposed on the ground that it was reasonably foreseeable or, alternatively, on the ground that it was natural or necessary or probable. The two grounds have been treated as coterminous, and so they largely are. But, where they are not, the question arises to which the wrong answer was given in *Polemis*. For, if some limitation must be imposed upon the consequences for which the negligent actor is to be held responsible — and all are agreed that some limitation there must be — why should that test (reasonable foreseeability) be rejected which, since he is judged by what the reasonable man ought to foresee, corresponds with the common conscience of mankind, and a test (the "direct" consequence) be substituted which leads to nowhere but the never-ending and insoluble problems of causation. "The lawyer," said Sir Frederick Pollock, "cannot afford to adventure himself with philosophers in the logical and metaphysical controversies that beset the idea of cause." Yet this is just what he has most unfortunately done and must continue to do if the rule in *Polemis* is to prevail. A conspicuous example occurs when the actor seeks to escape liability on the ground that the "chain of causation" is broken by a nova causa or novus actus interveniens. . . .

In the same connection may be mentioned the conclusion to which the Full Court finally came in the present case. Applying the rule in *Polemis* and holding therefore that the unforeseeability of the damage by fire afforded no defence, they went on to consider the remaining question. Was it a "direct" consequence? Upon this Manning, J., said: "Notwithstanding that, if regard is had separately to each individual occurrence in the chain of events that led to this fire, each occurrence was improbable and, in one sense, improbability was heaped upon improbability, I cannot escape from the conclusion that if the ordinary man in the street had been asked, as a matter of common sense, without any detailed analysis of the circumstances, to state the cause of the fire at Morts Dock, he would unhesitatingly have assigned such cause to spillage of oil by the appellant's employees." Perhaps he would, and probably he would have added: "I never should have thought it possible." But with great respect to the Full Court this is surely irrelevant, or, if it is relevant, only serves to show that the *Polemis* rule works in a very strange way. After the event even a fool is wise. But it is not the hindsight of a fool; it is the foresight of the reasonable man which alone can determine responsibility. The *Polemis* rule by substituting "direct" for "reasonably foreseeable" consequence leads to a conclusion equally illogical and unjust.

[Appeal allowed.]

NOTES

1. *Foresight v. directness:* Wagon Mound (No. 2). The abstract debate over the proper standard for remoteness of damage often obscures what is at stake in the two positions. An instructive way to approach this dispute over proximate cause is to ask whether *Wagon Mound (No. 1)* can be reconciled with *In re Polemis* even under the "direct consequences" test. To do so, it is necessary to examine the precise sequence of events between defendant's wrongful conduct and plaintiff's harm. In *Polemis* no human act intervened between the dropping of the plank and the burning of the ship; the only causal complication was the antecedent presence of fumes in the ship's hold. In *Wagon Mound (No. 1)*, however, the causal chain contained at least two human acts between the oil spill from defendant's ship and the destruction of plaintiff's wharf: first, the consultations by plaintiff's dock supervisor with CalTex's manager, and second, the ignition of the fire by the oxyacetylene torches used by plaintiff's servants. If the conduct of plaintiff's servants amounts to either assumption of risk or contributory negligence, it is possible both to keep the directness test of *Polemis* and to defend the result in *Wagon Mound (No. 1)*. Note too that if either defense is feasible, the plaintiff must proceed gingerly on foreseeability, for if defendant's servants could have foreseen the harm, so too could the plaintiff's.

The importance of plaintiff's conduct is illustrated by the Privy Counsel's subsequent decision in Overseas Tankship (U.K.) Ltd. v. The Miller Steamship Co., [1967] 1 A.C. 617, 642-643, better known as *Wagon Mound (No. 2)*. The facts in that case were the same as in *Wagon Mound (No. 1)* except that the plaintiff in *Wagon Mound (No. 2)* was the owner of a ship destroyed by the fire in *Wagon Mound (No. 1)*. The plaintiff shipowner was not, of course, bound by the prior decision; nor was he hampered by possible charges of contributory negligence or assumption of risk. As against the plaintiff, the conduct of the servants of Morts Dock (plaintiff in *Wagon Mound (No. 1)*) only went to the question of causal connection, where in the modern view it could not, as intervening negligence, be decisive. See *supra* at 509. Plaintiff, therefore, introduced evidence to show that some risk of harm by fire was reasonably foreseeable by defendant's engineer. Lord Reid, speaking for the Privy Council, distinguished *Wagon Mound (No. 1)* and affirmed a judgment for plaintiff. He noted that the plaintiff lost in Bolton v. Stone, *supra* at 154, because the risk of harm was small and the activity that caused the harm was lawful:

> In the present case there was no justification whatever for discharging the oil into Sydney Harbour. Not only was it an offence to do so, but it involved considerable loss financially. If the ship's engineer had thought about the matter, there could have been no question of balancing the advantages and disadvantages. From every point of view it was both his duty and his interest to stop the discharge immediately. . . .
>
> The findings show that he [the ship's engineer] ought to have known that it is possible to ignite this kind of oil on water, and that the ship's engineer probably ought to have known that this had in fact happened before. The most that can be said to justify inaction is that he would have known that this could only happen in very exceptional circumstances. But that does not mean that a reasonable man would dismiss such a risk from his mind and do nothing when it was so easy to prevent it.

Does Lord Reid's argument amount to a repudiation of Bolton v. Stone? An adoption of the Hand formula for negligence? A belated acceptance of the judgment of Nares, J., in Scott v. Shepherd, Chapter 2, *supra* at 115? On the progression from *Polemis* to *Wagon Mound*, see Levmore *The Wagon Mound Cases*: Foreseeability, Causation, and Mrs. Palsgraf, in Tort Stories 129, 142 (Rabin & Sugarman ed., 2003), suggesting that on grounds of causation the outcome of the two cases could easily be reversed.

2. *The passing of causation.* The proponents of the foresight test insist that it allows the courts to dispense with the technical and nearly insoluble conundrums of causation. Even if the argument is sound (is it?), the foresight test raises unique problems of its own. Chief among them is the task of describing the events that led to the plaintiff's harm. Professor Morris discusses this point in Torts 174-177 (1953):

> Once misconduct causes damage, a specific accident has happened in a particular way and has resulted in a discrete harm. When, after the event, the question is asked, "Was the particular accident and the resulting damages foreseeable?", the cases fall into the three classes:
>
> (1) In some cases damages resulting from misconduct are so typical that judge and jurors cannot possibly be convinced that they were unforeseeable. . . .
>
> (2) In some cases freakishness of the facts refuses to be downed and any description that minimizes it is viewed as misdescription. For example, in a recent Louisiana case [Lynch v. Fisher, 41 So. 2d 692 (La. App. 1949)] a trucker negligently left his truck on the highway at night without setting out flares. A car crashed into the truck and caught fire. A passerby came to the rescue of the car occupants — a man and wife. After the rescuer got them out of the car he returned to the car to get a floor mat to pillow the injured wife's head. A pistol lay on the mat rescuer

wanted to use. He picked it up and handed it to the husband. The accident had unbeknownst to the rescuer, temporarily deranged the husband, and he shot rescuer in the leg. Such a consequence of negligently failing to guard a truck with flares is so unarguably unforeseeable that no judge or juror would be likely to hold otherwise. (Incidentally the Louisiana court held the trucker liable to the rescuer on the ground that foreseeability is not a requisite of liability.)

(3) Between these extremes are cases in which consequences are neither typical nor wildly freakish. In these cases unusual details are arguably — but only arguably significant. If they are held significant, then the consequences are unforeseeable; if they are held unimportant then the consequences are foreseeable.

Into which class does *Polemis* fall? *Wagon Mound*? Need the defendant only foresee "in a general way" the consequences of his act, and not the "precise details of its occurrence"?

3. *A foreseeable kind of damage.* In the aftermath of *Wagon Mound (No. 1)* the English courts struggled to determine whether the harm suffered by plaintiff was foreseeable. In Doughty v. Turner Manufacturing Co., Ltd., [1964] 1 Q.B. 518, one of defendant's employees knocked an asbestos cement cover into a vat of extremely hot solution of sodium cyanide — eight times as hot as boiling water. His conduct was negligent since the falling cover might have splashed some of the molten substance on someone standing nearby. In fact, nobody was hurt by the splash; but after a short time the asbestos cement cover caused an explosion in the vat that hurled the molten substance into the air, some of it hurting the plaintiff, who stood fairly nearby. No one had any reason to suspect that this cover, when immersed, would explode. The trial judge allowed recovery given defendant's negligence, but the court of appeal reversed because the damage was the consequence of a risk or hazard about which defendant had not been negligent. Does *Doughty* present any problems of causal intervention?

Contrast *Doughty* with Hughes v. Lord Advocate, [1963] A.C. 837. Defendant's servants were working on an underground cable to which they had access through an open manhole nine feet deep. The manhole was covered by a shelter-tent. When defendant's servants left the work area, they lighted four paraffin warning lamps, left a ladder near the manhole, and pulled a tarpaulin over the entrance to the tent. Plaintiff, aged eight, and his uncle, aged ten, came by and started to play with the equipment with a view toward descending into the manhole. Plaintiff tripped over one of the paraffin lamps, which then fell into the hole. An explosion ensued when, as best could be determined, "paraffin escaped from the tank, formed vapour and was ignited by the flame." The respondents argued that the explosion was unforeseeable even if some harm from burning by the lamp was foreseeable. The House of Lords rejected the argument, holding that the damage was not of a different type from that which was foreseeable given that paraffin lamps were a "known source of danger." Is the distinction between burning and explosion "too fine to warrant acceptance"? If so, why accept the distinction between splashing and exploding? Does *Hughes* present the troublesome questions of causal intervention referred to in *Wagon Mound (No. 1)*? In this connection note that defendant, on appeal, did not claim that plaintiff's trespass barred his recovery.

4. *The thin skull rule, or "You take your victim as you find him."* One rule of tort law left unshaken by *Wagon Mound (No. 1)* is that the defendant takes his victim as he finds him. In Smith v. Brain Leech & Co. Ltd., [1962] 2 Q.B. 405, plaintiff's deceased was burned on his lip by splashing molten metal because defendant negligently failed to provide an adequate guard. Because of prior exposures of another kind in the past, deceased had (according to the court) developed a tendency toward cancer. In any event, the burned lip did develop a cancer from which he died. The court acknowledged that death by cancer was unforeseeable, but notwithstanding *Wagon Mound (No. 1)* allowed recovery, expressing certainty that the Privy Council had no intention of changing the "take plaintiff as he is" principle or denying recovery to the plaintiff with a thin skull.

On the thin skull rule and its relationship to the problems of causal intervention, see Seavey, Mr. Justice Cardozo and the Law of Torts, 39 Colum. L. Rev. 20, 32-33; 52 Harv. L. Rev. 372, 384-385; 48 Yale L.J. 390, 402-403 (1939):

> [W]here the defendant has negligently struck a person whose skull is so fragile that it is broken by the comparatively slight blow, all courts are agreed that the defendant is liable for the wholly unexpected breaking. This is true not only with reference to physical harm but also other forms of harm. If a person were negligently to incapacitate another who has a yearly earning capacity of a hundred thousand dollars, there is liability for the resulting loss though so great a loss could not have been anticipated. It may be that this is a possible explanation for the reaction of the King's Bench in its famous but doubtful decision of the *Polemis* case, in which the defendant whose workman negligently dropped a plank into the hold of a ship filled with gasoline vapor was made liable for the destruction of the ship resulting from the ensuing explosion. In this, as in other cases, the courts are agreed that the negligent person takes his victims as they are.

The causal complications of the thin skull rule are graphically illustrated by Steinhauser v. Hertz Corp., 421 F.2d 1169, 1172 (2d Cir. 1970). Plaintiff, a 14-year-old child, was a passenger in her parents' car when it was tortiously struck by the driver of defendant's car. The plaintiff suffered no physical injuries, but shortly thereafter she began to behave strangely; she became "highly agitated," "glassy-eyed," and "nervous." As her condition worsened, she was institutionally treated for schizophrenia. Even after her release she required further medical treatment, with reinstitutionalization a likely prospect. Two years prior to the accident, the plaintiff had suffered a mild concussion. Plaintiff's attorney argued that the accident was a "precipitating cause of a quiescent disease." The trial judge instructed the jury that recovery was permissible only if plaintiff were normal before the accident, but not if "this plaintiff had this disease all along." Proximate cause was in the words of the trial judge "a big word" for what ordinary people call cause. The jury's verdict for defendant was reversed on appeal, with Friendly, J., writing as follows:

> The testimony was that before the accident Cynthia was *neither* a "perfectly normal child" *nor* a schizophrenic, but a child with some degree of pathology which was activated into schizophrenia by an emotional trauma although it otherwise might not have blossomed. Whatever the medical soundness of this theory may or may not be, and there does not seem in fact to have been any dispute about it, plaintiffs were entitled to have it fairly weighed by the jury. They could not properly be pinioned on the dilemma of having either to admit that Cynthia was already suffering from active schizophrenia or to assert that she was wholly without psychotic tendencies.

5. *American response to* Polemis *and* Wagon Mound (No. 1). Friendly, J., also commented on the English debate over proximate cause in Petition of Kinsman Transit Co., 338 F.2d 708, 723-725 (2d Cir. 1964). A January thaw on the Buffalo River released large cakes of ice that, because of high water, banged into and loosened a negligently tied and improperly tended ship so that it started downstream, careening into another ship and knocking it loose. Both ships then drifted on and crashed into a drawbridge maintained by the city of Buffalo at a point before the river flows into Lake Erie. The two ships and the drawbridge made an effective dam against which floating ice accumulated, causing flooding for miles. This action was brought against the owner of the first ship and the city. The above events all occurred at night, when no traffic was expected on the river.

The crew tending the drawbridge was, or so the court held, under a statutory duty to raise the drawbridge not only for ships passing by in the course of navigation but also for drifting vessels. If the crew had displayed the required alertness by raising the bridge in time, all of the harm in issue could have been avoided. By a two-to-one vote the court held both defendants jointly liable for plaintiff's damages. Judge Friendly made these observations about the rejection of *Polemis* in *Wagon Mound (No. 1)*:

> [We] find it difficult to understand why one who had failed to use the care required to protect others in the light of expectable forces should be

exonerated when the very risks that rendered his conduct negligent produced other and more serious consequences to such persons than were fairly foreseeable when he fell short of what the law demanded. Foreseeability of danger is necessary to render conduct negligent where as here the damage was caused by just those forces whose existence required the exercise of greater care than was taken — the current, the ice, and the physical mass of the Shiras, the incurring of consequences other and greater than foreseen does not make the conduct less culpable or provide a reasoned basis for insulation. The oft-encountered argument that failure to limit liability to foreseeable consequences may subject the defendant to a loss wholly out of proportion to his fault seems scarcely consistent with the universally accepted rule that the defendant takes the plaintiff as he finds him and will be responsible for the full extent of the injury even though a latent susceptibility of the plaintiff renders this far more serious than could reasonably have been anticipated. . . .

The weight of authority in this country rejects the limitation of damages to consequences foreseeable at the time of the negligent conduct when the consequences are "direct," and the damage, although other and greater than expectable, is of the same general sort that was risked. . . . Other American courts, purporting to apply a test of foreseeability to damages, extend that concept to such unforeseen lengths as to raise serious doubt whether the concept is meaningful; indeed, we wonder whether the British courts are not finding it necessary to limit the language of The Wagon Mound as we have indicated.

We see no reason why an actor engaging in conduct which entails a large risk of small damage and a small risk of other and greater damage, of the same general sort, from the same forces, and to the same class of persons, should be relieved of responsibility for the latter simply because the chance of its occurrence, if viewed alone, may not have been large enough to require the exercise of care. By hypothesis, the risk of the lesser harm was sufficient to render his disregard of it actionable; the existence of a less likely additional risk that the very forces against whose action he was required to guard would produce other and greater damage than could have been reasonably anticipated should inculpate him further rather than limit his liability.

Why is plaintiff's harm direct damage in *Kinsman*?

6. *Poetic Interlude*. These matters of causation have prompted this poetic interlude offered by Eleanor Fox:

The Key to Proximate Cause

Lend me your ears. Hold the applause.
Here is the secret to proximate cause.

In *Gorris v. Scott*, where the sheep risked contagion,
no proximate cause, though a pen would have saved them.

The hazard that happened was pulls of the sea —
a hazard that prudent men wouldn't foresee.

In *Wagon Mound I* there was no risk of fire.
We know that was so; it was found by the trier
(and proof au contraire was to no one's desire).
The harm did not rise from the slippery scare
that gave rise to precautions to exercise care
and therefore the negligence was "in the air."

But in *Wagon Mound II* one *would* fire foresee,
and therefore the negligence was in the sea.
The oil that spilled since the leak wasn't fixed
gave rise to the hazard improperly risked.

In *Kinsman* the hazard was free-flying vessel.
The prudent beforehand will see that a mess'll
result from release of the boat
when it breaks from its moorings and charges, afloat.
The injury — flooding — arose from the snare
of the hazard that dictated duty of care.
As soon as we know that this force was released
and thus that the wheels of misfortune were greased,
we've satisfied "risk" as a point in the game
and move to the length and the strength of the chain.

And now we have yet a new point for the court:
Was the chain so direct; was it reasonably short?
Was no intervention of such independence
that it became *the* cause and freed the defendants?
If reasoning people can take different tacks,
It goes to the jury as question of facts.

And this is the story of causation prox as told by Judge Friendly
with glosses
   By Fox

Newer verses continue to be added to the lore of proximate cause. How does the counterpoint between foresight and directness play out in the next two cases?

Virden v. Betts and Beer Construction Company
656 N.W.2d 805 (Iowa 2003)

NEUMAN, J., Plaintiff, Ron Virden, worked in the maintenance department of Indianola High School. On the first day of school in 1997, Virden's supervisor asked him to reinstall an angle iron that had fallen from the ceiling of the school's new wrestling room. As Virden was bolting the angle iron into place, he fell from the top of the ten-foot ladder on which he was standing. He sustained severe injuries to his left leg, requiring several surgeries.

Virden sued the contractors, defendants Betts & Beer Construction and Stroh Corporation, who earlier in the year had installed the wrestling room ceiling. Over Virden's objection, the district court granted these defendants summary judgment. It held their negligence, if any, was not the proximate cause of Virden's injuries. Virden appealed and the court of appeals reversed. We granted further review and, now, vacate the court of appeals decision and affirm the judgment of the district court.

I.   SCOPE OF REVIEW/ISSUE ON APPEAL.

[The Court noted that summary judgment on the question of proximate cause is granted only in exceptional cases, of which this is one.]

II.   ANALYSIS.

. . . The summary judgment record makes plain that neither Virden nor his employer contacted the defendants about the fallen angle iron before attempting to effect repairs. Virden also concedes that he sought no help in positioning or securing the ladder, even though several pieces of weight-lifting equipment hampered clear access to the repair site. With this record in mind, we turn to the disputed elements of Virden's claim: duty and causation.

A.   DUTY.

[As a building or construction contractor] the defendants had a duty to Virden, and others using the room, to construct a ceiling that did not fall apart and injure someone.

Virden did not suffer, however, from being hit by the angle iron or tripping over it once it fell from the ceiling. In his words, he was injured when the ladder he stood on to replace the fallen hardware "suddenly kicked out from under [him] and [he] fell." That brings us to the crux of the case.

B.   CAUSATION.

Defendants' breach of their duty of care only constitutes actionable negligence if it is "also the proximate cause of the injury." There are two components to the proximate-cause inquiry: "(1) the defendant's conduct must have in fact caused the damages; and (2) the policy of the law must require the defendant to be legally responsible for them."

With respect to the first component, a plaintiff must at a minimum prove that the damages would not have occurred *but for* the defendant's negligence. Here, viewing the facts in the light most favorable to Virden, we assume that but for the faulty weld in the angle iron he would not have been perched precariously upon a ladder attempting to fix it. So, minimally, the but-for test of causation would survive defendants' motion for summary judgment.

The but-for test is not the end of the inquiry, however. . . . Virden must also tender proof that defendants' negligent welding of the angle iron was a *substantial factor* in bringing about his injury. . . .

Here, the district court assessed defendants' role in Virden's mishap as remote rather than foreseeable. Its conclusion stemmed from the undisputed fact that the instrumentality causing Virden's injury was a tipping or collapsing ladder, not a defective angle iron. We agree.

. . . [w]e observe that the duty to construct a solid ceiling is not to protect repairmen from perching on tall ladders but to prevent collapsing parts of the ceiling from falling on persons below.

To summarize, the unfortunate outcome of Virden's self-help remedy cannot be said to fall naturally within the scope of the probable risk created by the defendants' failure to properly install the ceiling. Because Virden's fall was not a reasonably foreseeable or probable consequence of *defendants'* negligence, the district court correctly granted judgment in their favor. We therefore vacate the court of appeals' contrary decision and affirm the judgment of the district court.

Hebert v. Enos
806 N.E.2d 452 (Mass. App. 2004)

KAFKER, J., The plaintiff William Hebert (Hebert) brought an action to recover for personal injuries he suffered as a result of receiving a severe electric shock while lawfully on the defendant Carl Enos's property to water the defendant's flowers. Hebert claimed that the defendant's faulty repairs of a second-floor toilet caused the toilet to overflow. The flooding water then reacted with the home's electrical system, creating an electrical current that shocked and injured Hebert when he touched the outside water faucet. Hebert asserted a claim for negligence in his complaint, and his wife sought damages for loss of consortium. The defendant moved for summary judgment on the ground that Hebert's injuries were not a reasonably foreseeable consequence of any negligence on the defendant's part. The judge allowed the defendant's motion for summary judgment, finding that "the injury to [Hebert] was highly extraordinary and 'so remote in everyday life' as to preclude a finding that the alleged negligence was a legal cause of [Hebert's] injuries." We affirm.

. . . In their opposition to the defendant's motion for summary judgment, the plaintiffs provided an expert's report prepared by a professional engineer. It was the expert's opinion that "in the several days the water was flowing through the house, the water caused good [or already deteriorated] insulation on wires to break down allowing leakage current to flow into a grounded surface and thence through the water piping system."

When Hebert "came into contact with the water piping system (i.e. the turn-on handle)," he became "part of the electric circuit." Because Hebert was wet from perspiration and from having watered his own flowers, the amount of electricity that would have flowed through him was much greater than it would have been had he been dry. The expert opined to a "reasonable degree of engineering certainty" that the electrical current flowing through Hebert's body and causing his injury was "a direct result of the water overflow and accompanying flooded condition of the house." . . .

Discussion. When the facts and reasonable inferences therefrom are viewed in the light most favorable to the plaintiffs, we conclude that the plaintiffs submitted sufficient evidence to establish that faulty repairs of the toilet by the defendant resulted in flooding and severe electric shock to Hebert when he touched the faucet. Summary judgment is still appropriate, however, if a plaintiff has no reasonable expectation of proving that "the injury to the plaintiff was a foreseeable result of the defendant's negligent conduct." house to the defendant. . . .

In the instant case, when we consider the likelihood, character, and location of the harm, we conclude as matter of law that the injuries sustained by Hebert were a "highly extraordinary" consequence of a defective second-floor toilet. . . . We therefore conclude that Hebert's severe and unfortunate injuries were the consequence of the type of unforeseeable accident for which we do not hold the defendant responsible in tort. The harm Hebert suffered, even when the facts and reasonable inferences that could be drawn therefrom are viewed in the light most favorable to him, was so highly extraordinary that the defendant cannot be required to guard against it. . . .

We briefly touch upon various subsidiary arguments raised by the plaintiffs. The plaintiffs argue that water and electricity have distinct places in the law, and that the motion judge should have recognized the foreseeability of the risk of injury due to the mixture of electricity and water "as a matter of common sense." We conclude that the motion judge held the defendant to the "proper standard of care [which] is . . . the usual one of traditional negligence theory: 'to exercise care that was reasonable in the circumstances.'"

Finally, the plaintiffs appear to suggest that so long as the defendant's negligence can be connected in an unbroken causal chain to the resultant harm, and no third party's negligence can be blamed for the injury, the harm is by definition proximate. This is not the law of proximate cause in Massachusetts, nor is it supported by the commentary upon which the plaintiffs rely. Here, the defendant could not have reasonably foreseen the harm that befell Hebert.

Judgment affirmed.

NOTE

A choice of theories? *Virden* and *Hebert* both result in summary judgments for the defendant. Yet in a sense they are polar opposites of each other. In *Virden* the dangerous condition was well known to the plaintiff who had a wide range of choices on whether, and if so how, to proceed in repairing the angle iron. In *Hebert* the dangerous condition was wholly concealed from the plaintiff who acted in complete ignorance of the peril that befell him. How then do both of these cases result in the same outcome? How should these cases come out if one looks at the question of whether a voluntary and independent act of the defendant severed causal connection? If foresight of harm by the defendant is the appropriate test? Should it make a difference in *Hebert* that Hebert was doing a favor for Enos?

2. Emotional Distress

Thus far, the question of proximate causation has been addressed largely with physical injuries. In this section we ask whether other consequences, such as mental shock or emotional distress, can flow from wrongful conduct. As with physical injury claims, the first line of defense simply denies the connection between the distress and the defendant's conduct, blaming some other event for the plaintiff's emotional harm. The second line of defense, however, holds that even if defendant's conduct is the cause in fact of plaintiff's injury, that conduct is not the proximate cause. Over the past century, liability in emotional distress cases has expanded, but the area still retains its distinctive limitations on recovery.

Mitchell v. Rochester Railway
45 N.E. 354 (N.Y. 1896)

MARTIN, J. The facts in this case are few, and may be briefly stated. On the 1st day of April, 1891, the plaintiff was standing upon a cross walk on Main Street, in the city of Rochester, awaiting an opportunity to board one of the defendant's cars which had stopped upon the street at that place.

While standing there, and just as she was about to step upon the car, a horse car of the defendant came down the street. As the team attached to the car drew near, it turned to the right, and came close to the plaintiff, so that she stood between the horses' heads when they were stopped. She testified that from fright and excitement caused by the approach and proximity of the team she became unconscious, and also that the result was a miscarriage, and consequent illness. Medical testimony was given to the effect that the mental shock which she then received was sufficient to produce that result. Assuming that the evidence tended to show that the defendant's servant was negligent in the management of the car and horses, and that the plaintiff was free from contributory negligence, the single question presented is whether the plaintiff is entitled to recover for the defendant's negligence which occasioned her fright and alarm, and resulted in the injuries already mentioned. While the authorities are not harmonious upon this question, we think the most reliable and better-considered cases, as well as public policy, fully justify us in holding that the plaintiff cannot recover for injuries occasioned by fright, as there is no immediate personal injury. If it be admitted that no recovery can be had for fright occasioned by the negligence of another, it is somewhat difficult to understand how a defendant would be liable for its consequences. Assuming that fright cannot form the basis of an action, it is obvious that no recovery can be had for injuries resulting therefrom. That the result may be nervous disease, blindness, insanity, or even a miscarriage, in no way changes the principle. These results merely show the degree of right or the extent of the damages. The right of action must still depend upon the question whether a recovery may be had for fright. If it can, then an action may be maintained, however slight the injury. If not, then there can be no recovery, no matter how grave or serious the consequences. Therefore, the logical result of the respondent's concession would seem to be, not only that no recovery can be had for mere fright, but also that none can be had for injuries which are the direct consequences of it. If the right of recovery in this class of cases should be once established, it would naturally result in a flood of litigation in cases where the injury complained of may be easily feigned without detection, and where the damages must rest upon mere conjecture or speculation. The difficulty which often exists in cases of alleged physical injury, in determining whether they exist, and if so, whether they were caused by the negligent act of the defendant, would not only be greatly increased, but a wide field would be opened for fictitious or speculative claims. To establish such a doctrine would be contrary to principles of public policy.

Moreover, it cannot be properly said that the plaintiff's miscarriage was the proximate result of the defendant's negligence. Proximate damages are such as are the ordinary and natural results of the negligence charged, and those that are usual and may, therefore, be expected. It is quite obvious that the plaintiff's injuries do not fall within the rule as to proximate damages. The injuries to the plaintiff were plainly the result of an accidental or unusual combination of circumstances, which could not have been reasonably anticipated, and over which the defendant had no control, and, hence, her damages were too remote to justify a recovery in this action. These considerations lead to the conclusion that no recovery can be had for injuries sustained by fright occasioned by the negligence of another, where there is no immediate personal injury.

[Reversed and dismissed.]

NOTES

1. *Coping with the physical injury rule.* Why should plaintiff's fright count as a superseding cause of the plaintiff's miscarriage? The early opposition to allowing recovery for negligently inflicted emotional distress rested on two distinct grounds. The first was that the damages were too "remote" and the second was the fear that allowing emotional distress claims would lead to a flood of fabricated claims. Which argument is stronger for disallowing recovery in the mere fright cases?

Historically, however, whenever the plaintiff showed actual impact, courts turned that impact, however slight, into the foundation for plaintiff's claim for emotional distress. In effect, courts treated the emotional distress as parasitic damages upon the most nominal of invasions. In Comstock v. Wilson, 177 N.E. 431 (N.Y. 1931), recovery was allowed for a slight jolt in a very minor automobile collision. In Porter v. Delaware, L. & W. R.R., 63 A. 860 (N.J. 1906), the plaintiff recovered when "something" slight hit her neck and she got dust in her eyes. In Kenney v. Wong Len, 128 A. 343 (N.H. 1925), the requisite impact was found when a mousehair in a spoonful of stew touched the roof of the plaintiff's mouth. And finally, in Christy Bros. Circus v. Turnage, 144 S.E. 680 (Ga. App. 1928), the hapless plaintiff recovered when one of defendant's horses "evacuated his bowels" in plaintiff's lap, "in full view of many people . . . all of whom laughed at the occurrence."

2. *Within the zone of danger.* While some courts extended the impact rule, other courts reexamined its foundations. In Dulieu v. White & Sons, [1901] 2 K.B. 669, 677, 681 the court rejected both the proximate cause and floodgates arguments. The plaintiff gave premature birth to her child after nearly being run over by the defendant's team of horses while working behind the counter in her husband's public house. Kennedy, J., rejected *Mitchell,* making these observations about remoteness of damage:

> Why is the accompaniment of physical injury essential? For my own part, I should not like to assume it to be scientifically true that a nervous shock which causes serious bodily illness is not actually accompanied by physical injury, although it may be impossible, or at least difficult, to detect the injury

at the time in the living subject. I should not be surprised if the surgeon or the physiologist told us that nervous shock is or may be in itself an injurious affection of the physical organism. Let it be assumed, however, that the physical injury follows the shock, but that the jury are satisfied upon proper and sufficient medical evidence that it follows the shock as its direct and natural effect, is there any legal reason for saying that the damage is less proximate in the legal sense than damage which arises contemporaneously?

Thereafter Kennedy, J., rejected any concern about spurious claims, saying:

I should be sorry to adopt a rule which would bar all such claims on grounds of policy alone, and in order to prevent the possible success of unrighteous or groundless actions. Such a course involves the denial of redress in meritorious cases, and it necessarily implies a certain degree of distrust, which I do not share, in the capacity of legal tribunals to get at the truth in this class of claim. My experience gives me no reason to suppose that a jury would really have more difficulty in weighing the medical evidence as to the effects of nervous shock through fright, than in weighing the like evidence as to the effects of nervous shock through a railway collision or a carriage accident, where, as often happens, no palpable injury, or very slight palpable injury, has been occasioned at the time.

Accordingly, Kennedy, J., nonetheless did impose this limitation: The plaintiff was not "entitled to maintain this action if the nervous shock was produced, not by the fear of bodily injury to herself, but by horror or vexation arising from the sight of mischief being threatened or done either to some other person, or to her own or her husband's property, by the intrusion of the defendant's van and horses." Defensible on proximate cause grounds?

3. *Empirical complications.* Is the concern with fraud or error in nervous shock cases understated in *Dulieu*? In 1944, a doctor-lawyer surveyed all cases brought for physical injuries resulting from negligently inflicted fright and concluded: "On the basis of all available factors, we thought at least 7/10 or 21/30 of the 301 cases examined should have been decided in defendant's favor. In practice, defendants were able to obtain jury verdicts in 7 cases only, to get directed verdicts in 25, and on appeal to prevail in but 19 additional cases. Thus, defendant prevailed in only 51 cases or 5/30 of the total series. In all, plaintiff won or still might win, 25/30 of the 301 cases. . . . Law, in a commendable desire to be forward looking, outran scientific standards. Taking all cases decided between 1850 and 1944, the net balance of justice would have been greater had all courts denied damages for injury imputed to psychic stimuli alone." Smith, Relation of Emotions to Injury and Disease: Legal Liability for Psychic Stimuli, 30 Va. L. Rev. 193, 284-285 (1944).

Dillon v. Legg
441 P.2d 912 (Cal. 1968)

[The defendant driver struck and killed Erin Lee Dillon, a child, as she was crossing a public street. Her death precipitated three separate claims. First, decedent's mother and minor sister, Cheryl, sued for wrongful death. Second, her mother sued for nervous shock and serious mental and physical pain suffered in consequence of defendant's negligence. Third, the minor sister, Cheryl, also sued for emotional and physical suffering. The evidence established that the mother was in "close proximity" to Erin Lee at the time of the collision, but that defendant's car never threatened her safety since she was outside the "zone of danger." The trial court dismissed the mother's action for emotional distress under Amaya v. Home Ice, Fuel & Supply Co., 379 P.2d 513 (Cal. 1963) because her fright and distress did not arise out of fear for her own safety. However, Cheryl's parallel action was not dismissed because she might have been in the zone of danger or feared for her own safety. The mother appealed.

Noting that her claim rested on considerations of "natural justice," the court held it should not be "frustrated" because of judicial fears of fraudulent claims that "would involve the courts in the hopeless task of defining the extent of the tortfeasor's liability." It then critiqued *Amaya*.]

TOBRINER, J.* . . . [W]e can hardly justify relief to the sister for trauma which she suffered upon apprehension of the child's death and yet deny it to the mother merely because of a happenstance that the sister was some few yards closer to the accident. The instant case exposes the hopeless artificiality of the zone-of-danger rule. In the second place, to rest upon the zone-of-danger rule when we have rejected the impact rule becomes even less defensible. We have, indeed, held that impact is not necessary for recovery. The zone-of-danger concept must, then, inevitably collapse because the only reason for the requirement of presence in that zone lies in the fact that one within it will fear the danger of *impact*. At the threshold, then, we point to the incongruity of the rules upon which any rejection of plaintiff's recovery must rest.

We further note, at the outset, that defendant has interposed the defense that the contributory negligence of the mother, the sister, and the child contributed to the accident. If any such defense is sustained and defendant found not liable for the death of the child because of the contributory negligence of the mother, sister or child, we do not believe that the mother or sister should recover for the emotional trauma which they allegedly suffered. In the absence of the primary liability of the tort-feasor for the

---

* Tobriner, J., while on the California Court of Appeals, wrote the opinion in *Amaya*, later reversed by the California Supreme Court, allowing the plaintiff to recover for nervous shock even though he was beyond the zone of danger. 23 Cal. Rptr. 131 (1962). — ED.

death of the child, we see no ground for an independent and secondary liability for claims for injuries by third parties. The basis for such claims must be the adjudicated liability and fault of defendant; that liability and fault must be the foundation for the tort-feasor's duty of due care to third parties who, as a consequence of such negligence, sustain emotional trauma.

We turn then to an analysis of the concept of duty, ...

The history of the concept of duty in itself discloses that it is not an old and deep-rooted doctrine but a legal device of the latter half of the nineteenth century designed to curtail the feared propensities of juries toward liberal awards.

1. *This court in the past has rejected the argument that we must deny recovery upon a legitimate claim because other fraudulent ones may be urged. . . .*

Indubitably juries and trial courts, constantly called upon to distinguish the frivolous from the substantial and the fraudulent from the meritorious, reach some erroneous results. But such fallibility, inherent in the judicial process, offers no reason for substituting for the case-by-case resolution of causes an artificial and indefensible barrier. Courts not only compromise their basic responsibility to decide the merits of each individually but destroy the public's confidence in them by using the broad broom of "administrative convenience" to sweep away a class of claims a number of which are admittedly meritorious. The mere assertion that fraud is possible, "a possibility [that] exists to some degree in all cases," does not prove a present necessity to abandon the neutral principles of foreseeability, proximate cause and consequential injury that generally govern tort law.

Indeed, we doubt that the problem of the fraudulent claim is substantially more pronounced in the case of a mother claiming physical injury resulting from seeing her child killed than in other areas of tort law in which the right to recover damages is well established in California. For example, a plaintiff claiming that fear for his own safety resulted in physical injury makes out a well recognized case for recovery.

Moreover, damages are allowed for "mental suffering," a type of injury, on the whole, less amenable to objective proof than the physical injury involved here; the mental injury can be in aggravation of, or "parasitic to," an established tort. In fact, fear for another, even in the absence of resulting physical injury, can be part of these parasitic damages. And emotional distress, if inflicted intentionally, constitutes an independent tort. The danger of plaintiffs' fraudulent collection of damages for nonexistent injury is at least as great in these examples as in the instant case.

In sum, the application of tort law can never be a matter of mathematical precision. In terms of characterizing conduct as tortious and matching a money award to the injury suffered as well as in fixing the extent of injury, the process cannot be perfect. Undoubtedly, ever since the ancient case of the tavern-keeper's wife who successfully avoided the hatchet cast by an irate customer (I. de S. et ux v. W. de S., Y.B. 22 Edw. iii, f. 99, pl. 60 (1348)), defendants have argued that plaintiffs' claims of injury from emotional trauma might well be fraudulent. Yet we cannot let the difficulties of adjudication frustrate the principle that there be a remedy for every substantial wrong.

2. *The alleged inability to fix definitions for recovery on the different facts of future cases does not justify the denial of recovery on the specific facts of the instant case; in any event, proper guidelines can indicate the extent of liability for such future cases....*

Since the chief element in determining whether defendant owes a duty or an obligation to plaintiff is the foreseeability of the risk, that factor will be of prime concern in every case. Because it is inherently intertwined with foreseeability such duty or obligation must necessarily be adjudicated only upon a case-by-case basis. We cannot now predetermine defendant's obligation in every situation by a fixed category; no immutable rule can establish the extent of that obligation for every circumstance of the future. We can, however, define guidelines which will aid in the resolution of such an issue as the instant one.

We note, first, that we deal here with a case in which plaintiff suffered a shock which resulted in physical injury and we confine our ruling to that case. In determining, in such a case, whether defendant should reasonably foresee the injury to plaintiff, or, in other terminology, whether defendant owes plaintiff a duty of due care, the courts will take into account such factors as the following: (1) Whether plaintiff was located near the scene of the accident as contrasted with one who was a distance away from it. (2) Whether the shock resulted from a direct emotional impact upon plaintiff from the sensory and contemporaneous observance of the accident, as contrasted with learning of the accident from others after its occurrence. (3) Whether plaintiff and the victim were closely related, as contrasted with an absence of any relationship or the presence of only a distant relationship.

The evaluation of these factors will indicate the degree of the defendant's foreseeability: obviously defendant is more likely to foresee that a mother who observes an accident affecting her child will suffer harm than to foretell that a stranger witness will do so. Similarly, the degree of foreseeability of the third person's injury is far greater in the case of his contemporaneous observance of the accident than that in which he subsequently learns of it. The defendant is more likely to foresee that shock to the nearby, witnessing mother will cause physical harm than to anticipate that someone distant from the accident will suffer more than a temporary emotional reaction. All these elements, of course, shade into each other; the fixing of obligation, intimately tied into the facts, depends upon each case.

In light of these factors the court will determine whether the accident and harm was *reasonably* foreseeable. Such reasonable foreseeability does not turn on whether the particular defendant as an individual would have in actuality foreseen the exact accident and loss; it contemplates that courts, on a case-to-case basis, analyzing all the circumstances, will decide what the ordinary man under such circumstances should reasonably have foreseen. The courts thus mark out the areas of liability, excluding the remote and unexpected.

In the instant case, the presence of all the above factors indicates that plaintiff has alleged a sufficient prima facie case. Surely the negligent driver who causes the death of a young child may reasonably expect that the mother will not be far distant and will upon witnessing the accident suffer emotional trauma. . . .

The fear of an inability to fix boundaries has not impelled the courts of England to deny recovery for emotional trauma caused by witnessing the death or injury of another due to defendant's negligence. We set forth the holdings of some English cases merely to demonstrate that courts can formulate and apply such limitations of liability.

[The court then reviewed the English cases which are favorable to recovery in nervous shock cases.]

Thus we see no good reason why the general rules of tort law, including the concepts of negligence, proximate cause, and foreseeability, long applied to all other types of injury, should not govern the case now before us. . . .

In short, the history of the cases does not show the development of a logical rule but rather a series of changes and abandonments. Upon the argument in each situation that the courts draw a Maginot Line to withstand an onslaught of false claims, the cases have assumed a variety of postures. At first they insisted that there be no recovery for emotional trauma at all. Retreating from this position, they gave relief for such trauma only if physical impact occurred. They then abandoned the requirement for physical impact but insisted that the victim fear for her own safety, holding that a mother could recover for fear for her children's safety if she simultaneously entertained a personal fear for herself. They stated that the mother need only be in the "zone of danger." The final anomaly would be the instant case in which the sister, who observed the accident, would be granted recovery because she was in the "zone of danger," but the *mother*, not far distant, would be barred from recovery.

The successive abandonment of these positions exposes the weakness of artificial abstractions which bar recovery contrary to the general rules. . . .

Yet for some artificial reason this delimitation of liability is alleged to be unworkable in the most egregious case of them all: the mother's emotional trauma at the witnessed death of her child. If we stop at this point, however, we must necessarily question and reject not merely recovery here, but the viability of the judicial process for ascertaining liability for tortious conduct itself. To the extent that it is inconsistent with our ruling here, we therefore overrule Amaya v. Home Ice, Fuel & Supply Co.

To deny recovery would be to chain this state to an outmoded rule of the 19th century which can claim no current credence. No good reason compels our captivity to an indefensible orthodoxy.

The judgment is reversed.

TRAYNOR, C.J. I dissent for the reasons set forth in Amaya v. Home Ice, Fuel & Supply Co. In my opinion that case was correctly decided and should not be overruled.

BURKE, J. [dissenting, questioned the guidelines set forth in the majority opinion] . . . What if the plaintiff was honestly *mistaken* in believing the third person to be in danger or to be seriously injured? What if the third person had assumed the risk involved? How "close" must the relationship be between the plaintiff and the third person? I.e., what if the third person was the plaintiff's beloved niece or nephew, grandparent, fiancé, or lifelong friend, more dear to the plaintiff than her immediate family? Next, how "near" must the plaintiff have been to the scene of the accident, and how "soon" must shock have been felt? Indeed, what is the magic in the plaintiff's being actually present? Is the shock any less real if the mother does not know of the accident until her injured child is brought into her home? On the other hand, is it any less real if the mother is physically present at the scene but is nevertheless unaware of the danger or injury to her child until after the accident has occurred? No answers to these questions are to be found in today's majority opinion. Our trial courts, however, will not so easily escape the burden of distinguishing between litigants on the basis of such artificial and unpredictable distinctions.

NOTES

1. *Foreseeability in emotional distress cases.* In Tobin v. Grossman, 249 N.E.2d 419, 422-423 (N.Y. 1969), the plaintiff suffered "physical injuries caused by shock and fear" when her two-year-old son was seriously injured in an automobile accident. The plaintiff did not see the accident, but heard the screech of brakes and arrived on the scene, only a few feet away, moments later. In denying recovery for negligent infliction of emotional distress, or NIED, Breitel, J., took direct issue with *Dillon's* heavy reliance on foreseeability, and predicted that actions, if allowed, could not in principle or practice be confined to close family members who witnessed the accident.

> On foreseeability, it is hardly cogent to assert that the negligent actor if he could foresee injury to the child that he should not also foresee at the same time harm to the mother who, especially in the case of children of tender years, is likely to be present or about. But foreseeability, once recognized, is

not so easily limited. Relatives, other than the mother, such as fathers or grandparents, or even other caretakers, equally sensitive and as easily harmed, may be just as foreseeably affected. Hence, foreseeability would, in short order, extend logically to caretakers other than the mother, and ultimately to affected bystanders. . . .

The final and most difficult factor is any reasonable circumscription, within tolerable limits required by public policy, of a rule creating liability. Every parent who loses a child or whose child of any age suffers an injury is likely to sustain grievous psychological trauma, with the added risk of consequential physical harm. Any rule based solely on eyewitnessing the accident could stand only until the first case comes along in which the parent is in the immediate vicinity but did not see the accident. Moreover, the instant advice that one's child has been killed or injured, by telephone, word of mouth, or by whatever means, even if delayed, will have in most cases the same impact. The sight of gore and exposed bones is not necessary to provide special impact on a parent.

Judge Breitel underestimated the resolve of the California courts on its dual requirements of close relationship and direct observation. Elden v. Sheldon, 758 P.2d 582 (Cal. 1988), denied claims for the negligent infliction of emotional distress (and loss of consortium) to an unmarried cohabitant involved in an automobile accident, who not only witnessed his cohabitant's death but was injured himself. The court in *Elden* construed *Dillon*'s third prong—that the plaintiff be "closely related" to the victim—to cover only spouses and siblings. It held, however, that *Dillon*'s general foreseeability language did not include a "close friend" and concluded that unmarried cohabitants stood in no better position, given the "state's interest in promoting marriage."

In Thing v. La Chusa, 771 P.2d 814, 815 (Cal. 1989), the court refused to buckle on the direct observation requirement by denying recovery for emotional distress to a mother who had not witnessed the automobile accident that injured her child. Eagleson, J., rejected *Dillon*'s assertion that "foreseeability" was the touchstone of duty, treating the concept as "amorphous." Instead he opted for a "bright line" rule. "In so doing we balance the impact of arbitrary lines which deny recovery to some victims whose injury is very real against that of imposing liability out of proportion to culpability for negligent acts. We also weigh in the balance the importance to the administration of justice of clear guidelines under which litigants and trial courts may resolve disputes."

In the absence of physical injury or impact to the plaintiff himself, damages for emotional distress should be recoverable only if the plaintiff: (1) is closely related to the injury victim; (2) is present at the scene of the injury-producing event at the time it occurs and is then aware that it is causing injury to the victim, and (3) as a result suffers emotional distress beyond that which would be anticipated in a disinterested witness.

Another Maginot line?

2. Dillon's *reception outside California. Dillon* and its progeny have been subject to intensive examination in other states. The tally on one recent scorecard reads: 3 states continue to stick to the impact test; some 10 states follow the Second Restatement's zone of danger test; 29 states follow *Dillon*, and 3 states go beyond *Dillon* to allow recovery for foreseeable harms that do not meet the three conditions set out in *Thing*. See Engler v. Illinois Farmers Insurance Co., 706 N.W.2d 764, 771 (Minn. 2005), which announced that it was sticking with the zone of danger test for the reasons announced in the Second Restatement, §§313, 436, chiefly because "it provides a bright line to limit recovery." In *Engler* the plaintiff experienced fright because the driver of the other car had threatened both her and her son. Blatz, C.J., allowed her to recover for the fright that she experienced, but not for the post-traumatic distress that she suffered because of the severe injuries to her son. Blatz, C.J., stated that NIED claims were allowable only:

> if the plaintiff can prove that she: (1) was in the zone of danger of physical impact; (2) had an objectively reasonable fear for her own safety; (3) had severe emotional distress with attendant physical manifestations; and (4) stands in a close relationship to the third-party victim. In addition, to succeed with such a claim, the plaintiff also must establish that the defendant's negligent conduct-the conduct that created an unreasonable risk of physical injury to the plaintiff-caused serious bodily injury to the third-party victim.

In his concurrence, Anderson, J., claimed that the majority position was too loose insofar as it allowed anyone with a "close relationship" to the injured person to recovery, and would have permitted recovery only to a "spouse, parent, child, grandparent, grandchild, or sibling of the plaintiff."

Other courts following *Dillon* have read it restrictively. Hawaii first adopted the *Dillon* rule in Rodrigues v. State, 472 P.2d 509 (Haw. 1970). Yet, in Kelley v. Kokua Sales and Supply, Ltd., 532 P.2d 673 (Haw. 1975), a divided court denied recovery in the case of a decedent, a California resident, who died of a heart attack shortly after being informed by telephone that his daughter and grandchild had been killed in a road accident. The court, unquestionably motivated by the fear of unlimited liability, invoked the language of "duty of care" and "foresight of consequences" to justify its denial of recovery. In Dziokonski v. Babineau, 380 N.E.2d 1295, 1302 (Mass. 1978), the court held that "allegations concerning a parent who sustains substantial physical harm as a result of severe mental distress over some peril or harm to his minor child caused by the defendant's negligence state a claim for which relief might be granted, where the parent either witnesses the accident or soon comes on the scene while the child is still there."

Similarly, the class of eligible plaintiffs has been narrowly construed. In Trombetta v. Conkling, 626 N.E.2d 653, 654 (N.Y. 1993), the court denied an emotional distress claim brought by a niece who witnessed the death of her aunt who had raised her from age 11, concluding baldly: "[r]ecovery of damages by bystanders for the negligent infliction of emotional distress should be limited only to the immediate family." Further, in Grotts v. Zahner, 989 P.2d 415 (Nev. 1999), the court concluded "Immediate family members of the victim qualify for standing to bring NIED claims as a matter of law." Even here new obstacles emerge. In Lee v. State Farm Mutual Insurance Co., 533 S.E.2d 82 (Ga. 2000), the plaintiff was involved in an accident that resulted in the death of her daughter and serious physical injuries to herself. The court sought to split the difference, holding that it is "for the finder of fact to determine whether the parent suffered emotional distress from witnessing the child's suffering and death apart from the grief which would naturally arise from a parent's loss of a child." Good luck.

In Dunphy v. Gregor, 642 A.2d 372 (N.J. 1994), the New Jersey Supreme Court also split the difference. As in *Dillon,* it required a plaintiff to have observed the death or injury of another person, but it repudiated *Elden,* by allowing the action to an unmarried cohabitant. "The State's interest in marriage would not be harmed if unmarried cohabitants are permitted to prove on a case-by-case basis that they enjoy a steadfast relationship that is equivalent to a legal marriage and thus equally deserves legal protection."

The Third Restatement takes much the same view:

§47.   NEGLIGENT INFLICTION OF EMOTIONAL DISTURBANCE RESULTING FROM
         BODILY HARM TO A THIRD PERSON

An actor who negligently causes serious bodily injury to a third person is subject to liability for serious emotional disturbance thereby caused to a person who:

(a) perceives the event contemporaneously, and

(b) is a close family member of the person suffering the bodily injury.

3. The "at risk" plaintiff: of drugs and toxic torts. One important variation on NIED cases involves individuals who are exposed to dangerous drugs or toxic substances and suffer distress, for fear of future harm to themselves. The Third Restatement notes the powerful judicial sentiment against awarding damages, for example, in cancer phobia, in part for the fear of multiple law suits—one for the fear and a second for the injury. RTT:LPH §46, comment *h.* For example, an "at-risk" claim for emotional distress was rejected in Payton v. Abbott Labs, 437 N.E.2d 171, 181 (Mass. 1982), when brought by DES daughters who stood between 1 in 1,000 and 1 in 10,000 chance of getting adenocarcinoma, a very serious form of cancer. The court insisted that the proper measure of damage was that which would be experienced by "a reasonable person, normally constituted," and then only for physical harm that "must be manifested by objective symptomatology and substantiated by expert medical testimony." Similarly, in Metro-North Commuter R.R. Co. v. Buckley, 521 U.S. 424 (1997), the court disallowed a claim alleging fear of cancer after exposure to cancer, and the court in In re Rezulin Products Liability Litigation, 361 F. Supp. 2d 268, 275 (S.D.N.Y. 2005), held the same in litigation over Rezulin, an anti-diabetes drug previously withdrawn from the market.

A parallel NIED claim arose in Potter v. Firestone Tire & Rubber Co., 863 P.2d 795, 800, 810, 826 (Cal. 1993), in which the defendant's local employees, in conscious violation of federal and state statutes, and internal company policy, dumped certain toxic wastes into an unauthorized dumpsite to cut costs. Firestone's toxins (unique to its manufacturing processes) made their way into the plaintiffs' wells. Informed of this risk, the plaintiff owners claimed relief for emotional distress even though none of them suffered from cancerous or precancerous conditions. They sought recovery because exposure to defendant's toxins led to some "significant increase in the risk of cancer." Defendants sought to limit recovery to persons who manifested some sign of physical injury from the ingested toxic substances.

Baxter, J., rejected both extremes and required, as in *Payton,* that the plaintiff "pleads and proves that the fear stems from a knowledge, corroborated by reliable medical and scientific opinion, that it is more likely than not that the feared cancer will develop in the future due to the toxic exposure." Generally, the court thought that in NIED cases only this limitation would confine liability to manageable limits, control insurance costs, and leave funds available for future serious cases of cancer. But owing to the defendant's malicious conduct the court allowed recovery even though plaintiffs' toxic intake from smoking was 2,500 times that found in the defendant's waste. Why credit the plaintiff's fears of the former to the exclusion of the latter?

4. *Direct victims.* The Third Restatement in RTT:LPH §46(b) holds that an NIED claim may also be bought when it "(b) occurs in the course of specified categories of activities, undertakings or relationships in which negligent conduct is especially likely to cause serious emotional disturbance." In these cases, there is no requirement of the direct observation of a harm to some third person. "Specifically, courts have imposed liability on hospitals and funeral homes for negligently mishandling a corpse and on telegraph companies for negligently mistranscribing or misdirecting a telegram that informs the recipient, erroneously, about the death of a loved one." *Id.* at comment *b.* Liability under this provision has also been extended to cover other cases in which the recipient of information is a "direct victim" of the harm. In Molien v. Kaiser Foundation Hospitals, 616 P.2d 813, 817 (Cal. 1980), the defendant's employee, Dr. Kilbridge,

negligently provided the plaintiff's wife with an erroneous report that she had contracted an infectious type of syphilis. She in turn had to undergo unnecessary medical treatment and became "upset and suspicious that her husband had engaged in extramarital sexual activities." Their marriage broke up from the ensuing tension and hostility, and the husband's suit for emotional distress was allowed, notwithstanding the limitations in *Dillon,* on the ground that the plaintiff was a "direct victim" of the defendant's erroneous report. Mosk, J., wrote:

> In the case at bar the risk of harm to plaintiff was reasonably foreseeable to defendants. It is easily predictable that an erroneous diagnosis of syphilis and its probable source would produce marital discord and resultant emotional distress to a married patient's spouse; Dr. Kilbridge's advice to Mrs. Molien to have her husband examined for the disease confirms that plaintiff was a foreseeable victim of the negligent diagnosis. Because the disease is normally transmitted only by sexual relations, it is rational to anticipate that both husband and wife would experience anxiety, suspicion, and hostility when confronted with what they had every reason to believe was reliable medical evidence of a particularly noxious infidelity.

In post-*Molien* cases, foresight is no longer the touchstone of duty. Instead, the California court asks whether the defendant has assumed some direct duty to the plaintiff. In Huggins v. Longs Drug Stores California, Inc., 862 P.2d 148, 152-153 (Cal. 1993), the court found that no direct relationship existed between the defendant pharmacy, which dispensed five times the prescribed dosage, and the parents whose child was harmed by the overdose. Likewise in Schwarz v. Regents of University of California, 276 Cal. Rptr. 470, 483 (Cal. App. 1990), a father was not the direct victim of emotional distress when the psychotherapist he hired to treat his son facilitated and concealed the mother's removal of the boy to England. But in Marlene F. v. Affiliated Psychiatric Medical Clinic, Inc., 770 P.2d 278 (Cal. 1989), a defendant psychotherapist that had treated both the plaintiff mothers and their sons for intrafamily difficulties owed duties to both.

7

AFFIRMATIVE DUTIES

SECTION A. INTRODUCTION

The previous six chapters have been largely, but not exclusively, devoted to understanding the rules for personal injury and property damage that result from the defendant's positive acts such as hitting another person or creating dangerous conditions that result in their harm. In this chapter the focus shifts from liability for misfeasance (literally, misdeeds) to liability for nonfeasance, or failure to act. The difference between these two cases is often expressed in terms of duty. For cases of misfeasance, the basic duty is for all individuals to abstain from hurting other persons, both strangers and persons with whom the defendant has some special relationship. In the stranger setting, under strict liability any invasion of the plaintiff's person or space by the defendant sets up a prima facie obligation to compensate. And in the negligence system, the usual reference to a duty of care is to take care to avoid harm to another person. Within consensual arrangements, most strict liability obligations drop out. In contrast, for cases of nonfeasance, the idea of negligence is subtly modified for now the notion of care refers not to taking precautions to avoid contact, but to rendering material aid or support to other persons. That duty of affirmative care is neatly divided in two halves: The first is directed to strangers and the second to individuals with whom the defendant stands in what is commonly termed a special relationship. These two concepts of duty are reflected in the Third Restatement, which discusses the duty question in connection with positive acts in §7, and the affirmative duties to aid in §§37 to 44.

In line with this distinction, the first part of this chapter examines a hardy problem of enduring philosophical interest: When are individuals liable for failing to rescue strangers in imminent peril of life or limb? The so-called good Samaritan cases are prominent in this area, in which the defendant was in no sense responsible for creating the dangerous condition or situation that brought forth the need to rescue in the first place. Thereafter, the discussion is extended to less controversial cases in which the defendant, either tortiously or nontortiously, has created the dangerous situation requiring rescue.

The second set of issues concerns the duties that landowners and occupiers owe to persons who enter their premises. These entries may be unlawful, as with trespassers, or lawful, as with persons who have received permission from the landowner. Despite fluctuations in judicial attitude, the law generally holds that the trespasser takes, at the very least, the risk of purely accidental injuries even if he is entitled to recover for deliberate and perhaps recklessly inflicted injuries. In contrast, the landowner clearly owes some duty to care for persons lawfully on the premises. The critical issues are how much care and to which persons. The traditional common law cases distinguished between social guests (called "licensees") and business visitors (called "invitees"), and imposed a lower duty to the former — merely to warn of known latent defects — than it did to the latter — to take reasonable care to both discover danger and to keep the premises safe. Many states today reject this status distinction and impose a uniform duty of reasonable care for the benefit of licensees and invitees alike. In addition, courts have more frequently addressed how far the duties of occupiers extend beyond making the premises safe, as by providing emergency assistance to persons in various states of distress.

The third set of issues involves gratuitous undertakings by the defendant to benefit or assist the plaintiff. These cases are, in a sense, contractual as they rest upon the defendant's promise, express or implied, to the plaintiff. But the defendant's undertakings have not been bargained for by the plaintiff, and, for that reason, these cases have historically been treated as part of the tort law.

The fourth set of issues arises whenever the defendant owes a duty to prevent harm to the plaintiff's person or property because the defendant stands in some sort of "special relationship" either with the plaintiff or with the person who threatens harm to the plaintiff. The first subclass of special relationship cases is an outgrowth of the premise liability cases and concerns, for example, the duties a landlord owes to his tenant, a hotel to its guests, a club to its members, or a university to its students. In these cases, the defendant may be called upon to guard against various contingencies, ranging from the simple loss or destruction of property entrusted to its care to the defective conditions of premises under its control, or, in today's most contentious area, to the criminal's act of a third party. The second subclass of special relationship cases arises when prisons and hospitals have charge of persons who, once released, commit acts of violence against third parties. Until recently, contemporary tort law had expanded the class of affirmative duties that large (and not-so-large) social institutions — schools, hotels, hospitals, landlords, common carriers — owe their customers and clients, but today the law shows evidence of stabilization and perhaps modest contraction.

SECTION B.   THE DUTY TO RESCUE

Luke 10:30-37 (King James Translation)

A certain man went down to Jerusalem to Jericho, and fell among thieves which stripped him of his raiment, and wounded him, and departed, leaving him half dead. And by chance there came down a certain priest that way: and when he saw him, he passed by on the other side. And likewise a Levite, when he was at the place, came and looked at him, and passed by on the other side. But a certain Samaritan, as he journeyed, came where he was: and when he saw him, he had compassion on him, and went to him, and bound up his wounds, pouring in oil and wine, and set him on his own beast, and brought him to an inn, and took care of him. And on the morrow when he departed, he took out two pence, and gave them to the host and said unto him, Take care of him; and whatsoever thou spendest more, when I come again, I will repay thee. Which of these three, thinkest thou, was neighbour unto him that fell among the thieves. And he said, He that shewed mercy on him. Then said Jesus unto him, Go, do thou likewise.

Buch v. Amory Manufacturing Co.
44 A. 809 (N.H. 1897)

[The plaintiff, aged eight years, trespassed in defendant's mill, where weaving machinery was in operation. An overseer observed him there and told him to leave. Plaintiff did not go because he did not understand English. Nonetheless the overseer did not put him out, although it was apparent that the running machinery presented an obvious hazard to a child of plaintiff's age. Plaintiff had his hand crushed in a machine that his brother, aged 13, an employee, was trying to teach him to run. The trial court denied a motion for a directed verdict. Defendant appealed. Verdict for plaintiff set aside and judgment for defendant.]

CARPENTER, C.J. Assuming, then, that the plaintiff was incapable either of appreciating the danger or of exercising the care necessary to avoid it, is he, upon the facts stated, entitled to recover? He was a trespasser in a place dangerous to children of his age. In the conduct of their business and management of their machinery the defendants were without fault. The only negligence charged upon, or attributed to, them is that, inasmuch as they could not make the plaintiff understand a command to leave the premises, and ought to have known that they could not, they did not forcibly eject him. Actionable negligence is the neglect of a legal duty. The defendants are not liable unless they owed to the plaintiff a legal duty which they neglected to perform. With purely moral obligations the law does not deal. For example, the priest and Levite who passed by on the other side were not, it is supposed, liable at law for the continued suffering of the man who fell among thieves, which they might and morally ought to have prevented or relieved. Suppose *A*, standing close by a railroad, sees a two-year-old babe on the track and a car approaching. He can easily rescue the child with entire safety to himself, and the instincts of humanity require him to do so. If he does not, he may, perhaps, justly be styled a ruthless savage and a moral monster; but he is not liable in damages for the child's injury, or indictable under the statute for its death. . . .

What duties do the owners owe to a trespasser upon their premises? They may eject him, using such force and such only as is necessary for the purpose. They are bound to abstain from any other or further intentional or negligent acts of personal violence, — bound to inflict upon him by means of their own active intervention no injury which by due care they can avoid. They are not bound to warn him against hidden or secret dangers arising from the condition of the premises, or to protect him against any injury that may arise from his own acts or those of other persons. In short, if they do nothing, let him entirely alone, in no manner interfere with him, he can have no cause of action against them for any injury that he may receive. On the contrary, he is liable to them for any damage that he by his unlawful meddling may cause them or their property. What greater or other legal obligation was cast on these defendants by the circumstance that the plaintiff was (as is assumed) an irresponsible infant?

If landowners are not bound to warn an adult trespasser of hidden dangers, — dangers which he by ordinary care cannot discover and, therefore, cannot avoid, — on what ground can it be claimed that they must warn an infant of open and visible dangers which he is unable to appreciate? No legal distinction is perceived between the duties of the owners in one case and the other. The situation of the adult in front of secret dangers which by no degree of care he can discover, and that of the infant incapable of comprehending danger, is in a legal aspect exactly the same. There is no apparent reason for holding that any greater or other duty rests upon the owners in one case than in the other.

There is a wide difference — a broad gulf — both in reason and in law, between causing and preventing an injury; between doing by negligence or otherwise a wrong to one's neighbor, and preventing him from injuring himself; between protecting him against injury by another and guarding him from injury that may accrue to him from the condition of the premises which he has unlawfully invaded. The duty to do no wrong is a legal duty. The duty to protect against wrong is, generally speaking and excepting certain intimate relations in the nature of a trust, a moral obligation only, not recognized or enforced by law. Is a spectator liable if he sees an intelligent man or an unintelligent infant running into danger and does not warn or forcibly restrain him? What difference does it make whether the danger is on another's land, or upon his own, in case the man or infant is not there by his express or implied invitation? If *A* sees an eight-year-old boy beginning to climb into his garden over a wall stuck with spikes and does not warn him or drive him off, is he liable in damages if the boy meets with injury from the spikes? I see my neighbor's two-year-old babe in dangerous proximity to the machinery of his windmill in his yard, and easily might, but do not, rescue him. I am not liable in damages to the child for his injuries, nor, if the child is killed, punishable for manslaughter by the common law or under the statute (P.S., c. 278, S. 8), because the child and I are strangers, and I am under no legal duty to protect him. Now suppose I see the same child trespassing in my own yard and meddling in like manner with the dangerous machinery of my own windmill. What additional obligation is cast upon me by reason of the child's trespass? The mere fact that the child is unable to take care of himself does not impose on me the legal duty of protecting him in the one case more than in the other. Upon what principle of law can an infant by coming unlawfully upon my premises impose upon me the legal duty of a guardian? None has been suggested, and we know of none.

An infant, no matter of how tender years, is liable in law for his trespasses. . . . If, then, the defendants' machinery was injured by the plaintiff's act in putting his hand in the gearing, he is liable to them for the damages in an action of trespass and to nominal damages for the wrongful entry. It would be no answer to such an action that the defendants might by force have prevented the trespass. It is impossible to hold that while the plaintiff is liable to the defendants in trespass, they are liable to him in case for neglecting to prevent the act which caused the injury both to him and them. Cases of enticement, allurement, or invitation of infants to their injury, or setting traps for them, and cases relating to the sufficiency of public ways, or to the exposure upon them of machinery attractive and dangerous to children, have no application here.

Danger from machinery in motion in the ordinary course of business cannot be distinguished from that arising from a well, pit, open scuttle, or other stationary object. The movement of the works is a part of the regular and normal condition of the premises. . . . The law no more compels the owners to shut down their gates and stop their business for the protection of a trespasser than it requires them to maintain a railing about an open scuttle or to fence in their machinery for the same purpose.

Hurley v. Eddingfield
59 N.E. 1058 (Ind. 1901)

BAKER, J. — Appellant sued appellee for $10,000 damages for wrongfully causing the death of his intestate. The court sustained appellee's demurrer to the complaint; and this ruling is assigned as error.

The material facts alleged may be summarized thus: At and for years before decedent's death appellee was a practicing physician at Mace in Montgomery county, duly licensed under the laws of the State. He held himself out to the public as a general practitioner of medicine. He had been decedent's family physician. Decedent became dangerously ill and sent for appellee. The messenger informed appellee of decedent's violent sickness, tendered him his fees for his services, and stated to him that no other physician was procurable in time and that decedent relied on him for attention. No other physician was procurable in time to be of any use, and decedent did rely on appellee for medical assistance. Without any reason whatever, appellee refused to render aid to decedent. No other patients were requiring appellee's immediate service, and he could have gone to the relief of decedent if he had been willing to do so. Death ensued, without decedent's fault, and wholly from appellee's wrongful act.

The alleged wrongful act was appellee's refusal to enter into a contract of employment. Counsel do not contend that, before the enactment of the law regulating the practice of medicine, physicians were bound to render professional service to every one who applied. The act regulating the practice of medicine provides for a board of examiners, standards of qualification, examinations, licenses to those found qualified, and penalties for practicing without license. The act is a preventive, not a compulsive, measure. In obtaining the State's license (permission) to practice medicine, the State does not require, and the licensee does not engage, that he will practice at all or on other terms than he may choose to accept. Counsel's analogies, drawn from the obligations to the public on the part of innkeepers, common carriers, and the like, are beside the mark.

Judgment affirmed.

NOTE

My brother's tormentor. Yania v. Bigan, 155 A.2d 343, 345, 346 (Pa. 1959), also manifests the same hostility toward the creation of affirmative duties. The decedent and defendant were operators of nearby strip mines. One day Yania was visiting Bigan's land to discuss business. Located on the land was a worked-out strip mine in which about 8 to 10 feet of water stood in a cut some 16 or 18 feet deep. Yania jumped into the cut and drowned, and the complaint in the wrongful death action that ensued charged Bigan "with three-fold negligence: (1) by urging, enticing, taunting and inveigling Yania to jump into the water; (2) by failing to warn Yania of a dangerous condition on the land; i.e., the cut wherein lay 8 to 10 feet of water; (3) by failing to go to Yania's rescue after he jumped into the water."

Jones, J., then dismissed all three parts of the claim. The first count failed because the

> complaint does not allege that Yania slipped or that he was pushed or that Bigan made any *physical* impact on his person. On the contrary, the only inference deducible from the facts alleged in the complaint is that Bigan, by the employment of cajolery and inveiglement, caused such a *mental* impact on Yania that the latter was deprived of his volition and freedom of choice and placed under a compulsion to jump into the water. Had Yania been a child of tender years or a person mentally deficient then it is conceivable that taunting and enticement could constitute actionable negligence if it resulted in harm. However to contend that such conduct directed to an adult in full possession of all his mental faculties constitutes actionable negligence is not only without precedent but completely without merit.

On the second count, Jones, J., held that Yania, as a strip-mine operator, was well aware of the obvious dangers of jumping into the water. The judge addressed the third claim as follows: "Lastly, it is urged that Bigan failed to take the necessary steps to rescue Yania from the water. The mere fact that Bigan saw Yania in a position of peril in the water imposed upon him no legal, although a moral, obligation or duty to go to his rescue unless Bigan was legally responsible in whole or in part, for placing Yania in the perilous position." It was his own fault for undertaking a dangerous and reckless course of action. How should the law respond to these various situations?

Bohlen, The Moral Duty to Aid Others as a Basis of Tort Liability
56 U. Pa. L. Rev. 217, 218-220 (1908)

There is no distinction more deeply rooted in the common law and more fundamental than that between misfeasance and non-feasance, between active misconduct working positive injury to others and passive inaction, a failure to take positive steps to benefit others, or to protect them from harm not created by any wrongful act of the defendant. This distinction is founded on that attitude of extreme individualism so typical of anglo-saxon thought.

Ames, Law and Morals
22 Harv. L. Rev. 97, 110-113 (1908)

The law is utilitarian. It exists for the realization of the reasonable needs of the community. If the interest of an individual runs counter to this chief object of the law, it must be sacrificed. That is why, in [some cases], the innocent suffer and the wicked go unpunished. . . .

It remains to consider whether the law should ever go so far as to give compensation or to inflict punishment for damage which would not have happened but for the wilful inaction of another. I exclude cases in which, by reason of some relation between the parties like that of father and child, nurse and invalid, master and servant and others, there is a recognized legal duty to act. In the case supposed the only relation between the parties is that both are human beings. As I am walking over a bridge a man falls into the water. He cannot swim and calls for help. I am strong and a good swimmer, or, if you please, there is a rope on the bridge, and I might easily throw him an end and pull him ashore. I neither jump in nor throw him the rope, but see him drown. Or, again, I see a child on the railroad track too young to appreciate the danger of the approaching train. I might easily save the child, but do nothing, and the child, though it lives, loses both legs. Am I guilty of a crime, and must I make compensation to the widow and children of the man drowned and to the wounded child? Macaulay, in commenting upon his Indian Criminal Code, puts the case of a surgeon refusing to go from Calcutta to Meerut to perform an operation, although it should be absolutely certain that this surgeon was the only person in India who could perform it, and that, if it were not performed, the person who required it would die.

We may suppose again that the situation of imminent danger of death was created by the act, but the innocent act, of the person who refuses to prevent the death. The man, for example, whose eye was penetrated by the glancing shot of the careful pheasant hunter, stunned by the shot, fell face downward into a shallow pool by which he was standing. The hunter might easily save him, but lets him drown.

In the first three illustrations, however revolting the conduct of the man who declined to interfere, he was in no way responsible for the perilous situation, he did not increase the peril, he took away nothing from the person in jeopardy, he simply failed to confer a benefit upon a stranger. As the law stands today there would be no legal liability, either civilly or criminally, in any of these cases. The law does not compel active benevolence between man and man. It is left to one's conscience whether he shall be the good Samaritan or not.

But ought the law to remain in this condition? Of course any statutory duty to be benevolent would have to be exceptional. The practical difficulty in such legislation would be in drawing the line. But that difficulty has continually to be faced in the law. We should all be better satisfied if the man who refuses to throw a rope to a drowning man or to save a helpless child on the railroad track could be punished and be made to compensate the widow of the man drowned and the wounded child. We should not think it advisable to penalize the surgeon who refused to make the journey. These illustrations suggest a possible working rule. One who fails to interfere to save another from impending death or great bodily harm, when he might do so with little or no inconvenience to himself, and the death or great bodily harm follows as a consequence of his inaction, shall be punished criminally and shall make compensation to the party injured or to his widow and children in case of death. The case of the drowning of the man shot by the hunter differs from the others in that the hunter, although he acted innocently, did bring about the dangerous situation. Here, too, the lawyer who should try to charge the hunter would lead a forlorn hope. But it seems to me that he could make out a strong case against the hunter on common law grounds. By the early law, as we have seen, he would have been liable simply because he shot the other. In modern times the courts have admitted as an affirmative defense the fact that he was not negligent. May not the same courts refuse to allow a defense, if the defendant did not use reasonable means to prevent a calamity after creating the threatening situation? Be that as it may, it is hard to see why such a rule should not be declared by statute, if not by the courts.

Epstein, A Theory of Strict Liability
2 J. Legal Stud. 151, 198-200 (1973)

Under Ames' good Samaritan rule, a defendant in cases of affirmative acts would be required to take only those steps that can be done "with little or no inconvenience." But if the distinction between causing harm and not preventing harm is to be disregarded, why should the difference in standards between the two cases survive the reform of the law? The only explanation is that the two situations are regarded at bottom as raising totally different issues, even for those who insist upon the immateriality of this distinction. Even those who argue, as Ames does, that the law is utilitarian must in the end find some special place for the claims of egoism which are an inseparable byproduct of the belief that individual autonomy — individual liberty — is a good in itself not explainable in terms of its purported social worth. It is one thing to *allow* people to act as they please in the belief that the "invisible hand" will provide the happy congruence of the individual and the social good. Such a theory, however, at bottom must regard individual autonomy as but a means to some social end. It takes a great deal more to assert that men are *entitled* to act as they choose (within the limits of strict liability) even though it is certain that there will be cases where individual welfare will be in conflict with the social good. Only then is it clear that even freedom has its costs: costs revealed in the acceptance of the good Samaritan doctrine.

But are the alternatives more attractive? Once one decides that as a matter of statutory or common law duty, an individual is required under some circumstances to act at his own cost for the exclusive benefit of another, then it is very hard to set out in a principled manner the limits of social interference with individual liberty. Suppose one claims, as Ames does, that his proposed rule applies only in the "obvious" cases where everyone (or almost everyone) would admit that the duty was appropriate: to the case of the man upon the bridge who refuses to throw a rope to a stranger drowning in the waters below. Even if the rule starts out with such modest ambitions, it is difficult to confine it to those limits. Take a simple case first. *X* as a representative of a private charity asks you for $10 in order to save the life of some starving child in a country ravaged by war. There are other donors available but the number of needy children exceeds that number. The money means "nothing" to you. Are you under a legal obligation to give the $10? Or to lend it interest-free? Does $10 amount to a substantial cost or inconvenience within the meaning of Ames' rule? It is true that the relationship between the gift to charity and the survival of an unidentified child is not so apparent as is the relationship between the man upon the bridge and the swimmer caught in the swirling seas. But lest the physical imagery govern, it is clear that someone will die as a consequence of your inaction in both cases. Is there a duty to give, or is the contribution a matter of charity?

Consider yet another example where services, not cash, are in issue. Ames insists that his rule would not require the only surgeon in India capable of saving the life of a person with a given affliction to travel across the subcontinent to perform an operation, presumably because the inconvenience and cost would be substantial. But how would he treat the case if some third person were willing to pay him for all of his efforts? If the payment is sufficient to induce the surgeon to act, then there is no need for the good Samaritan doctrine at all. But if it is not, then it is again necessary to compare the costs of the physician with the benefits to his prospective patient. It is hard to know whether Ames would require the forced exchange under these circumstances. But it is at least arguable that under his theory forced exchanges should be required, since the payment might reduce the surgeon's net inconvenience to the point where it was trivial.

Once forced exchanges, regardless of the levels of payment, are accepted, it will no longer be possible to delineate the sphere of activities in which contracts (or charity) will be required in order to procure desired benefits and the sphere of activity in which those benefits can be procured as of right. Where tests of "reasonableness" — stated with such confidence, and applied with such difficulty — dominate the law of tort, it becomes impossible to tell where liberty ends and obligation begins; where contract ends, and tort begins. In each case, it will be possible for some judge or jury to decide that there was something else which the defendant should have done, and he will decide that on the strength of some cost-benefit formula that is difficult indeed to apply. These remarks are conclusive, I think, against the adoption of Ames' rule by judicial innovation, and they bear heavily on the desirability of the abandonment of the good Samaritan rule by legislation as well. It is not surprising that the law has, in the midst of all the clamor for reform, remained unmoved in the end, given the inability to form alternatives to the current position.

Posner, Epstein's Tort Theory: A Critique
8 J. Legal Stud. 457, 460 (1979)

Suppose that if all the members of society could somehow be assembled they would agree unanimously that, as a reasonable measure of mutual protection, anyone who can warn or rescue someone in distress at negligible cost to himself (in time, danger, or whatever) should be required to do so. These mutual promises of assistance would create a contract that Epstein would presumably enforce since he considers the right to make binding contracts a fundamental one. However, there are technical obstacles—in this case insurmountable ones—to the formation of an actual contract among so many people. Transaction costs are prohibitive. If, moved by these circumstances, a court were to impose tort liability on a bystander who failed to assist a person in distress, such liability would be a means of carrying out the original desires of the parties just as if it were an express contract that was being enforced.

The point of this example is that tort duties can sometimes (perhaps, as we shall see, generally) be viewed as devices for vindicating the principles that underlie freedom of contract. It may be argued, however, that the contract analogy is inapplicable because the bystander would not be compensated for coming to the rescue of the person in distress. But this argument overlooks the fact that the consideration for the rescue is not payment when the rescue is effected but a commitment to reciprocate should the roles of the parties some day be reversed. Liability would create a mutual protective arrangement under which everyone was obliged to attempt a rescue when circumstances dictated and, in exchange, was entitled to the assistance of anyone who might be able to help him should he ever find himself in a position of peril.

Bender, A Lawyer's Primer on Feminist Theory and Tort
38 J. Legal Educ. 34-35 (1988)

How would this drowning-stranger hypothetical look from a new legal perspective informed by a feminist ethic based upon notions of caring, responsibility, interconnectedness, and cooperation? If we put abstract reasoning and autonomy aside momentarily, we can see what else matters. In defining duty, what matters is that someone, a human being, a part of us, is drowning and will die without some affirmative action. This seems more urgent, more imperative, more important than any possible infringement of individual autonomy by the imposition of an affirmative duty. If we think about the stranger as a human being for a moment, we may realize that much more is involved than balancing one person's interest in having his life saved and another's interest in not having affirmative duties imposed upon him in the absence of a special relationship, although even then the balance seems to me to weigh in favor of imposing a duty or standard of care that requires action. The drowning stranger is not the only person affected by the lack of care. He is not detached from everyone else. He no doubt has people who care about him — parents, spouse, children, friends, colleagues; groups he participates in — religious, social, athletic, artistic, political, educational, work-related; he may even have people who depend upon him for emotional or financial support. He is interconnected with others. If the stranger drowns, many will be harmed. It is not an isolated event with one person's interests balanced against another's. When our legal system trains us to understand the drowning-stranger story as a limited event between two people, both of whom have interests at least equally worth protecting, and when the social ramifications we credit most are the impositions on personal liberty of action, we take a human situation and translate it into a cold, dehumanized algebraic equation. We forget that we are talking about human death or grave physical harms and their reverberating consequences when we equate the consequences with such things as one person's momentary freedom not to act. People are decontextualized for the analysis, yet no one really lives an acontextual life. What gives us the authority to take contextual, actual problems and encode them in a language of numbers, letters, and symbols that represents no reality in any actual person's life?

. . . Why should our autonomy or freedom not to rescue weigh more heavily in law than a stranger's harms and the consequent harms to people with whom she is interconnected?

NOTES

1. *An affirmative duty to rescue.* Judge Posner returned to the good Samaritan problem in Stockberger v. United States, 332 F.3d 479 (7th Cir. 2003):

> Various rationales have been offered for the seemingly hardhearted common law rule: people should not count on nonprofessionals for rescue; the

circle of potentially liable nonrescuers would be difficult to draw (suppose a person is drowning and no one on the crowded beach makes an effort to save him — should all be liable?); altruism makes the problem a small one and liability might actually reduce the number of altruistic rescues by depriving people of credit for altruism (how would they prove they hadn't acted under threat of legal liability?); people would be deterred by threat of liability from putting themselves in a position where they might be called upon to attempt a rescue, especially since a failed rescue might under settled common law principles give rise to liability, on the theory that a clumsy rescue attempt may have interfered with a competent rescue by someone else.

That said, he refused, following Indiana law, to impose liability on co-workers of a hypoglycemic employee at a federal prison for allowing him to undertake his fatal drive home. The coworkers were familiar with the decedent's condition and had supplied him with Ensure, a nutritious liquid food substitute, which made him strong enough to start the drive home. Why treat this as a stranger case at all?

On the complications of creating a generalized duty of rescue, see Epstein, Causation and Corrective Justice, A Reply to Two Critics, 8 J. Legal Stud. 477, 490-492 (1979). For the affirmative case for the duty of easy rescue, see Weinrib, The Case for a Duty to Rescue, 90 Yale L.J. 247 (1980); Hasen, The Efficient Duty to Rescue, 15 Intl. Rev. Law & Econ. 141 (1995).

2. *Restitution and rescue.* As a common law matter, is it better to approach the rescue problem with restitution instead of tort doctrines? Whereas the tort solution requires a large judgment against the able defendant who does not rescue, the restitution solution gives a much smaller payment to the enterprising person who does rescue. The restitution scheme reduces the level of legal intervention, and it eliminates the vexing problems of multiple causation that arise whenever many persons are in a position to undertake a rescue (or to call the police) and none in fact does. Yet how are the levels of compensation to be fixed? Is it sound policy to pay rescuers out of public funds? See the thoughtful article by Dawson, Rewards for the Rescue of Human Life, in The Good Samaritan and the Law (Ratcliffe ed. 1966), which takes a cautious attitude toward creating restitution remedies. Note restitution remedies have been favored for professional rescuers who might be discouraged by the threat of tort suits from making the heavy investments necessary to carry out rescues at sea. See Landes and Posner, Salvors, Finders, Good Samaritans, and Other Rescuers: An Economic Study of Law and Altruism, 7 J. Legal Stud. 83, 119-127 (1978).

3. *Legislation and the good Samaritan.* Legislative responses to the good Samaritan problem have typically been designed either to induce rescue by insulating the rescuer against liability for ordinary negligence or by imposing affirmative duties to rescue, subject to the payment of fines. In both cases the rescuer remains liable for willful misconduct.

For example, Kan. Stat. Ann. §§65-2891(a) & (d) provide:

> (a) Any health care provider who in good faith renders emergency care or assistance at the scene of an emergency or accident including treatment of a minor without first obtaining the consent of the parent or guardian of such minor shall not be liable for any civil damages for acts or omissions other than damages occasioned by gross negligence or by willful and wanton acts or omissions by such persons in rendering emergency care.
>
> (d) Any provision herein contained notwithstanding, the ordinary standards of care and rules of negligence shall apply in those cases wherein emergency care and assistance is rendered in any physician's or dentist's office, clinic, emergency room or hospital with or without compensation.

A New Jersey statute, N.J.S.A. 2A:62A-1 provided similar protection but did not explicitly exempt from its purview emergency care rendered in a hospital. In Valazquez v. Jiminez, 798 A.2 51, 63 (N.J. 2002), the court read this exception into the statute in light of its purposes:

> That narrowly tailored interpretation does the least violence to our citizens' common-law right to institute tort actions against those whose negligence injures them. It thus conforms to our rules regarding the interpretation of statutes in derogation of the common law and statutes granting immunity.
>
> Moreover, it gives full throat to the goals underlying the legislation: to encourage the rendering of medical care to those who would not otherwise receive it, by physicians who come upon such patients by chance, without the benefit of the expertise, assistance, equipment or sanitation that is available in a hospital or medical setting.

Similar immunities for similar reasons have been extended to laypersons who supply emergency care. Thus, in Swenson v. Waseca Mutual Insurance Co., 653 N.W.2d 794, 798 (Minn. App. 2002), the defendant's insured attempted to transport an injured snowboarder to the hospital, but her car was hit by a speeding tractor-trailer, resulting in her death. Albrecht, J., sustained the defendant's summary judgment, noting that "the purpose of the statute is to encourage laypersons to help those in need, even when they are under no legal obligation to do so, by providing immunity from liability claims arising out of an attempt to assist a person in peril." Does it make sense to supply this protection to a defendant whose rescue efforts do not require him to accept any heightened risk?

A very different approach to the good Samaritan problem was adopted in Vermont, in 1972. Vermont Statute title 12, §519 (2006) provides:

> (a) A person who knows that another is exposed to grave physical harm shall, to the extent that the same can be rendered without danger or peril to himself or without interference with important duties owed to others, give

reasonable assistance to the exposed person unless that assistance or care is being provided by others.

(b) A person who provides reasonable assistance in compliance with subsection (a) of this section shall not be liable in civil damages unless his acts constitute gross negligence or unless he will receive or expects to receive remuneration. Nothing contained in this subsection shall alter existing law with respect to tort liability of a practitioner of the healing arts for acts committed in the ordinary course of his practice.

(c) A person who willfully violates subsection (a) of this section shall be fined not more than $100.00.

Does the Vermont statute adopt a straight negligence approach in rescue cases? Does it authorize the creation of a private cause of action? Note that litigation under the statute has been on collateral points. As of 2007, no reported actions, civil or criminal, have been brought for failure to rescue under section (a). See, on the statute, Franklin, Vermont Requires Rescue: A Comment, 25 Stan. L. Rev. 51 (1972).

The movement for statutory duties to rescue has provoked this response in Hyman, Rescue Without Law: An Empirical Perspective on the Duty to Rescue, 84 Texas L. Rev. 653, 712 (2006).

> During the past decade, there have been an average of 1.6 documented cases of non-rescue each year in the entire United States. Every year, Americans perform at least 946 non-risky rescues and 243 risky rescues. Every year, at least sixty-five times as many Americans die while attempting to rescue someone else as die from a documented case of non-risky non-rescue. If a few isolated (and largely unverified and undocumented) cases of non-rescues have been deemed sufficient to justify legislative reform, one would think a total of approximately 1,200 documented cases of rescue every year should point rather decisively in the opposite direction. When it comes to the duty to rescue, leaving well enough alone is likely to be sufficient unto the day.

Uneasiness with the current law of rescue elicited a proposal to remove rescue cases from the tort liability system altogether by allowing victims to "recover compensatory damages under either a renter's or homeowner's insurance policy." See White, No Good Deed Goes Unpunished: The Case for Reform of Rescue Doctrine, 97 Nw. U. L. Rev. 507 (2002). Why can't insurance companies just voluntarily supply the coverage?

4. *Duties to rescue for public entities.* The reluctance to impose duties of reasonable care on rescuers in emergency situations also carries over to public entities. In Riss v. City of New York, 240 N.E.2d 860, 860-861 (N.Y. 1968), the plaintiff was blinded when a disgruntled former suitor hired someone to throw lye in her face after making repeated threats against her person that were largely ignored by local police officials. Breitel, J.,

refused, largely on separation of power grounds, to impose the duty of care on the city.

> [T]his case involves the provision of a governmental service to protect the public generally from external hazards and particularly to control the activities of criminal wrongdoers. The amount of protection that may be provided is limited by the resources of the community and by a considered legislative-executive decision as to how those resources may be deployed. For the courts to proclaim a new and general duty of protection in the law of tort, even to those who may be the particular seekers of protection based on specific hazards, could and would inevitably determine how the limited police resources of the community should be allocated and without predictable limits. This is quite different from the predictable allocation of resources and liabilities when public hospitals, rapid transit systems, or even highways are provided.
>
> Before such extension of responsibilities should be dictated by the indirect imposition of tort liabilities, there should be a legislative determination that that should be the scope of public responsibility . . .

In fact, most state legislation explicitly declines to impose this form of liability, see Chapter 17, Section D on municipal governments. The Third Restatement takes just this position when it notes that the "large potential liability that might be imposed on them for every undertaking" induced courts to take a go-slow attitude on imposing tort liability.

Efforts to impose affirmative duties of care as a matter of constitutional law have also received a frosty reception. In DeShaney v. Winnebago County Department of Social Services, 489 U.S 189, 196-197 (1989), which rejected a claim under the Due Process Clause of the Fourteenth Amendment against a state social service agency that failed to protect a small child who had been left permanently injured after being repeatedly and savagely beaten by his father even when employees in the state's social service department had actual knowledge of the dangerous situation. Rehnquist, C.J., held that the clause generally confers "no affirmative right to government aid, even where such aid may be necessary to secure life, liberty, or property interests of which the government itself may not deprive the individual." Nonetheless, in K.H. v. Morgan, 914 F.2d 846, 859 (7th Cir. 1990), Posner, J., was prepared to allow an action against state officials, finding a clear breach of duty when a child taken into state custody is "handed over by state officers to a foster parent or other custodian, private or public, *whom the state knows or suspects to be a child abuser.*" Similarly in Currier v. Doran, 242 F.3d 905, 918 (10th Cir. 2001), Murphy, J., held that *DeShaney* did not bar the Due Process claim of an abused child against social workers in New Mexico's Youth and Family Services Department, saying: "In this case, Anthony and Latasha [the abused children] were removed from their mother and placed with their father. In *DeShaney*, Joshua was removed from his father and then returned to his father. Anthony and Latasha would not have been exposed to the dangers from their father but for the affirmative acts of the state; the same cannot be said for Joshua in *DeShaney*." Why? How should liability be determined if it is necessary to balance financial restraints and the limits of professional judgment in the provision of child care?

Montgomery v. National Convoy & Trucking Co.
195 S.E. 247 (S.C. 1937)

[Defendants' trucks had stalled on an icy highway without their fault, blocking the road completely. About 15 minutes later plaintiff's car came over a hill and started down toward the trucks before either plaintiff or plaintiff's driver could see them. The trucks were about 50 feet away, not being previously visible because they were obscured by the hill. In view of the icy condition of the road, plaintiff's car could not be stopped. "The agents of the [defendants] operating the trucks knew, or had every reason to know, that once a car had passed the crest of the hill and started down the decline, . . . it would be impossible to stop such automobile or motor vehicle due to the icy condition of the highway, regardless of the rate of speed at which such automobile may be traveling." Defendants' drivers had ample time to place a warning signal at the top of the hill, where it could have been observed by the plaintiff's chauffeur who, well aware of the dangerous condition of the road, could have stopped before the collision that injured plaintiff. The defendants' motion for a directed verdict was refused, and the jury awarded plaintiff the full amount demanded, $3,000. The defendants appealed.]

BAKER, J. One may be negligent by acts of omission as well as of commission, and liability therefor will attach if the act of omission of a duty owed another, under the circumstances, is the direct, proximate and efficient cause of the injury. It is only where the evidence is susceptible of but one reasonable inference that the Court may declare what that inference is and take the case from the consideration of the jury. . . .

One of the acts of negligence alleged in the complaint is the failure of the appellants to warn approaching vehicles of the conditions existing, and this necessarily means that the warning should be given at a point where it would be effective. That appellants recognized that they owed a duty to others using the highway cannot be questioned, since they at some time put out flares and left the lights on their trucks. But if appellants owed a duty to others using the highway, and this cannot be disputed, the performance of such duty was not met by merely having lights at the point where the trucks blocked the highway, but it was incumbent on the appellants to take such precautions as would reasonably be calculated to prevent injury.

For the moment let us repeat some of the facts. There is a curve in the highway at the crest of a long hill. A short distance to the south of the curve and crest of the hill two trucks are stalled and block the entire road. It is a much-traveled highway. Respondent's chauffeur testified that due to the curve in the road and the hill, the lights of an automobile approaching from the north would not focus on the trucks until the automobile was within a little over fifty feet from the trucks. Once a car passed the crest of the hill and commenced to descend on the south side, it could not be stopped due to the ice on the highway — the slippery condition thereof, which was known or should have been known to appellants. No flagman nor warning of any description was placed at the crest of the hill to warn approaching cars. That a warning at the crest of the hill would have been effective and prevented the injury is fully demonstrated from other evidence had upon the trial. The danger of the situation was so self-evident that a jury could have concluded that the omission to warn approaching travelers from the north at a point where the warning would be effective, amounted not only to negligence, but to willfulness. However, the jury in this case have vindicated their intelligence and freedom from passion when they found only inadvertence.

NOTES

1. *Misfeasance and nonfeasance.* The distinction between misfeasance and nonfeasance articulated with such confidence by Bohlen was sorely tested in *Montgomery*. To be sure, that line is relatively clear when the defendant has not rescued the plaintiff from some peril that the defendant has not created. But it is more difficult to draw when the defendant fails to neutralize a dangerous condition that he has created as in *Montgomery* when defendants' stalled trucks, without fault, blocked the icy highway. How would Bohlen treat the case?

A similar situation arose in Newton v. Ellis, 119 Eng. Rep. 424 (K.B. 1855). The defendant, while under contract with the local board of health, dug a hole in a public highway that he left unlighted at night. Shortly thereafter the plaintiff, while driving, fell into the hole. The three judges who heard the case denied that the action was for nonfeasance. Coleridge, J., remarked: "This is not a case of not doing: the defendant does something, omitting to secure protection for the public. He is not sued for not putting up a light, but for the complex act." Erle, J., agreed, saying: "Here the cause of action is the making the hole, compounded with the not putting up a light. When these two are blended, the result is no more than if two positive acts were committed, such as digging the hole and throwing out the dirt: the two would make up one act." Suppose that *A*, while driving, hits *B* because *A* has failed to apply the brakes. Can *A* argue that this is a simple case of nonfeasance for which he is not responsible? Why not?

The Third Restatement has codified the rule in *Montgomery*:

§39.   DUTY BASED ON PRIOR CONDUCT CREATING A RISK OF PHYSICAL HARM
When an actor's prior conduct, even though not tortious, creates a
continuing risk of physical harm of a type characteristic of the conduct, the
actor has a duty to exercise reasonable care to prevent or minimize the harm.

Could this duty attach if the defendant had no knowledge, or reason to
know, of the physical injury to others? Is there any reason, if knowledge is
had, to limit the continuing duty of care to cases of "physical harm of a type
characteristic of the conduct?" Note that the parallel provision in the
Second Restatement only applied to a plaintiff who was rendered "helpless
and in danger of further harm." RST §322. Any reason for the helpless
limitation? Note that many state statutes impose particular obligations on
motorists to render "reasonable assistance" to other persons involved in an
accident, and to exchange information names and registration to facilitate
subsequent resolution of any future litigation. See California Vehicle Code
§20003 (2007).

2. *The duty to rescue under strict liability.* In *Montgomery* the duty to rescue
only arose because the defendant could not be held liable in negligence
for originally blocking the highway, which occurred without its fault.
Montgomery, however, comes out quite differently if strict liability governs
highway accidents. On that view, the defendant could not rely on the
inevitable accident defense when its trucks first stalled. Nonetheless, it
could escape or reduce its liability by showing that the plaintiff proceeded
too rapidly in light of the poor road conditions. Given its potentially
extensive liability under strict liability, the defendant has a strong incentive to post warnings at the top of the road, both to reduce the chances of
having its own property damaged in the collision and to bolster its assumption of risk or contributory negligence defenses against any
potential plaintiffs who saw, or could have seen, the warnings. Strict liability, therefore, narrows the need for creating any fresh duty in tort to
take affirmative care given the prior dangerous situation. What analysis
should apply if a bystander is in a position to warn oncoming cars of the
peril, but chooses to continue on his way?

A strict liability rule could also narrow the scope of the duty to rescue in
Louisville & Nashville R.R. v. Scruggs, 49 So. 399 (Ala. 1909). The defendant's freight train was stopped, blocking a fire engine as it drove up to
extinguish a fire in plaintiff's house just across the tracks. Defendant's
employees refused to move the train except on the dispatcher's orders and,
by the time the firemen came, plaintiff's house was destroyed. Because the
defendant's use of its land was "merely passive," the Alabama Supreme
Court denied recovery, adding that "[t]he law imposes no duty on one man
to aid another in the preservation of the latter's property, but only the duty

not to injure another's property in the use of his own." The court did concede that the defendant could be held liable for the loss of plaintiff's home if its engineer deliberately or negligently ran over a hose that already was laid across the tracks. One judge dissented, thinking the attitude of defendant's employees showed "an indifference to the situation and emergency that was little short of shocking." What if the local rules of the road give fire engines the right of way over all other traffic?

Scruggs provoked the following response in Hale, Prima Facie Torts, Combination, and Non-Feasance, 46 Colum. L. Rev. 196, 214 (1946):

> Perhaps judicial reluctance to recognize affirmative duties is based on one or both of two inarticulate assumptions. One of these is that a rugged, independent individual needs no help from others, save such as they may be disposed to render him out of kindness, or such as he can induce them to render by the ordinary process of bargaining, without having the government step in to make them help. All he is supposed to ask of the government is that it interfere to prevent others from doing him positive harm. The other assumption is that when a government *requires* a person to act, it is necessarily interfering more seriously with his liberty than when it places limits on his freedom to act — to make a man serve another is to make him a slave, while to forbid him to commit affirmative wrongs is to leave him still essentially a freeman. Neither of these assumptions is universally true. Neither was true in [*Scruggs*]. No matter how rugged the owner of the burning building, his property depended for its preservation on the affirmative acts of the railroad employees — acts which they were evidently not disposed to render out of kindness, and which he was in no position to induce them to perform by bargaining. Nor would a legal duty to move the train have subjected either the employees or the railroad company itself to anything having the slightest resemblance to slavery.

3. *Aid to the helpless: once begun, then undone.* In Zelenko v. Gimbel Bros., 287 N.Y.S. 134, 135 (N.Y. Sup. Ct. 1935), Lauer, J. wrote:

> . . . Plaintiff's intestate was taken ill in defendant's store. We will assume that the defendant owed her no duty at all; that defendant could have let her be and die. But if a defendant undertakes a task, even if under no duty to undertake it, the defendant must not omit to do what an ordinary man would do in performing the task.
>
> Here the defendant undertook to render medical aid to the plaintiff's intestate. Plaintiff says that defendant kept his intestate for six hours in an infirmary without any medical care. If defendant had left plaintiff's intestate alone, beyond doubt some bystander, who would be influenced more by charity than by legalistic duty, would have summoned an ambulance. Defendant segregated this plaintiff's intestate where such aid could not be given and then left her alone.

The plaintiff is wrong in thinking that the duty of a common carrier of passengers is the same as the duty of this defendant. The common carrier assumes its duty by its contract of carriage. This defendant assumed its duty by meddling in matters with which legalistically it had no concern. The plaintiff is right in arguing that when the duty arose, the same type of neglect is actionable in both cases.

Restatement (Second) of Torts:

> §324.   DUTY OF ONE WHO TAKES CHARGE OF ANOTHER WHO IS HELPLESS
> One who, being under no duty to do so, takes charge of another who is helpless adequately to aid or protect himself is subject to liability to the other for any bodily harm caused to him by
>   (a) the failure of the actor to exercise reasonable care to secure the safety of the other while within the actor's charge, or
>   (b) the actor's discontinuing his aid or protection, if by so doing he leaves the other in a worse position than when the actor took charge of him.

The Restatement Third takes the same position. RTT:LPH §44. Does it make sense to prefer lofty indifference to honest but inept efforts to aid? Compare the following two cases: In the first, *A*, coming upon the scene of an accident, picks up *B*, who is helpless, and starts to drive him to a hospital. En route she drives negligently and has a collision, and *B*'s injuries are aggravated. In the second, *A* comes upon the scene of an accident and picks up *B*, who is helpless, and starts to drive him to a hospital. A moment later, *A* changes her mind and returns *B* to the scene of the accident. What result in each case if prompt medical care would have greatly reduced the harm to *B* and that this was obvious to *A*?

4. *Cracks in the good Samaritan doctrine.* In Soldano v. O'Daniels, 190 Cal. Rptr. 310 (Cal. App. 1983), the decedent was in imminent danger of being shot at Happy Jack's Saloon when another patron ran across the street to the defendant's restaurant. He asked the defendant's bartender for use of the phone to call the police or, in the alternative, for the bartender to make the emergency call. The bartender refused both requests, and the decedent was killed. The court rebuffed the defendant's argument that there was no duty to aid or assist the plaintiff. It first agreed with Prosser that the common law rule denying the duty to rescue violates "common decency" and is "revolting to any moral sense." It then held that the defendant, while not required to rescue, did have "to permit the patron from Happy Jack's to place a call to the police or to place the call himself." Restatement (Second) of Torts §327 renders any person who "knows or has reason to know that a third person is giving or is ready to give another aid necessary to prevent physical harm to [an endangered person]" tortiously

liable if he "negligently prevents or disables the third person from giving such aid."

Soldano itself came under heavy criticism in Eric J. v. Betty M., 90 Cal. Rtpr. 2d 549, 560 (Cal. App. 1999) for its ostensible misreading of the RST §327: "The problem with the court's analysis is that it subtly equated the concepts of prevention and interference as used in section 327 of the Restatement Second of Torts with the fact that the bartender had *refused to allow* a saloon patron from across the street use the *restaurant's* phone. Interference and refusal to allow one's property to be commandeered, even for a good purpose, are simply two different things. If the English words 'prevent' and 'interfere' still mean anything, they necessarily convey the notion of some sort of affirmative action, not just refusal to turn one's property over to someone else." If the patron had reached for the phone and had been rebuffed by the defendant's bartender, why is that not a form of prevention or interference? Should *Soldano* be governed by the doctrine of private necessity in Vincent v. Lake Eric Transportation Co., *supra* at 71.

SECTION C.   DUTIES OF OWNERS AND OCCUPIERS

Robert Addie & Sons (Collieries), Ltd. v. Dumbreck
[1929] A.C. 358

[The defendant colliers operated a haulage system in their fields near a public road in order to remove coal ashes from the pithead, where mining operations were going on. The haulage system employed an endless wire cable; at one end of the system, near the mouth of the mine, there was an eight-horsepower engine used intermittently to operate the system. At the other end, which was not visible to anyone working the electrical motor, was a large, heavy horizontal wheel around which the cable passed at a rate of two to two and one-half miles per hour when the system was in use. The wheel in question was protected only by four boards placed upon its top, leaving a space of eight or nine inches between the boards and the bed of ashes beneath the wheel. The court below found that the wheel was dangerous and attractive to children.

The haulage system was located in a field surrounded by a hedge that contained a number of gaps, making it inadequate for keeping little children away from the wheel. In fact, many people used the field as a shortcut and many children played there. Though the defendant's servants from time to time warned children to stay out of the field and admonished adults not to cross, they knew their warnings had little or no effect. The defendant's servants did maintain a watch over the field, but to protect the defendant's property, not the persons who trespassed on it. There were two gates to the field, at one of which was posted a notice that read "Trespassers will be prosecuted."

The plaintiff's son was a four-year-old boy whom the plaintiff had warned not to go into the field and not to play with the wheel. The exact circumstances of his death were not determined, but it appeared that he had either been "sitting on the cover of the wheel or in a position in front of and in close proximity to the pulley and rope, being caught and drawn into the mechanism when it was set in motion by the defendant's servants."

The court below had awarded the plaintiff judgment on the ground that the accident was due to the fault of the defendant in not taking suitable precautions to avoid accidents to persons using the fields before activating the haulage system.

The defendant appealed.]

HAILSHAM, L.C. . . . The first and in my opinion the only question which arises for determination is the capacity in which the deceased child was in the field and at the wheel on the occasion of the accident. There are three categories in which persons visiting premises belonging to another person may fall; they may go

1.   By the invitation, express or implied, of the occupier;
2.   With the leave and license of the occupier; and
3.   As trespassers.

It was suggested in argument that there was a fourth category of persons who were not on the premises with the leave or license of the occupier, but who were not pure trespassers. I cannot find any foundation for this suggestion either in English or Scotch law, and I do not think that the category exists.

The duty which rests upon the occupier of premises towards the persons who come on such premises differs according to the category into which the visitor falls. The highest duty exists towards those persons who fall into the first category, and who are present by the invitation of the occupier. Towards such persons the occupier has the duty of taking reasonable care that the premises are safe.

In the case of persons who are not there by invitation, but who are there by leave and licence, express or implied, the duty is much less stringent — the occupier has no duty to ensure that the premises are safe, but he is bound not to create a trap or allow a concealed danger to exist upon the said premises, which is not apparent to the visitor, but which is known — or ought to be known — to the occupier.

Towards the trespasser the occupier has no duty to take reasonable care for his protection or even to protect him from concealed danger. The trespasser comes on to the premises at his own risk. An occupier is in such a case liable only where the injury is due to some wilful act involving something more than the absence of reasonable care. There must be some act done with the deliberate intention of doing harm to the trespasser, or at least some act done with reckless disregard of the presence of the trespasser. . . .

The only question, therefore, that remains for decision in this case is whether, upon the findings of fact of the Court of Session (which are not open to review), the respondent's son may properly be regarded as having been at the wheel at the time of the accident with the leave and license of the appellants. If this had been proved, I should have been prepared to hold that the wheel, which was at times stationary and which was started without any warning, and which was, in the words of the Court of Session, "dangerous and attractive to children and insufficiently protected at the time of the accident," amounted to a trap, and that the respondent would therefore have been entitled to recover. But in my opinion, the findings of fact effectually negative that view. It is found that the appellants warned children out of the field and reproved adults who came there, and all that can be said is that these warnings were frequently neglected and that there was a gap in the hedge through which it was easy to pass on to the field. I cannot regard the fact that the appellants did not effectively fence the field or the fact that their warnings were frequently disregarded as sufficient to justify an inference that they permitted the children to be on the field, and, in the absence of such a permission, it is clear that the respondent's child was merely a trespasser. The sympathy which one cannot help feeling for the unhappy father must not be allowed to alter one's view of the law, and I have no doubt that in law the respondent's son was a mere trespasser, and that as such the appellants owed him no duty to protect him from injury. On these grounds I am of opinion that this appeal succeeds and must be allowed with costs, and I move your Lordships accordingly.

VISCOUNT DUNEDIN . . . What I particularly wish to emphasize is that there are the three different classes — invitees, licensees, trespassers. I think, in the Scottish cases at least, there has been a little laxity in distinguishing between invitees and licensees. The best test of who is an invitee is, I think, given by Lord Kinnear in *Devlin*'s case. He must be on the land for some purpose in which he and the proprietor have a joint interest. A licensee is a person whom the proprietor has not in any way invited — he has no interest in his being there — but he has either expressly permitted him to use his lands or knowledge of his presence more or less habitual having been brought home to him, he has then either accorded permission or shown no practical anxiety to stop his further frequenting the lands. The trespasser is he who goes on the land without invitation of any sort and whose presence is either unknown to the proprietor or, if known, is practically objected to.

Now the line that separates each of these three classes is an absolutely rigid line. There is no half-way house, no no-man's land between adjacent territories. When I say rigid, I mean rigid in law. When you come to the facts it may well be that there is great difficulty — such difficulty as may give rise to difference of judicial opinion — in deciding into which category a particular case falls, but a judge must decide and, having decided, then the law of that category will rule and there must be no looking to the law of the adjoining category. I cannot help thinking that the use of epithets, "bare licensees," "pure trespassers" and so on, has much to answer for in obscuring what I think is a vital proposition that, in deciding cases of the class we are considering, the first duty of the tribunal is to fix once and for all into which of the three classes the person in question falls. . . .

Something has been said about fencing. There is no duty on a proprietor to fence his land against the world under sanction that, if he does not, those who come over it become licensees. Of course, a proprietor may do nothing at all to prevent people coming over his lands and they may come so often that permission will be held to be implied, or he may do something, but that something so half-heartedly as to be equivalent to doing nothing. For instance, a mere putting up of a notice "No Trespassers Allowed" or "Strictly Private," followed, when people often come, by no further steps, would, I think, leave it open for a judge or jury to hold implied permission. But when a proprietor protests and goes on protesting, turning away people when he meets them, as he did here, and giving no countenance in anything that he does to their presence there, then I think no Court has a right to say that permission must be implied. As I have said, circumstances vary infinitely and you cannot ab ante furnish a test which will fit every case; but it is permission that must be proved, not tolerance, though tolerance in some circumstances may be so pronounced as to lead to a conclusion that it was really tantamount to permission. I, therefore, find that the child who met with an accident in this case was a trespasser.

[Appeal allowed.]

NOTES

1. Willful and wanton exception. The three categories of land entrants outlined in *Addie* still organize the American law on the subject, which also accepts its central proposition that a trespasser is not owed a duty of care, but is only to be free of wilful and wanton conduct by the landowner. In Excelsior Wire Rope Co., Ltd. v. Callan, [1930] A.C. 404, decided the year after *Addie*, the House of Lords upheld a judgment on behalf of two infant plaintiffs whose hands had been crushed when caught between the wire rope and the pulley used to operate the defendant's haulage system. The House of Lords treated the plaintiffs as trespassers, but nonetheless distinguished *Addie* by holding that the defendant's servants had acted in reckless disregard of the plaintiffs' welfare. The haulage system was located in an open field next to a playground run by the local town corporation for the benefit of its children. The field was constantly "swarming" with children, who left the playground to play games on and about the defendant's machinery. The defendant's servants knew that the children constantly played upon the machinery, and the House of Lords found them in reckless disregard of their duty even though they first cleared the area of children. However, "they started the machinery without being clear that the wire was free from children." In distinguishing *Addie*, Lord Buckmaster held that the defendants were in breach of their duty because it was "well known" to them "that when this machine was going to start it was extremely likely that children would be there and, with the wire in motion, would be exposed to grave danger."

The "willful and wanton" exception also permitted recovery in Gould v. DeBeve, 330 F.2d 826 (D.C. Cir. 1964). The plaintiff, a two-year-old infant, and his mother were staying temporarily with a Mrs. Dodd, under an arrangement whereby Mrs. DeBeve reimbursed Mrs. Dodd for half the rent owed to the landlord. The landlord did not know of this arrangement, which was contrary to an express provision in Mrs. Dodd's lease that restricted occupation of her apartment to herself and to members of her immediate family. The day of the accident was extremely hot. The two women had left a bedroom window open even though its screen was warped and cracked, defective in almost every conceivable way. The plaintiff, while playing by the open window, knocked out the loose screen and fell to the ground, sustaining injuries. The court expressed an obvious distaste for a rule that treats alike all trespassers, from guileless infants to persistent poachers. While it did not upset the finding below that the plaintiff was a trespasser in the apartment, it upheld the jury verdict for the plaintiff by noting it was proper to find the defendants guilty of "wilful and wanton misconduct" in ignoring their statutory obligation to replace the defective screen after receiving urgent requests from Mrs. Dodd to do so. Although the statute only provided that the screens "be so maintained as to prevent effectively the entrance of flies and mosquitoes into the building," the court found that the defendant's statutory obligation "certainly comprehends, in the Washington summer when windows must be raised, screens which keep flies out and young children in."

2. *Attractive nuisance: origins.* The rigors of the common law rules regarding trespassers have also been eased by the widespread adoption of the attractive nuisance doctrine. This doctrine allows infant trespassers to recover when lured onto defendant's premises by some tempting condition created and maintained by the defendant, such as railway turntables, explosives, electrical conduits, smoldering fires, and rickety structures. Exposure to liability under the doctrine is, however, limited, for the case law tends to exclude "rivers, creeks, ponds, wagons, axes, plows, woodpiles, haystacks," and the like. Franich v. Great Northern Ry., 260 F.2d 599 (9th Cir. 1958).

During the nineteenth century some courts rejected the attractive nuisance doctrine on grounds that, once recognized, its scope could not be confined or limited. For example, Mitchell, J., in Twist v. Winona & St. Peter R.R., 39 N.W. 402, 404 (Minn. 1888), wrote:

> To the irrepressible spirit of curiosity and intermeddling of the average boy there is no limit to the objects which can be made attractive playthings. In the exercise of his youthful ingenuity, he can make a plaything out of almost anything, and then so use it as to expose himself to danger. If all this is to be charged to natural childish instincts, and the owners of property are to be required to anticipate and guard against it, the result would be that it would be unsafe for a man to own property, and the duty of the protection of children would be charged upon every member of the community except the parents or the children themselves.

Yet most courts, including the New Hampshire court in *Buch*, followed the lead of Sioux City & Pacific R.R. v. Stout, 84 U.S. 657, 661 (1873). The Supreme Court allowed the plaintiff, a six-year-old child, to recover when his foot was caught between the fixed rail of the roadbed and the turning rail of a turntable while playing with friends. The Court wrote that "if from the evidence given it might justly be inferred by the jury that the defendant, in the construction, location, management, or condition of its machine had omitted that care and attention to prevent the occurrence of accidents which prudent and careful men ordinarily bestow, the jury was at liberty to find for the plaintiff." See also Smith, Liability of Landowners to Children Entering Without Permission, 11 Harv. L. Rev. 349 (1898).

3. Restatement reformulation of the attractive nuisance doctrine. The Restatement (Second) of Torts continues to exert enormous influence on the law of attractive nuisance. It seeks to reconcile "the public interest in the possessor's free use of his own land for his own purposes" (comment *n*) with the general law of negligence.

§339. ARTIFICIAL CONDITIONS HIGHLY DANGEROUS TO TRESPASSING CHILDREN
A possessor of land is subject to liability for physical harm to children trespassing thereon caused by an artificial condition upon the land if

(a) the place where the condition exists is one upon which the possessor knows or has reason to know that children are likely to trespass, and

(b) the condition is one of which the possessor knows or has reason to know and which he realizes or should realize will involve an unreasonable risk of death or serious bodily harm to such children, and

(c) the children because of their youth do not discover the condition or realize the risk involved in intermeddling with it or in coming within the area made dangerous by it, and

(d) the utility to the possessor of maintaining the condition and the burden of eliminating the danger are slight as compared with the risk to children involved, and

(e) the possessor fails to exercise reasonable care to eliminate the danger or otherwise to protect the children.

In some sense, the rule marks a retreat from the broad position staked out in *Stout*. First, as stated, the rule only applies to "artificial conditions on the land." While the Restatement itself takes no position on whether §339 should apply to natural conditions, such as an ocean cove or steep cliff, most cases hold it does not.

Sometimes the categories get blurred. In Maalouf v. Swiss Confederation, 208 F. Supp. 2d 31, 41 (D.D.C. 2002), the plaintiff was a 12-year-old boy injured in a sledding accident that took place on the grounds of the Swiss Embassy when his sled struck a guy wire that was used to prop up a nearby tree. The Embassy had permitted sledding on its ground, and the plaintiff claimed that the guy wire was concealed from view. Assuming arguendo, that the plaintiff was a trespasser, Huvelle, J., allowed the case to go the jury on an attractive nuisance theory:

> defendant argues that the attractive nuisance doctrine does not apply because it covers only artificial, rather than natural, elements of the land. However, defendant blurs the distinction between the attractive condition that lures the child and the nuisance that threatens him, and the examples it cites of natural elements not found to be nuisances-such as a beach at high tide, rolling land, shrubs and trees, and an unguarded stream-all differ from the instant case because here, the nuisance itself is an artificial one placed on the hill by the defendant. Although plaintiff was attracted to defendant's land by a natural source (i.e., the hill), the nuisance-namely, the metal wire-was artificial. Under the attractive nuisance doctrine, the relevant element is not what attracts the child, but rather the nuisance itself.

What result if the plaintiff is classified a licensee?

Second, the section only applies when the owner "knows or has reason to know that children are likely to trespass." This phrase is used in opposition to the phrase "should know" and was adopted to make it clear that the possessor is under no duty to investigate the land to determine whether trespassing children are present.

Third, the assumption of risk language in clause (c) bars many claims. See, e.g., Holland v. Baltimore & Ohio R.R., 431 A.2d 597 (D.C. 1981), in which a defendant obtained a judgment notwithstanding the verdict against a nine-year-old plaintiff who was injured while jumping trains, on the ground that the dangers were obvious even to a child of his age. Similarly, in Merrill v. Central Maine Power Co., 628 A.2d 1062 (Me. 1993), a nine-year-old plaintiff could not recover when he climbed over a fence surrounding defendant's electrical power substation and badly burned himself while trying to cook an eel against a live wire.

Within this framework, the Restatement provisions offer, however, strong possibility for recovery by young children in more routine settings. In Carmona v. Hagerman Irrigation Co., 957 P.2d 44, 49 (N.M. 1998), the court reversed a summary judgment granted to the defendant irrigation company when a two-year-old boy drowned in a canal. Even though the court acknowledged that "it is virtually impossible to make an irrigation ditch inaccessible to trespassing children," it found genuine issues of fact under §339 that precluded holding that "all irrigation ditches are categorically exempted from the doctrine of attractive nuisance." In Kessler v. Mortenson, 16 P.3d 1225 (Utah 2000) the court let the jury find an attractive nuisance with a six-year-old boy at a residential construction site, noting that "homebuilders and landowners will be encouraged to minimize or eliminate dangers that trespassing children may be exposed to on the site." Finally, in Bennett v. Stanley, 748 N.E.2d 41 (Ohio 2001), the court embraced §339, holding that a swimming pool left unused for three years, filled with six feet of rainwater and covered with algae could constitute an attractive nuisance to a five-year-old child.

4. *Licensees versus invitees.* Even though classical common law devoted considerable ingenuity to refining the difference between a licensee and an invitee, a host of marginal cases remained. The late Professor Harper observed:

> When a customer goes into a store to buy something and actually makes the purchase, the problem is easy. But how about the person who is merely "shopping" or who accompanies a friend who makes a purchase or children who accompany their parents or one who drops into a hotel or store to go to the toilet or use the telephone, or to mail a letter? And what of a worker looking for a job which he may or may not get? Then there is the problem of public officials of one kind or another who enter another's premises, not with his permission, but because they have legal authority to do so in the discharge of their duties.

Harper, Laube v. Stevenson: A Discussion: Licensor-Licensee, 25 Conn. B. J. 123, 131 (1951).

One way to meet these difficulties is to focus not on the purpose of the visit but on the nature of the premises. Those who run business premises, or premises to which the public generally is invited, are subject to the rules for invitees; those who maintain private or residential premises are not. See Prosser, Business Visitors and Invitees, 26 Minn. L. Rev. 573 (1942), taking up this position, which has been adopted in the Restatement (Second) of Torts:

§332.   INVITEE DEFINED
(1) An invitee is either a public invitee or a business visitor.
(2) A public invitee is a person who is invited to enter or remain on land as a member of the public for a purpose for which the land is held open to the public.

(3) A business visitor is a person who is invited to enter or remain on land for a purpose directly or indirectly connected with business dealings with the possessor of the land.

Yet even under this view some hard cases remain because private understandings might be used to alter the background standard of care. In Lemon v. Busey, 461 P.2d 145 (Kan. 1969), a five-year-old child was brought to the defendant church by her grandmother, a part-time church employee. The arrangement was "for the convenience of her grandmother and parents" and the church at no time supervised the child. While her grandmother was busy at work, the child wandered off and fell to her death from a roof that she had probably reached through an unlocked elevator door or fire escape. The court held that she was a licensee and denied recovery.

With *Lemon* contrast Post v. Lunney, 261 So. 2d 146 (Fla. 1972). The plaintiff had paid five dollars to tour defendant Marjorie Merriweather Post's home where she "tripped on a piece of transparent vinyl which had been placed over a valuable oriental rug, and she fractured her hip." The trial judge called the plaintiff a licensee because the visit was not, as the older conception of invitee required, to their mutual economic advantage given that the five dollars paid by the plaintiff did not go to the defendant. The Florida Supreme Court rejected that contention and treated the plaintiff as a public invitee. Should it make any difference whether the vinyl was placed over the oriental rug solely in preparation for the tour?

Finally, in Knorpp v. Hale, 981 S.W.2d 469 (Tex. App. 1998), the court held that a decedent killed while cutting down the dead tree on the property of his girlfriend's family in anticipation of a New Year's Eve bonfire should not, as a matter of law, be treated as an invitee but a social guest who was not expecting payment for cutting down a tree located on private property. Would a professional, paid tree-cutter be barred by the assumption of risk defense even if classified as an invitee?

5. *Duties to licensees and invitees — slip-and-fall-cases.* Slip and fall cases offer a vivid contrast between the duties to licensees and invitees. The sources of danger in slip-and-fall cases are typically short-lived phenomena, such as spilled fluids. A licensor typically has no knowledge of these evanescent conditions and no duty to inspect for them, but lives instead in a self-help regime. The invitee's host has, however, an explicit duty to seek out and correct these conditions within a reasonable time after their occurrence. "Whether a dangerous condition has existed long enough for a reasonably prudent person to have discovered it is a question of fact for the jury, and the cases do not impose exact time limitations." Ortega v. Kmart Corp., 36 P.3d 11, 16 (Cal. 2001). That approach was also taken in Peterson v. Wal-Mart, 241 F.3d 603, 605 (7th Cir. 2001), where Posner, J., held that the jury should decide whether the employees in a busy Wal-Mart

store should be expected to clean up spilled fluids within ten minutes after they occurred. "There is no evidence that any of Wal-Mart's employees were aware of the spillage that caused the plaintiff's injury and failed to clean it up; and there is, as we have pointed out, no duty of continuous inspection. But neither is there any flat rule in Illinois that ten minutes is always too short a period for a duty of inspection and clean up to arise. . . ."

6. *Duties to firefighters, police officers, and other public officials.* The question of classification has also proved difficult for public officials who enter private property to discharge public duties without obtaining the landowner's consent. Given the difficulty of classifying public officials as either licensees or invitees, some writers have suggested that they be treated as a class of entrants sui generis. See, e.g., Bohlen, The Duty of a Landowner Towards Those Entering His Premises of Their Own Right, 69 U. Pa. L. Rev. 142, 237, 340 (1921). Today courts tend to classify public officials who arrive under ordinary circumstances — to collect garbage or to make routine inspections — as business visitors. Thus, in treating a police officer delivering a summons as an implied invitee, the court in Mounsey v. Ellard, 297 N.E.2d 43, 47 (Mass. 1973), observed:

> It seems logical to contend that if the trashman and mailman can rely on the appearance of safety of an intended mode of approach which they necessarily use in the performance of their official duties, the police officer should be afforded the same right. At the very least, [our cases] have established the occupier's and landowner's obligation to keep the access routes to his house in reasonably safe condition for those who are required to use them in the performance of their official duties. The mere fact that a policeman rather than a mailman delivered the criminal summons should not affect the standard of care owed by the occupier or owner. Thus, we could rest our decision in the instant case on the narrow ground that the plaintiff was an implied invitee to whom the defendants owed a duty to keep the route of access to their premises in reasonably safe condition.

The court went on to reject the common law classification of invitees and licensees, following the lead of the next case.

Rowland v. Christian
443 P.2d 561 (Cal. 1968)

[On November 30, 1963, the defendant, Nancy Christian, invited James Rowland to her apartment. While he was using the bathroom fixtures, the porcelain handle on one of the water faucets broke, severing the nerves and tendons of his right hand. The defendant knew of the crack in the faucet and two weeks before the incident had asked her landlord to repair it, but she did not warn the plaintiff of its dangerous condition. The defendant's affidavits did not show that the defect was "obvious or even nonconcealed" or that the plaintiff knew or had reason to know of the defect. The defendant moved for a summary judgment, alleging first that the plaintiff was a social guest and, second, that the twin defenses of assumption of risk and contributory negligence barred the action. The trial court granted the motion. Reversed.]

PETERS, J. . . . Section 1714 of the Civil Code provides: "Every one is responsible, not only for the result of his willful acts, but also for an injury occasioned to another by his want of ordinary care or skill in the management of his property or person, except so far as the latter has, willfully or by want of ordinary care, brought the injury upon himself. . . ." This code section, which has been unchanged in our law since 1872, states a civil law and not a common law principle.

Nevertheless, some common law judges and commentators have urged that the principle embodied in this code section serves as the foundation of our negligence law. Thus in a concurring opinion, Brett, M.R., in Heaven v. Pender (1883) 11 Q.B.D. 503, 509, states: "whenever one person is by circumstances placed in such a position with regard to another that every one of ordinary sense who did think would at once recognise that if he did not use ordinary care and skill in his own conduct with regard to those circumstances he would cause danger of injury to the person or property of the other, a duty arises to use ordinary care and skill to avoid such danger."

Although it is true that some exceptions have been made to the general principle that a person is liable for injuries caused by his failure to exercise reasonable care in the circumstances, it is clear that in the absence of statutory provision declaring an exception to the fundamental principle enunciated by section 1714 of the Civil Code, no such exception should be made unless clearly supported by public policy.

A departure from this fundamental principle involves the balancing of a number of considerations; the major ones are the foreseeability of harm to the plaintiff, the degree of certainty that the plaintiff suffered injury, the closeness of the connection between the defendant's conduct and the injury suffered, the moral blame attached to the defendant's conduct, the policy of preventing future harm, the extent of the burden to the defendant and consequences to the community of imposing a duty to exercise care with resulting liability for breach, and the availability, cost, and prevalence of insurance for the risk involved.

One of the areas where this court and other courts have departed from the fundamental concept that a man is liable for injuries caused by his carelessness is with regard to the liability of a possessor of land for injuries to persons who have entered upon that land. It has been suggested that the special rules regarding liability of the possessor of land are due to historical considerations stemming from the high place which land has traditionally held in English and American thought, the dominance and prestige of the landowning class in England during the formative period of the rules governing the possessor's liability, and the heritage of feudalism.

The departure from the fundamental rule of liability for negligence has been accomplished by classifying the plaintiff either as a trespasser, licensee, or invitee and then adopting special rules as to the duty owed by the possessor to each of the classifications. Generally speaking a trespasser is a person who enters or remains upon land of another without a privilege to do so; a licensee is a person like a social guest who is not an invitee and who is privileged to enter or remain upon land by virtue of the possessor's consent, and an invitee is a business visitor who is invited or permitted to enter or remain on the land for a purpose directly or indirectly connected with business dealings between them.

Although the invitor owes the invitee a duty to exercise ordinary care to avoid injuring him, . . . the general rule is that a trespasser and licensee or social guest are obliged to take the premises as they find them insofar as any alleged defective condition thereon may exist, and that the possessor of the land owes them only the duty of refraining from wanton or willful injury. The ordinary justification for the general rule severely restricting the occupier's liability to social guests is based on the theory that the guest should not expect special precautions to be made on his account and that if the host does not inspect and maintain his property the guest should not expect this to be done on his account.

An increasing regard for human safety has led to a retreat from this position, and an exception to the general rule limiting liability has been made as to active operations where an obligation to exercise reasonable care for the protection of the licensee has been imposed on the occupier of land. . . . In an apparent attempt to avoid the general rule limiting liability, courts have broadly defined active operations, sometimes giving the term a strained construction in cases involving dangers known to the occupier.

Thus in Hansen v. Richey, 46 Cal. Rptr. 909 [1965], an action for wrongful death of a drowned youth, the court held that liability could be predicated not upon the maintenance of a dangerous swimming pool but upon negligence "in the active conduct of a party for a large number of youthful guests in the light of knowledge of the dangerous pool." . . .

Another exception to the general rule limiting liability has been recognized for cases where the occupier is aware of the dangerous condition, the condition amounts to a concealed trap, and the guest is unaware of the trap. In none of these cases, however, did the court impose liability on the basis of a concealed trap; in some liability was found on another theory, and in others the court concluded that there was no trap. A trap has been defined as a "concealed" danger, a danger with a deceptive appearance of safety. It has also been defined as something akin to a spring gun or steel trap. . . . [I]t is pointed out that the lack of definiteness in the application of the term "trap" to any other situation makes its use argumentative and unsatisfactory.

The cases dealing with the active negligence and the trap exceptions are indicative of the subtleties and confusion which have resulted from application of the common law principles governing the liability of the possessor of land. Similar confusion and complexity exist as to the definitions of trespasser, licensee, and invitee.

In refusing to adopt the rules relating to the liability of a possessor of land for the law of admiralty, the United States Supreme Court stated: "The distinctions which the common law draws between licensee and invitee were inherited from a culture deeply rooted to the land, a culture which traced many of its standards to a heritage of feudalism. In an effort to do justice in an industrialized urban society, with its complex economic and individual relationships, modern common-law courts have found it necessary to formulate increasingly subtle verbal refinements, to create subclassifications among traditional common-law categories, and to delineate fine gradations in the standards of care which the landowner owes to each. Yet even within a single jurisdiction, the classifications and subclassifications bred by the common law have produced confusion and conflict. As new distinctions have been spawned, older ones have become obscured. Through this semantic morass the common law has moved, unevenly and with hesitation, towards 'imposing on owners and occupiers a single duty of reasonable care in all circumstances.'" (Footnotes omitted.) (Kermarec v. Compagnie Generale, 358 U.S. 625, 630-631 (1959). . . .

There is another fundamental objection to the approach to the question of the possessor's liability on the basis of the common law distinctions based upon the status of the injured party as a trespasser, licensee, or invitee. Complexity can be borne and confusion remedied where the underlying principles governing liability are based upon proper considerations. Whatever may have been the historical justifications for the common law distinctions, it is clear that those distinctions are not justified in the light of our modern society and that the complexity and confusion which has arisen is not due to difficulty in applying the original common law rules — they are all too easy to apply in their original formulation — but is due to the attempts to apply just rules in our modern society within the ancient terminology.

Without attempting to labor all of the rules relating to the possessor's liability, it is apparent that the classifications of trespasser, licensee, and invitee, the immunities from liability predicated upon those classifications, and the exceptions to those immunities, often do not reflect the major factors which should determine whether immunity should be conferred upon the possessor of land. Some of those factors, including the closeness of the connection between the injury and the defendant's conduct, the moral blame attached to the defendant's conduct, the policy of preventing future harm, and the prevalence and availability of insurance, bear little, if any, relationship to the classifications of trespasser, licensee, and invitee and the existing rules conferring immunity.

Although in general there may be a relationship between the remaining factors and the classifications of trespasser, licensee, and invitee, there are many cases in which no such relationship may exist. Thus, although the foreseeability of harm to an invitee would ordinarily seem greater than the foreseeability of harm to a trespasser, in a particular case the opposite may be true. The same may be said of the issue of certainty of injury. The burden to the defendant and consequences to the community of imposing a duty to exercise care with resulting liability for breach may often be greater with respect to trespassers than with respect to invitees, but it by no means follows that this is true in every case. In many situations, the burden will be the same, i.e., the conduct necessary upon the defendant's part to meet the burden of exercising due care as to invitees will also meet his burden with respect to licensees and trespassers. The last of the major factors, the cost of insurance, will, of course, vary depending upon the rules of liability adopted, but there is no persuasive evidence that applying ordinary principles of negligence law to the land occupier's liability will materially reduce the prevalence of insurance due to increased cost or even substantially increase the cost.

Considerations such as these have led some courts in particular situations to reject the rigid common law classifications and to approach the issue of the duty of the occupier on the basis of ordinary principles of negligence. (E.g., Gould v. DeBeve, 330 F.2d 826, 829-830 (1964).) And the common law distinctions after thorough study have been repudiated by the jurisdiction of their birth. (Occupiers' Liability Act, 1957, 5 and 6 Eliz. 2, ch. 31.)

A man's life or limb does not become less worthy of protection by the law nor a loss less worthy of compensation under the law because he has come upon the land of another without permission or with permission but without a business purpose. Reasonable people do not ordinarily vary their conduct depending upon such matters, and to focus upon the status of the injured party as a trespasser, licensee, or invitee in order to determine the question whether the landowner has a duty of care, is contrary to our modern social mores and humanitarian values. The common law rules obscure rather than illuminate the proper considerations which should govern determination of the question of duty. . . .

We decline to follow and perpetuate such rigid classifications. The proper test to be applied to the liability of the possessor of land in accordance with section 1714 of the Civil Code is whether in the management of his property he has acted as a reasonable man in view of the probability of injury to others, and, although the plaintiff's status as a trespasser, licensee, or invitee may in the light of the facts giving rise to such status have some bearing on the question of liability, the status is not determinative.

Once the ancient concepts as to the liability of the occupier of land are stripped away, the status of the plaintiff relegated to its proper place in determining such liability, and ordinary principles of negligence applied, the result in the instant case presents no substantial difficulties. As we have seen, when we view the matters presented on the motion for summary judgment as we must, we must assume defendant Miss Christian was aware that the faucet handle was defective and dangerous, that the defect was not obvious, and that plaintiff was about to come in contact with the defective condition, and under the undisputed facts she neither remedied the condition nor warned plaintiff of it. Where the occupier of land is aware of a concealed condition involving in the absence of precautions an unreasonable risk of harm to those coming in contact with it and is aware that a person on the premises is about to come in contact with it, the trier of fact can reasonably conclude that a failure to warn or to repair the condition constitutes negligence. Whether or not a guest has a right to expect that his host will remedy dangerous conditions on his account, he should reasonably be entitled to rely upon a warning of the dangerous condition so that he, like the host, will be in a position to take special precautions when he comes in contact with it. . . .

The judgment is reversed.

TRAYNOR, C.J., and TOBRINER, MOSK, and SULLIVAN, JJ., concur.

BURKE, J., dissenting. I dissent. In determining the liability of the occupier or owner of land for injuries, the distinctions between trespassers, licensees and invitees have been developed and applied by the courts over a period of many years. They supply a reasonable and workable approach to the problems involved, and one which provides the degree of stability and predictability so highly prized in the law. The unfortunate alternative, it appears to me, is the route taken by the majority in their opinion in this case that such issues are to be decided on a case by case basis under the application of the basic law of negligence, bereft of the guiding principles and precedent which the law has heretofore attached by a virtue of the relationship of the parties to one another.

Liability for negligence turns upon whether a duty of care is owed, and if so, the extent thereof. Who can doubt that the corner grocery, the large department store, or the financial institution owes a greater duty of care to one whom it has invited to enter its premises as a prospective customer of its wares or services than it owes to a trespasser seeking to enter after the close of business hours and for a nonbusiness or even an antagonistic purpose? I do not think it unreasonable or unfair that a social guest (classified by the law as a licensee, as was plaintiff here) should be obliged to take the premises in the same condition as his host finds them or permits them to be. Surely a homeowner should not be obliged to hover over his guests with warnings of possible dangers to be found in the condition of the home (e.g., waxed floors, slipping rugs, toys in unexpected places, etc., etc.). Yet today's decision appears to open the door to potentially unlimited liability despite the purpose and circumstances motivating the plaintiff in entering the premises of another, and despite the caveat of the majority that the status of the parties may "have some bearing on the question of liability . . . ," whatever the future may show that language to mean.

In my view, it is not a proper function of this court to overturn the learning, wisdom and experience of the past in this field. Sweeping modifications of tort liability law fall more suitably within the domain of the Legislature, before which all affected interests can be heard and which can enact statutes providing uniform standards and guidelines for the future.

I would affirm the judgment for defendant.

NOTES

1. *Response to Rowland v. Christian.* Is it necessary to abolish the distinction between licensees and invitees in order to deny the defendant's motion for summary judgment? Should Burke, J.'s, decision properly have been a concurrence? Note that prior to Rowland v. Christian, California had not accepted the standard view stated in §342 of the Restatement (Second) of Torts that the possessor of real property was under a duty to warn a licensee of concealed dangerous conditions. See, e.g., Fisher v. General Petroleum Corp., 267 P.2d 841 (Cal. App. 1954); Hansen v. Richey, 46 Cal. Rptr. 909 (Cal. App. 1965). On remand in *Rowland,* will the plaintiff be able to prevail if the defendant can show that the defect was patent? Will the defendant escape liability if the defect was concealed? Does it make a difference if Rowland's apartment was a pigsty when she moved in so that the crack in the faucet was concealed under grime? For a discussion of the origins and influence of the case, see Rabin, *Rowland v. Christian*: Hall Mark of an Expansionary Era, in Torts Stories 73 (2003).

Rowland v. Christian has received a mixed response elsewhere. In Mallet v. Pickens, 522 S.E.2d 436 (W. Va. 1999), West Virginia abandoned the invitee/licensee distinction, while preserving the traditional common law rules for trespassers. It summarized the current state of authority as follows:

> Broad generalizations about the state of premises liability law in other jurisdictions are always subject to caveats and limitations. Several states have special rules for invited social guests; others limit landowner liability via recreational use statutes, or employ a distinction between "active" and "passive" negligence. Having said that, our research reveals that at least 25 jurisdictions have abolished or largely abandoned the licensee/invitee distinction. Among these 25 jurisdictions that have broken with past tradition, at least 17 have eliminated or fundamentally altered the distinction. Another eight of the 25 have eliminated even the trespasser distinction. And, of those retaining the old scheme, judges in at least five of those states have authored vigorous dissents or concurrences arguing for change.

The courts that have defended the older distinctions have tended to do so without an elaborate statement of reasons. Thus, in Gladon v. Greater Cleveland Regional Transit Authority, 662 N.E.2d 287 (Ohio 1996), the court noted that it was "not inclined to reject" the classic distinctions. It held that a railroad passenger who exceeded the scope of his invitation by entering areas near the track lost his status as an invitee, and was properly treated as either a licensee or trespasser.

Those who have been critical of the established order have been more vocal. Thus, in Nelson v. Freeland, 507 S.E.2d 882, 888 (N.C. 1998), the court wrote:

> [J]urisdictions retaining the trichotomy fear that plaintiff-oriented juries — like feudal juries composed mostly of land entrants — will impose unreasonable burdens upon defendant-landowners. This argument, however, fails to take into account that juries have properly applied negligence principles in all other areas of tort law and there has been no indication that defendants in other areas have had unreasonable burdens placed upon them. Moreover, given that modern jurors are more likely than feudal jurors to be landowners themselves, it is unlikely that they would be unwilling to place a burden upon a defendant that they would be unwilling to accept upon themselves.
>
> Another fear held by jurisdictions retaining the trichotomy is that by substituting the negligence standard of care for the common-law categories, landowners will be forced to bear the burden of taking precautions such as the expensive cost associated with maintaining adequate insurance policies. This argument, however, ignores the fact that every court which has abolished the trichotomy has explicitly stated that its holding was not intended to make the landowner an absolute insurer against all injuries suffered on his property....

The court then asserted that the complexity of the older order robbed it of its predictability.

2. *Landlord's liability.* The application of the common law categories creates special problems with leased premises. In Sargent v. Ross, 308 A.2d 528, 531 (N.H. 1973), the court abolished the distinction between licensees and invitees, holding that a landlord owes a general duty of care to all persons on his premises. The previous law held the landlord liable in tort for injuries "resulting from defective and dangerous conditions in the premises if the injury [was] attributable to (1) a hidden danger in the premises of which the landlord but not the tenant is aware, (2) premises leased for public use, (3) premises retained under the landlord's control, such as common stairways, or (4) premises negligently repaired by the landlord." The New Hampshire Supreme Court completed the conversion to *Rowland* in Ouellette v. Blanchard, 364 A.2d 631, 634 (N.H. 1976), noting it was "not disposed to limit our holding to abolishment of two-thirds of the trichotomy and to retain the category of trespassers as a legal

area of immunity." But it did qualify its result by saying that "a landowner cannot be expected to maintain his premises in a safe condition for a wandering tramp or a person who enters against the known wishes of the landowner."

Under *Rowland*, should courts adopt a strict liability standard of landlord liability for the protection of tenants? In Becker v. IRM Corp., 698 P.2d 116, 122-123 (Cal. 1985), plaintiff slipped and fell against an untempered shower door and severely lacerated his arm. It was undisputed that the defect was latent and that a door made of tempered glass would have substantially reduced the risk of injury. The plaintiff settled his suit against the door assembler and the builder, and proceeded on a strict liability action against the defendant landlord, who had purchased the building from a prior owner. Broussard J., held the landlord strictly liable for latent defects by analogy to the product liability cases. *Becker* left open two questions: first, whether the doctrine of strict liability applies to patent defects, and second, whether "the landlord is strictly liable for defects in the property which develop after the property is leased." The California Court of Appeals refused to extend *Becker*'s strict liability rule to commercial lessors in Muro v. Superior Court (Anjac Fashion Building, Inc., RPI), 229 Cal. Rptr. 383 (Cal. App. 1986), noting the abundance of commercial real estate. Peterson v. Superior Court (Banque Paribus, RPI), 899 P.2d 905, 906 (Cal. 1995), overruled *Becker* and returned California to the general negligence rule.

> [W]e conclude that we erred in *Becker* in applying the doctrine of strict products liability to a residential landlord that is not a part of the manufacturing or marketing enterprise of the allegedly defective product that caused the injury in question. . . . [W]e also conclude that it would be improper to impose strict liability under products liability principles upon a hotel proprietor for injuries caused by an alleged defect in the hotel premises that the hotel proprietor did not create or market. Accordingly, we overrule that portion of our decision in *Becker* imposing strict products liability, and hold that neither landlords nor hotel proprietors are strictly liable on a products liability theory for injuries to their respective tenants and guests caused by a defect in the premises.

Why?

3. *Duties to trespassers after Rowland v. Christian.* As noted above, *Rowland* has met with greater resistance on its extension of the ordinary duty of care to trespassers. Thus, the Minnesota Supreme Court, in Peterson v. Balach, 199 N.W.2d 639, 642 (Minn. 1972), observed:

> [T]he considerations governing a landowner's or occupant's liability to trespassers may be fundamentally different from his duty to those whom he has expressly or by implication invited onto his property. Burglars are trespassers; vandals are trespassers. We have criminal statutes governing

trespassers. Minn. St. 609.605. Sweeping away all distinction between trespassers and social guests and business invitees is a drastic step to take because there may be, and often is, good reason to distinguish between a trespasser and a social guest. There is little or no reason to distinguish between a social guest and a business invitee.

The Massachusetts Supreme Judicial Court, however, cast its lot with *Rowland* in Pridgen v. Boston Housing Authority, 308 N.E.2d 467, 476-477 (Mass. 1974). The plaintiff, an 11-year-old boy, lifted an escape hatch in the ceiling of an elevator and climbed into the elevator shaft. He slipped off the elevator roof and became trapped. His mother, having learned of her son's predicament, asked one of the defendant's servants to turn off "the lights" to keep her son from being injured, but he failed to shut down the power in time to prevent the boy's legs from being crushed by the moving elevator. The court, much troubled by the influence of the good Samaritan doctrine on the common law, observed:

> In the context of the relationship between an owner or occupier (owner) of the property and a trapped, imperiled and helpless trespasser thereon, we reject any rule which would exempt the owner from liability if he knowingly refrains from taking reasonable action which he is in a position to take and which would prevent injury or further injury to the trespasser. It should not be, it cannot be, and surely it is not now the law of this Commonwealth that the owner in such a situation is rewarded with immunity from liability as long as he ignores the plight of the trapped trespasser and takes no affirmative action to help him. Thus, in the case before us it is unthinkable to have a rule which would hold the authority liable if one of its employees, acting in the course of his employment, pushed the "go" button on the elevator although he knew Joseph Pridgen was trapped in the elevator shaft, but would not hold it liable if, being reasonably able to do so, the employee knowingly failed or refused to turn off the switch to the electrical power for the same elevator.

Is the result in *Pridgen* consistent with the statutory treatment of the good Samaritan problem, *supra* at 575, which only holds a rescuer liable on proof of willful misconduct, recklessness, or gross negligence? How ought *Pridgen* be decided under Addie v. Dumbreck or under Excelsior Wire Rope Ltd. v. Callan?

Still other states have flip-flopped on the question. Thus, in Mariorenzi v. Joseph DiPonte, Inc., 333 A.2d 127, 133 n.4 (R.I. 1975), the court stressed the malleable nature of the categories to abolish the special rules toward trespassers.

> A canvasser who comes on your premises without your consent is a trespasser. Once he has your consent, he is a licensee. Not until you do business with him is he an invitee. Even when you have done business with him, it

seems rather strange that your duty towards him should be different when he comes up to your door from what it is when he goes away. Does he change his colour in the middle of the conversation? What is the position when you discuss business with him and it comes to nothing? No confident answer can be given to these questions. Such is the morass into which the law has floundered in trying to distinguish between licensees and invitees.

Twenty years later, in Tantimonico v. Allendale Mutual Insurance Co., 637 A.2d 1056, 1061 (R.I. 1994), the boundary questions did not look so pressing, and the court backed off with respect to trespassers. It denied recovery to two trespassing motorcyclists who apparently collided head-on while riding in opposite directions on defendant's circular trail. "It is almost impossible to entertain the notion that anyone other than plaintiffs themselves is responsible for their injuries. To hold the property owner liable for injuries brought about by a plaintiff's negligent behavior would be patently ludicrous."

4. *Statutory abolition of the invitee/licensee distinction.* In some cases, the abolition of the categories is done by statute. The first move in this direction took place in England with the Occupiers' Liability Act, 1957 (5 & 6 Eliz. II, c. 31), which abolished the distinction between invitees and licensees but left untouched the rules governing the occupier's liability to trespassers. Likewise Illinois (740 Ill. Comp. Stat. Ann. 130/2 (2007)) abolishes the distinction between invitees and licensees and toughens up on the standard of liability, by noting that "[t]he duty of reasonable care under the circumstances which an owner or occupier of land owes to such entrants does not include any of the following: a duty to warn of or otherwise take reasonable steps to protect such entrants from conditions on the premises that are known to the entrant, are open and obvious, or can reasonably be expected to be discovered by the entrant; a duty to warn of latent defects or dangers or defects or dangers unknown to the owner or occupier of the premises; or a duty to protect such entrants from their own misuse of the premises or anything affixed to or located on the premises."

In Ward v. K-Mart Corp., 554 N.E.2d 223, 230-231, 233 (Ill. 1990), the plaintiff sustained injuries to his face and partial loss of vision when he walked into a concrete post located about 19 inches from the rear wall of the K-Mart store. On entering the store, plaintiff had noticed the post, but he had forgotten about it momentarily while leaving the store carrying a large bathroom mirror that obscured his view. A jury verdict for the plaintiff for $68,000 was overruled by the trial court, but was reinstated by the Illinois Supreme Court. Ryan, J., refused to hold that the defendant had automatically discharged its duty of care for dangerous conditions that are open and obvious, saying:

> [I]n the case at bar it was reasonably foreseeable that a customer would collide with the post while exiting defendant's store carrying merchandise

which could obscure view of the post. . . . It should be remembered that the post was located immediately outside the entrance to the Home Center section of defendant's store. Defendant had every reason to expect that customers would carry large, bulky items through that door, particularly where, as here, the large overhead door was closed. The burden on the defendant of protecting against this danger would be slight. A simple warning or a relocation of the post may have sufficed. It is also relevant that there were no windows or transparent panels on the customer entrance doors to permit viewing of the posts from the interior of the store.

Could this defect be treated as latent to the plaintiff even if patent to the world?

5. *Recreational land statutes.* Many states have also passed statutes that relax the liability of owners for recreational or rural lands. In 1963, California passed a "premises guest statute," Civil Code §846 (2007), under which "the landowner's duty to the nonpaying, uninvited recreational user is, in essence, that owed a trespasser under the common law as it existed prior to Rowland v. Christian." Ornelas v. Randolph, 847 P.2d 560, 562, 564 (Cal. 1993). *Ornelas*, then held that "'recreational' injury may result as readily from playing on a manmade object as on a natural edifice. Therefore, for our purposes here, clambering about on farm equipment is no different in kind from scaling a cliff or climbing a tree."

Another statute in this class, N.J. Stat. Ann. §§2A:42A-3 et seq. (West 2007), provides:

> a. An owner, lessee or occupant of premises, whether or not posted . . . and whether or not improved or maintained in a natural condition, or used as part of a commercial enterprise, owes no duty to keep the premises safe for entry or use by others for sport and recreational activities, or to give warning of any hazardous condition of the land or in connection with the use of any structure or by reason of any activity on such premises to persons entering for such purposes;
>
> b. An owner, lessee or occupant of premises who gives permission to another to enter upon such premises for a sport or recreational activity or purpose does not thereby (1) extend any assurance that the premises are safe for such purpose, or (2) constitute the person to whom permission is granted an invitee to whom a duty of care is owed, or (3) assume responsibility for or incur liability for any injury to person or property caused by any act of persons to whom the permission is granted.

"Sport and recreational activities" as statutory terms are to "be liberally construed to serve as an inducement to the owners, lessees and occupants of property, that might otherwise be reluctant to do so for fear of liability, to permit persons to come onto their property for sport and recreational activities." *Id.* §2A:42A-5.1 This statute did not, however, protect a landowner against suit by a good Samaritan who drowned while trying to rescue two 15-year-old boys who had fallen through thin ice on the defendant's reservoir on the first day of the skating season because the rescuer was not engaged in recreational activities. Harrison v. Middlesex Water Co., 403 A.2d 910, 914 (N.J. 1979).

See generally Barrett, Good Sports and Bad Lands: The Application of Washington's Recreational Use Statute Limiting Landowner Liability, 53 Wash. L. Rev. 1 (1977).

6. *Duties to strangers after Rowland v. Christian. Rowland* has also impacted the liability of owners and occupiers to persons who have not entered their land. As in attractive nuisance cases, a critical distinction is between natural and artificial conditions upon the land. Artificial conditions raise no special problems because they satisfy the normal "act" requirement of both negligence and strict liability theories. Natural conditions are more problematic because now the "act" requirement is not (at least not obviously) satisfied. Nor can any stranger rely upon affirmative duties born of the informal consensual arrangements with invitees and licensees. In consequence, the duty issue becomes a stumbling block in the path of the stranger's recovery.

Most American cases refuse to impose liability for natural conditions, except harm caused by falling trees. See, e.g., Taylor v. Olsen, 578 P.2d 779 (Or. 1978). See also Noel, Nuisances from Land in Its Natural Condition, 56 Harv. L. Rev. 772, 796-797 (1943), in which the author observed: "Where a planted tree has become dangerous to persons on the highway or on adjoining land, and causes harm, the fault lies not in the planting of the tree but in permitting it to remain after it has become unsafe."

The judicial acceptance of a no-liability regime for natural conditions has decreased in recent years, at least in urban settings. In Sprecher v. Adamson Co., 636 P.2d 1121, 1125, 1126 (Cal. 1981), the court was prepared to impose an affirmative duty on one Malibu landowner to prevent a mudslide after heavy rains that would damage the home of his downhill neighbor. Bird, C.J., showed her obvious hostility to the misfeasance-nonfeasance distinction at common law and placed heavy reliance upon Rowland v. Christian. "In rejecting the common law rule of non-liability for natural conditions, the courts have recognized the inherent injustice involved in a rule which states that 'a landowner may escape all liability for serious damage to his neighbors [or those using a public highway], merely by allowing nature to take its course.' . . . Whatever the rule may once have been, it is now clear that a duty to exercise due care can arise out of possession alone." Richardson, J., concurring, found it "exceedingly difficult to imagine what respondents *reasonably* could have done to prevent or reduce the damage caused by the natural condition here present." *Id.* at 1136.

Sprecher was relied on in Whitt v. Silverman, 788 So. 2d 210 (Fla. 2001), which involved a much more conventional problem. One pedestrian was killed and another injured when struck by a driver leaving the defendant's gas station. The driver's view of the highway was obscured by heavy foliage located exclusively on the defendant's property. The court refused to follow the so-called agrarian rule, whereby a landowner owes no duty of care to a stranger for harm caused by the natural condition of his land. The owners of ordinary businesses have specific knowledge of the "continuous flow of traffic entering and exiting the premises for the commercial benefit of the landowners," where their control over their own premises undercuts any claim "that it would have been unduly burdensome for the landowners to have maintained this foliage consistent with the safe egress and ingress of vehicles attracted to the business and persons affect thereby."

SECTION D. GRATUITOUS UNDERTAKINGS

Coggs v. Bernard
92 Eng. Rep. 107 (K.B. 1703)

[The action was brought in assumpsit, Latin, for "he has undertaken," which allowed for the recovery of damages for breach of a simple contract. The defendant had moved casks of brandy owned by the plaintiff from one cellar to another. Through the defendant's negligence, some of the casks were split open and great quantities of brandy were lost. The defendant sought to overturn the judgment in plaintiff's favor because plaintiff had not alleged that the defendant was a common porter or that he had received any reward or consideration. Notwithstanding, the plaintiff had judgment.]

GOULD, J. I think this is a good declaration. The objection that has been made is, because there is not any consideration laid. But I think it is good either way, and that any man, that undertakes to carry goods, is liable to an action, be he a common carrier, or whatever he is, if through his neglect they are lost, or come to any damage: and if a praemium be laid to be given, then it is without question so. The reason of the action is, the particular trust reposed in the defendant, to which he has concurred by his assumption, and in the executing which he has miscarried by his neglect. But if a man undertakes to build a house, without any thing to be had for his pains, an action will not lie for non-performance, because it is nudum pactum. . . .

HOLT, C.J. . . .

[After his review of the different types of bailments, discussed *supra* at 175, he continues]: [i]f it had appeared that the mischief happened by any person that met the cart in the way, the bailee had not been chargeable. As if a drunken man had come by in the streets, and had pierced the cask of brandy; in this case the defendant had not been answerable for it, because he was to have nothing for his pains. Then the bailee having undertaken to manage the goods and having managed them ill, and so by his neglect a damage had happened to the bailor, which is the case in question, what will you call this?

In Bracton, lib. 3,100, it is called *mandatum*. It is an obligation which arises *ex mandato*. It is what we call in English an acting commission. And if a man acts by his commission for another and in executing his commission behaves himself negligently, he is answerable . . . [I]t is supported by good reason and authority. The reasons are, first, because in such a case, a neglect is a deceit to the bailor. For when he intrusts the bailee upon his undertaking to be careful, he has put a fraud upon the plaintiff by being negligent, his pretence of care being the persuasion that induced the plaintiff to trust him. And a breach of a trust undertaken voluntarily will be a ground for an action. . . .

But secondly it is objected, that there is no consideration to ground this promise upon, and therefore the undertaking is but *nudum pactum*. But to this I answer, that the owner's trusting him with the goods is a sufficient consideration to oblige him to a careful management. Indeed if the agreement had been executory, to carry these brandies from the one place to the other such a day, the defendant had not been bound to carry them. But this is a different case, for *assumpsit* does not only signify a future agreement, but in such a case as this, it signifies an actual entry upon the thing, and taking the trust upon himself. And if a man will do that, and miscarries in the performance of his trust, an action will lie against him for that, though no body could have compelled him to do the thing.

NOTES

1. Contract without consideration. Coggs v. Bernard, discussed *supra* at 175, Note 2, on the issue of degrees of negligence, bears as well on the question of whether gratuitous promises can be a source of affirmative duties. Holt, C.J., attacks this point in two ways. He first claims that the case has overtones of deceit and pretence, both of which seem to be unlikely on the facts on the case. But if the former were proved, then the second issue, the absence of consideration, would be of no avail. Yet precisely because the allegation of deceit is fictionalized, the crux of the matter turns on consideration. Is the court right that consideration can be "found" in this essentially gratuitous transaction given that the general formula requires a benefit to the promisor or a detriment to the promisee? Note too that civil law treats these cases as contract cases without invoking the idea of consideration. Thus, the Roman learning on bailments, extensively relied upon by Lord Holt in Coggs v. Bernard, allows the plaintiff to recover on contractual grounds for the improper performance of the duty even though the promisor can withdraw if he changes his mind before performance was due. The doctrine of consideration, which in its heyday was the exclusive test for enforceable contractual promises at the common law, functions in the civil law mainly as the test for enforceability of fully executory agreements, not as the test of whether there was a contract at all.

The interaction between tort and contract is illustrated again by the famous early case of Thorne v. Deas, 4 Johns. Cas. 84 (N.Y. Sup. Ct. 1809). The plaintiff was captain of a ship and, as he was about to leave on a voyage, he suggested to his co-owner, the defendant, that they insure the ship before leaving. Defendant told plaintiff to go ahead and sail—that he would insure the ship on plaintiff's departure. Relying on defendant's promise, plaintiff left port. Defendant failed to insure the ship, which was subsequently wrecked. On his return home, plaintiff sued defendant for his loss. The court denied recovery, Chief Justice Kent, following the rule announced by Gould, J., noted that this was "an action on the case, for a *non-feasance*" and that it could not lie because of "the want of a consideration for the promise." Kent observed, however, that the plaintiff's case was good under Roman contract law. As mentioned in *Coggs,* the contract of mandate—a gratuitous promise to undertake something to the benefit of the promisee or a third party—gave rise to a good prima facie case even with the absence of consideration.

Because the contract option was foreclosed by the English consideration rules, the plaintiff tried to frame his action in tort. Kent held that the law could not first deny recovery for breach of a promise unsupported by consideration and turn around and allow recovery on the same facts by calling defendant's conduct a tort. However, plaintiff could recover, according to Kent, by showing that defendant had engaged in misfeasance—had actually started to perform and had done so negligently. Would the actions (incorrectly filling out papers) of the defendant have been tortious without reference to the former promise? If not, why does the ineffective promise make these ministerial mishaps actionable? What if defendant fails to finish the job he started, as by failing to supply the insurer with a certificate of title?

2. *Promissory estoppel.* Section 90 of the Restatement (Second) of Contracts provides:

§90. PROMISE REASONABLY INDUCING ACTION OR FORBEARANCE

   (1) A promise which the promisor should reasonably expect to induce action or forbearance on the part of the promisee or a third person and which does induce such action or forbearance is binding if injustice can be avoided only by enforcement of the promise. The remedy granted for breach may be limited as justice requires.

Does this section help the plaintiff in Coggs v. Bernard or Thorne v. Deas? On §90 and this area in general see Seavey, Reliance upon Gratuitous Promises or Other Conduct, 64 Harv. L. Rev. 913, 926-927 (1951), who observed: "The colloquial explanation for the rule of the section is that it creates 'promissory estoppel.' Estoppel is basically a tort doctrine and the rationale of the section is that justice requires the defendant to pay for the harm caused by foreseeable reliance upon the performance of his promise. The wrong is not primarily in depriving the plaintiff of the promised reward but in causing the plaintiff to change position to his detriment. . . . In a case like Thorne v. Deas, however, the continuing representation becomes fraudulent when the promisor decides not to perform and does not inform the plaintiff, knowing that he still relies upon performance." What if the defendant simply forgot his promise?

The question of reliance is usually raised in connection with simple promises from one person to another with respect to future undertakings. How should the ideas of reliance on voluntary undertakings be applied when made to the public at large? When made to individuals whom the defendant has already harmed? The next two cases address these points.

Erie Railroad Co. v. Stewart
40 F.2d 855 (6th Cir. 1930)

HICKENLOOPER, C.J. Stewart, plaintiff below, was a passenger in an automobile truck, sitting on the front seat to the right of the driver, a fellow employee of the East Ohio Gas Company. He recovered a judgment in the District Court for injuries received when the truck was struck by one of the defendant's trains at the 123d Street crossing in the city of Cleveland. Defendant maintained a watchman at this crossing, which was admittedly heavily traveled, but the watchman was either within the shanty or just outside of it as the train approached, and he gave no warning until too late to avoid the accident. . . .

The second contention of appellant presents the question whether the court erred in charging the jury that the absence of the watchman, where one had been maintained by the defendant company at a highway crossing over a long period of time to the knowledge of the plaintiff, would constitute negligence as a matter of law. In the present case it is conceded that the employment of the watchman by the defendant was voluntary upon its part, there being no statute or ordinance requiring the same, and that plaintiff had knowledge of this practice and relied upon the absence of the watchman as an assurance of safety and implied invitation to cross. We are not now concerned with the extent of the duty owing to one who had no notice of the prior practice, nor, in this aspect of the case, with the question of contributory negligence and the extent to which the plaintiff was relieved from the obligation of vigilance by the absence of the watchman. The question is simply whether there was any positive duty owing to the plaintiff in respect to the maintenance of such watchman, and whether a breach of such duty is so conclusively shown as to justify a peremptory charge of negligence. The question whether such negligence was the proximate cause of the injury was properly submitted to the jury.

Where the employment of a watchman or other precaution is required by statute, existence of an absolute duty to the plaintiff is conclusively shown, and failure to observe the statutory requirement is negligence per se.... Conversely, where there is no duty prescribed by statute or ordinance, it is usually a question for the jury whether the circumstances made the employment of a watchman necessary in the exercise of due care. Where the voluntary employment of a watchman was unknown to the traveler upon the highway, the mere absence of such watchman could probably not be considered as negligence toward him as a matter of law, for in such case there is neither an established duty positively owing to such traveler as a member of the general public, nor had he been led into reliance upon the custom. The question would remain simply whether the circumstances demanded such employment. But where the practice is known to the traveler upon the highway, and such traveler has been educated into reliance upon it, some positive duty must rest upon the railway with reference thereto. The elements of invitation and assurance of safety exist in this connection no less than in connection with contributory negligence. The company has established for itself a standard of due care while operating its trains across the highway, and, having led the traveler into reliance upon such standard, it should not be permitted thereafter to say that no duty required, arose from or attached to these precautions.

This duty has been recognized as not only actual and positive, but as absolute, in the sense that the practice may not be discontinued without exercising reasonable care to give warning of such discontinuance, although the company may thereafter do all that would otherwise be reasonably necessary. Conceding for the purposes of this opinion that, in cases where a watchman is voluntarily employed by the railway in an abundance of precaution, the duty is not absolute, in the same sense as where it is imposed by statute, still, if there be some duty, it cannot be less than that the company must use reasonable care to see that reliance by members of the educated public upon its representation of safety is not converted into a trap. Responsibility for injury will arise if the service be negligently performed or abandoned without other notice of that fact....

So, in the present case, the evidence conclusively establishes the voluntary employment of a watchman, knowledge of this fact and reliance upon it by the plaintiff, a duty, therefore, that the company, through the watchman, will exercise reasonable care in warning such travelers as plaintiff, the presence of the watchman thereabouts, and no explanation of the failure to warn. Therefore, even though the duty be considered as qualified, rather than absolute, a prima facie case was established by plaintiff, requiring the defendant to go forward with evidence to rebut the presumption of negligence thus raised, or else suffer a verdict against it on this point. . . . No such evidence was introduced by defendant. No other inference than that of negligence could therefore be drawn from the evidence. If, perhaps, the rule was stated more broadly than this in the charge, the error, if any, was harmless as applied to the present case. . . .

[Affirmed.]

TUTTLE, J. I concur in the result reached by the opinion of the majority of the court. I cannot, however, concur in the views, expressed in that opinion, which would make the actionable negligence of the defendant dependent upon the knowledge of the plaintiff, previous to his injury, of the custom of the defendant in maintaining a watchman at the crossing where such injury occurred. It is settled law that a railroad company operating trains at high speed across a public highway owes to travelers properly using such highway the duty to exercise reasonable care to give such warning of approaching trains as may be reasonably required by the particular circumstances. It is equally well settled that the standard of duty thus owed to the public, at least where not otherwise prescribed by statutory law, consists of that care and prudence which an ordinarily prudent person would exercise under the same circumstances. I am satisfied that where, as here, a railroad company has established a custom, known to the general public, of maintaining a watchman at a public crossing with instructions to warn the traveling public of the approach of trains, such railroad company, in the exercise of that reasonable care which it owes to the public, should expect, and is bound to expect, that any member of the traveling public approaching such crossing along the public highway is likely to have knowledge of and to rely upon the giving of such warning. Such knowledge, with the consequent reliance, may be acquired by a traveler at any time, perhaps only a moment before going upon the crossing, and this also the railroad company is bound to anticipate. Having, in effect, given notice to the public traveling this highway that it would warn them of trains at this crossing, I think that it was bound to assume (at least in the absence of knowledge to the contrary) that every member of such public would receive, and rely on, such notice. Under such circumstances such a railroad company, in my opinion, owes to every traveler so approaching this crossing a duty to give such a warning, if reasonably possible, and a reasonably prudent railroad company would not fail, without sufficient cause, to perform that duty. It follows that the unexplained failure, as in the present case, of the defendant to give this customary warning to the plaintiff, a traveler on the highway approaching this crossing, indicates, as a matter of law, actionable negligence for which it is liable. While undoubtedly lack of reliance by plaintiff upon the custom of the defendant has an important bearing and effect upon the question whether the plaintiff was guilty of contributory negligence, it seems to me clear that the knowledge or lack of knowledge of the plaintiff, unknown to the defendant, concerning such customs cannot affect the nature or extent of the duty owed to the plaintiff by the defendant or the performance of such duty. As therefore the conclusions expressed in the opinion of a majority of the court are, to the extent which I have thus indicated, not in accord with my own views in this connection, I have felt it my duty to briefly state such views in this separate concurring opinion.

NOTE

The scope of voluntary undertakings. What exactly is the point of disagreement between Judges Hickenlooper and Tuttle? If reliance is required in cases where promises or representations are made to a single person, should any member of the public who is injured be required to show that she was aware of the prior practice in order to make good her claim for "negative" reliance.

The limits of *Erie Railroad* are evident in Martin v. Twin Falls School District #411, 59 P.3d 317 (Idaho 2002). There the plaintiff children were struck by a pick-up truck driven by one Ryan Canoy as they were walking through a designated school crossing, properly equipped with signs and flashing lights, located about two blocks from their school. The plaintiffs claimed that the School District had a duty to supply crossing guards at this intersection because it had provided crossing guards at other intersections. Eismann, J., rejected that contention, noting: "By providing crossing guards at certain intersections or pedestrian crossings, the school district did not thereby assume the duty to provide guards at any other intersections or crossings." This decision is approved in the Third Restatement, which notes: The scope of an undertaking can be determined only from the facts and circumstances of the case. When reasonable minds can differ about whether the risk or negligence was within the scope of the undertaking, it is a question of fact for the factfinder. RTT:LPH §42, comment *g*.

Marsalis v. LaSalle
94 So. 2d 120 (La. App. 1957)

McBRIDE, J. Plaintiffs bring this suit for damages against Shelby P. LaSalle, the defendant, as a result of Mrs. Marsalis' having been bitten or scratched by a Siamese cat on January 12, 1953, in a store in Jefferson Parish, of which the defendant is proprietor, the occurrence having taken place while Mrs. Marsalis, who was accompanied by her husband, was shopping. The cat is the pet of defendant's minor son. Mrs. Marsalis is asserting her claim for personal injuries and her husband is seeking reimbursement of the cost of the medical treatment of his wife. From a judgment in favor of plaintiffs, defendant appeals.

While the testimony on the point is in conflict, we believe that it preponderates to the effect that after Mrs. Marsalis sustained her injury, Marsalis requested defendant to keep the cat under observation for fourteen days until it could be determined whether the animal was rabid and what medical precautions Mrs. Marsalis should take against being infected by rabies. We quote Marsalis' words: . . .

"I asked him to keep the cat up, to lock it up, and he said he would. . . ."

At any rate, on the evening of the fourth or fifth day after the episode in the grocery store the cat escaped and the only explanation given is by Mrs. LaSalle, who testified that this occurred as she and some friends were making their exit via the basement door. The cat was gone for about a month, and in the meantime its whereabouts was not known. Upon returning home the animal gave no evidence whatever of being infected.

Two days after she had sustained the injuries, Mrs. Marsalis sought advice from her friend and neighbor, Dr. Homer Kirgis, whose specialty is in the medical field of neurosurgery. He thought Mrs. Marsalis should first determine whether the cat had been inoculated and then consult her family physician. When it was learned a few days later that the animal had strayed from defendant's premises, Dr. Kirgis urged Mrs. Marsalis to see her family doctor and admonished her to contact the Pasteur Treatment Ward of the Charity Hospital in New Orleans. However, Dr. Kirgis subsequently undertook to administer the Pasteur treatment himself at his home, the first injection being made about January 23, 1953. This treatment consists of a number of injections of a prophylactic vaccine for rabies and we are informed that some persons are extremely allergic to the serum. Mrs. Marsalis was evidently in this category as she suffered a noxious reaction to the serum which brought about some ill effects. . . .

It is uncontroverted that there is no liability in defendant merely because the cat bit or scratched Mrs. Marsalis. Never before had the animal exhibited any vicious traits or tendencies and it had been, as the court found, a gentle and well-behaved pet and defendant was guilty of no negligence in allowing it to frequent his premises.

[The court then referred to a number of cases standing for the proposition "that one who voluntarily undertakes to care for, or to afford relief or assistance to, an ill, injured, or helpless person is under a legal obligation to use reasonable care and prudence in what he does."]

Our belief is that the above-discussed rule with respect to the duties of one who voluntarily undertakes to care for or to afford relief or assistance to an injured or distressed person is broad enough to have full application to the instant case. Perhaps the defendant, LaSalle, initially owed no duty whatever to Mrs. Marsalis, but when he once agreed to restrain and keep the cat under observation, he was bound to use reasonable care and prudence in doing so and to assume and exercise reasonable care and common humanity. It may be that Mrs. Marsalis had open to her some other course by which she could have had the cat incarcerated and examined in order to determine if it was rabid, but she unquestionably and in good faith relied upon defendant to carry out the agreement which he voluntarily made, thus foregoing such other possible available protection. It was of extreme importance to know if the cat had rabies so she could regulate her course of conduct with reference to the injury. We do not doubt for one moment that both defendant and his wife were fully cognizant that such injuries could be quite serious and exceedingly dangerous in the event the offending animal was infected with rabies. In fact we feel sure of our ground in saying this because of the statement of Mrs. LaSalle: "I have got that much sense to know that if a cat ever scratches anybody — ."

LaSalle's liability would then depend on whether he used reasonable care with reference to keeping the cat, for as it developed later the Pasteur treatment was entirely unnecessary and the escape of the cat was the direct and proximate cause of the necessity for the injections and the ill effects which Mrs. Marsalis suffered as a result thereof.

Neither defendant nor his wife took any especial steps or means to prevent the cat from straying from their premises. The cat, which was three years old, had always been kept in the basement and was allowed access to the yard from time to time. No change whatever in the animal's usual routine was undertaken and we must hold that defendant failed to use ordinary or reasonable care to see to it that the animal was kept secure, and, hence, defendant is liable unto plaintiffs for whatever damages they sustained as a result of such lack of care. [The court then discussed some of the medical testimony and proceeded as follows:]

However, Dr. Kirgis' testimony is sufficient to show that Mrs. Marsalis reacted unfavorably during the course of the injections, and it appears that she suffered headaches, fever, disorientation and nausea, and, of course, she is entitled to recover damages from the defendant, not only because she was compelled to submit to the fourteen injections, but also because of the effects of her reaction. The trial judge set her recovery at $3,000, but we believe that this award is excessive in view of the failure of Mrs. Marsalis to prove that her hospital stays and the attention rendered her by Dr. Mattingly were a result of the administration of the Pasteur injections.

NOTE

Reliance in action. In light of the decision in *Montgomery* and RTT §39, *supra* at 579, is the voluntary undertaking necessary to impose the duty of care on the LaSalles? What result in *Marsalis* if the defendant's cat had in fact been rabid?

The Restatement (Second) of Torts provides:

§323.   NEGLIGENT PERFORMANCE OF UNDERTAKING TO RENDER SERVICES

One who undertakes, gratuitously or for consideration, to render services to another which he should recognize as necessary for the protection of the other's person or things, is subject to liability to the other for physical harm resulting from his failure to exercise reasonable care to perform his undertaking, if

(a) his failure to exercise such care increases the risk of such harm, or

(b) the harm is suffered because of the other's reliance upon the undertaking.

See also RTT:LPH §42. This principle is frequently invoked today in suits against the government for breach of its various regulatory duties. In the leading case of Indian Towing v. United States, 350 U.S. 61, 64-65 (1955), the U.S. Coast Guard operated a lighthouse whose light was negligently allowed to go out, whereupon the plaintiff's barge ran aground. The plaintiff brought suit under the Federal Tort Claims Act that imposes upon the government the duties of a private party acting under like circumstances. Frankfurter, J., allowed the cause of action, noting that "it is hornbook tort law that one who undertakes to warn the public of danger and thereby induces reliance must perform his 'good Samaritan' task in a careful manner."

Moch Co. v. Rensselaer Water Co.
159 N.E. 896 (N.Y. 1928)

CARDOZO, C.J. The defendant, a water works company under the laws of this State, made a contract with the city of Rensselaer for the supply of water during a term of years. Water was to be furnished to the city for sewer flushing and street sprinkling; for service to schools and public buildings; and for service at fire hydrants, the latter service at the rate of $42.50 a year for each hydrant. Water was to be furnished to private takers within the city at their homes and factories and other industries at reasonable rates, not exceeding a stated schedule. While this contract was in force, a building caught fire. The flames, spreading to the plaintiff's warehouse near by, destroyed it and its contents. The defendant according to the complaint was promptly notified of the fire, "but omitted and neglected after such notice, to supply or furnish sufficient or adequate quantity of water, with adequate pressure to stay, suppress or extinguish the fire before it reached the warehouse of the plaintiff, although the pressure and supply which the defendant was equipped to supply and furnish, and had agreed by said contract to supply and furnish, was adequate and sufficient to prevent the spread of the fire to and the destruction of the plaintiff's warehouse and its contents." By reason of the failure of the defendant to "fulfill the provisions of the contract between it and the city of Rensselaer," the plaintiff is said to have suffered damage, for which judgment is demanded. A motion, in the nature of a demurrer, to dismiss the complaint, was denied at Special Term. The Appellate Division reversed by a divided court.

Liability in the plaintiff's argument is placed on one or other of three grounds. The complaint, we are told, is to be viewed as stating: (1) A cause of action for breach of contract within Lawrence v. Fox (20 N.Y. 268 [1859]); (2) a cause of action for a common-law tort, within MacPherson v. Buick Motor Company (217 N.Y. 382 [1916]); or (3) a cause of action for the breach of a statutory duty. These several grounds of liability will be considered in succession.

(1) We think the action is not maintainable as one for breach of contract.

No legal duty rests upon a city to supply its inhabitants with protection against fire. That being so, a member of the public may not maintain an action under Lawrence v. Fox against one contracting with the city to furnish water at the hydrants, unless an intention appears that the promisor is to be answerable to individual members of the public as well as to the city for any loss ensuing from the failure to fulfill the promise. No such intention is discernible here. On the contrary, the contract here is significantly divided into two branches: One a promise to the city for the benefit of the city in its corporate capacity, in which branch is included the service at the hydrants; and the other a promise to the city for the benefit of private takers, in which branch is included the service at their homes and factories. In a broad sense it is true that every city contract, not improvident or wasteful, is for the benefit of the public. More than this, however, must be shown to give a right of action to a member of the public not formally a party. The benefit, as it is sometimes said, must be one that is not merely incident and secondary. It must be primary and immediate in such a sense and to such a degree as to bespeak the assumption of a duty to make reparation directly to the individual members of the public if the benefit is lost. The field of obligation would be expanded beyond reasonable limits if less than this were demanded as a condition of liability. A promisor undertakes to supply fuel for heating a public building. He is not liable for breach of contract to a visitor who finds the building without fuel, and thus contracts a cold. . . .

[Cardozo then notes that the overwhelming authority treats the benefit to the public under these contracts as incidental and secondary.] An intention to assume an obligation of indefinite extension to every member of the public is seen to be the more improbable when we recall the crushing burden that the obligation would impose. . . . If the plaintiff is to prevail, one who negligently omits to supply sufficient pressure to extinguish a fire started by another assumes an obligation to pay the ensuing damage, though the whole city is laid low. A promisor will not be deemed to have had in mind the assumption of a risk so overwhelming for any trivial reward. . . .

(2) We think the action is not maintainable as one for a common-law tort.

"It is ancient learning that one who assumes to act, even though gratuitously, may thereby become subject to the duty of acting carefully, if he acts at all" (Glanzer v. Shepard, 233 N.Y. 236, 239 [1922]). The plaintiff would bring its case within the orbit of that principle. The hand once set to a task may not always be withdrawn with impunity though liability would fail if it had never been applied at all. A time-honored formula often phrases the distinction as one between misfeasance and nonfeasance. Incomplete the formula is, and so at times misleading. Given a relation involving in its existence a duty of care irrespective of a contract, a tort may result as well from acts of omission as of commission in the fulfillment of the duty thus recognized by law. What we need to know is not so much the conduct to be avoided when the relation and its attendant duty are established as existing. What we need to know is the conduct that engenders the relation. It is here that the formula, however incomplete, has its value and significance. If conduct has gone forward to such a stage that inaction would commonly result, not negatively merely in withholding a benefit, but positively or actively in working an injury, there exists a relation out of which arises a duty to go forward. So the surgeon who operates without pay is liable though his negligence is in the omission to sterilize his instruments; the engineer, though his fault is in the failure to shut off steam; the maker of automobiles, at the suit of some one other than the buyer, though his negligence is merely in inadequate inspection (*MacPherson*). The query always is whether the putative wrongdoer has advanced to such a point as to have launched a force or instrument of harm, or has stopped where inaction is at most a refusal to become an instrument for good.

The plaintiff would have us hold that the defendant, when once it entered upon the performance of its contract with the city, was brought into such a relation with every one who might potentially be benefited through the supply of water at the hydrants as to give to negligent performance, without reasonable notice of a refusal to continue, the quality of a tort. . . . We are satisfied that liability would be unduly and indeed indefinitely extended by this enlargement of the zone of duty. The dealer in coal who is to supply fuel for a shop must then answer to the customers if fuel is lacking. The manufacturer of goods, who enters upon the performance of his contract, must answer, in that view, not only to the buyer, but to those who to his knowledge are looking to the buyer for their own sources of supply. Everyone making a promise having the quality of a contract will be under a duty to the promisee by virtue of the promise, but under another duty, apart from contract, to an indefinite number of potential beneficiaries when performance has begun. The assumption of one relation will mean the involuntary assumption of a series of new relations, inescapably hooked together. Again we may say in the words of the Supreme Court of the United States: "The law does not spread its protection so far" (Robins Dry Dock & Repair Co. v. Flint, 275 U.S. 303 [1927]; cf. Byrd v. English, 117 Ga. 191 [1903]). We do not need to determine now what remedy, if any, there might be if the defendant had withheld the water or reduced the pressure with a malicious intent to do injury to the plaintiff or another. We put aside also the problem that would arise if there had been reckless and wanton indifference to consequences measured and foreseen. Difficulties would be present even then, but they need not now perplex us. What we are dealing with at this time is a mere negligent omission, unaccompanied by malice or other aggravating elements. The failure in such circumstances to furnish an adequate supply of water is at most the denial of a benefit. It is not the commission of a wrong.

(3) We think the action is not maintainable as one for the breach of a statutory duty.

The defendant, a public service corporation, is subject to the provisions of the Transportation Corporations Act. The duty imposed upon it by that act is in substance to furnish water, upon demand by the inhabitants, at reasonable rates, through suitable connections at office, factory or dwelling, and to furnish water at like rates through hydrants or in public buildings upon demand by the city, all according to its capacity. We find nothing in these requirements to enlarge the zone of liability where an inhabitant of the city suffers indirect or incidental damage through deficient pressure at the hydrants. The breach of duty in any case is to the one to whom service is denied at the time and at the place where services to such one is due. The denial, though wrongful, is unavailing without more to give a cause of action to another. We may find a helpful analogy in the law of common carriers. A railroad company is under a duty to supply reasonable facilities for carriage at reasonable rates. It is liable, generally speaking, for breach of a duty imposed by law if it refuses to accept merchandise tendered by a shipper. The fact that its duty is of this character does not make it liable to some one else who may be counting upon the prompt delivery of the merchandise to save him from loss in going forward with his work. If the defendant may not be held for a tort at common law, we find no adequate reason for a holding that it may be held under the statute.

The judgment should be affirmed with costs.

NOTES

1. The privity limitation and the waterworks cases. *Moch* represents an uneasy mixture of a gratuitous and commercial transaction. On the one hand the contract provided for reimbursement to the water company for the services provided. Yet on the other hand, the plaintiff, a stranger to the contract, did not pay for any services even as a taxpayer of the local community that funded the contract. Cardozo addresses both sides of the dilemma, first by negating liability in contract by refusing to recognize the plaintiff as a third-party beneficiary, and then by refusing to impose upon the defendant a duty to act carefully assuming that it has acted gratuitously.

The decision has met with a divided press, and was criticized in Seavey, Reliance upon Gratuitous Promises or Other Conduct, 64 Harv. L. Rev. 913, 920-921 (1951), on the ground that "it is difficult to differentiate this type of case from that where a person has negligently broken a water main and is held responsible for harm caused by the consequent lack of pressure. The earlier cases, however, were decided at a time when nonfeasance and lack of privity were sufficient to prevent liability and the subsequent cases have followed these precedents. Even Cardozo, in what is perhaps his most unsatisfactory opinion in the field of torts, rested his decision, in part, upon the nonfeasance of the waterworks company." On the other side, Professor Gregory, Gratuitous Undertakings and the Duty of Care, 1 DePaul L. Rev. 30, 59-60 (1951), defended *Moch* on the grounds that it placed the burden of the loss on the fire insurance companies who would otherwise assert their subrogation rights — which allow it to stand in the shoes of the insured after it pays the claim — against the water company. "Cardozo thought the sum of $42.50 insufficient to warrant the conclusion that a negligent water company should be made to relieve a fire insurance company from bearing the ultimate risk of loss by fire. . . ." Would Gregory's logic preclude liability even if the water company's own employee accidentally broke the water main while making repairs?

Should the plaintiff in *Moch* be able to recover on the strength of §42(a) or (b)?

RTT:LPH §42. DUTY BASED ON UNDERTAKING

An actor who undertakes to render services to another that the actor knows or should know reduce the risk of physical harm to the other has a duty of reasonable care to the other in conducting the undertaking if:

(a) the failure to exercise such care increases the risk of harm beyond that which existed without the undertaking, or

(b) the person to whom the services are rendered or another relies on the actor's exercising reasonable care in the undertaking.

Does this provision apply in *Moch* given that the breakdown in services was in the water supply to the plaintiff's neighbor? RTT:LPH §42, comment *f* observes: "This [reliance] requirement is often met because the plaintiff or another relied on the actor's performing the undertaking in a nonnegligent manner and declined to pursue an alternative means for protection."

Note that the comments to the Third Restatement explicitly question *Moch's* nonfeasance rationale:

> The difficulty with [*Moch*] is that the provision of utilities fundamentally changes the landscape, creating an expectation of and reliance on continued service. When the utility ceases to supply service, the omission is much like ceasing to provide warning signals at a railroad crossing. Put another way, reliance on the utility's continuing to provide its services is a cause of the harm. Moreover, the policies supporting the no-duty-to-rescue rule do not apply to a commercial enterprise that is engaged in the business of supplying services to customers.
>
> The better explanation for limitations on the duty of public utilities is concern about the huge magnitude of liability to which a utility might be exposed from a single failure to provide service that affects hundreds, thousands, or, in the case of an electrical blackout, millions of people. In addition, when the harm is property damage, often the plaintiff will have first-party insurance that covers the loss.

2. *Judicial developments since* Moch. The judicial developments since *Moch* anticipated the uneasiness now expressed in the Third Restatement. Most notably, in Doyle v. South Pittsburgh Water Co., 199 A.2d 875, 878 (Pa. 1964), Musmanno, J., held that the waterworks cases fell "squarely within the rule that where a party to a contract assumes a duty to the other party to the contract, and it is foreseeable that a breach of that duty will cause injury to some third person not a party to the contract, the contracting party owes a duty to all those falling within the foreseeable orbit of risk of harm."

New York courts have, however, followed *Moch*. Strauss v. Belle Realty Co., 482 N.E.2d 34, 38 (N.Y. 1985), arose out of the great New York power failure of 1977, for which the defendant, Consolidated Edison, had been found grossly negligent. The power failure cut off the pumps used to circulate water upstairs in defendant Belle Realty's building. The plaintiff, a 77-year-old tenant in Belle's building, was injured when he fell in the dark on some defective basement stairs in search of water. Both the plaintiff and Belle were customers of Con Ed, but only Belle had a direct contractual relation with the utility. The court refused to extend the utility's liability in negligence to the plaintiff tenant:

> [W]e deal here with a system-wide power failure occasioned by what has already been determined to be the utility's gross negligence. If liability could

be found here, then in logic and fairness the same result must follow in many similar situations. For example, a tenant's guests and invitees, as well as persons making deliveries or repairing equipment in the building, are equally persons who must use the common areas, and for whom they are maintained. Customers of a store and occupants of an office building stand in much the same position with respect to Con Edison as tenants of an apartment building. In all cases the numbers are to a certain extent limited and defined, and while identities may change, so do those of apartment dwellers. While limiting recovery to customers in this instance can hardly be said to confer immunity from negligence on Con Edison, permitting recovery to those in plaintiff's circumstances would, in our view, violate the court's responsibility to define an orbit of duty that places controllable limits on liability. . . .

3. *Affirmative duties and the role of insurance.* The possibility of insurer's subrogation rights led to a partial retreat from Cardozo's no duty rule in Weinberg v. Dinger, 524 A.2d 366, 378 (N.J. 1987). The court first noted its concern with the high insurance costs that water companies might have to bear, and wrote as follows:

> We believe that the imposition on a water company of liability for subrogation claims of carriers who pay fire losses caused by the company's negligent failure to maintain adequate water pressure would inevitably result in higher water rates paid by the class of consumers that paid for the fire insurance. The result of imposing subrogation-claim liability on water companies in such cases would be to shift the risk from the fire-insurance company to the water company, and, ultimately, to the consumer in the form of increased water rates. Thus, the consumer would pay twice — first for property insurance premiums, and then in the form of higher water rates to fund the cost of the water company's liability insurance. We find this result contrary to public policy.
>
> Accordingly, we abrogate the water company's immunity for losses caused by the negligent failure to maintain adequate water pressure for fire fighting only to the extent of claims that are uninsured or underinsured. To the extent that such claims are insured and thereby assigned to the insurance carrier as required by statute, *N.J.S.A.* 17:36-5:20, we hold that the carrier's subrogation claims are unenforceable against the water company.

Note that the water company contract at issue in *Weinberg* provided as follows:

> 8. The Company will use due diligence at all times to provide continuous service of the character or quality proposed to be supplied but in case the service shall be interrupted or irregular or defective or fail, the Company shall be liable and obligated only to use reasonably diligent efforts in light of the circumstances then existing to restore or correct its characteristics. . . .

10. The standard terms and conditions contained in this tariff are a part of every contract for service entered into by the Company and govern all classes of service where applicable.

What result if homeowner fire insurance contracts are redrafted to provide that no coverage shall exist when the fire in question could have been avoided by the due care of the water company?

The tariff limitation referred to above played a prominent role in Los Angeles Cellular Telephone Company v. Superior Court (Spielholz RPI), 76 Cal. Rptr. 2d 894 (Cal. App. 1998), Spielholz called 911 on defendant's cellular system as she was pursued by two men, one of whom subsequently shot her. The defendant company interposed its tariff that had been approved by the state's Public Utility Commission. That tariff explicitly and unambiguously limited the defendant's liability to $5,000 per incident. The Court, without resort to common law principles of nonfeasance, unhesitatingly applied the damage limitation noting: "A condition imposed by a tariff binds a utility's customers without regard to whether a contract is signed by the customer and without regard to the customer's actual knowledge of the tariff." Would *Moch* have come out the same way if its tariff had contained a similar dollar maximum?

4. Privity, leases and third-party suppliers. In Cullings v. Goetz, 176 N.E. 397, 397-398 (N.Y. 1931), Cardozo also invoked privity limitation to prevent the guest of a tenant from suing a landlord who had breached its covenant of repair to leased premises within the tenant's exclusive possession. *Cullings* was overruled in Putnam v. Stout, 345 N.E.2d 319, 325-326 (N.Y. 1976), which, following RST §357, held the landlord responsible to the tenant's guest so long as the breach of the covenant to repair has created "an unreasonable risk to persons on the land." The restrictive influence of *Moch* surfaced in Eaves Brooks Costume Co. v. Y.B.H. Realty Corp., 556 N.E.2d 1093 (N.Y. 1990), where the court denied the tenant's recovery against the company that had been hired to maintain and inspect its sprinkler system, when the sprinklers malfunctioned and flooded its premises. The plaintiff was neither a third-party beneficiary nor a person who had detrimentally relied on the contract. In Palka v. Servicemaster Management Service Corp., 634 N.E.2d 189 (N.Y. 1994), the court switched gears and allowed a nurse to recover from the hospital's maintenance company on the ground that it had maintained "comprehensive and exclusive" control over the facilities and thus owed a duty to "noncontracting individuals reasonably within the zone and contemplation of the intended safety services." Yet, in Espinal v. Melville Snow Contactors, Inc. 773 N.E.2d 485 (N.Y. 2002), *Moch* was again very much in evidence when an employee, who slipped and fell on the ice in her employer's parking lot, was barred as a matter of law from suing the snow removal contractor who had only limited and defined duties under the contract.

What result if suits are brought against the occupier in all these cases?

SECTION E.   SPECIAL RELATIONSHIPS

Restatement (Second) of Torts

§315.   GENERAL PRINCIPLE

There is no duty so to control the conduct of a third person as to prevent him from causing physical harm to another unless

(a) a special relation exists between the actor and the third person which imposes a duty upon the actor to control the third person's conduct, or

(b) a special relation exists between the actor and the other which gives the other a right to protection.

NOTE

On the borderland of nonfeasance. In Weirum v. RKO General Inc., 539 P.2d 36, 40-41 (Cal. 1975), the defendant's disk jockey, the Real Don Steele, staged a novel promotional contest. He would drive around town announcing that he "had bread to spread" and give his location on the air. The first contestant to reach that location and answer some simple quiz questions correctly would win small prizes. Two teenage drivers got into an 80-miles-per-hour drag race in an effort to reach Steele at his new location and forced decedent's car off the highway, where it overturned, killing him. The California Court of Appeals, over a dissent, reversed plaintiff's judgment against the radio station, saying that the station "had no control, or right to control, over the conduct of the drivers of other cars on the highway." 119 Cal. Rptr. 468 (1975). The California Supreme Court reinstated the plaintiff's judgment in a unanimous decision, insisting that liability here did not open up a Pandora's box:

We are not persuaded that the imposition of a duty here will lead to unwarranted extensions of liability. Defendant is fearful that entrepreneurs will henceforth be burdened with an avalanche of obligations: an athletic department will owe a duty to an ardent sports fan injured while hastening to purchase one of a limited number of tickets; a department store will be liable to injuries incurred in response to a "while-they-last" sale. This argument, however, suffers from a myopic view of the facts presented here.

The giveaway contest was no commonplace invitation to an attraction available on a limited basis. It was a competitive scramble in which the thrill of the chase to be the one and only victor was intensified by the live broadcasts which accompanied the pursuit. In the assertedly analogous situations described by defendant, any haste involved in the purchase of the commodity is an incidental and unavoidable result of the scarcity of the commodity itself. In such situations there is no attempt, as here, to generate a competitive pursuit on public streets, accelerated by repeated importuning by radio to be the very first to arrive at a particular destination. Manifestly the "spectacular" bears little resemblance to daily commercial activities.

The court then rebuffed an effort to use §315 to limit liability, noting that its main purpose was to codify the common law "good Samaritan rule" applicable to cases of nonfeasance only.

Here, there can be little doubt that we review an act of misfeasance to which section 315 is inapplicable. Liability is not predicated upon defendant's failure to intervene for the benefit of decedent but rather upon its creation of an unreasonable risk of harm to him. Defendant's reliance upon cases which involve the failure to prevent harm to another is therefore misplaced . . .

Kline v. 1500 Massachusetts Avenue Apartment Corp.
439 F.2d 477 (D.C. Cir. 1970)

WILKEY, J. The appellee apartment corporation states that there is "only one issue presented for review . . . whether a duty should be placed on a landlord to take steps to protect tenants from foreseeable criminal acts committed by third parties." The District Court as a matter of law held that there is no such duty. We find that there is, and that in the circumstances here the applicable standard of care was breached. We therefore reverse and remand to the District Court for the determination of damages for the appellant.

I

The appellant, Sarah B. Kline, sustained serious injuries when she was criminally assaulted and robbed at approximately 10:15 in the evening by an intruder in the common hallway of an apartment house at 1500 Massachusetts Avenue. This facility, into which the appellant Kline moved in October 1959, is a large apartment building with approximately 585 individual apartment units. It has a main entrance on Massachusetts Avenue, with side entrances on both 15th and 16th Streets. At the time the appellant first signed a lease a doorman was on duty at the main entrance twenty-four hours a day, and at least one employee at all times manned a desk in the lobby from which all persons using the elevators could be observed. The 15th Street door adjoined the entrance to a parking garage used by both the tenants and the public. Two garage attendants were stationed at this dual entranceway; the duties of each being arranged so that one of them always was in position to observe those entering either the apartment building or the garage. The 16th Street entrance was unattended during the day but was locked after 9:00 P.M.

By mid-1966, however, the main entrance had no doorman, the desk in the lobby was left unattended much of the time, the 15th Street entrance was generally unguarded due to a decrease in garage personnel, and the 16th Street entrance was often left unlocked all night. The entrances were allowed to be thus unguarded in the face of an increasing number of assaults, larcenies, and robberies being perpetrated against the tenants in and from the common hallways of the apartment building. These facts were undisputed. . . . The landlord had notice of these crimes and had in fact been urged by appellant Kline herself prior to the events leading to the instant appeal to take steps to secure the building.

Shortly after 10:00 P.M. on November 17, 1966, Miss Kline was assaulted and robbed just outside her apartment on the first floor above the street level of this 585 unit apartment building. This occurred only two months after Leona Sullivan, another female tenant, had been similarly attacked in the same commonway.

II

At the outset we note that of the crimes of violence, robbery, and assault which had been occurring with mounting frequency on the premises at 1500 Massachusetts Avenue, the assaults on Miss Kline and Miss Sullivan took place in the hallways of the building, which were under the exclusive control of the appellee landlord. Even in those crimes of robbery or assault committed in individual apartments, the intruders of necessity had to gain entrance through the common entry and passageways. These premises fronted on three heavily traveled streets, and had multiple entrances. The risk to be guarded against therefore was the risk of unauthorized entrance into the apartment house by intruders bent upon some crime of violence or theft.

While the apartment lessees themselves could take some steps to guard against this risk by installing extra heavy locks and other security devices on the doors and windows of their respective apartments, yet this risk in the greater part could only be guarded against by the landlord. No individual tenant had it within his power to take measures to guard the garage entranceways, to provide scrutiny at the main entrance of the building, to patrol the common hallways and elevators, to set up any kind of a security alarm system in the building, to provide additional locking devices on the main doors, to provide a system of announcement for authorized visitors only, to close the garage doors at appropriate hours, and to see that the entrance was manned at all times.

The risk of criminal assault and robbery on a tenant in the common hallways of the building was thus entirely predictable; that same risk had been occurring with increasing frequency over a period of several months immediately prior to the incident giving rise to this case; it was a risk whose prevention or minimization was almost entirely within the power of the landlord; and the risk materialized in the assault and robbery of appellant on November 17, 1966.

III

In this jurisdiction, certain duties have been assigned to the landlord because of his *control* of common hallways, lobbies, stairwells, etc., used by all tenants in multiple dwelling units. This Court in Levine v. Katz, 407 F.2d 303, 304 (D.C. Cir. 1968), pointed out that:

> It has long been well settled in this jurisdiction that, where a landlord leases separate portions of property and reserves under his own control the halls, stairs, or other parts of the property for use in common by all tenants, he has a duty to all those on the premises of legal right to use ordinary care and diligence to maintain the retained parts in a reasonably safe condition.

While Levine v. Katz dealt with a physical defect in the building leading to plaintiff's injury, the rationale as applied to predictable criminal acts by third parties is the same. The duty is the landlord's because by his control of the areas of common use and common danger he is the only party who has the *power* to make the necessary repairs or to provide the necessary protection.

As a general rule, a private person does not have a duty to protect another from a criminal attack by a third person. We recognize that this rule has sometimes in the past been applied in landlord-tenant law, even by this court. Among the reasons for the application of this rule to landlords are: judicial reluctance to tamper with the traditional common law concept of the landlord-tenant relationship; the notion that the act of a third person in committing an intentional tort or crime is a superseding cause of the harm to another resulting therefrom; the oftentimes difficult problem of determining foreseeability of criminal acts; the vagueness of the standard which the landlord must meet; the economic consequences of the imposition of the duty; and conflict with the public policy allocating the duty of protecting citizens from criminal acts to the government rather than the private sector.

But the rationale of this very broad general rule falters when it is applied to the conditions of modern day urban apartment living, particularly in the circumstances of this case. The rationale of the general rule exonerating a third party from any duty to protect another from a criminal attack has no applicability to the landlord-tenant relationship in multiple dwelling houses. The landlord is no insurer of his tenants' safety, but he certainly is no bystander. And where, as here, the landlord has notice of repeated criminal assaults and robberies, has notice that these crimes occurred in the portion of the premises exclusively within his control, has every reason to expect like crimes to happen again, and has the exclusive power to take preventive action, it does not seem unfair to place upon the landlord a duty to take those steps which are within his power to minimize the predictable risk to his tenants. . . .

In the case at bar we place the duty of taking protective measures guarding the entire premises and the areas peculiarly under the landlord's control against the perpetration of criminal acts upon the landlord, the party to the lease contract who has the effective capacity to perform these necessary acts.

[The court then noted that innkeepers were held liable to their guests for assaults and molestations by third parties, "be they innkeeper's employees, fellow guests or intruders."] Other relationships in which similar duties have been imposed include landowner-invitee, businessman-patron, employer-employee, school district-pupil, hospital-patient, and carrier-passenger. In all, the theory of liability is essentially the same: that since the ability of one of the parties to provide for his own protection has been limited in some way by his submission to the control of the other, a duty should be imposed upon the one possessing control (and thus the power to act) to take reasonable precautions to protect the other one from assaults by third parties which, at least, could reasonably have been anticipated. However, there is no liability normally imposed upon the one having the power to act if the violence is sudden and unexpected provided that the source of the violence is not an employee of the one in control.

We are aware of various cases in other jurisdictions following a different line of reasoning, conceiving of the landlord and tenant relationship along more traditional common law lines, and on varying fact situations reaching a different result from that we reach here. Typical of these is a much cited (although only a 4-3) decision of the Supreme Court of New Jersey, Goldberg v. Housing Authority of Newark [186 A.2d 291(N.J. 1962)], relied on by appellee landlord here. There the court said:

> Everyone can foresee the commission of crime virtually anywhere and
> at any time. If foreseeability itself gave rise to a duty to provide "police"

protection for others, every residential curtilage, every shop, every store, every manufacturing plant would have to be patrolled by the private arm of the owner. And since hijacking and attack upon occupants of motor vehicles are also foreseeable, it would be the duty of every motorist to provide armed protection for his passengers and the property of others. Of course, none of this is at all palatable.

This language seems to indicate that the court was using the word *foreseeable* interchangeably with the word *possible*. In that context, the statement is quite correct. It would be folly to impose liability for mere possibilities. But we must reach the question of liability for attacks which are foreseeable in the sense that they are *probable* and *predictable*. . . . As between tenant and landlord, the landlord is the only one in the position to take the necessary acts of protection required. He is not an insurer, but he is obligated to minimize the risk to his tenants. Not only as between landlord and tenant is the landlord best equipped to guard against the predictable risk of intruders, but even as between landlord and the police power of government, the landlord is in the best position to take the necessary protective measures. Municipal police cannot patrol the entryways and the hallways, the garages and the basements of private multiple unit apartment dwellings. They are neither equipped, manned, nor empowered to do so. In the area of the predictable risk which materialized in this case, only the landlord could have taken measures which might have prevented the injuries suffered by appellant.

We note that in the fight against crime the police are not expected to do it all; every segment of society has obligations to aid in law enforcement and to minimize the opportunities for crime. . . .

IV

We now turn to the standard of care which should be applied in judging if the landlord has fulfilled his duty of protection to the tenant. Although in many cases the language speaks as if the standard of care itself varies, in the last analysis the standard of care is the same — reasonable care in all the circumstances. . . .

We therefore hold in this case that the applicable standard of care in providing protection for the tenant is that standard which this landlord himself was employing in October 1959 when the appellant became a resident on the premises at 1500 Massachusetts Avenue. The tenant was led to expect that she could rely upon this degree of protection. While we do not say that the precise measures for security which were then in vogue should have been kept up (e.g., the number of people at the main entrances might have been reduced if a tenant-controlled intercom-automatic latch system had been installed in the common entryways), we do hold that the same relative degree of security should have been maintained. [The court then held that liability was "clear" on the face of the record and remanded the case to the district court on the issue of damages only.]

Having said this, it would be well to state what is *not* said by this decision. We do not hold that the landlord is by any means an insurer of the safety of his tenants. His duty is to take those measures of protection which are within his power and capacity to take, and which can reasonably be expected to mitigate the risk of intruders assaulting and robbing tenants. The landlord is not expected to provide protection commonly owed by a municipal police department; but as illustrated in this case, he is obligated to protect those parts of his premises which are not usually subject to periodic patrol and inspection by the municipal police. We do not say that every multiple unit apartment house in the District of Columbia should have those same measures of protection which 1500 Massachusetts Avenue enjoyed in 1959, nor do we say that 1500 Massachusetts Avenue should have precisely those same measures in effect at the present time. Alternative and more up-to-date methods may be equally or even more effective.

Granted, the discharge of this duty of protection by landlords will cause, in many instances, the expenditure of large sums for additional equipment and services, and granted, the cost will be ultimately passed on to the tenant in the form of increased rents. This prospect, in itself, however, is no deterrent to our acknowledging and giving force to the duty, since without protection the tenant already pays in losses from theft, physical assault and increased insurance premiums.

The landlord is entirely justified in passing on the cost of increased protective measures to his tenants, but the rationale of compelling the landlord to do it in the first place is that he is the only one who is in a position to take the necessary protective measures for overall protection of the premises, which he owns in whole and rents in part to individual tenants.

Reversed and remanded to the District Court for the determination of damages.

MACKINNON, J., dissenting. [The dissent first argued that liability was not established on the record, so that the case should, even on the court's view of the substantive law, be retried de novo, because the evidence on the number and frequency of previous criminal attacks was insufficient, as only one of the 20 incidents involved both an assault and robbery. It also argued that the notice to the landlord was only of theft, and that there was no evidence in the record that the landlord knew of the previous assault upon Leona Sullivan. It continued:]

The evidence introduced by the plaintiff is also deficient in my opinion in not proving that the alleged negligence was the proximate cause of the assault or that it contributed to it in any way. Plaintiff's evidence did not negate that it was a tenant, guest or person properly on the property who committed the offense, and while the panel opinion throughout asserts that an "intruder" committed the offense, there is no proof of that fact. So plaintiff's evidence failed to prove a nexus between the alleged deficiencies of the appellee and the cause of any damage to appellant. . . .

As for the claim that appellant was led to believe she would get the same standard of protection in 1966 that was furnished in 1959, there is obviously nothing to this point. She was not led to expect that. She personally observed the changes which occurred in this respect. They were obvious to her each day of her life. And since her original lease had terminated and her tenancy in 1966 was on a month to month basis, whatever contract existed was created at the beginning of the month and since there was no evidence of any alteration in the security precautions during the current month, there is no basis for any damage claim based on contract. . . .

In my opinion the decision in Goldberg v. Housing Authority of Newark, 186 A.2d 291 (N.J. 1962), answers all appellant's arguments. It is just too much, absent a contractual agreement, to require or expect a combination office-apartment building such as is involved here to provide police patrol protection or its equivalent in the block-long, well-lighted passageways. Yet nothing short of that will meet the second guessing standard of protection the panel opinion practically directs. If tenants expect such protection, they can move to apartments where it is available and presumably pay a higher rental, but it is a mistake in my judgment to hold an office-apartment building to such a requirement when the tenant knew for years that such protection was not being afforded.

NOTES

1. Contract or special relationship? If the defendant landlord could have taken effective steps to prevent crimes in common areas at a lower cost than its tenants, why didn't it assume that liability in its standard residential lease? Should the court have taken into account such precautions as entering and leaving only with a friend? If the promise were voluntarily made, could liquidated damages be imposed on recovery as in *Los Angeles Cellular?* In dealing with the contract alternative, should the court in *Kline* take into account the question of administrative costs? Contributory negligence? Error rates in litigation?

Whatever the answer to these questions, the *Kline* approach has met with widespread approval insofar as it reverses the older common law rule that imposed no duty on a landlord to shield tenants from the criminal attacks of strangers. But the content of that duty may well be limited. In Nivens v. 7-11 Hoagy's Corner, 943 P.2d 286, 291, 292, 293 (Wash. 1997), the court "explicitly" endorsed the use of §315 for business invitees, but nonetheless held that the defendant had no duty "to provide security personnel to prevent criminal behavior on the business premises. . . . To do so would unfairly shift the responsibility for policing, and the attendant costs, from government to the private sector." Similarly, in Shadday v. Omni Hotels Management Corp., 477 F.3d 511 (7th Cir. 2007), Posner, J. held that a hotel did not violate any duty of care because it was highly unlikely that a male guest would rape a female guest whom he accosted in an elevator.

2. *Proximate causation.* The issues of proximate causation stressed in MacKinnon J.'s, dissent explicitly surfaced in Burgos v. Aqueduct Realty Corp., 706 N.E.2d 1163, 1166 (N.Y. 1998), plaintiff was leaving her apartment unit when she was forced back into it by two men who beat and robbed her. In her action against the landlord for inadequate security, Kaye, C.J., held that

> the necessary causal link between a landlord's culpable failure to provide adequate security and a tenant's injuries resulting from a criminal attack in the building can be established only if the assailant gained access to the premises through a negligently maintained entrance. . . . Without such a requirement, landlords would be exposed to liability for virtually all criminal activity in their buildings. By the same token, because victims of criminal assaults often cannot identify their attackers, a blanket rule precluding recovery whenever the attacker remains unidentified would place an impossible burden on tenants.

Kaye, C.J., then held that, although the plaintiff bore the burden of proof on the causation issue, she could reach the jury on the question of proximate causation, when she testified that the assailants did not wear masks and that none of the building's entrances had functioning locks because the jury could infer that persons known to plaintiff would have covered their faces, and that access through unlocked doors was easy. What about the possibility that friends of tenants had assaulted plaintiff?

3. *Contributory negligence.* What role does an injured plaintiff have in *Kline* situations? In Wassell v. Adams, 865 F.2d 849, 855 (7th Cir. 1989), the plaintiff was raped and sodomized when, hearing a knock, she opened the door to her hotel room in the middle of the night under the mistaken belief that her fiancé was outside. The plaintiff argued that the defendants, operators of the motel, had failed to warn her of the risks of staying in a motel in a high-crime area. The jury assessed the plaintiff's damages at $850,000, but found her 97 percent negligent, leaving an award of $25,500, roughly the expenses of her therapy for posttraumatic stress. Posner, J., upheld the award:

> [I]t is absurd to think that hoteliers are required to give so *obvious* a warning any more than they must warn guests not to stick their fingers into the electrical outlets. Everyone, or at least the average person, knows better

than to open his or her door to a stranger in the middle of the night. The problem was not that Susan thought that she *should* open her bedroom door in the middle of the night to anyone who knocked, but that she wasn't thinking clearly. A warning would not have availed against a temporary, sleep-induced lapse.

4. The procession of liability. The new liability first raised in *Kline* has generated a flood of subsequent litigation about the institutional responsibilities to protect against crime.

a. Colleges and universities. In Peterson v. San Francisco Community College District, 685 P.2d 1193, 1197 (Cal. 1984), the California Supreme Court held that a community college district had a duty to protect a college student against a foreseeable criminal assault that took place in broad daylight on campus — here, on a stairway in a parking lot — on the strength of its special relationship with the student. "There is no question that if the defendant district here were a private landowner operating a parking lot on its premises it would owe plaintiff a duty to exercise due care for her protection." The court let the plaintiff reach the jury on two counts of negligence: first, had the defendant properly trimmed the hedge and foliage that concealed the perpetrator before he committed the crime and, second, did the school have a duty to warn the plaintiff about the hazards it left uncorrected. How might such a warning be given? Be updated?

b. Common carriers. In Lopez v. Southern California Rapid Transit District, 710 P.2d 907, 910-911 (Cal. 1985), held that a duty of care in favor of its passengers would not impose "colossal financial burden" on a public transportation district. Even without demanding "an armed security guard on every bus," the district could train drivers to eject unruly passengers who did not heed warnings to quiet down, to radio the police for assistance, or equip buses with alarm lights to warn of threatened or actual criminal activity. What causal complications are created by each such theory?

c. Condominiums. In Frances T. v. Village Green Owners Association, 723 P.2d 573 (Cal. 1986), the plaintiff was "molested, raped and robbed" by an unidentified assailant who entered her condominium unit at night after the condominium board refused to allow plaintiff to install lights by her unit for her own self-protection. The court held that the liability imposed on landlords in *Kline* should be extended to condominium boards and to their individual members who function as the de facto landlord of the premises. In dissent Mosk, J., rejected any parallels between a condominium board and an ordinary landlord and denied the existence of special relationship between a condominium association and its unit members. Will potential liability deter association members from serving gratis on condominium boards?

d. Shopping malls. In Ann M. v. Pacific Plaza Shopping Center, 863 P.2d 207, 210, 215-216 (Cal. 1993), the court refused to allow the plaintiff, who had been raped inside her place of employment in the defendant's shopping mall, to sue her employer's landlord. The plaintiff's employer had signed a lease that gave defendant exclusive control over all common areas. Plaintiff was raped around 8:00 A.M. by a customer who entered the store from the mall when she was alone in her shop. There was some evidence that the tenants in the shopping mall had complained of lack of security and the presence of transients, but the merchants association decided not to hire walking guards because the tenants could not afford the prohibitive rent increases that would be passed through under the leases. Instead, alternative arrangements were made for another security company to drive by three or four times a day. Panelli, J., concluded that "a high degree of foreseeability is required in order to find that the scope of a landlord's duty of care includes the hiring of security guards. We further conclude that the requisite degree of foreseeability rarely, if ever, can be proven in the absence of prior similar incidents of violent crime on the landlord's premises. To hold otherwise would be to impose an unfair burden upon landlords and, in effect, would force landlords to become the insurers of public safety, contrary to well established policy in this state."

e. Off-premises liability. More recently in twin cases, Delgado v. Trax Bar & Grill, 113 P.3d 1159 (Cal. 2005), and Morris v. De La Torre, 113 P.3d 1182, 1188 (Cal. 2005), restaurant patrons were attacked while leaving the premises in plain view of the restaurant employees. In *Delgado*, the defendant's bouncer did not accompany the plaintiffs to their car, and in *Morris*, the employees did not call 911 after one criminal assailant broke into the restaurant to steal a knife that he used to stab one of the plaintiffs. The Court allowed both cases to go to the jury. George, J.,writing in *Morris*, explicitly distinguished *Ann M.*, writing:

> as we explained in *Delgado*, even if a proprietor, such as the bar in that case, has no special-relationship-based duty to provide security guards or other similarly burdensome measures designed to prevent future criminal conduct (which measures are required only upon a showing of "heightened foreseeability"), such a proprietor nevertheless owes a special-relationship-based duty to undertake reasonable and minimally burdensome measures to assist customers or invitees who face danger from imminent or ongoing criminal assaultive conduct occurring upon the premises. In this regard, we noted in *Delgado* that restaurant proprietors owe a special-relationship-based duty to provide "assistance [to] their customers who become ill or need medical attention and that they are liable if they fail to act."
>
> In any event, . . . foreseeability analysis in a case such as this — involving a proprietor's duty to *respond* reasonably to criminal conduct that is *imminent* or even *ongoing* in his or her presence- contrasts fundamentally with the type of foreseeability at issue in cases such as Ann M., which involve a proprietor's duty to take *preventative* measures to guard against possible *future* criminal conduct.

Note in its earlier decision in KFC of California v. Brown, 927 P.2d 1260 (Cal. 1997), the Court also distinguished *Ann M.* when the defendant's employee stalled for time before opening the safe while the plaintiff was held at gunpoint. The court agreed with KFC and its amici that creating a duty to capitulate criminal threats could prove counterproductive because "there is no basis for an assumption that complying with a robber's demands would guarantee the safety of a hostage. Robbers are unpredictable and often injure victims and others even though there has been no resistance." The court left open the question of the extent to which the employees could be liable to patrons by active resistance to a robbery. Could anything more be required beyond a good faith effort to minimize loss under the emergency doctrine?

5. *Other duties on occupiers.* *Klein* bridged the gap between the traditional cases, such as *Levine*, that held an occupier responsible for physical defects in the premises, and those that involved criminal assaults. These two categories are not only vastly different from each other, but they also invite consideration of other kinds of risks that might be cast on occupiers for the benefit of their tenants and guests. For the most part, recent cases have shown a decided reluctance to branch out into new areas. In Drew v. Le Jay's Sportmen's Café, Inc., 806 P.2d 301 (Wy. 1991), the decedent choked to death while eating a meal in defendant's restaurant. The court held that the proprietor owed his invitee the duty to "promptly call" for first aid assistance, but did not include "the actual administration of first aid until qualified medical assistance arrives." In particular, the defendant was not required to have employees certified in cardiopulmonary resuscitation or the Heimlich maneuver (which forces up food by applying pressure below the chest). Likewise in Atcovitz v. Gulph Mills Tennis Club, Inc., 812 A.2d 1218 (Pa. 2002), the defendant tennis club was not required to maintain an automated external defillibrator for the benefit of a paying customer with a history of heart disease, who collapsed while playing tennis. Finally, in Mastriano v. Blyer, 779 A.2d 951 (Me. 2001), a cab driver who transported a tipsy passenger was only obliged to see that he had a "safe exit" at his chosen destination, but was not required to see that he did not drive his own automobile while intoxicated.

Tarasoff v. Regents of University of California
551 P.2d 334 (Cal. 1976)

TOBRINER, J. On October 27, 1969, Prosenjit Poddar killed Tatiana Tarasoff. Plaintiffs, Tatiana's parents, allege that two months earlier Poddar confided his intention to kill Tatiana to Dr. Lawrence Moore, a psychologist employed by the Cowell Memorial Hospital at the University of California at Berkeley. They allege that on Moore's request, the campus police briefly detained Poddar, but released him when he appeared rational. They further claim that Dr. Harvey Powelson, Moore's superior, then directed that no further action be taken to detain Poddar. [Elsewhere in the opinion it was noted: "Poddar had persuaded Tatiana's brother to share an apartment with him near Tatiana's residence; shortly after her return from Brazil, Poddar went to her residence and killed her." By way of additional background, Poddar was an "untouchable" Bengali who had little or no contact with women in India. He had come to Berkeley to study naval architecture and found it difficult to adapt to American mores. Tatiana was of Russian extraction, born in China and raised in Brazil, with a much more liberal upbringing. The trouble began when she kissed Poddar on New Year's Eve 1968, but thereafter was unresponsive to his attentions. She in turn had sexual relations with other men, which sent Poddar into a tailspin until his personal life and university work unraveled. He saw Dr. Moore some seven times, who diagnosed his condition as "paranoid schizophrenic reaction, acute and severe." Moore recommended that he be involuntarily committed for the safety of others. Moore's superior may have ordered him not to get further involved in the case. It is clear that no one took any steps to warn Tatiania of any danger. She returned from Brazil in September 1969, making Poddar's pain all the more acute. In late October 1969, Poddar tracked her to her family home, shot her with a pellet gun and stabbed her seventeen times with a kitchen knife.[*]] No one warned plaintiffs of Tatiana's peril.

Concluding that these facts set forth causes of action against neither therapists and policemen involved, nor against the Regents of the University of California as their employer, the superior court sustained defendants' demurrers to plaintiffs' second amended complaints without leave to amend. This appeal ensued. . . .

Plaintiffs' complaints predicate liability on two grounds: defendants' failure to warn plaintiffs of the impending danger and their failure to bring about Poddar's confinement pursuant to the Lanterman-Petris-Short Act (Welf. & Inst. Code, 5000ff.). Defendants, in turn, assert that they owed no duty of reasonable care to Tatiana and that they are immune from suit under the California Tort Claims Act of 1963 (Gov. Code, §810ff.). . . .

2. Plaintiffs Can State a Cause of Action Against Defendant Therapists for Negligent Failure to Protect Tatiana

The second cause of action can be amended to allege that Tatiana's death proximately resulted from defendant's negligent failure to warn

---

[*] These and other gory details are contained in *Tarasoff v Regents of the University of California:* The Therapist's Dilemma, in Tort Stories 99 (2003).

Tatiana or others likely to apprise her of her danger. Plaintiffs contend that as amended, such allegations of negligence and proximate causation, with resulting damages, establish a cause of action. Defendants, however, contend that in the circumstances of the present case they owed no duty of care to Tatiana or her parents and that, in the absence of such duty, they were free to act in careless disregard of Tatiana's life and safety.

In analyzing this issue, we bear in mind that legal duties are not discoverable facts of nature, but merely conclusory expressions that, in cases of a particular type, liability should be imposed for damage done. As stated in Dillon v. Legg, 441 P.2d 912, 916 (Cal. 1968): "The assertion that liability must . . . be denied because defendant bears no 'duty' to plaintiff 'begs the essential question — whether the plaintiff's interests are entitled to legal protection against the defendant's conduct. . . . [Duty] is not sacrosanct in itself, but only an expression of the sum total of those considerations of policy which lead the law to say that the particular plaintiff is entitled to protection.' (Prosser, Law of Torts [3d ed. 1964] at pp. 332-333.)"

[Tobriner, J., then explicitly relies on the general statements on duties to care from the landmark cases of Rowland v. Christian, and Heaven v. Pender, *supra* at 593, to conclude]: We depart from "this fundamental principle" only upon the "balancing of a number of considerations"; major ones "are the foreseeability of harm to the plaintiff, the degree of certainty that the plaintiff suffered injury, the closeness of the connection between the defendant's conduct and the injury suffered, the moral blame attached to the defendant's conduct, the policy of preventing future harm, the extent of the burden to the defendant and consequences to the community of imposing a duty to exercise care with resulting liability for breach, and the availability, cost and prevalence of insurance for the risk involved."

The most important of these considerations in establishing duty is foreseeability. As a general principle, a "defendant owes a duty of care to all persons who are foreseeably endangered by his conduct, with respect to all risks which make the conduct unreasonably dangerous." As we shall explain, however, when the avoidance of foreseeable harm requires a defendant to control the conduct of another person, or to warn of such conduct, the common law has traditionally imposed liability only if the defendant bears some special relationship to the dangerous person or to the potential victim. Since the relationship between a therapist and his patient satisfies this requirement, we need not here decide whether foreseeability alone is sufficient to create a duty to exercise reasonable care to protect a potential victim of another's conduct.

Although, as we have stated above, under the common law, as a general rule, one person owed no duty to control the conduct of another the courts have carved out an exception to this rule[5] in cases in which the defendant stands in some special relationship to either the person whose conduct needs to be controlled or in a relationship to the foreseeable victim of that conduct. Applying this exception to the present case, we note that a relationship of defendant therapists to either Tatiana or Poddar will suffice to establish a duty of care [under RST §315, *supra* at 623].

Although plaintiff's pleadings assert no special relation between Tatiana and defendant therapists, they establish as between Poddar and defendant therapists the special relation that arises between a patient and his doctor or psychotherapist. Such a relationship may support affirmative duties for the benefit of third persons. Thus, for example, a hospital must exercise reasonable care to control the behavior of a patient which may endanger other persons.[7] A doctor must also warn a patient if the patient's condition or medication renders certain conduct, such as driving a car, dangerous to others.

Although the California decisions that recognize this duty have involved cases in which the defendant stood in a special relationship *both* to the victim and to the person whose conduct created the danger,[9] we do not think that the duty should logically be constricted to such situations. Decisions of other jurisdictions hold that the single relationship of a doctor to his patient is sufficient to support the duty to exercise reasonable care to protect others against dangers emanating from the patient's illness. The courts hold that a doctor is liable to persons infected by his patient if he negligently fails to diagnose a contagious disease, or, having diagnosed the illness, fails to warn members of the patient's family.

Since it involved a dangerous mental patient, the decision in Merchants Nat. Bank & Trust Co. of Fargo v. United States, 272 F. Supp. 409 (D.N.D.

---

5. This rule derives from the common law's distinction between misfeasance and nonfeasance, and its reluctance to impose liability for the latter. (See Harper & Kime, The Duty to Control the Conduct of Another (1934) 43 Yale L.J. 886, 887.) Morally questionable, the rule owes its survival to "the difficulties of setting any standards of unselfish service to fellow men, and of making any workable rule to cover possible situations where fifty people might fail to rescue. . . . " (Prosser, Torts (4th ed. 1971) §56, p. 341.) Because of these practical difficulties, the courts have increased the number of instances in which affirmative duties are imposed not by direct rejection of the common law rule, but by expanding the list of special relationships which will justify departure from that rule.

7. When a "hospital has notice or knowledge of facts from which it might reasonably be concluded that a patient would be likely to harm himself *or others* unless preclusive measures were taken, then the hospital must use reasonable care in the circumstances to prevent such harm." (Vistica v. Presbyterian Hospital, 432 P.2d 193, 196 (Cal. 1967).) (Emphasis added.) A mental hospital may be liable if it negligently permits the escape or release of a dangerous patient. Greenberg v. Barbour (E.D. Pa. 1971) 322 F. Supp. 745, upheld a cause of action against a hospital staff doctor whose negligent failure to admit a mental patient resulted in that patient assaulting the plaintiff.

9. Ellis v. D'Angelo, 253 P.2d 675 (Cal. App. 1953), upheld a cause of action against parents who failed to warn a babysitter of the violent proclivities of their child; Johnson v. State of California, 447 P.2d 352 (Cal. 1968), upheld a suit against the state for failure to warn foster parents of the dangerous tendencies of their ward; Morgan v. City of Yuba, 41 Cal. Rptr. 508 (Cal. App. 1964), sustained a cause of action against a sheriff who had promised to warn decedent.

1967) comes closer to the issue. The Veterans Administration arranged for the patient to work on a local farm, but did not inform the farmer of the man's background. The farmer consequently permitted the patient to come and go freely during nonworking hours; the patient borrowed a car, drove to his wife's residence and killed her. Notwithstanding the lack of any "special relationship" between the Veterans Administration and the wife, the court found the Veterans Administration liable for the wrongful death of the wife. . . .

Defendants contend, however, that imposition of a duty to exercise reasonable care to protect third persons is unworkable because therapists cannot accurately predict whether or not a patient will resort to violence. In support of this argument amicus representing the American Psychiatric Association and other professional societies cites numerous articles which indicate that therapists, in the present state of the art, are unable reliably to predict violent acts; their forecasts, amicus claims, tend consistently to overpredict violence, and indeed are more often wrong than right. Since predictions of violence are often erroneous, amicus concludes, the courts should not render rulings that predicate the liability of therapists upon the validity of such predictions. . . .

We recognize the difficulty that a therapist encounters in attempting to forecast whether a patient presents a serious danger of violence. Obviously we do not require that the therapist, in making that determination, render a perfect performance; the therapist need only exercise "that reasonable degree of skill, knowledge, and care ordinarily possessed and exercised by members of [that professional specialty] under similar circumstances." Within the broad range of reasonable practice and treatment in which professional opinion and judgment may differ, the therapist is free to exercise his or her own best judgment without liability; proof, aided by hindsight, that he or she judged wrongly is insufficient to establish negligence.

In the instant case, however, the pleadings do not raise any question as to failure of defendant therapists to predict that Poddar presented a serious danger of violence. On the contrary, the present complaints allege that defendant therapists did in fact predict that Poddar would kill, but were negligent in failing to warn.

Amicus contends, however, that even when a therapist does in fact predict that a patient poses a serious danger of violence to others, the therapist should be absolved of any responsibility for failing to act to protect the potential victim. In our view, however, once a therapist does in fact determine, or under applicable professional standards reasonably should have determined, that a patient poses a serious danger of violence to others, he bears a duty to exercise reasonable care to protect the foreseeable victim of that danger. While the discharge of this duty of due care will necessarily vary with the facts of each case,[11] in each instance the adequacy of the therapist's conduct must be measured against the traditional negligence standard of the rendition of reasonable care under the circumstances. . . .

The risk that unnecessary warnings may be given is a reasonable price to pay for the lives of possible victims that may be saved. We would hesitate to hold that the therapist who is aware that his patient expects to attempt to assassinate the President of the United States would not be obligated to warn the authorities because the therapist cannot predict with accuracy that his patient will commit the crime. . . .

We recognize the public interest in supporting effective treatment of mental illness and in protecting the rights of patients to privacy, and the consequent public importance of safeguarding the confidential character of psychotherapeutic communication. Against this interest, however, we must weigh the public interest in safety from violent assault. The Legislature has undertaken the difficult task of balancing the countervailing concerns. In Evidence Code section 1014, it established a broad rule of privilege to protect confidential communications between patient and psychotherapist. In Evidence Code section 1024, the Legislature created a specific and limited exception to the psychotherapist-patient privilege: "There is no privilege . . . if the psychotherapist has reasonable cause to believe that the patient is in such mental or emotional condition as to be dangerous to himself or to the person or property of another and that disclosure of the communication is necessary to prevent the threatened danger."

We realize that the open and confidential character of psychotherapeutic dialogue encourages patients to express threats of violence, few of which are ever executed. Certainly a therapist should not be encouraged routinely to reveal such threats; such disclosures could seriously disrupt the patient's relationship with his therapist and with the persons threatened. To the contrary, the therapist's obligations to his patient require that he not disclose a confidence unless such disclosure is necessary to avert danger to others, and even then that he do so discreetly, and in a fashion that would preserve the privacy of his patient to the fullest extent compatible with the prevention of the threatened danger. (See Fleming & Maximov, The Patient or His Victim: The Therapist's Dilemma (1974) 62 Cal. L. Rev. 1025, 1065-1066.)

The revelation of a communication under the above circumstances is not a breach of trust or a violation of professional ethics as stated in the

---

11. Defendant therapists and amicus also argue that warnings must be given only in those cases in which the therapist knows the identity of the victim. We recognize that in some cases it would be unreasonable to require the therapist to interrogate his patient to discover the victim's identity, or to conduct an independent investigation. But there may also be cases in which a moment's reflection will reveal the victim's identity. The matter thus is one which depends upon the circumstances of each case, and should not be governed by any hard and fast rule.

Principles of Medical Ethics of the American Medical Association (1957) section 9: "A physician may not reveal the confidence entrusted to him in the course of medical attendance . . . *unless he is required to do so by law or unless it becomes necessary in order to protect the welfare of the individual or of the community.*" (Emphasis added.) We conclude that the public policy favoring protection of the confidential character of patient-psychotherapist communications must yield to the extent to which disclosure is essential to avert danger to others. The protective privilege ends where the public peril begins.

Our current crowded and computerized society compels the interdependence of its members. In this risk-infested society we can hardly tolerate the further exposure to danger that would result from a concealed knowledge of the therapist that his patient was lethal. If the exercise of reasonable care to protect the threatened victim requires the therapist to warn the endangered party or those who can reasonably be expected to notify him, we see no sufficient societal interest that would protect and justify concealment. The containment of such risks lies in the public interest. For the foregoing reasons, we find that plaintiffs' complaints can be amended to state a cause of action against defendants Moore, Powelson, Gold, and Yandell and against the Regents as their employer, for breach of a duty to exercise reasonable care to protect Tatiana.

[The court then held that defendant therapists were not immune from liability for their failure to warn under the discretionary function exception to the California Tort Claims Act. It further held that both defendant therapists and defendant police officers were immune from liability for failure to confine Poddar. Finally, the court concluded that the police defendants "do not have any such special relationship to either Tatiana or to Poddar sufficient to impose upon such defendants a duty to warning respecting Poddar's violent intentions."]

WRIGHT, C.J., and SULLIVAN and RICHARDSON, JJ., concur.

MOSK, J., concurring in part and dissenting in part. I concur in the result in this instance only because the complaints allege that defendant therapists did in fact predict that Poddar would kill and were therefore negligent in failing to warn of that danger. Thus the issue here is very narrow: we are not concerned with whether the therapists, pursuant to the standards of their profession, "should have" predicted potential violence; they allegedly did so in actuality. Under these limited circumstances I agree that a cause of action can be stated. . . .

CLARK, J., dissenting. Until today's majority opinion, both legal and medical authorities have agreed that confidentiality is essential to effectively treat the mentally ill, and that imposing a duty on doctors to disclose patient threats to potential victims would greatly impair treatment. Further, recognizing that effective treatment and society's safety are necessarily intertwined, the Legislature has already decided effective and confidential treatment is preferred over imposition of a duty to warn.

The issue whether effective treatment for the mentally ill should be sacrificed to a system of warnings is, in my opinion, properly one for the Legislature, and we are bound by its judgment. Moreover, even in the absence of clear legislative direction, we must reach the same conclusion because imposing the majority's new duty is certain to result in a net increase in violence.

NOTES

1. Tarasoff's *California aftermath*. The duty of reasonable care announced in *Tarasoff* has been widely accepted, see RTT:LPH §41 & comment g. Under its rationale, is the plaintiff's case easier or more difficult because the defendants were medical professionals instead of ordinary individuals? Does it make a difference whether we focus on the competence of psychiatrists to detect dangerous persons or the need for confidentiality in patient-psychiatrist relationships? How should the law reflect the differences between dangerous persons who are or who are not in custody?

Tarasoff's limits were tested in Beauchene v. Synanon Foundation, Inc., 151 Cal. Rptr. 796 (Cal. App. 1979), which held that a *private* rehabilitation center owed no duty of care to members of the public at large when it accepted individuals referred to it by the state prison system as a condition of their parole. The court held that the absence of a duty of care was fatal to both plaintiff's claims, to wit, that the assailant had been improperly admitted into the program and that he had been improperly supervised once admitted. Should the same result apply when a private institution treats patients without a criminal conviction?

In the subsequent California Supreme Court case of Thompson v. County of Alameda, 614 P.2d 728, 736 (Cal. 1980), a juvenile with a long and sorrowful personal history of violence and sexual abuse was released into the custody of his mother, even though the county knew that the youth had "indicated that he would, if released, take the life of a young child residing in the neighborhood." Although no particular person was identified, the released juvenile in fact murdered the plaintiff's son in the plaintiff's mother's garage within 24 hours of his release. The plaintiffs argued that warnings should have been issued to (a) the police, (b) the parents in the neighborhood, and/or (c) the juvenile's mother. The contention was rejected by the court:

> Unlike members of the general public, in *Tarasoff* . . . the potential victims were specifically known and designated individuals. The warnings which we therein required were directed at making those individuals aware of the danger to which they were uniquely exposed. The threatened targets were precise. In such cases, it is fair to conclude that warnings given discreetly and to

a limited number of persons would have a greater effect because they would alert those particular targeted individuals of the possibility of a specific threat pointed at them. In contrast, the warnings sought by plaintiffs would of necessity have to be made to a broad segment of the population and would be only general in nature. In addition to the likelihood that such generalized warnings when frequently repeated would do little as a practical matter to stimulate increased safety measures, as we develop below, such extensive warnings would be difficult to give.

Tobriner, J., dissented on the ground that warnings should have been given to the mother, who "might" have taken additional steps to control the conduct of her son.

The issue of the therapist's care in California is today governed by California Civil Code §43.92, which provides:

> (a) There shall be no monetary liability on the part of, and no cause of action shall arise against, any person who is a psychotherapist . . . in failing to warn of and protect from a patient's threatened violent behavior or failing to predict and warn of and protect from a patient's violent behavior except where the patient has communicated to the psychotherapist a serious threat of physical violence against a reasonably identifiable victim or victims.
>
> (b) If there is a duty to warn and protect under the limited circumstances specified above, the duty shall be discharged by the psychotherapist making reasonable efforts to communicate the threat to the victim or victims and to a law enforcement agency.

2. *Beyond California.* Notwithstanding the California statute, the influence of *Tarasoff* has extended far beyond California. The duties are especially strict on defendants whose steps facilitate attacks by persons within their care on innocent plaintiffs. One particularly chilling example is Lundgren v. Fultz, 354 N.W.2d 25, 29 (Minn. 1984), in which a psychiatrist interceded on behalf of his patient, who had been diagnosed and committed as a paranoid schizophrenic, to secure the return of his guns that had been confiscated by the police. The court noted that "a jury could conclude that the psychiatrist's letter caused the police to return these guns and, thus, materially increased the danger that Fultz posed. . . . There is a limit to the protection given the discretion in a professional relationship. That limit is exceeded where a psychiatrist places the gun in a potential assassin's hand under the guise of fostering trust between patient and psychiatrist." Liability is more closely contested when a psychiatrist has only limited interactions with psychiatric individuals on an outpatient basis. In Estates of Morgan v. Fairfield Family Counseling Center, 673 N.E.2d 1311, 1323 (Ohio 1997), Matt Morgan's severe schizophrenic disorders were only diagnosed and treated after his moody and abusive behavior forced him to

leave his parents' home in Ohio. While homeless, he received psychiatric care at Jefferson Hospital in Pennsylvania. After a 12-week hospitalization and a course of treatment with Navane, an antipsychotic drug, he was allowed to return home to his parents on the condition that he remain under medical supervision. Once home, he was seen three times by a psychiatrist, Dr. Brown, who suspected him of malingering for a disability claim. Brown took him off Navane and turned him over for care to the FFCC under the supervision of Nancy Lambert, a vocational counselor. He instructed Lambert to contact him should Matt's condition deteriorate. When Matt's behavior became more abusive, his parents sought to have him involuntarily committed, but were unable to do so in part because the FFCC did not support their application. Dr. Brown was not brought back into the case. Some nine months after Dr. Brown last saw Matt, Matt killed his parents and wounded his sister. He was acquitted of charges of murder and felonious assault by reason of insanity. Following *Tarasoff*, Resnick, J., allowed an action for negligence against Dr. Brown, Ms. Lambert, and the FFCC, relying in part on §319 of the Second Restatement:

> One who takes charge of a third person whom he knows or should know to be likely to cause bodily harm to others if not controlled is under a duty to exercise reasonable care to control the third person to prevent him from doing such harm.

She then noted that a psychiatrist "takes charge" of a patient who is not subject to "actual constraint or confinement" so long as the patient is treated in an "outpatient setting" where "anticipatory measures" could be taken to prevent the occurrence of violent episodes. An anguished dissent protested the loose tests adopted by the majority and asked "under the tenuous facts of this case, are all persons employed in the psychotherapy field now strictly liable for the acts of their patients?"

Finally, in Long v. Broadlawns Medical Center, 656 N.W.2d 71 (Iowa 2002), the decedent, Jillene Long, was killed by her husband, Gerald, a psychiatric patient who had been released from the defendant medical center. The husband had a long history of spousal abuse. During his commitment, the decedent agreed with hospital officials that she would remain at the marital residence, but that Broadlawns would call her on the day of her husband's discharge. That call was never made, and Cady, J., after extensive consideration of *Tarasoff*, held that the basic issue was "whether Broadlawns failed to exercise reasonable care in performing a promise to warn Jillene of Gerald's discharge thereby increasing the risk of harm to her or resulting in harm to her because of her reliance on the promised warning." The cause of action was allowed because the plaintiff could show the causal relevance of this breach of duty. "[S]ubstantial evidence exist[ed] to support a finding that Jillene would not have been at the marital residence had she known Gerald was discharged and essentially free to return there himself." Gerald's conduct did not count as a superseding cause because his acts fell "squarely within the scope of the original risk."

For a exhaustive bibliography on these issues, see, RTT:LPH §41, comment *g* and its Reporter's Note.

3. A Tarasoff *Retrospective.* One reason *Tarasoff* has always raised difficult problems is that it is not amenable to easy contractual solutions for, unlike *Long*, the three parties are not in privity with each other. Hence no one doubts the legitimate state interest in seeking to prevent death or serious injury by imposing some form of liability on the psychiatrists and institutions who provide care for seriously deranged patients. Disturbed persons are not easily deterrable, and they have few if any resources to answer tort claims. Yet at the same time the fear that potential disclosure will drive disturbed individuals from the care they so desperately need has placed a break on the liability. When *Tarasoff* came down there were many predictions of systematic professional doom, but these have moderated with time. Thus, notable critics such as Alan Stone, an expert in law and psychiatry, first denounced *Tarasoff,* Stone, *The* Tarasoff *Decision: Suing Psychotherapists to Safeguard Society,* 90 Harv. L. Rev. 358 (1976). But on reflection he later wrote "the duty to warn is not as unmitigated a disaster for the enterprise of psychotherapy as it once seemed to critics like myself." Stone, Law Psychiatry and Morality: Essays and Analysis 181 (1984). Progress, if not a full-throated endorsement.

But why? Three explanations seem relevant. First, many states, like California, have codified the duty in ways that soften its sharpest edges. Second, the courts have tended in practice to be cautious about imposing the duty on persons who are not in custody. Third, the duty tends to bite most powerfully in three situations: 1) where the potential target has been identified by the disturbed person, as in *Tarasoff* itself; 2) where the psychiatrist has somehow facilitated the commission of the crime, as in *Lundgren*; and 3), where the psychiatrist or institution has breached some explicit promise to the future victim, as in *Long*. Not perfect, perhaps. But not a bad application of traditional principles.

8

TRADITIONAL STRICT LIABILITY

SECTION A. INTRODUCTION

One major theme of this casebook concerns the recurrent tension between negligence and strict liability. This chapter pursues one facet of that theme by looking in detail at those areas of the tort law that resisted incorporation into a general negligence framework even when its influence was at its peak. The historical bastions of strict liability, grouped together in this chapter, involve liability for animals, for so-called ultrahazardous or abnormally dangerous activities, and for nuisance. These tort liabilities are quite ancient and were, it will be recalled, treated by Judge Blackburn as instances of the "true rule" (of strict liability for bringing, keeping, and collecting) that he announced in Rylands v. Fletcher. The second head of liability — ultrahazardous activities — has developed in the United States in large measure from efforts to rationalize and generalize from *Rylands*. Thus, *Rylands* provides the most convenient point of departure for determining how these rules relate to each other and to *Rylands* itself. In order to place the subject matter in perspective, it is helpful at this point to reread the opinions in Rylands v. Fletcher, *supra* at 127.

SECTION B. ANIMALS

Gehrts v. Batteen
620 N.W.2d 775 (S.D. 2001)

GILBERTSON, J. Gehrts was bitten by a St. Bernard owned by Nielsen. Gehrts sued Nielsen in strict liability and in negligence. The trial court

645

granted summary judgment as to both claims. Gehrts appeals and we affirm.

FACTS AND PROCEDURE

On July 29, 1995, Cindy Nielsen (Nielsen) visited the home of Jessica Gehrts (Gehrts) to pick up a wreath made by Gehrts' mother. Nielsen had come directly from dog obedience school with her eight-month-old dog, Wilbur, a St. Bernard. Wilbur was secured in the back of Nielsen's pickup by a harness attached to a restraining device that had been installed in the pickup box. This device allowed Wilbur to move freely between the sides of the box, but limited his movement between the front and back. While the parties were near the truck, Gehrts asked Nielsen if she could pet Wilbur. Nielsen allowed her to do so. As Gehrts reached up to pet Wilbur, he bit her in the face, causing injuries to her nose and forehead. Gehrts received extensive medical treatment as a result of those injuries.

Gehrts sued Nielsen and her husband, Jon Batteen, to recover for her injuries. In her complaint, Gehrts alleged that Nielsen was negligent in failing to restrain or control her dog. Nielsen moved for summary judgment, which was granted. Gehrts appeals the trial court's ruling and we affirm.

ANALYSIS AND DECISION

1. NEGLIGENCE

When wild animals, such as a bear or wolf, are kept as pets, an owner is liable for injuries caused by the animal. This results even if the owner had no prior knowledge of the animal's propensity to cause harm, and even if the owner has exercised the utmost care in preventing harm.

Owners of domesticated animals may also be held liable for harm caused by their pet if the owner knows or has reason to know that the animal has abnormally dangerous propensities. Again, this liability attaches regardless of the amount of care exercised by the owner. However, this liability is not strict liability. Rather, the failure to act upon the knowledge of an animal's abnormally dangerous propensities establishes a breach of the duty of care owed by the owner to those that come in contact with the animal. As it is a cause of action sounding in negligence, the defenses of contributory negligence and assumption of the risk are available to temper this liability. Before this breach of duty will affix to an owner, the plaintiff must establish that the owner knew or should have known of that animal's dangerous propensities. This knowledge is generally imputed to the owner when there is evidence of at least one attack by the animal.[1] In the case of a dog, evidence of the owner's knowledge that it constantly barked, bared its teeth, and strained at its leash is sufficient to establish dangerous propensities, absent an actual attack.

However, in certain instances a cause of action for negligence can survive without the owner's actual knowledge of an animal's dangerous propensities. When the owner does not know of the animal's dangerous propensities, the ordinary negligence standard of foreseeability will still be applied. To recover, the plaintiff must establish that a duty existed between the owner and the victim and that there was a breach of that duty. Thus, when no actual knowledge of dangerousness exists, the plaintiff must establish that as an ordinary, prudent person, the owner should have foreseen the event that caused the injury and taken steps to prevent the injury. Such liability may arise "depending upon the kind and character of the particular animal concerned, the circumstances in which it is placed, and the purposes for which it is employed or kept."

In the present action, there has been no evidence presented that Nielsen had any knowledge that Wilbur had dangerous propensities. The parties agree that, by nature, St. Bernards are gentle dogs. Nielsen and her husband testified in their depositions that Wilbur had never previously growled, bared his teeth, tried to bite or act aggressively toward any person. In addition, Gehrts admitted that she did not know of any incidents that would have alerted Nielsen to any dangerous propensities. Gehrts argues that the act of an unprovoked biting is evidence of the animal's dangerous propensity. While other jurisdictions may allow juries to determine after the fact whether the animal had dangerous propensities, such reasoning has been expressly rejected in South Dakota.

Nevertheless, Gehrts will still be allowed to recover if she can show that Nielsen failed to use reasonable care in the circumstances in that Nielsen as a prudent person should have foreseen the danger. In support of this claim, Gehrts produced an affidavit from a dog expert who concluded that Nielsen acted in an unreasonable manner when she failed to properly restrain Wilbur. This affidavit was based largely on the fact that the Gehrts family kept a dog at their home, its scent would be on Gehrts, and Nielsen should have known that the smell of a strange dog would make Wilbur act aggressively. However, there is no evidence in the record that Nielsen was aware that Gehrts owned a dog or that the scent of the dog would be on Gehrts. Beyond the assertions in the affidavit, there is no evidence or reason to believe that Nielsen knew, or as a prudent person should

---

1. There is no requirement that the attack cause injury to the victim to establish dangerous propensities. The common law "one free bite rule" was expressly rejected in *Ross v. Hanson*, 200 N.W.2d 255, 256 (S.D. 1972).

have known, that the scent of a strange dog would cause Wilbur to attack Gehrts.

Gehrts also claims that Nielsen was negligent in failing to restrain and have control over Wilbur while he was being petted by Gehrts. Wilbur was attached to a harness in the back of the pickup. This harness was specifically designed to secure a large dog. Gehrts claims that Nielsen should have released Wilbur from the harness, taken him out of the truck bed and allowed Gehrts to pet him while Nielsen held the leash. Whether this would have prevented the injury is speculative. It may actually have exacerbated the situation. If Wilbur had become sufficiently agitated to pull free of Nielsen's control, Gehrts' injuries may have been much more severe. . . .

There is simply no evidence that Nielsen violated the reasonable person standard of care in her handling of Wilbur. Therefore, Gehrts' cause of action for negligence cannot survive.

2. STRICT LIABILITY

Nielsen also urges us to follow the lead of the South Carolina Supreme Court by judicially adopting a strict liability standard for injuries caused by dogs. See Hossenlopp v. Cannon, 329 S.E.2d 438 (SC 1985). We decline to do so. The overwhelming majority of states that impose strict liability for injuries caused by dogs have done so through legislative mandate. See . . . Cal. Civil Code §3342 (West 1997) . . . . Our legislature has already imposed strict liability on dog owners for damages inflicted upon "poultry or domestic animal[s]." SDCL 40-34-2. While one may question the application of strict liability for damages to livestock, but not for injuries to children, the legislature is the proper place to decide such public policy issues.

[Affirmed.]

SABERS, J., dissenting.

I disagree with the premature conclusion that the facts of this case warrant summary judgment for Nielson. "This Court has stated on numerous occasions that summary judgment is generally not appropriate in negligence actions." . . .

Whether Nielson was negligent: 1) in restraining the dog, 2) allowing the fourteen year old girl to pet the dog, 3) failing to release the dog from the harness, or 4) whether Nielson knew that her co-worker, Gehrts' mother, owned a dog at that house are genuine issues of material fact that should be resolved by a jury. The facts of this case can not be resolved by summary judgment or rubber stamped by appellate review. The majority opinion's finding that Nielson was not negligent for failing to release the dog from the harness is a function best left to the jury.

NOTES

1. Basis of liability for animals.   The decision in *Gehrts* states the dominant English and American view that the liability rules tend to be strict, at least for animals classified as dangerous by nature, often called "animals ferae naturae" in the older cases. For wild animals, the Third Restatement subjects the owner or possessor to strict liability for physical harm. RTT:LPH §22. The category "wild animals" includes most of the obvious suspects such as lions and tigers, but has also been extended to cover elephants, monkeys, and camels. The basic test, adopted in the Third Restatement, confirms the obvious and treats as wild any animal "that belongs to a category of animals that have not been generally domesticated and that are likely, unless restrained, to cause personal injury." What about property damage?

For animals that are tame by nature (animals mansuetae naturae), the rules are a bit more complex. Normally, the owner is only liable for negligence, but a strict liability rule applies to domestic animals that, as individuals, have shown dangerous propensities even if they have not bitten. The common statement that every dog is entitled to one free bite is not an accurate reflection of the general law; a demonstrated tendency to bite is enough. RST §509, comment *g*. Where there is common law doubt on the question, the one free bite rule is often rejected by statute. See, e.g., N.H. Rev. Stat. Ann. §466:19 (2007). Some rare cases address the question of whether a particular animal is wild or tame. In Harper v. Robinson, 589 S.E.2d 295 (Ga. App. 2003), the defendant's dog, Natsayia, picked up the plaintiffs' infant and carried her into the kitchen, resulting in her death. The plaintiffs claimed that the animal had exhibited certain wolf-like characteristics and thus should be classified as wild. But the court held that plaintiffs' subjective beliefs did not raise a jury question when the defendant "presented evidence of Natsayia's direct pedigree as a dog."

Why should the line between wild and tame matter anyhow? What is wrong with a unified prima facie case that holds that "your dog (or other animal) bit me"? The Third Restatement rejects the vicarious liability intuition behind this approach by noting that "the language of trespass is analytically imperfect: a cow is obviously incapable of committing a tort. For that reason, any idea of vicarious liability is also inapt: there is no tort on the part of the cow that can be imputed to the owner." RTT:LPH §21, comment *b*.

Why can't cattle trespass? Is it because they cannot form intentions? Understand the significance of boundary lines? Note that following the Restatement lead, it is often said the gist of the strict liability cause of action is not the biting or kicking of the animal as such, but the breach of an absolute duty on the part of the owner or possessor to keep it contained. The different accounts of the formulations can result in different outcomes, especially when the animal is in the custody of someone who is not the owner. In Baker v. Snell, [1908] 2 K.B. 825, the defendant owned a dog known to be vicious, which he entrusted to his potman, or servant, to take care of each morning. While in the kitchen with the plaintiff, defendant's maidservant, the potman, "presumably by way of a foolish practical joke, said, 'I will bet the dog will not bite any one,' and then, 'Go it, Bob,' whereupon the dog bit the plaintiff." The county court judge dismissed the cause of action "on the ground that the conduct of the barman who had the dog in charge amounted to an assault by him." At the first stage of appeal, a new trial was ordered to on the question of scope of the potman's employment; Channell, J., said that the key question about the incitement by the potman was

> whether the man's wrongful act was done in the course of his employment, or whether it was done for purposes of his own. If it could be shewn that the man did it maliciously to gratify some grudge against the plaintiff, his master would be not be liable. But there was no evidence of that. In my view the potman's act amount to nothing more than a foolish and wanton act done in neglect of his duty to keep the dog safe; and if that is the right view, the defendant would be responsible. But the question is one of fact which ought to have been left to the jury.

Cozens-Hardy, M.R., accepted that position but made it clear that he did not think that the characterization of the potman's act was decisive.

> If a man keeps an animal whose nature is ferocious, or an animal of a class not generally ferocious, but which is know to the owner to be dangerous, is the owner of that animal liable only if he neglects his duty of keeping it safe or is negligent in the discharge of that duty, or is he bound to keep it secure at his peril? In my opinion the latter is the correct proposition of law. . . .

What result if lightning breaks the chains restraining the dog, who breaks free and does mischief to a stranger? If the dog is in the custody of someone who is not the defendant's employee?

Compare the view on causation under the Third Restatement, which provides as follows:

§23.   ABNORMALLY DANGEROUS ANIMALS

An owner or possessor of an animal that the owner or possessor knows or has reason to know has dangerous tendencies abnormal for the animal's category is subject to strict liability for physical harm caused by the animal if the harm ensues from that dangerous tendency.

The restriction of liability to the owner and possessor proved decisive for the defendant in Woods-Leber v. Hyatt Hotels of Puerto Rico, 124 F.3d 47 (1st Cir. 1997). A rabid mongoose leaped out of the woods and bit the plaintiff while she was sunbathing at the defendant's posh, luxury hotel. The strict liability case failed because the plaintiff could not show "at a bare minimum" that the hotel had possessed or owned the animal. The negligence claim failed because there was no warning or anticipation of a possible infestation of mongooses.

2. *Affirmative defenses for wild animals.* The strict liability principle works best when wild animals attack or injure strangers. However, this rule has been relaxed in a variety of controlled settings. In City and County of Denver v. Kennedy, 476 P.2d 762 (Colo. App. 1970), the Colorado Court of Appeals held that its state's general rule of strict liability (Collins v. Otto, 369 P.2d 564 (Colo. 1962)) did not apply to animals kept in public zoos. It agreed in general that the keeping or harboring of an animal is "in defiance of the safety and desires of the surrounding society." Nonetheless, it concluded that it would be improper to apply that rule to a zoo, which is maintained and operated "in response to the public's obvious desires," and "unrealistic" to hold that the operation of the zoo "exposes the public to an inordinate risk" of harm. It therefore held that negligence principles governed. On appeal, the state supreme court held that the plaintiff made out a jury case in negligence by showing that the defendant's zebra pit was constructed so that a person could easily reach over the barriers and come in direct physical contact with the animals. Kennedy v. City and County of Denver, 506 P.2d 764 (Colo. 1972).

In Rubenstein v. United States, 338 F. Supp. 654 (N.D. Cal. 1972), *aff'd,* 488 F.2d 1071 (9th Cir. 1973), the court reached the same conclusion for animals in national parks. The plaintiff, while sleeping in his tent in Yellowstone Park, was attacked and mauled by a bear. Before the incident took place, the plaintiff had received written warnings from the park authorities about the dangers of camping out in the park. The court held that the defendants had not been negligent, having discharged their duty to warn. The same result follows on strict liability, since the written warnings compel the finding that the plaintiff assumed the risk of injury.

3. *Notice of vicious tendencies.* Courts have much mooted the question of whether a tame animal has exhibited the vicious tendencies that would subject it to the strict liability regime for animals. In the usual case, actual knowledge that the animal has exhibited dangerous behaviors or has been involved in prior incidents is required. Thus, in Collier v. Zambito, 807 N.E.2d 254, 256 (N.Y. 2004), the 12-year-old Collier was visiting his friend when he was bitten in an unprovoked attack by the family dog, Cecil. The dog had been barking in the kitchen, and Ms. Zambito had placed him on a leash and invited Collier to let the dog smell him when the attack took place. The court denied any liability given that the defendant had no knowledge its vicious tendencies:

> Knowledge of vicious propensities may of course be established by proof of prior acts of a similar kind of which the owner had notice. In addition, a

triable issue of fact as to knowledge of a dog's vicious propensities might be raised—even in the absence of proof that the dog had actually bitten someone-by evidence that it had been known to growl, snap or bare its teeth. Also potentially relevant is whether the owner chose to restrain the dog, and the manner in which the dog was restrained. The keeping of a dog as a guard dog may give rise to an inference that an owner had knowledge of the dog's vicious propensities. . . .

The evidence submitted by plaintiff was simply insufficient to raise an issue of fact as to whether Cecil had vicious propensities that were known, or should have been known, to defendants. Cecil was kept as a family pet, not as a guard dog. Although the dog was restricted to the kitchen area, uncontroverted deposition testimony indicated that he was confined only because he would bark when guests were at the house. There was no evidence that Cecil was confined because the owners feared he would do any harm to their visitors. There was no evidence that the dog's behavior was ever threatening or menacing. Indeed, the dog's actions—barking and running around—are consistent with normal canine behavior. Barking and running around are what dogs do.

How should *Collier* come out under a regime of strict liability with an assumption of risk defense? What rule should apply with respect to pit bulls and other animals that are bred to promote aggressive behaviors? At least one court has refused to act on its own initiative. "At the summary judgment hearing, plaintiff invited the trial justice to take judicial notice that pitbull terriers are inherently dangerous by virtue of their breed. That would have, in effect, created a new cause of action by imposing strict liability upon pitbull owners. The hearing justice properly declined to accept the invitation, because the creation of a new cause of action should be left to the Legislature." Ferrara v. Marra, 823 A.2d 1134, 1137 (R.I. 2003). Many states have indeed passed special "breed laws" to answer that question.

4. Cattle trespass. The rules governing cattle trespass contain several distinctive features, as is set out in the Third Restatement:

§21.   INTRUSION BY LIVESTOCK OR OTHER ANIMALS

An owner or possessor of livestock or other animals, except for dogs and cats, that intrude upon the land of another is subject to strict liability for physical harm caused by the intrusion.

When the animal's owner entrusts it to someone else for safekeeping, the Third Restatement concludes: "Both the owner and the possessor are sufficiently responsible for the animal as to make their [joint] liability appropriate. Furthermore, the owner and the possessor remain free to work out between themselves the ultimate allocation of liability." *Id.*, comment *f.* The position is otherwise if the possessor has taken the animal without the owner's consent. *Id.* The possessor is then manifestly liable.

In general, the owner or possessor of the animal is responsible for any damage it does to the plaintiff's real property and to animals peacefully grazing there. See, e.g., Lee v. Riley, 144 Eng. Rep. 629 (C.B. 1865). Yet, causation problems may arise in deciding whether certain harms fall within the class of those that make the animal dangerous. The Second Restatement §504, for example, states that the strict liability of the "possessor" of trespassing livestock does "not extend to harm . . . not reasonably to be expected from the intrusion." Section 504, comment *g*, notes that "any trespassing bull may be expected to attack and gore any other animal, or any person who gets in his way." But are other defenses available? In Williams v. Goodwin, 116 Cal. Rptr. 200, 208 (Cal. App. 1974), the plaintiff was working in his garden when, without provocation, he was attacked by the defendant's trespassing bull. The defendant's motion for nonsuit was granted by the trial judge, but recovery was allowed on appeal.

> The sequence of events from entry upon the land to attack upon plaintiff, without interposition of any independent operative agency, compels the conclusion that plaintiff's injuries were the direct consequence of the trespass. Moreover, to conclude under these circumstances that an attack such as occurred with resulting injury was not reasonably to be expected would require a departure from logic. The manifest danger that inheres in exposure of the person to the immediate presence of an uncontrolled bull is strongly suggested by human experience and common sense. Thus, it is of no significance that defendant's bull did not pause to forage plaintiff's crop either before the attack, after the attack, or at all, or that plaintiff's injuries were not sustained in the course of an effort to expel the animal or to protect his property.

5. *Distress damage feasant.* "Distress damage feasant" refers to "the taking of chattels, whether animate or inanimate, that are doing damage to or (perhaps) encumbering land, or depasturing chattels, and the retaining of them by way of security until compensation is paid." G. Williams, Liability for Animals 7 (1939). This self-help remedy was critical in most disputes between farmers arising from trespassing cattle, and it offers a partial explanation for the dominance of the strict liability rule for trespassing animals. In Marshall v. Welwood, 38 N.J.L. 339, 341 (1876), Beasley, C.J., argued that "the right to plead that the escape had occurred by inevitable accident would have seriously impaired, if it did not entirely frustrate, the process of distress damage feasant. Custom has had much to do in giving shape to the law, and what is highly convenient readily runs into usage, and is accepted as a rule. It would but rarely occur that cattle would escape from a vigilant owner. . . ."

Note also that in England, a proposal to govern cattle trespass by negligence rules, Report of the Committee on the Law of Civil Liability for Damage Done by Animals, CMD 8746, & ¶3 (1953), was rejected in large measure because of the protests of the farmers themselves. As the report stated, "This class of liability is of interest only to farmers and landowners and the general public are not affected thereby."

6. *Animals on the public highway.* What duties, if any, do owners of cattle have to prevent them from straying onto the public highway? In Gibbs v. Jackson, 990 S.W.2d 745 (Tex. 1999), the plaintiff was driving her car on a "farm-to-market" road. Her car was totaled when she collided with and killed the defendant's horse, Tiny, that had wandered on to the public road. Abbot, J., refused to impose liability on the owner in light of extensive exceptions that the legislature had established to the "free-range" rule. "Under the English common law inherited by the United States, an owner of a domestic animal had a duty to prevent the animal from trespassing onto a neighbor's land, but had no duty to prevent the animal from straying onto a public roadway, unless the owner had prior knowledge that the animal had vicious propensities. . . . It is the right of every owner of domestic animals in this state, not known to be diseased, vicious, or 'breachy,' to allow them to run at large." Why? The rule in Mississippi appears to be by statute that the owner of animals, as defendant, has the burden to show that he took reasonable care when an animal strayed on a paved designated federal or state highway, but that on non-statutory roads, the burden is on the plaintiff to plead and prove negligence. Barrett v. Parker, 757 So.2d 182 (Miss. 2000). Again, why?

7. *"Fencing in" and "fencing out."* In Garcia v. Sumrall, 121 P.2d 640, 644 (Ariz. 1942), Lockwood, C.J., said:

> Under the common law it was presumed to be the duty of the owners of animals to keep the same properly enclosed and under control, and if they failed to do so and the animals trespassed upon the property of another, fenced or unfenced, the owners of the animals were liable for damages. This rule, however, has been greatly modified in America, and particularly in what is commonly referred to as the grazing states. The situation in these states may be briefly stated as follows:
>
> A very large percentage of the land therein is owned by the United States government, only an extremely small portion being under private ownership. Much of this land is valuable only for the pasturage of meat animals. The federal government for many years recognized the custom existing of allowing such animals to run at large upon the land and acquiesced therein, but forbade its enclosure by fences. The result was that if the old common law rule of trespass was applied, it would have been practically impossible to use these federal lands for grazing, for the animals running at large thereon, due to their natural instincts, would be practically certain to trespass upon any privately owned lands lying adjacent to the open range. For this reason many, if not most, of the western states adopted statutes similar to ours above referred to. The obvious purpose and effect of these statutes was to change the common law rule and to make the owner of private premises fence his land to keep animals out, rather than to compel the owner of the animals to

fence the land upon which they were grazing in order to keep them in. But notwithstanding this, it was practically universally held in the states having such laws that they did not have the effect of permitting those grazing animals upon the public domain to commit acts of willful trespass by deliberately and intentionally causing their animals to trespass upon private property.

Does a defendant who simply lets his animals roam the open fields with the knowledge that they might enter another's land commit a willful trespass? *Garcia* noted the division of authority on the question and opted for a higher standard, taking the view adopted in Colorado and Wyoming that requires the plaintiff to show "some overt and unlawful act on the part of the defendant which tends to increase the natural propensity of cattle to wander and to direct them upon the premises of another." Other cases, however, hold that the cattle owner on an open range commits an intentional tort only when he places cattle on his own land in a manner and location that makes it substantially certain that they will stray. E.g., Lazarus v. Phelps, 152 U.S. 81 (1894).

8. *Fencing out: historical, economic, and social complications.* "Fencing out" statutes depart from the usual principles of property law by requiring a plaintiff to take affirmative action to protect the exclusive use of land. The Third Restatement §21, comments *c* and *d*, explores in some depth the diversity of positions on the fencing out question. It notes that use of the English fencing-in rule is more common when farmers outnumber ranchers, especially since fencing-in helps the cattle owner protect his herd against a variety of perils running from rustlers and snakes to unwanted insemination.

The issue now lies at the tail end of fierce political conflicts during much of the nineteenth century. This early history has been well documented. See, e.g., R. Ellickson, Order Without Law: How Neighbors Settle Disputes chs. 2 & 3 (1991); Vogel, The Coase Theorem and California Animal Trespass Law, 16 J. Legal Stud. 149 (1987). Open-range regimes requiring landowners to fence out have slowly given way to the closed-range alternatives now favored in the Third Restatement.

This choice between open and closed range not only has dramatic economic consequences for both ranchers and farmers, but also influences the pattern of negotiations over the use of land. As Vogel points out, moving from open-range rules (favoring the rancher) to closed-range rules (favoring the farmer) reduces the costs of negotiating a change in the patterns of land use. Under an open-range system, a single landowner cannot in practice buy off some ranchers and hope to preserve his land for agricultural uses. Those ranchers not bound by the agreement could still let their cattle roam at will. Yet, when the rights to exclude belong to the farmer, a voluntary agreement can allow some ranchers limited grazing rights, without opening the land up to all ranchers. Placing exclusive rights in the farmer facilitates consensual reassignments of rights better than the open range rules. Thus, land remains open range when virtually all its users are cattle ranchers who benefit when animals can run freely. But once land is used more intensively, the balance of advantage shifts to the closed-range system, which encourages more specialized land uses. See also RTT:LPH §21, comment *d*, which notes that coordination costs tend to favor open-range regimes when ranchers dominate, and closed-range regimes when they do not.

SECTION C.   ULTRAHAZARDOUS OR ABNORMALLY DANGEROUS ACTIVITIES

Spano v. Perini Corp.
250 N.E.2d 31 (N.Y. 1969)

FULD, C.J. The principal question posed on this appeal is whether a person who has sustained property damage caused by blasting on nearby property can maintain an action for damages without a showing that the blaster was negligent. Since 1893, when this court decided the case of Booth v. Rome, W. & O.T.R.R. Co., [35 N.E. 592 (N.Y. 1893),] it has been the law of this State that proof of negligence was required unless the blast was accompanied by an actual physical invasion of the damaged property — for example, by rocks or other material being cast upon the premises. We are now asked to reconsider that rule.

The plaintiff Spano is the owner of a garage in Brooklyn which was wrecked by a blast occurring on November 27, 1962. There was then in that garage, for repairs, an automobile owned by the plaintiff Davis which he also claims was damaged by the blasting. Each of the plaintiffs brought suit against the two defendants who, as joint venturers, were engaged in constructing a tunnel in the vicinity pursuant to a contract with the City of New York. The two cases were tried together, without a jury, in the Civil Court of the City of New York, New York County, and judgments were rendered in favor of the plaintiffs. The judgments were reversed by the Appellate Term and the Appellate Division affirmed that order, granting leave to appeal to this court.

It is undisputed that, on the day in question (November 27, 1962), the defendants had set off a total of 194 sticks of dynamite at a construction site which was only 125 feet away from the damaged premises. Although both plaintiffs alleged negligence in their complaints, no attempt was made to show that the defendants had failed to exercise reasonable care or to take necessary precautions when they were blasting. Instead, they chose to rely, upon the trial, solely on the principle of absolute liability either on a tort theory or on the basis of their being third-party beneficiaries of the defendants' contract with the city. At the close of the plaintiff Spano's case, when defendants' attorney moved to dismiss the action on the ground, among others, that no negligence had been proved, the trial judge expressed the view that the defendants could be held liable even though they were not shown to have been careless. The case then proceeded, with evidence being introduced solely on the question of damages and proximate cause. Following the trial, the court awarded damages of some $4,400 to Spano and of $329 to Davis.

On appeal, a divided Appellate Term reversed that judgment, declaring that it deemed itself concluded by the established rule in this State requiring proof of negligence. Justice Markowitz, who dissented, urged that the Booth case should no longer be considered controlling precedent.

The Appellate Division affirmed; it called attention to a decision in the Third Department in which the court observed that "[i]f *Booth* is to be overruled, 'the announcement thereof should come from the authoritative source and not in the form of interpretation or prediction by an intermediate appellate court.'"

In our view, the time has come for this court to make that "announcement" and declare that one who engages in blasting must assume responsibility, and be liable without fault, for any injury he causes to neighboring property.

The concept of absolute liability in blasting cases is hardly a novel one. The overwhelming majority of American jurisdictions have adopted such a rule. . . .

We need not rely solely, however, upon out-of-state decisions in order to attain our result. Not only has the rationale of the *Booth* case been overwhelmingly rejected elsewhere but it appears to be fundamentally inconsistent with earlier cases in our own court which had held, long before *Booth* was decided, that a party was absolutely liable for damages to neighboring property caused by explosions. (See, e.g., Hay v. Cohoes Co., 2 N.Y. 159 [(1849)]; Heeg v. Licht, 80 N.Y. 579 [(1880).]) In the *Hay* case, for example, the defendant was engaged in blasting an excavation for a canal and the force of the blasts caused large quantities of earth and stones to be thrown against the plaintiff's house, knocking down his stoop and part of his chimney. The court held the defendant *absolutely* liable for the damage caused, stating:

> It is an elementary principle in reference to private rights, that every individual is entitled to the undisturbed possession and lawful enjoyment of his own property. The mode of enjoyment is necessarily limited by the rights of others — otherwise it might be made destructive of their rights altogether. Hence the maxim sic utere tuo, &c. The defendants had the right to dig the

canal. The plaintiff the right to the undisturbed possession of his property. If these rights conflict, the former must yield to the latter, as the more important of the two, since, upon grounds of public policy, it is better that one man should surrender a particular use of his land, than that another should be deprived of the beneficial use of his property altogether, which might be the consequence if the privilege of the former should be wholly unrestricted. The case before us illustrates this principle. For if the defendants in excavating their canal, in itself a lawful use of their land, could, in the manner mentioned by the witnesses, demolish the stoop of the plaintiff with impunity, they might, for the same purpose, on the exercise of reasonable care, demolish his house, and thus deprive him of all use of his property.

Although the court in *Booth* drew a distinction between a situation — such as was presented in the *Hay* case — where there was "a physical invasion" of, or trespass on, the plaintiff's property and one in which the damage was caused by "setting the air in motion, or in some other unexplained way," it is clear that the court, in the earlier cases, was not concerned with the particular manner by which the damage was caused but by the simple fact that any explosion in a built-up area was likely to cause damage. Thus, in Heeg v. Licht the court held that there should be absolute liability where the damage was caused by the accidental explosion of stored gunpowder, even in the absence of a physical trespass:

> The defendant had erected a building and stored materials therein, which from their character were liable to and actually did explode, causing injury to the plaintiff. The fact that the explosion took place tends to establish that the magazine was dangerous and liable to cause damage to the property of persons residing in the vicinity. . . . The fact that the magazine was liable to such a contingency, which could not be guarded against or averted by the greatest degree of care and vigilance, evinces its dangerous character, . . . In such a case, the rule which exonerates a party engaged in a lawful business, when free from negligence, has no application.

Such reasoning should, we venture, have led to the conclusion that the *intentional* setting off of explosives — that is, blasting — in an area in which it was likely to cause harm to neighboring property similarly results in absolute liability. However, the court in the *Booth* case rejected such an extension of the rule for the reason that "[t]o exclude the defendant from blasting to adapt its lot to the contemplated uses, at the instance of the plaintiff, would not be a compromise between conflicting rights, but an extinguishment of the right of the one for the benefit of the other." The court expanded on this by stating, "This sacrifice, we think, the law does not exact. Public policy is promoted by the building up of towns and cities and the improvement of property. Any unnecessary restraint on freedom of action of a property owner hinders this."

This rationale cannot withstand analysis. The plaintiff in *Booth* was not seeking, as the court implied, to "exclude the defendant from blasting" and thus prevent desirable improvements to the latter's property. Rather, he was merely seeking compensation for the damage which was inflicted upon his own property as a result of that blasting. The question, in other words, was not *whether* it was lawful or proper to engage in blasting but *who* should bear the cost of any resulting damage—the person who engaged in the dangerous activity or the innocent neighbor injured thereby. Viewed in such a light, it clearly appears that *Booth* was wrongly decided and should be forthrightly overruled.

In more recent cases, our court has already gone far toward mitigating the harsh effect of the rule laid down in the *Booth* case. Thus, we have held that negligence can properly be inferred from the mere fact that a blast has caused extensive damage, even where the plaintiff is unable to show "the method of blasting or the strength of the charges or the character of the soil or rock." (Schlansky v. Augustus V. Riegel, Inc., [174 N.E.2d 730 (N.Y. 1961)].) But, even under this liberal interpretation of *Booth,* it would still remain possible for a defendant who engages in blasting operations—which he realizes are likely to cause injury—to avoid liability by showing that he exercised reasonable care. Since blasting involves a substantial risk of harm no matter the degree of care exercised, we perceive no reason for ever permitting a person who engages in such an activity to impose this risk upon nearby persons or property without assuming responsibility therefor.

Indeed, the defendants devote but brief argument in defense of the *Booth* rule. The principal thrust of their argument is directed not to the requisite standard of care to be used but, rather, to the sufficiency of the plaintiffs' pleadings and the proof adduced on the issue of causation. [The court then disposed of both these points in plaintiff's favor.]

[Reversed and remanded.]

NOTE

Influence of the forms of action. The rule in Booth v. Rome, discussed in *Spano,* rested in part on the distinction between trespass and case, discussed earlier in Chapter 2, Section C. The argument there was that the physical entry of rocks or other materials upon the plaintiff's land was a direct invasion by the defendant and thus a trespass, to which strict liability applied. The soundness of this view rests on the eminently defensible view that mechanical devices (like guns) that fall under the exclusive control of the defendant do not negate the assertion that the defendant has directly applied force to the plaintiff's person or property. In contrast to blasting, damage caused only by vibration or concussion was "indirect" and thus fell under trespass on the case, with a negligence requirement. Fuld's Chief

Justice opinion echoes Holmes's argument in The Common Law, *supra* at 146, that the substantive ground for relief should not turn on the procedural requirements of the forms of action. Note how history has afforded Holmes only partial vindication of his views because the uniform theory is one of strict liability and not of negligence. To what extent does Fuld's argument anticipate the highly influential treatment of the subject in the Second Restatement?

American Law Institute, Restatement (Second) of Torts (1977)

§519.   GENERAL PRINCIPLE

(1) One who carries on an abnormally dangerous activity is subject to liability for harm to the person, land or chattels of another resulting from the activity, although he has exercised the utmost care to prevent the harm.

(2) This strict liability is limited to the kind of harm, the possibility of which makes the activity abnormally dangerous.

Comment c.

The word "care" includes care in preparation, care in operation and skill both in operation and preparation.

Comment on Subsection (2):

e. Extent of protection. The rule of strict liability stated in Subsection (1) applies only to harm that is within the scope of the abnormal risk that is the basis of the liability. One who carries on an abnormally dangerous activity is not under strict liability for every possible harm that may result from carrying it on. For example, the thing that makes the storage of dynamite in a city abnormally dangerous is the risk of harm to those in the vicinity if it should explode. If an explosion occurs and does harm to persons, land or chattels in the vicinity, the rule stated in Subsection (1) applies. If, however, there is no explosion and for some unexpected reason a part of the wall of the magazine in which the dynamite is stored falls upon a pedestrian on the highway upon which the magazine abuts, the rule stated in Subsection (1) has no application. In this case the liability, if any, will be dependent upon proof of negligence in the construction or maintenance of the wall. So also, the transportation of dynamite or other high explosives by truck through the streets of a city is abnormally dangerous for the same reason as that which makes the storage of the explosives abnormally dangerous. If the dynamite explodes in the course of the transportation, a private person transporting it is subject to liability under the rule stated in Subsection (1), although he has exercised the utmost care.

On the other hand, if the vehicle containing the explosives runs over a pedestrian, he cannot recover unless the vehicle was driven negligently.

§520.   ABNORMALLY DANGEROUS ACTIVITIES

In determining whether an activity is abnormally dangerous, the following factors are to be considered:

(a) existence of a high degree of risk of some harm to the person, land or chattels of others;

(b) likelihood that the harm that results from it will be great;

(c) inability to eliminate the risk by the exercise of reasonable care;

(d) extent to which the activity is not a matter of common usage;

(e) inappropriateness of the activity to the place where it is carried on and;

(f) extent to which its value to the community is outweighed by its dangerous attributes.

Comment:

d. Purpose of activity. In the great majority of the cases that involve abnormally dangerous activities the activity is carried on by the actor for purposes in which he has a financial interest, such as a business conducted for profit. This, however, is not necessary for the existence of such an activity. The rule here stated is equally applicable when there is no pecuniary benefit to the actor. Thus a private owner of an abnormally dangerous body of water who keeps it only for his own use and pleasure as a swimming pool is subject to the same liability as one who operates a reservoir of water for profit.

e. Not limited to the defendant's land. In most of the cases to which the rule of strict liability is applicable the abnormally dangerous activity is conducted on land in the possession of the defendant. This, again, is not necessary to the existence of such an activity. It may be carried on in a public highway or other public place or upon the land of another. . . .

Comment on Clause (c):

h. Risk not eliminated by reasonable care. Another important factor to be taken into account in determining whether the activity is abnormally dangerous is the impossibility of eliminating the risk by the exercise of reasonable care. Most ordinary activities can be made entirely safe by the taking of all reasonable precautions; and when safety cannot be attained by the exercise of due care there is reason to regard the danger as an abnormal one. . . .

Comment on Clause (d):

i. Common usage. An activity is a matter of common usage if it is customarily carried on by the great mass of mankind or by many people in the community. It does not cease to be so because it is carried on for a purpose peculiar to the individual who engages in it. Certain activities, notwithstanding their recognizable danger, are so generally carried on as to be regarded as customary. Thus automobiles have come into such general use that their operation is a matter of common usage. This, notwithstanding the residue of unavoidable risk of serious harm that may result even from their careful operation, is sufficient to prevent their use from being regarded as an abnormally dangerous activity. On the other hand, the operation of a tank or any other motor vehicle of such size and weight as to be unusually difficult to control safely, or to be likely to damage the ground over which it is driven, is not yet a usual activity for many people, and therefore the operation of such a vehicle may be abnormally dangerous.

Although blasting is recognized as a proper means of excavation for building purposes or of clearing woodland for cultivation, it is not carried on by any large percentage of the population, and therefore it is not a matter of common usage. Likewise the manufacture, storage, transportation and use of high explosives, although necessary to the construction of many public and private works, are carried on by only a comparatively small number of persons and therefore are not matters of common usage. So likewise, the very nature of oil lands and the essential interest of the public in the production of oil require that oil wells be drilled, but the dangers incident to the operation are characteristic of oil lands and not of lands in general, and relatively few persons are engaged in the activity. . . .

Comment on Clause (f):

k. Value to the community. Even though the activity involves a serious risk of harm that cannot be eliminated with reasonable care and it is not a matter of common usage, its value to the community may be such that the danger will not be regarded as an abnormal one. . . .

Comment:

l. Function of court. Whether the activity is an abnormally dangerous one is to be determined by the court, upon consideration of all the factors listed in this Section, and the weight given to each that it merits upon the facts in evidence. In this it differs from questions of negligence [in which questions of liability are normally left to the jury].

American Law Institute, Restatement (Third) of Torts: Liability for Physical Harm
(Proposed Final Draft No. 1, 2005)

§20.   ABNORMALLY DANGEROUS ACTIVITIES

(a) An actor who carries on an abnormally dangerous activity is subject to strict liability for physical harm resulting from the activity.

(b) An activity is abnormally dangerous if:

(1) the activity creates a foreseeable and highly significant risk of physical harm even when reasonable care is exercised by all actors; and

(2) the activity is not one of common usage.

Comment:

b. Relationship to negligence.... [A] prerequisite for the strict-liability rule identified in this section is not merely a highly significant risk associated with the activity itself, but a highly significant risk that remains with the activity even when all actors exercise reasonable care. Accordingly, at least at a general level, the issue of strict liability emerges at about the point at which the assignment of liability and losses in accordance with all actors' apparent negligence leaves off.

NOTES

1. *Definition of abnormally dangerous activities.* There is a peculiar progression on strict liability for abnormally dangerous activities. Sections 519 and 520 of the Restatement (Second) of Torts modify provisions of the first Restatement that in 1934 endorsed strict liability for all "ultrahazardous activities." The Second Restatement adds a set of elaborate conditions under §520, most of which are excised from §20 of the Third Restatement. For all their differences, these three sections do have at least some points in common. They all make judgments about *classes* of activities, such as drilling for oil, see Green v. General Petroleum Corp., 270 P. 952 (Cal. 1928); fumigation, see Luthringer v. Moore, 190 P.2d 1 (Cal. 1948); and more recently, gasoline storage, Bowers v. Wurzburg, 528 S.E.2d 475 (W. Va. 1999), that are covered by the provisions. See also RTT:LPH §20, comment *e*, reaffirming strict liability for blasting. The recent scorecard in In re Hanford Nuclear Reservation Litigation, 350 F. Supp. 2d 871, 876 (E.D. Wash. 2004), reads:

> In Washington, an assessment of the §520 factors has resulted in the imposition of strict liability for fire work displays; pile driving where injury occurred to the property on an adjacent lot; for aerial spraying of crops; and for a common carriers' transportation of large quantities of gasoline.... Washington courts have [also] held that the following activities are not abnormally dangerous including the transmission of electricity; the selling of handguns; ground damage caused by the crash landing of aircraft; and the transmission of natural gas.

Why is a categorical approach adopted for strict liability when negligence liability is usually determined on a case-by-case basis? How successful are the authors of either the Second or Third Restatements in working the basic classificatory effort between ordinary and "abnormally danger-ous" activities? Is there any ordinary activity that can be made *entirely* safe by taking all *reasonable* precautions? More generally, should the general Hand formula for negligence apply to all abnormally dangerous activities? For a view that judges rightly perceive that negligence law covers the entire field, see Boston, Strict Liability for Abnormally Dangerous Activities: The Negligence Barrier, 36 San Diego L. Rev. 597 (1999). Boston posits the negligence barrier represents the renewed judicial conviction that the "negligence system functions effectively to deter the serious risks posed by the activities involved." See also Henderson, Why Negligence Dominates Tort, 50 UCLA L. Rev. 377 (2002), for the view that strict liability has to pick limited spots, as "broad-based strict liability would not be viable be-cause it would generate unadjudicable disputes."

2. *Aviation as abnormally dangerous activity.* Should aviation be regarded as an abnormally dangerous activity? The 1934 Restatement regarded it so on the ground that "one of the risks of aviation is that the plane being flown at a high altitude and over a large area may encounter dangerous weather conditions which would be altogether abnormal on the surface of the earth." This explanation is untenable today when more lives are lost per passenger mile in automobile accidents — governed by negligence principles under the Restatement — than in airplane accidents. The strict liability principles of §§519 and 520 do not reach the airplane any more than they reach the automobile. Thus, in Boyd v. White, 276 P.2d 92 (Cal. App. 1954), the court denied recovery, concluding "the operation of an airplane in the year 1954 is not such a dangerous activity that it can be placed in this category." Similarly in Wood v. United Air Lines, Inc., 223 N.Y.S.2d 692, 695 (N.Y. Sup. Ct. 1961), the court held that a mid-air collision, which caused personal injuries to plaintiff and damage to her apartment, could not be treated as "trespass as a matter of law" in the absence of an intention to invade defendant's land. "In the instant case it would seem to be apparent that there was no intent to crash."

Notwithstanding these cases, §520A of the Second Restatement adopted a strict liability rule for all ground damage from aircraft "caused by the ascent, descent or flight of aircraft, or by the dropping or falling of an object from the aircraft." The Third Restatement equivocates on the matter, ob-serving that several states have passed statutes that provide that "aviation ground-damage cases should be decided 'in accordance with the rules of law applicable to torts on land.'" RTT:LPH §20, Reporters' Note to comment *k*. However, the Restatement also notes that even with the small risk of harm from commercial aviation, "one rationale for strict liability relates to the defendant's exclusive control over the instrumentality of harm, and this rationale is impressively applicable in aviation ground-damage cases." *Id.* Should falling planes be treated differently from falling water or falling barrels of flour? See Schwartz, The Vitality of Negligence and the Ethics of

Strict Liability, 15 Ga. L. Rev. 963, 1000 (1981), in which the author observed that "airplane flying being an activity which is normally very safe, an ordinary-language inquiry into causation would almost certainly concern itself with identifying the specific non-normal feature that could explain why the particular crash occurred." Does that also apply to *Rylands*?

3. *Common usage.* What is the function of the common usage requirement set out in RST §520(d)? If it is taken seriously, how can blasting, fumigating, or the manufacturing of explosives not be matters of common usage? One notable effort to make sense out of the Second Restatement's common usage requirement is found in Fletcher, Fairness and Utility in Tort Theory, 85 Harv. L. Rev. 537, 541-542, 547-548 (1972):

> I shall propose a specific standard of risk that makes sense of the Restatement's emphasis on uncommon, extra-hazardous risks, but which shows that the Restatement's theory is part of a larger rationale of liability that cuts across negligence, intentional torts, and numerous pockets of strict liability. The general principle expressed in all of these situations governed by diverse doctrinal standards is that a victim has a right to recover for injuries caused by a risk greater in degree and different in order from those created by the victim and imposed on the defendant — in short, for injuries resulting from nonreciprocal risks. Cases of liability are those in which the defendant generates a disproportionate, excessive risk of harm, relative to the victim's risk-creating activity. For example, a pilot or an airplane owner subjects those beneath the path of flight to nonreciprocal risks of harm. Conversely, cases of nonliability are those of reciprocal risks, namely those in which the victim and the defendant subject each other to roughly the same degree of risk. For example, two airplanes flying the same vicinity subject each other to reciprocal risks of a mid-air collision. . . .
>
> The rationale of nonreciprocal risk-taking accounts as well for pockets of strict liability outside the coverage of the Restatement's sections on extra-hazardous activities. For example, an individual is strictly liable for damage done by a wild animal in his charge, but not for damage committed by his domesticated pet. Most people have pets, children, or friends whose presence creates some risk to neighbors and their property. These are risks that offset each other; they are, as a class, reciprocal risks. Yet bringing an unruly horse into the city goes beyond the accepted and shared level of risks in having pets, children, and friends in one's household. If the defendant creates a risk that exceeds those to which he is reciprocally subject, it seems fair to hold him liable for the results of his aberrant indulgence. Similarly, according to the latest version [Second] of the Restatement, airplane owners and pilots are strictly liable for ground damage, but not for mid-air collisions. Risk of ground damage is nonreciprocal; homeowners do not create risks to airplanes flying overhead. The risks of mid-air collisions, on the other hand, are generated reciprocally by all those who fly the air lanes. Accordingly, the threshold of liability for damage resulting from mid-air collisions is higher than mere involvement in the activity of flying.

Fletcher's norm of reciprocity works well with repeat low-level inter-ferences that might be characterized as reciprocal, see *infra* at 685, Note 3, but it works less well with personal injuries, in which the harms are both infrequent and substantial. Often, as with dangerous animals, both actions are allowed instead of neither. How do we decide whether two actions or none is superior? In some cases, however, the outcome seems clear: In In re Hanford Nuclear Reservation Litigation, 350 F. Supp. 2d 871, 881 (E.D. Wash. 2004), excerpted earlier, the defendants' nuclear product process required complex forms of chemical separation, which released radioactive I-131 (iodine, with atomic weight of 131) into the atmosphere. The plaintiffs sought to hold the defendants liable under a strict liability theory after being diagnosed with thyroid disease that could stem from the ra-dioactive iodine. Nielsen, J., held that a strict liability theory was available after an exhaustive analysis of the factors set out in the Second Restate-ment. On common usage, he wrote:

> Plaintiffs argue that the production process certainly was not a common usage during the time period at issue in this case. In response, the Defen-dants argue that while the production of plutonium for use in atomic weapons was not a common activity, the chemical separation and air dilution and venting through a tall stack were common endeavors based on the science of the time. As to I-131, the Defendants argue also that existing knowledge was used to make the emissions safe. . . . Although radiation had seen medical usage and chemical separation had been used before, it is still undisputed that the weapons grade plutonium production which included chemical separation that released I-131 was an activity in which few people were engaged. As such it was not one of common usage and this factor weighs in favor of a finding of an abnormally dangerous activity.

Nielsen, J., then concluded that each factor under §520 favored the abnormally dangerous classification.

4. *Social utility of defendant's activity.* The Second Restatement's willing-ness to take into account the social value of an activity in determining whether it is abnormally dangerous was ably criticized in Koos v. Roth, 652 P.2d 1255, 1261-1262 (Or. 1982). Linde, J., upholding a strict liability action for fire damage, observed:

> There are at least two reasons not to judge civil liability for unintended harm by a court's views of the utility or value of the harmful activity. One reason lies in the nature of the judgment. Utility and value often are subjective and controversial. They will be judged differently by those who profit from an activity and those who are endangered by it, and between one locality and another. The use of explosives to remove old buildings for a new highway or shopping center may be described as slum clearance or as the destruction of historic landmarks and neighborhoods. On a smaller scale, it may celebrate a

traditional holiday which some may value more highly than either buildings or roads. Highly toxic materials may be necessary to the production of agricultural pesticides, or of drugs, or of chemical or bacteriological weapons, or of industrial products of all sorts; does liability for injury from their storage or movement depend on the utility of these products? Judges, like others, may differ about such values; they can hardly be described as conclusions of law. . . .

The second reason why the value of a hazardous activity does not preclude strict liability for its consequences is that the conclusion does not follow from the premise. In the prior cases, the court did not question the economic value of blasting, cropdusting, or storing natural gas. In an action for damages, the question is not whether the activity threatens such harm that it should not be continued. The question is who shall pay for harm that has been done. The loss has occurred. It is a cost of the activity whoever bears it. To say that when the activity has great economic value the cost should be borne by others is no more or less logical than to say that when the costs of an activity are borne by others it gains in value.

Should *Koos* lead to a reconsideration of those cases, such as Cadena v. Chicago Fireworks Manufacturing Co., 697 N.E.2d 802 (Ill. App. 1998), which held that fireworks displays were *not* ultrahazardous in part because under factor (f) "the general public enjoys fireworks displays to celebrate every July 4, [and] they are of some social utility to communities"? The Third Restatement responded to the criticism in *Koos* by scratching the social utility factor from the list of relevant factors for determining abnormally dangerous activities. See Reporter's Note to comment *h*. In regards to the manufacturing of nuclear weapons, Nielsen, J., tartly remarked on factor (f): "the benefit accrued to the entire nation but the risk and the potential harm was endured only by the people downwind of Hanford." In re Hanford, 350 F. Supp. 2d at 883.

Indiana Harbor Belt R.R. v. American Cyanamid Co.
916 F.2d 1174 (7th Cir. 1990)

POSNER, J.
[The American Cyanamid Company, a large diversified chemical manufacturer, leased from the Missouri Pacific Railroad a railroad car which it filled with 20,000 gallons of liquid acrylonitrile, a highly toxic chemical, possibly carcinogenic, that is flammable at 30 degrees Fahrenheit. The car was routed to a Cyanamid plant in New Jersey through the Blue Island Yard, located on the outskirts of Chicago and run by the Indiana Harbor Belt Railroad, which specialized in shifting cars between major railroad lines. Several hours after the car arrived in the plaintiff's Blue Island yard, several of its employees noted the leak from the Cyanamid car. Local

authorities, fearing that all 20,000 gallons may have leaked, ordered an evacuation of the yard, which lasted for several hours. When the car was moved to another portion of the lot, it was discovered that only about a quarter of its load had leaked. Nonetheless the Illinois Department of Environmental Protection ordered decontamination measures that cost plaintiff close to $1 million. Plaintiff brought its §529 action against Cyanamid, which won in the district court on summary judgment. On review, Posner, J., first noted that the district court's conclusion of law received no deference and continued.]

The roots of section 520 are in nineteenth-century cases. The most famous one is Rylands v. Fletcher[, *supra* at 127], but a more illuminating one in the present context is Guille v. Swan, 19 Johns. (N.Y.) 381 (1822) [, *supra* at 118]. A man took off in a hot-air balloon and landed, without intending to, in a vegetable garden in New York City. A crowd that had been anxiously watching his involuntary descent trampled the vegetables in their endeavor to rescue him when he landed. The owner of the garden sued the balloonist for the resulting damage, and won. Yet the balloonist had not been careless. In the then state of ballooning it was impossible to make a pinpoint landing.

Guille is a paradigmatic case for strict liability. (a) The risk (probability) of harm was great, and (b) the harm that would ensue if the risk materialized could be, although luckily was not, great (the balloonist could have crashed into the crowd rather than into the vegetables). The confluence of these two factors established the urgency of seeking to prevent such accidents. (c) Yet such accidents could not be prevented by the exercise of due care; the technology of care in ballooning was insufficiently developed. (d) The activity was not a matter of common usage, so there was no presumption that it was a highly valuable activity despite its unavoidable riskiness. (e) The activity was inappropriate to the place in which it took place — densely populated New York City. The risk of serious harm to others (other than the balloonist himself, that is) could have been reduced by shifting the activity to the sparsely inhabited areas that surrounded the city in those days. (f) Reinforcing (d), the value to the community of the activity of recreational ballooning did not appear to be great enough to offset its unavoidable risks.

These are, of course, the six factors in section 520. They are related to each other in that each is a different facet of a common quest for a proper legal regime to govern accidents that negligence liability cannot adequately control. . . . Shavell, Strict Liability versus Negligence, 9 J. Legal Stud. 1 (1980). By making the actor strictly liable — by denying him in other words an excuse based on his inability to avoid accidents by being more careful — we give him an incentive, missing in a negligence regime, to experiment with methods of preventing accidents that involve not greater exertions of care, assumed to be futile, but instead relocating, changing, or reducing (perhaps to the vanishing point) the activity giving rise to the accident. The greater the risk of an accident ((a)) and the costs of an accident if one occurs ((b)), the more we want the actor to consider the possibility of making accident-reducing activity changes; the stronger, therefore, is the case for strict liability. Finally, if an activity is extremely common ((d)), like driving an automobile, it is unlikely either that its hazards are perceived as great or that there is no technology of care available to minimize them; so the case for strict liability is weakened.

The largest class of cases in which strict liability has been imposed under the standard codified in the Second Restatement of Torts involves the use of dynamite and other explosives for demolition in residential or urban areas. Restatement, supra, §519, comment d. Explosives are dangerous even when handled carefully, and we therefore want blasters to choose the location of the activity with care and also to explore the feasibility of using safer substitutes (such as a wrecking ball), as well as to be careful in the blasting itself. Blasting is not a commonplace activity like driving a car, or so superior to substitute methods of demolition that the imposition of liability is unlikely to have any effect except to raise the activity's costs.

Against this background we turn to the particulars of acrylonitrile. Acrylonitrile is one of a large number of chemicals that are hazardous in the sense of being flammable, toxic, or both; acrylonitrile is both, as are many others. [Judge Posner then summarizes a list of 125 such substances, some more and some less dangerous than acrylonitrile. He then notes that under plaintiff's theory,] [e]very shipper of any of these materials would therefore be strictly liable for the consequences of a spill or other accident that occurred while the material was being shipped through a metropolitan area. . . .

No cases recognize so sweeping a liability. Several reject it, though none has facts much like those of the present case. [A discussion of some cases not following the Restatement rule is omitted.]

Siegler v. Kuhlman, 502 P.2d 1181 (Wash. 1972), also imposed strict liability on a transporter of hazardous materials, but the circumstances were again rather special. A gasoline truck blew up, obliterating the plaintiff's decedent and her car. The court emphasized that the explosion had destroyed the evidence necessary to establish whether the accident had been due to negligence; so, unless liability was strict, there would be no liability — and this as the very consequence of the defendant's hazardous activity. . . .

So we can get little help from precedent, and might as well apply section 520 to the acrylonitrile problem from the ground up. To begin with, we have been given no reason, whether the reason in *Siegler* or any other, for believing that a negligence regime is not perfectly adequate to remedy and deter, at reasonable cost, the accidental spillage of acrylonitrile from rail cars. Acrylonitrile could explode and destroy evidence, but of course did not here, making imposition of strict liability on the theory of the *Siegler* decision premature. More important, although acrylonitrile is flammable even at relatively low temperatures, and toxic, it is not so corrosive or otherwise destructive that it will eat through or otherwise damage or weaken a tank car's valves although they are maintained with due (which essentially means, with average) care. No one suggests, therefore, that the leak in this case was caused by the inherent properties of acrylonitrile. It was caused by carelessness—whether that of the North American Car Corporation in failing to maintain or inspect the car properly, or that of Cyanamid in failing to maintain or inspect it, or that of the Missouri Pacific when it had custody of the car, or that of the switching line itself in failing to notice the ruptured lid, or some combination of these possible failures of care. Accidents that are due to a lack of care can be prevented by taking care; and when a lack of care can (unlike *Siegler*) be shown in court, such accidents are adequately deterred by the threat of liability for negligence.

It is true that the district court purported to find as a fact that there is an inevitable risk of derailment or other calamity in transporting "large quantities of anything." This is not a finding of fact, but a truism: anything can happen. The question is, how likely is this type of accident if the actor uses due care? For all that appears from the record of the case or any other sources of information that we have found, if a tank car is carefully maintained the danger of a spill of acrylonitrile is negligible. If this is right, there is no compelling reason to move to a regime of strict liability, especially one that might embrace all other hazardous materials shipped by rail as well. This also means, however, that the amici curiae who have filed briefs in support of Cyanamid cry wolf in predicting "devastating" effects on the chemical industry if the district court's decision is affirmed. If the vast majority of chemical spills by railroads are preventable by due care, the imposition of strict liability should cause only a slight, not as they argue a substantial, rise in liability insurance rates, because the incremental liability should be slight. The amici have momentarily lost sight of the fact that the feasibility of avoiding accidents simply by being careful is an argument against strict liability. . . .

The district judge and the plaintiff's lawyer make much of the fact that the spill occurred in a densely inhabited metropolitan area. Only 4,000 gallons spilled; what if all 20,000 had done so? Isn't the risk that this might happen even if everybody were careful sufficient to warrant giving the shipper an incentive to explore alternative routes? Strict liability would supply that incentive. But this argument overlooks the fact that, like other transportation networks, the railroad network is a hub-and-spoke system. And the hubs are in metropolitan areas. Chicago is one of the nation's largest railroad hubs. In 1983, the latest year for which we have figures, Chicago's railroad yards handled the third highest volume of hazardous-material shipments in the nation. East St. Louis, which is also in Illinois, handled the second highest volume. With most hazardous chemicals (by volume of shipments) being at least as hazardous as acrylonitrile, it is un-likely—and certainly not demonstrated by the plaintiff—that they can be rerouted around all the metropolitan areas in the country, except at pro-hibitive cost. Even if it were feasible to reroute them one would hardly expect shippers, as distinct from carriers, to be the firms best situated to do the rerouting. Granted, the usual view is that common carriers are not subject to strict liability for the carriage of materials that make the trans-portation of them abnormally dangerous, because a common carrier can-not refuse service to a shipper of a lawful commodity. Restatement, supra, §521. Two courts, however, have rejected the common carrier exception. If it were rejected in Illinois, this would weaken still further the case for imposing strict liability on shippers whose goods pass through the densely inhabited portions of the state.

The difference between shipper and carrier points to a deep flaw in the plaintiff's case. Unlike *Guille*, and unlike *Siegler*, and unlike the storage cases, beginning with *Rylands* itself, here it is not the actors—that is, the transporters of acrylonitrile and other chemicals—but the manufacturers, who are sought to be held strictly liable. A shipper can in the bill of lading designate the route of his shipment if he likes, 49 U.S.C. §11710(a)(1), but is it realistic to suppose that shippers will become students of railroading in order to lay out the safest route by which to ship their goods? Anyway, rerouting is no panacea. Often it will increase the length of the journey, or compel the use of poorer track, or both. When this happens, the probability of an accident is increased, even if the consequences of an accident if one occurs are reduced; so the expected accident cost, being the product of the probability of an accident and the harm if the accident occurs, may rise. It is easy to see how the accident in this case might have been prevented at reasonable cost by greater care on the part of those who handled the tank car of acrylonitrile. It is difficult to see how it might have been prevented at reasonable cost by a change in the activity of transporting the chemical. This is therefore not an apt case for strict liability. . . .

The relevant activity is transportation, not manufacturing and shipping. This essential distinction the plaintiff ignores. But even if the plaintiff is treated as a transporter and not merely a shipper, it has not shown that the transportation of acrylonitrile in bulk by rail through populated areas is so hazardous an activity, even when due care is exercised, that the law should seek to create—perhaps quixotically—incentives to relocate the activity to nonpopulated areas, or to reduce the scale of the activity, or to switch to transporting acrylonitrile by road rather than by rail, perhaps to set the stage for a replay of Siegler v. Kuhlman. It is no more realistic to propose to reroute the shipment of all hazardous materials around Chicago than it is to propose the relocation of homes adjacent to the Blue Island switching yard to more distant suburbs. It may be less realistic. Brutal though it may seem to say it, the inappropriate use to which land is being put in the Blue

Island yard and neighborhood may be, not the transportation of hazardous chemicals, but residential living. The analogy is to building your home between the runways at O'Hare. . . .

At argument . . . the plaintiff's lawyer invoked distributive considerations by pointing out that Cyanamid is a huge firm and the Indiana Harbor Belt Railroad a fifty-mile-long switching line that almost went broke in the winter of 1979, when the accident occurred. Well, so what? A corporation is not a living person but a set of contracts the terms of which determine who will bear the brunt of liability. Tracing the incidence of a cost is a complex undertaking which the plaintiff sensibly has made no effort to assume, since its legal relevance would be dubious. We add only that however small the plaintiff may be, it has mighty parents: it is a jointly owned subsidiary of Conrail and the Soo line.

The case for strict liability has not been made. Not in this suit in any event. We need not speculate on the possibility of imposing strict liability on shippers of more hazardous materials, such as . . . bombs . . . any more than we need differentiate (given how the plaintiff has shaped its case) between active and passive shippers. . . .

The judgment is reversed (with no award of costs in this court) and the case remanded for further proceedings, consistent with this opinion, on the plaintiff's claim for negligence.

Reversed and remanded, with directions.

NOTES

1. The strict liability alternative. In Siegler v. Kuhlman, 502 P.2d 1181, 1184-1185 (Wash. 1972), the court defended using the strict liability regime of Rylands v. Fletcher for gasoline transported on public highways:

> In many respects, hauling gasoline as freight is no more unusual, but more dangerous, than collecting water. When gasoline is carried as cargo — as distinguished from fuel for the carrier vehicle — it takes on uniquely hazardous characteristics, as does water impounded in large quantities. Dangerous in itself, gasoline develops even greater potential for harm when carried as freight — extraordinary dangers deriving from sheer quantity, bulk and weight, which enormously multiply its hazardous properties. And the very hazards inhering from the size of the load, its bulk or quantity and its movement along the highways presents another reason for application of the Fletcher v. Rylands rule not present in the impounding of large quantities of water — the likely destruction of cogent evidence from which negligence or want of it may be proved or disproved. It is quite probable that the most important ingredients of proof will be lost in a gasoline explosion and fire. Gasoline is always dangerous whether kept in large or small quantities because of its volatility, inflammability and explosiveness. But when several

thousand gallons of it are allowed to spill across a public highway — that is, if, while in transit as freight, it is not kept impounded — the hazards to third persons are so great as to be almost beyond calculation.

Do the different properties of acrylonitrile justify a different response? Note that in *Indiana Harbor Belt R.R.* the action was brought against the shipper but not the carrier. How does the Second Restatement rule apply to transporters? How should *Indiana Harbor* come out under the Third Restatement? How does the analysis change if the bottom of the car was punctured by debris on the track? If vandals damaged the car? See Sykes, Strict Liability versus Negligence in *Indiana Harbor*, 74 U. Chi. L. Rev. 1911 (2007).

2. *Back to negligence?* The refusal to treat the shipment of dangerous chemicals as an ultrahazardous activity still leaves the plaintiff with a negligence cause of action. Should the railroad be joined in the suit as a codefendant, and if so, does res ipsa loquitur apply?

In Foster v. City of Keyser, 501 S.E.2d 165, 175 (W. Va. 1997), the defendant excavating company dug around the pipeline of the defendant gas company, such that the movement of the soil "contributed to the failure of a compression coupling joining two sections of the gas line, which in turn led to the line's separation." The court declined to treat the ordinary transmission of gas as an ultrahazardous activity, noting its judgment was "largely predicated upon our conclusion that other principles of law — a high standard of care and *res ipsa loquitur* — can sufficiently address the concerns that argue for strict liability in gas transmission line leak/explosion cases." Similarly, in In re Chicago Flood Litigation, 680 N.E.2d 265, 280 (Ill. 1997), large segments of downtown Chicago were flooded by pile driving undertaken by a city contractor. The plaintiff class argued that this conduct was inherently dangerous "since pile driving produces uncontrollable vibrations and concussions similar to blasting." But the court rejected this argument on the ground that the plaintiff class had not demonstrated any of the first three Restatement factors. The court did hold, however, that pile driving was not in common usage, given that only a few persons engaged in the business; but that was not enough to tip the balance in the opposite direction. Finally, relying on *American Cyanamid*, the court in Marmo v. IBP, Inc., 362 F. Supp. 2d 1129, 1134 (D. Neb. 2005), held that the operation of the defendant's wastewater treatment facility, from which large quantities of hydrogen sulfide were emitted, should not be classified as an ultrahazardous activity because "there is ample proof that the risk of harm associated with the emission of hydrogen sulfide can be controlled or eliminated with due care." For good measure, it regarded these plants as "a common function of municipalities and of many industries . . . located in both rural and urban areas." Are we back to Booth v. Rome? With or without res ipsa?

3. Ultrahazardous activities: causal complications and affirmative defenses.
Even if strict liability principles apply to abnormally dangerous activities,
the plaintiff still must negotiate hurdles on proximate causation, as well as
a full range of potential affirmative defenses. The Second Restatement sets
forth these possibilities.

§522. CONTRIBUTING ACTIONS OF THIRD PERSONS, ANIMALS AND FORCES OF
          NATURE

One carrying on an ultrahazardous activity is liable for harm under the
rule stated in §519, although the harm is caused by the unexpectable

(a) innocent, negligent or reckless conduct of a third person, or

(b) action of an animal, or

(c) operation of a force of nature.

§523. ASSUMPTION OF RISK

The plaintiff's assumption of the risk of harm from an abnormally dangerous activity bars his recovery for the harm.

§524. CONTRIBUTORY NEGLIGENCE

(1) Except as stated in Subsection (2), the contributory negligence of the
plaintiff is not a defense to the strict liability of one who carries on an
abnormally dangerous activity.

(2) The plaintiff's contributory negligence in knowingly and unreasonably
subjecting himself to the risk of harm from the activity is a defense to the
strict liability.

§524A. PLAINTIFF'S ABNORMALLY SENSITIVE ACTIVITY

There is no strict liability for harm caused by an abnormally dangerous
activity if the harm would not have resulted but for the abnormally sensitive
character of the plaintiff's activity.

Have the difficulties that arise in these cases been encountered elsewhere?

In Madsen v. East Jordan Irrigation Co., 125 P.2d 794, 795 (Utah 1942),
the plaintiff's farm was used for breeding and raising mink for sale. One
hundred yards north of the farm, the defendant blasted with explosives in
order to repair its irrigation ditch. The noise from the blast so frightened
the mother mink that it "caused 108 of them to kill 230 of their 'kittens'
(offspring)." Pratt, J., conceded that blasting was governed by an absolute
liability rule, but held that the damages were too remote, observing:

> [H]e who fires explosives is not liable for every occurrence following the
> explosion which has a semblance of connection to it. Jake's horse might
> become so excited that he would run next door and kick a few ribs out of Cy's
> jersey cow, but is such a thing to be anticipated from an explosion? Whether

the cases are concussion or nonconcussion, the results chargeable to the nonnegligent user of explosives are those things ordinarily resulting from an explosion. Shock, air vibrations, thrown missiles are all illustrative of the anticipated result of explosives; they are physical as distinguished from mental in character. The famous *Squib*[, *supra* at 115] case does not mitigate what has been said in the preceding lines. That was a case where the mental reaction was to be anticipated as an instinctive matter of self-preservation. In the instant case, the killing of their kittens was not an act of self-preservation on the part of the mother mink but a peculiarity of disposition which was not within the realm of matters to be anticipated. Had a squib been thrown and suddenly picked up by a dog, in fun, and carried near another, it is ventured that we would not have had a famous *Squib* case, as such a result would not have been within the realm of anticipation.

Does it matter that military aircraft are routinely cautioned about flying over mink farms? The result in *Madsen* was endorsed in RST §519, illustration 1.

Human intervention often prompts a different response. In Yukon Equipment v. Fireman's Fund Insurance Co., 585 P.2d 1206, 1211 (Alaska 1978), the defendants were sued for damage caused by the explosion of their storage magazine, located in suburban Anchorage. The damage was caused by four young thieves who set off the explosives in order to conceal evidence of their theft. The court strict liability applied to the storage of explosives under the leading case of Exner v. Sherman Power Construction Co., 54 F.2d 510 (2d Cir. 1931), whose application was not defeated by virtue of the fact that the petitioners had located their plant in a remote part of town nearly one mile from the nearest public highway.

The petitioners also claimed that the conduct of the four thieves was a superseding cause that negated tortious liability. That argument was rejected because "incendiary destruction of premises by thieves to cover evidence of theft is not so uncommon an occurrence that it can be regarded as highly extraordinary." Is this decision consistent with *Madsen*?

SECTION D. NUISANCE

1. Private Nuisance

Vogel v. Grant-Lafayette Electric Cooperative
548 N.W.2d 829 (Wis. 1996)

BRADLEY, J. The plaintiffs, Dale and Alice Vogel, seek review of a decision of the court of appeals, reversing in part a judgment in their favor for damages caused by stray voltage from electricity distributed by the defendant, Grant-Lafayette Electric Cooperative (GLEC). The Vogels assert that the court of appeals erred in holding as a matter of law that stray voltage may not be considered a private nuisance. Because we conclude that private nuisance is a viable cause of action under the facts of this case, we reverse that portion of the court of appeals' decision directing the circuit court to strike the nuisance-related damages from the judgment. We further conclude that because the stray voltage constituted an unintentional invasion and was otherwise actionable under negligence, the circuit court properly considered the Vogels' contributory negligence when it reduced the total damage award.

The following background facts are undisputed. The Vogels were dairy farmers and members of GLEC, a cooperative association that distributes electricity to its members. Shortly after the Vogels built a new milking facility in 1970, they noticed problems with their herd. Many cows exhibited violent or erratic behavior while in the facility. The herd also suffered from excessive and chronic mastitis. As a result, the Vogels suffered a decline in their herd's milk production and cows were repeatedly culled from the herd. Despite the fact that the Vogels made various changes with their equipment and in the facility itself, these problems persisted in varying degrees over subsequent years.

In March of 1986, the Vogels contacted GLEC because they suspected that the cows were suffering from the effects of excessive stray voltage. The Vogels received their electricity via a distribution system referred to as a multi-grounded neutral system, based on the fact that neutral wires in both the provider's primary system and the farm's secondary wiring system are connected to metal grounding rods driven into the earth. Because the neutral wires in a typical farm's electrical system are connected to metal work in the barn for safety purposes in order to provide a path for electrical current to flow to earth, a cow that contacts grounded metal objects may provide a path for this "stray voltage" traveling on the farm's secondary system.

GLEC responded to the Vogels' concerns about possible stray voltage by installing an "isolator" at its transformer on the Vogel farm, which is intended to reduce the risk of excessive stray voltage. After the isolator was properly installed, the behavior of the herd and the other problems began to improve immediately. GLEC subsequently visited the farm on numerous occasions to conduct tests and respond to other concerns raised by the Vogels.

In 1992, the Vogels filed suit against GLEC on theories of negligence and nuisance [for the "annoyance and inconvenience" caused by the stray voltage.]

The case was tried to a jury, which found that GLEC was negligent and that it had created a nuisance. It awarded the Vogels $240,000 in economic damages on their negligence claim and $60,000 for annoyance and inconvenience damages on their nuisance claim. The jury also found that the Vogels were one-third causally negligent.

[The trial judge entered a verdict for $200,000. GLEC appealed, claiming that stray voltage could not be a private nuisance. The Vogels appealed, claiming that the defendant committed an "intentional nuisance" not subject to reduction for contributory negligence. The Wisconsin Court of Appeals held that the trial judge erred in submitting the nuisance claim to the jury and "struck the $60,000 in damages awarded for annoyance and inconvenience attributed to the nuisance."]

I. PRIVATE NUISANCE ACTION FOR STRAY VOLTAGE

... This court has previously adopted the definition of private nuisance set forth in the Restatement (Second) of Torts (1979). The Restatement defines nuisance as "a nontrespassory invasion of another's interest in the private use and enjoyment of land." Restatement (Second) of Torts §821D.

GLEC argues that the concept of invasion in the Restatement necessarily involves a "unilateral encroachment." It contends that a nuisance is produced by an activity under the defendant's control to which the plaintiff objects, and not by activity which the plaintiff has requested and facilitated. According to GLEC, the Vogels' act of requesting electrical service and cooperating in the receipt of electricity by connecting its system to GLEC's distribution system negates the concept of unilateral invasion and thus defeats a claim for nuisance.

The court of appeals agreed with GLEC and concluded as a matter of law that the provision of electricity to the Vogels' farm cannot be considered a nuisance because it does not constitute the type of invasion on which nuisance liability is typically predicated. According to the court of appeals, "[a]s users of an instrumentality they invited onto their land, and have in many ways benefited from over the years, we do not think they now may be heard to claim that the instrumentality has illegally 'invaded' their property."[3] ...

We agree with the Vogels that their request for electric service itself does not negate the invasion element of nuisance. Both GLEC and the court of appeals fail to distinguish between electrical service generally and excessive levels of stray voltage which may accompany it. While the Vogels requested

3. The court of appeals and GLEC cite the following cases to support the propositions that the invasion must be unilateral and not be requested by the plaintiffs: Fortier v. Flambeau Plastics Co., 476 N.W.2d 593 (Wis. App. 1991) (toxic chemicals deposited in a landfill which seeped or leached onto the plaintiffs' property and contaminated their well water was the type of "invasion" that would subject the defendants to nuisance liability); Crest Chevrolet-Oldsmobile-Cadillac, Inc. v. Willemsen, 384 N.W.2d 692 (Wis. 1986) (diversion of surface water onto the plaintiff's property); Krueger v. Mitchell, 332 N.W.2d 733 (Wis. 1983) (excessive noise from an airport interfering with the operation of a neighboring business); ... Jost v. Dairyland Power Coop., 172 N.W.2d 647 (Wis. 1969) (discharge of sulphur dioxide gases from an electrical generating plant onto adjoining cropland).

electric service, they did not request excessive stray voltage to flow through their farm. Similarly, while they received benefit from the electrical service generally, the evidence presented at trial indicates that they hardly benefited from excessive stray voltage. . . .

We also disagree with the court of appeals that previous nuisance cases in Wisconsin compel the conclusion that stray voltage does not constitute the type of invasion on which nuisance liability is predicated. The court of appeals erroneously focuses on private nuisance as an invasion of land. . . .

Although some of the nuisance cases identified by the court of appeals involve a physical invasion of land, the Restatement uses the phrase "interest in the use and enjoyment of land" broadly to include more than freedom from detrimental change in the physical condition of the land itself: [it "comprehends the pleasure, comfort and enjoyment that a person normally derives from the occupancy of land." RST §821D, comment *b.*]

. . . This court has previously characterized the common law doctrine of private nuisance as being both "broad" to meet the wide variety of possible invasions, and "flexible" to adapt to changing social values and conditions. An interpretation of nuisance as only arising from a unilateral action and a physical invasion of land restricts the essential flexibility of the nuisance doctrine. We decline to do so here.

We conclude that nuisance law is applicable to stray voltage claims because excessive levels of stray voltage may invade a person's private use and enjoyment of land. Although excessive levels of stray voltage may be found to constitute a nuisance in certain circumstances, we do not hold that it constitutes a nuisance under all circumstances. The determination of whether stray voltage unreasonably interferes with a person's interest in the private use and enjoyment of land is reserved for the trier of fact.

II. "INTENTIONAL INVASION" NUISANCE

. . .

The Vogels argue that the uncontradicted testimony of their expert was that GLEC knew that a portion of its electric current would travel to the earth through the farm and its structures based on its use of the multi-grounded system with interconnected neutrals. They assert that although GLEC may not have intended to cause harm, the invasion is intentional under §825(b) because GLEC knew that the stray voltage was substantially certain to result from its conduct by application of basic laws of electricity. GLEC contends that even if it was substantially certain that some level of current would travel through the farm's structures, there is no evidence that any interference with the Vogels' use and enjoyment was certain to result.

We agree with GLEC that the mere fact that the systems were interconnected does not create an intentional invasion. . . . It is the unreasonable

levels of stray voltage that may give rise to liability for an intentional invasion, not the use of a multi-grounded delivery system with interconnecting
neutrals. The Vogels fail to identify any evidence in the record that GLEC
had knowledge prior to March of 1986 that its system was imposing unreasonable levels of stray voltage onto the Vogels' farm.

The Vogels also argue that GLEC's conduct constitutes an intentional
invasion because it was a continuing invasion of which they had knowledge. . . . [RST §825, comment *d.*] The Vogels maintain that in this case,
stray voltage arising from a multi-grounded distribution system necessarily
involves a continuing invasion because the utility knows that a portion of its
current is going to the earth through the farm's structures and the cows.

This argument fails in part for the same reason stated above. Intentionally supplying electrical current with the resulting stray voltage may be
an invasion of the land but it does not constitute a legal cause of action in
nuisance. In order for a nuisance to exist in this fact situation, there must be
an unreasonable amount of stray voltage that affects the person's interest in
the private use and enjoyment of land. Therefore, GLEC may be liable for
an intentional invasion under the continuing invasion rationale expressed
in the Restatement if it continued to impose excessive levels of stray voltage
onto the Vogels' farm that might endanger their cows after it had knowledge of the problem. However, that is not the case here. In fact, the record
indicates the opposite.

It is undisputed that GLEC was first notified about the Vogels' stray
voltage concerns in March of 1986. The evidence indicates that GLEC
immediately responded and worked to alleviate any problems with its delivery system. For example, it installed an isolator on the system sometime
in March after the Vogels' initial complaint. According to Mr. Vogel, the
problems with their herd improved immediately. Further, Mr. Vogel acknowledged at trial that he "could very well have" observed GLEC
employees working on the system in the vicinity of his farm at least 50 to 60
times after notifying GLEC of his concerns, and that GLEC representatives
were actually on his farm "less than half" of that many times.

Based on the record in this case, we conclude as a matter of law that the
trial court did not err by construing the nuisance action as an unintentional
invasion and otherwise actionable under negligence, and by not submitting
the question of intentional invasion to the jury. . . .

The decision of the court of appeals ordering the circuit court to strike
nuisance-related damages from the judgment is reversed.

NOTES

1. Stray voltage cases. Should *Vogel* be treated as an instance of a nuisance
between strangers given that the defendant was supplying services for the

mutual benefit of both parties, as in Carstairs v. Taylor, *supra* at 138, which engrafted this exception into the strict liability rule of Rylands v. Fletcher? Note this rationale might not apply in all stray voltage cases. Therefore defendants have sought other protections from liability. Thus, defendant proved successful in Kuper v. Lincoln-Union Electric Co., 557 N.W.2d 748, 761 (S.D. 1996) because a state statute exempted rural electrical cooperatives required to construct, operate and maintain electrical facilities, from the law of nuisance. The court concluded that "[i]n granting an exemption from nuisance actions to statutorily authorized activities, our legislature obviously adopted a public policy that private interests must endure some inconvenience for the general populace to receive the benefits of utilities." Should the negligence action survive? Does it make a difference whether the plaintiff was in the defendant's service grid? In Martins v. Interstate Power Co., 652 N.W.2d 657, 665 (Iowa 2002), the court rejected an invitation to "adopt a similar stance in the name of public policy," holding that it is the legislature's job to exempt groups from nuisance law. If it did, would it constitute a taking? Note that a condemnation claim was denied in Public Service Co. of Colorado v. Van Wyk, 27 P.3d 377, 386 (Colo. 2001), *supra* at 12, for intangible as opposed to physical invasions, at least if they do not interfere with the use and enjoyment of property. What if they do?

2. *Nuisance generally.* Stray voltage cases are a subset of the larger class of nuisances, which have both the common definition offered in *Vogel* and its statutory variations. Compare the definition of a nuisance given in the Restatement with that provided by the California Civil Code (West 2007):

> §3479.   NUISANCE DEFINED
>
> Anything which is injurious to health, including, but not limited to, the illegal sale of controlled substances, or is indecent or offensive to the senses, or an obstruction to the free use of property, so as to interfere with the comfortable enjoyment of life or property, or unlawfully obstructs the free passage or use, in the customary manner, of any navigable lake, or river, bay, stream, canal, or basin, or any public park, square, street, or highway, is a nuisance.

The reference to the sale of controlled substances was added in 1996. The rest of the statute dates from 1872. What prompted the change?

In some cases, the key question is not whether conduct is actionable, but whether it is actionable as a trespass or a nontrespassory nuisance. In Martin v. Reynolds Metals Co., 342 P.2d 790 (Or. 1959), the defendants had released quantities of fluoride gas that became airborne and settled on adjacent land, rendering it unfit for cattle grazing and watering. The defendants claimed that the plaintiff's cause of action sounded in nuisance, with a two-year statute of limitations. The court, however, ruled that the defendant's conduct amounted to an actionable trespass, to which a six-year statute of limitations applied. The court also noted that the question of trespass or nuisance could be important on substantive issues as well, pointing out that the defense of "coming to the nuisance," *infra* at 697, is, almost by definition, inapplicable to a trespass case. If trespass involves the direct and immediate application of force against the person or property of another, can the court's position in *Martin* be defended? See Merrill, Trespass, Nuisance, and the Costs of Determining Property Rights, 14 J. Legal Stud. 13 (1985). How does *Martin* come out under the California statute?

3. *Reasonableness in the law of nuisance.* Like *Vogel*, most accounts of nuisance law provide that the defendant's invasive conduct is actionable only if it constitutes an "unreasonable" interference with the plaintiff's use and enjoyment of her property. One view is that this reasonableness language imports general negligence principles into the law of nuisance, so that the ultimate question is whether the expected benefits of the challenged activities exceed their expected costs. Thus, §826 of the Restatement (Second) provides:

> §826. UNREASONABLENESS OF INTENTIONAL INVASION
> An intentional invasion of another's interest in the use and enjoyment of land is unreasonable if
>> (a) the gravity of the harm outweighs the utility of the actor's conduct, or
>> (b) the harm caused by the conduct is serious and the financial burden of compensating for this and similar harm to others would not make the continuation of the conduct not feasible.

This view appears to have been adopted in Copart Industries, Inc. v. Consolidated Edison Co. of New York, Inc., 362 N.E.2d 968, 971 (N.Y. 1977). There the plaintiff, an operator of a new car storage and preparation business, alleged that the emissions from the smokestacks of a nearby Con Ed plant damaged the finishes on his and his customers' cars, forcing him out of business. The court of appeals affirmed the judgment for the defendant below, noting the limited basis of liability in nuisance cases:

> Despite early private nuisance cases, which apparently assumed that the defendant was strictly liable, today it is recognized that one is subject to liability for a private nuisance if his conduct is a legal cause of the invasion of the interest in the private use and enjoyment of land and such invasion is (1) intentional and unreasonable, (2) negligent or reckless, or (3) actionable under the rules governing liability for abnormally dangerous conditions or activities.

A more hostile reception to negligence principles in nuisance cases is found in Jost v. Dairyland Power Coop., 172 N.W.2d 647, 650-652 (Wis. 1969), cited in *Vogel*, in which discharges of sulfur dioxide resulted in substantial damages to the plaintiff's land. The court adopted a strict liability rule for damages, which the jury had found "substantial":

> Plaintiffs' attorney from the outset made it clear that liability was predicated on the *fact* that sulphur dioxide gases were emitted into the atmosphere, despite complaints over a period of several years. There was no attempt to hinge plaintiffs' case on the theory that the defendant was not exercising due care. Under the plaintiffs' theory, which we deem to be a correct one, it is irrelevant that defendant was conforming to industry standards of due care if its conduct created a nuisance.

Pestey v. Cushman, 788 A.2d 496, 507 (Conn. 2002), presents another variation on the same theme, when plaintiff complained of a variety of objectionable odors coming from the defendant's extensive farming operations. The defendant argued that the use of his property was reasonable, but to no avail: "while an unreasonable use and an unreasonable interference often coexist, the two concepts are not equivalent, and it is possible to prove that a defendant's use of his property, while reasonable, nonetheless constitutes a common-law private nuisance because it unreasonably interferes with the use of property by another person." Read together, it appears that *Jost* and *Pestey* take the position that once the defendant's invasion crosses some threshold level, liability becomes strict. What happens for nuisance-like invasions below that level?

4. *Actual harm under nuisance law.* The traditional cases of nuisance were often directed at physical invasions that were harmful to the senses, rather than invasions that caused obvious damage to real property. In recent years, many nuisance claims have been brought for forms of physical contamination that have not produced any overt signs of harm. In Smith v. Carbide & Chemicals Corp., 298 F. Supp. 2d 561 (W.D. Ky. 2004), the court held, applying Kentucky law, that the plaintiff's nuisance and trespass claims foundered when they could not show that the low levels of radioactive waste from the defendant's Paducah Gaseous Diffusion Plant operations, which caused a decline in the market value of their properties, creating a significant health risk to the occupants. In so doing, it disagreed with the earlier decision in Cook v. Rockwell International Corp., 273 F. Supp. 2d 1175, 1207 (D. Colo. 2003), which rejected the defense's view that "a normal member of the affected community would not and could not experience fear, annoyance or discomfort amounting to substantial interference with the use and enjoyment of property unless current science has determined the contamination poses a 'real' and unacceptable level of health risk." If trace elements of nuclear wastes can spark a cleanup under Superfund, why should the defendant not have to pay damages under tort law?

The absence of any physical invasion is generally sufficient to defeat a nuisance action. Thus the court in Adkins v. Thomas Solvent Co., 487

N.W.2d 715, 721 (Mich. 1992), denied recovery to landowners for the loss of market value attributable to unfavorable publicity and the *unfounded* belief, contradicted by expert evidence on both sides, that such contamination might take place. Boyle, J., concluded that "negative publicity resulting in unfounded fear about dangers in the vicinity of the property does not constitute a significant interference with the use and enjoyment of land." Similarly, in Golen v. The Union Corporation, 718 A.2d 298 (Pa. Super. Ct. 1998), the court denied a nuisance action to a plaintiff who was unable to sell his property because the defendant's nearby contaminated property was listed on the Superfund National Priority List. Fearing that it might open the "floodgates" of litigation, the court held that fluctuations in market value did not matter as plaintiff's use and enjoyment was unchanged. Is that result correct if future contamination were a real possibility? If it deterred the plaintiff from improving her property?

Michalson v. Nutting
175 N.E. 490 (Mass. 1931)

WAIT, J. The plaintiffs brought this bill in equity alleging that roots from a poplar tree growing upon the land of the defendants had penetrated the plaintiffs' land and had filled up sewer and drain pipes there, causing expense in digging them up and clearing them, and also had grown under the cement cellar of the plaintiffs' house, causing the cement to crack and crumble and threatening seriously to injure the foundation of the dwelling. They sought a mandatory injunction compelling the removal of the roots, a permanent injunction restraining the defendants from allowing the roots to encroach on the plaintiffs' land, and damages. The trial judge found that, as alleged, roots had extended from a poplar tree set out on the land of the defendants into the plaintiffs' land; had entered and clogged the sewer so that several times the plaintiffs had been compelled to dig up the pipes and remove the roots at an expense for the last cleaning of $42.28; had extended under ground to the cement foundation wall of their house and had caused it to move slightly but as yet without serious harm; that, at the time of the first clogging of the sewer, notice had been given defendants and request made that the roots be removed but that they had refused and refrained from so doing. He ruled that upon the facts admitted and found to be true there was no liability on the part of the defendants for the clogging of the sewer and the moving of the wall by the roots of the tree the trunk of which stood on the defendants' land, and he ordered a decree dismissing the bill with costs. The case is before us upon the plaintiffs' appeal from a final decree entered in accord with that order.

There is no error. The law of Massachusetts was stated in Bliss v. Ball, 99 Mass. 597, 598 [1868], by Chapman, C.J., to be "As against adjoining proprietors, the owner of a lot may plant shade trees upon it, or cover it with a thick forest, and the injury done to them by the mere shade of the trees is *damnum absque injuria*. It is no violation of their rights." We see no distinction in principle between damage done by shade, and damage caused by overhanging branches or invading roots. The principle involved is that an owner of land is at liberty to use his land, and all of it, to grow trees. Their growth naturally and reasonably will be accompanied by the extension of boughs and the penetration of roots over and into adjoining property of others. . . .

The neighbor, though without right of appeal to the courts if harm results to him, is, nevertheless, not without remedy. His right to cut off the intruding boughs and roots is well recognized. His remedy is in his own hands. The common sense of the common law has recognized that it is wiser to leave the individual to protect himself, if harm results to him from this exercise of another's right to use his property in a reasonable way, than to subject that other to the annoyance, and the public to the burden, of actions at law, which would be likely to be innumerable and, in many instances, purely vexatious. . . .

Decree affirmed.

NOTES

1. *Does the law of nuisance contain an act requirement?* For ordinary torts, the defendant must normally be guilty of some positive action before liability can be imposed. What about nuisance cases? Is that requirement satisfied in the tree cases? See Chapter 2, at page 108, if the defendant planted the tree? Decided not to trim it?

The act requirement manifests itself in other ways. In Puritan Holding Co. v. Holloschitz, 372 N.Y.S.2d 500 (N.Y. Sup. Ct. 1975), the court held the defendant liable in nuisance when she abandoned and left in disrepair a building she owned in an urban renewal area in which property values had shown a marked increase. The court noted her conduct violated the local administrative ordinance that required vacant buildings to be guarded or sealed. It further stated that her conduct might not constitute a nuisance in an area that had already deteriorated, and measured plaintiff's damages by the loss in market value attributable to the defendant's nuisance.

The act requirement was also tested in Merriam v. McConnell, 175 N.E.2d 293 (Ill. App. 1961), in which the court held that the bugs infesting the plaintiff's trees did not constitute a nuisance because the defendant had not placed them there. See also Robinson v. Whitelaw, 364 P.2d 1085 (Utah 1961), which denied an action for damage caused by sand and dirt deposited on plaintiff's property after the defendant cut the sagebrush and natural growth off his land to make way for future cultivation he never undertook.

The court noted that the "defendant would have difficulty in stopping the wind or replacing the sagebrush." What result if the land were cleared in order to vex the plaintiff? Finally in Carvalho v. Wolfe, 140 P.3d 1161, 1164 (Or. App. 2006), the court held that the defendants did not commit an actionable nuisance when the roots of trees on their land crossed the boundary and damaged the foundation of plaintiff's house. "Plaintiffs also allege that defendants have not taken any action to ensure that the trees have been killed and the growth of their roots permanently stopped, but they do not allege either that the growth is continuing or that defendants know or should know that it is continuing." How could the plaintiffs not know of the growth? How does this rationale differ from that in *Michalson*?

2. *Absolute property rights.* *Michalson* sidesteps the question of whether the defendant caused the nuisance by treating the harm as *damnum absque injuria*, Latin for harm without legal injury. The phrase is odd because poplars did cause real harm. But the court offered two powerful justifications for why this harm should not be actionable. The first was that each landowner had the right of self-help even if it appears that cutting the roots kills the trees. The second was that the harms in question are typically *reciprocal*, in that each landowner is likely to have trees on his property that encroach on that of a neighbor. More generally, the rhetoric of absolute property rights, often dominant in the law of trespass to land, is muted in the law of nuisance. Sharp property boundaries are softened to accommodate to the high frequency of low level nuisance invasions, which make it quite undesirable to give universal redress for all these events. For an elaboration of concern, see Epstein, Nuisance Law: Corrective Justice and Its Utilitarian Constraints, 8 J. Legal Stud. 49, 74-79, 82-90 (1979), in which the following considerations are used to explain why ex ante all landowners are better off with the relaxation of the otherwise absolute common law right to be wholly free from physical interference:

1. High administrative costs for claim resolution;
2. High transaction costs for voluntary reassignment of rights;
3. Low value to the interested parties of the ownership rights whose rearrangement is mandated by the public rule; and
4. Presence of implicit in-kind compensation from all to all that precludes any systematic redistribution of wealth among the interested parties.

3. *Live and let live.* One discrete application of this approach is found in the "live and let live" rule as articulated by Bramwell, B., in Bamford v. Turnley, 122 Eng. Rep. 27, 32-33 (Ex. 1862):

> The instances put during the argument, of burning weeds, emptying cesspools, making noises during repairs, and other instances which be nuisances

if done wantonly or maliciously, nevertheless may be lawfully done. It cannot be said that such acts are not nuisances, because, by the hypothesis they are; and it cannot be doubted that, if a person maliciously and without cause made close to a dwelling-house the same offensive smells as may be made in emptying a cesspool, an action would lie. Nor can these cases be got rid of as extreme cases, because such cases properly test a principle. Nor can it be said that the jury settle such questions by finding there is no nuisance, though there is. . . .

There must be, then, some principle on which such cases must be excepted. It seems to me that that principle may be deduced from the character of these cases, and is this, viz., that those acts necessary for the common and ordinary use and occupation of land and houses may be done, if conveniently done, without submitting those who do them to an action. . . . There is an obvious necessity for such a principle as I have mentioned. It is as much for the advantage of one owner as of another for the very nuisance the one complains of, as the result of the ordinary use of his neighbour's land, he himself will create in the ordinary use of his own, and the reciprocal nuisances are of a comparatively trifling character. The convenience of such a rule may be indicated by calling it a rule of give and take, live and let live. . . .

The public consists of all the individuals of it, and a thing is only for the public benefit when it is productive of good to those individuals on the balance of loss and gain to all. So that if all the loss and all the gain were borne and received by one individual, he on the whole would be the gainer. But whenever this is the case, — whenever a thing is for the public benefit, properly understood, — the loss to the individuals of the public who lose will bear compensation out of the gains of those who gain. It is for the public benefit there should be railways, but it would not be unless the gain of having the railway was sufficient to compensate the loss occasioned by the use of the land required for its site; and accordingly no one thinks it would be right to take an individual's land without compensation to make a railway.

Bramwell's endorsement of the "live and let live" principle shows the link between the requirement of just compensation and the principle of reciprocity. Since all interferences are "reciprocal" in character, virtually *all* parties are left better off under the regime of "live and let live" for minimal harms. As stated, moreover, the rule contains its own limitations. Substantial damages make it more likely, first, that the parties will not suffer inconveniences of equal magnitude and, second, that the administrative costs of dispute resolution will shrink relative to the amount in controversy. In those cases, as with taking a land for a railway, explicit compensation helps insure that the taking operates for the benefit of all.

For the classic discussion of the impact of transaction costs on market transactions, see Coase, The Problem of Social Cost, 3 J.L. & Econ. 1 (1960). For the connection between Bramwell's general views and the modern tests of social welfare, see Coleman, Efficiency, Utility and Wealth Maximization, 8 Hofstra L. Rev. 509 (1980). For the connection between nuisance law and eminent domain, see R. Epstein, Takings: Private Property and the Power of Eminent Domain 199-202, 229-238 (1985).

4. Locality rule. Reciprocity also helps explain another feature of nuisance law with no parallel in the law of trespass, the so-called locality rule. Its underpinnings are well articulated by Earl, J., in Campbell v. Seaman, 63 N.Y. 568, 576-577 (1876), when the fumes from the defendant's brick factory destroyed the trees and vegetation upon the plaintiff's land.

> Persons living in organized communities must suffer some damage, annoyance and inconvenience from each other. For these they are compensated by all the advantages of civilized society. If one lives in the city he must expect to suffer the dirt, smoke, noisome odors, noise and confusion incident to city life. . . .
>
> . . . As to what is a reasonable use of one's own property cannot be defined by any certain general rules, but must depend upon the circumstances of each case. A use of property in one locality and under some circumstances may be lawful and reasonable, which, under other circumstances, would be unlawful, unreasonable and a nuisance. To constitute a nuisance, the use must be such as to produce a tangible and appreciable injury to neighboring property, or such as to render its enjoyment specially uncomfortable or inconvenient.
>
> Within the rules thus referred to, that defendant's brick burning was a nuisance to plaintiffs cannot be doubted.

Fontainebleau Hotel Corp. v. Forty-Five Twenty-Five, Inc.
114 So. 2d 357 (Fla. App. 1959)

PER CURIAM. This is an interlocutory appeal from an order temporarily enjoining the appellants from continuing with the construction of a fourteen-story addition to the Fontainebleau Hotel, owned and operated by the appellants. Appellee, plaintiff below, owns the Eden Roc Hotel, which was constructed in 1955, about a year after the Fontainebleau, and adjoins the Fontainebleau on the north. Both are luxury hotels, facing the Atlantic Ocean. The proposed addition to the Fontainebleau is being constructed twenty feet from its north property line, 130 feet from the mean high water mark of the Atlantic Ocean, and 76 feet 8 inches from the ocean bulkhead line. The 14-story tower will extend 160 feet above grade in height and is 416 feet long from east to west. During the winter months, from around two o'clock in the afternoon for the remainder of the day, the shadow of the addition will extend over the cabana, swimming pool, and sunbathing areas of the Eden Roc, which are located in the southern portion of its property.

In this action, plaintiff-appellee sought to enjoin the defendants-appellants from proceeding with the construction of the addition to the

Fontainebleau (it appears to have been roughly eight stories high at the time suit was filed), alleging that the construction would interfere with the light and air on the beach in front of the Eden Roc and cast a shadow of such size as to render the beach wholly unfitted for the use and enjoyment of its guests, to the irreparable injury of the plaintiff; further, that the construction of such addition on the north side of defendant's property, rather than the south side, was actuated by malice and ill will on the part of the defendants' president toward the plaintiff's president; and that the construction was in violation of a building ordinance requiring a 100-foot setback from the ocean. It was also alleged that the construction would interfere with the easements of light and air enjoyed by plaintiff and its predecessors in title for more than twenty years and "impliedly granted by virtue of the acts of the plaintiff's predecessors in title, as well as under the common law and the express recognition of such rights by virtue of Chapter 9837, Laws of Florida 1923. . . ." Some attempt was also made to allege an easement by implication in favor of the plaintiff's property, as the dominant, and against the defendants' property, as the servient, tenement.

The defendants' answer denied the material allegations of the complaint, pleaded laches and estoppel by judgment.

The chancellor heard considerable testimony on the issues made by the complaint and the answer and, as noted, entered a temporary injunction restraining the defendants from continuing with the construction of the addition. His reason for so doing was stated by him, in a memorandum opinion, as follows:

> In granting the temporary injunction in this case the Court wishes to make several things very clear. The ruling is not based on any alleged presumptive title nor prescriptive right of the plaintiff to light and air nor is it based on any deed restrictions nor recorded plats in the title of the plaintiff nor of the defendant nor of any plat of record. It is not based on any zoning ordinance nor on any provision of the building code of the City of Miami Beach nor on the decision of any court, nisi prius or appellate. It is based solely on the proposition that no one has a right to use his property to the injury of another. In this case it is clear from the evidence that the proposed use by the Fontainebleau will materially damage the Eden Roc. There is evidence indicating that the construction of the proposed annex by the Fontainebleau is malicious or deliberate for the purpose of injuring the Eden Roc, but it is scarcely sufficient, standing alone, to afford a basis for equitable relief.

This is indeed a novel application of the maxim sic utere tuo ut alienum non laedas. This maxim does not mean that one must never use his own property in such a way as to do any injury to his neighbor. It means only that one must use his property so as not to injure the lawful *rights* of another. . . .

No American decision has been cited, and independent research has revealed none, in which it has been held that—in the absence of some contractual or statutory obligation—a landowner has a legal right to the free flow of light and air across the adjoining land of his neighbor. Even at common law, the landowner had no legal right, in the absence of an easement or uninterrupted use and enjoyment for a period of 20 years, to unobstructed light and air from the adjoining land. And the English doctrine of "ancient lights" has been unanimously repudiated in this country.

There being, then, no legal right to the free flow of light and air from the adjoining land, it is universally held that where a structure serves a useful and beneficial purpose, it does not give rise to a cause of action, either for damages or for an injunction under the maxim sic utere tuo ut alienum non laedas, even though it causes injury to another by cutting off the light and air and interfering with the view that would otherwise be available over adjoining land in its natural state, regardless of the fact that the structure may have been erected partly for spite.

We see no reason for departing from this universal rule. If, as contended on behalf of plaintiff, public policy demands that a landowner in the Miami Beach area refrain from constructing buildings on his premises that will cast a shadow on the adjoining premises, an amendment of its comprehensive planning and zoning ordinance, applicable to the public as a whole, is the means by which such purpose should be achieved. (No opinion is expressed here as to the validity of such an ordinance, if one should be enacted pursuant to the requirements of law. But to change the universal rule—and the custom followed in this state since its inception—that adjoining landowners have an equal right under the law to build to the line of their respective tracts and to such a height as is desired by them (in the absence, of course, of building restrictions or regulations) amounts, in our opinion, to judicial legislation. . . .)

[Reversed.]

NOTES

1. *Cast a giant shadow: an easement of light.* As *Fontainebleau* states, American courts traditionally rejected a common law easement for the light and air that pass over a neighbor's property because that rule would inhibit the growth of both towns and industry. The height restrictions often imposed by legislation have, however, uniformly been sustained against challenges under the takings clause of the Constitution. On the vexed relationship between the law of nuisance and the law of eminent domain, see generally Michelman, Property, Utility, and Fairness: Comments on the Ethical Formulations of "Just Compensation" Law, 80 Harv. L. Rev. 1165 (1967); see also Miller v. Schoene, 276 U.S. 272 (1928).

A very different approach to the easement of light was taken in Prah v. Maretti, 321 N.W.2d 182, 189-191 (Wis. 1982). There the plaintiff and the defendant owned adjoining plots in a subdivision, with the defendant's land located to the south of the plaintiff's. The defendant wished to construct a house on his plot that conformed to all applicable subdivision and zoning restrictions. The plaintiff sought to enjoin the proposed construction until the defendant relocated it on the site, claiming that the defendant's proposed house would impair the efficiency of the plaintiff's solar heating system by blocking off the sunlight during part of the year.

The Wisconsin Supreme Court overturned defendant's summary judgment in trial court, explicitly repudiating *Fontainebleau*, holding that an "unreasonable obstruction of access to sunlight might be a private nuisance." The court noted that easements of light could be acquired by prescription under the English doctrine of "ancient lights" and everywhere by express grant. It justified the judicial recognition of solar easements by noting the sharp rise in land use regulation, and by insisting that "the policy of favoring unhindered private development in an expanding economy is no longer in harmony with the realities of our society." The court then concluded that summary judgment was inappropriate: "[t]he application of the reasonable use standard in nuisance cases normally requires a full exposition of all underlying facts and circumstances. Too little is known in this case of such matters as the extent of the harm to the plaintiff, the suitability of solar heat in that neighborhood, the availability of remedies to the plaintiff, and the costs to the defendant of avoiding the harm." A lengthy dissent insisted, first, that there was no "invasion" by the defendant, second, that solar energy had not proved itself in the marketplace, and, third, that the elaborate legislative scheme in place should not be displaced by a parallel judicial innovation. Why wouldn't the original developer of the tract have the right incentives to decide whether to grant solar easements to individual tract owners?

In Tenn v. 889 Associates, Ltd., 500 A.2d 366, 371 (N.H. 1985), the court sought to steer a middle course between *Fontainebleau* and *Prah*. The court first rejected the hard-line proposition that the doctrine of ancient lights could never limit a neighbor's right to build, and held that "there is no reason in principle why the law of nuisance should not be applied to claims for the protection of a property owner's interests in light and air." Nonetheless, on the facts of the case, it refused to enjoin defendant's plans to construct a six-story office building at the property line just south of the plaintiff's own six-story building.

> The sites were in the downtown commercial area of Manchester, where buildings commonly buttress and block the sides of adjacent structures. Moreover, the defendant proposed to do no more than the plaintiff's own predecessor had done, by building right to the lot line and to a height of six

stories. If, as the plaintiff claimed, this would require expenditures for additional artificial lighting and ventilation systems, she failed to present any evidence that the costs would exceed what was customarily necessary for such buildings.

On private nuisances and solar easements, see generally Williams, Solar Access and Property Rights: A Maverick Analysis, 11 Conn. L. Rev. 430, 443 (1979); Goble, Solar Access and Property Rights: Reply to a "Maverick" Analysis, 12 Conn. L. Rev. 270 (1980).

2. Spite fences. It has often been held that "a fence erected maliciously, and with no other purpose than to shut out the light and air from a neighbor's window, is a nuisance." Flaherty v. Moran, 45 N.W. 381 (Mich. 1890). This proposition tracks the logic of the live and let live rule insofar as it rests on the belief that all individuals are better off if each is denied the right to construct fences solely out of malice. Yet even those courts that regard spite fences as actionable nuisances are quick to qualify their conclusions. Thus, in Kuzniak v. Kozminski, 65 N.W. 275 (Mich. 1895), the defendant moved his coal and wood shed close to the plaintiff's property line, where it blocked the light and air to plaintiff's windows, partly out of malice. Nonetheless the court refused to extend the spite fence doctrine because the shed served some "useful purpose." What about spite fences with useful functions? How might *Prah* be distinguished from the spite fence cases?

3. Noninvasive nuisances: of ugly things and beautiful views. Is it a nuisance if the defendant paints his house the most horrendous shade of pink, thereby driving down the value of the neighboring houses? May aesthetic blight be so inconsistent with the character of a neighborhood that it becomes a nuisance? In Mathewson v. Primeau, 395 P.2d 183 (Wash. 1964), the court, while willing to enjoin the raising of hogs on the defendant's land because their odors reached the plaintiff's property, nonetheless refused to require the defendant to remove the collection of junk from his land. It held the law of nuisance was not concerned with aesthetics.

A tougher attitude toward aesthetic nuisances was taken in Rattigan v. Wile, 841 N.E.2d 680, 691-692 (Mass. 2006). A long struggle began when the defendant outbid the plaintiffs to purchase a 2.9 acre beachfront lot next to plaintiffs' own luxurious Edgewater property. The plaintiffs then sought unsuccessfully to block the defendant's efforts to get building permits and access rights. In retaliation, the defendant conducted sporadically for a period of years a set of harassing activities, including piloting a low-flying helicopter, and piling unsightly objects higher than the six-foot fence that the plaintiffs had erected to block out the view of junk previously left on the ground near the boundary line. The trial judge found that the local community was "intolerant" of the defendant's activities, awarded plaintiffs $532,035.05 in damages, including lost rentals, and issued an injunction, which when modified on appeal, provided "the defendant shall not leave unattended any objects more than six feet in height within forty feet of the plaintiffs' boundary line, such as tents, portable toilets, construction and industrial materials, trailers, and warning signs, except reasonable vegetation. The defendant shall not operate, or cause to be operated, a helicopter on his property or within the zone of interest above the property."

Note that condominium associations often impose extensive aesthetic restrictions. Should zoning laws be allowed to do the same?

Rogers v. Elliott
15 N.E. 768 (Mass. 1888)

[The facts of the case, somewhat abbreviated, are as follows: The defendant operated a large church bell in a small Massachusetts town, which he rang regularly each day. The plaintiff was recovering from a serious case of sunstroke in a house located not far from the church. One Saturday the plaintiff suffered severe convulsions attributed by his physician to the bell's noise. After the Saturday episode the physician informed the defendant of his patient's condition and predicted that the plaintiff would have further convulsions if the defendant rang the bell the next day. After receiving this warning, the defendant said he would ring his bell as usual the next day because he had no love for the plaintiff. He added that he would ring it even if his mother were ill. The next day the defendant rang his bell and the plaintiff suffered further damage, for which he brought this action.]

KNOWLTON, J. The defendant was the custodian and authorized manager of property of the Roman Catholic Church used for religious worship. The acts for which the plaintiff seeks to hold him responsible were done in the use of this property, and the sole question before us is whether or not that use was unlawful. The plaintiff's case rests upon the proposition that the ringing of the bell was a nuisance. The consideration of this proposition involves an inquiry into what the defendant could properly do in the use of the real estate which he had in charge, and what was the standard by which his rights were to be measured.

It appears that the church was built upon a public street in a thickly settled part of the town, and if the ringing of the bell on Sundays had materially affected the health or comfort of all in the vicinity, whether residing or passing there, this use of the property would have been a public nuisance, for which there would have been a remedy by indictment. Individuals suffering from it in their persons or their property could have recovered damages for a private nuisance.

In an action of this kind, a fundamental question is, by what standard, as against the interests of a neighbor, is one's right to use his real estate to be measured. In densely populated communities the use of property in many ways which are legitimate and proper necessarily affects in greater or less degree the property or persons of others in the vicinity. In such cases the inquiry always is, when rights are called in question, what is reasonable under the circumstances. If a use of property is objectionable solely on account of the noise which it makes, it is a nuisance, if at all, by reason of its effect upon the health or comfort of those who are within hearing. The right to make a noise for a proper purpose must be measured in reference to the degree of annoyance which others may reasonably be required to submit to. In connection with the importance of the business from which it proceeds, that must be determined by the effect of noise upon people generally, and not upon those, on the one hand, who are peculiarly susceptible to it, or those, on the other, who by long experience have learned to endure it without inconvenience; not upon those whose strong nerves and robust health enable them to endure the greatest disturbances without suffering, nor upon those whose mental or physical condition makes them painfully sensitive to everything about them.

That this must be the rule in regard to public nuisances is obvious. It is the rule as well, and for reasons nearly if not quite as satisfactory, in relation to private nuisances. Upon a question whether one can lawfully ring his factory bell, or run his noisy machinery, or whether the noise will be a private nuisance to the occupant of a house near by, it is necessary to ascertain the natural and probable effect of the sound upon ordinary persons in that house, — not how it will affect a particular person, who happens to be there to-day, or who may chance to come tomorrow. St. Helen's Smelting Co. v. Tipping, [11 Eng. Rep. 1485 (H.L.E. 1865)]. In the case of Westcott v. Middleton, 11 A. 490 (N.J. Eq. 1887), 478, it appeared that the defendant carried on the business of an undertaker, and the windows of the plaintiff's house looked out upon his yard, where boxes which had been used to preserve the bodies of the dead were frequently washed, and where other objects were visible and other work was going on, which affected the tender sensibilities of the plaintiff, and caused him great discomfort. Vice-Chancellor Bird, in dismissing the bill for an injunction against carrying on the business there, said: ". . . A wide range has indeed been given to courts of equity in dealing with these matters; but I can find no case where the court has extended aid unless the act complained of was, as I have above said, of a nature to affect all reasonable persons, similarly situated, alike."

If one's right to use his property were to depend upon the effect of the use upon a person of peculiar temperament or disposition, or upon one suffering from an uncommon disease, the standard for measuring it would be so uncertain and fluctuating as to paralyze industrial enterprises. The owner of a factory containing noisy machinery, with dwelling-houses all about it, might find his business lawful as to all but one of the tenants of the houses, and as to that one, who dwelt no nearer than the others, it might be a nuisance. The character of his business might change from legal to illegal, or illegal to legal, with every change of tenants of an adjacent estate or with an arrival or departure of a guest or boarder at a house near by or even with the wakefulness or the tranquil repose of an invalid neighbor on a particular night. Legal rights to the use of property cannot be left to such uncertainty. When an act is of such a nature as to extend its influence to those in the vicinity, and its legal quality depends upon the effect of that influence, it is as important that the rightfulness of it should be tried by the experience of ordinary people, as it is, in determining a question as to negligence, that the test should be the common care of persons of ordinary prudence, without regard to the peculiarities of him whose conduct is on trial.

In the case at bar it is not contended that the ringing of the bell for church services in the manner shown by the evidence materially affected the health or comfort of ordinary people in the vicinity, but the plaintiff's claim rests upon the injury done him on account of his peculiar condition. However his request should have been treated by the defendant upon considerations of humanity, we think he could not put himself in a place of exposure to noise, and demand as of legal right that the bell should not be used.

The plaintiff, in his brief, concedes that there was no evidence of express malice on the part of the defendant, but contends that malice was implied in his acts. In the absence of evidence that he acted wantonly, or with express malice, this implication could not come from his exercise of his legal rights. How far and under what circumstances malice may be material in cases of this kind, it is unnecessary to consider.

Judgment on the verdict.

NOTES

1. *Extrasensitive plaintiffs under the law of nuisance*. Can the result in Rogers v. Elliott be reconciled with the general rule, applicable in trespass and negligence cases, that the defendant takes his victim as he finds him? If it had been found in Rogers v. Elliott that an ordinary person would have suffered substantial discomfort but no physical injuries from the ringing of the bells, could the plaintiff have recovered for the full extent of his injuries? Could the defendant claim a prescriptive easement, based on long use, against the public at large?

The Restatement (Second) of Torts follows the rule in *Rogers* by stating in §821F: "There is liability for a nuisance only to those to whom it causes significant harm, of a kind that would be suffered by a normal person in the community or by property in normal condition and used for a normal purpose." *Rogers* is explicitly approved in RST §821, comment *d*, which also provides that a person without a sense of smell can recover for obnoxious odors, unendurable by a normal person, but from which he is not "personally troubled." Why?

2. *The extrasensitive use of plaintiff's property.* The extrasensitivity issue in nuisance cases arises not only with personal injuries, but also with property damage. In Belmar Drive-In Theater Co. v. Illinois State Toll Highway Commission, 216 N.E.2d 788 (Ill. 1966), the defendants operated a toll-road service center that was adjoined to the plaintiff's outdoor movie theater. The charge in the complaint was that the "brilliant artificial lights" used in the service area "dispelled" the darkness, making it impossible for the plaintiff to exhibit his outdoor movies, reducing the value of his theater. The court denied the plaintiff's cause of action, relying on the extrasensitivity test. For an endorsement of *Belmar*, see RST §821F, illustration 2. What if the defendant could have constructed its tollway service center so as not to cast light on the plaintiff's theater? Suppose the defendant was not a governmental agency?

Belmar was expressly distinguished in Page County Appliance Center v. Honeywell, Inc., 347 N.W.2d 171, 175, 176 (Iowa 1984). The defendant Honeywell installed a computer in a local travel agency as part of defendant ITT's plan to lease computers to retail travel outlets nationwide. The computer leaked extensive amounts of radiation, which interfered with the images on the television sets on display in plaintiff's nearby appliance store. Honeywell's efforts to fix the computers were to no avail because the "interference-causing radiation was a design and not a service problem." The jury awarded the plaintiff $221,000 in damages ($71,000 compensatory, $150,000 exemplary), and the judge required Honeywell to make full indemnity to ITT. The judgment was affirmed on appeal by Reynoldson, C.J.:

> In the case before us, ITT asserts the Appliance Center's display televisions constituted a hypersensitive use of its premises as a matter of law, and equates this situation to cases involving light thrown on outdoor theater screens in which light-throwing defendants have carried the day. *See Belmar.* . . .
>
> We cannot equate the rare outdoor theater screen with the ubiquitous television that exists, in various numbers in almost every home. Clearly, the presence of televisions on any premises is not such an abnormal condition that we can say, as a matter of law, that the owner has engaged in a *peculiarly* sensitive use of the property.

On extrasensitivity, see generally Ellickson, Alternatives to Zoning: Covenants, Nuisance Rules, and Fines as Land Use Controls, 40 U. Chi. L. Rev. 681, 751-757 (1973).

Ensign v. Walls
34 N.W.2d 549 (Mich. 1948)

CARR, J. Defendant herein has for some years past carried on at 13949 Dacosta Street, in the City of Detroit, the business of raising, breeding and boarding St. Bernard dogs. Plaintiffs are property owners and residents in the immediate neighborhood. Claiming that the business conducted by defendant constituted a nuisance as to them and their property, plaintiffs brought suit for injunctive relief. The bill of complaint alleged that obnoxious odors came from defendant's premises at all times, that the continual barking of the dogs interfered with and disturbed plaintiffs in the use and enjoyment of their respective properties, that the premises were infested with rats and flies, and that on occasions dogs escaped from defendant's premises and roamed about the neighborhood. Defendant in her answer denied that her business was conducted in such a manner as to constitute a nuisance, and claimed further that she had carried on the business at the premises in question since 1926, that she had invested a considerable sum of money in the purchase of the property and in the subsequent erection of buildings thereon, and that under the circumstances plaintiffs were not entitled to the relief sought. . . .

[The court concluded that the evidence supported the finding that the defendant's business constituted a nuisance to the plaintiffs and that the defendant had not acquired by prescriptive use the right to continue the nuisance.]

The record discloses that the plaintiffs, or the majority of them at least, have moved into the neighborhood in recent years. In view of this situation it is claimed by defendant that, inasmuch as she was carrying on her business of raising, breeding and boarding dogs on her premises at the time plaintiffs established their residences in the neighborhood, they cannot now be heard to complain. Such circumstance may properly be taken into account in a proceeding of this nature in determining whether the relief sought ought, in equity and good conscience, to be granted. Doubtless under such circumstances courts of equity are more reluctant to restrain the continued operation of a lawful business than in instances where it is sought to begin in a residential district a business of such character that it will constitute a nuisance. The Supreme Court of Pennsylvania in Wier's Appeal, 74 Pa. 230 [(1873)], declared the commonly accepted rule as follows:

> There is a very marked distinction to be observed in reason and equity between the case of a business long established in a particular locality, which has become a nuisance from the growth of population and the erection of dwellings in proximity to it, and that of a new erection threatened in such a vicinity. Carrying on an offensive trade for any number of years in a place

remote from buildings and public roads, does not entitle the owner to continue it in the same place after houses have been built and roads laid out in the neighborhood, to the occupants of which and travellers upon which it is a nuisance. As the city extends, such nuisances should be removed to the vacant grounds beyond the immediate neighborhood of the residences of the citizens. This, public policy, as well as the health and comfort of the population of the city, demand. It certainly ought to be a much clearer case, however, to justify a court of equity in stretching forth the strong arm of injunction to compel a man to remove an establishment in which he has invested his capital and been carrying on business for a long period of time, from that of one who comes into a neighborhood proposing to establish such a business for the first time, and who is met at the threshold of his enterprise by a remonstrance and notice that if he persists in his purpose, application will be made to a court of equity to prevent him. . . .

Defendant cites and relies on prior decisions of this court in each of which consideration was given to the circumstance that the parties seeking relief had established residences near the business the operation of which was sought to be enjoined. That such a circumstance may properly be considered in any case of this character in determining whether equitable relief should be granted is scarcely open to question. However it is not necessarily controlling. Looking to all the facts and circumstances involved, the question invariably presented is whether the discretion of the court should be exercised in favor of the parties seeking relief. In the case at bar the trial court came to the conclusion that the nuisance found by him to exist ought to be abated, and that such action was necessary in order to protect the plaintiffs in their rights and in the use and enjoyment of their homes. It may be assumed that new residences will be built in the community in the future, as they have been in the past, and that in consequence the community will become more and more thickly populated. This means of course that the injurious results of the carrying on of defendant's business, if the nuisance is not abated, will be greater in the future than it has been in the past. Such was obviously the view of the trial judge, and we cannot say that he abused his discretion in granting relief. On the contrary we think his conclusions were fully justified by the record.

The decree of the Circuit Court is affirmed. Plaintiffs may have costs.

NOTES

1. Coming to the nuisance. Ensign v. Walls adopts the general view that it is no categorical defense to show that the plaintiff came to the nuisance, so that trial courts do not abuse their discretion by issuing injunctions in these cases. The majority position finds its basis in the plaintiff's right to the exclusive use and control of his own land and holds that the defendant is not entitled to acquire by her unilateral conduct an easement to cause damage to the plaintiff's property. The case, briefly put, is that an acceptance of the coming to the nuisance defense allows the "theft" of an incorporeal interest in real property. Why not mandate the injunction in all cases?

The minority view on the coming to the nuisance question usually rests on some version of assumption of risk. In Bove v. Donner-Hanna Coke Corp., 258 N.Y.S. 229, 234 (App. Div. 1932), the plaintiff sought to enjoin the operation of defendant's coke oven, which was located on the opposite side of the street. The region was industrialized when the plaintiff moved into it, but a hickory grove was located on the site of the defendant's coke oven. The court rejected the plaintiff's request for an injunction because the plaintiff moved into the area "with full knowledge that this region was especially adapted for industrial rather than residential purposes, and that factories would increase in the future . . . ." The opinion concluded with a marked deference to local zoning authorities, by noting that it was inappropriate for a court to "condemn as a nuisance a business which is being conducted in an approved and expert manner, at the very spot where the council said it might be located."

Note the equivocation in the Second Restatement. Section 840C provides that assumption of risk should be a defense in nuisance actions "to the same extent as in other tort actions." Thereafter, §840D puts this gloss on coming to the nuisance: "The fact that the plaintiff has acquired or improved his land after a nuisance interfering with it has come into existence is not in itself sufficient to bar his action, but is a factor to be considered in determining whether the nuisance is actionable."

Echoes of *Bove* may be found in Utah Code Ann. 78-38-5 (2007):

> (1) . . . [N]o manufacturing facility or the operation thereof shall be or become a nuisance, private or public, by virtue of any changed conditions in and about the locality thereof after the same has been in operation for more than three years when such manufacturing facility or the operation thereof was not a nuisance at the time the operation thereof began; provided, the manufacturing facility does not increase the condition asserted to be a nuisance and that the provisions of this subsection shall not apply whenever a nuisance results from the negligent or improper operation of any such manufacturing facility.

Finally, the limits of the coming to the nuisance doctrine were tested in Amaral v. Cuppels, 831 N.E.2d 915, 919 (Mass. App. 2005), which held that the coming to the nuisance defense was not available to the owner of a golf course who was sued for a continuing trespass when players near the ninth hole bombarded landowners' homes, which were subsequently built nearby. Green, J., held that the discretionary principles applicable to coming to the nuisance cases did not apply because there is "no cognate notion of 'coming to a trespass.'" Why the difference?

2. *Economic analysis and the coming to the nuisance rule.* A spirited attack on the coming to the nuisance rule is found in Baxter & Altree, Legal Aspects of Airport Noise, 15 J.L. & Econ. 1 (1972), who claim that a law and economics approach suggests that the optimum use of land will be achieved with the following liability rule: "of two incompatible land uses the one which had but did not take the opportunity to avoid creating costs of incompatibility should bear the costs." From this premise it follows in general that the first party to invest in a given area should be protected and, to use the authors' phrase, "the unavoidable reciprocal costs" that arise when a second party makes an incompatible use of his own land should be borne by the second party. The temporal element is given dominance under this formulation that under the traditional nuisance law was reserved for the spatial element.

The Baxter-Altree rule is meant to discourage any wasteful investment that the second user might otherwise make if he knew he could collect full damages or enjoin the prior use. But it does not indicate what restrictions, if any, should be placed on the *initial* decision by the first user. If their proposal is followed, the plaintiff is left without a remedy in the standard coming to the nuisance case, which gives any landowner a strong incentive to develop quickly if only to preserve legal rights. Further, the second use could prove more beneficial to society, but be blocked by the incompatible land uses. The coming to the nuisance rule is therefore understood as an implicit bargain between two landowners in which the first allows the second to operate on the condition that the second waives any statute of limitations objection should the former develop his land. That rule postpones any litigation and holds open the prospect that the initial builder will abandon his obnoxious use when the developed region makes other uses more attractive. Note that the statute of limitations played an important role in Sturges v. Bridgman, 11 Ch. D. 852 (1879), in which Jessel, M.R., enjoined an established confectioner from the use of his mortar and pestle when the plaintiff physician built his examining room on the opposite side of the party wall.

The entire question of coming to the nuisance has been much debated in the academic literature. See Ellickson, Alternatives to Zoning, 40 U. Chi. L. Rev. 681, 758-761 (1973); Michelman, Property, Utility and Fairness, 80 Harv. L. Rev. 1165, 1235-1245 (1967). For a recent account of *Sturges*, see Simpson, Coase v. Pigou Reexamined, 25 J. Legal Stud. 53 (1996); Coase, Law and Economics and A.W. Brian Simpson, 25 J. Legal Stud. 103 (1996); and in reply, Simpson, An Addendum, 25 J. Legal Stud. 99 (1996); R. Epstein, Principles of a Free Society: Reconciling Individual Liberty with the Common Good 202-206 (1998).

Boomer v. Atlantic Cement Co.
257 N.E.2d 870 (N.Y. 1970)

BERGAN, J. Defendant operates a large cement plant near Albany. These are actions for injunction and damages by neighboring land owners alleging injury to property from dirt, smoke and vibration emanating from the plant. A nuisance has been found after trial, temporary damages have been allowed; but an injunction has been denied.

The public concern with air pollution arising from many sources in industry and in transportation is currently accorded ever wider recognition accompanied by a growing sense of responsibility in State and Federal Governments to control it. Cement plants are obvious sources of air pollution in the neighborhoods where they operate.

But there is now before the court private litigation in which individual property owners have sought specific relief from a single plant operation. The threshold question raised by the division of view on this appeal is whether the court should resolve the litigation between the parties now before it as equitably as seems possible; or whether, seeking promotion of the general public welfare, it should channel private litigation into broad public objectives.

A court performs its essential function when it decides the rights of parties before it. Its decision of private controversies may sometimes greatly affect public issues. Large questions of law are often resolved by the manner in which private litigation is decided. But this is normally an incident to the court's main function to settle controversy. It is a rare exercise of judicial power to use a decision in private litigation as a purposeful mechanism to achieve direct public objectives greatly beyond the rights and interests before the court.

Effective control of air pollution is a problem presently far from solution even with the full public and financial powers of government. In large measure adequate technical procedures are yet to be developed and some that appear possible may be economically impracticable.

[The court then notes that the scientific, financial and political implications are not easily addressed and lie in] an area beyond the circumference of one private lawsuit. It is a direct responsibility for government and should not thus be undertaken as an incident to solving a dispute between property owners and a single cement plant — one of many — in the Hudson River valley.

The cement making operations of defendant have been found by the court at Special Term to have damaged the nearby properties of plaintiffs in these two actions. That court, as it has been noted, accordingly found defendant maintained a nuisance and this has been affirmed at the Appellate Division. The total damage to plaintiffs' properties is, however, relatively small in comparison with the value of defendant's operation and with the consequences of the injunction which plaintiffs seek.

The ground for the denial of injunction, notwithstanding the finding both that there is a nuisance and that plaintiffs have been damaged substantially, is the large disparity in economic consequences of the nuisance and of the injunction. This theory cannot, however, be sustained without overruling a doctrine which has been consistently reaffirmed in several leading cases in this court and which has never been disavowed here, namely that where a nuisance has been found and where there has been any substantial damage shown by the party complaining an injunction will be granted.

The rule in New York has been that such a nuisance will be enjoined although marked disparity be shown in economic consequence between the effect of the injunction and the effect of the nuisance.

The problem of disparity in economic consequence was sharply in focus in Whalen v. Union Bag & Paper Co.[, 101 N.E. 804 (N.Y. 1913)]. A pulp mill entailing an investment of more than a million dollars polluted a stream in which plaintiff, who owned a farm, was "a lower riparian owner." The economic loss to plaintiff from this pollution was small. This court, reversing the Appellate Division, reinstated the injunction granted by the Special Term against the argument of the mill owner that in view of "the slight advantage to plaintiff and the great loss that will be inflicted on defendant" an injunction should not be granted. "Such a balancing of injuries cannot be justified by the circumstances of this case," Judge Werner noted. He continued: "Although the damage to the plaintiff may be slight as compared with the defendant's expense of abating the condition, that is not a good reason for refusing an injunction."

Thus the unconditional injunction granted at Special Term was reinstated. The rule laid down in that case, then, is that whenever the damage resulting from a nuisance is found not "unsubstantial," viz., $100 a year, injunction would follow. This states a rule that had been followed in this court with marked consistency.

Although the court at Special Term and the Appellate Division held that injunction should be denied, it was found that plaintiffs had been damaged in various specific amounts up to the time of the trial and damages to the respective plaintiffs were awarded for those amounts. The effect of this was, injunction having been denied, plaintiffs could maintain successive actions at law for damages thereafter as further damage was incurred.

The court at Special Term also found the amount of permanent damage attributable to each plaintiff, for the guidance of the parties in the event both sides stipulated to the payment and acceptance of such permanent damage as a settlement of all the controversies among the parties. The total of permanent damages to all plaintiffs thus found was $185,000. This basis of adjustment has not resulted in any stipulation by the parties.

This result at Special Term and at the Appellate Division is a departure from a rule that has become settled; but to follow the rule literally in these cases would be to close down the plant at once. This court is fully agreed to avoid that immediately drastic remedy; the difference in view is how best to avoid it.

One alternative is to grant the injunction but postpone its effect to a specified future date to give opportunity for technical advances to permit defendant to eliminate the nuisance; another is to grant the injunction conditioned on the payment of permanent damages to plaintiffs which would compensate them for the total economic loss to their property present and future caused by defendant's operations. For reasons which will be developed the court chooses the latter alternative.

If the injunction were to be granted unless within a short period — e.g., 18 months — the nuisance be abated by improved methods, there would be no assurance that any significant technical improvement would occur.

The parties could settle this private litigation at any time if defendant paid enough money and the imminent threat of closing the plant would build up the pressure on defendant. If there were no improved techniques found, there would inevitably be applications to the court at Special Term for extensions of time to perform on showing of good faith efforts to find such techniques.

Moreover, techniques to eliminate dust and other annoying by-products of cement making are unlikely to be developed by any research the defendant can undertake within any short period, but will depend on the total resources of the cement industry Nationwide and throughout the world. The problem is universal wherever cement is made.

For obvious reasons the rate of the research is beyond control of defendant. If at the end of 18 months the whole industry has not found a technical solution a court would be hard put to close down this one cement plant if due regard be given to equitable principles.

On the other hand, to grant the injunction unless defendant pays plaintiffs such permanent damages as may be fixed by the court seems to do justice between the contending parties. All of the attributions of economic loss to the properties on which plaintiffs' complaints are based will have been redressed.

The nuisance complained of by these plaintiffs may have other public or private consequences, but these particular parties are the only ones who have sought remedies and the judgment proposed will fully redress them. The limitation of relief granted is a limitation only within the four corners of these actions and does not foreclose public health or the public agencies from seeking proper relief in a proper court.

It seems reasonable to think that the risk of being required to pay permanent damages to injured property owners by cement plant owners would itself be a reasonable effective spur to research for improved techniques to minimize nuisance.

The power of the court to condition on equitable grounds the continuance of an injunction on the payment of permanent damages seems undoubted. . . .

Thus it seems fair to both sides to grant permanent damages to plaintiffs which will terminate this private litigation. The theory of damage is the "servitude on land" of plaintiffs imposed by defendant's nuisance. (See United States v. Causby, 328 U.S. 256, 261, 262, 267 (1946), where the term "servitude" addressed to the land was used by Justice Douglas relating to the effect of airplane noise on property near an airport.)

The judgment, by allowance of permanent damages imposing a servitude on land, which is the basis of the actions, would preclude future recovery by plaintiffs or their grantees.

This should be placed beyond debate by a provision of the judgment that the payment by defendant and the acceptance by plaintiffs of permanent damages found by the court shall be in compensation for a servitude on the land. . . .

The orders should be reversed, without costs, and the cases remitted to Supreme Court, Albany County to grant an injunction which shall be vacated upon payment by defendant of such amounts of permanent damage to the respective plaintiffs as shall for this purpose be determined by the court.

JASEN, J., dissenting. I agree with the majority that a reversal is required here, but I do not subscribe to the newly enunciated doctrine of assessment of permanent damages, in lieu of an injunction, where substantial property rights have been impaired by the creation of a nuisance.

It has long been the rule in this State, as the majority acknowledges, that a nuisance which results in substantial continuing damage to neighbors must be enjoined. To now change the rule to permit the cement company to continue polluting the air indefinitely upon the payment of permanent damages is, in my opinion, compounding the magnitude of a very serious problem in our State and Nation today.

In recognition of this problem, the Legislature of this State has enacted the Air Pollution Control Act (Public Health Law, §§1264-1299m) declaring that it is the State policy to require the use of all available and reasonable methods to prevent and control air pollution.

The harmful nature and widespread occurrence of air pollution have been extensively documented. Congressional hearings have revealed that air pollution causes substantial property damage, as well as being a contributing factor to a rising incidence of lung cancer, emphysema, bronchitis and asthma.

The specific problem faced here is known as particulate contamination because of the fine dust particles emanating from defendant's cement plant. The particular type of nuisance is not new, having appeared in many cases for at least the past 60 years. It is interesting to note that cement production has recently been identified as a significant source of particulate contamination in the Hudson Valley. This type of pollution, wherein very small particles escape and stay in the atmosphere, has been denominated as the type of air pollution which produces the greatest hazard to human health. We have thus a nuisance which not only is damaging to the plaintiffs, but also is decidedly harmful to the general public.

I see grave dangers in overruling our long-established rule of granting an injunction where a nuisance results in substantial continuing damage. In permitting the injunction to become inoperative upon the payment of permanent damages, the majority is, in effect, licensing a continuing wrong. It is the same as saying to the cement company, you may continue to do harm to your neighbors so long as you pay a fee for it. Furthermore, once such permanent damages are assessed and paid, the incentive to alleviate the wrong would be eliminated, thereby continuing air pollution of an area without abatement.

It is true that some courts have sanctioned the remedy here proposed by the majority in a number of cases, but none of the authorities relied upon by the majority are analogous to the situation before us. In those cases, the courts, in denying an injunction and awarding money damages, grounded their decision on a showing that the use to which the property was intended to be put was primarily for the public benefit. Here, on the other hand, it is clearly established that the cement company is creating a continuing air pollution nuisance primarily for its own private interest with no public benefit.

This kind of inverse condemnation may not be invoked by a private person or corporation for private gain or advantage. Inverse condemnation should only be permitted when the public is primarily served in the taking or impairment of property. The promotion of the interests of the polluting cement company has, in my opinion, no public use or benefit.

Nor is it constitutionally permissible to impose servitude on land, without consent of the owner, by payment of permanent damages where the continuing impairment of the land is for a private use. This is made clear by the State Constitution (art. I, §7, subd. [a]) which provides that "[p]rivate property shall not be taken for *public* use without just compensation" (emphasis added). It is, of course, significant that the section makes no mention of taking for a *private* use. . . .

I would enjoin the defendant cement company from continuing the discharge of dust particles upon its neighbors' properties unless, within 18 months, the cement company abated this nuisance.

NOTES

1. Permanent and temporary damages. Injunctions aside, plaintiffs may seek damages in a nuisance action. If so, frequently the court must decide between periodic payments or a single lump sum to cover the plaintiff's loss. As might be expected, both approaches have their advantages and disadvantages. Temporary damages allow the court to make more accurate assessments of actual harm without having to speculate about the course of future events. But they impose high administrative costs and burden the plaintiff with the inconvenience of having to bring multiple actions to redress one continuing wrong. Permanent damages raise the converse problems, for the risk of one inaccurate valuation is the price for avoiding a multiplicity of subsequent actions. Note that permanent damages do not offer a once and for all solution if the defendant increases its interference with the plaintiff's land beyond expected levels. How does one measure damages in such a case? Determine when the statute of limitations starts to run? Given the difficulties in choosing between permanent and temporary damages, should the plaintiff be given an election of remedies?

2. *Mitigation of damages.* With either permanent or temporary damages, the plaintiff is under a duty to mitigate damages. In Belkus v. City of Brockton, 184 N.E. 812 (Mass. 1933), the plaintiff's land had been flooded at various times in the six years prior to suit. The court allowed the plaintiff to recover the costs of raising the level of his basement in order to prevent its repeated flooding from a culvert that the defendant municipality improperly maintained. Should the costs of extensive renovations be allowed after a single flooding? In Stratford Theater, Inc. v. Town of Stratford, 101 A.2d 279 (Conn. 1953), the plaintiff's theater had been "frequently" flooded from a broken sewer line. The plaintiff recovered the expense, not of altering his own property, but of repairing the defendant's broken line. If the plaintiff had not chosen to make the repairs, could it recover for anticipated future losses, even if greater than the cost of repairs?

A hostile attitude toward mitigation is forcefully asserted in an oft-quoted, but little-followed, passage in H. Wood, The Law of Nuisances §844, 435 (3d ed. 1893):

> A person injured by a nuisance, is not precluded from a recovery by the fact that he might, by small exertion and a small expenditure, have prevented the injury, the rule being, that as it was the defendant's duty to abstain from the creation of the nuisance, and having created it adjoining owners are not bound to guard against the consequences ensuing therefrom, when in order to do so they are required to expend time or money. . . . A party is not bound to expend a dollar, or to do any act to secure for himself the exercise or enjoyment of a legal right of which he is deprived by reason of the wrongful acts of another.

3. *Permanent injunctions.* Wood's position represents the strongest manifestation of the autonomy principle for completed harms. The same principle justifies routine injunctive relief for individuals who have been substantially inconvenienced by the defendant's nuisance. In practice, as

both *Ensign* and *Boomer* suggest, courts do not follow an inflexible rule that requires an immediate injunction in all cases. Nonetheless, courts are typically quite cautious in denying injunctive relief. In some cases an injunction is awarded because of a serious risk of defendant's insolvency. In other cases the injunction usefully protects innocent third parties who did not find it cost effective to sue, even though they suffered nontrivial losses. See Menell, A Note on Private Versus Social Incentives to Sue in a Costly Legal System, 12 J. Legal Stud. 41 (1983). In addition, the injunction reduces the need for the court (which may still, however, be needed to assess interim damages) to determine accurately the plaintiff's subjective valuation of privacy and seclusion.

These factors have inclined most courts to treat injunctions as a presumptive, if not an absolute, remedy. But before and after *Boomer*, courts have balked at granting injunctive relief in cases of extreme disparity. Thus, in Madison v. Ducktown Sulphur, Copper & Iron Co., 83 S.W. 658, 666, 667 (Tenn. 1904), the plaintiffs were all owners of "thin mountain lands, of little agricultural value." The defendants operated two large copper smelting plants that the plaintiffs sought to shut down. The court refused to close the plants, worth nearly $2 million, in order to protect property worth $1,000. The injunction would ultimately "destroy half of the taxable values of a county, and drive more than 10,000 people from their homes." Should it make a difference that mining operations, unlike manufacturing operations, are often immobile? Less dramatically in Escobar v. Continental Baking Co., 596 N.E.2d 394, 396 (Mass. App. 1992), the court refused to enjoin deliveries to defendant's bakeries between 12 A.M. and 7 A.M. on the grounds that the $36,000 in damages from lost sleep was far less than the $1.7 million that it would cost the defendant to build a new distribution site. With an eye toward coming to the nuisance the court added: "The plaintiffs knew there was a bakery business next door when they bought their property for $35,900 in 1977. The 1977 price reflected the property's location and the defendant's business activities." Why doesn't the purchaser stand in the shoes of the prior owner?

Madison, in particular, offers a graphic illustration of strategic bargaining behavior in cases of enormous disparity between defendant's loss and plaintiff's gain. More specifically, granting the injunction gives both parties incentives to renegotiate the deal. Since the defendant's property was worth $2 million and the plaintiff's but $1,000, any bargain to dissolve the injunction that paid the plaintiff more than $1,000 but less than $2 million would leave both sides better off. The huge bargaining range ($1,999,000) invites the plaintiffs to hold out for a large portion of the gain as the price for letting the defendants resume their activities.

Injunctive relief thus poses two major risks: First, parties might waste enormous resources in bargaining over the surplus and, second, they might not be able to reach any agreement at all given the tendency to bluff and bluster. (Review the private necessity cases in Chapter 1.) The damage remedy forestalls that because the plaintiff is at most entitled to $1,000, which the defendant would happily pay. Note, however, that the social desirability of injunctive relief increases as the disparity between the parties' interests is reduced. Similarly, plaintiff's interest in injunction gets stronger as its value increases. At some point on the continuum, therefore, the injunctive relief begins to dominate damages. Accordingly, no one can propound a hard and fast rule as to when injunctive relief should yield to damages, even though the polar cases are tolerably easy to identify. On the proper mix between injunctions and damages, see Polinsky, Resolving Nuisance Disputes: The Simple Economics of Injunctive and Damage Remedies, 32 Stan. L. Rev. 1075 (1980).

4. Injunctions for threatened harms. Injunctive relief is ordinarily allowed against both ongoing and imminent harms. But suppose the defendant's activities only increase the risk of some future actionable harm? The general tendency is to deny an immediate injunction, both because injunctive relief is still available in the future should the harm become imminent, and damages serve as a backstop against and a deterrent to consummated harms.

Suppose the plaintiff seeks to enjoin the operation of a prison, pest house, fraternity, reform school, or housing for the homeless or people with AIDS. Quite often she fails because she cannot establish that the mere operation of the facility is in itself a nuisance. See, e.g., Nicholson v. Connecticut Half-Way House, Inc., 218 A.2d 383 (Conn. 1966), in which the plaintiffs, residents of a middle-class neighborhood, were unsuccessful in their efforts to enjoin the operation of a half-way house for parolees from state prisons. The court noted that the defendant's plans called for strict control upon the number of persons living in the house, for the exclusion of sex offenders, drug addicts, and alcoholics, and for extensive supervision of the parolees. Moreover, the court did not deny that the defendant's facility introduced fear and unhappiness into the neighborhood or that it lowered the values of the surrounding property. It also did not rule out the possibility of future relief on proof that the actual operation of the facility interfered with the peace and comfort of the neighborhood.

5. Discretion to issue injunctions. In exercise of their undeniable power to issue injunctions in nuisance cases, courts may, at their discretion, refuse to enjoin an activity or, in the alternative, enjoin it only if certain conditions are satisfied. In Pendoley v. Ferreira, 187 N.E.2d 142 (Mass. 1963), the court delayed enforcing an injunction against the continued operation of defendants' piggery to allow the defendants to engage in "an orderly, rather than a hurried, liquidation of their pigs," and have an "opportunity to find new premises." It is also possible to permit a defendant to continue in business, but only on condition that it take specific measures to eliminate the objectionable features of its enterprise. Thus, in Quinn v. American Spiral Spring &

Manufacturing Co., 141 A. 855 (Pa. 1928), the defendant was allowed to continue using its factory, but only on the condition that it rearrange its heavy machinery in order to reduce the inconvenience to the plaintiff. And in Hansen v. Independent School District No. 1, 98 P.2d 959 (Idaho 1939), the defendant school board could continue to schedule night baseball games on the school's athletic fields, but only if it controlled the illumination of its lights, terminated the games at a reasonable hour, and limited the parking in the neighborhood. Finally, in Edmunds v. Sigma Chapter of Alpha Kappa Lambda Fraternity, Inc., 87 S.W.3d 21 (Mo. App. 2002), the defendants used their rural land to stage large parties for 700 guests, "with 'music blaring' and 'tires spinning,' in the early hours of the morning." Sometimes the guests entered plaintiff's lands, screaming. The injunction required defendant to erect and maintain a four-barbed wire fence, to keep the gate shut at night, and to restrict the property's use to 200 persons to prevent "inappropriate noise levels." On "balancing the equities," see generally Developments in the Law—Injunctions, 78 Harv. L. Rev. 994 (1965); Note, An Economic Analysis of Land Use Conflicts, 21 Stan. L. Rev. 293 (1969).

6. *Purchased injunctions.* Thus far, we have considered three possible solutions to the nuisance problem: damages, injunctions (permanent or temporary), and, of course, no remedy at all. A fourth solution, often missed by courts and commentators alike, is a "purchased injunction." The plaintiff may enjoin the defendant, but only if she is prepared to compensate the defendant for the loss incurred. The rule first surfaced in Calabresi & Melamed, Property Rules, Liability Rules, and Inalienability: One View of the Cathedral, 85 Harv. L. Rev. 1089, 1115-1123 (1972), where the authors suggested a rule that states "Marshall may stop Taney from polluting, but if he does he must compensate Taney." Does the rule make sense if Taney is hitting Marshall?

Almost simultaneously, Spur Industries, Inc. v. Del E. Webb Development Co., 494 P.2d 700, 707-708 (Ariz. 1972), proposed a variation of this rule. There the defendants operated a cattle feedlot on the outskirts of Phoenix. The plaintiff development corporation purchased land in the vicinity of the defendant's feed lot that it developed into a tract of private homes. The initial houses were not near the defendant's feedlot, but its later homes were. The odors and flies from the feedlot made it impossible for the new residents to enjoy the outdoor amenities promised by the plaintiff, rendering unmarketable the plaintiff's unsold homes near the defendant's feedlot. The court held that the defendant's activities constituted an actionable nuisance and enjoined its operation. The court noted, however, that it would have accepted the coming to the nuisance defense if the plaintiff had not sold some of the units to individual purchasers. It continued:

> There was no indication in the instant case at the time Spur and its predecessors located in western Maricopa County that a new city would spring

up, fullblown, alongside the feeding operation and that the developer of that city would ask the court to order Spur to move because of the new city. Spur is required to move not because of any wrongdoing on the part of Spur, but because of a proper and legitimate regard of the courts for the rights and interests of the public.

Del Webb, on the other hand, is entitled to the relief prayed for (a permanent injunction), not because Webb is blameless, but because of the damage to the people who have been encouraged to purchase homes in Sun City. It does not equitably or legally follow, however, that Webb, being entitled to the injunction, is then free of any liability to Spur if Webb has in fact been the cause of the damage Spur has sustained. It does not seem harsh to require a developer, who has taken advantage of the lesser land values in a rural area as well as the availability of large tracts of land on which to build and develop a new town or city in the area, to indemnify those who are forced to leave as a result.

Having brought people to the nuisance to the foreseeable detriment of Spur, Webb must indemnify Spur for a reasonable amount of the cost of moving or shutting down.

Should Spur be allowed to recover for lost profits? Should the purchasers of the individual units be required to help pay for Spur's closing and relocation costs.

7. *Bargaining after injunctions.* One theoretical argument in favor of injunctions is that the parties to the dispute can thereafter use private bargains to correct any uneconomic assignment of property rights made by judicial decree. One empirical examination of the question suggests that these after-the-fact corrections never take place, even when renegotiation involves only two parties in low-transaction costs environments. Farnsworth, Do Parties to Nuisance Cases Bargain After Judgment? A Glimpse Inside the Cathedral, 66 U. Chi. L. Rev. 373, 421-422 (1999), reports as follows:

A study of twenty old-fashioned nuisance cases litigated to judgment revealed no bargaining after judgment in any of them. Nor did any of the lawyers contacted believe that bargaining after judgment would have occurred if the loser had won. They attributed the lack of bargaining after judgment to acrimony between the parties and to attitudes the parties held toward their rights that made them reluctant to bargain. . . .

These results raise a number of questions worthy of further exploration. Why might parties have the attitudes toward cash exchanges that the lawyers in these cases describe? To what extent do similar attitudes toward cash exchanges exist in other nonmarket contexts? What stance should the law take toward the parties' feelings in cases like these? . . .

[I]f it turns out that parties do not bargain over their rights when transaction costs are low (or if we know they wouldn't because we see them refusing to bargain for reasons that have nothing to do with transaction costs in the sense of feasibility problems), then the broad project of using law to create bargains for parties when transaction costs are high becomes more complicated to defend.

2. *Public Nuisance*

Anonymous
Y.B. Mich. 27 Hen. 8, f. 27, pl. 10 (1536)

One brought a Writ sur son cas [on his case] against another. He alleged that, whereas the plaintiff had used to have a way from his house to a close over the King's highway for carriage and re-carriage, etc., the defendant had stopped the King's highway, so that the plaintiff could not go to his aforesaid close, to his tort and damage.

BALDWIN, C.J. It seems to me that this action does not lie to the plaintiff for the stopping of the highway; for the King has the punishment of that, and he has his plaint in the Leet and there he has his redress, because it is a common nuisance to all the King's lieges, and so there is no reason for a private particular person to have an accion sur son cas; for if one person shall have an action for this, by the same reason every person shall have an action, and so he will be punished a hundred times on the same case.

FITZHERBERT, J., to the contrary. I agree well that each nuisance done in the King's highway is punishable in the Leet and not by an action, unless it be where one man has suffered greater hurt or inconvenience than the generality have; but he who has suffered such greater displeasure or hurt can have an action to recover the damage which he has by reason of this special hurt. So if one makes a ditch across the highway, and I come riding along the way in the night and I and my horse are thrown into the ditch so that I have great damage and displeasure thereby, I shall have an action here against him who made this ditch across the highway, because I have suffered more damage than any other person. So here the plaintiff had more convenience by this highway than any other person had, and so when he is stopped he suffers more damage because he has no way to go to his close. Wherefore it seems to me that he shall have this action pour ce special matiere [for his special harm]: but if he had not suffered greater damage than all others suffered, then he would not have the action. Quod Nota. [Which was noted.]

NOTE

Public nuisances. S.C. Code Ann. §49-1-10 (2007) treats all navigable streams as common highways, and defines their obstruction as a public nuisance, but it says nothing about what private actions could be maintained in the event of breach. In Overcash v. South Carolina Electric & Gas Co., 614 S.E.2d 619, 621 (S.C. 2005), the plaintiff was seriously injured in a boating accident involving a dock obstruction in public waters. Burnett, J., denied the cause of action.

> The dissent by Justice Fitzherbert in a 1536 King's Bench decision [*supra*] derailed the course of nuisance law as a branch of the common law, which once dealt only with harm to real property. Justice Fitzherbert argued against the contemporaneous understanding of the law in advocating an individual's action for special or particular damage, including personal injury, should be recognized under a cause of action for public nuisance. Although Justice Fitzherbert's view has been widely followed by other courts, we decline to recognize a common law cause of action under the doctrine of public nuisance for purely personal injuries.

Does it make sense to allow an action for the damage to a horse but not to its rider? To a boat but not its owner? As noted most jurisdictions hew to the distinction between public and private nuisances that Fitzherbert, J., articulated in 1536. RST §§821B-821E. General damages from public nuisances are controlled exclusively by direct public action, usually administrative regulation or criminal prosecution. The private action is maintainable only for "special," "peculiar," or "disproportionate" harm to the individual plaintiff. The reasons for this division lie less in matters of justice and more in matters of administration. General damages are of low intensity and are widely diffused across an extended population. Private actions for admitted grievances are therefore simply too costly to maintain. The enforcement function is centralized to preserve the deterrent and control objectives of the tort law, even though direct compensation to aggrieved parties is necessarily abandoned. When, however, the harms are "special," private actions may again be maintained, as in all ordinary tort situations, for now the administrative burdens are far smaller relative to the size of the stakes. See generally Epstein, Nuisance Law: Corrective Justice and Its Utilitarian Constraints, 8 J. Legal Stud. 49, 98-102 (1979). What is the relationship between public nuisances and the live-and-let-live doctrine in the law of private nuisances?

Within this framework, where is the line drawn between general and special damages? Although general formulas are hard to state, it is clear that private actions have always been appropriate in at least two classes of cases: total loss of access to private land and personal injuries. At the other extreme, no private action may be brought for delays in traffic, even if they disrupt important business or personal plans. One difficult intermediate case involves partial loss of street access. In Smith v. City of Boston, 61 Mass. 254, 255-256 (1851), Boston closed down a street to make way for a new railroad line. The plaintiff, in consequence, lost access to the closed street, though he retained access to other nearby streets. Shaw, C.J., denied the action on the ground that "[t]he damage complained of in this case, though it may be greater in degree, in consequence of the proximity of the petitioner's estates, does not differ in kind from that of any other members of the community who would have had occasion more or less frequently to pass over the discontinued highway." Does Shaw's reasoning apply to a gas station that receives 90 percent of its business from the closed street? What result if the closure results in major economic dislocations to many people?

532 Madison Avenue Gourmet Foods, Inc. v. Finlandia Center, Inc.
750 N.E.2d 1097 (N.Y. 2001)

KAYE, C.J.
The novel issues raised by these appeals — arising from construction-related disasters in midtown Manhattan — concern first, a landholder's duty in negligence where plaintiffs' sole injury is lost income and second, the viability of claims for public nuisance.

Two of the three appeals involve the same event. On December 7, 1997, a section of the south wall of 540 Madison Avenue, a 39-story office tower, partially collapsed and bricks, mortar and other material fell onto Madison Avenue at 55th Street, a prime commercial location crammed with stores and skyscrapers. The collapse occurred after a construction project, which included putting 94 holes for windows into the building's south wall, aggravated existing structural defects. New York City officials directed the closure of 15 heavily trafficked blocks on Madison Avenue — from 42nd to 57th Street — as well as adjacent side streets between Fifth and Park Avenues. The closure lasted for approximately two weeks, but some businesses nearest to 540 Madison remained closed for a longer period.

In 532 Madison Ave. Gourmet Foods v. Finlandia Ctr., plaintiff operates a 24-hour delicatessen one-half block south of 540 Madison, and was closed for five weeks. The two named plaintiffs in the companion case, 5th Ave. Chocolatiere v. 540 Acquisition Co., are retailers at 510 Madison Avenue, two blocks from the building, suing on behalf of themselves and a putative class of "all other business entities, in whatever form, including but not limited to corporations, partnerships and sole proprietorships, located in the Borough of Manhattan and bounded geographically on the west by Fifth Avenue, on the east by Park Avenue, on the north by 57th Street and on the South by 42nd Street." Plaintiffs allege that shoppers and others were unable to gain access to their stores during the time Madison Avenue was closed to traffic. Defendants in both cases are Finlandia Center (the building owner), 540 Acquisition Company (the ground lessee) and Manhattan Pacific Management (the managing agent).

Goldberg Weprin & Ustin v. Tishman Constr. involves the July 21, 1998 collapse of a 48-story construction elevator tower on West 43rd Street between Sixth and Seventh Avenues—the heart of bustling Times Square. [Plaintiff class actions for businesses and residents "in the vicinity of Broadway and 42nd Street" were brought for gross negligence, strict liability, and public and private nuisance. All theories of recovery were dismissed at trial. The Appellate Division affirmed the dismissal of Goldberg Weprin but reinstated the public nuisance and negligence claims in *532 Madison* and *5th Ave. Chocolatiere*, for economic loss.]

We now reverse in *532 Madison* and *5th Ave. Chocolatiere* and affirm in *Goldberg Weprin & Ustin*.

[Kaye, C.J., first dismissed the negligence claims in part on the authority of Strauss v. Belle Realty Co., *supra* at 620.] We have never held, however, that a landowner owes a duty to protect an entire urban neighborhood against purely economic losses.

PLAINTIFFS' PUBLIC NUISANCE CLAIMS

Plaintiffs contend that they stated valid causes of action for public nuisance, alleging that the collapses forced closure of their establishments, causing special damages beyond those suffered by the public.

A public nuisance exists for conduct that amounts to a substantial interference with the exercise of a common right of the public, thereby offending public morals, interfering with the use by the public of a public place or endangering or injuring the property, health, safety or comfort of a considerable number of persons. A public nuisance is a violation against the State and is subject to abatement or prosecution by the proper governmental authority.

A public nuisance is actionable by a private person only if it is shown that the person suffered special injury beyond that suffered by the community at large. This principle recognizes the necessity of guarding against the multiplicity of lawsuits that would follow if everyone were permitted to seek redress for a wrong common to the public.

A nuisance is the actual invasion of interests in land, and it may arise from varying types of conduct. In the cases before us, the right to use the public space around Madison Avenue and Times Square was invaded not only by the building collapses but also by the City's decision, in the interest of public safety, to close off those areas. Unlawful obstruction of a public street is a public nuisance, and a person who as a consequence sustains a special loss may maintain an action for public nuisance. Indeed, "in a populous city, whatever unlawfully turns the tide of travel from the sidewalk directly in front of a retail store to the opposite side of the street is presumed to cause special damage to the proprietor of that store, because diversion of trade inevitably follows diversion of travel."

The question here is whether plaintiffs have suffered a special injury beyond that of the community so as to support their damages claims for public nuisance. We conclude that they have not.

In Burns Jackson [Miller Summit & Spitzer v. Lindner, 451 N.E.2d 459 (N.Y. 1983),] we refused to permit a public nuisance cause of action by two law firms seeking damages for increased expenses and lost profits resulting from the closure of the New York City transit system during a labor strike. We concluded that, because the strike was so widespread, every person, firm and corporation conducting a business or profession in the City suffered similar damage and thus the plaintiffs could not establish an injury different from that of the public at large.

While not as widespread as the transit strike, the Madison Avenue and Times Square closures caused the same sort of injury to the communities that live and work in those extraordinarily populous areas. As the trial court in *Goldberg Weprin & Ustin* pointed out, though different in degree, the hot dog vendor and taxi driver suffered the same kind of injury as the plaintiff law firm. Each was impacted in the ability to conduct business, resulting in financial loss. . . .

Leo v. General Elec. Co. (145 A.D.2d 291 [(1989)]) is inapposite. In *Leo*, the Appellate Division recognized a private right of action by plaintiff commercial fishermen who contended that defendant's pollution of the Hudson River with toxic polychlorinated biphenyls (commonly known as PCBs), created a public nuisance that had a devastating effect on their ability to earn a living. Plaintiffs were able to establish that their injuries were special and different in kind, not merely in degree: a loss of livelihood was not suffered by every person who fished the Hudson. By contrast, every person who maintained a business, profession or residence in the heavily populated areas of Times Square and Madison Avenue was exposed to similar economic loss during the closure periods. Thus, in that the economic loss was "common to an entire community and the plaintiff[s] suffer[ed] it only in a greater degree than others, it is not a different kind of harm and the plaintiff[s] cannot recover for the invasion of the public right" (Restatement [Second] of Torts §821C, comment *h*).

[All of plaintiffs' counts were dismissed.]

NOTES

1. *Large or special losses?* What result if the major construction mishap had blocked access to only a single business? What if the average business lost $100,000 in profits during the period of closure? The traditional require-

ment of special damages for public nuisance was intended to exclude large numbers of small claims, by achieving the appropriate deterrence through direct administrative actions. In these cases, with large numbers of large claims, will the defendants have incentives to take due care if only subject to administrative fines that constitute only a small fraction of the economic losses attributable to defendant's actions? Should it make a difference if these plaintiffs carried business interruption insurance? Is *532 Madison Avenue* a modern rerun of Ryan v. New York Central R.R., *supra* at 497?

2. *Destruction of natural wildlife as a public nuisance.* Was Kaye, C.J., correct to distinguish *532 Madison Avenue* from *Leo*? One notable early case, Union Oil Co. v. Oppen, 501 F.2d 558 (9th Cir. 1974), entertained negligence and public nuisance claims by commercial fisherman who sued Union Oil for the loss of catch attributable to its pollution of the Santa Barbara Channel. The court adopted an economic approach that required it "to fix the identity of the party who can avoid the costs most cheaply. Once fixed, this determination then controls liability." See, e.g., Calabresi, The Cost of Accidents, 69-73 (1970). If the least cost avoider cannot be determined, who is the "party who can best correct any error in allocation, if such there be, by acquiring the activity to which the party has been made liable"? Sneed, J., suggested that on this second criteria "there is no contest — the defendants' capacity is superior." How is the buyout possible if the class of fisherman constantly shifts in its composition? Note the parallel to the farmer's difficulty in bargaining with ranchers under an open range regime.

One complication in *Oppen* involves ownership of the fish. "The plaintiffs who do not own the fish cannot complain if the Union Oil company captures them. As they cannot complain of capture, they cannot complain of destruction after capture. As they cannot complain of destruction after capture, they cannot complain of destruction before capture." Epstein, Nuisance Law: Corrective Justice and Its Utilitarian Constraints, 8 J. Legal Stud. 49, 52 (1979). This position overlooks, however, the problem of the common pool — i.e., that resources not subject to private ownership will be destroyed or consumed too rapidly. Since the fish are unowned, any individual actor motivated by self-interest will not take into account the social losses that premature capture and destruction work on the common pool. See generally Sweeney, Tollison & Willett, Market Failure, the Common-Pool Problem, and Ocean Resource Exploitation, 17 J.L. & Econ. 179 (1974). *Oppen* fills the gap by providing the tort action to the nonowners who suffer disproportionate impact. In Pruitt v. Allied Chemical Corp., 523 F. Supp. 975 (E.D. Va. 1981), the district court allowed the suits of the commercial fishermen and the marina, boat, tackle, and bait shop owners who were damaged by the spillage of kepone into the James River and the Chesapeake Bay. However, it denied the actions of the various seafood wholesalers, retailers, and distributors who purchased and marketed the seafood of the commercial fishermen whose harm was deemed "insufficiently direct." It also refused to allow actions by employees of the various groups named. Similarly, in In Re Exxon Valdez, 104 F.3d 1196, 1198 (9th Cir. 1997), stemming from the massive oil spill of the *Exxon Valdez* oil tanker, the court allowed the plaintiff class of Alaska natives to recover economic damage from loss of fishing resources, but refused to permit their claim for "cultural damage" to their "subsistence way of life."

3. Public regulation and the protection of the common pool. The dangers of overconsumption or destruction of common pool resources furnishes one of the most powerful justifications for state regulation. But is a private action for commercial fishermen preferable to a hefty government fine that might punish both pollution and chronic overfishing? Since 1980, the Comprehensive Environmental Response, Compensation, and Liability Act of 1980 (CERCLA), 42 U.S.C. §§9601-9675 (2007), has created an extensive scheme of regulation that, inter alia, requires parties to provide the government with notice, first, of any discharge of pollutants into the environment, and second, of the storage or collection of any dangerous substance in a "facility," broadly defined under the statute. CERCLA also specifically authorizes the Environmental Protection Agency (EPA), alone or in cooperation with state agencies, to clean up pollution spills and dumpsites and to recover its cost from the responsible parties.

CERCLA's remedial scheme carries considerable wallop, including an aggressive regime of joint and several liability, discussed *supra* Chapter 5. In United States v. Alcan Aluminum Corp., 964 F.2d 252 (3d Cir. 1992), Alcan unlawfully released into the Susquehanna River a treated waste emulsion that contained minute quantities of copper, chromium, lead, and zinc — all hazardous substances under CERCLA. These amounts were far below permissible release levels under applicable environmental regulations, and were "indeed, [on] orders of magnitude below ambient or naturally occurring background levels." Greenberg, J., nonetheless held that CERCLA set no minimum level of release to trigger private liability for cleanup costs under the statute. Once a release was established, the government, as plaintiff under CERCLA, "need not establish a direct causal connection between the defendant's hazardous substances and the release or the plaintiff's incurrence of response costs." He remanded for further determination as to whether Alcan's releases were sufficiently "divisible" from pollution caused by other sources so that it could be held accountable only for its distinct harm. Why not just tax each polluter an amount that approximates the losses it causes, without offering direct compensation to the plaintiff, on the old public nuisance model? How does one determine the level of any such tax? What to do with the proceeds? Whether to treat rich and poor alike? Are there some pollutants for which a total ban is appropriate, such as high-sulfur fuel in home furnaces in urban areas or lead in gasoline? Note that the trade off between taxes and bans is as difficult as that between damages and injunction in the private nuisance law. Taxes induce private parties to abandon their valuable activities. Injunctions could prevent serious systemic harms, and may of course be subject to conditions, so that a firm may burn coal, but only if it installs scrubbers in its chimneys. Aronovsky, Federalism and CERCLA: Rethinking the Role of Federal Law in Private Cleanup Cost Disputes, 33 Ecology L.Q. 1 (2006).

See also Harris & Milan, Avoiding Joint and Several Liability Under CERCLA, 23 Env. L. Rptr. 1726 (1992); Polinsky, Controlling Externalities and Protecting Entitlements: Property Right, Liability Rule, and Tax-Subsidy Approaches, 8 J. Legal Stud. 1 (1979).

4. Hi-tech public nuisances: modified seed. In In re Starlink Corn Products Liability Litigation, 212 F. Supp. 2d 828, 848 (N.D. Ill. 2002), the defendant Aventis genetically modified a corn seed that produced a protein known as Cry9C that proved toxic to certain insects. The product received only a limited registration from the EPA for use in animal feed, ethanol production and seed increase, but not for human consumption. The EPA also required certain safeguards to prevent cross-pollination with non-Starlink corn plants. Plaintiff brought suit, claiming defendant's crop contaminated the entire U.S. corn supply. Moran, J., relied on the fishery cases to justify the plaintiff's public nuisance claim for contamination of their crops. "Here, plaintiffs are commercial corn farmers. While the general public has a right to safe food, plaintiffs depend on the integrity of the corn supply for their livelihood." Should the action be allowed in the absence of any EPA statute if the market differentiates between the two kinds of corn? Note that the public nuisance claim failed in Sample v. Monsanto Co., 283 F. Supp. 2d 1088 (E.D. Mo. 2003), for plaintiffs whose crops were not contaminated, where the harm claimed was loss of sales to the European Union, which boycotted all American corn and soy given its opposition to genetically modified organisms. Note that there is also a close interconnection between public nuisance cases and pure economic loss cases, covered in Chapter 16, Section C.

Camden County Board of Chosen Freeholders v. Beretta, U.S.A. Corp.
273 F.3d 536 (3rd Cir. 2001).

PER CURIAM.

The Camden County Board of Chosen Freeholders (hereinafter "Camden County") contends that handgun manufacturers, because of their marketing and distribution policies and practices, are liable under a public nuisance theory for the governmental costs associated with the criminal use of handguns in Camden County. The District Court, in a 53-page opinion, dismissed the complaint. See Camden County Board of Chosen

Freeholders v. Beretta U.S.A., Corp., 123 F. Supp. 2d 245 (D.N.J. 2000). We affirm the order of the District Court.

I.

In its Second Amended Complaint, Camden County alleged that Defendants' conduct — the marketing and distribution of handguns — created and contributed to the widespread criminal use of handguns in the County. The County invoked three theories of liability: negligence, negligent entrustment, and public nuisance. The County requested several forms of relief, including compensation for the additional costs incurred by the County to abate the alleged public nuisance (costs borne by the County's prosecutor, sheriff, medical examiner, park police, correctional facility, and courts); an injunction requiring the manufacturers to change their marketing and distribution practices; and other compensatory and punitive damages. . . .

The District Court rejected all three of Camden County's theories of liability and granted the defendants' motion to dismiss the complaint. It dismissed the two negligence claims after its thorough six-factor analysis found proximate cause lacking. It also found that the public nuisance claim was defective because the County had not alleged "the required element that the defendants exercised control over the nuisance to be abated."

On appeal, Camden County has dropped the two negligence claims and pursues only the public nuisance claim. . . .

The County makes the following pertinent factual allegations: the manufacturers release into the market substantially more handguns than they expect to sell to law-abiding purchasers; the manufacturers continue to use certain distribution channels, despite knowing (often from specific crime-gun trace reports produced by the federal Bureau of Alcohol, Tobacco, and Firearms) that those channels regularly yield criminal end-users; the manufacturers do not limit the number, purpose, or frequency of handgun purchases and do not supervise these sales or require their distributors to do so; the manufacturers' contracts with distributors do not penalize distributor practices that facilitate criminal access to handguns; the manufacturers design, produce, and advertise handguns in ways that facilitate sales to and use by criminals; the manufacturers receive significant revenue from the crime market, which in turn generates more sales to law-abiding persons wishing to protect themselves; and the manufacturers fail to take reasonable measures to mitigate the harm to Camden County. The County makes no allegation that any manufacturer violated any federal or state statute or regulation governing the manufacture and distribution of firearms, and no direct link is alleged between any manufacturer and any specific criminal act.

The manufacturers respond that the County's factual allegations amount to the following attenuated chain of events: (1) the manufacturers produce firearms at their places of business; (2) they sell the firearms to federally licensed distributors; (3) those distributors sell them to federally licensed dealers; (4) some of the firearms are later diverted by unnamed third parties into an illegal gun market, which spills into Camden County; (5) the diverted firearms are obtained by unnamed third parties who are not entitled to own or possess them; (6) these firearms are then used in criminal acts that kill and wound County residents; and (7) this harm causes the County to expend resources to prevent or respond to those crimes. The manufacturers note that in this chain, they are six steps removed from the criminal end-users. Moreover, the fourth link in this chain consists of acts committed by intervening third parties who divert some handguns into an illegal market.

II.

Because this appeal presents a question of state law, we do not find it necessary to write at length. In brief, we agree with the District Court that the County has failed to state a valid public nuisance claim under New Jersey law.

A.

A public nuisance is "'an unreasonable interference with a right common to the general public.'" Philadelphia Elec. Co. v. Hercules, Inc., 762 F.2d 303, 315 (3d Cir. 1985) (quoting Restatement (Second) of Torts §821B(1) (1979)). For the interference to be actionable, the defendant must exert a certain degree of control over its source.

Traditionally, the scope of nuisance claims has been limited to interference connected with real property or infringement of public rights. . . .

Whatever the precise scope of public nuisance law in New Jersey may be, no New Jersey court has ever allowed a public nuisance claim to proceed against manufacturers for lawful products that are lawfully placed in the stream of commerce. On the contrary, the courts have enforced the boundary between the well-developed body of product liability law and public nuisance law. Otherwise, if public nuisance law were permitted to encompass product liability, nuisance law "would become a monster that would devour in one gulp the entire law of tort." Tioga Public Sch. Dist. v. U.S. Gypsum Co., 984 F.2d 915, 921 (8th Cir. 1993). If defective products are not a public nuisance as a matter of law, then the non-defective, lawful products at issue in this case cannot be a nuisance without straining the law to absurdity.

B.

Within the narrower context of similar tort actions against handgun manufacturers around the country, a majority of courts have rejected these claims as a matter of law. In a few other courts, the claim was not dismissed outright, but each such case is distinguishable from the instant case. To extend public nuisance law to embrace the manufacture of handguns would be unprecedented under New Jersey state law and unprecedented nationwide for an appellate court.

Even if public nuisance law could be stretched far enough to encompass the lawful distribution of lawful products, the County has failed to allege that the manufacturers exercise sufficient control over the source of the interference with the public right. The District Court found this to be the "fatal defect" of the County's claim. The County argues that proximate cause, remoteness, and control are not essential to a public nuisance claim, i.e., that conduct that merely contributes to the source of the interference can be sufficient. But the relevant case law shows that, even if the requisite element is not always termed "control," the New Jersey courts in fact require a degree of control by the defendant over the source of the interference that is absent here.

To connect the manufacture of handguns with municipal crime-fighting costs requires, as noted above, a chain of seven links. This causal chain is simply too attenuated to attribute sufficient control to the manufacturers to make out a public nuisance claim. . . .

A public-nuisance defendant can bring its own conduct or activities at a particular physical site under control. But the limited ability of a defendant to exercise control beyond its sphere of immediate activity may explain why public nuisance law has traditionally been confined to real property and violations of public rights. In the negligence context, this Court recently held that a defendant has no duty to control the misconduct of third parties. See Port Auth. v. Arcadian Corp., 189 F.3d 305, 312-17 (3rd. Cir. 1999). We agree with the District Court that this logic is equally compelling when applied in the public nuisance context. If independent third parties cause the nuisance, parties that have not controlled or created the nuisance are not liable.

Public nuisance is a matter of state law, and the role of a federal court ruling on a matter of state law in a diversity case is to follow the precedents of the state's highest court and predict how that court would decide the issue presented. It is not the role of a federal court to expand or narrow state law in ways not foreshadowed by state precedent. Here, no New Jersey precedents support the County's public nuisance claim or provide a sound basis for predicting that the Supreme Court of New Jersey would find that claim to be valid. While it is of course conceivable that the Supreme Court of New Jersey may someday choose to expand state public nuisance law in the manner that the County urges, we cannot predict at this time that it will do so.

AFFIRMED.

NOTE

Modern public nuisance cases. Shortly after this initial decision, the Third Circuit faced a revised version of the public nuisance complaint in City of Philadelphia v. Beretta U.S.A. Corp., 277 F.3d 415, 424 (3d Cir. 2002). Greenberg, J., rebuffed the defendant's effort to finesse *Camden County*:

> Plaintiffs try to shorten the causal chain by arguing that the "thriving illegal market . . . injures [them], even before any guns acquired in the illegal market are actually used in the commission of a crime." Appellants' Br. at 75. This statement, however, does not reduce the links that separate a manufacturer's sale of a gun to a licensee and the gun's arrival in the illegal market through a distribution scheme that is not only lawful, but also is prescribed by statute with respect to the manufacturers' conduct. We reiterate that gun manufacturers first ship their guns to independent, federally licensed distributors and dealers. Only then may the licensed dealer sell the gun to a purchaser who has been cleared by the Federal Bureau of Investigation and approved by the Pennsylvania state police. Although the purchaser may be a "straw" purchaser (a friend, relative or accomplice who acts as purchaser of the weapon for another) who then traffics the gun to prohibited purchasers for illicit purposes, the straw's dealings are not with the manufacturers. Moreover, straw purchases are not the only means by which guns allegedly reach the "illegal market," and the chain is likely much longer and more varied.

Both decisions were in turn relied on in District of Columbia v. Beretta, U.S.A., Corp., 872 A.2d 633, 650 (D.C. 2005), where the plaintiffs were rebuffed in efforts to circumvent a doomed public nuisance action on a negligence theory. Farrell, J., observed that these claims against manufacturers were not for negligent entrustment, but only sought to hold defendants responsible for the "'aggregate of the criminal acts of many individuals over whom they have no control.' In keeping with our own decisions and others we have found persuasive, we decline to relax the common-law limitations of duty, foreseeability, and direct causation so as to recognize the broad claim of public nuisance the District has alleged." One way to understand these results is to note that frequently no other defendant is responsible if the public nuisance claim is denied, as in *532 Madison*. But in the gun cases, downstream parties, including both retailers (who must check eligible purchasers) and the actual users of the guns are of course liable.

Other cases have proved more receptive to the public nuisance claim. In Johnson v. Bryco Arms, 304 F. Supp. 2d 383, 391 (E.D.N.Y. 2004), Weinstein, J., allowed a shooting victim to sue a gun manufacturer, wholesaler, distributor, and retailer on a public nuisance theory.

> Under New York law, a claim for public nuisance may lie against members of the gun industry whose marketing and sales practice lead to the diversion of large numbers of firearms into the illegal secondary gun market. . . . [E]xtensive discovery and detailed expert testimony demonstrated that gun manufacturers, importers and distributors were responsible for the creation of a public nuisance and that they could, voluntarily and through easily implemented changes, substantially reduce the harm occasioned by the illegal possession and use of handguns.

For a similar result, see Ileto v. Glock Inc., 349 F.3d 1191 (9th Cir. 2003). If the public nuisance claim goes forward, may the gun companies introduce evidence that the defensive use of guns offers an important deterrent against gun violence? See J. Lott, More Guns, Less Crime: Understanding Crime and Gun-Control Laws (1998). If the general distribution of guns is a public nuisance, is every individual gun death necessarily private nuisance?

9

PRODUCTS LIABILITY

SECTION A. INTRODUCTION

Products liability law has become so important today that it is virtually a
legal field unto itself. This field is conveniently defined in contrast to the
abnormally dangerous activities examined in Chapter 8, which dealt
with the liability of defendants with direct control over dangerous instrumentalities at the time they caused injury. The gist of products liability
law is that it governs the activities of the full panoply of manufacturers,
distributors, and sellers who have placed a product in the stream of commerce and therefore are *no longer* in possession of it at the time that it
causes damages.

   As befits its complexity, products liability law has a rich and dense history, which can be roughly divided into four periods. The first period ran
approximately from the mid-nineteenth century to the early twentieth
century. During this time, the major debate was whether to allow any suits at
all against product manufacturers or sellers. Courts often held that the
"privity" limitation prevented the injured party — whether consumer, user,
or bystander — from suing the "remote" supplier of the product in question. An injured consumer or user could sue only the immediate vendor of
the product; an injured bystander could sue only the party in possession of
the product just before the injury occurred. The last half of the nineteenth
century witnessed a steady, but limited, erosion of this privity limitation as
exceptions were created, roughly speaking, for products known to hold
hidden dangers that manifested themselves in ordinary use.

   The second period starts with MacPherson v. Buick Motor Co., 111 N.E.
1050 (N.Y. 1916), which rejected the privity limitation by imposing liability

for negligence on a remote seller, that is, one who has no direct contractual relationship with the injured party. The third stage of products liability law was inaugurated with the famous concurring opinion of Justice Traynor in Escola v. Coca Cola Bottling Co., 150 P.2d 436, 440-444 (Cal. 1944), which argued that strict liability, and not negligence principles, should govern the manufacturer's liability. Initially idiosyncratic, Traynor's view gained adherents in the early 1960s and quickly became the dominant view by 1965. At this time, the American Law Institute incorporated a general principle of strict liability into §402A of the Restatement (Second) of Torts. On the early development of strict liability through the Second Restatement, see also R. Epstein, Modern Products Liability Law (1980); Prosser, The Assault Upon the Citadel (Strict Liability to the Consumer), 69 Yale L.J. 1099 (1960).

Just when the Second Restatement was adopted, the law entered into a period of rapid expansion. The three dominant themes in debates over the Second Restatement focused on the role of manufacturers: their market power, their capacity to obtain insurance, and their ability to internalize the costs of accidents associated with their products. Taken together, these three issues pointed to "absolute liability. The presuppositions themselves do not incorporate any conceptual limit to manufacturer's liability." Priest, The Invention of Enterprise Liability: A Critical History of the Intellectual Foundations of Modern Tort Law, 14 J. Legal Stud. 461, 527 (1985).

The fourth and present stage of products liability law began with a series of important, and what are now widely known as, defective design and duty to warn cases that were decided in the decade after the 1965 Restatement. These cases, which ironically enough have expanded liability within the traditional framework of negligence law, form the centerpiece of modern products liability law.

In 1998, in response to these major developments after 1965, the American Law Institute issued a Third Restatement devoted exclusively to products liability law. "This [third] Restatement is, therefore, an almost total overhaul of Restatement Second as it concerns the liability of commercial sellers of products." RTT:PL at 3. At present it remains unclear whether the longer Third Restatement will displace or supplement the earlier, but more concise, Second Restatement. It will therefore be necessary to study both Restatements throughout this chapter. But no matter which way this question comes out, it is now evident that, as a *doctrinal* matter, the last generation has been a period of consolidation, if not some modest retrenchment. The constant string of plaintiff's breakthroughs that were par for the course between 1965 and 1980—the rise of crashworthiness theories, the decline of the open and obvious defense, the expansive definitions of product defect—have slowed down to a trickle. Many of the most important decisions, e.g., on manufacturer gun liability, have resulted in defendant's victories, which, while they have not rolled back the law, have prevented its further expansion. Henderson and Eisenberg, The Quiet

Revolution in Products Liability: An Empirical Study of Legal Change, 37 UCLA L. Rev. 479, 481 (1990) (noting the lack of expansion); Schwartz, The Beginning and the Possible End of the Rise of Modern American Tort Law, 26 Ga. L. Rev. 601, 604 (1992) (noting the steady state).

The newest development in this field goes beyond the traditional contours of the tort law to determine the extent to which direct forms of federal regulation, so common with motor vehicles, pharmaceuticals, and toxic chemicals, can supersede or preempt direct private rights of action under state law. The stakes here are enormous. Without question, the major developments in the product liability area since 2000 have concerned the preemption question, which forces tort lawyers to negotiate the treacherous shoals of federalism and administrative law.

Any examination of these developments makes clear that products liability law is big business. Therefore, it is useful to give some sense of its overall scope before turning to discrete legal issues. The first and most obvious fact is that litigation has soared since the adoption of the Second Restatement in 1965. The total number of products liability actions in federal court was 2,393 in 1975, the date corresponding to the first crisis in the products liability insurance market. It rose to 7,755 in 1980; to 19,428 in 1990; peaked at 33,649 in 1997; and tailed off to 27,775 in 1998. These gross figures, however, tell only a part of the whole story. Information about the kinds of products that generated this litigation is incomplete. In recent years, a relatively large number of suits have been brought in the marine, airline, and motor vehicle categories; but well over half the product liability suits are simply listed as "other," without any indication of the product line involved. The one startling exception to that pattern is the group of asbestos-related cases on the federal docket. No asbestos suits were reported as filed in federal court in 1980; yet by 1997, over 7,000 new suits were filed, amounting to 21 percent of new product liability cases. That percentage rose by nearly one-third by 1998, when over 9,000 new asbestos-related suits were brought. In 2002, after some relative calm, the number of asbestos-related claims soared in anticipation of possible major tort reform that would limit access to the courts. Finally, some note should be made about the number of product liability class actions brought: 1,560 in 1980; 922 in 1990; 1,475 in 1997; and 1,881 in 1998. From these numbers, it should come as no surprise that products liability actions now constitute over 10 percent of the docket of new filings in federal civil cases, up from under 5 percent in 1980. The increase in products liability actions has far outstripped the general increase of activity in federal courts. Complete data has not been collected for all years, but the trends on litigation are made evident by the data presented in Table 9.1. See Judicial Business of the United States Courts.

These figures tell an instructive tale. The number of lawsuits that involve various kinds of equipment — airplane, marine, and motor vehicle — has

Table 9-1. U.S. District Courts — Civil Cases Commenced, by Nature of Suit, During the Twelve-Month Periods Ending September 30, 1997 Through 2001

Nature of Suit	1994	1995	1996	1997	1998	1999	2000	2001	2002	2003	2004	2005	2006
Personal Injury, Total	44,306	50,565	55,647	53,940	46,496	40,497	32,621	29,789	58,997	39,563	50,594	47,364	64,743
Personal Injury/Product Liability, Total	22,288	27,547	27,584	32,856	26,886	18,781	14,428	12,307	41,135	21,611	34,100	29,537	48,739
Airplane	115	155	135	161	177	163	164	118	120	101	100	79	74
Marine	42	53	55	43	68	48	54	39	42	34	32	46	37
Motor Vehicle	534	566	550	537	438	433	421	654	564	609	618	531	561
Asbestos	6,518	6,916	7,289	7,143	9,111	8,948	7,187	5,041	26,818	1,562	1,471	1,243	16,547
Other	15,079	19,857	19,555	24,972	17,092	9,189	6,602	6,455	13,591	19,305	31,879	27,638	31,520
Other Personal Injury, Total	22,018	23,018	28,063	21,084	19,610	21,716	18,193	17,482	17,862	17,952	16,494	17,827	16,004
Airplane	557	683	809	740	733	678	747	714	846	659	483	351	294
Marine	2,330	2,277	2,172	2,298	2,110	4,995	2,006	2,164	1,978	1,814	1,841	1,667	1,584
Motor Vehicle	5,087	5,374	5,330	5,126	4,933	4,901	4,690	4,535	4,525	4,480	4,229	4,091	3,938
Assault, Libel, and Slander	783	826	848	859	767	825	801	623	693	892	668	647	587
Federal Employer's Liability Act	2,092	1,903	2,225	1,943	1,635	1,264	1,108	1,067	944	975	782	748	700
Medical Malpractice	1,332	1,328	1,330	1,368	1,322	1,447	1,526	1,429	1,463	1,607	1,313	1,221	1,221
Other	9,837	10,627	15,349	8,750	8,110	7,606	7,315	6,950	7,413	7,525	7,178	9,102	7,680

been quite constant, notwithstanding growth in population and usage. All of the action at the major level has taken place with asbestos and the category of other. The asbestos cases have been filed in bursts that reflect political or strategic reasons with little connection to changes in legal doctrine. The "other" category now accounts for two-thirds of the filings, with a near five-fold increase from its low point in 2000, and represents the large number of fen-phen, Vioxx, Baycol, manganism (from manganese welding fumes), and silicosis cases that have been filed in recent years. Both asbestosis and silicosis represent "cumulative trauma" cases that should be closely correlated with levels of exposure, at least in theory.

Interestingly, the volume of litigation has sharply increased even though the amount of workplace exposure has decreased. The National Institute for Occupational Safety and Health reports that deaths attributable to silicosis have steadily declined from 1,157 deaths in 1968 to 187 deaths in 1999. www.cdc.gov/niosh/docs/2003-111/pdfs/2003-111d.pdf. The increase in claims bears no relationship to the underlying health statistics. For example, about 120 silicosis claims were filed in Mississippi in 2000 and 2001. That number jumped to 10,642 claims in 2002 even though Mississippi had one of the lowest silicosis mortality rates in the nation, as lawyers worked to file claims before a Mississippi tort reform statute went into effect. After defendants removed these claims to federal court, these cases were consolidated into one federal MDL (multidistrict litigation) proceeding, and Judge Janice Jack found, in an exhaustive opinion, that most of the claims rested on shaky or fraudulent medical evidence where physicians had been paid to make false positive diagnoses for silicosis. Specifically, she noted the peculiar prevalence of silicosis diagnoses in patients who had been previously diagnosed with asbestosis for prior litigation, a medical rarity, especially considering that "a golfer is more likely to hit a hole-in-one than an occupational medicine specialist is to find a single case of both silicosis and asbestosis" in one person. In writing about the onslaught of claims, Jack, J., noted that if they had not been fraudulent, they would have represented one of the worst industrial disasters in recorded history, which would have gone strangely unreported in the media. In re Silica Products Liability Litigation, 398 F. Supp. 2d 563, 571, 603 (S.D. Tex. 2005). Having found that over 10,000 of these claims were "manufactured for money," she remanded these cases back to the Mississippi courts from which they originated, where many were summarily dismissed. For a vocal and detailed critique of the asbestos and silicosis scandals, see Brickman, Disparities between Asbestosis and Silicosis Claims Generated by Litigation Screenings and Clinical Studies, Cardozo Law Review, 29 Cardozo L. Rev. (2007); Brickman, On the Theory Class's Theories of Asbestos Litigation: The Disconnect Between Scholarship and Reality, 31 Pepp. L. Rev. 33 (2003-2004). In Ohio, a state court handling 35,000 asbestos claims and 900 silica claims is considering calling hearings to depose the doctors the same way Jack did, and similar activities are happening in other places.

The massive changes in the asbestos is and silicosis cases should be contrasted with the very different profile of traditional types of product liability litigation. Here the rapid increase in the overall level of products litigation has been matched by a long and steady decline in accident levels. From 1930 to 1985, workplace accidents have declined from 15 to 5 per 100,000, while home accident and vehicular accident rates have fallen dramatically as well. On this issue, the relationship between the improved accident picture and the changes in tort liability area seems weak at best. The decline in accident rates started before the expansion in tort liability and continued uniformly even as the doctrinal expansion in the field halted around 1990. See generally Priest, Products Liability Law and the Accident Rate, in Liability: Perspectives and Policy (R. Litan & C. Winston eds., 1988). The simplest explanation appears to be that technological improvements in safety are desired for their own sake, wholly apart from the choice of product liability regimes, to whose evolution we now turn.

SECTION B.   EXPOSITION

Winterbottom v. Wright
152 Eng. Rep. 402 (Ex. 1842)

[The defendant contracted with the Postmaster-General to supply coaches to carry the mail and to see that the coaches would "be kept in a fit, proper, safe, and secure state and condition for said purpose," and under this contract he assumed "the sole and exclusive duty, charge, care, and burden of the repairs, state, and condition" thereof. Atkinson, knowing of this contract, personally contracted with the Postmaster-General to supply horses and drivers for the defendant's coaches. The plaintiff, one of Atkinson's drivers, was driving a coach serviced by defendant, and was hurt when a latent defect caused the coach to break down, throwing him to the ground and injuring him. The defendant demurred to the plaintiff's action.]

ABINGER, C.B. I am clearly of opinion that the defendant is entitled to our judgment. We ought not to permit a doubt to rest upon this subject, for our doing so might be the means of letting in upon us an infinity of actions. This is an action of the first impression, and it has been brought in spite of the precautions which were taken, in the judgment of this Court in the case of Levy v. Langridge[, 150 Eng. Rep. 863 (Ex. 1836)], a case of fraudulent representation by the seller to the purchaser, to obviate any notion that such an action could be maintained. We ought not to attempt to extend the principle of that decision, which, although it has been cited in support of this action, wholly fails as an authority in its favour; for there the gun was bought for the use of the son, the plaintiff in that action, who could not make the bargain himself, but was really and substantially the party contracting. Here the action is brought simply because the defendant was a contractor with a third person; and it is contended that thereupon he became liable to everybody who might use the carriage. If there had been any ground for such an action, there certainly would have been some precedent of it; but with the exception of actions against innkeepers, and some few other persons, no case of a similar nature has occurred in practice. That is a strong circumstance, and is of itself a great authority against its maintenance. It is however contended, that this contract being made on the behalf of the public by the Postmaster-General, no action could be maintained against him, and therefore the plaintiff must have a remedy against the defendant. But that is by no means a necessary consequence — he may be remediless altogether. There is no privity of contract between these parties; and if the plaintiff can sue, every passenger, or even any person passing along the road, who was injured by the upsetting of the coach, might bring a similar action. Unless we confine the operation of such contracts as this to the parties who entered into them, the most absurd and outrageous consequences, to which I can see no limit, would ensue. Where a party becomes responsible to the public, by undertaking a public duty, he is liable, though the injury may have arisen from the negligence of his servant or agent. So, in cases of public nuisances, whether the act was done by the party as a servant, or in any other capacity, you are liable to an action at the suit of any person who suffers. Those, however, are cases where the real ground of the liability is the public duty, or the commission of the public nuisance. There is also a class of cases in which the law permits a contract to be turned into a tort; but unless there has been some public duty undertaken, or public nuisance committed, they are all cases in which an action might have been maintained upon the contract. Thus, a carrier may be sued either in assumpsit [contract] or case [tort]; but there is no instance in which a party, who was not privy to the contract entered into with him, can maintain any such action. The plaintiff in this case could not have brought an action on the contract; if he could have done so, what would have been his situation, supposing the Postmaster-General had released the defendant? That would, at all events, have defeated his claim altogether. By permitting this action, we should be working this injustice, that after the defendant had done everything to the satisfaction of his employer, and after all matters between them had been adjusted, and all accounts settled on the footing of their contract, we should subject them to be ripped open by this action of tort being brought against him.

NOTE

The American reception of Winterbottom v. Wright. During the nineteenth century, Winterbottom v. Wright was a leading case both in England and in the United States. Several late nineteenth-century cases, however, carved out exceptions to its categorical prohibition. The overall position in the United States was summarized by Sanborn, J., in Huset v. J. I. Case Threshing Machine Co., 120 F. 865, 866-871 (8th Cir. 1903):

> [T]he natural and probable effect of the negligence of the contractor or manufacturer will generally be limited to the party for whom the article is constructed, or to whom it is first sold, and, perhaps more than all this, for the reason that a wise and conservative public policy has impressed the courts with the view that there must be a fixed and definite limitation to the liability of manufacturers and vendors for negligence in the construction and sale of complicated machines and structures which are to be operated or used by the intelligent and the ignorant, the skillful and the incompetent, the watchful and the careless, parties that cannot be known to the manufacturers or vendors, and who use the articles all over the country hundreds of miles distant from the place of their manufacture or original sale, a general rule has been adopted and has become established by repeated decisions of the courts of England and of this country that in these cases the liability of the contractor or manufacturer for negligence in the construction or sale of the articles which he makes or vends is limited to the persons to whom he is liable under his contracts of construction or sale. The limits of the liability for negligence and for breaches of contract in cases of this character are held to be identical. The general rule is that a contractor, manufacturer, or vendor is not liable to third parties who have no contractual relations with him for negligence in the construction, manufacture, or sale of the articles he handles. But while this general rule is both established and settled, there are, as is usually the case, exceptions to it as well defined and settled as the rule itself. There are three exceptions to this rule.
>
> The first is that an act of negligence of a manufacturer or vendor which is imminently dangerous to the life or health of mankind, and which is committed in the preparation or sale of an article intended to preserve, destroy, or affect human life, is actionable by third parties who suffer from the negligence. . . .
>
> The second exception is that an owner's act of negligence which causes injury to one who is invited by him to use his defective appliance upon the owner's premises may form the basis of an action against the owner. . . .
>
> The third exception to the rule is that one who sells or delivers an article which he knows to be imminently dangerous to life or limb to another without notice of its qualities is liable to any person who suffers an injury therefrom which might have been reasonably anticipated, whether there were any contractual relations between the parties or not.

The court then held that the complaint alleged a cause of action under the third exception: the plaintiff alleged that the defendant's threshing machine was constructed so that the cylinder covering upon which its operator had to walk could not support his weight, that defect was latent in that it could not be discovered by ordinary inspection, and that this defective condition was known by the defendant. The court remanded the case for trial, noting that it was "perhaps improbable" that the defendant had knowledge of the imminently dangerous character of the machine at the time of delivery.

Some cases did succeed under this third exception. In Kuelling v. Roderick Lean Manufacturing Co., 75 N.E. 1098, 1101 (N.Y. 1905), the defendants sold a roller to a dealer who resold it to the plaintiff. The roller was made out of weak wood and contained a knot that prevented a safe hook-up of the roller to the team of horses that pulled it. The defect was deliberately concealed by putty and paint. Bartlett, J., allowed the action:

> In the case at bar we have not only fraudulent deceit and concealment, but what amounts to an affirmative representation that the tongue of the roller was sound, as the manufacturer by filling the defect with putty and painting the entire surface so that the eye could not detect any weakness by reason of the knot, knothole filled up, the kind of wood employed and the fact that it was cross-grained, must be held to have represented that the roller as offered for sale was in a perfectly marketable condition.

MacPherson v. Buick Motor Co.
111 N.E. 1050 (N.Y. 1916)

CARDOZO, J. The defendant is a manufacturer of automobiles. It sold an automobile to a retail dealer. The retail dealer resold to the plaintiff. While the plaintiff was in the car, it suddenly collapsed. He was thrown out and injured. One of the wheels was made of defective wood, and its spokes crumbled into fragments. The wheel was not made by the defendant; it was bought from another manufacturer. There is evidence, however, that its defects could have been discovered by reasonable inspection, and that inspection was omitted. There is no claim that the defendant knew of the defect and willfully concealed it. The case, in other words, is not brought within the rule of Kuelling v. Lean Mfg. Co. The charge is one, not of fraud, but of negligence. The question to be determined is whether the defendant owed a duty of care and vigilance to any one but the immediate purchaser.

The foundations of this branch of the law, at least in this state, were laid in Thomas v. Winchester (6 N.Y. 397 (1852)). A poison was falsely labeled. The sale was made to a druggist, who in turn sold to a customer. The customer recovered damages from the seller who affixed the label. "The defendant's negligence," it was said, "put human life in imminent danger." A poison falsely labeled is likely to injure anyone who gets it. Because the danger is to be foreseen, there is a duty to avoid the injury. . . .

Thomas v. Winchester became quickly a landmark of the law. In the application of its principle there may at times have been uncertainty or even error. There has never in this state been doubt or disavowal of the principle itself. The chief cases are well known, yet to recall some of them will be helpful. Loop v. Litchfield (42 N.Y. 351 (1870)) is the earliest. It was the case of a defect in a small balance wheel used on a circular saw. The manufacturer pointed out the defect to the buyer, who wished a cheap article and was ready to assume the risk. The risk can hardly have been an imminent one, for the wheel lasted five years before it broke. In the meanwhile the buyer had made a lease of the machinery. It was held that the manufacturer was not answerable to the lessee. Loop v. Litchfield was followed in Losee v. Clute (51 N.Y. 494 (1873)), the case of the explosion of a steam boiler. That decision has been criticised but it must be confined to its special facts. It was put upon the ground that the risk of injury was too remote. The buyer in that case had not only accepted the boiler, but had tested it. The manufacturer knew that his own test was not the final one. The finality of the test has a bearing on the measure of diligence owing to persons other than the purchaser.

These early cases suggest a narrow construction of the rule. Later cases, however, evince a more liberal spirit. First in importance is Devlin v. Smith (89 N.Y. 470 (1882)). The defendant, a contractor, built a scaffold for a painter. The painter's servants were injured. The contractor was held liable. He knew that the scaffold, if improperly constructed, was a most dangerous trap. He knew that it was to be used by the workmen. He was building it for that very purpose. Building it for their use, he owed them a duty, irrespective of his contract with their master, to build it with care.

From Devlin v. Smith we pass over intermediate cases and turn to the latest case in this court in which Thomas v. Winchester was followed. That case is Statler v. Ray Mfg. Co. (195 N.Y. 478, 480 (1909)). The defendant manufactured a large coffee urn. It was installed in a restaurant. When heated, the urn exploded and injured the plaintiff. We held that the manufacturer was liable. We said that the urn "was of such a character inherently that, when applied to the purposes for which it was designed, it was liable to become a source of great danger to many people if not carefully and properly constructed."

It may be that Devlin v. Smith and Statler v. Ray Mfg. Co. have extended the rule of Thomas v. Winchester. If so, this court is committed to the extension. The defendant argues that things imminently dangerous to life are poisons, explosives, deadly weapons — things whose normal function it is to injure or destroy. But whatever the rule in Thomas v. Winchester may once have been, it has no longer that restricted meaning. A scaffold (Devlin v. Smith, *supra*) is not inherently a destructive instrument. It becomes destructive only if imperfectly constructed. A large coffee urn . . . may have within itself, if negligently made, the potency of danger, yet no one thinks of it as an implement whose normal function is destruction. What is true of the coffee urn is equally true of bottles of aerated water (Torgeson v. Schultz, 192 N.Y. 156 (1908)). We have mentioned only cases in this court. But the rule has received a like extension in our courts of intermediate appeal. . . .

[Cardozo, J., then reviewed the parallel English decisions.]

We hold, then, that the principle of Thomas v. Winchester is not limited to poisons, explosives, and things of like nature, to things which in their normal operation are implements of destruction. If the nature of a thing is such that it is reasonably certain to place life and limb in peril when negligently made, it is then a thing of danger. Its nature gives warning of the consequences to be expected. If to the element of danger there is added knowledge that the thing will be used by persons other than the purchaser, and used without new tests, then, irrespective of contract, the manufacturer of this thing of danger is under a duty to make it carefully. That is as far as we are required to go for the decision of this case. There must be knowledge of a danger, not merely possible, but probable. It is *possible* to use almost anything in a way that will make it dangerous if defective. That is not enough to charge the manufacturer with a duty independent of his contract. Whether a given thing is dangerous may be sometimes a question for the court and sometimes a question for the jury. There must also be knowledge that in the usual course of events the danger will be shared by others than the buyer. Such knowledge may often be inferred from the nature of the transaction. But it is possible that even knowledge of the danger and of the use will not always be enough. The proximity or remoteness of the relation is a factor to be considered. We are dealing now with the liability of the manufacturer of the finished product, who puts it on the market to be used without inspection by his customers. If he is negligent, where danger is to be foreseen, a liability will follow. We are not required at this time to say that it is legitimate to go back of the manufacturer of the finished product and hold the manufacturers of the component parts. To make their negligence a cause of imminent danger, an independent cause must often intervene; the manufacturer of the finished product must also fail in *his* duty of inspection. It may be that in those circumstances the negligence of the earlier members of the series is too remote to constitute, as to the ultimate user, an actionable wrong. . . . We leave that question open. We shall have to deal with it when it arises. The difficulty which it suggests is not present in this case. There is here no break in the chain of cause and effect. In such circumstances, the presence of a known danger, attendant upon a known use, makes vigilance a duty. We have put aside the notion that the duty to safeguard life and limb, when the consequences of negligence may be foreseen, grows out of contract and nothing else. We have put the source of the obligation where it ought to be. We have put its source in the law.

From this survey of the decisions, there thus emerges a definition of the duty of a manufacturer which enables us to measure this defendant's liability. Beyond all question, the nature of an automobile gives warning of probable danger if its construction is defective. This automobile was designed to go fifty miles an hour. Unless its wheels were sound and strong, injury was almost certain. It was as much a thing of danger as a defective engine for a railroad. The defendant knew the danger. It knew also that the car would be used by persons other than the buyer. This was apparent from its size; there were seats for three persons. It was apparent also from the fact that the buyer was a dealer in cars, who bought to resell. The maker of this car supplied it for the use of purchasers from the dealer just as plainly as the contractor in Devlin v. Smith supplied the scaffold for use by the servants of the owner. The dealer was indeed the one person of whom it might be said with some approach to certainty that by him the car would not be used. Yet the defendant would have us say that he was the one person whom it was under a legal duty to protect. The law does not lead us to so inconsequent a conclusion. Precedents drawn from the days of travel by stage coach do not fit the conditions of travel today. The principle that the danger must be imminent does not change, but the things subject to the principle do change. They are whatever the needs of life in a developing civilization require them to be.

In reaching this conclusion, we do not ignore the decisions to the contrary in other jurisdictions. . . . The earlier cases are summarized by Judge Sanborn in Huset v. J. I. Case Threshing Machine Co. (120 Fed. Rep. 865). . . . Judge Sanborn says . . . that the contractor who builds a bridge, or the manufacturer who builds a car, cannot ordinarily foresee injury to other persons than the owner as the probable result. We take a different view. We think that injury to others is to be foreseen not merely as a possible, but as an almost inevitable result. Indeed, Judge Sanborn concedes that his view is not to be reconciled with our decision in Devlin v. Smith. The doctrine of that decision has now become the settled law of this state, and we have no desire to depart from it.

[Cardozo, J., then reviewed the English cases from *Winterbottom* onward and continued:] From these cases a consistent principle is with difficulty extracted. The English courts, however, agree with ours in holding that one who invites another to make use of an appliance is bound to the exercise of reasonable care. That at bottom is the underlying principle of Devlin v. Smith. The contractor who builds the scaffold invites the owner's workmen to use it. The manufacturer who sells the automobile to the retail dealer invites the dealer's customers to use it. The invitation is addressed in the one case to determinate persons and in the other to an indeterminate class, but in each case it is equally plain, and in each its consequences must be the same. . . .

. . . Subtle distinctions are drawn by the defendant between things inherently dangerous and things imminently dangerous, but the case does not turn upon these verbal niceties. If danger was to be expected as reasonably certain, there was a duty of vigilance, and this whether you call the danger inherent or imminent. In varying forms that thought was put before the jury. We do not say that the court would not have been justified in ruling as a matter of law that the car was a dangerous thing. If there was any error, it was none of which the defendant can complain.

We think the defendant was not absolved from a duty of inspection because it bought the wheels from a reputable manufacturer. It was not merely a dealer in automobiles. It was a manufacturer of automobiles. It was responsible for the finished product. It was not at liberty to put the finished product on the market without subjecting the component parts to ordinary and simple tests. Under the charge of the trial judge nothing more was required of it. The obligation to inspect must vary with the nature of the thing to be inspected. The more probable the danger, the greater the need of caution. . . .

The judgment should be affirmed with costs.

BARTLETT, C.J., dissenting. . . . [In Thomas v. Winchester,] Chief Judge Ruggles, who delivered the opinion of the court, distinguished between an act of negligence imminently dangerous to the lives of others and one that is not so, saying: "If A. build a wagon and sell it to B., who sells it to C. and C. hires it to D., who in consequence of the gross negligence of A. in building the wagon is overturned and injured, D. cannot recover damages against A., the builder. A.'s obligation to build the wagon faithfully, arises solely out of his contract with B. The public have nothing to do with it. . . . So, for the same reason, if a horse be defectively shod by a smith, and a person hiring the horse from the owner is thrown and injured in consequence of the smith's negligence in shoeing the smith is not liable for the injury.". . .

I do not see how we can uphold the judgment in the present case without overruling what has been so often said by this court and other courts of like authority in reference to the absence of any liability for negligence on the part of the original vendor of an ordinary carriage to any one except his immediate vendee. The absence of such liability was the very point actually decided in the English case of Winterbottom v. Wright, and the illustration quoted from the opinion of Chief Judge Ruggles in Thomas v. Winchester assumes that the law on the subject was so plain that the statement would be accepted almost as a matter of course. In the case at bar the defective wheel on an automobile moving only eight miles an hour was not any more dangerous to the occupants of the car than a similarly defective wheel would be to the occupants of a carriage drawn by a horse at the same speed; and yet unless the courts have been all wrong on this question up to the present time there would be no liability to strangers to the original sale in the case of the horse-drawn carriage.

NOTES

1. A landmark case. The trial record of *MacPherson* yields a somewhat different view of the facts of this case. The eyewitnesses all testified that

MacPherson was traveling (in 1911) at over 30 miles per hour when the accident took place, not the leisurely 8 miles per hour stated in the dissent. As James Henderson notes, "The problem with MacPherson's story was that it was premised on a physical impossibility. Uncontradicted expert testimony from defendant's experts showed that, at such a low speed in high gear, the Buick would have stalled in its tracks — the engine could not possibly have continued to operate in four inches of gravel — and the car would have come to a stop almost immediately." Henderson, MacPherson v. Buick Motor Company: Simplifying the Facts While Reshaping the Law 45-46 (2003). The nature of the collision offers a compelling explanation as to why the wheel broke as it did. If the defect had been built in from the beginning, the wheel surely would have collapsed sooner under the pressure of driving on back country roads. None of these details came out in the appellate litigation, as Buick preferred to concentrate on the legal issues surrounding the appeal. If the facts had come out, would the case for the privity limitation been stronger or weaker? On its actual facts, could MacPherson get to the jury *today*?

MacPherson, however, comes down to us not as it happened but as it was tried on appeal. As such, it counts as a great landmark in the history of our law. Before it came down, the opinion of Sanford, J., in Huset v. J. I. Case stated the law in virtually all jurisdictions, including New York. After MacPherson v. Buick, one jurisdiction after another abandoned the privity rule in cases involving physical injuries caused by defective products. Other cases incrementally extended the scope of *MacPherson*. Thus, in Smith v. Peerless Glass Co., 181 N.E. 576 (N.Y. 1932), the court allowed a direct action for negligence to be brought against the manufacturer of a component part, such as the wheel maker in *MacPherson*. Today, every jurisdiction in the United States follows the *MacPherson* rule. Great Britain also abandoned *Winterbottom* in Donoghue v. Stevenson, [1932] A.C. 562, 580, 599 (Scot.), when the plaintiff was allowed to sue, even without privity, the maker of a ginger beer bottle for the physical harm that allegedly resulted when she drank the remains of a decomposed snail left in an opaque bottle of its brew. While the House of Lords went out of its way to avoid overruling Winterbottom v. Wright, it took exception to its view of privity.

> [A] manufacturer of products which he sells in such a form as to show that he intends them to reach the ultimate consumer in the form in which they left him, with no reasonable possibility of intermediate examination, and with the knowledge that the absence of reasonable care in the preparation or putting up of the products is likely to result in injury to the consumer's life or property, owes a duty to the consumer to take that reasonable care.

Could MacPherson have recovered under this formulation of the rule in light of his ability to inspect the wheel?

2. The warranty side of the line, privity in contract law. In *Huset*, Sanborn, J., noted that products liability claims often sounded in contract as well as in negligence. Often, the plaintiff's strategy is to claim that the defendant made an express or implied warranty that the product in question was fit for its intended purpose. This theory has to surmount two obstacles: privity and the law of warranties.

The first question asked whether the plaintiff could rely on this warranty theory when she did not purchase the product directly from the defendant. In Chysky v. Drake Brothers Co., 139 N.E. 576, 578 (N.Y. 1923), the plaintiff, a waitress, was given a piece of the defendant's cake for lunch. She bit on a concealed nail that had been baked into the cake and suffered injuries to her mouth. Section 96 of the New York Personal Property Code provided that "there is no implied warranty or condition as to the quality or fitness for any particular purpose of goods supplied under a contract to sell or a sale, except as follows: 1. Where the buyer, expressly or by implication, makes known to the seller the particular purpose for which the goods are required, and it appears that the buyer relies on the seller's skill or judgment (whether he be the grower or manufacturer or not), there is an implied warranty that the goods shall be reasonably fit for such purpose." Even after *MacPherson*, the Court of Appeals held that the plaintiff's cause of action failed under this section, stating that "[t]he general rule is that a manufacturer or seller of food, or other articles of personal property, is not liable to third persons, under an implied warranty, who have no contractual relations with him. The reason for this rule is that privity of contract does not exist between the seller and such third persons, and unless there be privity of contract, there can be no implied warranty."

The privity barrier was overcome in Baxter v. Ford Motor Co., 12 P.2d 409, 412 (Wash. 1932). There the plaintiff was injured in the eye when a small rock shattered the front windshield of his car that was manufactured by Ford and sold to the plaintiff by the defendant dealer, St. Johns Motors. The Washington Supreme Court allowed the dealer to escape liability because of a contractual provision in the contract of sale that excluded all warranties. But, relying on Thomas v. Winchester, it held that Ford could be responsible for its representations in catalogues and printed materials that St. John distributed to its customers about its "Tri-plex shatter-proof glass windshield."

> The rule in such cases does not rest upon contractual obligations, but rather on the principle that the original act of delivering an article is wrong, when, because of the lack of those qualities which the manufacturer represented it as having, the absence of which could not be readily detected by the consumer, the article is not safe for the purposes for which the consumer would ordinarily use it.
>
> Since the rule of *caveat emptor* was first formulated, vast changes have taken place in the economic structures of the English speaking peoples.

Methods of doing business have undergone a great transition. Radio, bill boards and the products of the printing press have become the means of creating a large part of the demand that causes goods to depart from factories to the ultimate consumer. It would be unjust to recognize a rule that would permit manufacturers of goods to create a demand for their products by representing that they possess qualities which they, in fact, do not possess; and then, because there is no privity of contract existing between the consumer and the manufacturer, deny the consumer the right to recover if damages result from the absence of those qualities, when such absence is not readily noticeable.

Note that in *Baxter*, the direct contract limited the liability of the dealer. For those plaintiffs who were in privity with their sellers, a key question was whether any of the legal rules restricting the scope of warranties could block the plaintiff's cause of action in the absence of any express warranty. Or put otherwise, should the case come out for the defendant if the manufacturer had joined the contract with the dealer? In McCabe v. L.K. Liggett Drug Co., 112 N.E.2d 254, 256-257 (Mass. 1953), the plaintiff was injured by a metal coffee maker, the "Lucifer Lifetime," sold (but not manufactured) by the defendant in a sealed cardboard box and assembled by the plaintiff in accordance with the instructions. The plaintiff's expert testified that the "notches" in the coffee maker's filtration system were "inadequate to provide for the release of the pressure which developed from the boiling water," especially if they became clogged by the "congealing" of the coffee grounds. As a result, the coffee maker blew up and injured the plaintiff. Williams, J., brushed aside other defenses as follows:

> The sale carried an implied warranty by the seller that the appliance was a coffee maker of merchantable quality. G. L. (Ter. Ed.) c. 106, §17 (2). Merchantable quality means that goods are reasonably suitable for the ordinary uses for which goods of that description are sold. . . .
>
> The fact that the apparatus violently burst apart in the manner described showed that the accumulating pressure was not being released and in the absence of explanation was itself evidence of a defective condition. The jury could find that the explosion was caused by the failure of the water to rise into the upper bowl and from an examination of the notches in the filter that this failure was due to an inadequate outlet and the clogging effect of coffee grounds which would collect around the notches.
>
> If the coffee maker was so imperfect in design that it could not be used without the likelihood of an explosion it could be found that the appliance was not reasonably fit for making coffee and therefore not merchantable. The plaintiff was not deprived of her right to rely upon the implied warranty either by a failure to inspect or by an inspection before use, as it could have been found that the defect in design would not be obvious to an ordinary person on inspection.

The judge was not justified in entering the verdict for the defendant on the ground that, as contended by the defendant, the notice required by G. L. (Ter. Ed.) c.106, §38, was insufficient, in not stating the exact date of the purchase or the name of the purchaser. Information as to the exact date of the sale was here of little if of any importance to the seller. The defendant had been selling these coffee makers over a period of a week. Presumably all were constructed alike. No claim was made that there was a defect in the particular appliance which was not common to all. The notice indicated a date of purchase within the period when they were being sold and was sufficient to enable the defendant to examine into any fault in their common design. The name of the person who actually made the purchase did not enter into the transaction with the defendant and the failure to state it did not invalidate the notice.

After *MacPherson*, how would a defense lawyer attack plaintiff's story? Is there any difference between a defective and an unmerchantable appliance? Why shouldn't this action be brought against the manufacturer? How do the parallel lines of warranty and tort evolve?

Escola v. Coca Cola Bottling Co. of Fresno
150 P.2d 436 (Cal. 1944)

[The plaintiff was a waitress. As part of her job, she was placing into the restaurant's refrigerator bottles of Coca Cola that had been delivered to the restaurant at least 36 hours earlier. As she put the fourth bottle into the refrigerator, it exploded in her hand, causing severe injuries. The plaintiff alleged that the defendant had been negligent in selling "bottles containing said beverage which on account of excessive pressure of gas or by reason of some defect in the bottle was dangerous . . . and likely to explode."

The jury entered a verdict for the plaintiff that was affirmed on appeal. Gibson, J., wrote as follows: "The bottle was admittedly charged with gas under pressure, and the charging of the bottle was within the exclusive control of the defendant. As it is a matter of common knowledge that an overcharge would not ordinarily result without negligence, it follows under the doctrine of res ipsa loquitur that if the bottle was in fact excessively charged an inference of defendant's negligence would arise."]

TRAYNOR, J. I concur in the judgment, but I believe the manufacturer's negligence should no longer be singled out as the basis of a plaintiff's right to recover in cases like the present one. In my opinion it should now be recognized that a manufacturer incurs an absolute liability when an article that he has placed on the market, knowing that it is to be used without inspection, proves to have a defect that causes injury to human beings. MacPherson v. Buick Motor Co. established the principle, recognized by this court, that irrespective of privity of contract, the manufacturer is responsible for an injury caused by such an article to any person who comes in lawful contact with it. In these cases the source of the manufacturer's liability was his negligence in the manufacturing process or in the inspection of component parts supplied by others. Even if there is no negligence, however, public policy demands that responsibility be fixed wherever it will most effectively reduce the hazards to life and health inherent in defective products that reach the market. It is evident that the manufacturer can anticipate some hazards and guard against the recurrence of others, as the public cannot. Those who suffer injury from defective products are unprepared to meet its consequences. The cost of an injury and the loss of time or health may be an overwhelming misfortune to the person injured, and a needless one, for the risk of injury can be insured by the manufacturer and distributed among the public as a cost of doing business. It is to the public interest to discourage the marketing of products having defects that are a menace to the public. If such products nevertheless find their way into the market it is to the public interest to place the responsibility for whatever injury they may cause upon the manufacturer, who, even if he is not negligent in the manufacture of the product, is responsible for its reaching the market. However intermittently such injuries may occur and however haphazardly they may strike, the risk of their occurrence is a constant risk and a general one. Against such a risk there should be general and constant protection and the manufacturer is best situated to afford such protection.

The injury from a defective product does not become a matter of indifference because the defect arises from causes other than the negligence of the manufacturer, such as negligence of a submanufacturer of a component part whose defects could not be revealed by inspection, or unknown causes that even by the device of res ipsa loquitur cannot be classified as negligence of the manufacturer. The inference of negligence may be dispelled by an affirmative showing of proper care. If the evidence against the fact inferred is "clear, positive, uncontradicted, and of such a nature that it cannot rationally be disbelieved, the court must instruct the jury that the nonexistence of the fact has been established as a matter of law." An injured person, however, is not ordinarily in a position to refute such evidence or identify the cause of the defect, for he can hardly be familiar with the manufacturing process as the manufacturer himself is. In leaving it to the jury to decide whether the inference has been dispelled, regardless of the evidence against it, the negligence rule approaches the rule of strict liability. It is needlessly circuitous to make negligence the basis of recovery and impose what is in reality liability without negligence. If public policy demands that a manufacturer of goods be responsible for their quality regardless of negligence there is no reason not to fix that responsibility openly.

In the case of foodstuffs, the public policy of the state is formulated in a criminal statute. . . . Statutes of this kind result in a strict liability of the manufacturer in tort to the member of the public injured.

The statute may well be applicable to a bottle whose defects cause it to explode. In any event it is significant that the statute imposes criminal liability without fault, reflecting the public policy of protecting the public from dangerous products placed on the market, irrespective of negligence in their manufacture. While the Legislature imposes criminal liability only with regard to food products and their containers, there are many other sources of danger. It is to the public interest to prevent injury to the public from any defective goods by the imposition of civil liability generally.

The retailer, even though not equipped to test a product, is under an absolute liability to his customer, for the implied warranties of fitness for proposed use and merchantable quality include a warranty of safety of the product. This warranty is not necessarily a contractual one; see 1 Williston on Sales, 2d ed., §§197-201, for public policy requires that the buyer be insured at the seller's expense against injury. The courts recognize, however, that the retailer cannot bear the burden of this warranty, and allow him to recoup any losses by means of the warranty of safety attending the wholesaler's or manufacturer's sale to him. . . . Such a procedure, however, is needlessly circuitous and engenders wasteful litigation. Much would be gained if the injured person could base his action directly on the manufacturer's warranty.

The liability of the manufacturer to an immediate buyer injured by a defective product follows without proof of negligence from the implied warranty of safety attending the sale. Ordinarily, however, the immediate buyer is a dealer who does not intend to use the product himself, and if the warranty of safety is to serve the purpose of protecting health and safety it must give rights to others than the dealer. In the words of Judge Cardozo in the *MacPherson* case: "The dealer was indeed the one person of whom it might be said with some approach to certainty that by him the car would not be used. Yet, the defendant would have us say that he was the one person whom it was under a legal duty to protect. The law does not lead us to so inconsequent a solution." While the defendant's negligence in the *MacPherson* case made it unnecessary for the court to base liability on warranty, Judge Cardozo's reasoning recognized the injured person as the real party in interest and effectively disposed on the theory that the liability of the manufacturer incurred by his warranty should apply only to the immediate purchaser. It thus paves the way for a standard of liability that would make the manufacturer guarantee the safety of his product even when there is no negligence.

This court and many others have extended protection according to such a standard to consumers of food products, taking the view that the right of a consumer injured by unwholesome food does not depend "upon the intricacies of the law of sales" and that the warranty of the manufacturer to the consumer in absence of privity of contract rests on public policy. Dangers to life and health inhere in other consumers' goods that are defective and there is no reason to differentiate them from the dangers of defective food products.

In the food products cases the courts have resorted to various fictions to rationalize the extension of the manufacturer's warranty to the consumer: that a warranty runs with the chattel; that the cause of action of the dealer is assigned to the consumer; that the consumer is a third party beneficiary of the manufacturer's contract with the dealer. They have also held the manufacturer liable on a mere fiction of negligence: "Practically he must know it [the product] is fit, or bear the consequences if it proves destructive." Such fictions are not necessary to fix the manufacturer's liability under a warranty if the warranty is severed from the contract of sale between the dealer and the consumer and based on the law of torts as a strict liability. Warranties are not necessarily rights arising under a contract. An action on a warranty "was, in its origin, a pure action of tort," and only late in the historical development of warranties was an action in assumpsit allowed. (Ames, The History of Assumpsit, 2 Harv. L. Rev. 1, 8; 4 Williston on Contracts (1936) §970.) . . .

As handicrafts have been replaced by mass production with its great markets and transportation facilities, the close relationship between the producer and consumer of a product has been altered. Manufacturing processes, frequently valuable secrets, are ordinarily either inaccessible to or beyond the ken of the general public. The consumer no longer has means or skill enough to investigate for himself the soundness of a product, even when it is not contained in a sealed package, and his erstwhile vigilance has been lulled by the steady efforts of manufacturers to build up confidence by advertising and marketing devices such as trademarks. (See Thomas v. Winchester, 6 N.Y. 697; Baxter v. Ford Motor Co.[, 2 P.2d 409 (Wash. 1932)].) Consumers no longer approach products warily but accept them on faith, relying on the reputation of the manufacturer or the trademark. Manufacturers have sought to justify that faith by increasingly high standards of inspection and a readiness to make good on defective products by way of replacements and refunds. (See Bogert and Fink, Business Practices Regarding Warranties in the Sale of Goods, 25 Ill. L. Rev. 400.) The manufacturer's obligation to the consumer must keep pace with the changing relationship between them; it cannot be escaped because the marketing of a product has become so complicated as to require one or more intermediaries. Certainly there is greater reason to impose liability on the manufacturer than on the retailer who is but a conduit of a product that he is not himself able to test.

The manufacturer's liability should, of course, be defined in terms of the safety of the product in normal and proper use, and should not extend to injuries that cannot be traced to the product as it reached the market.

NOTES

1. Command decision. At a factual level, does the switch to a theory of strict liability resolve the question of whether the Coke bottles were excessively charged in the factory or were mishandled by subsequent parties? As a theoretical matter, how sound are the various rationales for strict liability that Traynor, J., offers?

a. *Loss minimization.* One rationale insists that the manufacturer is in the best position to minimize the losses that arise out of the general use of its product. If correct, should we also require strict liability for defective premises owned by commercial enterprises, or for that matter, strict liability for automobile accidents, at least when business enterprises are defendants? Recall Hammontree v. Jenner, *supra* at 163. On this rationale, what adjustments should be made if the plaintiff or some downstream third party is in a better position to take the desired precautions? If the plaintiff shook the bottle in use, or stored it in a hot place? Is it consistent with the loss minimization rationale to allow the manufacturer to contract out of liability with the consumer? Does a negligence rule fail to create the necessary incentives for the manufacturer to take appropriate cost-justified precautions?

For an early criticism of strict liability in products cases, see Plant, Strict Liability of Manufacturers for Injuries Caused by Defects in Products — An Opposing View, 24 Tenn. L. Rev. 938, 945 (1957), in which it is noted that "[t]he element which is most disturbing to manufacturers is not the potential judgment of legal liability but the injury which is done to the reputation of the product and its producers." Note that modern "event studies" establish that the decline in the value of the shares of a publicly traded company after a major product incident go down more than the anticipated amount of the liability.

b. *Loss spreading.* A second defense of the strict liability rule in *Escola* rests upon the ability of the defendant to spread and to cushion the "overwhelming misfortune" to the injured person or his family. This risk-spreading rationale for strict liability was challenged in Wights v. Staff Jennings, Inc., 405 P.2d 624, 628 (Or. 1965), where the court observed:

> The rationale of risk spreading and compensating the victim has no special relevancy to cases involving injuries resulting from the use of defective goods. The reasoning would seem to apply not only in cases involving personal injuries arising from the *sale* of defective goods, but equally to any case where an injury results from the risk creating conduct of the seller in any stage of the production and distribution of goods. Thus a manufacturer would be strictly liable even in the absence of fault for any injury to a person struck by one of the manufacturer's trucks being used in transporting his goods to market. It seems to us that the enterprise liability rationale

employed in the *Escola* case proves too much and that if adopted would compel us to apply the principle of strict liability in all future cases where the loss could be distributed.

c. Elimination of proof complications. Traynor, J., also defends strict liability in *Escola* because it simplifies the law by eliminating the need to resort to res ipsa loquitur — the same reason used to defend strict liability in Rylands v. Fletcher. See Chapter 2, *supra* at 127. In all contexts, a strict liability rule switches the residual risk of unavoidable accidents from the plaintiff to the defendant. With exploding pop bottles, that risk is generally quite small given the stringent quality control and inspection devices incorporated into the manufacturing process. How does res ipsa loquitur apply when misconduct by the plaintiff or a third party is also in issue? Should it make any difference that the plaintiff in *Escola* could not produce the pieces of the broken bottle for inspection and examination?

d. The foodstuffs analogy. A fourth defense of strict liability rests on the analogy between adulterated foodstuffs and product defects. In this regard, the law after *MacPherson* and before *Escola* drew a distinction between foodstuffs that were and were not sold in sealed containers. For goods sold in sealed containers, the law exempted the retailer from liability but allowed a direct suit against the manufacturer, albeit on a negligence theory. See, e.g., Richenbacher v. California Packing Corp., 145 N.E. 281 (Mass. 1924), sustaining the use of res ipsa loquitur when the plaintiff's mouth was cut by some heavy gray glass found in a container of spinach. In contrast, when goods were not so packaged, the general rule imposed a negligence liability, if at all, on the retailer but not on the original supplier of the food. Is *Richenbacher* an easier case for res ipsa loquitur than *Escola*? Why?

e. Corrective justice. One last argument for strict liability in products cases — one not pressed by Traynor — tracks a key reason for strict liability in ordinary trespass cases, or even under the rule in Rylands v. Fletcher. Once plaintiff establishes the causal connection to the defendant's act (here, the defective bottling under pressure that caused harm), then prima facie, the loss should be placed upon the party who created that condition, not the party who suffered from it. Note, however, one structural difference between the two types of cases. With abnormally dangerous activities, the defendant is virtually always in possession of the dangerous instrumentality just before it causes the accident, so the class of defenses based upon plaintiff's conduct remains quite small. See *supra* Chapter 2, Note 2, at 159, and Chapter 8 at 674. With products liability, the defendant is *never* in possession of the dangerous product when it causes injury so that the older privity limitation becomes a sensible way for liability to track possession (and hence control), save in those few cases in which a party out of possession is in a better position to avoid the loss. See Epstein, The Historical

Origins and Economic Structure of Workers' Compensation Law, 16 Ga. L.
Rev. 775, 806-808 (1982), defending privity for workplace injuries on the
ground that employer's liability is both cheaper and more efficient than
manufacturer's liability.

2. *Implied warranty — elimination of privity in contract law.* The early privity
limitation in Chysky v. Drake, *supra* at 737, was overruled 38 years later in
Greenberg v. Lorenz, 173 N.E.2d 773 (N.Y. 1961). There the plaintiff was
injured when she ate some canned salmon, containing sharp metal slivers,
sold by the defendant retail food dealer to her father. The court below
dismissed the plaintiff's complaint because the plaintiff had not purchased
the salmon. The Court of Appeals promptly reversed. Just about that time,
the warranty provisions of the law of sales were reworked under the then
new Uniform Commercial Code, which offers three possible approaches to
the scope of the warranty.

§2-318. THIRD PARTY BENEFICIARIES OF WARRANTIES EXPRESS OR IMPLIED . . .
Alternative A
   A seller's warranty whether express or implied extends to any natural
person who is in the family or household of his buyer or who is a guest in his
home if it is reasonable to expect that such person may use, consume or be
affected by the goods and who is injured in person by breach of the warranty.
A seller may not exclude or limit the operation of this section.

Alternative B
   A seller's warranty whether express or implied extends to any natural
person who may reasonably be expected to use, consume or be affected by
the goods and who is injured in person by breach of the warranty. A seller
may not exclude or limit the operation of this section.

Alternative C
   A seller's warranty whether express or implied extends to any person who
may reasonably be expected to use, consume or be affected by the goods and
who is injured by breach of the warranty. A seller may not exclude or limit
the operation of this section with respect to injury to the person of an
individual to whom the warranty extends.

New York originally adopted alternative A. In 1975, however, it adopted
alternative B (N.Y. U.C.C. Law §2-318 (McKinney 2002)). If *X* steals a roll
from *Y*, who had purchased it from *Z*, should *X* recover from *Z* under the
variations of §2-318 when injured by a piece of sharp metal baked into the
roll? Why should the parties, unlike the dealer in *Baxter*, be unable to
contract out of this provision?

3. *Implied warranty with a vengeance: Henningsen v. Bloomfield Motors,
Inc.*, 161 A.2d 69 (N.J. 1960). Henningsen purchased a new Plymouth
automobile, manufactured by the defendant Chrysler Corporation, from

defendant Bloomfield Motors, Inc. Henningsen gave the car to his wife, after indicating to the dealer his intention to make a gift. The contract of sale between Mr. Henningsen and the two defendants expressly disclaimed all warranties by the dealer or manufacturer, except one that limited the liability of the defendants *to the original purchaser* to the replacement of defective parts within 90 days or 4,000 miles, whichever occurred first. Shortly after the car was purchased, the plaintiff, Mrs. Henningsen, was driving along a clear road when the steering mechanism suddenly went awry. The car went out of control and veered off the road and into a wall, injuring her. She sued on theories of negligence and warranty. After the trial court dismissed the negligence claim, the jury found for the plaintiff against both defendants on the warranty claim and the defendants appealed. In his very lengthy opinion, Judge Francis examined how the courts had extended the implied warranty of merchantability to individuals who were not party to the original sales agreement, a development he found absolutely necessary since manufacturers distanced themselves from sales act liability to consumers by a complex web of contracts. He insisted that the limited protection to the plaintiff under this express warranty was a "sad commentary" on the marketing practices of automobile manufacturers.

Although he thought the ordinary warranty of merchantability might technically survive this disclaimer clause, Judge Francis did not rely on any interpretative techniques. Instead, he voided the disclaimer clause on the ground that it "was not fairly obtained." It therefore followed that the benefit of the implied warranty ran to the plaintiff, even in the absence of privity so long as the defendant "puts a new automobile in the stream of trade and promotes its purchase by the public."

A breakthrough for its time, *Henningsen*'s importance appears to have waned somewhat, not because courts have rejected its outcome, but ironically because its implied warranty theory tied products liability actions too closely to the law of sales. Modern cases, however, still occasionally allow a jury to find liability under a warranty theory while denying recovery under a tort theory. In Denny v. Ford Motor Co., 662 N.E.2d 730, 736 (N.Y. 1995), plaintiff was injured when her Ford Bronco, owing to its high center of gravity, rolled over after she slammed on the brakes. The jury found that the vehicle was not "defective" but awarded her $1,200,000 in damages on an implied warranty theory. The court rejected Ford's contention that tort had "completely subsumed" warranty theory, noting that the "negligence-like risk/benefit component of the defect element differentiates strict products liability claims from U.C.C.-based breach of implied warranty claims in cases involving design defects."

Can a product without a defect flunk the merchantability test? More recently in Castro v. QVC Network, 139 F.3d 114, 118 (2d Cir. 1998), the plaintiff was badly burned when her 25-pound Thanksgiving turkey fell on her legs and ankles, causing second and third-degree burns, after it slipped out of a roaster manufactured by defendant U.S.A. T-Fal Corp., and sold by defendant QVC over its home-shopping network. The trial judge refused to offer separate instructions on both strict liability and warranty counts, but after the jury found for the defendants, Calabresi, J., relied on *Denny* to grant a new trial: "The imposition of strict liability for an alleged design 'defect' is determined by a risk-utility standard. The notion of 'defect' in a U.C.C.-based breach of warranty claim focuses, instead, on consumer expectations." What is the difference if the claimed defect is that the handles to the pan were too small to allow the plaintiff to grip them firmly?

4. *Strict liability in torts: the* Greenman *reformulation.* Shortly after *Henningsen*, the tort side of product liability also gravitated toward strict liability. In Greenman v. Yuba Power Products, Inc., 377 P.2d 897, 900-901 (Cal. 1963), the plaintiff's wife gave him a product manufactured by the defendant. It was a Shopsmith combination power tool that could be used as a saw, a drill, and a wood lathe. The plaintiff read the manufacturer's brochure, which contained the following statements: "(1) WHEN SHOPSMITH IS IN HORIZONTAL POSITION — Rugged construction of frame provides rigid support from end to end. Heavy centerless-ground steel tubing insures perfect alignment of components. (2) SHOPSMITH maintains its accuracy because every component has positive locks that hold adjustments through rough or precision work." In the course of working the lathe, a piece of wood "suddenly flew out of the machine and struck him on the forehead, inflicting serious injury." There was substantial evidence that the plaintiff's injuries were caused by the defective construction of the Shopsmith whose set screws were of insufficient strength to hold the wood in place while the lathe was being operated. (What concept of defect is involved?) The plaintiff recovered damages from the manufacturer for negligence and breach of both express and implied warranties.

One of defendant's contentions on appeal was that the plaintiff's cause of action was barred because he failed to give notice of his injury within a "reasonable time" as required by §1769 of the California Civil Code. Justice Traynor, speaking for the entire court, sidestepped the "intricacies" of the warranty provisions by opting for strict liability in tort:

> A manufacturer is strictly liable in tort when an article he places on the market, knowing that it is to be used without inspection for defects, proves to have a defect that causes injury to a human being. Recognized first in the case of unwholesome food products, such liability has now been extended to a variety of other products that create as great or greater hazards if defective.
>
> Although in these cases strict liability has usually been based on the theory of an express or implied warranty running from the manufacturer to the plaintiff, the abandonment of the requirement of a contract between them, the recognition that the liability is not assumed by agreement but imposed by law, and the refusal to permit the manufacturer to define the scope of its own responsibility

for defective products make clear that the liability is not one governed by the law of contract warranties but by the law of strict liability in tort. Accordingly, rules defining and governing warranties that were developed to meet the needs of commercial transactions cannot properly be invoked to govern the manufacturer's liability to those injured by their defective products unless those rules also serve the purposes for which such liability is imposed.

We need not recanvass the reasons for imposing strict liability on the manufacturer. The purpose of such liability is to insure that the costs of injuries resulting from defective products are borne by the manufacturers that put such products on the market rather than by the injured persons who are powerless to protect themselves. Sales warranties serve this purpose fitfully at best. In the present case, for example, plaintiff was able to plead and prove an express warranty only because he read and relied on the representations of the Shopsmith's ruggedness contained in the manufacturer's brochure. Implicit in the machine's presence on the market, however, was a representation that it would safely do the jobs for which it was built. Under these circumstances, it should not be controlling whether plaintiff selected the machine because of the statements in the brochure, or because of the machine's own appearance of excellence that belied the defect lurking beneath the surface, or because he merely assumed that it would safely do the jobs it was built to do. It should not be controlling whether the details of the sales from manufacturer to retailer and from retailer to plaintiff's wife were such that one or more of the implied warranties of the sales act arose. (Civ. Code, §1735.) "The remedies of injured consumers ought not to be made to depend upon the intricacies of the law of sales." To establish the manufacturer's liability it was sufficient that plaintiff proved that he was injured while using the Shopsmith in a way it was intended to be used as a result of a defect in design and manufacture of which plaintiff was not aware that made the Shopsmith unsafe for its intended use.

SECTION C.   THE RESTATEMENTS

1.   *A Tale of Two Texts*

American Law Institute, Restatement (Second) of Torts
(1966)

§402A.   SPECIAL LIABILITY OF SELLER OF PRODUCT FOR PHYSICAL HARM
            TO USER OR CONSUMER

(1) One who sells any product in a defective condition unreasonably dangerous to the user or consumer or to his property is subject to liability for physical harm thereby caused to the ultimate user or consumer, or to his property, if

(a) the seller is engaged in the business of selling such a product, and

(b) it is expected to and does reach the user or consumer without substantial change in the condition in which it is sold.

(2) The rule stated in Subsection (1) applies although

(a) the seller has exercised all possible care in the preparation and sale of his product, and

(b) the user or consumer has not bought the product from or entered into any contractual relation with the seller.

Caveat:

The Institute expresses no opinion as to whether the rules stated in this Section may not apply

(1) to harm to persons other than users or consumers

(2) to the seller of a product expected to be processed or otherwise substantially changed before it reaches the user or consumer or

(3) to the seller of a component part of a product to be assembled.

Comments: . . .

f. Business of selling. The rule stated in this Section applies to any person engaged in the business of selling products for use or consumption. It therefore applies to any manufacturer of such a product, to any wholesale or retail dealer or distributor, and to the operator of a restaurant. . . .

The rule does not, however, apply to the occasional seller of food or other such products who is not engaged in that activity as a part of his business. Thus it does not apply to the housewife who, on one occasion, sells to her neighbor a jar of jam or a pound of sugar. Nor does it apply to the owner of an automobile who, on one occasion, sells it to his neighbor, or even sells it to a dealer in used cars, and this even though he is fully aware that the dealer plans to resell it. The basis for the rule is the ancient one of the special responsibility for the safety of the public undertaken by one who enters into the business of supplying human beings with products which may endanger the safety of their persons and property, and the forced reliance upon that undertaking on the part of those who purchase such goods. This basis is lacking in the case of the ordinary individual who makes the isolated sale, and he is not liable to a third person, or even to his buyer, in the absence of his negligence. . . .

g. Defective condition. The rule stated in this Section applies only where the product is, at the time it leaves the seller's hands, in a condition not contemplated by the ultimate consumer, which will be unreasonably dangerous to him. The seller is not liable when he delivers the product in a safe condition, and subsequent mishandling or other causes make it harmful by the time it is consumed. The burden of proof that the product was in a defective condition at the time that it left the hands of the particular seller is upon the injured plaintiff and unless evidence can be produced which will support the conclusion that it was then defective, the burden is not sustained.

Safe condition at the time of delivery by the seller will, however, include proper packaging, necessary sterilization, and other precautions required to permit the product to remain safe for a normal length of time when handled in a normal manner.

h. A product is not in defective condition when it is safe for normal handling and consumption. If the injury results from abnormal handling, as where a bottled beverage is knocked against a radiator to remove the cap, or from abnormal preparation for use, as where too much salt is added to food, or from abnormal consumption, as where a child eats too much candy and is made ill, the seller is not liable. . . .

The defective condition may arise not only from harmful ingredients, not characteristic of the product itself either as to presence or quantity, but also from foreign objects contained in the product, from decay or deterioration before sale, or from the way in which the product is prepared or packed. No reason is apparent for distinguishing between the product itself and the container in which it is supplied; and the two are purchased by the user or consumer as an integrated whole. Where the container is itself dangerous, the product is sold in a defective condition. Thus a carbonated beverage in a bottle which is so weak, or cracked, or jagged at the edges, or bottled under such excessive pressure that it may explode or otherwise cause harm to the person who handles it, is in a defective and dangerous condition. . . .

i. Unreasonably dangerous. The rule stated in this Section applies only where the defective condition of the product makes it unreasonably dangerous to the user or consumer. Many products cannot possibly be made entirely safe for all consumption, and any food or drug necessarily involves some risk of harm, if only from over-consumption. Ordinary sugar is a deadly poison to diabetics, and castor oil found use under Mussolini as an instrument of torture. That is not what is meant by "unreasonably dangerous" in this Section. The article sold must be dangerous to an extent beyond that which would be contemplated by the ordinary consumer who purchases it, with the ordinary knowledge common to the community as to its characteristics. Good whiskey is not unreasonably dangerous merely because it will make some people drunk, and is especially dangerous to alcoholics; but bad whiskey, containing a dangerous amount of fusel oil, is unreasonably dangerous. Good tobacco is not unreasonably dangerous merely because the effects of smoking may be harmful; but tobacco containing something like marijuana may be unreasonably dangerous. Good butter is not unreasonably dangerous merely because, if such be the case, it deposits cholesterol in the arteries and leads to heart attacks; but bad butter, contaminated with poisonous fish oil, is unreasonably dangerous.

j. Directions or warning. In order to prevent the product from being unreasonably dangerous, the seller may be required to give directions or warning, on the container, as to its use. The seller may reasonably assume that those with common allergies, as for example to eggs or strawberries, will be aware of them, and he is not required to warn against them. Where, however, the product contains an ingredient to which a substantial number of the population are allergic, and the ingredient is one whose danger is not generally known, or if known is one which the consumer would reasonably not expect to find in the product, the seller is required to give warning against it, if he has knowledge, or by the application of reasonable, developed human skill and foresight should have knowledge, of the presence of the ingredient and the danger. Likewise in the case of poisonous drugs, or those unduly dangerous for other reasons, warning as to use may be required. But a seller is not required to warn with respect to products, or ingredients in them, which are only dangerous or potentially so, when consumed in excessive quantity, or over a long period of time, when the danger, or potentiality of danger, is generally known and recognized. Again the dangers of alcoholic beverages are an example, as are also those of foods containing such substances as saturated fats, which may over a period of time have a deleterious effect upon the human heart. Where warning is given, the seller may reasonably assume that it will be read and heeded; and a product bearing such a warning, which is safe for use if it is followed, is not in defective condition, nor is it unreasonably dangerous.

k. Unavoidably unsafe products. There are some products which, in the present state of human knowledge, are quite incapable of being made safe for their intended and ordinary use. These are especially common in the field of drugs. An outstanding example is the vaccine for the Pasteur treatment of rabies, which not uncommonly leads to very serious and damaging consequences when it is injected. Since the disease itself invariably leads to a dreadful death, both the marketing and the use of the vaccine are fully justified, notwithstanding the unavoidable high degree of risk which they involve. Such a product, properly prepared, and accompanied by proper directions and warning, is not defective, nor is it *unreasonably* dangerous. The same is true of many other drugs, vaccines, and the like, many of which for this very reason cannot legally be sold except to physicians, or under the prescription of a physician. It is also true in particular of many new or experimental drugs as to which, because of lack of time and opportunity for sufficient medical experience, there can be no assurance of safety, or perhaps even of purity of ingredients, but such experience as there is justifies the marketing and use of the drug notwithstanding a medically recognizable risk. The seller of such products, again with the qualification that they are properly prepared and marketed, and proper warning is given, where the situation calls for it, is not to be held to strict liability for unfortunate consequences attending their use, merely because he has undertaken to supply the public with an apparently useful and desirable product, attended with a known but apparently reasonable risk.

m. "Warranty." . . . The rule stated in this Section does not require any reliance on the part of the consumer upon the reputation, skill, or judgment of the seller who is to be held liable, nor any representation or undertaking on the part of that seller. The seller is strictly liable although, as is frequently the case, the consumer does not even know who he is at the time of consumption. The rule stated in this Section is not governed by the provisions of the Uniform Sales Act, or those of the Uniform Commercial Code, as to warranties; and it is not affected by limitations on the scope and content of warranties, or by limitation to "buyer" and "seller" in those statutes. Nor is the consumer required to give notice to the seller of his injury within a reasonable time after it occurs, as is provided by the Uniform Act. . . .

n. Contributory negligence. Since the liability with which this Section deals is not based upon negligence of the seller, but is strict liability, the rule applied to strict liability cases (see §524) applies. Contributory negligence of the plaintiff is not a defense when such negligence consists merely in a failure to discover the defect in the product, or to guard against the possibility of its existence. On the other hand the form of contributory negligence which consists in voluntarily and unreasonably proceeding to encounter a known danger, and commonly passes under the name of assumption of risk, is a defense under this Section as in other cases of strict liability. If the user or consumer discovers the defect and is aware of the danger, and nevertheless proceeds unreasonably to make use of the product and is injured by it, he is barred from recovery.

NOTES

1. *Restatement of Torts section 402A.* Until the adoption of the Third Restatement of Products Liability, §402A and its comments formed the basic text of modern products liability law. At its inception, §402A was noted for its adoption of a broad strict liability rule for product defects. Earlier drafts were originally confined to foodstuffs and products intended for intimate body use, but by 1965 the strict liability was extended to all products. The endless diversity of products in turn made it more difficult to devise a single rule to cover, for example, the unique issues raised by pharmaceuticals. Accordingly, Prosser and other drafters of the Restatement addressed many hard questions only in the comments to the basic text, which, over time, have become as important as the basic provision itself. Even today, the Third Restatement has not displaced the Second across the board, so it is critical to gain mastery over both. On the adoption

of §402A, see R. Epstein, Modern Products Liability Law ch. 6 (1980); Priest, The Invention of Enterprise Liability: A Critical History of the Intellectual Foundations of Modern Tort Law, 14 J. Legal Stud. 461, 505-519 (1985).

2. *Bystander's recovery.* Today the case law has outstripped the Second Restatement by allowing injured bystanders to sue the original manufacturer. The initial hesitation in the bystander cases rested in part on the uncertainty whether any implied warranty or misrepresentation theory could hold the defendant accountable to the injured bystander. The bystander is not lured into using the product by the defendant's representations. Neither is she an immediate or ultimate beneficiary of any seller or manufacturer warranty. The bystander's case for strict liability in tort is far stronger: As with abnormally dangerous activities, the bystander is best able to claim having been hurt by a process that was in no sense her making because she never used the product at all. Today the liability of the manufacturer or seller to the bystander is universally allowed. See, e.g., Elmore v. American Motors Corp., 451 P.2d 84 (Cal. 1969); Codling v. Paglia, 298 N.E.2d 622 (N.Y. 1973); Noel, Defective Products: Extension of Strict Liability to Bystanders, 38 Tenn. L. Rev. 1 (1970). In practice, however, bystander cases are relatively infrequent compared to the numerous actions brought by injured product consumers or users.

The American Law Institute, Restatement (Third) of the Law of Products Liability
(1998)

§1. LIABILITY OF COMMERCIAL SELLER OR DISTRIBUTOR FOR HARM CAUSED BY DEFECTIVE PRODUCTS

One engaged in the business of selling or otherwise distributing products who sells or distributes a defective product is subject to liability for harm to persons or property caused by the defect.

§2. CATEGORIES OF PRODUCT DEFECTS

[For purposes of determining liability under section 1:]

A product is defective when, at the time of sale or distribution, it contains a manufacturing defect, is defective in design, or is defective because of inadequate instructions or warnings. A product:

   (a) contains a manufacturing defect when the product departs from its intended design even though all possible care was exercised in the preparation and marketing of the product;

(b) is defective in design when the foreseeable risks of harm posed by the product could have been reduced or avoided by the adoption of a reasonable alternative design by the seller or other distributor, or a predecessor in the commercial chain of distribution, and the omission of the alternative design renders the product not reasonably safe;

(c) is defective because of inadequate instructions or warnings when the foreseeable risks of harm posed by the product could have been reduced or avoided by the provision of reasonable instructions or warnings by the seller or other distributor, or a predecessor in the commercial chain of distribution, and the omission of the instructions or warnings renders the product not reasonably safe.

NOTE

Into the next generation. The Third Restatement reflects the transformation of products liability law after 1965. For example, §402A's caveats on bystander liability have disappeared. In addition, the Third Restatement adopts the now regnant classification of construction, design, and warning defects, and establishes a distinct liability rule for each class. It keeps the original strict liability rule for products with manufacturing defects, but imposes only the more limited obligation to make product designs, warnings, and instructions "reasonably safe." Many of the old rules, however, still carry over, such as the exclusion of "casual sellers" from the operation of this provision. See §1, comment *c*. Subsequent provisions of the Third Restatement examine each class of defects, and contain additional provisions to deal with prescription drugs, issues of causation, and affirmative defenses. These provisions will be set out, as needed, in connection with the specific topics they examine. For an early discussion of the revisions of the Second Restatement, see Henderson & Twerski, A Proposed Revision of Section 402A of the Restatement (Second) of Torts, 77 Cornell L. Rev. 1512 (1992), whose views take on special significance since they served as the joint reporters for the ALI revision. For an acceptance of the Third Restatement over the Second, see Wright v. Brooke Group, Ltd., 652 N.W.2d 159 (Iowa 2002); for the preference of the Second Restatement over the Third, see Green v. Smith & Nephew AHP, Inc., 629 N.W.2d 727 (Wis. 2001).

2. The Theory of Products Liability: Tort or Contract?

The early history of products liability law reveals a consistent tension between the contract-based theory of implied warranty and the tort theory sounding either in strict liability or negligence. The adoption of the

Restatement (Second) of Torts in 1965 seemed to presage the dominance of tort theories. While that prediction has proved largely true with respect to traditional forms of personal injury, the picture with respect to various forms of property damage has proved much less clear in practice. The source of the difficulty stems from the general view that, even after the adoption of the Second Restatement, matters of "economic loss" should best be left to voluntary agreement between the parties. At this point, it becomes necessary to define what these losses are. The clear cases of economic loss involve those disappointed expectations when products sold do not perform in the way in which they were intended, such as a truck that constantly stalls out on the highway, causing its owner to make late deliveries. But the class of such harms can go even further to cover the economic losses that flow, at least in some instances, from physical damage to the product that is sold. The following materials explore the difficulties that arise in policing the line between those types of damages that are governed by product liability and contract law respectively.

Casa Clara Condominium Association, Inc. v. Charley Toppino & Sons, Inc.
620 So. 2d 1244 (Fla. 1993)

McDONALD, J. . . . . The issue is whether a homeowner can recover for purely economic losses from a concrete supplier under a negligence theory. We agree with the district court that such a recovery cannot be had. . . .

Charley Toppino & Sons, Inc., a dissolved corporation, supplied concrete for numerous construction projects in Monroe County. Apparently, some of the concrete supplied by Toppino contained a high content of salt that caused the reinforcing steel inserted in the concrete to rust, which, in turn, caused the concrete to crack and break off. The petitioners own condominium units and single-family homes built with, and now allegedly damaged by, Toppino's concrete. In separate actions the homeowners sued numerous defendants and included claims against Toppino for breach of common law implied warranty, products liability, negligence, and violation of the building code. The circuit court dismissed all counts against Toppino in each case. On appeal the district court applied the economic loss rule and held that, because no person was injured and no other property damaged, the homeowners had no cause of action against Toppino in tort. The district court also held that Toppino, a supplier, had no duty to comply with the building code.

Plaintiffs find a tort remedy attractive because it often permits the recovery of greater damages than an action on a contract and may avoid the conditions of a contract. The distinction between "tort recovery for physical injuries and warranty recovery for economic loss" rests on an understanding of the nature of the responsibility a manufacturer must undertake in distributing his products. He can appropriately be held liable for physical injuries caused by defects by requiring his goods to match a standard of safety defined in terms of conditions that create unreasonable risks of harm. *He cannot be held for the level of performance of his products in the consumer's business unless he agrees that the product was designed to meet the consumer's demands.*

Seely v. White Motor Co., 403 P.2d 145, 151 (Cal. 1965) (emphasis supplied). An individual consumer, on the other hand,

> should not be charged at the will of the manufacturer with bearing the risk of physical injury when he buys a product on the market. He can, however, be fairly charged with the risk that the product will not match his economic expectations unless the manufacturer agrees that it will.

Id. *Seely* sets out the economic loss rule, which prohibits tort recovery when a product damages itself, causing economic loss, but does not cause personal injury or damage to any property other than itself. E.g., East River Steamship Corp. v. Transamerica Delaval, Inc., 476 U.S. 858 (1986); . . .

Economic loss has been defined as "damages for inadequate value, costs of repair and replacement of the defective product, or consequent loss of profits — without any claim of personal injury or damage to other property." Note, Economic Loss in Products Liability Jurisprudence, 66 Colum. L. Rev. 917, 918 (1966). It includes "the diminution in the value of the product because it is inferior in quality and does not work for the general purposes for which it was manufactured and sold." Comment, Manufacturers' Liability to Remote Purchasers for "Economic Loss" Damages — Tort or Contract?, 114 U. Pa. L. Rev. 539, 541 (1966). In other words, economic losses are "disappointed economic expectations," which are protected by contract law, rather than tort law. This is the basic difference between contract law, which protects expectations, and tort law, which is determined by the duty owed to an injured party. For recovery in tort "there must be a showing of harm above and beyond disappointed expectations. A buyer's desire to enjoy the benefit of his bargain is not an interest that tort law traditionally protects." Redarowicz v. Ohlendorf, 441 N.E.2d 324, 327 (Ill. 1982).

The homeowners are seeking purely economic damages — no one has sustained any physical injuries and no property, other than the structures built with Toppino's concrete, has sustained any damage. They argue that holding them to contract remedies is unfair and that homeowners in general should be excepted from the operation of the economic loss rule. We disagree.

In tort a manufacturer or producer of goods "is liable whether or not it is negligent because 'public policy demands that responsibility be fixed

wherever it will most effectively reduce the hazards to life and health inherent in defective products that reach the market.'" *East River,* 476 U.S. at
866 (quoting Escola v. Coca Cola Bottling Co. (Traynor, J., concurring)). . . . The purpose of a duty in tort is to protect society's interest in
being free from harm, and the cost of protecting society from harm is borne
by society in general. Contractual duties, on the other hand, come from
society's interest in the performance of promises. When only economic
harm is involved, the question becomes "whether the consuming public as a
whole should bear the cost of economic losses sustained by those who failed
to bargain for adequate contract remedies."

We are urged to make an exception to the economic loss doctrine for
homeowners. Buying a house is the largest investment many consumers
ever make, and homeowners are an appealing, sympathetic class. If a house
causes economic disappointment by not meeting a purchaser's expectations, the resulting failure to receive the benefit of the bargain is a core
concern of contract, not tort, law. There are protections for homebuyers,
however, such as statutory warranties, the general warranty of habitability,
and the duty of sellers to disclose defects, as well as the ability of purchasers
to inspect houses for defects. Coupled with homebuyers' power to bargain
over price, these protections must be viewed as sufficient when compared
with the mischief that could be caused by allowing tort recovery for purely
economic losses. Therefore, we again "hold contract principles more
appropriate than tort principles for recovering economic loss without an
accompanying physical injury or property damage." *Florida Power & Light,*
510 So. 2d at 902. If we held otherwise, "contract law would drown in a sea
of tort." *East River.* We refuse to hold that homeowners are not subject to
the economic loss rule.

The homeowners also argue that Toppino's concrete damaged "other"
property because the individual components and items of building material, not the homes themselves, are the products they purchased. We disagree. The character of a loss determines the appropriate remedies, and, to
determine the character of a loss, one must look to the product purchased
by the plaintiff, not the product sold by the defendant. Generally, house
buyers have little or no interest in how or where the individual components
of a house are obtained. They are content to let the builder produce the
finished product, i.e., a house. These homeowners bought finished products—dwellings—not the individual components of those dwellings.
They bargained for the finished products, not their various components.
The concrete became an integral part of the finished product and, thus, did
not injure "other" property.

We also disagree with the homeowners that the mere possibility that the
exploding concrete will cause physical injury is sufficient reason to abrogate
the economic loss rule. This argument goes completely against the principle that injury must occur before a negligence action exists. Because an

injury has not occurred, its extent and the identity of injured persons is
completely speculative. Thus, the degree of risk is indeterminate, with no
guarantee that damages will be reasonably related to the risk of injury, and
with no possibility for the producer of a product to structure its business
behavior to cover that risk. Agreeing with the homeowners' argument
would make it difficult "to maintain a realistic limitation on damages." *East
River*.

Therefore, we approve the district court's opinions and hold that the
economic loss rule applies to the purchase of houses. The cases in conflict
incorrectly refused to apply the economic loss rule to what should have
been contract actions, and we disapprove them. We also agree with the
district court that the homeowners cannot recover against Toppino under a
building code.

It is so ordered.

BARKETT, CHIEF JUSTICE, concurring in part, dissenting in part.

If the allegations of the homeowners in this case are true, their homes are
literally crumbling around them because the concrete supplied by Toppino
was negligently manufactured. The homeowners assert that the concrete is
now cracking and breaking apart and poses a danger of serious injury. The
courts, including this one, have said "too bad."

I find that answer unacceptable. . . .

Their claim for breach of implied warranty has been denied (they lack
privity with Toppino); their claim that Toppino violated the Florida
Building Codes Act has been denied (Toppino, as a material supplier, is not
governed by the Standard Building Code); and now their claim in tort has
been denied because, notwithstanding their alleged ability to prove that
their houses are falling down around them, they have not suffered any
damage to their property on the basis that homes are "products."

A key premise underlying the economic loss rule is that parties in a
business context have the ability to allocate economic risks and remedies as
part of their contractual negotiations. That premise does not exist here.
Moreover, I cannot subscribe to the majority's view that the defective
concrete has not damaged "other property" in the form of the houses'
individual components. . . .

SHAW, JUSTICE, concurring and dissenting . . .

While I agree with the majority opinion that parties who have freely
bargained and entered a contract relative to a particular subject matter
should be bound by the terms of that contract including the distribution of
loss, I feel that the theory is stretched when it is used to deny a cause of
action to an innocent third party who the defendant knew or should have
known would be injured by the tortious conduct. Toppino knew that the
concrete that was the subject matter of the bargain between Toppino and
the general contractor would be incorporated into homes that would be
bought and occupied by innocent third parties.

When the concrete proved to be contaminated, damages were not limited to simply the loss of concrete; innocent third parties suffered various degrees of damage to structures using the concrete. In my mind, the economic loss theory was never intended to defeat a tort cause of action that would otherwise lie for damages caused to a third party by a defective product.

NOTES

1. *Tort or contract: the minority view and intermediate views.* The narrow definition of physical damages in *Casa Clara* has been followed in other cases. Adams-Arapahoe School District No. 28-J v. GAF Corp., 959 F.2d 868, 872 (10th Cir. 1992), refused to allow the plaintiff to recover the cost of removal for asbestos that posed no immediate risk of harm. Blahd v. Richard B. Smith, Inc., 108 P.3d 996 (Idaho 2005), held that the economic loss rule prevented recovery for the settling of a house built on a bad foundation.

The harder question posed by *Casa Clara* is to explain why the logic of contract applies only to economic losses but not personal injury or property damage. Thus, if contractual solutions bind parties for economic losses of $1,000,000, why do they break down for physical damage worth $1,000? Does it make a difference if the transactions are between merchants? With consumers? Conversely, if the bargaining impediments for physical damage justify overriding disclaimers for liability for physical injury, then why not for economic loss? Peters, J., dissenting in *Seely*, 403 P.2d 145, 153-154, has so argued:

> Given the rationale of Greenman v. Yuba Power Products, Inc., it cannot properly be held that plaintiff may not recover the value of his truck and his lost profits on the basis of strict liability. The nature of the damage sustained by the plaintiff is immaterial, so long as it proximately flowed from the defect. What *is* important is not the nature of the damage but the relative roles played by the parties to the purchase contract and the nature of their transaction. . . .
>
> In *Greenman* we allowed recovery for "personal injury" damages. It is well established that such an award may include compensation for past loss of time and earnings due to the injury, for loss of future earning capacity, and for increased living expenses caused by the injury. There is no logical distinction between these losses and the losses suffered by plaintiff here. All involve economic loss, and all proximately arise out of the purchase of a defective product. I find it hard to understand how one might, for example, award a traveling salesman lost earnings if a defect in his car causes his *leg* to break in an accident but deny that salesman his lost earnings if the defect instead disables only his *car* before any accident occurs. The losses are exactly the same; the chains of causation are slightly different, but both

are "proximate." Yet the majority would allow recovery under strict liability in the first situation but not in the second. This, I submit, is arbitrary.

Notwithstanding these objections, the economic loss rule in *Casa Clara* represents the majority position in the United States, and controls in admiralty cases as well. Thus, in East River Steamship Corp. v. Transamerica Delaval, Inc., 476 U.S. 858 (1986), the Court refused to allow a tort action against the manufacturer of turbine engines that malfunctioned once installed into oil-transporting supertankers. More recently, however, in Saratoga Fishing Co. v. J.M. Martinac & Co., 520 U.S. 875 (1997), the Court treated the loss of "extra equipment (a skiff, a fishing net, spare parts) added by the initial user after the first sale and then resold as part of the ship" as "other property" for which an action in tort was appropriate. Justice Breyer argued that the contractual remedy was ineffective in the context of resale after initial use "because, as other courts have suggested, the Subsequent User does not contract directly with the Manufacturer (or distributor)." In 2-J Corporation v. Tice, 126 F.3d 539, 544 (3d Cir. 1997), the court, predicting Pennsylvania law, relied on *Saratoga Fishing* to allow plaintiff to recover for the goods that were damaged when defendant's warehouse collapsed. But in Seal-Land Service, Inc. v. General Electric Co., 134 F.3d 149 (3d Cir. 1998), defective replacement GE engine rods installed in a GE engine were treated as part of the "integrated" original product, since purchasers of the original product are "aware" of the need for routine replacements. What if a different manufacturer supplied the replacement rod?

In Gunkel v. Renovations, Inc., 822 N.E.2d 150, 155-156 (Ind. 2005), the defendant installed a stone and masonry exterior to plaintiff's preexisting home. The work proved defective and caused extensive damage to the structure and furnishings within the house. The court refused to let the economic loss doctrine bar plaintiff's tort action. "If a component is sold to the first user as a part of the finished product, the consequences of its failure are fully within the rationale of the economic loss doctrine. It therefore is not 'other property.' But property acquired separately from the defective good or service is 'other property,' whether or not it is, or is intended to be, incorporated into the same physical object." In other words, the cases that have invoked the economic loss doctrine "have typically involved claims by a first user of a finished product that includes a component supplied by the defendant where the purchaser had no dealings with the defendant." The scope of the economic loss doctrine was also limited in Indemnity Insurance Co. of North America v. American Aviation, Inc., 891 So. 2d 532, 534 (Fla. 2004). The defendant had negligently maintained and serviced the landing gear of an airplane that the plaintiff subsequently purchased. The Court held that "[b]ecause the defendant in this case is neither a manufacturer nor distributor of a product, and the parties are not in privity of contract, this negligence action is not barred by the economic loss rule." If the original owner could not sue under contract, why is that defense not available to a subsequent purchaser?

The Third Restatement follows the majority position. Section 1 limits the scope of the Restatement to "harms to persons or property" and these are defined in §21 to include only "the plaintiff's property other than the defective product itself." RTT:PL §21(a) states that cases of "'pure economic loss' are more appropriately assigned to contract law and the remedies set forth in Articles 2 and 2A of the Uniform Commercial Code. When the Code governs a claim, its provisions regarding such issues as statutes of limitation, privity, notice of claim, and disclaimer ordinarily govern the litigation." *Id.*, comment *a*.

2. *Express warranties in physical injury cases.* In most express warranty cases, the defendant invokes contract disclaimers to limit the scope of liability. Occasionally, however, the plaintiff seeks to sue on express warranty theories when the defendant has made a specific undertaking, without incorporating into the contract any limitation on consequential damages. In Hauter v. Zogarts, 534 P.2d 377 (Cal. 1975), the defendant sold a "Golfing Gizmo" consisting of a golf ball attached to a cotton and elastic cord. The gizmo was supposed to allow the user to improve his swing without risking physical injury. The defendant's literature urged the user to "drive the ball with full power" and further stated: "COMPLETELY SAFE BALL WILL NOT HIT PLAYER." Plaintiff, a 13-year-old boy, struck the ball at an inopportune angle and was struck as the ball came back. The court upheld his claim for breach of express warranty and misrepresentation, rejecting the defendant's arguments that the statements made were simple "puffing" and that the device — designed for learners — was warranted as safe only for experienced or skilled golf players.

Section 2-313 of the Uniform Commercial Code provides:

> (1) Express warranties by the seller are created as follows:
> (a) Any affirmation of fact or promise made by the seller to the buyer which relates to the goods and becomes part of the basis of the bargain creates an express warranty that the goods shall conform to the affirmation or promise.
> (b) Any description of the goods which is made part of the basis of the bargaining creates an express warranty that the goods shall conform to the description. . . .

Hauter turned on the proper interpretation of the "basis of the bargain" language, which, as Tobriner, J., noted, was subject to two possible interpretations. The more modest view holds that the language "merely shifts the burden of proving non-reliance to the seller." The more radical view holds that the language "eliminates the concept of reliance altogether." Tobriner, J., did not choose between these two positions because the plaintiff could recover under either test given that he "read and relied upon defendants' representation." Which view is preferable?

3. *Tort or warranty: the statute of limitations.* Claims for breach of warranty are barred by the statute of limitations, which under U.C.C. §2-725 runs four years from the date of sale. In contrast, the tort statute of limitations runs at the earliest from the date of the injury and in most jurisdictions only from the date at which the plaintiff has discovered, or through the exercise of reasonable diligence could have discovered, that injury. Today the tort rule trumps the U.C.C. The court in Victorson v. Bock Laundry Machine Co., 335 N.E.2d 275, 279 (N.Y. 1975), opted for the tort approach on the ground that "it is all but unthinkable that a person should be time-barred from prosecuting a cause of action before he ever had one." In the course of its opinion, the court observed: "One can observe that while passage of time may work a deterioration of the manufacturer's capability to defend, by similar token it can be expected to complicate the plaintiff's problem of proving, as he must, that the alleged defect existed at the time the product left the manufacturer's plant. In any event this consideration, of varying weight from case to case, cannot be accorded such significance as to dictate the outcome."

The concern with long-lived products that cause damage long after their initial sale has led many states to adopt so-called statutes of repose. In 2005, Ohio passed the Tort Reform Act (SB 80), which contains a ten-year "statute of repose" (O.R.C. §2305.131) for architects, engineers and builders. The Pennsylvania version of the statute, for example, provides, with minor exceptions, that any action "brought against any person lawfully performing or furnishing the design, planning, supervision or observation of construction, or construction of any improvement to real property must be commenced within twelve years after completion of construction of such improvement to recover damages . . . " 42 Pa. Cons. Stat. §5536(a) (1981 & Supp. 2007). In McConnaughey v. Building Components, Inc., 637 A.2d 1331, 1334 (Pa. 1994), trusses manufactured and supplied by defendant in 1970 for the construction of plaintiff's barn collapsed in 1986, killing 37 dairy cows. Defendant sought refuge under the statute. Papadakos, J., concluded:

> We find that the clear and unambiguous language of the statute of repose establishes that a manufacturer who does nothing other than supply a defective product which is later incorporated into an improvement to real property by others is not within the purview of the statute. . . . The Pennsylvania statute of repose was not intended to apply to manufacturers and suppliers of products, but only to the kinds of economic actors who perform acts of "individual expertise" akin to those commonly thought to be performed by builders.

Indiana Code §34-20-3-1(b) bars all product liability suits for injuries sustained more than ten years after the seller delivers it to its "initial user or consumer." In McIntosh v. Melroe Co., 729 N.E.2d 972 (Ind. 2000), the court sustained this provision against various constitutional challenges by holding that it was "rationally related to the General Assembly's reasonable determination that, in the vast majority of cases, failure of products over ten years old is due to wear and tear or other causes not the fault of the manu-facturer . . ." Why does this rationale not apply to the Pennsylvania statute as well?

At the federal level, the General Aviation Revitalization Act of 1994, Pub. L. No. 103-298, 49 U.S.C. §40101 (2000), creates an 18-year statute of repose designed to breathe life into a dormant general aviation industry. The protection so afforded extends only to the manufacturer "in its capacity as a manufacturer," thereby excluding from coverage subsequent services and maintenance. Nor does the statute's protection apply when (1) the manufacturer knowingly misrepresented or deliberately concealed relevant information to the FAA on a design feature or component that was "causally related" to the claimant's harm; (2) the injured person "is a pas-senger for purposes of receiving treatment for a medical or other emer-gency"; (3) the injured party is not on board the aircraft at the time of the accident; or (4) the action is for breach of an express warranty.

4. Limitations on damages in express warranties. In Collins v. Uniroyal, Inc., 315 A.2d 16 (N.J. 1974), the defendant tire company sold its Royal Master Tire under a guarantee against "blowouts, cuts, bruises, and similar injury rendering the tire unserviceable," covering the tires as long as they were not "punctured or abused." The guarantee went on to exclude, in italics, all liability for "consequential damage," obligating the tire company only to repair or replace the tire. The decedent was killed in an unexplained tire blowout, and plaintiff's tort recovery was blocked by the inability to identify any tire defect. The court, however, allowed the plaintiff an action for full damages on the warranty provision, holding the defendant to the warranty provided in the first clause of the guarantee but denying it the benefit of the limitation of liability contained in the italicized clause.

The court relied in part upon U.C.C. §2-719, which provides: "Conse-quential damages may be limited or excluded unless the limitation or exclusion is unconscionable. Limitation of consequential damages for in-jury to the person in the case of consumer goods is prima facie uncon-scionable, but limitation of damages where the loss is commercial is not." What is the force of the words "prima facie unconscionable"? Should the presumption be overridden here given that Uniroyal had no obligation to provide any comprehensive guarantee for its product at all? For criticism of *Collins* and of the general unconscionability doctrine, see Epstein, Un-conscionability: A Critical Reappraisal, 18 J.L. & Econ. 293 (1975).

3.   *Proper Defendants under Section 402A*

Cafazzo v. Central Medical Health Services, Inc.
668 A.2d 521 (Pa. 1995)

MONTEMURO, J. In this case of first impression, we are presented with the question of whether a hospital and a physician can be held subject to strict liability under the Restatement of Torts (Second) §402A, for defects in a product incidental to the provision of medical services.

In 1986, appellant Albert Cafazzo underwent surgery for implantation of a mandibular prosthesis. In 1992, some time after it was discovered that this device was defective, a complaint was filed against appellees, the physician who performed the surgery and the hospital where the operation took place, claiming that "all defendants sell, provide or use certain prosthetic devices," and that they should be held strictly liable as having "provided, sold or otherwise placed in the stream of commerce products manufactured by Vitek, Inc., known as Proplast TMJ Implants." The complaint alleged that the prosthesis was defectively designed, unsafe for its intended use, and lacked any warning necessary in order to ensure safety. . . .

Whether appellees are sellers for the purposes of 402A is the central issue in this matter, and, therefore, appellants' assertion that appellees are in fact, sellers, need not be accepted out of hand. . . .

This Court finds that the answer to the initial question is a negative, and further holds that even if appellees could be shown to have "marketed" the prothesis, strict liability does not apply.

[The Court sets out §402A.]

While we do not slavishly adhere to the language of 402A, the rule enunciated there, as with other non-statutory declarations, is a common law pronouncement by the court, which "always retains the right and the duty to test the reason behind a common law rule in determining the applicability of such a rule to the facts before it." . . .

In this instance, the manufacturer is in bankruptcy, and unable to sustain liability. Thus, an alternative, and solvent, payor was sought. All other considerations were subordinated to this objective, hence the unequivocal necessity, in appellants' view, for appellees to be designated as sellers irrespective of the actual facts of this matter. However, to ignore the ancillary nature of the association of product with activity is to posit surgery, or indeed any medical service requiring the use of a physical object, as a marketing device for the incorporated object. This is tantamount to deciding that the surgical skills necessary for the implantation of, e.g., mandibular prostheses, are an adjunct to the sale of the implants. Moreover, under such a theory, no product of which a patient in any medical setting is the ultimate consumer, from CT scanners to cotton balls, could escape the assignment of strict liability. Clearly, the relationship of hospital and/or doctor to patients is not dictated by the distribution of such products, even if there is some surcharge on the price of the product. As the New York Court of Appeals has aptly stated,

> Concepts of purchase and sale cannot be separately attached to the healing materials . . . supplied by the hospital for a price as part of the medical services. That the property or title to certain items of medical material may be transferred, so to speak, from the hospital to the patient during the course of medical treatment does not serve to make such a transaction a sale. "Sale" and "transfer" are not synonymous, and not every transfer of personal property constitutes a sale.

The thrust of the inquiry is thus not on whether a separate consideration is charged for the physical material used in the exercise of medical skill, but what service is performed to restore or maintain the patient's health. The determinative question becomes not what is being charged, but what is being done. See Hoff v. Zimmer, 746 F. Supp. 872 (W.D. Wis. 1990) (strict liability not applied to hospital for failure of hip prosthesis); Easterly v. HSP of Texas, Inc., 772 S.W.2d 211 (Tex. Ct. App. 1989); . . . Magrine v. Krasnica, 250 A.2d 129 (N.J. 1969) (strict liability not applied to dentist whose drill broke while in use on patient).

The cases cited above have been labeled by some the exponents of a "service exception" to 402A. However, the very term "service exception" is misleading, since it presupposes that the distinction drawn where medical personnel/hospitals are involved is an artificial one. The cases, however, make clear that provision of medical services is regarded as qualitatively different from the sale of products, and, rather than being an exception to 402A, is unaffected by it. . . .

In this connection, it must be noted that the "seller" need not be engaged solely in the business of selling products such as the defective one to be held strictly liable. An example supporting this proposition appears in comment *f* of the Restatement (Second) of Torts, §402A and concerns the owner of a motion picture theater who offers edibles such as popcorn and candy for sale to movie patrons. The analogue to the instant case is valid in one respect only: both the candy and the TMJ implant are ancillary to the primary activity, viewing a film or undergoing surgery respectively. However, beyond that any comparison is specious. A movie audience is free to purchase or not any food items on offer, and regardless of which option is exercised the primary activity is unaffected. On the other hand, while the implant was incidental to the surgical procedure here, it was a necessary adjunct to the treatment administered, as were the scalpel used to make the incision, and any other material objects involved in performing the operation, all of which fulfill a particular role in provision of medical service, the primary activity. [The court then addresses the policy arguments for strict liability in this context.]

The test was posited by this Court in Francioni v. Gibsonia Trucking Corp., 372 A.2d 736 (Pa. 1977), to determine whether a particular supplier of products, whose status as a supplier is already determined, is to be held liable for damages caused by defects in the products supplied. It was first concluded that a lessor of hauling equipment could properly be considered a supplier after the application of a four part inquiry, which focuses initially on which members of the marketing chain are available for redress; then asks whether imposition of liability would serve as an incentive to safety; whether the supplier is in a better position than the consumer to prevent the circulation of defective products; and, finally, whether the supplier can distribute the cost of compensation for injuries by charging for it in his business. . . .

First, as to the availability of some entity for redress, medical personnel and hospitals are already subject to liability, albeit only where the quality or quantity of the services they provide may be called into question. It is perfectly reasonable to assume, for example, that a physician or hospital possesses the necessary skill and expertise to select a product for use in medical treatment which is fit for its intended purpose. An error of choice might indeed be attributed to negligence or ignorance. However, no allegation has been made that the selection of the Vitek TMJ was made either carelessly or intentionally despite knowledge of its defects. To assign liability for no reason other than the ability to pay damages is inconsistent with our jurisprudence. Where the liability is sought to be imposed on a party which is not a seller under 402A, such liability would indeed be assigned for no reason at all.

Next comes the matter of whether applying strict liability would provide an incentive to safety. As the Superior Court correctly pointed out, the safety of the product depends on the judgment of those connected to the research, development, manufacture, marketing and sale of the product. Moreover, the safety testing and licensing for use of medical devices is a responsibility specifically undertaken by the federal government. Therefore, imposing liability for a poorly designed or manufactured product on the hospitals and doctors who use them on the assurances of the FDA is highly unlikely to effect changes of this sort. Again, selection of the wrong product becomes a matter of professional negligence for which recovery is available.

As to the related matter of restricting circulation of defective products, appellees and those similarly situated have no control over distribution. In Musser v. Vilsmeier Auction Co., Inc., 562 A.2d 279 (Pa. 1989), this Court noted that the "[control] factor implies the existence of some ongoing relationship with the manufacturer from which some financial advantage inures to the benefit of the latter and which confers some degree of influence on the [putative seller.]" 562 A.2d at 282.

The influence described is that of the putative seller, i.e., doctor/hospital, on the manufacturing process. However, in finding the relationship between auctioneer and product too tenuous to justify assignment of liability, the *Musser* Court notes that the catalogue of items for sale listed more than ninety different tractors, for each of which the auctioneer would have to be held strictly liable were 402A applied in the auction context. The list is easily comparable to the many items employed in surgery, which includes but is not limited to surgical instruments, medical devices such as the implant, anesthesia machine and accoutrements, drugs, bandages and dressings, surgical apparel and operating suite furniture, such as the table on which the procedure is performed. . . .

The fourth question posed is whether the supplier of the product can distribute the cost of compensating for injuries resulting from defects by spreading the charges therefor. The Superior Court, in addressing this element in conjunction with redress for potential plaintiffs, notes that the only considerations for extending strict liability, ability to pay plaintiffs and ability to charge others, would result in absolute rather than strict liability, and further observed that relying on cost factors alone without a logical basis would confine the focus of the 402A principle to the search for a deep pocket. The net effect of this cost spreading would further endanger the already beleaguered health care system. As a practical matter costs would merely be absorbed by the insurers of physicians and hospitals, whose charges would reflect the increase in policy rates without corresponding improvement to any aspect of the health care system. Rather, research and innovation in medical equipment and treatment would be inhibited. . . . In short, medical services are distinguished by factors which make them significantly different in kind from the retail marketing enterprise at which 402A is directed. . . .

[Affirmed.]

[The dissenting opinion of Cappy, J., is omitted.]

NOTES

1. *Sales v. services.* The Third Restatement follows in the footsteps of the Second by holding that "[s]ervices, even when provided commercially, are not products," RTT:PL §19(b), including those services that are designed to inspect, repair, and maintain machinery of the original product seller. A replacement part therefore is subject to product liability, but its installation is not.

The greatest difficulty in this area arises in the proper classification of hybrid transactions. In Murphy v. E.R. Squibb & Sons, Inc., 710 P.2d 247 (Cal. 1985), Mosk, J., held that a pharmacist who filled a prescription for DES was engaged in the provision of a service and not the sale of a product in light of the "stringent educational and professional requirements for obtaining and retaining a license."

> A pharmacist must not only use skill and care in accurately filling and labelling a prescribed drug, but he must be aware of problems regarding the medication, and on occasion he provides doctors as well as patients with advice regarding such problems. In counseling patients, he imparts the same kind of information as would a medical doctor about the effects of the drugs prescribed. A key factor is that the pharmacist who fills a prescription is in a different position from the ordinary retailer because he cannot offer a prescription for sale except by order of the doctor. In this respect, he is providing a service to the doctor and acting as an extension of the doctor in the same sense as a technician who takes an X-ray or analyzes a blood sample on a doctor's order. . . .
>
> If pharmacies were held strictly liable for the drugs they dispense, some of them, to avoid liability, might restrict availability by refusing to dispense drugs which pose even a potentially remote risk of harm, although such medications may be essential to the health or even the survival of patients. Furthermore, in order to assure that a pharmacy receives the maximum protection in the event of suit for defects in a drug, the pharmacist may select the more expensive product made by an established manufacturer when he has a choice of several brands of the same drug.

For a modern affirmation of this position see Madison v. American Home Products Corp., 595 S.E.2d 493 (2004). In light of these obligations, should the pharmacist be subject to a duty to warn? See *infra* at 806.

2. Liability of retailers and distributors. Product liability law does, however, uniformly apply to all ordinary product retailers and distributors within the initial chain of distribution. The rationale for this position was first stated by Traynor, J., in Vandermark v. Ford Motor Co., 391 P.2d 168, 171-172 (Cal. 1964), holding an automobile dealer strictly liable for product defects.

> Retailers like manufacturers are engaged in the business of distributing goods to the public. They are an integral part of the overall producing and marketing enterprise that should bear the cost of injuries resulting from defective products. In some cases the retailer may be the only member of that enterprise reasonably available to the injured plaintiff. In other cases the retailer himself may play a substantial part in insuring that the product is safe or may be in a position to exert pressure on the manufacturer to that end; the retailer's strict liability thus serves as an added incentive to safety. Strict liability on the manufacturer and retailer alike affords maximum protection to the injured plaintiff and works no injustice to the defendants, for they can adjust the costs of such protection between them in the course of their continuing business relationship. . . .

Why doesn't the rationale in *Vandermark* require liability in *Murphy*?

By analogy to retailers, product liability has been extended to the builders of mass-produced homes, Schipper v. Levitt & Sons, Inc., 207 A.2d 314 (N.J. 1965); to wholesalers and distributors, Barth v. B.F. Goodrich Tire Co., 71 Cal. Rptr. 306 (Cal. App. 1968); and to lessors and bailors of personal property, Cintrone v. Hertz Truck Leasing & Rental Service, 212 A.2d 769 (N.J. 1965), and Price v. Shell Oil Co., 466 P.2d 722 (Cal. 1970).

3. Beyond retailers and distributors. Other cases have also grappled with the identification of product sellers under §402A. Shaffer v. Victoria Station, Inc., 588 P.2d 233 (Wash. 1978), applied §402A to injuries caused by a broken wine glass at a restaurant dinner, brushing aside the "gloomy view" that similar products liability actions would often be brought against "busboys and waiters" and restaurants generally for all manner of ills. Kosters v. Seven-Up Co., 595 F.2d 347 (6th Cir. 1979), classified a franchisor as a seller liable in tort for "floating" its products into the stream of commerce, because it "exercised control over the 'type, style, size and design' of the carton in which its product was to be marketed."

The Third Restatement follows the lead of the Second. The product sellers include "nonmanufacturing sellers and distributors such as wholesalers and retailers," RTT:PL §1 comment *e*, even when they act as mere conduits that do nothing to make the products dangerous. In addition, §20 of the Third Restatement treats commercial lessors and bailors as product sellers, such that a dealer will be held to the same rules when he allows a test drive as when he sells a car. §20, comment *f*. Section 2, comment *o*, acknowledges that nonmanufacturing sellers "often are not in a good position feasibly to adopt safer product designs or better instructions or warnings." But it reiterates that nonmanufacturing sellers are nonetheless subject to the same standards applicable to manufacturers: "As long as the plaintiff establishes that the product was defective when it left the hands of a given seller in the distributive chain, liability will attach to that seller." §2, comment *c*. "Thus, strict liability is imposed on a wholesale or retail seller who neither knew nor should have known of the relevant risks, nor was in a position to have taken action to avoid them, so long as a predecessor in the chain of distribution could have acted reasonably to avoid the risks." §2, comment *o*. Should there be *any* liability if the retailer has no control over the manufacture, design, or warnings associated with a given product? What if the retailer remains in business after the manufacturer has become insolvent?

4. Casual sellers. Both Restatements insulate the casual seller from liability for defective products. In Sprung v. MTR Ravensburg, 788 N.E.2d 620, 623 (N.Y. 2003), that exception was not available to the defendant who provided General Electric a custom-made sheet metal for a retractable floor that failed, causing injuries to its plaintiff employee. Kaye, J., rejected the argument that a strict liability regime did not apply, with only some uneasiness:

> True, when a custom fabricator builds a product to suit a customer's specific needs, there may well be less informational disparity between the producer and the user than in the mass production setting. Such disparity is, however, only one of the several policy reasons underpinning strict liability. Like other manufacturers, custom fabricators engaged in the regular course of their business hold themselves out as having expertise in manufacturing their custom products, have the opportunity and incentive to ensure safety in the process of making those products, and are better able to shoulder the costs of injuries caused by defective products than injured consumers or users.

The court then distinguished Sukljian v. Ross & Son Co., 503 N.E.2d 1358 (N.Y. 1986) on the ground that "a third-party defendant's sale of a surplus 11-year-old mill on an 'as-is' basis was a casual or occasional sale, not subject to a claim of strict products liability, because it was wholly incidental to the seller's regular business." When the defendant's product is built to customer specifications, who is in the best position to avert the harm?

5. *Used and reconditioned products.* The scope of product liability law has also been litigated with respect to the sale of used or reconditioned products. Often the sellers of these products do not purchase them from the original manufacturer, but obtain them in the open market at the request of a particular client. In Tillman v. Vance Equipment Co., 596 P.2d 1299, 1303-1304 (Or. 1979), the plaintiff was injured by a 24-year-old used crane that his employer had purchased from the defendant, a used equipment dealer, on an "as is" basis. As with *Sukljian,* the court refused to apply the strict liability rule of §402A to this defendant:

> We conclude that holding every dealer in used goods responsible regardless of fault for injuries caused by defects in his goods would not only affect the prices of used goods; it would work a significant change in the very nature of used goods markets. Those markets, generally speaking, operate on the apparent understanding that the seller, even though he is in the business of selling such goods, makes no particular representation about their quality simply by offering them for sale. If a buyer wants some assurance of quality, he typically either bargains for it in the specific transaction or seeks out a dealer who routinely offers it (by, for example, providing a guarantee, limiting his stock of goods to those of a particular quality, advertising that his used goods are specially selected, or in some other fashion). The flexibility of this kind of market appears to serve legitimate interests of buyers as well as sellers. . . .
>
> As to the risk-reduction aspect of strict products liability, the position of the used-goods dealer is normally entirely outside the original chain of distribution of the product. As a consequence, we conclude, any risk reduction which would be accomplished by imposing strict liability on the dealer in used goods would not be significant enough to justify our taking

that step. The dealer in used goods generally has no direct relationship with either manufacturers or distributors. Thus, there is no ready channel of communication by which the dealer and the manufacturer can exchange information about possible dangerous defects in particular product lines or about actual and potential liability claims.

In Crandell v. Larkin & Jones Appliance Co., 334 N.W.2d 31 (S.D. 1983), the court accepted *Tillman* for simple sellers of used products, but imposed strict liability on sellers who rebuilt or reconditioned those products. Should the rule apply to defects in the original design or just defects in the reconditioning?

For the complex provisions of the Third Restatement, see RTT:PL §8, which, roughly speaking, follows the earlier law by limiting liability of the seller of used products to those defects that it created, or those created by predecessors in the same commercial chain of distribution. The Third Restatement also requires the reseller of used products to comply with all applicable regulations in force at the time of resale. *Id.* §8(d).

6. *Successor liability.* One question, much litigated in recent years, has been whether a corporation that acquires either the assets or the shares of a separate product seller can be sued for its predecessor's torts after the liquidation of the original corporation. The leading case in support of successor liability is Ray v. Alad Corp., 560 P.2d 3, 9 (Cal. 1977), in which the new defendant corporation simply took over the business of the prior corporation and exploited its good will without any change in operation or control. The court rested its case for successor liability on three separate grounds:

> (1) the virtual destruction of the plaintiff's remedies against the original manufacturer caused by the successor's acquisition of the business, (2) the successor's ability to assume the original manufacturer's risk-spreading role, and (3) the fairness of requiring the successor to assume a responsibility for defective products that was a burden necessarily attached to the original manufacturer's good will being enjoyed by the successor in the continued operation of the business.

Ray was not followed in Leannais v. Cincinnati, Inc., 565 F.2d 437, 439 (7th Cir. 1977), in which the management of the selling corporation had nothing to do with the operation of the new business after the sale. The court held that the transaction did not fall within any of the four exceptions to Wisconsin's general rule of no successor liability:

> (1) when the purchasing corporation expressly or impliedly agreed to assume the selling corporation's liability; (2) when the transaction amounts to a consolidation or merger of the purchaser and seller corporations; (3) when the purchaser corporation is merely a continuation of the seller corporation; or (4) when the transaction is entered into fraudulently to escape liability for such obligations.

These exceptions are now incorporated in RTT:PL §12.

In Nissen Corp. v. Miller, 594 A.2d 564, 568 (Md. 1991), the Maryland Supreme Court also refused to extend successor liability beyond these four exceptions in a 1981 asset purchase by Nissen Corporation, the buyer, from American Tredex, the seller. "[T]he contract expressly excluded assumption of liability for injuries arising from any product previously sold by American Tredex." American Tredex also agreed to maintain its corporate existence for a five-year period after the sale. The asset price reflected their full fair market value. In October 1986, the plaintiff was injured on a treadmill purchased from American Tredex, which had liquidated earlier that year. The court rejected the plaintiff's argument that the successor had to take the bitter with the sweet, concluding that the current rules "have functioned well to balance the rights of creditors and successor corporations by preserving traditional principles of corporate law and promoting the free alienability of business assets while maintaining adequate protection for the interests of consumers and creditors from fraudulent and unjust corporate transactions."

The rule in *Nissen* also has an efficiency justification. Requiring a successor corporation to indefinitely assume the tort obligations of its seller would kill off deals when the seller's contingent tort liabilities exceed the value of its assets. In that event, the selling corporation could either liquidate its business — thus leaving all its potential tort claimants in the lurch — or it could continue to run the business, but probably less efficiently than its would-be purchaser. For a proposal that all corporations wishing to go out of business by either sale or liquidation be required to get asset insurance, see Green, Successor Liability: The Superiority of Statutory Reform to Protect Products Liability Claimants, 72 Cornell L. Rev. 17 (1986). For a defense of using successor liability to induce corporate purchasers to exact greater diligence in their corporation purchases, see Cupp, Redesigning Successor Liability, 1999 Ill. L. Rev. 845 (1999).

SECTION D. PRODUCT DEFECTS

1. *Manufacturing Defects*

American Law Institute, Restatement (Third) of the Law of Products Liability

§3. CIRCUMSTANTIAL EVIDENCE SUPPORTING INFERENCE OF PRODUCT DEFECT

It may be inferred that the harm sustained by the plaintiff was caused by a product defect existing at the time of sale or distribution, without proof of a specific defect, when the incident that harmed the plaintiff:

(a) was of a kind that ordinarily occurs as a result of product defect; and

(b) was not, in the particular case, solely the result of causes other than product defect existing at the time of sale or distribution.

Speller v. Sears, Roebuck and Co.
790 N.E.2d 252 (N.Y. 2003)

GRAFFEO, J. In this products liability case, defendants — a product manufacturer and retailer — were granted summary judgment dismissing plaintiffs' complaint. Because we conclude that plaintiffs raised a triable issue of fact concerning whether a defective refrigerator caused the fire that resulted in plaintiffs' injuries, we reverse and reinstate the complaint against these defendants.

Plaintiffs' decedent Sandra Speller died in a house fire that also injured her seven-year-old son. It is undisputed that the fire originated in the kitchen. Plaintiffs commenced this action against Sears, Roebuck & Co., Whirlpool Corporation and the property owner alleging negligence, strict products liability and breach of warranty. Relevant to this appeal, plaintiffs asserted that the fire was caused by defective wiring in the refrigerator, a product manufactured by Whirlpool and sold by Sears.

After discovery, defendants Sears and Whirlpool moved for summary judgment seeking dismissal of the complaint. Relying principally on a report issued by the New York City Fire Marshall, defendants rejected the refrigerator as the source of the fire, instead contending that a stovetop grease fire was the cause of the conflagration. Thus, they argued that their product was outside the chain of causation that resulted in plaintiffs' damages.

In opposition to defendants' motion for summary judgment, plaintiffs submitted excerpts from the depositions of two experts and an affidavit from a third, as well as other materials. Plaintiffs' experts refuted the conclusions reached in the Fire Marshall's report, opining that the fire started in the upper right quadrant of the refrigerator, an area with a concentration of electrical wiring. All three rejected the stove as the source of the fire. Plaintiff also submitted portions of the deposition of a Whirlpool engineer retained as an expert by defendants. Although the engineer disputed that the fire originated in the refrigerator, he acknowledged that a fire would not occur in a refrigerator unless the product was defective. . . .

A party injured as a result of a defective product may seek relief against the product manufacturer or others in the distribution chain if the defect was a substantial factor in causing the injury. . . .

In this case, plaintiffs' theory was that the wiring in the upper right quadrant of the refrigerator was faulty, causing an electrical fire which then spread to other areas of the kitchen and residence. Because that part of the refrigerator had been consumed in the fire, plaintiffs noted that it was impossible to examine or test the wiring to determine the precise nature of the defect. Thus, plaintiffs sought to prove their claim circumstantially by establishing that the refrigerator caused the house fire and therefore did not perform as intended.

New York has long recognized the viability of this circumstantial approach in products liability cases. Indeed its origins can be traced back to Codling v Paglia (298 N.E.2d 622 [(N.Y. 1973)]), where this Court stated that a plaintiff "is not required to prove the specific defect" and that "proof of necessary facts may be circumstantial." In order to proceed in the absence of evidence identifying a specific flaw, a plaintiff must prove that the product did not perform as intended and exclude all other causes for the product's failure that are not attributable to defendants.

In this regard, New York law is consistent with [Restatement (Third) of Torts: Products Liability §3 [1998] which it adopts.]

Of course, if a plaintiff's proof is insufficient with respect to either prong of this circumstantial inquiry, a jury may not infer that the harm was caused by a defective product unless plaintiff offers competent evidence identifying a specific flaw.

Here, in their motion for summary judgment, defendants focused on the second prong of the circumstantial inquiry, offering evidence that the injuries were not caused by their product but by an entirely different instrumentality—a grease fire that began on top of the stove. This was the conclusion of the Fire Marshall who stated during deposition testimony that his opinion was based on his interpretation of the burn patterns in the kitchen, his observation that one of the burner knobs on the stove was in the "on" position, and his conversation with a resident of the home who apparently advised him that the oven was on when the resident placed some food on the stovetop a few hours before the fire.

In order to withstand summary judgment, plaintiffs were required to come forward with competent evidence excluding the stove as the origin of the fire. To meet that burden, plaintiffs offered three expert opinions: the depositions of an electrical engineer and a fire investigator, and the affidavit of a former Deputy Chief of the New York City Fire Department. Each concluded that the fire originated in the refrigerator and not on the stove.

In his extensive deposition testimony, the electrical engineer opined that the fire started in the top-right-rear corner of the refrigerator, an area that housed the air balancing unit, thermostat, moisture control and light control. He stated that the wiring in this part of the appliance had been destroyed in the fire, making it impossible to identify the precise mechanical failure and, thus, he could only speculate as to the specific nature of the defect. He testified that the "most logical probability" was that a bad connection or bad splice to one of the components in that portion of the unit caused the wire to become "red hot" and to ignite the adjacent plastic. He tested the combustibility of the plastic and confirmed that the "plastic lights up very easily, with a single match" and continues to burn like candle wax. The engineer observed that the doors of the refrigerator were "slightly bellied out," indicating they were blown out from the expanding hot gases inside the refrigerator. The wall behind the refrigerator was significantly damaged and the upper right quadrant was burned to such a degree that it was not likely to have been caused by an external fire. Interpreting the burn patterns differently from the Fire Marshall, the electrical engineer found that the cabinets above the stove, although damaged, were not destroyed to the extent he expected to find if there had been a stovetop grease fire.

Plaintiffs' fire investigator similarly opined that the fire originated in the refrigerator's upper right corner, in part basing his conclusion on his observations of the scene three days after the fire and his examination of the appliances. He also interviewed a witness to the fire. He testified that he eliminated the stove as the source of the fire after his examination of that appliance and the cabinets above it. Contrary to the testimony of the Fire Marshall, he observed that all of the burner knobs on the stove were in the same position, either all "off" or all "on." He further examined the burn patterns, noting that if the blaze had been caused by a grease fire on the stove, the cabinets directly above would have been consumed in the fire. Instead, they were merely damaged. He acknowledged that he did not know exactly how the fire started inside the refrigerator but indicated he suspected there had been a poor connection in the wiring that caused the wire to smolder until it ignited the highly combustible foam insulation inside the unit.

The former Deputy Chief of the New York City Fire Department asserted in his affidavit that the "fire damage to the area around the refrigerator when compared to that of the stove clearly shows the longer and heavier burn at the refrigerator," indicating the fire originated there. He also stated that he had ruled out all other possible origins of the fire.

Upon review of these expert depositions and affidavit, we conclude that plaintiffs raised a triable question of fact by offering competent evidence which, if credited by the jury, was sufficient to rebut defendants' alternative cause evidence. In other words, based on plaintiffs' proof, a reasonable jury could conclude that plaintiffs excluded all other causes of the fire.

We therefore disagree with the Appellate Division's characterization of plaintiffs' submissions as equivocal. Plaintiffs' experts consistently asserted that the fire originated in the upper right quadrant of the refrigerator and each contended the stove was not the source of the blaze. Both parties supported their positions with detailed, non-conclusory expert depositions and other submissions which explained the bases for the opinions.

Defendants contend that after they came forward with evidence suggesting an alternative cause of the fire, plaintiffs were foreclosed from establishing a product defect circumstantially but were then required to produce evidence of a specific defect to survive summary judgment. We reject this approach for two reasons. First, such an analysis would allow a defendant who offered minimally sufficient alternative cause evidence in a

products liability case to foreclose a plaintiff from proceeding circumstantially without a jury having determined whether defendant's evidence
should be credited. Second, it misinterprets the court's role in adjudicating
a motion for summary judgment, which is issue identification, not issue
resolution. . . . [P]laintiffs directly rebutted defendants' submissions with
competent proof specifically ruling out the stove as the source of the blaze.
Because a reasonable jury could credit this proof and find that plaintiff
excluded all other causes of the fire not attributable to defendants, this case
presents material issues of fact requiring a trial.

[Reversed.]

NOTES

1. Proof of manufacturing defect. What role, if any, did the decedent or his
mother play in bringing about the fire? Even if the fire started in the refrigerator, did plaintiffs introduce any evidence of a defect in the equipment? If so, was it a construction or a design defect? As should be evident,
the switch from negligence to strict liability in manufacturing defect cases
does not eliminate difficult causal questions. Many of the hardest cases arise
when the plaintiff's conduct occupies an uncertain place in the chain of
causation as is exemplified with long-lived products that receive intensive
and protracted use. In Jagmin v. Simonds Abrasive Co., 211 N.W.2d 810
(Wis. 1973), the plaintiff was injured when struck in the face by a grinding
wheel that broke into pieces while he was operating it. The plaintiff established that the wheel was of the defendant's manufacture. He further testified that he had used the wheel in the proper manner, that he had not
placed undue stress on it, that he had no evidence suggesting that any other
person had used the wheel while he was away from his job, and that the wheel
had several hours of life left at the time the accident took place. The wheel
itself was destroyed after it broke. The trial court refused to allow the case
to go to the jury, ruling that there was insufficient evidence on the question
of "defect." The state supreme court reversed, allowing an "exceedingly
close" case to reach the jury on a modified version of res ipsa loquitur. The
plaintiff's evidence tended to exclude the possibility of any responsible
cause of the injury apart from an original product defect even though that
defect could not be identified. Does the plaintiff's evidence negate the
possibility that the wheel was damaged in shipment or in installation? Does
the plaintiff's evidence explain why the wheel worked as long as it did? Does
Henderson's account of the *MacPherson* facts, *supra* at 736, argue in favor of
requiring a specific identification of a product defect in manufacturing
cases?

See generally Hoffman, Res Ipsa Loquitur and Indeterminate Product
Defects: If They Speak for Themselves, What Are They Saying?, 36 S. Tex.
L. Rev. 353 (1995).

2. Manufacturing defects in food cases. As was evident in *Escola*, food cases were one of the original battlegrounds for a theory of strict liability. In particular, the early common law held the manufacturer strictly liable for any "foreign object" that was found within the food, be it a sliver of tin or some waste impurities from animals. But by the same token, the earlier cases refused to hold manufacturers liable under any theory for substances "natural" to the product served. Thus, the leading case of Mix v. Ingersoll Candy Co., 59 P.2d 144 (Cal. 1936), held that "[b]ones which are natural to the type of meat served cannot legitimately be called a foreign substance, and a consumer who eats meat dishes ought to anticipate and be on his guard against the presence of such bones."

More modern cases have uniformly rejected this approach in favor of a reasonable expectations test. In Schafer v. JLC Food Systems, 695 N.W.2d 570, 575 (Minn. 2005), the plaintiff took a bite from a pumpkin muffin served a defendant's restaurant only to experience a sharp pain in her throat, which later turned into a serious infection. Page, J., wrote:

> Under the Restatement [Third] approach, consumer expectations are based on culturally defined, widely shared standards allowing a seller's liability to be resolved by judges and triers of fact based on their assessment of what consumers have a right to expect from preparation of the food in question. §7 cmt. b . . .
>
> Instead of drawing arbitrary distinctions between foreign and natural substances that caused harm, relying on consumers' reasonable expectations is likely to yield a more equitable result. After all, an unexpected natural object or substance contained in a food product, such as a chicken bone in chicken soup, can cause as much harm as a foreign object or substance, such as a piece of glass in the same soup.

Page, J., next held that the plaintiff could get to the jury even though she could not "present evidence identifying the object that cause the alleged harm," relying again on the strict liability analog to res ipsa loquitur, whereby, as in *Jagmin*, the plaintiff's task is to exclude all other causes of harm. Should this test be adopted in cases of food poisoning that manifest themselves a day after eating in the restaurant?

2. Design Defects

Campo v. Scofield
95 N.E.2d 802, 804 (N.Y. 1951).

FULD, J. If a manufacturer does everything necessary to make the machine function properly for the purpose for which it is designed, if the machine is without any latent defect, and if its functioning creates no danger or peril that is not known to the user, then the manufacturer has satisfied the law's demands. We have not yet reached the state where a manufacturer is under the duty of making a machine accident proof or foolproof. Just as the manufacturer is under no obligation, in order to guard against injury resulting from deterioration, to furnish a machine that will not wear out, so he is under no duty to guard against injury from a patent peril or from a source manifestly dangerous.

To illustrate, the manufacturer who makes, properly and free of defects, an axe or a buzz saw or an airplane with an exposed propeller, is not to be held liable if one using the axe or the buzz saw is cut by it, or if some one working around the airplane comes in contact with the propeller. In such cases, the manufacturer has the right to expect that such persons will do everything necessary to avoid such contact, for the very nature of the article gives notice and warning of the consequences to be expected, of the injuries to be suffered.

2 Harper and James, Torts §28.5
(1956)

The bottom does not logically drop out of a negligence case against the maker when it is shown that the purchaser knew of the dangerous condition. Thus if the product is a carrot-topping machine with exposed moving parts, or an electric clothes wringer dangerous to the limbs of the operator, and if it would be feasible for the maker of the product to install a guard or safety release, it should be a question for the jury whether reasonable care demanded such a precaution, though its absence is obvious. Surely reasonable men might find here a great danger, even to one who knew the condition and since it was so readily avoidable they might find the maker negligent.

Wade, On the Nature of Strict Tort Liability for Products
44 Miss. L.J. 825, 836-837 (1973)

If there is agreement that the determination of whether a product is unreasonably dangerous, or is not duly safe, involves the necessary application of a standard, it will, like the determination of negligence or of strict liability for an abnormally dangerous activity, require the consideration and weighing of a number of factors. I offer here a revised list of factors which seem to me to be of significance in applying the standard.

(1) The usefulness and desirability of the product — its utility to the user and to the public as a whole.

(2) The safety aspects of the product — the likelihood that it will cause injury, and the probable seriousness of the injury.

(3) The availability of a substitute product which would meet the same need and not be as unsafe.

(4) The manufacturer's ability to eliminate the unsafe character of the product without impairing its usefulness or making it too expensive to maintain its utility.

(5) The user's ability to avoid danger by the exercise of care in the use of the product.

(6) The user's anticipated awareness of the dangers inherent in the product and their availability, because of general public knowledge of the obvious condition of the product, or of the existence of suitable warnings or instructions.

(7) The feasibility, on the part of the manufacturer, of spreading the loss by setting the price of the product or carrying liability insurance.

NOTE

Two (or is it three?) views of design defect. The passages quoted above set up the possible approaches to design defect litigation. The open and obvious test of *Campo* dominated the law until the adoption of the (Second) Restatement, in which a design defect was determined by the consumer expectations test. RST §402A, comments *g* and *i*. The influential criticism of Professors Harper and James insisted that a negligence cause of action was not necessarily defeated by the obvious nature of the defect. Professor Wade's influential formulation of the risk-utility standard offers a strict liability version of the relevant cost benefit analysis. All three versions of design defect liability have ebbed and flowed in the past 40 years. The next case deals with the rise of the negligence standard in an important class of design defect cases, those dealing with the crashworthiness of automobiles.

Volkswagen of America, Inc. v. Young
321 A.2d 737 (Md. 1974)

[The decedent had stopped his 1968 Volkswagen Beetle at a red light when he was hit from behind by a 1967 Ford, negligently driven by William Benson. As a result, decedent's car was pushed forward. The seat bracketing pieces and seat adjustment mechanisms broke away from the body of the car. In the ensuing "second collision" the decedent was hurled into the rear of the car and was killed by head and torso injuries sustained on impact. The plaintiff sued Volkswagen in federal district court. She alleged that the Beetle was "defectively designed, manufactured, and marketed with defects which rendered it structurally hazardous, not merchantable, and not fit for the purpose intended" in that its entire seat assembly was "unreasonably vulnerable to separation from the floor upon collision." Pursuant to Maryland's Certification of Questions of Law Act, the district court certified this question to the Maryland Court of Appeals:

> Whether or not, under Maryland law, the definition of the "intended use" of a motor vehicle includes the vehicle's involvement in a collision; and thus in turn, whether a cause of action is stated against the manufacturer or importer of said vehicle in breach of warranty or negligence or absolute liability or misrepresentation by allegations that the design and manufacture of the vehicle unreasonably increased the risk of injury to occupants following a collision not caused by any defect of the vehicle.

The Maryland court answered the question in the affirmative, holding that the "intended use" of an automobile was not only to provide transportation but also reasonably safe transportation, and that the plaintiff's complaint stated a cause of action in negligence under Maryland law.]

ELDRIDGE, J. . . . This is the first case to reach this Court concerning the extent of an automobile manufacturer's liability for a design defect resulting in enhanced injuries in a motor vehicle accident, where the defect did not cause the initial impact or movement of the injured person. Such cases are often called "second collision" cases or "automobile crashworthiness" cases. They differ from other products liability cases involving defective automobiles by the combination of two factors. First, the alleged defect is in the design of the automobile rather than a negligent deviation during the construction or assembly process from the manner in which the vehicle was supposed to be made. The latter is usually called a "construction defect." Second, the defect is not the cause of the initial impact. Typically, the actions of the driver of the car in which the plaintiff is riding, or the actions of the driver of another vehicle, or the actions of some third person, cause an initial disruption or impact which in turn results in the plaintiff's colliding with the interior (or occasionally the exterior) of the car. The plaintiff's collision with the car is the so-called "second collision." The issue of whether the automobile manufacturer has a duty to take reasonable steps to design its vehicles so as to minimize the injuries caused by "second collisions" has engendered much controversy and comment throughout the nation.

The principal case holding that an automobile manufacturer has no duty to design its cars so as to minimize the injuries suffered in automobile accidents is Evans v. General Motors Corporation, 359 F.2d 822 (7th Cir. 1966). The plaintiff [the decedent] in *Evans* was killed when his 1961 Chevrolet station wagon was struck broadside by another car. He claimed that General Motors was negligent in designing the frame of his car, inasmuch as an "X" type frame rather than a box or perimeter type frame was used, contrary to the construction of some other cars. The claim was that an "X" type frame without side rails would not adequately protect occupants during a side impact collision, and that the defendant manufacturer had created an unreasonable risk of serious injury. The trial court, applying Indiana law, dismissed the complaint for failure to state a claim on which relief could be granted, and the dismissal was affirmed by the United States Court of Appeals for the Seventh Circuit. The Court of Appeals held that the critical question was the nature of the manufacturer's duty. It went on to conclude that a manufacturer has a duty only to design a car reasonably fit for its intended purpose, and that "[t]he intended purpose of an automobile does not include its participation in collisions with other objects, despite the manufacturer's ability to foresee the possibility that such collisions may occur. As defendant argues, the defendant also knows that its automobiles may be driven into bodies of water, but it is not suggested that defendant has a duty to equip them with pontoons." (Id. at 825.)

The Court of Appeals for the Seventh Circuit also stated as grounds for its decision that a "manufacturer is not under a duty to make his automobile accident-proof or fool-proof" and that requiring "manufacturers to construct automobiles in which it would be safe to collide . . . [is] a legislative function. . . ."

The seminal case on the other side of the issue is Larsen v. General Motors Corporation, 391 F.2d 495 (8th Cir. 1968). The plaintiff in *Larsen* suffered severe bodily injuries while driving a 1963 Corvair which collided head-on with another car. The impact caused the steering mechanism to thrust forward into the plaintiff's head. The suit against General Motors charged negligence in the design of the steering assembly and the placement of the component parts of the steering assembly into the structure of the car. It was alleged that General Motors was also negligent in not warning the user of this latent condition. The specific defect relied upon by the plaintiff was that the solid steering shaft was so designed as to extend "without interruption from a point 2.7 inches in front of the leading surface of the front tires to a position directly in front of the driver," exposing him "to an unreasonable risk of injury from the rearward displacement of that shaft in the event of a left-of-center head-on collision. So positioned it receives the initial impact of forces generated by a left-of-center head-on collision. The unabsorbed forces of the collision in this area are transmitted directly toward the driver's head, the shaft acting as a spear aimed at a vital part of the driver's anatomy." Id. at 497, n.2. The plaintiff also pointed out that other cars were designed so as to protect against such rearward displacement, in that the steering column did not protrude beyond the forward surface of the front tires. The lower court in *Larsen* granted General Motors' motion for summary judgment on the theory that the manufacturer had no duty to design a vehicle which would protect the plaintiff from injury in a collision. On appeal, the United States Court of Appeals for the Eighth Circuit reversed, holding that the plaintiff had made out a sufficient case for consideration by the jury.

[The court in *Larsen* gave a broad interpretation to "intended use," stating:]

> Automobiles are made for use on the roads and highways in transporting persons and cargo to and from various points. This intended use cannot be carried out without encountering in varying degrees the statistically proved hazard of injury-producing impacts of various types. The manufacturer should not be heard to say that it does not intend its product to be involved in any accident when it can easily foresee and when it knows that the probability over the life of its product is high, that it will be involved in some type of injury-producing accident. . . .

The Court of Appeals concluded that an automobile manufacturer "is under a duty to use reasonable care in the design of its vehicle to avoid subjecting the user to an unreasonable risk of injury in the event of a collision." (Ibid.)

The *Larsen* court then emphasized the limitations of its holding that it was not making automobile manufacturers "insurers"; that it was merely applying common law principles of negligence; that the standard for manufacturers was "reasonable care"; and that an automobile did not have to be absolutely crash-proof but only designed to provide "a reasonably safe vehicle in which to travel." 391 F.2d at 503.* . . .

In our view, Larsen v. General Motors Corporation, *supra*, and the cases following it, are more in accord with traditional negligence principles than Evans v. General Motors Corporation, *supra*. . . .

That the design defect does not cause the initial collision should make no difference if it is a cause of the ultimate injury. Where the injuries to an occupant of a motor vehicle resulted from both the negligence of a driver as well as a negligent condition created by some other entity, this Court has held that both negligent actors may be liable. . . .

In sum, "traditional rules of negligence" lead to the conclusion that an automobile manufacturer is liable for a defect in design which the manufacturer could have reasonably foreseen would cause or enhance injuries on impact, which is not patent or obvious to the user, and which in fact leads to or enhances the injuries in an automobile collision.

The arguments advanced by Volkswagen in the instant case for creating an exception to the application of traditional negligence principles in

---

* The defendant in *Larsen* received a unanimous verdict after a three-week trial, having introduced scientific evidence that the plaintiff had not been hit by the steering column. For a discussion of the expert evidence introduced at trial, see Bowman, Defense of an Auto Design Negligence Case, 10 For the Defense, No. 5, May, 1969. — ED.

"second collision" cases are not persuasive. They are essentially the same reasons set forth by the United States Court of Appeals for the Seventh Circuit in *Evans* and the other cases following *Evans*. Volkswagen's principal arguments are: (1) that the intended purpose of an automobile is transportation and does not include its participation in collisions; (2) that "a manufacturer is not required to produce accident-proof or injury-proof cars"; (3) that manufacturers are not insurers; and (4) that "[d]esign requirements are a legislative, not a judicial function. . . ."

While the intended purpose of an automobile may not be to participate in collisions, the intended purpose includes providing a reasonable measure of safety when, inevitably, collisions do occur. For many years automobiles have been equipped with safety glass, bumpers, windshield wipers, etc. More recently, and largely as a result of governmental action, automobiles are equipped with additional safety devices such as seat belts, shoulder harnesses, padded dashboards, padded visors, non-protruding knobs, etc. Frequent collisions are foreseeable, and the intended purpose of all of these parts of the vehicle is to afford reasonable safety when those collisions occur.

The arguments that there is no duty to design "accident-proof" or "injury-proof" vehicles, and that automobile manufacturers are not insurers, are "straw men." No case has ever held that an automobile manufacturer must design an "accident-proof" or "injury-proof" vehicle or that the manufacturer is an insurer. Concerning two of the examples most often used by the advocates of non-liability for design defects, no one has suggested that an automobile must be designed to withstand a high speed head-on collision with a truck or to float if it leaves the road and goes into a body of water. . . .

The standard to be applied is the traditional one of reasonableness.

The contention that the design of automobiles involves a legislative function and not a judicial function, similarly furnishes no sound reason for exempting automobile "second collision" cases from the normal principles of tort liability. Legislative or administrative requirements that persons or businesses conduct their operations in a particular manner, and adhere to specified standards, have never been viewed as supplanting tort liability. On the contrary, such statutory or regulatory requirements are deemed to furnish standards by which courts or juries determine, along with other circumstances, whether or not conduct is negligent. Failure to adhere to those standards is evidence of negligence for the court or jury to consider. Moreover, the most significant legislation dealing with motor vehicle safety standards makes it clear that Congress did not view the question of safe motor vehicle design as solely a legislative problem. The National Traffic and Motor Vehicle Safety Act of 1966 specifically provided that "Compliance with any Federal motor vehicle safety standard issued under this subchapter does not exempt any person from any liability under common law." 15 U.S.C. 1397(c). . . .

In addition, there can be no recovery if the danger inherent in the particular design was obvious or patent to the user of the vehicle. . . .

[The court then refuses to apply the strict liability theory of §402A to design defect cases.] Consequently, the tort liability under Maryland law of a manufacturer or supplier of a motor vehicle, for a defective design which enhances injuries in a collision, depends upon traditional principles of negligence.

NOTES

1. Determining standards for design defects. As *Young* indicates, design defect liability grew up under the aegis of negligence. As such, can the court accept the negligence doctrine and allow a complete defense for any dangers that were "obvious or patent" to the user of the vehicle? Could a jury regard a Volkswagen van, with its engine in the rear, as defective? A convertible? A cigarette lighter? For a negative answer on the first query, see Dreisonstok v. Volkswagenwerk A.G., 489 F.2d 1066 (4th Cir. 1974); for a negative answer on the second, see Delvaux v. Ford Motor Co., 764 F.2d 469 (7th Cir. 1985); and for a negative answer on the third, see Todd v. Societe Bic, 21 F.3d 1402, 1407 (7th Cir. 1994). When the defects are obvious, how should the cost benefit analysis be conducted?

Conversely, how would *Young* play out under §402A of the Second Restatement? Note that strict liability works well to protect strangers against the defendant's use of force, but it seems inappropriate to require any defendant to protect the plaintiff against any use (or misuse) of force initiated by either the plaintiff, a third party or an act of God. A motorcycle gasoline tank might be made "totally" safe against impact, but its weight and unwieldiness would make the motorcycle unmovable. Once absolute protection is rejected as unworkable, reasonableness standards take over.

Accordingly, setting the standard becomes the critical task. In some instances standards are set by legislation. See, e.g., The National Traffic and Motor Vehicle Safety Act, 49 U.S.C. §§30101-30170, wherein, for example, 49 C.F.R. §571.216 (2002) ("Roof Crush Resistance — Passenger Cars") provides that a force equal to one and one-half times a car's weight or 22,240 newtons (5,000 pounds), whichever is less, should not move the roof more than 127 millimeters (five inches) when applied to either of its front corners. Once statutory compliance does not provide an absolute defense in a design defect case, courts typically turn to cost-benefit tests to determine the applicable design standard. But how? For an early skeptical response, see Henderson, Judicial Review of Manufacturer's Conscious Design Choices: The Limits of Adjudication, 73 Colum. L. Rev. 1531 (1973), stressing the "polycentric nature" of design decisions, which requires a design engineer to find the proper balance of "such factors as market price, functional utility, and aesthetics, as well as safety." Henderson urged these are matters that cannot be adequately reexamined in litigation because "courts are not institutionally suited to establishing safety standards." For the early impetus on liability for design defects, see Nader & Page, Automobile Design and Judicial Process, 55 Cal. L. Rev. 645 (1967).

2. *Enhancement of injury.* The defendant in a crashworthiness case is not responsible for the unavoidable injuries associated with the original impact, but only for those harms that were "enhanced or aggravated" by the defective design. In light of the implicit division on causation, who bears the burden of proof on the question of enhancement? One position requires the plaintiff to prove that "it is more probable than not that the alleged defect aggravated or enhanced the injuries resulting from the initial collision." See Caiazzo v. Volkswagenwerk A.G., 647 F.2d 241 (2d Cir. 1981). *Caiazzo* was promptly rejected in Mitchell v. Volkswagenwerk A.G., 669 F.2d 1199, 1204-1205 (8th Cir. 1982):

> The primary difficulty we have with this analysis is that it forces not only the parties but the jury as well to try a hypothetical case. Liability and damage questions are difficult enough within orthodox principles of tort law without extending consideration to a case of a hypothetical victim. More realistically, the parties and juries should direct their attentions to what actually happened rather than what might have happened.
>
> By placing the burden of proof on a plaintiff to prove that the designer was the sole cause of not only an enhanced indivisible injury, but, in addition, that he would not otherwise have received injuries absent a defect, the injured victim is relegated to an almost hopeless state of never being able to succeed against a defective designer. The public interest is little served. We write to reaffirm that *Larsen* was not intended to create a rule which requires the plaintiff to assume an impossible burden of proving a negative fact.

Is the defendant ever the sole responsible party in any crashworthiness case? How can a jury avoid trying the "hypothetical case" once the defendant introduces evidence that the defect did not cause all or some of the harms? Does the burden of production ever switch back to the plaintiff? Whatever the force of these objections, the Third Restatement takes the same view. Even though the theory of proximate causation holds the defendant liable only for the "increased harm," the full loss falls on the defendant "[i]f proof does not support a determination . . . of the harm that would have resulted in the absence of the product defect." RTT:PL §16(c).

3. *Crashworthiness cases: acceptance, disquiet, and reform?* The crashworthiness doctrine of *Larsen* and *Young* is today the law in every state of the union and explicitly embraced in the Third Restatement. See RTT:PL §16, comment *a*. But some courts have expressed misgivings about its potential scope. In Dawson v. Chrysler Corp., 630 F.2d 950, 962-963 (3d Cir. 1980), the plaintiff, a police officer, was hurrying to answer a burglar alarm when

his Dodge Monaco patrol car slipped off a rain-soaked highway into an "unyielding" steel pole some 15 inches in diameter. The pole ripped through the side of the car, crushed the plaintiff, and left him a quadriplegic. The plaintiff urged that the car was defective because it did not have "a full continuous steel frame extending through the door panels," which would have kept the pole from penetrating the passenger space. The defendant's expert testified that the plaintiff's proposed changes would have added between 200 and 250 pounds of weight to the car and cost some $300. He also noted that "deformation" of a car in a crash is in general desirable because it absorbs the impact that would otherwise be transmitted to the occupant. Adams, J., uneasily affirmed the plaintiff's jury verdict under New Jersey law:

> The result of such arrangement is that while the jury found Chrysler liable for not producing a rigid enough vehicular frame, a factfinder in another case might well hold the manufacturer liable for producing a frame that is too rigid. Yet, as pointed out at trial, in certain types of accidents — head-on collisions — it is desirable to have a car designed to collapse upon impact because the deformation would absorb much of the shock of the collision, and divert the force of deceleration away from the vehicle's passengers. In effect, this permits individual juries applying varying laws in different jurisdictions to set nationwide automobile safety standards and to impose on automobile manufacturers conflicting requirements. It would be difficult for members of the industry to alter their design and production behavior in response to jury verdicts in such cases, because their response might well be at variance with what some other jury decides is a defective design. Under these circumstances, the law imposes on the industry the responsibility of insuring vast numbers of persons involved in automobile accidents. . . .

Even though courts have created this problem, Congress sets the national standards, and can be explicit in preempting state law (see Chapter 9, Section F). The level of cynicism about this "damned-if-you-do-damned-if-you-don't" problem surfaced in Blankenship v. General Motors Corp., 406 S.E.2d 781, 783, 784 (W. Va. 1991). Neely, J., joined the crashworthiness parade for reasons that had little to do with the intrinsic merits of the doctrine. After noting the dangers of inviting juries to "second-guess the safety standards promulgated by the National Highway Traffic Safety Administration," he nonetheless offered this strategic defense of his decision:

> West Virginia is a small rural state with .66 percent of the population of the United States. Although some members of this court have reservations about the wisdom of many aspects of the tort law, as a court we are utterly powerless to make the *overall* tort system for cases arising in interstate commerce more rational: Nothing that we do will have any impact whatsoever on the set of economic trade-offs that occur in the *national* economy. And, ironically, trying

unilaterally to make the American tort system more rational through being uniquely responsible in West Virginia will only punish our residents severely without, in any regard, improving the system for anyone else. . . .

So long as West Virginians have to pay premiums on General Motors cars sold around the world it would be "foolish and irresponsible" not to allow West Virginians to collect on their implicit insurance policies for accidents to them. Note that the crashworthiness cases got their start because the courts refused to protect the defendant when the risks in question were open and obvious. When are consumer expectations likely to prove decisive?

4. *The decline of open and obvious.* Automobiles were not the only product for which liability expanded dramatically in the 1970s. The design liability for machine tools and other equipment exploded as well. Specifically, *Campo* was explicitly overruled in Micallef v. Miehle Co., 348 N.E.2d 571 (N.Y. 1976). There the plaintiff sought to "chase a hickie" (that is, remove a foreign object) that had made its way onto a high-speed printing press manufactured by the defendant. Without shutting down the press (which would have cost valuable production time), he tried to remove the hickie with an eight-inch piece of plastic, and his finger got caught in the nip-point of the machine. Plaintiff tried to turn off the press but the shut-off button was beyond his reach. Cooke, J., accepted the proposition that the machine could be defective in design even when the dangerous condition was open and obvious:

> Apace with advanced technology, a relaxation of the *Campo* stringency is advisable. A casting of increased responsibility upon the manufacturer, who stands in a superior position to recognize and cure defects, for improper conduct in the placement of finished products into the channels of commerce furthers the public interest. To this end, we hold that a manufacturer is obligated to exercise that degree of care in his plan or design so as to avoid any unreasonable risk of harm to anyone who is likely to be exposed to the danger when the product is used in the manner for which the product was intended as well as an unintended yet reasonably foreseeable use.
>
> What constitutes "reasonable care" will, of course, vary with the surrounding circumstances and will involve "a balancing of the likelihood of harm, and the gravity of harm if it happens, against the burden of the precaution which would be effective to avoid the harm." Under this approach, "the plaintiff endeavors to show the jury such facts as that competitors used the safety device which was missing here, or that a 'cotter pin costing a penny' could have prevented the accident. The defendant points to such matters as cost, function, and competition as narrowing the design choices. He stresses 'trade-offs.' If the product would be unworkable when the alleged missing feature was added, or would be so expensive as to be priced out of the market, that would be relevant defensive matter." (Rheingold, Expanding Liability of the Product Supplier: A Primer, 2 Hofstra L. Rev. 521, 537.)

Restatement Third Section 2, comment *d* follows the now dominant position: "The fact that a danger is open and obvious is relevant to the issue of defectiveness, but does not necessarily preclude a plaintiff from establishing that a reasonable alternative design should have been adopted that would have reduced or prevented injury to the plaintiff." The Third Restatement approves of *Micallef*. See §2, illustration 3.

Barker v. Lull Engineering Co.
573 P.2d 443 (Cal. 1978)

TOBRINER, C.J. In August 1970, plaintiff Ray Barker was injured at a construction site at the University of California at Santa Cruz while operating a high-lift loader manufactured by defendant Lull Engineering Co. and leased to plaintiff's employer by defendant George M. Philpott Co., Inc. Claiming that his injuries were proximately caused, inter alia, by the alleged defective design of the loader, Barker instituted the present tort action seeking to recover damages for his injuries. The jury returned a verdict in favor of defendants, and plaintiff appeals from the judgment entered upon that verdict, contending primarily that in view of this court's decision in Cronin v. J. B. E. Olson Corp. 501 P.2d 1153 (Cal. 1972), the trial court erred in instructing the jury "that strict liability for a defect in design of a product is based on a finding that the product was unreasonably dangerous for its intended use. . . . "

As we explain, we agree with plaintiff's objection to the challenged instruction and conclude that the judgment must be reversed. . . .

[W]e have concluded from this review that a product is defective in design either (1) if the product has failed to perform as safely as an ordinary consumer would expect when used in an intended or reasonably foreseeable manner, or (2) if, in light of the relevant factors discussed below, the benefits of the challenged design do not outweigh the risk of danger inherent in such design. In addition, we explain how the burden of proof with respect to the latter "risk-benefit" standard should be allocated.

This dual standard for design defect assures an injured plaintiff protection from products that either fall below ordinary consumer expectations as to safety, or that, on balance, are not as safely designed as they should be. At the same time, the standard permits a manufacturer who has marketed a product which satisfies ordinary consumer expectations to demonstrate the relative complexity of design decisions and the tradeoffs that are frequently required in the adoption of alternative designs. Finally, this test reflects our continued adherence to the principle that, in a product liability action, the trier of fact must focus on the *product,* not on the *manufacturer's conduct,* and that the plaintiff need not prove that the manufacturer acted unreasonably or negligently in order to prevail in such an action. . . .

1.   THE FACTS OF THE PRESENT CASE

[Barker, a substitute driver, was injured while using a Lull High-Lift Loader, which was designed to be kept level on a sloping terrain. He had received only limited instruction in the use of the loader. While attempting to lift a load of lumber 18 or so feet on uneven ground, he sought to maneuver the forks on the base of the load to compensate for sloping ground. As he lost control of the loader, he attempted to jump away from it, and was struck and seriously injured by some falling timber.

The plaintiff claimed that the loader was defective in several respects: first, that it was not equipped with seat belts or a roll-bar; second, that it was not equipped with "outriggers" that might have given it greater lateral stability; third, that it was not equipped with an automatic locking device on its leveling mechanism; and, fourth, that it was not equipped with a separate park gear. In response to this assignment of defects, the defendant argued as follows: first, seat belts or roll-bars were in fact dangerous because they prevented any quick escape from the loader; second, that the outriggers were not needed if the loader was operated on level terrain as was intended, that none of the defendant's competitors had such outriggers, and that a regular crane should have been called in if work on uneven terrain was required; third, that the leveling device used was the most convenient and safe for the operator; and, fourth, that none of the transmissions manufactured for loaders incorporated a park position. The defendant also argued that the plaintiff's inexperience and panic were the sole source of his injury.

The jury returned a verdict for the defendant by a vote of ten to two.] . . .

3.   A TRIAL COURT MAY PROPERLY FORMULATE INSTRUCTIONS TO
ELUCIDATE THE "DEFECT" CONCEPT IN VARYING CIRCUMSTANCES. IN
PARTICULAR, IN DESIGN DEFECT CASES, A COURT MAY PROPERLY
INSTRUCT A JURY THAT A PRODUCT IS DEFECTIVE IN DESIGN IF (1) THE
PLAINTIFF PROVES THAT THE PRODUCT FAILED TO PERFORM AS SAFELY
AS AN ORDINARY CONSUMER WOULD EXPECT WHEN USED IN AN
INTENDED OR REASONABLY FORESEEABLE MANNER, OR (2) THE PLAINTIFF
PROVES THAT THE PRODUCT'S DESIGN PROXIMATELY CAUSED INJURY
AND THE DEFENDANT FAILS TO PROVE, IN LIGHT OF THE RELEVANT
FACTORS, THAT ON BALANCE THE BENEFITS OF THE CHALLENGED
DESIGN OUTWEIGH THE RISK OF DANGER INHERENT IN SUCH
DESIGN. . . .

As this court has recognized on numerous occasions, the term defect as utilized in the strict liability context is neither self-defining nor susceptible to a single definition applicable in all contexts.[8] . . . [T]he concept of defect raises considerably more difficulties in the design defect context than it does in the manufacturing or production defect context.

In general, a manufacturing or production defect is readily identifiable because a defective product is one that differs from the manufacturer's intended result or from other ostensibly identical units of the same product line. For example, when a product comes off the assembly line in a sub-standard condition it has incurred a manufacturing defect. . . . A design defect, by contrast, cannot be identified simply by comparing the injury-producing product with the manufacturer's plans or with other units of the same product line, since by definition the plans and all such units will reflect the same design. Rather than applying any sort of deviation-from-the-norm test in determining whether a product is defective in design for strict liability purposes, our cases have employed two alternative criteria in ascertaining, in Justice Traynor's words, whether there is something "wrong, if not in the manufacturer's manner of production, at least in his product." (Traynor, The Ways and Meanings of Defective Products and Strict Liability, 32 Tenn. L. Rev. 363, 366 [1965].)

First, our cases establish that a product may be found defective in design if the plaintiff demonstrates that the product failed to perform as safely as an ordinary consumer would expect when used in an intended or reason-ably foreseeable manner. This initial standard, somewhat analogous to the Uniform Commercial Code's warranty of fitness and merchantability (Cal. U. Com. Code, §2314), reflects the warranty heritage upon which California product liability doctrine in part rests. As we noted in *Greenman*, "implicit in [a product's] presence on the market . . . [is] a representation that it [will] safely do the jobs for which it was built." When a product fails to satisfy such ordinary consumer expectations as to safety in its intended or reasonably foreseeable operation, a manufacturer is strictly liable for resulting injuries. . . .

As Professor Wade has pointed out, however, the expectations of the ordinary consumer cannot be viewed as the exclusive yardstick for evalu-ating design defectiveness because "[i]n many situations . . . the consumer would not know what to expect, because he would have no idea how safe the product could be made." . . . Numerous California decisions have implicitly recognized this fact and have made clear, through varying linguistic for-mulations, that a product may be found defective in design, even if it

---

8. One commentator has observed that, in addition to the deficiencies in the "unreasonably dangerous" terminology noted in *Cronin*, the Restatement's language is potentially misleading because "[i]t may suggest an idea like ultrahazardous, or abnormally dangerous, and thus give rise to the impression that the plaintiff must prove that the product was unusually or extremely dangerous." (Wade, On the Nature of Strict Tort Liability for Products 44 Miss. L.J. 825, 832 (1973).) We agree with this criticism and believe it constitutes a further reason for refraining from utilizing the "unreasonably dangerous" terminology in defining a defective product.

satisfies ordinary consumer expectations, if through hindsight the jury determines that the product's design embodies "excessive preventable danger," or, in other words, if the jury finds that the risk of danger inherent in the challenged design outweighs the benefits of such design. . . .

A review of past cases indicates that in evaluating the adequacy of a product's design pursuant to this latter standard, a jury may consider, among other relevant factors, the gravity of the danger posed by the challenged design, the likelihood that such danger would occur, the mechanical feasibility of a safer alternative design, the financial cost of an improved design, and the adverse consequences to the product and to the consumer that would result from an alternative design. . . .

Although our cases have thus recognized a variety of considerations that may be relevant to the determination of the adequacy of a product's design, past authorities have generally not devoted much attention to the appropriate allocation of the burden of proof with respect to these matters. . . . The allocation of such burden is particularly significant in this context inasmuch as this court's product liability decisions, from *Greenman* to *Cronin,* have repeatedly emphasized that one of the principal purposes behind the strict product liability doctrine is to relieve an injured plaintiff of many of the onerous evidentiary burdens inherent in a negligence cause of action. Because most of the evidentiary matters which may be relevant to the determination of the adequacy of a product's design under the "risk-benefit" standard — e.g., the feasibility and cost of alternative designs — are similar to issues typically presented in a negligent design case and involve technical matters peculiarly within the knowledge of the manufacturer, we conclude that once the plaintiff makes a prima facie showing that the injury was proximately caused by the product's design, the burden should appropriately shift to the defendant to prove, in light of the relevant factors, that the product is not defective. Moreover, inasmuch as this conclusion flows from our determination that the fundamental public policies embraced in *Greenman* dictate that a manufacturer who seeks to escape liability for an injury proximately caused by its product's design on a risk-benefit theory should bear the burden of persuading the trier of fact that its product should not be judged defective, the defendant's burden is one affecting the burden of proof, rather than simply the burden of producing evidence. . . .

Because the jury may have interpreted the erroneous instruction given in the instant case as requiring plaintiff to prove that the highlift loader was ultrahazardous or more dangerous than the average consumer contemplated, and because the instruction additionally misinformed the jury that the defectiveness of the product must be evaluated in light of the product's "intended use" rather than its "reasonably foreseeable use" . . . , we cannot find that the error was harmless on the facts of this case. In light of this conclusion, we need not address plaintiff's additional claims of error, for such issues may not arise on retrial.

The judgment in favor of defendants is reversed.

NOTES

1. What is a design defect? The two-pronged *Barker* formulation represents the dominant norm today. In Tran v. Toyota Motor Corp., 420 F.3d
1310, 1314 (11th Cir. 2005), the plaintiff became a quadriplegic in 1998
due to a head-on collision with another vehicle. She claimed that her 1983
Toyota Cressida was defective because its passive constraint shoulder belt
rode too high her neck, considering that she was a short person between 5
foot 2 inches and 5 foot 4 inches tall. The trial judge gave only the risk
benefit instruction on which the jury returned a defendant's verdict.
Wilson, J., nevertheless ruled that this instruction was in error:

> We emphasize that we do not hold that the consumer expectations test jury
> instruction is required in all product liability cases. We merely hold . . . that the
> instruction is proper as an independent basis for liability under Florida law
> when the product in question is one about which an ordinary consumer could
> form expectations. Under Florida law, seatbelts are such a product.

Although the *Barker* two-tier test seems dominant today, other design
defect tests were propounded during the late 1970s. In Azzarello v. Black
Bros. Co., Inc., 391 A.2d 1020, 1027 (Pa. 1978), the plaintiff's hand was
injured when caught between two rubber rollers in a coating machine
manufactured by the defendant. The court noted the need to control "giant
corporate structures" and, following *Cronin* and *Barker*, rejected "the unreasonably dangerous" limitation on product defects. It held that although
the supplier was not "an insurer of all injuries caused by the product," it
nonetheless was cast "in the role of a guarantor of his product's safety."

> For the term guarantor to have any meaning in this context the supplier
> must at least provide a product which is designed to make it safe for the
> intended use. Under this standard, in this type case, the jury may find a
> defect where the product left the supplier's control lacking any element
> necessary to make it safe for its intended use or possessing any feature that
> renders it unsafe for the intended use. It is clear that the term "unreasonably
> dangerous" has no place in the instructions to a jury as to the question of
> "defect" in this type of case. We therefore agree with the court en banc that
> the use of the term "unreasonably dangerous" in the charge was misleading
> and that the appellee was entitled to a new trial.

If a manufacturer makes economy and deluxe models of a chain saw,
both intended for the same general uses, is the economy model necessarily
defective under the *Azzarello* formulation? Presumptively defective? Is the

Azzarello formulation of product defect narrower than that in *Barker*, owing to its repeated reference to intended, as distinguished from foreseeable, use?

A more restrictive approach to the test for design defect was taken in Wilson v. Piper Aircraft Corp., 577 P.2d 1322, 1327-1328 (Or. 1978), a wrongful death action brought by the representatives of two passengers who died in the crash of a Piper Cherokee airplane manufactured by the defendants. The plaintiffs' claimed that the defective design was the engine's susceptibility to icing because (1) the aircraft was not equipped with an injection-type fuel system; (2) the carburetor was not designed and equipped to provide a proper fuel-air mixture under icing conditions; (3) the aircraft was not supplied with an adequate carburetor-heating system; and (4) the aircraft was not equipped with a carburetor heat gauge.

The defendant in turn urged that the product was not defective because its design had been approved by the Federal Aviation Administration (FAA) and had received an FAA certificate of airworthiness. The court first noted that by the statute's own terms, the FAA standard was "minimum" only, and did not provide the defendant with an automatic safe harbor from liability. It then parted with *Barker* by imposing stringent requirements on the plaintiff in a design defect case that required the plaintiff to present evidence "from which the jury could find the suggested alternatives are not only technically feasible but also practicable in terms of cost and the over-all design and operation of the product." It further held that the plaintiff had not offered any evidence on how fuel injection would alter the price or performance of the airplane. In addition, it concluded that while it would not give conclusive force to the FAA regulation, it nonetheless believed "that in a field as closely regulated as aircraft design and manufacture, it is proper to take into consideration, in determining whether plaintiffs have produced sufficient evidence of defect to go to the jury, the fact that the regulatory agency has approved the very design of which they complain after considering the dangers involved."

2. State of the art: time of sale or time of trial? In setting the appropriate design standard for product safety, many judicial decisions look in part to the state of the art in the product supplier's trade or business. The state of the art is generally understood to refer to something more stringent than the "common practice" in the industry, and to embrace the scientific, technological and safety standards that are reasonably feasible at the time of product design. Carter v. Massey-Ferguson, Inc. 716 F.2d 344 (5th Cir. 1983); RTT:PL §2, comment *d*. Most courts today do not allow compliance with the state of the art to resolve the design defect question in defendant's favor, but nonetheless treat it as a factor to consider, which "is both necessary and probative on the issue of 'unreasonably dangerous.'" Reed v. Tiffin Motor Homes, 697 F.2d 1192, 1197 (4th Cir. 1982). In Bruce v. Martin-Marietta Corp., 544 F.2d 442 (10th Cir. 1976), the court measured the state of the art at the time the defendant's airplane seats entered the stream of commerce in 1952, not at the time of the crash, October 1970. The record also showed that the seats did meet all FAA standards as well as the applicable state of the art for 1952. In the court's view, the crucial test was the "expectations of the ordinary consumer," who "would not expect a Model T to have safety features which are incorporated in automobiles today." See *The T.J. Hooper, supra* at 224. For a defense of the common practice standard, see R. Epstein, Modern Products Liability Law 74-90 (1980); for an analysis of *Barker*, see Schwartz, Forward: Understanding Products Liability, 67 Cal. L. Rev. 435 (1979).

3. *Subsequent improvements.* The substantive dispute in *Bruce* also has its evidentiary side: can evidence of subsequent design changes be introduced to show the defectiveness of defendant's basic design? In Ault v. International Harvester Co., 528 P.2d 1148, 1151-1152 (Cal. 1974), the California Supreme Court allowed the evidence, saying:

> The contemporary corporate mass producer of goods, the normal products liability defendant, manufactures tens of thousands of units of goods; it is manifestly unrealistic to suggest that such a producer will forego making improvements in its product, and risk innumerable additional lawsuits and the attendant adverse effect upon its public image, simply because evidence of adoption of such improvement may be admitted in an action founded on strict liability for recovery on an injury that preceded the improvement.

Since that time a well nigh uniform line of decisions has refused to admit the evidence. Federal Rule of Evidence 407 now provides:

> When, after an injury or harm allegedly caused by an event, measures are taken that, if taken previously, would have made the injury or harm less likely to occur, evidence of the subsequent measures is not admissible to prove negligence, culpable conduct, a defect in a product, a defect in a product's design, or a need for a warning or instruction. This rule does not require the exclusion of evidence of subsequent measures when offered for another purpose, such as proving ownership, control, or feasibility of precautionary measures, if controverted, or impeachment.

In Cann v. Ford Motor Co., 658 F.2d 54, 60 (2d Cir. 1981), Meskill, J., relied on Rule 407 to exclude evidence of Ford's redesigned transmission, even under a strict liability theory:

> Rule 407 is prompted by the fear that people will be less likely to take subsequent remedial measures if evidence of their repairs or improvements may be used against them in lawsuits arising out of prior accidents. Appellants point out that a negligence action places in issue whether the defendant's conduct

was reasonable while a strict liability action involves whether the product was defective; they note that the jury focuses on the *defendant* in a negligence action, but solely upon the *product* in a strict liability action. However, the defendant must pay the judgment in both situations, regardless of where the jury's attention focused when they found against him. Since the policy underlying Rule 407 not to discourage persons from taking remedial measures is relevant to *defendants* sued under either theory, we do not see the significance of the distinction. A potential defendant must be equally concerned regardless of the theoretical rubric under which this highly prejudicial, and extremely damaging, evidence is admitted.

More recently, in Diehl v. Blaw-Knox, 360 F.3d 426, 430 (3d Cir. 2004), the court refused to apply Rule 407 when the improvement in question was not made by the defendant but a third party, in this instance, the plaintiff's employer. The court noted that Rule 407 is intended to encourage defendants to make improvements by insulating them from liability: "[t]his policy is not implicated where the evidence concerns remedial measures taken by an individual or entity that is not a party to the lawsuit. The admission of remedial measures by a non-party necessarily will not expose that non-party to liability, and therefore will not discourage the non-party from taking the remedial measures in the first place. It is noteworthy that each of the circuits to address this issue has concluded that Rule 407 does not apply to subsequent remedial measures taken by a non-party."

4. *Product modification.* Much litigation has focused on the question of whether a product alteration made after a manufacturer has shipped goods constitutes a superseding cause sufficient to relieve the original manufacturer of tort liability for design defects. Young v. Aeroil Products Co., 248 F.2d 185 (9th Cir. 1957), was a case that protected the manufacturer from liability due to subsequent alterations. There the decedent had been crushed to death when the portable elevator he had been operating toppled. The decedent's employer had previously added additional equipment to the elevator, causing its imbalance. Even though the defendant had sold the elevator with the express warranty that it was balanced, the court held that the warranty was unavailing because "[t]he thing being used was not the thing sold."

Subsequent to *Barker*, courts have expanded the manufacturer's liability for products with subsequent modifications. In Soler v. Castmaster, Div. of H.P.M. Corp., 484 A.2d 1225, 1231, 1232 (N.J. 1984), the defendant manufacturer sold a manually operated die casting machine that was not equipped with any automatic safety gate or interlock device. Subsequently, the plaintiff's employer modified the machine in two ways: It added a trip wire to the machine to make it cycle automatically without operator activation, and at the same time it added a safety gate. As the plaintiff tried to remove a cast from the molding, his hand was crushed in the machine. The court first concluded that a jury could find the original machine design defective under the risk-utility analysis, and then allowed the jury to decide whether the changes made by the plaintiff's employer insulated the defendant from liability. "The critical question then is whether the original defect in the design of the machine — the absence of a safety gate with interlock — constitutes a proximate cause of the accident, notwithstanding the subsequent substantial alteration." The court further observed that "in applying strict liability in torts for design defects, manufacturers cannot escape liability on the grounds of misuse or abnormal use if the actual use proximate to the injury was objectively foreseeable. Foreseeable misuse or abnormal use can be extended by analogy to foreseeable substantial change of the product from its original design."

In the companion case of Brown v. United States Stove Co., 484 A.2d 1234, 1244 (N.J. 1984), the New Jersey court held that an employer's product modification exonerated the original manufacturer as a matter of law. The plaintiff was seriously burned while standing near an unvented, freestanding space heater manufactured by the defendant for home use. Some 15 years before the accident, the plaintiff's employer had removed its thermocouple valve, gas safety shut-off valve, and pilot light tube, increasing the flow through the heater 100-fold. The plaintiff's expert testified that these space heaters were often abused when, as here, they were moved between construction sites. He therefore suggested that either the unit should have been redesigned to bear the higher rate of gas flow or, alternatively, that the defendant could have used "noncommercial left-handed threading and inverted flange connectors, which were available in the 1950's and 1960's" to make the heaters more tamper resistant. A defendant's employee testified that the right-handed threading was used for "serviceability and market convenience." On appeal the court first held that the product alterations were objectively foreseeable, but next awarded defendant judgment on the ground that its original defect, if any, was too remote a cause of the plaintiff's harm because "the record discloses that the heater was deliberately altered for the specific purpose of operating it beyond its safe capacity, and, further, it was wilfully, persistently and intensively misused in this fashion for an extraordinarily long period of time, perhaps for as long as fifteen years."

A Connecticut statute provides that "[a] product seller shall not be liable for harm that would not have occurred but for the fact that his product was altered or modified by a third party unless: (1) The alteration or modification was in accordance with the instructions or specifications of the product seller; (2) the alteration or modification was made with the consent of the product seller; or (3) the alteration or modification was the result of conduct that reasonably should have been anticipated by the product seller." Conn. Gen. Stat. Ann. §52-572p(a) (West 1991 & Supp. 2007). The Third Restatement recognizes that product alteration and modification could defeat or diminish defendant's responsibility, but develops no specialized rules to deal with them, treating them (along with product misuse) as parts of the broader questions of product defect, causation, and plaintiff's conduct. RTT:PL §2 comment *p*.

5. *The government contractor defense.* Broad-based design defect liability raises special complications when products procured for government use must meet precise specifications, thereby precluding any manufacturer's design choice. In Boyle v. United Technologies Corp., 487 U.S. 500, 512 (1988), the decedent was killed when he was unable to exit from a helicopter escape hatch that he claimed was negligently designed. The Supreme Court, per Scalia, J., refused to allow the plaintiff to try the case under state law, because "the imposition of tort liability will directly affect the terms of Government contracts" by inducing the contractor to decline work or to increase its prices. Scalia, J., subsequently held:

> Liability for design defects in military equipment cannot be imposed pursuant to state law, when (1) the United States approved reasonably precise specifications; (2) the equipment conformed to those specifications; and (3) the supplier warned the United States about the dangers in the use of the equipment that were known to the supplier but not to the United States. . . . The third condition is necessary because, in its absence, the displacement of state tort law would create some incentive for the manufacturer to withhold knowledge of risks, since conveying that knowledge might disrupt the contract but withholding it would produce no liability.

Justice Brennan dissented on the ground that the Court's government contractor defense might be satisfied by "perhaps no more than a rubberstamp from a federal procurement officer who might or might not have noticed or cared about the defects, or even had the expertise to discover them." Should the government contractors defense apply when the United States purchases stock items?

Linegar v. Armour of America
909 F.2d 1150 (8th Cir. 1990)

BOWMAN, J. This action was brought as a products liability case and heard under the District Court's diversity jurisdiction. Armour of America, Inc. (Armour) appeals a judgment based on a jury verdict in favor of the widow and children of Jimmy Linegar, a Missouri State Highway Patrol trooper who was killed in the line of duty. The jury found that the bullet-resistant vest manufactured by Armour and worn by Linegar at the time of the murder was defectively designed, and it awarded his family $1.5 million in damages. We reverse.

[The decedent was killed during a routine traffic stop by David Tate, later convicted of capital murder.] None of the shots that hit the contour-style, concealable protective vest Linegar was wearing — there were five such shots — penetrated the vest or caused injury. The wounds Linegar suffered all were caused by shots that struck parts of his body not protected by the vest.

The Missouri State Highway Patrol issued the vest to Linegar when he joined the Patrol in 1981. The vest was one of a lot of various sizes of the same style vest the Patrol purchased in 1979 directly from Armour. The contour style was one of several different styles then on the market. It provided more protection to the sides of the body than the style featuring rectangular panels in front and back, but not as much protection as a wrap-around style. The front and back panels of the contour vest, held together with Velcro closures under the arms, did not meet at the sides of the wearer's body, leaving an area along the sides of the body under the arms exposed when the vest was worn. This feature of the vest was obvious to the Patrol when it selected this vest as standard issue for its troopers and could only have been obvious to any trooper who chose to wear it. The bullet that proved fatal to Linegar entered between his seventh and eighth ribs, approximately three-and-one-fourth inches down from his armpit, and pierced his heart. . . .

We conclude that, as a matter of law, the contour vest Trooper Linegar was wearing when he was murdered was not defective and unreasonably dangerous. . . .

The Missouri cases leave the meaning of the phrase "unreasonably dangerous" largely a matter of common sense, the court's or the jury's. . . . The conditions under which a bullet-resistant vest will be called upon to perform its intended function most assuredly will be dangerous, indeed life-threatening, and Armour surely knew that. It defies logic, however, to suggest that Armour reasonably should have anticipated that anyone would wear its vest for protection of areas of the body that the vest obviously did not cover.

[Under Restatement (Second) of Torts §402A, comment *i* (1965)], the consumer expectation test focuses attention on the vest's wearer rather than on its manufacturer. The inherent limitations in the amount of coverage offered by Armour's contour vest were obvious to this Court, observing a demonstration from the bench during oral argument, as they would be to anyone with ordinary knowledge, most especially the vest's wearer. A person wearing the vest would no more expect to be shielded from a shot taken under the arm than he would expect the vest to deflect bullets aimed at his head or neck or lower abdomen or any other area not covered by the vest.

Plaintiff insists that the user's expectations should not be considered by us, since doing so would effectively afford Armour the benefit of the "open and obvious" defense, inappropriate, they say, in a defective design strict products liability action. We disagree. Although not conclusive, "[t]he obviousness of a defect or danger is material to the issue whether a product is 'unreasonably dangerous.'" McGowne v. Challenge-Cook Bros., 672 F.2d 652, 663 (8th Cir. 1982). Here, the vest's purported dangerous defect — its lack of closure at the sides — could not have been more open and obvious. An otherwise completely effective protective vest cannot be regarded as dangerous, much less unreasonably so, simply because it leaves some parts of the body obviously exposed.[6] . . .

We have no difficulty in concluding as a matter of law that the product at issue here was neither defective nor unreasonably dangerous. Trooper Linegar's protective vest performed precisely as expected and stopped all of the bullets that hit it. No part of the vest nor any malfunction of the vest caused Linegar's injuries. The vest was designed to prevent the penetration of bullets where there was coverage, and it did so; the amount of coverage was the buyer's choice. The Missouri Highway Patrol could have chosen to buy, and Armour could have sold the Patrol, a vest with more coverage; no one contests that. But it is not the place of courts or juries to set specifications as to the parts of the body a bullet-resistant garment must cover. A manufacturer is not obliged to market only one version of a product, that being the very safest design possible. If that were so, automobile manufacturers could not offer consumers sports cars, convertibles, jeeps, or compact cars. All boaters would have to buy full life vests instead of choosing a ski belt or even a flotation cushion. Personal safety devices, in particular, require personal choices, and it is beyond the province of courts and juries to act as legislators and preordain those choices.

In this case, there obviously were trade-offs to be made. A contour vest like the one here in question permits the wearer more flexibility and mobility and allows better heat dissipation and sweat evaporation, and thus is more likely to be worn than a more confining vest. It is less expensive than styles of vests providing more complete coverage. If manufacturers like Armour are threatened with economically devastating litigation if they market any vest style except that offering maximum coverage, they may decide, since one can always argue that more coverage is possible, to get out of the business altogether. Or they may continue to market the vest style that, according to the latest lawsuit, affords the "best" coverage. Officers who find the "safest" style confining or uncomfortable will either wear it at risk to their mobility or opt not to wear it at all. . . . Law enforcement agencies trying to work within the confines of a budget may be forced to purchase fewer vests or none at all. How "safe" are those possibilities? "The

---

6. The wrap-around vest style advocated by appellees as preferable still must have an armhole that will be open some distance below the armpit to allow freedom of movement. See, e.g., Transcript Vol. II at 334 (testimony of Missouri Highway Patrol Trooper Don Phillips that his wrap-around-style vest left a four-inch opening beneath his armpit).

core concern in strict tort liability law is safety." We are firmly convinced that to allow this verdict to stand would run counter to the law's purpose of promoting the development of safe and useful products, and would have an especially pernicious effect on the development and marketing of equipment designed to make the always-dangerous work of law enforcement officers a little safer.

The death of Jimmy Linegar by the hand of a depraved killer was a tragic event. We keenly feel the loss that this young trooper's family has suffered, and our sympathies go out to them. But we cannot allow recovery from a blameless defendant on the basis of sympathy for the plaintiffs. To hold Armour liable for Linegar's death would cast it in the role of insurer for anyone shot while wearing an Armour vest, regardless of whether any shots penetrated the vest. That a manufacturer may be cast in such a role has been soundly rejected by courts applying Missouri law.

[Reversed.]

NOTES

1. *The resurgence of open and obvious?* In *Linegar*, Judge Bowman made two separate claims. First, that the condition in question was patent; and second, that the trade-offs it embodied were reasonable. Why the second condition? What result if Armour had sold only the protective vest model worn by Linegar? The Third Restatement that approved of the decision in *Micallef* also approved of *Linegar*, RTT:PL §2, illustration 10. Consistent? Did the court in *Linegar* make an implicit analysis that no alternative design was superior to that offered by Armour?

2. *Alternative designs.* The question of alternative design has been explicitly addressed in the Restatement (Third) of Torts largely in response to the New Jersey case of O'Brien v. Muskin Corp., 463 A.2d 298, 302-303, 305-306 (N.J. 1983). Muskin sold a pool to Arthur Henry, which, when assembled, had an embossed vinyl bottom and a depth of about three feet. The plaintiff, 23 years old, dove into the pool from either a nearby platform or from the eight-foot-high roof of the Henrys' garage. "As his outstretched hands hit the vinyl-lined pool bottom, they slid apart, and O'Brien struck his head on the bottom of the pool, thereby sustaining injuries." The plaintiff's expert claimed that the pool design was dangerous because wet vinyl was more than twice as slippery as rubber latex, which is used to line in-ground pools. The trial court excluded that testimony when the expert admitted that he knew of no above-ground pool lined with a material other than vinyl. On appeal the court allowed the design defect count to go to the jury on Wade's risk-utility test, noting that for the plaintiff to reach the jury under a risk-utility test, "it was not necessary for plaintiff to prove the existence of alternative, safer designs."

In New Jersey, *Muskin* was altered by statute, which provided, among other things, that "the manufacturer or seller shall not be liable if: (1) At the time the product left the control of the manufacturer, there was not a practical and technically feasible alternative design that would have prevented the harm without substantially impairing the reasonably anticipated or intended function of the product." N.J. Stat. Ann. §2A:58C-3 (West 2000). The Third Restatement takes much the same line by requiring "that the plaintiff show a reasonable alternative design . . . even though the plaintiff alleges that the category of product sold by the defendant is so dangerous that it should not have been marketed at all." RTT:PL §2, comment *d*. It explicitly disapproved of *Muskin* because "the vinyl pool liner that [the manufacturer] utilized was the best and safest liner available and that no alternative, less slippery liner was feasible." RTT:PL §2, illustration 4. Is it appropriate for a jury to decide that above-ground pools should not be marketed at all? In dealing with its alternative design conception, §2, comment *f* of the Third Restatement observes:

> A broad range of factors may be considered in determining whether an alternative design is reasonable and whether its omission renders a product not reasonably safe. The factors include, among others, the magnitude and probability of the foreseeable risks of harm, the instructions and warnings accompanying the product, and the nature and strength of consumer expectations regarding the product, including expectations arising from product portrayal and marketing. The relative advantages and disadvantages of the product as designed and as it alternatively could have been designed may also be considered. Thus, the likely effects of the alternative design on production costs; the effect of alternative design on product longevity, maintenance, repair, and esthetics; and the range of consumer choice among products are factors that may be taken into account.

3. *Judicial reception of the Third Restatement.* The alternative design requirement set out in the Third Restatement received a mixed reception in Potter v. Chicago Pneumatic Tool Co., 694 A.2d 1319, 1332, 1334-1335 (Conn. 1997), which took the position that a plaintiff may, but need not, prove an alternative design to prevail. There the plaintiffs claimed that they had suffered "permanent vascular and neurological impairments" from using pneumatic hand tools that the defendants had manufactured. Katz, J., first noted that a majority of states did not in fact impose the Third Restatement's alternative design requirement, and refused to do so, lest the law place an "undue burden" on plaintiffs by requiring them to use expert evidence in every design defect case. He then observed that "the manufacturer may be strictly liable for a design defect notwithstanding the fact that there are no safer alternative designs in existence. . . ." Connecticut's strict liability test for a product defect required an interplay between the consumer expectation and risk-utility tests. The reasonable

expectation test is "appropriate when the everyday experience of a particular product's users permits the inference that the product did not meet minimum safety expectations. . . . Conversely, the jury should engage in the risk-utility balancing required by our modified consumer expectation test when the particular facts do not reasonably permit the inference that the product did not meet the safety expectations of the ordinary consumer. . . . The availability of a feasible alternative design is a factor that the plaintiff may, rather than must, prove in order to establish that a product's risks outweigh its utility" Katz, J., then reviewed the evidence which showed that a large number of defendant's tools were not in conformity with the safety standards of the American Conference of Governmental and Industrial Hygienists and the American National Standards Institutes, and that its equipment did not incorporate the various techniques of "isolation, dampening and balancing, available to reduce the deleterious effects of vibration." Has the plaintiff shown enough to establish an alternative design? To show that the defendant's tools were not in accord with the common practice of the time?

The need for an alternative design was embraced, however, in Unrein v. Timesavers, Inc., 394 F.3d 1008, 1010, 1012 (8th Cir. 2005), where the plaintiff's hand was badly damaged when caught in a sanding device manufactured by a third-party defendant Foley-Martens Co. Dr. Tarold Kvalseth, plaintiff's expert and a professor of mechanical engineering at the University of Minnesota, testified that the sander had been improperly designed because it its emergency stop-buttons were not easily accessible, and because proper guards had not been installed. The expert then suggested that the "preferred and appropriate design solution" would have required the installation of "a continuous safety trip cord along the outside of each of the three sides of the infeed area of the sander." Murphy, J., held that the trial court was right to give the defendant a summary judgment under the *Daubert* standards of admissibility.

> Our cases do not require that experts manufacture a new device or prototype in order for their opinion to be admitted. . . . We conclude that Dr. Kvalseth's proffered opinion lacked indicia of reliability for other reasons. Although he proposed using a safety trip cord, a commonly used device, he did not prepare drawings showing how it would be integrated into the Timesavers sander or present photographs showing its use with similar machines. . . . Dr. Kvalseth provided even less information about how the brake would function. An expert proposing safety modifications must demonstrate by some means that they would work to protect the machine operators but would not interfere with the machine's utility.

Why not return to the open and obvious test of *Campo*?

4. *The Third Restatement on defective drug design.* Criticism of the Third Restatement's design defect test was also voiced in Bryant v.

Hoffman-LaRoche, 585 S.E.2d 723, 727-728 (Ga. App. 2003), where the plaintiff sued the defendant on the ground that its heart medication, Posicor, had killed his wife because it was defectively designed and inter-acted poorly with other drugs she had taken. The defendant urged that the case should be governed by Restatement (Third) Torts, §6(c), which provides:

> A prescription drug or medical device is not reasonably safe due to defective design if the foreseeable risks of harm posed by the drug or medical device are sufficiently great in relation to its foreseeable therapeutic benefits that reasonable health-care providers, knowing of such foreseeable risks and therapeutic benefits, would not prescribe the drug or medical device for any class of patients.

Comment *b* to §6(c) provides that "a drug is defectively designed only when it provides no net benefit to any class of patients." The court rejected this view in favor of comment *k* to the Second Restatement, noting:

> [Section] 6(c) has been criticized for its failure to reflect existing case law, its lack of flexibility with regard to drugs involving differing benefits and risks, its unprecedented application of a reasonable physician standard, and the fact that a consumer's claim could easily be defeated by expert opinion that the drug had some use for someone, despite potentially harmful effects on a large class of individuals. [Freeman v. Hoffman-LaRoche, 618 N.W.2d 827 (2000)]. To date, no court has adopted the Third Restatement's strict liability test for prescription drugs, and one court [*Freeman*] has explicitly refused to adopt the test . . .
>
> Moreover, we agree with the majority of courts that Comment *k* serves as an affirmative defense and that the defense has no application to claims of manufacturing defect or failure to warn.

Does §6(c) create an absolute immunity for all FDA-approved drugs?

For further criticism of the "complete overhaul" of the design defect provisions in the Third Restatement, see Conk, Is There a Design Defect in the Restatement (Third) of Torts: Products Liability?, 109 Yale L.J. 1087 (2000).

Halliday v. Sturn, Ruger & Co.
792 A.2d 1145 (Md. 2002)

WILNER, J. This case arises from the tragic death of Jordan Garris. In June, 1999, Jordan shot himself while playing with his father's handgun. Jordan's mother, petitioner here, seeks to hold the manufacturer of the handgun, respondent Sturm, Ruger & Co. (Sturm Ruger), liable for Jordan's death.

The Circuit Court for Baltimore City, by granting respondent's motion for summary judgment, found no liability. A divided Court of Special Appeals affirmed. We shall do likewise.

BACKGROUND

The handgun in question is a Ruger P89 semi-automatic pistol. To fire the gun, one must place a loaded magazine into it, pull the slide at the top of the gun as far to the rear as possible and then release it, ensure that a safety lever is in the "fire" position, and then pull the trigger. Even when loaded, the gun will not fire unless the trigger is pulled with the safety lever in the "fire" position.

Jordan's father, Clifton Garris, purchased the gun in March, 1999, from On Target, Inc., a retail firearms store. With the purchase of the gun came an instruction manual, the offer of a free safety course, which Garris declined, a pamphlet entitled "Youth Handgun Safety Act Notice" published by the Federal Bureau of Alcohol, Tobacco and Firearms, a lock box in which to store the gun and the magazine, and a padlock for the box.

[The instruction manual supplied detailed instructions and warnings in capital letters on the proper use and handling of the gun, all of which were deemed adequate. The decedent's father disregarded all the warnings and left the gun under his mattress and a loaded magazine on the bookshelf in the same room. Jordan, aged 3, found the two pieces and from watching television was able to assemble them, only to shoot himself in the head. The plaintiff abandoned all duty to warn counts against Sturm Ruger and On-Target. Only the design defect claims remained.]

Petitioner alleged that the gun was defective and unreasonably dangerous because its design "failed to incorporate reasonable devices to prevent its use by young children," in particular "one or more of the following: a grip safety, a heavy trigger-pull, a child-resistant manual safety, a built-in lock, a trigger lock, and/or personalized gun technology that would have substantially reduced the likelihood that a child could fire the gun. . . ." Citing data released by the Centers for Disease Control and Prevention to the effect that 1,641 children under ten were accidentally killed by handguns between 1979 and 1996, petitioner averred in her complaint that "[i]t was foreseeable that the gun would be found and handled by a young child, and that it would be fired by a young child, with resulting foreseeable grievous or fatal injury to the child and/or others." Petitioner contended that the handgun industry was aware of the problem of young children finding and injuring themselves with handguns and, in the 1880's, had developed a childproof grip safety, but that Sturm Ruger manufactured the gun without that, or any other, childproof device. . . .

The essence of petitioner's case was that, when dealing with design defects in a strict liability claim, the court should apply a "risk-utility" analysis in lieu of a "consumer expectation" test and hold that the gun in question failed that preferred test because (1) the risk of excluding child safety features outweighs the utility of that exclusion, and (2) alternative safer designs could have been adopted economically.

DISCUSSION

[The Court exhaustively reviewed the history of these two tests and continued:]

We revisited the issue of which test to apply in Kelley v. R.G. Industries, Inc., 497 A.2d 1143 (Md. 1985), in connection with handguns. [In *Kelley*, the court held that normally gun makers are only liable when their products malfunction, but in addition the court] determined that there was a "limited category of handguns which clearly is not sanctioned as a matter of public policy" and that to impose strict liability upon the manufacturers and marketers of those handguns, which we denoted as "Saturday Night Specials," would *not* be contrary to the public policy set by the General Assembly. Those kinds of guns, characterized by short barrels, low weight, easy concealability, cheap quality, inaccuracy, and unreliability, rendered them particularly attractive for criminal use but virtually useless for any legitimate purpose. After surveying both Federal and State legislation, we determined that those types of guns really were in a separate category, that their use for criminal purposes was entirely foreseeable by their manufacturers and marketers, and that holding such manufacturers and marketers strictly liable for injuries to innocent persons from the criminal misuse of those guns would be consistent with public policy. Whether a particular gun fell within that limited category, we said, was an issue of fact for a trial court to determine. . . .

The courts still seem to be split with respect to gun cases. Some follow the approach of *Kelley*, apply the consumer expectation test, and hold that a manufacturer may not be held liable for design defect on a risk-utility analysis unless the gun malfunctions. In some States, Texas and California among them, that approach is governed by statute. Others have, as petitioner urges, adopted a risk-utility analysis without regard to malfunction and held gun manufacturers liable, even when the gun operates precisely as intended, for failure to attach an available safety feature that might have precluded the gun from firing. We have discerned no significant shift or coalescence of views in this regard since our decision in *Kelley*.

The one arena in which *Kelley*, itself, and the question of gun safety in general, has produced the most significant and relevant debate has been the Maryland General Assembly. [A 1988 statute created a Handgun Roster Board to determine what guns could be legally sold within Maryland. A 1992 statute made it criminal to store or leave a loaded handgun accessible to children. A number of subsequent bills proposed the adoption of specific performance standards for child resistant guns, but did not pass.]

About a dozen bills are pending in the current 2002 session of the General Assembly dealing with handgun safety and with the right to sue for damages caused by handguns. Some would strengthen the penalties attached to the 1992 law dealing with the storage of loaded guns where children might find them. One (SB 381) would reserve to the State alone the right to sue gun manufacturers and dealers for damages or other relief.

CONCLUSION

It is clear that, under the consumer expectation test that we applied in *Kelley*, no cause of action had been stated in this case. There was no malfunction of the gun; regrettably, it worked exactly as it was designed and intended to work and as any ordinary consumer would have expected it to work. The gun is a lawful weapon and was lawfully sold. What caused this tragedy was the carelessness of Jordan's father in leaving the weapon and the magazine in places where the child was able to find them, in contravention not only of common sense but of multiple warnings given to him at the time of purchase.

. . . Given the controversy that continues to surround the risk-utility standard articulated for design defect cases in §2 of the RESTATEMENT (THIRD), we are reluctant at this point to cast aside our existing jurisprudence in favor of such an approach on any broad, general basis. Nor is there a need to do so in this case, which deals with more specific issues that have been presented on several occasions to the General Assembly and have been considered and debated in that arena. So far, the Legislature has chosen not to place these burdens on gun manufacturers but has attempted to deal with the problem in other ways. We shall respect that policy choice.

[Affirmed.]

3. The Duty to Warn

Implicit in many design defect decisions is the view that it is cheaper to design out certain dangerous conditions than it is to warn consumers and users of their dangers. Although that rule works well for most various forms of equipment, it works far less well with pharmaceutical and chemical products where small changes in molecular composition can negate the effectiveness of the product for its intended purpose, or require a new round of approvals from, say, either the Food and Drug Administration or some branch of the Environmental Protection Agency. In these cases the use of product warnings may offer the sensible compromise, especially for potential harms that are not apparent to a product user from the appearance of the product or from common knowledge about its lurking dangers. What legal standards should apply in these warning cases?

MacDonald v. Ortho Pharmaceutical Corp.
475 N.E.2d 65 (Mass. 1985)

ABRAMS, J. This products liability action raises the question of the extent of a drug manufacturer's duty to warn consumers of dangers inherent in the use of oral contraceptives. The plaintiffs brought suit against the defendant, Ortho Pharmaceutical Corporation (Ortho), for injuries allegedly caused by Ortho's birth control pills, and obtained a jury verdict in their favor. The defendant moved for a judgment notwithstanding the verdict. The judge concluded that the defendant did not owe a duty to warn the plaintiffs, and entered judgment for Ortho. The plaintiffs appealed. We transferred the case to this court on our own motion and reinstate the jury verdict.

We summarize the facts. In September, 1973, the plaintiff Carole D. MacDonald (MacDonald), who was twenty-six years old at the time, obtained from her gynecologist a prescription for Ortho-Novum contraceptive pills, manufactured by Ortho. As required by the then effective regulations promulgated by the United States Food and Drug Administration (FDA), the pill dispenser she received was labeled with a warning that "oral contraceptives are powerful and effective drugs which can cause side effects in some users and should not be used at all by some women," and that "[t]he most serious known side effect is abnormal blood clotting which can be fatal." The warning also referred MacDonald to a booklet which she obtained from her gynecologist, and which was distributed by Ortho pursuant to FDA requirements. The booklet contained detailed information about the contraceptive pill, including the increased risk to pill users that vital organs such as the brain may be damaged by abnormal blood clotting. [The warning supplied listed the death and injury rates to women of various ages from taking the pill and noted "that women who have had blood clots in the legs, lungs, or brain [should] not use oral contraceptives."] The word "stroke" did not appear on the dispenser warning or in the booklet.

MacDonald's prescription for Ortho-Novum pills was renewed at subsequent annual visits to her gynecologist. The prescription was filled annually. On July 24, 1976, after approximately three years of using the pills, MacDonald suffered an occlusion of a cerebral artery by a blood clot, an injury commonly referred to as a stroke [or a "cerebral vascular accident"]. The injury caused the death of approximately twenty per cent of MacDonald's brain tissue, and left her permanently disabled. She and her husband initiated an action in the Superior Court against Ortho, seeking recovery for her personal injuries and his consequential damages and loss of consortium.

MacDonald testified that, during the time she used the pills, she was unaware that the risk of abnormal blood clotting encompassed the risk of stroke, and that she would not have used the pills had she been warned that stroke is an associated risk. [The court noted that the amended FDA regulations listed "the serious side effects of oral contraceptives, such as thrombophlebitis, pulmonary embolism, myocardial infarction, retinal artery thrombosis, *stroke,* benign hepatic adenomas, induction of fetal abnormalities, and gallbladder disease" (emphasis added [by court—ED.]). See 21 C.F.R. §310.501(a)(2)(iv) (1984).] The case was submitted to a jury on the plaintiffs' theories that Ortho was negligent in failing to warn adequately of the dangers associated with the pills and that Ortho breached its warranty of merchantability. These two theories were treated, in effect, as a single claim of failure to warn. The jury returned a special verdict, finding no negligence or breach of warranty in the manufacture of the pills. The jury also found that Ortho adequately advised the gynecologist of the risks inherent in the pills;[7] the jury found, however, that Ortho was negligent and in breach of warranty because it failed to give MacDonald sufficient warning of such dangers. The jury further found that MacDonald's injury was caused by Ortho's pills, that the inadequacy of the warnings to MacDonald was the proximate cause of her injury, and that Ortho was liable to MacDonald and her husband.

After the jury verdict, the judge granted Ortho's motion for judgment notwithstanding the verdict, concluding that, because oral contraceptives are prescription drugs, a manufacturer's duty to warn the consumer is satisfied if the manufacturer gives adequate warnings to the prescribing physician, and that the manufacturer has no duty to warn the consumer directly.

The narrow issue, on appeal, is whether, as the plaintiffs contend, a manufacturer of birth control pills owes a direct duty to the consumer to warn her of the dangers inherent in the use of the pill. We conclude that such a duty exists under the law of this Commonwealth.

1. EXTENT OF DUTY TO WARN. . . .

[The court first noted that the general rule was that the defendant must warn all "persons who it is foreseeable will come in contact with, and

---

7. MacDonald stated at trial that her gynecologist had informed her only that oral contraceptives might cause bloating, and had not advised her of the increased risk of stroke associated with consumption of birth control pills. The physician was not joined as a defendant in this action, and no questions relating to any potential liability on his part are before us. MacDonald further testified at trial that she had read both the warning on the Dialpak tablet dispenser as well as the booklet which she received from her gynecologist.

consequently be endangered by, that product." It then recognized a "narrow" exception, as set out in Restatement (Second) of Torts §388, comment *n*, when warnings have been given to a responsible intermediary "so that the manufacturer has no duty directly to warn the consumer." It continued:]

The rule in jurisdictions that have addressed the question of the extent of a manufacturer's duty to warn in cases involving prescription drugs is that the prescribing physician acts as a "learned intermediary" between the manufacturer and the patient, and "the duty of the ethical drug manufacturer is to warn the doctor, rather than the patient, [although] the manufacturer is directly liable to the patient for a breach of such duty." McEwen v. Ortho Pharmaceutical Corp., 528 P.2d 522 (Or. 1974). Oral contraceptives, however, bear peculiar characteristics which warrant the imposition of a common law duty on the manufacturer to warn users directly of associated risks. Whereas a patient's involvement in decision-making concerning use of a prescription drug necessary to treat a malady is typically minimal or nonexistent, the healthy, young consumer of oral contraceptives is usually actively involved in the decision to use "the pill," as opposed to other available birth control products, and the prescribing physician is relegated to a relatively passive role.

Furthermore, the physician prescribing "the pill," as a matter of course, examines the patient once before prescribing an oral contraceptive and only annually thereafter. At her annual checkup, the patient receives a renewal prescription for a full year's supply of the pill. Thus, the patient may only seldom have the opportunity to explore her questions and concerns about the medication with the prescribing physician. Even if the physician, on those occasions, were scrupulously to remind the patient of the risks attendant on continuation of the oral contraceptive, "the patient cannot be expected to remember all of the details for a protracted period of time." 35 Fed. Reg. 9002 (1970).

Last, the birth control pill is specifically subject to extensive Federal regulation [which, inter alia, requires that "users of these drugs should, without exception, be furnished with written information telling them of the drug's benefits and risks."]

The oral contraceptive thus stands apart from other prescription drugs in light of the heightened participation of patients in decisions relating to use of "the pill"; the substantial risks affiliated with the product's use; the feasibility of direct warnings by the manufacturer to the user; the limited participation of the physician (annual prescriptions); and the possibility that oral communications between physicians and consumers may be insufficient or too scanty standing alone fully to apprise consumers of the product's dangers at the time the initial selection of a contraceptive method is made as well as at subsequent points when alternative methods may be considered. We conclude that the manufacturer of oral contraceptives is not justified in relying on warnings to the medical profession to satisfy its common law duty to warn, and that the manufacturer's obligation encompasses a duty to warn the ultimate user. Thus, the manufacturer's duty is to provide to the consumer written warnings conveying reasonable notice of the nature, gravity, and likelihood of known or knowable side effects, and advising the consumer to seek fuller explanation from the prescribing physician or other doctor of any such information of concern to the consumer.[13]

2. ADEQUACY OF THE WARNING

Because we reject the judge's conclusion that Ortho had no duty to warn MacDonald, we turn to Ortho's separate argument, not reached by the judge, that the evidence was insufficient to warrant the jury's finding that Ortho's warnings to MacDonald were inadequate. Ortho contends initially that its warnings complied with FDA labeling requirements, and that those requirements preempt or define the bounds of the common law duty to warn. We disagree. The regulatory history of the FDA requirements belies any objective to cloak them with preemptive effect. In response to concerns raised by drug manufacturers that warnings required and drafted by the FDA might be deemed inadequate by juries, the FDA commissioner specifically noted that the boundaries of civil tort liability for failure to warn are controlled by applicable State law. 43 Fed. Reg. 4214 (1978). Although the common law duty we today recognize is to a large degree coextensive with the regulatory duties imposed by the FDA, we are persuaded that, in instances where a trier of fact could reasonably conclude that a manufacturer's compliance with FDA labeling requirements or guidelines did not adequately apprise oral contraceptive users of inherent risks, the manufacturer should not be shielded from liability by such compliance. Thus, compliance with FDA requirements, though admissible to demonstrate lack of negligence, is not conclusive on this issue, just as violation of FDA requirements is evidence, but not conclusive evidence, of negligence. We therefore concur with the plaintiffs' argument that even if the conclusion that Ortho complied with FDA requirements were inescapable, an issue we need not decide, the jury nonetheless could have found that the lack of a reference to "stroke" breached Ortho's common law duty to warn.

The common law duty to warn, like the analogous FDA "lay language" requirement, necessitates a warning "comprehensible to the average user

---

13. This opinion does not diminish the prescribing physician's duty to "disclose in a reasonable manner all significant medical information that the physician possesses or reasonably should possess that is material to an intelligent decision by the patient whether to take 'the pill.'" Harnish v. Children's Hosp. Medical Center, 439 N.E.2d 240 (Mass. 1982).

and . . . convey[ing] a fair indication of the nature and extent of the danger to the mind of a reasonably prudent person."

Whether a particular warning measures up to this standard is almost always an issue to be resolved by a jury; few questions are "more appropriately left to a common sense lay judgment than that of whether a written warning gets its message across to an average person." Ferebee v. Chevron Chem. Co., 552 F. Supp. 1293, 1304 (D.D.C. 1982). A court may, as a matter of law, determine "whether the defendant has conformed to that standard, in any case in which the jury may not reasonably come to a different conclusion," Restatement (Second) of Torts §328B(d) and Comment *g* (1965), but judicial intrusion into jury decision-making in negligence cases is exceedingly rare. Further, we must view the evidence in the light most favorable to the plaintiffs. The test is whether "anywhere in the evidence, from whatever source derived, any combination of circumstances could be found from which a reasonable inference could be drawn in favor of the plaintiff."

Ortho argues that reasonable minds could not differ as to whether MacDonald was adequately informed of the risk of the injury she sustained by Ortho's warning that the oral contraceptives could cause "abnormal blood clotting which can be fatal" and further warning of the incremental likelihood of hospitalization or death due to blood clotting in "vital organs, such as the brain." We disagree . . . We cannot say that this jury's decision that the warning was inadequate is so unreasonable as to require the opposite conclusion as a matter of law. The jury may well have concluded, in light of their common experience and MacDonald's testimony, that the absence of a reference to "stroke" in the warning unduly minimized the warning's impact or failed to make the nature of the risk reasonably comprehensible to the average consumer. Similarly, the jury may have concluded that there are fates worse than death, such as the permanent disablement suffered by MacDonald, and that the mention of the risk of death did not, therefore, suffice to apprise an average consumer of the material risks of oral contraceptive use.

We reverse the judgment, which the judge ordered notwithstanding the verdict, and remand the case to the Superior Court for the entry of judgment for the plaintiffs.

So ordered.

O'CONNOR, J. (dissenting). . . . I would hold that, as a matter of law, by adequately informing physicians of the risks associated with its product and by complying with applicable FDA regulations, a contraceptive pill manufacturer fulfils the duty to warn that it owes consumers. . . .

I believe that the "prescription drug" rule, combined with the *Harnish* rule most fairly and efficiently allocates among drug manufacturers, physicians, and drug users, the risks and responsibilities involved with the use of prescription drugs. Furthermore, I believe that those rules best ensure that a prescription drug user will receive in the most effective manner the information that she needs to make an informed decision as to whether to use the drug. The rules place on drug manufacturers the duty to gather, compile, and provide to doctors data regarding the use of their drugs, tasks for which the manufacturers are best suited, and the rules place on doctors the burden of conveying those data to their patients in a useful and understandable manner, a task for which doctors are best suited. Doctors, unlike printed warnings, can tailor to the needs and abilities of an individual patient the information that that patient needs in order to make an informed decision whether to use a particular drug. Manufacturers are not in position to give adequate advice directly to those consumers whose medical histories and physical conditions, perhaps unknown to the consumers, make them peculiarly susceptible to risk. Prescription drugs — including oral contraceptives — differ from other products because their dangers vary widely depending on characteristics of individual consumers. Exposing a prescription drug manufacturer to liability based on a jury's determination that, despite adequately informing physicians of the drug's risks and complying with FDA regulations, the manufacturer failed reasonably to warn a particular plaintiff-consumer of individualized risks is not essential to reasonable consumer protection and places an unfair burden on prescription drug manufacturers.

NOTES

1. *Physicians as learned intermediaries.* To what extent is the decision in *MacDonald* strengthened or weakened by the wide availability of all forms of product warnings on the web? In contrast to *MacDonald*, the learned intermediary rule held firm in Harrison v. American Home Products, 165 F.3d 374 (5th Cir. 1999), when the plaintiffs complained of adverse side effects from the contraceptive Norplant, a long-term birth control method. Jolly, J., stressed the "significant role" that physicians played "in prescribing Norplant and in educating their patients about the benefits and disadvantages to using it." He also rejected the view that AHP's aggressive direct-to-consumer marketing campaign undercut the physicians duty to warn in the absence of any evidence that the plaintiffs "actually saw, let alone relied, on" any AHP marketing materials. What result if they had so relied? In contrast, the court in Perez v. Wyeth Laboratories, 734 A.2d 1245 (N.J. 1999), did impose a direct duty to warn on Wyeth because of its "massive advertising campaign for Norplant in 1991, which it directed at women rather than at their doctors," through such women's magazines as Glamour, Mademoiselle and Cosmopolitan. In so doing, the court relied on the Restatement (Third) of Torts §6(d), which reads:

A prescription drug or medical device is not reasonably safe due to inadequate instructions or warnings if reasonable instructions or warnings regarding foreseeable risks of harm are not provided to:

(1) prescribing and other health-care providers who are in a position to reduce the risks of harm in accordance with the instructions or warnings; or

(2) the patient when the manufacturer knows or has reason to know that health-care providers will not be in a position to reduce the risks of harm in accordance with the instructions or warnings.

On the status of the learned intermediary doctrine in birth control and mass vaccination cases, the Third Restatement takes a studious pass: "The Institute leaves to developing case law whether exceptions to the learned intermediary rule in these or other situations should be recognized." RTT: PL §6, comment *e*. How does *MacDonald* come out under the Third Restatement test? Should Wyeth's direct promotional activities with other drugs be factored into the mix under §6(d)(2)?

2. *Pharmacists' duty to warn.* In McKee v. American Home Products Corp., 782 P.2d 1045, 1051 (Wash. 1989), the court refused to subject a pharmacist to the duties to warn normally imposed on prescribing physicians:

In deciding whether to use a prescription drug, the patient relies primarily on the expertise and judgment of the physician. Proper weighing of the risks and benefits of a proposed drug treatment and determining what facts to tell the patient about the drug requires an individualized medical judgment based on knowledge of the patient and his or her medical condition. The physician is not required to disclose all risks associated with a drug, only those that are material. It is apparent that a pharmacist would not be qualified to make such a judgment as to materiality. Moreover, circumstances may exist justifying nondisclosure of even material risks. Requiring the pharmacist to warn of potential risks associated with a drug would interject the pharmacist into the physician-patient relationship and interfere with ongoing treatment. We believe that duty, and any liability arising therefrom, is best left with the physician.

The court also held that a pharmacist could be held liable for prescribing drugs that to his personal knowledge were contraindicated for this particular patient—perhaps because of alcoholism—or for dispensing drugs without a label indicating the maximum safe dosage, given the standard practice to the contrary. *McKee* is followed in the Third Restatement §6(e), which restricts the liability of retail sellers of drugs and medical devices to cases of manufacturing defects (why?) or for failing "to exercise reasonable care and such failure causes harm to persons." *McKee* has also been followed in Massachusetts, notwithstanding *MacDonald*. In Cottam v. CVS Pharmacy, 764 N.E.2d 814 (Mass. 2002), the court noted that any generalized duty to warn poses excessive burdens on pharmacists to retain records, and might tempt pharmacists to barrage their patients with warnings that might induce patients to disregard the advice of their physicians. Consistent with *McKee*, the duty to warn was, however, imposed in Happel v. Wal-Mart Stores, Inc., 766 N.E.2d 1118, 1124 (Ill. 2002). There the defendant maintained a registry that warned of possible adverse drug interactions or allergic reactions for all of its customers. "The burden on defendant of imposing this duty is minimal. All that is required is that the pharmacist telephone the physician and inform him or her of the contraindication. Alternatively, the pharmacist could provide the same information to the patient." What incentives does this case give to pharmacies that have registries? Should pharmacies be allowed first to undertake to supply this additional service, but disclaim or limit their liability for breach? Should all pharmacists be required routinely to collect this information? Are these cases consistent with the view in *Murphy, supra* at 767, that pharmacists supply services, not products?

3. *Mass vaccination cases.* The issue of warnings has proved critically important to mass immunization programs. Davis v. Wyeth Laboratories, Inc., 399 F.2d 121, 129-131 (9th Cir. 1968), and Reyes v. Wyeth Laboratories, Inc., 498 F.2d 1264 (5th Cir. 1974), are the watershed cases involving liability for the Sabin live virus polio vaccine. In *Davis*, the plaintiff was vaccinated as part of a mass immunization program administered by the local pharmacist, as no physician was available to do the job. The program for immunization was promoted by one of the defendant's representatives whose expenses were reimbursed by the local medical organization. The court held that the defendant did not meet its duty to warn when it failed to inform the plaintiff of the one-in-a-million chance that even when properly prepared and administered the vaccine could cause polio.

> Ordinarily in the case of prescription drugs warning to the prescribing physician is sufficient. . . .
>
> Here, however, although the drug was denominated a prescription drug it was not dispensed as such. It was dispensed to all comers at mass clinics without an individualized balancing by a physician of the risks involved. In such cases (as in the case of over-the-counter sales of nonprescription drugs) warning by the manufacturer to its immediate purchaser will not suffice. . . . In such cases, then, it is the responsibility of the manufacturer to see that warnings reach the consumer, either by giving warning itself or by obligating the purchaser to give warning. Here appellee knew that warnings were not reaching the consumer. Appellee had taken an active part in setting up the mass immunization clinic program for the society and well knew that the program did not make any such provision, either in advertising prior to the clinics or at the clinics themselves. On the contrary, it attempted to assure all members of the community that they should take the vaccine . . .

This duty does not impose an unreasonable burden on the manufacturer. When drugs are sold over the counter to all comers warnings normally can be given by proper labeling. Such method of giving warning was not available here, since the vaccine came in bottles never seen by the consumer. But other means of communication such as advertisements, posters, releases to be read and signed by recipients of the vaccine, or oral warnings were clearly available and could easily have been undertaken or prescribed by appellee.

In *Reyes*, the court then let the jury decide whether the vaccine was the physical cause of the injury and whether an adequate warning would have led the plaintiff to change his behavior. "In the absence of evidence rebutting the presumption, a jury finding that the defendant's product was the producing cause of the plaintiff's injury would be sufficient to hold him liable." Does this presumption make sense if the background rate of infection from the "wild-strain" is known on average to be 10 or 100 times as great as that from vaccines?

Reyes and *Davis* were first-generation cases in which no warnings had been provided. Subsequent litigation focused on the adequacy of the warnings. In Givens v. Lederle, 556 F.2d 1341, 1343 (5th Cir. 1977), another Sabin vaccine case — the defendant Lederle's warning to physicians stated in full:

> Paralytic disease following the ingestion of live polio virus vaccines has been reported in individuals receiving the vaccine, and in some instances, in persons who were in close contact with subjects who had been given live oral polio virus vaccine. Fortunately, such occurrences are rare, and it could not be definitely established that any such case was due to the vaccine strain and was not coincidental with infection due to naturally occurring poliomyelitis, or other enteroviruses.

The package insert also noted that the risk, if any, was 1 in 3 million. The physician who had inoculated the plaintiff's daughter gave the plaintiff no warning of the risk because he thought that the insert was too "nebulous" to require it. On appeal, the court held that this testimony, together with evidence showing that such infections had occurred, supported the jury's verdict that the warning was inadequate, especially because the warning denied any definite connection between the vaccine and the disease. Dr. Sabin had testified for the defendant that his vaccine could not possibly cause polio. What result if the FDA has approved this warning?

4. Reforming mass torts. The number of large damage awards have substantially increased the costs of vaccines. See Manning, Changing Rules of Tort Law and the Market for Childhood Vaccines, 37 J.L. & Econ. 247, 248 (1994), whose econometric analysis shows that the price of the DPT vaccine between 1975 and 1990 increased by over 2,000 percent, of which over 96 percent went to litigation costs. Numbers like these have given rise to much scholarly criticism of the law. See Huber, Safety and the Second Best: The Hazards of Public Risk Management in the Courts, 85 Colum. L. Rev. 277 (1985):

> Which brings us to the whooping cough vaccine, one for which especially precise risk figures are available. In recent decades the vaccine has been used to immunize almost every child in the United States. According to a report by two scientists at the Centers for Disease Control, use of the vaccine prevents an estimated 322,000 cases of whooping cough per year. An estimated 457 persons per year would die of the disease without the vaccination program; use of the vaccine reduces annual mortality to 44, for a net annual savings of 413 lives. Tragically, however, about 1 in every 310,000 recipients experiences serious, long term brain damage. Without the vaccine there would be 29 such cases per year; vaccine raises that figure to 54 cases, an increase of 25 cases per year. The aggregate figures could scarcely be less ambiguous; receiving the vaccine increases the risk of one particular form of injury a little, but drastically reduces the risk of another.

Huber notes that notwithstanding FDA approval and encouragement of the vaccine program, Wyeth has ceased to produce it solely because of the risk of tort liability, notwithstanding its net social benefits.

One possible reform would allow the parties by contract to limit the damages payable for adverse events on the ground that high damages are misguided so long as compensation is paid for all injuries, whether or not caused by the vaccine. The cap on damages would reduce the sale price and thus induce consumers to use vaccines that promise some net advantage. See for the proposal, Rubin, Tort Reform by Contract 62-63 (1993).

In response to the crisis, Congress passed the National Childhood Vaccine Injury Act of 1986, which provides for a complex system of no-fault compensation of up to $250,000 for persons who suffer particular side effects from certain vaccine programs within specified time limits. 42 U.S.C. §300aa (2000). The details of the statute are discussed in Chapter 12, Section C, and raise many of the hard issues of proof of causation found in other settings. The vaccine statute covers only a small sliver of cases, and the question is whether other devices might sensibly limit the potential scope of duty to warn cases in all situations involving drugs and medical devices.

5. *Standardized warnings.* The decisions in both *MacDonald* and *Givens* that allows juries to treat FDA warnings as statutory minimums has provoked much response at both the state and federal level.

Consider the Michigan Revised Judicature Act of 1961, Mich. Stat. Ann. §600.2946 (5)(West 2007):

(5) In a product liability action against a manufacturer or seller, a product that is a drug is not defective or unreasonably dangerous, and the manufacturer or seller is not liable, if the drug was approved for safety and efficacy by the United States food and drug administration, and the drug and its labeling were in compliance with the United States food and drug administration's approval at the time the drug left the control of the manufacturer or seller. However, this subsection does not apply to a drug that is sold in the United States after the effective date of an order of the United States food and drug administration to remove the drug from the market or to withdraw its approval. This subsection does not apply if the defendant at any time before the event that allegedly caused the injury does any of the following:

    (a) Intentionally withholds from or misrepresents to the United States food and drug administration information concerning the drug that is required to be submitted under the federal food, drug, and cosmetic act . . . , and the drug would not have been approved, or the United States food and drug administration would have withdrawn approval for the drug if the information were accurately submitted.

The stakes of this legislative intervention are huge. Without such a provision, the adequacy of all drug warnings is largely left to the jury. With this provision, a pharmaceutical defendant gets summary judgment unless one of the exceptions applies, thereby stopping most duty to warn cases in their tracks even after the statutory exceptions are taken into account. The defenders of the statute point to the excessive risk aversion that the FDA has on the question of new drug approval. The attackers of the statute point to the Vioxx and Avandia cases to demonstrate the serious gaps in the FDA approval process. For a review of the huge literature on this topic, see Struve, The FDA and the Tort System: Postmarketing Surveillance, Compensation, and the Role of Litigation, 5 Yale J. Health Pol'y L. & Ethics 587 (2005) (critical of the statute); Noah, Rewarding Regulatory Compliance: The Pursuit of Symmetry in Products Liability, 8 Geo. L.J. 2147 (2000) (supportive of statute).

How long will the Michigan statute remain on the books if other states do not follow suit, given the political dynamics outlined in *Blankenship*, at *supra* 786? Quite naturally, since this debate depends at least in part of the scope of FDA rules and regulations, the matter has migrated to intense disputes at the federal level, discussed *infra* at 842.

Vassallo v. Baxter Healthcare Corp.
696 N.E.2d 909 (Mass. 1998)

GREANEY, J. In this products liability case, the plaintiff Florence Vassallo claimed that the defendants, Baxter Healthcare Corporation and Baxter

International, Inc., were liable to her for damages because silicone breast implants, manufactured by a predecessor company to the defendants (Heyer-Schulte Corporation), that had been implanted in her were negligently designed, accompanied by negligent product warnings, and breached the implied warranty of merchantability, with the consequence that she was injured. The plaintiff Vincent Vassallo claimed a loss of consortium. The plaintiffs also asserted a claim for violation of G.L. c. 93A, §§2(a) and 9. [The court affirmed the judgment for the plaintiff below on the negligence and statutory claims.]

We conclude, however, that we should change our products liability law to conform to the clear majority rule regarding what has to be shown to recover in a breach of warranty claim for failure to warn of risks associated with a product, and we do so in Part 3 of this opinion.

The jury could have based their verdicts on the following evidence. In February, 1977, at the age of forty-eight, Mrs. Vassallo underwent breast implantation surgery. The silicone gel breast implants that Mrs. Vassallo received were manufactured by Heyer-Schulte Corporation in October, 1976. Through a series of corporate transactions, the defendants assumed responsibility for breast implant products manufactured by Heyer-Schulte.

In 1992, Mrs. Vassallo underwent a mammogram after complaining of chest pains that extended up under her left armpit. The mammogram revealed that her breast implants possibly had ruptured. The silicone gel implants were subsequently removed in April, 1993, and were replaced with saline implants. During the course of the explant surgery, the surgeon noted severe, permanent scarring of Mrs. Vassallo's pectoral muscles which she attributed to the silicone gel. The implants themselves were encapsulated in scar tissue with multiple nodules of silicone granulomas. Dissection of the scar tissue capsules revealed that the left implant had ruptured, releasing free silicone gel, while the right implant was intact, but had several pinholes through which silicone gel could escape.

[The court reviewed plaintiff's expert evidence on the harm caused by the slow release of silicone gel. It also examined "extensive testimony that Heyer-Schulte knew of the risk of rupture and of its adverse consequences. In 1976 the defendant's president issued a letter to doctors that did not address all of the adverse consequences that the leakage could have on an implant user, including those going to the "risks of chronic inflammation, permanent tissue scarring, or possible effects on the immune system."]

Mrs. Vassallo stated that, if she had known that the implants could cause permanent scarring, chronic inflammation, and problems with her immune system, she would not have gone ahead with the implantation procedure. We now turn to the issues appropriate for discussion.

[The court extensively reviewed and rejected defendant's objections to the admission of plaintiff's expert witnesses and documentary evidence.]

We take this opportunity, however, to consider the defendants' argument that we should change our products liability law concerning the implied warranty of merchantability from what is stated in Hayes v. Ariens Co., 462 N.E.2d 273 (Mass. 1984), and that the law should be reformulated to adopt a "state of the art" standard that conditions a manufacturer's liability on actual or constructive knowledge of the risks.

Our current law, regarding the duty to warn under the implied warranty of merchantability, presumes that a manufacturer was fully informed of all risks associated with the product at issue, regardless of the state of the art at the time of the sale, and amounts to strict liability for failure to warn of these risks. This rule has been justified by the public policy that a defective product, "unreasonably dangerous due to lack of adequate warning[s], [is] not fit for the ordinary purposes for which [it is] used regardless of the absence of fault on [a defendant's] part." At trial, [the judge followed *Hayes* by refusing to issue a "jury instruction that a manufacturer need only warn of risks 'known or reasonably knowable in light of the generally accepted scientific knowledge available at the time of the manufacture and distribution of the device.'"] While the judge's instruction was a correct statement of our law, we recognize that we are among a distinct minority of States that applies a hindsight analysis to the duty to warn.[17] . . .

The thin judicial support for a hindsight approach to the duty to warn is easily explained. The goal of the law is to induce conduct that is capable of being performed. This goal is not advanced by imposing liability for failure to warn of risks that were not capable of being known.

The Restatement (Third) of Torts: Products Liability §2(c) (1998), recently approved by the American Law Institute, reaffirms the principle expressed in Restatement (Second) of Torts, *supra* at §402A comment *j*, by stating that a product "is defective because of inadequate instructions or warnings when the foreseeable risks of harm posed by the product could have been reduced or avoided by the provision of reasonable instructions or warnings . . . and the omission of the instructions or warnings renders the product not reasonably safe." The rationale behind the principle is explained by stating that "[u]nforeseeable risks arising from foreseeable product use . . . by definition cannot specifically be warned against." Restatement (Third) of Torts: Products Liability, *supra* at §2 comment *m*, at 34. However, comment m also clarifies the manufacturer's duty "to perform reasonable testing prior to marketing a product and to discover risks and risk-avoidance measures that such testing would reveal. A seller is charged with knowledge of what reasonable testing would reveal." Id. . . .

---

17. The Reporters' Note to the Restatement (Third) of Torts: Products Liability §2(c) comment *m*, at 106 (1998), lists four States taking the position that a manufacturer is charged with a duty to warn of risks without regard to whether the manufacturer knew or reasonably should have known of the risks, including Massachusetts; Hawaii; Pennsylvania; Washington.

In recognition of the clear judicial trend regarding the duty to warn in products liability cases, and the principles stated in Restatement (Third) of Torts: Products Liability, *supra* at §2 and comment *m*, we hereby revise our law to state that a defendant will not be held liable under an implied warranty of merchantability for failure to warn or provide instructions about risks that were not reasonably foreseeable at the time of sale or could not have been discovered by way of reasonable testing prior to marketing the product. A manufacturer will be held to the standard of knowledge of an expert in the appropriate field, and will remain subject to a continuing duty to warn (at least purchasers) of risks discovered following the sale of the product at issue. In accordance with the usual rule governing retroactivity in this type of action, the standard just expressed will apply to all claims on which a final judgment has not been entered, or as to which an appeal is pending or the appeal period has not expired, and to all claims on which an action is commenced after the release of this opinion. [The court noted that the defendant could not take advantage of this change in law because of the adverse jury verdict on the negligence count, and the jury's apparent conclusion that defendant did have actual or constructive notice of the risks associated with their silicone implants.]

[Affirmed.]

NOTES

1. *The silicone breast implant controversy.* The modern disputes over silicone implants began in 1992 when then FDA Commissioner David Kessler announced a ban of silicone-gel-filled breast implants for cosmetic purposes on the ground that they had not been proven safe. The ban was announced after between 1 and 2 million women had already received these breast implants, raising questions of whether these implants should be removed and replaced or simply watched. In consequence of the ban, the onslaught of litigation against the implant manufacturers frequently resulted in large verdicts (not always affirmed fully on appeal) in individual cases and a huge class action suit against implant manufacturers that resulted in a complex settlement of $4.25 billion. In May 1995, Dow-Corning, one of the largest implant manufacturers, filed for bankruptcy. At the same time, an emerging and widespread professional consensus within the scientific community denied any association between silicone implants and any connective tissue disorder. This evidence is necessarily statistical in nature because connective tissue disorder is found both in women who did and did not receive breast implants. The class settlement itself unraveled because of the large number of individual claims filed after its announcement. For an exhaustive and highly critical account of this litigation, see M. Angell, Science on Trial: The Clash of Medical Evidence

and the Law in the Breast Implant Case (1996). For a defense of his original decision, see Kessler, The Basis for the FDA's Decision on Breast Implants, 326 N. Engl. J. Med. 1713 (1992). These implants now have been allowed back on the market both for medical reasons and for breast augmentation, but have been subject to extensive post-marketing review. See http://www.fda.gov/cdrh/breastimplants/qa2006.html#2.The FDA now takes the position in line with the Institute of Medicine that no convincing evidence links breast implants with either connective tissue disease or cancer. See generally http://www.fda.gov/cdrh/breastimplants/siliconegel.html.

2. *Unavoidably dangerous products.* Closely related to §402A, comment *j*, is comment *k*, which deals with products known to be unavoidably dangerous. In these cases, it is impractical to remove the product from the market or to alter its composition because removing the adverse side effects undermines the effectiveness of the treatment. In consequence, a warning that allows informed consumer choice is the only workable alternative. This use of warnings has arisen in a number of important contexts.

a. Hepatitis. At one time courts flirted with a strict liability standard for transfusions of contaminated blood. In Brody v. Overlook Hospital, 296 A.2d 668 (N.J. Super. Ct. Law Div. 1972), the decedent died from hepatitis caused by a blood transfusion. At the time of the transfusion, it was known that blood could be contaminated with the hepatitis virus, but no test could detect it. The trial court held that the "imposition of strict tort liability may well spur the hospital to take a more active role in influencing the bank's collection processes, i.e. more careful screening of donors." The court also thought that strict liability sensibly spread the loss "among all parties, i.e. donors, blood banks, perhaps its patients. This 'allocative effect' will be felt if hospitals allocate their hepatitis costs as a charge on each unit of blood actually used: physicians will automatically more carefully weigh the risks of surgery and transfusions."

In *Brody* the plaintiff's victory was short-lived, as the decision was reversed in Brody v. Overlook Hospital, 317 A.2d 392, 395 (N.J. Super. Ct. App. Div. 1974). The court noted, first, that "in December 1966 (when the blood was transfused) there was no known scientific or medical test for determining whether blood drawn from a donor contained serum hepatitis virus," and used comment *k* to reject the strict liability theory. It also rejected "loss spreading" and "allocative effect" rationales, concluding that this theory "has some weight but not nearly enough when laid beside other more basic considerations. It plays only the part of a makeweight argument." The New Jersey Supreme Court affirmed the appellate division in a brief per curiam opinion, 332 A.2d 596 (N.J. 1975).

More than 40 states have enacted legislation adopting the negligence standard in hepatitis cases, including Illinois, 745 Ill. Comp. Stat. 40/1-3 (West 2007). The Illinois statute first noted that whole blood, plasma, and other body parts are of great importance to the "health and welfare" of the people of the state and that a strict liability rule "inhibits the exercise of sound medical judgment and restricts the availability of important scientific knowledge, skills and materials." It then provided that a party supplying blood need only "warrant" to the recipient of the blood or related product that "he has exercised due care and followed professional standards of care in providing the service according to the current state of the medical arts," and has complied with applicable labeling provisions. The Idaho variation adopts a general negligence standard but imposes a strict liability rule on any "paid blood, organ or tissue donor, or a blood, organ or tissue bank operated for profit." Idaho Code §39-3702 (2002). Is there any reason to suppose that the commercial provision of blood results in a systematic reduction in the quality of the blood furnished?

Since *Brody* was decided reliable tests have been developed to detect the hepatitis virus in blood. Is there any way in which this technological breakthrough could be related to the particular rule of liability? Does the widespread availability of the test point to the superiority of either a negligence or a strict liability rule?

For early responses to the hepatitis question see generally Kessel, Transfused Blood, Serum Hepatitis, and The Coase Theorem, 17 J.L. & Econ. 265 (1974).

b. Asbestos. The single most controversial application of comment *k* is in the numerous suits for asbestos-related diseases. Asbestos fits within the category of unavoidably dangerous products because it is both highly useful as an insulation product and because it undeniably causes many fatal conditions — chief among them asbestosis, mesothelioma, and bronchiogenic carcinoma. The watershed case is Borel v. Fibreboard Paper Products Corp., 493 F.2d 1076 (5th Cir. 1973), which affirmed a jury verdict against asbestos manufacturers on behalf of an insulation worker who had extensive contact with asbestos for more than 30 years. Wisdom, J., in an exhaustive opinion, found sufficient evidence of the dangers of asbestos in the medical literature to impose upon manufacturers — here held to the standard of "experts" in the field — a duty to warn all workers coming in contact with the product to allow them to make an informed choice of whether to expose themselves to asbestos.

Before *Borel* no plaintiff had ever recovered from an asbestos manufacturer. The decision unleashed a veritable avalanche of suits against asbestos suppliers. By most reckonings they constituted the single largest body of cases in the federal system and by their sheer numbers have overwhelmed the operation of the system. See Table 9-1, *supra* at 726. The first generation of asbestos cases was brought against the manufacturers of asbestos products, virtually all of whom have been driven into bankruptcy. One early case suggested manufacturers could have been held responsible for unknowable defects, see Beshada v. Johns-Manville Products Corp., 447 A.2d 539 (N.J. 1982). This push for strict liability died for asbestos just as it died for medical products in *Vassello*. See, e.g., Anderson v. Owens-Corning Fiberglas Corp., 810 P.2d 549, 558-559 (Cal. 1991). However, as with medical products, plaintiffs consistently won on negligence theories, often obtaining hefty punitive damages.

The second wave of litigation, which began in the late 1990s, has been far broader. The typical modern lawsuit often pits thousands of plaintiffs against dozens of typically second-tier defendants, such as firms that operated premises on which asbestos products were used or which incorporated asbestos into their own products, e.g., brake linings. The recent cases typically do not involve asbestos, but pleural plaque cases. "Pleural plaques have been described as 'discrete, elevated, opaque, shiny, rounded lesions, . . . diffuse or nodular,' of the parietal pleura or diaphragm. They strongly indicate asbestos exposure." Schuck, The Worst Should Go First: Deferral Registries in Asbestos Litigation, 15 Harv. J.L. & Pub. Pol'y 541 (1992). Although these plaques illustrate exposure, they do not increase the risk of deadly asbestosis or any other deadly disease. See Weiss, Asbestos-Related Pleural Plaques and Lung Cancer, 103 Chest. 1854 (1993). An effort to forge a class action settlement of these cases was rejected in Amchem Products, Inc. v. Windsor, 521 U.S. 591 (1997), partly on the ground that it did not provide adequate safeguards for future injured persons. See also Ortiz v. Fibreboard Corp., 527 U.S. 815 (1999). The matter has now spilled over into the political arena, but Congress has been unable to fashion any solution that satisfied the plaintiffs, the various asbestos defendants and their insurers. The key bill was S. 1125, the "Fairness in Asbestos Injury Resolution (FAIR) Act of 2003." On this Act, see Report, The Fairness in Asbestos Injury Resolution Act of 2003, 108 Cong. 1 Sess. Report 108-118, stating various views on the bill. One stumbling block concerned the question of whether any suitable political settlement would respond to charges that fraudulent claims have overwhelmed the system. For an exhaustive indictment of a "malignant" enterprise on this system, see Brickman, On the Theory Class's Theories of Asbestos Litigation: The Disconnect Between Scholarship and Reality, 31 Pepperdine L. Rev. 33 (2003). For judicial evidence of sharp practices on medical evidence, see In re Silica Products Liability Litigation, 398 F. Supp. 2d 563, 571, 602 (S.D. Tex. 2005), *supra* at 727.

c. DES. In Enright by Enright v. Eli Lilly & Co., 570 N.E.2d 198 (N.Y. 1991), the court refused to extend the duty to warn to the unborn grandchildren of DES women on the ground that a "pre-conception tort" was not viable under either a negligence or strict liability theory. Wachtler, C.J., first noted the difficulties in proving causation across two or more generations, and limited recovery to persons injured in utero:

> More important, however, is recognition that public policy favors the availability of prescription drugs even though most carry some risks. That is not to say that drug manufacturers should enjoy immunity from liability

stemming from their failure to conduct adequate research and testing prior to the marketing of their products. They do not enjoy such immunity, as evidenced by our recognition of liability in favor of those who have been injured by ingestion or in utero exposure to DES. But we are aware of the dangers of overdeterrence — the possibility that research will be discouraged or beneficial drugs withheld from the market. These dangers are magnified in this context, where we are asked to recognize a legal duty toward generations not yet conceived.

d. AIDS. The unavoidably dangerous drug limitation has also held firm in AIDS cases. In Doe v. Miles Laboratories, 927 F.2d 187, 191 (4th Cir. 1991), plaintiff contracted AIDS in September 1983 when given a blood clotting agent, Koyne. This agent was prepared by concentrating blood plasma donations from about 13,000 individual plasma donors. Koyne was administered because plaintiff had sustained severe vaginal bleeding after giving birth. The court upheld a comment *k* defense because Koyne was administered before it was certain that AIDS was a blood-borne virus, when no test existed to identify the HIV virus, and when the clotting agent was medically essential. The court also held that "we cannot expect [drug companies] to have implemented a blood donor screening program when they did not know that the HIV virus was transmissible through blood or blood products."

Hood v. Ryobi America Corp.
181 F.3d 608 (4th. 1999)

WILKINSON, C.J. Wilson M. Hood lost part of his thumb and lacerated his leg when he removed the blade guards from his new Ryobi miter saw and then used the unguarded saw for home carpentry. Hood sued Ryobi, alleging that the company failed adequately to warn of the saw's dangers and that the saw was defective. Applying Maryland products liability law, the district court granted summary judgment to Ryobi on all claims.

The saw and owner's manual bore at least seven clear, simple warnings not to operate the tool with the blade guards removed. The warnings were not required to spell out all the consequences of improper use. Nor was the saw defective — Hood altered and used the tool in violation of Ryobi's clear warnings. Thus we affirm the judgment.

I.

Hood purchased a Ryobi TS-254 miter saw in Westminster, Maryland on February 25, 1995, for the purpose of performing home repairs. The saw was fully assembled at the time of purchase. It had a ten-inch diameter blade mounted on a rotating spindle controlled by a finger trigger on a handle near the top of the blade. To operate the saw, the consumer would use that handle to lower the blade through the material being cut.

Two blade guards shielded nearly the entire saw blade. A large metal guard, fixed to the frame of the saw, surrounded the upper half of the blade. A transparent plastic lower guard covered the rest of the blade and retracted into the upper guard as the saw came into contact with the work piece.

A number of warnings in the operator's manual and affixed to the saw itself stated that the user should operate the saw only with the blade guards in place. For example, the owner's manual declared that the user should "KEEP GUARDS IN PLACE" and warned: "ALWAYS USE THE SAW BLADE GUARD. Never operate the machine with the guard removed"; "NEVER operate this saw without all guards in place and in good operating condition"; and "WARNING: TO PREVENT POSSIBLE SERIOUS PER-SONAL INJURY, NEVER PERFORM ANY CUTTING OPERATION WITH THE UPPER OR LOWER BLADE GUARD REMOVED." The saw itself carried several decals stating "DANGER: DO NOT REMOVE ANY GUARD. USE OF SAW WITHOUT THIS GUARD WILL RESULT IN SERIOUS INJURY"; "OPERATE ONLY WITH GUARDS IN PLACE"; and "WARNING . . . DO NOT operate saw without the upper and lower guards in place."

The day after his purchase, Hood began working with the saw in his driveway. While attempting to cut a piece of wood approximately four inches in height Hood found that the blade guards prevented the saw blade from passing completely through the piece. Disregarding the manufac-turer's warnings, Hood decided to remove the blade guards from the saw. Hood first detached the saw blade from its spindle. He then unscrewed the four screws that held the blade guard assembly to the frame of the saw. Finally, he replaced the blade onto the bare spindle and completed his cut.

Rather than replacing the blade guards, Hood continued to work with the saw blade exposed. He worked in this fashion for about twenty minutes longer when, in the middle of another cut, the spinning saw blade flew off the saw and back toward Hood. The blade partially amputated his left thumb and lacerated his right leg.

Hood admits that he read the owner's manual and most of the warning labels on the saw before he began his work. He claims, however, that he believed the blade guards were intended solely to prevent a user's clothing or fingers from coming into contact with the saw blade. He contends that he was unaware that removing the blade guards would permit the spinning blade to detach from the saw. But Ryobi, he claims, was aware of that possibility. In fact, another customer had sued Ryobi after suffering a similar accident in the mid-1980s. . . .

II.

A manufacturer may be liable for placing a product on the market that bears inadequate instructions and warnings or that is defective in design. Hood asserts that Ryobi failed adequately to warn of the dangers of using the saw without the blade guards in place. Hood also contends that the design of the saw was defective. We disagree on both counts.

A.

Hood first complains that the warnings he received were insufficiently specific. Hood admits that Ryobi provided several clear and conspicuous warnings not to operate the saw without the blade guards. He contends, however, that the warnings affixed to the product and displayed in the operator's manual were inadequate to alert him to the dangers of doing so. In addition to Ryobi's directive "never" to operate a guardless saw, Hood would require the company to inform of the actual consequences of such conduct. Specifically, Hood contends that an adequate warning would have explained that removing the guards would lead to blade detachment.

We disagree. Maryland does not require an encyclopedic warning. Instead, "a warning need only be one that is reasonable under the circumstances." Levin v. Walter Kidde & Co., 248 A.2d 151, 153 (Md. 1968). A clear and specific warning will normally be sufficient—"the manufacturer need not warn of every mishap or source of injury that the mind can imagine flowing from the product." Liesener v. Weslo, Inc., 775 F. Supp. 857, 861 (D. Md. 1991); see *Levin*, 248 A.2d at 154 (declining to require warning of the danger that a cracked syphon bottle might explode and holding "never use cracked bottle" to be adequate as a matter of law). In deciding whether a warning is adequate, Maryland law asks whether the benefits of a more detailed warning outweigh the costs of requiring the change.

Hood assumes that the cost of a more detailed warning label is minimal in this case, and he claims that such a warning would have prevented his injury. But the price of more detailed warnings is greater than their additional printing fees alone. Some commentators have observed that the proliferation of label detail threatens to undermine the effectiveness of warnings altogether. As manufacturers append line after line onto product labels in the quest for the best possible warning, it is easy to lose sight of the label's communicative value as a whole. Well-meaning attempts to warn of every possible accident lead over time to voluminous yet impenetrable labels—too prolix to read and too technical to understand.

By contrast, Ryobi's warnings are clear and unequivocal. Three labels on the saw itself and at least four warnings in the owner's manual direct the user not to operate the saw with the blade guards removed. Two declare that "serious injury" could result from doing so. This is not a case where the manufacturer has failed to include any warnings at all with its product. Ryobi provided warnings sufficient to apprise the ordinary consumer that it is unsafe to operate a guardless saw — warnings which, if followed, would have prevented the injury in this case.

It is apparent, moreover, that the vast majority of consumers do not detach this critical safety feature before using this type of saw. Indeed, although Ryobi claims to have sold thousands of these saws, Hood has identified only one fifteen-year-old incident similar to his. Hood has thus not shown that these clear, unmistakable, and prominent warnings are insufficient to accomplish their purpose. Nor can he prove that increased label clutter would bring any net societal benefit. We hold that the warnings Ryobi provided are adequate as a matter of law.

B.

Hood's defective design claim is likewise unpersuasive [on the ground that the product alterations defeat liability].

AFFIRMED.

NOTES

1. *Warnings, design modification, and the heeding presumption.* In Liriano v. Hobart Corp., 700 N.E.2d 303, 308 (N.Y. 1998), the 17-year-old plaintiff caught his right hand and lower arm in a commercial meat grinding machine from which the employer had removed the safety guard. Unlike *Hood*, no warnings stated that it was dangerous to remove the guard. On an advisory opinion to the Second Circuit, Ciparik, J., held that a duty to warn cause of action could survive even in cases where a product modification blocked liability under a design defect theory. The court noted if the injured person is "fully aware of the hazard through general knowledge, observation or common sense, or participated in the removal of the safety device whose purpose is obvious, lack of a warning about that danger may well obviate the failure to warn as a legal cause of an injury resulting from that danger. . . . Similarly, a limited class of hazards need not be warned of as a matter of law because they are patently dangerous or pose open and obvious risks." Nonetheless, the court then returned the failure to warn cause of action for a "fact-specific" inquiry in the Second Circuit. In Liriano v. Hobart Corp., 170 F.3d 264 (2d Cir. 1999), Calabresi, J., upheld a jury verdict for the plaintiff (subject to a one-third reduction for comparative negligence) because the youthful plaintiff had only recently migrated to the United States, had worked for his employer, Super, for only a week, and

had never been given instructions on how to operate the grinder, which he had used only two or three times. In light of the variation in product users, some users might not discover dangers that others find obvious. Accordingly, he held that the "jury could reasonably find that there exist people who are employed as meat grinders and who do not know (a) that it is feasible to reduce the risk with safety guards, (b) that such guards are made available with grinders, and (c) that the grinders should be used only with the guards." He further held that on the question of causation, the burden of proof shifted to the defendant: "When a defendant's negligent act is deemed wrongful precisely because it has a strong propensity to cause the type of injury that ensued, that very causal tendency is evidence enough to establish a *prima facie* case of cause-in-fact. The burden then shifts to the *defendant* to come forward with evidence that its negligence was *not* such a but-for cause."

What result if the employer who removed the guard also covered up the initial warning affixed to the machine? Or if that warning had been placed on the removed guard? How do we know that if an adequate warning had been given, it would have been heeded? See Pavlik v. Lane Limited/ Tobacco Exporters International, 135 F.3d 876, 883-884 (3d Cir. 1998), which gave the plaintiff the benefit of a "heeding presumption as a logical corollary to comment *j*" (RST §402A). There, the decedent died from self-administered inhalation of butane distributed and manufactured by the defendants in 5.3-ounce cans. The heeding presumption was allowed to stand even though there was testimony that he had been warned of the risk of butane inhalation by his mother and further evidence that he had read the much more detailed warnings on butane gas sold by other suppliers. If the evidence on causation is in possession of the plaintiff, why put the burden on the defendant?

2. When must a warning be given? Latent defects. The adequacy of warnings has also been litigated in cases involving all types of household products. *Hood* dealt with what a warning must illustrate, but a threshold question in these cases is whether the circumstances of a case call for any duty to warn at all. In Ayers v. Johnson & Johnson Co., 818 P.2d 1337, 1341 (Wash. 1991), David Ayers, then aged 15 months, had taken an unmarked bottle of Johnson's baby oil out of the purse of his 13-year-old sister. Just as he began to drink the oil, his mother yelled at him, causing him to gasp and inhale the oil in his lungs. Once there, the baby oil coated his air sacs and quickly led to oxygen deprivation that resulted in serious injuries: His leg motions became spastic; he had limited control over his head movements; and he suffered retardation, seizures, and lost any ability to speak.

Both sides agreed that once David inhaled the baby oil, no medical attention could have prevented these injuries. Plaintiff contended that a warning on the bottle was needed to alert users of this risk in order to keep baby oil out of the reach of infants in the first place. The plaintiff's mother testified that she read warnings, and kept dangerous products away from her young children, and instructed her teenage daughters to do the same. Both mother and daughters testified that they thought baby oil could cause diarrhea or stomach upset, but not more serious injuries. Johnson & Johnson argued that it was rank speculation to claim that the additional knowledge would have led to different conduct since all members of the Ayers family knew that the baby oil was only for external use, and was dangerous if taken internally. The jury found for the plaintiff, and its verdict was sustained on appeal:

> On the basis of this evidence, the jury was entitled to infer that if the Ayerses had known of the dangers of aspiration, they would have treated the baby oil with greater care; that they would have treated it with the caution they used in relation to items they recognized as highly dangerous, like cleaning products; and that had they done so, the accident would have never occurred. We conclude that the evidence of causation presented to the jury was sufficient to sustain the jury's verdict.

Should Johnson & Johnson change the warnings on its bottles? On its package inserts? If a warning should be included, what should it say?

3. *Duty to warn: patent defects.* The risks in *Ayers* were both latent and remote. What ought to be done with respect to generic properties of common substances known to cause harm, as with alcohol? In Garrison v. Heublein, Inc., 673 F.2d 189 (7th Cir. 1982), the court rejected the plaintiff's claim for "physical and mental injuries as a result of consuming the defendant's product [Smirnoff vodka] over a twenty year period," holding that the defendant had no duty to warn of risks that were common knowledge. Common knowledge, however, did not allow the defendant to obtain a summary judgment in Hon v. Stroh Brewery Co., 835 F.2d 510, 511 (3d Cir. 1987). The plaintiff's husband had died of pancreatitis that the plaintiff alleged had resulted mainly from his consuming about 8 to 12 cans of the defendant's beer each week over a period of several years. The court accepted the plaintiff's claim that a warning was required because it was not common knowledge that "*either* excessive *or* prolonged, even though moderate, use of alcohol may result in diseases of many kinds, including pancreatic disease." The defendant's comment *j* defense was rejected in part because the jury could find that Stroh's advertising campaign linked the consumption of large quantities of beer to the "good life." The Court wrote that "comment *j* does not say that whenever alcohol is consumed over a long period of time the dangers are necessarily generally known. Rather it says that *when* the danger is generally known, no warning is required." Note that recent federal regulations, 27 C.F.R. §16.21 (2002), now require the following warning label to be attached conspicuously to containers of alcoholic beverages sold:

GOVERNMENT WARNING: (1) According to the Surgeon General, women should not drink alcoholic beverages during pregnancy because of the risk of birth defects. (2) Consumption of alcoholic beverages impairs your ability to drive a car or operate machinery, and may cause health problems.

4. Warnings or design? The impatience with warnings received a very different spin in Latin, Good Warnings, Bad Products, and Cognitive Limitations, 41 UCLA L. Rev. 1193 (1994). Latin rejects the "Rational Risk Calculator Model" of human behavior, often championed by economists, in favor of the rival "Mistake and Momentary Inattention" model. This model draws more heavily on the psychological and sociological literature to support the view that even cautious actors are subject to momentary lapses in judgment or attention. Latin strongly supports this second perspective, which clearly implies that even "good" warnings should not be respected when cheap design alternatives are available to protect the users of products from the disastrous consequences of not heeding a warning. Latin's attack is Restatement §402A, comment *j*: "Where warning is given, the seller may reasonably assume that it will be read and heeded." If the Mistake and Momentary Inattention Model is correct, Latin argues the law should require design changes no matter how strong or "good" the warnings are.

Latin criticizes Skyhook Corp. v. Jasper, 560 P.2d 934 (N.M. 1977) (overruled in Klopp v. Wackenhut Corp., 824 P.2d 293 (N.M. 1992)), in which defendant's warning that its crane should never be brought within ten feet of a high-voltage line barred recovery in a wrongful death action stemming from an electrocution when the crane operator moved the crane into the danger zone. Oman, C.J., relied not only on the presumption of comment *j*, but also on the additional facts that the crane had been used without incident for five years, and that both crane operators had been personally told of the risks of letting the crane go near these wires.

Latin's prescriptions have been followed in Uniroyal Goodrich Tire Co. v Martinez, 977 S.W.2d 328, 337 (Tex. 1998), in which the plaintiff mechanic was injured when a 16-inch tire exploded while he sought to mount it on a 16.5-inch wheel. The plaintiff ignored detailed warnings on a label attached to the tire that contained a list of stern "NEVERS," beginning with "never mount a 16″ size diameter tire on a 16.5″ rim. Mounting a 16″ tire on a 16.5″ inch rim can cause severe injury or death." These "nevers" were followed by warnings about the proper procedures for mounting tires, all of which plaintiff ignored. Plaintiff claimed the tire was "defective because it failed to incorporate a safer alternative bead design that would have kept the tire from exploding." Phillips, C.J., rejected the test of §402A, comment *j*, and, citing Latin, adopted the position of the Third Restatement, §2, comment *l*, requiring the design change.

> We do not hold, as the dissenting justices claim, that "a product is defective whenever it could be more safely designed without substantially impairing its utility," or that "warnings are irrelevant in determining whether a product is reasonably safe." Rather, . . . we agree with the new Restatement that warnings and safer alternative designs are factors, among others, for the jury to consider in determining whether the product as designed is reasonably safe. While the dissenting judges say that they also agree with the Restatement's approach, they would, at least in this case, remove the balancing process from the jury.

Who's right? As a variation on the warnings question, what should be done with Q-Tips or other cotton swabs whose standard warnings instruct people never to insert them into the ear? Is the correct remedy to redesign the Q-Tip, strengthen the warning, take the product off the market, or leave things as they are?

5. *Duty to warn of dangerous products made by others.* In Adams v. Northern Illinois Gas Co., 809 N.E.2d 1248, 1262-1263 (Ill. 2004), the decedent was killed when she turned on the light switch while entering her own home. Her house had been filled with natural gas that leaked out of a faulty connector between the main gas line on the kitchen stove. The leak had resulted from the predictable corrosion in a flexible connector hose manufactured years before by the Cobra Hose Company, which went out of business in 1979. The connector was attached to household appliances by a "brazing" process that relied on a mix of phosphorous and copper in the hose. That phosphorous reacted with the sulfur contained in ethyl mercaptin, which gas companies routinely add to give a smell to natural gas, which is otherwise odorless and deadly. NI knew of the dangers of these connectors, which a voluntary trade group, the American National Standards Institute, had long banned from the market in 1968. From time to time, NI had issued warnings to customers about the dangers of these fittings, but these warnings had not reached the decedent or anyone in her household.

Adams is a product liability case only in the sense that the defendant's natural gas is a product supplied to homes. But that product contained no defect. Nonetheless, majority of the Illinois Court held that NI had a duty to warn the homeowner of the dangers of appliances made by others in selling its own product. Freeman, J., held that it did not matter that the defendant gas company neither manufactured nor owned the defective equipment, or that it had no knowledge of this particular premise leak.

> [T]here is no dispute that NI-Gas had actual knowledge of the danger. NI-Gas knew that sulfides in the gas corroded brazed connectors, ultimately causing the connectors to leak gas; it was only a question of when the connector would fail. Based on its superior knowledge and the fact that it helped to create

the dangerous condition, we hold that NI-Gas owed a common law duty of reasonable care with respect to the brazed connectors. . . . We repeat plaintiff's clarification at oral argument that NI-Gas' duty of reasonable care in this case consists only of warning and not inspection.

Note that generally gas companies have a duty to fix those leaks of which they have actual or constructive knowledge. Who should bear the costs of inspecting older homes to see if they are equipped with defective hoses?

SECTION E. PLAINTIFF'S CONDUCT

Daly v. General Motors Corp.
575 P.2d 1162 (Cal. 1978)

RICHARDSON, J. The most important of several problems which we consider is whether the principles of comparative negligence expressed by us in Li v. Yellow Cab Co., apply to actions founded on strict products liability. We will conclude that they do. . . .

[The decedent was driving his Opel southbound on the Harbor Freeway between 50 and 70 miles per hour when it struck the metal divider. The car spun around and the decedent was forcibly thrown from the car, sustaining fatal head injuries. The plaintiffs alleged that the door lock was defectively design because of its exposed push button, which, it was claimed, was forced open during the original collision.]

Over plaintiffs' objections, defendants were permitted to introduce evidence indicating that: (1) the Opel was equipped with a seat belt-shoulder harness system, and a door lock, either of which if used, it was contended, would have prevented Daly's ejection from the vehicle; (2) Daly used neither the harness system nor the lock; (3) the 1970 Opel owner's manual contained warnings that seat belts should be worn and doors locked when the car was in motion for "accident security"; and (4) Daly was intoxicated at the time of collision, which evidence the jury was advised was admitted for the limited purpose of determining whether decedent had used the vehicle's safety equipment. After relatively brief deliberations the jury returned a verdict favoring all defendants, and plaintiffs appeal from the ensuing adverse judgment.

STRICT PRODUCTS LIABILITY AND COMPARATIVE FAULT. . . .

Those counseling against the recognition of comparative fault principles in strict products liability cases vigorously stress, perhaps equally, not only the conceptual, but also the semantic difficulties incident to such a course. The task of merging the two concepts is said to be impossible, that "apples and oranges" cannot be compared, that "oil and water" do not mix, and that strict liability, which is not founded on negligence or fault, is inhospitable to comparative principles. The syllogism runs, contributory negligence was only a defense to negligence, comparative negligence only affects contributory negligence, therefore comparative negligence cannot be a defense to strict liability.... While fully recognizing the theoretical and semantic distinctions between the twin principles of strict products liability and traditional negligence, we think they can be blended or accommodated.

The inherent difficulty in the "apples and oranges" argument is its insistence on fixed and precise definitional treatment of legal concepts. In the evolving areas of both products liability and tort defenses, however, there has developed much conceptual overlapping and interweaving in order to attain substantial justice. The concept of strict liability itself, as we have noted, arose from dissatisfaction with the wooden formalisms of traditional tort and contract principles in order to protect the consumer of manufactured goods. Similarly, increasing social awareness of its harsh "all or nothing" consequences led us in *Li* to moderate the impact of traditional contributory negligence in order to accomplish a fairer and more balanced result. We acknowledged an intermixing of defenses of contributory negligence and assumption of risk and formally effected a type of merger....

Furthermore, the "apples and oranges" argument may be conceptually suspect. It has been suggested that the term "contributory negligence," one of the vital building blocks upon which much of the argument is based, may indeed itself be a misnomer since it lacks the first element of the classical negligence formula, namely, a duty of care owing to another....

Given all of the foregoing, we are, in the wake of *Li*, disinclined to resolve the important issue before us by the simple expedient of matching linguistic labels which have evolved either for convenience or by custom. Rather, we consider it more useful to examine the foundational reasons underlying the creation of strict products liability in California to ascertain whether the purposes of the doctrine would be defeated or diluted by adoption of comparative principles. We imposed strict liability against the manufacturer and in favor of the user or consumer in order to relieve injured consumers "from *problems of proof* inherent in pursuing negligence ... and warranty ... remedies...."As we have noted, we sought to place the burden of loss on manufacturers rather than "... injured persons *who are powerless to protect themselves* ..." ([we promote the "*protection of otherwise defenseless victims* of manufacturing defects and the spreading throughout society of the cost of compensating them";] italics added).

The foregoing goals, we think, will not be frustrated by the adoption of comparative principles. Plaintiffs will continue to be relieved of proving that the manufacturer or distributor was negligent in the production, design, or dissemination of the article in question. Defendant's liability for injuries caused by a defective product remains strict. The principle of protecting the defenseless is likewise preserved, for plaintiff's recovery will be reduced *only* to the extent that his own lack of reasonable care contributed to his injury. The cost of compensating the victim of a defective product, albeit proportionately reduced, remains on defendant manufacturer, and will, through him, be "spread among society." However, we do not permit plaintiff's own conduct relative to the product to escape unexamined, and as to that share of plaintiff's damages which flows from his own fault we discern no reason of policy why it should, following *Li,* be borne by others. Such a result would directly contravene the principle announced in *Li,* that loss should be assessed equitably in proportion to fault.

We conclude, accordingly, that the expressed purposes which persuaded us in the first instance to adopt strict liability in California would not be thwarted were we to apply comparative principles. What would be forfeit is a degree of semantic symmetry. However, in this evolving area of tort law in which new remedies are judicially created, and old defenses judicially merged, impelled by strong considerations of equity and fairness we seek a larger synthesis. If a more just result follows from the expansion of comparative principles, we have no hesitancy in seeking it, mindful always that the fundamental and underlying purpose of *Li* was to promote the equitable allocation of loss among all parties legally responsible in proportion to their fault.

A second objection to the application of comparative principles in strict products liability cases is that a manufacturer's incentive to produce safe products will thereby be reduced or removed. While we fully recognize this concern we think, for several reasons, that the problem is more shadow than substance. First, of course, the manufacturer cannot avoid its continuing liability for a defective product even when the plaintiff's own conduct has contributed to his injury. The manufacturer's liability, and therefore its incentive to avoid and correct product defects, remains; its exposure will be lessened only to the extent that the trier finds that the victim's conduct contributed to his injury. Second, as a practical matter a manufacturer, in a particular case, cannot assume that the user of a defective product upon whom an injury is visited will be blameworthy. Doubtless, many users are free of fault, and a defect is at least as likely as not to be exposed by an entirely innocent plaintiff who will obtain full recovery. In such cases the manufacturer's incentive toward safety both in design and production is wholly unaffected. Finally, we must observe that under the present law, which recognizes assumption of risk as a complete defense to products liability, the curious and cynical message is that it profits the manufacturer to make his product so defective that in the event of injury he can argue that the user had to be aware of its patent defects. To that extent the incentives are inverted. We conclude, accordingly, that no substantial or significant impairment of the safety incentives of defendants will occur by the adoption of comparative principles.

In passing, we note one important and felicitous result if we apply comparative principles to strict products liability. This arises from the fact that under present law when plaintiff sues in negligence his own contributory negligence, however denominated, may diminish but cannot wholly defeat his recovery. When he sues in strict products liability, however, his "assumption of risk" *completely bars* his recovery. Under *Li*, as we have noted, "assumption of risk" is merged into comparative principles. . . . The consequence is that after *Li* in a negligence action, plaintiff's conduct which amounts to "negligent" assumption of risk no longer defeats plaintiff's recovery. Identical conduct, however, in a strict liability case acts as a complete bar under rules heretofore applicable. Thus, strict products liability, which was developed to free injured consumers from the constraints imposed by traditional negligence and warranty theories, places a consumer plaintiff in a worse position than would be the case were his claim founded on simple negligence. This, in turn, rewards adroit pleading and selection of theories. The application of comparative principles to strict liability obviates this bizarre anomaly by treating alike the defenses to both negligence and strict products liability actions. In each instance the defense, if established, will reduce but not bar plaintiff's claim.

A third objection to the merger of strict liability and comparative fault focuses on the claim that, as a practical matter, triers of fact, particularly jurors, cannot assess, measure, or compare plaintiff's negligence with defendant's strict liability. We are unpersuaded by the argument and are convinced that jurors are able to undertake a fair apportionment of liability. . . . [The court then noted that comparative principles had functioned smoothly in the unseaworthiness cases tried in admiralty, even though unseaworthiness is a strict liability concept.]

We find equally unpersuasive a final objection that the merger of the two principles somehow will abolish or adversely affect the liability of such intermediate entities in the chain of distribution as retailers . . . and bailors. . . . We foresee no such consequence. Regardless of the identity of a particular defendant or of his position in the commercial chain the basis for his liability remains that he has marketed or distributed a defective product. If, as we believe, jurors are capable of assessing fully and fairly the legal responsibility of a manufacturer on a strict liability basis, no reason appears why they cannot do likewise with respect to subsequent distributors and vendors of the product.

We note that the majority of our sister states which have addressed the problem, either by statute or judicial decree, have extended comparative principles to strict products liability.

Our research discloses that of the more than 30 states which have adopted some form of comparative negligence, three (including California) have done so judicially. . . . [The court noted that its position enjoys considerable academic support, and that the proposed Uniform Comparative Fault Act embraces a comparative fault principle in strict liability actions. It concluded that it also covered assumption of risk, to the extent that it is a form of contributory negligence.]

JEFFERSON, J., concurring and dissenting. . . . What the majority envisions as a fair apportionment of liability to be undertaken by the jury will constitute nothing more than an *unfair reduction* in the plaintiff's total damages suffered, resulting from a jury process that necessarily is predicated on speculation, conjecture and guesswork. . . .

MOSK, J., dissenting. I dissent.

This will be remembered as the dark day when this court, which heroically took the lead in originating the doctrine of products liability [in *Greenman*] and steadfastly resisted efforts to inject concepts of negligence into the newly designed tort (Cronin v. J. B. E. Olson Corp.), inexplicably turned 180 degrees and beat a hasty retreat almost back to square one. The pure concept of products liability so pridefully fashioned and nurtured by this court for the past decade and a half is reduced to a shambles.

The majority inject a foreign object — the tort of negligence — into the tort of products liability by the simple expedient of calling negligence something else: on some pages their opinion speaks of "comparative fault," on others reference is to "comparative principles," and elsewhere the term "equitable apportionment" is employed, although this is clearly not a proceeding in equity. But a rose is a rose and negligence is negligence; thus the majority find that despite semantic camouflage they must rely on Li v. Yellow Cab Co., even though *Li* is purely and simply a negligence case which merely rejects contributory negligence and substitutes therefor comparative negligence.

. . . [I]n *Cronin* we stressed that "the very purpose of our pioneering efforts in this field was to relieve the plaintiff from problems of proof inherent in pursuing negligence." And in Luque v. McLean, 501 P.2d 1163 (Cal. 1972), this court unanimously declared that "contributory negligence does not bar recovery in a strict liability action." . . .

The bench and bar have abided by this elementary rule. They have learned to avoid injecting negligence — whether of the defendant or the plaintiff — into a products liability case. And they have understood the reason behind the distinction between negligence of any party and products liability. It was expressed over three decades ago by Justice Traynor in his concurring opinion in Escola v. Coca-Cola Bottling Co.[, *supra* at 739.] . . .

Transferring the liability, or part of the liability, from the party responsible for putting the article in the stream of commerce to the consumer is precisely what the majority propose to do. They do this by employing a euphemism: the victim's recovery is to be "proportionately reduced." The result, however delicately described, is to dilute the defect of the article by elevating the conduct of the wounded consumer to an issue of equal significance. We can be as certain as tomorrow's daylight that every defendant charged with marketing a defective product will hereafter assert that the injured plaintiff did something, anything, that conceivably could be deemed contributorily negligent: he drove the vehicle with a defective steering mechanism 56 miles an hour instead of 54; or he should have discovered a latent defect hidden in the machinery; or perhaps he should not have succumbed to the salesman's persuasion and purchased the defective object in the first instance. I need no crystal ball to foresee that the pleading of affirmative defenses alleging contributory negligence — or the currently approved substitute terminology — will now become boilerplate. . . .

The defective product is comparable to a time bomb ready to explode; it maims its victims indiscriminately, the righteous and the evil, the careful and the careless. Thus when a faulty design or otherwise defective product is involved, the litigation should not be diverted to consideration of the negligence of the plaintiff. The liability issues are simple: was the product or its design faulty, did the defendant inject the defective product into the stream of commerce, and did the defect cause the injury? The conduct of the ultimate consumer-victim who used the product in the contemplated or foreseeable manner is wholly irrelevant to those issues. . . .

The majority note one "felicitous result" of adopting comparative negligence to products liability: the merger of assumption of risk — which they term a "bizarre anomaly" — into their innovative defense. I find that result neither felicitous nor tenable. In Barker v. Lull Engineering Co., we defined a defective product as one which failed to perform safely when used in an intended or foreseeable manner. If a consumer elects to use a product patently defective when other alternatives are available, or to use a product in a manner clearly not intended or foreseeable, he assumes the risks inherent in his improper utilization and should not be heard to complain about the condition of the object. One who employs a power saw to trim his fingernails — and thereafter finds the number of his fingers reduced — should not prevail to any extent whatever against the manufacturer even if the saw had a defective blade. I would retain assumption of risk as a total defense to products liability, as it always has been.

I would affirm the judgment.

NOTES

1. *Contributory negligence in products cases.* Is there any reason why contributory negligence should not be a defense in products liability cases if allowed in other types of actions? In Melia v. Ford Motor Co., 534 F.2d 795 (8th Cir. 1976), the decedent was killed in an intersection collision when she was thrown through the unlocked door on the driver's side of the

car. The court first held that it was a jury question whether the design of the door assembly was defective. It then refused to admit evidence on any of the three assignments of contributory negligence raised by the defendant in plaintiff's strict liability action: (1) entering the intersection through a red light, (2) driving with the door unlocked, (3) not using the seat belt. In state court, the plaintiff's contributory negligence had previously barred her cause of action against the other driver. Melia v. Svoboda, 214 N.W.2d 476 (Neb. 1974).

The question of seatbelt use also arose in Morgen v. Ford Motor Co., 797 N.E.2d 1146, 1148-1149 (Ind. 2003), where the plaintiff sustained serious spinal cord injuries while riding in the back of a Ford car without a seatbelt. Indiana law did not require backseat passengers to use seatbelts, and its codification of products liability law provides: "It is a defense that a cause of the physical harm is a misuse of the product by the claimant or any other person not reasonably expected by the seller at the time the seller sold or otherwise conveyed the product to another party." Ind. Code §34-20-6-4 (1998). The court held that the question of misuse should be left to the jury. "While we agree with Morgen that his failure to use the seat belt did not constitute a misuse as a matter of law, so too do we agree with Ford that the question of misuse was a matter for the jury, not the court, to decide. We believe this result serves to encourage manufacturers to equip their products with safety devices irrespective of whether the devices' use is mandatory or even widespread." What benefits arise from the uncertainty over the status of the misuse defense in seatbelt cases? If a per se rule is used, which way should it cut?

2. *Foreseeable misuse.* In most crashworthiness cases, plaintiff's misconduct goes far beyond the "normal and proper use" contemplated in *Escola*. In LeBouef v. Goodyear Tire & Rubber Co., 623 F.2d 985, 989 (5th Cir. 1980), decedent purchased "a new, 1976 Mercury Cougar equipped with a 460 cubic-inch, 425 horsepower engine, and with Goodyear HER78-15 Custom Polysteel Radial Tires." The car was capable of going 100 miles per hour, but Goodyear had tested the tires for safety only for speeds of 85 mph. Ford's only warning was "a statement in the Cougar owner's manual that '[c]ontinuous driving over 90 mph requires using high-speed-capability tires'; the manual did not state whether the tires in question were or were not of high-speed-caliber." The decedent was killed when the car veered off the road while driving intoxicated at speeds of 100 to 105 mph. The trial court, sitting without a jury, found that the tire, although properly manufactured, was defective because of its insufficient warnings about the risk of tread separation at high speeds. It also found that "while Leleux's [the decedent's] excessive speed was a contributory cause of the accident, his intoxication was not." It also rejected the contributory negligence and assumption of risk defenses. On appeal, the decision was affirmed, and the court had this to say about the misuse defense:

Certainly the operation of the Cougar in excess of 100 miles per hour was not "normal" in the sense of being a routine or intended use. "Normal use," however, is a term of art in the parlance of Louisiana products liability law, delineating the scope of a manufacturer's duty and consequent liability; it encompasses all *reasonably foreseeable* uses of a product. . . . The sports car involved here was marketed with an intended and recognized appeal to youthful drivers. The 425 horsepower engine with which Ford had equipped it provided a capability of speeds over 100 miles per hour, and the car's allure, no doubt exploited in its marketing, lay in no small measure in this power and potential speed. It was not simply foreseeable, but was to be readily expected, that the Cougar would, on occasion, be driven in excess of the 85 miles per hour proven maximum safe operating speed of its Goodyear tires. Consequently, Ford cannot, on the basis of abnormal use, escape its duty either to provide an adequate warning of the specific danger of tread separation at such high speeds or to ameliorate the danger in some other way.

The foreseeable misuse standard has been criticized as creating a "moral hazard" problem by increasing the probability of accidents. In addition, foreseeable misuse creates an implicit transfer of wealth from careful to careless drivers because the manufacturer cannot differentiate in price charged between a retiree and a traveling salesman, or between the careful driver who has never had a ticket and the teenage hot-rodder. See Epstein, Products Liability as an Insurance Market, 14 J. Legal Stud. 645 (1985), noting that first party insurers routinely make risk classifications that cannot be made when tort insurance is tied to the sale of a product. Should the law expand the role of the misuse defense in a comparative negligence regime?

3. *Misuse in other contexts.* It is difficult to track the judicial responses to different forms of misuse. The plaintiff gained the upper hand in Hernandez v. Barbo Machinery Co., 957 P.2d 147, 150, 153 (Or. 1998), in which defendant designed a saw with a fully concealed blade operated by a difficult to locate on/off switch. The saw contained no limit switch that would turn off the saw when the access panel was open, and it sported no decal warning the user to check that the saw was inoperative. Plaintiff, a maintenance mechanic, was unfamiliar with the saw design. He could not find the on/off switch and, placing his hand over the panel housing, was unable to detect any vibration. He then opened the access panel, slipped on some sawdust, and the whirring blade mangled his hand. The jury found the plaintiff 50.5 percent negligent, which denied him recovery under Oregon's modified (50 percent cut-off) comparative negligence statute. The court, however, held that it was reversible error not to segregate out that fraction of plaintiff's "alleged negligence [that] consists in the kind of unobservant, inattentive, ignorant, or awkward failure to discover or to guard against the defect that goes toward making the product dangerously defective in the first place." Citing comment *n* of the Second

Restatement, the court concluded that the 1975 codification of Oregon's modified comparative negligence rule did not disturb "the long-established principle that a plaintiff's incidental carelessness or negligent failure to discover or guard against a product defect is not an appropriate defense to that plaintiff's products liability action for injuries suffered because of the product defect."

In Jeld-Wen, Inc. v. Gamble, 501 S.E.2d 393 (Va. 1998), the 13-month-old plaintiff fell through defendant's screen window when his father left him momentarily unattended on the family couch as he moved to adjust the blinds to allow his son to wave goodbye to his mother. The window screen was designed for ordinary use and was kept in place by two spring loaded pins on the lower left and right sides of the frame. The left pin was defectively manufactured so that it could not be inserted into the slot that allowed it to be held in place, resulting in a "false latch." The plaintiff argued that the defendant knew or should have known that a child could make "casual contact with the screen and cause the screen to fall out of the frame," and thereafter the child could fall through the open window. The court rejected this position, holding that the key inquiry "is not the occurrence of the 'gentle touch, but the misuse of the screen to provide balance and restraining support . . . " It then held that "manufacturers of ordinary window screens are not charged with a duty to safeguard against the misuse of their products as body restraints as this misuse is not considered reasonably foreseeable despite, or perhaps even because of, the obvious nature of the danger the misuse presents. . . . " It then held "it is irrelevant that, absent this defect, Jeld-Wen's screen might have provided some level of restraint, since, as we have already determined, the misuse of the screen for balance and restraining support, however modest, was not reasonably foreseeable."

Do plaintiffs have a stronger case here than in the crashworthiness situations given the latent nature of the defect?

4. *The Restatement position.* The Restatement (Third) of Torts, §17 and comment *d* follows *Daly* in what has become the majority position.

§17. APPORTIONMENT OF RESPONSIBILITY BETWEEN OR AMONG PLAINTIFF,
        SELLERS AND DISTRIBUTORS OF DEFECTIVE PRODUCTS, AND OTHERS

(a) A plaintiff's recovery of damages for harm caused by a product defect may be reduced if the conduct of the plaintiff combines with the product defect to cause the harm and plaintiff's conduct fails to conform to generally applicable rules establishing appropriate standards of care.

(b) The manner and extent of the reduction under Subsection (a) and the apportionment of plaintiff's recovery among multiple defendants are governed by generally applicable rules concerning responsibility.

In essence, the Third Restatement declines to treat as independent defenses product misuse, alteration, or assumption of risk when it operates its contributory negligence regime. Rather, to the extent that these are traced to the plaintiff's conduct, they are governed by the comparative fault system in effect within the jurisdiction, usually pure comparative negligence or the 50 percent cut-off rule. Prior to the Third Restatement many states followed a rule that provided that the plaintiff was under no duty to discover latent defects contained in the defendant's product. See Kassouf v. Lee Brothers, Inc., 26 Cal. Rptr. 276 (Cal. App. 1962), in which plaintiff ate, without inspection, a chocolate bar that contained worms and maggots. But once again, under the influence of comparative negligence, this defense may be allowed, at least in some cases: "when the defendant claims that the plaintiff failed to discover a defect, there must be evidence that the plaintiff's conduct in failing to discover a defect did, in fact, fail to meet a standard of reasonable care." RTT:PL §17, comment *d*.

5. *Contractual defenses to product liability actions.* In many settings express assumption of risk by contract is a complete defense to a tort action. One vital question is whether product sellers should be able, directly or through intermediaries, to contract out of their liability with potential product users and consumers. The contractual regime could redefine product defect, cap damages, or eliminate liability altogether. Starting with *Henningsen* that approach has been uniformly rejected by the courts, and it receives a very chilly reception in the Third Restatement, as §18 categorically states: "Disclaimers and limitations of remedies by product sellers or other distributors, waivers by product purchasers, and other similar contractual exculpations, oral or written, do not bar or reduce otherwise valid products liability claims against sellers or other distributors of new products for harm to persons." The explanation for this sweeping prohibition is found in comment *a*: "It is presumed that the ordinary product user or consumer lacks sufficient information and bargaining power to execute a fair contractual limitation of rights to recover." The rule does not apply to cases of purely economic loss usually covered under the U.C.C. Nor does it necessarily apply to cases in which product users and consumers are "represented by informed and economically powerful consumer groups or intermediaries." "When such contracts are accompanied by alternative nontort remedies that serve as an adequate quid pro quo for reducing or eliminating rights to recover in tort, arguments may support giving effect to such agreements. Such contractual arrangements raise policy questions different from those raised by this Section and require careful consideration by the courts." RTT:PL §18, comment *d*. Does a reduction in price or increase in product or service access count as the necessary quid pro quo? How would the law of product liability have to be rewritten if the contractual waivers were freely accepted in all cases of physical injury or property damage?

SECTION F.   FEDERAL PREEMPTION

United States Constitution
Article VI, Section 2

This Constitution, and the Laws of the United States which shall be made in Pursuance thereof; and all Treaties made, or which shall be made, under the Authority of the United States, shall be the supreme Law of the Land: and the Judges in every State shall be bound thereby, any Thing in the Constitution or Law of any State to the contrary notwithstanding.

It may seem odd that the Supremacy Clause of the United States Constitution finds its way into a chapter on products liability. But it is undoubtedly the case today that much major tort litigation is concerned with the interaction between direct forms of federal regulation and the common law of product liability. The Supremacy Clause provides that any federal statute or regulation shall take precedence over an inconsistent state law. In some instances the federal statute makes the conflict explicit, but often the conflict gives rise to complex matters of statutory construction. In Rice v. Santa Fe Elevator, 331 U.S. 218, 230-231 (1947), the Supreme Court opted for a presumption that insulated state tort law from federal preemption when it wrote:

> [W]e start with the assumption that the historic police powers of the States [to regulate safety and health] were not to be superseded by the Federal Act unless that was the clear and manifest purpose of Congress. Such a purpose may be evidenced in several ways. The scheme of federal regulation may be so pervasive as to make reasonable the inference that Congress left no room for the States to supplement it. Or the Act of Congress may touch a field in which the federal interest is so dominant that the federal system will be assumed to preclude enforcement of state laws on the same subject. Likewise, the object sought to be obtained by the federal law and the character of obligations imposed by it may reveal the same purpose. Or the state policy may produce a result inconsistent with the objective of the federal statute.

In standard terminology the doctrine of implied preemption can apply in three circumstances: 1) when the state law is inconsistent with the federal statute; 2) when the federal statute is sufficiently comprehensive to occupy the field; and 3) when the enforcement of the state law frustrates the federal scheme. Working out the implications of this basic system is no easy task given the modern proliferation of design, warning, and liability theories that have proliferated at the state law level. For a recent discussion of these issues, see the collection of essays in Federal Preemption: States' Powers,

National Interests (Epstein & Greve, eds. 2007). The following case is a recent Supreme Court effort.

Geier v. American Honda Motor Co.
529 U.S. 861 (2000)

BREYER, J. This case focuses on the 1984 version of a Federal Motor Vehicle Safety Standard promulgated by the Department of Transportation under the authority of the National Traffic and Motor Vehicle Safety Act of 1966, 80 Stat. 718, 15 U.S.C. §1381 et seq. (1988 ed.). The standard, FMVSS 208, required auto manufacturers to equip some but not all of their 1987 vehicles with passive restraints. We ask whether the Act pre-empts a state common-law tort action [for a design defect] in which the plaintiff claims that the defendant auto manufacturer, who was in compliance with the standard, should nonetheless have equipped a 1987 automobile with airbags. We conclude that the Act, taken together with FMVSS 208, pre-empts the lawsuit.

I

In 1992, petitioner Alexis Geier, driving a 1987 Honda Accord, collided with a tree and was seriously injured. The car was equipped with manual shoulder and lap belts which Geier had buckled up at the time. The car was not equipped with airbags or other passive restraint devices.

[Breyer, J. outlines the procedural history of the case and notes the sharp split of opinion in the lower federal and state courts.]

We granted certiorari to resolve these differences. We now hold that this kind of "no airbag" lawsuit conflicts with the objectives of FMVSS 208, a standard authorized by the Act, and is therefore pre-empted by the Act.

In reaching our conclusion, we consider three subsidiary questions. First, does the Act's express pre-emption provision pre-empt this lawsuit? We think not. Second, do ordinary pre-emption principles nonetheless apply? We hold that they do. Third, does this lawsuit actually conflict with FMVSS 208, hence with the Act itself? We hold that it does.

II

We first ask whether the Safety Act's express pre-emption provision pre-empts this tort action. The provision reads as follows:

> "Whenever a Federal motor vehicle safety standard established under this subchapter is in effect, no State or political subdivision of a State shall have any authority either to establish, or to continue in effect, with respect to any

motor vehicle or item of motor vehicle equipment[,] any safety standard applicable to the same aspect of performance of such vehicle or item of equipment which is not identical to the Federal standard." 215 U.S.C. §1392(d) (1988 ed.).

American Honda points out that a majority of this Court has said that a somewhat similar statutory provision in a different federal statute — a provision that uses the word "requirements" — may well expressly pre-empt similar tort actions. Petitioners reply that this statute speaks of pre-empting a state-law "safety *standard*," not a "requirement," and that a tort action does not involve a safety *standard*. Hence, they conclude, the express pre-emption provision does not apply.

We need not determine the precise significance of the use of the word "standard," rather than "requirement," however, for the Act contains another provision, which resolves the disagreement. That provision, a broad "savings" clause, says that "[c]ompliance with" a federal safety standard "does not exempt any person from any liability under common law." 15 U.S.C. §1397(k) (1988 ed.). The saving clause assumes that there are some significant number of common-law liability cases to save. And a reading of the express pre-emption provision that excludes common-law tort actions gives actual meaning to the saving clause's literal language, while leaving adequate room for state tort law to operate — for example, where federal law creates only a floor, *i.e.*, a minimum safety standard. See, *e.g.*, Brief for United States as Amicus Curiae 21 (explaining that common-law claim that a vehicle is defectively designed because it lacks antilock brakes would not be pre-empted by 49 CFR §571.105 (1999), a safety standard establishing minimum requirements for brake performance). Without the saving clause, a broad reading of the express pre-emption provision arguably might pre-empt those actions, for, as we have just mentioned, it is possible to read the pre-emption provision, standing alone, as applying to standards imposed in common-law tort actions, as well as standards contained in state legislation or regulations. And if so, it would pre-empt all nonidentical state standards established in tort actions covering the same aspect of performance as an applicable federal standard, even if the federal standard merely established a minimum standard. On that broad reading of the pre-emption clause little, if any, potential "liability at common law" would remain. And few, if any, state tort actions would remain for the saving clause to save. We have found no convincing indication that Congress wanted to pre-empt, not only state statutes and regulations, but also common-law tort actions, in such circumstances. Hence the broad reading cannot be correct. The language of the pre-emption provision permits a narrow reading that excludes common-law actions. Given the presence of the saving clause, we conclude that the pre-emption clause must be so read.

III

We have just said that the saving clause at least removes tort actions from the scope of the express pre-emption clause. Does it do more? In particular, does it foreclose or limit the operation of ordinary pre-emption principles insofar as those principles instruct us to read statutes as pre-empting state laws (including common-law rules) that "actually conflict" with the statute or federal standards promulgated thereunder? . . .

Nothing in the language of the saving clause suggests an intent to save state-law tort actions that conflict with federal regulations. The words "[c]ompliance" and "does not exempt," sound as if they simply bar a special kind of defense, namely, a defense that compliance with a federal standard automatically exempts a defendant from state law, whether the Federal Government meant that standard to be an absolute requirement or only a minimum one. See Restatement (Third) of Torts: Products Liability §4(b), Comment e (1997) (distinguishing between state-law compliance defense and a federal claim of pre-emption). It is difficult to understand why Congress would have insisted on a compliance-with-federal-regulation precondition to the provision's applicability had it wished the Act to "save" all state-law tort actions, regardless of their potential threat to the objectives of federal safety standards promulgated under that Act. . . .

Why, in any event, would Congress not have wanted ordinary pre-emption principles to apply where an actual conflict with a federal objective is at stake? Some such principle is needed. In its absence, state law could impose legal duties that would conflict directly with federal regulatory mandates, say, by premising liability upon the presence of the very windshield retention requirements that federal law requires. . . .

IV

The basic question, then, is whether a common-law "no airbag" action like the one before us actually conflicts with FMVSS 208. We hold that it does.

In petitioners' and the dissent's view, FMVSS 208 sets a minimum airbag standard. As far as FMVSS 208 is concerned, the more airbags, and the sooner, the better. But that was not the Secretary's view. The Department of Transportation's (DOT's) comments, which accompanied the promulgation of FMVSS 208, make clear that the standard deliberately provided the manufacturer with a range of choices among different passive restraint devices. Those choices would bring about a mix of different devices introduced gradually over time; and FMVSS 208 would thereby lower costs, overcome technical safety problems, encourage technological development, and win widespread consumer acceptance—all of which would promote FMVSS 208's safety objectives.

A.

[A review of the history of the regulation is omitted.]

B.

Read in light of this history, DOT's own contemporaneous explanation of FMVSS 208 makes clear that the 1984 version of FMVSS 208 reflected the following significant considerations. First, buckled up seatbelts are a vital ingredient of automobile safety. . . . Second, despite the enormous and unnecessary risks that a passenger runs by not buckling up manual lap and shoulder belts, more than 80% of front seat passengers would leave their manual seatbelts unbuckled. Third, airbags could make up for the dangers caused by unbuckled manual belts, but they could not make up for them entirely.

Fourth, passive restraint systems had their own disadvantages, for example, the dangers associated with, intrusiveness of, and corresponding public dislike for, nondetachable automatic belts. Fifth, airbags brought with them their own special risks to safety, such as the risk of danger to out-of-position occupants (usually children) in small cars. . . .

Sixth, airbags were expected to be significantly more expensive than other passive restraint devices, raising the average cost of a vehicle price $320 for full frontal airbags over the cost of a car with manual lap and shoulder seatbelts (and potentially much more if production volumes were low). And the agency worried that the high replacement cost — estimated to be $800 — could lead car owners to refuse to replace them after deployment. . . .

FMVSS 208 reflected these considerations in several ways. Most importantly, that standard deliberately sought variety — a mix of several different passive restraint systems. It did so by setting a performance requirement for passive restraint devices and allowing manufacturers to choose among different passive restraint mechanisms, such as airbags, automatic belts, or other passive restraint technologies to satisfy that requirement. And DOT explained why FMVSS 208 sought the mix of devices that it expected its performance standard to produce. DOT wrote that it had *rejected* a proposed FMVSS 208 "all airbag" standard because of safety concerns (perceived or real) associated with airbags, which concerns threatened a "backlash" more easily overcome "if airbags" were "not the only way of complying." It added that a mix of devices would help develop data on comparative effectiveness, would allow the industry time to overcome the safety problems and the high production costs associated with airbags, and would facilitate the development of alternative, cheaper, and safer passive restraint systems. And it would thereby build public confidence, necessary to avoid another interlock-type fiasco.

The 1984 FMVSS 208 standard also deliberately sought a *gradual* phase-in of passive restraints. . . .

In effect, petitioners' tort action depends upon its claim that manufacturers had a duty to install an airbag when they manufactured the 1987 Honda Accord. Such a state law — *i.e.*, a rule of state tort law imposing such a duty — by its terms would have required manufacturers of all similar cars to install airbags rather than other passive restraint systems, such as automatic belts or passive interiors. It thereby would have presented an obstacle to the variety and mix of devices that the federal regulation sought.

[Affirmed.]

STEVENS, J., dissenting.

Airbag technology has been available to automobile manufacturers for over 30 years. There is now general agreement on the proposition "that, to be safe, a car must have an airbag." Indeed, current federal law imposes that requirement on all automobile manufacturers. The question raised by petitioners' common-law tort action is whether that proposition was sufficiently obvious when Honda's 1987 Accord was manufactured to make the failure to install such a safety feature actionable under theories of negligence or defective design. The Court holds that an interim regulation motivated by the Secretary of Transportation's desire to foster gradual development of a variety of passive restraint devices deprives state courts of jurisdiction to answer that question. I respectfully dissent from that holding, and especially from the Court's unprecedented extension of the doctrine of pre-emption. . . .

NOTES

1. *Preemption on the march.* *Geier* represents a relatively broad reading of the scope of federal preemption. In the face of the evident conflict between the preemption clause and the savings clause for common law actions, Breyer, J. adopted the standard of conflict preemption in order to preserve the elaborate administrative compromise for the introduction of air bags. *Geier* itself was sharply distinguished by a unanimous Supreme Court in Sprietsma v. Mercury Marine, 537 U.S. 51 (2002), which held that the Federal Boat Safety Act of 1971, 46 U.S.C. §§4301-4311 (2000), and the regulations promulgated under it, did not preempt a state tort action brought on behalf of a decedent who was killed when she fell overboard from "an 18-foot ski boat equipped with a 115-horsepower outboard motor manufactured by [defendant]." As in *Geier* the FBSA contained both a preemption clause that forbade the state imposition of requirements that were not "identical" to those contained in the federal regulation. That

clause was coupled with a savings clause for common law actions. As in *Geier,* the Secretary of Transportation conducted an exhaustive safety study, only to refuse to issue any regulations that mandated propeller guards because it feared that "given current technology, feasible propeller guards might prevent penetrating injuries but increase the potential for blunt trauma caused by collision with the guard, which enlarges the boat's underwater profile." Nonetheless Justice Stevens allowed the action to go forward out of deference to the Agency decision. "The agency is likely to have a thorough understanding of its own regulation and its objectives and is 'uniquely qualified' to comprehend the likely impact of state require-ments. In the case before us today, the Solicitor General, joined by counsel for the Coast Guard, has informed us that the agency does not view the 1990 refusal to regulate or any subsequent regulatory actions by the Coast Guard as having any pre-emptive effect." Should it make a difference that this announcement was only made at the eleventh hour in the Supreme Court?

2. Preemption in warning cases. The preemption question arises as much with warnings as it does in design cases. In Cipollone v. Liggett Group, Inc., 505 U.S. 504, 521, 524 (1992), the Court held that plaintiff's duty to warn claims against cigarette manufacturers were preempted under the Public Health Cigarette Smoking Act, 15 U.S.C. §§1331-1340, which in section 5 provided:

> (b) No requirement or prohibition based on smoking and health shall be imposed under State law with respect to the advertising or promotion of any cigarettes the packages of which are labeled in conformity with the provi-sions of this Act.

It rebuffed plaintiff's claim that this provision only preempted state legislation and administrative rules, holding that "those words easily en-compass obligations that take the form of common law rules." Thereafter, the Court concluded that plaintiff's failure to warn claims insofar as they "require a showing that respondents' post-1969 advertising or promotions should have included additional, or more clearly stated, warnings, . . . are pre-empted." But this ruling did not preempt, for example, design defect, express warranty, or fraud claims.

The preemption issue in warnings cases surfaced anew in Bates v. Dow Agrosciences LLC, 544 U.S. 431, 442, 445, 454 (2005). There the peti-tioners, Texas peanut farmers, sued Dow claiming that their crops were damaged during the 2000 growing season when treated with Dow's "Strongarm" pesticide, which they claimed stunted their crops and did not kill weeds. Strongarm was marketed with a warning that said: "Use of Strongarm is recommended in all areas where peanuts are grown." The plaintiffs alleged that Strongarm was only appropriate in soils with a pH below 7.0, and not in Texas where the soil had a pH of 7.2. After the initiation of the plaintiffs' suit, Dow changed its warning to read: "Do not apply Strongarm to soils with a pH of 7.2 or greater." Justice Stevens held that the Federal Insecticide, Fungicide, and Rodenticide Act (FIFRA), 7 U.S.C. §136 *et seq.* (2000 ed. and Supp. II) did not preempt the plaintiff's claim. Its preemption provision provided in section 136v:

> (b) Uniformity
> Such State shall not impose or continue in effect any requirements for labeling or packaging in addition to or different from those required under this subchapter. . . .

Overturning the decisions of the lower courts, Stevens, J., held that this provision did not preempt all the plaintiffs' actions. He concluded first that under the preemption provision the states have "ample authority" to impose additional sanctions "for violating state rules that merely duplicate federal requirements." He further noted that *Cipollone* was correct when it noted that state common law actions were covered by the standard preemption language. Nonetheless, he concluded: "The prohibitions in §136v(b) apply only to 'requirements.' An occurrence that merely motivates an optional decision does not qualify as a requirement. The Court of Appeals was therefore quite wrong when it assumed that any event, such as a jury verdict, that might 'induce' a pesticide manufacturer to change its label should be viewed as a requirement." In addition, he observed that "[n]one of these common-law rules requires that manufacturers label or package their products in any particular way. Thus, petitioners' claims for defective design, defective manufacture, negligent testing, and breach of express warranty are not pre-empted." Finally, he remanded the case to see if the plaintiff's duty to warn claims were preempted with these observations:

> For example, a failure-to-warn claim alleging that a given pesticide's label should have stated "DANGER" instead of the more subdued "CAUTION" would be pre-empted because it is inconsistent with 40 C.F.R. §156.64 (2004), which specifically assigns these warnings to particular classes of pesticides based on their toxicity.
> In undertaking a pre-emption analysis at the pleadings stage of a case, a court should bear in mind the concept of equivalence. To survive pre-emption, the state-law requirement need not be phrased in the *identical* language as its corresponding FIFRA requirement; indeed, it would be surprising if a common-law requirement used the same phraseology as FIFRA. If a case proceeds to trial, the court's jury instructions must ensure that nominally equivalent labeling requirements are *genuinely* equivalent.

Would any of these various claims survived if Strongarm had been originally marketed with a warning that said the product was not be used in soil whose pH was over 7.2? If not, then why doesn't the comprehensive federal control over warnings trigger the application of field or conflict preemption?

3. FDA Preemption. The same tension over the scope of express preemption provisions is evident in the high-stakes litigation that has taken place in connection with the extensive federal regulatory scheme for new drugs and medical devices. The saga starts with Medtronic, Inc. v. Lohr, 518 U.S. 470, 489 (1996), in which the plaintiff sued on a variety of duty to warn and design defect theories when her pacemaker failed, requiring emergency surgery. The Medical Device Amendment Act (MDA) 21 U.S.C. §360k(a), reads:

> no State or political subdivision of a State may establish or continue in effect with respect to a device intended for human use any requirement (1) which is different from, or in addition to, any requirement applicable under [the MDA] to the device, and (2) which relates to the safety or effectiveness of the device or to any other matter included in a requirement applicable to the device under [the MDA].

The premarket notification process is an abbreviated review of the product lasting an average of 20 hours, under which the FDA undertakes no tests or systematic review of product safety, but allows for the marketing of the product so long as it is "substantially equivalent" to a pre-1976 product already on the market, at least until the earlier product is required to undergo a premarket approval (PMA) process. Justice Stevens relied on *Rice's* presumption against preemption to hold that the premarket notification process did not preempt either the duty to warn or manufacturing defect claims, and only prohibited those design defect actions that specifically targeted medical devices for special treatment. "Given the ambiguities in the statute and the scope of the preclusion that would occur otherwise, we cannot accept Medtronic's argument that by using the term 'requirement,' Congress clearly signaled its intent to deprive States of any role in protecting consumers from the dangers inherent in many medical devices."

The Supreme Court did, however, afford the MDA preemptive effect in Riegel v. Medtronic, Inc., 552 U.S.___(2008 WL 440744) (2008). There the plaintiff was injured when a cardiologist used Medtronic's FDA-approved Evergreen Balloon Catheter to perform an angioplasty—a procedure to clear clogged arteries—at a pressure of 10 atmospheres when the catheter was only rated for use at eight atmospheres. The overinflated balloon ruptured inside the plaintiff, causing serious injuries. Scalia, J., held, distinguishing *Lohr*, that the premarket approval, as opposed to premarket notification, preempted all state law claims for damages. Unlike premarket notification, the PMA process required an exhaustive review of Medtronic's product design and data, because its catheter was classified as a potentially dangerous, or Class III, device that posed serious risk to human life and health. On average about 1,200 hours are spent reviewing each application. Once approved, moreover, Medtronic could only make further design changes with explicit FDA approval. Scalia, J., affirmed that the statutory prohibition on any requirements "different from or additional to" the FDA's included common law actions. "State tort law that requires a manufacturer's catheters to be safer, but hence less effective, than the model the FDA has approved disrupts the federal scheme no less than state regulatory law to the same effect." Stevens, J., concurred on the ground that the statutory language left no ambiguity. Ginsburg, J., dissented, arguing that the MDA was not intended to deny injured parties a second tier protection through common law damage actions.

The federal statutes contain no explicit preemption provision that deals with the PMA of drugs, which is every bit as rigorous a process as it is with devices. The question here is whether, and if so, to what extent, the complex FDA procedures preempt private rights of action in drug cases. In Buckman Co., v. Plaintiffs' Legal Committee, 531 U.S. 341, 347-348, 353-354 (2001), the plaintiffs claimed that fraudulent representations that the defendants made to the FDA to obtain approval for a surgical screw counted as a "but-for" cause of subsequent injuries. Rehnquist, C.J., found that since the gist of the complaint had to do with approval practice before the FDA, "federalism concerns and the historic primacy of state regulation in matters of health and safety" did not support *Rice*'s presumption against preemption. He concluded that state damage actions were not needed because "the federal statutory scheme amply empowers the FDA to punish and deter fraud against the Administration," and that this authority is used by the Administration to achieve a somewhat delicate balance of statutory objectives. The balance sought by the Administration can be skewed by allowing fraud-on-the-FDA claims under state tort law. In a brief concurrence, Stevens, J., urged that the private action should be allowed if "the FDA had determined that petitioner had committed fraud" on the FDA during the approval process. "In such a case, a plaintiff would be able to establish causation without second-guessing the FDA's decisionmaking or overburdening its personnel, thereby alleviating the Government's central concerns regarding fraud-on-the-agency claims."

Buckman was applied in Garcia v. Wyeth-Ayerst Labs, 385 F.3d 961 (6th Cir. 2004). There the plaintiffs claimed that the Michigan tort statute, *supra* 816, was entirely preempted because *Buckman* prevented the implementation of the full scheme by blocking any plaintiff from proving fraud on the FDA. Kennedy, J., rejected the claim by holding that a more faithful reading of the Michigan law would preserve most of the reform act by allowing the plaintiff to make claims only if the FDA had found the defendant had issued a fraudulent application. That position was in turn rejected by Calabresi, J., in Desiano v. Warner-Lambert Co., 467 F.3d 85 (2d Cir. 2006). There Calabresi, J., interpreted *Buckman* narrowly, insisting that the decision covered only causes of action based "solely" on fraud, which in his view did not include claims based on the exception contained in the Michigan statute. The Second Circuit also dismissed *Buckman*'s concerns that state law litigation on the matter of fraud could disrupt the actions before the FDA. The Supreme Court granted certiorari in *Desiano* in *Warner-Lambert v. Kent,* 128 S. Ct. 31 (2007).

A still larger fight is now brewing over the question of whether an FDA agency determination that its warnings should be conclusive in private tort actions should be afforded the kind of judicial deference announced in *Sprietsma.* In January 2006, the FDA issued a preamble to a report devoted to other labeling issues that stated that the "FDA believes that under existing preemption principles, FDA approval of labeling under the act, whether it be in the old or new format, preempts conflicting or contrary State law." Department of Health and Human Services, Food and Drug Administration, Requirements on Content and Format of Labeling for Human Prescription Drug and Biological Products, 71 Fed. Reg. 3922, 3934 (2006). In reversing its earlier position against preemption, see *MacDonald, supra* at 807, the FDA's key concern was to immunize its own scientific expertise from counterattacks before multiple juries. In addition, the FDA took issue with the established case law. "Another misunderstanding . . . is that FDA labeling requirements represent a minimum safety standard. In fact, FDA interprets the act to establish both a 'floor' and a 'ceiling.' . . . " Prior to issuing its regulation, the FDA had advanced that position in several amicus curia briefs, and it was accepted in Horn v. Thoratec Corp., 376 F.3d 163, 178 (3d Cir. 2004). The announcement itself received a far frostier reception in dicta in *Desiano*, 467 F.3d at 97 n.9. See Sharkey, Catherine M., Preemption by Preamble: Federal Agencies and the Federalization of Tort Law, 56 DePaul L. Rev. 227 (2007). For different views on the matter of federal preemption, see Nagareda, FDA Preemption: When Tort Law Meets the Administrative State, 1 J. Tort Law, art. 4 (2006), which generally defends the status quo, and proposes that FDA preemption be conditioned on the willingness of drug companies to supply further information about their products to the public at large. In response, see Epstein, Why the FDA Must Preempt Tort Litigation: A Critique of *Chevron* Deference and A Response to Richard Nagareda, 1 J. Tort Law, art. 5 (2006). Should a federal agency receive the same deference when it preempts state tort actions as when it allows them?

10

DAMAGES

Sullivan v. Old Colony Street Ry.
83 N.E. 1091, 1092 (Mass. 1908)

RUGG, C.J. The rule of damages is a practical instrumentality for the administration of justice. The principle on which it is founded is compensation. Its object is to afford the equivalent in money for the actual loss caused by the wrong of another. Recurrence to this fundamental conception tests the soundness of claims for the inclusion of new elements of damage.

Zibbell v. Southern Pacific Co.
116 P. 513, 520 (Cal. 1911)

HENSHAW, J. No rational being would change places with the injured man for an amount of gold that would fill the room of the court, yet no lawyer would contend that such is the legal measure of damages.

SECTION A. INTRODUCTION

Proof of damages is an essential element of the plaintiff's case in most civil litigation. When liability is clear, both sides will judge their success by the size of the verdict. The plaintiff will suffer a major defeat if she receives a low verdict when a high one was expected. The converse is true for the defendant. In this day of potential million-dollar verdicts, it is routine for both sides to have medical and economic experts testify on three critical elements of damages: pain and suffering, medical expenses, and lost earnings attributable to the accident. For each head of damages, a jury must take into account both past and future losses. Often substantial concrete evidence is available for past losses, but only estimates, often verging on guesswork, are available for future injuries, whose duration and severity may be unknown.

The difficulties in making damage calculations should not cause us to lose sight of their essential function within the tort system. Within a system of corrective justice, ideally damages are meant, as Rugg, C.J., suggests, to place the plaintiff in the position that she would have enjoyed if the tort had never been committed. Over a wide range of cases, it works fairly well, but in extreme cases (of which death is only one) no amount of money serves that function, even if some amount must be chosen by a jury and ratified by a court. Damages are also crucial to the deterrence function of tort law because they set the "prices" defendants must pay for engaging in their chosen activities. Low damage awards, by allowing defendants to escape full responsibility for the losses they create, may induce overinvestment in socially costly activities. Yet excessive damage awards could induce potential defendants *not* to engage in activities that promise great private and social benefits. To be sure, too much can be made of the deterrent and control function of damages, given the host of other sanctions—injunctions, licenses, inspections, and fines—that serve to curb harmful behavior. But even though these sanctions from time to time intrude, the tort damage remedy remains one constant feature in our system of social control. Does the ideal amount of damages in, say, a wrongful death case compute the same way under a compensatory and a deterrent theory? If not, which approach should be followed and why?

The topic of damages also intersects a number of critical institutional features of the tort system. In the typical tort action today, the plaintiff's lawyer receives compensation in the form of a contingency fee taken out of the moneys that plaintiff is awarded, either by settlement or judgment. To what extent should damage awards be adjusted to reflect these legal fees? Many cases also raise questions of mitigation of damages and set-offs for payments from collateral sources, such as first-party health plans. It is also necessary to consider the special rules governing the loss of consortium, wrongful death, and—with ever greater constitutional over-tones—punitive damages.

SECTION B. RECOVERABLE ELEMENTS OF DAMAGES

1. *Pain and Suffering*

McDougald v. Garber
536 N.E.2d 372 (N.Y. 1989)

WACHTLER, CHIEF JUDGE. This appeal raises fundamental questions about the nature and role of nonpecuniary damages in personal injury litigation. By nonpecuniary damages, we mean those damages awarded to compensate an injured person for the physical and emotional consequences of the injury, such as pain and suffering and the loss of the ability to engage in certain activities. Pecuniary damages, on the other hand, compensate the victim for the economic consequences of the injury, such as medical expenses, lost earnings and the cost of custodial care.

The specific questions raised here deal with assessment of nonpecuniary damages and are (1) whether some degree of cognitive awareness is a prerequisite to recovery for loss of enjoyment of life and (2) whether a jury should be instructed to consider and award damages for loss of enjoyment of life separately from damages for pain and suffering. We answer the first question in the affirmative and the second question in the negative.

I.

On September 7, 1978, plaintiff Emma McDougald, then 31 years old, underwent a Caesarean section and tubal ligation at New York Infirmary. Defendant Garber performed the surgery; defendants Armengol and Kulkarni provided anesthesia. During the surgery, Mrs. McDougald suffered oxygen deprivation which resulted in severe brain damage and left her in a permanent comatose condition. This action was brought by Mrs. McDougald and her husband, suing derivatively, alleging that the injuries were caused by the defendants' acts of malpractice.

A jury found all defendants liable and awarded Emma McDougald a total of $9,650,102 in damages, including $1,000,000 for conscious pain and suffering and a separate award of $3,500,000 for loss of the pleasures and pursuits of life. The balance of the damages awarded to her were for pecuniary damages—lost earnings and the cost of custodial and nursing care. Her husband was awarded $1,500,000 on his derivative claim for the loss of his wife's services. On defendants' posttrial motions, the Trial Judge reduced the total award to Emma McDougald to $4,796,728 by striking the entire award for future nursing care ($2,353,374) and by reducing the separate awards for conscious pain and suffering and loss of the pleasures and pursuits of life to a single award of $2,000,000. Her husband's award was left intact. On cross appeals, the Appellate Division affirmed and later granted defendants leave to appeal to this court.

II.

We note at the outset that the defendants' liability for Emma McDougald's injuries is unchallenged here.

Also unchallenged are the awards in the amount of $770,978 for loss of earnings and $2,025,750 for future custodial care — that is, the pecuniary damage awards that survived defendants' posttrial motions.

What remains in dispute, primarily, is the award to Emma McDougald for nonpecuniary damages. At trial, defendants sought to show that Mrs. McDougald's injuries were so severe that she was incapable of either experiencing pain or appreciating her condition. Plaintiffs, on the other hand, introduced proof that Mrs. McDougald responded to certain stimuli to a sufficient extent to indicate that she was aware of her circumstances. Thus, the extent of Mrs. McDougald's cognitive abilities, if any, was sharply disputed.

The parties and the trial court agreed that Mrs. McDougald could not recover for pain and suffering unless she were conscious of the pain. Defendants maintained that such consciousness was also required to support an award for loss of enjoyment of life. The court, however, accepted plaintiffs' view that loss of enjoyment of life was compensable without regard to whether the plaintiff was aware of the loss. Accordingly, because the level of Mrs. McDougald's cognitive abilities was in dispute, the court instructed the jury to consider loss of enjoyment of life as an element of nonpecuniary damages separate from pain and suffering. . . .

We conclude that the court erred, both in instructing the jury that Mrs. McDougald's awareness was irrelevant to their consideration of damages for loss of enjoyment of life and in directing the jury to consider that aspect of damages separately from pain and suffering.

III.

We begin with the familiar proposition that an award of damages to a person injured by the negligence of another is to compensate the victim, not to punish the wrongdoer. The goal is to restore the injured party, to the extent possible, to the position that would have been occupied had the wrong not occurred. To be sure, placing the burden of compensation on the negligent party also serves as a deterrent, but purely punitive damages — that is, those which have no compensatory purpose — are prohibited unless the harmful conduct is intentional, malicious, outrageous, or otherwise aggravated beyond mere negligence.

Damages for nonpecuniary losses are, of course, among those that can be awarded as compensation to the victim. This aspect of damages, however, stands on less certain ground than does an award for pecuniary damages. An economic loss can be compensated in kind by an economic gain; but recovery for noneconomic losses such as pain and suffering and loss of enjoyment of life rests on "the legal fiction that money damages can compensate for a victim's injury." We accept this fiction, knowing that although money will neither ease the pain nor restore the victim's abilities, this device is as close as the law can come in its effort to right the wrong. We have no hope of evaluating what has been lost, but a monetary award may provide a measure of solace for the condition created.

Our willingness to indulge this fiction comes to an end, however, when it ceases to serve the compensatory goals of tort recovery. When that limit is met, further indulgence can only result in assessing damages that are punitive. The question posed by this case, then, is whether an award of damages for loss of enjoyment of life to a person whose injuries preclude any awareness of the loss serves a compensatory purpose. We conclude that it does not.

Simply put, an award of money damages in such circumstances has no meaning or utility to the injured person. An award for the loss of enjoyment of life "cannot provide [such a victim] with any consolation or ease any burden resting on him. . . . He cannot spend it upon necessities or pleasures. He cannot experience the pleasure of giving it away." (Flannery v. United States, 4th Cir., 718 F.2d 108, 111 (1983)).

We recognize that, as the trial court noted, requiring some cognitive awareness as a prerequisite to recovery for loss of enjoyment of life will result in some cases "in the paradoxical situation that the greater the degree of brain injury inflicted by a negligent defendant, the smaller the award the plaintiff can recover in general damages." The force of this argument, however — the temptation to achieve a balance between injury and damages — has nothing to do with meaningful compensation for the victim. Instead, the temptation is rooted in a desire to punish the defendant in proportion to the harm inflicted. However relevant such retributive symmetry may be in the criminal law, it has no place in the law of civil damages, at least in the absence of culpability beyond mere negligence.

Accordingly, we conclude that cognitive awareness is a prerequisite to recovery for loss of enjoyment of life. We do not go so far, however, as to require the fact finder to sort out varying degrees of cognition and determine at what level a particular deprivation can be fully appreciated. With respect to pain and suffering, the trial court charged simply that there must be "some level of awareness" in order for plaintiff to recover. We think that this is an appropriate standard for all aspects of nonpecuniary loss. No doubt the standard ignores analytically relevant levels of cognition, but we resist the desire for analytical purity in favor of simplicity. A more complex instruction might give the appearance of greater precision but, given the limits of our understanding of the human mind, it would in reality lead only to greater speculation.

We turn next to the question whether loss of enjoyment of life should be considered a category of damages separate from pain and suffering.

IV.

There is no dispute here that the fact finder may, in assessing nonpecuniary damages, consider the effect of the injuries on the plaintiff's capacity to lead a normal life. [The court reviewed the movement, within and outside of New York, to treat loss of enjoyment of life as a separate category, in part to facilitate the appellate review of damage awards.]

We do not dispute that distinctions can be found or created between the concepts of pain and suffering and loss of enjoyment of life. If the term "suffering" is limited to the emotional response to the sensation of pain, then the emotional response caused by the limitation of life's activities may be considered qualitatively different. But suffering need not be so limited — it can easily encompass the frustration and anguish caused by the inability to participate in activities that once brought pleasure. Traditionally, by treating loss of enjoyment of life as a permissible factor in assessing pain and suffering, courts have given the term this broad meaning.

If we are to depart from this traditional approach and approve a separate award for loss of enjoyment of life, it must be on the basis that such an approach will yield a more accurate evaluation of the compensation due to the plaintiff. We have no doubt that, in general, the total award for nonpecuniary damages would increase if we adopted the rule. That separate awards are advocated by plaintiffs and resisted by defendants is sufficient evidence that larger awards are at stake here. But a larger award does not by itself indicate that the goal of compensation has been better served.

The advocates of separate awards contend that because pain and suffering and loss of enjoyment of life can be distinguished, they must be treated separately if the plaintiff is to be compensated fully for each distinct injury suffered. We disagree. Such an analytical approach may have its place when the subject is pecuniary damages, which can be calculated with some precision. But the estimation of nonpecuniary damages is not amenable to such analytical precision and may, in fact, suffer from its application. Translating human suffering into dollars and cents involves no mathematical formula; it rests, as we have said, on a legal fiction. The figure that emerges is unavoidably distorted by the translation. Application of this murky process to the component parts of nonpecuniary injuries (however analytically distinguishable they may be) cannot make it more accurate. If anything, the distortion will be amplified by repetition.

[The court ordered a] new trial on the issue of nonpecuniary damages to be awarded to plaintiff Emma McDougald....

TITONE, JUDGE (dissenting).

The majority's holding represents a compromise position that neither comports with the fundamental principles of tort compensation nor furnishes a satisfactory, logically consistent framework for compensating nonpecuniary loss. Because I conclude that loss of enjoyment of life is an objective damage item, conceptually distinct from conscious pain and suffering, I can find no fault with the trial court's instruction authorizing separate awards and permitting an award for "loss of enjoyment of life" even in the absence of any awareness of that loss on the part of the injured plaintiff. Accordingly, I dissent....

[T]he compensatory nature of a monetary award for loss of enjoyment of life is not altered or rendered punitive by the fact that the unaware injured plaintiff cannot experience the pleasure of having it. The fundamental distinction between punitive and compensatory damages is that the former exceed the amount necessary to replace what the plaintiff lost....

NOTES

1. Recovery for pain and suffering. In *McDougald* both the majority and dissent agreed that recovery for pain and suffering is generally proper in tort actions. Typically, the elements of pain and suffering include worry, anguish, and grief, all notoriously difficult to quantify. There is also, even in the usual case of a conscious plaintiff, extensive disagreement as to how to present the issue of pain and suffering to the jury. In Rounds v. Rush Trucking Corp., 211 F.3d 185, 190 (2d Cir. 2000), the plaintiff suffered serious and permanent injuries when her pickup truck was rammed in the rear by one of defendant's tractor-trailers. The jury awarded the plaintiff $350,000 for past and future mental suffering and $350,000 for past and future emotional distress. On appeal, Walker, J., struck the second award on the ground that *McDougald* embraces both forms of loss under a single heading.

> Despite our ability to distinguish between loss of enjoyment of life and the emotional distress at issue in this case, we follow the reasoning of the New York Court of Appeals and find that emotional distress is no more amenable to analytical precision than loss of enjoyment of life. There is no plausible basis for limiting *McDougald* to its facts and holding, as Rounds

urges, that pain and suffering does not also encompass emotional distress, which is just as difficult to measure.

Accordingly, Walker, J., ordered a new trial unless the plaintiff agreed to a reduction of $350,000 in damages in light of the duplicative instructions. What about the possibility that the jury already reduced the award for pain and suffering precisely because a separate head was allowed for emotional distress? "If Rounds is convinced that a properly charged jury would award in excess of $350,000 for pain and suffering, including emotional distress, she is free to reject remittitur and re-present the case to a jury." The original liability determination would remain undisturbed.

McDougald and *Rounds* raise the larger question whether the difficulties in valuation should preclude any recovery for pain and suffering, no matter how packaged. The most famous critique of this sort is Jaffe, Damages for Personal Injury: The Impact of Insurance, 18 Law & Contemp. Probs. 219, 224-225 (1953):

> But why we may ask *should* the plaintiff be compensated in money for an experience which involves no financial loss? It cannot be on the principle of returning what is his own. Essentially that principle rests on an economic foundation: on maintaining the integrity of the economic arrangements which provide the normally expectable basis for livelihood in our society. Pain is a harm, an "injury," but neither past pain nor its compensation has any consistent economic significance. The past experience is not a loss except in so far as it produced present deterioration. . . .
>
> I am aware, however, that though the premise may elude detection, some deep intuition may claim to validate this process of evaluating the imponderable. One who has suffered a violation of his bodily integrity may feel a sense of continuing outrage. This is particularly true where there has been disfigurement or loss of a member (even though not giving rise to economic loss). Because our society sets a high value on money; it uses money or price as a means of recognizing the worth of non-economic as well as economic goods. If, insists the plaintiff, society really values my personality, my bodily integrity, it will signify its sincerity by paying me a sum of money. Damages thus may somewhat reestablish the plaintiff's self-confidence, wipe out his sense of outrage. Furthermore, though money is not an equivalent it may be a consolation, a solatium. . . .

Even if an exact evaluation of the value of pain and suffering is unattainable, does it follow that it should be assigned a zero value under the tort law, with or without insurance? Would plaintiff pay nothing to be rid of pain? Would she accept nothing to endure it voluntarily? Should it matter if, as has been suggested, most surveys find that ordinary people oppose compensation for pain and suffering? Does it make any difference if the defendant has insurance? For continued skepticism about pain and suffering awards, see Avraham, Putting a Price on Pain-and-Suffering Damages: A Critique of the Current Approaches and a Preliminary Proposal for Change, 100 Nw. U. L. Rev. 87 (2006).

2. *Hedonic damages.* An extensive new literature casts some doubt on the conventional practice of awarding hedonic damages, as in *McDougald*, that go beyond pain and suffering. That view has been challenged on the ground that individual preferences are highly adaptive, such that these awards overestimate the situation on the ground. Even though most people without disabilities think of having a disability as being unbearable, "[a] rich psychological literature demonstrates that disability does not inherently limit enjoyment of life to the degree that these courts suggest. Rather, people who experience disabling injuries tend to adapt to their disabilities. To the extent that they experience continuing hedonic loss, it is physical pain, loss of societal opportunities, and social stigma—*not* anything inherent in the disability—that is the major contributor." Bagenstos & Schlanger, Hedonic Damages, Hedonic Adaptation, and Disability, 60 Vand. L. Rev. (forthcoming 2007). Is survey evidence that seriously disabled people report higher levels of happiness than expected enough to clinch this case? What if disabled people spend, when possible, large sums to eliminate their disabilities?

3. *The "per diem" rule.* Even if attention is concentrated on pain and suffering, how is that information translated into dollars? One ingenious suggestion about how to solve these valuation difficulties was first advanced in M.Belli, The Use of Demonstrative Evidence in Achieving the More Adequate Award 33-35 (1952).

> This is the key: You must break up the 30-year life expectancy into *finite* detailed periods of time. You must take these small periods of time, seconds and minutes, and determine in dollars and cents what each period is worth. You must start with the seconds and minutes rather than at the other end of thirty years. You cannot stand in front of a jury and say, "Here is a man horribly injured, permanently disabled, who will suffer excruciating pain for the rest of his life, he is entitled to a verdict of $225,000."
>
> You must start at the beginning and show that pain is a continuous thing, second by second, minute by minute, hour by hour, year after year for thirty years. You must interpret one second, one minute, one hour, one year of pain and suffering into dollars and cents and then multiply to your absolute figure to show how you have achieved your result of an award approaching adequacy at $225,000. If you throw a novel figure at a jury or an appellate court of $225,000, without breaking it down, you are going to frighten both your trier of facts and your reviewer of facts. . . .

Although Belli's numerical examples have been eroded by inflation, his approach to valuation still retains much of its punch. Would it work for hedonic damages? As might be expected, the propriety of Belli's argument has been much debated in the appellate opinions. The use of the per diem argument was initially prohibited in Botta v. Brunner, 138 A.2d 713 (N.J. 1958). Today, however, some jurisdictions allow the jury to hear per diem calculations, subject to a cautionary instruction this approach is argument, not evidence. See, e.g., Vanskike v. ACF Industries, Inc., 665 F.2d 188 (8th Cir. 1981). Other courts have condemned per diem instructions to the jury but have permitted the trial judge to allow plaintiff to use that approach in closing argument. E.g., Manning v. Lunda Construction Co., 953 F.2d 1090, 1093 (8th Cir. 1992).

The per diem rule was put to novel use in Miller v. Rohling, 720 N.W.2d 562, 570 (Iowa 2006), a nuisance action arising out of defendant's operation of grain silos:

> The court calculated the plaintiffs' damages for loss of use and enjoyment using a rate of $6 per hour for 16 hours a day for 90 days a year.
>
> The defendants claim this reasoning was erroneous, citing our cases stating that damages for pain and suffering cannot be measured by any exact or mathematical standard. It is true no precise formula exists for determining damages for physical or mental pain and suffering. Nonetheless, the use of a mathematical formula, while not required, is not forbidden.
>
> This court has refused to find any error in counsel's use of a per diem formula to support the amount requested by a plaintiff for intangible damages in personal injury cases. . . .
>
> We see no distinction here where a per diem calculation was used by the court in determining reasonable compensation for loss of use and enjoyment of property. The court did not commit reversible error in relying on a mathematical formula to compute the plaintiffs' damages.

4. *Increased risk of future injury.* The proper treatment of probabilistic assessments of future pain and suffering divided the court in DePass v. United States, 721 F.2d 203, 210 (7th Cir. 1983). There the plaintiff suffered a traumatic amputation of his left leg below the knee. In addition to the usual elements of pain and suffering, plaintiff's expert witness testified, largely on the strength of an extensive National Institute of Health study of World War II veterans, that there was "a statistical connection between traumatic limb amputations and future cardiovascular problems and decreased life expectancy." The expert estimated an 11-year reduction in plaintiff's life expectancy. The government did nothing to counter that evidence, and the trial judge rejected as speculative damages for these potential losses. Flaum, J., affirmed on the ground that the study was "inconclusive" and that "Illinois law is not settled as to whether increased risk of future injury is compensable." A spirited dissent by Posner, J., argued that it was clearly erroneous to refuse to award damages for this type of loss:

The district judge's rejection of such evidence, if widely followed, would lead to systematically undercompensating the victims of serious accidents and thus to systematically underdeterring such accidents. Accidents that require the amputation of a limb, particularly a leg, are apparently even more catastrophic than one had thought. They do not just cause a lifetime of disfigurement and reduced mobility; they create a high risk of premature death from heart disease. The goal of awarding damages in tort law is to put the tort victim as nearly as possible in the position he would have occupied if the tort had not been committed. This goal cannot be attained or even approached if judges shut their eyes to consequences that scientists have found are likely to follow from particular types of accident, merely because the scientists' evidence is statistical.

5. *Scheduled damages.* The high variation in pain and suffering awards for individuals whose conditions are rated as having approximately the same level of severity has led to reform proposals that are described in Bovbjerg, Sloan & Blumstein, Valuing Life and Limb in Tort: Scheduling "Pain and Suffering," 83 Nw. U. L. Rev. 908, 923-924 (1989):

> Within an individual severity level, the highest valuation can be scores of times larger than the lowest. Awards for the most serious permanent injuries [such as those involving quadriplegia] . . . range in value from a low of $147,000 to a high of $18,100,000. Even considering only the spread between the top and bottom quartiles, the range is great. All the awards in the top 25% of [permanent significant injury cases, such as deafness, loss of limb, loss of eye, or loss of one kidney or lung], for example, are at least six times larger than any of the bottom 25%; the ranges are even larger for lower severity cases. Very large awards are also disproportionately present; the distributions skew to the high end of values, as mean values always far exceed medians. Much of this variation may legitimately reflect claimants' precise individual circumstances, as the tort system intends. [This evidence does] not, for instance, control for the age of the claimant, a factor that strongly influences duration of permanent injury. Nor does it control for pre-injury earnings, or the amount of medical care received. Including many other factors in a multiple regression analysis in addition to severity as valuation predictors helps explain some of the differences in awards within individual severity categories. It is not possible to fully and objectively adjust for other circumstances that plausibly influence a jury's valuation, such as the subjective nature of how an injury occurred. No amount of adjusting, however, is likely to fully account for the extreme values.

What if compromise verdicts are involved?

Given these jury extremes, the authors urge courts to use "scheduled" damages for pain and suffering and other forms of noneconomic loss, preferably by developing a matrix that classifies injuries by severity and age. A second approach informs the jury of the range of awards in past similar cases as nonbinding benchmarks for recovery. A third approach sets floors and ceilings to constrain awards.

Scheduled damages in workers' compensation systems typically make no independent award for pain and suffering nor do the no-fault automobile insurance plans that many states use to supplement the tort system. Elimination of damages for pain and suffering is common in various first party insurance schemes, including Social Security Disability Income as well as Medicare and Medicaid. These omissions have been treated as evidence that in first party markets injured parties are generally unwilling to purchase insurance against possible future pain and suffering. See Danzon, Tort Reform and the Role of Government in Private Insurance Markets, 13 J. Legal Stud. 517 (1984). Why? Would anyone sell this insurance? Even if Danzon's point is true, does it follow that damages in tort actions should ignore pain and suffering?

6. *Fair compensation.* Why might informed persons in a voluntary market wish to limit their recoverable damages (and hence their damages for pain and suffering) in tort? One theoretical explanation is developed in Friedman, What Is "Fair Compensation" For Death or Injury?, 2 Int. Rev. Law & Econ. 81, 82 (1982):

> [The basic way of putting the point] is to say that bodily injury makes the victim worse off in two ways. It lowers his effective income by reducing his earning power and imposing costs (a seeing eye dog, hospital bills, etc.). In addition it lowers the value to him of any given income by eliminating the ways in which he can spend it. Death is the extreme case; not only does it lower the victim's income to zero, it simultaneously reduces to zero the benefit he can get by spending any form of income — including damage payments.
>
> One thing this argument suggests is that 'full compensation' — a level of payment for damages which restores the victim to the level of welfare he had before the injury — is in a sense inefficient.

Friedman attributes this inefficiency to the initial preference of most individuals, prior to accident, to use the money on other consumption expenditures in his uninjured state. Accordingly, Friedman suggests that the law should permit any person to *sell* insurance on his life, that is, to receive payments for today in exchange for transferring to other persons the right to collect damages in the event of death at some future time. Is Friedman's thesis consistent with the award of very large tort damages in personal injury cases in which, for example, extensive life-support and custodial care are needed to keep someone alive?

2. Economic Losses

O'Shea v. Riverway Towing Co.
677 F.2d 1194 (7th Cir. 1982)

POSNER, J. This is a tort case under the federal admiralty jurisdiction. We are called upon to decide questions of contributory negligence and damage assessment, in particular the question — one of first impression in this circuit — whether, and if so how, to account for inflation in computing lost future wages.

On the day of the accident, Margaret O'Shea was coming off duty as a cook on a towboat plying the Mississippi River. A harbor boat operated by the defendant, Riverway Towing Company, carried Mrs. O'Shea to shore and while getting off the boat she fell and sustained the injury complained of. The district judge found Riverway negligent and Mrs. O'Shea free from contributory negligence, and assessed damages in excess of $150,000. Riverway appeals only from the finding that there was no contributory negligence and from the part of the damage award that was intended to compensate Mrs. O'Shea for her lost future wages. [The court held that the plaintiff was free of contributory negligence.]

The more substantial issues in this appeal relate to the computation of lost wages. Mrs. O'Shea's job as a cook paid her $40 a day, and since the custom was to work 30 days consecutively and then have the next 30 days off, this comes to $7200 a year although, as we shall see, she never had earned that much in a single year. She testified that when the accident occurred she had been about to get another cook's job on a Mississippi towboat that would have paid her $60 a day ($10,800 a year). She also testified that she had been intending to work as a boat's cook until she was 70 — longer if she was able. An economist who testified on Mrs. O'Shea's behalf used the foregoing testimony as the basis for estimating the wages that she lost because of the accident. He first subtracted federal income tax from yearly wage estimates based on alternative assumptions about her wage rate (that it would be either $40 or $60 a day); assumed that this wage would have grown by between six and eight percent a year; assumed that she would have worked either to age 65 or to age 70; and then discounted the resulting lost-wage estimates to present value, using a discount rate of 8.5 percent a year. These calculations, being based on alternative assumptions concerning starting wage rate, annual wage increases, and length of employment, yielded a range of values rather than a single value. The bottom of the range was $50,000. This is the present value, computed at an 8.5 percent discount rate, of Mrs. O'Shea's lost future wages on the assumption that her starting wage was $40 a day and that it would have grown by six percent a year until she retired at the age of 65. The top of the range was $114,000, which is the present value (again discounted at

8.5 percent) of her lost future wages assuming she would have worked till she was 70 at a wage that would have started at $60 a day and increased by eight percent a year. The judge awarded a figure — $86,033 — near the midpoint of this range. . . .

There is no doubt that the accident disabled Mrs. O'Shea from working as a cook on a boat. The break in her leg was very serious: it reduced the stability of the leg and caused her to fall frequently. It is impossible to see how she could have continued working as a cook, a job performed mostly while standing up, and especially on a boat, with its unsteady motion. But Riverway argues that Mrs. O'Shea (who has not worked at all since the accident, which occurred two years before the trial) could have gotten some sort of job and that the wages in that job should be deducted from the admittedly higher wages that she could have earned as a cook on a boat.

The question is not whether Mrs. O'Shea is totally disabled in the sense, relevant to social security disability cases but not tort cases, that there is no job in the American economy for which she is medically fit. It is whether she can by reasonable diligence find gainful employment, given the physical condition in which the accident left her. Here is a middle-aged woman, very overweight, badly scarred on one arm and one leg, unsteady on her feet, in constant and serious pain from the accident, with no education beyond high school and no work skills other than cooking, a job that happens to require standing for long periods which she is incapable of doing. It seems unlikely that someone in this condition could find gainful work at the minimum wage. True, the probability is not zero; and a better procedure, therefore, might have been to subtract from Mrs. O'Shea's lost future wages as a boat's cook the wages in some other job, discounted (i.e., multiplied) by the probability — very low — that she would in fact be able to get another job. But the district judge cannot be criticized for having failed to use a procedure not suggested by either party. The question put to him was the dichotomous one, would she or would she not get another job if she made reasonable efforts to do so? This required him to decide whether there was a more than 50 percent probability that she would. We cannot say that the negative answer he gave to that question was clearly erroneous.

Riverway argues next that it was wrong for the judge to award damages on the basis of a wage not validated, as it were, by at least a year's employment at that wage. Mrs. O'Shea had never worked full time, had never in fact earned more than $3600 in a full year, and in the year preceding the accident had earned only $900. But previous wages do not put a cap on an award of lost future wages. If a man who had never worked in his life graduated from law school, began working at a law firm at an annual salary of $35,000, and was killed the second day on the job, his lack of a past wage history would be irrelevant to computing his lost future wages. The present case is similar if less dramatic. Mrs. O'Shea did not work at all until 1974, when her husband died. She then lived on her inheritance and worked at a variety of part-time jobs till January 1979, when she started working as a cook on the towboat. According to her testimony, which the trial judge believed, she was then working full time. It is immaterial that this was her first full-time job and that the accident occurred before she had held it for a full year. Her job history was typical of women who return to the labor force after their children are grown or, as in Mrs. O'Shea's case, after their husband dies, and these women are, like any tort victims, entitled to damages based on what they would have earned in the future rather than on what they may or may not have earned in the past. . . .

We come at last to the most important issue in the case, which is the proper treatment of inflation in calculating lost future wages. Mrs. O'Shea's economist based the six to eight percent range which he used to estimate future increases in the wages of a boat's cook on the general pattern of wage increases in service occupations over the past 25 years. During the second half of this period the rate of inflation has been substantial and has accounted for much of the increase in nominal wages in this period; and to use that increase to project future wage increases is therefore to assume that inflation will continue, and continue to push up wages. Riverway argues that it is improper as a matter of law to take inflation into account in projecting lost future wages. Yet Riverway itself wants to take inflation into account — one-sidedly, to reduce the amount of the damages computed. For Riverway does not object to the economist's choice of an 8.5 percent discount rate for reducing Mrs. O'Shea's lost future wages to present value, although the rate includes an allowance — a very large allowance — for inflation.

To explain, the object of discounting lost future wages to present value is to give the plaintiff an amount of money which, invested safely, will grow to a sum equal to those wages. So if we thought that but for the accident Mrs. O'Shea would have earned $7200 in 1990, and we were computing in 1980 (when this case was tried) her damages based on those lost earnings, we would need to determine the sum of money that, invested safely for a period of 10 years, would grow to $7200. Suppose that in 1980 the rate of interest on ultra-safe (i.e., federal government) bonds or notes maturing in 10 years was 12 percent. Then we would consult a table of present values to see what sum of money invested at 12 percent for 10 years would at the end of that time have grown to $7200. The answer is $2318. But a moment's reflection will show that to give Mrs. O'Shea $2318 to compensate her for lost wages in 1990 would grossly undercompensate her. People demand 12 percent to lend money risklessly for 10 years because they expect their principal to have much less purchasing power when they get it back at the end of the time. In other words, when long-term interest rates are high, they are high in order to compensate lenders for the fact that they will be repaid in cheaper dollars. In periods when no inflation is anticipated, the risk-free interest rate is between one and three percent. See references in Doca v. Marina Mercante Nicaraguense, S.A., 634 F.2d 30, 39 n.2 (2d Cir. 1980). Additional percentage points above that level reflect inflation anticipated over the life of the loan. But if there is inflation it will affect wages as well as prices. Therefore to give Mrs. O'Shea $2318 today because that is the present value of $7200 10 years hence, computed as a discount rate — 12 percent — that consists mainly of an allowance for anticipated inflation, is in fact to give her less than she would have been earning then if she was earning $7200 on the date of the accident, even if the only wage increases she would have received would have been those necessary to keep pace with inflation.

There are (at least) two ways to deal with inflation in computing the present value of lost future wages. One is to take it out of both the wages and the discount rate — to say to Mrs. O'Shea, "we are going to calculate your probable wage in 1990 on the assumption, unrealistic as it is, that there will be zero inflation between now and then and, to be consistent, we are going to discount the amount thus calculated by the interest rate that would be charged under the same assumption of zero inflation." Thus, if we thought Mrs. O'Shea's real (i.e., inflation-free) wage rate would not rise in the future, we would fix her lost earnings in 1990 as $7200 and, to be consistent, we would discount that to present (1980) value using an estimate of the real interest rate. At two percent, this procedure would yield a present value of $5906. Of course, she would not invest this money at a mere two percent. She would invest it at the much higher prevailing interest rate. But that would not give her a windfall; it would just enable her to replace her lost 1990 earnings with an amount equal to what she would in fact have earned in that year if inflation continues, as most people expect it to do. (If people did not expect continued inflation, long-term interest rates would be much lower; those rates impound investors' inflationary expectations.)

An alternative approach, which yields the same result, is to use a (higher) discount rate based on the current risk-free 10-year interest rate, but apply that rate to an estimate of lost future wages that includes expected inflation. Contrary to Riverway's argument, this projection would not require gazing into a crystal ball. The expected rate of inflation can, as just suggested, be read off from the current long-term interest rate. If that rate is 12 percent, and if as suggested earlier the real or inflation-free interest rate is only one to three percent, this implies that the market is anticipating 9-11 percent inflation over the next 10 years, for a long-term interest rate is simply the sum of the real interest rate and the anticipated rate of inflation during the term.

Either approach to dealing with inflation is acceptable (they are, in fact, equivalent) and we by no means rule out others; but it is illogical and indefensible to build inflation into the discount rate yet ignore it in calculating the lost future wages that are to be discounted. That results in systematic undercompensation, just as building inflation into the estimate of future lost earnings and then discounting using the real rate of interest would systematically overcompensate. . . .

[Posner, J., then upheld the economist's methodology and noted that his calculations were favorable for the defendant because he did not build in any increase in real wages that Mrs. O'Shea could expect to earn as she gained experience. He also faulted the economist for his failure to take into account the risk that Mrs. O'Shea might not be in the labor market in 1990 because of death or injury. However, he affirmed the award below because this objection was not pressed by the defendant. He concluded that the calculation of lost earnings "can and should be an analytical rather than an intuitive undertaking," and "for the future" asked "the district judges in this circuit to indicate the steps by which they arrive at damage awards for lost future earnings."]

Judgment affirmed.

NOTES

1. *Discounting to present value.* As *O'Shea* makes clear, discounting to present value is an essential task in determining the proper awards for any future item of recovery, whether lost earnings or, by extension, medical expenses. The requirement for discounting future income streams can be justified by a single proposition: A dollar today is worth more than a dollar next year. The reason for the difference should be apparent: If a person is in possession of the dollar at the present time, he will be able at the end of the year to enjoy both the dollar and the interest earned on it. If he gets the dollar at the end of the year, the interest on it will benefit the actor (say, the bank) who has had the use of the dollar in the interim. The value of that one year's use of the dollar is, uncertainty to one side, a function of the going rate of interest for the use of money. As interest rates increase, the demand for immediate cash, relative to future payments, increases as well. Accordingly, the discount rate will be steeper. Indeed, the present value of a future payment of $1.00 is a function of the current rate of interest and the elapsed time until payment is made. It is estimated by the formula

$$PV_{\$1.00} = \$1.00 \div (1 + i)^n$$

where $PV_{\$1.00}$ equals the present value of the future payment of $1.00, n equals the number of years until this payment is made, and i equals the uniform rate of interest applicable during the period. Inspection of the formula reveals that the discount for a future payment depends both on the interest rate and on the length of time before payment is due. The longer a creditor must wait for payment, the greater its discounted value today. Should future pain and suffering be discounted to present value? For a negative answer, see Brant v. Bockholt, 532 N.W.2d 801 (Iowa 1995), following RST §913A.

The value of $1.00 payable at some future time can be calculated by the analogous formula:

$$FV_{\$1.00} = \$1.00 \times (1 + i)^n$$

In effect a dollar today will grow exponentially with time. Both discounting to present value and projecting future values are an essential portion of the damage enterprise. Should the same logic require discounting future pain and suffering?

2. *Inflation.* Both discounting and projecting become more difficult with inflation. As a general economic proposition, inflation means that it will take more dollars tomorrow than it takes today to purchase the same market basket of goods. A lender, then, in order to preserve his real economic position over time, will have to receive a payment above and beyond the "real rate" of interest—i.e., the level of interest appropriate when the inflation rate is zero. Most economic studies estimate that the real rate of interest is somewhere between 1.5 and 3 percent, with 2 percent being perhaps the most commonly cited figure. See, e.g., Gibson, Interest Rates and Inflationary Expectations: New Evidence, 62 Am. Econ. Rev. 854 (1972). As Newman, J., observed in Doca v. Marina Mercante Nicaraguense, S.A., 634 F.2d 30, 38 (2d Cir. 1980), "it is entirely feasible to take inflation into account without making any prediction as to the specific level of future inflation rates. All that is needed is a prediction that in the future inflation rates will bear approximately the same relationship to long-term interest rates that they have in the past."

Neither *O'Shea* nor *Doca* demands that the district courts always use the 2 percent discount rate, with Newman, J., noting that "[l]itigants are free to account for inflation in other ways, or to offer evidence of a rate more appropriate than 2 percent." In In re Federal-Mogul Global, Inc., 330 B.R. 133, 163 (D. Del. 2005), a massive asbestos bankruptcy case, the court followed established precedent an announced that "we do not believe a trial court . . . should be reversed if it adopts a rate between 1 and 3% and explains its choice." If inflation is constant across all cases, why allow the discount rate to vary from case to case? For a defense of fixed rates, see Bowers, Courts, Contracts, and the Appropriate Discount Rate: A Quick Fix for the Legal Lottery, 63 U. Chi. L. Rev. 1099 (1996). Perhaps the best economic estimations are made if inflation and discounting are ignored altogether. In Kaczkowski v. Bolubasz, 421 A.2d 1027, 1038-1039 (Pa. 1980), the Pennsylvania Supreme Court held that "future inflation shall be presumed equal to future interest rates with these factors offsetting. Thus, the courts of this Commonwealth are instructed to abandon the practice of discounting lost future earnings."

That result finds support in Carter & Palmer, Real Rates, Expected Rates, and Damage Awards, 20 J. Legal Stud. 439, 461 (1991), who concluded "that there is, on average, no need to try to estimate nominal or real interest rates, inflation rates, or the aggregate growth of labor productivity in legal cases involving a loss of earning capacity over time. These terms all cancel out in the equation for calculating the present value of the stream of losses." The authors did not control for the tax effects of damages, nor take into account the possibility that productivity increases will decrease or disappear as workers approach conventional retirement ages.

In Richardson v. Chapman, 676 N.E.2d 621 (Ill. 1997), the defendant's truck struck the car in which the plaintiff rode, rendering her a quadriplegic at age 23. In calculating the present value of her future medical expenses, the plaintiff's expert, Professor Linke, "testified that the present cash value of her future medical expenses had a lower bound of $7,371,914 and an upper bound of $9,570,034. The lower bound figure assumed a discount rate one percentage point higher than the growth rate [of wages and prices]; the upper bound figure assumed that the two rates would be equal." He used similar calculations for lost earnings. Relying on *O'Shea*, the court held that "Professor Linke's approach was a reasonable one; by using a differential between the two rates, he did not have to make a prediction of future growth and inflation rates. Professor Linke was consistent in his treatment of inflation, and he did not adopt a method that would undercompensate or overcompensate the plaintiff." What should be done if increases in the cost of medical services are systematically higher than the rate of inflation? If future expensive medical advances allow new therapies and treatments to be applied?

In Aldridge v. Baltimore & Ohio Railroad, 789 F.2d 1061, 1067 (4th Cir. 1986), the court held, citing to the Ninth Circuit, that "the party who would benefit from the application of a particular economic formula has the burden of producing competent evidence to prove it."

3. *Prejudgment interest.* At common law, the general rule was that interest for a successful tort plaintiff ran only from the time of judgment, i.e., that moment when the unliquidated amount of the damages imposed by the tort law was fixed by litigation. One obvious objection to this rule is that it allows the defendant, by delay, to reduce the amount paid to the plaintiff, and thereby to frustrate the common law objective of full compensation to the plaintiff. To meet this objection, the court in In re Air Crash Disaster Near Chicago, 644 F.2d 633 (7th Cir. 1981), held that prejudgment interest was recoverable under the Illinois wrongful death statute, today 740 Ill. Comp. Stat. 180/2, which calls for "fair and just compensation" for pecuniary losses in death cases. Prejudgment interest is sometimes mandated by statute, see Colo. Rev. Stat. Ann. §13-21-101(1) (West 2007), which makes it the "duty of the court" to add interest "calculated from the date such suit was filed to the date of satisfying the judgment." This interest counts as taxable income. See Brabson v. United States, 73 F.3d 1040 (10th Cir. 1996). In still other cases, the plaintiff's award is increased on appeal, in which case the usual rule starts the interest running from the

date of the original judgment, not the appeal. See Lakin v. Senco Products, 987 P.2d 476 (Or. 1999).

4. *Expected life calculations.* As Posner, J., pointed out, ambiguity lurks in the proposition that a plaintiff of a certain age has, say, 20 years of productive work left before retirement. Few people die right on schedule, so any award for future earnings should take into account the possibility of the plaintiff's death or disability before retirement in order not to misstate systematically lost earnings. The proper procedure thus asks (1) the expected (discounted) earnings of each future year, and (2) the probability that the plaintiff will actually be in the work force in that year. While the probability that the plaintiff would have worked the next year may be close to 100 percent, the same cannot be said of employment 10 or 20 years later. The results achieved by this annualized methodology differ from the results achieved by assuming that a person will live to her life expectancy.

To see why, consider a highly stylized case in which the plaintiff whose annual income is $100 has a 20 percent probability of dying at the end of each of five consecutive years. On this assumption the plaintiff has an expected life of exactly three years

$$(0.2 \times 1) + (0.2 \times 2) + (0.2 \times 3) + (0.2 \times 4) + (0.2 \times 5) = 3.0$$

One simple way to evaluate the lost earnings is to assume that the plaintiff lived exactly three years. The present value of $100 paid three years from now, with a constant 10 percent discount rate is $75.13 (or $100/1.10^3$) such that her cumulative earnings for three years would equal $225.39. That number is lower than the actual lost wages determined by calculating her total wages on the assumption that she had 20 percent chance of dying at the end of each working year. Thus, plaintiff is sure to collect $90.91, equal to the present discounted value of her first year wage. But she has only an 80 percent chance of collecting the second year's wage whose discounted value is $82.64, for $66.12. Similarly, she has only a 60 percent chance of collecting her third year's wage whose discounted value is $75.13, for $45.08. In the fourth period, she stands only a 40 percent chance of getting her discounted wage of $68.30, or $27.32, and last she has only a 20 percent chance of earning $62.09, or $12.42 for the fifth period. On this view the total expected earnings for the five years are

$$\$90.91 + \$66.12 + \$45.08 + \$27.32 + \$12.42 = \$241.85$$

The additional $16.46 collected under the correct method is attributable to higher likelihood of survival in the earlier years, which more than offsets the less steep arithmetical decline in expected wages for each successive year. Getting these calculations right matters in a case like *O'Shea*, given the substantial possibility that a woman in her fifties with both weight and health problems will not be able to work, at least at current capacity, until 70 years of age. Nonetheless, the Supreme Court in Jones & Laughlin Steel Corp. v. Pfeifer, 462 U.S. 523, 533-534 (1983), noted the common perception that these calculations are not made in practice. "Given the complexity of trying to make an exact calculation, litigants frequently follow the relatively simple course of assuming that the worker would have continued to work up to a specific date certain." In calculating the likelihood of future death or disability, should a court confine its attention only to general insurance mortality and disability tables, or should it take into account the individual condition of each particular plaintiff?

5. *Mitigation of damages.* In tort law, as in contract law, the plaintiff normally has a duty to mitigate damages, that is, to take steps that minimize the expected losses from an accident. Hence the inquiry in *O'Shea* as to whether the plaintiff could find alternative land-based employment which should be suitable for the plaintiff but not so onerous that she is worse off than before.

The mitigation issue raises even more serious questions with medical interventions. In principle, it seems easy to conclude that the plaintiff should spend $1,000 of her own money on medical treatment to save the defendant $10,000 of his. The plaintiff is no worse off from mitigation so long as she receives the $1,000 from the defendant, who is left better off by $9,000. Thus, mitigation operates as a barrier against waste by making the plaintiff a fiduciary of sorts for the defendant. However, the outcome of a surgical intervention, for example, is often highly uncertain. Thus, if the operation for $1,000 turns out to be a success, the defendant could save $9,000. But if the patient dies or is permanently injured, the plaintiff is a big loser even if the defendant must compensate for the inferior outcome, which creates real danger whenever risky treatment is elected. Sensing this conflict of interest, most courts give the plaintiff the benefit of the doubt so long as she acts in good faith in deciding whether to accept or reject treatment. See, e.g., McGinley v. United States, 329 F. Supp. 62 (E.D. Pa. 1971), in which the court held that the plaintiff did not have to undergo further surgery with a two-thirds chance of success in order to alleviate pain in his back, after he had undertaken several other procedures. Wood, J., explained:

> It is, of course, settled law that if injuries may be cured or alleviated by a simple and safe surgical operation, then refusal to submit thereto should be considered in mitigation of damages. This is not true, however, where the operation is a serious one, or one attended by grave risk of death or failure. A plaintiff has a duty to submit to reasonable medical treatment and the test of reasonableness is to be determined by the triers of fact.

What result if the plaintiff accepts the surgery and has a bad outcome? A good one?

6. *Taxation of tort damage awards.* The Internal Revenue Code does not tax damage awards received in compensation for personal injuries, even when they are a substitute for lost taxable income. I.R.C. §104(a). In contrast, punitive damages, which are viewed more as a windfall, are taxable. See O'Gilvie v. United States, 519 U.S. 79 (1996).

One recurrent question is whether actual damage awards for lost earnings should be reduced to offset their tax-free status. An early negative answer to that question was offered by Friendly, J., in McWeeney v. New York, New Haven & Hartford Railroad Co., 282 F.2d 34, 36 (2d Cir. 1960), who feared that any reference to the Internal Revenue Code could only make personal injury litigation more speculative and prolonged than it already is: "Is the jury in each case to speculate, or hear testimony, on the procreative proclivities and potentialities of the plaintiff and his spouse?"

The opposite view was taken in Norfolk & Western Ry. v. Liepelt, 444 U.S. 490, 494 (1980), where Justice Stevens allowed these tax issues into evidence in FELA cases, saying:

> Admittedly there are many variables that may affect the amount of a wage earner's future income-tax liability. The law may change, his family may increase or decrease in size, his spouse's earnings may affect his tax bracket, and extra income or unforeseen deductions may become available. But future employment itself, future health, future personal expenditures, future interest rates, and future inflation are also matters of estimate and prediction. Any one of these issues might provide the basis for protracted expert testimony and debate. But the practical wisdom of the trial bar and the trial bench has developed effective methods of presenting the essential elements of an expert calculation in a form that is understandable by juries that are increasingly familiar with the complexities of modern life. We therefore reject the notion that the introduction of evidence describing a decedent's estimated after-tax earnings is too speculative or complex for a jury.

Justice Blackmun's dissent supported the older practice of ignoring taxes in torts cases:

> In my view, by mandating adjustment of the award by way of reduction for federal income taxes that would have been paid by the decedent on his earnings, the Court appropriates for the tortfeasor a benefit intended to be conferred on the victim or his survivors. And in requiring that the jury be instructed that a wrongful-death award is not subject to federal income tax, the Court opens the door for a variety of admonitions to the jury not to "misbehave," and unnecessarily interjects what is now to be federal law into the administration of a trial in a state court.

The administrative complexities of taking taxes into account provoked a different response in New York, where by statute it is now provided that in medical malpractice cases, evidence of the taxation of lost earnings "shall be admissible for consideration by the court, outside of the presence of the jury." The rule further provides that the jury should be instructed that any adjustments for taxes shall be made "if warranted" by the court, which has the power to reduce the award to take into account "the amount of federal, state and local personal income taxes which the court finds, with reasonable certainty, that the plaintiff would have been obligated by law to pay." N.Y. C.P.L.R. §4546 (McKinney 2007). What is wrong with an alternative proposal that reduces all damage awards for lost income by a fixed figure, say, 20 percent? Note that the loss in precision is offset by the consistency in results and the reduction in administrative costs.

7. *Imputed income: additions to market losses.* Imputed income from non-market activities is another element that must be included in damages. The benefits are said to be "imputed" because there is no explicit market transaction to give direct evidence of their worth. In the law of damages, the most important aspect of imputed income lies in the value of lost services for persons not engaged in ordinary market activities. For example, serious personal injuries to a housewife may disable her from performing services of great value to herself and her family, and require her to hire replacement services. See, e.g., Cummins v. Rachner, 257 N.W.2d 808 (Minn. 1977), in which the court affirmed an award of $225,000 to the next of kin in a wrongful death action. The 37-year-old decedent was a housewife, "a truly remarkable and exceptional woman." She had been married for 19 years and had had full charge of a household with seven children, including one with learning disabilities. She was active in church and civic affairs and still found time to complete two years of college education before her death. Is the proper measure of damages what she could have earned in the marketplace, less the taxes paid thereon? For a development of this theme see Komesar, Toward a General Theory of Personal Injury Loss, 3 J. Legal Stud. 457 (1974).

Duncan v. Kansas City Southern Railway
773 So. 2d 670 (La. 2000)

JOHNSON, J. This case arises out of a collision between a locomotive and a church van at a railroad crossing in Beauregard Parish. There were three passengers, all sisters, riding in the church van. As a result of the collision, one sister was killed, a second was rendered a quadriplegic, and the third suffered less serious injuries. Plaintiffs, parents of the three passengers, filed suit to recover damages. A jury found the driver of the van and the railroad liable for the accident, apportioning fault between the two. The decision was affirmed by the court of appeal. We granted certiorari to review the correctness of this decision. . . .

The plaintiffs were awarded damages totaling $27,876,813.31. Included in the award were future medical expenses in the amount of $17,000,000.00 and general damages for physical pain and suffering, mental anguish, and loss of enjoyment of life in the amount of $8,000,000.00 to Rachel Duncan. . . .

EXCESSIVE DAMAGES

Finally, we turn our attention to the last assignment of error raised by KCS [defendant], whether the jury's award of damages was so excessive as to be set aside. According to KCS, the jury was prejudiced in its award by the plaintiffs' bringing Rachel Duncan in and out of the courtroom during the trial. Sympathy for this quadriplegic child resulted in the general damage award of $8 million dollars and the $17 million dollar award for future medical care. KCS contends these awards are unprecedented, grossly excessive, and not supported by the evidence. . . .

GENERAL DAMAGES

General damages are those which may not be fixed with pecuniary exactitude; instead, they "involve mental or physical pain or suffering, inconvenience, the loss of intellectual gratification or physical enjoyment, or other losses of life or life-style which cannot be definitely measured in monetary terms." Vast discretion is accorded the trier of fact in fixing general damage awards. This vast discretion is such that an appellate court should rarely disturb an award of general damages. Thus, the role of the appellate court in reviewing general damage awards is not to decide what it considers to be an appropriate award, but rather to review the exercise of discretion by the trier of fact. . . .

The initial inquiry, in reviewing an award of general damages, is whether the trier of fact abused its discretion in assessing the amount of damages. Only after a determination that the trier of fact has abused its "much discretion" is a resort to prior awards appropriate and then only for the purpose of determining the highest or lowest point which is reasonably within that discretion.

RACHEL DUNCAN

In the present case, the trial court awarded $8 million in general damages to Rachel Duncan for her physical pain and suffering, mental anguish, and loss of enjoyment of life. According to KCS, this award far exceeds the highest reasonable awards in cases involving similar injuries.

However, our initial determination is not guided by awards for similar injuries; rather, our initial inquiry is whether the instant award is beyond that which a reasonable trier of fact could assess for the effects of the particular injury to the particular plaintiff under the particular circumstances. KCS contends the jury's award was based on sympathy for Rachel, who was brought in and out of the courtroom during the trial in a special, self-propelled wheelchair. While the sight of Rachel in her self-propelled wheelchair may have elicited some sympathetic feelings from the jury, the evidence presented more than amply demonstrates the effects of this accident on Rachel Duncan.

Prior to the accident, Rachel was an active eleven-year-old girl, she enjoyed outdoor activities, she was excelling academically in her sixth-grade class, she had many friends, and she was planning to attend college someday. As a result of the accident, Rachel's whole life has changed. The injuries she sustained when she was thrown from the church van have left her a quadriplegic who is totally dependent on others for all her care needs. Rachel's medical diagnosis and impairments include C5 ASIA A tetraplegia, traumatic brain injury, scoliosis, a tracheostomy, neurogenic bladder, neurogenic bowel, muscle spasms, contractures of upper and lower extremities, pulmonary insufficiency, a non-functioning left lung, left-sided hearing loss, severe headaches, anorexia, severe malnutrition and depression. She also suffers from recurrent pulmonary infections, recurrent bladder infections, and is in constant danger of developing decubitus ulcers and autonomic dysreflexia.

In addition to having to cope with the injuries she sustained in the accident, Rachel is also coping with the fact that her older sister was killed in the accident and her younger sister was injured in the accident. She is no longer able to attend school with her friends, she spends the majority of her day in either her bed or her wheelchair, she can no longer go on the family fishing and camping trips she enjoyed before the accident, and she is aware of the effect her injuries have had on her family. While Rachel still plans on attending college, she will not be able to go off to college like other college freshmen. Even if she decides to move out of her parents home when she becomes an adult, she will require a specially designed home and 24-hour care. Even when all these factors are considered, we find that the general damage award of $8,000,000 is excessive and the trial court abused its discretion in fixing the general damage award to Rachel Duncan. A review of cases involving similar injuries reveals that the highest amount that could reasonably be awarded under the facts of this case is $6,000,000. Therefore, we reduce the general damage award from $8,000,000 to $6,000,000.

[Other assignments of error are omitted.]

Lastly, KCS contends that the $17 million award for Rachel's future medical care is clearly excessive. According to KCS, if this award is invested conservatively so as to obtain only a five percent return, it would still produce an annual interest income of $850,000. Future medical expenses must be established with some degree of certainty. Awards will not be made in the absence of medical testimony that they are indicated and setting out their probable cost.

In the matter at hand, the jury was presented with medical testimony by plaintiffs', as well as, defendant's experts. [T]he [plaintiffs' expert's] plan provides for a treatment program with individual counseling, family counseling, occupational therapy, physical therapy, speech therapy, weekly review by a registered nurse ("RN"), and 24-hour attendant care by either a licensed practical nurse ("LPN") or a RN. The LPN or RN would be provided by a home health agency, and their activities would be supervised by a case manager. [The plan was based] on Rachel having the same life expectancy as persons her age without spinal cord injuries, that is 81 years. . . .

[Defendant's expert's] plan . . . recommends evaluations by physicians specializing in physical medicine and rehabilitation, pulmonology, urology, internal medicine, orthopedics, and psychiatry. [This plan] further recommends educational counseling, physical therapy, and occupational therapy, as well as, 16 to 24 hour attendant care by a home health aide.

[The court reviews the different mixes of attendant care, either registered nurses or home health aides, on either 16-hour or 24-hour cycles. It further discusses what life expectancy should be used: a 57-year life expectancy, based on statistics for people with spinal cord injuries, or an 81-year life expectancy based on general actuarial tables.]

Rachel Duncan has been diagnosed as a C5 tetraplegic and her age at the time of trial was 14.6 years. [A] 15-year old in the C5 neurologic category has a life expectancy of 42.6 years. The record does include accurate evidence with reference to Rachel's life expectancy. Dr. Zidek's [Rachel's treating physician] predicted 57-year life expectancy for Rachel is more realistic than the 81-year life expectancy predicted by Dr. Voogt [plaintiffs' expert]. Furthermore, the 57-year life expectancy is also the more scientifically accurate prediction. [The court reduced the recovery for future medical expenses from $17 million to $10,528,722, based on the jury's estimate of the cost of annual care for the 57-year life expectancy instead of the longer life expectancy erroneously introduced.]

NOTES

1. *Excessive damages as an abuse of discretion.* If the standard for the appellate review of damage awards is abuse of discretion, how should the court decide that $8 million is too much and $6 million is about right? Note that cases of serious injury routinely give rise to the questions raised in *Duncan*. Historically, most courts applied some variation of the "shock

the conscience standard," which offered only a limited power to review jury awards in cases, for example, in which there was a clear "miscarriage of justice." See, e.g., Johnson v. Parrish, 827 F.2d 988 (4th Cir. 1987). Under this deferential standard, most courts have sustained large verdicts for gruesome injuries. See, e.g., Firestone v. Crown Center Redevelopment Corp., 693 S.W.2d 99 (Mo. 1985) (active 34-year-old woman left quadriplegic in Hyatt Skyway collapse awarded $15,000,000); Wry v. Dial, 503 P.2d 979 (Ariz. App. 1973) (affirming a $3,500,000 award for a brilliant scientist terribly maimed in an automobile accident); Murphy v. Colorado Aviation, Inc., 588 P.2d 877 (Colo. App. 1978) (affirming a $2,500,000 wrongful death award to the widow of Audie Murphy, a famous actor and decorated war hero).

2. *Remittitur and additur.* One common way that courts have exercised some control over damage awards in personal injury cases is through remittitur or additur. Under remittitur, the court does not simply lower the award below what the jury had provided. Rather it gives the plaintiff the option to avoid the cost and expense of a new trial by accepting a reduction in the size of the jury award. Under additur, the defendant can avoid the cost of a new trial by consenting to a larger verdict equal, perhaps, to the smallest verdict the court would sustain against a charge of inadequacy. This power is limited in federal courts by the Seventh Amendment, which provides that "no fact tried by a jury, shall be otherwise reexamined in any Court of the United States, than according to the rules of the common law." The reexamination clause has been held to prevent an appellate court from reducing the size of an award on its own motion. Instead, it must remand the case and allow the plaintiff the option of a new trial if it finds the reduced amount too small. In Hetzel v. Prince William County, 523 U.S. 208, 211 (1998), an employment discrimination case, the Supreme Court in a per curiam opinion held that "[t]he Court of Appeals' writ of mandamus, requiring the District Court to enter judgment for a lesser amount than that determined by the jury without allowing petitioner the option of a new trial, cannot be squared with the Seventh Amendment."

Different states have experimented with different modes of controlling juries. The Missouri Supreme Court in *Firestone, supra,* abolished the practice of remittitur as an invasion of the province of the jury that has "been fraught with confusion and inconsistency." In contrast, the New York legislature increased the judicial power to trim excessive damage awards, and incidentally, to boost up inadequate ones by displacing a "shock the conscience" standard with N.Y. C.P.L.R. §5501(c) (McKinney 2007), which reads:

In reviewing a money judgment . . . in which it is contended that the award is excessive or inadequate and that a new trial should have been granted unless a stipulation is entered to a different award, the appellate division shall determine that an award is excessive or inadequate if it deviates materially from what would be reasonable compensation.

Implementing this provision has not proved easy. In Consorti v. Armstrong World Industries, Inc., 9 F. Supp. 2d 307, 313 (S.D.N.Y. 1998), the plaintiff contracted incurable mesothelioma, from which he eventually died at age 51. The jury awarded him $12 million for pain and suffering, $8 million of which covered about 23 months of past pain and suffering and $4 million covered the anticipated pain and suffering for the estimated nine remaining months of his life. After the case went to the Second Circuit and the Supreme Court, on remand in the district court, Sweet, J., ordered a remittitur to $5 million under the New York statute. In making this judgment, he looked to jury awards in comparable cases. "Given the availability of remitted verdicts in cases where plaintiffs suffered from mesothelioma due to asbestos exposure, . . . broadening the comparison group to nonasbestos cases would cloud the issue and increase the proba-bility of reaching an amount that may not be within the 'reasonable' range for mesothelioma victims. Moreover, Consorti has more in common with those plaintiffs who suffered the same disease due to the same causal agent than, for example, a middle-aged man who suffered a leg amputation." The court noted that $100,000 per month of suffering had been regarded as appropriate compensation in 1990, but that the number had been increased to $129,000 by the mid 1990s. Taking specific circumstances into account, a $5 million remittitur works out to about $156,000 per month. What, if anything, does or should prevent an upward award creep?

3. *Structured settlements.* One way that the pressure of large verdicts manifests itself is in the increased use of structured settlements. These settlements pay plaintiff's damages in periodic installments rather than in a single lump sum. The structured settlement reduces the need for the parties to make a joint estimate of future inflation rates since future pay-ments can be geared to inflation if and when it occurs. Structured settle-ments in big cases help reduce the uncertainty in projecting both lost earnings and future medical expenses, either of which can be sizable sums. Their use in smaller cases is, however, sharply limited because of their high administrative costs.

Structured settlements may be used by mutual agreement of the parties even if the common law rule provides only for lump sum damages. The more controversial question is whether one party may demand them as of right over the opposition of the other. For example, legislation may allow one side to require their use. A 1985 Illinois law (735 Ill. Comp. Stat. 5/2-1705-1718 (2007)), applicable to medical malpractice actions only, allows either plaintiff or defendant by pretrial motion to elect a structured settlement whenever a good-faith estimate places future economic damages over $250,000. The statute requires the court to award lump sum payments for present economic damages and noneconomic damages. Periodic payments are made for future economic loss. Payment of attorney's fees to the plaintiff's lawyer takes the form of a lump sum, calculated with reference to both the past and future damage awards, and deducted proportionately from both parts of the award. These damage provisions were sustained against various constitutional challenges in Bernier v. Burris, 497 N.E.2d 763 (Ill. 1986). A similar provision is found in Cal. Civ. Proc. Code §667.7 (West 2007), which states that when future damages awarded against any "health care provider" exceed $50,000, either party may request that it be paid in whole or in part in periodic payments and not in lump sum. In construing this section, the court in Deocampo v. Ahn, 125 Cal. Rptr. 2d 79, 89 (Cal. App. 2002) wrote:

> Section 667.7 is intended to enable courts to provide for the needs of injured plaintiffs and their dependents for the length of time such monetary compensation is necessary. The goal is to prevent early dissipation of an award, and ensure that when the plaintiff incurs losses or expenses in the future, the money awarded to him will be there. While a precise match between future needs and the periodic payments is not necessary, there must be evidence to support the payment schedule developed by the court.
>
> Section 667.7 also addresses plaintiffs who die prematurely after entry of a judgment providing for such periodic payments. Section 667.7 prevents such a plaintiff's survivors from receiving the periodic payments that the plaintiff would have received for his or her future care if he or she had not died prematurely, thus preventing the survivors from receiving a windfall of such money which would no longer be needed for the plaintiff's care. Section 667.7 does not place such a blanket restriction, however, on the periodic payments for the future lost *wages* awarded to the plaintiff.

Why the difference between wages and medical expenses? For a defense of the lump sum common law system of payments, see Rea, Lump-Sum Versus Periodic Damage Awards, 10 J. Legal Stud. 131 (1981).

4. *Caps on damages.* The dramatic increase in the level of damages awarded to successful plaintiffs in tort actions has brought forth a strong legislative response in many states: capping damages, especially in medical malpractice cases. This reform, in its many variations, has met with a mixed fate when subjected to constitutional challenges.

An early acquiescence to these limits is found in Fein v. Permanente Medical Group, 695 P.2d 665, 683 (Cal. 1985), in which the California Supreme Court upheld §3333.2 of the California Civil Code, which limited recovery for pain and suffering to $250,000. The court adopted the deferential "rational basis" standard of review as appropriate to this challenge. It first noted that the statute placed no restrictions on recovery for economic losses, and it observed that many scholars (including Jaffe, *supra* at page 860) have attacked the award for pain and suffering in tort cases as matter of first principle. The court continued:

> Nor can we agree with amicus' contention that the $250,000 limit is un-constitutional because the Legislature could have realized its hoped-for cost savings by mandating a fixed-percentage reduction of all noneconomic damage awards. The choice between reasonable alternative methods of achieving a given objective is generally for the Legislature, and there are a number of reasons why the Legislature may have made the choice it did. One of the problems identified in the legislative hearing was the unpre-dictability of the size of large noneconomic damage awards, resulting from the inherent difficulties in valuing such damages and the great disparity in the price tag which different juries placed on such losses. The Legislature could reasonably have determined that an across-the-board limit would provide a more stable base on which to calculate insurance rates. Further-more, as one amicus suggests, the Legislature may have felt that the fixed $250,000 limit would promote settlements by eliminating "the unknown possibility of phenomenal awards for pain and suffering that can make liti-gation worth the gamble." Finally, the Legislature simply may have felt that it was fairer to malpractice plaintiffs in general to reduce only the very large noneconomic damage awards, rather than to diminish the more modest recoveries for pain and suffering and the like in the great bulk of cases. Each of these grounds provides a sufficient rationale for the $250,000 limit.

Unlike California, several courts have struck down caps on damages. With *Fein* compare Best v. Taylor Machine Works, 689 N.E.2d 1057, 1076 (Ill. 1997), in which the court struck down a $500,000 cap on general damages as special legislation. 735 ILCS 5/2-1115.1 (West 1996). McMorrow, J., explained:

> We do not disagree with defendants' assertion that damages for noneco-nomic injuries are difficult to assess. We simply determine that it does not follow that the difficulty in quantifying compensatory damages for noneco-nomic injuries is alleviated by imposing an arbitrary limitation or cap in all cases, without regard to the facts or circumstances. . . . There is universal agreement that the compensatory goal of tort law requires that an injured plaintiff be made whole. In this case, the arbitrary and automatic cap on compensatory damages for noneconomic injuries in only certain tort cases parallels the harm of the arbitrary classifications stricken by this court [in previous cases]. Therefore, the $500,000 limit does not reestablish the credibility of the tort system, and does nothing to assist the trier of fact in determining appropriate damages for noneconomic injuries. The limitation actually undermines the stated goal of providing consistency and rationality to the civil justice system.

Still other cases invite genuine disputes over the proper interpretation of a particular statutory cap. Thus, in Bartholomew v. Wisconsin Patients

Compensation Fund & Compcare Health Services Insurance Corp., 717 N.W.2d 216, 241 (Wis. 2006), the question was whether Wisconsin's $422,632 ($350,000, indexed for inflation) cap on noneconomic damages imposed a single limitation on noneconomic damages for personal injuries prior to death for a wrongful death action. Overturning earlier precedent, a sharply splintered court concluded that the interpretation of

> Wisconsin's medical malpractice and wrongful death statutes to impose a single global wrongful death cap on all noneconomic damages is flawed because it failed to take into account the well-established distinction in Wisconsin tort law between actions for predeath damages and actions for postdeath damages (wrongful death actions). [Three justices] further conclude that the legislature adopted two caps: a medical malpractice cap for noneconomic damages for predeath claims and a wrongful death cap for noneconomic damages for postdeath loss of society and companionship. Claimants can thus recover for the different damages up to the separate limits of the applicable respective cap.

5. *Empirical estimation of the effects of medical malpractice reform.* The imposition of caps on damages has led to an extensive debate over whether these have had any influence on the frequency and severity of medical malpractice claims. One recent study, Avraham, An Empirical Study of the Impact of Tort Reforms on Medical Malpractice Settlement Payments, 36 J. Legal Stud. (forthcoming 2007), draws on a large data set from the National Practitioner Data Bank, including both settlements and final judgments, to conclude that caps on damages for pain and suffering had significant negative effect on both total payments and individual award size, but caps on noneconomic damages had at most some modest effect of annual payments. The use of structured settlements also tended to reduce reward size.

SECTION C. CONTINGENCY FEES, FEE-SHIFTING DEVICES, SALES OF TORT CLAIMS, AND LITIGATION INSURANCE

Bringing and defending a modern tort claim is a costly venture. The underlying rules of tort liability are often very complex, the facts of a given case highly uncertain, and the potential damages at stake enormous. Expert witnesses are usually needed to establish critical elements on liability and damages. This combination of high stakes and high uncertainty raises the cost of bringing an ordinary tort action beyond the means of

884

the ordinary individual and, especially when done en masse, may test the financial capability of the individuals and firms forced to defend them.

In the context of the tort system, therefore, it is useful to make a quick survey of the standard fee arrangements for tort litigation. Four items require special attention. First, the plaintiff's lawyer in a damage suit is universally retained on a contingent fee arrangement, while the defendant's lawyer is commonly hired (whether by a firm or an insurance company) on an hourly wage. Second, under the American system, each side typically bears its own costs in litigation whether it wins or loses the case. Third, although contingent fee contracts are routinely allowed, an injured party is usually prohibited from making an outright sale of a tort claim to any third party, either before or after it has matured. Finally, litigation insurance can help cover these costs, but it is rarely used.

1. *Contingency Fees*

Under the contingent fee system, the plaintiff's attorney agrees to take compensation for services rendered only out of the funds that the plaintiff recovers from the defendant, either by settlement or judgment. If the action is lost, the plaintiff's attorney receives nothing for time and effort expended and cannot recoup his out-of-pocket expenses of investigative work, expert witnesses, and the like. These contingent fees originated in the United States, but recently they have been approved in other jurisdictions that had long regarded their use as an "unethical practice." In England for example, pursuant to the Courts and Legal Services Act 1990, §58(4), contingent fees were introduced for personal injury, insolvency, and human rights actions by the Conditional Agreements Fee Order 1995 (SI 1995/1674). In 1998, these fee arrangements were extended to all civil cases, excluding family matters, which in turn has been modified on several occasions. The current position is governed by The Conditional Fee Agreements (Revocation) Regulations 2005 (SI 2005/2305), http://www.legislation.gov.uk/si/si2005/uksi_20052305_en.pdf, which makes it easier to implement contingent fee agreements. The relaxation of the prohibitions against contingent fees has also taken place in Canada, as in British Columbia. See R.S.B.C. c. 9, for individual suits, and c. 50 for representative, or class, actions. The proponents of the contingent fee system argue that it enables individuals to press forward with meritorious claims that would otherwise remain unprosecuted for want of funds. They claim, moreover, that feared abuses are not likely to occur since lawyers have a strong incentive to choose those cases with the greatest chance of success: They receive no compensation for their services and expenses from suits that fail. The opponents of the system argue, though with less theoretical justification, that it stirs up needless litigation. For the efficiency case on contingent fees, see Dana & Spier, Expertise and Contingent Fees: The Role of Asymmetric Information in Attorney Compensation, 9 J. L. Econ. & Org. 349 (1993), which extols the virtues of the contingent fee system, especially when the plaintiff's attorney has superior knowledge about the value of a case than the accident victim.

The dispute over contingent fees has been particularly intense with medical malpractice cases (in which the contingency for the lawyer may range anywhere from 25 to 50 percent), and proposals are frequently made to limit the size of the fees the plaintiff's attorney can recover in successful cases. The New Jersey rules, for example, allow (1) 33 1/3 percent on the first $500,000 recovered, (2) 30 percent on the next $500,000, (3) 25 percent on the next $500,000, (4) 20 percent on the next $500,000 recovered, and (5) a "reasonable fee" beyond that. N.J. Rules of Court 1:21-7(c) (2007). Moreover, the rules provide that if an attorney considers his fee to be inadequate, "an application on written notice to the client may be made to the Assignment Judge for the hearing and determining of a reasonable fee in light of all the circumstances." N.J. Rules of Court 1:21-7(f) (2007). The power of the court or legislature to regulate these fees has been sustained against challenges that they improperly restrict the access of injured parties to legal services. Thus, Canon 2 of the New York Lawyer's Code of Professional Responsibility reads, "A Lawyer Should Assist the Legal Profession in Fulfilling its Duty to Make Legal Counsel Available," and Ethical Consideration (EC) 2-20 states:

> Contingent fee arrangements in civil cases have long been commonly accepted in the United States in proceedings to enforce claims. The historical bases of their acceptance are that (1) they often, and in a variety of circumstances, provide the only practical means by which one having a claim against another can economically afford, finance, and obtain the services of a competent lawyer to prosecute a claim, and (2) a successful prosecution of the claim produces a fund out of which the fee can be paid. Although a lawyer generally should decline to accept employment on a contingent fee basis by one who is able to pay a reasonable fixed fee, it is not necessarily improper for a lawyer, where justified by the particular circumstances of a case, to enter into a contingent fee contract in a civil case with any client who, after being fully informed of all relevant factors, desires that arrangement. Because of the human relationships involved and the unique character of the proceedings, contingent fee arrangements in domestic relations matters are rarely justified. In administrative agency proceedings, contingent fee contracts should be governed by the same considerations as in other civil cases. Public policy properly condemns contingent fee arrangements in criminal cases, largely on the ground that legal services in criminal cases do not produce a fund out of which the fee can be paid.

Online   at   http://www.nysba.org/Content/NavigationMenu/Attorney_
Resources/Lawyers_Code_of_Professional_Responsibility/Lawyers.Code.pdf
Accepting the Canon, see Gair v. Peck, 160 N.E.2d 43 (N.Y. 1959).

See also In re The Florida Bar, 349 So. 2d 630 (Fla. 1977), in which the
court noted its disagreement with the New Jersey approach and concluded
that "due to the absence of competent evidence demonstrating any significant abuse of the contingent fee arrangements within the State, we
reject the proposed amendment [to the state code of professional responsibility,] which would impose a maximum contingent fee schedule and
thereby impinge upon the constitutional guarantee of freedom of contract." The court did, however, approve rules requiring disclosure of any
division of fees with referring lawyers and the preparation of a closing
statement summarizing the distribution of funds received in the case. In
addition, the law in Florida and elsewhere imposes in particular contract
disputes a burden on the attorney to prove the reasonableness of the
contingent fee arrangement by clear and convincing evidence. In re Estate
of Kindy v. Krongold & Bass, 310 So. 2d 349 (Fla. App. 1975).

Contingent fees in Florida have recently become a matter of politics as a
state referendum limited these fees in medical liability cases to 30 percent
of the first $250,000, plus 10 percent of any recovery in excess of that
amount. F.S.A. Const. Art. 1 §26. In In re Amendment to the Rules Regulating the Florida Bar, 939 So. 2d 1032, 1039 (Fla. 2006), the state supreme court rejected the "Grimes petition" filed by numerous Florida
lawyers who asked that informed waivers of the constitutional limitation be
allowed, but only with explicit approval of a court that had examined the
facts and circumstances of each case. The court, per curiam, adopted the
alternative proposal of the bar, which allowed voluntary waivers subject to
full disclosure upon completion of detailed forms. "Upon review, we reject
these proposed restrictions [of the Grimes petition] because we do not find
it appropriate to place the courts in the position of unduly restricting the
right of a competent adult client to waive his or her rights under article I,
section 26. Instead, we believe the court's role, when appropriate, is to
ensure that any waiver is made knowingly and voluntarily." What result if
article I, §26 is explicitly made nonwaivable?

What complex malpractice case could be brought with the 10 percent
contingent fee from which expert witnesses have to be paid?

One important issue concerning the contingent fee is its relative efficacy
compared to alternative fee arrangements, most notably the hourly fee and
the fixed fee arrangements. The relative superiority of the contingent fee
for the ordinary tort damage action depends critically on its ability to
minimize the structural conflict of interests between lawyer and client. A
description of the nature of these conflicts and their possible resolution is
forcefully set out by Judge Easterbrook in Kirchoff v. Flynn, 786 F.2d 320,
324-325 (7th Cir. 1986):

The market for legal services uses three principal plans of compensation: the hourly fee, the fixed fee, and the contingent fee. The contingent fee serves in part as a financing device, allowing people to hire lawyers without paying them in advance (or at all, if they lose). It also serves as a monitoring device. In any agency relation, the agent may pursue his own goals at the expense of the principal's. A fixed fee creates the incentive to shirk; a lawyer paid a lump sum, win or lose, may no longer work hard enough to present his client's case. Fixed fees therefore are used only in cases where the client can monitor the results and the lawyer's work (did the lawyer secure the divorce or not?) or where the client (or the client's general counsel) is sufficiently sophisticated to assess what the lawyer has accomplished.

An hourly fee creates an incentive to run up hours, to do too much work in relation to the stakes of the case. An hourly fee may be appropriate where it is hard to define output (in litigation, for example, the outcome turns on the merits and not simply the lawyer's skill and dedication), so the hourly method measures and prices the inputs, the attorney's hours. . . .

The contingent fee uses private incentives rather than careful monitoring to align the interests of lawyer and client. The lawyer gains only to the extent his client gains. This interest-alignment device is not perfect. When the lawyer gains 40 cents to the client's dollar, the lawyer tends to expend too little effort; unless concern for his reputation dominates, he would not put in an extra $600 worth of time to obtain an extra $1,000 for his client, because he would receive only $400 for his effort. But imperfect alignment of interests is better than a conflict of interests, which hourly fees may create. The unscrupulous lawyer paid by the hour may be willing to settle for a lower recovery coupled with a payment for more hours. Contingent fees eliminate this incentive and also ensure a reasonable proportion between the recovery and the fees assessed to defendants. Except in grudge litigation, no client, however wealthy, pays a lawyer more than a dollar to pursue a dollar's worth of recovery.

Contingent fee arrangements also contain other provisions to reduce the conflict of interest between client and lawyer. Thus, it is generally regarded as a violation of the standards of professional ethics for a lawyer to reject a settlement offer or to settle an outstanding case without first obtaining the approval of the client. See ABA Model Rules of Professional Conduct, Rule 1.2(a). In addition, the standard contract typically allows the client to discharge the attorney if the client is dissatisfied with the handling of the case. Wholly apart from legal threats, concerns for professional reputation and the desire to obtain future business through word-of-mouth advertising often keep the plaintiff's lawyer hard at work.

Standing alone, these provisions would seem to place all the cards in the hand of the client, but this balance is redressed in several ways. First, when a client discharges a lawyer without cause, the court may allow that lawyer, after the underlying claim is resolved, to recover a fee based upon the value of work previously done. The client, moreover, is usually reluctant to switch lawyers in the middle of a case because it is difficult to hire a second lawyer who must come up to speed in ongoing litigation shaped by another attorney. In addition, the standard contract also allows the lawyer to withdraw from the case if he thinks that it is unwise to pursue the matter further, which might happen if discovery reveals evidence adverse to the client's case. Yet even here withdrawal is normally allowed only with approval of the court, which, although usually granted, may occasionally be denied. For accounts of the contractual features of contingent fee arrangements, see Miller, Some Agency Problems in Settlement, 16 J. Legal Stud. 189 (1987). For models of the contingent fee arrangement, see Schwartz & Mitchell, An Economic Analysis of the Contingent Fee in Personal Injury Litigation, 22 Stan. L. Rev. 1125 (1970), and the exhaustive study in Clermont & Currivan, Improving on the Contingent Fee, 63 Cornell L. Rev. 529 (1978).

Notwithstanding these safeguards, a more skeptical view of the contingent fee believes that it allows lawyers to collect enormous payments when settling easy cases. A study by L. Brickman, J. O'Connell & M. Horowitz, Rethinking Contingency Fees: A Proposal to Align the Contingency Fee System with Its Policy Roots and Ethical Mandates (1994), claims that the de facto compensation for plaintiff's attorneys reaches $25,000 per hour in cases that carry little risk and that require little skill. The Brickman proposal seeks to counter this risk by allowing defendants a guaranteed opportunity to make settlement offers within 60 days of suit. If accepted, the plaintiff's attorney's compensation could be based on an hourly rate of return, or on some modest percentage of the total recovery, say, 10 percent. If the offer is refused, however, it then becomes the benchmark against which a contingent fee is calculated in any subsequent settlement. For example, if the settlement offer is for $90,000, and the final settlement is for $100,000, the contingent fee is based on the marginal improvement of $10,000 instead of the full $100,000 in recovery. This system encourages defendants to make a good first offer, knowing that a low offer, if rejected, could well result down the road in a higher contingent fee to the lawyer and hence less for the plaintiff, who thus will demand even more money to settle. For a further reprise, see Brickman, Effective Hourly Rates of Contingency-Fee Lawyers: Competing Data and Non-Competitive Fees, 81 Wash. U. L.Q. 653 (2003); for a defense of contingent fees, see Kritzer, Seven Dogged Myths Concerning Contingency Fees, 80 Wash. U. L.Q. 739 (2002).

The issue of contingent fees is also the subject of an exhaustive study of the American Bar Association. See A.B.A. Tort Trial & Ins. Practice Section Task Force on Contingent Fees, Report on Contingent Fees in Medical Malpractice Litigation 3 (2004), available at http://www.abanet.org/tips/contingent/MedMalReport092004DCW2.pdf, insisting that the contingent fee arrangement gives incentives against bringing frivolous law suits, and that limitations on contingent fees should not be enacted because they will deny clients access to the civil justice system. That study is in turn critiqued in Dwyer, An Empirical Examination of the Equal Protection Challenge to Contingency Fee Restrictions in Medical Malpractice Reform Statutes, 56 Duke L.J. 611, 624 (2006), claiming that the ABA methodology was flawed. Dwyer claims that a constant or declining rate of new filings since 2000 is not evidence of the desirability of contingent fees since the contingent fees have been in place both before and after that time.

Whatever the merits of the contingent fee in ordinary tort actions, it is not ideally suited to all situations. There is, for example, no obvious way to value a lawyer's services when injunctive relief is obtained. Since no lawyer wants one-third of the injunction, an hourly fee system is typically required. More important for ordinary tort damage actions is the presumptive belief that contingent fee arrangements will not work for compensating the *defendant's* lawyer in a tort action. Until recently, the defendant's lawyer was normally reimbursed on a straight hourly basis for services rendered, even though the hourly fee does not give defense lawyers the same incentives for success as the contingent fee provides for the plaintiff's lawyer. The defense lawyer who obtains, for example, a summary judgment in a difficult case receives relatively little in compensation, while the defense lawyer who loses a large verdict after a protracted trial receives far higher compensation.

Hourly fee arrangements, however, are still common. When these are used in tort defense work, the pull of repeat business helps keep the relationship in line, as the unexpected successes in some cases offset the unwanted failures in others. Typically, however, clients must monitor defense lawyers more closely than plaintiff lawyers. It is not uncommon for a defense lawyer's hourly bills to be revised after the fact to take into account exceptional failures or exceptional successes. In principle, of course, there is, and ought to be, no legal prohibition against the use of contingent fee arrangements on the defendant's side, and there is mounting evidence (in the oral tradition) that some large corporations have experimented with their use. Using contingent fees on the defendant's side has often been frustrated by the inability to set a suitable baseline against which to measure the recovery, comparable to $0.00, usually deployed by plaintiffs. On the defendant's side, however, the contingent fee must be calculated as some fraction of the savings realized from some baseline set to reflect the anticipated verdict or settlement. If the defendant and the lawyer both knew that the proper value of the claim was $1,000,000, the lawyer's fee could equal one-third of any judgment or settlement below that level. (Thus, the million-dollar case that settles for $400,000 would net the lawyer a fee of $200,000, or one-third of $600,000 saved.)

In practice that baseline usually cannot be determined in a precise manner. The ad damnum clause in the complaint is apt to be inflated, and it is often difficult to put any estimated value on a case even after its merits have been investigated. When the defendant is insured, the reserve value that the insurer places on a claim for regulatory purposes might serve as the baseline. But that figure itself is at best an equal mixture of hunch and experience that may have to be revised frequently over the life of the lawsuit. And there is always the risk that a litigated case will yield an outcome greater than the reservation price. Notwithstanding these difficulties, as of late more and more firms have been experimenting with other kinds of fee arrangements, both for tort and other litigation. A defendant may *pay* the lawyer a sum of money up front, in exchange for the lawyer assuming a fraction of the legal liability of the case. The legal fee becomes the difference between the amount that the lawyer receives from the client (plus interest) and the amount that it loses on the case, either through labor or settlement. But unlike the plaintiff's contingent fee arrangement, the defense lawyer could *lose* if its share of the total judgment exceeds the amount it was paid up front. It is possible, of course, to mix and match arrangements so that the law firm receives some hourly compensation and some lump-sum payment along with the contingent arrangement. But once the firm is on the hook for its own dollars, the tendency to pad cases with lengthy memos and squads of associates and paralegals is said to disappear, as if by magic.

2.   Fee Shifting

The second critical feature of the American legal system concerns the allocation of costs and attorney's fees. Although the losing side must often compensate the winning side for its "costs," this term has been defined quite narrowly so that usually it includes only such incidental expenses as court filing fees. The largest item of expense in any litigation, however, is attorney's fees, followed in many cases by expert witness fees. Under the American rule these costs are borne by the respective parties, win or lose. In ordinary tort litigation, attorney's fees are rarely awarded, only when the prevailing party can clearly demonstrate that the other side advanced a claim or defense that was frivolous or malicious. Cases of malicious prosecution are very difficult to bring. "Suits for malicious prosecution cannot be maintained in Illinois unless the plaintiff alleges and proves that the plaintiff in the original tort action acted maliciously and without probable cause; that the prior cause terminated in the plaintiff's favor; and that some special injury not necessarily resulting in any and all suits prosecuted to recover for like causes of action was suffered." Berlin v. Nathan, 381 N.E.2d 1367, 1371 (Ill. App. 1978), denying a malicious prosecution claim to a physician who had prevailed in an earlier malpractice claim.

Hence, except in extraordinary circumstances, each party bears its own costs in the ordinary tort damage claim in the American system. The American practice on this point stands virtually alone among the advanced industrialized nations. Both the English and the Continental systems use fee shifting, which entitles the winning party to recover its "reasonable" attorney's fees (usually as determined by a taxing master) from the losing party as a matter of course.

The choice of fee-shifting arrangements has profound effects on the willingness of parties to settle or litigate a claim. The standard analysis treats a litigant as a rational party that seeks to maximize its expected gain through litigation. Accordingly, the plaintiff will litigate only when the expected return from litigation is greater than its expected cost. Similarly, the defendant will normally litigate (instead of settle) only when the additional expenditures on litigation promise a larger reduction in the expected amount of ultimate payment by settlement or verdict.

Under this model, both sides face strong pressures to settle cases short of ultimate verdict. Settlement reduces the total costs of litigation for both sides, and therefore leaves a larger pie for the two sides to divide. Settlement also reduces the inherent uncertainty associated with the prosecution of any claim or defense, a clear gain to risk-averse parties.

Within this framework the choice of fee shifting rules is critical because it influences the willingness to litigate or settle. The relative merits of that choice are revealed in several examples set out in Shavell, Suit, Settlement and Trial: A Theoretical Analysis Under Alternative Methods for the Allocation of Legal Costs, 11 J. Legal Stud. 35, 58-60 (1982):

> . . . *under the American system, the plaintiff will bring suit if and only if his expected judgment would be at least as large as his legal costs.* To illustrate, consider
>
> Example 1: The plaintiff's legal costs from a trial would be $1,000, and he believes that if he prevails he would obtain a judgment for $10,000. Thus, if he thinks the likelihood of prevailing is, say, 75 percent, he will bring suit, for then his expected judgment from a trial would be $7,500 (i.e., 75 percent × $10,000), which would exceed his legal costs of $1,000. However, if he believes the chance of success is only, say, 5 percent, he will not bring suit, since his expected judgment would be $500, which would be less than his legal costs.
>
> Similarly, under the British system, the plaintiff will bring suit if and only if his expected judgment would be at least as large as his expected legal costs — that is, the total legal costs discounted by his probability of losing at trial. Consider now
>
> Example 2: The plaintiff's legal costs and beliefs concerning a judgment are as in the previous example, and the defendant's legal costs from a trial would be $1,500. Consequently, if the plaintiff thinks the probability of prevailing is 75 percent, his expected judgment of $7,500 would exceed his expected legal costs of $625 (i.e., 25 percent x sign; $2,500), so that he would bring suit. But if he thinks the probability is 5 percent, his expected judgment of $500 would be below his expected legal costs of $2,375 (i.e., 95 percent x; $2,500), so that he would not bring suit.

Comparing the two systems, it is apparent that *the frequency of suit will be greater under the British system when the plaintiff believes the likelihood of prevailing is sufficiently high — above a "critical" level — and the frequency will be greater under the American system when the likelihood is below the critical level.* This is so because when the plaintiff is relatively optimistic about prevailing, his expected legal costs will be relatively low under the British system — he will be thinking about the possibility of not having to pay any such costs — whereas under the American system he must bear his own costs with certainty. Thus he will be likely to find suit a more attractive prospect under the British system. But when the plaintiff is not optimistic, converse reasoning explains why he would be expected to sue more often under the American system.

The analysis of course becomes even more complicated for several reasons. The evaluation of a claim is not made once and for all at the outset of a suit, so both parties will have to revise their calculations going forward as new information alters beliefs about the chances of success or the size of the claim. In addition, simple multiplication does not capture the subjective gain or loss when either or both sides to the litigation are risk-averse, perhaps to different degrees. A risk-averse party fears uncertainty and thus has a stronger impulse to settle than a risk-neutral party. Therefore, when a risk-averse plaintiff (the ordinary tort claimant, a large fraction of whose wealth is tied up in an individual claim) is pitted against a (relatively) risk-neutral defendant (an insurance company with a large portfolio of cases), the plaintiff is likely to settle for a somewhat lower payment than a risk-neutral analysis suggests. Similarly, litigation will be somewhat less frequent since plaintiffs will hesitate to sue in the face of uncertainty. *Id.*, at 61-62. The contingent fee arrangement reduces the plaintiff's reluctance to sue, for part of the risk is now shifted to the lawyer, who is likely to be more risk-neutral given his portfolio of claims and greater familiarity with litigation.

A statutory variation on this basic theme calls for "one-way" fee shifting in favor of the prevailing plaintiff. Thus, the defendant who wins pays his own fees, while the defendant who loses pays both his fees and the plaintiff's. How does this asymmetry influence litigation strategies? For an exhaustive analysis of fee shifting in its private and public contexts, see Symposium, Attorney Fee-Shifting, 47 Law & Contemp. Probs. 1-346 (1984); Symposium, 47 DePaul L. Rev. 227-477 (1998).

The choice of fee structures and fee-shifting rules may also subtly influence the development of the substantive law. Risky claims are more likely to be initiated in the United States, because the risks of failure are born in part by the successful defendants. Once these claims are established, they are more likely to be imitated in England and other common law jurisdictions that follow a winner-take-all rule. See Prichard, A Systemic Approach to Comparative Law: The Effect of Cost, Fee and Financing Rules on the Development of the Substantive Law, 17 J. Legal Stud. 451 (1988).

3. Sales of Tort Claims

Today the tort law forbids the outright assignment of unliquidated tort claims in contrast to the rules that allow for the free assignments of the right to collect debt. In some sense, the contingent fee moderates this prohibition by functioning as a partial sale of a tort claim after the accident has occurred. Two questions arise: Why should total sales be prohibited when partial sales are allowed, and why should the only eligible purchaser of claims be a contingent fee lawyer? Removing these two restrictions would in effect create an open market for the sale of matured tort claims, unregulated by the current statutes that make maintenance, champerty, and barratry all criminal offenses. The argument for removing that restriction is found in Shukaitis, A Market in Personal Injury Tort Claims, 16 J. Legal Stud. 329, 329-330, 339-340 (1987):

> Allowing victims to sell their claims to third parties, that is, allowing a market in personal injury tort claims, would have significant advantages for tort victims. Compared with litigation, tort victims would be able to receive immediate and certain compensation by selling their claims to purchasers in the market. Compared with settlement, tort victims would receive compensation at a market price closer to what they would expect from a court judgment. Thus compensation by the tort system would be made less dependent on the tort victim's ability to withstand delay and uncertainty. Victims who now do not pursue their claims because of ignorance of their rights or a lack of resources might receive compensation. Some of the incentive problems of hiring an attorney on either a contingent fee or an hourly arrangement would be lessened. And, by increasing the costs of tortfeasors, a market would increase deterrence against harm-causing activities.

Shukaitis then compares the sale of a tort claim with standard fee arrangements:

> There is one important market impediment for the outright sale of tort claims, however. The amount of recovery in a personal injury suit may depend not only on the efforts of the attorney but also on the efforts of the tort victim. After a tort victim sold his interest in a claim, he would have little incentive to appear sympathetic and deserving before a jury. To the extent the tort victim's lack of incentive reduces the expected recovery, the development of a market in claims could be inhibited. Either a purchaser would have to reduce the amount offered for a claim, or he would have to find a way to motivate the tort victim.

A tort claim purchaser has several ways to structure the transaction to minimize this incentive problem. For instance, purchasers could require tort victims to cooperate as a condition of purchase; such cooperation clauses are routinely found in standard insurance contracts, which raise the mirror problem with the defense of claims. Purchasers might also pay the purchase price in installments, with some payments at least contingent on cooperation. Finally, purchasers might condition part of the purchase price on the amount of recovery. A purchaser thus might purchase only 90 percent of the claim, leaving the tort victim with 10 percent of the risk as an incentive to cooperate in pursuing the claim.

If sales of matured tort claims are allowed, why prohibit the sale of unmatured tort claims? That proposal was first raised by Friedman, *supra* at 864, and received explicit endorsement in Cooter, Towards a Market in Unmatured Tort Claims, 75 Va. L. Rev. 383, 387 (1989).

> A market for UTCs [unmatured tort claims] can be defended solely because it gives people more options. UTCs are no exception to the proposition that both parties benefit in a voluntary exchange. Perhaps less obviously, the market for UTCs may also be defended as a superior vehicle for achieving tort law's two proclaimed goals — deterrence and insurance. If a market in UTCs were established . . . potential victims would substitute cheaper first party insurance for the tort system's current third party insurance scheme. Additionally, competitive pricing of UTCs would result in appropriate deterrence of potential tortfeasors. Because the price of UTCs should vary according to the likelihood and severity of potential torts, the potential tortfeasor faced with purchasing the UTC or risking litigation should take the optimal amount of precaution.

As Cooter points out, his proposal might ironically reintroduce through the back door many of the standard doctrines of nineteenth-century tort law. Thus, if an employer buys a UTC from its employee, the final position approaches the classical doctrine of assumption of risk. If prospective patients can sell their rights to recover for pain and suffering to an employer, they can be bundled and resold to a health care provider and thereby eliminate pain and suffering as an element in malpractice actions. Should the legal system allow these sales by persons who have no insurance for personal injury or disability?

Finally, what happens to potential defendants in a world where injured parties can sell either matured or unmatured claims? Shukaitis and Cooter both believe that the present rules of tort liability impose optimal incentives on potential tortfeasors. If that judgment is incorrect, as many believe it to be in both medical malpractice and products liability cases, will the sale of claims exacerbate or mitigate the defects of the present system?

4. Litigation Insurance

Another way to provide for legal fees is through litigation insurance that covers the ordinary costs of suit. At present no legal impediments block the sale of this form of insurance, but it is practically unknown in the United States owing to the dominant position of the contingent fee. Where the contingent fee is prohibited, as in Germany, litigation insurance is commonly sold. In principle, this insurance could fall prey to the standard risks of adverse selection: The only buyers are people who plan to sue or who expect to be sued. Or it could fall prey to moral hazard: Once individuals acquire insurance they become more willing to litigate. The German experience suggests that these problems have not been strong enough to destroy the market for litigation insurance. The increase in claim frequency tends to be slight, perhaps because litigation requires huge amounts of personal time and emotion, even if legal fees are covered by others. For discussion, see Gross, We Could Pass a Law . . . What Might Happen If Contingent Legal Fees Were Banned, 47 DePaul L. Rev. 321, 330-334 (1998).

SECTION D.   COLLATERAL BENEFITS

Harding v. Town of Townshend
43 Vt. 536 (1871)

[The plaintiff sued for injuries caused "by reason of an insufficiency of a highway of the defendant." The plaintiff had received payment of $130 from an insurance policy that he purchased for $7. The court charged the jury that it should reduce the amount of recovery by the net proceeds of the insurance, $123.]

PECK, J. There is no technical ground which necessarily leads to the conclusion that the money received by the plaintiff of the accident insurance company should operate as a defense, or enure to the benefit of the defendant. The insurer and the defendant are not joint tortfeasors or joint debtors so as to make a payment or satisfaction by the former operate to the benefit of the latter. Nor is there any legal privity between the defendant and the insurer so as to give the former a right to avail itself of a payment by the latter. The policy of insurance is collateral to the remedy against the defendant, and was procured solely by the plaintiff and at his expense, and to the procurement of which the defendant was in no way contributory. It is in the nature of a wager between the plaintiff and a third person, the insurer, to which the defendant was in no measure privy, either by relation of the parties or by contract or otherwise. It cannot be said that the plaintiff took out the policy in the interest or behalf of the defendant; nor is there any legal principle which seems to require that it be ultimately appropriated to the defendant's use and benefit.

But it is urged, on the part of the defense, that the plaintiff is entitled to but one satisfaction for the injury he has sustained. If we assume this to be a correct proposition, the question arises whether the defendant stands in a condition to make this objection. This depends on the question who, as between the insurer and the defendant, ought to pay the damage — which of the two ought primarily to make compensation to the plaintiff and ultimately to bear the loss? If the insurer ought ultimately to bear the loss, the defendant is entitled in this action to have the benefit of that payment; but if the defendant should ultimately bear the loss, then the payment by the insurer and the collection of the entire damage of the defendant only creates an equity between the plaintiff and the insurer, to be ultimately adjusted between them, in which the defendant has no interest, and with which he has no concern. . . . [A]s between the insurer and the wrong-doer, in reason and justice the burden of making compensation to the injured party ought to be ultimately borne by the party thus in fault. . . . It would seem to be a perversion of justice to subrogate the wrong-doer, who has caused the loss, to the rights of the injured party as to his remedy against the insurer. But it is not uncommon that the insurer, who has paid the loss, is put in place of the insured and subrogated to his rights in respect to his remedies against others for the injury.

Judgment of the county court reversed, and judgment for the plaintiff for the amount of the verdict, and the $123 to be added thereto.

NOTES

1. *Varieties of collateral benefits.* Collateral source payments include more than insurance payments made directly to the plaintiff, including salary, Motts v. Michigan Cab Co., 264 N.W. 855 (Mich. 1936), payments from the Welfare Fund of the United Mine Workers, Conley v. Foster, 335 S.W.2d 904 (Ky. 1960), and sick or vacation pay, Davidson v. Vogler, 507 S.W.2d 160 (Ky. 1974). The principle has been hotly contested in those instances where an injured plaintiff receives a discount from list price from Medicare, Medicaid, or some private insurer, only to claim that the tort recovery should be calibrated by the list and not the discounted price — arguing in effect that under the collateral source rule neither the defendant nor its insurer is entitled to the benefit of plaintiff's market prowess or good fortune. Recent courts have sharply split on this question. In Arthur v. Catour, 833 N.E.2d 847 (Ill. 2005), Freeman, J., held that the plaintiff could introduce into evidence the total health care bills charged to her insurer even if these exceeded the amounts actually paid. "The only relevant question in the litigation between plaintiff and defendants is the reasonable value of the services rendered." The same line was taken in Bynum v. Magno, 101 P.3d 1149, 1162 (Haw. 2004), where Acoba, J., protested that "limiting medical expenses to the pecuniary loss suffered by a plaintiff would mean, for example, that injured plaintiffs who received gratuitous medical services, were treated at a veteran's hospital, or were

covered by medical insurance plans such as offered to Kaiser Hospital patients would not be entitled to recover any monetary amount from the tortfeasor." In Bozeman v. State, 879 So. 2d 692, 705-706 (La. 2004), the injured plaintiff had about $613,000 in medical expenses "written off" to about $345,000. Johnson, J., held that "Medicaid recipients are unable to collect the Medicaid 'write-off' amounts as damages because no consideration is provided for the benefit. Thus, plaintiff's recovery is limited to what was paid by Medicaid. However, in those instances, where plaintiff's patrimony has been diminished in some way in order to obtain the collateral source benefits, then plaintiff is entitled to the benefit of the bargain, and may recover the full value of his medical services, including the 'write-off' amount." How should the value be computed if these discounts are routinely accepted by health care providers? If different prices for identical services are charged to government and private insurers?

2. *Government benefits and the collateral source rule.* The collateral source rule gives rise to special complications when the government is both a tortfeasor liable under the Federal Torts Claims Act and the supplier of first party benefits under, for example, both Social Security and veterans benefits programs. With mixed success, the government typically claims that payments under other government programs do not count as collateral payments, and hence should be used to reduce the government's tort obligation. In Steckler v. United States, 549 F.2d 1372, 1379 (10th Cir. 1977), the government sought to set off both veterans benefits and Social Security from the tort award. The court deducted veterans benefits in order to prevent the plaintiff from recovering "double payment" for the same injury from the same source. The court refused, however, to allow the government a total setoff for Social Security. "The part contributed by the worker and the employers has the aspects of social insurance and as such is collateral to monies contributed by the government." The part of Social Security from general government contributions, however, was not collateral, and hence was set off against tort damages, like veterans benefits. *Steckler* then placed the burden on the plaintiff to determine what fraction of the Social Security payment counted as a nondeductible collateral source. *Steckler* was modified by Berg v. United States, 806 F.2d 978, 985 (10th Cir. 1986). "We are now convinced that it is in fact impossible to distinguish accurately which part of a fund that has been produced by millions of contributors is attributable to the government and which part is attributable to a particular injured party. Therefore we require that the plaintiff bear the burden of showing only that he or she contributed to a special fund that is separate and distinct from general government revenues." The court held that Medicare benefits, funded under Social Security, so qualified as collateral sources. That approach was followed in Molzof v. United States, 6 F.3d 461, 465, 466 (7th Cir. 1993), in which Cudahy, J., applying Wisconsin law, refused to allow the government to set off benefits it paid out through its Veterans Administration program against

damages awarded against it under the Federal Torts Claims Act, on the ground that the two funds were different sources even if the defendant was the same. What if the social security or veteran's benefits were by statute or by agreement explicitly setoff from tort awards?

3. *Statutory modification of the collateral source rule.* The ongoing expansion of tort liability has ushered in many statutory exceptions to the collateral source rule, especially for health care providers.

CALIFORNIA CIVIL CODE (2007)
§3333.1. NEGLIGENCE OF HEALTH CARE PROVIDER; EVIDENCE OF BENEFITS
          AND PREMIUMS PAID; SUBROGATION

(a) In the event the defendant so elects, in an action for personal injury against a health care provider based upon professional negligence, he may introduce evidence of any amount payable as a benefit to the plaintiff as a result of the personal injury pursuant to the United States Social Security Act, any state or federal income disability or worker's compensation act, any health, sickness or income-disability insurance, accident insurance that provides health benefits or income-disability coverage, and any contract or agreement of any group, organization, partnership, or corporation to provide, pay for, or reimburse the cost of medical, hospital, dental, or other health care services. Where the defendant elects to introduce such evidence, the plaintiff may introduce evidence of any amount which the plaintiff has paid or contributed to secure his right to any insurance benefits concerning which the defendant has introduced evidence.

What should be done with the information once introduced? A New York statute, N.Y. C.P.L.R. §4545(a) (McKinney 2007), reduces recovery for any present or future payment, subject to reasonable estimation. That amount recoverable is increased by an amount equal to (1) the cost of keeping the benefit in place during the previous two years plus (2) the projected contractual cost of keeping the benefits in place in the future. The purpose of the New York statute is to return the plaintiff to the same position she would have been in if she had not acquired any collateral coverage at all.

For an attack on the various statutory exceptions to the collateral source rule, see Marshall & Fitzgerald, The Collateral Source Rule and Its Abolition: An Economic Perspective, 15 Kan. J. L. & Pub. Pol'y 57, 58 (2005).

4. *Subrogation and reimbursement.* As noted above, a second way to avoid double payments for collateral sources is to allow injured parties to recover their amounts paid from the tort damage award. Systems of this sort can come in two varieties. First, subrogation grants the collateral source the power to participate in, or even control, the tort litigation, and to recover its expenses directly from the tort claimant. Second, reimbursement leaves the injured party in full control over the litigation so that the insurer only recovers its expenses from the proceeds of recovery. Should subrogation

rights survive when state law has abrogated the collateral source rule in whole or in part? New Jersey law provides that collateral benefits (except workers' compensation benefits and life insurance), "shall be disclosed to the court and the amount thereof which duplicates any benefit contained in the award shall be deducted from any award recovered by the plaintiff, less any premium paid to an insurer directly by the plaintiff or by any member of the plaintiff's family on behalf of the plaintiff for the policy period during which the benefits are payable." N.J. Stat. Ann. §2A:15-97 (West 2007). In Perreira v. Rediger, 778 A.2d 429 (N.J. 2001), the court held that this statute trumped a first party insurer's subrogation rights. Thus suppose that an insured, with $20 worth of medical expenses, recovers $100 in damages from the tortfeasor. The New Jersey statute reduces that amount to $80. If the subrogation right kicks in, the plaintiff is left only with $60, which is plainly at variance with the scheme. In the face of the statutory silence on subrogation rights, Long, J., first decided that N.J. Stat. Ann. §2A:15-97 was intended "to favor liability carriers" at the expense of subrogees. Accordingly, the court overruled the insurance commissioner's decision to authorize subrogation and reimbursement rights under the statute, subject to a statutory override. Just that override is found in Conn. Gen. Stat. Ann. §52-225 (2007), which reinstates the traditional collateral source rule when a third party is subrogated to the plaintiff's right of recovery.

5. *Collusive settlements to defeat subrogation and reimbursement claims.* One question common to subrogation and reimbursement concerns the priorities in payouts when the amount paid by the tortfeasor is insufficient to cover both damages for pain and suffering and for lost medical expenses, where the subrogee has a right to the second but not to the first. The normal default rule appears to compensate the injured party in full for pain and suffering damages before the subrogee is entitled to any reimbursement for medical expenses. Should the parties by contract be allowed to reverse that order so that subrogation or reimbursement "comes first" even if the injured party has not made a full recovery? A clause of that sort was invalidated on both contractual and "equitable" grounds in Powell v. Blue Cross and Blue Shield, 581 So. 2d 772, 777 (Ala. 1990), on the ground that "full compensation to the injured" necessarily came first. *Powell* in turn was overruled in Ex parte State Farm Fire and Casualty Co., 764 So. 2d 543 (Ala. 2000), where the court brushed aside concerns with stare decisis and allowed contractual variation. That last result is supported in Sykes, Subrogation and Insolvency, 30 J. Legal Stud. 383, 386 (2001), which addresses the question of priority between insurer and insured as follows:

> [F]rom the standpoint of optimal risk allocation, the fortuitous presence of an injurer who is liable for the insured's losses does not affect the risk that

the insured should optimally bear. Thus, if it is optimal for the insured to bear the risk of uncovered losses associated with accidents in which no injurer is liable, the insured should bear the same risk in accidents in which an injurer is liable. Accordingly, no violence is done to optimal risk sharing if the insurer is reimbursed first by the partially insolvent injurer.

Whenever subrogation contracts are valid, resourceful tort litigants seek to structure their settlements to cut off the claims of the plaintiff's first party insurer. In Westendorf v. Stasson, 330 N.W.2d 699, 702 (Minn. 1983), the tort settlement provided that all "payments to be made hereunder are solely attributable to the pain and suffering and permanent injury" of the plaintiff and the loss of consortium to her spouse. Simonett, J., contrasted the settlement situation with one in which a jury makes findings as to the amounts recoverable for pain and suffering and medical expenses, and refused to give this collusive clause effect against the insurer:

> When, however, plaintiffs' claim is settled without a verdict, the application of the reimbursement provision is more problematic. In such a case, any allocation is left to the bargaining of the parties to the tort action, and it is not surprising if the parties give little solicitude to the reimbursement rights of the health care provider. The enrollee, even though entitled to recover medical expenses from a third party, may elect not to do so here. . . . Because the parties to the settlement agreement have characterized their settlement as excluding any damages for medical expenses, it does not follow, however, that this characterization is binding on the HMO provider. The effect of the HMO's reimbursement clause should not depend on a settlement bargain to which it was not privy. The settlement agreement should not be determinative of how the proceeds are allocated.

If the settlement excludes compensation for medical expenses, can the health care provider also have a direct action against the tort defendant? For the position that such actions are excluded by the prohibition on assignment of tort claims (and splitting of causes of action), see Allstate Insurance Co. v. Druke, 576 P.2d 489 (Ariz. 1978).

6. *Subrogation and the independent cause of action.* As a matter of contract law, a subrogee's claim takes the form of an assignment, subject to all defenses that the defendant can raise against the injured party. That rule would prevent, for example, a health plan from recovering its expenses in treating victims of lung cancer from tobacco companies unless the victims themselves could overcome assumption of risk and contributory negligence defenses. "Where the insured has no right of recovery, the insurer has no enforceable right of subrogation." Gibbs v. Hawaiian Eugenia Corp., 966 F.2d 101, 106 (2d Cir. 1992). To circumvent these subrogation limitations,

many insurers assert "direct" or "independent" claims against the tobacco defendants. Generally, these actions are blocked by the rule that "[a]n insurance company cannot recover from a wrongdoer, who causes the loss insured against, the money paid to satisfy such loss." 1 J.G. Sutherland, A Treatise on the Law of Damages 55 (1883). These independent claims have proved successful, however, for state Medicaid programs that have persuaded courts that their public duty to provide care to tort victims authorizes direct actions for their own expenses, free of defenses that could be asserted against the tobacco smokers. See State of Texas v. American Tobacco Co., 14 F. Supp. 2d 956 (E.D. Tex. 1997). Yet private labor unions and health plans have been generally rebuffed when they have sought to unhinge their reimbursement claims for RICO claims for racketeering and fraudulent misrepresentation from the underlying tort actions. See Laborers Local 17 Health and Benefit Fund v. Philip Morris, Inc., 191 F.3d 229 (2d Cir. 1999), *infra* at 1222.

SECTION E. WRONGFUL DEATH AND LOSS OF CONSORTIUM

The close connection between claims for wrongful death and loss of consortium justifies their unified treatment. Both types of suit vindicate the "relational" interest of the plaintiff to the person injured or killed. This relational interest rests on the evident social fact that individuals have obligations of duty and support to other persons: husband and wife to each other; parent to child; and servant to employer. The protection of relational interests adds another layer of complexity to the law, for now the legal system must coordinate the actions of the injured party with those who bring derivative claims through that party.

The common law protected relational interests through in two ways. The first was the action quod servitium amiserit ("because the service has been lost"), which was given only to a man whenever the defendant injured his wife, child, or servant, thereby preventing them from rendering him valuable services. 3 Bl. Comm.; 142 Kendrick v. McCrary, 11 Ga. 603 (1852). The basic action was subject to two limitations. First, the action for loss of services could not be brought by a wife or a child. Second, the action for loss of services did not cover cases of wrongful death. The efforts to overcome these two limitations did not proceed in an orderly fashion. Accordingly, we turn first to the history of actions for wrongful death and related causes. Thereafter, we will turn to the loss of consortium.

1. *Wrongful Death*

a. History

The orderly development of wrongful death actions at common law was stymied by Lord Ellenborough's famous, if ill-considered, opinion in Baker v. Bolton, 170 Eng. Rep. 1033 (K.B. 1808), which held that a husband suffered no damage when his wife was not merely injured, but killed, by the defendant's wrongful conduct. The plaintiff could recover damages for the loss of his wife's services and consortium only for the month between injury and death, but was denied damages for both lost after her death. Relying on scattered precedents, Lord Ellenborough treated the matter as though it had long been settled on the highest authority: "In a civil court," he said, "the death of a human being could not be complained of as an injury; and in this case the damages as to the plaintiff's wife must stop with the period of her existence." See Holdsworth, Origin of the Rule in Baker v. Bolton, 32 Law Q. Rev. 431 (1916).

The situation stood unchanged in England until the passage of Lord Campbell's Act of 1846 (Fatal Accidents Act, 9 & 10 Vict. c. 93 (1846)). The statutory preamble treated Baker v. Bolton as decisive authority against allowing the action at the common law. However, its operative provision then provided that "whenever the death of a person is caused by the wrongful act, neglect or default of another, such as would (if death had not ensued) have entitled the injured person to sue and recover damages in respect thereof, then the person who would have been liable if death had not ensued shall be liable to an action for damages, although the death shall have been caused under circumstances as amount to a felony." The last clause was inserted to make it clear that the plaintiff in the wrongful death action did not have to first prosecute the defendant for any possible felony. The statute designated the class of dependents (since expanded by the Fatal Accidents Act, 1959 §1(1)) entitled to the action: husband, wife, parent, child, grandparent, or grandchild of the deceased. The action was not transmissible by will, and did not follow the usual rules for the distribution of assets in case of intestacy.

Lord Campbell's statute subjects plaintiffs to any defenses that would have been available against the decedent had she lived, including her contributory negligence and assumption of risk. The English statute does not establish a specific measure of damages, but only provides that damages, however assessed, should be divided among eligible beneficiaries as the jury sees fit. But in subsequent judicial opinions, the English courts apportioned damages "in reference to a reasonable expectation of pecuniary benefit as of right, or otherwise, from the continuance of the life." Franklin v. South Eastern Ry., 157 Eng. Rep. 448 (Ex. 1858).

After passage of the statute, some plaintiffs sued at common law to recover elements of damages not listed in the wrongful death statutes, but without luck. Thus, in Osborn v. Gillett, L.R. 8 Ex. 88 (1873), the plaintiff was denied recovery for burial expenses, then not provided for under the statute. In Admiralty Commissioners v. S.S. Amerika, [1917] A.C. 38, the plaintiffs failed to recover the ex gratiae pensions they had paid out to the relatives of crew members lost when the defendant ship sank an admiralty submarine. Baker v. Bolton loomed large in both cases, where it effectively foreclosed any common law development in England long after its errors were openly acknowledged. The courts declined to tread where Parliament had intervened, partly out of deference to Parliament and partly out of fear of the complications that a dual scheme for wrongful death actions could create.

The history of wrongful death in the United States exhibits the same complex interaction between common law and legislation. In the early colonial period, particularly in Massachusetts, local tribunals probably made awards for wrongful death that were not sanctioned by statute or at common law. Even after Baker v. Bolton, some courts seemed prepared to develop wrongful death actions on their own. See, e.g., Plummer v. Webb, 19 Fed. Cas. 894 (No. 11234) (1825); Ford v. Monroe, 20 Wend. 210 (N.Y. Sup. Ct. 1838). But the rarity of such actions suggests that they were not well established. Indeed Baker v. Bolton was not even cited in an American court until 1848. In that year, however, the Massachusetts Supreme Judicial Court, in Carey v. Berkshire R.R., 55 Mass. 475 (1848), relied on Baker v. Bolton to deny the plaintiff a common law action for wrongful death. The companion case of Skinner v. Housatonic R.R., 55 Mass. 475 (1848), refused to allow a wrongful death action when a father sued to recover for the loss of services of his deceased son. Eight years before *Carey*, Massachusetts had passed a statute that authorized wrongful death actions for between $500 and $5,000 to the families of deceased railway passengers whose death was caused by the negligence of the railroad. The deceased in *Carey* was an employee, not a passenger, and thus not covered by the statute. He lost because the court did not wish to create its own wrongful death action in parallel with the legislature's. State after state followed *Carey*'s logic, with only Georgia willing to face the problems of policing and coordinating two different systems of wrongful death actions. See Shields v. Yonge, 15 Ga. 349 (1854). For an excellent history of the early evolution of wrongful death actions, see Malone, The Genesis of Wrongful Death, 17 Stan. L. Rev. 1043 (1965).

A similar pattern developed in maritime cases. The Harrisburg, 119 U.S. 199 (1886), held that maritime law did not provide relief in cases of wrongful death. In 1920, Congress passed the Jones Act, 46 U.S.C. §30104 (2007), which applies only to seamen, the Death on the High Seas Act, current version at 46 U.S.C. §§30302 et seq. (2007), which covered all persons for both unseaworthiness and negligence, who were killed "beyond a marine league from the shore of any State" (now 12 nautical miles). Both of these actions allow damages for pecuniary losses, but neither allows them for the general loss of society. Finally, the 1927 Longshore and Harbor Workers Compensation Act, 33 U.S.C. §§901-950 (2007) creates a workers' compensation scheme for employees that explicitly preserves third-party actions.

The situation remained unchanged until 1972 when the Supreme Court in Moragne v. States Marine Lines, Inc., 398 U.S. 375 (1970), first allowed a nonstatutory cause of action, but limited it to breaches of the maritime duty of seaworthiness. Thereafter in Miles v. Apex Marine Corp., 498 U.S. 19 (1990), the Supreme Court held that the plaintiffs in such a general maritime action under *Moragne* could not recover damages for loss of society. "[I]t would be inconsistent with [the Court's] place in the constitutional scheme . . . to sanction more expansive remedies in a judicially created cause of action in which liability is without fault than Congress has allowed in cases of death resulting from negligence." Next in Norfolk Shipbuilding & Drydock Corp. v. Garris, 532 U.S. 811 (2001), the Supreme Court unanimously held that wrongful death actions also lay for breach of general duties of negligence—the decedent was killed while sandblasting aboard a vessel that was berthed in the navigable waters of the United States—just as they did for lack of seaworthiness. Scalia, J., was still concerned with the question of whether a new maritime action would conflict with any of scheme that Congress created in the exercise of its admiralty power, and ultimately concluded that it did not. Questions about the coordination of the various systems still arise, as in In re American River Transportation Co., 490 F.3d 351, 356 (5th Cir. 2007), which answered in the negative the question of whether "the non-dependent survivors of a deceased longshoreman or harborworker may recover for loss of society when the death occurs in state waters," thus refusing to create a larger class of beneficiaries under the general maritime law than existed under the particular state statutes.

b. Measure of Damages

As indicated above, the various maritime actions for wrongful death contain limitations on recovery by type of damage, allowing recovery for pecuniary losses, but not for loss of society. Those decisions do not, of course, control the evolution of wrongful death actions under state law, which have taken a different path. Each state statute sets its own measure of damages for wrongful death actions. Most early wrongful death statutes placed stringent ceilings on the amount of damages permitted the surviving plaintiff, largely out of fear of the jury's passion and sympathy for the aggrieved plaintiff. Courts held that plaintiffs had to take the bitter with the sweet. So long as any recovery was by legislative grace, the recipients could not protest any attached conditions. Nonetheless, over time, these limitations became anachronistic. Twenty-two states had ceilings on wrongful death claims in 1893. By 1965 that number dropped to 12, and by 1974 the number had dwindled to 4. Today, no state has a hard dollar cap on damages in wrongful death actions, although a few states retain special limitations for certain types of cases.

But what measure of damages is appropriate? No state attempts the impossible, which is to put the decedent in the position that she would have enjoyed if the tort had never happened. And no state is able to overcome the profound irony — and puzzle for the economic theory of tort law — that it is cheaper for a defendant to kill his victim than it is to maim her for life. Medical expenses are not part of a wrongful death action per se. That said, most statutes fall into one of two camps: loss-to-survivors and loss-to-estate. Under a loss-to-survivors standard, the defendant must pay damages only if some beneficiary depends upon the decedent for support. Under the loss-to-estate standard, damages will be awarded against the defendant even if the decedent had no dependents at the time of death. Most jurisdictions have adopted a loss-to-survivors test as the measure of damages. Which standard is better from the point of view of deterrence?

Calculating damages in wrongful death cases is fraught with many of the same difficulties in administration found in serious personal injury cases. The pure wrongful death action awards nothing for the decedent's pain and suffering or medical expenses. Nonetheless enormous controversy can arise over both the suffering of the survivors and the estimation of lost earnings, especially for children who had never assumed any definable niche in life. Thus, in Wycko v. Gnodtke, 105 N.W.2d 118 (Mich. 1960), the court allowed the parents of a reliable and trustworthy boy of 14 to recover $15,000 in damages, dismissing the objection that the parents were entitled to recover only for their pecuniary loss. The court noted the general progress in the social treatment of children since the passage of Lord Campbell's Act in 1846, but rejected "as prayed by appellant, the child-labor measure of the pecuniary loss suffered through the death of a minor child, namely, his probable wages less the cost of his keep." The court then awarded two types of damages. First, on analogy to the costs of maintenance service and repairs for machinery, it allowed the parents damages for the "expenses of birth, of food, of clothing, of medicines, of instruction, of nurture and of shelter." Second, by treating the family as a functioning social unit, it allowed "the value of mutual society and protection, in a word, companionship." Michigan law now provides: "[T]he court or jury may award damages as the court or jury shall consider fair and equitable, under all the circumstances including reasonable medical, hospital, funeral, and burial expenses for which the estate is liable; reasonable compensation for the pain and suffering, while conscious, undergone by the deceased during the period intervening between the time of the injury and death; and damages for the loss of financial support and the loss of the society and companionship of the deceased." Mich. Comp. Laws Ann. §600.2922(6) (West 2007). For an account of the deviation between the evaluation of a lost life in tort and administrative law, see E. Posner & Sunstein, Dollars and Death, 72 U. Chi. L. Rev. 537 (2005), urging major reforms in the tort law, including granting damages for the welfare loss to the decedent.

2. Survival of Personal Injury Actions

One other feature of the common law treatment of death in tort cases deserves mention. From at least the fifteenth century, the common law maxim actio personalis moritur cum persona—a personal action dies with the person—provided that any tort action, including one for personal injuries or property damage (but not to recover property), was extinguished by the death of either the plaintiff or the defendant. The right of action created by the defendant's wrong was treated as exclusively personal between the two original parties; as death severed that personal relationship, so it destroyed any cause of action predicated upon it.

Abandonment of the early position came slowly. Today such survival of actions is well nigh universal except perhaps for actions for deceit or defamation, and even these actions pass in a few states. Under the typical survivor statute, compensation is allowed for the pain and suffering of the decedent before his death, as that item of damages is not covered under the wrongful death statutes proper. See Leebron, Final Moments: Damages for Pain and Suffering Prior to Death, 64 N.Y.U. L. Rev. 256 (1989), where the author concludes that the primary justification for such awards must be deterrence and not compensation. Leebron notes that, empirically, the variation in awards under this head of damages is exceptionally high and recommends more judicial supervision to iron out the anomalies in the area. The issue continues to be litigated today. In Ghotra v. Bandila Shipping, Inc., 113 F.3d 1050 (9th Cir. 1997), the decedent fell to his death while inspecting a cargo hold. The court refused to allow pain and suffering on the supposition that the decedent might have been conscious of his fatal injuries for about ten seconds, noting that only pain and suffering that lasts an "appreciable period of time" is recoverable. But in Maracallo v. Board of Education of New York, 769 N.Y.S.2d 717 (N.Y. Sup. Ct. 2003), the court held that a jury award of $6 million for about six minutes of suffering before a 14-year-old drowned in defendant's wave pool was excessive and ordered a new trial if the plaintiff did not agree to a reduction of damages to $2 million. Does it follow that damages of $20 million are appropriate if slow asphyxiation lasts just over one hour?

3. *Actions for Loss of Consortium*

The historical development of the action for loss of consortium has not followed the course of wrongful death actions. After their early acceptance of the doctrine, the English courts came to regard all actions for loss of consortium as misconceived. In Best v. Samuel Fox & Co. Ltd, [1952] A.C. 716, the House of Lords, with evident discomfort, refused to grant the action to the wife for her loss of the services and comfort of her husband. In 1982, Parliament finished the job by abolishing the action for loss of consortium for husbands, parents, children and menial servants. 30 & 31 Eliz. 2 §2 (1982).

The American cases, however, took the opposite course. Today they universally allow wives as well as husbands to sue for loss of consortium. The new era was ushered in by Hitaffer v. Argonne Co., 183 F.2d 811 (D.C. Cir. 1950), which has been followed everywhere in this country. See RST §693(1), which provides that liability in these cases covers "the resulting loss of the society and services of the first spouse, including impairment of capacity for sexual intercourse, and for reasonable expense incurred by the second spouse in providing medical treatment." In a self-conscious break with the past, the court in *Hitaffer* first argued that although the element of lost services was important in a consortium case, elements of "companionship, love, felicity and sexual relations" were of equal if not greater importance. It then rejected arguments that the wife's action should be barred because her injuries were too "indirect," too "remote," or too "consequential." If these arguments are good against the wife's claim, they could be lodged with equal force against the husband's action as well. Should both claims be barred on the grounds that persons deprived of society and services can adapt to their change of circumstances?

The debate over the action for loss of consortium has now shifted from suits by the spouse to suits by children whose parents have been injured or killed. Wrongful death actions are allowed to children in part because of the forcible disruption of their advantageous relationships with their parents. The same type of relational loss, albeit of different extent, also exists when the parent is not killed but injured. If one spouse may sue when the other is killed or injured, and children may sue (for wrongful death) when parents are killed, why shouldn't children be able to sue when their parents are injured? Note, however, substantial administrative costs are entailed by the recognition of such actions. Although the decedent had only one spouse, he or she could have many children (not to mention grandchildren and more distant relations). It is easy to envision severe difficulties in estimating damages owed to each claimant and in coordinating the recovery of the injured party with that of the dependents. The leading case against the child's consortium action is Borer v. American Airlines, Inc., 563 P.2d 858,

860-861 (Cal. 1977), in which Tobriner, J., rejected the damage claims of the injured party's nine children:

> Judicial recognition of a cause of action for loss of consortium, we believe, must be narrowly circumscribed. Loss of consortium is an intangible injury for which money damages do not afford an accurate measure or suitable recompense; recognition of a right to recover for such losses in the present context, moreover, may substantially increase the number of claims asserted in ordinary accident cases, the expense of settling or resolving such claims, and the ultimate liability of the defendants. Taking these considerations into account, we shall explain why we have concluded that the payment of damages to persons for the lost affection and society of a parent or child neither truly compensates for such loss nor justifies the social cost in attempting to do so. We perceive significant differences between the marital relationship and the parent-child relationship that support the limitation of a cause of action for loss of consortium to the marital situation; we shall therefore further elaborate our reasons for concluding that a child cannot maintain a cause of action for loss of parental consortium. In similar fashion we conclude in the companion case of Baxter v. Superior Court[, 563 P.2d 871 (Cal. 1977)] that a parent cannot maintain a cause of action for loss of a child's consortium.

Subsequent cases have been mixed. A divided Connecticut court refused to recognize in children an action for loss of consortium, even though they can recover for emotional distress if they witness the death of a parent. See Mendillo v. Board of Education of the Town of East Haddam, 717 A.2d 1177 (Conn. 1998). In contrast, many states have allowed children to bring actions for the loss of companionship of their parents. See, e.g., Berger v. Weber, 303 N.W.2d 424 (Mich. 1981). Similarly, these courts have also recognized an action in the parents for the loss of filial companionship of their children. Yet the court in Sizemore v. Smock, 422 N.W.2d 666 (Mich. 1988), held that Michigan "does not recognize a parent's action for the loss of a child's society and companionship, and that any decision to further extend a negligent tortfeasor's liability for consortium damages should be determined by the Legislature." A somewhat different pattern emerged in Arizona, where the court now freely allows both children and parents to bring actions for loss of consortium. See Villareal v. Arizona, 774 P.2d 213 (Ariz. 1989). The Arizona rule, moreover, allows parents to recover for the loss of companionship of their adult children, even though the parents were not dependent upon those adult children for financial support. See Howard Frank, M.D., P.C. v. Superior Court, 722 P.2d 955, 960 (Ariz. 1986). There the court stressed that the damage action should not be denied on "an archaic and outmoded pecuniary theory of parental rights" that misses the importance of companionship, love, and support. The court brushed aside the defendant's objections that the new action will "spawn increased litigation," noting that courts can deal with these administrative complications as they arise without heeding "the fabled cry of wolf," which usually proves groundless. Finally, in Barnes v. Outlaw, 964 P.2d 484 (Ariz. 1998), the court extended the action for loss of consortium to purely emotional harms, holding that "a marriage may be damaged by emotional trauma" as well as by physical injury. One device used to prevent double recovery has been to require joinder of the loss of consortium claim with the underlying tort action whenever feasible. See Ueland v. Reynolds Metals Co., 691 P.2d 190 (Wash. 1984). Finally, a complex intermediate position was taken in Fernandez v. Walgreen Hastings Co., 968 P. 2d 774 (N.M. 1998). The court held that a triable question of fact arose when a grandparent brought an action for the loss of consortium of her 22-month-old child as long as the victim was a minor and the grandparent occupied the role of "familial care-taker . . . who lived with and cared for the child for a significant period of time prior to the injury or death."

At a substantive level, many courts have balked at extending actions for loss of consortium to unmarried couples who are living together. In Elden v. Sheldon, 758 P.2d 582 (Cal. 1988), the court stressed "the state's interest in promoting the responsibilities of marriage and the difficulty of assessing the emotional, sexual and financial relationship of cohabiting parties to determine whether their arrangement was the equivalent of marriage." One exception to that dominant rule is Lozoya v. Sanchez, 66 P.3d 948, 958 (N.M. 2003). The plaintiff and her husband were unmarried at the time of his first accident, but had lived together for about 15 years in a home they had jointly purchased and had three children together. The first accident disrupted their social and sexual arrangements, but they nonetheless married before their second accident. Minzner, J., held that the couple virtually met the standards for a common law marriage, so that the action for loss of consortium was proper.

> They held themselves out as a married couple. Further, they testified as to their mutual dependence on each other in their day to day lives. Every single factor we have enunciated for determining whether they had an intimate familial relationship also appears to cut in their favor. We believe that the evidence presented demonstrates that Sara may be able to present a cognizable claim for loss of consortium. She should therefore be allowed to present this claim to the jury.

Sensible in the light of an ever greater variety of living arrangements? See Note, Like Family: Rights of Nonmarried Cohabitational Partners in Loss of Consortium Actions, 46 B.C. L. Rev. 391 (2005)

SECTION F. PUNITIVE DAMAGES

Kemezy v. Peters
79 F.3d 33 (7th Cir. 1996)

POSNER, C.J.

Jeffrey Kemezy sued a Muncie, Indiana policeman named James Peters under 42 U.S.C. §1983, claiming that Peters had wantonly beaten him with the officer's nightstick in an altercation in a bowling alley where Peters was moonlighting as a security guard. The jury awarded Kemezy $10,000 in compensatory damages and $20,000 in punitive damages. Peters' appeal challenges only the award of punitive damages, and that on the narrowest of grounds: that it was the plaintiff's burden to introduce evidence concerning the defendant's net worth for purposes of equipping the jury with information essential to a just measurement of punitive damages.

[Posner, C.J., notes that a majority of courts have rejected Peters's contention.] [W]e think the majority rule, which places no burden of production on the plaintiff, is sound, and we take this opportunity to make clear that it is indeed the law of this circuit.

The standard judicial formulation of the purpose of punitive damages is that it is to punish the defendant for reprehensible conduct and to deter him and others from engaging in similar conduct. This formulation is cryptic, since deterrence is a purpose of punishment, rather than, as the formulation implies, a parallel purpose, along with punishment itself, for imposing the specific form of punishment that is punitive damages. An extensive academic literature, however, elaborates on the cryptic judicial formula, offering a number of reasons for awards of punitive damages. Some of these reasons are mentioned in our cases. A review of the reasons will point us toward a sound choice between the majority and minority views.

1. Compensatory damages do not always compensate fully. Because courts insist that an award of compensatory damages have an objective basis in evidence, such awards are likely to fall short in some cases, especially when the injury is of an elusive or intangible character. If you spit upon another person in anger, you inflict a real injury but one exceedingly difficult to quantify. If the court is confident that the injurious conduct had no redeeming social value, so that "overdeterring" such conduct by an "excessive" award of damages is not a concern, a generous award of punitive damages will assure full compensation without impeding socially valuable conduct.

2. By the same token, punitive damages are necessary in such cases in order to make sure that tortious conduct is not underdeterred, as it might be if compensatory damages fell short of the actual injury inflicted by the tort . . .

3. Punitive damages are necessary in some cases to make sure that people channel transactions through the market when the costs of voluntary

transactions are low. We do not want a person to be able to take his neighbor's car and when the neighbor complains tell him to go sue for its value. We want to make such expropriations valueless to the expropriator and we can do this by adding a punitive exaction to the judgment for the market value of what is taken. . . .

4. When a tortious act is concealable, a judgment equal to the harm done by the act will underdeter. Suppose a person who goes around assaulting other people is caught only half the time. Then in comparing the costs, in the form of anticipated damages, of the assaults with the benefits to him, he will discount the costs (but not the benefits, because they are realized in every assault) by 50 percent, and so in deciding whether to commit the next assault he will not be confronted by the full social cost of his activity.

5. An award of punitive damages expresses the community's abhorrence at the defendant's act. We understand that otherwise upright, decent, law-abiding people are sometimes careless and that their carelessness can result in unintentional injury for which compensation should be required. We react far more strongly to the deliberate or reckless wrongdoer, and an award of punitive damages commutes our indignation into a kind of civil fine, civil punishment.

Some of these functions are also performed by the criminal justice system. Many legal systems do not permit awards of punitive damages at all, believing that such awards anomalously intrude the principles of criminal justice into civil cases . . .

6. Punitive damages relieve the pressures on the criminal justice system. They do this not so much by creating an additional sanction, which could be done by increasing the fines imposed in criminal cases, as by giving private individuals — the tort victims themselves — a monetary incentive to shoulder the costs of enforcement.

7. If we assume realistically that the criminal justice system could not or would not take up the slack if punitive damages were abolished, then they have the additional function of heading off breaches of the peace by giving individuals injured by relatively minor outrages a judicial remedy in lieu of the violent self-help to which they might resort if their complaints to the criminal justice authorities were certain to be ignored and they had no other legal remedy.

What is striking about the purposes that are served by the awarding of punitive damages is that none of them depends critically on proof that the defendant's income or wealth *exceeds* some specified level. The more wealth the defendant has, the smaller is the relative bite that an award of punitive damages not actually geared to that wealth will take out of his pocketbook, while if he has very little wealth the award of punitive damages may exceed his ability to pay and perhaps drive him into bankruptcy. To a very rich person, the pain of having to pay a heavy award of damages may be a mere pinprick and so not deter him (or people like him) from continuing to engage in the same type of wrongdoing. What in economics is called the principle of diminishing marginal utility teaches, what is anyway obvious, that losing $1 is likely to cause less unhappiness (disutility) to a rich person than to a poor one. . . . But rich people are not famous for being indifferent to money, and if they are forced to pay not merely the cost of the harm to the victims of their torts but also some multiple of that cost they are likely to think twice before engaging in such expensive behavior again. Juries, rightly or wrongly, think differently, so plaintiffs who are seeking punitive damages often present evidence of the defendant's wealth. The question is whether they *must* present such evidence — whether it is somehow unjust to allow a jury to award punitive damages without knowing that the defendant really is a wealthy person. The answer, obviously, is no. . . .

It ill becomes *defendants* to argue that plaintiffs *must* introduce evidence of the defendant's wealth. Since most tort defendants against whom punitive damages are sought are enterprises rather than individuals, the effect of such a rule would be to encourage plaintiffs to seek punitive damages whether or not justified, in order to be able to put before the jury evidence that the defendant has a deep pocket and therefore should be made to pay a large judgment regardless of any nice calculation of actual culpability. . . . Individual defendants, as in the present case, are reluctant to disclose their net worth in any circumstances, so that compelling plaintiffs to seek discovery of that information would invite a particularly intrusive and resented form of pretrial discovery and disable the defendant from objecting. Since, moreover, information about net worth is in the possession of the person whose net wealth is in issue, the normal principles of pleading would put the burden of production on the defendant — which, as we have been at pains to stress, is just where defendants as a whole would want it. . . .

Affirmed.

NOTES

1. *Punitive damages at common law.* Does anything prevent the plaintiff from discovering evidence about the defendant's net worth in order to increase the level of punitive damages?

Punitive damages have long been awarded at common law. In Day v. Woodworth, 54 U.S. 363, 371 (1852), the plaintiff brought a trespass action against the defendants for tearing down and destroying his mill-dam, more than was necessary to protect the operation of their own mill-dam. Grier, J., affirmed an award of punitive damages, noting:

> In actions of trespass, where the injury has been wanton and malicious, or gross and outrageous, courts permit juries to add to the measured compensation of the plaintiff that he would have been entitled to recover, had

the injury been inflicted without design or intention, something farther by way of punishment or example, which has sometimes been called "smart money." This has been always left to the discretion of the jury, as the degree of punishment to be thus inflicted must depend on the peculiar circumstances of each case.

Modern punitive damage actions against institutional defendants, in complex products liability litigation, test the traditional concepts of malice and oppression against parties that never harbor any personal animus toward anonymous plaintiffs. In Owens-Corning Fiberglas Corp. v. Garrett, 682 A.2d 1143, 1166-1167 (Md. 1996), the court answered this abstract question by requiring the plaintiff to prove, by clear and convincing evidence, that the defendant has "actual knowledge of the defect and deliberate disregard of the consequences" of the danger of its product to its ordinary users. It set aside a punitive damage award to the plaintiff, who argued that the defendant had not quickly removed its Kaylo insulation product from the marketplace. The court stressed that at the time of the defendant's actions, from 1968-1972, no one, "not even the medical experts who were researching and discovering the links between asbestos and cancer, believed, or at least voiced any belief, that asbestos needed to be immediately eliminated entirely." The dissent rested in part on the argument that OCF delayed the introduction of a nonasbestos insulation to preserve the higher profit margins on its existing product lines.

Many defendants in asbestos cases have fared less well on the question of punitive damages. In the earlier rounds of litigation, plaintiffs could point to written correspondence among high officials in asbestos manufacturing during the 1930s and 1940s that stressed their desire to keep from the public the risks of asbestos disclosure, before these were commonly known. Thus, in Fischer v. JohnsManville Corp., 512 A.2d 466, 476-478 (N.J. 1986), Clifford, J., refused to excuse the corporation simply because none of the executives who made the key decisions were around to answer for them, noting that the primary purpose of deterrence is "well served regardless of changes in personnel within the offending corporation." He also rejected the argument that punitive damages were inappropriate because of the harm that they wrought on "innocent shareholders," noting that compensatory damages create the same risk. "Also, we would not consider it harmful were shareholders to be encouraged by decisions such as this to give close scrutiny to corporate practices in making investment decisions." In addition, he continued:

> [We are also concerned with] the possibility that asbestos defendants' assets may become so depleted by early awards that the defendants will no longer be in existence and able to pay compensatory damages to later plaintiffs. Again, it is difficult if not impossible to ascertain the additional impact of

punitive damages as compared to the impact of mass compensatory damages alone. . . .

Accepting the possibility of punitive damage "overkill," we turn to means of addressing that problem. Because the problem is nationwide, several possible remedial steps can be effective only on a nationwide basis, and hence are beyond our reach. One such solution is the setting of a cap on total punitive damages against each defendant. Such a cap would be ineffective unless applied uniformly. To adopt such a cap in New Jersey would be to deprive our citizens of punitive damages without the concomitant benefit of assuring the availability of compensatory damages for later plaintiffs. This we decline to do.

None of these devices have staved off financial ruin to the first generation of asbestos defendants. In recent years the number of actions against the so-called secondary asbestos defendants — the firms that incorporated asbestos into brakes and other friction products, for example — has increased far beyond the levels of the 1980s, without bringing about any legislative or judicial solution, even if the face of extensive fraud charges. See Chapter at page 725.

2. *Statutory reform of punitive damages.* The extensive common law litigation on punitive damages has brought forth a wide range of legislative reforms. New Hampshire's law provides simply: "No punitive damages shall be awarded in any action, unless otherwise provided by statute." N.H. Rev. Stat. Ann. §507:16 (2007). Other states have capped punitive damages as a multiple of actual damages, at least in some areas. For example, Conn. Gen. Stat. Ann. §52-240b (West 2007) caps punitive damages at twice compensatory damages in products liability cases. Fla. Stat. §768.73 (1) (2007) has an elaborate step system. First, it imposes an across the board cap on punitive damages equal either to three times compensatory damages or $500,000, whichever is greater. Next, it allows an award of either four times compensatory damages or $2 million, whichever is greater, "[w]here the fact finder determines that the wrongful conduct proven under this section was motivated solely by unreasonable financial gain and determines that the unreasonably dangerous nature of the conduct, together with the high likelihood of injury resulting from the conduct, was actually known by the managing agent, director, officer, or other person responsible for making policy decisions on behalf of the defendant. . . . " Finally "where the fact finder determines that at the time of injury the defendant had a specific intent to harm the claimant and determines that the defendant's conduct did in fact harm the claimant, there shall be no cap on punitive damages." In addition, some states have ordered bifurcated trials of liability and damages in punitive damage cases. See Cal. Civ. Code §3295(d) (2007), where on the application of the defendant, the court shall not admit evidence of the defendant's "profits or

financial condition" until the jury has made an award of actual damages. See also Kan. Stat. Ann. §60-3701(a) (2007), under which the trier of fact determines the defendant's liability for punitive damages and the court determines its amount, based on the likelihood of harm, the defendant's awareness thereof, the profitability of the defendant's misconduct, its duration and concealment, if any, the attitude of the defendant upon discovery of the misconduct, and the financial position of the defendant. For a full account of these statutes as of 1996, see the Appendix to Justice Ginsburg's dissent in BMW of North America v. Gore, 517 U.S. 559, 618 (1996). See also L. Schlueter & K. Redden, Punitive Damages §9.12 (5th ed. 2005).

On a second front, Florida law also pays 35 percent of any punitive damage award to various state funds, on the ground that some portion of payments for quasi-criminal conduct should be paid to the state. The provision was held constitutional against both due process and takings challenges in Gordon v. State, 608 So. 2d 800 (Fla. 1992). With *Gordon*'s constitutional approach, contrast Kirk v. Denver Publishing Co., 818 P.2d 262, 269 (Colo. 1991), which struck down a Colorado statute (6A Colo. Rev. Stat. §13-21-102(4) (1987)) requiring one-third of any punitive damage award to be paid to the state as an unconstitutional taking of private property without just compensation. More recently, the Oregon Supreme Court sustained a similar statute, Or. Rev. Stat. §31.735 (2007), which provides that 60 percent of all punitive damage awards go to a Criminal Injuries Compensation Account, against a variety of challenges. See DeMendoza v. Huffman, 51 P.3d 1232 (Ore. 2002). See also Dardinger v. Anthem Blue Cross and Blue Shield, 781 N.E.2d 121, 146 (Ohio 2002), where Pfeifer, J., on his own initiative directed that two-thirds of a $30 million punitive damages award against a health plan provider should to the Esther Dardinger Fund at the Cancer Hospital and Research Center at Ohio State University, where she was treated:

> The final net amount remaining after the prescribed payments [to Dardinger, and various fees] should go to a place that will achieve a societal good, a good that can rationally offset the harm done by the defendants in this case. Due to the societal stake in the punitive damages award, we find it most appropriate that it go to a state institution. In this case we order that the corpus of the punitive damages award go to a cancer research fund, to be called the Esther Dardinger Fund, at the James Cancer Hospital and Solove Research Institute at the Ohio State University.

Should potential beneficiaries be allowed to intervene at trial for a share of any punitive damage awards? For a sympathetic response to *Dardinger*, see Sharkey, Punitive Damages As Societal Damages, 113 Yale L.J. 347 (2003). Given the presence of some statutory reforms, should constitutional limitations be imposed on punitive damage awards?

State Farm Mutual Automobile Insurance Co. v. Campbell
538 U.S. 408 (2003)

KENNEDY, J.:

We address once again the measure of punishment, by means of punitive damages, a State may impose upon a defendant in a civil case. The question is whether, in the circumstances we shall recount, an award of $145 million in punitive damages, where full compensatory damages are $1 million, is excessive and in violation of the Due Process Clause of the Fourteenth Amendment to the Constitution of the United States.

I

In 1981, Curtis Campbell (Campbell) was driving with his wife, Inez Preece Campbell, in Cache County, Utah. He decided to pass six vans traveling ahead of them on a two-lane highway. Todd Ospital was driving a small car approaching from the opposite direction. To avoid a head-on collision with Campbell, who by then was driving on the wrong side of the highway and toward oncoming traffic, Ospital swerved onto the shoulder, lost control of his automobile, and collided with a vehicle driven by Robert G. Slusher. Ospital was killed, and Slusher was rendered permanently disabled. The Campbells escaped unscathed.

In the ensuing wrongful death and tort action, Campbell insisted he was not at fault. Early investigations did support differing conclusions as to who caused the accident, but "a consensus was reached early on by the investigators and witnesses that Mr. Campbell's unsafe pass had indeed caused the crash." 65 P.3d 1134, 1141 (Utah 2001). Campbell's insurance company, petitioner State Farm Mutual Automobile Insurance Company (State Farm), nonetheless decided to contest liability and declined offers by Slusher and Ospital's estate (Ospital) to settle the claims for the policy limit of $50,000 ($25,000 per claimant). State Farm also ignored the advice of one of its own investigators and took the case to trial, assuring the Campbells that "their assets were safe, that they had no liability for the accident, that [State Farm] would represent their interests, and that they did not need to procure separate counsel." To the contrary, a jury determined that Campbell was 100 percent at fault, and a judgment was returned for $185,849, far more than the amount offered in settlement.

At first State Farm refused to cover the $135,849 in excess liability. Its counsel made this clear to the Campbells: "'You may want to put for sale signs on your property to get things moving.'" Nor was State Farm willing to post a supersedeas bond to allow Campbell to appeal the judgment against him. Campbell obtained his own counsel to appeal the verdict. During the pendency of the appeal, in late 1984, Slusher, Ospital, and the

Campbells reached an agreement whereby Slusher and Ospital agreed not to seek satisfaction of their claims against the Campbells. In exchange the Campbells agreed to pursue a bad faith action against State Farm and to be represented by Slusher's and Ospital's attorneys. The Campbells also agreed that Slusher and Ospital would have a right to play a part in all major decisions concerning the bad-faith action. No settlement could be concluded without Slusher's and Ospital's approval, and Slusher and Ospital would receive 90 percent of any verdict against State Farm.

In 1989, the Utah Supreme Court denied Campbell's appeal in the wrongful-death and tort actions. State Farm then paid the entire judgment, including the amounts in excess of the policy limits. The Campbells nonetheless filed a complaint against State Farm alleging bad faith, fraud, and intentional infliction of emotional distress. [State Farm defended on the ground that it had made an honest mistake. At trial, the plaintiff received an award of $2.6 million in compensatory damages and $145 million in punitives. The trial judge reduced those figures to $1 million and $25 million respectively. The Utah Supreme Court affirmed the $1 million award for compensatory damages and reinstated the $145 million in punitive damages on the ground that "State Farm's decision to take the case to trial was a result of a national scheme to meet corporate fiscal goals by capping payouts on claims company wide. This scheme was referred to as State Farm's 'Performance, Planning and Review,' or PP & R, policy. To prove the existence of this scheme, the trial court allowed the Campbells to introduce extensive expert testimony regarding fraudulent practices by State Farm in its nation-wide operations" over a 20-year period. It pointed to State Farm's "massive wealth," and the low probability of detection — estimated at 1 case in 50,000 — for actions that each carried various criminal and civil penalties, "including $10,000 for each act of fraud, the suspension of its license to conduct business in Utah, the disgorgement of profits, and imprisonment."] We granted certiorari.

II

We recognized in Cooper Industries, Inc. v. Leatherman Tool Group, Inc., 532 U.S. 424, (2001), that in our judicial system compensatory and punitive damages, although usually awarded at the same time by the same decisionmaker, serve different purposes. Compensatory damages "are intended to redress the concrete loss that the plaintiff has suffered by reason of the defendant's wrongful conduct." By contrast, punitive damages serve a broader function; they are aimed at deterrence and retribution.

While States possess discretion over the imposition of punitive damages, it is well established that there are procedural and substantive constitutional limitations on these awards. The Due Process Clause of the Fourteenth Amendment prohibits the imposition of grossly excessive or arbitrary punishments on a tortfeasor. The reason is that "[e]lementary notions of fairness enshrined in our constitutional jurisprudence dictate that a person receive fair notice not only of the conduct that will subject him to punishment, but also of the severity of the penalty that a State may impose." To the extent an award is grossly excessive, it furthers no legitimate purpose and constitutes an arbitrary deprivation of property.

Although these awards serve the same purposes as criminal penalties, defendants subjected to punitive damages in civil cases have not been accorded the protections applicable in a criminal proceeding. This increases our concerns over the imprecise manner in which punitive damages systems are administered. We have admonished that "[p]unitive damages pose an acute danger of arbitrary deprivation of property. Jury instructions typically leave the jury with wide discretion in choosing amounts, and the presentation of evidence of a defendant's net worth creates the potential that juries will use their verdicts to express biases against big businesses, particularly those without strong local presences." Honda Motor [Co. v Oberg, 512 U.S. 415, 432 (1994)]. Our concerns are heightened when the decisionmaker is presented, as we shall discuss, with evidence that has little bearing as to the amount of punitive damages that should be awarded. Vague instructions, or those that merely inform the jury to avoid "passion or prejudice," do little to aid the decisionmaker in its task of assigning appropriate weight to evidence that is relevant and evidence that is tangential or only inflammatory.

In light of these concerns, in [BMW of North America v. Gore, 517 U.S. 559 (1996)], we instructed courts reviewing punitive damages to consider three guideposts: (1) the degree of reprehensibility of the defendant's misconduct; (2) the disparity between the actual or potential harm suffered by the plaintiff and the punitive damages award; and (3) the difference between the punitive damages awarded by the jury and the civil penalties authorized or imposed in comparable cases. We reiterated the importance of these three guideposts in *Cooper Industries* and mandated appellate courts to conduct *de novo* review of a trial court's application of them to the jury's award. Exacting appellate review ensures that an award of punitive damages is based upon an "'application of law, rather than a decisionmaker's caprice.'"

III

Under the principles outlined in BMW of North America, Inc. v. Gore, this case is neither close nor difficult. It was error to reinstate the jury's $145 million punitive damages award. We address each guidepost of *Gore* in some detail.

A

"[T]he most important indicium of the reasonableness of a punitive damages award is the degree of reprehensibility of the defendant's conduct." We have instructed courts to determine the reprehensibility of a defendant by considering whether: the harm caused was physical as opposed to economic; the tortious conduct evinced an indifference to or a reckless disregard of the health or safety of others; the target of the conduct had financial vulnerability; the conduct involved repeated actions or was an isolated incident; and the harm was the result of intentional malice, trickery, or deceit, or mere accident. The existence of any one of these factors weighing in favor of a plaintiff may not be sufficient to sustain a punitive damages award; and the absence of all of them renders any award suspect. It should be presumed a plaintiff has been made whole for his injuries by compensatory damages, so punitive damages should only be awarded if the defendant's culpability, after having paid compensatory damages, is so reprehensible as to warrant the imposition of further sanctions to achieve punishment or deterrence.

Applying these factors in the instant case, we must acknowledge that State Farm's handling of the claims against the Campbells merits no praise. The trial court found that State Farm's employees altered the company's records to make Campbell appear less culpable. State Farm disregarded the overwhelming likelihood of liability and the near-certain probability that, by taking the case to trial, a judgment in excess of the policy limits would be awarded. State Farm amplified the harm by at first assuring the Campbells their assets would be safe from any verdict and by later telling them, postjudgment, to put a for-sale sign on their house. While we do not suggest there was error in awarding punitive damages based upon State Farm's conduct toward the Campbells, a more modest punishment for this reprehensible conduct could have satisfied the State's legitimate objectives, and the Utah courts should have gone no further.

This case, instead, was used as a platform to expose, and punish, the perceived deficiencies of State Farm's operations throughout the country. The Utah Supreme Court's opinion makes explicit that State Farm was being condemned for its nationwide policies rather than for the conduct directed toward the Campbells. This was, as well, an explicit rationale of the trial court's decision in approving the award, though reduced from $145 million to $25 million. . . .

A State cannot punish a defendant for conduct that may have been lawful where it occurred. Nor, as a general rule, does a State have a legitimate concern in imposing punitive damages to punish a defendant for unlawful acts committed outside of the State's jurisdiction. Any proper adjudication of conduct that occurred outside Utah to other persons would require their inclusion, and, to those parties, the Utah courts, in the usual case, would need to apply the laws of their relevant jurisdiction.

Here, the Campbells do not dispute that much of the out-of-state conduct was lawful where it occurred. They argue, however, that such evidence was not the primary basis for the punitive damages award and was relevant to the extent it demonstrated, in a general sense, State Farm's motive against its insured. This argument misses the mark. Lawful out-of-state conduct may be probative when it demonstrates the deliberateness and culpability of the defendant's action in the State where it is tortious, but that conduct must have a nexus to the specific harm suffered by the plaintiff. A jury must be instructed, furthermore, that it may not use evidence of out-of-state conduct to punish a defendant for action that was lawful in the jurisdiction where it occurred. A basic principle of federalism is that each State may make its own reasoned judgment about what conduct is permitted or proscribed within its borders, and each State alone can determine what measure of punishment, if any, to impose on a defendant who acts within its jurisdiction.

For a more fundamental reason, however, the Utah courts erred in relying upon this and other evidence: The courts awarded punitive damages to punish and deter conduct that bore no relation to the Campbells' harm. A defendant's dissimilar acts, independent from the acts upon which liability was premised, may not serve as the basis for punitive damages. A defendant should be punished for the conduct that harmed the plaintiff, not for being an unsavory individual or business. Due process does not permit courts, in the calculation of punitive damages, to adjudicate the merits of other parties' hypothetical claims against a defendant under the guise of the reprehensibility analysis, but we have no doubt the Utah Supreme Court did that here. Punishment on these bases creates the possibility of multiple punitive damages awards for the same conduct; for in the usual case nonparties are not bound by the judgment some other plaintiff obtains.

The same reasons lead us to conclude the Utah Supreme Court's decision cannot be justified on the grounds that State Farm was a recidivist. . . .

. . . The Campbells attempt to justify the courts' reliance upon this un-related testimony on the theory that each dollar of profit made by under-paying a third-party claimant is the same as a dollar made by underpaying a first-party one. For the reasons already stated, this argument is unconvincing. The reprehensibility guidepost does not permit courts to expand the scope of the case so that a defendant may be punished for any malfeasance, which in this case extended for a 20-year period. In this case, because the Campbells have shown no conduct by State Farm similar to that which harmed them, the conduct that harmed them is the only conduct relevant to the reprehensibility analysis.

B

Turning to the second *Gore* guidepost, we have been reluctant to identify concrete constitutional limits on the ratio between harm, or potential harm, to the plaintiff and the punitive damages award. We decline again to impose a bright-line ratio which a punitive damages award cannot exceed. Our jurisprudence and the principles it has now established demonstrate, however, that, in practice, few awards exceeding a single-digit ratio between punitive and compensatory damages, to a significant degree, will satisfy due process. In [Pacific Mutual Life Insurance Co. v.] Haslip [499 U.S. 1, 23-24 (1991)], in upholding a punitive damages award, we concluded that an award of more than four times the amount of compensatory damages might be close to the line of constitutional impropriety. We cited that 4-to-1 ratio again in *Gore*. The Court further referenced a long legislative history, dating back over 700 years and going forward to today, providing for sanctions of double, treble, or quadruple damages to deter and punish. While these ratios are not binding, they are instructive. They demonstrate what should be obvious: Single-digit multipliers are more likely to comport with due process, while still achieving the State's goals of deterrence and retribution, than awards with ratios in range of 500 to 1, or, in this case, of 145 to 1....

In sum, courts must ensure that the measure of punishment is both reasonable and proportionate to the amount of harm to the plaintiff and to the general damages recovered. In the context of this case, we have no doubt that there is a presumption against an award that has a 145-to-1 ratio. The compensatory award in this case was substantial; the Campbells were awarded $1 million for a year and a half of emotional distress. This was complete compensation. The harm arose from a transaction in the economic realm, not from some physical assault or trauma; there were no physical injuries; and State Farm paid the excess verdict before the complaint was filed, so the Campbells suffered only minor economic injuries for the 18-month period in which State Farm refused to resolve the claim against them. The compensatory damages for the injury suffered here, moreover, likely were based on a component which was duplicated in the punitive award. Much of the distress was caused by the outrage and humiliation the Campbells suffered at the actions of their insurer; and it is a major role of punitive damages to condemn such conduct....

[Kennedy, J., rejected the specific justifications that the Utah Supreme Court offered to justify the 145 multiple: State Farm's massive wealth and the rate of concealment.]

C

The third guidepost in *Gore* is the disparity between the punitive damages award and the "civil penalties authorized or imposed in comparable cases." We note that, in the past, we have also looked to criminal penalties that could be imposed. The existence of a criminal penalty does have bearing on the seriousness with which a State views the wrongful action. When used to determine the dollar amount of the award, however, the criminal penalty has less utility. Great care must be taken to avoid use of the civil process to assess criminal penalties that can be imposed only after the heightened protections of a criminal trial have been observed, including, of course, its higher standards of proof. Punitive damages are not a substitute for the criminal process, and the remote possibility of a criminal sanction does not automatically sustain a punitive damages award.

Here, we need not dwell long on this guidepost. The most relevant civil sanction under Utah state law for the wrong done to the Campbells appears to be a $10,000 fine for an act of fraud, an amount dwarfed by the $145 million punitive damages award. The Supreme Court of Utah speculated about the loss of State Farm's business license, the disgorgement of profits, and possible imprisonment, but here again its references were to the broad fraudulent scheme drawn from evidence of out-of-state and dissimilar conduct. This analysis was insufficient to justify the award.

IV

[Reversed and remanded for a redetermination of punitive damages by the Utah Courts.]

SCALIA, J., dissenting.

I adhere to the view expressed in my dissenting opinion in [*Gore*] that the Due Process Clause provides no substantive protections against "excessive" or "'unreasonable'" awards of punitive damages. I am also of the view that the punitive damages jurisprudence which has sprung forth from [*Gore*] is insusceptible of principled application; accordingly, I do not feel justified in giving the case *stare decisis* effect. I would affirm the judgment of the Utah Supreme Court.

[In *Gore*, Scalia, J., had written in dissent: "What the Fourteenth Amendment's procedural guarantee assures is an opportunity to contest the reasonableness of a damages judgment in state court; but there is no federal guarantee a damages award actually *be* reasonable."]

THOMAS, J., dissenting.

I would affirm the judgment below because "I continue to believe that the Constitution does not constrain the size of punitive damages awards." Accordingly, I respectfully dissent.

GINSBURG, J. dissenting. . . .

In *Gore*, I stated why I resisted the Court's foray into punitive damages "territory traditionally within the States' domain." I adhere to those views, and note again that, unlike federal habeas corpus review of state-court convictions under 28 U.S.C. §2254, the Court "work[s] at this business [of checking state courts] alone," unaided by the participation of federal district courts and courts of appeals. It was once recognized that "the laws of the particular State must suffice [to superintend punitive damages awards] until judges or legislators authorized to do so initiate system-wide change." I would adhere to that traditional view.

NOTES

1. *Punitive damages in the Supreme Court.* State Farm represents the most authoritative Supreme Court decision on the appropriate constitutional standards for evaluating punitive damages. Its basic thrust was confirmed more recently in Philip Morris USA v. Williams, 127 S. Ct. 1057, 1064 (2007). After much litigation in a tobacco case, the Oregon Supreme Court affirmed a jury award of $79.5 in punitive damages in a wrongful death action that awarded the plaintiff $800,000 in noneconomic damages. That court rejected Philip Morris's argument that the Constitution prevents a party "from using punitive damages to punish a defendant for harm to nonparties," and sustained the award even though it was over 100 times actual damages. Justice Breyer vacated the judgment:

> In our view, the Constitution's Due Process Clause forbids a State to use a punitive damages award to punish a defendant for injury that it inflicts upon nonparties or those whom they directly represent, i.e., injury that it inflicts upon those who are, essentially, strangers to the litigation. . . . [A] defendant threatened with punishment for injuring a nonparty victim has no opportunity to defend against the charge, by showing, for example in a case such as this, that the other victim was not entitled to damages because he or she knew that smoking was dangerous or did not rely upon the defendant's statements to the contrary.
>
> For another, to permit punishment for injuring a nonparty victim would add a near standardless dimension to the punitive damages equation. How many such victims are there? How seriously were they injured? Under what circumstances did injury occur? The trial will not likely answer such questions as to nonparty victims. The jury will be left to speculate. And the fundamental due process concerns to which our punitive damages cases refer — risks of arbitrariness, uncertainty and lack of notice — will be magnified.

He then refused to pass on the question of whether the 100-to-1 ratio was excessive, preferring to wait to see the outcome of a new trial.

Philip Morris represents only the latest chapter in the Supreme Court's generation-long effort to impose constitutional limitations on punitive damages. In its initial foray, Browning Ferris Industries of Vermont, Inc. v. Kelco Disposal, Inc., 492 U.S. 257 (1989), the Court held that a punitive damages award did not violate the Eighth Amendment prohibition against the imposition of "excessive fines." In Pacific Mutual Life Insurance Co. v. Haslip, 499 U.S. 1 (1991), the Court refused to strike down a punitive damage award of over $1,000,000 awarded against an insurance company that had canceled a group insurance policy after an independent agent had failed to remit payments due Pacific under its policy. Next, in TXO Production Corp. v. Alliance Resources Corp., 509 U.S. 443, 460 (1993), the Supreme Court refused to set aside a punitive damage award of $10,000,000 when the actual damages in the underlying slander of title action amounted to only $19,000. Stevens, J., speaking for a plurality of the Court, noted that it "is appropriate to consider the magnitude of the *potential* harm that the defendant's conduct would have caused to its intended victim if the wrongful plan had succeeded, as well as the possible harm to other victims that might have resulted if similar future behavior were not deterred."

Thereafter, the tide of battle shifted in favor of defendants. In Honda Motor Co., Ltd. v. Oberg, 512 U.S. 415 (1994), the Court struck down an Oregon law which, unlike the rules in all other states, required that the plaintiff show the customary elements for punitive damages by clear and convincing evidence, but prohibited judicial review of any jury award "unless the court can affirmatively say there is no evidence to support the verdict." Stevens, J., found that this abbreviated appellate review violated due process norms by failing to provide sufficient procedural safeguards against "the danger of arbitrary awards." Next, in BMW of North America v. Gore, 517 U.S. 559 (1996), the court finally struck down a punitive damage award as excessive. Plaintiff recovered $2 million in punitive damages under Alabama law when he had not been told that he had purchased a damaged and repainted BMW that reduced the resale value of the car by at most $4,000. The decision set out the three factors discussed at length in *State Farm*. With regard to reprehensibility, Stevens, J., noted the loss was only economic and not physical; that the defendant had engaged in at most nondisclosure without either concealment or fraud; and that the punitive damages could not be used to deter conduct that was legal in the other states where it was performed. Further, Stevens, J., noted the award was over 500 times the actual damages, and criminal fines were at most $10,000, often with breaks for first offenders. Finally, in Cooper Industries v. Leatherman Tool Group, Inc., 532 U.S. 424 (2001), the Supreme Court vacated and remanded a punitive damage award of $4.5 million given on top of a $50,000 award in an unfair competition case. It did so on the ground "that court of appeals should apply a *de novo* standard of review when passing on district courts' determinations of the constitutionality of punitive damages awards."

2. *Punitive damages in the lower courts.* The recent Supreme Court decisions have had important effects on the behavior of both state and lower federal courts. In Romo v. Ford Motor Co., 122 Cal. Rptr. 2d 139 (Cal. App. 2002), the court dealt with a 1993 rollover accident involving a used 1978 Ford Bronco that killed three passengers and injured three more. Ford paid nearly $5 million in actual damages for its share of the actual damages, and was assessed $290 million in punitive damages on the ground that its roof, which was steel in the front and weaker fiberboard in the rear, had been designed to look sturdier than it was. Vartabedian, P.J., refused to reduce punitive damages, holding that the false appearance of sturdiness counted as "'malicious or despicable' conduct," even though it was 48 times the actual damage. After *State Farm*, the Supreme Court vacated the judgment and remanded the case to the California Appellate Court "for further consideration in light of [*State Farm*]." Ford Motor Co. v. Romo, 123 S. Ct. 2072 (2003). Thereafter an award of about $23.7 million in punitive damages, about five times total compensatory damages, was upheld on appeal. Romo v. Ford Motor Co., 6 Cal. Rptr. 3d 793 (Cal. App. 2003).

In re Exxon Valdez, 472 F.3d 600, 618 (9th Cir. 2006), presented the question of how much punitive damages should be awarded against Exxon for spilling 11 million gallons of crude oil into Prince William Sound and Lower Cook Inlet when it ran aground on Bligh Reef in 1989 while under the command of Captain Hazelwood, whom the court described as a "relapsed alcoholic." After multiple hearings, the Court reduced the last punitive damage award from $4.5 billion to $2.5 billion to correct for errors below in determining the reprehensibility of defendant's conduct under *State Farm*, including its efforts to mitigate the losses by extensive clean-up efforts after the spill. In reaching that decision it made an exhaustive evaluation of five factors that bore on reprehensibility. It first looked at the difference between physical and economic harm and concluded:

> Placing a relapsed alcoholic in control of a supertanker was highly reprehensible conduct. As a result, Exxon disrupted the lives of thousands of people who depend on Prince William Sound for their livelihoods, and endangered its own crew and their rescuers. Over the span of three years, Exxon could and should have relieved Captain Hazelwood of command of supertankers, but it did not do so. At the same time, however, Exxon did not act with malice toward plaintiffs or anyone else; Exxon did not intend to damage plaintiffs' livelihoods or cause them the emotional grief that went with the economic loss.
>
> Thus, Exxon's conduct is in the higher realm of reprehensibility, but not in the highest realm. In addition Exxon's post-grounding efforts to mitigate

the harm serve materially to reduce the reprehensibility of the original misconduct. They reduce the reprehensibility for purposes of our review to, at most, a mid range.

The Court then rejected Exxon's argument that the appropriate base for punitive damages was not the $500 million+ in actual damages, less the nearly $500 million voluntarily spent in clean up costs and settlement, which in Exxon's view would have reduced punitive damages to about $25 million. Instead, for this midrange case it accepted a five-fold multiple under *State Farm*. Browning, J., would have affirmed the higher reward because on appellate review "our sole duty is to ensure its imposition does not violate due process."

3. Theoretical basis for punitive damages. Spurred on in part by the spate of Supreme Court cases, an extensive academic literature has examined the theoretical basis and practical operation of punitive damages in tort cases. Polinsky & Shavell, Punitive Damages: An Economic Analysis, 111 Harv. L. Rev. 869 (1998), adopted a strict efficiency model stressing the need for a damage multiplier to take into account the risk that a wrongdoer will escape punishment. That rationale seems to apply with equal force in cases of negligent infliction of harm where it is hard to identify the wrongdoer, and thus tends to slight the mental requirements for punitive damages in most cases. It received some judicial backing from Calabresi, J., in Ciraolo v. City of New York, 216 F.3d 236, 243 (2d Cir. 2000), who noted: "Punitive damages can ensure that a wrongdoer bears all the costs of its actions, and is thus appropriately deterred from causing harm, in those categories of cases in which compensatory damages alone result in systematic under-assessment of costs, and hence in systematic underdeterrence." This theory does not, however, systematically take into account the risk of overdeterrence from the repetitive use of these multipliers.

In any event, the efficiency boomlet did not carry the day in the Supreme Court, as Stevens, J., wrote in *Cooper Industries*, 532 U.S. at 438, first, that "[h]owever attractive such an approach to punitive damages might be as an abstract policy matter, it is clear that juries do not normally engage in such a finely tuned exercise of deterrence calibration when awarding punitive damages." Secondly, he stated that "[c]itizens and legislators may rightly insist that they are willing to tolerate some loss in economic efficiency in order to deter what they consider morally offensive conduct albeit cost-beneficial morally offensive conduct," quoting Galanter & Luban, Poetic Justice: Punitive Damages and Legal Pluralism, 42 Am. U. L. Rev. 1393, 1449 (1993).

For his initial point, Stevens, J., relied on Sunstein, Schkade & Kahneman, Do People Want Optimal Deterrence?, 29 J. Legal Stud. 237 (2000), disputing the Polinsky and Shavell position that jurors actually increase punitive damages in hard-to-detect events. See also Sunstein, Kahneman &

Schkade, Assessing Punitive Damages (with Notes on Cognition and Valuation in Law), 107 Yale L.J. 2071 (1998). The authors examine the other dimensions of punitive damage awards, and note a wide consensus across social, geographical, and racial boundaries on the determinants of "shared outrage" in punitive damage cases. They then suggest that the wide variation in punitive damage awards given this apparent consensus stems from a common inability to translate moral judgments into dollar amounts. See Schkade, Sunstein & Kahneman, Deliberating About Dollars: The Severity Shift, 100 Colum. L. Rev. 1139 (2000).

Yet another take on punitive damages is offered in Eisenberg & Wells, The Predictability of Punitive Damages Awards in Published Opinions, the Impact of *BMW v. Gore* on Punitive Damages Awards, and Forecasting Which Punitive Damage Awards Will Be Reduced, 7 Sup. Ct. Econ. Rev. 59, 83 (1999). The authors first observe that the skewness in punitive damages is reduced if the logarithm of the award is used (which narrows the range: $10 = 10^1$, and $100 = 10^2$, so that using the logs 1 and 2 show a smaller dispersion), and conclude that the cases after *BMW* seem to come out much the way they did before.

Finally, punitive damages awards often present this dilemma: First, a court demands that a manufacturer make an explicit cost-benefit analysis in designing products. Second, juries then infer that a correct cost-benefit analysis shows the callous quantification of human life that calls for punitive damages. See Viscusi, Corporate Risk Analysis: A Reckless Act?, 52 Stan. L. Rev. 547, 556-557 (2000), noting, empirically, increases in punitive damage awards when corporations make cost-benefit analyses. One instance of conscious design choices was Grimshaw v. Ford Motor Co., 174 Cal. Rptr. 348 (Cal. App. 1981), where the jury awarded the plaintiff $125,000,000 in punitive damages against Ford. In designing the Pinto, Ford had made a number of cost-benefit calculations that involved estimating the value of a human life. In dealing with that issue, should it make a difference if the changes proposed (such as a bladder inside the gas tank of the Pinto) had never been used commercially in cars sold at any price? If the Pinto had a rate of burn deaths or injuries no greater than that of other comparably priced and sized cars? For an exhaustive analysis of the case see Schwartz, The Myth of the Ford Pinto Case, 43 Rutgers L. Rev. 1013 (1991).

11

THE INSTITUTION OF INSURANCE

SECTION A. INTRODUCTION

In this chapter we turn from the rules governing tortious liability for physical harm and to the institutional framework for the defense, settlement, and litigation of tort claims. Even when insurance coverage is not generally required, it is still carried by a huge number of individuals and firms who prefer the constant stream of steady but limited payments to the remote possibility of a large, and perhaps ruinous, financial loss. In both personal injury and property damage cases, an insurance company is apt to be at the center of the controversy since it is responsible both for the defense of the action and, within policy limits, for the satisfaction of any judgment entered against its insured.

The complex tripartite relationship among accident victim, insurance company, and insured was once played out chiefly in connection with automobile accidents. But in recent years, major insurance litigation has involved high stakes disputes concerning products liability and toxic torts, both in individual and in mass tort contexts. In dealing with this wealth of material, this chapter first examines some of the coverage disputes under the comprehensive general liability policy (CGL) in these hotly disputed areas. It then offers a brief overview of automobile liability insurance, still in the aggregate one of the largest lines of coverage. The second section of the chapter deals with the ancillary obligations of the insured, the duty to defend, and the duty to negotiate settlement in good faith, which have been staples in modern insurance litigation.

Before turning to these particulars, it is useful to briefly address the connection between tort liability and insurance. The basic problem that bedevils this area is that an insurance contract between a defendant and its insurer must regulate not only the relationship between the parties, but also their joint relationship to the injured plaintiff whose claim against the insured is typically covered by the tortfeasor's insurance. The instabilities of this three-cornered game are well illustrated by two early twentieth-century cases. Bain v. Atkins, 63 N.E. 414, 415 (Mass. 1902), involved a suit against an insurer who had written an indemnity policy on the insured that required it to pay a third party only to the extent that the insured was solvent. As written, the contract benefitted the insured and insurer, but not the injured party. When the plaintiff was unable to collect from the bankrupt insured, he sued the carrier, but in vain:

> [The policy] contains no agreement that the insurance shall enure to the benefit of the person accidentally injured, and no language from which such an understanding or intention can be implied. Atkins was under no obligation to procure insurance for the benefit of the plaintiff, nor did any relation exist between the plaintiff and Atkins which could give the latter the right to procure insurance for the benefit of the plaintiff. The only correct statement of the situation is simply that the insurance was a matter wholly between the company and Atkins, in which the plaintiff had no legal or equitable interest, any more than in any other property belonging absolutely to Atkins.

The counterattack against Bain, which eventually bore fruit, was that public policy should prevent an insurer from hiding behind the insolvency of its insured. The proposed cure was to read all indemnity contracts as authorizing third persons to recover from the insurer, whether or not the insured was solvent. The upshot was, therefore, to increase the effectiveness of tort liability insurance in compensating strangers for losses. See Laube, The Social Vice of Accident Indemnity, 80 U. Pa. L. Rev. 189 (1930).

At the same time, indemnity contracts were attacked from the opposite side, on the ground that they should be wholly void as a matter of public policy. The focus of this attack turned from the compensation of injuries after the fact to the deterrence of injury before the fact. In Breeden v. Frankfort Marine, Accident & Plate Glass Insurance Co., 119 S.W. 576, 608 (Mo. 1909), an injured worker sued his employer for personal injuries caused by the employer's negligence. The underlying suit was successful, and the question was whether the insurance indemnity contract was void as against public policy for encouraging sloth and indifference by employers who escaped the financial sting of any adverse judgment. An exhaustive initial judgment invalidated the indemnity contract, but was reversed on appeal, with the court, per Woodson, J., noting that

> such insurance does not lessen the employer's liability or responsibility, but increases his means of meeting both; . . . that the existence of an indemnity

fund does not directly or necessarily cause the master or carrier to relax his care and diligence to prevent injury to servants, passengers, or shippers; . . . that the employer, shipper, or passenger, instead of less security, has the added security of the vigilance, experience, and self-interest of the insurance company itself to prevent the use of negligent methods, negligently constructed or operated machines and appliances or other negligent exposure to injury; . . . [and] that there is no unvarying rule, of which judicial notice will be taken, that an indemnity against losses by negligence will, in and of itself, induce a master or carrier to omit the highest degree of care, and that (absent such rule) it does not logically follow that an indemnity contract is directly or incidentally repugnant to public policy.

For a detailed account of how tort liability meshes with liability insurance, see Schwartz, The Ethics and the Economics of Tort Liability Insurance, 75 Cornell L. Rev. 313 (1990).

SECTION B. THE SCOPE OF INSURANCE COVERAGE

1. Modern Tort Litigation

Dimmitt Chevrolet, Inc. v. Southeastern Fidelity Insurance Corp.
636 So. 2d 700 (Fla. 1993)

Per Curiam. This cause is before the Court on the following certified question of law from the United States Court of Appeals in Industrial Indemnity Insurance Co. v. Crown Auto Dealerships, Inc., 935 F.2d 240 (11th Cir. 1991) [on the scope of the pollution exclusion clause contained within the comprehensive general liability policy as it applies to environmental contamination.

Dimmitt Chevrolet operated two dealerships, which sold the used crankcase oil generated by its business to Peak Oil Company from 1974 to 1979. From 1974 to 1979 Peak had recycled oil from Dimmitt and other sources for sale as used oil. In 1983 the Environmental Protection Agency determined that substantial pollution at Peak's worksite had resulted from Peak's storage of its waste sludge in unlined bins. In addition to its suit against Peak, the EPA designated Dimmitt as a potentially responsible party (PRP) under CERCLA because it had generated and transported hazardous materials to the Peak site. Dimmitt agreed to undertake remedial measures without conceding its liability under CERCLA.]

Appellee Southeastern Fidelity Insurance Corporation ("Southeastern") provided comprehensive general liability ("CGL") insurance coverage to Dimmitt from 1972 through 1980. The policy covered Dimmitt for all sums which the INSURED shall become legally obligated to pay as DAMAGES because of A. BODILY INJURY or B. PROPERTY DAMAGE to which this insurance applies, caused by an occurrence, and the Company shall have the right and duty to defend any suit against the INSURED seeking DAMAGES on account of such BODILY INJURY or PROPERTY DAMAGE, even if any of the allegations of the suit are groundless. . . .

An "occurrence" is defined by the policy as

an accident including continuous or repeated exposure to conditions, which results in BODILY INJURY or PROPERTY DAMAGE neither expected nor intended from the standpoint of the INSURED. . . .

However, the policy excluded coverage for

BODILY INJURY or PROPERTY DAMAGE arising out of the discharge, dispersal, release or escape of smoke, vapors, soot, fumes, acids, alkalis, toxic chemicals, liquids, or gases, waste materials . . . into or upon land, the atmosphere or any water course or body of water; but this exclusion does not apply if such discharge, dispersal, release or escape is sudden and accidental. . . .

. . . The issue before us is whether Dimmitt's comprehensive liability insurance policy was intended to cover hazardous waste pollution under the circumstances set forth in the court of appeals' opinion. The question turns on the meaning of the term "sudden and accidental" within the pollution exclusion clause of Dimmitt's policy.

Dimmitt asserts that the term "sudden and accidental" is ambiguous because it is subject to multiple definitions. Thus, because ambiguous terms within an insurance policy should be construed in favor of the insured, the policy should be construed in Dimmitt's favor. Dimmitt argues that the word "sudden" does not have a temporal meaning and that the term was intentionally written so as to provide coverage for unexpected and unintended pollution discharge.

Southeastern Fidelity Insurance Corporation (Southeastern) contends that the clause excludes coverage for all pollution except when the discharge or dispersal of the pollutant occurs abruptly and accidentally. As such, Southeastern asserts that it had no duty to defend or indemnify Dimmitt because the pollution by the actual polluter, Peak Oil Company (Peak), was gradual and occurred over a period of several years.

Both sides also argue that the drafting history of pollution exclusion clauses favors their respective positions. In this regard, it should be noted that comprehensive general liability (CGL) policies are standard insurance policies developed by insurance industry trade associations, and these policies are the primary form of commercial insurance coverage obtained by businesses throughout the country. Before 1966, the standard CGL policy covered only property and personal injury damage that was caused by "accident." In 1966 the insurance industry switched to "occurrence-based" policies in which the term "occurrence" was defined as "'an accident, including continuous or repeated exposure to conditions, which results in bodily injury or property damage neither expected nor intended from the standpoint of the insured.'" Beginning in 1970, the pollution exclusion clause at issue in this case was added to the standard policy. Finally, the policy was again changed in 1984 by the addition of what has been called an "absolute exclusion clause," which totally excludes coverage for pollution clean-up costs that arise from governmental directives. Kenneth S. Abraham, Environmental Liability Insurance Law 161 (1991).

Dimmitt argues that because many state insurance commissioners approved the 1970 addition of the pollution exclusion clause without ordering a reduction in premiums, this indicates that the clause did little more than clarify coverage. Southeastern counters by saying that the reason there was no premium reduction in 1970 was because there had been no premium increase when the coverage was expanded in 1966 to cover occurrences. Both parties also rely on conflicting statements made by insurance representatives who had appeared before state insurance commissions, as well as statements made by other insurance experts.

The policy language at issue here has been the subject of extensive litigation throughout the United States. There is substantial support for both parties' positions. On the one hand, the supreme courts of Colorado, Georgia, West Virginia, and Wisconsin have found the pollution exclusion clause to be ambiguous. In reaching their conclusions, these courts refer to the varying dictionary definitions of the word "sudden." They are also persuaded by the drafting history that the words "sudden and accidental" were intended to mean "unexpected and unintended."

On the other hand, the supreme courts of Massachusetts, Michigan, North Carolina, and Ohio have held that the word "sudden" has a temporal context. Therefore, when the word "sudden" is combined with the word "accidental," the clause means abrupt and unintended. A majority of federal courts of appeal appear to have adopted this view in construing policies in states in which the supreme court of that state has not yet set forth its position.

We are persuaded that the federal district judge properly construed Southeastern's pollution exclusion clause. The ordinary and common usage of the term "sudden" includes a temporal aspect with a sense of immediacy or abruptness. . . .

Dimmitt points to dictionary definitions of "sudden" which also include the meaning of "happening or coming unexpectedly." Dictionaries are helpful insofar as they set forth the ordinary, usual meaning of words. However, as noted in New Castle County v. Hartford Accident & Indemnity

Co., dictionaries are "imperfect yardsticks of ambiguity." 933 F.2d 1162 at 1193-94 (3d Cir. 1991). Our duty is to determine whether the word "sudden" is ambiguous in the context of the specific insurance policy at issue.

The use of the word "sudden" can connote a sense of the unexpected. However, rather than standing alone in the pollution exclusion clause, it is an integral part of the conjunctive phrase "sudden and accidental." The term accidental is generally understood to mean unexpected or unintended. Therefore, to construe sudden also to mean unintended and unexpected would render the words sudden and accidental entirely redundant.

As expressed in the pollution exclusion clause, the word sudden means abrupt and unexpected.

We reject Dimmitt's suggestion that the policy is ambiguous because the term accident is included both within the definition of occurrence and in the pollution exclusion provision.

In the final analysis, we construe this policy to mean that (1) basic coverage arises from the occurrence of unintended damages, but (2) such damages as arise from the discharge of various pollutants are excluded from the basic coverage, except that (3) damages arising from the discharge of these pollutants will fall within the coverage of the policy where such discharge is sudden and accidental.

Because we conclude that the policy language is unambiguous, we find it inappropriate and unnecessary to consider the arguments pertaining to the drafting history of the pollution exclusion clause.

Applying the policy language to the facts of this case, we hold that the pollution damage was not within the scope of Southeastern's policy. The pollution took place over a period of many years and most of it occurred gradually. With respect to the pollution which resulted from oil spills and leaks at the site as well as from occasional runoff of contaminated rain water, we agree with the analysis of the federal district judge in this case when he said: These spills and leaks appear to be common place events which occurred in the course of daily business, and therefore cannot, as a matter of law, be classified as "sudden and accidental." That is, these "occasional accidental spills" are recurring events that took place in the usual course of recycling the oil. . . .

We answer the certified question in the affirmative and return the record to the Eleventh Circuit.

It is so ordered.

Grimes, Justice, concurring.

I originally concurred with the position of the dissenters in this case. I have now become convinced that I relied too much on what was said to be the drafting history of the pollution exclusion clause and perhaps subconsciously upon the social premise that I would rather have insurance companies cover these losses rather than parties such as Dimmitt who did not actually cause the pollution damage. In so doing, I departed from the basic rule of interpretation that language should be given its plain and ordinary meaning. Try as I will, I cannot wrench the words "sudden and accidental" to mean "gradual and accidental," which must be done in order to provide coverage in this case.

Overton, Justice, dissenting.

I dissent. In my view, the majority: (1) ignores key factors in determining that the term "sudden and accidental," as used in comprehensive liability insurance policies, is not ambiguous; (2) fails to consider the facts in this record concerning the intent of the insurance industry in using that term and, consequently, is wrong on the merits . . . .

The Definition of "Sudden and Accidental" . . .

In my view, the term "sudden and accidental" must be found to be ambiguous given that the term is, in fact, subject to more than one interpretation. Although the insurance industry asks that we find the term to be unambiguous, it is clear that the term can mean "unexpected and unintended," a definition not limited as to time of occurrence, in addition to Southeastern's asserted definition of "instantaneous or abrupt." This is especially true when considering the extreme divergence among the numerous jurisdictions considering this issue. As noted, even dictionaries cannot agree as to the primary and secondary meanings of the word "sudden." Notably, however, perhaps the most important illustration of this ambiguity is the definition that the insurance industry itself embraced in regulatory presentations. An examination of the pollution exclusion clause drafting history set forth below unquestionably supports the conclusion that the clause was included only to preclude coverage for intentionally caused pollution damage, not to preclude damage that was "unexpected and unintended."

The Drafting History of Comprehensive General Liability Policies and the Pollution Exclusion Clause

[The dissent retraces the evolution of the standard coverage provision from an accident to an occurrence policy.]

Statements by the insurance industry at that time indicate that the shift to an occurrence-based CGL policy was to "clarify the coverage provided by liability policies, and to avoid the confusion resulting from courts attempting to distinguish between accidental means and accidental results." Additionally, the shift was to clearly indicate that the term "occurrence" included damages caused by "'exposure to conditions which may [have] continue[d] for an unmeasured period of time.'" . . .

On March 17, 1970, the industry again proposed to amend CGL policies to include the pollution exclusion clause at issue in Dimmitt. When the pollution exclusion clause was proposed, representatives of the industry indicated that the new clause was not designed to reduce coverage; instead, it was to ensure that insureds who recklessly and intentionally polluted or who failed to take reasonable precautions to prevent pollution would not be afforded coverage.

[The dissent then reviewed the statements in support of this position made by representatives of the insurance industry in various states.]

The drafting history of the pollution exclusion clause leads to the inescapable conclusion that the insurance industry was attempting to exclude from coverage those polluters who committed their acts intentionally. The record of representations by the insurance industry itself clearly support this conclusion. The addition of the pollution exclusion clause, specifically the term "sudden and accidental" was presented by the insurance industries to the regulators to mean that coverage would continue for those events that were "unexpected and unintended"; the clause's purpose was simply to make clear that intentionally committed pollution would not be covered.

NOTES

1. The battle over the pollution coverage. As *Dimmitt* indicates, state and federal courts have fought a battle royal over the scope of the insurer's responsibility for pollution since the passage of CERCLA in 1980. In general, it appears that the position of the *Dimmitt* majority has been gaining ground. See, e.g., Buell Industries, Inc. v. Greater New York Mutual Insurance Co., 791 A.2d 489 (Conn. 2002): "We emphasize that the focus of the pollution exclusion is on the release or discharge of the pollutants, which must be 'sudden and accidental,' rather than on the damage caused by such an event." One difficulty of the dissenting position in *Dimmitt* is the so-called redundancy problem whereby reading "sudden" to mean "unexpected" adds nothing to the term "accidental," which itself refers to an unexpected happening. In Charter Oil Co. v. American Employers' Insurance Co., 69 F.3d 1160, 1165-1166 (D.C. Cir. 1995), Williams, J., observed:

> Further, even apart from the redundancy problem, reading "sudden" to mean only unexpected presents serious difficulties. In advocating that reading, for instance, the Supreme Court of Georgia reasoned: "[O]n reflection one realizes that, even in its popular usage, 'sudden' does not usually describe the duration of an event, but rather its unexpectedness: a sudden storm, a sudden turn in the road, sudden death." Claussen v. Aetna Casualty & Sur. Co., 380 S. E.2d 686, 688 (Ga. 1989). The instances cited seem unconvincing. A "sudden turn" connotes an abrupt change in direction, one that might still be described as "sudden" by a driver who had traveled the road many times and knew to expect the turn. Likewise, the other two usages seem likely in fact to apply only where the event is abrupt— a spike in an imaginary graph rather than a gentle slope— and any unexpected character seems in large part merely a typical concomitant of the event's being abrupt.

See also Dutton-Lainson v. The Continental Insurance Co., 716 N.W.2d 87, 96 (Neb. 2006), which noted that courts "that have considered the qualified pollution exclusion here presented have generally held that while the burden rests with the insurer to establish the initial applicability of the pollution exclusion by showing the discharge or release of a pollutant into the environment, the burden then shifts to the insured to show that the 'sudden and accidental' exception to that exclusion is applicable." *Dutton* then noted that many courts follow the position of the *Dimmett* dissent. Representative of these is Textron, Inc. v. Aetna Casualty & Surety, 754 A.2d 742, 650 (R.I. 2000), where the insured sued to recover the costs needed to clean up groundwater contamination under CERCLA. Unbeknownst to the plaintiff, some of its toxic waste had leaked from an artificial holding pond only to contaminate the surrounding groundwater. Flanders, J., rebuffed the insurer's effort to rely on a policy exclusion for the release of pollutants, except "if such discharge, dispersal, release or escape is sudden and accidental."

> When used in the context of an insurance policy's pollution-exclusion clause, the word "sudden," we hold, bars coverage for the intentional or reckless polluter but provides coverage to the insured that makes a good-faith effort to contain and to neutralize toxic waste but, nonetheless, still experiences unexpected and unintended releases of toxic chemicals that cause damage. Thus, coverage will be provided when the contamination was unexpected from the insured's standpoint: that is, when the insured reasonably believed that the waste-disposal methods in question were safe. The insured must show that it had no reason to expect the unintended damage and that it undertook reasonable efforts to contain the waste safely. In other words, a manufacturer that uses state-of-the-art technology, adheres to state and federal environmental regulations, and regularly inspects, evaluates, and upgrades its waste-containment system in accordance with advances in available technology should reap the benefits of coverage under our construction of this type of pollution-exclusion clause. But one that knowingly or recklessly disposes of waste without the necessary and advisable precautions will forfeit coverage under this clause.

2. Other coverage issues. The struggle over "suddenness" marks only one coverage battle among many. In some cases, the question is whether some basic coverage applies. One such issue is whether the disputed event falls within the pollution exemption in the first place. In Sulphuric Acid Trading Co, Inc. v. Greenwich Insurance Co., 211 S.W.3d 243, 245-246 (Tenn. 2006), the insured's employee was severely injured when 1,800 gallons of sulphuric acid were sprayed 26 feet into the air after a transloading coupler located on top of a rank tank car broke. The insurer refused to defend the case relying on the following provision:

> This insurance shall not apply to:
> (2) "Bodily injury", "property damage", "personal injury", or "advertising injury" arising out of or in any way related to exposure to pollutants, including but not limited to the inhaling or ingesting of pollutants; . . .

Pollutants means any solid, liquid, gaseous or thermal irritant or contaminant, including but not limited to smoke, vapor, soot, fumes, acid, alkalis, chemicals and waste. Waste includes material to be recycled, reconditioned or reclaimed.

The policyholder's request for a declaratory judgment of coverage was denied on summary judgment. Susano, J., held that:

The Court recognizes that exclusions in insurance contracts will be liberally interpreted in favor of the insured against the insurer if ambiguous . . .

This Court finds no ambiguity in the exclusion as applied to the instant case. The exclusion clearly applies to bodily injury or personal injury such as that suffered by James Gregory Johnson. This incident occurred because of the unintentional discharge or release or escape of a pollutant as defined by the contract, sulphuric acid. The definition of pollutant specifically includes acid. [The Owner] argues that sulphuric acid is not an acid within the definition of the policy. The Court is precluded from creating an ambiguity in an insurance contract where none exists and giving to words meanings other than those ordinarily understood.

Different issues arose in Boeing Co. v. Aetna Casualty & Surety Co., 784 P.2d 507, 511-512 (Wash. 1990), where the insurer claimed that clean up costs under CERCLA were not included in the CGL policy, which was limited to "all sums which the insured shall become legally obligated to pay as damages."

If the state were to sue in court to recover in traditional "damages," including the state's costs incurred in cleaning up the contamination, for the injury to the ground water, defendant's obligation to defend against the lawsuit and to pay damages would be clear. It is merely fortuitous from the standpoint of either plaintiff or defendant that the state has chosen to have plaintiff remedy the contamination problem, rather than choosing to incur the costs of clean-up itself and then suing the plaintiff to recover those costs. The damage to the natural resources is simply measured in the cost to restore the water to its original state.

It is instructive to contrast the coverage for clean-up damages in *Boeing* with the effort of power companies to gain coverage when, pursuant to federal mandate, they install new equipment to minimize their future emissions under the Clean Air Act. In Cinergy v. Associated Electric and Gas Insurance, Inc., 865 N.E.2d 571, 582 (Ind. 2007), Dickson, J., held that these costs were not covered for "the installation costs for equipment to prevent future emissions, is not caused by the *happening* of an accident, event, or exposure to conditions but rather result from the *prevention* of such an occurrence. . . . Notwithstanding our preference to construe ambiguous insurance policy language strictly and against the insurer, we discern no ambiguity here that would permit the occurrence requirement reasonably to be understood to allow coverage for damages in the form of installation costs for government-mandated equipment intended to reduce future emissions of pollutants and to prevent future environmental harm."

See generally Ballard and Manus, Clearing Muddy Waters: Anatomy of the Comprehensive General Liability Pollution Exclusion, 75 Cornell L. Rev. 610 (1990).

Next, in many coverage disputes courts are prepared to read in implied conditions that they think comport with the overall expectations of the parties. Thus, in Fayad v. Clarendon National Insurance Co, 899 So. 2d 1082, 1084 (2005), the insurer asserted that certain damage from blasting was covered by an exclusion for in a homeowner's policy for "earth movement, meaning earthquake, including land shock waves or tremors before, during or after a volcanic eruption; landslide; mine subsidence; mudflow; earth sinking, rising or shifting." The court, however, held that "well-established principles of insurance contract interpretation" required the exclusion to be limited to earth movements triggered by natural events, not human actions, including blasting. Accordingly, it held that the insurer's all-risk policy covered the claimed losses. Should it make a difference whether the third party is, or is not, liable for the blasting damage?

Last, will the absolute pollution exclusion cover liabilities for global warming attributable to carbon dioxide emissions, which are now in principle subject to direct regulation under by the Environmental Protection Agency, after Massachusetts v. EPA, 127 S. Ct. 1438 (2007)? For an argument that "most companies' Commercial General Liability ('CGL') policies will provide coverage for liabilities resulting from contributions to global warming, and that coverage for these liabilities will ultimately benefit consumers," see Note, The Price of Emission: Will Liability Insurance Cover Damages Resulting From Global Warming?, 19 Loyola Com. L Rev. 468 (2007).

3. *Triggers for coverage under the CGL.* The question of initial coverage for most injuries does not present any difficulty in the ordinary case of traumatic injury, which, like the "sudden and accidental" discharge, is confined to a single period. But finding the proper trigger or triggers for coverage gives rise to major interpretive difficulties in so-called cumulative trauma cases where the period between initial exposure and the first manifestation of bodily injury or property damage spans several policy periods. In general, it is possible to identify four distinct rules (each with its own variations) that could be used to resolve these coverage difficulties. First, the so-called exposure or pro-ration approach apportions the cost of indemnity over the entire period between the initial exposure and the first manifestation of illness or disease. See, e.g., Insurance Co. of North America v. Forty-Eight Insulations, Inc., 633 F.2d 1212 (6th Cir. 1980),

modified, 657 F.2d 814 (6th Cir. 1981), which prorated indemnity and defense coverage across the entire period from initial exposure to the defendant's asbestos to the manifestation of disease. It left the insured at risk for periods in which no coverage had been purchased or available coverage had been exhausted. A second approach ties the coverage to the moment at which the plaintiff first manifested symptoms of an asbestos-related disease and, as is the case with ordinary accidents, covers each tort dispute to a single insurance policy. See Eagle-Picher Industries, Inc. v. Liberty Mutual Insurance Co., 682 F.2d 12 (1st Cir. 1982). A third position — the continuous trigger or "triple trigger" view — championed in Keene v. Insurance Co. of North America, 667 F.2d 1034 (D.C. Cir. 1981), quickly became the industry benchmark for future settlement negotiations. The triple trigger lets the insured elect to assign the loss to any policy in effect at the time of initial exposure, at first manifestation, or at any time in between. Fourth, an injury in fact trigger ties coverage to that point in time where some actual injury to the person can be identified. In general, this position offers more limited protection than the basic continuous trigger test because it excludes from coverage at least some fraction of the exposure period.

Most courts have adopted some form of the exposure or continuous trigger approaches. In Montrose Chemical Corp. v. Admiral Insurance Co., 913 P.2d 878, 902-903 (Cal. 1995), Lucas, C.J., opted for the continuous trigger approach. He first noted that "courts will generally apply equitable considerations to spread the cost among the several policies and insurers," noted that the expanded coverage implied by the term "occurrence" meant that

> they specifically considered and rejected the suggestion that language establishing a manifestation or discovery trigger of coverage be incorporated into the standard form CGL policy. Among the reasons relied on for rejecting the incorporation of such limitations into the standard definitions in the coverage clauses were several stated equitable concerns: the difficulty of applying such limitations or requirements in cases of continuing damage or injury over the course of successive policy periods, the uncertainty of who would bear the burden of a discovery requirement (i.e., the insured or third party claimants), the arbitrariness, from the carrier's perspective, of telescoping all damage in a continuing injury case into a single policy period, and the fear that policyholders could be disadvantaged by such an approach. . . .
>
> Finally, we agree with Montrose that application of a manifestation trigger of coverage to an occurrence-based CGL policy would unduly transform it into a "claims made" policy. Claims made policies were specifically developed to limit an insurer's risk by restricting coverage to the single policy in effect at the time a claim was asserted against the insured, without regard to the timing of the damage or injury, thus permitting the carrier to establish reserves without regard to possibilities of inflation, upward-spiraling jury

awards, or enlargements of tort liability after the policy period. . . . We agree with the conclusion of the Court of Appeal below that to apply a manifestation trigger of coverage to Admiral's occurrence-based CGL policies would be to effectively rewrite Admiral's contracts of insurance with Montrose, transforming the broader and more expensive occurrence-based CGL policy into a claims made policy.

Note that under the triple trigger theory, the insurer that supplies coverage on January 1, 1990, for instance, must, if requested, supply full coverage for all cases in which any exposure prior to that date manifests itself in damages after that date no matter how short a time its policy was in effect. Does Lucas, C.J., explain why the triple trigger theory should be preferred to the proration theory of *Forty-Eight Insulations*? Should the triple trigger theory be rejected on the grounds that it allocates the insured to allocate losses to the most favorable coverage period after it knows the distribution and severity of all relevant claims? For a defense of the first manifestation position, see Epstein, The Legal and Insurance Dynamics of Mass Tort Litigation, 13 J. Legal Stud. 475, 495-505 (1984); for a defense of Keene's triple trigger see Note, Adjudicating Asbestos Insurance Liability: Alternatives to Contract Analysis, 97 Harv. L. Rev. 739 (1984). See generally, Fischer, Insurance Coverage for Mass Exposure Tort Claims: The Debate Over the Appropriate Trigger Rule, 45 Drake L. Rev. 625 (1997).

2. Automobile Insurance Coverage

a. The March to Compulsory Insurance

Notwithstanding the enormous coverage battles arising from modern pollution and mass torts, much of the day-to-day business of insurance coverage still involves disputes arising out of automobile accidents. Unlike the commercial disputes, individual drivers, having only limited resources, had strong incentives not to take out any coverage at all or, alternatively, to purchase indemnity policies of the sort upheld in Bain v. Atkins, 63 N.E. 414 (Mass. 1902), *supra* at 930. The broad dissatisfaction with indemnity policies led to a movement to require automobile insurance that gave genuine protection to injured third parties. Starting in the 1920s, many states passed so-called financial responsibility statutes that required individuals to show that they were financially able, within certain stated limits, to satisfy tort judgments against them. Since the mechanisms of enforcement were unclear, some states passed security responsibility statutes that allowed a driver to renew a driver's license only on a showing that they could make available assets above the stated limits to meet these tort claims.

These financial and security responsibility statutes did not explicitly require individuals to take out insurance, even though most people did. Starting in the 1930s, a compulsory insurance movement, which was promptly challenged on constitutional grounds, picked up steam,. These challenges were rebuffed as early as 1925 by the Massachusetts Supreme Judicial Court, which in In re Opinion of the Justices, 147 N.E. 681, 693, 694 (Mass. 1925), held that the general power to exclude automobiles from the public highways "includes the lesser power to grant the right to use public ways only upon the observance of prescribed conditions precedent." The court sanctioned this "extension of the police power into a new field" because the conditions imposed could not be "pronounced unreasonable" given the need to assure innocent persons full compensation for their accidents.

One major tension in compulsory insurance regime arises when an insured makes false and fraudulent statements to an insurer that are sufficient to allow for prompt cancellation of coverage. Yet once an accident has taken place, the common view is that, now that third party interests have intervened, the time for cancellation is past with respect to the statutory minimums, but not to any voluntary excess. See Odum v. Nationwide Mutual Insurance Co., 401 S.E.2d 87, 90 (N.C. App. 1991), construing N.C. Gen. Stat. §20-279.21(f), which stipulates that "the insurance required by this Article shall become absolute whenever injury or damage covered by said motor vehicle liability policy occurs." What recourse, if any, does the insurer have against the insured?

A second major problem with the compulsory insurance laws concerns the treatment of individuals whose risk profiles are so grim that they cannot purchase any insurance in the voluntary market. The usual legislative response places risky individuals in an "assigned risk" pool. All of the insurance companies doing business within the state must insure some fraction of the total pool, usually based on their market share within the state and at rates substantially above those charged to their regular customers. In California State Automobile Association Inter-Insurance Bureau v. Maloney, 341 U.S. 105 (1951), the Supreme Court upheld those assigned risk provisions (here in the context of the California financial responsibility statutes) against various constitutional challenges. It noted that the wisdom of those enactments was for the legislature to determine. Instead of requiring insurance companies to cover risky drivers, would it be better to ban all uninsured drivers? What happens if the rates set for the assigned risk pool are below that for the voluntary market for some drivers? For an account of the difficulties of rate regulation, see Epstein, A Clash of Two Cultures: Will the Tort System Survive Automobile Insurance Reform?, 25 Val. U. L. Rev. 173 (1991). See generally R. Keeton and A. Widiss, Insurance Law §4.10(b) (1988); Note, Withdrawal Restrictions in the Automobile Insurance Market, 102 Yale L.J. 1431 (1993). For an attack on insurance rate regulation, see Earhart, Lifting the Iron Curtain of Automobile Insurance Regulation, 49 S.C. L. Rev. 1193, 1201 (1998).

The strain that automobile insurance coverage placed on family budgets motivated California voters to adopt by a hard fought popular referendum, Proposition 103 in 1989, which extensively revised how insurance companies operated in California. The initiative was described in these terms by the California Supreme Court in Calfarm Insurance Co. v. Deukmejian, 771 P.2d 1247, 1250, 1254 (Cal. 1989):

> Insurance rates are to be immediately reduced to "at least 20 percent less" than those in effect on November 8, 1987 (approximately the date when the initiative was proposed, and one year prior to its enactment). All rate increases require the approval of the Insurance Commissioner, who may not approve rates which are "excessive, inadequate, unfairly discriminatory, or otherwise in violation of [the initiative]." Prior to November 8, 1989, however, rates may be increased only if the commissioner finds "that an insurer is substantially threatened with insolvency." "Certain procedures are specified for hearing applications for rate approval."

The California Supreme Court upheld the basic initiative, but struck down, as a taking under the due process clause, its critical provision allowing a rate increase before November 1989 only upon a showing of a substantial threat of insolvency.

> The insolvency standard of subdivision (b) refers to the financial position of the company as a whole, not merely to the regulated lines of insurance. Many insurers do substantial business outside of California, or in lines of insurance within this state which are not regulated by Proposition 103. If an insurer had substantial net worth, or significant income from sources unregulated by Proposition 103, it might be able to sustain substantial and continuing losses on regulated insurance without danger of insolvency. In such a case the continued solvency of the insurer could not suffice to demonstrate that the regulated rate constitutes a fair return.

More generally, what justification, if any, exists for imposing rate-of-return regulation in a competitive industry? For the Supreme Court's most recent pronouncements on the constitutionality of various systems of rate regulation, see Duquesne Light Co. v. Barasch, 488 U.S. 299 (1989); Verizon Communications, Inc. v. Federal Communications Commission, 535 U.S. 467 (2002).

b.   The Standard Provisions of the Automobile Insurance Contract

Automobile insurance polices contain specialized provisions that merit some brief attention.

i.   Omnibus Clauses

The so-called omnibus clause provides:

> The following are insureds [for tort liability] with respect to the owned au-
> tomobile, (1) the named insured and any resident of the same household;
> (2) any other person using such automobile with the permission of the
> named insured, provided his actual operation or (if he is not operating) his
> actual use thereof is within the scope of such permission. . . .

For one variation, see, e.g., Cal. Ins. Code §11580.1(4). As drafted, the
clause provides the owner protection under circumstances in which he
might be held vicariously liable as an employer. It also protects the owner
from any liability under either the owner consent statutes or the family
purpose doctrine, when some nonemployee uses the owner's vehicle with
his consent or for his benefit.

The distinctive feature of the clause, however, protects the owner when
his car is used with his permission by third parties, even if the owner is not
liable. It is a case of insurance beyond liability. In some cases, the injured
party seeks to reach the owner's policy under an omnibus clause when the
injury is caused by the negligence of someone who did not drive with
the owner's permission, but only with the permission of, as is common, the
owner's children who were prohibited from lending the car to third persons. In Hays v. Country Mutual Insurance Co., 192 N.E.2d 855, 859 (Ill.
1963), Schaefer, J., adopted the general principle that the contract controls
unless the state legislature overrides it for the benefit of third parties. He
thus refused to read

> the requirement of permission out of the insurance contract on the ground
> that it is wholly purposeless, technical, and fortuitous. When the insured
> purchases extended coverage he seeks to protect those whom he allows to
> use his car from the risks of financial disaster as he would guard them against
> danger from mechanical defects. Ordinarily he has no interest in buying
> protection for those who use his car without permission. The insurer, on the
> other hand, limits the risk assumed by requiring permission, since usually
> the insured will use discretion in permitting others to use his car, if only as a
> matter of self-interest in avoiding damage to his property. As a matter of
> probability based on experience with policyholders as a group, we cannot say
> that the limitation to users who have the insured's permission carries no
> actuarial significance.

Schaefer's approach was limited in Maryland Casualty Co. v. Iowa
National Mutual Insurance Co., 297 N.E.2d 163, 168 (Ill. 1973), which held
"that once the initial permission has been given by the named insured,

coverage is fixed, barring theft or the like." U.S. Fidelity & Guaranty Co. v. McManus, 356 N.E.2d 78 (Ill. 1976), subsequently held that once an owner gave initial permission to a third person, the insurer was liable when that person allowed still other people to use the car without the permission or knowledge of the automobile owner. For a discussion of the application of these insurance principles to rental companies, see Chapter 5, Section C.

How should the omnibus clause be interpreted whenever a driver who receives permission to use the car for one particular purpose uses it for quite another? The court in Branch v. United States Fidelity & Guaranty Co., 198 F.2d 1007, 1009 (6th Cir. 1952), responded as follows:

> The construction and application of the omnibus clause in automobile liability insurance policies have been the subject of much litigation throughout the country. The Courts are divided in their holdings into three general groups: (1) the so-called strict rule, which denies coverage if the driver departs from the intended purposes of the owner; (2) the minor deviation rule holding that the policy covers the driver of the car if the deviation is slight; and (3) the so-called liberal rule which holds that the policy covers the driver although he deviates from the intended purposes of the owner, if he originally obtained possession with the owner's permission.

The modern trend is clearly in favor of the broad initial permission rule. For a collection of cases on all sides of the issue, see Commercial Union Insurance Co. v. Johnson, 745 S.W.2d 589 (Ark. 1988).

ii.   "Drive the Other Car" Clauses

A "drive the other car clause" gives the owner of an insured car (and normally the owner's spouse) liability coverage while driving another car, usually on a casual or occasional basis. See, e.g., Hochgurtel v. San Felippo, 253 N.W.2d 526 (Wis. 1977). This clause is often in tension with the omnibus clause, which makes coverage run with the vehicle, while the drive the other car clause makes it run with the driver. If each insurance policy says that its liability is secondary to that contained in other policies, then the insured with two ostensible coverages might be left with no coverage at all. This conclusion has been stoutly resisted by the courts. See, e.g., American Automobile Insurance Co. v. Penn Mutual Indemnity Co., 161 F.2d 62 (3d Cir. 1947), which held that primary coverage lay with the "drive the other car" policy. The dispute is now resolved by the language of the standard automobile policy, under which the omnibus clause is treated as the primary policy. See generally I. Schermer & W. Schermer, Automobile Liability Insurance §3:9 (4th ed. 2004).

iii. Uninsured Motorist Coverage

Automobile insurance contracts now commonly provide that the insurance company will pay limited sums of money to its own insured who is harmed by an uninsured motorist, or UIM, who is legally responsible for the accident. To guard against the possibility of collusion between the insured and the uninsured motorist, these provisions stipulate that the insurance company is bound by a judgment that the insured obtains against the uninsured motorist only with its approval. The coverage runs in favor of the insured, his immediate family, and any other person injured while occupying the insured's automobile.

"Within uninsured motorist insurance, third-party liability rights are implemented through a first-party insurance system." G. Schwartz, A Proposal for Tort Reform: Reformulating Uninsured Motorist Plans, 48 Ohio St. L.J. 419, 425 (1987). Accordingly, coverage extends to pain and suffering and punitive damages, even though these are not normally purchased in first-party settings. To avoid these anomalies and reduce premiums, Schwartz suggests that this coverage be configured along the lines of standard first-party policies, since this insurance can serve no sensible deterrent function.

Uninsured motorist policies treat the *under*insured motorist like an uninsured motorist to the extent of the shortfall in coverage. Complications can arise if an injured person is harmed by two persons, one of whom is uninsured. In Victor v. State Farm Fire & Casualty Co., 908 P.2d 1043 (Alaska 1996), the uninsured motorist was responsible for $225,000 in losses. The motorist had recovered $50,000 from the second driver and had an uninsured motorist policy of $100,000. The court held that State Farm could not deduct the $50,000 paid by a second driver from its UIM policy limits. "Generally, the intent of the statutes mandating UIM coverage is to afford a person injured in an accident caused by an uninsured motorist the same benefits that the victim would have had if injured by an identifiable motorist covered by an applicable standard automobile liability insurance policy." Since that party could not claim any credit for the $50,000 paid over by the settling defendant, neither could the UIM carrier.

Coverage also applies in those cases in which "an unidentified accident-causing" motorist is involved, whether or not that party actually has insurance. See Lowing v. Allstate Insurance Co., 859 P.2d 724 (Ariz. 1993). The problem of underinsurance has been also addressed explicitly in legislation, with a small handful of states mandating the coverage while in most states the coverage need merely be offered. See, e.g., Ariz. Rev. Stat. Ann. 20-259.01 (2002). Punitive damages are not normally covered. See Bodner v. United Services Automobile Ass'n, 610 A.2d 1212 (Conn. 1992). See also 3 A. Widiss, Uninsured and Underinsured Motorist Insurance ch. 32 (3d ed. 2005).

One oft-litigated problem with the uninsured motorist provisions concerns the role of "stacking." Thus, an insured may take out two or more insurance policies each of which provides uninsured motorist coverage for an injured person paid for by a separate premium. If the driver of the other car is uninsured, is the insured entitled to recover the full amount from each policy both for general damages and particular medical expenses? In Descoteaux v. Liberty Mutual Insurance Co., 480 A.2d 14, 19 (N.H. 1984), the court allowed recovery of the full limits under both policies even though both policies contained language (in a drive the other car clause) that purported to limit the plaintiff to the coverage of a single policy without specifying which. "Since the legislature created an option for additional coverage, it intended that those choosing to buy increased protection should receive its benefits." Many statutes limit the uninsured motorist to the single policy with the highest limit. Tenn. Code Ann. §56-7-1201 (b)(1) (2007) . For a detailed examination of the many variations on this theme, see 3 A. Widiss, Uninsured and Underinsured Motorist Insurance §34 (3d ed. 2005).

iv. Medical Payments

Many current policies allow payment for medical expenses even before any dispute about liability is resolved. Thus, one common clause states that the insurance company will pay, within the limits specified by the policy, "expenses incurred by the insured for such immediate medical and surgical relief to others as shall be imperative at the time of an accident involving an automobile insured hereunder and not due to war...." Courts have often placed a liberal construction on the clause, noting that, in the words of an Illinois appellate court, "the basic purpose of medical pay provisions such as here involved is to make available a fund to assure prompt and adequate medical care when injury is incurred, to relieve the physical suffering of the insured and to relieve the insured of the anxiety of not knowing from what source the money to pay the bills is coming." Jackson v. Country Mutual Insurance Co., 190 N.E.2d 490, 492 (Ill. App. 1963). Typically, these payments are credited against any judgment or settlement, but they are not recoverable in the event that the insured is not held liable. Edwards v. Passarelli Bros. Automotive Service, Inc., 221 N.E.2d 708 (Ohio 1966).

A second form of medical benefit requires the insurance company to pay "all reasonable expenses incurred within one year from the date of accident for necessary medical, surgical, X-ray and dental services, including prosthetic devices and necessary ambulance, hospital, professional nursing and funeral services." Clauses of this sort contain explicit dollar limitations and benefit not only the insured and members of his immediate family, but also all persons in the insured's car with his permission, whether or not the insured is ultimately found at fault.

v. *Misrepresentation and Nondisclosure*

An insurance company is entitled to set aside any policy that the insured has obtained through either misrepresentation or nondisclosure of a material fact. These rules apply to all insurance contracts, and were first introduced with marine insurance under the general rubric of good faith, as way to combat the problem of asymmetrical information, where the insured was likely to know more about the status of the risk than the insurer. As stated by Bayley, J., "I think that in all cases of insurance, whether or ships, houses or lives the underwrite should be informed of every material circumstance within the knowledge of the assured; and that the proper question is, whether any particular circumstance was in fact material, not whether the party believed it to be so." Lindenau v. Desborough, 108 Eng. Rep. 1160, 1162 (K.B. 1828). Today, these obligations have contractual status as well because insurers reserve explicitly the right to rescind the policy if there has been misrepresentation or nondisclosure of a material fact. These contracts can usually be set aside if the applicant conceals the identity of all the owners of a vehicle, the driving history of the insured, the place where the car is garaged, or previous cancellations of coverage. See, e.g., Safeway Insurance Co. v. Duran, 393 N.E.2d 688 (Ill. App. 1979).

Judges often invoke a number of doctrines to cushion injured parties from the harsh consequences of the misrepresentation rules, most notably waiver and estoppel. In a waiver the insurer expressly, or by its conduct impliedly, gives up a known privilege or power otherwise available under the policy. For an estoppel the insured changes his position in reliance upon representations, by word or conduct, of the insurance company to make it inequitable to permit the insurer to deny the truth of the representations.

vi. *Notice and Cooperation*

Two of the most typical clauses found in insurance contracts govern notice and cooperation. The typical notice clauses provide as follows:

> *Notice of accident.* When an accident occurs written notice shall be given by or on behalf of the insured to the company or any of its authorized agents as soon as practicable. Such notice shall contain particulars sufficient to identify the insured and also reasonably obtainable information respecting the time, place and circumstances of the accident, the names and addresses of the injured and of available witnesses.

> *Notice of claim or suit.* If claim is made or suit is brought against the insured, the insured shall immediately forward to the company every demand, notice, summons or other process received by him or his representative.

These clauses allow an insurance company adequate time to investigate the accident or claim in question. The most commonly litigated question under them is whether an insurance company must show actual prejudice to decline coverage or whether prejudice should be presumed from the fact of delay. The automatic rule avoids an expensive inquiry into causation, but at the price of allowing an insurer to avoid coverage for an insured's inconsequential delay in notification. What should be said for (or against) a rule that any failure to notify within 30 days shall be treated as immaterial, while any failure to notify after 30 days shall be treated as prejudicial?

The typical cooperation clause found in a standard insurance policy reads as follows:

> *Assistance and cooperation of the insured.* The insured shall cooperate with the company and, upon the company's request, shall attend hearings and trials and shall assist in effecting settlements, securing and giving evidence, obtaining the attendance of witnesses and in the conduct of suits. The insured shall not, except at his own cost, voluntarily make any payment, assume any obligation or incur any expense other than for such immediate medical and surgical relief to others as shall be imperative at the time of accident.

One common question under the cooperation clause is whether the insured has breached its terms by, for example, admitting liability either orally or in writing to the injured party, or fleeing the scene of an accident. A second question is whether the lack of cooperation prejudices the insurer, which brings forth the same division of opinion found with notice clauses: Does a minor breach by the insured excuses an insurer from all liability? The more common answer is that substantial prejudice must be shown to avoid liability on the policy. Thus, in M.F.A. Mutual Insurance Co. v. Cheek, 363 N.E.2d 809 (Ill. 1977), the court allowed coverage when an insured corrected his initial failure to notify in a "timely" fashion. In contrast, in Ramos v. Northwestern Mutual Insurance Co., 336 So. 2d 71, 75 (Fla. 1976), the insured never contacted the insurer after the accident, failed to report the accident, failed to notify the insurer of any change in address, and generally disappeared. The plaintiff urged that the insurer should be held liable regardless of the misbehavior of the insured to advance the objectives of Florida's financial responsibility laws. But the court adhered to its traditional view that released the insurer from its obligations, so long as the failure to cooperate "constitutes a material breach and substantially prejudices the right of the insurer in defense of the cause." For a detailed discussion of all these clauses, see R. Keeton and A. Widiss, Insurance Law §4.9 (1988).

SECTION C.   AMBIGUITIES IN THE POSITION OF THE LIABILITY INSURER

The ordinary liability policy provides not only that the company will pay on behalf of the insured all sums the insured becomes legally obligated to pay for personal injury or property damage, but, perhaps equally important, it also provides: "the company shall defend any suit alleging such bodily injury or property damage — even if any of the allegations of the suit are groundless, false or fraudulent; but the company may make such investigation and settlement of any claim or suit as it deems expedient."

As a result, there are two key consequences: (1) The insurer obligates itself to handle the claim and to defend against it even when the risk of ultimate liability is low; (2) The insurer obtains control of both litigation and settlement. These two consequences underscore a principal practical benefit in having liability insurance — an experienced party is in charge of litigation, and bonds its performance by agreeing to pay damages in the event of an adverse outcome. Usually, however, the insurer will not take on the risk of infinite liability, but imposes contractual limits on its assumed risk. These limitations create a conflict of interest between the insurer and insured, which may break the united front that they prefer to present to the tort plaintiff. The major source of conflict arises in setting the scope of the duty to defend and enforcing the insurer's obligation to settle claims in good faith.

1.   The Duty to Defend

One key question that faces an insurer is whether the underlying events of the accident fall within the policy's basic coverage and, if it does, whether it is covered by any policy exclusion. The problem is often difficult in practice because the decision to defend often has to be made before the full facts of the case are known, often on the strength of the allegations in the plaintiff's tort complaint. Just these problems were presented in Evanston Insurance Co. v. Adkins, 2006 U.S. Dist. LEXIS 73746 (N.D. Tex. 2006), where Adkins's small firm was doing welding work on a TXI site at which a fire broke out for which he was allegedly responsible. The fire originated when molten particles from the welding twice came in contact with an exposed "polypropylene mist eliminator" (or "demister"). The first blaze was detected and extinguished, but it was hypothesized that a second incident from which the fire later arose went undetected. The defendant insurer denied that it had a duty to defend Atkins on the ground that the underlying lawsuit by TXI only alleged "economic" damages which were not covered by the policy which did, however, cover various forms of "property" damage. The insurer also claimed that the policy's "absolute pollution exclusion," inter alia, similar to that in *Sulphuric Acid, supra* at 937, excluded the coverage for the waste that triggered the fire. In assessing Evanston's duty to defend, Lindsay, J., wrote:

> TXI seeks a declaration of coverage for the underlying state court claims. Evanston asserts that TXI's underlying lawsuit only alleges economic damages not covered by the policy or, alternatively, that four exclusions in the policy apply to exclude coverage. In determining whether an insurer has a duty to defend, the court must examine the pleading upon which the insurer based its refusal to defend the action. Texas courts follow the "eight corners" rule, which requires the trier of fact to examine only the allegations in the underlying complaint and the insurance policy, without reference to their veracity.
>
> In reviewing the underlying pleadings, the court must focus on the factual allegations that show the origin of the damages rather than on the legal theories alleged. The allegations in the underlying petition are to be interpreted liberally, resolving any doubt in favor of the insured. The duty to defend arises when the facts alleged in the petition, if taken as true, potentially state a cause of action within the terms of the policy. Thus, it is the insured's burden to show that the claim against it is potentially within the policy's coverage. An insurer has an obligation to defend an insured if the petition alleges at least one cause of action within the policy's coverage. If, however, under the facts alleged, there is a *prima facie* showing that the claim is not covered under the policy, the insurer has no duty to defend.

Applying this standard, the court held that the duty to defend arose for factual allegations contained in the complaint explicitly "alleges *physical* damage to TXI property and a loss of use of that property for twenty-seven days," such that coverage attached, even if some elements of damage were caught by the policy exclusions.

What ought to be done if the insurer takes up the defense while having genuine doubts on the question of coverage? In Maryland Casualty Co. v. Peppers, 355 N.E.2d 24, 28-29 (Ill. 1976), the insured, Peppers, shot Mims, a suspected burglar, and demanded protection under two policies, one issued by the St. Paul's Fire & Marine Insurance Company, and the other by Maryland Casualty. Each policy excluded from coverage harms that were intentionally inflicted by the insured. Ryan, J., first concluded that the insurer was obligated to defend so long as "one of which is within the coverage of a policy while the others may not be."

> It is generally held that an insurer may be estopped from asserting a defense of noncoverage when the insurer undertakes the defense of an action against the insured. However, it is also the general rule that the undertaking must result in some prejudice to the insured. . . .
>
> Whether an insured is prejudiced by an insurer's conduct in entering an appearance and assuming the defense of an action is a question of fact. Prejudice will not be conclusively presumed from the mere entry of appearance and assumption of the defense. If, however, by the insurer's assumption of the defense the insured has been induced to surrender his right to control his own defense, he has suffered a prejudice which will support a finding that the insurer is estopped to deny policy coverage.

He then concluded that the trial judge could find that the insurer was not estopped because "[t]here is nothing in the record to establish that Peppers was not at all times represented by his own attorney, Massa, or that in reliance on the attorneys hired by St. Paul he was induced to surrender the right to conduct his own defense."

The scope of the defense obligation extends to all claims, not only valid or strong ones. In reversing the judgment below denying the duty to defend, Mikva, J., gave this explanation of the coverage provision in Continental Casualty Co. v. Cole, 809 F.2d 891, 898 (D.C. Cir. 1987):

> The main purpose of the defense clause and the "groundless, false, and fraudulent allegations" language is to shift to the insurer the burden of defending against any and all attempts to assess liability against the insured which are based on covered activities. To follow the district court's reasoning would, in those instances in which an ultimate award of damages appears unlikely, place the insured in the difficult position of having to choose between two unappealing alternatives: pay for its own defense to protect against the possibility, no matter how remote, that damages might be awarded; or sit idle and do nothing in uneasy reliance on the insurer's promises that damages cannot possibly be awarded. The insured, who has paid for coverage, should not be required to make this choice.

When the insurer has wrongly refused to defend, and the insured has settled the case on its own account, what damages can the insured recover from its own insurer? In American Motorists Insurance Co. v. Trane Co., 718 F.2d 842, 845 (7th Cir. 1983), the court affirmed a district court's order providing for "indemnification for covered claims and costs associated with defending" them. The court refused to require the insurance carrier to pay the full extent of the insured's damages where these exceeded the face value of the policy, noting that insurers "may refuse to defend suits and seek declaratory judgments without risking liability for the underlying suit's entire judgment—a risk so high as to coerce insurers to defend actions that they are not obligated to defend." What result when the insurer refuses to settle a covered claim within policy limits?

2. The Obligation to Act in Good Faith

Crisci v. Security Insurance Co.
426 P.2d 173 (Cal. 1967)

Peters, J. In an action against The Security Insurance Company of New Haven, Connecticut, the trial court awarded Rosina Crisci $91,000 (plus interest) because she suffered a judgment in a personal injury action after Security, her insurer, refused to settle the claim. . . . Security has appealed.

[Mrs. Crisci's tenants, June Dimare and her husband, brought suit for physical injuries and severe psychosis when Dimare was hurt on the premises after she fell through a broken step and was left hanging 15 feet above the ground. Mrs. Crisci had an insurance policy with Security for $10,000 with the usual defense obligations. After much negotiation, Security refused to settle the case for the policy limit even though the underlying claim was for $400,000. At trial, the jury awarded Mrs. Dimare $100,000 and her husband $1,000. Security paid its $10,000 policy limit. Mrs. Crisci could not pay the remaining $91,000 in cash, so she entered into a settlement in which she transferred some property to Mrs. DiMare, including her right to sue Security for the $91,000 in excess of policy limits.]

The liability of an insurer in excess of its policy limits for failure to accept a settlement offer within those limits was considered by this court in Comunale v. Traders & General Ins. Co., 328 P.2d 198 (Cal. 1958). It was there reasoned that in every contract, including policies of insurance, there is an implied covenant of good faith and fair dealing that neither party will do anything which will injure the right of the other to receive the benefits of the agreement; that it is common knowledge that one of the usual methods by which an insured receives protection under a liability insurance policy is by settlement of claims without litigation; that the implied obligation of good faith and fair dealing requires the insurer to settle in an appropriate case although the express terms of the policy do not impose the duty; that in determining whether to settle the insurer must give the interests of the insured at least as much consideration as it gives to its own interests; and that when "there is great risk of a recovery beyond the policy limits so that the most reasonable manner of disposing of the claim is a settlement which can be made within those limits, a consideration in good faith of the insured's interest requires the insurer to settle the claim."

In determining whether an insurer has given consideration to the interests of the insured, the test is whether a prudent insurer without policy limits would have accepted the settlement offer. . . .

Several cases, in considering the liability of the insurer, contain language to the effect that bad faith is the equivalent of dishonesty, fraud, and concealment. Obviously a showing that the insurer has been guilty of actual dishonesty, fraud, or concealment is relevant to the determination whether it has given consideration to the insured's interest in considering a settlement offer within the policy limits. The language used in the cases, however, should not be understood as meaning that in the absence of evidence establishing actual dishonesty, fraud, or concealment no recovery may be had for a judgment in excess of the policy limits. *Comunale* makes it clear that liability based on an implied covenant exists whenever the insurer refuses to settle in an appropriate case and that liability may exist when the insurer unwarrantedly refuses an offered settlement where the most reasonable manner of disposing of the claim is by accepting the settlement. Liability is imposed not for a bad faith breach of the contract but for failure to meet the duty to accept reasonable settlements, a duty included within the implied covenant of good faith and fair dealing. Moreover, examination of the balance of [our prior] opinions makes it abundantly clear that recovery may be based on unwarranted rejection of a reasonable settlement offer and that the absence of evidence, circumstantial or direct, showing actual dishonesty, fraud, or concealment is not fatal to the cause of action.

Amicus curiae argues that, whenever an insurer receives an offer to settle within the policy limits and rejects it, the insurer should be liable in every case for the amount of any final judgment whether or not within the policy limits. As we have seen, the duty of the insurer to consider the insured's interest in settlement offers within the policy limits arises from an implied covenant in the contract, and ordinarily contract duties are strictly enforced and not subject to a standard of reasonableness. Obviously, it will always be in the insured's interest to settle within the policy limits when there is any danger, however slight, of a judgment in excess of those limits. Accordingly the rejection of a settlement within the limits where there is any danger of a judgment in excess of the limits can be justified, if at all, only on the basis of interests of the insurer, and, in light of the common knowledge that settlement is one of the usual methods by which an insured receives protection under a liability policy, it may not be unreasonable for an insured who purchases a policy with limits to believe that a sum of money equal to the limits is available and will be used so as to avoid liability on his part with regard to any covered accident. In view of such expectation an insurer should not be permitted to further its own interests by rejecting opportunities to settle within the policy limits unless it is also willing to absorb losses which may result from its failure to settle.

The proposed rule is a simple one to apply and avoids the burdens of a determination whether a settlement offer within the policy limits was reasonable. The proposed rule would also eliminate the danger that an insurer, faced with a settlement offer at or near the policy limits, will reject it and gamble with the insured's money to further its own interests. Moreover, it is not entirely clear that the proposed rule would place a burden on insurers substantially greater than that which is present under existing law. The size of the judgment recovered in the personal injury action when it exceeds the policy limits, although not conclusive, furnishes an inference that the value of the claim is the equivalent of the amount of the judgment and that acceptance of an offer within those limits was the most reasonable method of dealing with the claim.

Finally, and most important, there is more than a small amount of elementary justice in a rule that would require that, in this situation where the insurer's and insured's interests necessarily conflict, the insurer, which may reap the benefits of its determination not to settle, should also suffer the detriments of its decision. On the basis of these and other considerations, a number of commentators have urged that the insurer should be liable for any resulting judgment where it refuses to settle within the policy limits. . . .

We need not, however, here determine whether there might be some countervailing considerations precluding adoption of the proposed rule because, under Comunale v. Traders & General Ins. Co., and the cases following it, the evidence is clearly sufficient to support the determination that Security breached its duty to consider the interests of Mrs. Crisci in proposed settlements [owing to the inherent uncertainty in all psychiatric evidence].

The trial court found that defendant "knew that there was a considerable risk of substantial recovery beyond said policy limits" and that "the defendant did not give as much consideration to the financial interests of its said insured as it gave to its own interests." That is all that was required. The award of $91,000 must therefore be affirmed.

NOTES

1. *Conflicts of interest between insurer and insured.* Should the insurer's liability be confined only to bad faith behavior, or should it embrace a more stringent duty to look after the interests of the assured in light of the potential conflicts of interest? Some courts have followed *Crisci* in rejecting the position that "proof of malice or ill will is necessary to find a breach of the implied obligation of good faith and fair dealing." See, e.g., deVries v. St. Paul Fire and Marine Insurance Co., 716 F.2d 939, 942 (1st Cir. 1983) (New Hampshire law), allowing the jury to find for the plaintiff if he proved by a preponderance of the evidence that the acts of the insurer "in investigating and adjusting the claim here amounted to a calculated and

not inadvertent unreasonable denial of payment" in violation of "the contractual obligation of good faith and fair dealing." Is this a negligence standard? With *deVries* contrast Awrey v. Progressive Casualty Insurance Co., 728 F.2d 352, 357 (6th Cir. 1984) (Michigan law), which held that "it is not enough to show that the insurer 'ignored completely' and 'did not consider' the insured's position in order to prove bad faith on the part of the insurer. [Michigan law] requires a showing that the insurer engaged in the 'conscious doing of wrong because of dishonest purpose or moral obliquity' for a finding of bad faith."

The California Court of Appeals in Merritt v. Reserve Insurance Co., 110 Cal. Rptr. 511, 519-520 (Cal. App. 1973), contains an excellent discussion of the conflicts of interest between insurer and insured, in a case in which defendant had a policy that provided only the minimum allowable coverage of $15,000 per injury and the plaintiff sought $50,000 in damages. Generally speaking, the basic tension arises because the insurance company bears all the costs of litigation under the standard policy, even though an insured with limited coverage may have to shoulder the bulk of the financial loss if liability is established. The insurance company that looks only to its own financial interest will compare its costs of defense with the $15,000 policy maximum regardless of the size of the verdict. Thus, if litigation costs $5,000, with a 50 percent chance of liability, the insurance company will refuse to settle for $15,000. That $15,000 settlement is greater than its expected losses from fighting the suit, which would equal $12,500 (the $5,000 in litigation expenses incurred in all cases, plus $7,500 in damages, equal to the 50 percent chance of losing $15,000). The prudential decision for the insurance company may, however, have ruinous consequences for the insured. Settling the case for the $15,000 policy limit completely insulates the insured from any possibility of liability. Litigating it at the insurer's expense exposes the insured to a 50 percent chance of $35,000 in liability, an expected loss of $17,500 for a risk-neutral insured.

To resolve this conflict, Peters, J., seems to suggest once the risk of piercing policy limits is known, then a strong presumption arises in favor of the duty to settle. But there is a more precise way of dealing with the question that asks how the insurance company would behave if its policy limits were in excess of the anticipated $50,000 liability so that it bore all the loss from either settlement or litigation. Now the company would settle the case because a $15,000 payment is less than the anticipated liability of $30,000 ($5,000 in legal fees plus the 50 percent chance of having to pay $50,000). If the company would settle a case under a no-limits policy, it has a duty to settle that case under a policy that contains occurrence or aggregate limits. But suppose that the plaintiff only has a 5 percent chance of winning in the underlying litigation. Here the insured will still prefer for the insurer to settle for the policy limit of $15,000 because it faces no loss with a settlement and a loss of $1,750 (5 percent of $35,000). But from the combined point of view the settlement makes no sense because the expected costs of the suit are only $7,500 (5 percent of $50,000 plus $5,000 in litigation expenses). So long as "the test is whether a prudent insurer without policy limits would have accepted the settlement offer," a per se duty to compensate for all verdicts in excess of policy limits appears to be mistaken. See generally K. Abraham, Distributing Risk: Insurance, Legal Theory, and Public Policy 191-192 (1986).

Eliminating this conflict of interest, however, is both tricky and expensive so long as both parties want policies that contain explicit limitations on the underlying indemnity obligation. The court in *Merritt* noted that having the insured hire independent counsel is no cure-all because the control of the lawsuit normally remains in the control of the insurer.

> Nor can the liability of the assured be divided into separate segments, about which the carrier and the assured may make their separate evaluations and go their separate ways. Patently, the carrier cannot settle its share of the assured's liability and turn the assured adrift, exposed to a suit for excess liability financed by the carrier's settlement. Nor can the assured settle the claim for excess liability and abandon the carrier to defend a suit financed by the assured's settlement. For better or worse, like a married couple, assured and carrier must make the best of each other.

One additional solution is for the insured to pay an additional premium then and there so that the insurer assumes the full liability for any eventual verdict.

2. *A two-way street?* The prospect of bad-faith actions often induces some nifty maneuvers by the tort plaintiff and the tort defendant against the latter's insurer. In Hamilton v. Maryland Casualty Co., 41 P.3d 128, 132 (Cal. 2002), the insured VLC was sued by several of its clients, including Hamilton, for invasion of privacy. Maryland Casualty agreed to accept the defense of the case under two successive liability policies for $1 million each. The tort plaintiffs demanded $1 million to settle with Maryland, and rejected Maryland's counteroffer of $150,000. Thereafter, the plaintiffs, the insured, and its codefendants agreed to a global settlement without Maryland's participation or consent. That deal called for $2 million in payment from VLC's various codefendants. VLC paid nothing toward that judgment, but agreed that it was liable for a stipulated judgment of $3 million. VLC assigned its rights to bring its bad faith claims against Maryland to the Hamilton group, which agreed not to execute the judgment against VLC. (This decision was made against the backdrop of California law, which prevents the tort claimant from bringing any bad faith action against the insurer of the tort defendant. Moradi-Shalal v. Fireman's Fund Insurance Co., 758 P.2d 58, 66 (Cal. 1988)). The entire settlement was approved by the special master pursuant to Civil Procedure

Rule 877.6 (which is designed to make sure that the allocations are fair between joint tortfeasors), and the Hamilton group sued Maryland for $3 million. Werdegar, J., rebuffed the action.

> Plaintiffs maintain that a stipulated judgment, despite the covenant not to execute, creates a rebuttable presumption of the insured's damages, at least where it has been confirmed as reached in good faith pursuant to Code of Civil Procedure section 877.6. We disagree. . . . [W]here the insurer has accepted defense of the action, no trial has been held to determine the insured's liability, and a covenant not to execute excuses the insured from bearing any actual liability from the stipulated judgment, the entry of a stipulated judgment is insufficient to show, even rebuttably, that the insured has been injured to any extent by the failure to settle, much less in the amount of the stipulated judgment. In these circumstances, the judgment provides no reliable basis to establish damages resulting from a refusal to settle, an essential element of plaintiffs' cause of action.

After this bad faith settlement is rejected in Hamilton, what duties, if any, remain with Maryland Casualty? Can it walk from the litigation? Must it pay the $150,000 it offered? Should the terms of the insurance contract be allowed to specify the conditions for a bad faith action? Limit the damages? Bar the action altogether? Note that the conflict of interest identified in *Crisci* and *Merritt* is one of the many costs of doing business. Are the administrative inconveniences of a bad faith action greater or less than those generated by the basic conflict? R. Keeton and A. Widiss, Insurance Law §7.8 (1988).

Practices such as that found in *Hamilton* (which were also adopted in *State Farm*, Chapter 10 at page 916) show how plaintiffs' lawyers can use bad faith actions as a lever to extract settlements from the defendant in excess of a claim's fair value. "Practice manuals on settlement advise plaintiffs' lawyers to encourage settlement by fixing the claim above policy limits, and by sending a detailed demand letter to the insurer together with a request for a response in a brief period." Syverud, The Duty to Settle, 76 Va. L. Rev. 1113, 1169 n. 146 (1990). As an example of a "set-up" letter, Syverud refers to Baton v. Transamerica Insurance Co., 584 F.2d 907 (9th Cir. 1978), in which the tort plaintiff offered to settle a case for the lower of $110,000 or the policy limits, but only if the offer was accepted within ten days. How much protection does *Hamilton* afford against that practice?

In light of these complications, it is not surprising that few, if any insurers voluntarily agree to be bound by the good faith obligation as it has evolved since *Crisci*, even in exchange for a higher premium. It could therefore well be that the older view, which flatly denied actions for bad faith, better served the interests of the insured from an ex ante perspective. Without the threat of the tort defendant assigning the bad faith action to the tort plaintiff, an insurance company can bargain hard against the tort plaintiff without fear of retaliation if its tough strategy fails. On the other hand, this gain to the insurer and the insured might unduly frustrate claim collection by injured plaintiff. Hence, in a modern day rerun of the indemnity disputes in *Bain*, the bad faith action has been defended less as a mode of protection of the insured and more to protect the injured party. For the elaboration of this argument, see Meurer, The Gains from Faith in an Unfaithful Agent: Settlement Conflicts between Defendants and Liability Insurers, 8 J. L. Econ. & Org. 502 (1992).

3. Excess insurance. An insurer's duty to settle a case within its policy limits has been extensively debated in the context of excess insurance. Excess insurance usually covers catastrophic losses beyond the limits of the primary policy. Typically the excess carrier insists that its insured have some approved primary coverage (why?), but does not establish a direct contractual relationship with the primary carrier or with any of its reinsurers, that is, companies to whom the primary insurer "cedes" risk by paying them a premium. When the primary carrier does not settle a case within policy limits, does it owe the same good faith duties to the excess carrier as it does to the primary insured? Commercial Union Assurance v. Safeway Stores, 610 P.2d 1038, 1043 (Cal. 1980), held that an insured owed no such settlement obligation to an excess carrier. *Commercial Union* was confined to actions for breach of the implied covenant of good faith. "If an excess carrier wishes to insulate itself from liability for an insured's failure to accept what it deems to be a reasonable settlement offer, it may do so by appropriate language in the policy." Would that stipulation bind the insured's primary insurer?

The result in *Commercial Union* could be doubted for needlessly exposing the excess carrier to a strategic decision of the primary carrier to proceed to suit instead of settling within policy limits. Cudahy, J., outlines one possible response to that risk in Fire Insurance Co. v. General Star Indemnity Co., 183 F.3d 578 (7th Cir. 1999):

> The duty that a primary insurer owes to an excess insurer is derivative of the duty to the insured; an excess insurer can use the doctrine of equitable subrogation to assert the insured's right to insist that the primary insurer use due care to avoid an excess judgment against the insured. Because equitable subrogation allows one party to step into the legal shoes of another, the excess insurer (the subrogee) acquires no greater or lesser rights than those of the insured (the subrogor). "Thus the actions of the insured, who no longer possesses a financial stake in the outcome of the litigation against it, can defeat the excess insurer's right of recovery by failing to cooperate with the primary insurer or otherwise acting to supply the primary insurer with a defense to a bad faith action." Certain Underwriters of Lloyd's v. General Accident Ins. Co., 909 F.2d 228, 232-33 (7th Cir. 1990).

The high stakes involved are made evident in New England Insurance Co. v. Health Care Underwriters Mutual Insurance Co., 295 F.3d 232 (2d Cir. 2002). There the underlying hospital defendant faced potentially huge liabilities for a mismanaged delivery, which left the plaintiff with a high conceptual ability (I.Q. 145) but no ability to walk or to talk. As the case progressed, the parents of the injured child made successively greater demands for settlement. The primary insurer had a $1 million policy limit, but refused to settle within policy limits even when the excess carrier repeatedly urged it to do so in light of the potentially explosive level of damages. Berman, J., rejected any rule which held that the good faith duty to an excess carrier was triggered only in cases of "clear liability," and thus required the primary carrier to compensate the excess carrier for its damages when a jury awarded the injured plaintiff huge sums.

In light of the multiple cross-currents with excess policy, what rule is most desirable? Note also that some of these conflicts can be avoided if the primary carrier pays the excess carrier a premium to assume all potential defense and indemnity obligations, or for that matter running the deal in reverse. The conflict of interest problem going forward is resolved because the sole remaining insurer internalizes all costs and benefits of the decision. The transaction is also a win/win for both insurers if in expectation the payment received is sufficient to fund the additional liabilities. What obstacles lie in the path of these settlements? And which party should soldier on alone?

12

THE NO-FAULT SYSTEMS

SECTION A.   INTRODUCTION

This chapter examines the various "no-fault" alternatives to the tort system. The first of these is workers' compensation, which has received relatively little attention in academic circles, notwithstanding its universal adoption and great practical importance. In recent years, the study of workers' compensation has gained new urgency for two reasons. First, the workers' compensation system is big business. There are over 128 million covered workers. The premiums collected to run the system have been sharply up in recent years, exceeding $88.0 billion in 2005. Of that figure, about $55 billion is in payouts to covered workers, of which about $26 billion are for medical expenses and $29 billion for cash payouts for direct payments to covered workers. The remaining $33 billion covers various administrative costs. Stated otherwise, the total amount collected for running the system amounts to about 1.70 percent of wages, but the amount received amounts to about 1.06 percent of wages. The spread between premiums collected and benefits paid declined slightly from 2004, even though that spread had increased sharply in previous years. This movement is not attributable to any increase in accident rates or to substantial increases in benefit levels. Rather, the industry had suffered losses in previous years so that firms raised premiums to cover their reserves. For an exhaustive compilation of the insurance data, see National Academy of Social Insurance, Workers' Compensation: Benefits, Coverage, and Costs, 2005 (2007), http://www. nasi.org/usr_doc/NASI_Workers_Comp_2005_Full_Report.pdf.

Second, workers' compensation has served as the model for a number of contemporary no-fault systems of liability, including those for injuries arising out of the use of automobiles, the distribution of consumer products, the provision of medical services, childhood vaccine programs, and, most recently, the now completed special 9/11 fund for victims at the World Trade Center and other sites. Each of these areas presents special and unique problems of its own. Workers' compensation law, with its oft controversial history of no-fault liability, presents the best benchmark for evaluating the more modern no-fault schemes.

A brief list of their common points helps show the close kinship of the various no-fault systems. Workers' compensation and modern no-fault systems provide compensation for individual injuries that are everywhere noncompensable at common law; all make use of broad coverage formulas (arising out of employment or the use of an automobile, consumer product, vaccine treatment, or so forth); all systems contemplate sharp limitations on damages, with little or no recovery for pain and suffering; and all require some coordination with the common law tort rules retained after the adoption of the plan. Accordingly, we start with the workers' compensation system and conclude by examining its modern offshoots.

SECTION B.   WORKERS' COMPENSATION

1.   *Historical Origins*

The emergence of workers' compensation laws follows a long and tortuous path that can be summarized only briefly here. Before 1837 there were no recorded cases in which an employee sought damages from an employer for a work-related injury. Matters changed with the English case of Priestley v. Fowler, 150 Eng. Rep. 1030 (Ex. 1837), and the leading American case of Farwell v. Boston & W.R.R., 45 Mass. (4 Met.) 49 (1842), after which workers began to sue employers on negligence theories for workplace accidents, only to be met with the famous trinity of common law defenses: common employment, assumption of risk, and contributory negligence. See Chapter 4, *supra* at 361. Efforts to deal with these legal barriers followed two distinct courses. First, private firms and their (often unionized) workers entered into private arrangements that expressly contracted out of the common law rules for industrial accidents and frequently substituted in their place, not a total employer immunity from all responsibility, but a complex voluntary compensation system on which modern workers' compensation laws were patterned. See, e.g., Griffiths v. Earl of Dudley, 9 Q.B. 357 (1882); Clements v. London & N.E. Ry., [1894] 2 Q.B. 482. Second, explicit legislative intervention modified the common law rules of tort liability for industrial accidents. The first of these statutes — the Employer's

Liability Act, 1880, 43 & 44 Vict. ch. 42 — eliminated the defense of common employment and also provided for the general liability of the employer to his workers on the grounds of negligence. The English courts in *Griffiths* and *Clements* held that this Act allowed employers and employees to contract out of its coverage provisions into a compensation-like system.

The 1880 English statute became the model for many American state statutes on employment relations. See, e.g., Massachusetts Employer's Liability Act, 1887 Mass. Acts 566; California Employer's Liability Act, 1907 Cal. Stat. 119. At the federal level the common law rules were also displaced by the Federal Employer's Liability Act, 35 Stat. 65 (1908). It applied to the employees of interstate common carriers, and withstood constitutional challenge in the Second Employer's Liability Cases, 223 U.S. 1 (1912), after some earlier constitutional doubts. The American statutes did not accept the contractual defenses of assumption of risk, and thus are properly regarded as regulatory schemes. The FELA is still in effect today, as amended, 45 U.S.C. §§51-60 (2007), and has generated extensive litigation. See, e.g., Wilkerson v. McCarthy, *supra* at 294, Note 2.

For very different views on the early history, see L. Friedman, A History of American Law ch. 14 (2d ed. 1985); Epstein, The Historical Origins and Economic Structure of the Workers' Compensation Act, 16 Ga. L. Rev. 775 (1982); Fishback, Liability Rules and Accident Prevention in the Workplace: Empirical Evidence from the Early Twentieth Century, 16 J. Legal Stud. 305 (1987); P.V. Fishback and S.E. Kantor, A Prelude to the Welfare State: The Origins of Workers' Compensation (2000).

The adoption of the various employer's liability acts marked the first stage in the transformation of the law of industrial accidents. In England the 1880 statute was supplanted in 1897 by the first modern workers' compensation act, the Workmen's Compensation Act, 1897, 60 & 61 Vict. ch. 37, which served as a blueprint for the American statutes. The 1897 Act explicitly banned any contractual waiver of the protection afforded workers. That Act in turn set the stage for an extensive debate over these laws in the United States, which reached a turning point when New York passed the first American workers' compensation statute in 1910, 1910 N.Y. Laws 625, to implement the recommendations of the Wainwright Commission, which summarized its conclusions as follows:

> *First*, that the present system in New York rests on a basis that is economically unwise and unfair, and that in operation it is wasteful, uncertain and productive of antagonism between workmen and employers.
>
> *Second*, that it is satisfactory to none and tolerable only to those employers and workmen who practically disregard their legal rights and obligations, and fairly share the burden of accidents in industries.
>
> *Third*, that the evils of the system are most marked in hazardous employments, where the trade risk is high and serious accidents frequent.

Fourth, that, as a matter of fact, workmen in the dangerous trades do not, and practically cannot, provide for themselves adequate accident insurance, and therefore, the burden of serious accidents falls on the workmen least able to bear it, and brings many of them and their families to want.

The legislation was immediately challenged in the courts on constitutional grounds and was overturned by the New York Court of Appeals in the famous case of Ives v. South Buffalo Ry., 94 N.E. 431, 436, 439-440, 449 (N.Y. 1911). *Ives* described the workers' compensation law in terms that in broad outline are still accurate today.

> The statute, judged by our common-law standards, is plainly revolutionary. Its central and controlling feature is that every employer who is engaged in any of the classified industries shall be liable for any injury to a workman arising out of and in the course of the employment by "a necessary risk or danger of the employment or one inherent in the nature thereof, . . . provided that the employer shall not be liable in respect of any injury to the workman which is caused in whole or in part by the serious and willful misconduct of the workman." This rule of liability, stated in another form, is that the employer is responsible to the employee for every accident in the course of the employment, whether the employer is at fault or not, and whether the employee is at fault or not, except when the fault of the employee is so grave as to constitute serious and willful misconduct on his part. The radical character of this legislation is at once revealed by contrasting it with the rule of the common law, under which the employer is liable for injuries to his employee only when the employer is guilty of some act or acts of negligence which caused the occurrence out of which the injuries arise, and then only when the employee is shown to be free from any negligence which contributes to the occurrence.

The court then addressed the objections to the statute and concluded that it was constitutionally permissible to abolish the employer's "trinity" of common law defenses in personal injury actions: the fellow servant doctrine (whereby the injured party could not recover from the employer for harm caused by the negligence of a fellow servant), assumption of risk, and contributory negligence. Yet in spite of the impressive economic and sociological brief made on behalf of the statute, the court struck it down as an impermissible exercise of the police power because it bore no relationship to the health, safety, or morals of employees. The court also found that the statutory imposition of "liability without fault" was an unconstitutional deprivation of property without due process of law:

> The right of property rests not upon philosophical or scientific speculations nor upon the commendable impulses of benevolence or charity, nor yet upon the dictates of natural justice. The right has its foundation in the fundamental law. That can be changed by the people, but not by legislatures.

In a government like ours theories of public good or necessity are often so plausible or sound as to command popular approval, but courts are not permitted to forget that the law is the only chart by which the ship of state is to be guided. Law as used in this sense means the basic law and not the very act of legislation which deprives the citizen of his rights, privileges or property. Any other view would lead to the absurdity that the Constitutions protect only those rights which the legislatures do not take away. If such economic and sociologic arguments as are here advanced in support of this statute can be allowed to subvert the fundamental idea of property, then there is no private right entirely safe, because there is no limitation upon the absolute discretion of legislatures, and the guarantees of the Constitution are a mere waste of words. . . . If the argument in support of this statute is sound we do not see why it cannot logically be carried much further. Poverty and misfortune from every cause are detrimental to the state. It would probably conduce to the welfare of all concerned if there could be a more equal distribution of wealth. Many persons have much more property than they can use to advantage and many more find it impossible to get the means for a comfortable existence. If the legislature can say to an employer, "you must compensate your employee for an injury not caused by you or by your fault," why can it not go further and say to the man of wealth, "you have more property than you need and your neighbor is so poor that he can barely subsist; in the interest of natural justice you must divide with your neighbor so that he and his dependents shall not become a charge upon the State?" The argument that the risk to an employee should be borne by the employer because it is inherent in the employment, may be economically sound, but it is at war with the legal principle that no employer can be compelled to assume a risk which is inseparable from the work of the employee, and which may exist in spite of a degree of care by the employer far greater than may be exacted by the most drastic law. If it is competent to impose upon an employer, who has omitted no legal duty and has committed no wrong, a liability based solely upon a legislative fiat that his business is inherently dangerous, it is equally competent to visit upon him a special tax for the support of hospitals and other charitable institutions, upon the theory that they are devoted largely to the alleviation of ills primarily due to his business. In its final and simple analysis that is taking the property of *A* and giving it to *B*, and that cannot be done under our Constitutions.

Cullen, C.J., echoed similar themes in his concurrence:

I know of no principle on which one can be compelled to indemnify another for loss unless it is based upon contractual obligation or fault. It might as well be argued in support of a law requiring a man to pay his neighbor's debts, that the common law requires each man to pay his own debts, and the statute in question was a mere modification of the common law so as to require each to pay his neighbor's debts.

This early judicial setback was short-lived. Pursuant to a suggestion made by the court in *Ives*, the state passed a constitutional amendment that authorized passage of the workers' compensation statute. In New York Central R.R. v. White, 243 U.S. 188, 202-204, 208 (1916), a unanimous United States Supreme Court upheld the new statute against federal constitutional challenges. Justice Pitney wrote:

Of course, we cannot ignore the question whether the new arrangement is arbitrary and unreasonable, from the standpoint of natural justice. Respecting this, it is important to be observed that the act applies only to disabling or fatal personal injuries received in the course of hazardous employment in gainful occupation. Reduced to its elements, the situation to be dealt with is this: Employer and employee, by mutual consent, engage in a common operation intended to be advantageous to both; the employee is to contribute his personal services, and for these is to receive wages, and ordinarily nothing more; the employer is to furnish plant, facilities, organization, capital, credit, is to control and manage the operation, paying the wages and other expenses, disposing of the product at such prices as he can obtain, taking all the profits, if any there be, and of necessity bearing the entire losses. In the nature of things, there is more or less of a probability that the employee may lose his life through some accidental injury arising out of the employment, leaving his widow or children deprived of their natural support or that he may sustain an injury not mortal but resulting in his total or partial disablement, temporary or permanent, with corresponding impairment of earning capacity. The physical suffering must be borne by the employee alone; the laws of nature prevent this from being evaded or shifted to another, and the statute makes no attempt to afford an equivalent in compensation. But, besides, there is the loss of earning power; a loss of that which stands to the employee as his capital in trade. This is a loss arising out of the business, and, however it may be charged up, is an expense of the operation, as truly as the cost of repairing broken machinery or any other expense that ordinarily is paid by the employer. Who is to bear the charge? It is plain that, on grounds of natural justice, it is not unreasonable for the State, while relieving the employer from responsibility for damages measured by common-law standards and payable in cases where he or those for whose conduct he is answerable are found to be at fault, to require him to contribute a reasonable amount, and according to a reasonable and definite scale, by way of compensation for the loss of earning power incurred in the common enterprise, irrespective of the question of negligence, instead of leaving the entire loss to rest where it may chance to fall — that is, upon the injured employee or his dependents. Nor can it be deemed arbitrary and unreasonable, from the standpoint of the employee's interest, to supplant a system under which he assumed the entire risk of injury in ordinary cases, and in others had a right to recover an amount more or less speculative upon proving facts of negligence that often were difficult to prove, and substitute a system under which in all ordinary cases of accidental injury he is sure of a definite and easily ascertained compensation, not being obliged to assume the entire loss in any case but in all cases assuming any loss beyond the prescribed scale.

Much emphasis is laid upon the criticism that the act creates liability without fault. This is sufficiently answered by what has been said, but we may add that liability without fault is not a novelty in the law. The common-law liability of the carrier, of the inn-keeper, of him who employed fire or other dangerous agency or harbored a mischievous animal, was not dependent altogether upon questions of fault or negligence. Statutes imposing liability without fault have been sustained. . . .

We conclude that the prescribed scheme of compulsory compensation is not repugnant to the provisions of the Fourteenth Amendment.

What is the nature of the "bargain between workers and employers set by the workmen's compensation statutes"? If that bargain benefits all concerned, why must it be imposed by legislation?

The challenges to workers' compensation went beyond the constitutional issues. As early as 1913, Professor Jeremiah Smith, Sequel to Workmen's Compensation Acts, 27 Harv. L. Rev. 235, 252-253 (1913), argued that workers' compensation could not be justified on grounds of "justice and expediency." In so doing, he addressed the common argument that workers should receive special protection from the state because the employer "will reap the net profit of the business," as follows:

> The employee is himself a part of the undertaking. He has, in one sense, voluntarily participated in it; and is deriving benefit from it. Whereas outsiders have nothing to do with the undertaking. Frequently they "are exposed, without any choice on their side, to more or less risk of injury arising from what is done in the conduct of it by the owner or his servants." An outsider is not a participant in the business and "derives no direct benefit from its carrying on."
>
> Why single out workmen employed in the undertaking and constitute them a specially protected class, while overlooking other persons whose claim stands on at least equal ground? . . .

One further clarification is in order before taking a closer look at the workers' compensation laws. "Liability without fault" (which plays a large role in stranger cases) has often been misconstrued to represent a belated triumph of the strict liability of the old common law in the field of industrial relations. Thus, in *White*, for example, Justice Pitney grappled with cases of fire or mischievous animals, precisely because of the strict character of the rules that govern these cases. Likewise, Jeremiah Smith could conclude: "If the Workmen's Compensation Act is regarded as right in principle and the common law of A.D. 1900 as wrong in principle, then the argument is strong in favor of repudiating the common law of A.D. 1900 and going back to the common law of A.D. 1400." 27 Harv. L. Rev. 344, 368 (1913).

Yet the words "liability without fault" in the context of workers' compensation refers to a system that differs as much from common law strict liability as it does from common law negligence. In the first place, common law strict liability, properly conceived, makes allowance for affirmative defenses based on plaintiff's conduct, including both assumption of risk and contributory negligence, that are expressly abolished or restricted by the workers' compensation statutes. Only the willful misconduct of the worker will remove or limit in some circumstances coverage under these acts. A second difference is equally important. The modern workers' compensation law imposes upon employers liability for injuries, to use the time-honored phrase, "arising out of and in the course of employment." That test for compensation largely eliminates the requirement of a causal nexus between defendant's (particular) acts and the plaintiff's harm that is so central to the traditional common law theory of strict liability. Thus, with common law strict liability for damage caused by fire, the plaintiff must demonstrate that the defendant, or perhaps his guests or servants, set the fire in question. If the defendant is an "insurer" under this scheme, he is an insurer only for the consequences of his own acts or those on his premises with his permission, not for the plaintiff's harms attributable to an independent source. The workers' compensation scheme, however, focuses on the injuries to the worker. The emphasis is on where and when the worker suffered the harm by fire—it is of no importance whether or not the employer or a fellow employee set the fire. "Liability without fault" in the context of workers' compensation means not only liability without defendant's negligence, but also liability without the strict causal connection to defendant's conduct required under the strict liability rules, and most definitely includes harms for which the plaintiff is the sole cause of her own harms.

We are now in a position to look more closely at the "arising out of and in the course of employment" language of the workers' compensation statutes. The formula is central to the administration of workers' compensation, as thousands of cases that have litigated its outer limits illustrate. For an exhaustive treatment of the subject, see A. Larson, Workmen's Compensation Law, chs. 3-29 (2007). After evaluating the coverage formula, we will turn to two other distinctive features of workers' compensation laws: its rules for damages and its coordination with the common law rules of tort.

2.   The Scope of Coverage: "Arising Out of and in the Course of Employment"

Clodgo v. Industry Rentavision, Inc.
701 A.2d 1044 (Vt. 1997)

GIBSON, J. On July 22, 1995, claimant was working as manager of Rentavision's store in Brattleboro. During a lull between customers, claimant began firing staples with a staple gun at a co-worker, who was sitting on a couch watching television. The co-worker first protested, but then, after claimant had fired twenty or thirty staples at him, fired three staples back at claimant. As claimant ducked, the third staple hit him in the eye.

[The defendant argued] that claimant was engaged in noncompensable horseplay at the time of the injury. Following a hearing in March 1996, the Commissioner awarded permanent partial disability and vocational rehabilitation benefits, medical expenses, and attorney's fees and costs. This appeal followed. . . .

The question certified for review is whether claimant's horseplay bars him from recovery for the resulting injury under Vermont's Workers' Compensation Act. Rentavision contends the Commissioner misapplied the law in concluding that claimant's horseplay-related injury was compensable. We agree. An injury arises out of employment if it would not have occurred but for the fact that the conditions and obligations of the employment placed claimant in the position where he or she was injured. Thus, claimant must show that "but for" the employment and his position at work, the injury would not have happened.

Although the accident here would not have happened but for claimant's participation in the horseplay and therefore was not exclusively linked to his employment, it also was not a purely personal risk that would have occurred regardless of his location and activity on that day. He was injured during work hours with a staple gun provided for use on the job, and thus the findings support a causal connection between claimant's work conditions and the injury adequate to conclude that the accident arose out of his employment.

Nonetheless, claimant must also show that the injury occurred in the course of the employment. An accident occurs in the course of employment when it was within the period of time the employee was on duty at a place where the employee was reasonably expected to be *while fulfilling the duties of the employment contract*. Thus, while some horseplay among employees during work hours can be expected and is not an automatic bar to compensation, the key inquiry is whether the employee deviated too far from his or her duties.

The Commissioner must therefore consider (1) the extent and seriousness of the deviation; (2) the completeness of the deviation (i.e., whether the activity was commingled with performance of a work duty or was a complete abandonment of duty); (3) the extent to which the activity had become an accepted part of the employment; and (4) the extent to which the nature of the employment may be expected to include some horseplay. The Commissioner found that although shooting staples was common among employees, such activity was not considered acceptable behavior by Rentavision. She made no finding concerning whether Rentavision knew that staple-shooting occurred at work, but did find that claimant made material misrepresentations of fact designed to avoid an inference of horseplay or inappropriate behavior in order that he might obtain workers' compensation benefits. Claimant makes no showing that shooting staples at fellow employees was an accepted part of claimant's employment or furthered Rentavision's interests. . . .

The facts show that the accident was unrelated to any legitimate use of the staplers at the time, indicating there was no commingling of the horseplay with work duties. The Commissioner focused on the slack time inherent in claimant's job, but this factor alone is not dispositive. Although some horseplay was reasonably to be expected during idle periods between customers, the obvious dangerousness of shooting staples at fellow employees and the absence of connection between duties as a salesperson and the horseplay events indicates the accident occurred during a substantial deviation from work duties. Therefore, we reverse the Commissioner's award.

MORSE, J., dissenting. I respectfully dissent. . . .

With respect to the extent and seriousness of the deviation, as well as its completeness, the Commissioner found that claimant and his fellow employee had completed virtually all the work that needed to be done in the absence of customers and that business was very slow that day. When the injury occurred, claimant and his fellow employee were in a period of enforced idleness while they waited for customers. They were not actively pursuing any specific tasks and were passing the time as required by their jobs. As Larson points out, when there is a lull in work, there are no duties to abandon. During such periods, the deviation can be more substantial than at other times when an employee may be actively pursuing a task directly related to employment. The Commissioner could thus reasonably conclude that the horseplay in this case did not constitute an abandonment of duties or even a serious deviation from the demands of work at that time of day.

Regarding the extent to which such horseplay had become an accepted activity, the Commissioner found that it had been a commonplace occurrence at the store. Although the executive assistant to defendant's president testified that claimant's horseplay was not considered acceptable behavior, he acknowledged that an employee would not be fired for engaging in such activity. The Commissioner thus reasonably concluded that the horseplay as engaged in by claimant, while not condoned by the employer, was a tacit part of employment.

NOTES

1. *Injuries arising out of and in the course of employment. Clodgo* is one of literally thousands of cases that have probed the outer limits of coverage

under the workers' compensation statutes. In a sense, the unending stream of litigation under the statute shows that these laws cannot escape the high volume of case-by-case adjudication found under negligence law in employer liability cases. The more generous coverage formula of the workers' compensation statute rendered easy many liability questions that were vexed at common law. But by expanding the class of compensable events, the law ushered in a new class of contested cases, of which injury during an employee's horseplay is only one. The standard view of the subject treats "arising out of" and "in the course of" employment as distinct requirements. "The words 'in the course of' refer to the time, place, and circumstances of the injury. The term 'arising out of' refers to the cause and origin of the injury." Miedema v. Dial Corporation, 551 N.W.2d 309 (Iowa 1996). With those words spoken, the court held that an employee who strained his back after making a trip to the employer's restroom while getting ready for work was injured in the course of employment, but that his injury did not arise out of his employment. He could not show that the incident did not "coincidentally [occur] while at work," because neither "the design of the restroom or of the toilet Dial provided for its employees contributed to [his] injury. . . . The risk of a back injury in this circumstance is in no way connected to nor increased by his employment with Dial." These two elements also govern the countless separate coverage questions.

2. *Employee theft.* In Matter of Richardson v. Fiedler, 493 N.E.2d 228, 229, 231, 233 (N.Y. 1986), the decedent, a waterproofer and roofing mechanic, fell to his death while attempting to steal copper downspouts from the roof of his job site. Simons, J., held that the death was covered under the workers' compensation law even though antithetical to the employer's interests.

> The Board found from the evidence in this case that it was common practice in the industry for roofers to remove copper downspouts and sell them for scrap. It further found that this employer not only knew of the practice but also frequently had been required to pay for or replace downspouts stolen by its employees. Despite this experience, the employer had never disciplined or discharged an employee for these thefts, and after it learned that decedent and his co-worker had been stealing downspouts on the day of the accident, it did not discipline or discharge the coemployee. Accordingly, the Board found that decedent's activities while waiting for necessary work materials to arrive did not constitute a deviation from, or an abandonment of, his employment and that the death arose out of and in the course of decedent's employment. These finding are supported by substantial evidence and thus are conclusive on the court. . . .
>
> Although the appellants' argument is based on moral grounds — the need to prevent parties from profiting from illegal acts — the suspicion is that the concern has more to do with dollars and cents than morality. The way for an

employer to express dissatisfaction with its employees' acts and also avoid paying benefits for such claims, however, is not for the Board to disqualify innocent dependents but for the employer to make clear to its employees that illegal conduct on the job will not be tolerated.

The dissent of Titone, J., argued that it was "totally unacceptable" to award coverage "where an employer tolerates conduct blatantly in violation of the Penal Law." What result in *Richardson* if the employer had disciplined or discharged workers found to have stolen copper downspouts from the workplace?

3. *Sexual harassment.* In Anderson v. Save-A-Lot, Ltd. 989 S.W.2d 277 (Tenn. 1999), the plaintiff alleged that her supervisor had sexually harassed her on a daily basis from which she suffered severe post-traumatic stress disorder and depression, with the consequent medical expenses and loss of work. The court found that the accident occurred within the course of employment, but did not arise out of the employment. The decision rested in part on the belief that the harassment in question was done for the sole benefit of the supervisor and had not been condoned by the employer. Yet in part the decision rested on the fear that allowing the compensation claim would block, under the exclusive remedy provision of the workers' compensation law, a worker's action under the Tennessee Human Rights Act. Such actions were allowed under the Florida Human Rights Act and Title VII of the Civil Rights act in Byrd v. Richardson-Greenshields Securities, Inc., 552 So. 2d 1099 (Fla. 1989).

4. *Workers' compensation for acts of third parties.* Workers' compensation statutes have universally extended coverage for injuries to workers caused by third persons while they are on the job — a leading cause of death in the United States today. In Martinez v. Worker's Compensation Appeals Board, 544 P.2d 1350, 1352 (Cal. 1976), the injured worker had been hired to operate a beer stand at a fiesta operated by the Roman Catholic Church between noon and 4:30 P.M. While strolling through the fiesta with his family after work, he heard reports that some teenagers had pilfered beer from the church's supplies. At 8:00 P.M. he encountered a group of boys with beer that he believed to be stolen and tried to grab it from them, at which point he was brutally beaten. The hearing examiner denied compensation because the injuries occurred after hours and because the employee had not been hired as a security guard. On appeal the court held that the plaintiff's injuries were emergency actions for the employer's benefit covered by workers' compensation because a reasonable employee might "attempt" to prevent theft even if not explicitly hired to do so.

In Grant v. Grant Textiles, 641 S.E.2d 869, 872 (S.C. 2007), a vice president in the family business was injured when he drove his company-owned truck to the Clinton House to meet his father and some potential customers. As he approached the Clinton House, he swerved to avoid what appeared to be an animal lying in the road. He then insisted on helping a Clinton House employee clean up the debris when he was hit by a pickup truck. The claimant testified that his offer to help was made to prevent further injury to his father and his customers. The Compensation Commission denied the claim. Moore, J., reversed, saying:

> The full commission erred by finding that the accident did not have a causal connection with Claimant's employment. The accident would not have happened but for Claimant's business trip to the Clinton House to meet his employer's customers. Because removing road hazards was not part of Claimant's job duties, he could have ignored the hazard in the road; however, he chose to remove the hazard to benefit himself, his co-worker father, and his customers. . . . Claimant's act, while outside his regular duties, was undertaken in good faith to advance his employer's interest and, therefore, was within the course of his employment.

5. *Personal work.* Under the workers' compensation law how should the line be drawn between activities that pertain to the personal affairs of the worker and those that pertain to the job? In Orsini v. Industrial Commission, 509 N.E.2d 1005, 1009 (Ill. 1987), the plaintiff mechanic who used his employer's service bay to repair his own car was injured because a missing transmission pin in his car caused the vehicle to lurch forward, pinning his legs between the car and a workbench. The court held that the accident was personal and noncompensable. It was not "a risk peculiar to the work or a risk to which the employee is exposed to a greater degree than the general public by reason of his employment." The court explained its decision as follows:

> In the instant case, the risk of harm to Orsini was not increased by any condition of the employment premises. Unlike [other cases] cited by the appellee, where the harm to the employee came about as a result of a defect in the employer's premises, the injury here came about solely as a result of a defect in Orsini's own car—the missing retainer pin. It is undisputed that the malfunction on Orsini's car could have occurred anytime or anywhere, and only coincidentally occurred at the Wilmette Texaco service station. Nor is there any suggestion here that the tools provided by Wilmette Texaco and used by Orsini in repairing his car were in any way defective. Further, under the terms of his employment, Orsini was not required to work on his personal automobile during working hours, and Wilmette Texaco could just as well have permitted him to do nothing while he was waiting for the additional brake parts needed to complete the job he was performing for his employer.

6. *Acts of God under workers' compensation.* Workers' compensation cases have also had to determine coverage for injuries caused by acts of God. In

Electro-Voice, Inc. v. O'Dell, 519 S.W.2d 395, 397 (Tenn. 1975), the claimant was awarded disability benefits when she suffered a violent allergic reaction after being stung by a bee while working on an assembly line. In demonstrating that the injury "arose out of" her employment, the claimant showed that the conditions in the plant "increased the risk or hazard" of suffering bee stings by proving that "bees often entered walls of buildings in the warm summer months and came out later in the year," and that the walls in the employer's building had been treated twice in the past two years in order to kill the bees that lived in them.

Electro-Voice adopted what is known as the "actual risk" test, whereby the claimant is allowed to recover only by showing that the employment increased (perhaps "materially") the risk of the harm beyond the levels to which an ordinary member of the public is exposed. In contrast, the so-called positional risk theory adopted by a minority of jurisdictions allows compensation under a "but for" test if the employer's activities require the employee to work in a position to suffer the harm. This positional risk approach is gaining some ground. See, e.g., National Fire Insurance Co. v. Edwards, 263 S.E.2d 455, 456 (Ga. App. 1979), in which the plaintiff, injured when a tornado struck the building in which he was working, was allowed to recover. "[F]or the injury to be compensable it is only necessary for the claimant to prove that his work brought him within range of the danger by requiring his presence in the locale when the peril struck, even though any other person present would have also been injured irrespective of his employment." See generally 1 A. Larson, Part 2: 'Arising Out of the Employment'.

7. *Drunkenness.* Although the workers' compensation statutes have removed contributory negligence and assumption of risk from the catalogue of available defenses, they have not, as *Richardson* makes plain, eliminated all defenses based on the employee's misconduct since the employee's willful misconduct, drunkenness, and aggression may either bar or reduce recovery. §3600 of the California Labor Code (2007), for example, parallels section 10 of the New York statute by denying compensation for an injury caused by the intoxication of the injured employee for an injury that is intentionally self-inflicted, and "where the employee has willfully and deliberately caused his own death." Is there any reason why the drunkenness rule should apply only to injury and not to death?

In some cases, the hard question is whether drunkenness is personal or work-related. In Van Vleet v. Montana Association of Counties Workers' Compensation Trust, 103 P.3d 544, 548 (Mont. 2004), the decedent, Shawn Van Vleet, who was a deputy sheriff at the time of his death, fell from a balcony. Earlier that night he had drunk liquor at a hospitality suite organized by his employer, but continued to drink after the suite had been closed. The Workers' Compensation Commission denied recovery since both the death and some drinking occurred after the hospitality suite was closed. Regnier, J., reversed:

> It must be remembered that the issue is not Shawn's drinking and intoxi-
> cation. The WCC concluded, and the parties agree, Shawn's intoxication
> during the conference did not bar Van Vleet's claim. The pivotal question
> under these facts, according to the WCC, is whether Shawn's later half-hour
> of drinking, up until the time of his fall, constituted a substantial deviation
> from his earlier six hours of drinking, which was established as "employment
> related matters."

Suppose Shawn had drunk for six hours after the suite were closed and only one hour during it?

8. *Beyond accidents.* The original compensation statutes tended to limit compensation to "personal injury by accident" where the last two words limited compensable injuries to those caused by a sudden and unexpected blow. Statutory coverage has been expanding by giving accidental injuries a broader construction so that it is no longer necessary to establish a definite time, place, and cause. Thus, in Johannesen v. New York City Department of Housing Preservation and Development, 638 N.E.2d 981, 984-985 (N.Y. 1994), the claimant suffered "two sudden and traumatic asthmatic attacks at work" when she had been exposed to high levels of secondhand smoke in a closed work environment. She had kept the position for ten years although her physicians had recommended a transfer. Bellacosa, J., held that the injuries were accidental because the exposures, from a common sense point of view, had "an exacerbative and excessive quality. . . . Claimant worked in an office where the tools of her trade are papers, pens, files, computers and telephones. Cigarette smoke is surely not a natural by-product of the Department of Housing Preservation and Development's activities and her employment role." On the scope of "by accident," see A. Larson §§42.01-42.03.

Constant stress and exposure can result not only in asthma attacks but also in injuries as diverse as a bad back from lifting heavy weights to a heart attack from stress on the job. In principle these cumulative trauma cases are as work-related as a sudden injury, but they raise formidable questions of work-relatedness when, for example, a heart attack is suffered on the job by a worker who already suffered from arteriosclerotic heart disease. In Kostamo v. Marquette Iron Mining Co., 274 N.W.2d 411, 415 (Mich. 1979), Levin, J., addressed the coverage challenge as follows:

> The workers' compensation law does not provide compensation for a person
> afflicted by an illness or disease not caused or aggravated by his work or
> working conditions. Nor is a different result required because debility has
> progressed to the point where the worker cannot work without pain or injury.

Accordingly, compensation cannot be awarded because the worker may suffer heart damage which would be work-related if he continued to work. Unless the work has accelerated or aggravated the illness, disease or deterioration and, thus, contributed to it, or the work, coupled with the illness, disease or deterioration, in fact causes an injury, compensation is not payable.

Arteriosclerosis is an ordinary disease of life which is not caused by work or aggravated by the stress of work. However, stress that would not adversely affect a person who does not have arteriosclerosis may cause a person who has that disease to have a heart attack.

The medical evidence necessary to establish that work aggravated, accelerated, or precipitated a heart attack is, of course, expensive to assemble and difficult to evaluate. Furthermore, Levin, J., insisted that the matter is not exclusively one of medical evidence, so that the Workers' Compensation Appeal Board could properly consider such factors as the "[t]emporal proximity of the cardiac episodes to the work experience, the hot and dusty conditions of employment, the repeated return to work after each episode, and the mental stress" to which the worker was subjected.

In recent years, explicit statutes have regulated compensation in these exertion cases. N.J. Stat. Ann. §34:15-7.2 (West 2007) provides:

> In any claim for compensation for injury or death from cardiovascular or cerebral vascular causes, the claimant shall prove by a preponderance of the credible evidence that the injury or death was produced by the work effort or strain involving a substantial condition, event or happening in excess of the wear and tear of the claimant's daily living and in reasonable medical probability caused in a material degree the cardiovascular or cerebral vascular injury or death resulting therefrom.
>
> Material degree means an appreciable degree or a degree substantially greater than de minimis.

However difficult the causation problem in heart attack and other traumatic injury cases, it is even more difficult for cumulative trauma where no clear temporal division separates non-work-related from work-related causes. See, e.g., Pullman Kellogg v. Workers' Compensation Appeals Board, 605 P.2d 422, 424 (Cal. 1980), in which the California Supreme Court grappled with the apportionment rules for cases of chronic bronchitis and emphysema aggravated by the claimant's heavy smoking over the entire length of the employment period. The court concluded that under the California statute "the board must allow compensation not only for the disability resulting solely from the employment, but also for that which results from the acceleration, aggravation, or 'lighting up' of a prior nondisabling disease." How should the rule be applied in asbestos cases when smoking can increase the risk of disease 30-fold?

Wilson v. Workers' Compensation Appeals Board
545 P.2d 225 (Cal. 1976)

CLARK, J. Applicant seeks review of a Workers' Compensation Appeals Board decision vacating a referee's compensation award and holding that her injury did not arise "out of and in the course of the employment." (Lab. Code, §3600.) We affirm the board's order.

After driving her children to their school, applicant, a grade school teacher, sustained injury in an automobile accident driving to her school. Her car contained a small bag of thread spools for use in art class, materials graded at home the previous evening, and a few books, including her teaching manual.

The employing school district did not require instructors to commute in their personal cars. The school grounds were unitary and teachers did not travel elsewhere during the day. Public transportation was available and regularly used by at least one teacher. Since the class schedule did not include a specific period for planning lessons or grading papers, instructors commonly performed these duties at school outside class periods or at home in the evening. Teachers could complete class preparation at school but usually chose to work at home for their own convenience. . . .

The board denied benefits after making the following principal findings: (1) applicant's home was not a second job site because her activities outside school hours were matters of personal choice, (2) only convenience motivated applicant's automobile trip, and (3) the "transportation of the work-related items was not a major part of the trip, nor even a significant alternative reason for the trip."

The "going and coming" rule provides that workers' compensation does not ordinarily compensate injuries sustained while the employee travels to or from work. . . .

Applicant contends that, although the accident occurred during her regular commute, she is entitled to exemption from the going and coming rule because exceptional circumstances are established by her performing work at home the night before the accident and by her transporting work-related items—the graded materials and the spools—to class.

Work done at home may exempt an injury occurring during a regular commute from the going and coming rule if circumstances of the employment—and not mere dictates of convenience to the employee—make the home a second jobsite. . . . However, if work is performed at home for the employee's convenience, the commute does not constitute a business trip, since serving the employee's own convenience in selecting an off-premise place to work is a personal and not business purpose.

The record compels the board's determination that applicant's home did not constitute a second jobsite warranting exemption from the going and coming rule. The explicit job requirements demanded only that she report to the school grounds—nowhere else. Her employer's implicit requirement to work beyond classroom hours did not require labor at home. Teachers often worked after 3:15 in the school building unless their broad personal freedom vis-à-vis the nature and hours of class preparation led them home for the sake of convenience. There is no claim that facilities at school were not sufficient to permit completion of the preparatory chores.

That applicant's type of work regularly is performed at home must not disturb the board's determination. The contemporary professional frequently takes work home. There, the draftsman designs on a napkin, the businessman plans at breakfast, the lawyer labors in the evening. But this hearthside activity—while commendable—does not create a white-collar exception to the going and coming rule.

[Tobriner, J., joined by Mosk, J., dissented on the ground that the case fell into one of the "special" exceptions to the "going and coming" rule because the employee was expressly or implicitly "required or expected to furnish [her] own means of transportation to the job."]

NOTES

1. *The "going and coming" rule.* A great mass of litigation has helped establish the precise contours of the basic going and coming rule and its many exceptions. As a first approximation, the going and coming rule only bars recovery to those employees who, with fixed hours and places of employment, are injured while *off* the employer's premises. The rule itself is, however, subject to elaborate qualifications in most jurisdictions.

Thus, in Fred Meyer, Inc. v. Hayes, 943 P.2d 197 (Or. 1997), the plaintiff was assaulted in her employer's parking lot after leaving work. The court held that the injury was within the course of employment under the "parking lot" exception to the going and coming rule. Should it make a difference that she shopped for a few minutes in the employer's store for personal items before leaving the premises? Does the accident arise out of employment because plaintiff was required to park in the lot? In La Croix v. Omaha Public Schools, 582 N.W.2d 283 (Neb. 1998), the court recognized an exception to the going and coming rule on behalf of a plaintiff who fell in a parking lot located off premises. The employer encouraged her to park there and offered free shuttle services back to the workplace. "By providing transportation, the employer created a condition under which its employees will necessarily encounter hazards while traveling to the premises where they work," thereby establishing the necessary causal link.

Additional complications arise for an employee with no single fixed place of work. Hinojosa v. Workmen's Compensation Appeals Board, 501 P.2d 1176, 1181 (Cal. 1972), involved a farm laborer whose employer owned several noncontiguous ranches. As a condition of his employment, the plaintiff was required to find transportation between worksites. He therefore arranged to be driven by a fellow worker, whom he paid $3.00 to cover his share of the operating expenses. The employee's accident occurred in a collision while he was being driven home from one of the employer's ranches. The court awarded compensation because the trips in question were "the extraordinary transits that vary from the norm because the employer requires a special, different transit, means of transit, or use of a car, for some particular reason of his own." Should compensation be awarded when the routine commute is over hazardous roads? When the employee is required to work long hours of overtime before returning home?

2. *Personal injuries while away from work.* Defining the course of employment often gives rise to intractable difficulties when the injury is suffered by an employee away from the employer's premises. Thus, in Capizzi v. Southern District Reporters, 459 N.E.2d 847, 849 (N.Y. 1984), the claimant, a court reporter, was injured when she slipped and fell while getting out of a hotel bathtub while out of town on a business trip. The traditional New York rule in this area allowed compensation only when the claimant was injured "while traveling on behalf of his employer." Nonetheless, the court rejected its earlier cases and awarded compensation.

> Given the expanded theory of compensability with respect to injuries sustained by traveling employees involving incidents other than dressing or bathing, it is difficult to reconcile a compensation award to an employee who, when returning to her hotel after dinner, slipped and fell on a sidewalk with the denial of an award to a claimant in the present matter, who slipped and fell in a hotel bathtub in preparation for her return to her place of employment in New York City. Both employees sent by their employers on a business trip were removed from their normal environments, thereby increasing the risk of injury; and, as a result, were injured while engaged in "personal acts" attendant to their employment, although not participating in the actual duties of their employment.

Similarly in Meredith v. Jefferson County Property Valuation Administrator, 19 S.W.3d 106 (Ky. 2000), a field representative who traveled from bank to bank was held to be within the course of employment when, just before his first client call, he slipped and fell while having a cup of coffee in a restaurant located near the client's office, sustaining a severe back injury. The court held that substantial "down-time" was the norm, so that the detour for coffee did not count as "a departure from his duties."

3. *Fraud and abuse on the system.* The workers' compensation system has periodically faced large cost increases because of fraud and abuse, especially for mental distress claims that do not result in such discrete episodes as asthma or heart attacks. These so-called mental-mental stress claims were unrecognized before 1971, but have mushroomed under the broader

state interpretations of the phrase "compensable injury." See generally A. Larson §§56.04, 56.06[1]. These claims have invited an elaborate *institutional* network of fraud against the system. Schwartz, Waste, Fraud, and Abuse in Workers' Compensation: The Recent California Experience, 52 Md. L. Rev. 983 (1993), offers a detailed account of the situation as it existed before 1992.

The process often began when a "capper"—who received between $150 and $450 per case—approached a worker, typically on the unemployment line or outside plants that are laying off workers, and told her that she could obtain compensation far in excess of unemployment benefits. A waiting car whisked the worker away for interviews with lawyers and a barrage of medical tests that could easily cost $10,000 or $15,000, all of which, under California law, were charged to the employer whether or not the claim was valid. Often this network of lawyers, physicians, cappers, and handlers tried to persuade the employee that she suffered from various ailments in order to file bogus claims or obtain more medical work. Often weak claims were settled for around $1,500 with some claims obviously bringing more. At its peak, Schwartz reports the estimate for California was "that ten percent of all workers' compensation claims are fraudulent and that twenty-five percent of all employer payments are the result of either fraudulent claims or the deliberate padding of otherwise valid claims."

Statutory reform proved difficult. Demanding workers show that at least 10 percent of the emotional distress was tied to "actual events" on the job, Cal. Lab. Code §3208.3(b) (West. Supp. 2003), was widely regarded as a joke by the bar and easily evaded in practice. Criminal prosecution for fraud and insurance company racketeering claims under RICO against certain workers' compensation mills had greater effect, and Schwartz's subsequent informal investigations found that the fraud mills had been closed down by the various reform measures. See the discussion of the asbestosis and silicosis cases, Chapter 9, *supra* at 727.

3.   Benefits Under the Workers' Compensation Statutes

It is most instructive to compare the benefits received under workers' compensation to common law damages. The common law imposes no maximum limitation on tort damages, and allows full recovery of lost earnings, medical expenses, and pain and suffering. In contrast, all workers' compensation awards have a statutory base that is geared not to the severity of the claimant's injuries as such but only to its resulting "disability," that is, the degree to which it impairs the worker's earning capacity. The worker who is able to carry on without loss of income notwithstanding some physical impairment may be injured, but has not ordinarily sustained any compensable disability under the statutes.

Workers' compensation schemes also impose, albeit with wide variation, strict limitations on the amount of compensation recoverable from the employer. In all states the benefits payable to the employee are usually calculated in terms of the average weekly wage (AWW). The definition of the AWW provided under the New York Work. Comp. Law §14 (McKinney 1992 & Supp. 2003) is typical. That statute provides:

§14.   WEEKLY WAGES BASIS OF COMPENSATION
Except as otherwise provided in this chapter, the average weekly wages of the injured employee at the time of the injury shall be taken as the basis upon which to compute compensation or death benefits, and shall be determined as follows:

1. If the injured employee shall have worked in the employment in which he was working at the time of the accident, whether for the same employer or not, during substantially the whole of the year immediately preceding his injury, his average annual earnings shall consist of three hundred times the average daily wage or salary for a six-day worker, and two hundred sixty times the average daily wage or salary for a five-day worker, which he shall have earned in such employment during the days when so employed;

2. If the injured employee shall not have worked in such employment during substantially the whole of such year, his average annual earnings, if a six-day worker, shall consist of three hundred times the average daily wage or salary, and, if a five-day worker, two hundred and sixty times the average daily wage or salary, which an employee of the same class working substantially the whole of such immediately preceding year in the same or in a similar employment in the same or a neighboring place shall have earned in such employment during the days when so employed.

The statute also provides that where neither of these methods is applicable, the AWW should be calculated by taking into account "the previous earnings of the injured employee and of other employees of the same or most similar class, working in the same or most similar employment." Cases in this class are subject to enormous difficulties, just as tort cases are, especially when injured workers have just started a new career, have changed jobs or locations, or have recently reentered the workforce. See A. Larson, ch. 93.

The workers' compensation laws typically place work-related injuries in one of four categories: temporary partial, temporary total, permanent partial, and permanent total. The disability is treated as temporary when it is believed that the employee, within some period set by statute, will be able to return to work with his capabilities undiminished by the accident. The disability is regarded as permanent when the employee's capacities remain impaired even after the recuperation period. Total and partial are more or less self-defining terms. Finally, the death cases receive separate treatment from the disability cases.

The statutes in every state set out in some detail the levels of compensation appropriate for the different categories of injuries. With permanent total benefits, for example, an initial calculation determines the weekly wage earned by the typical worker. Most states set compensation at a figure equal to two-thirds that wage, although some states set benefits presumptively equal to 80 percent of spendable earnings. Thereafter, this individual weekly wage figure is subject to both statutory minimums and maximums. In California, for example, the figures run as follows. As of January 2006, the payments for temporary total benefits are set at two-thirds the worker's wage and two-thirds AWW. They run from a minimum of $126 (or full AWW if less) to a maximum of $840, up from a $112 minimum and $224 maximum in 1987. The benefits run for the duration of the disability. The lowest state on the totem pole is Georgia, whose compensation benefits are also set at two-thirds of the worker's wage, with a minimum of $50 (or full AWW if less) and a maximum of $500, where benefits run for only 400 weeks. Iowa sets the standard for generosity at the high end, with benefits calculated at 80 percent of the workers' weekly wage, from a minimum of $229 or actual wage if it is less, up to a high of $1311, for the duration of the disability. Similar calculations are made for permanent partial disabilities, although in some states the maximum figures allowable in these cases are lower than those permitted for permanent total disabilities. Finally, most states have special tables for death benefits. These award some multiple of the AWW wage, typically in the neighborhood of 400 or 500 weeks. For the detailed calculations, see A. Larson, Tables 7 (permanent total), 8 (permanent partial), 6 (temporary total), and 12 (death benefits), as periodically updated.

The tables, of course, do not resolve all factual disputes in setting the partial and total benefits for permanent disabilities. In general these benefits are measured by the expected loss in earning power attributable to the worker's medical impairment, up to some specified statutory maximum. For a broad class of undifferentiated injuries (e.g., backaches and occupational diseases), the calculation of benefits turns on a number of factors, each material but none decisive. One part of the picture is the medical condition itself and its amenability to improvement over time. A second part is whether the particular employee has engaged in useful employment after the injury. Where such employment is established, account must be taken of the wages earned in order to determine the diminution of earning capacity. Where, however, there is no further employment, it must be determined whether the employee is fit for any further employment and whether the employer has offered him work that is appropriate to his current condition. For an exhaustive summary of these rules, see A. Larson, ch. 81.

A full appreciation of the benefits systems created by the workers' compensation laws requires some brief discussion of "scheduled benefits." For the loss or destruction of an organ or limb, the benefits awarded to the victim are not calculated anew in terms of wage loss attributable to the injury. Instead, reference is made to some schedule of damages either set out or authorized by statute. Here, not only is the nature of the disability (e.g., loss of sight in one eye, loss of leg below knee but above ankle) taken into account, but also the employee's occupation, age, and sometimes, as in California, number of dependents. Scheduled damages are not set out in dollar figures, but are typically expressed as some multiple of the AWW. Thus, the New York Workers' Compensation statute provides, in §15(3) (McKinney 1993 & Supp. 2003), as follows:

	Member lost	Number of weeks' compensation		Member lost	Number of weeks' compensation
a.	Arm	312	h.	Great toe	38
b.	Leg	288	i.	Second finger	30
c.	Hand	244			
d.	Foot	205	j.	Third finger	25
e.	Eye	160	k.	Toe other than great toe	16
f.	Thumb	75			
g.	First finger	46	l.	Fourth finger	15

The basic theme is embellished by setting an appropriate number of weeks for persons who suffer multiple disabilities, e.g., a loss of a hand plus loss of an eye. Thereafter, further adjustments are made for moneys received from collateral sources, such as social security disability payments. See §15(3)(u)-(v) of the New York statute.

The benefits calculated under these formulas belong to the worker and are in no event tied to any actual wage loss. The worker who by good fortune can earn as much after the injury as before is, in effect, compensated for the extra effort needed to perform the job. When the evidence establishes an impairment in use, but not a total disability, statutory awards are reduced to reflect the partial nature of the permanent disability. Thus, for a 50 percent loss in the use of an arm, the claimant under section 15(3)(a) of the New York statute will be entitled to receive 166 weeks of compensation given that 312 weeks of benefits are awarded for permanent total disability. On scheduled benefits, see A. Larson, ch. 86.

4. Exclusive Remedy

Rainer v. Union Carbide Corporation
402 F.3d 608 (6th Cir. 2005)

GILMAN, Circuit Judge. Workers at a uranium-enrichment plant near Paducah, Kentucky were exposed over many years to dangerous radioactive substances without their knowledge. Although not yet suffering from any symptoms of a clinical disease, four such workers and members of their families have sued General Electric (GE), the supplier of the spent uranium fuel to the plant, and the plant's three successive operators (the defendant-operators) on various state and federal grounds. In a series of orders, the district court rejected all of the plaintiffs' claims on the basis that no present harm has been shown and that the Kentucky Workers' Compensation Act provides the exclusive remedy for the former workers. For the reasons set forth below, we AFFIRM the judgment of the district court.

I. BACKGROUND

A. FACTUAL BACKGROUND

The Paducah Gas Diffusion Plant (PDGP) is a sprawling industrial plant located on a 3,425-acre tract of land in western Kentucky. It was built by the federal government in the early 1950s as part of an initial foray into uranium processing. Although the Department of Energy (DOE) retains full ownership of the plant, the PGDP has been managed since its construction by three successive operators all who have all been named as defendants in this suit. They are Union Carbide (1950-1984), Martin Marietta (1984-1995), and Lockheed Martin Utilities Services (1995 to the present). Approximately 1,800 individuals have been employed by the PGDP at any one time.

The primary purpose of the PGDP is and always has been to enrich uranium. [The court then describes how uranium is processed and reprocessed, yielding spent uranium that contains two unwanted byproducts, both highly radioactive: neptunium-237 and plutonium-239, which have contaminated the PGDP since 1959 in quantities "well beyond the amount considered safe for a plant the size of the PGDP."]

The rank-and-file PGDP employees were apparently kept ignorant about the presence of transuranics at the plant. One manager testified during a deposition that, despite his ten-year tenure, he could not recall whether workers were ever informed about the presence of either neptunium or plutonium. Company documents also reveal a disregard for worker safety. A 1960 memo written by a medical researcher, for example, noted that management hesitated to have approximately 300 workers examined because of the "union's use of this as an excuse for hazard pay." The same researcher noted that he had "watched one man push up his mask and smoke a cigarette using potentially contaminated hands and gloves." Another memo commented that analyzing neptunium exposure through urine samples would be too "tedious and expensive." Workers were not required to wash their hands and, into the late 1970s, not required to use respirators. . . .

Despite the fact that these transuranics are dangerous carcinogens, however, the plaintiffs have yet to display any salient clinical symptoms. . . .

The plaintiffs nevertheless assert that they have suffered certain subcellular damage to their DNA and chromosomes. [The court then reviews the expert evidence.]

B.   PROCEDURAL BACKGROUND

. . . The plaintiffs commenced suit in September of 1999. In an order dated March 30, 2001, the district court dismissed the claims brought by [these] plaintiffs, concluding that the Kentucky Workers' Compensation Act, Ky. Rev. Stat. Ann. §342.610(4) (2004), provided the exclusive remedy for claims brought by employees against their employers. . . . The relevant provision of the Act states as follows:

> If an employer secures payment of compensation as required by this chapter, the liability of such employer under this chapter shall be exclusive and in place of all other liability of such employer to the employee, his legal representative, husband or wife, parents, dependents, next of kin, and anyone otherwise entitled to recover damages from such employer at law or in admiralty on account of such injury or death.

The plaintiffs acknowledge the normal exclusivity of the Kentucky Workers' Compensation Act, but contend that their claim falls under one of the Act's main exceptions, which reserves a cause of action to a worker who is injured "through the deliberate intention of his employer to produce such injury or death." Ky. Rev. Stat. Ann. §342.610(4) (2004). In so arguing, the plaintiffs assert that the phrase "deliberate intention" must "include conduct undertaken with the knowledge that it will produce a certain result, or is substantially certain to do so." They claim that a narrower interpretation "would mean that a landscaping employer who ordered his workers to mow grass and plant trees in a garden filled with land mines . . . would not be liable under the common law due to the exclusive remedy provisions of the Kentucky Workers' Compensation Act."

We do not find the plaintiffs' hypothetical to be analogous to the facts before us, nor is their position supported by Kentucky law. In Fryman v. Electric Steam Radiator Corp., 277 S.W.2d 25 (Ky. 1955), the first case to directly address the specific meaning of Ky. Rev. Stat. Ann. §342.610(4)'s "deliberate intention" language, the Kentucky Supreme Court considered the case of a employee injured while operating a defective metal press. The court dismissed the worker's claims, concluding that the employer had not possessed the "deliberate intention" to injure as required by Ky. Rev. Stat. Ann. §342.610(4) and noting that "the phrase 'deliberate intention' implies that the employer must have determined to injure the employee." Id. at 26. . . .

This narrow reading of "deliberate intention" has been adopted by subsequent Kentucky cases addressing the question. In McCray v. Davis H. Elliott Co., 419 S.W.2d 542 (Ky. 1967), for example, the estate of a deceased worker claimed that the employer had demonstrated a "deliberate intention" to injure the worker by forcing him to work on a tall, dangerous electrical pole on which he was electrocuted. The Kentucky Supreme Court rejected the estate's claim, citing *Fryman* in declining the invitation to "to equate wanton and gross negligence with 'deliberate intention' as used in KRS [§342.610(4)]." . . .

. . . The plaintiffs nonetheless point to a number of cases from other jurisdictions and to secondary authorities that support the proposition that "deliberate intention" may also include instances where the employer acts with the knowledge that harm might follow. But even if this is the appropriate standard in other jurisdictions and in other fields of law, this is not the Kentucky Supreme Court's interpretation of the Kentucky Workers' Compensation Act. As the district court noted in its lengthy and persuasive assessment, "the definition of 'deliberate intention to produce injury' as used in the [Kentucky Workers' Compensation Act] is much narrower than 'intent' in general tort law, where the substantial certainty analysis is proper. And . . . although a few states have either legislatively or judicially adopted the substantial certainty standard for their intent-based exclusivity exception, none had their genesis in a federal court."

In sum, Kentucky caselaw is dispositive of the claims brought by [these] plaintiffs. Cases like *Fryman* have established that the "deliberate intention" exception to the Kentucky Workers' Compensation Act is viable only when the employer has "determined to injure an employee and used some means appropriate to that end, and there must be a specific intent." *Fryman.* Because no proof has been presented in this case to demonstrate that the defendants possessed the specific intention to injure the PGDP employees, the district court did not err in dismissing [these claims].

NOTES

1. Intentional wrongs by the employer. The decision in *Rainer* takes a narrow view of the intentional harm exception. A broader view was taken in Beauchamp v. Dow Chemical Co., 398 N.W.2d 882, 891-892 (Mich. 1986), where plaintiffs alleged that "Dow intentionally misrepresented and fraudulently concealed the potential danger" associated with exposure to Agent Orange. In dealing with this question, Levin, J., adopted the substantial certainty test from the Second Restatement of Torts.

The "substantial certainty" line of cases defines intentional tort more broadly. An intentional tort "is not . . . limited to consequences which are desired. If the actor knows that the consequences are certain, or substantially certain, to result from his act, and still goes ahead, he is treated by the law as if he had in fact desired to produce the result." It does not matter whether the employer wishes the injury would not occur or does not care whether it occurs. If the injury is substantially certain to occur as a consequence of actions the employer intended, the employer is deemed to have intended the injuries as well. The substantial certainty test tracks the Restatement definition of an intentional tort. . . .

The recent *People v. Film Recovery Systems* case decided in Illinois adds a new perspective to the different intentional tort standards. The facts in the case were as follows: Film Recovery Systems went into the business of recovering silver from film negatives. This was done by placing the negatives into vats of cyanide. Hydrogen cyanide gas would bubble up from the vats and there was inadequate ventilation. The employer knew about the dangers. The labels on the chemicals being used contained adequate warnings; as a result, the employer hired only employees who could not speak or read English. The workers complained about the fumes daily. In 1981, an inspector had warned that the operation had outgrown the plant. The employer's response was to move the executive offices while tripling the size of the operations. Eventually one worker died and several others were seriously injured because of hydrogen cyanide poisoning. The corporate officers were convicted of involuntary manslaughter.

In *Beauchamp*, Levin., J., explicitly rejected the effort to equate "substantial certainty" with "substantial likelihood" as was done in Jones v. VIP Development Co., 472 N.E.2d 1046, 1051 (Ohio 1984). There the plaintiff charged that "the defendant employer 'intentionally, maliciously, willfully and wantonly' removed the safety cover from the discharge chute." The court used the broad Restatement definitions of intent to define the exception to the exclusive remedy rule.

> Thus, a specific intent to injure is not an essential element of an intentional tort where the actor proceeds despite a perceived threat of harm to others which is *substantially certain*, not merely likely to occur. It is this element of substantial certainty which distinguishes a merely negligent act from intentionally tortious conduct. Where a defendant acts despite his knowledge that the risk is appreciable, his conduct is negligent. Where the risk is great, his actions may be characterized as reckless or wanton, but not intentional. The actor must know or believe that harm is a substantially certain consequence of his act before an intent to injure will be inferred.

As applied, *Jones* appears to convert every failure to warn case into an intentional tort, thereby gutting the exclusive remedy provision. In 1986, the Ohio Legislature extensively revised its statute to undo the *Jones* line of cases, Ohio Rev. Code Ann. §4121.80, but that statute was overruled in its entirety in Brady v. Safety-Kleen Corp., 576 N.E.2d 722, 729 (Ohio 1991), where the court held that intentional torts always fall outside the scope of employment. The Ohio Legislature tried again to limit the scope of its intentional harm exception in Ohio R.C. 2745.01, which requires a claimant to "prove by clear and convincing evidence that the employer deliberately committed all the elements of an employer intentional tort." This tort covered "an act committed by an employer in which the employer deliberately and intentionally injures, causes an occupational disease of, or causes the death of any employee." But in Johnson v. BP Chemicals, 707 N.E.2d 1107, 1112 (Ohio 1999), the Ohio Supreme Court, by a five to four decision, followed *Brady*, striking the statute down, saying that intentional torts "will always take place outside [the employment] relationship."

2. *Dual capacity.* A second important exception to the exclusive remedy provisions is the so-called dual capacity doctrine. In Duprey v. Shane, 249 P.2d 8, 15 (Cal. 1952), the defendant chiropractor mistreated his nurse when she came to him for treatment for a work-related injury. The court held that the defendant was a "person other than the employer" and allowed her tort action on the ground that since "Dr. Shane—bore towards his employee two relationships—that of employer and that of a doctor—there should be no hesitancy in recognizing this fact as a fact."

Duprey has received a rocky reception elsewhere. In Suburban Hospital, Inc. v. Kirson, 763 A.2d 185, 204 (Md. 2000), the plaintiff, an employee of the defendant hospital, suffered a work-related injury that required medical treatment, which the hospital supplied. While recovering from surgery, the plaintiff suffered additional harms from the admitted post-operative negligence of one of defendant's patient care technicians. After an exhaustive review of the cases the court sided with the majority of states that had declined to follow *Duprey*. It held that the plaintiff's position undermined "the social contract on which workers' compensation is based. . . . We hold, however, that in exchange for the imposition of no fault limited liability for workplace accidents, Suburban bought peace from being considered as a third party when rendering hospital services to Kirson in fulfillment of its obligation under the Act to 'provide medical care.'" *Kirson* was rejected in Wymer v. JH Hospitals, 50 S.W.3d 195 (Ky. 2001). For a sustained evaluation of the dual capacity test, see A. Larson, ch. 113.

3. *Tort actions against fellow employees.* In Fuerschbach v. Southwest Airlines Co. 439 F.3d 1197 (10th Cir. 2006), the plaintiff had just completed her probation period at Southwest Airlines. As a graduation prank, two of Southwest's supervisors persuaded two Albuquerque police officers to stage a mock arrest of the plaintiff, which included handcuffing her for a supposed prior offense in front of her coworkers. This "joke gone bad" caused alleged psychological injuries for which the plaintiff sought tort

damages against the two supervisors and Southwest. Lucero, C.J., held that workers compensation was the plaintiff's sole remedy, saying:

> Fuerschbach, however, argues that the incident giving rise to this case was so egregious that it cannot be considered horseplay. Although we agree that [the supervisors' request of the officers] was ill-considered, the horseplay jurisprudence is broad enough to encompass it. Analogous cases from other jurisdictions show that diverse and even more repugnant workplace incidents have properly been considered compensable. See, e.g., Nelson v. Winnebago Indus., 619 N.W.2d 385 (Iowa 2000) (suit claiming false imprisonment and battery, where plaintiff was duct taped from head to toe "like a mummy" in a prank to commemorate his transfer); Diaz v. Newark Industrial Spraying, Inc., 35 N.J. 588, 174 A.2d 478 (N.J. 1961) (co-employee threw bucket of lacquer thinner on plaintiff; thinner was immediately ignited by nearby flame causing serious injuries). . . .

4. *Tort actions against a third-party defendant.* A uniform line of cases has held that employees are not barred by the exclusive remedy provision of the workers' compensation acts from bringing tort actions against unrelated third parties. Courts have treated third-party automobile drivers and product manufacturers, for example, as strangers to the workers' compensation bargain who are not entitled to any benefit from it. See generally A. Larson, ch. 110. The hard question asks whether the exclusive remedy provision then protects the employer against an action for indemnity and contribution by a third party defendant found liable to the plaintiff. In the early case of Westchester Lighting Co. v. Westchester County Small Estates Corp., 15 N.E.2d 567, 569 (N.Y. 1938), the court allowed the action on a theory of implied indemnity based on the "independent obligation" of care that the employer owes the third party. *Westchester Lighting* was followed under the Federal Employees Compensation Act (FECA) in Lockheed Aircraft Corp. v. United States, 460 U.S. 190 (1983). There a civilian employee of the United States was killed when a C-5A transport, operated by the United States and manufactured by Lockheed, crashed outside of Saigon in April 1975. The employee sued Lockheed for its defective manufacture of the aircraft and Lockheed in turn sought indemnity from the United States, which argued that Lockheed's suit was barred by §8116(c) of the FECA, which, on the model of the New York statute, provided that liability under the statute is "exclusive . . . to the employee, his legal representative, spouse, dependents, next of kin [or] any other person otherwise entitled to recover tort damages against the United States." The Supreme Court held that the words "any other person" were not broad enough to encompass the third party claim of Lockheed and allowed the action to go forward.

5. *Breaking the eternal triangle.* Under the current law, the employee's successful third-party action also works for the benefit of the employer who

is normally allowed to recoup workers' compensation benefits already paid to the worker, in order to prevent the injured party from obtaining a double recovery. An alternative approach stipulates that in third party actions, the injured worker may recover only damages in excess of the amounts paid or payable for such injury under the workers' compensation statutes. The employer would then remain liable in full under such statutes but would be denied any workers' compensation lien against the employee's (reduced) tort recovery against a third-party. This plan also eliminates the need for any third party indemnity actions against the employer. For a defense of this compensation setoff, see Epstein, The Coordination of Workers' Compensation Benefits with Tort Damage Awards, 13 Forum 464 (1978).

6. *The plaintiff's side: derivative or independent actions?* Generally, the exclusive remedy provision bars not only the tort claim of the employee, but also any derivative actions brought by the employee's dependents, including actions for loss of the employee's services, loss of consortium, and even actions for emotional distress suffered by a spouse who witnessed an employee's injuries. See Cole v. Fair Oaks Fire Protection District, 729 P.2d 743 (Cal. 1987). In Snyder v. Michael's Stores, Inc., 945 P.2d 781, 786 (Cal. 1997), the court refused to extend this line of cases to bar a child's actions for prenatal injuries arising from her mother's workplace exposures:

> Biologically, fetal and maternal injury have no necessary relationship. The processes of fetal growth and development are radically different from the normal physiological processes of a mature human. Whether a toxin or other agent will cause congenital defects in the developing embryo or fetus depends not on whether the mother herself is injured, but on the exact stage of the embryo or fetus's development at the time of exposure, as well as on the degree to which maternal exposure results in embryonic or fetal exposure. Even when the mother *is* injured, moreover, the derivative injury rule does not apply, unless the child's claim can be considered merely collateral to the mother's work-related injury, a conclusion that rests on the legal or logical basis of the claim rather than on the biological cause of the fetal injury.

Should the risk of tort damages allow employers to keep pregnant women or women under 45 out of certain dangerous workplaces?

SECTION C.   NO-FAULT INSURANCE

1.   *Automobile No-Fault Insurance*

Proposals to extend workers' compensation principles to cover *non-industrial* accidents date back to the early days of workers' compensation laws. Ballantine, A Compensation Plan for Railway Accident Claims, 29 Harv. L. Rev. 705 (1916), identifies the two elements that lie at the root of most modern no-fault proposals. First, liability, irrespective of negligence, "is founded upon conviction that the cost of transportation service should include the expense of insuring the passenger against all risks peculiar to the service for which he pays his fare." The second principle, that of a fixed and limited schedule of damages, "is founded upon the belief that exact money compensation for physical injury, now supposed to be determined by juries, is impossible, and that if companies are held as insurers and not as wrongdoers there is no reason why the entire risk involved in the transportation service should be borne by the transportation agency."

Although Ballantine envisioned his no-fault scheme for railway accidents, in fact his article established the basic pattern for the no-fault automobile insurance proposal offered by the Columbia Plan of 1932. See Report of Committee to Study Compensation for Automobile Accidents (Columbia Reports) (1932). The Columbia Plan followed the pattern of tort law insofar as it envisioned a system of third party insurance: "[e]very owner of a motor vehicle shall pay compensation for disability or death from personal injury caused by the operation of such motor vehicle, without regard to fault as a cause of the injury or death. . . ." The basic rule was then qualified by limited exceptions: persons who intentionally brought about their own injuries could not recover; coverage did not extend to people who drove without the owner's permission, express or implied. When published, the plan was subject to considerable discussion and debate. It received serious study in Connecticut, New York, Virginia, and Wisconsin but was never adopted in any jurisdiction.

The next wave of no-fault automobile legislation peaked in the 1960s and shifted to a system of first-party coverage. The most influential defense of this system was R. Keeton and J. O'Connell, Basic Protection for the Accident Victim (1965). This work also contained a "Basic Protection Plan" for personal injuries, which often involved the payment of periodic damages, without the use of scheduled damages found in the workers' compensation cases. The key feature of these plans is a partial exemption provision which purports to eliminate the tort system for less serious injuries, while allowing plaintiffs with major injuries to get two sources of recovery when the defendant is found liable, and one if he is not. Judge Keeton later defended this program on the ground that "the no-fault laws effect a distinct improvement in the reparations system to the extent that they correct the inequity of relatively poorer treatment for the more severely injured persons." Keeton, Compensation Systems and Utah's No-Fault Statute, 1973 Utah L. Rev. 383, 398. In addition, the no-fault system was defended in an extensive government report, U.S. Department of Transportation, Motor Vehicle Crash Losses and Their Compensation in the United States, 94-129 (1971). It argued that the first-party system would substitute the convenience of homeowners and health insurance for the dangers of an adversarial relationship, and would include in its coverage all those individuals who could not prove fault under the traditional tort system. More concretely, it has been claimed that the tort system fails because:

> Only 45% of all those killed or seriously injured in auto accidents benefited in any way under the tort liability system. . . .
> Tort liability insurance would appear to cost in the neighborhood of $1.07 in total system expenses to deliver $1.00 in net benefits to victims. . . .

How might these charges be answered?

American Bar Association, Special Committee on Automobile Insurance Legislation, Automobile No-Fault Insurance 13-17 (1978)*

WHY THE STATISTICAL STUDIES CRITICAL OF THE FAULT SYSTEM ARE FATALLY FLAWED

[Each of the above mentioned] "findings" is seriously misleading, if not demonstrably incorrect. The first, that only 45 percent of those seriously injured in automobile accidents received any benefits under the tort liability system, is meaningless once it is recognized that tort liability is not intended as a system of insurance that can properly be evaluated under a criterion of comprehensiveness. Since not all accidents are the result of culpable fault solely on the part of the injurer, it is not surprising that not all accident victims recover under the tort system. Indeed, if all did, that would be evidence that judges and juries had converted the tort system into an insurance scheme, contrary to its purposes. This illustrates the dilemma of tort liability, when evaluated as if it were an insurance system: if a low percentage of victims recover, this fact can be used as evidence that liability provides inadequate compensation; but if a high percentage recover, this fact can be used as evidence that liability has been converted into, and hence should be replaced by, explicit insurance.

The 45 percent figure is also misleading in ignoring the degree to which victims of automobile accidents obtain compensation outside of the tort system — from life, collision, disability, accident, medical, and other first-party insurance, and from wage-replacement sources such as sick leave and workers' compensation. When these sources of compensation are included,

---

* The preface to the report indicates that Professor Richard A. Posner was "primarily responsible" for its drafting.

as DOT acknowledged, of those suffering serious injury or death in automobile accidents, "about 9 out of 10 recovered some losses." This is twice the percentage recovering in tort alone. It suggests that a combination of tort liability with voluntary first-party insurance and other sources of compensation provides compensation for almost all victims of automobile accidents. . . .

One of the most frequently cited statements in the DOT studies is that it costs about $1.07 in administrative expenses for each $1.00 in net benefits delivered to the accident victim. This may seem a high ratio of expense to pay-out — until it is remembered that a major benefit of tort liability which is not counted in the benefits received by victims is the reduction in the accident rate that is brought about by adherence to the standard of care established by the fault system. This effect of tort liability has not been adequately measured, nor its monetary equivalent computed, but to ignore it completely is to give a specious plausibility to DOT's statistical demonstration that the expenses of the system exceed its benefits.

Epstein, Automobile No-Fault Plans: A Second Look at First Principles
13 Creighton L. Rev. 769, 789-790 (1980)

[It is also important to examine the] soundness of the automobile no-fault plans when set in opposition to their nontort rival, the total abolition of the tort system without any substitute compulsory first party protection. In this connection the benefits of the no-liability system must be stressed. One of its great attractions is that it neatly avoids the troublesome question of how to make a collective determination of the level of payments for certain injuries, and the corresponding question of how to distribute the premium burden amongst those who will be conscripted to finance the system. To the contrary, it is a little noticed but important feature of most automobile no-fault plans that they achieve their universality of coverage by the *compulsory* purchase of the benefits in question, thereby committing all individuals to take a certain set of benefits in accordance with a predetermined set of coverage formulas. As I have in general a strong basic preference for voluntary markets, both on efficiency and liberty grounds, I think that there is much to be said for the system that allows individuals to choose the nature and type of benefits in light of their own estimation of their personal circumstances and needs. Those who wish to buy deep coverage with high deductibles should be allowed to do so, while those who want first dollar coverage with shallow protection should be free to do so as well. Those who want group coverage are free to explore that possibility. It may well be that the case is made for the abolition of all tort liability, but it does not follow that those same arguments require instituting compulsory first party insurance.

The real quid pro quo for losing the benefits of being a tort plaintiff is being freed from the burden of being a tort defendant. It is *not* the surrender of a tort claim for the receipt of a set of benefits that are not requested, and which perhaps ill suit the needs of the party to whom they are provided.

References. W. Blum and H. Kalven, Jr., Public Law Perspectives on a Private Law Problem — Auto Compensation Plans (1965); Calabresi, Fault, Accidents and the Wonderful World of Blum and Kalven, 75 Yale L.J. 216 (1965); Blum and Kalven, The Empty Cabinet of Dr. Calabresi: Auto Accidents and General Deterrence, 34 U. Chi. L. Rev. 239 (1967); Symposium: Alternative Compensation Schemes and Tort Theory, 73 Cal. L. Rev. 548 (1985); Trebilcock, Incentive Issues in the Design of "No-Fault" Compensation Systems, 39 U. Toronto L.J. 19 (1989).

Pinnick v. Cleary
271 N.E.2d 592 (Mass. 1971)

REARDON, J. [The plaintiff alleged he was injured in an automobile accident caused solely by the negligence of the defendant. His common-law tort action sought damages in excess of those allowed under the Massachusetts no-fault statute, c. 670. After the defendant interposed the statute as an affirmative defense, the plaintiff brought his bill in equity to the Massachusetts Supreme Judicial Court, challenging the no-fault statute on the grounds that it unconstitutionally deprived him of "his right to full recovery in tort."]

SUMMARY OF CHAPTER 670

[The court starts with an extensive account of the basic provisions of the statute, noting that] it appears that the statute affords the citizen the security of prompt and certain recovery to a fixed amount of the most salient elements of his out-of-pocket expenses and an increased flexibility in avoiding duplicate coverage, at double premiums, for the same expenses. In return for this he surrenders the possibly minimal damages for pain and suffering recoverable in cases not marked by serious economic loss or objective indicia of grave injury and the outside chance that through a generous settlement or a liberal award by a judge or jury in such a case he may be able to reap a monetary windfall out of his misfortune. . . .

The key concept embodied in c. 670 is that of personal injury protection insurance, which is required of all owners of motor vehicles registered in

Massachusetts. Under this coverage, personal injury protection benefits are paid by the insurer, as the expenses they cover accrue, to the insured, members of his household, authorized operators or passengers of his motor vehicle including guest occupants, and any pedestrians struck by him, regardless of fault in the causation of the accident [up to $2,000.] . . .

The only limitation imposed by c. 670 on the potential plaintiff's prior right of recovery at common law is the elimination of damages for "pain and suffering, including mental suffering associated with . . . injury" except in certain specified categories of cases. Section 5 of c. 670 provides generally that the reasonable and necessary medical expenses incurred by a plaintiff in the treatment of his injuries must be over $500 to permit recovery for pain and suffering. However, recognizing that certain types of injuries could entail considerable pain and suffering which would warrant monetary compensation regardless of medical expense incurred, the Legislature provided by way of exception to the general rule that damages for pain and suffering could be sought in all cases involving five designated types of injuries. These are a fracture, injury causing death, injury consisting in whole or in part of loss of a body member, permanent and serious disfigurement, and injury resulting in loss of sight or hearing as elsewhere defined in the General Laws. The victim whose injury falls outside these categories and whose medical expenses are less than $500 cannot recover at all for pain and suffering. However, it is still possible for the person who desires to assure for himself recovery in excess of his out-of-pocket costs to do so. Just as he may elect a deductible if he has medical payments insurance to avoid duplicate recovery for medical expenses, so he may choose to keep both forms of insurance in full precisely to allow himself double recovery of these expenses. Other forms of duplicate coverage are equally possible. It is true that the amount of excess he will receive thereby will bear no necessary relation to the value of his pain and suffering as arbitrarily set by a jury but, on the other hand, he is assured of some profit over out-of-pocket expenses in every motor vehicle accident. This certainty he was never afforded by his prior "right" to recovery for pain and suffering in a suitable case, which in order to be realized even in such a case had to be actively pursued at considerable expense. . . .

NATURE OF RIGHTS AFFECTED

. . . The plaintiff claims that c. 670 has impaired a cause of action which is on a higher, more sacrosanct level than the "ordinary" common law cause of action. Two alternative reasons are advanced in support of this contention: first, that the tort action has the status of a "vested property right," and, second, that the function of the cause of action is to safeguard the fundamental "right of personal security and bodily integrity" which, although not mentioned in the Bill of Rights of the United States Constitution, is nonetheless protected by it. We find both grounds unpersuasive.

In arguing that the cause of action affected by c. 670 constitutes a vested property right, the plaintiff seems to ignore the distinction between a cause of action which has accrued and the expectation which every citizen has if a legal wrong should occur to find redress according to the rules of statutory and common law applicable at that time. The Legislature is admittedly restricted in the extent to which it can retroactively affect common law rights of redress which have already accrued. However, there is authority in abundance for the proposition that "[n]o person has a vested interest in any rule of law entitling him to insist that it shall remain unchanged for his benefit." New York Cent. R.R. v. White, 243 U.S. 188 [1916], 198; Munn v. Illinois, 94 U.S. 113, 134 [1876]. . . .

DUE PROCESS ISSUES

A. APPLICABLE PRINCIPLES

We will deal first with the propriety of c. 670 under the due process clause. The overall test under this clause is whether the statute bears a reasonable relation to a permissible legislative objective. . . . In the application of this test, the statute is accorded a presumption of constitutionality, a corollary of which is that if a state of facts could exist which would justify the legislation, it must be presumed to have existed when the statute was passed. . . .

Such actions in other contexts have been sustained because it was felt that the Legislature was acting "to attain a permissible legislative object." Silver v. Silver, 280 U.S. 117, 122 ("guest statute," taking away right of gratuitous passenger in automobile to sue driver on account of mere negligence). . . .

In the instant case, however, the Legislature has not attempted to abolish the preexisting right of tort recovery and leave the automobile accident victim without redress. On the contrary, as was pointed out above, the statute has affected his substantive rights of recovery only in one respect and has simply altered his method of enforcing them in all others. Therefore, c. 670 may be judged by the stricter test which the plaintiff urges upon us and for which there is considerable authority in workmen's compensation cases: whether the statute provides an adequate and reasonable substitute for preexisting rights. New York Cent. R.R. v. White, 243 U.S. 188, 201 (New York workmen's compensation statute). The similarity between c. 670 and the workmen's compensation statutes, in the nature of their purposes and the means chosen to achieve them, also leads us to conclude that the reasonable and adequate substitute test is appropriate to apply here even if its application is not constitutionally required. . . .

B. DOES C. 670 BEAR A RATIONAL RELATION TO A LEGITIMATE LEGISLATIVE OBJECTIVE?

[The court concluded that the individual provisions of chapter 670 withstand challenges under the due process clause, and that the statute taken as a whole did not deprive the plaintiff of his rights under the equal protection clause.]

C. DOES C. 670 PROVIDE A REASONABLE SUBSTITUTION FOR PRIOR RIGHTS?

[The court relied heavily on New York Central R.R. v. White, *supra* at 966, which had sustained the workers' compensation bargain of broader coverage with lower damages.]

In considering the effect of c. 670, we cannot view it from the point of view of plaintiffs and defendants, for these are not preexisting categories as are the employers and employees affected by a workmen's compensation act. Every driver is a potential plaintiff and, equally, a potential defendant. The desired effect of c. 670 on all motorists alike is initially to make available to them compulsory insurance at lower rates due to the savings to insurance companies in administrative expenses and total payments which are expected to follow from c. 670. If injury occurs on the road, motorists are assured of the probability of quick and efficient payment of the first $2,000 of defined losses incurred. In cases of accidents in which the motorist was not negligent, he avoids the uncertainty, delay and cost of a tort proceeding. He still retains the option of recovering more by litigation if he so wishes and the facts so warrant. Although c. 670 may also have the effect of depriving him of his damages for pain and suffering in such an instance, the exchange of rights involved with respect to the driver in an accident in which he was not negligent bears considerable resemblance to that effected by the statute in the *White* case with respect to employees.

This exchange of rights cannot be viewed in isolation, however, for non-negligent drivers are not a distinct class. To it must be added the effect of c. 670 on the driver in a case where he has been negligent or where negligence cannot be determined. In this situation, rather than no compensation for his own injuries, c. 670 accords him the same benefits he would have if he were non-negligent.[17] In addition, he is afforded immunity from liability to the extent other injured parties are eligible for benefits. And,

---

17. The day has long since passed when legal negligence in the automobile accident situation could be equated with moral culpability. The whole concept of negligence has in fact become something of a fiction, since in many cases fault cannot meaningfully be placed on any one of the parties more than on another. The new comparative negligence statute is a recognition of this inherent difficulty of assigning fault to one party only. The legally negligent driver is therefore morally as entitled to compensation as the other parties. It should be noted in addition that in defined cases where he is clearly culpable, the injured party is denied benefits under c. 670.

just as his right to sue for pain and suffering is limited when he is non-negligent, so he is protected from comparable claims where he has been negligent. The effect of c. 670 on Massachusetts motorists thus is to provide benefits in return for affected rights at least as adequate as those provided to New York employers and employees in return for rights taken by the act in the *White* case. . . .

[The court holds that the inclusion of pedestrian harms does not invalidate c. 670 since they too receive the benefit of] the certainty of a prompt recovery of a limited amount and limited exemption from liability instead of the necessity of tort proceedings or no compensation at all and liability to an unlimited amount. . . .

NOTES

1. *Constitutional issues.* The strong presumption of constitutionality operative in Pinnick v. Cleary was also adopted in other states that sustained their own no-fault plans. Montgomery v. Daniels, 340 N.E.2d 444 (N.Y. 1975); Opinion of the Justices, 304 A.2d 881 (N.H. 1973). Where the no-fault schemes have been struck down, courts have usually relied on the specific language of state constitutions and not on the broad principles of the due process or equal protection clauses. Thus, in Grace v. Howlett, 283 N.E.2d 474 (Ill. 1972), the Illinois Supreme Court struck down the state no-fault scheme as offending several state constitutional provisions, including one that required that no "special law" be passed when a "general law" could be made applicable. Likewise, the Florida court in Kluger v. White, 281 So. 2d 1 (Fla. 1973), invalidated the property no-fault provisions of the Florida law as violative of the state constitutional provisions guaranteeing that the courts "shall be open for redress of any injury." This legislation did not provide any "reasonable alternative" remedy to protect the rights of individuals whose property was damaged or destroyed by the acts of another.

2. *The varieties of no-fault plans.* Although no-fault plans typically provide first-party compensation not based on fault, they differ in their treatment of limits, deductibles, options, collateral sources, and the like. Thus, total benefits in New York can reach $50,000, subject to further limits on income loss and worker expenses, which are payable to a level of $1,000 per month for a three-year period. Kentucky provides for $10,000 in benefits while Minnesota allows $20,000 for medical expenses and $20,000 for economic losses. In some jurisdictions optional coverage may be purchased for an additional premium. Pennsylvania, for example, allows optional benefits of $100,000 for medical expenses, $2,500 per month to a maximum of $50,000 for lost income, and a $25,000 death benefit. This bewildering array of plans resists any simple summarization or generalization, and the

particulars in any event are often changed by legislation. For capsule summaries of the various auto no-fault plans, see W. Schermer & I. Schermer, Automobile Liability Insurance chs. 65-86 (4th ed. 2007 rev.), in which it takes over 200 pages to outline the details of each plan presently in effect. See also 3 Harper, James & Gray, Torts §13.8 for a selective summary of some key plan features.

3. *Performance of the no-fault plans.* Given the wide range of no-fault plans, it is difficult to assess how they have fared in practice. Overall, somewhat blandly, the dominant impression is that they have not done as well as their supporters have hoped nor as badly as their detractors have feared. In the political arena the massive push for automobile no-fault peaked in the early 1970s, and since then no new plans have been enacted, although several have been repealed, and others (e.g., Florida, Massachusetts, and Pennsylvania) have undergone extensive reform since their introduction. The system today is best described as one in steady-state, with little current activity.

On theoretical grounds, no-fault plans have been attacked as inefficient because they allow careless drivers to impose costs on others, and induce careful drivers to engage in cautious defensive tactics. Support for that position is found in Elisabeth Landes, Insurance, Liability, and Accidents: A Theoretical and Empirical Investigation of No-Fault Accidents, 25 J.L. & Econ. 49 (1982). Controlling for such variables as age, race and sex, her study concluded that for the years 1967 to 1976 "a medical expense threshold of $500 implies about a 4 percent increase in fatal accident rates; a medical expense threshold of $1,500 implies an increase in fatal accidents of *more than 10 percent*." For a reply to Landes, see O'Connell and Levmore, A Reply to Landes: A Faulty Study of No-Fault's Effect on Fault, 48 Mo. L. Rev. 649 (1983). For a more recent review of the evidence, see Schwartz, Auto No-Fault and First-Party Insurance: Advantages and Problems, 73 S. Cal. L. Rev. 611 (2000), which notes that no-fault systems reverse the premiums for heavy and light vehicles. Under the tort system, the lion's share of the loss goes to drivers of large vehicles owing to the harm that they cause. But under a first-party system this loss is shifted to the lighter vehicles that are hit. Which regime sets the appropriate baseline, and why?

4. *Litigation under automobile no-fault.* Unlike litigation under workers' compensation, the coverage disputes under automobile no-fault plans have been largely humdrum. Representative of the disputes that fall on either side of the line are two Michigan cases. The basic Michigan statute, for example, holds that an insurer "is liable to pay benefits for accidental bodily injury arising out of the ownership, operation maintenance or use of a motor vehicle as a motor vehicle." Mich. Comp. Laws Ann. §500.3105(1) (2007). In McKenzie v. Auto Club Insurance Association, 580 N.W.2d 424 (Mich. 1998), the court denied coverage to two plaintiffs who were nearly asphyxiated by carbon monoxide fumes from their air heater

while sleeping in a camper/trailer attached to plaintiff's pick-up truck because the injury did not arise out of the use of a motor vehicle "as a motor vehicle." The court distinguished the earlier case of Putkamer v. Transamerica Insurance Corp. of America, 563 N.W.2d 683 (Mich. 1997), which held that injuries sustained while entering a motor vehicle were so closely tied to its transportation function that they were covered under the act. See generally I. Schermer, Automobile Liability Insurance ch. 5 (2d ed. 1989).

5. *The tort threshold.* As of 2002 nine states—Arkansas, Delaware, Maryland, New Hampshire, Oregon, South Dakota, Texas, Virginia, and Washington—and the District of Columbia had add-on statutes, in which the plaintiff's right to maintain a tort action was not limited by the adoption of the no-fault plan. See, e.g., R. Joost, Automobile Insurance and No Fault Law (2d ed. 2002). In 13 other states, various thresholds were required before the tort action could be pursued. The various automobile no-fault provisions have different types of tort thresholds. One type of threshold is simply monetary and lets the injured party enter the tort system so long as the medical costs of injury exceed the amount designated in the statute, which as of 1991 varied from a low of $1,000 in Kentucky to a high of $5,000 in Hawaii. Many states have a mix of this monetary threshold with what is known as a verbal threshold. Five states—Florida, Michigan, New Jersey, New York, and Pennsylvania— have a verbal threshold only. In some states—Colorado, Georgia, Kansas, Kentucky, Minnesota, and Utah—permanent disfigurement is required. In others— Florida, Michigan, New Jersey, and Pennsylvania—the verbal formula calls for permanent and significant disfigurement. New York requires significant disfigurement while Massachusetts and North Carolina refer to "permanent and serious" disfigurement. See I. Schermer, Automobile Liability Insurance ch. 10 (2d ed. 1994 rev.); R. Joost, Automobile Insurance and No Fault, ch. 6 (2002).

Choosing the right tort threshold affects the overall operation of the no-fault system. Numerical thresholds act as magnets and encourage parties (as with the workers' compensation system) to inflate their medical costs in order to obtain the keys to the tort kingdom. Verbal thresholds are much more immune from manipulation, but more subject to disputation. Thus, it appears that relatively few claims make it into the tort system over the strong verbal threshold that is found in New York, while in states like California that preserve the traditional tort system, many more personal injury claims make it into the tort system. As one measure of the difference, note that in 1989 for each 100 property damage claims there were 56 claims for bodily injury in California and only 11 in New York. For discussion of this and similar issues, see O'Connell, Carroll, Horowitz & Abrahamse, Consumer Choice in the Auto Insurance Market, 52 Md. L. Rev. 1016 (1993). For an exhaustive survey of the evidence, see S. Carroll,

J. Kakalik, N. Pace & J. Adams, No-Fault Approaches to Compensating People Injured in Automobile Accidents (RAND 1991).

6. *Fraud rings in no-fault auto insurance.* The problem of mass fraud, noted in connection with workers' compensation, has surfaced in New York where the lure of up to $50,000 in free medical care has generated thousands of staged crashes and fraudulent claims. Apparently, "crash dummies"—that is, participants in the fraud ring—drive their cars in front of cars driven by elderly people or women with children. They then stop abruptly to create a crash. The crash dummies fill their car with friends and relations who were paid $1,500 per "patient" to join the scam. The payoff came when an elaborate ring of doctors, lawyers, and acupuncturists, often operating out of fake clinics, billed the insurance companies for the generous New York benefits. The scheme cost an estimated $432 million in New York, adding around $177 to each driver's bill. Five hundred sixty-seven criminal indictments have been issued, with more to come. For the gory details, see Patrick Healy, Investigators Say Fraud Ring Staged Thousands of Crashes, The New York Times, August 13, 2003, at A1. Apparently no ordinary tort suits were filed.

2. *No-Fault Insurance for Medical and Product Injuries*

The widespread adoption of automobile no-fault plans in the early 1970s spurred on proposals to extend no-fault plans into both the medical malpractice and products liability arenas. Unlike automobile no-fault plans, these plans necessarily rely on the third-party coverage mechanisms originally championed by Ballantine for no-fault railway insurance. During the 1970s, one such no-fault proposal was put forward on an elective or voluntary basis. O'Connell, Ending Insult to Injury: No-Fault Insurance for Products and Services 97 (1975):

> Any enterprise should be allowed to elect, if it chooses, to pay from then on for injuries it causes on a no-fault basis, thereby foreclosing claims based on fault or a defect. Under such an option, payment would be made regardless not only of lack of fault or defect on the payer's part but also, as under no-fault auto insurance and workers' compensation, regardless of any fault on the victim's part. In other words, elective no-fault liability would be true no-fault insurance, with the fault of neither the injurer nor the injured having a bearing on payment. The enterprise would be allowed to select all or, if it chose, just certain risks of personal injury it typically creates, for which it could agree to pay for out-of-pocket losses when injury results from those risks. To the extent—and only to the extent—a guarantee of no-fault payment exists at the time of the accident, as under no-fault auto or workers' compensation insurance, no claim based on fault or a defect would be allowed against the party electing to be covered under no-fault liability insurance.

The idea garnered little support, even by those who favored automobile no-fault insurance. One obstacle is that product manufacturers (especially of component products) cannot easily notify the ultimate user or consumer that it has elected coverage under the plan. Indeed, that notice is wholly impossible with bystander injuries. In addition, it is difficult to coordinate this new no-fault coverage with tort liability, workers' compensation, and first-party insurance. Most importantly, the plan lacks any concept of product defect, which expands the class of product-related injuries beyond recognition. Thus, Professor Blum has asked *who* should provide coverage when a worker wearing slippery shoes falls off a well-constructed ladder after drinking a few beers. Blum, Review of O'Connell's *Ending Insult to Injury*, 43 U. Chi. L. Rev. 217 (1975).

While proposals for comprehensive no-fault coverage have largely disappeared in the products area, they have had some influence in the area of medical and hospital injuries. As before, the basic no-fault bargain offers broader coverage and lower administrative expenses in exchange for reduced coverage awards on either an elective or a mandatory basis. And, as before, the central challenge has been to develop a workable definition of a compensable event, which is especially hard to define with respect to missed medical diagnoses. See Epstein, Medical Malpractice: The Case for Contract, 1 Am. Bar Found. Res. J. 87, 141-147 (1976). If these are covered, the expansion of liability under the medical no-fault system is enormous, where the most skilled physicians will face huge exposure. But if they are entirely excluded, even serious diagnostic blunders would no longer count as compensable events. One proposed intermediate solution ties compensation for diagnostic errors back to the reasonable care standard of the negligence system. See Weiler, The Case for No-Fault Medical Liability, 52 Md. L. Rev. 908 (1993), acknowledging that a comprehensive no-fault system must "reinstate the fault principle as the basis for compensating at least this category of iatrogenic injuries."

The interpretative conundrums of broad coverage definitions have brought forth proposals to limit the program by building lists of designated compensable events, or DCEs, in consultation with medical professionals. See Havighurst and Tancredi, "Medical Adversity Insurance" — A No-Fault Approach to Medical Malpractice and Quality Assurance, The Milbank Memorial Fund Quarterly/Health and Society (Spring 1973), reprinted in 613 Ins. L.J. 69 (1974), and developed at greater length in Commission of Medical Professional Liability of the ABA, Designated Compensable Event System: A Feasibility Study (1979). This type of system requires an enormous front-end investment, for lists are needed for each specialty. These lists must be constantly updated, and they face the nasty problem of disentangling responsibility for the adverse consequences of surgery from those of anesthesiology. The use of the DCE system has been criticized in

P. Danzon, Medical Malpractice: Theory, Evidence and Public Policy 217-219 (1985), for also creating odd incentives for both doctor and patient if negligence actions survive for adverse events that might not count as DCEs. Much like the exclusive remedy provisions of the workers' compensation laws, patients will claim that items are not listed if they think they have a strong negligence claim, but will insist that they are DCEs if they do not. She therefore fears that the complexities could simply discourage physicians from taking on high-risk patients in the first place.

One area in which a no-fault scheme has made headway is a highly particularistic, but important, legislative initiative, the National Childhood Vaccine Injury Act of 1986, which was passed in response to a sharp increase in the price of vaccines that threatened to drive many vaccine makers out of the marketplace. As most vaccines are administered to children, the NCVIA in fact covers a large portion of the overall market. Its basic provisions provide for a complex system of no-fault compensation of up to $250,000 for persons who suffer particular side effects from certain vaccine programs within specified time limits. 42 U.S.C. §300aa (2000). In many cases, the statute employs explicit tests for determining whether compensation is owed. For example, the recipient of a measles vaccine who suffers an anaphylactic shock within 24 hours of inoculation can receive payment. The statute also provides that persons who have met the conditions for no-fault recovery may nonetheless choose to reject the payment and sue for tort damages. The largest award under the statute has been $8.4 million, and the average award has been around $833,000. Between 1988 and 2007, about 150 claims were filed per year, covering a wide range of cases of which close to a third received compensation. The issues of coverage in these cases turn heavily on the question of causation in fact, which brings to the fore many of the issues raised in Chapter 6, Section B. Recovery is based on the deceptively simple question of whether the vaccine in question caused the conditions for which the plaintiff seeks damages.

Pafford v. Secretary of Health and Human Services
451 F.3d 1352 (Fed. Cir. 2006) (en banc)

Rader, C.J.

Richelle Pafford (Pafford) alleges that her DTaP [diphtheria, tetanus (commonly known as lockjaw), and pertussis (commonly known as whooping cough)] MMR [measles, mumps, and rubella] and OPV [oral poliovirus] vaccinations resulted in the onset of systematic Juvenile Rheumatoid Arthritis. Because the Special Master correctly interpreted and applied the relevant statutory test for proving causation in off-table cases, this court affirms.

II.

This court reviews the United States Court of Federal Claims' review of the Special Master's decision without deference. Thus, this court examines the Special Master's legal determinations under a "not in accordance with law" standard and factual determinations under an "arbitrary and capricious" standard.

Generally a petitioner can obtain compensation under the vaccine injury program in two ways. In a "table" case, the petitioner has an initial burden to prove an injury listed in the Vaccine Injury Table within the prescribed time period under the [statutory] requirements. . . . Upon satisfying this initial burden, the petitioner earns a presumption of causation. At that point, the burden shifts to the respondent to prove that a factor unrelated to the vaccination actually caused the illness, disability, injury, or condition.

The other avenue for compensation does not involve the presumption of causation conferred by the table. In an "off-table" case (also known as a "causation-in-fact" claim), the petitioner cannot obtain a presumption of causation. Rather, the petitioner in an off-table case has the burden to prove the vaccination in question "caused" the illness, disability, injury, or condition. Pafford does not allege she suffered a table injury. Thus, Pafford must prove causation-in-fact or that the vaccine was actually the cause of her injuries.

Under this court's precedent, Pafford must prove by preponderant evidence both that her vaccination were a substantial factor in causing the illness, disability, injury or condition and that the harm would not have occurred in the absence of the vaccination [under the Restatement's substantial factor test].

This court recently articulated an alternative three-part test. To show causation in fact, the petitioner must show:

(1) a medical theory causally connecting the vaccination and the injury;

(2) a logical sequence of cause and effect showing that vaccination the was the reason for the injury; and (3) . . . a proximate temporal relationship between the vaccine and injury.

The Special Master applied [our] tests . . . correctly in this case. Specifically, the Special Master indicated:

First, a petitioner must provide a reputable medical theory causally connecting the vaccination and the injury. *In fine*, can [the] vaccine(s) at issue cause the type of injury alleged? *Second*, a petitioner must also prove that the vaccine actually caused the alleged symptoms in her particular case.

III.

Applying the causation test to the facts before the court, the Special Master determined that Pafford proved only one of the two prongs of his test by preponderant evidence. Specifically, the Special Master noted, while "it is biologically plausible that one or more of the vaccinations at issue could cause the onset of Still's disease Pafford did not prove that the vaccinations were a but-for cause of her contracting Still's disease." The Special Master was particularly troubled by the lack of evidence demonstrating "any defined time period in which one would expect to see the onset of Still's disease subsequent to a triggering event."

To the Special Master, the absence of temporal linkage evidence prevented him from finding that a vaccination was the reason for the injury rather than other contemporaneous events unrelated to the vaccinations. ("[A]bsent an appropriate time frame, the Court cannot find the mere temporal proximity of the vaccination and injury dispositive."). These contemporaneous events included: (1) a positive test for mycoplasma (a type of bacteria); (2) x-rays showing a thickening of the sinus membrane consistent with a sinus infection; (3) an earlier bout of tonsillitis; and (4) an earlier cold accompanied by diarrhea. Thus, according to the Special Master, Pafford did not prove by preponderant evidence that one or more of her vaccinations were a "but-for" cause of her contracting Still's disease.

[The Court then distinguished Shyface v. Secretary of Health & Human Services, 165 F.3d 1344 (Fed. Cir. 1999).] *Shyface* was a vaccine injury case involving an infant's April 1, 1993 DPT [an older version of the DTaP vaccination.] Four days after inoculation, the infant was taken to a hospital with a fever hovering between 109° and 110° F; tragically the infant died from the fever the same day. Subsequent tests revealed the presence of a bacterial infection that could not be ruled out as the cause of death. Thus, at trial, petitioners' expert theorized the DPT vaccination "caused" the infant's fever, which was then significantly exacerbated by the infection. In other words, petitioners' expert argued there were two "but-for" causes, the vaccination and the infection, each of the "but-for" causes being a substantial factor in the infant's death. When presented with this theory, the Special Master found preponderant evidence linking the DPT vaccination to the infant's death, but still rejected petitioners' claim because "it is impossible to know with any degree of confidence, which source is the predominant cause of death."

On appeal, this court reversed. This court held that, in order to establish a *prima facie* case, the petitioners had to show "that the DPT vaccine was both a but-for cause of and a substantial factor in [the infant's] death." The court went on to explain that, while the vaccination must be a "substantial factor" in the infant's death, it need not be the sole factor or even the predominant factor. Thus, the court reversed the Special Master's decision in favor of respondent; the Special Master should have awarded compensation to the petitioners who had proven the DPT vaccine was both a but-for cause of and a substantial factor in the infant's death.

Unlike *Shyface*, the petitioner here never established that the vaccinations were a but-for cause of her contracting Still's disease. Thus, this case does not feature several "but-for" causes, one of which is a vaccination. Rather, the Special Master concluded he was unable to tell whether any of the vaccinations made any contribution to her contracting Still's disease due, in part, to the absence of "evidence indicating an appropriate time frame in which Still's disease will manifest subsequent to a triggering event." "Without such a defined time period, the link between the vaccinations and the injury is tenuous."

Evidence demonstrating petitioner's injury occurred within a medically acceptable time frame bolsters a link between the injury alleged and the vaccination at issue under the "but-for" prong of the causation analysis. If, for example, symptoms normally first occur ten days after inoculation but petitioner's symptoms first occur several weeks after inoculation, then it is doubtful the vaccination is to blame. In contrast, if symptoms normally first occur ten days after inoculation and petitioner's symptoms do, in fact, occur within this period, then the likelihood increases that the vaccination is at least a factor. Strong temporal evidence is even more important in cases involving contemporaneous events other than the vaccination, because the presence of multiple potential causative agents makes it difficult to attribute "but-for" causation to the vaccination. After all, credible medical expertise may postulate that any of the other contemporaneous events may have been the sole cause of the injury. Thus, it was entirely proper for the Special Master to require Pafford to prove but-for causation, including some showing of temporal relationship between the vaccination(s) and the onset of injury.

[The Court then held that the plaintiff's expert, Dr. Levin, proved only that the vaccine could have, in principle, caused the plaintiff's condition but did not] provide any evidence about a medically acceptable time frame for the onset of the disease following the vaccination. . . . Dr. Levin also did not discuss in detail the other contemporaneous events unrelated to the vaccinations. Thus, the Special Master properly concluded, under our arbitrary and capricious standard of review, that Dr. Levin's testimony standing alone was not sufficient to prove the medically acceptable time frame or to link the onset of Still's disease to the vaccinations in this case.

Dyk, J. dissenting:

[T]he statute clearly contemplates that causation in fact may be established in off-Table cases without showing the "medically accepted temporal relationship" listed in the Table.

This purpose would be directly thwarted if proof of a medically accepted timeframe were required to show causation in off-Table cases. But that is exactly what the majority requires here. In this case, there was substantial evidence regarding the biological mechanism of causation, even though the experts did not identify a medically accepted temporal relationship.

Under the majority's holding, any petitioner who fails to establish a medically accepted temporal relationship automatically lacks an essential element of their *prima facie* case for causation in fact. That holding is inconsistent with the clear provisions of the statute and our prior holdings interpreting it.

NOTES

1. *Compensable events under the NCVIA.* The (relative) success of the NCVIA rests on two key design elements. First, vaccines are administered in controlled environments with accurate records so that there is little dispute that a particular child has been vaccinated. That contrasts dramatically with the haphazard administration of many prescription and nonprescription drugs where often a hotly disputed question is one of simple identification: Did the plaintiff take a particular medicine and, if so, how much? Second, even if it the vaccine was administered, what are its effects? In some cases, the vaccine produces "signature" injuries so that inferences of causation are relatively straightforward. But in off-table cases, as *Pafford* indicates, the occurrence of a disease or harmful condition, like juvenile arthritis, raises an elaborate causation inquiry similar to those found in ordinary product liability cases against drug companies. Even if the warning issue disappears from NCVIA cases, physical causation does not. The various schemes to extend no-fault liability for drugs have gained little traction because of the large risks of false positives on both the identification and physical causation issues.

2. *The thimerosal autism link.* In recent years, the major struggle under the NCVIA has been over whether thimerosal, a mercury-based preservative, has been responsible for the sharp increase in observed autism cases from 1 in every 2,500 children a generation ago to 1 in 166 children today. Thimerosal was much favored because it functioned as a binding agent that allowed for many different vaccines to be administered at one time, lowering the number of office visits and increasing the early-infant protection that vaccines offer against childhood diseases. In 1999, the American Academy of Pediatrics requested removal of thimerosal from all pediatric vaccines because of its possible, if undocumented, link with autism. In 2001, the Institute of Medicine, citing insufficient evidence, claimed that it was unable to prove or disprove any link between thiomerosal and autism. However, it concluded that a causal connection between thiomersal and autism is "biologically plausible." http://www.fda.gov/cber/vaccine/thimerosal.htm. In 2004, the IOM rejected the hypothetical causative link between for thimerosal and autism.

The disconnect between the IOM recommendation and NCVIA litigation is striking. Between 1988 and 2000, an average of 147.6 non-autism claims were filed. The number of autism claims filed during that same period was 0. From 2001 to 2007, the average number of non-autism claims filed remained steady at 156.43 (with 32% of the claims being compensated) and the average number of autism claims was 735, but *none* of these claims have been compensated because of a lack of scientific proof of causal connection. The bulk of scientific evidence appears to deny the causal relationship between thimerosal and autism; the theory, however, enjoys strong support, especially among activist groups. Is evidence of the tenfold increase sufficient to overcome that negative conclusion? For a continuous update on the issue, see Thimerosal Controversy, Wikipedia, http://en.wikipedia.org/wiki/Thiomersal_controversy. Is it proper to give up the use of thimerosal without proof of harm if the result could be an increase in childhood diseases? If the IOM is correct, then why pull thimerosal from the market? Epstein, It Did Happen Here: Fear and Loathing on the Vaccine Trial, 24 Health Affairs 740 (May/June 2005).

3. No-fault plans for birth-related neurological injuries. The no-fault approach used under the NCVIA has also been tried at the state level for medical injuries. Virginia in 1987 enacted the Virginia Birth-Related Neurological Injury Compensation Act, Va. Code Ann. §§38.2-5000-5001 (2007). In 1988, Florida (where premiums for obstetricians were far higher) enacted a similar statute patterned on the Virginia Act. Fla. Stat. Ann. §§766.301-316 (West 2007). The Virginia statute makes participation in the program elective with physicians and hospitals, who do not (it appears) have to notify their patients that they have opted for the coverage. Once in the program, the statute specifies compensation formulas that closely track those for the workers' compensation statutes. No compensation is awarded for pain and suffering and compensation for lost future earnings is limited to 50 percent of the average weekly wage. The statute is funded through fixed charges on participating hospitals ($50 per delivery, with a maximum of $150,000 per year) and covered physicians ($5,000 per year), which cannot be raised by administrative action in subsequent years. The statute also imposes a general tax on most non-participating physicians of $250 per year. If these charges cannot cover the costs of running the program, a general levy on all insurance companies in the state, regardless of whether they sell medical malpractice coverage, is supposed to make up the shortfall.

> The core of the Virginia Act defines "a birth-related neurological injury" to mean: injury to the brain or spinal cord of an infant caused by the deprivation of oxygen or mechanical injury occurring in the course of labor, delivery or resuscitation in the immediate post-delivery period in a hospital which renders the infant permanently motorically disabled and (i) developmentally disabled or (ii) for infants sufficiently developed to be cognitively evaluated, cognitively disabled. In order to constitute a "birth-related neurological injury" within the meaning of this chapter, such disability shall cause the infant to be permanently in need of assistance in all activities of

daily living. This definition shall apply to live births only and shall not include disability or death caused by genetic or congenital abnormality, degenerative neurological disease, or maternal substance abuse.

Proving coverage under the act has proved no easy task. In Wolfe v. Virginia Birth-Related Neurological Injury Compensation Board, 580 S.E.2d 467 (Va. App. 2003), the court reviewed in exquisite detail the evidence of a half-dozen expert witnesses, before it sustained the 2 to 1 decision by the Compensation Board that rejected a claim for compensation by a cerebral palsy child who could neither speak nor walk, chiefly on the ground that the absence of any trouble signs during delivery of a child born with "normal heart and normal color" meant that the plaintiff had not proved oxygen deprivation during delivery.

For a critical account of the Virginia law, see Epstein, Market and Regulatory Approaches to Medical Malpractice: The Virginia Obstetrical No-Fault Statute, 74 Va. L. Rev. 1451 (1988); for its qualified defense, see O'Connell, Pragmatic Constraints on Market Approaches: A Response to Professor Epstein, 74 Va. L. Rev. 1475 (1988). See also Bovbjerg and Sloan, No-Fault For Medical Injury: Theory and Evidence, 67 U. Cin. L. Rev. 53 (1998), for a comprehensive evaluation of these two programs. Between 1989 and 1992, they report that obstetricians' malpractice premiums fell 26.5 percent in Florida (from $106,000 to $78,000) and 28.9 percent in Virginia (from $35,500 to $25,300). They also found that parties delayed filing their claims, perhaps because they were waiting to see if they could obtain recovery under the tort system, but that once these claims were filed they tended to be resolved more quickly than in the tort system. More recently, a 2003 report on the Virginia program has paid out the $25 million in claimant expenses for the entire 1988 to 2002 period, but has about an $88 million in unfunded liabilities that for the next 25 years at least should be met by future contributions to the fund at current rates. The Report also estimated that the tort awards in 2002 would have totaled about $4.3 million less than the actual costs of running the no-fault program during the same period. Virginia Joint Legislative and Audit Review Commission 4, 5 (2003) http://jlarc.state.va.us/Summary/Sum284.pdf. In contrast, Florida's Office of Program Policy Analysis and Government Accountability (OPPAGA) reported that the state's no-fault program was fully funded http://nica.com/downloads/OPPAGAreport.pdf, 4 (2004).

SECTION D.   THE 9/11 COMPENSATION FUND

Eleven days after the September 11, 2001, attack on the World Trade Center, the Pentagon, and the airlines, Congress passed the Air Transportation

Safety and System Stabilization Act of 2001, Publ. L. No. 107-42, 115 Stat. 230 (2001) (codified at 49 U.S.C. §§40101). Title IV of that Act creates the Victim Compensation Fund for any person who was killed or injured in the September 11th terrorist attack. Pursuant to the Act, President Bush appointed Kenneth Feinberg to administer the victim compensation program. Feinberg was charged with setting out the rules and regulations by which compensation was to be paid without regard to the negligence of any party. To participate in the fund, the claimants had to waive all suits against any airline, airline manufacturer, airport sponsor, or property holder of the World Trade Center. Tort actions were preserved against the knowing participants in the hijacking conspiracy. Unlike tort damages, the recoveries in question were offset by payments from collateral sources, but allowed for the recovery of all forms of economic and noneconomic losses, without a maximum dollar limitation. These recoveries were not governed by any set rule, but were to be based only on the "facts of the claim," including evidence on the extent of harm.

To facilitate his work, Feinberg divided the cases on two tracks. The first track set out an elaborate grid that allowed claimants to recover under a formula that contained both an economic and noneconomic loss component. The economic losses were based on their average income between 1998 and 2000, but only up to the 98th percentile, or about $231,000 per year. Noneconomic losses per decedent were set at $250,000, with an additional $100,000 for a spouse and each dependent. These presumptive awards were payable, no questions asked, within 120 days of filing. Alternatively, claimants who were dissatisfied with the presumptive levels of compensation could ask for an individual determination of their claim. In Colaio v. Feinberg, 262 F. Supp. 2d 273, 301 (S.D.N.Y. 2003), a number of high-income earners challenged Feinberg's presumptive structure of awards because of "the sharp truncation of potential damage awards at the top of the earnings distribution," which hit hard traders whose incomes were far above those amounts. Hellerstein, J. had no trouble in disposing of these claims:

> In enacting the Victim Compensation Fund, Congress and the President
> sought to provide some measure of recompense for the irreparable loss of
> the thousands who died and were injured. They granted to the Department
> of Justice and the Special Master the authority to promulgate regulations,
> exercise wise discretion in justly and efficiently administering the Fund, and
> the ability to craft and implement policies and instructions with respect to
> that administration. After thorough review, I have found that the regulations,
> duly promulgated as required by law, reasonably and properly implement the
> provisions of the Act. Similarly, the interpretive methodologies and policies of
> the Special Master are reasonable and proper implementations of the Act and
> regulations. The duty of a judge is to give deference to the Department of

Justice's regulations and respect to the Special Master's policies to the extent that they are rooted in law. I hold that the regulations and policies are lawful and valid.

Note, of course, that Feinberg could have structured the fund to replicate the distribution of outcomes that would have been obtained in a tort action against the terrorists. But it is debatable whether the Congressional payments should be bound to that model when none of the deterrence or compensation issues of a normal tort system are at stake. Thus, suppose a charitable organization had to decide how to distribute a limited fund to the victims of a terrorist attack or, for that matter, a natural disaster; it is doubtful that it would follow the tort model. For early commentary on the fund structure, see, e.g., Weinstein, Some 9-11 Injured Left Out by Victims Fund, Wall Street Journal, June 11, 2003, at B.1, noting that of the 3,025 people eligible for compensation as of that date only 895 had filed claims. By the end of the process, however, more people came into the fold so that $7 billion in compensation was paid out, with an average award of $1.8 million to 97 percent of the families that filed claims. Of that total some 1,600 asked for individual hearings. Feinberg personally conducted over 900 of these hearings. For his own account of the process, see Feinberg, What is Life Worth?: The Unprecedented Effort to Compensate the Victims of 9/11 (2005). His bottom line: "There is not one family member I've met who wouldn't gladly give back the check, or, in many cases, their own lives to have that loved one back. 'Happy' never enters into this equation."

One question that remained was whether individuals who claimed compensation through the fund could still maintain tort actions. That effort was soundly rebuffed in Virgilio v. City of New York, 407 F.3d 105, 112-113 (2d Cir. 2005), when personal representatives of the deceased firefighters sued both Motorola and New York City for their intentional and/or negligent provision of radio-transmission services to the firefighters who were trapped inside the twin towers. Their argument was that the Air Stabilization Act was meant only to protect the airline industry from ruinous liability, and did not extend its protection to other culpable parties. Wesley, J., disagreed:

> In our view, the waiver provision is unambiguous. The language of the waiver provision clearly states that Fund claimants waive their right to bring civil actions resulting from any harm caused by the 9/11 attacks: "[u]pon the submission of a claim . . . , the claimant waives the right to file a civil action . . . in any Federal or State court for damages sustained as a result of the terrorist-related aircraft crashes of September 11, 2001." Air Stabilization Act §405(c)(3)(B)(i). The waiver provision plainly requires litigants to choose between risk-free compensation and civil litigation. If this waiver

provision is ambiguous as plaintiffs suggest, few if any statutory provisions could be viewed as clear....

It is clear to us that plaintiffs' claims are within the scope of the waiver provision. Here, plaintiffs damages arose "as a result" of the terrorist-related attacks. Plaintiffs assert that the waiver should not reach defendants' alleged tortious conduct. In plaintiffs' view, defendants' acts independently caused plaintiffs' injuries. But, in fact, the injuries to plaintiffs and their loved ones resulted from a series of interrelated events that began with the terrorist attack. Even assuming independent, successive tortious acts by both the terrorists and defendants, as we must on this motion to dismiss, we are hard pressed to find plaintiffs' damages did not *result*—at least in part— from the terrorist attacks.

SECTION E.   THE NEW ZEALAND PLAN

The New Zealand Accident Compensation Act (as amended by the Accident Compensation Amendment (no. 2) Act of 1973) is the most radical no-fault plan. Under it, virtually all actions for personal injuries or death have been abolished and their place taken by a comprehensive insurance scheme that awards benefits to all persons who suffer "personal injury by accident," where the words "by accident" were meant largely to exclude compensation for death or injury caused by sickness. The definition of accident under the Act is generally decided from the point of view of the injured party, so that compensation is awarded to victims of intentional torts (including criminal assaults), as well as those who have been harmed in automobile accidents and product-related injuries. Also covered under the statute are certain occupational diseases, including deafness. In 1972, amendments to the original Accident Compensation Act extended coverage to "medical, surgical, dental or first aid misadventure," (§2(1)(a)(ii)) without further elaboration.

The justifications for the New Zealand plan were outlined in 1967 in the Report of the Royal Commission of Inquiry, Compensation for Personal Injury in New Zealand, more commonly known as the Woodhouse Report after the commission's chairman, Justice Owen Woodhouse. Chief among these justifications was the criticism that the negligence system was a "lottery," and coverage under workers' compensation and social security was spotty at best in dealing with the 100,000 accidents large and small in New Zealand. In order to respond to these difficulties, the no-fault plan was designed to meet five objectives: community responsibility, comprehensive entitlement, complete rehabilitation, real compensation, and administrative efficiency. These were elaborated as follows:

Report of the Royal Commission of Inquiry, Compensation for Personal Injury in New Zealand
19-22, 26 (1967)

. . .

5. Community Responsibility — If the well-being of the work force is neglected, the economy must suffer injury. For this reason the nation has not merely a clear duty but also a vested interest in urging forward the physical and economic rehabilitation of every adult citizen whose activities bear upon the general welfare. This is the plain answer to any who might query the responsibility of the community in the matter. Of course, the injured worker himself has a moral claim, and further a more material claim based upon his earlier contribution, or his readiness to contribute to the national product. But the whole community has a very real stake in the matter. There is nothing new in this idea. It is something which for 30 years in New Zealand has been recognized for every citizen in the country in the area of medical and health services.

6. Injury, not Cause, is the Issue — Once the principle of community responsibility is recognized the principle of comprehensive entitlement follows automatically. Few would attempt to argue that injured workers should be treated by society in different ways depending upon the cause of injury. Unless economic reasons demanded it the protection and remedy society might have to offer could not in justice be concentrated upon a single type of accident to the exclusion of others. With the admirable exception of the health services this has occurred in the past. There has been such concentration upon the risks faced by men during the working day that the considerable hazards they must face during the rest of each 24 hours (particularly on every road in the country) have been virtually disregarded. But workers do not change their status at 5 P.M., and if injured on the highway or at home they are the same men, and their needs and the country's need of them are unchanged.

7. The Self-employed and the Housewives — Exactly similar considerations clearly apply to every other gainfully employed person such as independent contractors and others who are self-employed. The same considerations must apply, also, to the women in the population who as housewives make it possible for the productive work to be done. The need is for an integrated solution with comprehensive entitlement for every man and woman, and coverage in respect of every type of accident. This is the central recommendation of our Report.

8. Incentive — Incentive must be the driving purpose of any effective scheme. Incentive offered by effective rehabilitation to get well; incentive to return to work by leaving to each man a fair margin for independent effort; incentive which is not restricted by averaging benefits or begrudging help for long-term incapacities. Real compensation must be the aim, tailored to

the severity of the injury and to the needs of citizens at all levels of employment and every normal level of income. . . .

9. The Cost — It will be asked, we do not doubt, whether we have kept in mind the need to balance the ideal with the practical. Even if the country were entirely free from current economic pressures, the money argument would weigh heavily upon an inquiry concerned, as this is, with systems of social insurance. The proposals we make for unifying and widening the scope of present arrangements must, of course, pass the economic test. And although difficulty has arisen from a dearth of statistical information, our proposals do this. In fact it seems that in overall terms the rationalization put forward avoids new large expenditures and yet permits at the same time greatly increased relief where it is needed most — for the losses which are greatest.

17. Sickness and Disease — It may be asked how incapacity arising from sickness and disease can be left aside. In logic there is no answer. A man overcome by ill health is no more able to work and no less afflicted than his neighbour hit by a car. In the industrial field certain diseases are included already. But logic on this occasion must give way to other considerations. First, it might be thought unwise to attempt one massive leap when two considered steps can be taken. Second, the urgent need is to co-ordinate the unrelated systems at present working in the injury field. Third, there is a virtual absence of the statistical signposting which alone can demonstrate the feasibility of the further move. And finally, the proposals now put forward for injury leave the way entirely open for sickness to follow whenever the relevant decision is taken.

18. Summary — On the basis of the principles outlined, the scheme proposed —

would provide immediate compensation without proof of fault for every injured person, regardless of his or her fault, and whether the accident occurred in the factory, on the highway, or in the home;

would entitle that person to compensation both for permanent physical disability and also for income losses on an income-related basis;

would provide for regular adjustment in the level of payment to accord with variations in the value of money;

would provide benefits, if necessary, for life, and in certain circumstances they would be commutable in whole or in part to lump sum payments;

would lift the present weekly maximum rate of compensation to $120 and thus safeguard the interests of persons on every normal level of income;

would be geared to urge forward their physical and vocational rehabilitation; and in all these ways it would provide them with effective insurance for all the risks of the day. If the scheme can be said to have a single purpose it is 24-hour insurance for every member of the work force, and for the housewives who sustain them.

Accident Compensation: Options for Reform 9-12
Credit Suisse First Boston (1998)

At its introduction, the ACS was promoted as a comprehensive pro-
gramme to protect New Zealanders from losses incurred due to personal
injury by accident. It was meant to establish a model of effective accident
compensation that would be emulated by other countries seeking to avoid
the problems associated with schemes based on common law. It was claimed
that the centralised monopoly structure would reduce costs to society of
accidents, encourage rehabilitation, and facilitate collection of detailed
information for research. The proponents of the ACS were so convinced of
the merits of a social insurance approach that they sought to extend it to all
forms of incapacity.

The consensus 25 years later is that the ACS has failed to meet expectations. Rehabilitation has not been a priority. Claims have largely been
rubber-stamped to minimise administrative costs, yet total ACS costs have
escalated well beyond projections since the scheme began. The Corporation has failed to develop a useful information database. Coverage levels
have been a never-ending source of dispute and political pressure. The
Corporation itself is perceived as failing to meet basic standards of pro-
fessionalism. Media reports suggest a great deal of successful rent-seeking
by professionals associated with the scheme and by opportunistic claimants.
Cross-subsidies within and between industries distort incentives. Total ACS
expenditure has increased at an annual average growth rate of 8 percent
since 1985. A significant tail of long-term claimants and a massive unfunded liability of $7.5 billion complete the picture. . . .

[The Report then reviews the Woodhouse Report and continues:]

The Royal Commission regarded accidents as acts of God, with individuals having no ability to influence their incidence. The principle of
'comprehensive entitlement' meant that the focus of the approach was on
the outcome of an accident, not on its cause. In addition, the Royal Commission ruled out private insurance. . . .

Employees were not given the option of receiving, through higher wages,
the cost savings associated with abolition of the right to sue — to spend on
insurance premiums, or otherwise, as they individually saw fit. Instead, the
state put the savings toward the funding of a one-size-fits-all monopoly
scheme. . . .

In keeping with its emphasis on compensating accident victims rather
than providing incentives for employers and individuals to prevent accidents, the Royal Commission recommended that employers be charged a
flat rate for accident compensation, regardless of their activity, arguing that
charging different rates did not "recognise that all industrial activity
is interdependent." This recommendation was not implemented. However,
the small number of premium classes resulted in comparatively safe

industries subsidising unsafe injuries. Safety records of individual employers were ignored in setting premia, removing one of the most important incentives for employers to take account of workplace safety.

NOTES

1. Assessment of the no-fault plan. It should be evident from the critique of the New Zealand Plan offered in the Credit Suisse report that the major difficulties stemmed less from the changes in the substantive tort law as such, and more from the state-run insurance system that received a monopoly over the insurance system. On the former, one reason why the ACS made relatively little difference is that New Zealand tort law was far less expansive than its American equivalent. Liability, especially in problem areas like medical malpractice and product liability is much more restrictive than in the United States. And in those cases in which the plaintiff prevailed, damages were far lower than under the American norm. The abolition of the tort law, therefore, abolished far less than would have been the case here. Yet the second half of the equation dealing with administration and cost-containment is a different matter. No one quite knew the extent of the ACS's activities, the breadth of which is revealed by a quick tour of its Web site (http://www.acc.co.nz/index.htm). The expansive coverage does not come cheap, and the general public, while sympathetic to the program in the abstract, has been deeply troubled by its failure in cost-containment, which led to a 1986 premium increase of 192 percent for employers and 265 percent for self-employed enrollees. See Law Commission, Personal Injury: Prevention and Recovery, Report No. 4, 16-22 (1988).

The cost increases had two major causes. First, large claims in the early years took a long time to resolve and thus were recorded only after the plan was in operation. More critical perhaps was the shift in its internal accounting methods. Until 1982 the system was fully funded, which meant that the premiums collected in any single year were sufficient to cover all costs for claims arising in that year, including payments to be made in future years. In 1982, the system shifted to "pay as you go" financing, whereby only enough money was collected to pay the bills for that year, without reserving funds to pay the future expenses associated with current accidents. In the early years of this plan, the convention led to a reduction in costs as only the current expenditures of, say, a 1983 claim had to be covered in 1984. But in 1984, it was necessary to cover the second year of the outstanding 1983 claims and the first year of the 1984 claims. Each additional year brought on ever larger amounts of deferred costs for earlier claims until the accrued liabilities from past years led to the sharp increase in premiums in 1986. The $7.5 billion deficit followed a decade later. For a detailed account of the 1980s episode, see Miller, The Future of New Zealand's Accident Compensation Scheme, 11 U. Haw. L. Rev. 1 (1989).

By way of reform, the Credit Suisse Report recommends that the government withdraw from the insurance business and "be fully exposed to competition from private insurers and be sold at the end of a transition period." It further recommended that the purchase of accident insurance be "voluntary, instead of mandatory." With regard to liability rules, it recommended that "consideration be given, wherever possible to allowing contracting parties to determine what remedies will apply," and in stranger cases, it advocated consideration of a system of strict liability for road accidents, in which compliance with the rules of the road, and not the antecedent negligence of either party, governed. Sound? The first of its recommendations, allowing private insurance companies to supply work-related accident insurance was introduced by the National (conservative) government in July, 1999, but was repealed a year later by the Labour government that reinstated the ACC's monopoly over accident insurance.

For a summary and defense of the Woodhouse Report, see also Franklin, Personal Injury Accidents in New Zealand and the United States: Some Striking Similarities, 27 Stan. L. Rev. 653 (1975). For an exhaustive account of the New Zealand plan and the unsuccessful efforts to secure its introduction in Australia, see G. Palmer, Compensation for Incapacity: A Study of Law and Social Change in New Zealand and Australia (1979). For an analysis by New Zealand's National Minister of Labour, in charge of the program, see W.F. Birch, Accident Compensation: A Fairer Scheme (1991). For an insider's account of the New Zealand experience, see Palmer, New Zealand's Accident Compensation Scheme: Twenty Years On, 44 U. Toronto L. Rev. 223 (1994).

2. Administration of the system. The New Zealand plan has also generated its fair share of tricky coverage disputes. In ACC v. Auckland Hospital Board, [1980] 2 N.Z.L.R. 748, 751, the court awarded damages to a claimant who became pregnant when a tubal ligation failed because the surgeon without negligence had been unable to close her fallopian tubes with his available forceps, subsequently replaced with a more modern variety. The court found medical misadventure because the unsatisfactory outcome was not "within the normal range of medical or surgical failure attendant upon even the most felicitous treatment."

Similarly in MacDonald v. Accident Compensation Corp., [1985] 5 N.Z.A.R. 276, the plaintiff, who suffered a leaky bowel (a small but predictable risk) from a properly performed operation, was awarded compensation because the event had "turned out badly" and thus constituted a medical misadventure under the statute. For an account of these developments, see generally Gellhorn, Medical Malpractice Litigation (U.S.) — Medical Mishap Compensation (N.Z.), 73 Cornell L. Rev. 170 (1988). Cases of this sort led to the formulation of a two-page definition of the bad outcomes compensable in the context of medical treatment that raise all the difficulties found in connection with schemes for no-fault medical liability in this country. See Accident Rehabilitation and Compensation Insurance Act of 1992 No. 13, §1.

3. A final evaluation. The one common feature of all these no-fault plans is that they seek to displace the common law rules of negligence with some other standard of compensable event. The defenders of these systems have been quick to note the difficulties of the general negligence system, but wrong on balance to think that the shift to any no-fault program will solve one problem without introducing another in its place. Thus, the workers' compensation system eliminates the hard line between negligence and pure accident within the workplace, but now substitutes in its stead the equally complex problem of drawing the line between personal and work-related injuries. The vaccine and obstetrical no-fault compensation programs remove the negligence from the equation but introduce the equally vexing question of whether causation was from a natural event outside the compensation or from something within it. There is in short no obvious panacea even if there are marginal improvements. But in thinking about the question of global reforms for accident compensation, the urge to make systemic changes should not be allowed to obscure the possibility that sensible reforms in the tort system — such as greater reliance on bright-line rules in highway cases — might shift the relative balance of advantage back to a traditional tort remedy. In addition, the greater use of contractual limitations on liability could also ease the burden in areas like medical malpractice and product liability. Indeed one irony is this: Some of the success of the New Zealand Accident Compensation System stems from the fact that by limiting tort liability it approaches in an oblique fashion the contractual system of limited liability.

PART TWO
TORTS AGAINST NONPHYSICAL INTERESTS

13

DEFAMATION

SECTION A. INTRODUCTION

Iago:
> Good name in man and woman, dear my lord,
> Is the immediate jewel of their souls:
> Who steals my purse steals trash; 'tis something, nothing;
> 'Twas mine, 'tis his, and has been slave to thousands;
>
> But he that filches from me my good name
> Robs me of that which not enriches him,
> And makes me poor indeed.
> *Othello*, Act III, scene iii

Of all the areas of tort law, defamation is perhaps the most difficult to organize and to understand. At one time defamation was, with only occasional statutory intervention, a common law subject. Starting from the premise that an individual's reputation should be protected against false words, the common law judges developed an elaborate set of rules to determine what statements were defamatory, when they were actionable or privileged, and what damages could be recovered for them.

The common law of defamation is still important today, but its uncontested supremacy has been undermined starting with the epochal (no lesser word will do) Supreme Court decision in New York Times v. Sullivan, 376 U.S. 254 (1964), which, for the first time, invoked the First Amendment guarantee of freedom of speech to limit the common law of defamation. More specifically, *New York Times* held that public officials could maintain actions in defamation only upon proof that the defendant's statement was made with "actual malice," defined by the Supreme Court as "knowledge that it [the statement] was false or with reckless disregard of whether it was false or not." Malice in the sense of spite or ill will harbored toward the plaintiff was rendered constitutionally irrelevant, at least in suits brought by public officials against media defendants. The actual malice rule was extended to public figures in the important case of Curtis Publishing Co. v. Butts, 388 U.S. 130 (1967). Finally, the third of the great constitutional trilogy, Gertz v. Robert Welch, Inc., 418 U.S. 323 (1974), constitutionalized much of the law of defamation that relates to private plaintiffs against media defendants so that today each of the common law rules (and any legislated variants) must be scrutinized under the First Amendment's guarantees of freedom of speech and of the press. The 1980s witnessed many complex and contentious First Amendment cases in which by and large the media defendants came out on top, owing in large measure to their fierce defense in virtually every case. Today there are relatively few high-profile defamation suits, so the basic constitutional ground rules have remained unchanged for the past generation.

The constitutionalization of large portions of the law of defamation did not mark, however, the end of the traditional common law inquiries. Even when public officials sue media defendants, it is still necessary to determine whether the statements made were defamatory, whether they were true, and whether they caused damage to the plaintiff. A complex network of common law issues weaves its way through the modern constitutional fabric so that the skilled defamation lawyer must be a master of two intersecting legal systems. In addition, as suits by public officials and public figures have dwindled, recent years have witnessed an increased frequency of defamation actions in other contexts, including suits brought against colleges and universities for statements made concerning various personnel matters. Also, suits against Internet service providers for messages posted by others, although largely unsuccessful, have multiplied in recent years.

The shifting patterns of litigation should not be allowed to conceal the significant differences between the constitutional and common law orientations. Everyone agrees that the central task of the modern law of defamation is to reconcile the interest in reputation with that in freedom of speech. Today no one thinks that the appropriate balance permits the complete protection of one interest to the exclusion of the other. The disagreement is over the proper balance. Roughly speaking, the common law set its initial presumption in favor of reputation, while the Supreme Court has tilted the constitutional balance in favor of freedom of speech. As a result, defamation (and for similar reasons, privacy) stand virtually alone in modern tort law. As the plaintiff's right to recover has been vigorously expanded in other areas, in defamation cases the balance has shifted, often quite dramatically, in favor of the defendant.

The rapid changes in the law of defamation suggest two possible approaches to the subject. The first begins with New York Times v. Sullivan and the constitutional materials, and works backwards to the common law doctrines as the need arises. Although that approach highlights dramatic and memorable disputes, on balance it suffers from the greater handicap of requiring us to jump midstream into a most troubled area of the law without the benefit of a (more or less) systematic presentation of its historical development, and without a sense of its special character and language. This chapter, for the sake of historical continuity and analytical clarity, starts with the common tort before turning to the constitutional overlay. These traditional inquiries include: What is publication? What is defamation? What is the distinction between libel and slander, and why is it important? What is the basis of liability in defamation — strict liability, negligence, or intention to harm? What are general and special damages? What privileges are available to make defamatory statements in both the private and the public spheres, and are these privileges "absolute" or "qualified"? Only thereafter is the constitutional material taken up in its historical sequence. There is no neat division between the materials in different portions of the chapter, and the student may need to read them several times before they can be mastered.

SECTION B.   PUBLICATION

Doe v. Gonzaga University
24 P.3d 390 (Wash. 2001)

IRELAND, J. . . . In late 1992, while John Doe was an elementary education student at Gonzaga University (Gonzaga), he had a sexually intimate relationship with Jane Doe, a student who was studying special education at Gonzaga. [Both Does are pseudonyms.]

In October 1993, Roberta League (League), Gonzaga's teacher certification specialist, overheard student Julia Lynch (Lynch) talking with another student about Lynch's dissatisfaction with the way the school dealt with complaints of date rape. Lynch said that when she had been a resident assistant, she had observed Jane Doe in obvious physical pain, which Jane Doe said was the result of having sex with "John." Lynch was angry that no one from Gonzaga had bothered to find out what had happened.

League recognized the name "John"; she knew John Doe was a student teacher in the education program at Gonzaga. Two days later, League told Dr. Susan Kyle (Kyle), Gonzaga's director of field experience for student teachers, what she had overheard. Kyle and League decided that they needed to investigate the situation. League was concerned that the allegations she had overheard about John Doe might affect the dean's ability to submit an affidavit supporting John Doe's application for teacher certification.

The two women met with Lynch on October 14, 1993. According to Lynch, Jane Doe told Lynch that John Doe had sexually assaulted her three times in late November or December 1992. . . .

[League instituted an extensive investigation of the possibility of date rape, which was conducted by Adelle Nore, an investigator for the Office of the Superintendent of Public Instruction (OSPI). The school investigated the crime with multiple witnesses, including Jane Doe. But school officials also decided not to inform John Doe of the investigation or to ask him for his view of the events. Several witnesses noted that Jane Doe had stated that she had been forced to have sex with John Doe, but Jane Doe herself equivocated on the question saying at one time, "I guess I don't really know what rape is," and, further, "I promised [John] I wouldn't tell." Jane Doe refused to make any formal statement. In February 1994, Dr. Corrine McGuigan, dean of the school of education, reviewed the assembled evidence and concluded that John Doe's "serious behavioral problem" precluded her from signing the required moral character affidavit for his teaching application. McGuigan only told John Doe of the decision a month later, but refused to tell him the source of the testimony against him, and also informed him that he had no right to appeal that decision. At the time of trial Jane Doe was married and out of state in graduate school. Her testimony (by videotaped deposition) backed up John Doe's story, and stated that there were false statements in many of the key declarations and that things had generally been blown out of proportion. The jury awarded $500,000 for defamation and lesser sums on other counts, including invasion of privacy.]

1. DEFAMATION

"In Washington, a defamation plaintiff must show four essential elements: falsity, an unprivileged communication, fault, and damages." Commodore v. Univ. Mech. Contractors, Inc., 839 P.2d 314 (Wash. 1992). Liability for defamation requires that the defamation be communicated to someone other than the person defamed; in other words, there must be a "publication" of the defamation. Pate v. Tyee Motor Inn, Inc., 467 P.2d 301 (Wash. 1970). The Court of Appeals vacated John Doe's defamation award and directed that the jury be instructed on remand that Gonzaga cannot be held liable for communications among its own employees. More than 80 years ago, this Court held that intracorporate communications are not "published" for purposes of defamation. "For a corporation . . . acting through one of its agents or representatives, to send a libelous communication to another of its agents or representatives cannot be a publication of the libel on the part of the corporation. It is but communicating with itself." Prins v. Holland-North Am. Mortgage Co., 181 P. 680 (Wash. 1919). The plaintiff there was a Seattle branch manager of a company headquartered in the Netherlands. The alleged defamation was contained in a letter sent by the main office and read only by the plaintiff's co-manager and a bookkeeper. The *Prins* court held that there had been no publication of the allegedly defamatory statements.

In the case before us, the Court of Appeals reasoned that, likewise, the conversations and memoranda between Gonzaga's employees regarding John Doe should be characterized as the university communicating with itself—not the kind of "publication" required to support a defamation claim.

John Doe contends that the common interests of a corporation's employees create only a qualified privilege. "A privileged communication involves the occasion where an otherwise slanderous statement is shared with a third person who has a common interest in the subject and is reasonably entitled to know the information." *Pate*. The plaintiffs in *Pate* were chambermaids who sued their employer and its supervisors for defamation. The alleged slander was a supervisor's statement that the plaintiffs were sneaking around joining a union—actions which amounted to Communism. The statement was made in a meeting attended by both the plaintiffs and nonunion housekeepers. The opinion noted that the supervisor had no duty to comment upon the ideology of unions in the ordinary course of her work, which took her statement outside the circumstances and principles of *Prins*.

Because the employees in *Prins* were clearly acting "within the limits of their employment," the court was not required to address the nature of any privilege on the communications among them. However, when the supervisor in *Pate* made comments not "[i]n the ordinary course of her work," she could be held liable for publishing a defamatory statement to third persons, even though the third persons were also employees of the corporation. Under these cases, intracorporate communications are not absolutely privileged. When a corporate employee, not acting in the ordinary course of his or her work, publishes a defamatory statement, either to another employee or to a nonemployee, there can be liability in tort for resulting damages.

In the instant case, from the evidence presented at trial, it could reasonably be found that Julia Lynch was not acting in the ordinary course of her work as an office assistant when she told another student that John Doe had injured Jane Doe during a sexual relationship. It could also be found that Roberta League was not acting in the ordinary course of her work as a certificate specialist when she eavesdropped on Lynch's conversation and shared her concerns of possible misconduct with Susan Kyle. Likewise, it could be found that Roberta League and Susan Kyle were not acting in the ordinary course of their work when they questioned Lynch about alleged sexual assaults of Jane Doe by John Doe and then disclosed John Doe's identity and details about his sexual relations to Adelle Nore at OSPI. . . .

There is a qualified privilege for communications made between coemployees, but that privilege may be lost if the employees are not acting in the ordinary course of their work. The trial court's instructions fully encompassed the principles of publication and qualified privilege in a corporate context as announced in *Pate*. Therefore, the jury was properly instructed.

When a defendant has a qualified privilege to communicate a potentially defamatory statement, the privilege may also be lost by showing that the defendant made the statement with actual malice. . . .

Under Washington law, the trial court properly instructed the jury regarding the defamation claim. There was sufficient evidence for the jury to find that communications among Gonzaga personnel and statements made to OSPI were not privileged. Therefore, the jury's verdict and damage award [of $500,000] for John Doe's defamation claim are reinstated.

NOTES

1. Publication, privilege, and the defamation triangle. If the plaintiff's damages came from the dean's refusal to certify his teaching application, how are they attributable to the defamatory statements made pursuant to the investigation? What result if the dean had returned an unfilled form to a state agency that had requested certification for Doe? Made no answer at all?

The publication requirement has important structural significance for the law of defamation. Without this requirement, defamation would be indistinguishable from the insult or deceit that arises when the defendant utters an abusive or false statement to the plaintiff directly. The publication requirement shows that the tort of defamation protects only the interest in reputation, not self-esteem. The publication requirement also accounts for much of the complexity of defamation law, for it insures that every defamation case must involve at least three people — the plaintiff, defendant, and the third party to whom the statement was made. Indeed, oftentimes defamation expands this simple triangle. For example, one defendant can defame a plaintiff to many third parties, each of whom interacts with the plaintiff in different ways.

How should *Doe* be decided under the Restatement (Second) of Torts, which provides:

§577. WHAT CONSTITUTES PUBLICATION

(1) Publication of defamatory matter is its communication intentionally or by a negligent act to one other than the person defamed.

(2) One who intentionally and unreasonably fails to remove defamatory
matter that he knows to be exhibited on land or chattels in his possession or
under his control is subject to liability for its continued publication.

Comment *e* to the section states:

The fact that the defamatory matter is communicated to an agent of the
defamer does not prevent it from being a publication sufficient to constitute
actionable defamation. The publication may be privileged, however, under
the rule stated in section 593. So too, the communication to a servant or
agent of the person defamed is a publication although if the communication
is in answer to a letter or a request from the other or his agent, the publication may not be actionable in defamation.

2. *Publication by default.* Section 577(2) is vividly illustrated by Hellar v.
Bianco, 244 P.2d 757, 758 (Cal. App. 1952), in which the "[r]espondents
were the proprietors of a public tavern and for the convenience of patrons
maintained a toilet room for men on the wall of which there appeared
on May 4, 1950, libelous matter indicating that appellant was an unchaste
woman who indulged in illicit amatory ventures. The writer recommended
that anyone interested should call a stated telephone number, which was
the number of the telephone in appellant's home, and 'ask for Isabelle,'
that being appellant's given name." Plaintiff was told of the writing by a
telephone call from a stranger requesting a date. The defendant did not
promptly remove the material when requested to do so by the plaintiff's
husband. The trial court nonsuited the plaintiff, and the appellate court
reversed, holding that knowingly permitting such matter to remain after a
reasonable opportunity to remove it made the owner of the tavern guilty of
a republication. Could a patron of the bar be charged with defamation if
he saw the statement and did not remove it?

3. *Republication by plaintiff.* A particularly troublesome question arises
when plaintiff himself shows defamatory material to others. Normally this
is held to be a publication by the plaintiff. The problem is acute in the area
of employment recommendations. In Lewis v. Equitable Life Assurance
Society, 389 N.W.2d 876, 888 (Minn. 1986), the defendant told the plaintiffs that they had been discharged for gross insubordination. The plaintiffs
in turn communicated this information to prospective employers in
response to inquiries why they had left their previous employers. The court
rejected the defendant's argument that the plaintiffs' defamation actions
were barred by their own voluntary republication of the libel.

The trend of modern authority persuades us that Minnesota law should
recognize the doctrine of compelled self-publication. We acknowledge that
recognition of this doctrine provides a significant new basis for maintaining

a cause of action for defamation and, as such, it should be cautiously applied. However, when properly applied, it need not substantially broaden the scope of liability for defamation. The principle of compelled self-publication does no more than hold the originator of the defamatory statement liable for damages caused by the statement where the originator knows, or should know, of circumstances whereby the defamed person has no reasonable means of avoiding publication of the statement or avoiding the resulting damages; in other words, in cases where the defamed person was compelled to publish the statement. In such circumstances, the damages are fairly viewed as the direct result of the originator's actions.

The court also imposed on plaintiffs a duty to mitigate damages, which was implemented by "requiring plaintiffs when they encounter a situation in which they are compelled to repeat a defamatory statement to take all reasonable steps to attempt to explain the true nature of the situation and to contradict the defamatory statement."

Lewis received a chilly reception in De Leon v. St. Joseph Hospital, Inc., 871 F.2d 1229, 1237 (4th Cir. 1989). Murnaghan, J., wrote that the doctrine was inadvisable because "otherwise, the theory of self-publication might visit liability for defamation on every Maryland employer each time a job applicant is rejected." But in Theisen v. Covenant Medical Center, 636 N.W.2d 74, 85 (Iowa 2001), the plaintiff security guard was fired when he refused to submit to a voice print test after he was accused of making obscene phone calls to a hospital nurse. Partially following *Lewis*, the court refused to give the employer total immunity from suit, but concluded instead that we "recognize and adopt a qualified privilege for statements made by employers to employees concerning the reasons for an employee's discharge regardless of whether the employer or employee publishes the statement. Without such a privilege, employers would be stymied in their ability to effectively deal with personnel matters and left with the choice of giving no reason for terminating employment or hoping an employee will not reveal the reasons for discharge to a prospective employer." The court then affirmed the dismissal of plaintiff's suit.

Firth v. State of New York
775 N.E.2d 463 (N.Y. 2002)

LEVINE, J. This appeal presents the first occasion for us to determine how our defamation jurisprudence, developed in connection with traditional mass media communications, applies to communications in a new medium — cyberspace — in the modern Information Age. Specifically, we must resolve the question whether, for statute of limitations purposes, the single publication rule is applicable to allegedly defamatory statements that are posted on an Internet site and, if so, whether an unrelated modification to a different portion of the Web site constitutes a republication.

Claimant George Firth was formerly employed by the Department of Environmental Conservation as Director of the Division of Law Enforcement. His responsibilities included weapons acquisition. At a press conference held on December 16, 1996, the Office of the State Inspector General issued a report entitled "The Best Bang for Their Buck," which was critical of claimant's managerial style and procurement of weapons. On the same day, the State Education Department posted an executive summary with links to the full text of the report on its Government Information Locator Service Internet site.

On March 18, 1998, more than one year after the report was first released and posted on the Internet, claimant filed a claim against the State alleging that the report defamed him. The State moved to dismiss on the ground that the claim was time-barred under the one-year statute of limitations for defamation. In opposition, claimant argued the merits of his defamation claim, failing to address the statute of limitations issue. . . .

The Court of Claims granted summary judgment to the State, rejecting claimant's argument that the ongoing availability of the report via the Internet constituted a continuing wrong or new publication. The court concluded that the statute of limitations began to run on December 16, 1996, when the report was first made available on the Internet. The court did not address whether the modification of the State's Web site by the addition of the report on the DMV constituted a republication of the report concerning claimant.

The Appellate Division affirmed. . . . Claimant now appeals as of right to this Court (see CPLR 5601[a]).

In Gregoire v. Putnam's Sons, we adopted the single publication rule, namely that

> the publication of a defamatory statement in a single issue of a newspaper, or a single issue of a magazine, although such publication consists of thousands of copies widely distributed, is, in legal effect, one publication which gives rise to one cause of action and that the applicable statute of limitation[s] runs from the date of that publication (81 N.E.2d 45, 47 [N.Y. 1948]; see RST §577A [3]).

Claimant argues that the single publication rule should not be applied verbatim to defamatory publications posted on the Internet in light of significant differences between Internet publications and traditional mass media. Instead, claimant maintains that because a Web site may be altered at any time by its publisher or owner and because publications on the Internet are available only to those who seek them, each "hit" or viewing of the report should be considered a new publication that retriggers the statute of limitations. We disagree.

Under the early common law of defamation, which claimant seeks to have applied in this case, each communication of a defamatory statement to a third person constituted a separate publication giving rise to a new cause of action. In *Gregoire*, we held that a publisher's sale from stock of a copy of a book containing libelous language did not constitute a new publication. We explained that if the multiple publication rule were applied to such a sale, "the [s]tatute of [l]imitation[s] would never expire so long as a copy of such book remained in stock and is made by the publisher the subject of a sale or inspection by the public. Such a rule would thwart the purpose of the Legislature . . . to bar completely and forever all actions which, as to the time of their commencement, overpass the limitation there prescribed upon litigation."

In addition to increasing the exposure of publishers to stale claims, applying the multiple publication rule to a communication distributed via mass media would permit a multiplicity of actions, leading to potential harassment and excessive liability, and draining of judicial resources. Further, the single publication rule actually reduces the possibility of hardship to plaintiffs by allowing the collection of all damages in one case commenced in a single jurisdiction. . . .

The policies impelling the original adoption of the single publication rule support its application to the posting of the Inspector General's report regarding claimant on the State's Web site. Communications accessible over a public Web site resemble those contained in traditional mass media, only on a far grander scale. . . . Communications posted on Web sites may be viewed by thousands, if not millions, over an expansive geographic area for an indefinite period of time.

Thus, a multiple publication rule would implicate an even greater potential for endless retriggering of the statute of limitations, multiplicity of suits and harassment of defendants. Inevitably, there would be a serious inhibitory effect on the open, pervasive dissemination of information and ideas over the Internet, which is, of course, its greatest beneficial promise. Thus, we hold that the single publication rule applies in this case.

Claimant alternatively argues that if the single publication rule governs, the State should be deemed to have republished the report within one year of the filing of the claim when it added an unrelated report of the Inspector General on the DMV to the Education Department's Web site in May 1997. We conclude as a matter of law that this modification of the State's Web site did not constitute a republication of the allegedly defamatory report at issue here.

Republication, retriggering the period of limitations, occurs upon a separate aggregate publication from the original, on a different occasion, which is not merely "a delayed circulation of the original edition." The justification for this exception to the single publication rule is that the subsequent publication is intended to and actually reaches a new audience. Thus, for example, repetition of a defamatory statement in a later edition of a book, magazine or newspaper may give rise to a new cause of action.

The mere addition of unrelated information to a Web site cannot be equated with the repetition of defamatory matter in a separately published edition of a book or newspaper. . . . The justification for the republication exception has no application at all to the addition of unrelated material on a Web site, for it is not reasonably inferable that the addition was made either with the intent or the result of communicating the earlier and separate defamatory information to a new audience.

We observe that many Web sites are in a constant state of change, with information posted sequentially on a frequent basis. For example, this Court has a Web site which includes its decisions, to which it continually adds its slip opinions as they are handed down. Similarly, Web sites are used by news organizations to provide readily accessible records of newsworthy events as they occur and are reported. Those unrelated additions are indistinguishable from the asserted DMV report modification of the State's Web site here. A rule applying the republication exception under the circumstances here would either discourage the placement of information on the Internet or slow the exchange of such information, reducing the Internet's unique advantages. In order not to retrigger the statute of limitations, a publisher would be forced either to avoid posting on a Web site or use a separate site for each new piece of information. These policy concerns militate against a holding that any modification to a Web site constitutes a republication of the defamatory communication itself.

[Affirmed.]

NOTES

1. *Mass publication. Firth* follows the Restatement (Second) of Torts §577A, which provides that "[a]ny one edition of a book or newspaper, or any one radio or television broadcast, exhibition of a motion picture or similar aggregate communication is a single publication" for which only one action in defamation may be maintained. The Restatement rule was explicitly endorsed by the Supreme Court in Keeton v. Hustler Magazine, Inc., 465 U.S. 770, 777 (1984), a case involving the minimum "contacts" necessary to allow a state court to assert its jurisdiction under the Due Process Clause. In *Keeton*, a New York resident sued Hustler Magazine, an Ohio corporation, in federal court in New Hampshire. Her sole purpose for suing in New Hampshire was to take advantage of its six-year statute of limitations, which had not yet run. Under the single publication rule, New Hampshire law allowed the plaintiff to recover for damage to her

reputation not only in New Hampshire, but anywhere in the United States. Reversing the lower court, the Supreme Court held, first, that the regular circulation of 10,000-15,000 copies of the magazine in New Hampshire established sufficient contacts for New Hampshire to assert its jurisdiction under the Due Process Clause. Thereafter, Rehnquist, J., praised the single publication rule as follows:

> New Hampshire also has a substantial interest in cooperating with other States, through the "single publication rule," to provide a forum for efficiently litigating all issues and damage claims arising out of a libel in a unitary proceeding. The rule reduces the potential serious drain of libel cases on judicial resources. It also serves to protect defendants from harassment resulting from multiple suits.

See generally Note, Cyber-Defamation and the Single Publication Rule, 81 Bost. U. L. Rev. 895 (2001).

2. *Republication by third parties.* Even before the advent of the Internet, the common law held the defendant liable for defamation only when he had both knowledge of what was published and discretion over whether to make or withhold publication. Neither of those requirements would be met, for example, if a public library rarely knew the contents of its many holdings, and could not refuse to check out a book that might contain some defamatory material. "Those who merely deliver or transmit defamatory material previously published by another will be considered to have published the material only if they knew, or had reason to know, that the material was false and defamatory. It is this rule that protects libraries and vendors of books, magazines, and newspapers." Church of Scientology of Minnesota v. Minnesota State Medical Association Foundation, 264 N.W.2d 152, 156 (Minn. 1978).

This rule has added urgency in connection with active internet sites. The Communications Decency Act of 1996, 47 U.S.C. §230(c)(1), states that "no provider or user of an interactive computer service shall be treated as the publisher or speaker of any information provided by another information content provider." In Carafano v. Metrosplash.com, Inc., 339 F.3d 1119 (9th Cir. 2003), the plaintiff Christianne Carafano was a well known actress who performed under the name Chase Masterson, starring in such television programs as Star Trek and General Hospital. Matchmaker.com is an internet dating service that supplies a detailed questionnaire that addresses a range of questions, some of which are sexually suggestive. An unknown person using a Berlin computer posted on the Matchmaker site a profile that suggested "Chase529 was looking for a 'hard and dominant' man with a 'strong sexual appetite,' and that she 'liked sort of be[]ing controlled by a man, in and out of bed.'" The posting then listed Carafano's home address and several pictures readily available from her acting career. It also included an internet site, which when contacted produced an automatic response that provided her home address and telephone number. After the material was posted, the plaintiff received a large number of abusive phone calls, voicemail messages, emails, and letters that led the plaintiff and her son to take refuge in hotels in and around Los Angeles during the next several months. Shortly after the material was posted, Matchmaker first blocked the profile at her request and then removed it from their web site.

The plaintiff claimed that the defendant was not protected by the CDA, but Thomas, J., disagreed:

> Congress enacted this provision as part of the Communications Decency Act of 1996 for two basic policy reasons: to promote the free exchange of information and ideas over the Internet and to encourage voluntary monitoring for offensive or obscene material . . . .
>
> In light of these concerns, reviewing courts have treated §230 immunity as quite robust, adopting a relatively expansive definition of "interactive computer service" and a relatively restrictive definition of "information content provider." Under the statutory scheme, an "interactive computer service" qualifies for immunity so long as it does not also function as an "information content provider" for the portion of the statement or publication at issue.
>
> The fact that some of the content was formulated in response to Matchmaker's questionnaire does not alter this conclusion. Doubtless, the questionnaire facilitated the expression of information by individual users. However, the selection of the content was left exclusively to the user. The actual profile "information" consisted of the particular options chosen and the additional essay answers provided. Matchmaker was not responsible, even in part, for associating certain multiple choice responses with a set of physical characteristics, a group of essay answers, and a photograph. Matchmaker cannot be considered an "information content provider" under the statute because no profile has any content until a user actively creates it.

This approach has been uniform in the cases. In Gentry v. eBay, 121 Cal. Rptr. 2d 703 (Cal. 2002), the CDA insulated the eBay.com auction website from liability for false material prepared by sellers using eBay's form. More strikingly, in Zeran v. America Online, Inc., 129 F.3d 327 (4th Cir. 1997), the court applied the CDA on behalf of AOL when an unknown third party posted messages on an AOL bulletin board falsely stating that the plaintiff was selling tasteless "naughty Oklahoma T-Shirts" celebrating the bombing of the Alfred P. Murrah Federal Building, which had killed 168 people in 1995. AOL did not remove the material from its site for some time despite promising to do so, exposing the plaintiff to death threats and other abusive communications. Nonetheless, Wilkinson, C.J., wrote:

Congress' purpose in providing the §230 immunity was thus evident. Interactive computer services have millions of users. The amount of information communicated via interactive computer services is therefore staggering. The specter of tort liability in an area of such prolific speech would have an obvious chilling effect. It would be impossible for service providers to screen each of their millions of postings for possible problems. Faced with potential liability for each message republished by their services, interactive computer service providers might choose to severely restrict the number and type of messages posted. Congress considered the weight of the speech interests implicated and chose to immunize service providers to avoid any such restrictive effect.

Why grant the immunity after the defendant has been informed of the defamatory material?

SECTION C.   FALSE OR DEFAMATORY STATEMENTS

Parmiter v. Coupland
151 Eng. Rep. 340, 342 (Ex. 1840)

PARKE, B. A publication, without justification or lawful excuse, which is calculated to injure the reputation of another, by exposing him to hatred, contempt, or ridicule, is a libel.

American Law Institute, Restatement (Second) of Torts
(1977)

§559.   DEFAMATORY COMMUNICATION DEFINED

A communication is defamatory if it tends so to harm the reputation of another as to lower him in the estimation of the community or to deter third persons from associating or dealing with him.

Muzikowski v. Paramount Pictures Corp.
322 F.3d 918 (7th Cir. 2003)

WOOD, J. [In 2000, defendant Paramount Pictures released a movie, *Hardball*, with the actor Keanu Reeves, which was based on a book written by Daniel Coyle, *Hardball: A Season in the Projects*, which recorded his experiences as a coach in the Little Leagues on the North Side of Chicago. The book was described as a work of non-fiction and contained throughout it various references to the plaintiff by name. In contrast to the book, the movie credits stated: "While this motion picture is in part inspired by actual events, persons and organizations, this is a fictitious story and no actual persons, events or organizations have been portrayed." The movie then chronicles the activities of other coaches in the league, including one fictitious coach named Conor O'Neill. Neither Robert Muzikowski's first or last name is used in the film. O'Neill's character was based in part on the plaintiff Muzikowski, but the movie attributed to O'Neill certain derogatory features that Muzikowski did not have. The accurate biographical information was that the O'Neill character had dropped out of college after the death of his father, had used illegal drugs and alcohol, had been arrested for participating in a bar brawl that left a scar on his left hand, had driven a blue station wagon, had from time to time "lost it," and had spoken at the funeral of one of his players who had been killed in a gang incident. After Paramount began promoting the movie in 2000, Muzikowski began getting telephone calls from all over the country from friends and acquaintances telling him that Paramount was about to make a movie about him. The defamation suit arose because of the negative features that *Hardball* had added to the historical record. It stated that O'Neill had not been able to break his drinking habit when, in reality, Muzikowski had not had a drink in 17 years. The movie depicted O'Neill as having committed various crimes such as "battery, theft, criminal destruction of property, disorderly conduct, and drinking on the public way," and depicted him as falsely representing himself as a broker when he did not hold a license. In the movie, O'Neill is a ticket scalper and gambler, and gets involved with the Little League in order to pay off a gambling debt when in fact Muzikowski had done so "solely out of a genuine concern for children."

The plaintiff's efforts to enjoin distribution of the film came to naught, and the district court dismissed his claim for damages on summary judgment. After disposing of some preliminary procedural matters, Wood, J., continued:]

III

The parties agree that Illinois law applies to the substance of Muzikowski's claim, and so (to the extent it is pertinent) we will confine our discussion accordingly. A defamatory statement is one that "tends to cause such harm to the reputation of another that it lowers that person in the eyes of the community or deters third persons from associating with him." Kolegas v. Heftel Broad. Corp., 607 N.E.2d 201, 206 (Ill. 1992). An Illinois defamation action may state a claim either for defamation *per se* (statements so harmful to reputation that damages are presumed) or defamation *per quod* (statements requiring extrinsic facts to show their defamatory meaning). Bryson v. News Am. Publ'ns, Inc., 672 N.E.2d 1207, 1214, (Ill. 1996).

The district court found that Muzikowski had not stated a claim for defamation *per se* because the statements Paramount made were reasonably capable of an "innocent construction" or of referring to somebody other than Muzikowski. It dismissed the *per quod* claim because, under FED. R. CIV. P. 9(g) (which applies to a state law defamation case in federal court), Muzikowski had not met the heightened pleading standard for special damages and pecuniary loss.

A

We begin with the defamation *per se* claim. In a *per se* action, Muzikowski may recover only if Paramount's statements fit into one of the limited categories of statements or imputations that Illinois considers actionable *per se*: (1) commission of a criminal offense; (2) infection with a venereal disease; (3) inability to perform or want of integrity in the discharge of duties of public office; (4) fornication or adultery; or (5) words that prejudice a party in her trade, profession, or business.

Even if a statement falls into a recognized category, it will not be actionable per se if the statement "may reasonably be innocently interpreted or reasonably be interpreted as referring to someone other than the plaintiff." Chapski v. Copley Press, 442 N.E.2d 195, 199 (Ill. 1982). In Illinois courts, this determination is made by the judge and it is regarded as a question of law. Allocation of functions between judge and jury in federal court, however, are a matter of federal law. Moreover, facts beyond those that appear in a federal complaint may be relevant to the reasonableness inquiry, which requires that statements be read in their natural sense, not in the light most favorable to the defendant. However, if a statement is capable of two reasonable constructions, one defamatory and one innocent, the innocent one will prevail.

Paramount provides two reasons why it is reasonable to construe the statements in question as referring to someone other than Muzikowski (namely O'Neill, an entirely fictional character). First, it points to material differences between Muzikowski and O'Neill, which Muzikowski himself identifies in his complaint. Second, it contends that because Hardball is a work of fiction, it cannot reasonably be interpreted to refer to Muzikowski.

The second contention is more easily dispensed with and so we turn to it first. "[S]imply because the story is labeled 'fiction' and, therefore, does not purport to describe any real person" does not mean that it may not be defamatory *per se*. In *Bryson*, the plaintiff sued a magazine publisher over an article appearing in its fiction section. The article featured a character who also had the last name of Bryson (but not the plaintiff's first name), and who was described as a "slut." The article was set in southern Illinois, where both the plaintiff and the author of the article resided, and the plaintiff alleged

25 other physical attributes and life experiences she shared with the character. Under these circumstances, the Illinois Supreme Court held that the plaintiff should have the opportunity to prove that the character bore "such a close resemblance to the plaintiff that reasonable persons would understand that the character was actually intended to portray the plaintiff." In light of *Bryson*, the mere fact that Paramount labeled its movie "fictitious" is not enough to shield it from an Illinois defamation action.

Paramount responds that its case is different from *Bryson* because Robert Muzikowski is never referenced by name in *Hardball*, and thus his pleading cannot be construed to support a claim for defamation *per se*. . . . [*Bryson* and other cases suggest] that there is no automatic ban on recovery if the plaintiff is not named, . . . but that instead that Illinois imposes a heightened pleading standard for complaints basing claims on publications that do not literally name the plaintiff.

That may be the Illinois pleading rule, but it of course does not apply in a federal court. . . . Even if Muzikowski's complaint would not have met Illinois's heightened pleading standard, we are satisfied that it was sufficient to put Paramount on notice of his claim. In his complaint, he lists in great detail many similarities between himself and O'Neill that could cause a reasonable person in the community to believe that O'Neill was intended to depict him and that Paramount intended *Hardball*'s mischaracterizations to refer to him.

Notwithstanding those details, Paramount argues that Muzikowski has failed to plead a category of speech that is defamatory *per se*. Muzikowski in response asserts that he fits within two of the five possible categories. First, Muzikowski claims Paramount's portrayal of O'Neill has injured him in his profession or business. In *Hardball*, O'Neill is lying when he tells people that he is a licensed securities broker. As a matter of substantive Illinois law, alleging or implying that a person is not a legitimate member of her profession is defamatory *per se*. Paramount is correct that some of Muzikowski's other allegations, such as his claim that he will be damaged because the movie asserts that his motives for coaching were pecuniary and not philanthropic, are statements of opinion which do not amount to defamation *per se*. But the narrow accusation that O'Neill/Muzikowski is an unlicensed broker fits squarely within the *per se* category.

Furthermore, Muzikowski has adequately alleged that Paramount has imputed to him the commission of a crime of moral turpitude. Such a crime cannot be a mere misdemeanor but must be punishable by imprisonment. Muzikowski describes numerous crimes that the O'Neill character commits, some of which (such as ticket scalping and drinking on the public way) are not punishable by imprisonment. Some of them, however, are more serious, such as the crime of theft, which has been held to be defamatory *per se*.

In the end, the most serious hurdle Muzikowski faces is the question whether he has in essence pleaded himself out of court, by showing that the federal trier of fact (whether judge or jury) would be compelled to find an innocent construction of the movie. Paramount argues that this is the case, and in support of its position it points to a number of differences between the real and the fictional man that are apparent on the face of the complaint. *Hardball* focuses on how O'Neill, a down-and-out gambler, finds redemption by coaching an inner-city baseball league. Muzikowski, in contrast, found redemption long before he became involved in Little League. O'Neill drinks alcohol, while Muzikowski no longer does. O'Neill gambles while Muzikowski does not, and O'Neill begins coaching only to pay for his gambling addiction while Muzikowski co-founded multiple inner-city leagues out of a genuine concern for children.

In our view, Muzikowski might be able to produce evidence showing that there is in fact no *reasonable* interpretation of the movie that would support an innocent construction. He may be able to show that no one could think that anyone but him was meant, and the changes to "his" character, far from supporting an innocent construction that O'Neill is a fictional or different person, only serve to defame him in the ways already discussed. We conclude that Muzikowski's allegations, read in the light most favorable to him, entitle him to the chance to prove his claim under a defamation *per se* theory. As the case develops further, of course, it is entirely possible that Paramount will be able to produce enough facts to support its "innocent construction" argument. At this stage, however, we believe it was premature to reject Muzikowski's case.

B

Muzikowski also urged that his complaint stated a claim for defamation *per quod*. In such an action, Muzikowski could have complained about any statements that caused him actual damage, not just those fitting into the narrow *per se* categories. In his opening brief before this court, however, Muzikowski raises no arguments contesting the district court's dismissal of his defamation *per quod* count and has therefore waived the claim. Even if we were to overlook this fact, Muzikowski concedes in his reply brief that he did not itemize his losses or plead specific damages of actual financial injury. This is a required element of a *per quod* claim. Because Muzikowski did not specifically state his damages, we affirm the judgment for Paramount on the *per quod* claim.

[Reversed and remanded.]

NOTES

1. Mitior sensus. As *Muzikowski* indicates, defamation law must set rules of construction for ambiguous statements. In the early common actions for slander, the maxim was: "Sensus verborum est duplex, mitis et asper, et verba semper sunt accipienda in mitiore sensu." (Loosely translated: "When words have two meanings, lenient and severe, they will always be construed in the more lenient sense"). An early work, G.S. Bower, Actionable Defamation 332, 333 (1908), recounted the extremes to which this rule had been taken:

> To take a few illustrations, it was solemnly held in one case that a 'coiner' *might* mean an officer in the Mint; in another, the expression 'forger' *might* conceivably import no more than the honourable industry of the metal-worker. . . .
>
> This curious doctrine originated at a period in the history of the English law of defamation when the devices employed by the courts of common law to recover their lost jurisdiction over actions of slander had achieved an embarrassing success, and similarly artificial methods had to be resorted to in order to keep within manageable bounds the ever rising flood of this species of litigation. The fact that the doctrine was never applied to libel, the courts not being burdened overmuch with actions of this description, betrays the opportunism of its origin, and so also does the fact that, as soon as the practical necessity for its application ceased to exist, the rule, like all other expedients "ad hoc," disappeared utterly.

For a modern account of this and other early developments in the law of defamation see R.H. Helmholz, Select Cases on Defamation to 1600 (1985).

2. *Ordinary meaning versus innocent construction.* The question of innocent construction often turns on time and circumstances. In *Bryson*, discussed in *Muzikowski*, the defendant described the plaintiff, using the term "slut," which Roby v. Murphy, 27 Ill. App. (1888) had held to be not defamatory in 1888.

> At the time *Roby* was decided, Webster's dictionary defined the term "slut" as "an untidy woman," "a slattern" or "a female dog," and stated that the term was "the same as 'bitch.'" Apparently, when *Roby* was decided, none of the dictionary definitions of "slut" implied sexual promiscuity. Moreover, the *Roby* court found that, even in its "common acceptance," the term "slut" did not amount to a charge of unchastity.
>
> We cannot simply assume that the term "slut" means the same thing today as it did a century ago. Many modern dictionaries include the definitions of the term "slut" cited in *Roby*, but add new definitions that imply sexual promiscuity. See, e.g., Webster's New World Dictionary (2d Coll. ed. 1975) ("a sexually immoral woman"); American Heritage Dictionary 1153 (2d Coll. ed. 1985) ("[a] woman of loose morals" "prostitute"). Moreover, in the present age, the term "slut" is commonly used and understood to refer to sexual promiscuity.

McMorrow, J., weighed in with this dissent:

> As a general rule, it is not actionable to call a woman a "slut" unless the word is used in such a manner as to impute whoredom. This rule recognizes that the word itself does not always impute a breach of chastity, but carries with it such nonactionable connotations as brazen or shameless. Indeed, as defendants point out, and the majority concedes, the American Heritage Dictionary contains several definitions of the word "slut," such as a "slovenly, dirty woman," "a woman of loose morals," a "prostitute," "a bold, brazen girl," or "a female dog." Consequently, because the word has many different meanings, most of which are not defamatory *per se*, context is crucial; for as noted above, if a word "may reasonably be innocently interpreted," it is not actionable *per se*.

The Supreme Court refused to apply any rule of innocent construction in Milkovich v. Lorain Journal Co., 497 U.S. 1, 21 (1990), when it rebuffed defendant's efforts to dismiss its statement that the plaintiff had perjured himself in a judicial proceeding as "loose, figurative or hyperbolic language" to which the opinion privilege would attach. Similarly, in Masson v. New Yorker Magazine, Inc., 501 U.S. 496, 513 (1991), the Supreme Court refused to afford the opinion privilege to allegedly fabricated quotations in which the plaintiff was said to have described himself as an "intellectual gigolo" — "you get pleasure from him, but don't take him out in public," during an interview with Janet Malcolm, the writer of the New Yorker story. Kennedy, J., noted that in a serious account published in a magazine which "seemed to enjoy a reputation for scrupulous factual accuracy," a reader could be expected to take these words at "face value." "A defendant may be able to argue to the jury that quotations should be viewed by the reader as nonliteral or reconstructions, but we conclude that a trier of fact in this case could find that the reasonable reader would understand the quotations to be nearly verbatim reports of statements made by the subject."

Masson finally came to closure 11 years after the publication of the original New Yorker story, when the jury found that two of Malcolm's statements were false, one of which was defamatory, but that none had been published with the actual malice necessary for awarding damages. For an account of the subdued ending to an epic struggle, see Margolick, Psychoanalyst Loses Libel Suit Against New Yorker Reporter, N.Y. Times, November 3, 1994, at A1.

3. Newspaper headlines. Unlike reviews and opinion pieces, context plays a diminished role with newspaper headlines, which are thereafter corrected by qualifications buried in the body of the text. A headline may be libelous even though the full story sufficiently explains it. The rule was justified in Sprouse v. Clay Communication, Inc., 211 S.E.2d 674, 686 (W. Va. 1975):

> Generally, where the headline is of normal size and does not lead to a conclusion totally unsupported by the body of the story, both story and

headline are to be considered together for their total impression. However, where oversized headlines are published which reasonably lead the average reader to an entirely different conclusion than [sic] the facts recited in the body of the story, and where the plaintiff can demonstrate that it was the intent of the publisher to use such misleading headlines to create a false impression on the normal reader, the headlines may be considered separately with regard to whether a known falsehood was published.

See also Restatement (Second) of Torts §563, comment *d*, which notes that the "context" of a defamatory newspaper headline does not "ordinarily" include the text of the article itself. These principles were applied in Kaelin v. Globe Communications Corp., 162 F.3d 1036 (9th Cir. 1998), in which the defendant published in the National Examiner a headline— COPS THINK KATO DID IT—one week after O.J. Simpson was acquitted of the murders of Nicole Brown Simpson and Ronald Goldman. The court held that the headline standing alone was capable of meaning that Kato Kaelin had committed the murders. It rejected the argument that a subheadline—he fears that they want him for perjury, says pals—and the story buried 17 pages in the interior of the National Examiner were sufficient to escape liability.

> Since the publication occurred just one week after O.J. Simpson's highly publicized acquittal for murder, we believe that a reasonable person, at that time, might well have concluded that the "it" in the first sentence of the cover and the internal headlines referred to the murders. Such a reading of the first sentence is not negated by or inconsistent with the second sentence as a mater of logic, grammar, or otherwise. In our view, an ordinary reader reasonably could have read the headline to mean that the cops think that Kato committed the murders *and* that Kato thinks that he is wanted for perjury.

The same principle has been applied to small disclaimers posted with respect to pictures of the plaintiff. In Stanton v. Metro Corp., 438 F.3d 119, 122 (1st Cir. 2006), DiClerico, J., reversing the court below, held that a triable question of defamation was raised when the defendant published a picture of plaintiff, "smiling faintly" in a group of five, next to an article on the "Mating Habits of the Suburban Teenager," which chronicled a rise in teenage sexual activity. The evident linkage between the placement of the picture and the story could not be overcome as a matter of law by posting a disclaimer in the smallest possible type that stated "the individuals pictured are unrelated to the people or events described in this story." Should the plaintiff be entitled to a judgment as a matter of law that the headline referred to her?

For analysis see R. Smolla, Law of Defamation §4.07 (2d ed. 2003).

4. *Of and concerning the plaintiff.* As indicated in *Muzikowski*, the plaintiff must show that she is the target of the defamatory utterance. Although this

is an easy task when the plaintiff is a well-known personage who is identified by name, it can prove more difficult when names are changed in
loosely fictionalized accounts that draw on real-life people. In addition, the
problem becomes more troublesome when the plaintiff is described by
some generic title, such as a commissioner or public official. On the
constitutional status of the "of and concerning" requirement, see New York
Times v. Sullivan, *infra* at 1097. For a balanced discussion of the pros and
cons of abolishing all liability for fiction, see R. Posner, Law and Literature: A Misunderstood Relation 320-329 (1988).

Wilkow v. Forbes, Inc.
241 F.3d 552 (7th Cir. 2001)

EASTERBROOK, J., *Forbes* Magazine runs a column on pending litigation of
interest to the business community. The October 5, 1998, issue of *Forbes*
covered the grant of certiorari in what was to become Bank of America
National Trust & Savings Ass'n v. 203 North LaSalle Street Partnership, 526
U.S. 434 (1999), which presented the question whether the absolute-priority
rule in bankruptcy has a new-value exception. The absolute-priority rule,
codified in 11 U.S.C. §1129(b)(2)(B)(ii), forbids confirmation of a plan of
reorganization over the objection of an impaired class of creditors unless
"the holder of any claim or interest that is junior to the claims of such
[impaired] class will not receive or retain under the plan on account of such
junior claim or interest any property." In other words, creditors may insist on
priority of payment: secured creditors must be paid in full before unsecured
creditors retain any interest, and unsecured creditors must be paid off before
equity holders retain an interest. But equity investors frequently argue that
this rule may be bent if they contribute new value as part of the plan.
Although this court had rejected other new-value arguments, in *203 North
LaSalle* we held that the equity investors could retain ownership of a commercial office building, in exchange for about $6 million in new capital over
a five-year period, even though the principal lender would fall about $38
million short of full repayment. This was the decision on which *Forbes* published a short column, seven months before the Supreme Court held the
plan "doomed, . . . without necessarily exhausting its flaws, by its provision
for vesting equity in the reorganized business in the Debtor's partners
without extending an opportunity for anyone else either to compete for that
equity or to propose a competing reorganization plan." 526 U.S. at 454.

The majority opinion in the Supreme Court required about 8,000 words
to resolve the case — and without reaching a final decision on the vitality of
the new-value exception (though the majority's analysis hog-tied the doctrine). The majority opinion in this court ran about 9,500 words, with 5,200
more in a dissent. A 670-word article such as the one *Forbes* published could

not present either the facts of the case or the subtleties of the law. What the article lacked in analysis, however, it made up for with colorful verbs and adjectives. Taking lenders' side, *Forbes* complained that "many judges, ever more sympathetic to debtors, are allowing unscrupulous business owners to rob creditors." According to the article, a partnership led by Marc Wilkow "stiffed" the bank, paying only $55 million on a $93 million loan while retaining ownership of the building. . . . Its core paragraph reads:

> By the mid-1990s, rents were not keeping up with costs. When the principal came due in January 1995, Wilkow and his partners pleaded poverty. To keep the bank from foreclosing, LaSalle Partnership filed for bankruptcy. Appraisals of the property came in at less than $60 million. In theory the bank was entitled to the entire amount. It suggested selling the property to the highest bidder. Determined to keep the building, LaSalle partners asked the bankruptcy court instead to accept a plan under which the bank would likely receive a fraction of what it was owed while the partners would keep the building. The bank, not the equity holder, would take the hit.

Wilkow replied with this libel suit under the diversity jurisdiction, contending that *Forbes* and Brigid McMenamin, the article's author, defamed him by asserting that he was in poverty (or, worse, "pleaded poverty" when he was solvent) and had filched the bank's money. According to Wilkow, *Forbes* should at least have informed its readers that the bank had lent the money without recourse against the partners, so that a downturn in the real estate market, rather than legal machinations, was the principal source of the bank's loss. . . .

[Easterbrook, J., addressed some procedural, choice of law, and constitutional issues, and continued:]

We don't think it necessary to consider either constitutional limits on liability for defamation or privileges under New York law, because this article is not defamatory under Illinois law in the first place. In Illinois, a "statement of fact is not shielded from an action for defamation by being prefaced with the words 'in my opinion,' but if it is plain that the speaker is expressing a subjective view, an interpretation, a theory, conjecture, or surmise, rather than claiming to be in possession of objectively verifiable facts, the statement is not actionable." Haynes v. Alfred A. Knopf, Inc., 8 F.3d 1222, 1227 (7th Cir. 1993).

Characterizations such as "stiffing" and "rob" convey McMenamin's objection to the new-value exception. She expostulates against judicial willingness to allow debtors to retain interests in exchange for new value, not particularly against debtors' seizing whatever opportunities the law allows. Nothing in the article implies that Wilkow did (or even proposed) anything illegal; *Forbes* informed the reader that the district court and this court *approved* Wilkow's proposed plan of reorganization. Every detail in the article (other than the quotation in the final paragraph) comes from public documents; the article does not suggest that McMenamin knows extra information implying that Wilkow pulled the wool over judges' eyes or engaged in other misconduct. Colloquialisms such as "pleaded poverty" do not imply that Wilkow was destitute and failing to pay his personal creditors, an allegation that would have been defamatory. Read in context, the phrase conveys the idea that the partnership could not repay the loan out of rents received from the building's tenants. After all, inability to pay one's debts as they come due is an ordinary reason for bankruptcy, and 203 North LaSalle Street Partnership *did* file a petition in bankruptcy. Filing a bankruptcy petition is one way of "pleading poverty."

Although the article drips with disapproval of Wilkow's (and the judges') conduct, an author's opinion about business ethics isn't defamatory under Illinois law, as *Haynes* and *Bryson* explain. Informing the reader about the nonrecourse nature of the loan might have made Wilkow look better, but it would not have drawn the article's sting: that the partners got to keep the property even though the bank lost $38 million. The original deal's fundamental structure was that the partnership would repay the loan from rental income, and that if revenue was insufficient the bank could choose to foreclose (cutting its loss and reinvesting at the market rate elsewhere), to renegotiate a new interest rate with the partners, or to forebear in the hope that the market would improve and the full debt could yet be paid. These options collectively would be worth more than the market value of the building on the date of default. Yet the partners refused to honor these promises to the bank. They persuaded judges to eliminate the bank's rights to foreclose, to renegotiate, or to forebear and retain the full security interest. The plan of reorganization stripped down the security interest, prevented the bank from foreclosing, and required it to finance the partnership's operations for the next decade, at a rate of interest below what the bank would have charged in light of the newly revealed riskiness of the loan. If the real estate market fell further during that time, so that the partnership could not repay even the reduced debt, then the bank was going to lose still more money. The present value of the promises made to the bank in the plan of reorganization therefore was less than the appraised value of the building. But the partners stood to make a great deal of money if the market turned up again (as it did), for they had shucked $38 million in secured debt while retaining most appreciation in the property's value. Whether that was a sound use of bankruptcy reorganization, independent of the plan's new-value aspects, is open to question.

A reporter is entitled to state her view that an ethical entrepreneur should have offered the lender a better bargain, such as allowing the bank to foreclose and take its $55 million with certainty, avoiding the additional risk that this plan fastened on the lender. Foreclosure would have had serious consequences for the partners, who would have lost about $20 million in recaptured tax benefits. These potential losses created room for negotiation. Armed with the new-value exception, however, the partners were able to retain the tax benefits, sharing none with the bank in exchange for its approval of a restructuring, while depriving the bank of a security interest that would have been valuable when the market recovered. Although a reader might arch an eyebrow at Wilkow's strategy, an allegation of greed is not defamatory; sedulous pursuit of self-interest is the engine that propels a market economy. Capitalism certainly does not depend on sharp practices, but neither is an allegation of sharp dealing anything more than an uncharitable opinion. Illinois does not attach damages to name-calling. See Stevens v. Tillman, 855 F.2d 394, 400-02 (7th Cir. 1988) (collecting cases, including examples such as "sleazy" and "rip-off"). Wilkow's current and potential partners would have read this article as an endorsement of Wilkow's strategy; they want to invest with a general partner who drives the hardest possible bargain with lenders. By observing that Wilkow used every opening the courts allowed, *Forbes* may well have improved his standing with investors looking for real estate tax shelters (though surely it did not help his standing with lenders). No matter the net effect of the article, however, it was not defamatory under Illinois law, so the judgment of the district court is AFFIRMED.

NOTES

1. *Reputation in the eyes of which beholder?* The last paragraph of Easterbrook's opinion notes that the *Forbes* story might be regarded as favorable by potential investors who are looking for a general partner willing to protect their interests. How should the law of defamation apply if a story wins the approbation of some of its readers and the disapproval of others? Does the general response in the larger community matter if only specialized individuals are likely to do business with Wilkow in the future?

The traditional American view allows the plaintiff to prevail if she can point to any subgroup of the population that would find the statement defamatory. In Peck v. Tribune Co., 214 U.S. 185, 189-190 (1909), an advertisement printed in the defendant's newspaper used the picture of the plaintiff, a nurse in real life, over the name of some other woman who had extolled the virtues of the malt whiskey promoted in the advertisement. Holmes, J., held, first, that the ad referred to the plaintiff, notwithstanding the incorrect name below the picture. He continued:

> It was pointed out that there was no general consensus of opinion that to drink whiskey is wrong or that to be a nurse is discreditable. It might have been added that very possibly giving a certificate and the use of one's portrait in aid of an advertisement would be regarded with irony, or a stronger

feeling, only by a few. But it appears to us that such inquiries are beside the point. It may be that the action for libel is of little use, but while it is maintained it should be governed by the general principles of tort. If the advertisement obviously would hurt the plaintiff in the estimation of an important and respectable part of the community, liability is not a question of a majority vote.

We know of no decision in which this matter is discussed upon principle. But obviously an unprivileged falsehood need not entail universal hatred to constitute a cause of action. No falsehood is thought about or even known by all the world. No conduct is hated by all. That it will be known by a large number and will lead an appreciable fraction of that number to regard the plaintiff with contempt is enough to do her practical harm.

Accordingly, Holmes held that the question of defamation should have been left to the jury. Should an offset to damages be allowed if the statement *improves* the reputation of the plaintiff in the eyes of another respectable segment of the community? The Restatement, following *Peck*, provides that a statement is defamatory only if it prejudices the plaintiff "in the eyes of a substantial and respectable minority" of the members of the community, but not if it simply offends "some individual or individuals with views sufficiently peculiar to regard as derogatory what the vast majority of persons regard as innocent." RST §559, comment *e*. Illustration 3 of §559 provides: "*A*, a member of a gang of hoodlums, writes to *B*, a fellow bandit, that *C*, a member of the gang, has reformed and is no longer to be trusted with the loot of the gang. *A* has not defamed *C*."

Is that result consistent with *Peck*? Should the action be denied because there is no damage to reputation or because the illegality of the plaintiff's conduct defeats any prima facie case on the ground that the law should never lend its hand to aid conspirators?

What result should happen where the defendant defames a plaintiff who already has a horrible reputation in the relevant community for acts unrelated to the particular charge of defamation? Cooper v. Greeley, 1 Denio 347, 364-365 (N.Y. 1845), involved a celebrity literary dispute between the writer James Fenimore Cooper and Horace Greeley, the editor of New York Tribune. When threatened with the action Greeley famously replied: "Mr. Cooper will have to bring his action to trial somewhere. He will not like to bring it in New York, for we are known here, nor in Otsego for he is known there." The court construed the newspaper remark to mean that plaintiff had such a poor reputation in Otsego that he would not risk filing suit there. The defendants pleaded in justification that plaintiff had acquired in Otsego "the reputation of a proud, captious, censorious, arbitrary, dogmatical, malicious, illiberal, revengeful and litigious man, wherefore the said plaintiff was in bad repute in the said county of Otsego." The court allowed defendant's plea, noting that: "Reputation is the estimate in which an individual is held by public fame in the place where he is known. And the existence of a good or bad reputation is, I think, a fact which may be directly put in issue." But why should this issue be pleaded as a justification, instead of a denial of harm flowing from the false statement? Is it possible for a plaintiff to have so bad a reputation as to become "libel-proof"?

2. *Group libel.* Yet another variation on this basic theme involves defamatory statements made about a group of which plaintiff is a member. Whether or not plaintiff succeeds in demonstrating a defamation "of and concerning" himself depends on the size of the group and on whether the defamatory comment speaks of all members of the group or merely of some. In general, recovery has been limited to cases in which the statement is made of all members of a small group. In Neiman-Marcus v. Lait, 13 F.R.D. 311 (S.D.N.Y. 1952), the defendants, in their book *U.S.A. Confidential*, charged that some models and saleswomen of the Neiman-Marcus store in Texas frequently served as "call girls" and that most of the male salesmen were homosexuals. Suit was brought by 9 models (constituting the entire staff of models at the time of publication), by 15 salesmen out of a group of 25 at the time of publication, and by 30 saleswomen out of a group of 382. The defendants probably did not contest the claims of the nine models, but moved to dismiss those of the salesmen and saleswomen. The court denied the motion as to the salesmen, emphasizing that the group was small and that the characterization was of "most" of them. It granted the motion to dismiss as to the saleswomen because of the size of the group, saying that "no reasonable man would take the writer seriously and conclude from the publication a reference to any individual saleswoman." More recently, the assertion that (exactly) one person in a group of nine employees had AIDS was held to be neither group nor individual libel because it implied that eight members of the group did not have AIDS. Chapman v. Byrd, 475 S.E.2d 734 (N.C. App. 1996).

For much of this century there has been considerable concern over the calculated defamation of large groups such as Jews, Catholics, and blacks. Yet in these cases a defamation action has been consistently denied. Thus, in Khalid Abdullah Tarig Al Mansour Faissal Fahd Al Talal v. Fanning, 506 F. Supp. 186, 187 (N.D. Cal. 1980), the plaintiff brought a class action on behalf of some 600 million Muslims, alleging that the film "Death of a Princess" was defamatory to all Muslims because "it depicts the public execution of a Saudi Arabian princess for adultery." The court denied the remedy, noting that "to permit an action to lie for the defamation of such a multitudinous group . . . would render meaningless the rights guaranteed by the First Amendment to explore issues of public import." For an argument that group libel rules should be automatically dismissed for groups over 25, see King, Reference to the Plaintiff Requirement in Defamatory Statements Directed at Groups, 35 Wake Forest L. Rev. 343 (2000).

3. *Injurious falsehood.* Should a plaintiff be allowed to recover special damages for harm caused by false but *non*defamatory statements? In

Cardiff v. Brooklyn Eagle, Inc., 75 N.Y.S.2d 222 (Sup. Ct. 1947), publication of the obituary of a living plaintiff was not defamatory because it did not expose the plaintiff to hatred, ridicule, or contempt. Had there been proof of special damages, however, should the plaintiff have been allowed to recover, if not for defamation, for a separate tort of injurious falsehood? As the large number of defamation suits in commercial settings shows, defamation can be most devastating when it induces third parties not to do business with a plaintiff. The injury to the plaintiff is, of course, every bit as serious when the diversion of business is induced by injurious but nondefamatory falsehoods. For example, in Radcliffe v. Evans, 2 Q.B. 524 [Q.B. 1892], the defendant newspaper reported that the plaintiff had ceased to carry on his business as an engineer and boilermaker. The jury found specially that the words did not reflect on the plaintiff's character and were not libelous. Judgment for plaintiff was affirmed, however, with Bowen, L.J., saying: "That an action will lie for written or oral falsehoods, not actionable per se nor even defamatory, where they are maliciously published, where they are calculated in the ordinary course of things to produce, and where they do produce, actual damage, is established law. Such an action is not one of libel or of slander, but an action on the case for damage willfully and intentionally done without just occasion or excuse, analogous to an action for slander of title."

If defamation is actionable without proof of malice, why require proof of malice in injurious falsehood cases? Should damages for emotional distress be allowed in injurious falsehood cases? See Prosser, Injurious Falsehood: The Basis of Liability, 59 Colum. L. Rev. 425 (1959).

SECTION D. LIBEL AND SLANDER

1. *The Common Law Distinction*

Historically, the common law drew a distinction between libel and slander. Libel was the proper theory when the defendant's statement was embodied in some permanent form, such as a book or a picture, or even a wax sculpture. Even public shadowing to prevent an individual from testifying against the defendant was treated as libelous because "[a]ctual pursuit and public surveillance of person and home are suggestive of criminality fatal to public esteem and productive of public contempt and ridicule." Schultz v. Frankfort Marine Accident & Plate Glass Insurance Co., 139 N.W. 386, 390 (Wis. 1913).

Slander, for its part, consists primarily of false spoken words. In addition, "the use of a mere transitory gesture commonly understood as a substitute for spoken words, such as a nod of the head, a wave of the hand, or a sign of the fingers, is slander rather than libel." RST §568, comment *d*. More generally, Restatement (Second) of Torts §568(3) provides: "The area of dissemination, the deliberate and premeditated character of its publication and the persistence of defamation are factors to be considered in determining whether a publication is a libel rather than a slander."

The libel-slander distinction rests on the perception that the permanence of libel made it a more dangerous form of misconduct. Accordingly, libels were ordinarily actionable per se without proof of special damages, while slander was generally actionable only upon proof of special damages (e.g., a lost business arrangement), except if the slander fell into one of four basic categories:

a. Loathsome diseases. The presumption of damage has been confined to diseases that are not merely contagious but also loathsome, such as plague, leprosy, and venereal disease, and therefore merit social ostracism. How should AIDS be classified?

b. Criminal conduct. Also slanderous per se at common law was the imputation of criminal activities, the law's concern apparently being that such a statement might expose plaintiff to criminal prosecution. However, all charges of criminal misconduct are not slanderous per se. Most jurisdictions now insist that the crime involve "moral turpitude." See, e.g., Wooten v. Martin, 131 S.W. 783 (Ky. 1910). Other jurisdictions follow the English rule and require that the words charge an offense punishable by death or imprisonment.

If plaintiff is accused of conduct that is criminal under the law in the state where the allegations are made, but not criminal where the conduct was performed, are the statements slanderous per se? Klumph v. Dunn, 66 Pa. 141 (1870), opted for the "law of the country where the words are spoken," because it is by those laws that the reputation of the plaintiff is judged.

c. Imputation of unchastity. The older common law did not treat as slanderous per se words that imputed unchastity to a woman. That result was reversed by statute in England in 1891 and in several states in the United States. States without such statutes sometimes granted recovery on the ground that the charge of fornication was criminal under local laws. Other states allowed the action regardless of whether there were imputations of criminal conduct. The first Restatement of Torts treated allegations of unchastity as slanderous per se. RT §574. See also 740 Ill. Comp. Stat. 145/1 (2007) that makes it actionable slander to publish or utter words that charge any person of being guilty of "fornication or adultery." The Second Restatement §574 now makes slanderous per se allegations of "serious sexual misconduct," which, as comment *c* now makes clear, applies to both men and women. How should false allegations of homosexuality be treated?

d. Slander of a person's trade or profession. This critical category includes such charges that a surgeon is a butcher, or a cashier has his hands in the till. More problematic are statements reflecting adversely upon plaintiff's character by charging dishonesty, sloth, immorality, or drunkenness. Also slanderous per se are unprivileged charges of dishonesty or corruption against public officials.

In Ravnikar v. Bogojavlensky, 782 N.E.2d 508, 512 (Mass. 2003), the plaintiff and defendant were both physicians working at a common facility. The defendant commented to a prospective new patient of the plaintiff that the plaintiff was dying of cancer when in fact she had been cured. The individual patient retained the plaintiff's service so that no special damages could be proved. Nonetheless, the court allowed her case for general damages.

> A statement that a physician is terminally ill can discourage potential patients by creating the natural inference that death is not far off and that the physician will be distracted by her medical condition and its treatment. A potential patient hearing this type of statement could quite reasonably conclude that any relationship formed with that physician would necessarily be a brief one, and, while the relationship lasts, that the physician's ability to provide care would be impaired. Such a statement, thus, has the potential to damage a physician's medical practice because patients are more likely to choose a physician on whom they can rely for quality care over the long term. Today physicians compete for patients just as businesspeople compete for customers, and a doctor who cannot offer stable and reliable care to her patients faces the same competitive disadvantage as any other business-person.

Why is this not a case of injurious falsehood?

In contrast, in Gahafer v. Ford Motor Co., 328 F.3d 859, 862-863 (6th Cir. 2003), the plaintiff's supervisor, Sabol, offered an obscenity-laced ti-rade accusing the plaintiff, a mid-manager employee, of fraud and casti-gating him for diverting time from his responsibilities as "dimensional control engineer" to work on another Ford project, 6-Sigma, for a different supervisor. The court refused to treat the tirade as slander per se.

> [N]othing in Sabol's statements directly or indirectly suggests that Gahafer is unfit, incompetent or otherwise unqualified to perform his job. Sabol's words did not attack Gahafer's skills, honesty, integrity or character. He did not accuse Gahafer of being useless and dispensable or a common parasite on Ford's financial resources. To the contrary, Sabol's poor choice of words reveals only that Gahafer's services and expertise were highly valued, as evidenced by the statement: "I need you here seven days a week to work dimension control and you don't have time to do anything else." Thus, Sabol's exclamations simply suggest frustration at Gahafer's time commit-ment to the 6-Sigma project; they do not cast doubt on his ability, fitness or qualification to effectively carry out his job duties.

For the classic criticism of the distinction between libel and slander see Veeder, The History and Theory of the Law of Defamation, 3 Colum. L. Rev. 546, 571-573 (1903).

In modern times, the main challenge to the distinction between libel and slander arose first with radio and television. In Hartmann v. Winchell, 73 N.E.2d 30 (N.Y. 1947), the court held that reading a defamatory statement on the radio from a prepared manuscript should be governed by the law of libel because the wide dissemination of the broadcast could reach a "far-flung" audience larger than that attained by a newspaper. *Hartmann* did not reach the question of how to treat spontaneous remarks on the air. The Restatement (Second) of Torts §568A states the modern position that "[b]roadcasting of defamatory matter by means of radio or television is libel, whether or not it is read from a manuscript." The English Defamation Act, 15 & 16 Geo. VI and Eliz. II. ch. 66, §§1, 16 (1952), adopts the same rule.

2.   *Libel Per Quod and Libel Per Se*

The elaborate common law distinction between libel per quod and libel per se, referred to in *Muzikowski, supra* at 1034, depends on whether the reference to the plaintiff can be derived from the statement itself, in which case it can be libel per se (in itself) or whether it requires some reference to extrinsic evidence, in which case it is libel per quod (through which). When the defendant mentions the plaintiff by name, the statement may be libel per se. But when the defendant says, "The person who stole my money lives in the house next door," extrinsic evidence is needed to establish that the statement refers to the plaintiff.

In other cases the identity of the plaintiff is undisputed, but extraneous facts are needed to establish the defamatory meaning. The basic problem is nicely illustrated by two old New York cases. In Smith v. Smith, 142 N.E. 292 (N.Y. 1923), defendant had made the following statement in applying for a marriage license in 1921: "Number of marriage, 1; is applicant a divorced person? No." The plaintiff, however, alleged the following additional facts: That she and defendant had been married and were divorced in 1911, that the statement in the application therefore meant that defendant had never been married to plaintiff, such that during the time they lived together she had been his mistress. The court held that with this amplification the complaint stated a cause of action. In Braun v. Armour & Co., 173 N.E. 845 (N.Y. 1930), defendant had issued an advertisement setting forth a list of dealers in its meat products, including plaintiff, stating: "These progressive dealers listed here sell Armour's Star Bacon in the new window-top carton." In the complaint plaintiff added that he was a dealer in kosher meat and that bacon was a non-kosher product. Again the court held that the complaint stated a cause of action.

The interaction between the rules on innuendo and those on libel and slander can be quite complex. Prosser, Libel Per Quod, 46 Va. L. Rev. 839 (1960), suggested that in most states when libel has been established per quod, that is, only by extrinsic evidence, the plaintiff must show special damages, as in ordinary slander cases. An exception to this rule involves words that, if spoken, would have been slanderous per se and therefore actionable without proof of special damages. Prosser's view was sharply challenged in Eldredge, The Spurious Role of Libel Per Quod, 79 Harv. L. Rev. 733 (1966), which argued that the majority of the states had retained the traditional rule that all libels, whether per se or per quod, were actionable without proof of special damages. See, e.g., Hinsdale v. Orange County Publications, Inc., 217 N.E.2d 650 (N.Y. 1966). In the end, with both Prosser and Eldredge participating, the Second Restatement adopted a compromise position that required proof of special damages only if the defendant was ignorant of the extrinsic facts that made his statements defamatory. Section 569 adopts the traditional position that all libels are actionable without proof of special damages.

SECTION E.   BASIS OF LIABILITY: INTENTION, NEGLIGENCE, AND STRICT LIABILITY IN DEFAMATION

E. Hulton & Co. v. Jones
[1910] A.C. 20

[The defendant newspaper ran an article written by its Paris correspondent that in part read as follows: "'Whist! There is Artemus Jones with a woman who is not his wife, who must be, you know — the other thing!' whispers a fair neighbor of mine excitedly to her bosom friend's ear. Really, is it not surprising how certain of our fellow-countrymen behave when they come abroad? Who would suppose by his goings on, that he is a church warden at Peckham?" Plaintiff was a lawyer named Thomas Artemus Jones of North Wales; he was not a church warden, nor did he reside at Peckham, but he had up to 1901 contributed signed articles to defendant's newspaper. Defendant's contention that they had never heard of plaintiff and had used the name Artemus Jones as a fictitious name was accepted as true by plaintiff at the trial. Plaintiff produced witnesses who said they had read the article and thought that it referred to plaintiff. The trial judge charged the jury that the issue was not what the writer had intended but how the statement would be understood. At the trial plaintiff recovered a jury verdict of £1,750. The court of appeal affirmed by a two-to-one vote and, on appeal, the House of Lords affirmed.

The issue was perhaps most succinctly put during argument in the House of Lords when defendant's counsel said: "The question is who was meant," and Lord Loreburn asked: "Is it not rather who was hit?" Counsel replied: "No. A man cannot be held responsible for remote and improbable results of his actions."]

LOREBURN, L.C. My Lords, I think this appeal must be dismissed. A question in regard to the law of libel has been raised which does not seem to me to be entitled to the support of your Lordships. Libel is a tortious act. What does the tort consist in? It consists in using language which others knowing the circumstances would reasonably think to be defamatory of the person complaining of and injured by it. A person charged with libel cannot defend himself by shewing that he intended in his own breast not to defame, or that he intended not to defame the plaintiff, if in fact he did both. He has none the less imputed something disgraceful and has none the less injured the plaintiff. A man in good faith may publish a libel believing it to be true, and it may be found by the jury that he acted in good faith believing it to be true, and reasonably believing it to be true, but that in fact the statement was false. Under those circumstances he has no defence to the action, however excellent his intention. If the intention of the writer be immaterial in considering whether the matter written is defamatory, I do not see why it need be relevant in considering whether it is defamatory of the plaintiff. The writing, according to the old form, must be malicious, and it must be of and concerning the plaintiff. Just as the defendant could not excuse himself from malice by proving that he wrote it in the most benevolent spirit, so he cannot shew that the libel was not of and concerning the plaintiff by proving that he never heard of the plaintiff. His intention in both respects equally is inferred from what he did. His remedy is to abstain from defamatory words. . . .

The damages are certainly heavy, but I think your Lordships ought to remember two things. The first is that the jury were entitled to think, in the absence of proof satisfactory to them (and they were the judges of it), that some ingredient of recklessness, or more than recklessness, entered into the writing and the publication of this article, especially as Mr. Jones, the plaintiff, had been employed on this very newspaper, and his name was well known in the paper and also well known in the district in which the paper circulated. In the second place the jury was entitled to say this kind of article is to be condemned. There is no tribunal more fitted to decide in regard to publications, especially publications in the newspaper Press, whether they bear a stamp and character which ought to enlist sympathy and to secure protection. If they think that the licence is not fairly used and that the tone and style of the libel is reprehensible and ought to be checked, it is for the jury to say so; and for my part, although I think the damages are certainly

high, I am not prepared to advise your Lordships to interfere, especially as
the Court of Appeal have not thought it right to interfere, with the verdict.

NOTES

1. *Strict liability and malicious intent.* Would Lord Loreborn have reduced
the plaintiff's damages if he had been convinced that the reference to
plaintiff was strictly accidental? If the plaintiff's name had been Tom Jones?

Hulton is followed today in the United States insofar as defamation cases
are governed by common law rules. "Actual malice, in the sense of spite or
ill will, is presumed and need not be proved if the words are defamatory on
their face." Tate v. Bradley, 837 F.2d 206 (5th Cir. 1988). Should defamation be a tort of strict liability if harms for physical injuries are governed
by a principle of negligence?

Before *New York Times*, the commentators were divided on the merits of
Hulton v. Jones. Jeremiah Smith pronounced it superior to all the alternatives. Smith, *Jones v. Hulton*: Three Conflicting Judicial Views as to a
Question of Defamation, 60 U. Pa. L. Rev. 365 (1912). Morris, Inadvertent
Newspaper Libel and Retraction, 32 Ill. L. Rev. 36 (1937), favored the strict
liability rule because it eliminates the need to prove the negligence that is
present in most cases of this sort. Holdsworth, A Chapter of Accidents in
the Law of Libel, 57 Law Q. Rev. 74 (1941), supported the negligence rule.

2. *Basis of liability for publication.* Even after *Hulton*, it seems widely agreed
that the defendant will be liable only if the publication was intentional or at
least negligent. Thus, the Restatement of Torts §577, comment *n*, excuses
the defendant for "accidental" publications. That rule applies when *A* writes
defamatory statements about *B*, which are stolen from a locked desk by a
thief who reads or publishes them. Similarly, if *A* sends a defamatory letter
about *B* to *B* through the mail, the publication is regarded as accidental if a
robber reads or publishes the stolen letter. Finally, if *A* sends a defamatory
letter to *B* marked "personal" which is opened and read by *B*'s secretary
there is no publication, unless *A* knew of the secretary's practice. Note that if
defendant is strictly liable for publication, he could escape responsibility so
long as the publication was made by some independent third person.

SECTION F. DAMAGES

1. Special Damages

"By 'actual damage' is meant what in the books is usually called 'special
damage.' This latter expression is either meaningless or misleading." G. S.
Bower, Actionable Defamation, Article 13, at 33 (1908).

Terwilliger v. Wands
17 N.Y. 54 (1858)

[Action for slander. Plaintiff proved that defendant told La Fayette Wands that plaintiff was having continued sexual intercourse with one Mrs. Fuller and that he — plaintiff — would do all he could to keep Mr. Fuller in the penitentiary so that he could continue to enjoy Mrs. Fuller's favors. Plaintiff proved that defendant had said much the same thing to one Neiper, a good friend of plaintiff's, who had told plaintiff about this statement. Also, he proved that Neiper had told him that this information about plaintiff was spreading all over the county. As a result of learning this information, plaintiff became very ill, both mentally and physically, had to have medical treatment, and could not do any work; subsequently his crops and business were neglected and he had to hire more help. The judgment for the defendant below was affirmed.]

STRONG, J. The words spoken by the defendant not being actionable of themselves, it was necessary in order to maintain the action to prove that they occasioned special damages to the plaintiff. The special damages must have been the natural, immediate and legal consequence of the words. . . . [The court first concluded that defendant was not responsible for a repetition of the words to plaintiff, and continued:]

But there is another ground upon which the judgment must be affirmed. The special damages relied upon are not of such a nature as will support the action. The action for slander is given by the law as a remedy for "injuries affecting a man's reputation or good name by malicious, scandalous and slanderous words, tending to his damage and derogation." (3 Bl. Com., 123.) It is injuries affecting the reputation only which are the subject of the action. In the case of slanderous words actionable per se, the law, from their natural and immediate tendency to produce injury, adjudges them to be injurious, though no special loss or damage can be proved. "But with regard to words that do not apparently and upon the face of them import such defamation as will of course be injurious, it is necessary that the plaintiff should aver some particular damage to have happened." (3 Bl. Com., 124.) As to what constitutes special damages, Starkie mentions the loss of a marriage, loss of hospitable gratuitous entertainment, preventing a servant or bailiff from getting a place, the loss of customers by a tradesman; and says that in general whenever a person is prevented by the slander from receiving that which would otherwise be conferred upon him, though gratuitously, it is sufficient. (1 Stark. on Sland., 195, 202.) In Olmsted v. Miller (1 Wend. 506) [(N.Y. Sup. 1828)], it was held that the refusal of civil entertainment at a public house was sufficient special damage. So in Williams v. Hill (19 Wend. 305 [N.Y. 1838]), was the fact that the plaintiff was turned away from the house of her uncle and charged not to return until she had cleared up her character. So in Beach v. Ranney, was the circumstance that persons, who had been in the habit of doing so, refused longer to provide fuel, clothing, &c. These instances are sufficient to illustrate the kind of special damage that must result from defamatory words not otherwise actionable to make them so; they are damages produced by, or through, impairing the reputation.

It would be highly impolitic to hold all language, wounding the feelings and affecting unfavorably the health and ability to labor, of another, a ground of action; for that would be to make the right of action depend often upon whether the sensibilities of a person spoken of are easily excited or otherwise; his strength of mind to disregard abusive, insulting remarks concerning him; and his physical strength and ability to bear them. Words which would make hardly an impression on most persons, and would be thought by them, and should be by all, undeserving of notice, might be exceedingly painful to some, occasioning sickness and an interruption of ability to attend to their ordinary avocations. There must be some limit to liability for words not actionable per se, both as to the words and the kind of damages; and a clear and wise one has been fixed by the law. The words must be defamatory in their nature; and must in fact disparage the character; and this disparagement must be evidenced by some positive loss arising therefrom directly and legitimately as a fair and natural result. In this view of the law words which do not degrade the character do not injure it, and cannot occasion loss. . . . In the present case the words were defamatory, and the illness and physical prostration of the plaintiff may be assumed, so far as this part of the case is concerned, to have been actually produced by the slander, but this consequence was not, in a legal view, a natural, ordinary one, as it does not prove that the plaintiff's character was injured. The slander may not have been credited by or had the slightest influence upon any one unfavorable to the plaintiff; and it does not appear that any body believed it or treated the plaintiff any different from what they would otherwise have done on account of it. The cause was not adapted to produce the result which is claimed to be special damages. Such an effect may and sometimes does follow from such a cause but not ordinarily; and the rule of law was framed in reference to common and usual effects and not those which are accidental and occasional. . . .

NOTE

Special damages today. Is there any reason to exclude recovery for mental anguish of the sort that would be suffered by a reasonable person in plaintiff's position? The modern case law still shows a certain resistance toward special damages. Zeran v. Diamond Broadcasting, Inc., 203 F.3d 714 (10th Cir. 2000), grew out of the same unfortunate incident as Zeran v. America Online, *supra* at 1033. Only this time, the plaintiff sued the radio station that had broadcast the show urging listeners to tell "Ken" Zeran what they thought of his tactics. Kimball, J., first held that the defamatory statements did not fall into any of the categories of slander per se, and thus required proof of special damages for two reasons:

Emotional distress is not a form of special damages, and Plaintiff's *de minimis* medical expenses, consisting of one visit to his physician and one prescription drug purchase, are insufficient to support the cause of action. Under . . . the *de minimis* doctrine, the law does not care for, or take notice of, very small or trifling matters. . . .

Plaintiff's defamation claim [also] fails because Plaintiff has not shown that any person thinks less of him, Kenneth Zeran, as a result of the broadcast. As the district court found, there was no evidence that anyone who called his number in response to the posting or the broadcast even knew his last name. In other words, under the facts of this case, there was an insufficient link between Plaintiff's business telephone number and Plaintiff himself for Plaintiff to have sustained damage to his reputation.

If Zeran had sustained more medical expenses, would these have been recoverable if his reputation in the community had not suffered? In Wood v. Wood, 693 A.2d 673, 674 (Vt. 1997), the court stated that "evidence of sleeping problems, loss of appetite, development of a temporary drinking problem, and deteriorating family relationships demonstrated actual harm. We have also recognized that proof of 'embarrassment and temporary injury to reputation' would be sufficient to support an award of general damages."

Ellsworth v. Martindale-Hubbell Law Directory, Inc.
280 N.W. 879 (N.D. 1938)

[In this action for libel plaintiff alleged that defendant misstated his professional and financial rating in the code form that it used in its directory. The directory itself was widely relied on by lawyers in many states and countries who needed to forward legal business. Plaintiff claimed that his rating in defendant's private key symbols was defamatory and that as a result his reputation was injured. In his pleadings he elaborately set forth the translation of this private key system, with which all members of his profession were presumably familiar. From 1907 through 1926, plaintiff received the rating "a v 5 g," of which "a" meant legal ability very high, "v," recommendations very high, "5," financial worth $10,000 to $20,000, and "g," promptness in paying bills very good. The defamation itself consisted of the ratings in the 1928 edition: "b w 5 f," of which "b" meant legal ability second class, "w," recommendations second class, "5," financial worth $10,000 to $20,000, and "f," promptness in paying bills fair. The defendant's 1929 edition left the rating of plaintiff blank, which plaintiff alleged meant that his rating was so low that it did not merit mention in the directory. It appeared that defendant had written a strong letter of protest after the 1928 edition.

When plaintiff's case was previously before the court, Ellsworth v. Martindale-Hubbell Law Directory, Inc., 268 N.W. 400 (N.D. 1936), the court held that the alleged defamation was not actionable per se and therefore required the plaintiff allege and prove special damages to maintain his action. The plaintiff's amended complaint offered allegations as to his professional income in 1928, the year prior to the alleged misstatements, and for the succeeding three years. During these years his earnings were substantially lower, allegedly because of defendant's publication, with damages over $2,500. Defendant appealed from an order overruling its demurrer to the amended complaint.]

NUESSLE, J. . . . The sole question on this appeal is as to whether this amended paragraph sufficiently sets forth the special damages claimed to have been suffered. The defendant contends that it does not. That it fails to set out the names of the clients lost by the plaintiff because of the publication of the alleged defamatory matter, and that it does not specify particularly the origin, character, and amount of the business the plaintiff has been deprived of because of its publication.

In substance, the amended complaint alleges that the plaintiff has been engaged in the practice of law for many years; that he has always borne a good reputation as a man and as a lawyer; that he has had a substantial law business that came to him largely from forwarders through a widely spread foreign territory; that he was personally unacquainted with such forwarders; that the defendant's publication in which the alleged defamatory matter was published, was circulated generally throughout such territory and among those who forwarded business to the plaintiff; that, as a consequence of the circulation of such matter and immediately following such publication and circulation, his practice decreased in the manner and to the extent as set out in that portion of the complaint quoted. . . .

. . . From the nature of the circumstances as disclosed by the pleading the plaintiff cannot describe the particular items of business which he has lost or give the names of particular individuals who would have become his clients had it not been for the publication. But he does show a diminution of his business and of the income therefrom by pleading what that business amounted to prior to the publication and what it was after the publication, and as a result thereof. As to whether he can make proof in support of the allegations contained in his pleading is another matter with which we are not now concerned. . . .

[In] Odgers, Libel & Slander, 5th ed. at page 382, it is stated:

> But it is not always necessary for the plaintiff to call as his witnesses those who have ceased to deal with him. He may be able to show by his account-books or otherwise, a general diminution of business as distinct from the loss of particular known customers or promised orders. He has still to connect that diminution of business with the defendant's words. Such a connection may sometimes be established by the nature of the words themselves. Where the defendant has published a statement about the plaintiff's business, which is

intended or reasonably calculated to produce, and in the ordinary course
of things does produce, a general loss of business, evidence of such loss of
business is admissible, and sufficient special damage to support the action,
although the words are not actionable per se, and although no specific
evidence is given at the trial of the loss of any particular customer or order by
reason of such publication.

[Affirmed.]

NOTES

1. *Business losses as special damages.* The Restatement (Second) of Torts
§575, comment *b*, offers an account of special damages that reflects the
decided cases:

> Thus, while a slander that has been so widely disseminated as to cause
> persons previously friendly to the plaintiff to refuse social intercourse with
> him is not of itself special harm, the loss of the material advantages of their
> hospitality is sufficient. Special harm may be a loss of presently existing
> advantage, as a discharge from employment. It may also be a failure to
> realize a reasonable expectation of gain, as the denial of employment which,
> but for the currency of the slander, the plaintiff would have received. It is not
> necessary that he be legally entitled to receive the benefits that are denied to
> him because of the slander. It is enough that the slander has disappointed
> his reasonable expectation of receiving a gratuity.

2. *Proof of special damages.* Plaintiff's attempt to establish special damages
can raise sharp questions of fact if defendant claims that plaintiff's loss was
caused not by defendant's defamatory statement but by some independent
event. In Touma v. St. Mary's Bank, 712 A.2d 619, 622 (N.H. 1998), the
defendant's foreclosure notice made it appear that plaintiff's restaurant
would be closed down because of the bank's takeover of the plaintiff's
landlord who had defaulted on his loan to the bank. Horton, J., conceded
that the notice was defamatory, but held, in affirming the denial of special
damages below, that the plaintiff had not established that any lost profits
were attributable to the defective foreclosure notice:

> Although the plaintiff contends that the foreclosure notice is the only
> explanation for the restaurant's decline in March 1993, the record estab-
> lishes that gross revenues actually began to decline several months earlier.
> Moreover, the trial court could reasonably have concluded that the plaintiff's
> rebuttal advertisements and continued operation of the restaurant should
> have halted any decline caused by the foreclosure notice; in fact, sales con-
> tinued to decline thereafter.

In Jones v. Western & Southern Life Insurance Co., 91 F.3d 1032, 1036 (7th Cir. 1996), the plaintiff was rebuffed in his efforts to recover for a lost job opportunity stemming from defamatory statements. Wood, J., observed:

> Jones is under the misapprehension that he did not need to prove that the job either existed or was worth any particular amount of money in order for this question to be submitted to the jury. . . . [Illinois law] allows a plaintiff to recover general compensatory damages (including non-quantifiable damages like humiliation or anxiety) under the doctrine of presumed damages. Illinois law does not, however, allow for recovery of economic damages, such as lost employment opportunities, unless these damages are pleaded and proved as special damages. Otherwise plaintiffs could make up practically any number and call it presumed damages. How do we know Dr. Moore was going to pay Jones only $125,000? Why not $150,000, or $500,000? With nothing but Jones' own testimony, both with respect to the existence of the job opportunity itself and with respect to the amount of money it was worth, the district court correctly refused to submit this item of damages to the jury.

In contrast, the plaintiff in Calero v. Del Chemical Corp., 228 N.W.2d 737 (Wis. 1975), was able to forge the causal link in his action against his former employer and another of its employees. The gist of the suit was that the defendants, after they had dismissed plaintiff, responded to inquiries from firms where plaintiff subsequently was employed or had applied for employment by stating that plaintiff had used company records to help start his own competing business. These reports made it difficult for the plaintiff to find or keep work. In one instance, the plaintiff was fired 15 minutes after his new employer had contacted the individual defendant to ask if plaintiff should be given a promotion. Plaintiff ultimately moved to Arizona because his references were "too harmful to overcome." The Wisconsin Supreme Court upheld a verdict of $10,000 in compensatory damages and $9,000 in punitive damages.

2. General Damages

McCormick, Damages
§116, p. 422 (1935)

When "special" damage need not be shown, "general" damage may be recovered. That such damage has been suffered need not be proved by the plaintiff, for it is presumed; however, it is customary to make proof of some of the items. The elements of "general" damage are: (1) injury to reputation; (2) loss of business; (3) wounded feelings and bodily suffering resulting therefrom.

Faulk v. Aware, Inc.
231 N.Y.S.2d 270 (Sup. Ct. 1962)

[Aware, Inc., is a "membership corporation whose purpose is to combat communism in the entertainment and communication industries." John Henry Faulk, a popular radio and TV performer, brought a libel action against Aware, Inc., and Vincent Hartnett, its founder and president, for statements made by them and widely distributed charging him with communist sympathies and affiliations.]

GELLER, J. In this libel action the jury rendered a verdict awarding compensatory damages of $1,000,000 against the three defendants and punitive damages of $1,250,000 each against defendants Aware, Inc., and Vincent Hartnett. . . .

The fact that the amounts awarded are very large does not necessarily render the verdict excessive as a matter of law. The question is whether there is a rational basis for the jury's awards in the evidence adduced and in the circumstances of this case. The court should not substitute its judgment for that of the jury, unless the amounts awarded are insupportable under any fair-minded view of the facts. . . .

However, since an award of damages always rests in the "sound discretion" of a jury, it is subject to court review. That discretion must be exercised in accordance with the applicable rules of law and on the basis of the evidence in the case.

The damages recoverable for a libel consist of two items [compensatory and punitive.]

We will consider each of these two types of awards separately, just as the jury was instructed to do in its deliberations and form of verdict.

I.   COMPENSATORY DAMAGES

. . .

The principal item of damages was plaintiff's claim that he had been rendered unemployable in the television and radio industry as the direct result of the alleged libel and the concerted acts of the defendants, depriving him of the opportunity to realize his earning capacities in his profession. . . .

There was substantial testimony, which was uncontradicted, that prior to the alleged libel in February, 1956, plaintiff, in addition to his regular radio show, had appeared on a large number of television programs and had shown particular talent for that medium, being especially suited for the game, fun and quiz shows which were extremely popular during the period here involved. There also was uncontradicted testimony of an upward trend during this period in the television industry and in the income earned by television performers.

Plaintiff offered proof of his earning capacity through experts in the industry familiar with his achievements and abilities, among whom were Mark Goodson, David Susskind and Garry Moore, well-known producers of television shows.

It is well settled that a person wrongfully injured is entitled to recover for deprivation of future earning capacity, without limitation to his actual earnings preceding the injury; and that opinion testimony with regard to his potential earnings in that field by experts familiar with his capacities, is admissible.

. . . [Plaintiff's expert witnesses] testified that he would have earned between $150,000 and $500,000 annually, giving the reasons for their opinion. Defendants offered no proof in contradiction of plaintiff's experts.

The minimal figure of plaintiff's experts would represent damages of $900,000 for the six years involved. Assuming that the jury accepted that figure, they could take into consideration the other elements of injury to plaintiff's reputation and his mental anguish and distress in public and private life arising from the nature of the charge made against him, and find basis for arriving at compensatory damages in the sum of $1,000,000. . . .

II. PUNITIVE DAMAGES . . .

[The court upheld the award of punitive damages against the claim that they were excessive.]

Faulk v. Aware, Inc.
244 N.Y.S.2d 259 (App. Div. 1963)

RABIN, J. . . . We are greatly concerned, however, with the size of the verdict — both as to compensatory and punitive damages. . . . We find the verdict to be grossly excessive and most unrealistic — even in the field of entertainment.

The plaintiff's prior earnings are an important factor in assessing the damage suffered when his earnings are cut off. His damage need not be limited to the level of his actual earnings at the time of the libel. His potential earnings may be taken into consideration when there is evidence to enable a jury to assess those potentialities. . . . In this case, the plaintiff's potential earnings were fixed by his witnesses in amounts ranging from $100,000.00 to $1,000,000.00 a year. The larger figure was arrived at by reference to the earnings of those who had reached the very top of the profession. We are mindful of the statement of our colleague, Mr. Justice

Breitel, in the *Grayson* case where he said: "[I]n the case of persons of rare and special talents many are called but few are chosen." While the plaintiff's experts testified that the plaintiff would, without doubt, be among the "chosen," it seems that none of these experts, although in the entertainment field, was perceptive enough to contract for his services even though his earnings were never more than about $35,000.00 a year.

Those who testified to potential earnings of between $100,000.00 and $250,000.00 arrived at that estimate based upon what comparable performers were receiving. Yet they gave no explanation as to why the plaintiff's earnings were so comparatively low. In short, the testimony of the experts left plenty of room for speculation.

Upon that testimony, the jury was justified in its obvious conclusion that the plaintiff's prospects for advancement in his profession were extremely good and that his income would rise correspondingly. Despite that however, there is hardly enough justification for the finding of compensatory damages in the amount of $1,000,000.00, even making allowance for his mental pain and suffering. It is interesting to note that at current savings bank interest rates, his yearly income for life would exceed the best of his past earnings. We believe that the compensatory damages should be fixed at a figure no higher than $400,000.00.

[The Court reduced the punitive damage award against Aware to $50,000 and against Hartnett to $100,000.]

NOTES

1. *Justification for general damages.* Courts use general damages in defamation cases to avoid the administrative and evidentiary problems that arise in seeking to prove special damages. The key premise is that a rough estimate is a better first approximation of the true state of affairs than the alternative presumption, which denies recovery altogether. In Tex Smith, The Harmonica Man, Inc. v. Godfrey, 102 N.Y.S.2d 251, 253 (Sup. Ct. 1951), the defendant, a famous media figure, had made disparaging remarks about the plaintiff's ukuleles on both television and radio. The court noted that Godfrey's words could be taken as reflecting ill upon the plaintiff or its products. If the former, damages could be recovered for slander per se. The court continued:

> If the words are regarded purely as a reflection on the instruments, the same result would be reached. Here the words only become actionable if it is shown that damage followed upon their utterance. There was a time when such damage had to be specifically shown — the loss of a contract, a position, or the like. It is practicably impossible for one selling to the general public at retail or by mail order to show loss of particular sales. Under such circumstances those

people were without remedy from the most groundless calumny. It is, however, now recognized that allegations and proof of a general loss of sales is sufficient, leaving it to the trier of the facts to determine whether the loss is properly to be attributed to the slander or not. The allegations of the complaint on this subject are sufficient by this standard.

2. *Proof of general damages.* In defamation cases proof of general damages does not in principle preclude proof of special damages as well. For example, in Bishop v. New York Times, 135 N.E. 845, 848 (N.Y. 1922), the court stated: "We are inclined to the view that a plaintiff is not compelled to rely upon a favorable presumption with which the law endows his cause of action, but that he may prove, if he can, that he has been avoided and shunned by former friends and acquaintances as the direct and well-connected result of the libel." In Macy v. New York World-Telegram Corp., 141 N.E.2d 566, 570 (N.Y. 1957), the defendant newspaper falsely charged the plaintiff, a prominent civic figure and a Congressman running for reelection, with threatening to make public a certain letter if plaintiff were not chosen as his party's senatorial nominee. On appeal the court vacated the plaintiff's jury award of $50,000 for general damages and granted the newspaper a new trial because the plaintiff had testified on his own behalf that he had been subject to personal attacks, expelled from his country club, and denied his seat in the House of Representatives. The court said that in some cases the plaintiff could rely on his own hearsay testimony to show the loss that followed from the libel, but it concluded that the "better practice would be to call as witnesses for plaintiff, subject to cross-examination, the persons who were supposed to have spoken or acted adversely to plaintiff and to demonstrate, if such demonstration be possible, a connection to the libel."

3. *Constitutional response.* The traditional common law views on general and punitive damages have been analyzed in a constitutional context in Gertz v. Robert Welch, Inc., 418 U.S. 323 (1974), *infra* at 1116, and Dun & Bradstreet, Inc. v. Greenmoss Builders, Inc., 472 U.S. 749 (1985), *infra* at 1123.

3. Other Remedies

a. Injunctions

Courts have long refused to enjoin either slander or libel. Historically, that equitable remedy was said to deprive defendants of the right to a jury trial when an "adequate" remedy at law was available. More recently, the rule rests squarely on the constitutional ground that injunctive relief would necessarily infringe on the freedom of speech protected under the First Amendment by denying the speaker the option of getting his message to the public at large. See Near v. Minnesota, 283 U.S. 697 (1931). See also R. Smolla, Law of Defamation §9:86-90 (2d. 2003).

The absolute nature of this prohibition was briefly tested in the unusual case of Tory v. Cochran, 544 U.S. 734 (2005). The famed lawyer Johnnie Cochran brought a defamation suit against Ulysses Tory and his codefendants who had engaged in a nonstop campaign to collect $10 million from Cochran by posting false, insulting, and obscene signs outside his office, and by chanting similar insults and threats on a continuous basis. The trial judge found that Tory's claim was utterly without foundation, and was conducted solely to "coerce" payment of money as a "tribute" for desisting in their defamatory activities. When informed that the defendants planned to continue their activity indefinitely, the trial judge issued an injunction that prevented Tory and his confederates from "picketing" or "displaying signs, placards or other written or printed material," and to cease from "orally uttering statements" about Cochran's law firm in "any public forum." Cochran died after the Supreme Court granted certiorari on a petition that raised this question:

> Whether a permanent injunction as a remedy in a defamation action, preventing all future speech about an admitted public figure, violates the First Amendment.

Breyer, J., first held that the case was not moot, but then refused to address this question because Cochran's death had rendered the injunction "overbroad" by depriving it of its central rationale: the effort to extort tribute from Cochran. The Court therefore remanded the case to see whether some narrower injunction was needed to protect the interests of Cochran's firm. Would it make sense to enjoin the picketing but not the oral statements? To distinguish between activities near the law offices, and those held elsewhere?

b. Retraction

Alternatively, the law could require the defendant to retract the defamatory utterance, usually by publishing a withdrawal of the libel in the same newspaper or broadcast that originally published it. At common law retraction was not considered a complete defense, but only mitigated damages. See, e.g., Webb v. Call Publishing Co., 180 N.W. 263 (Wis. 1920), holding that a retraction does not fully restore the plaintiff to the position enjoyed before the initial libel was published. Even if the retraction receives broad publicity, many people who read the original defamatory statement are likely to miss it. Further, the retraction itself may not erase lingering doubts that the original statement contained at least some grain of truth.

Recently many states have enacted retraction statutes that apply to either or both print and broadcast defendants. For example, Minnesota Statute §548.06 (2007) provides:

> In an action for damages for the publication of a libel in a newspaper, the plaintiff shall recover no more than special damages, unless a retraction be demanded and refused as hereinafter provided. The plaintiff shall serve upon the publisher at the principal place of publication, a notice, specifying the statements claimed to be libelous, and requesting that the same be withdrawn. If a retraction thereof be not published on the same page and in the same point type and the statement headed in 18-point type or larger "RETRACTION," as were the statement complained of, in a regular issue thereof published within one week after such service, the plaintiff may allege such notice, demand, and failure to retract in the complaint and recover both special and general damages if the cause of action be maintained. If such retraction be so published, the plaintiff may still recover general damages, unless the defendant shall show that the libelous publication was made in good faith and under a mistake as to the facts.

This statute represents an elegant compromise of conflicting interests in an effort to stop litigation before it begins. The statute first gives the plaintiff an incentive to seek the retraction: Unless that is done, she can only recover special damages. The statute does not set any specific time to request the retraction. Even so, the plaintiff has a strong incentive to do so quickly in order to correct the record while the issue is current. The statute next uses both carrots and sticks to get the defendant to respond quickly to the retraction demand. If the demand is not met, the defendant exposes himself to suit for both special and general damages. If it is honored, the plaintiff gets at most general damages, but even those are denied if the defendant can show that he made an honest mistake in publishing the facts. Publishing the retraction also blocks suits for punitive damages. Any retraction must be full and complete since evasive apologies could confirm in the minds of readers that the defendant still stands behind the original charges. These statutory procedures are routinely invoked today, making the corrections columns of most newspapers one of the widely read features of the modern newspaper. For an exhaustive tabulation of retraction statutes, see R. Sack, Sack on Defamation §11.2 (3d ed. 2003); for a general account, see R. Smolla, Law of Defamation §9:70-84 (2d ed. 2003).

c. Reply Statutes

In Miami Herald Publishing Co. v. Tornillo, 418 U.S. 241, 244, 257-258 (1974), a unanimous Supreme Court struck down a Florida "right of reply" statute that "provides that if a candidate for nomination or election is assailed regarding his personal character or official record by any newspaper, the candidate has the right to demand that the newspaper print, free of cost to the candidate, any reply the candidate may make to the newspaper's charges. The reply must appear in as conspicuous a place and in the same kind of type as the charges which prompted the reply, provided it does not take up more space than the charges. Failure to comply with the statute constitutes a first-degree misdemeanor."

As drafted the statute was not limited to defamatory statements. The Court held it unconstitutional in part because it increased the costs of printing and distributing a newspaper. Its decision rested, however, on more than pure economic considerations:

> Faced with the penalties that would accrue to any newspaper that published news or commentary arguably within the reach of the right-of-access statute, editors might well conclude that the safe course is to avoid controversy. Therefore, under the operation of the Florida statute, political and electoral coverage would be blunted or reduced. Government-enforced right of access inescapably "dampens the vigor and limits the variety of public debate," New York Times Co. v. Sullivan. . . .

> Even if a newspaper would face no additional costs to comply with a compulsory access law and would not be forced to forgo publication of news or opinion by the inclusion of a reply, the Florida statute fails to clear the barriers of the First Amendment because of its intrusion into the function of editors. A newspaper is more than a passive receptacle or conduit for news, comment, and advertising. The choice of material to go into a newspaper, and the decisions made as to limitations on the size and content of the paper, and treatment of public issues and public officials — whether fair or unfair — constitute the exercise of editorial control and judgment. It has yet to be demonstrated how governmental regulation of this crucial process can be exercised consistent with First Amendment guarantees of a free press as they have evolved to this time.

Should a right to reply be granted in the context of political broadcasts?

SECTION G.   NONCONSTITUTIONAL DEFENSES

1. Truth

Auvil v. CBS 60 Minutes
67 F.3d 816 (9th Cir. 1996)

PER CURIAM: Grady and Lillie Auvil et al., suing on behalf of themselves and other similarly situated Washington State apple growers ("growers"), appeal from the district court's summary judgment in favor of CBS "60 Minutes" ("CBS"). The district court held that the growers failed to prove the falsity of the message conveyed by the "60 Minutes" broadcast of "'A' is for Apple," which concerned the use of Alar, a chemical sprayed on apples. We . . . affirm because we agree that the growers have failed to raise a genuine issue of material fact as to the falsity of the broadcast.

BACKGROUND

On February 26, 1989, CBS's weekly news show "60 Minutes" aired a segment on daminozide, a chemical growth regulator sprayed on apples. The broadcast, entitled "'A' is for Apple," also addressed the slow pace of government efforts to recall the chemical. The broadcast was based largely on a Natural Resources Defense Council ("NRDC") report, entitled *Intolerable Risk: Pesticides in Our Children's Food* ("*Intolerable Risk*"), which outlined health risks associated with the use of a number of pesticides on fruit, especially the risks to children. "'A' is for Apple" focused on the NRDC report's findings concerning daminozide, as well as the EPA's knowledge of daminozide's carcinogenity. Scientific research had indicated that daminozide, more commonly known by its trade name, Alar, breaks down into unsymmetrical dimethylhydrazine (UDMH), a carcinogen.

The segment opened with the following capsule summary from Ed Bradley, a "60 Minutes" commentator:

> The most potent cancer-causing agent in our food supply is a substance sprayed on apples to keep them on the trees longer and make them look better. That's the conclusion of a number of scientific experts. And who is most at risk? Children, who may someday develop cancer from this one chemical called daminozide. Daminozide, which has been sprayed on apples for more than 20 years, breaks down into another chemical called UDMH.

During the broadcast, Bradley garnered a number of viewpoints on the Alar issue. Those interviewed included an Environmental Protection Agency ("EPA") administrator, an NRDC attorney, a U.S. congressman, a professor of pediatrics at Harvard Medical School, and a scientist from the Consumers Union, which publishes *Consumer Reports* magazine. After Bradley's opening synopsis, the broadcast segment began with the EPA administrator's admission that the EPA had known of cancer risks associated with daminozide for sixteen years, but that EPA regulations had hampered the removal of the chemical from the market. The U.S. Congressman rejected the EPA administrator's explanation that the laws were to blame for the EPA's hesitation. He thought that it was well within the EPA's power to remove daminozide from the market, and that the EPA's reluctance stemmed from its fear that Uniroyal, the company that manufactured daminozide, would sue the EPA. The broadcast segment continued with testimonials from the NRDC attorney, who discussed the findings published in *Intolerable Risk*, focusing on the cancer risks to children from ingestion of apples treated with daminozide. The NRDC's findings were corroborated both by the EPA administrator and the Harvard pediatrician. The broadcast ended with the statements of a Consumers Union scientist, who revealed that most manufacturers of apple products said they no longer use apples treated with daminozide but that the manufacturers were unsuccessful in keeping daminozide completely out of their products.

Following the "60 Minutes" broadcast, consumer demand for apples and apple products decreased dramatically. The apple growers and others dependent upon apple production lost millions of dollars. Many of the growers lost their homes and livelihoods.

In November 1990, eleven Washington State apple growers, representing some 4,700 growers in the Washington area, filed a complaint in Washington State Superior Court against CBS, local CBS affiliates, the NRDC, and Fenton Communications, Inc., a public relations firm used by the NRDC in 1989. The growers asserted, among others, a claim for product disparagement. . . .

DISCUSSION

We review the district court's summary judgment ruling *de novo*. To survive CBS's motion for summary judgment, the growers must set forth specific facts showing that there is a genuine issue for trial. . . .

[The court first held that the plaintiffs] whose products are disparaged face a higher burden of proof than do defamation plaintiffs. . . . Accordingly, for a product disparagement claim to be actionable, the plaintiff must prove, *inter alia*, the falsity of the disparaging statements. . . .

The growers offered evidence showing that no studies have been conducted to test the relationship between ingestion of daminozide and incidence of cancer in *humans*. Such evidence, however, is insufficient to show a genuine issue for trial regarding the broadcast's assertions that daminozide is a potent carcinogen. Animal laboratory tests are a legitimate means for assessing cancer risks to humans. . . .

The growers provide no other challenge to the EPA's findings, nor do they directly attack the validity of the scientific studies. All of the statements referenced above are factual assertions made by the interviewees, based on the scientific findings of the NRDC. These findings were corroborated by the EPA administrator and a Harvard pediatrician. The EPA, which often relies on the results of animal studies, acknowledged that it knew of the cancer risks associated with ingestion of daminozide and, in August 1985, classified daminozide as a "probable human carcinogen." Indeed, the EPA estimated that the dietary risk to the general population from UDMH, a metabolite of daminozide, was fifty times an acceptable risk and ultimately concluded that daminozide posed an unreasonable risk to the general population. . . .

On the subject of cancer risks to children from the use of daminozide on apples, the growers point to the following factual assertions to support their falsity claim:

> What we're talking about is a cancer-causing agent used on food that EPA knows is going to cause cancer for thousands of children over their lifetime.
>   [T]he Natural Resources Defense Council[ ] has completed the most careful study yet on the effect of daminozide and seven other cancer-causing pesticides on the food children eat.
>   [O]ver a lifetime, one child out of every 4,000 or so of our preschoolers will develop cancer just from these eight pesticides. [The NRDC study] says children are being exposed to a pesticide risk several hundred times greater than what the agency says is acceptable.

The growers offered evidence showing that no scientific study has been conducted on cancer risks to children from the use of pesticides. However, CBS based its statements regarding cancer and children on the NRDC's findings that the daminozide found on apples is more harmful to children because they ingest more apple products per unit of body weight than do adults. The growers have provided no affirmative evidence that daminozide does not pose a risk to children. The fact that there have been no studies conducted specifically on the cancer risks to children from daminozide does nothing to disprove the conclusion that, if children consume more of a carcinogenic substance than do adults, they are at higher risk for contracting cancer. The growers' evidence, therefore, does not create a genuine issue as to the falsity of the broadcast's assertion that daminozide is more harmful to children.

Despite their inability to prove that *statements* made during the broadcast were false, the growers assert that summary judgment for CBS was improper because a jury could find that the broadcast contained a provably false *message*, viewing the broadcast segment in its entirety. They further argue that, if they can prove the falsity of this implied message, they have satisfied their burden of proving falsity.

The growers' contentions are . . . unprecedented and inconsistent with Washington law. No Washington court has held that the analysis of falsity proceeds from an implied, disparaging message. It is the statements themselves that are of primary concern in the analysis. . . .

The Washington courts' view finds support in the Restatement, which instructs that a product disparagement plaintiff has the burden of proving the "falsity of the *statement*." Restatement (Second) of Torts §651(1)(c) (emphasis added). This standard refers to individual statements and not to any overall message. Therefore, we must reject the growers' invitation to infer an overall message from the broadcast and determine whether that message is false.

We also note that, if we were to accept the growers' argument, plaintiffs bringing suit based on disparaging speech would escape summary judgment merely by arguing, as the growers have, that a jury should be allowed to determine both the overall message of a broadcast and whether that overall message is false. Because a broadcast could be interpreted in numerous, nuanced ways, a great deal of uncertainty would arise as to the message conveyed by the broadcast. Such uncertainty would make it difficult for broadcasters to predict whether their work would subject them to tort liability. Furthermore, such uncertainty raises the spectre of a chilling effect on speech.

CONCLUSION

Because the growers have failed to raise a genuine issue of material fact regarding the falsity of statements made during the broadcast of "'A' is for Apple," the district court's decision granting CBS's motion for summary judgment is

Affirmed.

NOTES

1. The Alar "scare." Should the plaintiff or defendant bear the burden of proof on the truth issue? What if the plaintiffs in *Auvil* had introduced evidence showing no increased incidence of cancer among children who ate large numbers of apples? Airing the "60 Minutes" segment to 40 million people across the country was estimated to cause apple growers nationwide more than $100 million in lost sales. The story affected sales of all apples even though only about 15 percent of apples were treated with Alar. A few months after the original CBS story, Uniroyal Chemical Co. pulled Alar from the market and had its registration cancelled with the EPA. In 1991, C. Everett Koop, the former U.S. Surgeon General, concluded that, properly used, "Alar-treated apple products posed no hazard to the health of children or adults." A 1991 study of the National Cancer Institute concluded that the Alar flap was an "unfounded carcinogen scare." Wynder, Primary Prevention of Cancer: Planning and Policy Considerations, 83 J. Nat'l Cancer Inst. 475 (1991). For a retrospective on the controversy, see Ashton, After 10 Years, Debate Continues over Pesticide that Tainted Red Apples, Seattle Post-Intelligencer, March 1, 1999, at B4.

2. *Defamation and truth.* What is the proper relationship between defamation and truth? The conventional view holds that the prima facie case in defamation does not require a showing that the statement published is false. Instead, it is enough that the defendant published defamatory matter about ("of and concerning") the plaintiff that tends to lower the estimation of plaintiff in the eyes of third parties to whom it is directed. As Judge Learned Hand wrote in Burton v. Crowell Publishing Co., 82 F.2d 154, 156 (2d Cir. 1936), "The only reason why the law makes truth a defense is not because a libel must be false, but because the utterance of truth is in all circumstances an interest paramount to reputation; it is like a privileged communication, which is privileged only because the law prefers it conditionally to reputation." Truth is regarded as an absolute defense to the defamation so published, which is tantamount to an assertion that a statement is defamatory only if it is false. See RST §581A. Why should truthful statements of the defendant ever be regarded as libelous?

The allocation of truth as a defense suggests that the burden lies on the defendant to establish the defense. That orientation is consistent with the approach of the earlier common law, which was more hostile to the defense of truth than *Auvil*. In order to protect reputation, common law courts often read statements quite closely, rejecting the defense where there had been small and seemingly insignificant factual errors in the defendant's statement. The headnote in Sharpe v. Stevenson, 34 N.C. 348, 348 (1851), gives some hint of the level of precision that is required: "In an action of slander (under our statute) for charging that the plaintiff had criminal intercourse with one *A.* at a particular time and place, the defendant cannot justify by showing that she had such intercourse with *A.* at another time and place." That result was criticized in Courtney, Absurdities of the Law of Slander and Libel, 36 Am. L. Rev. 552, 563 (1902), in which the author observed: "A criminal abandon in the drawing-room as completely destroys all claim to a reputation for chastity as a lascivious embrace in the bushes." For a modern hint of the same point, see Haynes v. Alfred A. Knopf, Inc., 8 F.3d 1222, 1228 (7th Cir. 1993), in which Posner, C.J., observes: "The rule of substantial truth is based on a recognition that falsehoods which do no *incremental* damage to the plaintiff's reputation do not injure the only interest that the law of defamation protects."

3. *Known to be false.* In the usual case of defamation, the false information leads people to shun the plaintiff because they revise their opinion of her. But what should be done in those cases where the false statement leads people to hold the plaintiff in hatred, ridicule, and/or contempt when they *know* the statement to be false, but are titillated by it nonetheless? In Hustler Magazine v. Falwell, 485 U.S. 46 (1988), *supra* at 99, the Supreme Court held that the vicious nature of the defendant's parody

rendered it intrinsically unbelievable and therefore undercut the plaintiff's libel claim. *Falwell* has been followed with enthusiasm in lower court decisions that have held *deliberate* parody is outside the scope of defamation on the ground that no one could believe it to be true. In Dworkin v. Hustler Magazine, Inc., 867 F.2d 1188, 1191, 1193-1194 (9th Cir. 1989), the plaintiff, Andrea Dworkin, a prominent radical feminist, was targeted in a Hustler magazine cartoon that "depicts two women engaged in a lesbian act of oral sex with the caption, 'You remind me so much of Andrea Dworkin, Edna. It's a dog-eat-dog world.'" In a subsequent issue "[o]ne photograph, supposedly of a Jewish male, has a caption stating: 'While I'm teaching this little shiksa the joys of Yiddish, the Andrea Dworkin Fan Club begins some really *serious* suck-'n'-squat. Ready to give up the holy wafers for matzoh, yet, guys?'"

Hall, J., dispatched Dworkin's action for defamation on the ground that "Hustler's statements in this case are privileged opinion."

> An examination of a Hustler feature filed by appellants and amici Steinem and Brownmiller helps to illustrate this point. The work is entitled, "Hustler Interview: Gloria Steinem's Clit." This work contains a number of statements that by their terms can be read as statements of fact. Nevertheless, the article purports to be an interview of a body part, and therefore cannot be reasonably understood as making assertions of fact. By the same token, such phrases as "pus bloated walking sphincter," "wacko," or "bizarre paranoia" were not reasonably understood as attributions of physical or mental disease to the plaintiff in *Leidholt* [v. L.F.P. Inc., 860 F.2d 890, 894 (9th Cir. 1988)]. The statements about Dworkin contained in the Features are of the same ilk, and are not reasonably understood as statements of fact. Instead, they are privileged opinion.
>
> Dworkin errs by limiting "opinion" to high-minded discourse. In this context, the word "opinion" is a label differentiating statements containing assertions of fact from those that do not. To differentiate among statements not of a factual nature would be at odds with fundamental principles of first amendment law, which seeks to facilitate the "search for truth" by encouraging "uninhibited, robust, and wide open" public debate, *New York Times*, and is informed by the notion that "there is no such thing as a false idea." *Gertz*. We agree with counsel for Dworkin that this means that outrageous and outlandish statements are sometimes protected, but do not share their alarm over this prospect. Ludicrous statements are much less insidious and debilitating than falsities that bear the ring of truth. We have little doubt that the outrageous and the outlandish will be recognized for what they are.

For the constitutional dimension see Philadelphia Newspapers, Inc. v. Hepps, 475 U.S. 767 (1986), *supra* at 1125.

2. *Privileges in the Private Sphere*

Watt v. Longsdon
[1930] 1 K.B. 130

[Watt sued Longsdon for three separate defamatory publications. Plaintiff was the managing director at Casablanca, Morocco, of a British oil company of which the defendant was a director. At the time the various communications took place, the company was in the process of voluntary liquidation. In April 1928, Browne, who was the company's manager in Casablanca, wrote a letter to the defendant in England at about the time the plaintiff left Casablanca for Lisbon and after the plaintiff's wife had returned to England. Browne's letter charged that plaintiff had left a liquor bill of £88, which Browne doubted would ever get paid, and related in detail how the plaintiff's maid had been plaintiff's mistress for several months. Browne expressed his surprise, "especially as she is an old woman, stone deaf, almost blind, with dyed hair!!!" but stated that the maid was able to give corroborating details. Browne's letter stated further that servants had told him that the plaintiff had had "orgies" with dancing girls, that he had designs on Browne's wife, and that plaintiff had shown himself to be "a blackguard, a thief, a liar and . . . lives exclusively to satisfy his own passions and lust." In a postscript, Browne suggested that it would probably be better not to show the plaintiff's wife the letter but that Mr. Singer, chairman of the board of directors of the company, should be told. In May 1928, defendant sent Browne's letter to Singer; and this is the first act of defamation complained of.

Defendant at the same time wrote Browne a letter in which he shared Browne's general view of the plaintiff and asked Browne to obtain sworn statements from his informants, offering to pay any bribes necessary to obtain such statements; the letter further said he thought it his duty to inform plaintiff's wife but that he would not do so until he had the sworn statements in his hand. This letter from the defendant to Browne was the second act of defamation complained of.

A few days later, without having received further confirmation of the statements in Browne's letter, the defendant showed it to plaintiff's wife, with the result that plaintiff and his wife separated, and she began suit for divorce. The showing of Browne's letter to plaintiff's wife was the third act of defamation complained of.

Defendant did not defend the truth of the libels contained in the letters. Nevertheless, Horridge, J., gave judgment for the defendant, ruling that all three publications were privileged. The court of appeal reversed for the reasons indicated below.]

SCRUTTON, L.J. This case raises, amongst other matters, the extremely difficult question, equally important in its legal and social aspect, as to the circumstances, if any, in which a person will be justified in giving to one partner to a marriage information which that person honestly believes to be correct, but which is in fact untrue, about the matrimonial delinquencies of the other party to the marriage. . . .

By the law of England there are occasions on which a person may make defamatory statements about another which are untrue without incurring any legal liability for his statements. These occasions are called privileged occasions. A reason frequently given for this privilege is that the allegation that the speaker has "unlawfully and maliciously published," is displaced by proof that the speaker had either a duty or an interest to publish, and that this duty or interest confers the privilege. But communications made on these occasions may lose their privilege: (1.) they may exceed the privilege of the occasion by going beyond the limits of the duty or interest, or (2.) they may be published with express malice, so that the occasion is not being legitimately used, but abused. . . . The classical definition of "privileged occasions" is that of Parke B. in Toogood v. Spyring, a case where the tenant of a farm complained to the agent of the landlord, who had sent a workman to do repairs, that the workman had broken into the tenant's cellar, got drunk on the tenant's cider, and spoilt the work he was sent to do. The workman sued the tenant. Parke B. gave the explanation of privileged occasions in these words: "In general, an action lies for the malicious publication of statements which are false in fact, and injurious to the character of another (within the well-known limits as to verbal slander), and the law considers such publication as malicious, unless it is fairly made by a person in the discharge of some public or private duty, whether legal or moral, or in the conduct of his own affairs, in matters where his interest is concerned. In such cases, the occasion prevents the inference of malice, which the law draws from unauthorized communications, and affords a qualified defence depending upon the absence of actual malice. If fairly warranted by any reasonable occasion or exigency, and honestly made, such communications are protected for the common convenience and welfare of society; and the law has not restricted the right to make them within any narrow limits." It will be seen that the learned judge requires: (1.) a public or private duty to communicate, whether legal or moral; (2.) that the communication should be "fairly warranted by any reasonable occasion or exigency"; (3.) or a statement in the conduct of his own affairs where his interest is concerned. Parke B. had given several other definitions in slightly varying terms. [Later cases add] to the protection of his own interest spoken of in Toogood v. Spyring the protection of the interests of another where the situation of the writer requires him to protect those interests. This, I think, involves that his "situation" imposes on him a legal or moral duty. The question whether the occasion was privileged is for the judge, and so far as "duty" is concerned, the question is: Was there a duty, legal, moral, or social, to communicate? As to legal duty, the judge should have no difficulty; the judge should know the law; but as to moral or social duties of imperfect obligation, the task is far more troublesome. The judge has no evidence as to the view the community takes of moral or social duties. . . . Is the judge merely to give his own view of moral and social duty, though he thinks a considerable portion of the community hold a different opinion? Or is he to endeavour to ascertain what view "the great mass of right-minded men" would take? It is not surprising that with such a standard both judges and text-writers treat the matter as one of great difficulty in which no definite line can be drawn. . . .

[After considering various other English precedents, the court summarized the occasions giving rise to a privileged communication as follows:] [E]ither (1.) a duty to communicate information believed to be true to a person who has a material interest in receiving the information, or (2.) an interest in the speaker to be protected by communicating information, if true, relevant to that interest, to a person honestly believed to have a duty to protect that interest, or (3.) a common interest in and reciprocal duty in respect of the subject matter of the communication between speaker and recipient. . . .

In my opinion Horridge J. went too far in holding that there could be a privileged occasion on the ground of interest in the recipient without any duty to communicate on the part of the person making the communication. But that does not settle the question, for it is necessary to consider, in the present case, whether there was, as to each communication, a duty to communicate, and an interest in the recipient.

First as to the communication between Longsdon and Singer, I think the case must proceed on the admission that at all material times Watt, Longsdon and Browne were in the employment of the same company, and the evidence afforded by the answer to the interrogatory put in by the plaintiff that Longsdon believed the statements in Browne's letter. In my view on these facts there was a duty, both from a moral and material point of view, on Longsdon to communicate the letter to Singer, the chairman of his company, who, apart from questions of present employment, might be asked by Watt for a testimonial to a future employer. Equally, I think Longsdon receiving the letter from Browne, might discuss the matter with him, and ask for further information, on the ground of a common interest in the affairs of the company, and to obtain further information for the chairman. I should therefore agree with the view of Horridge J. that these two occasions were privileged, though for different reasons. Horridge J. further held that there was no evidence of malice fit to be left to the jury, and, while I think some of Longsdon's action and language in this respect was unfortunate, as the plaintiff has put in the answer that Longsdon believed the truth of the statements in Browne's and his own letter, like Lord Dunedin in Adam v. Ward, I should not try excess with too nice scales, and I do not dissent from his view as to malice. As to the communications to

Singer and Browne, in my opinion the appeal should fail, but as both my brethren take the view that there was evidence of malice which should be left to the jury, there must, of course, be a new trial as to the claim based on these two publications.

The communication to Mrs. Watt stands on a different footing. I have no intention of writing an exhaustive treatise on the circumstances when a stranger or a friend should communicate to husband or wife information he receives as to the conduct of the other party to the marriage. I am clear that it is impossible to say he is always under a moral or social duty to do so; it is equally impossible to say he is never under such a duty. It must depend on the circumstances of each case, the nature of the information, and the relation of speaker and recipient. It cannot, on the one hand, be the duty even of a friend to communicate all the gossip the friend hears at men's clubs or women's bridge parties to one of the spouses affected. On the other hand, most men would hold that it was the moral duty of a doctor who attended his sister in law, and believed her to be suffering from a miscarriage, for which an absent husband could not be responsible, to communicate that fact to his wife and the husband. . . . If this is so, the decision must turn on the circumstances of each case, the judge being much influenced by the consideration that as a general rule it is not desirable for any one, even a mother in law, to interfere in the affairs of man and wife. Using the best judgment I can in this difficult matter, I have come to the conclusion that there was not a moral or social duty in Longsdon to make this communication to Mrs. Watt such as to make the occasion privileged, and that there must be a new trial so far as it relates to the claim for publication of a libel to Mrs. Watt. The communications to Singer and Browne being made on a privileged occasion, there must be a new trial of the issue as to malice defeating the privilege. There must also be a new trial of the complaint as to publication to Mrs. Watt, the occasion being held not to be privileged. . . .

GREER, L.J. . . . In my judgment no right minded man in the position of the defendant, a friend of the plaintiff and his wife, would have thought it right to communicate the horrible accusations contained in Mr. Browne's letter to the plaintiff's wife. The information came to Mr. Browne from a very doubtful source, and in my judgment no reasonably right-minded person could think it his duty, without obtaining some corroboration of the story, and without first communicating with the plaintiff, to pass on these outrageous charges of marital infidelity of a gross kind, and drunkenness and dishonesty to the plaintiff's wife. As regards the publication to the plaintiff's wife, the occasion was not privileged, and it is unnecessary to consider whether there was evidence of express malice. As regards the publication to the chairman of the company, who owned nearly all the shares, and to Mr. Browne, I think on the facts as pleaded there was between the defendant and the recipients of the letters a common interest which would make the occasion privileged, but I also think there is intrinsic evidence in the letter to Browne, and evidence in the hasty and unjustifiable communication to the plaintiff's wife, which would be sufficient to entitle the plaintiff to ask for a verdict on these publications on the ground of express malice. . . .

I think the defendant's conduct in disseminating the gross charges that he did to the plaintiff's wife, and to Mr. Singer, and repeating and to some extent adding to them in his letter to Mr. Browne, and his offer to provide funds for procuring the evidence of the two women in Casablanca, affords some evidence of malice which ought to have been left to the jury. It is not for us to weigh the evidence. It will be for the jury to decide whether they are satisfied that in publishing the libels the defendant was in fact giving effect to his malicious or otherwise improper feelings towards the plaintiff, and was not merely using the occasion for the protection of the interests of himself and his two correspondents.

NOTES

1. *When is a communication privileged?* The common law has sought to identify those socially useful private communications that should be encouraged by relaxing the basic rule of liability, whether strict, or more recently, negligence. To achieve the proper balance most courts and commentators, both in England and the United States, have closely followed Baron Park's scheme outlined in Toogood v. Spyring, 149 Eng. Rep. 1044 (Ex. 1834), discussed in *Watt*. Under this scheme the existence of privileged occasions depends on the interest of the speaker, the interest of his audience, or a common interest between the speaker and his audience. See RST §§594-596, following the basic rule.

The claim of privilege is recognized for references (or "characters") of former servants, where the defendant is replying to an inquiry. In Gardner v. Slade, 116 Eng. Rep. 1467, 1470 (Q.B. 1849), a case involving a domestic servant, Wightman, J., said: "It is quite a mistake to treat questions of this kind as if the law allowed a privilege only for the benefit of the giver of the character. It is of importance to the public that characters should be readily given. The servant who applies for the character, and the person who is to take him, are equally benefited. Indeed, there is no class to whom it is of so much importance that characters should be freely given as honest servants." The privilege has been extended to many intragroup situations such as churches, fraternal organizations, labor unions, shareholders of a corporation, and, more recently, faculty evaluation committees, Colson v. Stieg, 433 N.E.2d 246 (Ill. 1982), student evaluation committees, see *Doe, supra* at 1023, and physicians and their health plans, with respect to the medical records of their patients, Kuwik v. Starmark Star Marketing & Administration, Inc., 619 N.E.2d 129, 134, 135 (Ill. 1993).

The potential dangers in this area, especially with references for former employees, has sparked an effort to regulate the matter by consent, which, when given, is generally understood to create only a qualified privilege. See RST §583: "one who agrees to submit his conduct to investigation, knowing that its results will be published, consents to the publication of honest findings of investigators." In many cases, the fear of defamation suits has led former employers to adopt a strict rule under which they only provide information as to dates of employment and last position held. Even salary information (which is hard to interpret with bonuses and the like) is often not disclosed. In Woodfield v. Providence Hospital, 779 A.2d 933 (D.C. 2001), the plaintiff received a conditional job offer from Suburban Hospital for which she signed a "Notification and Verification to Conduct Background Investigation." The provision was for the stated benefit of all persons who answered the inquiries. The court held the clause protected Providence Hospital when its personnel officer (in ignorance of the clause) stated by phone that the plaintiff had never been promoted because of a poor work record. It denied any inference of malice because the personnel officer's communication was consistent with the low evaluations that the plaintiff had received on the job. Do these consent forms do anything more than ratify the existence of the common law privilege? What result if they sought to create an absolute immunity for all parties giving references?

2. *Credit reports.* In Smith v. Thomas, 132 Eng. Rep. 146 (C.P. 1835), a case involving a credit reference, the court observed: "The publication is alleged to have taken place in the course of a confidential communication between one tradesman and another, as to the solvency of a third person, whom the inquirer was about to trust. If such communications are not protected by law from the danger of vexatious litigation in cases where they turn out to be incorrect in fact, the stability of men engaged in trade and commerce would be exposed to the greatest hazard, for no man would answer an inquiry as to the solvency of another." This privilege has also been extended to commercial credit agencies. In Shore v. Retailers Commercial Agency, 174 N.E.2d 376, 379 (Mass. 1961), Spaulding, J., wrote:

> We are of opinion that reports made by a mercantile agency to an interested subscriber should be conditionally privileged. Those about to engage in a commercial transaction like to know something about the persons with whom they are dealing. Often they are unable to get that information themselves and must obtain it through mercantile agencies. In furnishing such information the agencies are supplying a legitimate business need and ought to have the protection of the privilege. Without such protection few would undertake to furnish the information, and the cost would be high, if not prohibitive. For a good discussion of the reason supporting the privilege see Smith, Conditional Privilege for Mercantile Agencies, 14 Col. L. Rev.

187, 296, 306-310 [1914]. We are not to be understood as holding that there is a privilege where information is published by the agency generally to subscribers having no particular interest in the report. Restatement: Torts, §595, comment *g*.

Shore reflects the majority view in the United States, with only Georgia and Idaho denying a conditional privilege attaches to credit reports. See R. Sack, Sack on Defamation, §9.2.2.3 (3d ed. 2003). This area of privilege has generally not been affected by *New York Times*. See Dun & Bradstreet, Inc. v. Greenmoss Builders, 472 U.S. 749 (1985), *infra* at 1123, Note 2.

3. *Volunteers*. As *Watt* indicates, one troublesome problem arises when the defendant has volunteered communication to a third party without a request. Generally, a party is not necessarily protected in answering an inquiry; nor is he necessarily exposed by volunteering information. Rather, Restatement (Second) of Torts §595(2)(a) notes that it is an "important factor" that "the publication is made in response to a request rather than volunteered by the publisher."

In Count Joannes v. Bennett, 87 Mass. 169, 172 (1862), defendant, the family pastor and intimate friend, was persuaded by the father to write the daughter a letter urging her to call off her proposed marriage to plaintiff. The court held that the contents of the letter were not privileged, pointing out that the defendant, although he acted "from laudable motives in writing it," was no longer the daughter's pastor and was in no way related to her other than as a friend. The court said, in part: "It is obvious that if such communications could be protected merely on the ground that the party making them held friendly relations with those to whom they were written or spoken, a wide door would be left open by which indiscriminate asper-sion of private character could escape with impunity. Indeed, it would rarely be difficult for a party to shelter himself from the consequences of uttering or publishing a slander or libel under a privilege which could be readily made to embrace almost every species of communication. The law does not tolerate any such license of speech or pen." The same result under *Watt*?

4. *Defamation in self-defense*. Still another form of conditional privilege arises "when the person making the publication reasonably believes that his interest in his own reputation has been unlawfully invaded by another person and that the defamatory matter that he publishes about the other is reasonably necessary to defend himself," — "including the statement that his accuser is an unmitigated liar." RST §594, comment *k*. The boundaries of this privilege are not clearly established, which gives rise to questions reminiscent of those raised with self-defense against physical attack: How vigorous must the plaintiff's original aggression have been? Must the original attack have been defamatory? What if it was true or privileged? Again, how much verbal force may the defendant use in reply? Does the

privilege extend to the defense of third parties? Further, the doctrine has strong overtones of assumption of risk and contributory negligence because the plaintiff, having invited a reply, cannot complain when a vigorous one is given to a public already alert to controversy.

3. Privileges in the Public Sphere

a. Legal Proceedings and Reports Thereon

Kennedy v. Cannon
182 A.2d 54 (Md. 1962)

SYBERT, J. This appeal questions whether the trial court erred in directing a verdict for the defendant, an attorney, in a suit for slander on the grounds that the allegedly slanderous statement was privileged as part of the defendant's duty as counsel to his client, and that no malice on the part of the defendant had been shown.

[The defendant-appellee was the lawyer for a black man, Charles Humphreys, charged with raping the plaintiff-appellant, a white woman. He admitted to having had intercourse with her but claimed that she had consented to the act. The defendant spoke to the editor of the local paper, giving Humphreys' side of the story. The editor said it would be "impossible to print matter of that type and at such great length." The story in the afternoon paper recounted the plaintiff's charges against Humphreys, noted his admission of intercourse, and concluded with the defendant saying "He [Humphreys] emphatically denies the charge. He says that the woman submitted to his advances willingly."]

As a result of the publication of the statement appellant alleged she suffered humiliation and harassment by annoying phone calls from unknown persons and eventually was forced to move with her family out of the community and the State. She instituted a suit against appellee alleging that the words spoken by him to the newspaper charged her with the crime of adultery, were slanderous per se under Art. 88, §1, Code (1957), and were not privileged.

The appellee admitted on the witness stand that the newspaper article correctly quoted his statement to the editor. He sought to justify its publication on the ground that the physical safety of his client required it. He stated he feared the possibility of a lynching if only the material released by the State's Attorney were published. Recalling a lynching which had occurred in Salisbury under similar circumstances some 25 years previously, he said he felt that the account should include a denial of the charge based upon his client's claim of consent by the woman. At the conclusion of the testimony before a jury, the trial court granted appellee's motion for a directed verdict, expressing the opinion that when the State had under-taken to publish a statement about the case damaging to his client, the appellee was justified and privileged in replying as he did. Appellant appeals from the judgment for costs entered in favor of appellee. . . .

The privilege afforded an attorney in a judicial proceeding and its ratio-nale are discussed in the leading case of Maulsby v. Reifsnider, 69 Md. 143 (1888), where this Court stated:

> . . . All agree, that counsel are privileged and protected to a certain extent, at least, for defamatory words spoken *in a judicial proceeding*, and words thus spoken are not actionable, which would in themselves be actionable, if spoken elsewhere. He is obliged, in the discharge of a professional duty, to prosecute and defend the most important rights and interests, the life it may be, or the liberty or the property of his client, and it is absolutely essential to the administration of justice that he should be allowed the widest latitude in commenting on the character, the conduct and motives of parties and wit-nesses and other persons directly or remotely connected with the subject-matter in litigation. And to subject him to actions of slander by every one who may consider himself aggrieved, and to the costs and expenses of a harassing litigation, would be to fetter and restrain him in that open and fearless discharge of duty which he owes to his client, and which the demands of justice require. Not that the law means to say, that one, because he is counsel in the trial of a cause, has the right, abstractly considered, deliberately and maliciously to slander another, but it is the fear that if the rule were otherwise, actions without number might be brought against counsel who had not spoken falsely and maliciously. It is better therefore to make the rule of law so large that counsel acting bona fide in the discharge of duty, shall never be troubled, although by making it so large, others who have acted mala fide and maliciously, are included. The question whether words spoken by counsel were spoken maliciously or in good faith, are, and always will be, open questions, upon which opinion may differ, and counsel, however innocent, would be liable if not to judgments, to a vexatious and expensive litigation. The privilege thus recognized by law is not the privilege merely of counsel, but the privilege of clients, and the evil, if any, resulting from it must be endured for the sake of the greater good which is thereby secured. But this privilege is not an absolute and unqualified privilege, and cannot be extended beyond the reason and principles on which it is foun-ded. . . . (Emphasis added.)

[The court went on to hold that the words, to be privileged, must also be relevant to the judicial proceedings in which they were spoken.]

The statement just quoted reflects the view of a majority of the jurisdic-tions in this country, although the semantics in this area of tort law have changed somewhat since the date of the *Maulsby* case. What was character-ized in that case as a qualified privilege for communications, conditioned on their being pertinent or relevant to a judicial proceeding without regard to the motive of the speaker, is referred to by modern text writers and in case law as an absolute privilege. . . . This absolute immunity extends to the judge as well as to witnesses and parties to the litigation, for defamatory statements uttered in the course of a trial or contained in pleadings, affidavits, depositions, and other documents directly related to the case. . . . An absolute privilege is distinguished from a qualified privilege in that the former provides immunity regardless of the purpose or motive of the defendant, or the reasonableness of his conduct, while the latter is conditioned upon the absence of malice and is forfeited if it is abused. . . .

Appellee in this case contends that under the *Maulsby* case, his statement was absolutely privileged. It is not disputed that the statement was relevant to the criminal proceeding. The essential question to be answered is whether it was published in — that is, as part of — a "judicial proceeding."

The term "judicial proceeding" is broad enough to cover all steps in a criminal action, so that when Humphreys was arrested and charged with rape it would be a valid conclusion that the judicial proceeding had commenced. . . . However, this does not necessarily mean that every statement made by an attorney after the inception of a judicial proceeding will be privileged.

Appellee cites the oft quoted rule from 3 Restatement, Torts, §586:

> An attorney at law is absolutely privileged to publish false and defamatory matter of another in communications preliminary to a proposed judicial proceeding, or in the institution of, or during the course and as a part of a judicial proceeding in which he participates as counsel, if it has some relation thereto.

However, the extension of this absolute privilege to statements not made in the judicial proceeding itself is limited both by the comments on the rule of the Restatement itself, and by the decisions. The scope of the privilege is restricted to communications such as those made between an attorney and his client, or in the examination of witnesses by counsel, or in statements made by counsel to the court or jury. . . . Appellee cites no authorities which would extend the privilege beyond a communication to one actually involved in the proceeding, either as judge, attorney, party or witness. On the other hand, it has been held that such absolute privilege will not attach to counsel's extrajudicial publications, related to the litigation, which are made outside the purview of the judicial proceeding. . . . Nor will the attorney be privileged for actionable words spoken before persons in no way connected with the proceeding. [The court discusses several cases.]

All of the above cited cases make it obvious that aside from any question of ethics, an attorney who wishes to litigate his case in the press will do so at his own risk. We hold that appellee had no absolute privilege in regard to the statement made by him to the newspaper.

However, the argument is made (and the language of the trial court's opinion shows that it was persuasive there) that the forum had been chosen by the State's Attorney, and not by appellee, and that he had a right, perhaps even a duty to his client, to publish the statement in question. This argument raises indirectly the contention that because of the attorney-client relationship, at least a qualified privilege existed in the absence of a showing of malice or abuse of the privilege.

There may well be a qualified privilege based upon an attorney-client relationship which would justify an otherwise slanderous communication to certain other persons, to protect the rights of society or one to whom a legal or moral duty is owed. However, the communication must be made in a proper manner and to proper parties only, i.e., to parties having a corresponding interest or duty. . . . It may be conceded that appellee indeed had a duty to act upon the information he had gained as to the statement given by the State's Attorney to the newspaper, particularly in light of Humphreys' statement to him. However, the means he chose to fulfill that duty were not proper, nor did he release the communication to a party having a corresponding interest or duty in the matter; and it cannot be said that his action was within the scope of his professional acts as an attorney in a pending case. . . . Other steps more consonant with Canon 20, Canons of Professional Ethics, were open to appellee. He could have requested the transfer of Humphreys to the jail of another jurisdiction for safekeeping until trial. He could have sought to have the objectionable matter, contained in the proposed article, kept out of publication. Even if this attempt were unsuccessful, other tactics were possible to the attorney who eventually defended the case, e.g., a request for change of venue, voir dire examination of prospective jurors in regard to the article, and preservation of the question of the prejudicial effect of the article, for appellate review.

The solicitude of appellee for his client is understandable, and the initial act of the State's Attorney in releasing his statement to the press must be disapproved. Nevertheless, as we have stated, appellee's legal duty in no way justified the publication of his defamatory reply statement. To hold otherwise would open the door to the universally condemned "trial by press," a procedure forbidden to counsel and subversive of the fair and orderly conduct of judicial proceedings. . . .

We hold that as a matter of law appellee had neither an absolute nor a qualified privilege in regard to the defamatory statement. Since the words spoken were slanderous per se they required no proof of special damage and carried the implication of malice. However, even though appellee was not reasonably entitled to believe in the existence of privilege, since none existed at law under the circumstances of this case, the trier of facts, on retrial, may consider his testimony, if reoffered, that he acted in good faith and without malice, on the question of mitigation of damages. . . .

For the reasons stated, the granting of a directed verdict for appellee was erroneous and the case should have been submitted to the jury.

NOTES

1. Scope of the absolute privilege. The common law courts have long recognized that the absolute privilege extends without doubt to judges in the course of official business, to lawyers for conduct both preliminary to and in the course of judicial proceedings, and to parties to judicial proceedings. RST §§585-587. Many recent cases have grappled with the scope of the absolute privilege insofar as it pertains to legal proceedings. In Barker v. Huang, 610 A.2d 1341, 1345-1346 (Del. 1992), the court rebuffed plaintiff's invitation to create an exception for sham statements made in the course of litigation. Horsey, J., wrote: "To allow claims of defamation in the context of judicial proceedings to proceed to costly discovery in an attempt to ferret out facts purporting to show a sham nature to the litigation would largely defeat the purpose of the privilege. Moreover, sufficient sanctions already exist to deter and punish frivolous litigation. We therefore hold that no 'sham litigation' exception to the defense of absolute privilege exists under the law of Delaware." More recently, in Finkelstein, Thompson & Loughran v. Hemispherx Biopharma, Inc., 774 A.2d 332 (D.C. 2001), Enright, a member of the defendant class action law firm, sent an unsolicited email to a shareholder of plaintiff Hemispherx that contained defamatory assertions in order to induce him to bring a derivative or class action lawsuit against Hemispherx. The court held that the defendant's absolute privilege extends to "some statements that are made prior to the commencement of litigation, for instance 'in conferences and other communications preliminary to the proceeding.'"

2. Other governmental bodies. The larger debate in this area turns on the various kinds of bodies in which statements made are absolutely privileged. This basic question has been raised countless times in other bodies of the modern administrative state, most of which have complex internal procedures. Thus, in Craig v. Stafford Construction Co., 856 A.2d 372, 382 (Conn. 2004), the plaintiff Craig was a police officer who claimed that the defendant company and its employee "had defamed him when they filed a citizen complaint with the [internal affairs division of the Hartford police] department alleging that he had directed racial slurs toward them at a construction site." The plaintiff was charged with "conduct unbecoming of a police officer." The Court found that "[d]uring the investigatory process, Ramistella [the employee] made a false statement" regarding the incident, and thereafter withdrew his complaint. Several months later the plaintiff was found not guilty.

A unanimous Court held that the extensive procedures created a quasi-judicial proceeding which accorded the charging witnesses an absolute privilege. These procedures required the commander of the internal affairs division to empower either the officer's immediate supervisor or some independent member of internal affairs to investigate any complaint. In this case, the independent investigator took sworn statements from various witnesses as well as a statement from the accused officer. He then prepared a report that was reviewed first by the commander of the internal affairs division and then by the bureau commander, who then exercised his option to initiate an internal prosecution before a board consisting of three officers from within the division. "[A]lthough we recognize the debilitating affect that a false allegation of racial discrimination can have on a police officer, we conclude that the policy of encouraging citizens complaints against those people who wield extraordinary power within the community outweighs the need to protect the reputation of the police officer against whom the complaint is made." Should the rule be relaxed when the defendant admits to a false statement? Similarly, all reports that private individuals make to police officers about possible criminal activity of other private parties are also treated as communications "made preliminary to a proposed judicial proceeding," RST §587, comment *b*. See, e.g., Correllas v. Viverios, 572 N.E.2d 7, 13 (Mass. 1991), defending this rule on the ground that any witness has a strong incentive to tell the truth, for "[b]y implicating the plaintiff, the defendant knew that she would have to repeat her accusations at the plaintiff's trial, and do so under oath, subjecting herself to possible perjury for any false testimony."

The absolute privilege has been upheld in other administrative procedures. *Craig* relied on the earlier decision in Kelley v. Bonney, 606 A.2d 693 (Conn. 1992), which recognized an absolute privilege by treating proceedings instituted to revoke a teachers licenses as quasi-judicial. Western Mass. Blasting Corp. v. Metro. Prop. & Cas. Ins. Co., 783 A.2d 398 (R.I. 2001), afforded the same absolute privilege to statements made during an insurance arbitration proceeding. In Tobkin v. Jarboe, 710 So. 2d 975, 976 (Fla. 1998), the absolute privilege applied to complaints that clients lodged against their attorneys with the Florida Bar "in so far as the complainant makes no public announcement of the complaint outside of the grievance process, thus allowing the grievance procedure to run its natural course."

States have divided on the type of privilege accorded to hospital peer review committees that evaluate — often in response to individual complaints — the performance of staff physicians. Franklin v. Blank, 525 P.2d 945, 946 (N.M. App. 1974), held that both a letter written to initiate peer review and the peer review process at common law were shielded by an absolute privilege. "The appropriate professional societies, by exercising peer review, can and do perform a great public service by exercising control over those persons placed in a position of public trust but nevertheless unfit to bear that responsibility." But in DiMiceli v. Klieger, 206 N.W.2d 184 (Wis. 1973), the court recognized only a qualified privilege. Today most states have specific statutes that supply some privilege for peer review proceedings. Thus, Fla. Stat. Ann. §766.101 (West 2007) protects a peer review committee member, or health care provider who gives information to a peer review committee, when "the committee member or health care provider acts without intentional fraud." Further amendments limit the use that can be made in court of information presented to a peer review committee. In contrast, Cal. Civ. Code §47 (West 2007) extends the privilege to "any other official proceeding authorized by law," with unrelated exceptions.

For bodies that look less like courts and more like political fora, a conditional privilege is the norm. In Park Knoll Associates v. Schmidt, 451 N.E.2d 182 (N.Y. 1983), the court, with two judges dissenting, held that the president of a tenant's association did *not* enjoy absolute privilege from liability, as he was not an attorney, party, or witness in a judicial or quasi-judicial proceeding. Likewise, a claim for absolute privilege was rebuffed in Ezekiel v. Jones Motor Co., Inc., 372 N.E.2d 1281, 1285 (Mass. 1978), when the defendant's employee, testifying before a joint management-union grievance board, falsely accused the plaintiff of stealing company property.

> While a witness at a judicial proceeding is free to make defamatory statements without fear of being sued by the defamed person, the witness is nevertheless subject to the control of the judge. If he or she gives false testimony, prosecution for perjury or punishment for contempt may be forthcoming. Such protections against false testimony simply do not exist at a labor grievance hearing such as the one which took place here. A witness at a grievance hearing need not give sworn testimony, nor is he subject to the control of a judge to limit his testimony to competent relevant and material evidence. A conditional privilege provides sufficient incentive for the witness to speak openly, but does not remove the safeguards against communications which are deliberately false.

For the still classic discussion, see Veeder, Absolute Immunity in Defamation: Judicial Proceedings, 9 Colum. L. Rev. 463 (1909).

b. Reports of Public Proceedings or Meetings

Brown & Williamson Tobacco Corp. v. Jacobson
713 F.2d 262 (7th Cir. 1983)

POSNER, J.
This diversity suit brought by Brown & Williamson, the manufacturer of Viceroy cigarettes, charges CBS and Walter Jacobson with libel and other violations of Illinois law. Jacobson is a news commentator for WBBM-TV, a

Chicago television station owned by CBS. [In 1975, the Ted Bates advertising agency teamed up with the Kennan market-research firm to develop a strategy for selling Viceroys to young people by placing smoking in the same "illicit pleasure category" as "wine, beer, shaving, wearing a bra (or purposely not wearing one)." Brown & Williamson promptly rejected the entire approach and fired Ted Bates "primarily because of displeasure with the proposed strategy."]

Years later the Federal Trade Commission conducted an investigation of cigarette advertising, and in May 1981 it published a report of its staff on the investigation. The FTC staff report discusses the Kennan report, correctly dates it to May 1975, and after quoting from it the passages we have quoted states that "B & W adopted many of the ideas contained in this report in the development of a Viceroy advertising campaign." In support of this assertion the staff report quotes an internal Brown & Williamson document on "Viceroy Strategy," dated 1976, which states, "The marketing efforts must cope with consumers' attitudes about smoking and health, either providing them a *rationale* for smoking a full flavor VICEROY or providing a means of *repressing* their concerns about smoking a full flavor VICEROY." The staff report then quotes a description of three advertising strategies. Although the description contains no reference to young smokers or to "starters," the staff report states: "B & W documents also show that it translated the advice [presumably from the Kennan report] on how to attract young 'starters' into an advertising campaign featuring young adults in situations that the vast majority of young people probably would experience and in situations demonstrating adherence to a 'free and easy, hedonistic lifestyle.'" The interior quotation is from another 1976 Brown & Williamson document on advertising strategy.

On November 4, 1981, a reporter for WBBM-TV called Brown & Williamson headquarters and was put in touch with a Mr. Humber in the corporate affairs department. The reporter told Mr. Humber that he was preparing a story on the tobacco industry for Walter Jacobson's "Perspective" program and asked him about the part of the FTC staff report that dealt with the Viceroy advertising strategy. Humber replied that Brown & Williamson had rejected the proposals in the Kennan report and had fired Ted Bates in part because of dissatisfaction with those proposals.

Walter Jacobson's "Perspective" on the tobacco industry was broadcast on November 11 and rebroadcast on November 12 and again on March 5, 1982. In the broadcast, Jacobson, after stating that "pushing cigarettes on television is prohibited," announces his theme: "Television is off limits to cigarettes and so the business, the killer business, has gone to the ad business in New York for help, to the slicksters on Madison Avenue with a billion dollars a year for bigger and better ways to sell cigarettes. Go for the youth of America, go get 'em guys. . . . Hook 'em while they are young, make 'em start now—just think how many cigarettes they'll be smoking when they grow up." Various examples of how cigarette marketing attempts "to addict the children to poison" are given. The last and longest concerns Viceroy.

> The cigarette business insists, in fact, it will swear up and down in public, it is not selling cigarettes to children, that if children are smoking, which they are, more than ever before, it's not the fault of the cigarette business. "Who knows whose fault it is?" says the cigarette business. That's what Viceroy is saying, "Who knows whose fault it is that children are smoking? It's not ours."
>
> Well, there is a confidential report on cigarette advertising in the files of the Federal Government right now, a Viceroy advertising, the Viceroy strategy for attracting young people, starters they are called, to smoking — "FOR THE YOUNG SMOKER. . . . A CIGARETTE FALLS INTO THE SAME CATEGORY WITH WINE, BEER, SHAVING OR WEARING A BRA. . . ." says the Viceroy strategy — "A DECLARATION OF INDEPENDENCE AND STRIVING FOR SELF-IDENTITY." Therefore, an attempt should be made, says Viceroy, to ". . . PRESENT THE CIGARETTE AS AN INITIATION INTO THE ADULT WORLD," to ". . . PRESENT THE CIGARETTE AS AN ILLICIT PLEASURE . . . A BASIC SYMBOL OF THE GROWING-UP, MATURING PROCESS." An attempt should be made, say the Viceroy slicksters, "TO RELATE THE CIGARETTE TO 'POT', WINE, BEER, SEX. DO NOT COMMUNICATE HEALTH OR HEALTH-RELATED POINTS." That's the strategy of the cigarette slicksters, the cigarette business which is insisting in public, "We are not selling cigarettes to children."
>
> They're not slicksters, they're liars.

While Jacobson is speaking these lines the television screen is showing Viceroy ads published in print media in 1980. Each ad shows two packs of Viceroys alongside a golf club and ball. . . .

Under contemporary as under traditional Illinois law, Jacobson's broadcast is libelous per se. Accusing a cigarette company of what many people consider the immoral strategy of enticing children to smoke — enticing them by advertising that employs themes exploitive of adolescent vulnerability — is likely to harm the company. It may make it harder for the company to fend off hostile government regulation and may invite rejection of the company's product by angry parents who smoke but may not want their children to do so. These harms cannot easily be measured, but so long as some harm is highly likely the difficulty of measurement is an additional reason, under the modern functional approach of the Illinois courts, for finding libel per se rather than insisting on proof of special damage. . . .

The defendants also argue and the district court also found that the libel was privileged as a fair and accurate summary of the Federal Trade

Commission staff's report on cigarette advertising. The parties agree as they must that Illinois recognizes a privilege for fair and accurate summaries of, or reports on, government proceedings and investigations. They agree that the privilege extends to a public FTC staff report on an investigation. But they disagree over whether Jacobson's summary of the FTC staff report was "fair," that is, whether the overall impression created by the summary was no more defamatory than that created by the original. See Restatement (Second) of Torts §611, comment f (1977). Since this is a question of fact, and the case was dismissed on the pleadings, all we need decide is whether the fairness of the Jacobson summary emerges so incontrovertibly from a comparison of the FTC staff report with the broadcast that no rational jury considering these documents with the aid of whatever additional evidence Brown & Williamson might introduce could consider the summary unfair. . . .

The fact that there are discrepancies between a libel and the government report on which it is based need not defeat the privilege of fair summary. Unless the report is published verbatim it is bound to convey a somewhat different impression from the original, no matter how carefully the publisher attempts to summarize or paraphrase or excerpt it fairly and accurately. An unfair summary in the present context is one that amplifies the libelous effect that publication of the government report verbatim would have on a reader who read it carefully — that carries a "greater sting." The FTC staff report conveys the following message: six years ago a market-research firm submitted to Brown & Williamson a set of rather lurid proposals for enticing young people to smoke cigarettes and Brown & Williamson adopted many of its ideas (though not necessarily the specific proposals quoted in the report) in an advertising campaign aimed at young smokers which it conducted the following year. The Jacobson broadcast conveys the following message: Brown & Williamson currently is advertising cigarettes in a manner designed to entice children to smoke by associating smoking with drinking, sex, marijuana, and other illicit pleasures of youth. So at least a rational jury might interpret the source and the summary, and if it did it would be entitled to conclude that the summary carried a greater sting and was therefore unfair.

[Reversed and remanded.]

NOTES

1. **Brown & Williamson** *on remand*. At trial, Brown & Williamson recovered $3,000,000 in actual damages and $2,050,000 in punitive, of which $50,000 were against Jacobson personally and the rest against CBS. The trial judge reduced the compensatory damages to $1.00. On appeal compensatory damages were increased to $1,000,000 and the punitive

damages award was preserved. Brown & Williamson Tobacco Corp. v. Jacobson, 827 F.2d 1119 (7th Cir. 1987).

2. *English origins of the fair reporting privilege.* In general the privilege of "record libel"—the traditional term for the fair report privilege—is accorded to persons who publish to the world statements that previously have been made as a matter of public record. In one famous early case, Stockdale v. Hansard, 112 Eng. Rep. 1112 (Q.B. 1839), the court held that a parliamentary report, even though published by Hansard at the direct request of Parliament, was not privileged. That decision was immediately overturned by legislation; see Parliamentary Papers Act, 1840, s. 4. It was not, however, until Wason v. Walter, 4 Q.B. 73 (1868), that the privilege was extended to proceedings of Parliament voluntarily republished by the press. This decision smacked of judicial legislation since Parliament had twice previously refused to create a privilege for such reports. In his opinion Cockburn, C.J., noted that the privilege was well established for judicial proceedings, and that it was "of paramount public and national importance that the proceedings of the houses of parliament shall be communicated to the public" in order that "confidence" be maintained in the legislative process. Today in England the privilege extends not only to reports of parliamentary proceedings but to those of administrative bodies as well. See, e.g., Perera v. Peiris, [1949] A.C. 1 (P.C.).

3. *Scope of the privilege in the United States.* In this country the record libel privilege always applied to reports of legislative, judicial, and administrative proceedings, and it was quickly extended to various functions performed by "quasi-public" bodies. The Restatement (Second) of Torts defines the privilege as follows:

§611. REPORT OF OFFICIAL PROCEEDING OR PUBLIC MEETING
The publication of defamatory matter concerning another in a report of an official action or proceeding or of a meeting open to the public that deals with a matter of public concern is privileged if the report is accurate and complete or a fair abridgment of the occurrence reported.

Much litigation has also focused on the requirement that the defendant's statement be a fair and accurate statement or abridgment of the official proceedings. Clearly, the report of a complex trial need not be exhaustive in all respects, but if a newspaper reports the derogatory portions of a judicial proceeding one day, "it may not, after reporting the derogatory parts, fail to publish the further proceedings that tend to vindicate the person defamed." RST §611, comment *f*.

The record libel privilege at common law applies "even if the reporter of defamatory statements made in court believes or knows them to be false; the privilege is abused only if the report fails the test of fairness or accuracy." Rosenberg v. Helinski, 616 A.2d 866, 873 (Md. 1992). The reporter (or indeed any other person who narrates the event) does not lose the privilege because he refuses to become a commentator as well. But in many respects the privilege is closely circumscribed. In Moreno v. Crookston Times Printing Co., 610 N.W.2d 321 (Minn. 2000), the court applied the absolute privilege of RST §611 to a fair and accurate report of remarks made to the city council but refused to apply it insofar as the article "included material reporting on events other than those that occurred at the city council meeting." In addition, any report made about official proceedings is closely scrutinized for accuracy, and any errors they contain are not excused even if the inaccuracy in reporting was unintentional or the result of a mistake. The justification for requiring the defendant at his peril to report accurately the results of legal proceedings was given by the Kansas Supreme Court in Gobin v. Globe Publishing Co., 531 P.2d 76, 81-82 (Kan. 1975), in which the defendant was accused of falsely reporting that the plaintiff had pleaded guilty to a charge of cruelty to animals.

> [J]udicial proceedings are peculiarly susceptible to exact reporting; an account of that which transpired at trial is not contingent upon fallible or futile modes of investigation; court records are available and insofar as reports of in-progress proceedings are concerned, the threat of libel emanates only from incompetent reporting; moreover, because those participating in judicial proceedings enjoy an absolute immunity from suit for defamation, instances of defamation perpetrated by trial participants might well be compounded if reports of the proceedings enjoyed too protective a privilege.

However, this strict interpretation of the record libel privilege had been precluded by the Supreme Court's decision in *Gertz*, and the Kansas Supreme Court acknowledged that it was constrained henceforth to use a negligence standard in record libel cases. See RST §611, comment *b*.

c. Fair Comment: Artistic and Literary Criticism

The common law privilege of fair comment extended to all matters in the public eye, thereby allowing the defendant to express defamatory opinions on matters of public interest. The privilege extended to statements about public officials and candidates for public office, about educational, charitable, and religious institutions, about quasi-public institutions such as bar and medical associations, about sporting games and contests, and about artistic, literary, and scientific matters generally. The cardinal distinction under the common law privilege is between fact and opinion; the defense of fair comment applied only to the latter. For the line between fact and opinion, see Veeder, *infra* at 1094. To be sure, a substantial minority of states held that the privilege applied to false statements of fact as well as to statements of opinion. See Noel, Defamation of Public Officers and Candidates,

49 Colum. L. Rev. 875, 877-880 (1949). For the best exposition of this position at common law, see Coleman v. MacLennan, 98 P. 281 (Kan. 1908). The leading decision in support of the majority view was written by William Howard Taft, later President of the United States and Chief Justice of the United States Supreme Court, when he was a judge on the Court of Appeals. See Post Publishing Co. v. Hallman, 59 F. 530 (6th Cir. 1893).

The leading common law decision on fair comment was Carr v. Hood, 170 Eng. Rep. 981, 983 (K.B. 1808), a libel action that involved some savage criticism of Sir John Carr's book *The Stranger in Ireland*. Lord Ellenborough rebuffed the action as follows:

> Here the supposed libel has only attacked those works of which Sir John Carr is the avowed author; and one writer in exposing the follies and errors of another may make use of ridicule, however poignant. Ridicule is often the fittest weapon that can be employed for such a purpose. If the reputation or pecuniary interests of the person ridiculed suffer, it is damnum absque injuria. Where is the liberty of the press if an action can be maintained on such principles? Perhaps the plaintiff's *Tour through Scotland* is now unsaleable; but is he to be indemnified by receiving a compensation in damages from the person who may have opened the eyes of the public to the bad taste and inanity of his compositions? Who would have bought the works of Sir Robert Filmer after he had been refuted by Mr. Locke? But shall it be said that he might have sustained an action for defamation against that great philosopher, who was labouring to enlighten and ameliorate mankind? We really must not cramp observations upon authors and their works. They should be liable to criticism, to exposure, and even to ridicule, if their compositions be ridiculous; otherwise the first who writes a book on any subject will maintain a monopoly of sentiment and opinion respecting it. This would tend to the perpetuity of error. — Reflection on personal character is another thing. Shew me an attack on the moral character of this plaintiff, or any attack upon his character unconnected with his authorship, and I shall be as ready as any judge who ever sate here to protect him; but I cannot hear of malice on account of turning his works into ridicule.

Lord Ellenborough himself was taken for task for giving the privilege too narrow a scope in G. S. Bower, Actionable Defamation, 383 (1908):

> Nothing could be more misleading than the above [opinion], which assumes not that honest comment is justified, because it is comment, but that the author is to be punished for "the bad taste and inanity of his compositions," as Cinna the poet was "torn" for his "bad verses," and that, if the positions be reversed, — if the author is "labouring to enlighten mankind," and the critic's compositions are inane, — the immunity would not exist; whereas the whole foundation, and the sole justification, of the protection is the freedom of *any* man, however worthless his observations may be, to criticize with the severity he pleases (provided that he does not stray beyond the assigned

limits of comment into the region of personal imputation) the public conduct or the published work, however exalted or brilliant the rest of the world may deem it, of *any* other man. Sir Robert Filmer had the same right to criticize Locke, as Locke had to criticize him. The fact that one criticism may demolish the author, and another the critic himself, is utterly irrelevant to the question of the legal right.

The early decisions faithfully adhered to the distinction between criticisms of the book and the author. Thus, in Cherry v. Des Moines Leader, 86 N.W. 323, 323 (Iowa 1901), the court extended fair comment privilege to a vicious review of the plaintiff's three-sister vaudeville act, which described it as being performed by "strange creatures with painted faces and hideous mien." But in Triggs v. Sun Printing & Publishing Association, 71 N.E. 739 (N.Y. 1904), the court, consistent with *Carr*, let the jury decide whether comments about the private life of Professor Oscar Lovell Triggs of the English Department of the University of Chicago strayed into forbidden personal territory when they ridiculed his private life by stating, for example, "that he was unable to select a name for his baby until after a year of solemn deliberation." What happens to the public/private distinction after *New York Times*?

Veeder, Freedom of Public Discussion
23 Harv. L. Rev. 413, 419-420 (1910)

The distinction is fundamental, then, between comment upon given facts and the direct assertion of facts. And the significance of the distinction is plain. If the facts are stated separately, and the comment appears as an inference drawn from those facts, any injustice that the imputation might occasion is practically negatived by reason of the fact that the reader has before him the grounds upon which the unfavorable inference is based. When the facts are truthfully stated, comment thereon, if unjust, will fall harmless, for the former furnish a ready antidote for the latter. The reader is then in a position to judge whether the critic has not by his unfairness or prejudice libelled himself rather than the object of his animadversion. But if a bare statement is made in terms of a fact, or if facts and comment are so intermingled that it is not clear what purports to be inference and what is claimed to be fact, the reader will naturally assume that the injurious statements are based upon adequate grounds known to the writer. In one case, the insufficiency of the facts to support the inference will lead fairminded men to reject it; in the other, there is little, if any, room for the supposition that the injurious statement is other than a direct change of the fact, based upon grounds known to the writer, although not disclosed by him.

NOTES

1. The distinction at work. The elusive line between fact and opinion retains its importance today, for while a plaintiff may recover for false statements of fact upon proof of actual malice, statements of opinion are protected by an absolute privilege. In policing that line, courts continue to rely on Veeder's early formulation. By way of illustration, the Massachusetts Supreme Judicial Court wrote: "[I]f I write, without more, that a person is an alcoholic, I may well have committed a libel prima facie; but it is otherwise if I write that I saw the person take a martini at lunch and accordingly state that he is an alcoholic." National Association of Government Employees, Inc. v. Central Broadcasting Co., 396 N.E.2d 996, 1001 (Mass. 1979). That analogy proved persuasive in Beattie v. Fleet National Bank, 746 A.2d 717 (R.I. 2000). The defendant had issued a derogatory letter criticizing a real estate appraisal that Beattie had submitted to the bank, which

> faulted the comparable sales data he had relied upon to arrive at his valuation of the subject property. The bank's appraiser concluded the letter by stating that "in the aggregate, the data in this [appraisal] report combines to present such a misleading indication of the value of this property as to be considered fraudulent." The writer's opinion, however, was based upon disclosed, non-defamatory facts, including a seven-page memorandum enclosed with the letter that detailed the appraisal's perceived deficiencies. As a result, we hold that it did not constitute an actionable-defamatory communication.

2. Fact and opinion: political disputation. The stakes are often raised for the fact/opinion line in disputes with political overtones. Ollman v. Evans, 750 F.2d 970, 986 (D.C. Cir. 1984), arose out of an Evans and Novak column in November 1978, called "The Marxist Professor's Intentions," that protested the planned move of the plaintiff, a Marxist, to the Department of Government and Politics at the University of Maryland. The column first attacked Ollman for using the classroom as a forum to promote "revolution" and labeled him "an outspoken proponent of political Marxism." It recounted how he had finished last of 16 candidates in an election for the council to the American Political Science Association, running under the party name of the Caucus for a New Political Science. Further, it described Ollman's principal book, "Alienation: Marx's Conception of Man in Capitalist Society," as a "ponderous tome." Thereafter, in the passage specifically challenged as defamatory, the column said:

> Such pamphleteering is hooted at by one political scientist in a major eastern university, whose scholarship and reputation as a liberal are well known. "Ollman has no status within the profession, but is a pure and simple activist," he said. Would he say that publicly? No chance of it. Our Academic culture does not permit the raising of such questions.

Drawing heavily on common law precedents, Starr, J., proposed the following four-part test to elucidate the distinction between fact and opinion, with its clear constitutional overtones.

> Four constituent elements point to a given statement being one of fact: first, the proposition contains a "core meaning" understood by its intended audience; second, the proposition is "verifiable" by objective tests; third, the context increases the willingness to infer that the statement has a factual context; and fourth, the broader context is one that stresses fact or narrative, as opposed to editorials and reviews, where the reader expects greater latitude from the author.
>
> Relying upon the Restatement (Second) of Torts §566, the courts consider whether the opinion implies the existence of undisclosed facts as the basis for the opinion. If the opinion implied factual assertions, courts have held that it should not receive the benefit of First Amendment protection as an opinion. . . .
>
> The reasonable reader who peruses an Evans and Novak column on the editorial or Op-Ed page is fully aware that the statements found there are not "hard" news like those printed on the front page or elsewhere in the news sections of the newspaper. Readers expect that columnists will make strong statements, sometimes phrased in a polemical manner that would hardly be considered balanced or fair elsewhere in the newspaper. That proposition is inherent in the very notion of an "Op-Ed" page.

Bork, J., concurred to voice his worry about the onslaught of new libel actions, but expressed his impatience with "such things as four-factor frameworks, three-pronged tests, and two-tiered analyses," and urged a return to "first principles." "A judge who refuses to see new threats to an established constitutional value, and hence provides a crabbed interpretation that robs a provision of its full, fair and reasonable meaning, fails in his judicial duty." He concluded that the column should be protected because "a damage award would have a heavily inhibiting effect upon the journalism of opinion."

3. *Fact and opinion: restaurant reviews.* Ollman proved influential in Mr. Chow of New York v. Ste. Jour Azur, S.A., 759 F.2d 219, 227-228 (2d Cir. 1985). The defendant restaurant guide published a review (in French, of course) that castigated the plaintiff's restaurant because, inter alia, "It is impossible to have the basic condiments . . . on the table," "the sweet and sour pork contained more dough . . . than meat," "the green peppers . . . remained still frozen on the plate," and the Peking Duck "was made up of only one dish (instead of the three traditional ones)." The guide defended its review in part as containing statements of opinion and not of fact. An unpersuaded jury awarded the plaintiff $20,000 in actual damages and $5,000,000 in punitive damages, which were sustained by the trial judge. On appeal Meskill, J.,

applied the analysis of fact and opinion adopted by Starr, J., in *Ollman* and held that the review constituted protected opinion:

> Restaurant reviews are also [like the Evans and Novak column] the well recognized home of opinion and comment. Indeed, "by its very nature, an article commenting upon the quality of a restaurant or its food, like a review of a play or movie, constitutes the opinion of the reviewer." . . . The natural function of the review is to convey the critic's opinion of the restaurant reviewed: the food, the service, the decor, the atmosphere, and so forth. Such matters are to a large extent controlled by personal tastes. The average reader approaches a review with the knowledge that it contains only one person's views of the establishment. And importantly, "[a]s is essential in aesthetic criticism . . . the object of the judgment is available to the critic's audience." Appellee does not cite a single case that has found a restaurant review libelous. Appellants and *amici* on the other hand cite numerous decisions that have refused to do so. Although the rationale of each of these decisions is different, they all recognize to some extent that reviews, although they may be unkind, are not normally a breeding ground for successful libel actions.

The court then held that the statement about the Peking Duck was an assertion of fact. "The statement is not metaphorical or hyperbolic; it clearly is laden with factual content." Plaintiff's victory on the point was, however, bittersweet, because the false statement about the Peking Duck was found protected by the actual malice rule, applicable because the restaurant was considered a public figure.

What if the condiments were always on the table, the sweet and sour pork was encased in a thin, delicate dough, and the green peppers were cooked to a turn? Does it make a difference that customers are free to patronize the restaurant if none will spend $40 or more for a dinner after reading that review?

SECTION H.   CONSTITUTIONAL PRIVILEGES

1.   *Public Officials and Public Figures*

New York Times Co. v. Sullivan
376 U.S. 254 (1964)

BRENNAN, J. We are required in this case to determine for the first time the extent to which the constitutional protections for speech and press limit a State's power to award damages in a libel action brought by a public official against critics of his official conduct.

[The plaintiff-respondent, L.B. Sullivan, was one of three elected Commissioners of Montogomery, Alabama, who claimed that he was defamed in a full-page ad, costing $4,800, taken out in the New York Times on March 29, 1960. The ad was entitled "Heed Their Rising Voices," and it charged in part that an "unprecedented wave of terror" had been directed against those who participated in the civil rights movement in the South. The letter was signed by 64 prominent members of the civil rights movement and contained statements in two key paragraphs that were said to be defamatory:

Third paragraph:

"In Montgomery, Alabama, after students sang 'My Country, 'Tis of Thee' on the State Capitol steps, their leaders were expelled from school, and truckloads of police armed with shotguns and tear-gas ringed the Alabama State College Campus. When the entire student body protested to state authorities by refusing to re-register, their dining hall was padlocked in an attempt to starve them into submission."

Sixth paragraph:

"Again and again the Southern violators have answered Dr. King's peaceful protests with intimidation and violence. They have bombed his home almost killing his wife and child. They have assaulted his person. They have arrested him seven times — for 'speeding,' 'loitering' and similar 'offenses.' And now they have charged him with 'perjury' — a *felony* under which they could imprison him for *ten years*. . . . "

Although the ad did not mention Sullivan by name, he claimed that it referred to him by indirection because he had oversight responsibility of the police. Sullivan did not show that he suffered any special damages from the publication, but he claimed general damages for defamation. It was "uncontroverted" some of the particulars in the story were false: for example, the police had not ringed the campus, but were only deployed nearby; during the demonstration the students sang the National Anthem, not "My Country, 'Tis of Thee;" Dr. King had been arrested only four times, not seven; the nine students were expelled by the State Board of Education not for leading the demonstration, but "for demanding service at a lunchcounter at the Montgomery County Courthouse on another day." The jury awarded Sullivan $500,000 in damages and its decision was affirmed in the Alabama Supreme Court, 144 So. 2d 25 (1962).

Before publishing the ad, the Times had received a letter from A. Philip Randolph, chairman of the Committee, which certified that all the signatories had indeed signed the letter. The Times' Advertising Acceptability Department knew Mr. Randolph, and followed its established practice in accepting the letter as proper authorization. Some of the individuals, petitioners in this case, whose names were listed had not in fact authorized the use of their names but only found out about the ad when Sullivan had demanded a retraction. The manager of the Acceptability Department testified that he authorized publication of the ad because he did not have any reason to believe that its contents were false, but he admitted that he made no independent effort to check the report's accuracy. Sullivan demanded a retraction of the letter from all parties. The individual petitioners refused to retract the statements that they claimed they had never made; the New York Times wrote back, noting it was "puzzled" as to why Sullivan thought that the ad reflected adversely on him. This suit followed without further reply. The Times eventually published a retraction insofar as it applied to the Governor of Alabama whom it believed could be seen as "the embodiment of the State of Alabama." At trial the jury found the advertisement libelous per se, and hence actionable without proof of malice or special damages. The $500,000 award followed.]

Because of the importance of the constitutional issues involved, we granted the separate petitions for certiorari of the individual petitioners and of the Times. We reverse the judgment. We hold that the rule of law applied by the Alabama courts is constitutionally deficient for failure to provide the safeguards for freedom of speech and of the press that are required by the First and Fourteenth Amendments in a libel action brought by a public official against critics of his official conduct. We further hold that under the proper safeguards the evidence presented in this case is constitutionally insufficient to support the judgment for respondent.

[The Court first discussed two preliminary issues: whether there was state action and whether the defendant's statement, as an advertisement, was beyond the protection of the First Amendment. It decided that the common law rule in Alabama constituted sufficient state action and that the statement was not a "commercial" advertisement but an "editorial" advertisement on an issue "of the highest public interest and concern." It continued:]

Under Alabama law as applied in this case, a publication is "libelous per se" if the words "tend to injure a person . . . in his reputation" or to "bring [him] into public contempt"; the trial court stated that the standard was met if the words are such as to "injure him in his public office, or impute misconduct to him in his office, or want of official integrity, or want of fidelity to a public trust. . . ." The jury must find that the words were published "of and concerning" the plaintiff, but where the plaintiff is a public official his place in the government hierarchy is sufficient evidence to support a finding that his reputation has been affected by statements that reflect upon the agency of which he is in charge. Once "libel per se" has been established, the defendant has no defense as to stated facts unless he can persuade the jury that they were true in all their particulars. . . . His privilege of "fair comment" for expressions of opinion depends on the truth of the facts upon which the comment is based. Unless he can discharge the burden of proving truth, general damages are presumed, and may be awarded without proof of pecuniary injury. A showing of actual malice is apparently a prerequisite to recovery of punitive damages, and the defendant may in any event forestall a punitive award by a retraction meeting the statutory requirements. Good motives and belief in truth do not negate an inference of malice, but are relevant only in mitigation of punitive damages if the jury chooses to accord them weight.

The question before us is whether this rule of liability, as applied to an action brought by a public official against critics of his official conduct, abridges the freedom of speech and of the press that is guaranteed by the First and Fourteenth Amendments.

Respondent relies heavily, as did the Alabama courts, on statements of this Court to the effect that the Constitution does not protect libelous publications. Those statements do not foreclose our inquiry here. None of the cases sustained the use of libel laws to impose sanctions upon expression critical of the official conduct of public officials. . . . In deciding the question now, we are compelled by neither precedent nor policy to give any more weight to the epithet "libel" than we have to other "mere labels" of state law. Like insurrection, contempt, advocacy of unlawful acts, breach of the peace, obscenity, solicitation of legal business, and the various other formulae for the representation of expression that have been challenged in this Court, libel can claim no talismanic immunity from constitutional limitations. It must be measured by standards that satisfy the First Amendment. . . .

Thus we consider this case against the background of a profound national commitment to the principle that debate on public issues should be uninhibited, robust, and wide-open, and that it may well include vehement, caustic, and sometimes unpleasantly sharp attacks on government and public officials. The present advertisement, as an expression of grievance and protest on one of the major public issues of our time, would seem clearly to qualify for the constitutional protection. The question is whether it forfeits that protection by the falsity of some of its factual statements and by its alleged defamation of respondent.

Authoritative interpretations of the First Amendment guarantees have consistently refused to recognize an exception for any test of truth—whether administered by judges, juries, or administrative officials—and especially one that puts the burden of proving truth on the speaker. The constitutional protection does not turn upon "the truth, popularity, or social utility of the ideas and beliefs which are offered." N.A.A.C.P. v. Button, 371 U.S. 415, 445 (1963). As Madison said, "Some degree of abuse is inseparable from the proper use of everything; and in no instance is this more than in that of the press." 4 Elliot's Debates on the Federal Constitution (1876), p. 571. . . .

[E]rroneous statement is inevitable in free debate, and . . . it must be protected if the freedoms of expression are to have the "breathing space" that they "need . . . to survive," . . .

Injury to official reputation affords no more warrant for repressing speech that would otherwise be free than does factual error. Where judicial officers are involved, this Court has held that concern for the dignity and reputation of the courts does not justify the punishment as criminal contempt of criticism of the judge or his decision. Bridges v. California, 314 U.S. 252 (1941). This is true even though the utterance contains "half-truths" and "misinformation." Such repression can be justified, if at all, only by a clear and present danger of the obstruction of justice. If judges are to be treated as "men of fortitude, able to thrive in a hardy climate," surely the same must be true of other government officials, such as elected city commissioners. Criticism of their official conduct does not lose its constitutional protection merely because it is effective criticism and hence diminishes their official reputations.

If neither factual error nor defamatory content suffices to remove the constitutional shield from criticism of official conduct, the combination of the two elements is no less inadequate. This is the lesson to be drawn from the great controversy over the Sedition Act of 1798, 1 Stat. 596, which first crystallized a national awareness of the central meaning of the First Amendment. That statute made it a crime, punishable by a $5,000 fine and five years in prison, "if any person shall write, print, utter or publish . . . any false, scandalous and malicious writing or writings against the government of the United States, or either house of the Congress . . . , or the President . . . , with intent to defame . . . or to bring them, or either of them, into contempt or disrepute; or to excite against them, or either or any of them, the hatred of the good people of the United States." The Act allowed the defendant the defense of truth, and provided that the jury were to be judges both of the law and the facts. Despite these qualifications, the Act was vigorously condemned as unconstitutional in an attack joined in by Jefferson and Madison. In the famous Virginia Resolutions of 1798, the General Assembly of Virginia resolved that it "doth particularly protest against the palpable and alarming infractions of the Constitution, in the two late cases of the 'Alien and Sedition Acts,' passed at the last session of Congress. . . . [The Sedition Act] exercises . . . a power not delegated by the Constitution, but, on the contrary, expressly and positively forbidden by one of the amendments thereto — a power which, more than any other, ought to produce universal alarm, because it is levelled against the right of freely examining public characters and measures, and of free communication among the people thereon, which has ever been justly deemed the only effectual guardian of every other right." 4 Elliot's Debates, *supra* at 553-554. Madison prepared the Report in support of the protest.

Although the Sedition Act was never tested in this Court,[16] the attack upon its validity has carried the day in the court of history. Fines levied in its prosecution were repaid by Act of Congress on the ground that it was unconstitutional. See, e.g., Act of July 4, 1840, c. 45, 6 Stat. 802, . . .

There is no force in respondent's argument that the constitutional limitations implicit in the history of the Sedition Act apply only to Congress and not to the States. It is true that the First Amendment was originally addressed only to action by the Federal Government, and that Jefferson, for one, while denying the power of Congress "to control the freedom of the press," recognized such a power in the States. But this distinction was eliminated with the adoption of the Fourteenth Amendment and the application to the States of the First Amendment's restrictions. . . .

What a State may not constitutionally bring about by means of a criminal statute is likewise beyond the reach of its civil law of libel. The fear of damage awards under a rule such as that invoked by the Alabama courts here may be markedly more inhibiting than the fear of prosecution under a criminal statute. Alabama, for example, has a criminal libel law which subjects to prosecution "any person who speaks, writes, or prints of and concerning another any accusation falsely and maliciously importing the commission by such person of a felony, or any other indictable offense involving moral turpitude," and which allows as punishment upon conviction a fine not exceeding $500 and a prison sentence of six months. Alabama Code, Tit. 14, §350. Presumably a person charged with violation of this statute enjoys ordinary criminal-law safeguards such as the requirements of an indictment and of proof beyond a reasonable doubt. These safeguards are not available to the defendant in a civil action. The judgment awarded in this case—without the need for any proof of actual pecuniary loss—was one thousand times greater than the maximum fine provided by the Alabama criminal statute, and one hundred times greater than that provided by the Sedition Act. And since there is no double-jeopardy limitation applicable to civil lawsuits, this is not the only judgment that may be awarded against petitioners for the same publication.[18] Whether or not a newspaper can survive a succession of such judgments, the pall of fear and timidity imposed upon those who would give voice to public criticism is an atmosphere in which the First Amendment freedoms cannot survive. Plainly the Alabama law of civil libel is "a form of regulation that creates hazards to protected freedoms markedly greater than those that attend reliance upon the criminal law." Bantam Books, Inc. v. Sullivan, 372 U.S. 58, 70 (1963).

16. The Act expired by its terms in 1801.

18. The Times states that four other libel suits based on the advertisement have been filed against it by others who have served as Montgomery City Commissioners and by the Governor of Alabama; that another $500,000 verdict has been awarded in the only one of these cases that has yet gone to trial; and that the damages sought in the other three total $2,000,000.

The state rule of law is not saved by its allowance of the defense of truth. . . . A rule compelling the critic of official conduct to guarantee the truth of all his factual assertions — and to do so on pain of libel judgments virtually unlimited in amount — leads to . . . "self-censorship." Allowance of the defense of truth, with the burden of proving it on the defendant, does not mean that only false speech will be deterred. Even courts accepting this defense as an adequate safeguard have recognized the difficulties of adducing legal proofs that the alleged libel was true in all its factual particulars. . . . Under such a rule, would-be critics of official conduct may be deterred from voicing their criticism, even though it is believed to be true and even though it is in fact true, because of doubt whether it can be proved in court or fear of the expense of having to do so. They tend to make only statements which "steer far wider of the unlawful zone." The rule thus dampens the vigor and limits the variety of public debate. It is inconsistent with the First and Fourteenth Amendments.

The constitutional guarantees require, we think, a federal rule that prohibits a public official from recovering damages for a defamatory falsehood relating to his official conduct unless he proves that the statement was made with "actual malice" — that is, with knowledge that it was false or with reckless disregard of whether it was false or not. [See] Coleman v. MacLennan, 98 P. 281 (Kan. 1908). . . .

We hold today that the Constitution delimits a State's power to award damages for libel in actions brought by public officials against critics of their official conduct. Since this is such an action, the rule requiring proof of actual malice is applicable. While Alabama law apparently requires proof of actual malice for an award of punitive damages, where general damages are concerned malice is "presumed." Such a presumption is inconsistent with the federal rule. "The power to create presumptions is not a means of escape from constitutional restrictions," Bailey v. Alabama, 219 U.S. 219, 239 (1911); "the showing of malice required for the forfeiture of the privilege is not presumed but is a matter for proof by the plaintiff. . . ." Lawrence v. Fox, 97 N.W.2d 719, 725 (Mich. 1959). Since the trial judge did not instruct the jury to differentiate between general and punitive damages, it may be that the verdict was wholly an award of one or the other. But it is impossible to know, in view of the general verdict returned. Because of this uncertainty, the judgment must be reversed and the case remanded. . . .

Since respondent may seek a new trial, we deem that considerations of effective judicial administration require us to review the evidence in the present record to determine whether it could constitutionally support a judgment for respondent. . . .

[We] consider that the proof presented to show actual malice lacks the convincing clarity which the constitutional standard demands, and hence that it would not constitutionally sustain the judgment for respondent under the proper rule of law. The case of the individual petitioners requires little discussion. Even assuming that they could constitutionally be found to have authorized the use of their names on the advertisement, there was no evidence whatever that they were aware of any erroneous statements or were in any way reckless in that regard. The judgment against them is thus without constitutional support.

As to the Times, we similarly conclude that the facts do not support a finding of actual malice. The statement by the Times' Secretary that, apart from the padlocking allegation, he thought the advertisement was "substantially correct," affords no constitutional warrant for the Alabama Supreme Court's conclusion that it was a "cavalier ignoring of the falsity of the advertisement [from which] the jury could not have but been impressed with the bad faith of The Times, and its maliciousness inferable therefrom." [Justice Brennan then concluded that Times' evidence showed that its belief in the truth of the advertisement was "at least a reasonable one" and that no evidence had impeached the good faith of its witnesses. He further held that no inference of malice could be drawn from the fact that the Times offered a retraction to the governor but not the plaintiff, given the explanation the Times' Secretary, whose good faith was not impeached, had offered for it. He further concluded that the failure to check on the accuracy of the story was at most negligence, given its reasonable reliance on the assurances of A. Philip Randolph and other signatories of the letter.] . . .

We also think the evidence was constitutionally defective in another respect: it was incapable of supporting the jury's finding that the allegedly libelous statements were made "of and concerning" respondent. Respondent relies on the words of the advertisement and the testimony of six witnesses to establish a connection between it and himself. . . .

There was no reference to respondent in the advertisement, either by name or official position. A number of the allegedly libelous statements — the charges that the dining hall was padlocked and that Dr. King's home was bombed, his person assaulted, and a perjury prosecution instituted against him — did not even concern the police; despite the ingenuity of the arguments which would attach this significance to the word "They," it is plain that these statements could not reasonably be read as accusing respondent of personal involvement in the acts in question. The statements upon which respondent principally relies as referring to him are the two allegations that did concern the police or police functions: that "truckloads of police . . . ringed the Alabama State College Campus" after the demonstration on the State Capitol steps, and that Dr. King had been "arrested . . . seven times." . . . Although the statements may be taken as referring to the police, they did not on their face make even an oblique reference to respondent as an individual. . . .

The judgment of the Supreme Court of Alabama is reversed and the case is remanded to that court for further proceedings not inconsistent with this opinion.

Reversed and remanded.

BLACK, J., with whom DOUGLAS, J., joins, concurring. I concur in reversing this half-million-dollar judgment against the New York Times Company and the four individual defendants. . . . I base my vote to reverse on the belief that the First and Fourteenth Amendments not merely "delimit" a State's power to award damages to "public officials against critics of their official conduct" but completely prohibit a State from exercising such a power. The Court goes on to hold that a State can subject such critics to damages if "actual malice" can be proved against them. "Malice," even as defined by the Court, is an elusive, abstract concept, hard to prove and hard to disprove. The requirement that malice be proved provides at best an evanescent protection for the right critically to discuss public affairs and certainly does not measure up to the sturdy safeguard embodied in the First Amendment. Unlike the Court, therefore, I vote to reverse exclusively on the ground that the Times and the individual defendants had an absolute, unconditional right to publish in the Times advertisement their criticisms of the Montgomery agencies and officials. . . .

[The concurring opinion of Justice Goldberg has been omitted.]

NOTES

1. *The constitutionalization of the law of defamation.* New York Times v. Sullivan ushered in a new constitutional jurisprudence for all defamation cases brought by public officials against (to use the current expression) media defendants. In choosing to override the common law, was the Court more swayed by the predicament of the New York Times or by the weaknesses of the common law of defamation? What are the narrowest grounds on which the plaintiff's verdict could be overturned? For an argument that Alabama misapplied the common law of defamation on all relevant issues, see Epstein, Was *New York Times v. Sullivan* Wrong?, 53 U. Chi. L. Rev. 782 (1986).

2. *A jurisdictional escape.* In New York Times Co. v. Connor, 365 F.2d 567 (5th Cir. 1966), the court found that the plaintiff, Eugene "Bull" Connor, then one of Birmingham's city commissioners, had not made out actual malice against either the New York Times or Harrison Salisbury, then a staff member of the paper, who in April 1960 wrote an article entitled "Fear and Hatred Grip Birmingham." In a sense that finding was unnecessary because the court had previously held that under the Due Process Clause Alabama did not have jurisdiction over the Times solely because it mailed papers to individual subscribers and local wholesalers in Alabama. In its view the "minimum contacts" for suit were not established because the defendant published in New York, had no agents or employees in Alabama, had paid its Alabama stringers (part-time sources)

a total of $415, and derived from Alabama sources "approximately 25/1000 to 46/1000 of 1% of the total Times advertising revenue." Was the same argument open to the Supreme Court in New York Times v. Sullivan? Note that in footnote 3 of *New York Times*, omitted above, Justice Brennan observed: "Approximately 394 copies of the edition of the Times containing the advertisement were circulated in Alabama. Of these, about 35 copies were distributed in Montgomery County. The total circulation of the Times for that day was approximately 650,000 copies." What result if Sullivan or Connor sued in New York State?

3. The private conduct of public officials. In Monitor Patriot Co. v. Roy, 401 U.S. 265, 277 (1971), petitioner newspaper published a column characterizing senatorial candidate Roy as a "former small-time bootlegger." The jury found for respondent on the ground that the bootlegger charge was "in the private sector." The Court noted first that under *New York Times* "publications concerning candidates must be accorded at least as much protection under the First and Fourteenth Amendments as those concerning occupants of public office." It rejected respondent's contentions that *New York Times* applies only to a candidate's "official conduct," meaning "conduct relevant to fitness for office" and that the public-private issue is one for the jury. The Court held "as a matter of constitutional law that a charge of criminal conduct, no matter how remote in time or place, can never be irrelevant to an official's or a candidate's fitness for office for purposes of the 'knowing falsehood or reckless disregard' rule of New York Times Co. v. Sullivan."

4. References. The literature on *New York Times* is extensive. For an enthusiastic interpretation of *New York Times* as an occasion "for dancing in the streets," see Kalven, The *New York Times* Case: A Note on "The Central Meaning of the First Amendment," 1964 Sup. Ct. Rev. 191; see also Brennan, The Supreme Court and the Meiklejohn Interpretation of the First Amendment, 79 Harv. L. Rev. 1 (1965). For further commentary, see Symposium: New Perspectives in the Law of Defamation, 74 Cal. L. Rev. 3 (1986) (with contributions by Barrett, Bellah, Bezanson, Casper, Franklin, Post, Reston, Schauer, Shapiro, Skolnick, and Sunstein); Bezanson, Randall & Cranberg, Gilbert, Institutional Reckless Disregard for Truth in Public Defamation Actions Against the Press, 90 Iowa L. Rev. 887 (2005).

Curtis Publishing Co. v. Butts
388 U.S. 130 (1967)

[No. 37, Curtis Publishing Co. v. Butts, involved charges in the Saturday Evening Post that Wally Butts, coach of the University of Georgia football team, had conspired to fix a 1962 Georgia-Alabama game by giving to Paul Bryant, coach of the University of Alabama team, crucial information about

Georgia's offensive strategy. The article concluded: "The chances are that Wally Butts will never help any football team again. . . . The investigation by university and Southeastern Conference officials is continuing; motion pictures of other games are being scrutinized; where it will end no one so far can say. But careers will be ruined, that is sure." Butts sued for libel and a jury awarded him $60,000 in general damages and $3,000,000 in punitive damages. After *New York Times* was decided the defendant requested a new trial, but the motion was denied on two grounds — first, that *New York Times* was inapplicable because the plaintiff was not a public official and, second, that the record contained ample evidence from which a jury could have concluded that the article was published with reckless disregard for truth. The judgment of the trial court was affirmed on appeal. 351 F.2d 702 (5th Cir. 1965).

No. 150, Associated Press v. Walker, arose out of the distribution of a news dispatch giving an eyewitness account of events on the campus of the University of Mississippi on the night of September 30, 1962, when a massive riot erupted because of federal efforts to enforce a court decree ordering the enrollment of a Negro, James Meredith, as a student in the University. The dispatch stated that respondent Edwin Walker, who was present on the campus, had taken command of the violent crowd and had personally led a charge against federal marshals sent there to effectuate the court's decree and to assist in preserving order. Walker, a private citizen with a long and honorable military career, sued for libel claiming that he had "counseled restraint" to the students, had exercised no control over the crowd, and had not taken part in any charge against federal marshals. Some evidence showed that the Associated Press was negligent in assigning an inexperienced reporter to cover the story and had failed to catch minor discrepancies between an early oral dispatch and a later written dispatch. The jury awarded plaintiff $500,000 in compensatory and $300,000 in punitive damages, but the court refused to enter the award of punitive damages, concluding that the record contained at most evidence of negligence but not malice. Both sides appealed. The decision was affirmed by the Texas Civil Court of Appeals, 393 S.W.2d 671 (1965). The United States Supreme Court granted certiorari after the Supreme Court of Texas denied writ of error.

Both plaintiffs were public figures but not public officials. Four separate Supreme Court opinions, much condensed here, addressed the question of how the standards of *New York Times* applied.]

HARLAN, J. . . . We thus turn to a consideration, on the merits, of the constitutional claims raised by Curtis in *Butts* and by the Associated Press in *Walker*. Powerful arguments are brought to bear for the extension of the *New York Times* rule in both cases.

[Justice Harlan reviewed at length various leading precedents on free speech, and continued:]

In *New York Times* we were adjudicating in an area which lay close to seditious libel, and history dictated extreme caution in imposing liability. The plaintiff in that case was an official whose position in government was such "that the public [had] an independent interest in the qualifications and performance of the person who [held] it." Rosenblatt v. Baer, 383 U.S. 75, at 86 (1966). Such officials usually enjoy a privilege against libel actions for their utterances, see, e.g., Barr v. Matteo, 360 U.S. 564 (1960), and there were analogous considerations involved in *New York Times*. Thus we invoked "the hypothesis that speech can rebut speech, propaganda will answer propaganda, free debate of ideas will result in the wisest governmental policies," Dennis v. United States, 341 U.S. 494, 503 (1951), and limited recovery to those cases where "calculated falsehood" placed the publisher "at odds with the premises of democratic government and with the orderly manner in which economic, social, or political change is to be effected." Garrison v. Louisiana, 379 U.S. 64, 75 (1964). That is to say, such officials were permitted to recover in libel only when they could prove that the publication involved was deliberately falsified, or published recklessly despite the publisher's awareness of probable falsity. Investigatory failures alone were held insufficient to satisfy this standard.

In the cases we decide today none of the particular considerations involved in *New York Times* is present. These actions cannot be analogized to prosecutions for seditious libel. Neither plaintiff has any position in government which would permit a recovery by him to be viewed as a vindication of governmental policy. Neither was entitled to a special privilege protecting his utterances against accountability in libel. We are prompted, therefore, to seek guidance from the rules of liability which prevail in our society with respect to compensation of persons injured by the improper performance of a legitimate activity by another. Under these rules, a departure from the kind of care society may expect from a reasonable man performing such activity leaves the actor open to a judicial shifting of loss. In defining these rules, and especially in formulating the standards for determining the degree of care to be expected in the circumstances, courts have consistently given much attention to the importance of defendants' activities. The courts have also, especially in libel cases, investigated the plaintiff's position to determine whether he has a legitimate call upon the court for protection in light of his prior activities and means of self-defense. We note that the public interest in the circulation of the materials here involved, and the publisher's interest in circulating them, is not less than that involved in *New York Times*. And both Butts and Walker commanded a substantial amount of independent public interest at the time of the publications; both, in our opinion, would have been labeled "public figures" under ordinary tort rules. Butts may have attained that status by position alone and Walker by his purposeful activity amounting to a thrusting of his personality into the "vortex" of an important public controversy, but both commanded sufficient continuing public interest and had sufficient access to the means of counterargument to be able to "expose through discussion the falsehood and fallacies" of the defamatory statements. Whitney v. California, 274 U.S. 357, 377 (1927) (Brandeis, J., dissenting).

These similarities and differences between libel actions involving persons who are public officials and libel actions involving those circumstanced as were Butts and Walker, viewed in light of the principles of liability which are of general applicability in our society, lead us to the conclusion that libel actions of the present kind cannot be left entirely to state libel laws, unlimited by any overriding constitutional safeguard, but that the rigorous federal requirements of *New York Times* are not the only appropriate accommodation of the conflicting interests at stake. We consider and would hold that a "public figure" who is not a public official may also recover damages for a defamatory falsehood whose substance makes substantial danger to reputation apparent, on a showing of highly unreasonable conduct constituting an extreme departure from the standards of investigation and reporting ordinarily adhered to by responsible publishers.

Nothing in this opinion is meant to affect the holdings in *New York Times* and its progeny, including our recent decision in Time, Inc. v. Hill.

Having set forth the standard by which we believe the constitutionality of the damage awards in these cases must be judged, we turn now, as the Court did in *New York Times*, to the question whether the evidence and findings below meet that standard. We find the standard satisfied in No. 37, *Butts*, and not satisfied by either the evidence or the findings in No. 150, *Walker*.

[Justice Harlan reviewed the evidence in detail. He then examined defendants' challenge to the constitutionality of the punitive damages award and rejected it. His opinion concludes:]

The judgment of the Court of Appeals for the Fifth Circuit in No. 37 is affirmed. The judgment of the Texas Court of Civil Appeals in No. 150 is reversed and the case is remanded to that court for further proceedings not inconsistent with the opinions that have been filed herein by The Chief Justice, Justice Black, and Justice Brennan.

WARREN, C.J., concurring in the result. . . . To me, differentiation between "public figures" and "public officials" and adoption of separate standards of proof for each have no basis in law, logic, or First Amendment policy. Increasingly in this country, the distinctions between governmental and private sectors are blurred. Since the depression of the 1930's and World War II there has been a rapid fusion of economic and political power, a merging of science, industry, and government, and a high degree of interaction between the intellectual, governmental, and business worlds. Depression, war, international tensions, national and international markets, and the surging growth of science and technology have precipitated national and international problems that demand national and international solutions. While these trends and events have occasioned a consolidation of governmental power, power has also become much more organized in what we have commonly considered to be the private sector. In many situations, policy determinations which traditionally were channeled through formal political institutions are now originated and implemented through a complex array of boards, committees, commissions, corporations, and associations, some only loosely connected with the Government. This blending of positions and power has also occurred in the case of individuals so that many who do not hold public office at the moment are nevertheless intimately involved in the resolution of important public questions or, by reason of their fame, shape events in areas of concern to society at large.

Viewed in this context, then, it is plain that although they are not subject to the restraints of the political process, "public figures," like "public officials," often play an influential role in ordering society. And surely as a class these "public figures" have as ready access as "public officials" to mass media of communication, both to influence policy and to counter criticism of their views and activities. Our citizenry has a legitimate and substantial interest in the conduct of such persons, and freedom of the press to engage in uninhibited debate about their involvement in public issues and events is as crucial as it is in the case of "public officials." The fact that they are not amenable to the restraints of the political process only underscores the legitimate and substantial nature of the interest, since it means that public opinion may be the only instrument by which society can attempt to influence their conduct.

I therefore adhere to the *New York Times* standard in the case of "public figures" as well as "public officials." It is a manageable standard, readily stated and understood, which also balances to a proper degree the legitimate interests traditionally protected by the law of defamation. . . .

I have no difficulty in concluding that No. 150, Associated Press v. Walker, must be reversed since it is in a clear conflict with *New York Times*. . . .

But No. 37, Curtis Publishing Co. v. Butts, presents an entirely different situation. . . .

[The Chief Justice discussed the failure of the defendants to raise at the trial any First Amendment defense and noted that the decision of the Post to "change its image" in order to boost sagging sales and revenue supported the damage award, especially since the Post refused to investigate the matter further after Butts and his daughter stated that the story was absolutely untrue.]

I am satisfied that the evidence here discloses that degree of reckless disregard for the truth of which we spoke in *New York Times* and *Garrison*. Freedom of the press under the First Amendment does not include absolute license to destroy lives or careers.

[Justice Black, with whom Justice Douglas joined, concurred in the reversal of *Walker* and dissented from the affirmance of *Butts*:]

I think it is time for this Court to abandon New York Times Co. v. Sullivan and adopt the rule to the effect that the First Amendment was intended to leave the press free from the harassment of libel judgments.

[Mr. Justice Brennan, with whom Mr. Justice White joined, concurred in the reversal of *Walker* and dissented from the affirmance of *Butts*. He agreed with the Chief Justice that the evidence in *Butts* supported a jury award for the plaintiff under the *New York Times* rule, but thought it proper "to remand for a new trial since the charge to the jury did not comport with that standard."]

NOTES

1. An embarrassment of constitutional standards? At the end of the day, *Butts* and *Walker* extended the actual malice test of *New York Times* from public officials to public figures. Five members of the Court (Black and Douglas adopting for this purpose the Warren position) rejected the arguments put forward by Harlan, which would have allowed a public figure to override the constitutional defense by showing, in essence, the gross negligence of the defendant. For a criticism of the Harlan position as lacking in "constitutional dimensions," see Kalven, The Reasonable Man and the First Amendment, 1967 Sup. Ct. Rev. 267, 300. "For centuries it has been the experience of Anglo-American law that the truth never catches up with the lie, and it is because it does not that there has been a law of defamation. I simply do not see how the constitutional protection in this area can be rested on the assurance that counterargument will take the sting out of the falsehoods the law is thereby permitting. And if this premise is not persuasive, the whole Harlan edifice tumbles." Does Kalven's argument justify the extension of *New York Times* to public figures, or the return to the common law rules of fair comment for both public officials and public figures?

2. Actual malice. For both public officials and public figures, the Supreme Court has strictly applied its actual malice standard. For example, in St. Amant v. Thompson, 390 U.S. 727, 731-732 (1968), petitioner made a televised political speech in which he charged respondent, a deputy sheriff, with criminal conduct. The Supreme Court assumed that the charges were defamatory and false and that respondent was a public official under *New York Times*, but held that the evidence failed to support respondent's contention that petitioner had acted with reckless disregard of the truth.

It may be said that [the actual malice] test puts a premium on ignorance, encourages the irresponsible publisher not to inquire, and permits the issue to be determined by the defendant's testimony that he published the statement in good faith and unaware of its probable falsity. Concededly the reckless disregard standard may permit recovery in fewer situations than would a rule that publishers must satisfy the standard of the reasonable man or the prudent publisher. But *New York Times* and succeeding cases have emphasized that the stake of the people in public business and the conduct of public officials is so great that neither the defense of truth nor the standard of ordinary care would protect against self-censorship and thus adequately implement First Amendment policies. Neither lies nor false communications serve the ends of the First Amendment, and no one suggests their desirability or further proliferation. But to insure the ascertainment and publication of the truth about public affairs, it is essential that the First Amendment protect some erroneous publications as well as true ones. We adhere to this view and to the line which our cases have drawn between false communications which are protected and those which are not.

The defendant in a defamation action brought by a public official cannot, however, automatically insure a favorable verdict by testifying that he published with a belief that the statements were true. The finder of fact must determine whether the publication was indeed made in good faith. Professions of good faith will be unlikely to prove persuasive, for example, where a story is fabricated by the defendant, is the product of his imagination, or is based wholly on an unverified anonymous telephone call. Nor will they be likely to prevail when the publisher's allegations are so inherently improbable that only a reckless man would have put them in circulation. Likewise, recklessness may be found where there are obvious reasons to doubt the veracity of the informant or the accuracy of his reports.

3. Summary judgments under New York Times. Under *New York Times*, what quantum of evidence must the plaintiff present to survive a motion for summary judgment on the actual malice question? In Anderson v. Liberty Lobby, Inc., 477 U.S. 242, 254-255 (1986), Jack Anderson, the columnist, published three articles about the Liberty Lobby and its key officials that "portrayed the [plaintiffs] as neo-Nazi, anti-Semitic, racist, and fascist." All were public figures. In response to respondents' defamation suit, the defendant moved for summary judgment on the strength of affidavits by Anderson's key researcher that he had spent "substantial time" researching the articles. The precise issue in the case was whether "the clear-and-convincing-evidence requirement [of *New York Times*] must be considered by a court ruling on a motion for summary judgment." The Court, speaking through Justice White, held that it did:

> Just as the "convincing clarity" requirement is relevant in ruling on a motion for directed verdict, it is relevant in ruling on a motion for summary judgment. When determining if a genuine factual issue as to actual malice exists in a libel suit brought by a public figure, a trial judge must bear in mind the actual quantum and quality of proof necessary to support liability under

New York Times. For example, there is no genuine issue if the evidence presented in the opposing affidavits is of insufficient caliber or quantity to allow a rational finder of fact to find actual malice by clear and convincing evidence....

Our holding that the clear-and-convincing standard of proof should be taken into account on summary judgment motions does not denigrate the role of the jury. It by no means authorizes trial on affidavits. Credibility determinations, the weighing of the evidence, and the drawing of legitimate inferences from the facts are jury functions, not those of a judge, whether he is ruling on a motion for summary judgment or for a directed verdict. The evidence of the non-movant is to be believed, and all justifiable inferences are to be drawn in his favor.

The Court then remanded the case to the trial judge to sort out the situation. In separate dissents Justices Brennan and Rehnquist argued that the case should be left to the jury. In their view, using different standards for summary judgment would invade the province of the jury, induce trial judges to conduct exhaustive minitrials before making their decisions, and lead to confusion in the granting and denying of summary judgments.

4. *Discovery on mental state.* The issue of actual malice injects the delicate question of the defendant's mental state into many defamation cases. The modern rules of discovery, moreover, generally give the moving party broad latitude to "obtain discovery regarding any matter, not privileged, that is relevant to the claim or defense of any party" to the litigation. Fed. R. Civ. P. 26(b)(1). In Herbert v. Lando, 441 U.S. 153, 170 (1979), the defendant, an editor of the television show "60 Minutes," urged the court to hold (as was done in the Second Circuit below) that "when a member of the press is alleged to have circulated damaging falsehoods and is sued for injury to the plaintiff's reputation, the plaintiff is barred from inquiring into the editorial process of those responsible for the publication, even though the inquiry would produce evidence material to the proof of a critical element of his cause of action." The Court rejected the claim, in part for the following reasons:

In the first place, it is plain enough that the suggested privilege for the editorial process would constitute a substantial interference with the ability of a defamation plaintiff to establish the ingredients of malice as required by *New York Times*. As respondents would have it, the defendant's reckless disregard of the truth, a critical element, could not be shown by direct evidence through inquiry into the thoughts, opinions and conclusions of the publisher but could be proved only by objective evidence from which the ultimate fact could be inferred. It may be that plaintiffs will rarely be successful in proving awareness of falsehood from the mouth of the defendant himself, but the relevance of answers to such inquiries, which the District Court recognized and the Court of Appeals did not deny, can hardly be doubted. To erect an impenetrable barrier to the plaintiff's use of such evidence on his side of the case is a matter of some substance, particularly when defendants themselves are prone to assert their good-faith belief in the truth of their publications, and libel plaintiffs are required to prove knowing or reckless falsehood with "convincing clarity."

Justice Brennan dissented in part: "I would hold, however, that the First Amendment requires predecisional communication among editors to be protected by an editorial privilege, but that this privilege must yield if a public-figure plaintiff is able to demonstrate to the prima facie satisfaction of a trial judge that the publication in question constitutes defamatory falsehood." Litigation in the case continued for seven more years, ending with a summary judgment for the defendant on the actual malice question. See Herbert v. Lando, 781 F.2d 298 (2d Cir. 1986). On the Supreme Court decision, see generally Franklin, Reflections on *Herbert v. Lando*, 31 Stan. L. Rev. 1035 (1979); Friedenthal, *Herbert v. Lando*: A Note on Discovery, 31 Stan. L. Rev. 1059 (1979).

5. *Public figures in the Supreme Court.* The identification of public officials under the *New York Times* rule is, in general, a straightforward affair. The determination of who counts as a public figure presents, however, a trickier problem. To be sure, there are a host of simple cases: Former public officials, professional athletes, entertainers, and celebrities are treated as public figures (and here the ambiguity begins) most of the time and for most if not all purposes. Since *Butts* and *Walker*, the Supreme Court has frequently wrestled with this question. Thus, in Time, Inc. v. Firestone, 424 U.S. 448 (1976), the Supreme Court held that the wife of "the scion of one of America's wealthier industrial families" was not a public figure even though she held a news conference during a sensational and messy divorce trial. The Supreme Court also held that a research scientist who was awarded William Proxmire's "Golden Fleece" award was not a public figure even though — as the award itself suggests — the plaintiff had been successful in getting federal grant support. Hutchinson v. Proxmire, 443 U.S. 111 (1979). In the companion case of Wolston v. Reader's Digest Association, Inc., 443 U.S. 157 (1979), the plaintiff was listed in Reader's Digest as a Soviet agent along with (among others) Julius and Ethel Rosenberg and his uncle, Jack Soble. In fact, the plaintiff was not a Soviet agent, but had only refused to appear before a grand jury for questioning about his uncle. The Supreme Court, reversing the district court and court of appeals, held that the plaintiff was not a public figure because he was neither a person of general prominence nor had he "thrust himself to the forefront" of a particular public controversy simply because he had fled when pursued by the government. See also the discussion in *Gertz, infra* at 1116.

6. *Public figures in the lower courts.* The lower courts have also joined the chase. Persons who had former connections with public events have generally been held to be public figures. Thus, in Meeropol v. Nizer, 381 F. Supp. 29 (S.D.N.Y. 1974), Judge Tyler held that the two sons of Julius and Ethel Rosenberg were public figures, notwithstanding the fact that they "later may have renounced the public spotlight by changing their name to Meeropol," because "as children they were the subject of considerable public attention." Perry v. Columbia Broadcasting System, Inc., 499 F.2d 797 (7th Cir. 1974), held that plaintiff, who as Stepin Fetchit was a leading black actor and movie star in the 1920s and 1930s, was a public figure.

In addition, a long list of persons, large insurance companies, professional football players, navy officers during the Vietnam War, Johnny Carson, local mobsters, belly dancers, Nobel Prize winners, and debt collection agencies under public investigation have all been treated as public figures on a "limited basis" for those aspects of their conduct subjected to public scrutiny and review. In Reuber v. Food Chemical News, Inc., 925 F.2d 703, 706, 708 (4th Cir. 1991), the plaintiff was a research scientist at the National Cancer Institute who "disseminated his own research and took other actions which created the misleading impression that the NCI had reversed its official position that the pesticide malathion was a non-carcinogen." A letter from his supervisor rebuking his research and statements was published by the defendant. The Fourth Circuit held that the plaintiff was "a limited purpose" public figure because he had "injected" himself into the public arena by his previous publications on the problem. That element of injection has proved critical. In Khawar v. Globe International, Inc., 965 P.2d 696 (Cal. 1998), the plaintiff, who stood next to Robert Kennedy before he was assassinated was not a limited figure accused of doing the killing solely because he stood in the wrong place at the wrong time. He neither injected himself into the controversy nor had the effective means to reply to a defamatory newspaper account.

An intermediate case is Lohrenz v. Donnelly, 350 F.3d 1272, 1280-1281 (D.C. Cir. 2003). Carey Lohrenz was one of the first female combat pilots in the United States Navy. The defendant Elaine Donnelly had formed and served as president of the Center for Military Readiness. She used that organization to attack the plaintiff as "unqualified" to fly and the general program to include women as combat pilots as "politically driven." In consequence of these attacks, Lohrenz claimed that she was removed from flying F-14 combat jets, even though prior to the attacks she had received "above-average" ratings. Rogers, J., held that the District Court had rightly entered summary judgment against the plaintiff on the ground that she was a "voluntary limited-purpose public figure" because she was "well aware of the public controversy of women in combat roles." By choosing to fly F-14s "Lt. Lohrenz assumed the risk that if she succeeded in qualifying for a combat assignment . . . she would find herself at the center of the controversy as a result of the special prominence that she and only one other woman combat pilot attained upon receiving their F-14 assignments. That Lt. Lohrenz might have preferred a combat assignment that did not place her in the center of the public controversy is legally irrelevant."

See generally R. Sack, Sack on Defamation chs. 5-6 (3d ed. 2003); R. Smolla, Law of Defamation §2 (2d ed. 2003); Schauer, Public Figures, 25 Wm. & Mary L. Rev. 905 (1984); Comment, Defamation Law: Public Figures — Who Are They?, 45 Baylor L. Rev. 955 (1993).

2. *Private Parties*

Gertz v. Robert Welch, Inc.
418 U.S. 323 (1974)

[Petitioner, a reputable attorney, was retained by the Nelson family to represent them in a civil action against Nuccio, a Chicago policeman who had previously been convicted of second-degree murder for the death of young Nelson. As counsel for the family, petitioner attended the coroner's inquest into Nelson's death and initiated actions for damages, but he neither discussed Officer Nuccio with the press nor played any part in the criminal proceeding.

Respondent published *American Opinion*, a periodical of the John Birch Society. As part of its campaign to warn America of a communist conspiracy to discredit local law enforcement agencies, respondent published an article entitled "Frame-Up: Richard Nuccio and the War On Police" that purported to show that Nuccio was innocent, that his prosecution was a communist "frame-up," and that petitioner was an "architect of the frame-up." The article also falsely charged that Gertz was a communist who had engaged in communist activities. The managing editor of *American Opinion* had not independently investigated the article's charges but had relied on its author's "extensive research." The article was accompanied by a photograph of petitioner over the caption "Elmer Gertz of Red Guild harasses Nuccio."

Gertz filed a libel action in federal district court and won a jury verdict for $50,000. The court refused to enter judgment on the verdict on the ground that the *New York Times* standard protects discussion of any public issue without regard to the status of the person defamed. The court of appeals affirmed, adding that petitioner had failed to show that respondent acted with actual malice as defined by *New York Times*, "mere proof of failure to investigate, without more" being insufficient to establish reckless disregard for the truth. 471 F.2d 801 (7th Cir. 1972). The Supreme Court reversed.]

POWELL, J. . . . The principal issue in this case is whether a newspaper or broadcaster that publishes defamatory falsehoods about an individual who is neither a public official nor a public figure may claim a constitutional privilege against liability for the injury inflicted by those statements. The Court considered this question on the rather different set of facts presented in Rosenbloom v. Metromedia, Inc., 403 U.S. 29 (1971)....

The eight Justices who participated in *Rosenbloom* announced their views in five separate opinions, none of which commanded more than three votes....

[The Court then reviewed *New York Times*, *Butts*, and *Walker*, and continued:]

In his opinion for the plurality in Rosenbloom v. Metromedia, Inc., 403 U.S. 29 (1971), Mr. Justice Brennan took the *New York Times* privilege one step further. He concluded that its protection should extend to defamatory falsehoods relating to private persons if the statements concerned matters of general or public interest. He abjured the suggested distinction between public officials and public figures on the one hand and private individuals on the other. He focused instead on society's interest in learning about certain issues: "If a matter is a subject of public or general interest, it cannot suddenly become less so merely because a private individual is involved, or because in some sense the individual did not 'voluntarily' choose to become involved." Id., at 43. Thus, under the plurality opinion, a private citizen involuntarily associated with a matter of general interest has no recourse for injury to his reputation unless he can satisfy the demanding requirements of the *New York Times* test.

[The Court then examined the other opinions in *Rosenbloom.*]

We begin with the common ground. Under the First Amendment there is no such thing as a false idea. However pernicious an opinion may seem, we depend for its correction not on the conscience of judges and juries but on the competition of other ideas. But there is no constitutional value in false statements of fact. Neither the intentional lie nor the careless error materially advances society's interest in "uninhibited, robust, and wide-open" debate on public issues. They belong to that category of utterances which "are no essential part of any exposition of ideas, and are of such slight social value as a step to truth that any benefit that may be derived from them is clearly outweighed by the social interest in order and morality." Chaplinsky v. New Hampshire, 315 U.S. 568, 572 (1942).

[Powell, J., reviewed the reasons why *New York Times* calls for "breathing room" and the avoidance of self-censorship in order to promote open debate.]

The need to avoid self-censorship by the news media is, however, not the only societal value at issue. If it were, this Court would have embraced long ago the view that publishers and broadcasters enjoy an unconditional and indefeasible immunity from liability for defamation. Such a rule would, indeed, obviate the fear that the prospect of civil liability for injurious falsehood might dissuade a timorous press from the effective exercise of

First Amendment freedoms. Yet absolute protection for the communications media requires a total sacrifice of the competing value served by the law of defamation.

The legitimate state interest underlying the law of libel is the compensation of individuals for the harm inflicted on them by defamatory falsehood. We would not lightly require the State to abandon this purpose, for, as Mr. Justice Stewart has reminded us, the individual's right to the protection of his own good name "reflects no more than our basic concept of the essential dignity and worth of every human being—a concept at the root of any decent system of ordered liberty. . . ." Rosenblatt v. Baer, 383 U.S. 75, 92 (1966) (concurring opinion).

Some tension necessarily exists between the need for a vigorous and uninhibited press and the legitimate interest in redressing wrongful injury. . . . In our continuing effort to define the proper accommodation between these competing concerns, we have been especially anxious to assure to the freedoms of speech and press that "breathing space" essential to their fruitful exercise. To that end this Court has extended a measure of strategic protection to defamatory falsehood.

The *New York Times* standard defines the level of constitutional protection appropriate to the context of defamation of a public person. . . . We think that [the decisions under *New York Times*] are correct, but we do not find their holdings justified solely by reference to the interest of the press and broadcast media in immunity from liability. Rather, we believe that the *New York Times* rule states an accommodation between this concern and the limited state interest present in the context of libel actions brought by public persons. For the reasons stated below, we conclude that the state interest in compensating injury to the reputation of private individuals requires that a different rule should obtain with respect to them.

Theoretically, of course, the balance between the needs of the press and the individual's claim to compensation for wrongful injury might be struck on a case-by-case basis. . . . But this approach would lead to unpredictable results and uncertain expectations, and it could render our duty to supervise the lower courts unmanageable. Because an ad hoc resolution of the competing interests at stake in each particular case is not feasible, we must lay down broad rules of general application. Such rules necessarily treat alike various cases involving differences as well as similarities. Thus it is often true that not all of the considerations which justify adoption of a given rule will obtain in each particular case decided under its authority.

With that caveat we have no difficulty in distinguishing among defamation plaintiffs. The first remedy of any victim of defamation is self-help—using available opportunities to contradict the lie or correct the error and thereby to minimize its adverse impact on reputation. Public officials and public figures usually enjoy significantly greater access to the channels of effective communication and hence have a more realistic opportunity to counteract false statements than private individuals normally enjoy. Private individuals are therefore more vulnerable to injury, and the state interest in protecting them is correspondingly greater.

More important than the likelihood that private individuals will lack effective opportunities for rebuttal, there is a compelling normative consideration underlying the distinction between public and private defamation plaintiffs. An individual who decides to seek governmental office must accept certain necessary consequences of that involvement in public affairs. He runs the risk of closer public scrutiny than might otherwise be the case. And society's interest in the officers of government is not strictly limited to the formal discharge of official duties. . . .

Those classed as public figures stand in a similar position. Hypothetically, it may be possible for someone to become a public figure through no purposeful action of his own, but the instances of truly involuntary public figures must be exceedingly rare. For the most part those who attain this status have assumed roles of especial prominence in the affairs of society. Some occupy positions of such persuasive power and influence that they are deemed public figures for all purposes. More commonly, those classed as public figures have thrust themselves to the forefront of particular public controversies in order to influence the resolution of the issues involved. In either event, they invite attention and comment.

Even if the foregoing generalities do not obtain in every instance, the communications media are entitled to act on the assumption that public officials and public figures have voluntarily exposed themselves to increased risk of injury from defamatory falsehood concerning them. No such assumption is justified with respect to a private individual. He has not accepted public office or assumed an "influential role in ordering society." Curtis Publishing Co. v. Butts, (Warren, C.J., concurring in result). He has relinquished no part of his interest in the protection of his own good name, and consequently he has a more compelling call on the courts for redress of injury inflicted by defamatory falsehood. Thus, private individuals are not only more vulnerable to injury than public officials and public figures; they are also more deserving of recovery. . . .

We hold that, so long as they do not impose liability without fault, the States may define for themselves the appropriate standard of liability for a publisher or broadcaster of defamatory falsehood injurious to a private individual. This approach provides a more equitable boundary between the competing concerns involved here. It recognizes the strength of the legitimate state interest in compensating private individuals for wrongful injury to reputation, yet shields the press and broadcast media from the rigors of strict liability for defamation. At least this conclusion obtains where, as here, the substance of the defamatory statement "makes substantial danger to reputation apparent." This phrase places in perspective the conclusion we announce today. Our inquiry would involve considerations somewhat different from those discussed above if a State purported to condition civil liability on a factual misstatement whose content did not warn a reasonably prudent editor or broadcaster of its defamatory potential. Such a case is not now before us, and we intimate no view as to its proper resolution.

[The Court then stated that the state interest in the protection of reputation "extends no further than compensation for actual injury."] For the reasons stated below, we hold that the States may not permit recovery of presumed or punitive damages, at least when liability is not based on a showing of knowledge of falsity or reckless disregard for the truth.

The common law of defamation is an oddity of tort law, for it allows recovery of purportedly compensatory damages without evidence of actual loss. Under the traditional rules pertaining to actions for libel, the existence of injury is presumed from the fact of publication. Juries may award substantial sums as compensation for supposed damage to reputation without any proof that such harm actually occurred. The largely uncontrolled discretion of juries to award damages where there is no loss unnecessarily compounds the potential of any system of liability for defamatory falsehood to inhibit the vigorous exercise of First Amendment freedoms. Additionally, the doctrine of presumed damages invites juries to punish unpopular opinion rather than to compensate individuals for injury sustained by the publication of a false fact. More to the point, the States have no substantial interest in securing for plaintiffs such as this petitioner gratuitous awards of money damages far in excess of any actual injury.

We would not, of course, invalidate state law simply because we doubt its wisdom, but here we are attempting to reconcile state law with a competing interest grounded in the constitutional command of the First Amendment. It is therefore appropriate to require that state remedies for defamatory falsehood reach no farther than is necessary to protect the legitimate interest involved. It is necessary to restrict defamation plaintiffs who do not prove knowledge of falsity or reckless disregard for the truth to compensation for actual injury. We need not define "actual injury," as trial courts have wide experience in framing appropriate jury instructions in tort actions. Suffice it to say that actual injury is not limited to out-of-pocket loss. Indeed, the more customary types of actual harm inflicted by defamatory falsehood include impairment of reputation and standing in the community, personal humiliation, and mental anguish and suffering. Of course, juries must be limited by appropriate instructions, and all awards must be supported by competent evidence concerning the injury, although there need be no evidence which assigns an actual dollar value to the injury.

We also find no justification for allowing awards of punitive damages against publishers and broadcasters held liable under state-defined standards of liability for defamation. In most jurisdictions jury discretion over the amounts awarded is limited only by the gentle rule that they not be excessive. Consequently, juries assess punitive damages in wholly unpredictable amounts bearing no necessary relation to the actual harm caused. And they remain free to use their discretion selectively to punish expressions of unpopular views. Like the doctrine of presumed damages, jury discretion to award punitive damages unnecessarily exacerbates the danger of media self-censorship, but, unlike the former rule, punitive damages are wholly irrelevant to the state interest that justifies a negligence standard for private defamation actions. They are not compensation for injury. Instead, they are private fines levied by civil juries to punish reprehensible conduct and to deter its future occurrence. In short, the private defamation plaintiff who establishes liability under a less demanding standard than that stated by *New York Times* may recover only such damages as are sufficient to compensate him for actual injury.

[The Court rejected respondent's argument that plaintiff was a public official or public figure. The petitioner was not a public official even though he appeared at the inquest or had once served on a city housing committee; nor was he a public official even though he was a lawyer and therefore an officer of the court. Likewise, his general activities in community and professional affairs did not give him any "general fame or notoriety in the community" sufficient to make him a public figure.

Justice Blackmun concurred for two reasons. First, he thought that the Court's position gave the press sufficient protection against punitive damages. And second, although he supported the *Rosenbloom* plurality, he voted with the Court to make a majority for the Court "to come to rest in the defamation area."

Chief Justice Burger dissented, voting to reinstate the jury's verdict in favor of Gertz.

Justice Douglas dissented, for the reasons stated by Mr. Justice Black in *New York Times*.

Justice Brennan dissented, for the reasons stated in his *Rosenbloom* opinion.]

WHITE, J., dissenting. For some 200 years—from the very founding of the Nation—the law of defamation and right of the ordinary citizen to recover for false publication injurious to his reputation have been almost exclusively the business of state courts and legislatures. . . .

But now, using that Amendment as the chosen instrument, the Court, in a few printed pages, has federalized major aspects of libel law by declaring unconstitutional in important respects the prevailing defamation law in all or most of the 50 States. That result is accomplished by requiring the plaintiff in each and every defamation action to prove not only the defendant's culpability beyond his act of publishing defamatory material but also actual damage to reputation resulting from the publication. Moreover, punitive damages may not be recovered by showing malice in the traditional sense of ill will; knowing falsehood or reckless disregard of the truth will now be required.

[Justice White then reviewed the 1938 Restatement of Torts on defamation.]

The Court proceeds as though it were writing on tabula rasa and suggests that it must mediate between two unacceptable choices — on the one hand, the rigors of the *New York Times* rule which the Court thinks would give insufficient recognition to the interest of the private plaintiff, and, on the other hand, the prospect of imposing "liability without fault" on the press and others who are charged with defamatory utterances. Totally ignoring history and settled First Amendment law, the Court purports to arrive at an "equitable compromise," rejecting both what it considers faultless liability and *New York Times* malice, but insisting on some intermediate degree of fault. Of course, the Court necessarily discards the contrary judgment arrived at in the 50 States that the reputation interest of the private citizen is deserving of considerably more protection.

The Court evinces a deep-seated antipathy to "liability without fault." But this catch-phrase has no talismanic significance and is almost meaningless in this context where the Court appears to be addressing those libels and slanders that are defamatory on their face and where the publisher is no doubt aware from the nature of the material that it would be inherently damaging to reputation. He publishes notwithstanding, knowing that he will inflict injury. With this knowledge, he must intend to inflict that injury, his excuse being that he is privileged to do so — that he has published the truth. But as it turns out, what he has circulated to the public is a very damaging falsehood. Is he nevertheless "faultless"? Perhaps it can be said that the mistake about his defense was made in good faith, but the fact remains that it is he who launched the publication knowing that it could ruin a reputation.

In these circumstances, the law has heretofore put the risk of falsehood on the publisher where the victim is a private citizen and no grounds of special privilege are invoked. The Court would now shift this risk to the victim, even though he has done nothing to invite the calumny, is wholly innocent of fault, and is helpless to avoid his injury. I doubt that jurisprudential resistance to liability without fault is sufficient ground for employing the First Amendment to revolutionize the law of libel, and in my view, that body of legal rules poses no realistic threat to the press and its service to the public. The press today is vigorous and robust. To me, it is quite incredible to suggest that threats of libel suits from private citizens are causing the press to refrain from publishing the truth. I know of no hard facts to support that proposition, and the Court furnishes none.

[Justice White concluded that a concentrated communications industry was well-equipped to cope with the common law rules of defamation, and attacked the Court for its rejection of the common law rules on actual and punitive damages.]

NOTES

1. The negligence principle under Gertz. What are the contours of the negligence standard under *Gertz*? May the plaintiff invoke res ipsa loquitur, given the defendant's exclusive access to the preparation of the story? Is there a presumption of negligence if a story is defamatory of the plaintiff on its face? Is compliance with standard reporting practices a defense against negligence actions?

Some sense of the height of the negligence barrier can be gleaned from the subsequent history of *Gertz*. On retrial, the jury awarded the plaintiff $100,000 in compensatory damages and $300,000 in punitive damages, sums far in excess of those awarded in the original action. On appeal, in Gertz v. Robert Welch Inc., 680 F.2d 527 (7th Cir. 1982), both elements of the award were upheld over a number of objections regarding (1) the proof of actual malice, (2) the ability of the plaintiff to relitigate the malice question, and (3) the clarity of the instructions on both actual and punitive damages.

2. Presumed damages after Gertz. In Dun & Bradstreet, Inc. v. Greenmoss Builders, Inc., 472 U.S. 749, 760-761 (1985), the defendant Dun & Bradstreet (D&B) issued a credit report on the plaintiff to several of its customers that stated that Greenmoss had filed for voluntary bankruptcy. The report had been prepared by a 17-year-old high school student who had confused the bankruptcy petition of several of Greenmoss's former employees with the bankruptcy of the firm itself. The report, therefore, gave a highly inaccurate summary of the firm's financial position. When Greenmoss found out about the error, it asked D&B to send out an immediate correction and to give Greenmoss a list of the clients to whom the report had been sent. D&B promised only to look into the matter; a week later it sent to the five subscribers who had received the original report a correction letter, which noted the error in the earlier report, but did not give a complete appraisal of Greenmoss's actual financial position. When Greenmoss again protested that the notice was inaccurate, D&B refused to take any further steps. Greenmoss sued for defamation in Vermont State Court. At the trial D&B's employee testified that, although they routinely verified information with the firm that was the subject of the report, no verification had been attempted in this particular case. The jury awarded $50,000 in presumed damages and $300,000 in punitive damages. The Vermont Supreme Court affirmed the judgment below noting that *Gertz* was limited to media defendants, and did not include credit reporting firms.

On appeal, the Supreme Court, speaking through Justice Powell, addressed two questions. First, whether the presumed and punitive damage rule in *Gertz* applied "where the defamatory statements do not involve matters of public concern." Second, whether these statements were of public concern.

On the first question, Powell first observed that private speech poses no threat to the "free and robust" debate of public issues or to questions of self-government, and continued:

> In *Gertz*, we found that the state interest in awarding presumed and punitive damages was not "substantial" in view of their effect on speech at the core of First Amendment concern. This interest, however, *is* "substantial" relative to the incidental effect these remedies may have on speech of significantly less constitutional interest. The rationale of the common-law rules has been the experience and judgment of history that "proof of actual damage will be impossible in a great many cases where, from the character of the defamatory words and the circumstances of publication, it is all but certain that serious harm has resulted in fact." W. Prosser, The Law of Torts, §112 p. 765 (4th ed. 1971). As a result, courts for centuries have allowed juries to presume that some damage occurred from many defamatory utterances and publications. This rule furthers the state interest in providing remedies for defamation by ensuring that those remedies are effective. In light of the reduced constitutional value of speech involving no matters of public concern, we hold that the state interest adequately supports awards of presumed and punitive damages — even absent a showing of "actual malice."

The Court then held that the credit report was not directed to a public issue. "It was speech solely in the individual interest of the speaker and its specific business audience."

The Court was badly fractured on the question; only three justices (Powell, Rehnquist, and O'Connor) adopted this middle course. Two justices (Burger and White) concurred in the result. Justice White concluded his long opinion as follows: "The question before us is whether *Gertz* is to be applied in this case. For either of two reasons, I believe that it should not. First, I am unreconciled to the *Gertz* holding and believe that it should be overruled. Second, as Justice Powell indicates, the defamatory publication in this case does not deal with a matter of public importance." The dissent of the four remaining justices took exactly the opposite tack and urged that the speech involved in this case deserved explicit constitutional protection. "The credit reporting at issue here surely involves a subject matter of sufficient public concern to require the comprehensive protections of *Gertz*. Were this speech appropriately characterized as a matter of only private concern, moreover, the elimination of the *Gertz* restrictions on presumed and punitive damages would still violate basic First Amendment requirements."

3. *State law responses to* Gertz. *Gertz* treats the negligence standard as the minimum threshold in damage cases brought by private parties, but allows states to impose stringent requirements on plaintiffs. Nearly 40 states and the District of Columbia have at present chosen to follow the negligence standard of liability in cases that involve a suit by private figures against media defendants on issues of public concern, with only four states — Alaska, Colorado, Indiana, and New Jersey — requiring that the plaintiff prove

actual malice. See R. Smolla, Law of Defamation §§3.30-3.31 (2d ed. 2003). In addition, after *Dun & Bradstreet*, states may be able to return to a strict liability standard when private plaintiffs sue on matters of no public concern, although some states have decided to apply *Gertz* to nonmedia as well as media defendants. See, e.g., Jacron Sales Co. v. Sindorf, 350 A.2d 688 (Md. 1976). Massachusetts, fearing "excessive and unbridled jury verdicts," abolished punitive damage actions after *Gertz* "in any defamation action, on any state of proof, whether based in negligence or reckless or wilful conduct." Stone v. Essex County Newspapers, Inc., 330 N.E.2d 161 (Mass. 1975).

Philadelphia Newspapers v. Hepps
475 U.S. 767 (1986)

O'CONNOR, J. This case requires us once more to "struggl[e] . . . to define the proper accommodation between the law of defamation and the freedoms of speech and press protected by the First Amendment." In *Gertz*, the Court held that a private figure who brings a suit for defamation cannot recover without some showing that the media defendant was at fault in publishing the statements at issue. Here, we hold that, at least where a newspaper publishes speech of public concern, a private-figure plaintiff cannot recover damages without also showing that the statements at issue are false.

I

[The defendants published five stories between May 1975 and May 1976 about Hepps and the corporation of which he was principal stockholder. The stories claimed that they had links to organized crime and had used those connections "to influence the State's governmental processes, both legislative and administrative." The trial judge held that the plaintiff bore the burden of proving falsity, as distinguished from fault, but refused to issue any instructions on the whether plaintiff could draw any inference of falsity from the defendant's reliance on Pennsylvania's shield law, 42 Pa. Cons. Stat. §5942(a) (1982), which provides: "No person . . . employed by any newspaper of general circulation . . . or any radio or television station, or any magazine of general circulation, . . . shall be required to disclose the source of any information procured or obtained by such person, in any legal proceeding, trial or investigation before any government unit."]

[The Pennsylvania Supreme Court] viewed *Gertz* as simply requiring the plaintiff to show fault in actions for defamation. It concluded that a showing of fault did not require a showing of falsity, held that to place the burden of showing truth on the defendant did not unconstitutionally inhibit free

debate, and remanded the case for a new trial. We noted probable jurisdiction, and now reverse.. . .

II

[An extensive summary of *New York Times, Gertz,* and *Dun & Bradstreet* is
omitted.]

Our opinions to date have chiefly treated the necessary showings of fault
rather than of falsity. Nonetheless, as one might expect given the language
of the Court in *New York Times,* a public-figure plaintiff must show the falsity
of the statements at issue in order to prevail on a suit for defamation. . . .

Here, as in *Gertz,* the plaintiff is a private figure and the newspaper
articles are of public concern. In *Gertz,* as in *New York Times,* the common-
law rule was superseded by a constitutional rule. We believe that the common law's rule on falsity — that the defendant must bear the burden of
proving truth — must similarly fall here to a constitutional requirement
that the plaintiff bear the burden of showing falsity, as well as fault, before
recovering damages.

There will always be instances when the factfinding process will be unable
to resolve conclusively whether the speech is true or false; it is in those cases
that the burden of proof is dispositive. Under a rule forcing the plaintiff to
bear the burden of showing falsity, there will be some cases in which
plaintiffs cannot meet their burden despite the fact that the speech is in fact
false. The plaintiff's suit will fail despite the fact that, in some abstract sense,
the suit is meritorious. Similarly, under an alternative rule placing the
burden of showing truth on defendants, there would be some cases in which
defendants could not bear their burden despite the fact that the speech is in
fact true. Those suits would succeed despite the fact that, in some abstract
sense, those suits are unmeritorious. Under either rule, then, the outcome
of the suit will sometimes be at variance with the outcome that we would
desire if all speech were either demonstrably true or demonstrably false.

This dilemma stems from the fact that the allocation of the burden of proof
will determine liability for some speech that is true and some that is false, but
all of such speech is *unknowably* true or false. Because the burden of proof is
the deciding factor only when the evidence is ambiguous, we cannot know
how much of the speech affected by the allocation of the burden of proof is
true and how much is false. In a case presenting a configuration of speech
and plaintiff like the one we face here, and where the scales are in such an
uncertain balance, we believe that the Constitution requires us to tip them in
favor of protecting true speech. To ensure that true speech on matters of
public concern is not deterred, we hold that the common-law presumption
that defamatory speech is false cannot stand when a plaintiff seeks damages
against a media defendant for speech of public concern. . . .

We recognize that requiring the plaintiff to show falsity will insulate from liability some speech that is false, but unprovably so.... To provide "'breathing space'" for true speech on matters of public concern, the Court has been willing to insulate even demonstrably false speech from liability, and has imposed additional requirements of fault upon the plaintiff in a suit for defamation. We therefore do not break new ground here in insulating speech that is not even demonstrably false.

We note that our decision adds only marginally to the burdens that the plaintiff must already bear as a result of our earlier decisions in the law of defamation. The plaintiff must show fault. A jury is obviously more likely to accept a plaintiff's contention that the defendant was at fault in publishing the statements at issue if convinced that the relevant statements were false. As a practical matter, then, evidence offered by plaintiffs on the publisher's fault in adequately investigating the truth of the published statements will generally encompass evidence of the falsity of the matters asserted.

We recognize that the plaintiff's burden in this case is weightier because of Pennsylvania's "shield" law, which allows employees of the media to refuse to divulge their sources. But we do not have before us here the question of the permissible reach of such laws. Indeed, we do not even know the precise reach of Pennsylvania's statute. The trial judge refused to give any instructions to the jury as to whether it could, or should, draw an inference adverse to the defendant from the defendant's decision to use the shield law rather than to present affirmative evidence of the truthfulness of some of the sources. That decision of the trial judge was not addressed by Pennsylvania's highest court, nor was it appealed to this Court. In the situation before us, we are unconvinced that the State's shield law requires a different constitutional standard than would prevail in the absence of such a law.

For the reasons stated above, the judgment of the Pennsylvania Supreme Court is reversed, and the case is remanded for further proceedings not inconsistent with this opinion.

JUSTICE BRENNAN, with whom JUSTICE BLACKMUN joins, concurring.... I write separately only to note that, while the Court reserves the question whether the rule it announces applies to non-media defendants, I adhere to my view that such a distinction is "irreconcilable with the fundamental First Amendment principle that '[t]he inherent worth of ... speech in terms of its capacity for informing the public does not depend upon the identity of the source, whether corporation, association, union, or individual.'" Dun & Bradstreet, Inc. v. Greenmoss Builders, Inc. (Brennan, J., dissenting).

JUSTICE STEVENS, with whom THE CHIEF JUSTICE, JUSTICE WHITE, and JUSTICE REHNQUIST join, dissenting. The issue the Court resolves today will make a difference in only one category of cases — those in which a private individual can prove that he was libeled by a defendant who was at least negligent. For unless such a plaintiff can overcome the burden imposed by

Gertz v. Robert Welch, Inc., he cannot recover regardless of how the burden of proof on the issue of truth or falsity is allocated. By definition, therefore, the only litigants — and the only publishers — who will benefit from today's decision are those who act negligently or maliciously. . . .

I do not agree that our precedents require a private individual to bear the risk that a defamatory statement — uttered either with a mind toward assassinating his good name or with careless indifference to that possibility — cannot be proven false. By attaching no weight to the state's interest in protecting the private individual's good name, the Court has reached a pernicious result.

NOTES

1. *Truth*. *Hepps* is at sharp variance with the uniform common law view requiring the defendant to demonstrate the truth of his statements. Once the plaintiff had to establish the invasion of a protected interest, the defendant had to show that the invasion was indeed "justified." Historically, many common-law jurisdictions placed an additional obstacle in the defendant's path by treating an unsuccessful effort to demonstrate truth as a republication of the libel, entitling plaintiffs to additional damages. See Corabi v. Curtis Publishing Co., 273 A.2d 899 (Pa. 1971).

Wholly apart from the Constitution, however, there are good reasons to question the common law allocation of the burden of proof, see *supra* at 1072. Plaintiff has better access to information concerning her own conduct and therefore is in an excellent position to rebut the charges against her. Alternatively, placing the burden on the plaintiff could be justified on the ground that no one should be allowed to claim injury to reputation when a favorable reputation was undeserved in the first place.

2. *Reform of defamation law*. The initial reaction to *New York Times* was largely celebratory, not only for the boost that it gave to the civil rights movement, but also because of the implicit judgment that the actual malice rule could undo the litigation logjam in defamation cases. But starting in the 1970s and working through the 1980s, defamation suits resulted in mammoth struggles whose movements to and fro were avidly covered by the press. The expanded pace of civil litigation galvanized pressure for legislative action. During the 1980s, the *New York Times* actual malice rule came under attack from *both* sides. For the plaintiffs the chief grievance was that the actual malice rule allowed a defendant to escape liability even when admittedly false statements worked substantial damage to reputation. One traditional function of libel law — to provide official vindication to the plaintiff's reputation — is sidetracked by a motive-based privilege that prevents the plaintiff from setting the record straight. On the media side, the main concern is with the enormous cost and expense of

defending a defamation action. Here, ironically, the actual malice rule may well be part of the problem. Although it reduces the number of cases that can be brought, it increases the uncertainty of the outcome and the size of any potential recovery in successful suits since proof of actual malice might easily justify claims for punitive damages, with large and erratic awards. Litigation costs could easily escalate, as they did in the twin great cases of the 1980s, Sharon v. Time, Inc., 599 F. Supp. 538 (S.D.N.Y. 1984), and Westmoreland v. CBS, 10 Media L. Rep. 2417 (S.D.N.Y. 1984). Oddly enough, these titanic struggles have not been repeated during the last generation, and the Supreme Court has not heard an important defamation case in over 15 years. In a word, media defendants have proved so successful in blockbuster cases that few are brought today.

The current lull in defamation cases has reduced the discussions over the proper approach to legal reform. But when the issue was hot, a wide range of alternatives received serious public attention. One extreme suggestion was to abolish all defamation actions by public officials and public figures. A more modest version of the same idea was to prohibit punitive damages in all suits brought by public officials and public figures against media defendants. In this vein, see Lewis, *New York Times v. Sullivan* Reconsidered: Time to Return to "The Central Meaning of the First Amendment," 83 Colum. L. Rev. 603 (1983), advocating among other changes more frequent use of summary judgments, special verdicts, and a prohibition on recovery for mental anguish and punitive damages.

In the opposite direction, many scholars urged that the plaintiff be allowed to obtain a declaratory judgment on the question of truth or falsity without proof of actual malice, but only (under some versions of the proposal) by first waiving any right to damages. A declaratory judgment was achieved in a backhand manner in the *Sharon* case, in which, in response to specific questions propounded by special verdicts, the jury decided both that Time's statements were wrong and that the error was not actuated by actual malice. What is the reputational effect of such a verdict on Time?

For various detailed proposals for reform, see R. Adler, Reckless Disregard (1986); R. Bezanson, G. Cranberg, & J. Soloski, Libel Law and the Press: Myth and Reality ch. 8 (1987).

14

PRIVACY

SECTION A. INTRODUCTION

By all accounts the protection of individual interests in privacy is one of the essential tasks of any civilized order. Before the late nineteenth century, the tort law supplied no remedy for the invasion of privacy as such, but relied on other legal devices to maintain privacy protection. Thus, the basic rules of private ownership, backed by the common law of trespass to land, allowed individuals to wall off their lands or buildings to preserve some measure of privacy. In addition, confidentiality arrangements, both by explicit agreement and common practice, allowed people to keep private sensitive information and records that they shared with physicians, employers, and insurers. But the great question in this area is the extent to which these traditional tort and contract rules can take up the slack on the full range of privacy issues. Historically, the creation of a separate and distinct tort of privacy was long in coming. However, starting in the late nineteenth century, both commentators and judges began to move on this issue. The pattern of development was twofold from the outset. On one hand, the protection of the privacy interest was viewed defensively, whereby it allowed individuals to ward off the invasions of strangers. Elsewhere, privacy protection served the opposite purpose, which was to allow individuals the exclusive right to the commercial use of their name and likeness, in what has come to be called the right of publicity.

This chapter explores the interrelationship among these various themes. Section B traces the historical evolution of the privacy right from the classic article of Brandeis and Warren through the early development of the doctrine. The next four sections take up the four standard heads of privacy analysis that were articulated by Prosser in 1960: intrusion upon seclusion, public disclosure of embarrassing past facts, false light, and the right of publicity, that is, the right of each individual to control the use of his or her personal name or likeness.

SECTION B.   HISTORICAL BACKGROUND

Warren and Brandeis, The Right to Privacy
4 Harv. L. Rev. 193, 193-197 (1890)

That the individual shall have full protection in person and in property is a principle as old as the common law; but it has been found necessary from time to time to define anew the exact nature and extent of such protection. Political, social, and economic changes entail the recognition of new rights, and the common law, in its eternal youth, grows to meet the demands of society. Thus, in very early times, the law gave a remedy only for physical interference with life and property, for trespasses vi et armis. Then the "right to life" served only to protect the subject from battery in its various forms; liberty meant freedom from actual restraint; and the right to property secured to the individual his lands and his cattle. Later, there came a recognition of man's spiritual nature, of his feelings and his intellect. Gradually the scope of these legal rights broadened; and now the right to life has come to mean the right to enjoy life, — the right to be let alone; the right to liberty secures the exercise of extensive civil privileges; and the term "property" has grown to comprise every form of possession — intangible, as well as tangible.

Thus, with the recognition of the legal value of sensations, the protection against actual bodily injury was extended to prohibit mere attempts to do such injury; that is, the putting another in fear of such injury. From the action of battery grew that of assault. Much later there came a qualified protection of the individual against offensive noises and odors, against dust and smoke, and excessive vibration. The law of nuisance was developed. So regard for human emotions soon extended the scope of personal immunity beyond the body of the individual. His reputation, the standing among his fellow-men, was considered, and the law of slander and libel arose. Man's family relations became a part of the legal conception of his life, and the alienation of a wife's affections was held remediable. Occasionally the law halted, — as in its refusal to recognize the intrusion by seduction upon the honor of the family. But even here the demands of society were met. A mean fiction, the action per quod servitium amisit [through which the wife's services have been lost], was resorted to, and by allowing damages for injury to the parents' feelings, an adequate remedy was ordinarily afforded. Similar to the expansion of the right to life was the growth of the legal conception of property. From corporeal property arose the incorporeal rights issuing out of it; and then there opened the wide realm of intangible property, in the products and processes of the mind, as works of literature and art, goodwill, trade secrets, and trademarks.

This development of the law was inevitable. The intense intellectual and emotional life, and the heightening of sensations which came with the advance of civilization, made it clear to men that only a part of the pain, pleasure, and profit of life lay in physical things. Thoughts, emotions, and sensations demanded legal recognition, and the beautiful capacity for growth which characterizes the common law enabled the judges to afford the requisite protection, without the interposition of the legislature.

Recent inventions and business methods call attention to the next step which must be taken for the protection of the person, and for securing to the individual what Judge Cooley calls the right "to be let alone." Instantaneous photographs and newspaper enterprise have invaded the sacred precincts of private and domestic life; and numerous mechanical devices threaten to make good the prediction that "what is whispered in the closet shall be proclaimed from the house-tops." For years there has been a feeling that the law must afford some remedy for the unauthorized circulation of portraits of private persons; and the evil of the invasion of privacy by the newspapers, long keenly felt, has been but recently discussed by an able writer. . . .

Of the desirability — indeed of the necessity — of some such protection, there can, it is believed, be no doubt. The press is overstepping in every direction the obvious bounds of propriety and decency. Gossip is no longer the resource of the idle and of the vicious, but has become a trade, which is pursued with industry as well as effrontery. To satisfy a prurient taste the details of sexual relations are spread broadcast in the columns of the daily papers. To occupy the indolent, column upon column is filled with idle gossip, which can only be procured by intrusion upon the domestic circle. The intensity and complexity of life, attendant upon advancing civilization, have rendered necessary some retreat from the world, and man, under the refining influence of culture, has become more sensitive to publicity, so that solitude and privacy have become more essential to the individual; but modern enterprise and invention have, through invasions upon his privacy, subjected him to mental pain and distress, far greater than could be inflicted by mere bodily injury. Nor is the harm wrought by such invasions confined to the suffering of those who may be made the subjects of journalistic or other enterprise. In this, as in other branches of commerce, the supply creates the demand. Each crop of unseemly gossip, thus harvested, becomes the seed of more, and, in direct proportion to its circulation, results in a lowering of social standards and of morality. Even gossip apparently harmless, when widely and persistently circulated, is potent for evil. It both belittles and perverts. It belittles by inverting the relative importance of things, thus dwarfing the thoughts and aspirations of a people. When personal gossip attains the dignity of print, and crowds the space available for matters of real interest to the community, what wonder that the ignorant and thoughtless mistake its relative importance. Easy of comprehension, appealing to that weak side of human nature which is never wholly cast down by the misfortunes and frailties of our neighbors, no one can be surprised that it usurps the place of interest in brains capable of other things. Triviality destroys at once robustness of thought and delicacy of feeling. No enthusiasm can flourish, no generous impulse can survive under its blighting influence.

It is our purpose to consider whether the existing law affords a principle which can properly be invoked to protect the privacy of the individual; and, if it does, what the nature and extent of such protection is.

Prosser, Privacy
48 Cal. L. Rev. 383, 383-384 (1960)

In the year 1890 Mrs. Samuel D. Warren, a young matron of Boston, which is a large city in Massachusetts, held at her home a series of social entertainments on an elaborate scale. She was the daughter of Senator Bayard of Delaware, and her husband was a wealthy young paper manufacturer, who only the year before had given up the practice of law to devote himself to an inherited business. Socially Mrs. Warren was among the élite; and the newspapers of Boston, and in particular the *Saturday Evening Gazette*, which specialized in "blue blood" items, covered her parties in highly personal and embarrassing detail. It was the era of "yellow journalism," when the press had begun to resort to excesses in the way of prying that have become more or less commonplace today; and Boston was perhaps, of all of the cities in the country, the one in which a lady and a gentleman kept their names and their personal affairs out of the papers. The matter came to a head when the newspapers had a field day on the occasion of the wedding of a daughter, and Mr. Warren became annoyed. It was an annoyance for which the press, the advertisers and the entertainment industry of America were to pay dearly over the next seventy years.

Mr. Warren turned to his recent law partner, Louis D. Brandeis, who was destined not to be unknown to history. The result was a noted article, The Right to Privacy, in the Harvard Law Review, upon which the two men collaborated. It has come to be regarded as the outstanding example of the influence of legal periodicals upon the American law. In the Harvard Law School class of 1877 the two authors had stood respectively second and first, and both of them were gifted with scholarship, imagination, and ability.

Internal evidences of style, and the probabilities of the situation, suggest that the writing, and perhaps most of the research, was done by Brandeis; but it was undoubtedly a joint effort, to which both men contributed their ideas.

——————

In the material's excerpted above, Warren and Brandeis less than exact on the historical emergence of the new torts, as both the Roman and English law systems allowed actions for nuisance, mental distress and defamation from very early times. But the prior existence of all these wrongs set the stage for Warren and Brandeis to isolate the common law principle for invasion of privacy. They reject analogies to libel and slander, insisting that privacy is not concerned with plaintiff's reputation or "with the injury done to the individual in his external relations to the community." They also reject the view that the tort is designed to protect a person from "mere injury to feelings," by insisting that such harm is compensable only if the plaintiff is the victim of some "recognized" legal injury.

Warren and Brandeis then examine and reject the view that plaintiff's right to privacy rests solely on a fiduciary or contract theory, given that these theories only protect parties from the misuse of information by others with whom they have previously formed some consensual relationship, as by posing for a picture or by lecturing to students in a private hall. Implicit in these special relationships is a firm understanding that the picture taken or the information acquired will be used only for limited purposes. These consensual theories do not explain how the right of privacy can be vindicated against a stranger who, for example, takes, as "the latest advances in photographic art" allow, the plaintiff's picture "surreptitiously," or who tape records a lecture from outside the hall.

To Warren and Brandeis the "in rem" nature of the tort means that the right must be good against the entire world. Accordingly, they find the key analogy to the privacy right in the common law of copyright, which gives the owner control over access to his *unpublished* materials. "In every such case the individual is entitled to decide whether that which is his shall be given to the public." (*Id.* at 199.) Since the better rule protects even writing of no literary value as long as it is unpublished, they conclude: "The principle which protects personal writings and all other personal productions, not against theft and physical appropriation, but against publications in any form, is in reality not the principle of private property, but that of an inviolate personality." (*Id.* at 205.)

Having thus located the basic principle of protection, the authors identify six potential "limitations on this right to privacy" (*id.* at 214-219): It does not apply to oral communications in the absence of special damages; it inherits all the privileges of defamation; it is subject to a privilege for matter "which is of public or general interest"; truth, however, is not a defense; malice in the sense of ill will is not required; and the right ceases upon voluntary publication.

Kalven, Privacy in the Tort Law — Were Warren and Brandeis Wrong?
31 Law & Contemp. Probs. 326, 330-331 (1966)

While the article is admirable in the care with which it specifies certain limitations on the new right, it makes it apparent at the birth of the right that there are certain major ambiguities. These are all points which haunt the tort today and to which we will return, but we would note here that there is no effort to specify what will constitute a prima facie case; no concern with how damages are to be measured; no concern, other than to dismiss actual malice, with what the basis of liability will be; and finally there is the projection of a generous set of privileges but no effort to assess whether they do not engulf the cause of action. And, of course, there is no hint that any but gentlemen will ever be moved to use the new remedy.

———————————

Twelve years after Warren and Brandeis wrote, the right to privacy moved into the judicial arena in Roberson v. Rochester Folding Box Co., 64 N.E. 442, 443 (N.Y. 1902). The Franklin Mills Company purchased from its codefendant, the Rochester Folding Box Company, 25,000 lithographic prints, which it circulated widely in "stores, warehouses, saloons, and other public places." The defendants had, without her consent, reproduced on the prints a portrait of the plaintiff below the words "Flour of the Family," and above the words "Franklin Mills Flour," in large capital letters. The name of the defendant box company was printed in the lower right-hand corner of the picture. The plaintiff claimed that by the publication of the picture she had "been greatly humiliated by the scoffs and jeers of persons who have recognized her face and picture on this advertisement and her good name has been attacked, causing her great distress and suffering both in body and mind; that she was made sick and suffered a severe nervous shock, was confined to her bed and compelled to employ a physician, because of these facts."

The plaintiff's case reveals the two different sides to the privacy right. The first side rests on a theory of restitution under which the plaintiff demands that the defendant disgorge the profits it obtained from the unauthorized use of her picture. The analogy is to the general law of restitution that allows the recovery of gains from the defendant's unauthorized conversion of a physical asset. Alternatively, the plaintiff challenges the defendant's invasion of her private space, seeking compensation for anguish and loss of society derived from the attack on her reputation and good name. In this aspect the privacy tort is far closer to defamation. But Parker, J., had no patience with either claim:

The so-called right of privacy is, as the phrase suggests, founded upon the claim that a man has the right to pass through this world, if he wills, without having his picture published, his business enterprises discussed, his successful experiments written up for the benefit of others, or his eccentricities commented upon either in handbills, circulars, catalogues, periodicals or newspapers, and, necessarily, that the things which may not be written and published of him must not be spoken of him by his neighbors, whether the comment be favorable or otherwise. While most persons would much prefer to have a good likeness of themselves appear in a responsible periodical or leading newspaper rather than upon an advertising card or sheet, the doctrine which the courts are asked to create for this case would apply as well to the one publication as to the other. . . .

If such a principle be incorporated into the body of the law through the instrumentality of a court of equity, the attempts to logically apply the principle will necessarily result, not only in a vast amount of litigation, but in litigation bordering upon the absurd, for the right of privacy, once established as a legal doctrine, cannot be confined to the restraint of the publication of a likeness but must necessarily embrace as well the publication of a word-picture, a comment upon one's looks, conduct, domestic relations or habits. And were the right of privacy once legally asserted it would necessarily be held to include the same things if spoken instead of printed, for one, as well as the other, invades the right to be absolutely let alone. . . .

The legislative body could very well interfere and arbitrarily provide that no one should be permitted for his own selfish purpose to use the picture or the name of another for advertising purposes without his consent. In such event, no embarrassment would result to the general body of the law, for the rule would be applicable only to cases provided for by the statute. The courts, however, being without authority to legislate, are required to decide cases upon principle, and so are necessarily embarrassed by precedents created by an extreme, and, therefore, unjustifiable application of an old principle. . . .

The dissent of Gray, J., took sharp issue with the majority's reasoning:

[I]f it is to be permitted that the portraiture may be put to commercial, or other, uses for gain, by the publication of prints therefrom, then an act of invasion of the individual's privacy results, possibly more formidable and more painful in its consequences, than an actual bodily assault might be. Security of person is as necessary as the security of property; and for that complete personal security, which will result in the peaceful and wholesome enjoyment of one's privileges as a member of society, there should be afforded protection, not only against the scandalous portraiture and display of one's features and person, but against the display and use thereof for another's commercial purposes or gain.

Gray's dissent was quickly adopted in Pavesich v. New England Life Insurance Co., 50 S.E. 68 (Ga. 1905), another unauthorized advertisement case, and in Hinish v. Meier & Frank Co., 113 P.2d 438, 447 (Or. 1941), when the defendant signed plaintiff's name to a telegram urging a veto of certain legislation that would put the defendant out of business. Plaintiff sued because he feared that the telegram might cost him his job and pension with the federal government in light of a statutory prohibition against federal employee participation in political affairs. In allowing the cause of action, the Oregon Court emphatically rejected *Roberson*.

> The opinion of the court in the *Roberson* case, after an exaggerated statement, as we view it, of what is claimed for the right of privacy, dwelt upon the absurd consequences which it was conceived would follow from acceptance of the doctrine. "The attempt to logically apply the principle," it was said, "will necessarily result not only in a vast amount of litigation but in litigation bordering on the absurd." It was not stated that the litigation then before the court was absurd. It may be doubted whether any court today would render the decision that the New York court did in that case. . . . When a legal principle is pushed to an absurdity, the principle is not abandoned, but the absurdity avoided. The courts are competent, we think, to deal with difficulties of the sort suggested, and case by case, through the traditional process of inclusion and exclusion, gradually to develop the fullness of the principle and its limitations.

Why is *Hinish* not a case of defamation?

By 1960, many cases had recognized some form of the right to privacy, without articulating its basic structure. To fill that gap, without doing too much violence to the case law, Prosser proposed his seminal fourfold classification of privacy interests.

Prosser, Privacy
48 Cal. L. Rev. 383, 389, 407 (1960)

[The] law of privacy comprises four distinct kinds of invasion of four different interests of the plaintiff, which are tied together by the common name, but otherwise have almost nothing in common except that each represents an interference with the right of the plaintiff, in the phrase coined by Judge Cooley, "to be let alone." Without any attempt to exact definition, these four torts may be described as follows:

1. Intrusion upon the plaintiff's seclusion or solitude, or into his private affairs.
2. Public disclosure of embarrassing private facts about the plaintiff.
3. Publicity which places the plaintiff in a false light in the public eye.
4. Appropriation, for the defendant's advantage, of the plaintiff's name or likeness.

It should be obvious at once that these four types of invasion may be subject, in some respects at least, to different rules; and that when what is said as to any one of them is carried over to another, it may not be at all applicable, and confusion may follow. . . .

Judge Biggs has described the present state of the law of privacy as "still that of a haystack in a hurricane." Disarray there certainly is; but almost all of the confusion is due to a failure to separate and distinguish these four forms of invasion, and to realize that they call for different things. . . .

Taking them in order — intrusion, disclosure, false light, and appropriation — the first and second require the invasion of something secret, secluded or private pertaining to the plaintiff; the third and fourth do not. The second and third depend upon publicity, while the first does not, nor does the fourth, although it usually involves it. The third requires falsity or fiction; the other three do not. The fourth involves a use for the defendant's advantage, which is not true of the rest. . . .

NOTE

Prosser's classification has been adopted by many courts, and it forms the basis for the treatment of the subject in the Restatement (Second) of Torts §§652A-652L, of which Prosser was the original draftsman. For subsequent commentary, see Posner, The Right of Privacy, 12 Ga. L. Rev. 393 (1978); Epstein, Privacy, Property Rights, and Misrepresentations, 12 Ga. L. Rev. 455 (1978); Zimmerman, Requiem for a Heavyweight: A Farewell to Warren and Brandeis's Privacy Tort, 68 Cornell L. Rev. 291 (1983); Gormley, One Hundred Years of Privacy, 1992 Wis. L. Rev. 1335, analyzing the early cases.

This chapter follows Prosser's classification in order. In the first three torts, the plaintiff seeks to ward off the defendant. In the last, the plaintiff seeks to enter the marketplace by treating the right of publicity, as it is now commonly called, as a species of intellectual property ripe for commercial development.

SECTION C. INTRUSION UPON SECLUSION

American Law Institute, Restatement (Second) of the Law of Torts (1976)

§652B. INTRUSION UPON SECLUSION

One who intentionally intrudes, physically or otherwise, upon the solitude or seclusion of another, or his private affairs or concerns, is subject to liability to the other for invasion of his privacy, if the intrusion would be highly offensive to a reasonable person.

Nader v. General Motors Corp.
255 N.E.2d 765 (N.Y. 1970)

FULD, C.J. On this appeal, we are called upon to determine the reach of the tort of invasion of privacy as it exists under the law of the District of Columbia.

The complaint, in this action by Ralph Nader, pleads four causes of action against the appellant, General Motors Corporation, and three other defendants allegedly acting as its agents. The first two causes of action charge an invasion of privacy, the third is predicated on the intentional infliction of severe emotional distress and the fourth on interference with the plaintiff's economic advantage. This appeal concerns only the legal sufficiency of the first two causes of action, which were upheld in the courts below as against the appellant's motion to dismiss.

The plaintiff, an author and lecturer on automotive safety, has, for some years, been an articulate and severe critic of General Motors' products from the standpoint of safety and design. According to the complaint — which, for present purposes, we must assume to be true — the appellant, having learned of the imminent publication of the plaintiff's book "Unsafe at any Speed," decided to conduct a campaign of intimidation against him in order to "suppress plaintiff's criticism of and prevent his disclosure of information" about its products. To that end, the appellant authorized and directed the other defendants to engage in a series of activities which, the plaintiff claims in his first two causes of action, violated his right to privacy.

Specifically, the plaintiff alleges that the appellant's agents (1) conducted a series of interviews with acquaintances of the plaintiff, "questioning them about, and casting aspersions upon [his] political, social . . . racial and religious views . . . ; his integrity; his sexual proclivities and inclinations; and his personal habits"; (2) kept him under surveillance in public places for an unreasonable length of time; (3) caused him to be accosted by girls for the purpose of entrapping him into illicit relationships; (4) made threatening, harassing and obnoxious telephone calls to him; (5) tapped his telephone and eavesdropped, by means of mechanical and electronic equipment, on his private conversations with others; and (6) conducted a "continuing" and harassing investigation of him. . . .

[The court then held that the District of Columbia recognized Prosser's tort of intrusion upon seclusion.]

Quite obviously, some intrusions into one's private sphere are inevitable concomitants of life in an industrial and densely populated society, which the law does not seek to proscribe even if it were possible to do so. "The law does not provide a remedy for every annoyance that occurs in everyday life." However, the District of Columbia courts have held that the law should and does protect against certain types of intrusive conduct, and we must, therefore, determine whether the plaintiff's allegations are actionable as violations of the right to privacy under the law of that jurisdiction.

It should be emphasized that the mere gathering of information about a particular individual does not give rise to a cause of action under this theory. Privacy is invaded only if the information sought is of a confidential nature and the defendant's conduct was unreasonably intrusive. Just as a common-law copyright is lost when material is published, so, too, there can be no invasion of privacy where the information sought is open to public view or has been voluntarily revealed to others. In order to sustain a cause of action for invasion of privacy, therefore, the plaintiff must show that the appellant's conduct was truly "intrusive" and that it was designed to elicit information which would not be available through normal inquiry or observation.

The majority of the Appellate Division in the present case stated that *all of "[t]he activities complained of"* in the first two counts constituted actionable invasions of privacy under the law of the District of Columbia.[2] We do not agree with that sweeping determination. At most, only two of the activities charged to the appellant are, in our view, actionable as invasions of privacy under the law of the District of Columbia. . . .

Turning, then, to the particular acts charged in the complaint, we cannot find any basis for a claim of invasion of privacy, under District of Columbia law, in the allegations that the appellant, through its agents or employees, interviewed many persons who knew the plaintiff, asking questions about him and casting aspersions on his character. Although those inquiries may have uncovered information of a personal nature, it is difficult to see how they may be said to have invaded the plaintiff's privacy. Information about the plaintiff which was already known to others could hardly be regarded as private to the plaintiff. Presumably, the plaintiff had previously revealed the information to such other persons, and he would necessarily assume the risk that a friend or acquaintance in whom he had confided might breach the confidence. If, as alleged, the questions tended to disparage the plaintiff's character, his remedy would seem to be by way of an action for defamation, not for breach of his right to privacy.

Nor can we find any actionable invasion of privacy in the allegations that the appellant caused the plaintiff to be accosted by girls with illicit proposals, or that it was responsible for the making of a large number of threatening and harassing telephone calls to the plaintiff's home at odd hours. Neither of these activities, howsoever offensive and disturbing, involved intrusion for the purpose of gathering information of a private and confidential nature.

2. "The activities complained of:" wrote the Appellate Division majority, "the shadowing, the indiscriminate interviewing of third persons about features of his intimate life, the wiretapping and eavesdropping, the prying into his bank accounts, taxes, the alleged accosting by young women and the receipt of threatening phone calls, all are within the purview of these cases."

As already indicated, it is manifestly neither practical nor desirable for the law to provide a remedy against any and all activity which an individual might find annoying. On the other hand, where severe mental pain or anguish is inflicted through a deliberate and malicious campaign of harassment or intimidation, a remedy is available in the form of an action for the intentional infliction of emotional distress — the theory underlying the plaintiff's third cause of action. But the elements of such an action are decidedly different from those governing the tort of invasion of privacy, and just as we have carefully guarded against the use of the prima facie tort doctrine to circumvent the limitations relating to other established tort remedies we should be wary of any attempt to rely on the tort of invasion of privacy as a means of avoiding the more stringent pleading and proof requirements for an action for infliction of emotional distress.

Apart, however, from the foregoing allegations which we find inadequate to spell out a cause of action for invasion of privacy under District of Columbia law, the complaint contains allegations concerning other activities by the appellant or its agents which do satisfy the requirements for such a cause of action. The one which most clearly meets those requirements is the charge that the appellant and its codefendants engaged in unauthorized wiretapping and eavesdropping by mechanical and electronic means. The Court of Appeals in [Pearson v. Dodd, 410 F.2d 701 (D.C. 1969)] expressly recognized that such conduct constitutes a tortious intrusion and other jurisdictions have reached a similar conclusion. (See, e.g., Roach v. Harper, 105 S.E.2d 546 (W. Va. 1958).) In point of fact, the appellant does not dispute this, acknowledging that, to the extent the two challenged counts charge it with wiretapping and eavesdropping, an actionable invasion of privacy has been stated.

There are additional allegations that the appellant hired people to shadow the plaintiff and keep him under surveillance. In particular, he claims that, on one occasion, one of its agents followed him into a bank, getting sufficiently close to him to see the denomination of the bills he was withdrawing from his account. From what we have already said, it is manifest that the mere observation of the plaintiff in a public place does not amount to an invasion of his privacy. But, under certain circumstances, surveillance may be so "overzealous" as to render it actionable. Whether or not the surveillance in the present case falls into this latter category will depend on the nature of the proof. A person does not automatically make public everything he does merely by being in a public place, and the mere fact that Nader was in a bank did not give anyone the right to try to discover the amount of money he was withdrawing. On the other hand, if the plaintiff acted in such a way as to reveal that fact to any casual observer, then, it may not be said that the appellant intruded into his private sphere. In any event, though, it is enough for present purposes to say that the surveillance allegation is not insufficient as a matter of law. . . .

[Affirmed.]

BREITEL, J., concurring in result. [I]t is inappropriate to decide that several of the allegations as they now appear are referable only to the more restricted tort of intentional infliction of mental distress rather than to the common-law right of privacy upon which the first and second causes of action depend.

NOTES

1. *Invasions of privacy without trespass.* The invasion of privacy on public streets necessarily involves an element of balancing under yet another version of the live-and-let-live test, *supra* Chapter 8, at 685. Watching the comings and goings of other individuals is an inescapable part of public life from which all receive benefits that on average exceed their private burdens. It is only when extraordinary means are used in the public forum that a claim for invasion of privacy becomes viable. In some contexts, however, the choice of extreme means introduces an imbalance that does not work to the advantage of all, as when people seek to snoop or overhear conversations of others.

These tactics can also be applied against individuals on private property. As *Nader* recognizes, in this context the tort of invasion of privacy does not require a physical trespass on plaintiff's property, but may be accomplished by eavesdropping near an open window or by overhearing conversations by means of a parabolic microphone. The defense against recognizing this tort starts from the position "no physical invasion, no tort," which still controls in the blocking of light cases. See *Fontainebleau, supra* at 687. On privacy, however, the cases have consistently gone the other way. Blackstone himself condemned "eaves-droppers, or such as listen under walls and windows," but he did so not only for what they thought but also for "the slanderous and mischievous tales" they uttered. W. Blackstone, Commentaries on the Laws of England 169 (1769). The more modern approach condemns the intrusion, but downplays two elements in Blackstone's formulation: the physical entry and any subsequent defamatory publication. Rhodes v. Graham, 37 S.W.2d 46 (Ky. 1931), counts as a transitional case in which the action for invasion of privacy was allowed for phone conversations overheard by a technical trespass, the tapping of a telephone line. In Roach v. Harper, 105 S.E.2d 564 (W. Va. 1958), the court allowed an action for invasion of privacy when the defendant used a "hearing device" to overhear the plaintiff's private and confidential conversations in an apartment that he rented to her. In line with the case law movement, the modern dictionary definition excises all references to trespass in its definition of eavesdropping: "To listen, or try to listen, secretly, as to a private conversation."

Why the shift? Creating liability without trespass is best justified, perhaps, by asking again whether the general security promoted by an expanded right works to the long-term advantage of all individuals governed by the newer rule. That norm is reflected in settings where people voluntarily congregate in close quarters, as in the anti-snooping norm in crowded restaurants. By extension, the prohibition against snooping reduces the need for individuals to take elaborate precautions to fence themselves off from their neighbors, and thus allows for the more intensive use of land in crowded areas.

The soundness of the privacy right against intrusion has not been sharply contested in the private law, but it has generated much controversy in connection with the Fourth Amendment's guarantee against "unreasonable searches and seizures." Katz v. United States, 389 U.S. 347 (1967), rejected the government's argument that its tap on a public telephone booth did not amount to a search or seizure because the electronic device did not commit a common law trespass because it "did not happen to penetrate the wall of the booth. . . ." Subsequent Fourth Amendment cases have retreated from *Katz*'s broad holding. For example, in Smith v. Maryland, 442 U.S. 735 (1979), the Court refused to apply *Katz* when the police, without a warrant, used a device known as a "pen register" to record the numbers dialed from a particular phone and the times they were dialed, because no phone conversations were recorded. Does the legitimate interest of privacy test allow a distinction between *Katz* and *Smith*?

2. Trespass by fraudulent entry. In those intrusion cases that do involve an actual entry onto plaintiff's land, the dispute sometimes boils down to whether the plaintiff's consent to entry has been vitiated by the defendant's fraud. In the early case of De May v. Roberts, 9 N.W. 146, 149 (Mich. 1881), the plaintiff was granted an action for invasion of privacy against an attending physician who brought a young unmarried man into the plaintiff's apartment to observe the physician delivering her baby. "In obtaining admission at such a time and under such circumstances without fully disclosing his true character, both parties were guilty of deceit, and the wrong thus done entitles the injured party to recover the damages afterwards sustained, from shame and mortification upon discovering the true character of the defendants."

3. Remedies for intrusion. In Galella v. Onassis, 487 F.2d 986, 992, 998-999 (2d Cir. 1973), the defendant Donald Galella was a freelance photographer or "paparazzo," who repeatedly hounded Jacqueline Kennedy Onassis and her children in an effort to secure photographs for publication. He often eluded the United States Secret Service agents assigned to guard her, bribed doormen, and romanced a family servant to gain access to the family.

Onassis's initial temporary restraining order enjoined Galella from "harassing, alarming, startling, tormenting, touching the person of the defendant . . . or her children . . . and from blocking their movements in the public places and thoroughfares, invading their immediate zone of privacy by means of physical movements, gestures or with photographic equipment and from performing any act reasonably calculated to place the lives and safety of the defendant . . . and her children in jeopardy." After a full trial, "Galella was enjoined from (1) keeping the defendant and her children under surveillance or following any of them; (2) approaching within 100 yards of the home of defendant or her children, or within 100 yards of either child's school or within 75 yards of either child or 50 yards of defendant; (3) using the name, portrait or picture of defendant or her children for advertising; (4) attempting to communicate with defendant or her children except through her attorney."

On appeal, Smith, J., accepted the need for injunctive relief to forestall defendant's determined and intrusive coverage of plaintiff and her family, but then limited its scope.

> The injunction, however, is broader than is required to protect the defendant. Relief must be tailored to protect Mrs. Onassis from the "paparazzo" attack which distinguishes Galella's behavior from that of other photographers; it should not unnecessarily infringe on reasonable efforts to "cover" defendant. Therefore, we modify the court's order to prohibit only (1) any approach within twenty-five (25) feet of defendant or any touching of the person of the defendant Jacqueline Onassis; (2) any blocking of her movement in public places and thoroughfares; (3) any act foreseeably or reasonably calculated to place the life and safety of defendant in jeopardy; and (4) any conduct which would reasonably be foreseen to harass, alarm or frighten the defendant.
>
> Any further restriction on Galella's taking and selling pictures of defendant for news coverage is, however, improper and unwarranted by the evidence.
>
> Likewise, we affirm the grant of injunctive relief to the government modified to prohibit any action interfering with Secret Service agents' protective duties. Galella thus may be enjoined from (a) entering the children's schools or play areas; (b) engaging in action calculated or reasonably foreseen to place the children's safety or well being in jeopardy, or which would threaten or create physical injury; (c) taking any action which could reasonably be foreseen to harass, alarm, or frighten the children; and (d) from approaching within thirty (30) feet of the children. . . .

Timbers, J., dissented in part on the ground that deference should be accorded to the district court's determination of the sweep of injunctive relief, protesting, for example, "a wholly unexplained and anomalous 84% reduction of the distance Galella is required to keep away from Mrs. Onassis (from 50 *yards* to 25 *feet*), and an equally implausible 87% reduction of the distance he is required to keep away from the children (from 75 *yards* to 30 *feet*)."

Desnick v. American Broadcasting Co., Inc.
44 F.3d 1345 (7th Cir. 1995)

POSNER, C.J. The plaintiffs — an ophthalmic clinic known as the "Desnick Eye Center" after its owner, Dr. Desnick, and two ophthalmic surgeons employed by the clinic, Glazer and Simon — appeal from the dismissal of their suit against the ABC television network, a producer of the ABC program *PrimeTime Live* named Entine, and the program's star reporter, Donaldson. The suit is for trespass, defamation, and other torts arising out of the production and broadcast of a program segment of *PrimeTime Live* that was highly critical of the Desnick Eye Center. . . .

In March of 1993 Entine telephoned Dr. Desnick and told him that *PrimeTime Live* wanted to do a broadcast segment on large cataract practices. The Desnick Eye Center has 25 offices in four midwestern states and performs more than 10,000 cataract operations a year, mostly on elderly persons whose cataract surgery is paid for by Medicare. The complaint alleges — and in the posture of the case we must take the allegations to be true, though of course they may not be — that Entine told Desnick that the segment would not be about just one cataract practice, that it would not involve "ambush" interviews or "undercover" surveillance, and that it would be "fair and balanced." Thus reassured, Desnick permitted an ABC crew to videotape the Desnick Eye Center's main premises in Chicago, to film a cataract operation "live," and to interview doctors, technicians, and patients. Desnick also gave Entine a videotape explaining the Desnick Eye Center's services.

Unbeknownst to Desnick, Entine had dispatched persons equipped with concealed cameras to offices of the Desnick Eye Center in Wisconsin and Indiana. Posing as patients, these persons — seven in all — requested eye examinations. Plaintiffs Glazer and Simon are among the employees of the Desnick Eye Center who were secretly videotaped examining these "test patients."

The program aired on June 10. Donaldson introduces the segment by saying, "We begin tonight with the story of a so-called 'big cutter,' Dr. James Desnick. . . . [I]n our undercover investigation of the big cutter you'll meet tonight, we turned up evidence that he may also be a big charger, doing unnecessary cataract surgery for the money." Brief interviews with four patients of the Desnick Eye Center follow. One of the patients is satisfied ("I was blessed"); the other three are not — one of them says, "If you got three eyes, he'll get three eyes." Donaldson then reports on the experiences of the seven test patients. The two who were under 65 and thus not eligible for Medicare reimbursement were told they didn't need cataract surgery. Four of the other five were told they did. Glazer and Simon are shown recommending cataract surgery to them. Donaldson tells the viewer that *Prime-Time Live* has hired a professor of ophthalmology to examine the test patients who had been told they needed cataract surgery, and the professor tells the viewer that they didn't need it—with regard to one he says, "I think it would be near malpractice to do surgery on him." Later in the segment he denies that this could just be an honest difference of opinion between professionals.

[The show also broadcasted an interview with an ophthalmic surgeon who turned down a job with Desnick because of his inability to screen patients; a former marketing executive who noted that the firm took advantage of "people who had Alzheimer's, and people who did not know what planet they were on"; former patients who had unsatisfactory experiences at the clinic; and a former employee who said that Dr. Desnick altered vision tests to make it appear that people needed cataract operations. The show then detailed how Desnick "rigged" a glare machine to persuade people that they had cataracts.]

The plaintiffs' claims fall into two distinct classes. The first arises from the broadcast itself, the second from the means by which ABC and Entine obtained the information that they used in the broadcast. The first is a class of one. The broadcast is alleged to have defamed the three plaintiffs by charging that the glare machine is tampered with. [The Court holds that the evidence, as presented, is sufficient to reach the jury on defamation.]

The second class of claims in this case concerns, as we said, the methods that the defendants used to create the broadcast segment. There are four such claims: that the defendants committed a trespass in insinuating the test patients into the Wisconsin and Indiana offices of the Desnick Eye Center, that they invaded the right of privacy of the Center and its doctors at those offices (specifically Glazer and Simon), that they violated federal and state statutes regulating electronic surveillance, and that they committed fraud by gaining access to the Chicago office by means of a false promise that they would present a "fair and balanced" picture of the Center's operations and would not use "ambush" interviews or undercover surveillance.

To enter upon another's land without consent is a trespass. The force of this rule has, it is true, been diluted somewhat by concepts of privilege and of implied consent. But there is no journalists' privilege to trespass. And there can be no implied consent in any nonfictitious sense of the term when express consent is procured by a misrepresentation or a misleading omission. The Desnick Eye Center would not have agreed to the entry of the test patients into its offices had it known they wanted eye examinations only in order to gather material for a television exposé of the Center and that they were going to make secret videotapes of the examinations. Yet some cases, illustrated by Martin v. Fidelity & Casualty Co., 421 So. 2d 109, 111 (Ala. 1982), deem consent effective even though it was procured by fraud. There must be *something* to this surprising result. Without it a restaurant critic could not conceal his identity when he ordered a meal, or a browser pretend to be interested in merchandise that he could not afford to buy. Dinner guests would be trespassers if they were false friends who never would have been invited had the host known their true character, and a consumer who in an effort to bargain down an automobile dealer falsely claimed to be able to buy the same car elsewhere at a lower price would be a trespasser in the dealer's showroom. Some of these might be classified as privileged trespasses, designed to promote competition. Others might be thought justified by some kind of implied consent — the restaurant critic for example might point by way of analogy to the use of the "fair use" defense by book reviewers charged with copyright infringement and argue that the restaurant industry as a whole would be injured if restaurants could exclude critics. But most such efforts at rationalization would be little better than evasions. The fact is that consent to an entry is often given legal effect even though the entrant has intentions that if known to the owner of the property would cause him for perfectly understandable and generally ethical or at least lawful reasons to revoke his consent.

The law's willingness to give effect to consent procured by fraud is not limited to the tort of trespass. The Restatement gives the example of a man who obtains consent to sexual intercourse by promising a woman $100, yet (unbeknownst to her, of course) he pays her with a counterfeit bill and intended to do so from the start. The man is not guilty of battery, even though unconsented-to sexual intercourse is a battery. Restatement (Second) of Torts §892B, illustration 9, pp. 373-74 (1979). Yet we know that to conceal the fact that one has a venereal disease transforms "consensual" intercourse into battery. Seduction, standardly effected by false promises of love, is not rape; intercourse under the pretense of rendering medical or psychiatric treatment is, at least in most states. Trespass presents close parallels. If a homeowner opens his door to a purported meter reader who is in fact nothing of the sort — just a busybody curious about the interior of the home — the homeowner's consent to his entry is not a defense to a suit for trespass. And likewise if a competitor gained entry to a business firm's premises posing as a customer but in fact hoping to steal the firm's trade secrets. Rockwell Graphic Systems, Inc. v. DEV Industries, Inc., 925 F.2d 174, 178 (7th Cir. 1991); . . .

How to distinguish the two classes of case — the seducer from the medical impersonator, the restaurant critic from the meter-reader impersonator? The answer can have nothing to do with fraud; there is fraud in all the cases. It has to do with the interest that the torts in question, battery and trespass, protect. The one protects the inviolability of the person, the other the inviolability of the person's property. The woman who is seduced wants to have sex with her seducer, and the restaurant owner wants to have customers. The woman who is victimized by the medical impersonator has no desire to have sex with her doctor; she wants medical treatment. And the homeowner victimized by the phony meter reader does not want strangers in his house unless they have authorized service functions. The dealer's objection to the customer who claims falsely to have a lower price from a competing dealer is not to the physical presence of the customer, but to the fraud that he is trying to perpetuate. The lines are not bright — they are not even inevitable. They are the traces of the old forms of action, which have resulted in a multitude of artificial distinctions in modern law. But that is nothing new.

There was no invasion in the present case of any of the specific interests that the tort of trespass seeks to protect. The test patients entered offices that were open to anyone expressing a desire for ophthalmic services and videotaped physicians engaged in professional, not personal, communications with strangers (the testers themselves). The activities of the offices were not disrupted. . . . Nor was there any "inva[sion of] a person's private space," as in our hypothetical meter reader case, as in the famous case of De May v. Roberts, 46 Mich. 160, 9 N.W. 146 (Mich. 1881), . . . and as in Dietemann v. Time, Inc., 449 F.2d 245 (9th Cir. 1971), on which the plaintiffs in our case rely. *Dietemann* involved a home. True, the portion invaded was an office, where the plaintiff performed quack healing of nonexistent ailments. The parallel to this case is plain enough, but there is a difference. Dietemann was not in business, and did not advertise his services or charge for them. His quackery was private.

No embarrassingly intimate details of anybody's life were publicized in the present case. There was no eavesdropping on a private conversation; the testers recorded their own conversations with the Desnick Eye Center's physicians. There was no violation of the doctor-patient privilege. There was no theft, or intent to steal, trade secrets; no disruption of decorum, of peace and quiet; no noisy or distracting demonstrations. Had the testers been undercover FBI agents, there would have been no violation of the Fourth Amendment, because there would have been no invasion of a legally protected interest in property or privacy. "Testers" who pose as prospective home buyers in order to gather evidence of housing discrimination are not trespassers even if they are private persons not acting under color of law. The situation of the defendants' "testers" is analogous. Like testers seeking evidence of violation of anti-discrimination laws, the defendants' test patients gained entry into the plaintiffs' premises by misrepresenting their purposes (more precisely by a misleading omission to disclose those purposes). But the entry was not invasive in the sense of infringing the kind of interest of the plaintiffs that the law of trespass protects; it was not an interference with the ownership or possession of land. We need not consider what if any difference it would make if the plaintiffs had festooned the premises with signs forbidding the entry of testers or other snoops. Perhaps none, but that is an issue for another day.

What we have said largely disposes of two other claims — infringement of the right of privacy, and illegal wiretapping. The right of privacy embraces several distinct interests, but the only ones conceivably involved here are the closely related interests in concealing intimate personal facts and in preventing intrusion into legitimately private activities, such as phone conversations....

Affirmed in part, reversed in part, and remanded.

NOTES

1. Publication and fraudulent entry. With *Desnick*, compare Dietemann v. Time, Inc., 449 F.2d 245, 249 (9th Cir. 1971), in which plaintiff, "a disabled veteran with little education, was engaged in the practice of healing with clay, minerals, and herbs — as practiced, simply quackery." As part of an effort to expose the practices of plaintiff and those like him, two of defendant's reporters for Life magazine, Mr. Ray and Mrs. Metcalf, hatched a scheme with the local district attorney's office that allowed the pair to gain entry into plaintiff's house by falsely representing that they had been sent by a friend for treatment. By means of concealed equipment, Mrs. Metcalf transmitted the conversations between herself and plaintiff to a parked car occupied by a Life employee and two government officials. Mr. Ray took secret pictures of plaintiff, later used in the Life story, including one of "plaintiff with his hand on the upper portion of Mrs. Metcalf's breast while he was looking at some gadgets and holding what appeared to be a wand in his right hand." Four weeks later, plaintiff was arrested for practicing medicine without a license and, after the publication of the story, entered a plea of nolo contendere. Thereafter, he recovered $1,000 in a tort action for the invasion of privacy, and the verdict was affirmed on appeal. "The First Amendment has never been construed to accord newsmen immunity from torts or crimes committed during the course of newsgathering. The First Amendment is not a license to trespass, to steal, or to intrude by electronic means into the precincts of another's home or office." Does it make a difference that the Desnick Clinics were open to the general public and Dietemann operated out of his home? Could Desnick have excluded the defendants if he had known their true purpose from the outset?

A similar damage suit for investigative reporting was also rebuffed in Food Lion, Inc. v. Capital Cities/ABC, Inc., 194 F.3d 505 (4th Cir. 1999). The defendants, as producers of the show *PrimeTime Live*, developed a scheme whereby two of their investigators, Susan Barnett and Lynne Litt, fraudulently obtained positions in the meat department of a Food Lion store. They used hidden cameras to take footage of its operations that was subsequently used in a hard-hitting broadcast about the firm's dangerous health practices in a November 1992 episode of *PrimeTime Live*. The plaintiffs' claims for trespass and invasion of privacy were rebuffed on the ground that the "publication damages" that resulted from a substantial loss in business could not be recovered given the First Amendment. As a matter of tort law, are these publication damages proximately caused by the initial trespass? For a criticism of *Desnick* and *Food Lion*, see Epstein, Privacy, Publication, and the First Amendment: The Dangers of First Amendment Exceptionalism, 52 Stan. L. Rev. 1003, 1020-1023 (2000).

Even plaintiffs who are not the targets of investigation have lost cases for intrusion upon seclusion, in light of the First Amendment protections to the press. In Howell v. New York Post Co., Inc., 612 N.E.2d 699 (N.Y. 1993), the plaintiff was a patient at the Four Winds Hospital, a private psychiatric hospital. Her complaint (treated as true on appeal) alleged "that it was imperative to her recovery that the hospitalization remain a secret from all but her immediate family." A co-resident at the facility was Hedda Nussbaum, who had received massive publicity as the "adoptive" mother of six-year-old Lisa Steinberg, who had died of unrelenting child abuse. In September 1988, a Post photographer trespassed on the hospital grounds and used a telephoto lens to take pictures of a group of patients that included Nussbaum and the plaintiff. That evening the medical director of Four Winds pleaded with the Post not to run the picture. But the next day it appeared, showing a happy and recuperating Nussbaum in the company of friends, next to a picture of her bruised and disfigured face at the time of her arrest. The caption beneath the picture read: "The battered face above belongs to the Hedda Nussbaum people remember — the former live-in lover of Joel Steinberg. The serene woman in jeans at left is the same Hedda, strolling with a companion in the grounds of the upstate psychiatric center where her face and mind are healing from the terrible wounds Steinberg inflicted." Although the plaintiff's name was not used in the picture, her identity was easily discernible.

Kaye, C.J., wrote for a unanimous court and rejected both the claim for intentional infliction of emotional distress and for an invasion of privacy. She held that a real relationship between the public story and the inclusion of plaintiff in the picture blocked recognition of the privacy tort: "The visual impact would not have been the same had the *Post* cropped plaintiff out of the photograph, as she suggests was required." She then dispatched *Galella*, by noting that the journalist's trespassory conduct here did not "remotely approach" the required minimum, given that the picture was taken outdoors and from a distance.

The fortunes of war shifted yet again in Sanders v. American Broadcasting Co., Inc., 978 P.2d 67, 77 (Cal. 1999), involving yet another *PrimeTime Live* broadcast. An ABC employee took a position as an employee of a telepsychic company and secretly videotaped her conversations with plaintiff, another telepsychic. Even though these conversations were routinely witnessed by other employees, Werdegar, J., rejected the notion that privacy had "a binary, all-or-nothing characteristic," and concluded that "in the workplace, as elsewhere, the reasonableness of a person's expectation of visual and aural privacy depends not only who might have been able to observe the subject interaction, but on the identity of the claimed intruder and the means of intrusion." Accordingly, "a person who lacks a reasonable expectation of complete privacy in a conversation because it could be seen and overheard by coworkers (but not the general public) may nevertheless have a claim for invasion of privacy by intrusion based on a television reporter's covert videotaping of that conversation." *Desnick* was distinguished on the ground that *Sanders* is concerned "with interactions between coworkers rather than between a proprietor and a customer."

The California Court relied on *Sanders* in Taus v. Loftus, 151 P.3d 1185, 1216-1217 (Cal. 2007), where the plaintiff had, as "Jane Doe," been the subject of previous stories indicating how she had suffered serious child abuse at the hands of her mother. The defendant, Loftus, a prominent skeptic of "repressed memory" cases, published two articles that mentioned the plaintiff by name and disputed the accuracy of the original accounts. George, J., first held that the defendant had not invaded the plaintiff's privacy when she had discovered the plaintiff's identity by piecing together information from public sources. But he further held that the defendant did invade the plaintiff's privacy if, as alleged, she had secured an interview with the plaintiff's former foster mother by falsely pretending to be working with the physician who was currently treating the plaintiff. Accordingly, a violation of a person's reasonable expectation of privacy could occur "when a third party—for example, a private investigator—obtains access to personal information about the person . . . by utilizing improper and unanticipated means, particularly when such information would not have been disclosed by the relative or friend absent the third party's use of such means." Should the action allow for damages for the publication of that information?

2. Receipt—and publication—of stolen information. In Pearson v. Dodd, 410 F.2d 701, 705-706, 708 (D.C. Cir. 1969), the defendants, columnists Drew Pearson and Jack Anderson, received illegally made photocopies of numerous confidential documents from the offices of the plaintiff, Senator Thomas Dodd of Connecticut. The material concerned plaintiff's relationship to certain lobbyists for foreign interests, and the defendants used it to portray the plaintiff in an unflattering fashion. The court first noted that the plaintiff had not proved his charge that the defendants "had aided and abetted in the removal of the documents." It then dismissed the action, drawing a distinction between the damages caused by obtaining and by publishing the information:

> Of course, appellants did more than receive and peruse the copies of the documents taken from appellee's files; they published excerpts from them in the national press. But in analyzing a claimed breach of privacy, injuries from intrusion and injuries from publication should be kept clearly separate. Where

there is intrusion, the intruder should generally be liable whatever the content of what he learns. An eavesdropper to the marital bedroom may hear marital intimacies, or he may hear statements of fact or opinion of legitimate interest to the public; for purposes of liability that should make no difference. On the other hand, where the claim is that private information concerning plaintiff has been published, the question of whether that information is genuinely private or is of public interest should not turn on the manner in which it has been obtained. Of course, both forms of invasion may be combined in the same case.

In dismissing the action, the court noted that the material published was "of obvious public interest."

Judge Tamm, concurring, observed:

> Some legal scholars will see in the majority opinion — as distinguished from its actual holding — an ironic aspect. Conduct for which a law enforcement officer would be soundly castigated is, by the phraseology of the majority opinion, found tolerable; conduct which, if engaged in by government agents would lead to the suppression of evidence obtained by these means, is approved when used for the profit of the press. There is an anomaly lurking in this situation: the news media regard themselves as quasi-public institutions yet they demand immunity from the restraints which they vigorously demand be placed on government. That which is regarded as mortal taint on information secured by any illegal conduct of government would appear from the majority opinion to be permissible as a technique or modus operandi for the journalist.

Could Anderson and Pearson have been sued under *Dietemann* for the damages caused by the publication in their columns if they or their agents had personally obtained the material in question?

Shortly afterwards in New York Times Co. v. United States, 403 U.S. 713 (1971), the Supreme Court upheld the right of the press to publish classified information that had been stolen from the government by a third party so long as it related to matters of great public concern — in that case the motivations and justifications for the Vietnam War. *New York Times* left open the question of whether a party that had obtained the information lawfully could be held liable for disclosing information that he knew or had reason to know had been obtained illegally in the first instance. That question arose in Bartnicki v. Vopper, 532 U.S. 514, 530-531, 534 (2001). The plaintiffs Bartnicki and Kane were union leaders in the midst of contentious negotiations with the local school board. During a lengthy cell phone call, Kane told Bartnicki that "if they're [the Board] not gonna move for three percent, we're gonna have to go to their, their homes. . . . To blow off their front porches." An unknown person illegally intercepted the conversation, and then mailed a tape of the session to Yocum, the head of a local taxpayer's organization that had opposed the union demands. After the union won a favorable settlement, Yocum handed the tape over to Vopper, who broadcast it on his public affairs talk show. Federal and state law make it a crime for any person to "intentionally disclose" the contents of any phone communication which he knows or has reason to know was obtained in violation of federal law. However, the plaintiff's claim for invasion of privacy from the publication of the information failed because Vopper's publication was held protected under the First Amendment. Justice Stevens wrote:

> The normal method of deterring unlawful conduct is to impose an appropriate punishment on the person who engages in it. If the sanctions that presently attach to a violation of [the rule against illegal interceptions] do not provide sufficient deterrence, perhaps those sanctions should be made more severe. But it would be quite remarkable to hold that speech by a law-abiding possessor of the information can be suppressed in order to deter conduct by a non-law-abiding third party. . . .
>
> In this case, privacy concerns give way when balanced against the interest in publishing matters of public importance. As Warren and Brandeis stated in their classic law review article: "The right of privacy does not prohibit any publication of matter which is of public or general interest." One of the costs associated with participation in public affairs is an attendant loss of privacy.

Chief Justice Rehnquist's dissent criticized the court for speaking about "a matter of 'public concern,'" an amorphous concept that the Court does not even attempt to define. But the Court's decision diminishes, rather than enhances, the purposes of the First Amendment: chilling the speech of the millions of Americans who rely upon electronic technology to communicate each day." Why is it not a tort to receive goods known to be stolen?

SECTION D. PUBLIC DISCLOSURE OF EMBARRASSING PRIVATE FACTS

American Law Institute, Restatement (Second) of the Law of Torts
(1976)

§652D.   PUBLICITY GIVEN TO PRIVATE LIFE

One who gives publicity to a matter concerning the private life of another is subject to liability to the other for invasion of his privacy, if the matter publicized is of a kind that
    (a) would be highly offensive to a reasonable person, and
    (b) is not of legitimate concern to the public.

Comment

a. Publicity. The form of invasion of the right of privacy covered in this Section depends upon publicity given to the private life of the individual. "Publicity," as it is used in this Section, differs from "publication," as that term is used in §577 in connection with liability for defamation. "Publication," in that sense, is a word of art, which includes any communication by the defendant to a third person. "Publicity," on the other hand, means that the matter is made public, by communicating it to the public at large, or to so many persons that the matter must be regarded as substantially certain to become one of public knowledge. The difference is not one of the means of communication, which may be oral, written, or by any other means. It is one of a communication which reaches, or is sure to reach, the public. . . .

b. Private life. The rule stated in this Section applies only to publicity given to matters concerning the private, as distinguished from the public, life of the individual. There is no liability when the defendant merely gives further publicity to information about the plaintiff which is already public. Thus there is no liability for giving publicity to facts about the plaintiff's life that are matters of public record, such as the date of his birth, the fact of his marriage, his military record, the fact that he is admitted to the practice of medicine or is licensed to drive a taxicab, or the pleadings which he has filed in a lawsuit. On the other hand, if the record is one not open to public inspection, as in the case of income tax returns, it is not public, and there is an invasion of privacy when it is made so.

Sidis v. F-R Publishing Corp.
113 F.2d 806 (2d Cir. 1940)

CLARK, J. William James Sidis was the unwilling subject of a brief biographical sketch and cartoon printed in The New Yorker weekly magazine for August 14, 1937. Further references were made to him in the issue of December 25, 1937, and in a newspaper advertisement announcing the August 14 issue. He brought an action in the district court against the publisher, F-R Publishing Corporation. His complaint stated three "causes of action": The first alleged violation of his right of privacy as that right is recognized in California, Georgia, Kansas, Kentucky, and Missouri; the second charged infringement of the rights afforded him under §§50 and 51 of the N.Y. Civil Rights Law; the third claimed malicious libel under the laws of [nine states]. Defendant's motion to dismiss the first two "causes of action" was granted, and plaintiff has filed an appeal from the order of dismissal. . . .

William James Sidis was a famous child prodigy in 1910. His name and prowess were well known to newspaper readers of the period. At the age of eleven, he lectured to distinguished mathematicians on the subject of Four-Dimensional Bodies. When he was sixteen, he was graduated from Harvard College, amid considerable public attention. Since then, his name has appeared in the press only sporadically, and he has sought to live as unobtrusively as possible. Until the articles objected to appeared in The New Yorker, he had apparently succeeded in his endeavor to avoid the public gaze.

Among The New Yorker's features are brief biographical sketches of current and past personalities. In the latter department, which appears haphazardly under the title "Where Are They Now?" the article on Sidis was printed with a subtitle "April Fool." The author describes his subject's early accomplishments in mathematics and the wide-spread attention he received, then recounts his general breakdown and the revulsion which Sidis thereafter felt for his former life of fame and study. The unfortunate prodigy is traced over the years that followed, through his attempts to conceal his identity, through his chosen career as an insignificant clerk who would not need to employ unusual mathematical talents, and through the bizarre ways in which his genius flowered, as in his enthusiasm for collecting streetcar transfers and in his proficiency with an adding machine. The article closes with an account of an interview with Sidis at his present lodgings, "a hall bedroom of Boston's shabby south end." The untidiness of his room, his curious laugh, his manner of speech, and other personal habits are commented upon at length, as is his present interest in the lore of the Okamakammessett Indians. The subtitle is explained by the closing sentence, quoting Sidis as saying "with a grin" that it was strange, "but, you know, I was born on April Fool's Day." Accompanying the biography is a small cartoon showing the genius of eleven years lecturing to a group of astounded professors.

It is not contended that any of the matter printed is untrue. Nor is the manner of the author unfriendly; Sidis today is described as having "a certain childlike charm." But the article is merciless in its dissection of intimate details of its subject's personal life, and this in company with elaborate accounts of Sidis' passion for privacy and the pitiable lengths to which he has gone in order to avoid public scrutiny. The work possesses great reader interest, for it is both amusing and instructive; but it may be fairly described as a ruthless exposure of a once public character, who has since sought and has now been deprived of the seclusion of private life.

The article of December 25, 1937, was a biographical sketch of another former child prodigy, in the course of which William James Sidis and the recent account of him were mentioned. The advertisement published in the New York World-Telegram of August 13, 1937, read: "Out Today. Harvard Prodigy. Biography of the man who astonished Harvard at age 11. Where are they now? by J. L. Manley. Page 22. The New Yorker." . . .

All comment upon the right of privacy must stem from the famous article by Warren and Brandeis on The Right of [to] Privacy in 4 Harv. L. Rev. 193. [The court then quoted from those passages of the article set out *supra* at 1132.]

Warren and Brandeis realized that the interest of the individual in privacy must inevitably conflict with the interest of the public in news. Certain public figures, they conceded, such as holders of public office, must sacrifice their privacy and expose at least part of their lives to public scrutiny as the price of the powers they attain. But even public figures were not to be stripped bare. "In general, then, the matters of which the publication should be repressed may be described as those which concern the private life, habits, acts, and relations of an individual, and have no legitimate connection with his fitness for a public office. . . . Some things all men alike are entitled to keep from popular curiosity, whether in public life or not, while others are only private because the persons concerned have not assumed a position which makes their doings legitimate matters of public investigation."

It must be conceded that under the strict standards suggested by these authors plaintiff's right of privacy has been invaded. Sidis today is neither politician, public administrator, nor statesman. Even if he were, some of the personal details revealed were of the sort that Warren and Brandeis believed "all men alike are entitled to keep from popular curiosity."

But despite eminent opinion to the contrary, we are not yet disposed to afford to all of the intimate details of private life an absolute immunity from the prying of the press. Everyone will agree that at some point the public interest in obtaining information becomes dominant over the individual's desire for privacy. Warren and Brandeis were willing to lift the veil somewhat in the case of public officers. We would go further, though we are not yet prepared to say how far. At least we would permit limited scrutiny of the "private" life of any person who has achieved, or has had thrust upon him, the questionable and indefinable status of a "public figure." . . .

William James Sidis was once a public figure. As a child prodigy, he excited both admiration and curiosity. Of him great deeds were expected. In 1910, he was a person about whom the newspapers might display a legitimate intellectual interest, in the sense meant by Warren and Brandeis, as distinguished from a trivial and unseemly curiosity. But the precise motives of the press we regard as unimportant. And even if Sidis had loathed public attention at that time, we think his uncommon achievements and personality would have made the attention permissible. Since then Sidis has cloaked himself in obscurity, but his subsequent history, containing as it did the answer to the question of whether or not he had fulfilled his early promise, was still a matter of public concern. The article in The New Yorker sketched the life of an unusual personality, and it possessed considerable popular news interest.

We express no comment on whether or not the news worthiness of the matter printed will always constitute a complete defense. Revelations may be so intimate and so unwarranted in view of the victim's position as to outrage the community's notions of decency. But when focused upon public characters, truthful comments upon dress, speech, habits, and the ordinary aspects of personality will usually not transgress this line. Regrettably or not, the misfortunes and frailties of neighbors and "public figures" are subjects of considerable interest and discussion to the rest of the population. And when such are the mores of the community, it would be unwise for a court to bar their expression in the newspapers, books, and magazines of the day.

Plaintiff in his first "cause of action" charged actual malice in the publication, and now claims that an order of dismissal was improper in the face of such an allegation. We cannot agree. If plaintiff's right of privacy was not invaded by the article, the existence of actual malice in its publication would not change that result. Unless made so by statute, a truthful and therefore non-libelous statement will not become libelous when uttered maliciously. A similar rule should prevail on invasions of the right of privacy. "Personal ill-will is not an ingredient of the offence, any more than in an ordinary case of trespass to person or to property." Warren and Brandeis. Nor does the malice give rise to an independent wrong based on an intentional invasion of the plaintiff's interest in mental and emotional tranquility. This interest, however real, is one not yet protected by law.

If the article appearing in the issue of August 14, 1937, does not furnish grounds for action, then it is clear that the brief and incidental reference to it contained in the article of December 25, 1937, is not actionable.

[The Court then held that the plaintiff had no cause of action under §§50 and 51 of the N.Y. Civil Rights Law, *infra* at 1182, because the story was not done for commercial purposes.]

Affirmed.

NOTES

1. *The painful past.* On *Sidis* generally, see Karafiol, The Right to Privacy and the *Sidis* Case, 12 Ga. L. Rev. 513 (1978). For an account of Sidis's life, see http://en.wikipedia.org/wiki/William_James_Sidis. Evidently, Sidis did secure some settlement from the New Yorker in 1944, the year he died at age 46 of a cerebral hemorrhage. His IQ had been estimated "easily" at between 250 and 300, and as an adult he could master a new language in a day. Other early decisions were more receptive to allowing claims about truthful revelations of past actions. Melvin v. Reid, 297 P. 91, 93 (Cal. App. 1931), allowed the action of a former prostitute who had been tried for murder and acquitted against defendants who had published a film about her past that had ruined her marriage, exposed her to "obloquy, contempt, and ridicule, causing her

grievous mental and physical suffering." A similar solicitude for privacy was shown in Briscoe v. Reader's Digest Association, Inc., 483 P.2d 34, 40 (Cal. 1971), when a rehabilitated criminal was allowed to sue for the publication of a similar story in Reader's Digest, on the ground that while the facts of the incident fell within the public domain, the identification of the actor did not. Peters, J., distinguished *Sidis*, by noting that the plaintiff had no relevant past public name recognition. But *Briscoe* fell to the general newsworthiness privilege when it was overruled in Gates v. Discovery Communications, Inc. 101 P.3d 552 (Cal. 2004), as inconsistent with subsequent Supreme Court precedent, discussed *infra* at XXX.

2. *The painful present.* As might be expected, the newsworthiness privilege outlined in *Sidis* has undisputed clout in dealing with painful publication of present facts. In Sipple v. Chronicle Publishing Co., 201 Cal. Rptr. 665, 670 (Cal. App. 1984), the plaintiff "grabbed or struck" the arm of Sarah Jane Moore as she attempted to shoot President Gerald Ford in September 1975, possibly saving his life. Sipple received great publicity, including a Herb Caen's column in the San Francisco Chronicle that disclosed he was a homosexual, which when learned for the first time by members of his immediate family caused them to abandon him, causing him mental anguish, embarrassment, and humiliation.

Caldecott, P.J., affirmed the trial court's grant of summary judgment to the defendant under the newsworthiness privilege. None of the facts published about the plaintiff were private because, prior to the publication of the article, plaintiff's "homosexual orientation and participation in gay community activities had been known by hundreds of people in a variety of cities, including New York, Dallas, Houston, San Diego, Los Angeles and San Francisco." In addition, plaintiff's "friendship with Harvey Milk, another prominent gay, was well known and publicized in gay newspapers."

> In the case at bench the publication of [Sipple's] homosexual orientation which had been already widely known by many people in a number of communities was not so offensive even at the time of the publication as to shock the community notions of decency. Moreover, and perhaps even more to the point, the record shows that the publications were not motivated by a morbid and sensational prying into [Sipple's] private life, but rather were prompted by legitimate political considerations, i.e., to dispel the false public opinion that gays were timid, weak and unheroic figures and to raise the equally important political question whether the President of the United States entertained a discriminatory attitude or bias against a minority group such as homosexuals.

In *Melvin*, *Briscoe*, and *Sipple*, should it make a difference if the plaintiffs had lied to their families?

Sipple relied on Virgil v. Time, Inc., 527 F.2d 1122, 1128-1129 (9th Cir. 1975). *Virgil* stated:

> The privilege to publicize newsworthy matters is included in the definition of the tort set out in Restatement (Second) of Torts §652D. Liability may be imposed for an invasion of privacy only if "the matter publicized is of a kind which . . . is not of legitimate concern to the public." While the Restatement does not so emphasize, we are satisfied that this provision is one of constitutional dimension delimiting the scope of the tort and that the extent of the privilege thus is controlled by federal rather than state law.

Cox Broadcasting Corp. v. Cohn
420 U.S. 469 (1975)

WHITE, J. . . . The issue before us in this case is whether consistently with the First and Fourteenth Amendments a State may extend a cause of action for damages for invasion of privacy caused by the publication of the name of a deceased rape victim which was publicly revealed in connection with the prosecution of the crime.

In August 1971, appellee's 17-year-old daughter was the victim of a rape and did not survive the incident. Six youths were soon indicted for murder and rape. Although there was substantial press coverage of the crime and of subsequent developments, the identity of the victim was not disclosed pending trial, perhaps because of Ga. Code Ann. §26-9901, which makes it a misdemeanor to publish or broadcast the name or identity of a rape victim. In April 1972, some eight months later, the six defendants appeared in court. Five pled guilty to rape or attempted rape, the charge of murder having been dropped. The guilty pleas were accepted by the court, and the trial of the defendant pleading not guilty was set for a later date.

In the course of the proceedings that day, appellant Wassell, a reporter covering the incident for his employer, learned the name of the victim from an examination of the indictments which were made available for his inspection in the courtroom. That the name of the victim appears in the indictments and that the indictments were public records available for inspection are not disputed. Later that day, Wassell broadcast over the facilities of station WSB-TV, a television station owned by appellant Cox Broadcasting Corporation, a news report concerning the court proceedings. The report named the victim of the crime and was repeated the following day.

In May 1972, appellee brought an action for money damages against appellants, relying on §26-9901 and claiming that his right to privacy had been invaded by the television broadcasts giving the name of his deceased daughter. [Relying in part on *Briscoe*, the Georgia courts rejected Cox's claim of constitutional privilege and held that the plaintiff had stated a claim for invasion of privacy in the form of a tort of public disclosure of private facts, and left it to the jury whether the public disclosure of his daughter's name invaded his "zone of privacy."]

Georgia stoutly defends both §26-9901 and the State's common law privacy action challenged here. Its claims are not without force, for powerful arguments can be made, and have been made, that however it may be ultimately defined, there *is* a zone of privacy surrounding every individual, a zone within which the State may protect him from intrusion by the press, with all its attendant publicity. [The Court then referred to Warren and Brandeis; Prosser; Time, Inc. v. Hill; and Pavesich v. New England Life Insurance Co., a Georgia case.]

These are impressive credentials for a right of privacy, but we should recognize that we do not have at issue here an action for the invasion of privacy involving the appropriation of one's name or photograph, a physical or other tangible intrusion into a private area, or a publication of otherwise private information that is also false although perhaps not defamatory. The version of the privacy tort now before us—termed in Georgia "the tort of public disclosure," is that in which the plaintiff claims the right to be free from unwanted publicity about his private affairs, which, although wholly true, would be offensive to a person of ordinary sensibilities. Because the gravamen of the claimed injury is the publication of information, whether true or not, the dissemination of which is embarrassing or otherwise painful to an individual, it is here that claims of privacy most directly confront the constitutional freedoms of speech and press. The face-off is apparent, and the appellants urge upon us the broad holding that the press may not be made criminally or civilly liable for publishing information that is neither false nor misleading but absolutely accurate, however damaging it may be to reputation or individual sensibilities.

[The Court notes that public officials and public figures must show actual malice to succeed in a defamation action under New York Times *v. Sullivan*, but it left unresolved] the question whether truthful publication of very private matters unrelated to public affairs could be constitutionally proscribed.

Those precedents, as well as other considerations, counsel similar caution here. In this sphere of collision between claims of privacy and those of the free press, the interests on both sides are plainly rooted in the traditions and significant concerns of our society. Rather than address the broader question whether truthful publications may ever be subjected to civil or criminal liability consistently with the First and Fourteenth Amendments, or to put it another way, whether the State may ever define and protect an area of privacy free from unwanted publicity in the press, it is appropriate to focus on the narrower interface between press and privacy that this case presents, namely, whether the State may impose sanctions on the accurate publication of the name of a rape victim obtained from public records — more specifically, from judicial records which are maintained in connection with a public prosecution and which themselves are open to public inspection. We are convinced that the State may not do so.

In the first place, in a society in which each individual has but limited time and resources with which to observe at first hand the operations of his government, he relies necessarily upon the press to bring him in convenient form the facts of those operations. Great responsibility is accordingly placed upon the news media to report fully and accurately the proceedings of government, and official records and documents open to the public are the basic data of governmental operations. Without the information provided by the press most of us and many of our representatives would be unable to vote intelligently or to register opinions on the administration of government generally. With respect to judicial proceedings in particular, the function of the press serves to guarantee the fairness of trials and to bring to bear the beneficial effects of public scrutiny upon the administration of justice.

Appellee has claimed in this litigation that the efforts of the press have infringed his right to privacy by broadcasting to the world the fact that his daughter was a rape victim. The commission of crime, prosecutions resulting from it, and judicial proceedings arising from the prosecutions, however, are without question events of legitimate concern to the public and consequently fall within the responsibility of the press to report the operations of government.

The special protected nature of accurate reports of judicial proceedings has repeatedly been recognized. . . .

[The Restatement provides that there is no liability when the information in dispute is contained in public records.] Thus even the prevailing law of invasion of privacy generally recognizes that the interests in privacy fade when the information involved already appears on the public record. The conclusion is compelling when viewed in terms of the First and Fourteenth Amendments and in light of the public interest in a vigorous press. The Georgia cause of action for invasion of privacy through public disclosure of the name of a rape victim imposes sanctions on pure expression — the content of a publication — and not conduct or a combination of speech and nonspeech elements that might otherwise be open to regulation or prohibition. The publication of truthful information available on the public record contains none of the indicia of those limited categories of expression, such as "fighting" words, which "are no essential part of any exposition of ideas, and are of such slight social value as a step to truth that any benefit that may be derived from them is clearly outweighed by the social interest in order and morality." Chaplinsky v. New Hampshire, 315 U.S. 568, 572 (1942).

By placing the information in the public domain on official court records, the State must be presumed to have concluded that the public interest was thereby being served. Public records by their very nature are of interest to those concerned with the administration of government, and a public benefit is performed by the reporting of the true contents of the records by the media. The freedom of the press to publish that information appears to us to be of critical importance to our type of government in which the citizenry is the final judge of the proper conduct of public business. In preserving that form of government the First and Fourteenth Amendments command nothing less than that the States may not impose sanctions for the publication of truthful information contained in official court records open to public inspection.

We are reluctant to embark on a course that would make public records generally available to the media but forbid their publication if offensive to the sensibilities of the supposed reasonable man. Such a rule would make it very difficult for the press to inform their readers about the public business and yet stay within the law. The rule would invite timidity and self-censorship and very likely lead to the suppression of many items that would otherwise be put into print and that should be made available to the public. At the very least, the First and Fourteenth Amendments will not allow exposing the press to liability for truthfully publishing information released to the public in official court records. If there are privacy interests to be protected in judicial proceedings, the States must respond by means which avoid public documentation or other exposure of private information. Their political institutions must weigh the interests in privacy with the interests of the public to know and of the press to publish.[26] Once true information is disclosed in public court documents open to public inspection, the press cannot be sanctioned for publishing it. In this instance as in others reliance must rest upon the judgment of those who decide what to publish or broadcast.

Appellant Wassell based his televised report upon notes taken during the court proceedings and obtained the name of the victim from the indictments handed to him at his request during a recess in the hearing. Appellee has not contended that the name was obtained in an improper fashion or that it was not on an official court document open to public inspection. Under these circumstances, the protection of freedom of the press provided by the First and Fourteenth Amendments bars the State of Georgia from making appellants' broadcast the basis of civil liability. . . .

Reversed.

[Justice Powell concurred separately in order to state his views solely on the meaning of Gertz v. Robert Welch, Inc., which, he believed, constitu-

---

26. We mean to imply nothing about any constitutional questions which might arise from a state policy not allowing access by the public and press to various kinds of official records, such as records of juvenile-court proceedings.

tionally required that truth be an absolute defense in defamation actions brought by either public or private persons. Justice Rehnquist dissented on the ground that there had been no final judgment in the case from which an appeal could be taken to the Supreme Court.]

NOTES

1. *Privacy and the public record.* How should the Supreme Court decide the questions left unanswered in footnote 26? Does the decision accord constitutional status to §652D of the Restatement (Second)? What of the confidentiality of public records of adoption proceedings? In Doe v. Sundquist, 106 F.3d 702 (6th Cir. 1997), the court held that no constitutional right of privacy prevented Tennessee from passing a law that allowed adopted children access to previously confidential adoption records for the purpose of identifying their birth parents.

The Supreme Court has addressed the clash between the First Amendment and privacy interests in a number of Supreme Court cases since *Cox*. In Oklahoma Publishing Co. v. District Court, 430 U.S. 308, 311 (1977), the state court entered a pretrial order enjoining the publication of the name and picture of an 11-year-old boy charged with delinquency by second degree murder. The Court held under *Cox* the ban violated the First Amendment. "No objection was made to the presence of the press in the courtroom or to the photographing of the juvenile as he left the courthouse. There is no evidence that petitioner acquired the information unlawfully or even without the State's implicit approval. The name and picture of the juvenile here were 'publicly revealed in connection with the prosecution of the crime,' much as the name of the rape victim in *Cox Broadcasting* was placed in the public domain." Could reporters have been excluded from the court? See Globe Newspaper Co. v. Superior Court, 457 U.S. 596 (1982).

In The Florida Star v. B. J. F., 491 U.S. 524, 533 (1989), the plaintiff had filed a report with the local sheriff's department stating that she had been robbed and raped. The Florida Star obtained this report lawfully. Thereafter it published a short account of the rape using plaintiff's name in its "Police Reports" section in inadvertent violation of its own internal policies that barred the use of any rape victim's name. In a jury trial, the plaintiff recovered $75,000 in compensatory damages and $25,000 in punitive damages for the violation of Florida Statute §794.03 (1987), rendering it unlawful to "print, publish, or broadcast . . . in any instrument of mass communication the name, address, or other identifying fact or information of the victim of any sexual offense. . . . "

The Supreme Court threw out the jury awards for both compensatory and punitive damages. The Court refused to adopt any categorical rule making it constitutionally protected to publish the name of a rape victim, only to deny recovery on a more limited ground: "[I]f a newspaper lawfully obtains truthful information about a matter of public significance then state officials may not constitutionally punish publication of the information, absent a need to further a state interest of the highest order." The proper treatment for unlawfully obtained information was again left unsettled.

Justice White's dissent stressed that as a result of publication, "B. J. F. received harassing phone calls, required mental health counseling, was forced to move from her home, and was even threatened with being raped again." He distinguished his earlier opinion in *Cox* by noting that there the state did not undertake any effort to keep the information confidential, while in this instance the state did seek to keep the information quiet.

Note that one informal survey suggests that in practice over 90 percent of the newspapers in the country do not publish the names of rape victims. See Alex S. Jones, Rape Victim Is Still a Murky Issue for the Press, N.Y. Times, June 25, 1989, §1, at 18. Does the general practice help the majority or the dissent?

2. *Statutory response to* Cox. *Cox* provoked two modifications of the New York privacy statute. In 1979 the legislature adopted, and has since modified, N.Y. Civ. Rights Law §50-b (McKinney Supp. 2003), which states:

> The identity of any victim of a sex offense, . . . or of an offense involving the alleged transmission of the human immunodeficiency virus, shall be confidential. No report, paper, picture, photograph, court file or other documents, in the custody or possession of any public officer or employee, which identifies such a victim shall be made available for public inspection. No such public officer or employee shall disclose any portion of any police report, court file, or other document, which tends to identify such a victim except as provided in subdivision two of this section.

Subdivision 2 in turn allows access to this information only by obtaining a court order that "good cause exists for disclosure to that person." Other interested parties may appear at the hearing. The statute indicates that any victim must give consent to any disclosure, and makes it clear that the right does not operate for the benefit of the person charged with the sexual offense. A 1991 amendment to the statute, N.Y. Civ. Rights Law §50-c, creates a private right of action for damages suffered by "any person" injured by the disclosure, and allows the court in its discretion to award reasonable attorney's fees to the prevailing plaintiff. The statute does not apply to disclosures made by private persons who have no access to public records.

Haynes v. Alfred A. Knopf, Inc.
8 F.3d 1222 (7th Cir. 1993)

POSNER, C.J. Luther Haynes and his wife, Dorothy Haynes nee Johnson, appeal from the dismissal on the defendants' motion for summary judgment of their suit against Nicholas Lemann, the author of a highly praised, best-selling book of social and political history called *The Promised Land: The Great Black Migration and How It Changed America* (1991), and Alfred A. Knopf, Inc., the book's publisher. The plaintiffs claim that the book libels Luther Haynes and invades both plaintiffs' right of privacy. Federal jurisdiction is based on diversity, and the common law of Illinois is agreed to govern the substantive issues. The appeal presents difficult issues at the intersection of tort law and freedom of the press.

Between 1940 and 1970, five million blacks moved from impoverished rural areas and, after sojourns of shorter or greater length in the poor black districts of the cities, moved to middle-class areas. Others, despite the ballyhooed efforts of the federal government, particularly between 1964 and 1972, to erase poverty and racial discrimination, remained mired in what has come to be called the "urban ghetto." *The Promised Land* is a history of the migration. It is not history as a professional historian, a demographer, or a social scientist would write it. Lemann is none of these. He is a journalist and has written a journalistic history, in which the focus is on individuals whether powerful or representative. In the former group are the politicians who invented, executed, or exploited the "Great Society" programs. In the latter are a handful of the actual migrants. Foremost among these is Ruby Lee Daniels. Her story is the spine of the book. We are introduced to her on page 7; we take leave of her on page 346, within a few pages of the end of the text of the book.

[Posner, C.J., details the history of Daniel's life, starting from her early days in the 1940s as a sharecropper in Mississippi, through her migration to Chicago where she met and married Luther Haynes. The story describes his descent from a well-paid worker, a result of his drunkenness, adultery, temper, and irresponsibility throughout his marriage to Daniels. That marriage ended in divorce and thereafter Luther married another woman, Dorothy, with whom he lived a respectable life for 20 years. He now has a home, a steady job as a parking-lot attendant, and a position as deacon in his church.

Posner, C.J., first affirmed the dismissal of the defamation portions of the complaint on the ground that any deviations from the truth were too insubstantial to support an action for libel. He then addressed the privacy claims as follows.]

The branch of privacy law that the Hayneses invoke in their appeal is not concerned with, and is not a proper surrogate for legal doctrines that are concerned with, the accuracy of the private facts revealed. It is concerned with the propriety of stripping away the veil of privacy with which we cover the embarrassing, the shameful, the tabooed, truths about us. The revelations in the book are not about the intimate details of the Hayneses' life. They are about misconduct, in particular Luther's. (There is very little about Dorothy in the book, apart from the fact that she had had an affair with Luther while he was still married to Ruby and that they eventually became and have remained lawfully married.) The revelations are about his heavy drinking, his unstable employment, his adultery, his irresponsible and neglectful behavior toward his wife and children. So we must consider cases in which the right of privacy has been invoked as a shield against the revelation of previous misconduct.

[He then reviews *Melvin, Sidis,* and *Cox* and notes that, like the protagonists in the earlier cases,] Luther Haynes did not aspire to be a representative figure in the great black migration from the South to the North. People who do not desire the limelight and do not deliberately choose a way of life or course of conduct calculated to thrust them into it nevertheless have no legal right to extinguish it if the experiences that have befallen them are newsworthy, even if they would prefer that those experiences be kept private. The possibility of an involuntary loss of privacy is recognized in the modern formulations of this branch of the privacy tort, which require not only that the private facts publicized be such as would make a reasonable person deeply offended by such publicity but also that they be facts in which the public has no legitimate interest.

The two criteria, offensiveness and newsworthiness, are related. An individual, and more pertinently perhaps the community, is most offended by the publication of intimate personal facts when the community has no interest in them beyond the voyeuristic thrill of penetrating the wall of privacy that surrounds a stranger. The reader of a book about the black migration to the North would have no legitimate interest in the details of Luther Haynes's sex life; but no such details are disclosed. Such a reader does have a legitimate interest in the aspects of Luther's conduct that the book reveals. For one of Lemann's major themes is the transposition virtually intact of a sharecropper morality characterized by a family structure "matriarchal and elastic" and by an "extremely unstable" marriage bond to the slums of the northern cities, and the interaction, largely random and sometimes perverse, of that morality with governmental programs to alleviate poverty. Public aid policies discouraged Ruby and Luther from living together; public housing policies precipitated a marriage doomed to fail. No detail in the book claimed to invade the Hayneses' privacy is not germane to the story that the author wanted to tell, a story not only of legitimate but of transcendent public interest.

The Hayneses question whether the linkage between the author's theme and their private life really is organic. They point out that many social histories do not mention individuals at all, let alone by name. That is true.

Much of social science, including social history, proceeds by abstraction, aggregation, and quantification rather than by case studies; the economist Robert Fogel has won a Nobel prize for his statistical studies of economic history, including, not wholly unrelated to the subject of Lemann's book, the history of Negro slavery in the United States. But it would be absurd to suggest that cliometric or other aggregative, impersonal methods of doing social history are the only proper way to go about it and presumptuous to claim even that they are the best way. Lemann's book has been praised to the skies by distinguished scholars, among them black scholars covering a large portion of the ideological spectrum — Henry Louis Gates Jr., William Julius Wilson, and Patricia Williams. Lemann's methodology places the individual case history at center stage. If he cannot tell the story of Ruby Daniels without waivers from every person who she thinks did her wrong, he cannot write this book.

Well, argue the Hayneses, at least Lemann could have changed their names. But the use of pseudonyms would not have gotten Lemann and Knopf off the legal hook. The details of the Hayneses' lives recounted in the book would identify them unmistakably to anyone who has known the Hayneses well for a long time (members of their families, for example), or who knew them before they got married; and no more is required for liability either in defamation law or in privacy law. Lemann would have had to change some, perhaps many, of the details. But then he would no longer have been writing history. He would have been writing fiction. The non-quantitative study of living persons would be abolished as a category of scholarship, to be replaced by the sociological novel. That is a genre with a distinguished history punctuated by famous names, such as Dickens, Zola, Stowe, Dreiser, Sinclair, Steinbeck, and Wolfe, but we do not think that the law of privacy makes it (or that the First Amendment would permit the law of privacy to make it) the exclusive format for a social history of living persons that tells their story rather than treating them as data points in a statistical study. . . .

The Promised Land does not afford the reader a titillating glimpse of tabooed activities. The tone is decorous and restrained. Painful though it is for the Hayneses to see a past they would rather forget brought into the public view, the public needs the information conveyed by the book, including the information about Luther and Dorothy Haynes, in order to evaluate the profound social and political questions that the book raises. Given the *Cox* decision, moreover, all the discreditable facts about the Hayneses that are contained in judicial records are beyond the power of tort law to conceal; and the disclosure of those facts alone would strip away the Hayneses' privacy as effectively as *The Promised Land* has done. (This case, it could be argued, has stripped them of their privacy, since their story is now part of a judicial record — the record of this case.) We do not think it is an answer that Lemann got his facts from Ruby Daniels rather than from judicial records. The courts got the facts from Ruby. We cannot see what difference it makes that Lemann went to the source.

[Summary judgment was proper under *Cox* because "on the basis of the evidence obtained in pretrial discovery no reasonable jury could render a verdict for the plaintiff. . . ."]

Affirmed.

NOTE

The prosaic sources of newsworthiness. Unlike *Sidis*, the history recounted in *Haynes* involves ordinary people whom the author chooses to highlight, not those who are thrust into the public eye by their greatness or misfortunes. The newsworthiness privilege attaches to both kinds of involuntary public figures. In Shulman v. Group W Productions, Inc., 955 P.2d 469, 488 (Cal. 1998), Ruth and Wayne Shulman were two members of a family trapped in their car when it went off the highway. They were rescued by a medical transport and helicopter crew. The event was recorded by a video camera operator hired by a television producer who later incorporated the footage into a documentary television show, 'On Scene: Emergency Response,' covering the entire episode, which was aired without plaintiffs' consent. Werdegar, J., held that the newsworthiness privilege applied because the automobile accident was a subject of

> legitimate concern to much of the public, involving as it does a critical service that any member of the public may someday need. The story of Ruth's difficult extrication from the crashed car, the medical attention given her at the scene, and her evacuation by helicopter was of particular interest because it highlighted some of the challenges facing emergency workers dealing with serious accidents.
>
> The more difficult question is whether Ruth's appearance and words as she was extricated from the overturned car, placed in the helicopter and transported to the hospital were of legitimate public concern. . . . [W]e conclude the disputed material was newsworthy as a matter of law. One of the dramatic and interesting aspects of the story as a whole is its focus on flight nurse Carnahan, who appears to be in charge of communications with other emergency workers, the hospital base and Ruth, and who leads the medical assistance to Ruth at the scene. Her work is portrayed as demanding and important and as involving a measure of personal risk (e.g. in crawling under the car to aid Ruth despite warnings that gasoline may be dripping from the car.)

More recently in Veilleux v. National Broadcasting Co., 206 F.3d 92 (1st Cir. 2000), *Dateline NBC ran* an hour-long show about the long-distance trucking industry that focused on the dangers of fatigue in driving and featured the plaintiffs Veilleux and Kennedy. *Dateline NBC* revealed on its show that Kennedy failed a drug test. Campbell, J., rebuffed the plaintiffs' claim for invasion of privacy noting that "Kennedy's drug test results reasonably tend to illustrate the report's newsworthy themes of interstate truck driving, highway safety and relevant government regulation." Citing *Haynes*, he concluded that "we follow other circuit courts that have permitted journalists to portray individuals' personal circumstances in ways that reveal their identities where sufficiently related to a matter of public concern." Has the newsworthiness privilege swallowed the tort, as Kalven claimed? Is all the news that is printed now fit to print?

SECTION E. FALSE LIGHT

American Law Institute, Restatement (Second) of the Law of Torts (1976)

§652E.   PUBLICITY PLACING PERSON IN FALSE LIGHT

One who gives publicity to a matter concerning another that places the other before the public in a false light is subject to liability to the other for invasion of his privacy, if

 (a) The false light in which the other was placed would be highly offensive to a reasonable person, and

 (b) The actor had knowledge of or acted in reckless disregard as to the falsity of the publicized matter and the false light in which the other would be placed.

Caveat:

The Institute takes no position as to whether there are any circumstances under which recovery can be obtained under this Section if the actor did not know of or act with reckless disregard as to the falsity of the matter publicized and the false light in which the other would be placed but was negligent in regard to these matters.

Comment

b. Relation to defamation. The interest protected by this Section is the interest of the individual in not being made to appear before the public in an objectionable false light or false position, or in other words, otherwise than as he is. In many cases to which the rule stated here applies, the publicity given to the plaintiff is defamatory, so that he would have an action for libel or slander under the rules stated in Chapter 24. In such a case the action for invasion of privacy will afford an alternative or additional remedy, and the plaintiff can proceed upon either theory, or both, although he can have but one recovery for a single instance of publicity.

Time, Inc. v. Hill
385 U.S. 374 (1967)

BRENNAN, J. . . . The question in this case is whether appellant, publisher of *Life* magazine, was denied constitutional protections of speech and press by the application by the New York courts of §§50-51 of the New York Civil Rights Law to award appellee damages on allegations that Life falsely reported that a new play portrayed an experience suffered by appellee and his family.

[In September 1952, James Hill, his wife, and five Hill children were held hostage for 19 hours in their suburban Philadelphia home by three escaped convicts. The convicts released the Hill family untouched and unharmed, but the story made the front pages of the newspapers when the police, in a widely publicized encounter, subsequently killed two of the convicts and captured the third. Shortly after the incident, the Hills moved to Connecticut.]

In 1955 *Life* magazine, owned by defendant Time, Inc., published an article entitled "True Crime Inspires Tense Play" that told of a new Broadway thriller, *The Desperate Hours*. The article said that the experience of the Hill family, which had first been brought to attention in Joseph Hayes' novel *The Desperate Hours*, was now being "re-enacted" in a new play based on the original book. The article said the play showed that the family "rose in heroism" in its time of crisis. The article was accompanied by pictures of scenes from the play, reenacted in the Hill's suburban Philadelphia home. One showed a son being "roughed up" by a "brutish convict"; another, the "darling daughter" biting the hand of one of the convicts; and a third, of the father making a "brave try" to save his family.

Hill brought his action in the New York State Supreme Court under §§50 and 51 of the New York Civil Rights Law, [*infra* at 1182], alleging that the article was intended to, and in fact did, give the public the impression that the play was an accurate account of the experiences of the Hill family. Hill also alleged that the defendant knew that its article was "false and untrue." The defendant answered that the article was "a subject of legitimate news interest," that it was "a subject of general interest and of value and concern to the public" at the time it was published, and that it was "published in good faith without any malice whatsoever. . . . " The trial judge denied defendant's motion to dismiss and the jury awarded plaintiff $50,000 in actual and $25,000 in punitive damages. . . .

[The New York Court of Appeals affirmed on the ground that defendant's "fictionalized" account of plaintiff's personal life, used in this unauthorized biography, was not protected by the newsworthiness defense.]

We hold that the constitutional protections for speech and press preclude the application of the New York statute to redress false reports of matters of public interest in the absence of proof that the defendant published the report with knowledge of its falsity or in reckless disregard of the truth.

The guarantees for speech and press are not the preserve of political expression or comment upon public affairs, essential as those are to healthy government. One need only pick up any newspaper or magazine to comprehend the vast range of published matter which exposes persons to public view, both private citizens and public officials. Exposure of the self to others in varying degrees is a concomitant of life in a civilized community. The risk of this exposure is an essential incident of life in a society which places a primary value on freedom of speech and of press. . . . We create a grave risk of serious impairment of the indispensable service of a free press in a free society if we saddle the press with the impossible burden of verifying to a certainty the facts associated in news articles with a person's name, picture or portrait, particularly as related to nondefamatory matter. Even negligence would be a most elusive standard, especially when the content of the speech itself affords no warning of prospective harm to another through falsity. A negligence test would place on the press the intolerable burden of guessing how a jury might assess the reasonableness of steps taken by it to verify the accuracy of every reference to a name, picture or portrait.

In this context, sanctions against either innocent or negligent misstatement would present a grave hazard of discouraging the press from exercising the constitutional guarantees. Those guarantees are not for the benefit of the press so much as for the benefit of all of us. A broadly defined freedom of the press assures the maintenance of our political system and an open society. Fear of large verdicts in damage suits for innocent or merely negligent misstatement, even fear of the expense involved in their defense, must inevitably cause publishers to "steer . . . wider of the unlawful zone," and thus "create the danger that the legitimate utterance will be penalized."

But the constitutional guarantees can tolerate sanctions against *calculated* falsehood without significant impairment of their essential function. We held in *New York Times* that calculated falsehood enjoyed no immunity in the case of alleged defamation of a public official concerning his official conduct. Similarly, calculated falsehood should enjoy no immunity in the situation here presented us. . . .

Turning to the facts of the present case, the proofs reasonably would support either a jury finding of innocent or merely negligent misstatement by *Life*, or a finding that *Life* portrayed the play as re-enactment of the Hill family's experience reckless of the truth or with actual knowledge that the portrayal was false. [Justice Brennan then reviewed the evidence in great detail.]

The appellant argues that the statute should be declared unconstitutional on its face if construed by the New York courts to impose liability without proof of knowing or reckless falsity. Such a declaration would not be warranted even if it were entirely clear that this had previously been the view of the New York courts. The New York Court of Appeals . . . has been assiduous in construing the statute to avoid invasion of the constitutional protections of speech and press. We, therefore, confidently expect that the New York courts will apply the statute consistently with the constitutional command. Any possible difference with us as to the thrust of the constitutional command is narrowly limited in this case to the failure of the trial judge to instruct the jury that a verdict of liability could be predicated only on a finding of knowing or reckless falsity in the publication of the *Life* article.

The judgment of the Court of Appeals is set aside and the case is remanded for further proceedings not inconsistent with this opinion.

It is so ordered.

[Justice Black, with whom Justice Douglas joined, concurred, but reiterated his view in New York Times v. Sullivan that the First Amendment imposed a total bar on these suits.]

DOUGLAS J., concurring. . . . The episode around which this book was written had been news of the day for some time. The most that can be said is that the novel, the play, and the magazine article revived that interest. A fictionalized treatment of the event is, in my view, as much in the public domain as would be a watercolor of the assassination of a public official. It seems to me irrelevant to talk of any right of privacy in this context. Here a private person is catapulted into the news by events over which he had no control. He and his activities are then in the public domain as fully as the matters at issue in New York Times Co. v. Sullivan. Such privacy as a person normally has ceases when his life has ceased to be private. . . .

[HARLAN, J., concurring in part and dissenting in part, urged the adoption of a negligence standard, in part because of the inability of the Hills to use counterspeech to offset the errors found in the *Life Magazine* account.]

MR. JUSTICE FORTAS, with whom THE CHIEF JUSTICE and MR. JUSTICE CLARK join, dissenting.

[The instructions given at the trial were] close enough to this Court's insistence upon "knowing or reckless falsity" as to render a reversal arbitrary and unjustified. If the defendant *altered* or *changed* the true facts so that the article as published was a *fictionalized* version, this, in my judgment, was a knowing or reckless falsity. "Alteration" or "change" denotes a positive act — not a negligent or inadvertent happening. "Fictionalization" and "fiction" to the ordinary mind mean so departing from fact and reality as to be *deliberately* divorced from the fact — not merely in detail but in general and pervasive impact.

NOTES

1. *Time v. Hill today.* Time v. Hill was decided just before the Supreme Court held in *Butts* that the actual malice requirement applied to defamation suits brought by public figure against media defendants. Is there any reason to distinguish the false light from the defamation cases? The Court briefly reexamined Time v. Hill in Cantrell v. Forest City Publishing Co., 419 U.S. 245, 250-251 (1974), when it upheld a verdict for plaintiff in a false light case because the trial judge had properly instructed the jury that the plaintiff had the burden of showing that defendant's story was written with knowledge of its falsity or with a reckless disregard of its truth. The plaintiff in *Cantrell* was a private person, but the Court chose not reexamine Time v. Hill in light of Gertz v. Welch, decided earlier in the same term. Because the plaintiff had not objected to the jury instructions, the Court concluded that "this case presents no occasion to consider whether a State may constitutionally apply a more relaxed standard of liability for a publisher or broadcaster of false statements injurious to a private individual under a false-light theory of invasion of privacy, or whether the constitutional standard announced in Time, Inc. v. Hill applies to all false-light cases."

2. *False light in state courts.* Nothing in *Time* requires any state to adopt the false-light action in the first place, and many state courts have refused to recognize the tort. In Lake v. Wal-Mart Stores, Inc., 582 N.W.2d 231, 235-236 (Minn. 1998), the court accepted the privacy torts of seclusion, appropriation, and publication of private facts, but drew the line at false light:

> False light is the most widely criticized of the four privacy torts and has been rejected by several jurisdictions. Most recently the Texas Supreme Court [in Cain v. Hearst Corp., 878 S.W.2d 577 (Tex. 1994),] refused to recognize the tort of false light invasion of privacy because defamation encompasses most false light claims and false light "lacks many of the procedural limitations that accompany actions for defamation, thus unacceptably increasing the tension that already exists between free speech constitutional guarantees and tort law." Citing "numerous procedural and substantive hurdles" under Texas statutory and common law that limit defamation actions, such as privileges for public meetings, good faith, and important public interest and mitigation factors, the court concluded that these restrictions "serve to safeguard the freedom of speech." Thus to allow recovery under false light invasion of privacy, without such safeguards, would "unacceptably derogate constitutional free speech." The court rejected the solution of some jurisdictions — application of the defamation restrictions to false light — finding instead that any benefit to protecting nondefamatory false speech was outweighed by the chilling effect of free speech.

> . . . Most false light claims are actionable as defamation claims; because of the overlap with defamation and the other privacy torts, a case has rarely succeeded squarely on a false light claim.

For a defense of the defamation approach, see Schwartz, Explaining and Justifying a Limited Tort of False Light Invasion of Privacy, 41 Case W. Res. L. Rev. 885, 898 (1991).

For scholarly defense of the minority position, *see* Zimmerman, False Light Invasion of Privacy: The Light That Failed, 64 N.Y.U. L. Rev. 364 (1989).

Should *Roberson, supra* at 1136, be treated as a false-light case?

SECTION F.   COMMERCIAL APPROPRIATION OF PLAINTIFF'S NAME OR LIKENESS, OR THE RIGHT OF PUBLICITY

New York Civil Rights Law
§§50-51 (McKinney 1992 & Supp. 2003)

§50.   RIGHT OF PRIVACY

A person, firm or corporation that uses for advertising purposes, or for the purposes of trade, the name, portrait or picture of any living person without having first obtained the written consent of such person, or if a minor of his or her parent or guardian, is guilty of a misdemeanor.

§51.   ACTION FOR INJUNCTION AND FOR DAMAGES

Any person whose name, portrait, picture, or voice is used within this state for advertising purposes or for the purposes of trade without the written consent first obtained as above provided may maintain an equitable action in the supreme court of this state against the person, firm or corporation so using his name, portrait, picture or voice, to prevent and restrain the use thereof; and may also sue and recover damages for any injuries sustained by reason of such use and if the defendant shall have knowingly used such person's name, portrait, picture or voice in such manner as is forbidden or declared to be unlawful by section fifty of this article, the jury, in its discretion, may award exemplary damages. . . .

American Law Institute, Restatement (Second) of the Law of Torts
(1976)

§652C. APPROPRIATION OF NAME OR LIKENESS

One who appropriates to his own use or benefit the name or likeness of
another is subject to liability to the other for invasion of his privacy.

Comment

b. How invaded. The common form of invasion of privacy under the rule
here stated is the appropriation and use of the plaintiff's name or likeness
to advertise the defendant's business or product, or for some similar
commercial purpose. Apart from statute, however, the rule stated is not
limited to commercial appropriation. It applies also where the defendant
makes use of the plaintiff's name or likeness for his own purposes and
benefit, even though such use is not a commercial one, and even though the
benefit sought to be obtained is not a pecuniary one. Statutes in some states
have, however, limited the liability to commercial uses of name or likeness.

American Law Institute
Restatement (Third) of the Law, Unfair Competition
(1995)

§46. APPROPRIATION OF THE COMMERCIAL VALUE OF PERSON'S IDENTITY:
     THE RIGHT OF PUBLICITY

One who appropriates the commercial value of a person's identity by
using without consent the person's name, likeness, or other indicia of
identity for purposes of trade is subject to liability for the relief appropriate
under the rules stated in §§48, 49 [governing injunctions and monetary
relief respectively].

Doe a/k/a Twist v. TCI Cablevision
110 S.W.3d 363 (Mo. 2003)

LIMBAUGH J. Appellant Anthony Twist, also known as Tony Twist, is a
former professional hockey player in the National Hockey League. After
learning of the existence of a comic book, titled *Spawn*, that contained a
villainous character sharing his name, Twist brought misappropriation of
name and defamation claims against respondents, the creators, publishers
and marketers of *Spawn* and related promotional products. Respondents
defended on First Amendment grounds. The circuit court dismissed the

defamation count, but allowed the misappropriation of name count to go to trial, which resulted in a jury verdict in favor of Twist in the amount of $24,500,000. The circuit court, however, granted respondents' motion for judgment notwithstanding the verdict and, in the alternative, ordered a new trial in the event that its judgment notwithstanding the verdict was overturned on appeal. A request for injunctive relief was also denied. [The Court then decided to hear the case.]

I.

Tony Twist began his NHL career in 1988 playing for the St. Louis Blues, later to be transferred to the Quebec Nordiques, only to return to St. Louis where he finished his career in 1999, due to injuries suffered in a motor-cycle accident. During his hockey career, Twist became the League's pre-eminent "enforcer," a player whose chief responsibility was to protect goal scorers from physical assaults by opponents. In that role, Twist was noto-rious for his violent tactics on the ice. Describing Twist, a *Sports Illustrated* writer said: "It takes a special talent to stand on skates and beat someone senseless, and no one does it better than the St. Louis Blues left winger." The article goes on to quote Twist as saying, "I want to hurt them. I want to end the fight as soon as possible and I want the guy to remember it." *Id.*

Despite his well-deserved reputation as a tough-guy "enforcer," or per-haps because of that reputation, Twist was immensely popular with the hometown fans. He endorsed products, appeared on radio and television, hosted the "Tony Twist" television talk show for two years, and became actively involved with several children's charities. It is undisputed that Twist engaged in these activities to foster a positive image of himself in the community and to prepare for a career after hockey as a sports commen-tator and product endorser.

Respondent Todd McFarlane, an avowed hockey fan and president of Todd McFarlane Productions, Inc. (TMP), created *Spawn* in 1992. TMP employs the writers, artists and creative staff responsible for production of the comic book. *Spawn* is marketed and distributed monthly by Image Comics, Inc., which was formed by McFarlane and others.

Spawn is "a dark and surreal fantasy" centered on a character named Al Simmons, a CIA assassin who was killed by the Mafia and descended to hell upon death. Simmons, having made a deal with the devil, was transformed into the creature Spawn and returned to earth to commit various violent and sexual acts on the devil's behalf. In 1993, a fictional character named "Anthony 'Tony Twist' Twistelli" was added to the *Spawn* storyline. The fictional "Tony Twist" is a Mafia don whose list of evil deeds includes multiple murders, abduction of children and sex with prostitutes. The fictional and real Tony Twist bear no physical resemblance to each other and, aside from the common nickname, are similar only in that each can be characterized as having an "enforcer" or tough-guy persona.

Each issue of the *Spawn* comic book contains a section entitled "Spawning Ground" in which fan letters are published and McFarlane responds to fan questions. In the September 1994 issue, McFarlane admitted that some of the *Spawn* characters were named after professional hockey players, including the "Tony Twist" character: "Antonio Twistelli, a/k/a Tony Twist, is actually the name of a hockey player of the Quebec Nordiques." And, again, in the November 1994 issue, McFarlane stated that the name of the fictional character was based on Twist, a real hockey player, and further promised the readers that they "will continue to see current and past hockey players' names in my books."

In April 1996, *Wizard*, a trade magazine for the comic book industry, interviewed McFarlane. In the published article, "Spawning Ground: A Look at the Real Life People Spawn Characters Are Based Upon," McFarlane is quoted as saying that he uses the names of real-life people to create the identities of the characters. Brief biographies and drawings of the *Spawn* characters follow the McFarlane interview. The paragraph devoted to the "Tony Twist" character contained a drawing of the character accompanied by the following description:

> First Appearance: Spawn # 6
> Real-Life Persona: Tony Twist.
> Relation: NHL St. Louis Blues right winger.
> The Mafia don that has made life exceedingly rough for Al Simmons and his loved ones, in addition to putting out an ill-advised contract on the Violator, is named for former Quebec Nordiques hockey player Tony Twist, now a renowned enforcer (i.e. "Goon") for the St. Louis Blues of the National Hockey League.

Below the character description was a photo of a Tony Twist hockey trading card, in which Twist was pictured in his St. Louis Blues hockey jersey.

In 1997, Twist became aware of the existence of *Spawn* and of the comic book's use of his name for that of the villainous character. On one occasion, several young hockey fans approached Twist's mother with Spawn trading cards depicting the Mafia character "Tony Twist." Subsequently, at an autograph session Twist was asked to sign a copy of the *Wizard* article in which McFarlane was interviewed and Twist's hockey trading card was pictured. . . .

At trial, McFarlane denied that the comic book character was "about" the real-life Tony Twist despite the fact that the names were the same. McFarlane also denied that he or the other defendants had attained any benefit by using Twist's name. Twist, however, presented evidence that McFarlane and the other defendants had indeed benefited by using his name. For example, Twist introduced evidence suggesting that in marketing Spawn products, McFarlane directly targeted hockey fans—Twist's primary fan base—by producing and licensing Spawn logo hockey pucks, hockey jerseys and toy zambonis. On cross-examination, McFarlane admitted that on one occasion defendants sponsored "Spawn Night" at a minor league hockey game, where McFarlane personally appeared and distributed Spawn products, including products containing the "Tony Twist" character. Another "Spawn Night" was planned to take place at a subsequent NHL game, but the event never occurred. On the issue of damages, Twist, through purported expert testimony, offered a formula for determining the fair market value that McFarlane and the other defendants should have paid Twist to use his name. In addition, Twist introduced evidence that his association with the *Spawn* character resulted in a diminution in the commercial value of his name as an endorser of products. To that end, Sean Philips, a former executive of a sports nutrition company, testified that his company withdrew a $100,000 offer to Twist to serve as the company's product endorser after Philips learned that Twist's name was associated with the evil Mafia don in the *Spawn* comic book.

II.

In this case, Twist seeks to recover the amount of the fair market value that respondents should have paid to use his name in connection with Spawn products and for damage done to the commercial value—in effect the endorsement value—of his name. Therefore, Twist's case, though brought as a misappropriation of name action[, which would also allow recovery for intrusion on dignity and self-respect], is more precisely labeled a right of publicity action—a point that both parties appear to concede in their briefs.

Despite the differences in the types of damages that may be recovered, the elements of the two torts are essentially the same. To establish the misappropriation tort, the plaintiff must prove that the defendant used the plaintiff's name without consent to obtain some advantage. *Nemani v. St. Louis Univ.*, 33 S.W.3d 184, 185 (Mo. banc 2000). In a right of publicity action, the plaintiff must prove the same elements as in a misappropriation suit, with the minor exception that the plaintiff must prove that the defendant used the name to obtain a *commercial* advantage. Given the similarity of elements of the two actions, Missouri cases analyzing the tort of misappropriation of name are pertinent to our recognition of a right of publicity claim.

In *Nemani*, the plaintiff, a research professor, brought suit against St. Louis University after the university used plaintiff's name in support of a federal grant application. This Court, reviewing the claim as a misappropriation of name tort, held that a defendant is liable under the tort when it uses a plaintiff's name without consent to obtain an advantage. . . . In a right of publicity case, plaintiff must prove that defendant intended to obtain a commercial advantage, and it is not enough to show that defendant incidentally obtained a commercial advantage by using plaintiff's name or that defendant had some other purpose in using plaintiff's name other than to obtain a commercial advantage.

To summarize, the elements of a right of publicity action include: (1) That defendant used plaintiff's name as a symbol of his identity (2) without consent (3) and with the intent to obtain a commercial advantage. . . .

A.

Respondents' initial contention that Twist did not prove that his name was used as a "symbol of his identity" is spurious. To establish that a defendant used a plaintiff's name as a symbol of his identity, "the name used by the defendant must be understood by the audience as referring to the plaintiff." . . .

On this record, respondents cannot seriously maintain that a good many purchasers of *Spawn* did not readily understand that respondents' use of the name referred to appellant. . . .

B.

[The court below] held that the record was devoid of credible evidence that respondents intended 1) "to injure Twist's marketability," (2) "to capitalize on the market recognition of the name," or (3) "derived any pecuniary benefit whatsoever from the use of that name."

At the outset, two of the premises for the circuit court's rationale are incorrect: Twist was under no obligation to prove that respondents intended to injure Twist's marketability or that respondents actually derived a pecuniary benefit from the use of his name. As explained, the commercial advantage element of the right of publicity focuses on the defendant's intent or purpose to obtain a commercial benefit from use of the plaintiff's identity. But in meeting the commercial advantage element, it is irrelevant whether defendant intended to injure the plaintiff, or actually succeeded in obtaining a commercial advantage from using plaintiff's name. That said, it still was incumbent upon Twist to prove that respondents used his name intending to obtain a commercial advantage.

Twist contends, and this Court again agrees, that the evidence admitted at trial was sufficient to establish respondents' intent to gain a commercial advantage by using Twist's name to attract consumer attention to *Spawn* comic books and related products. As the Ninth Circuit noted in *Abdul-*

Jabbar v. General Motors Corp., 85 F.3d 407, 416 (9th Cir. 1996), "The first step toward selling a product or service is to attract the consumers' attention." . . . . At a minimum, respondents' statements and actions reveal their intent to create the impression that Twist was somehow associated with the *Spawn* comic book, and this alone is sufficient to establish the commercial advantage element in a right of publicity action.

But this is not all. At trial, Twist introduced evidence that respondents marketed their products directly to hockey fans. [The court then discusses the evidence outlined in the statement of facts about Spawn's active promotion to hockey fans.]

In support of the court's ruling that the evidence presented was insufficient to show that Twist's name was used to obtain a commercial advantage, respondents cite *Nemani*, . . . to demonstrate the kind of commercial advantage that must be shown and to highlight that Twist's evidence was dissimilar. In *Nemani* . . . , the defendants used the plaintiffs' names in grant applications for money; in *Munden v. Harris*, 134 S.W. 1076 (Mo. App 1911), the defendant used a picture of the plaintiff in an advertisement. Though it is true that respondents' intent to obtain a commercial advantage is not as obvious as that found in *Nemani*, and *Munden*, the fact remains that to the extent that the evidence suggests that respondents used Twist's name to attract attention to their product, they did so to obtain a commercial advantage. Therefore, this Court holds that Twist presented sufficient evidence to establish that respondents used his name for a commercial advantage.

III.

Having determined that Twist made a submissible case at trial, we next address whether the right of publicity claim is nevertheless prohibited by the First Amendment. Courts throughout the country have struggled with this issue. Of course, not all speech is protected under the First Amendment, and in cases like this, courts often will weigh the state's interest in protecting a plaintiff's property right to the commercial value of his or her name and identity against the defendant's right to free speech.

Zacchini v. Scripps Howard Broadcasting Co., 433 U.S. 562 (1977), is the first and only right of publicity case decided by the Supreme Court. The case involved the unauthorized broadcast of a videotape of the plaintiff's 15-second "human cannonball" act during a nightly news program. The plaintiff brought suit under the state-recognized tort of right of publicity, alleging that the unauthorized broadcast amounted to an "unlawful appropriation" of his "professional property," and the defendant broadcasting company defended on First Amendment grounds. In balancing the respective parties' interests, the Court held, "Wherever the line in particular situations is to be drawn between media reports that are protected and those that are not, we are quite sure that the First and Fourteenth Amendments do not immunize the media when they broadcast a performer's entire act without his consent." Because the *Zacchini* Court limited its holding to the particular facts of the case — the appropriation of plaintiff's "entire act" — it does not control the case at hand. Nonetheless, there are larger lessons that are certainly applicable.

First, the Court acknowledged, as had many lower courts previously, that the right of publicity is not always trumped by the right of free speech. Explaining the competing right of publicity interests, the Court observed that "the rationale for protecting the right of publicity is the straight-forward one of preventing unjust enrichment by the theft of goodwill. No social purpose is served by having the defendant get free some aspect of the plaintiff that would have market value and for which he would normally pay."

Second, the Court distinguished claims for right of publicity or name appropriateness from claims for defamation like those adjudicated in *New York Times v. Sullivan*, 376 U.S. 254, (1964), [*supra* at 1097] and *Hustler Magazine v. Falwell*, 485 U.S. 46, (1988), [*supra* at 99] and claims for "publicity that places plaintiff in a 'false light'" like that adjudicated in *Time, Inc. v. Hill*, 385 U.S. 374, (1967) [*supra* at 1171] Because property interests are involved in the former categories but not the latter, the Court refused to apply the *New York Times v. Sullivan* "actual malice" standard that speech is privileged unless it was "knowingly false or was published with reckless disregard for the truth." As the Court later made clear in *Hustler, Zacchini* stands for the proposition that "the 'actual malice' standard does not apply to the tort of appropriation of a right of publicity. . . ."

Right to publicity cases, both before and after *Zacchini*, focus instead on the threshold legal question of whether the use of a person's name and identity is "expressive," in which case it is fully protected, or "commercial," in which case it is generally not protected. For instance, the use of a person's identity in news, entertainment, and creative works for the purpose of communicating information or expressive ideas about that person is protected "expressive" speech. On the other hand, the use of a person's identity for purely commercial purposes, like advertising goods or services or the use of a person's name or likeness on merchandise, is rarely protected. *White v. Samsung Elec. Am., Inc.*, 971 F.2d 1395, 1397-99 (9th Cir. 1992); *Midler v. Ford Motor Co.*, 849 F.2d 460, 462-64 (9th Cir. 1988).

Several approaches have been offered to distinguish between expressive speech and commercial speech. The RESTATEMENT, for example, employs a "relatedness" test that protects the use of another person's name or identity in a work that is "related to" that person. The catalogue of "related" uses includes "the use of a person's name or likeness in news reporting, whether in newspapers, magazines, or broadcast news . . . use in entertainment and other creative works, including both fiction and non-fiction . . . use as part of an article published in a fan magazine or in a feature story broadcast on an entertainment program . . . dissemination of an unauthorized print or broadcast biography, [and use] of another's identity in a novel, play, or motion picture. . . . " RESTATEMENT (THIRD) OF UNFAIR COMPETITION sec. 47 cmt. c at 549. The proviso to that list, however, is that "if the name or likeness is used solely to attract attention to a work that is *not related* to the identified person, the user may be subject to liability for a use of the other's identity in advertising. . . . " *Id.* (Emphasis added.)

California courts use a different approach, called the "transformative test," that was most recently invoked in *Winters v. D.C. Comics*, 69 P.3d 473 (Cal. 2003), a case with a remarkably similar fact situation. In that case, Johnny and Edgar Winters, well-known musicians with albino complexions and long white hair, brought a right of publicity action against defendant D.C. Comics for its publication of a comic book featuring the characters "Johnny and Edgar Autumn," half-worm, half-human creatures with pale faces and long white hair. On appeal, the California Supreme Court considered whether the action was barred by the First Amendment and employed "'what is essentially a balancing test between the First Amendment and the right of publicity based on whether the work in question adds significant creative elements so as to be transformed into something more than a mere celebrity likeness or imitation.'" Concluding that the comic book characters "Johnny and Edgar Autumn" "are not just conventional depictions of plaintiffs but contain significant expressive content other than plaintiffs' mere likenesses," the Court held that the characters were sufficiently transformed so as to entitle the comic book to full First Amendment protection.

The weakness of the Restatement's "relatedness" test and California's "transformative" test is that they give too little consideration to the fact that many uses of a person's name and identity have both expressive and commercial components. These tests operate to preclude a cause of action whenever the use of the name and identity is in any way expressive, regardless of its commercial exploitation. Under the relatedness test, use of a person's name and identity is actionable only when the use is solely commercial and is otherwise unrelated to that person. Under the transformative test, the transformation or fictionalized characterization of a person's celebrity status is not actionable even if its sole purpose is the commercial use of that person's name and identity. Though these tests purport to balance the prospective interests involved, there is no balancing at all — once the use is determined to be expressive, it is protected. At least one commentator, however, has advocated the use of a more balanced balancing test — a sort of predominant use test — that better addresses the cases where speech is both expressive and commercial: . . .

The relative merit of these several tests can be seen when applied to the unusual circumstances of the case at hand. As discussed, Twist made a submissible case that respondents' use of his name and identity was for a commercial advantage. Nonetheless, there is still an expressive component in the use of his name and identity as a metaphorical reference to tough-guy "enforcers." And yet, respondents agree (perhaps to avoid a defamation claim) that the use was not a parody or other expressive comment or a fictionalized account of the real Twist. As such, the metaphorical reference to Twist, though a literary device, has very little literary value compared to its commercial value. On the record here, the use and identity of Twist's name has become predominantly a ploy to sell comic books and related products rather than an artistic or literary expression, and under these circumstances, free speech must give way to the right of publicity.

IV.

[The Court then held that errors in the court's instructions] allowed the jury to render a verdict for plaintiff without a finding that respondents *intended* to obtain a commercial advantage, and because the jury may well have determined that respondents obtained a commercial advantage even though they did not intend to do so, the verdict must be set aside.

V.

In addition to the misappropriation of name claim, Twist sought equitable relief from the circuit court in the form of a permanent injunction prohibiting respondents from using his "name, commercial image, persona, autograph and/or likeness *for any purpose* without his consent." (Emphasis added.) The court denied equitable relief concluding, *inter alia*, that the injunction sought was overbroad because it could "interfere with legitimate and proper action by the defendants in the future." This Court holds that the circuit court was correct in doing so, because, as respondents state in their brief, the requested injunction attempted to prohibit respondents "from engaging in a variety of expressive activities unrelated to the subject matter of this lawsuit and undoubtedly protected by the First Amendment—*e.g.*, a parody of plaintiff, a commentary on his fighting style, a factual report on this lawsuit."

VI.

[Reversed and remanded for a new trial. Order for an injunction denied.] All concur.

NOTES

1. *Rights of publicity and the reportage of public events.* As *Twist* indicates, misappropriation or right of publicity cases tend to be divided into three categories: those involving the reportage of public events, those which are pure commercial uses, and those which involve some mix between commercial and expressive uses.

Thus, at the first pole, courts have uniformly held that the right of publicity does not prohibit newspapers, whether or not operated for profit, from using anyone's name or likeness in an ordinary news story. In Tropeano v. Atlantic Monthly Co., 400 N.E.2d 847, 851 (Mass. 1980), the defendant published a picture of plaintiff in connection with its story "After the Sexual Revolution," without identifying her by name or discussing her. The court held that its publication did not amount to an appropriation of her likeness for advertisement and purposes of trade under Massachusetts law, but was simply part of a "sociological commentary." "The fact that the defendant is engaged in the business of publishing the Atlantic Monthly magazine for profit does not by itself transform the incidental publication of the plaintiff's picture into an appropriation for advertising or trade purposes." Indeed if it did, all news stories would be fair game for the right of publicity. Similarly, in Express One International, Inc. v. Steinbeck, 53 S.W.3d 895 (Tex. App. 2001), the court refused to apply the appropriation doctrine when the defendant posted critical comments about union supporters on Express One's Internet bulletin board. The defendant "Steinbeck intended to impugn Express One's reputation, rather than appropriate it," so that defamation was the proper remedy if any was available at all. Closer to the line perhaps, in Felsher v. University of Evansville, 755 N.E.2d 589 (Ind. 2001), the court held that the misappropriation wrong did not protect corporate entities because the various comments to the Restatement (such as the descendibility of the action at death) were available only to ordinary individuals. Although an invasion of seclusion does not seem to cover a corporate entity, is there any reason why the appropriation or publicity tort should not apply to corporations?

Nor does the outcome change when historical events are fictionalized in public broadcasts. In Tyne v. Time Warner Entertainment Co., 901 So. 2d 802 (Fla. 2005), the plaintiffs were survivors of the crewmembers of the *Andrea Gail* who perished in the 1991 storm which formed the basis of Sebastian Junger's best-selling book, *The Perfect Storm*. The defendants in this case made and distributed a fictionalized version of the book, labeled as such, without asking for the permission of any of the survivors, or paying them for the use of the historical material. The survivors did not sue under a false-light theory even though some of the scenes cast the decedents in a negative light, but they did sue for commercial misappropriation under Florida Statutes §540.08 (2000). The Florida Supreme Court recognized that one of the defendants' purposes in this case was to make money, but rebuffed the claim holding that "the term 'commercial purpose' as used in section 540.08(1) does not apply to publications, including motions pictures, that do not directly promote a product or service." In its view, any broader application of the statute ran into serious difficulties under the First Amendment. Although not in these words, the broad newsworthiness privilege available in other branches of privacy law covers these misappropriation cases as well.

   2. *Pure commercial appropriation.* At the opposite extreme, defendants receive no protection for acts of pure commercial appropriation. In Abdul-Jabbar v. General Motors Corp., 85 F.3d 407 (9th Cir. 1996), the court held that the publicity right protected Abdul-Jabbar's exclusive right to the use of his prior name, Lew Alcindor, under which he played while in college at U.C.L.A. The court reasoned that the tort protected not only the plaintiff's name, but also his identity. In White v. Samsung 971 F.2d 1395 (9th Cir. 1992), the plaintiff Vanna White, the popular hostess of the TV show *Wheel of Fortune*, sued Samsung when it used an image of a robot similar to Vanna White in an advertisement to promote its videocassette recorders. The ad depicted a robot, dressed in a wig, gown, and jewelry which Deutsch, Samsung's ad agency and codefendant, had consciously selected to resemble White's hair and dress. The robot was posed next to a game board that is instantly recognizable as the *Wheel of Fortune* game show set, in a stance for which White is famous. The caption of the ad read: "Longest-running game show. 2012 A.D." The Court allowed the action even though the robot did not amount to appropriation of her name or likeness, holding that the right of publicity "does not require that appropriations of identity be accomplished through particular means to be actionable." It therefore agreed with such decisions as Midler v. Ford Motor Co., 849 F.2d 460 (9th Cir. 1988), in which a "sound-alike's" performance of a song that had made Midler famous was found actionable, and Carson v. Here's Johnny Portable Toilets, Inc., 698 F.2d 831 (6th Cir. 1983), where the defendants improperly used the distinctive Carson introduction, "Here's Johnny," to market a line of portable toilets. The decision in *White* provoked a sharp dissent from Kozinski, J.:

> Saddam Hussein wants to keep advertisers from using his picture in unflattering contexts. Clint Eastwood doesn't want tabloids to write about him. Rudolf Valentino's heirs want to control his film biography. The Girl Scouts don't want their image soiled by association with certain activities. George Lucas wants to keep Strategic Defense Initiative fans from calling it "Star Wars." Pepsico doesn't want singers to use the word "Pepsi" in their songs. Guy Lombardo wants an exclusive property right to ads that show big bands playing on New Year's Eve. Uri Geller thinks he should be paid for ads showing psychics bending metal through telekinesis. Paul Prudhomme, that

household name, thinks the same about ads featuring corpulent bearded chefs. And scads of copyright holders see purple when their creations are made fun of.

Something very dangerous is going on here. Private property, including intellectual property, is essential to our way of life. It provides an incentive for investment and innovation; it stimulates the flourishing of our culture; it protects the moral entitlements of people to the fruits of their labors. But reducing too much to private property can be bad medicine. Private land, for instance, is far more useful if separated from other private land by public streets, roads and highways. Public parks, utility rights-of-way and sewers reduce the amount of land in private hands, but vastly enhance the value of the property that remains.

In light of subsequent decisions like *Twist*, is Kozinski, J., correct about the overexpansion of IP rights in this area?

3. Transformative and expressive uses. The core right of publicity cases is widely held to prohibit firms from marketing pictures of professional athletes without their permission even when the images are not being used to sell any separate product. But what should be done if the athletes' images are made subject to parody by the imposition of some additional creative element? In Cardtoons v. Major League Baseball Players Association, 95 F.3d 959, 971 (10th Cir. 1996), defendant produced "parody trading cards featuring caricatures of major league baseball players," which contained some humorous commentary on the players as well as information about such matters as salary and playing careers on the back. (Having San Francisco Giants star Barry Bonds "on your team is like having money in the bank.") In obvious tension with *Twist*, Tacha, J., rejected the request of the Major League Baseball Players Association to enjoin their sale, holding that the First Amendment protected their publication. After distinguishing *White*, she wrote:

> MLBPA maintains that there are many ways that Cardtoons could parody the institution of baseball that would not require use of player names and likenesses. Cardtoons could, for example, use generic images of baseball players to poke fun at the game. Second, MLBPA contends that Cardtoons could use recognizable players in a format other than trading cards, such as a newspaper or magazine, without infringing on its right of publicity. MLBPA argues that these alternative means of communication are adequate and, therefore, that we may uphold its property rights without seriously infringing upon Cardtoons' right to free expression. . . .
>
> In this case, Cardtoons' expression requires use of player identities because, in addition to parodying the institution of baseball, the cards also lampoon individual players. Further, Cardtoons' use of the trading card format is an essential component of the parody because baseball cards have traditionally been used to celebrate baseball players and their accomplishment.

Prior to its decision in *Winter*, discussed in *Twist*, the California Supreme Court adopted and extended the *Cardtoons'* approach in Comedy III Productions, Inc. v. Gary Saderup, Inc., 21 P.3d 797, 808 (Cal. 2001). The court enjoined the defendant from selling T-shirts that featured a precise rendition of the well-known comedy act, The Three Stooges. "When artistic expression takes the form of a literal depiction or imitation of a celebrity for commercial gain, directly trespassing on the right of publicity without adding significant expression beyond that trespass, the state law interest in protecting the fruits of artistic labor outweighs the expressive interests of the imitative artist." "On the other hand, when a work contains significant transformative elements, it is not only especially worthy of First Amendment protection, but it is also less likely to interfere with the economic interest protected by the right of publicity. . . . [W]orks of parody or other distortions of the celebrity figure are not, from the celebrity fan's viewpoint, good substitutes for conventional depictions of the celebrity and therefore do not generally threaten markets for celebrity memorabilia that the right of publicity is designed to protect." "In sum, when an artist is faced with a right of publicity challenge to his or her work, he or she may raise as affirmative defense that the work is protected by the First Amendment inasmuch as it contains significant transformative elements or that the value of the work does not derive primarily from the celebrity's fame." The transformative test developed in *Comedy III* was then applied to protect the defendants in Winter v. DC Comics, 69 P.3d 473 (Cal. 2003), criticized in *Twist*.

That same tension between the right of publicity and the First Amendment was also evident in Parks v. LaFace Records, 329 F.3d 437 (6th Cir. 2003). There the court held that the plaintiff, Rosa Parks, whose act of defiance precipitated the Montgomery Bus Boycott of 1956, raised at least a jury question on whether the defendant record company had misappropriated her name by making it the title of a hit single, Rosa Parks, which contained some racy lyrics that earned it a Parental Advisory warning. The defendants argued that the title of the song was designed to evoke the "symbolic" image of what it means to go to the back of the bus. On remand the question was whether the title of the song was "wholly unrelated" to the content of the song, so that it could be regarded as a "disguised commercial advertisement," or chosen "solely to attract attention" to the work. How does this case come out under *Twist*? Under the transformation test of *Comedy III*? Is the outcome in *Zacchini* consistent with the transformation test in *Comedy III*? Note also that Zacchini could not have sued for copyright infringement for the broadcast, because he had not, as the federal copyright law requires, "fixed" his act in some tangible medium of expression, as by filming it himself. The copyright law, however, also contains a "fair use" exception, "for purposes such as criticism, comment, news reporting, teaching (including multiple copies for classroom use), scholarship, and research," which are not regarded as infringements of copyright. See Copyright Act, 17 U.S.C. §107 (1977). Should *Zacchini* be decided on analogous "fair use" principles? If so, could the rebroadcast of the entire act be justified? For a discussion of the copyright analogies, see Note, Human Cannonballs and the First Amendment: *Zacchini v. Scripps-Howard Broadcasting Co.*, 30 Stan. L. Rev. 1185 (1978).

4. *The first sale doctrine.* The close affinity between the common law right of publicity and traditional forms of intellectual property, such as copyrights and patents, is revealed in the first sale doctrine. In Allison v. Vintage Sports Plaques, 136 F.3d 1443, 1448-1449 (11th Cir. 1998), the plaintiff's late husband, a well known race car driver, had assigned to Maxx Race Cards the right to "manufacture and market trading cards bearing his likeness in exchange for a royalty of 18% of sales receipts. . . ." The defendant purchased trading cards bearing the image of plaintiffs from manufacturers and distributors, which it mounted in a plaque bearing the name of the featured player or team. The defendant did not copy or alter the cards in any way. The so-called first sale doctrine in the law of patents and copyrights provides that the holder of an intellectual property right has no further right to control its subsequent resale or further disposition once it is placed in the market. Kravitch, J., held that this doctrine barred plaintiff's claim for violation of the right of publicity:

> [A]ccepting appellants' argument would have profoundly negative effects on numerous industries and would grant a monopoly to celebrities over their identities that would upset the delicate "balance between the interests of the celebrity and those of the public." *White*, 989 F.2d at 1515 (Kozinski, J., dissenting). . . . Indeed, a decision by this court not to apply the first-sale doctrine to right of publicity actions would render tortious the resale of sports trading cards and memorabilia and thus would have a profound effect on the market for trading cards, which now supports a multi-billion dollar industry. Such a holding presumably also would prevent, for example, framing a magazine advertisement that bears the image of a celebrity and reselling it as a collector's item, reselling an empty cereal box that bears a celebrity's endorsement, or even reselling a used poster promoting a professional sports team. Refusing to apply the first-sale doctrine to the right of publicity also presumably would prevent a child from selling to his friend a baseball card that he had purchased, a consequence that undoubtedly would be contrary to the policies supporting that right.
>
> A holding that the first-sale doctrine does limit the right of publicity, on the other hand, would not eliminate a celebrity's control over the use of her name or image; the right of publicity protects against unauthorized use of an image, and a celebrity would continue to enjoy the right to license the use of her image *in the first instance* — and thus enjoy the power to determine when, or if, her image will be distributed.

Note that the first sale doctrine need not necessarily reduce the plaintiff's total receipts, for that royalty charge for the initial use could reflect both present and future users of the object sold. The single lump sum thus displaces a series of smaller payments that would be, to say the least, difficult to collect. By using a single payment, however, the first sale rule prevents any price discrimination by plaintiff based on knowledge of the extra demand for the subsequent sale, as in *Allison* itself. That price discrimination often meets with an uncertain response. On the one hand, price discrimination allows a monopolist to sell to individuals who are willing and able to pay more than the marginal cost of production, but who cannot or will not pay any single price charged by a monopolist. But that price discrimination also undermines the parity of treatment between people who perceive themselves as equals. Price discrimination (without collusion) is allowed for patented products, especially pharmaceuticals, but has been subject to a sharp political backlash in recent years, in light of the huge price disparities that are found in international markets.

Factors Etc., Inc. v. Pro Arts, Inc.
579 F.2d 215 (2d Cir. 1978)

[The plaintiff in this action had received from Boxcars, Inc. — a corporation controlled by the late Elvis Presley and his business partner, Colonel Tom Parker — an exclusive license to commercially exploit the name and likeness of Elvis Presley. Factors Etc. had paid Boxcar $100,000 for the license against a guarantee of $150,000. Immediately upon learning of Presley's death, Pro Arts purchased the copyright of a Presley photograph from a staff reporter of the Atlanta (Georgia) Journal, which it published on a poster three days later. Above the picture were the words "IN MEMORY" and below it were the dates "1935-1977." Among the many purchasers of the posters was the New York codefendant, Stop and Shop Companies. Factors Etc. demanded in writing that Pro Arts cease marketing the poster and threatened suit if it did not. Pro Arts responded by filing a declaratory judgment action in the Northern District of Ohio. Factors Etc. brought suit in the Southern District of New York. The issue on appeal was whether the New York district court had properly issued a preliminary injunction against Pro Arts.]

INGRAHAM, J. . . . The injunction restrained Pro Arts during the pendency of the action from manufacturing, selling or distributing (1) any more copies of the poster labeled "IN MEMORY . . . 1935-1977," (2) any other posters, reproductions or copies containing any likeness of Elvis Presley, and (3) utilizing for commercial profit in any manner or form the name or likeness of Elvis Presley. The order also denied Pro Arts' motion to dismiss, stay or transfer. Pro Arts has duly perfected this interlocutory appeal from the order. . . .

On appeal, Pro Arts alleges two errors of law on the part of the trial court. According to Pro Arts, the trial court erred first in concluding that the right of publicity could survive the death of the celebrity. Second, Pro Arts argues that even if the right did so survive, Pro Arts was privileged, as a matter of law, in printing and distributing its "memorial poster" of Presley, because the poster celebrated a newsworthy event.

The first issue, the duration of the so-called "right of publicity," is one of state law, more specifically the law of the State of New York. Because of the dearth of New York case law in this area, however, we have sought assistance from federal court decisions interpreting and applying New York law, as well as decisions from courts of other states.

[The court then relied on *Zacchini* and the excerpt from the Kalven article quoted therein to establish that the right of publicity is designed to protect the plaintiff's right of commercial exploitation and thus is sharply distinguishable from the other forms of privacy which, in contrast, are designed "to minimize the intrusion or publication" of damaging information. It also noted that Haelan Laboratories, Inc. v. Tops Chewing Gum, Inc., 202 F.2d 866 (2d Cir. 1953), recognized that the right of publicity was transferable by its owner.]

There can be no doubt that Elvis Presley assigned to Boxcar a valid property right, the exclusive authority to print, publish and distribute his name and likeness. In so doing, he carved out a separate intangible property right for himself, the right to a certain percentage of the royalties which would be realized by Boxcar upon exploitation of Presley's likeness and name. The identification of this exclusive right belonging to Boxcar as a transferable property right compels the conclusion that the right survives Presley's death. The death of Presley, who was merely the beneficiary of an income interest in Boxcar's exclusive right, should not in itself extinguish Boxcar's property right. Instead, the income interest, continually produced from Boxcar's exclusive right of commercial exploitation, should inure to Presley's estate at death like any other intangible property right. To hold that the right did not survive Presley's death, would be to grant competitors of Factors, such as Pro Arts, a windfall in the form of profits from the use of Presley's name and likeness. At the same time, the exclusive right purchased by Factors and the financial benefits accruing to the celebrity's heirs would be rendered virtually worthless. . . .

Pro Arts' final argument is that even if Factors possesses the exclusive right to distribute Presley memorabilia, this right does not prevent Pro Arts from publishing what it terms a "memorial poster" commemorating a newsworthy event. In support of this argument, Pro Arts cites Paulsen v. Personality Posters, Inc., 299 N.Y.S.2d 501 (Sup. Ct. 1968), a case arising out of the bogus presidential candidacy of the television comedian Pat Paulsen. Paulsen sued defendant for publishing and distributing a poster of Paulsen with the legend "FOR PRESIDENT." The court refused to enjoin sale of the poster because Paulsen's choice of the political arena for satire made him "newsworthy" in the First Amendment sense. We cannot accept

Pro Arts' contention that the legend "IN MEMORY . . ." placed its poster in the same category as one picturing a presidential candidate, albeit a mock candidate. We hold, therefore, that Pro Arts' poster of Presley was not privileged as celebrating a newsworthy event. . . .

   Affirmed.

NOTES

1. Commercial life after death? The issue raised in the principal case received a very different treatment in Memphis Development Foundation v. Factors Etc., Inc., 616 F.2d 956, 958-960 (6th Cir. 1980). The Development Foundation offered an eight-inch statuette of Elvis Presley to persons who contributed $25.00 to the Foundation. The Foundation instituted a declaratory judgment action to establish that Factors' license did not preclude its distribution of the statue. Factors counterclaimed for damages and injunctive relief. In holding that the right of publicity did not survive the death of the actor, the court took issue with *Pro Arts* by examining some of the fundamental principles underlying private property and a market economy.

> Recognition of a post-mortem right of publicity would vindicate two possible interests: the encouragement of effort and creativity, and the hopes and expectations of the decedent and those with whom he contracts that they are creating a valuable capital asset. Although fame and stardom may be ends in themselves, they are normally by-products of one's activities and personal attributes, as well as luck and promotion. The basic motivations are the desire to achieve success or excellence in a chosen field, the desire to contribute to the happiness or improvement of one's fellows and the desire to receive the psychic and financial rewards of achievement. . . .
>   On the other hand, there are strong reasons for declining to recognize the inheritability of the right. A whole set of practical problems of judicial line-drawing would arise should the courts recognize such an inheritable right. How long would the "property" interest last? In perpetuity? For a term of years? Is the right of publicity taxable? At what point does the right collide with the right of free expression guaranteed by the First Amendment? Does the right apply to elected officials and military heroes whose fame was gained on the public payroll, as well as to movie stars, singers and athletes? Does the right cover posters or engraved likenesses of, for example, Farrah Fawcett Majors or Mahatma Gandhi, kitchen utensils ("Revere Ware"), insurance ("John Hancock"), electric utilities ("Edison"), a football stadium ("RFK"), a pastry ("Napoleon"), or the innumerable urban subdivisions and apartment complexes named after famous people? Our legal system normally does not pass on to heirs other similar personal attributes even though the attributes may be shared during life by others or have some commercial value. Titles, offices and reputation are not inheritable. Neither are trust or distrust and friendship or enmity descendible. An employment contract

during life does not create the right for heirs to take over the job. Fame falls in the same category as reputation; it is an attribute from which others may benefit but may not own.

The law of defamation, designed to protect against the destruction of reputation including the loss of earning capacity associated with it, provides an analogy. There is no right of action for defamation after death. . . .

There is no indication that changing the traditional common law rule against allowing heirs the exclusive control of the commercial use of their ancestor's name will increase the efficiency or productivity of our economic system. It does not seem reasonable to expect that such a change would enlarge the stock or quality of the goods, services, artistic creativity, information, invention or entertainment available. Nor will it enhance the fairness of our political and economic system. It seems fairer and more efficient for the commercial, aesthetic, and political use of the name, memory and image of the famous to be open to all rather than to be monopolized by a few. An equal distribution of the opportunity to use the name of the dead seems preferable. The memory, name and pictures of famous individuals should be regarded as a common asset to be shared, an economic opportunity available in the free market system.

After *Memphis Development*, the Second Circuit abandoned its earlier decision by giving "conclusive" effect "to a rule by a court of appeals deciding the law of a state within its circuit." Factors Etc., Inc. v. Pro Arts, Inc., 652 F.2d 278 (2d Cir. 1981). Why aren't the descendible interests just those that are protected during life by the right of publicity? On the descendibility question, see generally Felcher & Rubin, Privacy, Publicity, and Portrayal of Real People by the Media, 88 Yale L.J. 1577 (1979).

2. *Exploitation only after death?* Should the right of publicity descend if it had not been utilized during the lifetime of the original creator? The California Supreme Court answered that question in the negative in Lugosi v. Universal Pictures, 603 P.2d 425 (Cal. 1979). The decedent had not taken any steps while alive to exploit his famous Dracula image, developed in his movie roles for the defendant. The defendant thereafter licensed a number of other businesses to make an impressive assortment of clothes, trinkets, and memorabilia that utilized the Dracula image. The California court refused to allow Lugosi's heirs to enjoin the sales. The legislature responded to *Lugosi* by adoption of California Civil Code §3344.1(b), which provides: "The rights recognized under this section are property rights, freely transferable, in whole or in part, by contract or by means of trust or testamentary documents, . . ."

In Cairns v. Franklin Mint Co., 24 F. Supp. 2d 1013 (C.D. Cal. 1998), the court refused to apply that statute for the benefit of plaintiffs, trustees of the Princess Diana Memorial Fund, who brought suit to prevent this use of her name or likeness in conjunction with the sale of Princess Diana memorabilia because Great Britain, whose law applied in the case, does not recognize a descendible right of publicity. The court also held that the plaintiff was entitled to reach the jury on whether the defendant's activities constituted a false designation of origin or a false endorsement of product, actionable in this country under the Lanham Act. The death of Diana continues to reverberate to this day; Channel 4, over the protest of her two sons, Andrew and Edward, recently broadcast some newly discovered footage of the late princess on the day of her fatal crash. C4 Rebuffs Diana Photographs Plea, BBC News (May 2007) http://news.bbc.co.uk/2/hi/uk_news/6721789.stm.

15

MISREPRESENTATION

SECTION A. INTRODUCTION

All civil societies prohibit at least two forms of harmful conduct, aggression and deceit. Sometimes the two are very much intertwined: The assailant who feints before he throws a blow combines both together in a single act. Even with accidental harms, force and misrepresentation often work in tandem. Thus, a misrepresentation forms one link in the chain of causation when physical injuries are attributable to latent defects in the defendant's premises or products. By creating or maintaining the latent defect, the defendant's conduct misrepresents the condition of either his premises or product, which leads the plaintiff to use those premises or that product to her detriment. Similarly, informed consent suits against physicians and duty to warn cases against product manufacturers turn on, if not express misrepresentations, then inadequate disclosures when given a duty to speak. Finally, misrepresentations play a critical role in the law of defamation, in which the false statements of the defendant mislead a third party to avoid interacting with the plaintiff.

Oddly enough, none of these situations of physical injury or defamation is covered by the basic tort of misrepresentation, which starts from a somewhat different vantage point—that of the plaintiff who claims *pecuniary or commercial* loss because she acted, to her detriment, on the faith of the defendant's misrepresentation. See Restatement (Second) of Torts §531 (1976). Typical situations include entering into a losing contract or making cash advances in reliance upon the defendant's false statements. Usually the plaintiff is required to show not only that she was misled by the defendant's misstatements, but also that the defendant knew that his statements were false, or at least that he was indifferent to their truth or falsity. Restatement (Second) of Torts §525 sets out the elements of common law fraud as follows:

> One who fraudulently makes a misrepresentation of fact, opinion, intention or law for the purpose of inducing another to act or to refrain from action in reliance upon it, is subject to liability to the other in deceit for pecuniary loss caused to him by his justifiable reliance upon the misrepresentation.

The first section of the following materials is devoted to the law of fraud, and the second to the law of negligent misrepresentation.

SECTION B. FRAUD

Pasley v. Freeman
100 Eng. Rep. 450 (K.B. 1789)

[The plaintiffs were merchants who asked the defendant about the financial condition of John Christopher Falch before selling Falch a large amount of goods on credit. Plaintiffs alleged that the defendant "did wrongfully and deceitfully encourage and persuade the said John Pasley and Edward, to sell and deliver to the said John Christopher Falch divers other goods, wares and merchandizes, to wit, 16 other bags of cochineal of great value, to wit, of the value of [about £2,634] upon trust and credit; and did for that purpose then and there falsely, deceitfully, and fraudulently, assert and affirm to the said John Pasley and Edward, that the said John Christopher then and there was a person safely to be trusted and given credit in that respect." The plaintiffs further alleged that they sold the goods on credit, but that Falch, as the defendant had known all along, was a bad credit risk, wholly unable to pay for the goods; in fact he paid for no part of them. The plaintiff sued the defendant to recover from him the value of the goods sold and delivered to Falch. Verdict for the plaintiffs.]

The Court took time to consider of this matter, and now delivered their opinions seriatim.

GROSE, J. Upon the face of this count in the declaration, no privity of contract is stated between the parties. No consideration arises to the defendant; and he is in no situation in which the law considers him in any trust, or in which it demands from him any account of the credit of Falch. He appears not to be interested in any transaction between the plaintiffs and Falch, nor to have colluded with them; but he knowingly asserted a falsehood, by saying that Falch might be safely entrusted with the goods, and given credit to, for the purpose of inducing the plaintiffs to trust him with them, by which the plaintiffs lost the value of the goods. . . . It is admitted, that the action is new in point of precedent: but it is insisted that the law recognises principles on which it may be supported. The principle on which it is contended to lie is, that wherever deceit or falsehood is practised to the detriment of another, the law will give redress. . . . When this was first argued at the Bar, on the motion for a new trial, I confess I thought it reasonable that the action should lie: but, on looking into the old books for cases in which the old action of deceit has been maintained upon the false affirmation of the defendant, I have changed my opinion. . . . I have not met with any case of an action upon a false affirmation, except against a party to a contract, and where there is a promise, either express or implied, that the fact is true, which is misrepresented: and no other case has been cited at the Bar. Then if no such case has ever existed, it furnishes a strong objection against the action, which is brought for the first time for a supposed injury, which has been daily committed for centuries past; . . . A variety of cases may be put: suppose a man recommends an estate to another, as knowing it to be of greater value than it is; when the purchaser has bought it, he discovers the defect, and sells the estate for less than he gave; why may not an action be brought for the loss upon any principle that will support this action? And yet such an action has never been attempted. Or, suppose a person present at the sale of an horse asserts that he was his horse, and that he knows him to be sound and sure-footed, when in fact the horse is neither the one nor the other; according to the principle contended for by the plaintiffs, an action lies against the person present as well as the seller; and the purchaser has two securities. And even in this very case, if the action lies, the plaintiffs will stand in a peculiarly fortunate predicament, for then they will have the responsibility both of Falch and the defendant. And they will be in a better situation than they would have been if, in the conversation that passed between them and the defendant, instead of asserting that Falch might safely be trusted, the defendant had said, "If he do not pay for the goods, I will:" for then undoubtedly an action would not have lain against the defendant. . . . The misrepresentation stated in the declaration is respecting the credit of Falch; the defendant asserted that the plaintiffs might safely give him credit: but credit to which a man is entitled is matter of judgment and opinion, on which different men might form different opinions, and upon which the plaintiffs might form their own; to mislead which no fact to prove the good credit of Falch is falsely asserted. It seems to me therefore that any assertion relative to credit, especially where the party making it has no interest, nor is in any collusion with the person respecting whose credit the assertion is made, is . . . not an assertion of a fact peculiarly in the knowledge of the defendant. Whether Falch deserved credit depended on the opinion of many; for credit exists on the good opinion of many. Respecting this, the plaintiffs might have inquired of others, who knew as much as the defendant; it was their fault that they did not, and they have suffered damage by their own laches. It was owing to their own gross negligence that they gave credence to the assertion of the defendant, without taking pains to satisfy themselves that that assertion was founded in fact, as in the case of Bayly v. Merrel. I am therefore of opinion, that this action is as novel in principle as it is in precedent, that it is against the principles to be collected from analogous cases, and consequently that it cannot be maintained.

BULLER, J. The foundation of this action is fraud and deceit in the defendant, and damage to the plaintiffs. And the question is, whether an action thus founded can be sustained in a Court of Law? Fraud without damage, or damage without fraud, gives no cause of action; but where these two concur, an action lies. But it is contended, that this was a bare naked lie; that, as no collusion with Falch is charged, it does not amount to a fraud: and, if there were any fraud, the nature of it is not stated. And it was supposed by the counsel who originally made the motion, that no action could be maintained, unless the defendant, who made this false assertion, had an interest in so doing. I agree that an action cannot be supported for telling a bare naked lie; but that I define to be, saying a thing which is false, knowing or not knowing it to be so, and without any design to injure, cheat, or deceive, another person. Every deceit comprehends a lie; but a deceit is more than a lie on account of the view with which it is practised, it's being coupled with some dealing, and the injury which it is calculated to occasion, and does occasion, to another person. Deceit is a very extensive head in the law; and it will be proper to take a short view of some of the cases which have existed on the subject, to see how far the Courts have gone, and what are the principles upon which they have decided. [Buller, J., reviewed the precedents and concluded that proof of collusion or conspiracy was not necessary to make out an action for deceit.] Some general arguments were urged at the Bar, to shew that mischiefs and inconveniences would arise if this action were sustained; for if a man, who is asked a question respecting another's responsibility, hesitate, or is silent, he blasts the character of the tradesman: and if he say that he is insolvent, he may not be able to prove it. But let us see what is contended for: it is nothing less than that a man may assert that which he knows to be false, and thereby do an everlasting injury to his neighbour, and yet not be answerable for it. This is as repugnant to law as it is to morality. Then it is said, that the plaintiffs had no right to ask the question of the defendant. But I do not agree in that; for the plaintiffs had an interest in knowing what the credit of Falch was. It was not the inquiry of idle curiosity, but it was to govern a very extensive concern. The defendant undoubtedly had his option to give an answer to the question, or not: but if he gave none, or said he did not know, it is impossible for any Court of Justice to adopt the possible inferences of a suspicious mind as a ground for grave judgment. All that is required of a person in the defendant's situation is, that he shall give no answer, or that if he do, he shall answer according to the truth as far as he knows. . . . If the answer import insolvency, it is not necessary that the defendant should be able to prove that insolvency to a jury; for the law protects a man in giving that answer, if he does it in confidence and without malice. No action can be maintained against him for giving such an answer unless express malice can be proved. From the circumstance of the law giving that protection, it seems to follow, as a necessary consequence, that the law not only gives sanction to the question, but requires that, if it be answered at all, it shall be answered honestly. . . .

ASHHURST, J. . . . For the gist of the action is the injury done to the plaintiff, and not whether the defendant meant to be a gainer by it: what is it to the plaintiff whether the defendant was or was not to gain by it; the injury to him is the same. And it should seem that it ought more emphatically to lie against him, as the malice is more diabolical, if he had not the temptation of gain. For the same reason, it cannot be necessary that the defendant should collude with one who has an interest. But if collusion were necessary, there seems all the reason in the world to suppose both interest and collusion from the nature of the act; for it is to be hoped that there is not to be found a disposition so diabolical as to prompt any man to injure another without benefiting himself. . . . Another argument which has been made use of is, that this is a new case, and that there is no precedent of such an action. Where cases are new in their principle, there I admit that it is necessary to have recourse to legislative interposition in order to remedy the grievance: but where the case is only new in the instance, and the only question is upon the application of a principle recognized in the law to such new case, it will be just as competent to Courts of Justice to apply the principle to any case which may arise two centuries hence as it was two centuries ago; if it were not, we ought to blot out of our law books one fourth part of the cases that are to be found in them. . . .

LORD KENYON, C.J. . . . There are many situations in life, and particularly in the commercial world, where a man cannot by any diligence inform himself of the degree of credit which ought to be given to the persons with whom he deals; in which cases he must apply to those whose sources of intelligence enable them to give that information. The law of prudence leads him to apply to them, and the law of morality ought to induce them to give the information required. In the case of Bulstrode the carrier might have weighed the goods himself: but in this case the plaintiffs had no means of knowing the state of Falch's credit but by an application to his neighbours. . . . Then it was contended here that the action cannot be maintained for telling a naked lie: but that proposition is to be taken sub modo. If, indeed, no injury is occasioned by the lie, it is not actionable: but if it be attended with a damage, it then becomes the subject of an action. As calling a woman a whore, if she sustain no damage by it, is not actionable; but if she loses her marriage by it, then she may recover satisfaction in damages. But in this case the two grounds of the action concur: here are both the damnum et injuria. The plaintiffs applied to the defendant telling him that they were going to deal with Falch, and desiring to be informed of his credit, when the defendant fraudulently, and knowing it to be otherwise, and with a design to deceive the plaintiffs, made the false affirmation which is stated on the record, by which they sustained a considerable damage. Then can a doubt be entertained for a moment but that this is injurious to the plaintiffs? If this be not an injury, I do not know how to define the word. Then as to the loss, this is stated in the declaration, and found by the verdict. Several of the words stated in this declaration, and particularly "fraudulenter," did not occur in several of the cases cited. It is admitted that the defendant's conduct was highly immoral, and detrimental to society. And I am of opinion that the action is maintainable on the grounds of deceit in the defendant, and injury and loss to the plaintiffs.

[Judgment affirmed.]

NOTES

1. *The birth of an action.* What would have been the impact upon commercial life if Pasley v. Freeman had been decided the other way? Would Grose, J., have allowed the action if the plaintiff had paid the defendant for the information? Note that the early reception to *Pasley* was not always favorable. In Evans v. Bicknell, 31 Eng. Rep. 998, 1003 (Ch. 1801), Lord Eldon, stressing the difficulty of proof when plaintiff's "stout assertion" is met with defendant's "positive denial," thought that the protection of the Statute of Frauds was needed. Why not allow the action if there is testimony of a third-party witness who heard the exchange?

2. *An action for deceit.* Under *Pasley*, the action for deceit requires, as its name suggests, proof of deliberate lying. During the nineteenth century, courts from time to time sought to expand deceit to reach a defendant guilty only of "legal fraud" or "fraud in law" — i.e., a false statement of fact made without having any reasonable grounds for believing his statement to be true — in practice a form of negligence liability. The debate over whether an action for deceit reached negligent misrepresentations came to a head in the famous case of Derry v. Peek, 14 App. Cas. 337, 374, 375-376 (H.L.E. 1889). The defendants were directors of a corporation who issued a prospectus in which they claimed a special act of Parliament gave them "the right to use steam or mechanical motive power, instead of horses" to run their trams along public ways to the corporation's substantial financial advantage. The plaintiff invested in shares of the company on the faith of the representations, which proved false, as the corporation was entitled to use mechanical power only on a limited portion of its tracks. After the

company liquidated, the plaintiff sued the directors for deceit to recover the value of his original investment. The trial judge dismissed the plaintiff's cause of action, which was subsequently allowed by the court of appeal. Cotton, L.J., equated speaking "recklessly, or without care whether it is true or false" with speaking "without any reasonable ground for believing it to be true." Peek v. Derry, [1887] 37 Ch. 541, 566. The decision was reversed in the House of Lords, in which Lord Herschell first took issue with Cotton's suggestion that negligence and recklessness are "convertible expressions." "To make a statement careless whether it be true or false, and therefore without any real belief in its truth, appears to me to be an essentially different thing from making, through want of care, a false statement, which is nevertheless honestly believed to be true." Later, he summarized the law:

> I think the authorities establish the following propositions: First, in order to sustain an action of deceit, there must be proof of fraud, and nothing short of that will suffice. Secondly, fraud is proved when it is shewn that a false representation has been made (1) knowingly, or (2) without belief in its truth, or (3) recklessly, careless whether it be true or false. Although I have treated the second and third as distinct cases, I think the third is but an instance of the second, for one who makes a statement under such circumstances can have no real belief in the truth of what he states. To prevent a false statement being fraudulent, there must, I think, always be an honest belief in its truth. And this probably covers the whole ground, for one who knowingly alleges that which is false, has obviously no such honest belief. Thirdly, if fraud be proved, the motive of the person guilty of it is immaterial. It matters not that there was no intention to cheat or injure the person to whom the statement was made.

Lord Herschell added that "if I thought that a person making a false statement had shut his eyes to the facts, or purposely abstained from inquiring into them, I should hold that honest belief was absent and that he was just as fraudulent as if he had knowingly stated that which was false." Nonetheless, on the evidence he concluded that charges of fraud could not be sustained, only to express his misgivings about letting the defendant off scot-free on the ground that "those who put before the public a prospectus to induce them to embark their money in a commercial enterprise ought to be vigilant to see that it contains such representations only as are in strict accordance with fact. . . ." Parliament responded to this invitation with the Director's Liability Act, 1890, 53 & 54 Vict. ch. 64, which provides in part that a director or promoter of a corporation will be held liable for damages to purchasers of stocks and bonds unless the director or promoter can show that "he had reasonable ground to believe," and at all material times did believe, his statements to be true. The statute also contained special rules governing the liability of directors for statements in the prospectus that reflected the opinion of experts in the venture or the state of the public record. What is the appropriate standard of liability in these cases?

3. *Fraud and recklessness generally.* *Derry* remains extremely influential in American Courts in defining the appropriate scope of fraud. In Neurosurgery & Spine Surgery, S.C., v. Goldman, 790 N.E.2d 925, 933 (Ill. App. 2003), the court relied heavily on *Derry* when it "decline[d] to extend the tort of fraudulent misrepresentation to encompass noncommercial and nonfinancial dealings between parties." In other cases, courts have been careful not to erode the line between fraud and negligence. Thus, in In re Acosta, 406 F.3d 367, 372 (5th Cir. 2005), the question was whether a creditor's claim was nondischargable in bankruptcy on the ground that the debtor had fraudulently omitted to state two prior liens on the debtor's property. Vance, J., held that it was not. "An intent to deceive may be inferred from 'reckless disregard for the truth or falsity of a statement combined with the sheer magnitude of the resultant misrepresentation.' Nevertheless, an honest belief, even if unreasonable, that a representation is true and that the speaker has information to justify it does not amount to an intent to deceive. Thus, a 'dumb but honest' defendant does not have scienter." Nonetheless, recklessness can be found in those cases where a defendant holds out to a level of expertise that he does not in fact possess. Thus, in Skowronski v. Sachs, 818 N.E.2d 635 (Mass. App. Ct. 2004), a jeweler certified an inferior diamond as a stone of a higher grade when he had no knowledge of the proper procedures required of an expert in that area. The court found that the misrepresentations were reckless, and hence fraudulent, when the defendant did not disclose his want of expertise.

4. *Securities fraud today.* The problem of fraud continues to be the source of active litigation in wide variety of transactions in established securities markets. The Securities and Exchange Act of 1934, 15 U.S.C. §§78a-78mm (2000). Section 10(b), 15 U.S.C. §78j(b), also reaches these transactions by providing that it shall be unlawful "To use or employ, in connection with the purchase or sale of any security . . . any manipulative or deceptive device or contrivance in contravention of such rules and regulations as the Commission may prescribe as necessary or appropriate in the public interest or for the protection of investors." Pursuant to the statute, the SEC published Rule 10b-5, 17 C.F.R. §240.10b-5 (2007). It provides as follows:

EMPLOYMENT OF MANIPULATIVE AND DECEPTIVE DEVICES

It shall be unlawful for any person, directly or indirectly, by the use of any means or instrumentality of interstate commerce, or of the mails or of any facility of any national securities exchange,

(a) To employ any device, scheme, or artifice to defraud,

(b) To make any untrue statement of a material fact or to omit to state a material fact necessary in order to make the statements made, in the light of the circumstances under which they were made, not misleading, or

(c) To engage in any act, practice, or course of business which operates or would operate as a fraud or deceit upon any person, in connection with the purchase or sale of any security.

In Ernst & Ernst v. Hochfelder, 425 U.S. 185, 199 (1976), a reprise of *Derry*, the Supreme Court was asked to hold that negligent misrepresentations were actionable under the rule, because the effects were the same "regardless of whether the conduct is negligent or intentional." The Court rejected the invitation, noting that as a matter of ordinary English the commission's argument "simply ignores the use of the words 'manipulative,' 'device,' and 'contrivance' — terms that make unmistakable a Congressional intent to proscribe a type of conduct quite different from negligence. Use of the word 'manipulative' is especially significant. It is and was virtually a term of art when used in connection with securities markets. It connotes intentional or willful conduct designed to deceive or defraud investors by controlling or artificially affecting the price of securities."

Ernst & Ernst left open the question, decided in the affirmative in *Derry*, whether recklessness should be equated with fraud in the contexts of securities. Every Circuit Court that has considered the matter has held that reckless conduct meets the scienter requirement under the Securities Act, even if they differ in the level of recklessness required. See, e.g., Ottmann v. Hanger Orthopedic Group, Inc. 353 F.3d 338, 343 (4th Cir. 2003), which defined recklessness to mean "an act so highly unreasonable and such an extreme departure from the standard of ordinary care as to present a danger of misleading the plaintiff to the extent that the danger was either known to the defendant or so obvious that the defendant must have been aware of it."

The Supreme Court has yet to rule on whether recklessness constitutes a species of fraud, see Tellabs, Inc. v. Makro Issues & Rights, Ltd., 127 S.Ct. 2499 (2007), a securities fraud case brought against Tellabs and its chief executive officer. But it seems highly unlikely that it will deviate from the consensus in the Circuit Courts.

5. The Private Securities Litigation Reform Act of 1995. Tellabs also resolved a hotly disputed pleading issue under the PSLRA that, in an effort to curb what were regarded as abusive class actions, requires the plaintiff to "specify each statement alleged to have been misleading, the reason or reasons why the statement is misleading." Furthermore, in dealing with the defendant's state of mind, the PSLRA imposes two related requirements: First, "if an allegation regarding the statement or omission is made on information and belief, the complaint shall state with particularity all facts on which that belief is formed," and, second, the complaint must "state with particularity facts giving rise to a strong inference that the defendant acted with the required state of mind." 15 U.S.C. §78a.

Ginsburg, J., held that "the inference of scienter must be more than merely plausible or reasonable — it must be cogent and at least as compelling as any opposing inference of nonfraudulent intent." She then added that the proper inquiry "is whether *all* of the facts alleged, taken collectively given rise to a strong inference of scienter, not whether any individual allegation, scrutinized in isolation meets that standard."

Section 10-b-5 is not confined to the purchase and sale of stock in ordinary exchanges. In The Wharf (Holdings) Limited v. United International Holdings, Inc., 532 U.S. 588 (2001), a unanimous Supreme Court held that the defendant Wharf had engaged in manipulative and deceptive behavior when it sold an oral option to buy stock with the contemporaneous secret intention of never honoring its terms. Breyer, J., held that an oral option was covered by the act, which extends to "'any contract' for the purchase or sale of a security." He also deflected concerns that this action would swamp ordinary actions for breach of contract by noting that "United proved that secret intent with documentary evidence that went well beyond evidence of a simple failure to perform." What result if the plaintiff's claim was not supported by any documentary evidence?

Vulcan Metals Co. v. Simmons Manufacturing Co.
248 F. 853 (2d Cir. 1918)

[The defendant, Simmons Manufacturing, sold to the plaintiff, Vulcan Manufacturing Co., all of its patents, tools, dies, and equipment for the manufacture of vacuum cleaners, together with all machines and parts then on hand. During the sales negotiations, Simmons's agents made two sorts of representations to Albert Freeman, a promoter of the Vulcan Corporation. The first group included "commendations of the cleanliness, economy, and efficiency of the machine"; that it was superior to rival methods of cleaning, such as "beating and brushing"; that it was so simple that a child of six could use it; that it was durable and long-lasting; and that it promised its users perfect satisfaction, if properly adjusted. The second class of representations stated that the defendant "[c]ompany had not sold the machine, or made any attempt to sell it; that they had not shown it to any one; that it had never been on the market, and that no one outside the company officials and the men in the factory knew anything about it." Although 15,000 units were on hand, the defendant's agent said "it would be a mistake for them to attempt to sell these along with their ordinary line, which was furniture."

The plaintiff's action for deceit alleged that the purchase was made on the strength of these representations, but that "the machines and patents were totally inefficient and unmarketable." Simmons counterclaimed on the notes that Vulcan signed for part of the purchase price; Freeman had signed as a guarantor on the notes. The district court directed a verdict for

Simmons on both the original action and the counterclaim, finding that Vulcan had not proved any actionable fraud. The record showed that the machines, when exploited by Vulcan, were of little value and that "their manufacture was discontinued by that company not very long after they had undertaken it." There was also evidence that defendant's agents had made several efforts to sell the machines, which had proved unsuccessful because the machines could not create the vacuum necessary for their operation.]

L. HAND, J. [after stating the facts as above]. The first question is of the misrepresentations touching the quality and powers of the patented machine. These were general commendations, or, in so far as they included any specific facts, were not disproved; e.g., that the cleaner would produce 18 inches of vacuum with 25 pounds water pressure. They raise, therefore, the question of law how far general "puffing" or "dealers' talk" can be the basis of an action for deceit.

The conceded exception in such cases has generally rested upon the distinction between "opinion" and "fact"; but that distinction has not escaped the criticism it deserves. An opinion is a fact, and it may be a very relevant fact; the expression of an opinion is the assertion of a belief, and any rule which condones the expression of a consciously false opinion condones a consciously false statement of fact. When the parties are so situated that the buyer may reasonably rely upon the expression of the seller's opinion, it is no excuse to give a false one. And so it makes much difference whether the parties stand "on an equality." For example, we should treat very differently the expressed opinion of a chemist to a layman about the properties of a composition from the same opinion between chemist and chemist, when the buyer had full opportunity to examine. The reason of the rule lies, we think, in this: There are some kinds of talk which no sensible man takes seriously, and if he does he suffers from his credulity. If we were all scrupulously honest, it would not be so; but, as it is, neither party usually believes what the seller says about his own opinions, and each knows it. Such statements, like the claims of campaign managers before election, are rather designed to allay the suspicion which would attend their absence than to be understood as having any relation to objective truth. It is quite true that they induce a compliant temper in the buyer, but it is by a much more subtle process than through the acceptance of his claims for his wares.

So far as concerns statements of value, the rule is pretty well fixed against the buyer....

In the case at bar, since the buyer was allowed full opportunity to examine the cleaner and to test it out, we put the parties upon an equality. It seems to us that general statements as to what the cleaner would do, even though consciously false, were not of a kind to be taken literally by the buyer. As between manufacturer and customer, it may not be so; but this was the case of taking over a business, after ample chance to investigate. Such a buyer, who the seller rightly expects will undertake an independent and adequate inquiry into the actual merits of what he gets, has no right to treat as material in his determination statements like these. The standard of honesty permitted by the rule may not be the best; but, as Holmes, J., says in Deming v. Darling, 20 N.E. 107 (Mass. 1889), the chance that the higgling preparatory to a bargain may be afterwards translated into assurances of quality may perhaps be a set-off to the actual wrong allowed by the rule as it stands. We therefore think that the District Court was right in disregarding all these misrepresentations.

As respects the representation that the cleaners had never been put upon the market or offered for sale, the rule does not apply; nor can we agree that such representations could not have been material to Freeman's decision to accept the contract. The actual test of experience in their sale might well be of critical consequence in his decision to buy the business, and the jury would certainly have the right to accept his statement that his reliance upon these representations was determinative of his final decision. We believe that the facts as disclosed by the depositions of the Western witnesses were sufficient to carry to the jury the question whether those statements were false. It is quite true, as the District Judge said, that the number of sales was small, perhaps not 60 in all; but they were scattered in various parts of the Mountain and Pacific States, and the jury might conclude that they were enough to contradict the detailed statements of Simmons that the machines had been kept off the market altogether. . . .

The next question is as to whether any such misrepresentations were conclusively cured by the recital in the contract of purchase as follows:

> The party of the first part [the Simmons Company] has been engaged in the manufacture of a certain type of vacuum cleaning machines, and the parties of the first and second part [the National Suction Cleaner Company] have been engaged in the sale thereof.

We all agree that an adequate retraction of the false statement before Freeman executed the contract would be a defense. Whether this be regarded as terminating the consequences of the original wrong, or as a correction of it, is of little importance. Further, we agree that, even if Freeman had in fact never learned of the retraction, it would serve, if given under such circumstances as justified the utterer in supposing that he would. For example, a letter actually delivered into his hands containing nothing but a retraction would be a defense, though it abundantly appeared that he had never read it. His loss might still be the consequence, and the reasonable consequence, but for the letter, of the original fraud; but the writer would have gone as far as necessary to correct that fraud, and we should not be disposed to hold it as an insurer that its correction should be effective. Judge Ward and I, however, do not think that such a recital in such a place was certain to catch the eye of the reader, and that therefore neither was the defendant's duty of retraction inevitably discharged, nor, what is nearly the same thing, did the defendant show beyond question that Freeman actually saw it. . . .

It results from the foregoing that the judgment [for the defendant] in the action for deceit must be reversed. In the action [by Simmons] upon the notes the judgment upon the notes will be affirmed, because the Vulcan Metals Company, Incorporated, did not make any offer to return the machines, tools, and patents, which were not shown to be without any value, and consequently it was in no position to rescind.

[The dissent argued that the plaintiff should be "presumed to know what [the contract] means and says," and thus barred from suit.]

NOTES

1. *Puffing.* Why don't the provisions of the express contract allocate all risk associated with the overall sale to the buyer? If Simmons had offered to return all that it had received, could it have recovered the purchase price in full even if the value of the invention had declined in the interim? As noted in *Vulcan Metals*, Holmes, J., gave wide latitude for puffing in Deming v. Darling, 20 N.E. 107, 108-109 (Mass. 1889). The plaintiff purchased a railroad bond from the defendant's agent, who claimed that a railroad mortgage served as good security for the bond such that "the bond was of the very best and safest, and was an A No. 1 Bond." The jury was instructed to find for the defendant if the statement was made in good faith, but not if otherwise. On appeal from plaintiff's verdict, Justice Holmes refused to treat the defendant's "vague commendations of his wares" that did not contain false statement of facts, for in his view "[t]he rule of law is hardly to be regretted, when it is considered how easily and insensibly words of hope or expectation are converted by an interested memory into statements of quality and value when the expectation has been disappointed." Is the risk identified by Holmes present in the case at hand?

A more tolerant attitude towards puffing was evident in Speakers of Sport, Inc. v. ProServ, Inc., 178 F.3d 862 (7th Cir. 1999). ProServ lured Ivan Rodriguez, a star catcher for the Texas Rangers, from his contract at will with Speakers by promising to get him between $2 and $4 million in endorsements. ProServ was unable to deliver on that promise, and Rodriguez signed after one year with a third company. Speakers sued ProServ for fraud, for the loss of its client, alleging that ProServ knew it could not come through with the endorsements. Posner, J., denied the action:

> There would be few more effective inhibitors of the competitive process than making it a tort for an agent to promise the client of another agent to do better by him, which is pretty much what this case comes down to. It is true

that Speakers argues only that the competitor may not make a promise that he knows he cannot fulfill, may not, that is, compete by fraud. Because the competitor's privilege does not include a right to get business from a competitor by means of fraud, it is hard to quarrel with this position in the abstract, but the practicalities are different. If the argument were accepted and the new agent made a promise that was not fulfilled, the old agent would have a shot at convincing a jury that the new agent had known from the start that he couldn't deliver on the promise. Once a case gets to the jury, all bets are off. The practical consequence of Speakers' approach, therefore, would be that a sports agent who lured away the client of another agent with a promise to do better by him would be running a grave legal risk.

Could Rodriguez have sued ProServ for fraud? Would Speakers be allowed to pursue a fraud action for its losses if Rodriguez had successfully sued ProServ for fraud? If ProServ had lured Rodriguez away by saying that "a large endorsement contract with Nike is in the bag" when in fact it was not?

2. *Misrepresentations of law.* At common law the dominant rule once provided that the action for deceit did not lie for misrepresentations of law. One reason was that legal rules were generally matters of public record to which the plaintiff and defendant had equal access. Alternatively, the plaintiff could confirm those representations from an independent source if she desired. That rule has not, in general, been applied when a lawyer misrepresents the law to a lay adversary on the ground that it would be "unconscionable" to allow a lawyer for a bus company to procure a favorable settlement from a serviceman injured in hospital by a false statement of the relevant law. Sainsbury v. Pennsylvania Greyhound Lines, 183 P.2d 548, 550 (4th Cir. 1950).

In addition, the older rule has largely given way to allow fraud actions for "mixed" statements of fact and law. In National Conversion Corp. v. Cedar Building Corp., 246 N.E.2d 351, 355 (N.Y. 1969), the plaintiff tenant entered into a five-year lease with the defendant landlord after the he had represented in the lease that the zoning allowed the plaintiff to conduct business of converting restaurant garbage into fertilizer. The representations were false and the plaintiff was allowed to recover both the rentals paid prior to the rescission and the costs of the installation and removal of its equipment. Breitel, J., specifically rejected defendant's claim that its misrepresentations were not actionable:

> Most important it is that the law has outgrown the over-simple dichotomy between law and fact in the resolution of issues in deceit. It has been said that "a statement as to the law, like a statement as to anything else, may be intended and understood either as one of fact or one of opinion only, according to the circumstances of the case" (Prosser, [3d ed.] p. 741). The statements in this case, both before the execution of the lease, and in the body of the lease, exemplify ideally an instance in which the statements are not intended or

understood merely as an expression of opinion. Landlords said they knew the premises were in an unrestricted district. This meant that they knew as a fact, that the zoning resolution did not restrict the use of the particular premises, and tenant so understood it. When coupled with the further fact that tenant's lawyer was persuaded not to verify the status of the premises on the landlords' representation, it is equally clear that tenant understood the statement to be one of fact, namely, what the zoning resolution provided by description, map, and requirements as to the area in question. The misrepresented fact, if it is at all necessary to find misrepresented facts, was what the zoning resolution contained by way of description, map, and requirements, hardly opinions as to the law albeit matters to be found in a law.

Swinton v. Whitinsville Savings Bank
42 N.E.2d 808 (Mass. 1942)

QUA, J. The declaration alleges that on or about September 12, 1938, the defendant sold the plaintiff a house in Newton to be occupied by the plaintiff and his family as a dwelling; that at the time of the sale the house "was infested with termites, an insect that is most dangerous and destructive to buildings"; that the defendant knew the house was so infested; that the plaintiff could not readily observe this condition upon inspection; that, "knowing the internal destruction that these insects were creating in said house," the defendant falsely and fraudulently concealed from the plaintiff its true condition; that the plaintiff at the time of his purchase had no knowledge of the termites, exercised due care thereafter, and learned of them about August 30, 1940; and that, because of the destruction that was being done and the dangerous condition that was being created by the termites, the plaintiff was put to great expense for repairs and for the installation of termite control in order to prevent the loss and destruction of said house.

There is no allegation of any false statement or representation, or of the uttering of a half truth which may be tantamount to a falsehood. There is no intimation that the defendant by any means prevented the plaintiff from acquiring information as to the condition of the house. There is nothing to show any fiduciary relation between the parties, or that the plaintiff stood in a position of confidence toward or dependence upon the defendant. So far as appears the parties made a business deal at arm's length. The charge is concealment and nothing more; and it is concealment in the simple sense of mere failure to reveal, with nothing to show any peculiar duty to speak. The characterization of the concealment as false and fraudulent of course adds nothing in the absence of further allegations of fact.

If this defendant is liable on this declaration every seller is liable who fails to disclose any nonapparent defect known to him in the subject of the sale which materially reduces its value and which the buyer fails to discover.

Similarly it would seem that every buyer would be liable who fails to disclose any nonapparent virtue known to him in the subject of the purchase which materially enhances its value and of which the seller is ignorant. See Goodwin v. Agassiz, 186 N.E. 659 (Mass. 1933). The law has not yet, we believe, reached the point of imposing upon the frailties of human nature a standard so idealistic as this. That the particular case here stated by the plaintiff possesses a certain appeal to the moral sense is scarcely to be denied. Probably the reason is to be found in the facts that the infestation of buildings by termites has not been common in Massachusetts and constitutes a concealed risk against which buyers are off their guard. But the law cannot provide special rules for termites and can hardly attempt to determine liability according to the varying probabilities of the existence and discovery of different possible defects in the subjects of trade.

[Affirmed.]

NOTES

1. *Latent defects: liability for nondisclosure by a seller?* If the defendant had plastered over the parts of the woodwork where termites were present, could the action for concealment properly lie, even for Qua, J.? Note that other cases have long held that actions by defendant to cover up some defect count as fraud, even in the absence of words to that effect. Thus, in Croyle v. Moses, 90 Pa. 250 (1879), the defendant had committed fraud when he hitched up his horse short in order to conceal the fact that the animal was "a cribber and a windsucker." More recently, Osborn v. Gene Teague Chevrolet Co., 459 P.2d 988 (Or. 1969), sustained the plaintiff's verdict in a fraud case in which the defendant used car dealer had set back the odometer from 100,000 to 62,000 miles, without making any verbal misrepresentations.

Note that the no-duty rule in *Swinton* has eroded in recent years. See Obde v. Schlemeyer, 353 P.2d 672, 674-675 (1960), another termite case, which rejected *Swinton* saying: "Where there are concealed defects in demised premises, dangerous to the property, health, or life of the tenant, which defects are known to the landlord when the lease is made, but unknown to the tenant, and which a careful examination on his part would not disclose, it is the landlord's duty to disclose them." In addition, the Restatement (Second) of Torts §551 qualifies its general rule of nondisclosure with a long list of exceptions, the last of which requires disclosure of "facts basic to the transaction, if he [the defendant] knows that the other is about to enter into it under a mistake as to them, and that the other, because of the relationship between them, the customs of the trade or other objective circumstances, would reasonably expect a disclosure of those facts." The provision is illustrated as follows: "*A* sells to *B* a dwelling house, without disclosing to *B* the fact that the house is riddled with termites. This is a fact basic to the transaction." What evidence of community norms might be relevant to whether disclosure is required? If the standard contract for a home purchase contains an explicit warranty by the seller that a house is free of termites or other latent defects, is disclosure required when that contract is not used?

In reliance on §551, the duty to disclose has proved more difficult with respect to conditions external to the property sold. In Strawn v. Canuso, 657 A.2d 420, 431 (N.J. 1995), the court held that a defendant developer and broker were under a duty to disclose that the plaintiff's new home was located near a closed landfill site that contained many toxic substances so long as "the off-site physical conditions [are] known to it and unknown and not readily observable by the buyer if the existence of those conditions is of sufficient materiality to affect the habitability, use, or enjoyment of property and, therefore, render the property substantially less desirable or valuable to the objectively reasonable buyer." Yet in Hannah v. Sibcy Kline Realtors, 769 N.E.2d 876, 883, 884 (Ohio App. 3d 2001), the court held that the defendant broker, who had constantly evaded plaintiff's insistent request for information on the racial diversity of the neighborhood in which they bought their home, owed no duty "to inform a client whether a neighborhood was ethnically diverse or to direct the client to resources concerning this information. . . . The reason for the cautious attitude was that such comments could be misconstrued so as to result in claims that the agent had violated the Fair Housing Act." If the buyers know that the broker is evasive, must they look elsewhere? Would this evasion be tolerated if there were no exposure to liability under fair housing acts?

2. *Partial disclosures.* Even where there is no general duty to speak, partial disclosures are not allowed: "one who voluntarily elects to make a partial disclosure is deemed to have assumed a duty to tell the whole truth, i.e., to make full disclosure, even though the speaker was under no duty to make the partial disclosure in the first place." Union Pacific Resources Group, Inc. v. Rhone-Poulenc, Inc., 247 F.3d 574, 584 (5th Cir. 2001); see also RST §551(2)(b). What result if the information that is supplied by one party becomes obsolete with the passage of time? The general position indicates that the defendant who has led the plaintiff to believe in a certain state of affairs is under a duty to update that information to correct any earlier misimpressions. RST §551(2)(c). But there are clear limits on any such duty. In Hord v. Environmental Research Institute of Michigan, 617 N.W.2d 543 (Mich. 2000), the court held that an accurate 1991 operating summary of a firm's prospects did not generate an implicit duty to update the information when conditions changed thereafter. The court denied that "plaintiff had a right to rely on the 1991 summary as an accurate picture of the company's performance in fiscal year 1992, without some additional inquiry or affirmative representation by defendant."

Laidlaw v. Organ
15 U.S. 178 (1817)

[The plaintiff Organ was a New Orleans merchant in the tobacco trade. He had learned from a friend that peace had been concluded between the British and American forces fighting in the War of 1812. Before the information had been made public, he contracted to purchase a large order of tobacco from defendant Laidlaw. Before the sale was completed, Laidlaw had asked the plaintiff whether he knew of any information that would affect the price of the tobacco; from the record it is unclear whether the plaintiff had made any reply, or if so, what he had said. When the peace was announced, the price of tobacco rose between 30 and 50 percent, owing to the end of the British blockade. Laidlaw, who had delivered the tobacco to Organ, repossessed it by force. Organ brought suit for damages for the loss of the tobacco. The key question in the case was whether their prior agreement, pursuant to which the tobacco was transferred, was vitiated by fraud or nondisclosure. The jury found that Organ was entitled to the tobacco, whereupon Laidlaw appealed. After extensive argument Marshall, C.J., issued a brief opinion.]

MARSHALL, C.J. The question in this case is, whether the intelligence of extrinsic circumstances, which might influence the price of the commodity, and which was exclusively within the knowledge of the vendee, ought to have been communicated by him to the vendor? The court is of opinion that he was not bound to communicate it. It would be difficult to circumscribe the contrary doctrine within proper limits, where the means of intelligence are equally accessible to both parties. But at the same time, each party must take care not to say or do any thing tending to impose upon the other. The court thinks that the absolute instruction of the judge was erroneous, and that the question, whether any imposition was practised by the vendee upon the vendor ought to have been submitted to the jury. For these reasons the judgment must be reversed, and the cause remanded to the district court of Louisiana, with directions to award a venire facias de novo [new trial].

NOTES

1. Latent virtue: liability for nondisclosure by a buyer? Unlike the latent defect cases, the nondisclosure of a material fact may be made by a buyer who happens to have superior information about the subject matter of the contract. The situation can occur in contexts far removed from the stock market. Thus, the proprietor of a secondhand music store may sell a Stradivarius violin for a trifling price to a violin expert who happens to wander into the premises. Generally, the buyer is under no duty to disclose, even though the price would surely be higher if the seller knew the violin's pedigree. See RST §551, comment *k*, illustration 6.

A similar problem often arises with land purchases. Generally, the purchaser of farmland need not disclose that he is buying it because he believes that it contains oil. Similarly, the land developer who takes an option on farmland in trying to assemble a large parcel of land from several buyers for a major real estate development is normally under no duty to disclose the purpose of his venture, and may even act in a manner calculated to persuade his seller that he is in fact only interested in farmland for its own sake. In Guaranty Safe Deposit & Trust Co. v. Liebold, 56 A. 951, 953 (Pa. 1904), the option in question had been procured by the trust company in order to provide a site for a steel mill. The court held that the trust company had no duty to disclose.

> In this commercial age options are daily procured by those in possession of information from which they expect to profit, simply because those from whom the options are sought are ignorant of it. When the prospective seller knows as much as the prospective buyer, options can rarely, if ever, be procured, and the rule that counsel for appellant would have us apply would practically abolish them. The prospective buyer seeks an option instead of at once entering into a contract for the purchase of land, because, no matter what information he may possess exclusively, he is unwilling to act upon it until it becomes a certainty. In the meantime, on the contingency of its becoming so, he makes his contingent bargain to purchase. This is fair in law and in morals. If the appellee concealed anything it was his duty to disclose, or said anything to mislead or deceive the appellant, this rule, of course, would not apply; but they dealt at arm's length, as men always do under such circumstances, each trying to make what was supposed to be the best bargain for himself at the time.

The court then noted that its conclusion was especially apt because Liebold had increased the price for the land in response to a "rumor" that a large manufacturing company was contemplating setting up business in town.

2. Insider trading. The use of undisclosed information plays a central role whenever corporate insiders, typically directors, key officers, or major shareholders purchase common stock from outsiders. In Goodwin v. Agassiz, 186 N.E. 659, 661 (Mass. 1933), the defendants were directors of a corporation that purchased shares over the Boston Exchange from the plaintiff, himself an experienced trader who had kept records of his own transactions in the company stock. The plaintiff sought to rescind the sale or obtain other appropriate relief on the ground that the defendants did not disclose that they had received reports from a geologist that indicated that certain properties owned by the corporation might have valuable mineral deposits. The court barred the plaintiff's legal claim because he "made no inquiries of the defendant or of other officers of the company."

> Fiduciary obligations of directors ought not to be made so onerous that men of experience and ability will be deterred from accepting such office. Law in its sanctions is not coextensive with morality. It cannot take to put all parties to every contract on an equality as to knowledge, experience, skill and shrewdness. It cannot undertake to relieve against hard bargains made between competent parties without fraud. On the other hand, directors cannot rightly be allowed to indulge with impunity in practices which do violence to prevailing standards of upright business men. Therefore, where a director personally seeks a stockholder for the purpose of buying his shares without making disclosure of material facts within his peculiar knowledge and not within reach of the stockholder, the transaction will be closely scrutinized and relief may be granted in appropriate instances.

What might these instances be? Should the share purchase in *Goodwin* be judged by the same rules applicable to latent defects in real estate?

Today the federal regulation of insider trading under Rule 10b-5 of the Securities and Exchange Acts, *supra* at 1202, Note 4, has been read to require directors to make public disclosures before they trade on inside information. See, e.g., SEC v. Texas Gulf Sulfur Co., 401 F.2d 833 (2d Cir. 1968), another famous case involving mineral deposits. Under *Goodwin* should it make a difference if other transactions between unrelated parties took place on the day that the plaintiff sold to the defendants? Should the rule be different if the insider sells his shares or sells short because he has undisclosed information about the firm's incompetence? In principle, should the corporate charter be allowed to stipulate that insiders may trade without disclosure on the organized exchange? There is a huge amount of literature on insider trading; see, e.g., Carlton and Fischel, The Regulation of Insider Trading, 35 Stan. L. Rev. 857 (1983).

3. An economic account of nondisclosure. As these materials make clear, the entire question of nondisclosure between the parties often can be clarified by an agreement between them. A purchaser can always ask a seller point blank if the premises are infested with termites; a seller can always ask a buyer if he believes oil lies under the seller's farmland or whether the land is slated for industrial development. If the party so asked responds with a falsehood, the ordinary rules of fraud apply; and if he refuses to answer the direct question, the other party is on notice and can act accordingly. Within this environment, the law helps devise a set of default rules to govern in the absence of any explicit agreement. One notable effort to find a coherent set of principles to govern nondisclosure cases is found in Kronman, Mistake, Disclosure, Information, and the Law of Contracts, 7 J. Legal Stud. 1, 9 (1978), who argues:

> Where nondisclosure is permitted (or put differently, where the knowledgeable party's contract rights are enforced despite his failure to disclose a known mistake), the knowledge involved is typically the product of a costly

search. A rule permitting nondisclosure is the only effective way of providing an incentive to invest in the production of such knowledge. By contrast, in the cases requiring disclosure, and in those excusing a unilaterally mistaken promisor because the other party knew or had reason to know of his error, the knowledgeable party's special information is typically not the fruit of a deliberate search. Although information of this sort is socially useful as well, a disclosure requirement will not cause a sharp reduction in the amount of such information which is actually produced. If one takes into account the investment costs incurred in the deliberate production of information, the two apparently divergent lines of cases described above may both be seen as conforming (roughly) to the principle of efficiency, which requires that the risk of a unilateral mistake be placed on the most effective risk-preventer.

Kronman applies his analysis to most of the cases set out above. How good is the fit?

Edgington v. Fitzmaurice
29 Ch. 459 (1885)

[The plaintiff advanced £1,500 for debentures of a society of which the defendants were directors and officers. In the circular distributed to raise the funds, the defendants announced that they had acquired a valuable property that was "subject to the half yearly payment of £500 in redemption of a mortgage of which £21,500 is outstanding." Elsewhere in the prospectus the defendants stated they would use the moneys raised "to complete . . . altera-tions and additions to the buildings, and to purchase their own horses and vans," and "to further develop the arrangements at present existing for the direct supply of cheap fish from the coast."

The statements in the prospectus were impeached on the following grounds:

1. That the prospectus was so framed as to lead to the belief that the debentures would be a charge on the property of the company.
2. That the prospectus omitted to refer to a second mortgage for £5,000 to Messrs. Hores and Pattisson which had been made on the 10th of August, 1880.
3. That the prospectus stated that the property was subject to the half-yearly payment of £500 in redemption of the mortgage for £21,500, but omitted to state that on the 5th of April 1884, the whole balance of the mortgage that would then be due, namely, £18,000, might be at once called in.
4. That the real object of the issue of debentures was to pay off pressing liabilities of the company and not to complete the buildings or to purchase horses and vans or to develop the business of the company.

At trial, Denman, J., found for the plaintiffs. The defendants appealed.]

BOWEN, L.J. This is an action for deceit, in which the Plaintiff complains that he was induced to take certain debentures by the misrepresentations of the Defendants, and that he sustained damage thereby. The loss which the Plaintiff sustained is not disputed. In order to sustain his action he must first prove that there was a statement as to facts which was false; and secondly, that it was false to the knowledge of the Defendants, or that they made it not caring whether it was true or false. For it is immaterial whether they made the statement knowing it to be untrue, or recklessly, without caring whether it was true or not, because to make a statement recklessly for the purpose of influencing another person is dishonest. It is also clear that it is wholly immaterial with what object the lie is told. That is laid down in Lord Blackburn's judgment in Smith v. Chadwick[, 9 App. Cas. 187 (H.L.E. 1884)], but it is material that the defendant should intend that it should be relied on by the person to whom he makes it. But, lastly, when you have proved that the statement was false, you must further shew that the plaintiff has acted upon it and has sustained damage by so doing: you must shew that the statement was either the sole cause of the plaintiff's act, or materially contributed to his so acting. . . .

The alleged misrepresentations were three. First, it was said that the prospectus contained an implied allegation that the mortgage for £21,500 could not be called in at once, but was payable by instalments. I think that upon a fair construction of the prospectus it does so allege; and therefore that the prospectus must be taken to have contained an untrue statement on that point; but it does not appear to me clear that the statement was fraudulently made by the Defendants. It is therefore immaterial to consider whether the Plaintiff was induced to act as he did by that statement.

Secondly, it is said that the prospectus contains an implied allegation that there was no other mortgage affecting the property except the mortgage stated therein. I think there was such an implied allegation, but I think it is not brought home to the Defendants that it was made dishonestly; accordingly, although the Plaintiff may have been damnified by the weight which he gave to the allegation, he cannot rely on it in this action: for in an action of deceit the Plaintiff must prove dishonesty. Therefore if the case had rested on these two allegations alone, I think it would be too uncertain to entitle the Plaintiff to succeed.

But when we come to the third alleged misstatement I feel that the Plaintiff's case is made out. I mean the statement of the objects for which the money was to be raised. These were stated to be to complete the alterations and additions to the buildings, to purchase horses and vans, and to develope the supply of fish. A mere suggestion of possible purposes to which a portion of the money might be applied would not have formed a basis for an action of deceit. There must be a misstatement of an existing fact: but the state of a man's mind is as much a fact as the state of his digestion. It is true that it is very difficult to prove what the state of a man's mind at a particular time is, but if it can be ascertained it is as much a fact as anything else. A misrepresentation as to the state of a man's mind is, therefore, a misstatement of fact. Having applied as careful consideration to the evidence as I could, I have reluctantly come to the conclusion that the true objects of the Defendants in raising the money were not those stated in the circular. . . .

Then the question remains — Did this misstatement contribute to induce the Plaintiff to advance his money. Mr. Davey's argument has not convinced me that they did not. He contended that the Plaintiff admits that he would not have taken the debentures unless he had thought they would give him a charge on the property, and therefore he was induced to take them by his own mistake, and the misstatement in the circular was not material. But such misstatement was material if it was actively present to his mind when he decided to advance his money. The real question is, what was the state of the Plaintiff's mind, and if his mind was disturbed by the misstatement of the Defendants, and such disturbance was in part the cause of what he did, the mere fact of his also making a mistake himself could make no difference. It resolves itself into a mere question of fact. I have felt some difficulty about the pleadings, because in the statement of claim this point is not clearly put forward, and I had some doubt whether this contention as to the third misstatement was not an afterthought. But the balance of my judgment is weighed down by the probability of the case. What is the first question which a man asks when he advances money? It is, what is it wanted for? Therefore I think that the statement is material, and that the Plaintiff would be unlike the rest of his race if he was not influenced by the statement of the objects for which the loan was required. The learned Judge in the Court below came to the conclusion that the misstatement did influence him, and I think he came to a right conclusion.

NOTES

1. *Causation in fraud cases.* Will a defendant in a fraud case have a good causal defense if the plaintiff knew of the falsity at the time the statement was made? If the plaintiff had the means to learn of the falsity of the defendant's statements? Note that in litigating fraud cases, the best defense is often a good offense. One tactic is for the defendant to insist that the plaintiff, far from being deceived, is only a disgruntled investor trying to recoup an unfortunate business investment out of the defendant's hide. Alternatively, the defendant might portray the plaintiff as fraudulent in his relations with third parties, say, persons for whom the plaintiff received a finder's fee for persuading them to invest with the defendant. Complex webs of human interactions lead to protracted battles over causation in an

effort to understand the interaction of various oral and written statements, sometimes formal and sometimes not — whose meaning becomes ambiguous with the passage of time.

In *Egington* and most fraud cases, the plaintiff seeks to recover for the lost value of the investment or purchase made, to the extent that this is attributable to the defendant's fraud, which in turn must be distinguished from declines in the value attributable to other sources. The general Restatement (Second) rule read:

§549. MEASURE OF DAMAGES FOR FRAUDULENT MISREPRESENTATION
(1) The recipient of a fraudulent misrepresentation is entitled to recover as damages in an action of deceit against the maker the pecuniary loss to him of which the misrepresentation is a legal cause, including
(a) the difference between the value of what he has received in the transaction and its purchase price or other value given for it; and
(b) pecuniary loss suffered otherwise as a consequence of the recipient's reliance upon the misrepresentation.
(2) The recipient of a fraudulent misrepresentation in a business transaction is also entitled to recover additional damages sufficient to give him the benefit of his contract with the maker, if these damages are proved with reasonable certainty.

Note that §549 (2) is not often brought into play. In cases like *Pasley*, the expectation and reliance interests are often the same, as the creditor wants to recover the amount owed, with interest. Where the plaintiff seeks the benefit of the contract, the expectation damages sought are often available in the event of simple nonperformance wholly without regard to the allegation of fraud. One fraud case that gave the plaintiff the benefit of the bargain was Selman v. Shirley, 85 P.2d 384 (Or. 1938), where the buyers of land were not entitled to just their money back, but to the increment in value they would have enjoyed if the land, as represented, contained 4,000 cords of wood, worth $2,000, and had been crossed by a stream that supplied enough water to irrigate ten acres. Why would any owner, fraudulent or not, agree to part with land known to be worth more than the purchase price? In addition, the expectation measure of damages is hard to calculate with financial investments, which typically have a high variance, often attributable to factors unrelated to the fraud.

2. Materiality in fraud cases. For the reasons stated, the reliance interest tends to dominate fraud cases. Proving that reliance interest forces courts to choose either an objective or subjective standard of evaluation to decide whether the plaintiff's reliance was in fact "justifiable." At one extreme, the simple fact of plaintiff's reliance could be sufficient to complete the causal chain. Perhaps out of a fear of feigned suits, most courts impose an additional, objective, requirement that the plaintiff's reliance is justifiable only if the defendant's misrepresentation is of a "material" fact. Under the

Restatement (Second) of Torts §538, a matter is regarded as material if one of two conditions is satisfied: "(a) a reasonable man would attach importance to its existence or nonexistence in determining his choice of action in the transaction in question, or (b) the maker of the representation knows or has reason to know that its recipient regards or is likely to regard the matter as important in determining his choice of action, although a reasonable man would not so regard it." The requirement is often construed as a jury control device. "The court may withdraw the case from the jury if the fact misrepresented is so obviously unimportant that the jury could not reasonably find that a reasonable man would have been influenced by it." RST §538, comment *e*. If a particular representation is regarded as material, should it be presumed that the plaintiff in fact relied on it in a transaction?

The relationship between materiality and reliance has been much debated in cases arising under the securities law. In TSC Industries, Inc. v. Northway, Inc., 512 F.2d 324, 330 (7th Cir. 1975), which involved a complex joint proxy statement, the Seventh Circuit stated that omissions were material as a matter of law if they touched on "all facts which a reasonable stockholder *might* consider important." The Supreme Court, concerned that this lax standard might lead to endless disclosures of trivial facts, stated the applicable standard more narrowly: "An omitted fact is material if there is a substantial likelihood that a reasonable shareholder would consider it important in deciding how to vote." TSC Industries, Inc. v. Northway, Inc., 426 U.S. 438, 449 (1976). Which standard better conforms to the Restatement's account of materiality? Is the same set of rules on materiality applicable to omissions as to positive misstatements?

In Basic Inc. v. Levinson, 485 U.S. 224, 238, 239 (1988), the Supreme Court held that the definition of materiality in *TSC Industries* also applied to actions brought under Rule 10b-5, governing actions for securities fraud. Basic's president publicly announced that "management was unaware" of any reason for extensive trading in its stock, after it had been approached by a larger company seeking to acquire it. The Court rejected Basic's argument that its statements were proper as long as the parties had not entered into an "agreement-in-principle" for the acquisition. It wrote: "No particular event or factor short of closing the transaction need be either necessary or sufficient by itself to render merger discussions material." Rather, "materiality 'will depend at any given time upon a balancing of both the indicated probability that the event will occur and the anticipated magnitude of the event in the light of the totality of the company activities,'" which could include "board resolutions, instructions to investment bankers, and actual negotiations between principals or their intermediaries." The Court remanded the case for further consideration under its standard. What now?

3. *Loss causation in fraud on the market cases.* Strictly construed, the traditional reliance element of the tort of deceit would block the action. Should plaintiffs be able to overcome that barrier by showing that the defendant's

false statements had led to systematic market movements adverse to the interest of the plaintiffs? In *Basic, supra* at 1219, Note 2, the Supreme Court approved using the "fraud on the market" theory in federal securities cases. Quoting from Peil v. Speiser, 806 F.2d 1154, 1160-1161 (3d Cir. 1986), it observed:

> The fraud on the market theory is based on the hypothesis that, in an open and developed securities market, the price of a company's stock is determined by the available material information regarding the company and its business. . . . Misleading statements will therefore defraud purchasers of stock even if the purchasers do not directly rely on the misstatements. . . . The causal connection between the defendants' fraud and the plaintiffs' purchase of stock in such a case is no less significant than in a case of direct reliance on misrepresentations.

Basic then held that the fraud on the market theory created a "rebuttable presumption of reliance." "Requiring proof of individualized reliance from each member of the proposed plaintiff class effectively would have prevented respondents from proceeding with a class action, since the individual issues then would have overwhelmed the common ones." It therefore concluded that although individual proof of reliance might be appropriate in the "face-to-face transactions contemplated by early fraud cases," it was inappropriate for transactions in mass markets.

Justice White wrote a skeptical dissent. "But with no staff economists, no experts schooled in the 'efficient-capital-market hypothesis,' no ability to test the validity of empirical market studies, we are not well equipped to embrace novel constructions of a statute based on contemporary microeconomic theory." See generally Fischel, Use of Modern Finance Theory in Securities Fraud Cases, 38 Bus. Law. 1 (1982). On efficient markets generally, see Gilson and Kraakman, The Mechanisms of Market Efficiency, 70 Va. L. Rev. 549 (1984).

Proof of loss-causation in securities actions is now regulated by the PSLRA, 15 U.S.C. §78u-4(b)(4), as follows:

> (4) Loss causation. In any private action arising under this title, the plaintiff shall have the burden of proving that the act or omission of the defendant alleged to violate this title caused the loss for which the plaintiff seeks to recover damages.

This provision was instrumental in the Supreme Court's decision in Dura Pharmaceuticals, Inc. v. Broudo, 544 U.S. 336, 343-344 (2005), which refused plaintiff's invitation to state a securities claim simply by alleging in the complaint and subsequently establishing that "the price" of the security "on the date of purchase was inflated because of the misrepresentation." Those allegations were insufficient because they did not account for the circumstances between purchase and sale. "[I]f, say, the purchaser sells the shares quickly before the relevant truth begins to leak out, the misrepresentation will not have led to any loss. If the purchaser sells later after the truth makes its way into the marketplace, an initially inflated purchase price *might* mean a later loss. But that is far from inevitably so. When the purchaser subsequently resells such shares, even at a lower price, that lower price may reflect, not the earlier misrepresentation, but changed economic circumstances, changed investor expectations, new industry-specific or firm-specific facts, conditions, or other events, which taken separately or together account for some or all of that lower price."

That skeptical attitude toward the fraud-on-the-market theory in *Dura* and under the PSLRA was also evident in Oscar Private Equity Investments v. Allegiance Telecom Inc., 487 F.3d 261 (5th Cir. 2007). The defendant overstated the number of cable lines it added in its 2001 quarterly announcements because of a glitch in its computer system, but issued corrective statements thereafter, before the firm went bankrupt in the midst of a general downturn in the cable market. In dealing with loss causation, Higginbotham, J., held that even at the stage of class-certification (that is, before the merits), under *Basic* "[w]e now require more than proof of a material misstatement; we require proof that the misstatement *actually moved* the market." He then concluded that the plaintiff class could not carry that burden in absence of any evidence that the market moved downward in response to the defendant's corrective disclosure on the number of lines, in part because of the simultaneous publication of unrelated downward pressure from an analyst's negative statement about a potential violation of some of defendant's unrelated covenants. Dennis J., dissented on the ground that the aggressive application of the loss-causation doctrine at the certification stage stripped the plaintiff of the benefit of *Basic*'s rebuttable presumption.

4. Damages under a fraud on the market theory. Under the fraud on the market theory, how should damages be computed? Take a simple case in which a company places false statements in its prospectus in order to increase the price it can obtain for a new offering of its publicly traded stock. If a person both buys and sells shares in the firm before the fraud is unmasked, ordinarily damages should not be allowed. The extra money paid to purchase the shares is roughly offset by the extra money obtained on sale. But if an open-market purchase is made before the fraud is discovered, and the sale is made after the market breaks, then the downward adjustment in the share price (measurable, with difficulty, by statistical techniques) sets the level of the damages suffered by these share purchasers.

Using the fraud on the market approach makes it appear that all other market participants have suffered at the hands of the defendant. In many cases, however, many ignorant buyers or sellers *profit* incidentally from the defendant's fraud. Consider a person who already owns stock in a company that launches a new issue of stock with fraudulent statements that inflate the value of both its new shares and the existing shares. The owner might dispose of the shares before the fraud is revealed, thereby obtaining a higher price than if the fraud had never been committed. The buyer of those shares will in turn suffer losses once the fraud has been revealed. The gains and losses of buyer and seller will roughly net out. The fraud on the market theory, however, charges the buyer's losses to the issuer while ignoring the seller's gains. The theory, therefore, may in effect overdeter fraud by overstating the *social* losses that it causes. One possible escape is to set damages equal to the *gains* that the fraudulent defendant obtained from the fraud. Yet even these gains may be hard to measure, and, in some cases like *Basic,* appear to be nonexistent. On these damages problems, see Fischel, *supra* Note 3, at 1220, 38 Bus. Law. at 16-17.

5. *Contributory negligence in fraud cases.* In Seeger v. Odell, 115 P.2d 977, 980 (Cal. 1941), Traynor, J., noted: "Negligence on the part of the plaintiff in failing to discover the falsity of a statement is no defense when the misrepresentation was intentional rather than negligent." In Teamsters Local 282 Pension Trust Fund v. Angelos, 762 F.2d 522, 528 (7th Cir. 1985), Easterbrook, J., explained the rule in holding that the failure of a pension trustee to investigate did not relieve the defendant of liability for securities fraud.

> Securities law seeks to impose on issuers duties to disclose, the better to obviate the need for buyers to investigate. The buyer's investigation of things already known to the seller is a wasteful duplication of effort. If the securities laws worked perfectly there would be little need for investigation; sellers would disclose to the buyers and the market the information necessary for informed trading. Because some frauds will not be caught, and because people cannot interpret information flawlessly, this mechanism cannot work perfectly. This failure makes investigations by investors necessary and creates incentives for sellers to hire certifiers (such as auditors and investment bankers) to verify sellers' statements. But such investigations and other devices are distinctly second-best solutions to legal and practical problems, and we will not establish a legal rule under which investors must resort to the costly self-help approach of investigation on pain of losing the protection of the principal legal safeguard, the rule against fraud.
>
> This is just another way to state the common law rule that contributory negligence is not a defense to an intentional or reckless tort.

Laborers Local 17 Health and Benefit Fund v. Philip Morris, Inc.
191 F.3d 229 (2d Cir. 1999)

CARDAMONE, J. [Plaintiffs' funds were organized under ERISA to provide health care to their union members. These funds claimed that they were the victims of tobacco industry frauds on its patients, which induced them to overconsume cigarettes and therefore to increase their costs of providing health care under its plans to participants that suffered from illness related to cigarette smoking.

Among the causes of action pleaded were those alleging RICO violations and common law fraud, both which were held to present the same requirement for proof of proximate causation. Later in its opinion the court said: "These [RICO] principles also apply in general terms to the fraud and special duty causes of action asserted by plaintiffs under New York common law."]

The complaint seeks past and future damages to recover for "money expended . . . to provide medical treatment to [plaintiffs'] participants and beneficiaries who have suffered and are suffering from tobacco-related illnesses." As interpreted by the district court, the complaint also seeks damages inflicted on the Funds' infrastructure independent of the harm suffered by plan participants. These latter damages, alleged to be separate and wholly distinct from participants' medical costs, consist of losses suffered due to the Funds' inability to control costs, to promote the use of safer alternative products, and to establish programs to educate their participants not to use tobacco products.

Ordinarily, plaintiffs' right to sue for damages would be subrogated to the rights of those individual smokers for whom they provided health care benefits. In other words, plaintiffs would stand in the shoes of the injured participants and recoup damages from defendants, as tortfeasors, only to the extent defendants were liable to the participants themselves. But the Funds have not asserted such a subrogation action in this complaint. Instead, they have sued in their own right for the money spent for plan participants and [for infrastructure losses].

DISCUSSION

PROXIMATE CAUSE

The first certified question we are called upon to answer raises a question of proximate cause, namely, whether the chain of causation linking defendants' alleged wrongdoing to plaintiffs' alleged injuries is too remote to permit recovery as a matter of law. We begin by analyzing this subject in the context of plaintiffs' RICO claims.

I. *Proximate Cause as an Element of Standing Under RICO*

The RICO provision for civil actions states

> Any person injured in his business or property by reason of a violation of section 1962 of this chapter may sue therefor in any appropriate United States district court and shall recover threefold the damages he sustains and the cost of the suit, including a reasonable attorney's fee.

18 U.S.C. §1964(c) (1994). In *Holmes* [v. Securities Investor Protection Corp., 503 U.S. 258, 268 (1992)], the Supreme Court stated that a plaintiff's standing to sue under RICO requires "a showing that the defendant's violation not only was a 'but for' cause of his injury, but was the proximate cause as well." To determine in a given case whether proximate cause is present, common law principles are applied.

A. The concept in general. In everyday terms, the concept [of proximate cause] might be explained as follows: Because the consequences of an act go endlessly forward in time and its causes stretch back to the dawn of human history, proximate cause is used essentially as a legal tool for limiting a wrongdoer's liability only to those harms that have a reasonable connection to his actions. The law has wisely determined that it is futile to trace the consequences of a wrongdoer's actions to their ultimate end, if end there is.

B. Direct injury as a requirement of proximate cause. Over the passage of time, however, courts have somewhat clarified the definition of proximate cause by identifying several traditional common law principles limiting liability whose application, in aggregate, formulates the proximate cause analysis. As noted in *Holmes,* "'proximate cause' [is used] to label generically the judicial tools used to limit a person's responsibility for the consequences of that person's own acts.". . .

Among these "judicial tools," one notion traditionally included in the concept of proximate causation is the requirement that there be "some direct relation between the injury asserted and the injurious conduct alleged." For this reason, "a plaintiff who complain[s] of harm flowing merely from the misfortunes visited upon a third person by the defendant's acts [is] generally said to stand at too remote a distance to recover."

C. Applying the direct injury test to instant case. Ultimately, however, whether plaintiffs' injuries are labeled as "infrastructure harm" or "harm to financial stability," their damages are entirely derivative of the harm suffered by plan participants as a result of using tobacco products. Without injury to the individual smokers, the Funds would not have incurred any increased costs in the form of the payment of benefits, nor would they have experienced the difficulties of cost prediction and control that constituted the crux of their infrastructure harms. Being purely contingent on harm to third parties, these injuries are indirect. Consequently, because defendants' alleged misconduct did not proximately cause the injuries alleged, plaintiffs lack standing to bring RICO claims against defendants.

II.   Policy Considerations

Further, this conclusion is consistent with the three policy factors addressed by *Holmes,* which buttress the principle that plaintiffs with indirect injuries lack standing to sue under RICO. "First, the less direct an injury is, the more difficult it becomes to ascertain the amount of a plaintiff's damages attributable to the violation, as distinct from other, independent, factors." . . . It will be virtually impossible for plaintiffs to prove with any certainty: (1) the effect any smoking cessation programs or incentives would have had on the number of smokers among the plan beneficiaries; (2) the countereffect that the tobacco companies' direct fraud would have had on the smokers, despite the best efforts of the Funds; and (3) other reasons why individual smokers would continue smoking, even after having been informed of the dangers of smoking and having been offered smoking cessation programs. On a fundamental level, these difficulties of proving damages stem from the agency of the individual smokers in deciding whether, and how frequently, to smoke. In this light, the direct injury test can be seen as wisely limiting standing to sue to those situations where the chain of causation leading to damages is not complicated by the intervening agency of third parties (here, the smokers) from whom the plaintiffs' injuries derive.

These concerns become particularly pointed in a case, like the present one, where the injuries are alleged to derive not simply from defendants' affirmative misconduct but also from plaintiffs' fraudulently induced inaction. That is, it is often easier to ascertain the damages that flow from actual, affirmative conduct, than to speculate what damages arose from a party's failure to act. In the latter situation, as in the case at hand, it becomes difficult to distinguish among the multitude of factors that might have affected the damages. Here, for example, plaintiffs' alleged damages might have derived from inefficiencies in the Funds' own management, as well as from non-smoking related health problems suffered by the smokers, and it would be the sheerest sort of speculation to determine how these damages might have been lessened had the Funds adopted the measures defendants allegedly induced them not to adopt.

The complexity of these calculations makes the ultimate question of damages suffered by the Funds virtually impossible to determine. Indeed, this case seems to present precisely the type of large, complicated damages claims that *Holmes* . . . sought to avoid. Moreover, for us to rule otherwise could lead to a potential explosion in the scope of tort liability, which, while perhaps well-intentioned, is a subject best left to the legislature.

The second policy factor addressed in *Holmes* focuses on the possibility that "recognizing claims of the indirectly injured would force courts to adopt complicated rules apportioning damages among plaintiffs removed at different levels of injury from the violative acts, to obviate the risk of multiple recoveries." [The court then finds that the New York rules on collateral benefits do not eliminate the need to coordinate multiple payments.]

In the third policy factor discussed by *Holmes*, the Supreme Court concluded that the need to grapple with the problems of calculating and apportioning damages was unjustified where "directly injured victims can generally be counted on to vindicate the law as private attorneys general, without any of the problems attendant upon suits by plaintiffs injured more remotely." The Funds correctly note that these RICO causes of action could not be asserted by the smokers or by the Funds in a subrogation action because the RICO statute requires an injury to "business or property," whereas the smokers' injuries are personal in nature. Hence, the Funds conclude there are no more directly injured "private attorneys general" who could vindicate the law for these alleged RICO violations. The district court also found that because individual smokers would not be able to bring a RICO action, the harms alleged in plaintiffs' complaint would go unremedied were the Funds' action not allowed to continue.

Yet, to the contrary, our holding that plaintiffs lack standing under RICO need not bring about the result plaintiffs fear. The Funds may still bring a subrogation action to recover the medical costs paid out for the individual smokers, and the smokers themselves have sufficient independent incentive to pursue their own causes of action for such additional types of injuries as pain and suffering.

III. *Is a Defendant's Specific Intent to Harm a Plaintiff an Exception to the Direct-Injury Rule?*

Plaintiffs aver that even if their claims fail the direct injury test, they should still have standing to sue because an exception to this rule exists where the defendants specifically intend to harm plaintiffs.

[The Court then reviews the relevant cases.] As such, these decisions regarding specific intent do not support the proposition that an indirect injury is actionable where the injury was specifically intended by the defendant. In other words, an allegation of specific intent does not overcome the requirement that there must be a direct injury to maintain this action.

IV. *Common Law Fraud and Special Duty Claims*

[After an examination of the New York cases, the court concludes that] "analogous principles to those that doomed plaintiffs' RICO causes of action also bar plaintiffs' common law fraud and special duty actions."

Accordingly, we hereby reverse the district court's March 25, 1998 order with respect to causes of action I and II (the RICO claims), V (the fraud claim), and VI (the special duty claim). The case is remanded to the district court with directions to dismiss plaintiffs' complaint.

NOTES

1. *Causation and privity in fraud cases.* *Laborers Local 17* shows in vivid fashion how common law fraud actions often surface in modern contexts, here as virtual duplicates of the federal RICO claims. The need to limit

liability for words is in general greater than it is for deeds, because the number of persons who can rely on a defendant's public statements is potentially infinite. That said, how clear is the line between direct and indirect causation in fraud cases? If rejected, what should be substituted in its place? Should it make a difference in applying this analysis that individual smokers have largely failed in their common law actions to recover damages from tobacco companies? Whatever its soundness, the position taken in *Laborers Local 17* has been adopted in at least seven other circuits that have considered the issue. See, e.g., Service Employees International Union Health and Welfare Fund v. Philip Morris, Inc., 249 F.3d 1068, 1072 n.2 (D.C. Cir. 2001). See also Schwab v. Philip Morris USA, Inc., 449 F. Supp. 2d 992 (E.D.N.Y. 2006), where in a massive opinion Weinstein, J. denied defendant's summary judgment motion where plaintiffs had alleged that defendant had induced them to buy "light" cigarettes by falsely representing that they would face reduced health risks from lower amounts of tar and nicotine. In order to facilitate proofs, he held that, consistent with constitutional guarantees of due process, the plaintiffs could introduce statistical evidence to establish liability and damages.

Laborers Local 17 did not, however, bar the plaintiffs' suits in Desiano v. Warner-Lambert Co., 326 F.3d 339, 349-350 (2d Cir. 2003). The plaintiff class consisted of a group of health benefit plans (HBPs) that had paid for their members to purchase Rezulin, then an FDA-approved drug for treating Type II (adult onset) diabetes. Rezulin, which had gone through an arduous and controversial FDA approval process, remained on the market from February 1997 to March 2000, when it was withdrawn from the market after reports of a series of deaths from liver complications. The complaint alleged that the FDA had only approved the drug and kept it on the market as long as it did because the defendant had submitted fraudulent materials to the FDA both to obtain the initial approval and to keep it on the market. The class members did not consist of persons injured by the drugs, but of the HBPs who reimbursed the prescription costs for those individuals who had taken it successfully. The HBPs claimed a refund under New Jersey's Consumer Fraud Act, insisting that the defendant's fraud had induced them to buy the "Defendants' product, rather than available cheaper alternatives, had they not been misled by Defendants' misrepresentations." The district court held that "certainly the HBPs have no claim to recover the cost of providing the drug to patients who were not harmed." Calabresi, J., first noted that the requirements for proximate causation could be broader under New Jersey Law than they were under RICO, and that *Holmes* and *Laborers Local 17* were distinguishable:

> Defendants argue, however, that "if Rezulin had been effective in all diabetic patients without any side effects, plaintiffs would have no basis for a claim." But it is easy to see how Defendants' reasoning is flawed. Consider, for

example, a hypothetical in which a defendant drug company markets a "new," much more expensive drug claiming it is a great advancement (safer, more effective, etc. than metformin — the standard diabetes drug) when in fact the company is simply replicating the metformin formula and putting a new label on it. In other words, the only difference between metformin and the "new" drug is the new name and the higher prescription price (paid almost entirely by the insurance company). In that case, the "new drug" would be *exactly* as safe and effective as metformin, and thus there could be no injury to any of the insurance company's insured. Nevertheless, the insurance companies would be able to claim — precisely as they do here — that the defendants engaged in a scheme to defraud it, and that the company suffered direct economic losses as a result.

In the hypothetical stated, why wouldn't each patient have a direct action to recover the excess, so that the insurance company could proceed under ordinary principles of subrogation? What result if the patients who went off Rezulin did not go back to metformin, but to a newer drug (either Avadia or Actos), which operated in a fashion similar to Rezulin?

2. *Dealing with proximate causation.* Proximate causation has cropped up in other modern complex fraud cases. For example, in Litton Industries, Inc. v. Lehman Brothers Kuhn Loeb Inc., 967 F.2d 742, 749, 751 (2d Cir. 1992), Lehman employees used inside information to drive up the price of Itek stock from $42.50 to $48.00, forcing Litton to pay a premium for the shares acquired in its takeover bid in a friendly acquisition. The plaintiff did not rely on the actions of the defendant's employees, of which it had no knowledge, but it did look to the overall market price of the shares in calculating its $48 bid to the Itek board. Oakes, C.J., reversed a summary judgment for defendant below and allowed the case to go to the jury. He noted, "[a] rational bidder planning a tender offer seeks to estimate the minimum premium required to induce a sufficient percentage of the target's shareholders to tender their shares." Given that premise, he concluded that "[i]n a situation such as this, in which the thought processes of the Itek Board and the theory that best characterizes their conduct are at issue, caution must be exercised in granting summary judgment. Exercising such caution, we find . . . that a reasonable jury might find that market price was a substantial factor in the Itek Board's assessment of Litton's offer and that absent insider trading the Itek Board would have accepted less than $48 per share."

3. *Causation in nondisclosure cases.* In Affiliated Ute Citizens v. United States, 406 U.S. 128, 153-154 (1972), the Ute Distribution Corporation issued shares to its corporate assets to "mixed-blood" descendants of the Ute Tribes. The articles of incorporation required that any mixed-blood shareholder wanting to sell shares to outsiders had to first offer these shares to tribal members, but could sell to outsiders if no tribe member

was prepared to accept the offer. Employees of the First Security Bank purchased shares from mixed-blood shareholders without disclosing to them that the price they offered was below that which they could receive by selling the shares in outside markets. Blackmun, J., refused to deny liability on the ground that the tribe members could not establish causation.

> Under the circumstances of this case, involving primarily a failure to disclose, positive proof of reliance is not a prerequisite to recovery. All that is necessary is that the facts withheld be material in the sense that a reasonable investor might have considered them important in making this decision. This obligation to disclose and this withholding of a material fact establish the requisite element of causation in fact.

SECTION C. NEGLIGENT MISREPRESENTATION

Ultramares Corporation v. Touche
174 N.E. 441 (N.Y. 1931)

CARDOZO, C.J. The action is in tort for damages suffered through the misrepresentations of accountants, the first cause of action being for misrepresentations that were merely negligent and the second for misrepresentations charged to have been fraudulent.

In January, 1924, the defendants, a firm of public accountants, were employed by Fred Stern & Co., Inc., to prepare and certify a balance sheet exhibiting the condition of its business as of December 31, 1923. They had been employed at the end of each of the three years preceding to render a like service. Fred Stern & Co., Inc., which was in substance Stern himself, was engaged in the importation and sale of rubber. To finance its operations, it required extensive credit and borrowed large sums of money from banks and other lenders. All this was known to the defendants. The defendants knew also that in the usual course of business the balance sheet when certified would be exhibited by the Stern Company to banks, creditors, stockholders, purchasers, or sellers, according to the needs of the occasion, as the basis of financial dealings. Accordingly, when the balance sheet was made up, the defendants supplied the Stern company with thirty-two copies certified with serial numbers as counterpart originals. Nothing was said as to the persons to whom these counterparts would be shown or the extent or number of the transactions in which they would be used. In particular there was no mention of the plaintiff, a corporation doing business chiefly as a factor, which till then had never made advances to the Stern Company, though it had sold it merchandise in small amounts. The range of the transactions in which a certificate of audit might be expected to play a part was as indefinite and wide as the possibilities of the business that was mirrored in the summary.

By February 26, 1924, the audit was finished and the balance sheet made up. It stated assets in the sum of $2,550,671.88 and liabilities other than capital and surplus in the sum of $1,479,956.62, thus showing a net worth of $1,070,715.26. Attached to the balance sheet was a certificate as follows:

TOUCHE, NIVEN & CO.
Public Accountants
Eighty Maiden Lane
New York

February 26, 1924

Certificate of Auditors

We have examined the accounts of Fred Stern & Co., Inc., for the year ending December 31, 1923, and hereby certify that the annexed balance sheet is in accordance therewith and with the information and explanations given us. We further certify that, subject to provision for federal taxes on income, the said statement, in our opinion, presents a true and correct view of the financial condition of Fred Stern & Co., Inc., as at December 31, 1923.

Touche, Niven & Co.
Public Accountants

[Cardozo, C.J., noted that the accountant's statement was wrong in all material respects. Stern & Co. was in fact insolvent at the time the balance sheet was prepared, and the defendant auditors had been taken in by false statements of income and expenses prepared by Stern's officers. After an extensive review of the evidence, Cardozo, C.J., concluded that a skilled auditor would have followed up various leads and detected the fraud perpetrated by Stern & Co.'s chief officers. On the faith of the balance sheet certified by the defendant, the plaintiff, as part of its factoring business, advanced various sums to Stern & Co. throughout most of 1924. Stern & Co. collapsed in January 1925, leaving the plaintiff with a host of unpaid loans, both unsecured and inadequately secured. In November 1926, the plaintiffs sued the defendants for both negligence and fraud. The trial judge refused to allow the fraud count to go to the jury. The jury, however, found the defendant negligent and awarded the plaintiff some $187,500. The trial judge, who had reserved judgment on the sufficiency of the negligence claim, entered a judgment for the defendant on the ground that the plaintiff's claim for negligent misrepresentation did not state a cause of action. That decision was reversed by the appellate division. Cardozo, C.J., noted that the finding of negligence was supported by the evidence. "The reckoning was not wrong upon the evidence before us, if duty be assumed."]

We are brought to the question of duty, its origin and measure.

The defendants owed to their employer a duty imposed by law to make their certificate without fraud, and a duty growing out of contract to make it with the care and caution proper to their calling. Fraud includes the pretense of knowledge when knowledge there is none. To creditors and investors to whom the employer exhibited the certificate, the defendants owed a like duty to make it without fraud, since there was notice in the circumstances of its making that the employer did not intend to keep it to himself. A different question develops when we ask whether they owed a duty to these to make it without negligence. If liability for negligence exists, a thoughtless slip or blunder, the failure to detect a theft or forgery beneath the cover of deceptive entries, may expose accountants to a liability in an indeterminate amount for an indeterminate time to an indeterminate class. The hazards of a business conducted on these terms are so extreme as to enkindle doubt whether a flaw may not exist in the implication of a duty that exposes to these consequences. We put aside for the moment any statement in the certificate which involves the representation of a fact as true to the knowledge of the auditors. If such a statement was made, whether believed to be true or not, the defendants are liable for deceit in the event that it was false. The plaintiff does not need the invention of novel doctrine to help it out in such conditions. The case was submitted to the jury and the verdict was returned upon the theory that even in the absence of a misstatement of a fact there is a liability also for erroneous opinion. The expression of an opinion is to be subject to a warranty implied by law. What, then, is the warranty, as yet unformulated, to be? Is it merely that the opinion is honestly conceived and that the preliminary inquiry has been honestly pursued, that a halt has not been made without a genuine belief that the search has been reasonably adequate to bring disclosure of the truth? Or does it go farther and involve the assumption of a liability for any blunder or inattention that could fairly be spoken of as negligence if the controversy were one between accountant and employer for breach of a contract to render services for pay?

The assault upon the citadel of privity is proceeding in these days apace. How far the inroads shall extend is now a favorite subject of juridical discussion. . . . In the field of the law of contract there has been a gradual widening of the doctrine of Lawrence v. Fox (20 N.Y. 268 (1859)), until today the beneficiary of a promise, clearly designated as such, is seldom left without a remedy (Seaver v. Ransom[, 120 N.E. 639 (N.Y. 1918)]). Even in that field, however, the remedy is narrower where the beneficiaries of the promise are indeterminate or general. Something more must then appear than an intention that the promise shall redound to the benefit of the public or to that of a class of indefinite extension. The promise must be such as to "bespeak the assumption of a duty to make reparation directly to the individual members of the public if the benefit is lost" (Moch Co. v. Rensselaer Water Co). In the field of the law of torts a manufacturer who is negligent in the manufacture of a chattel in circumstances pointing to an unreasonable risk of serious bodily harm to those using it thereafter may be liable for negligence though privity is lacking between manufacturer and user (MacPherson v. Buick Motor Co., 217 N.Y. 382 (1916); American Law Institute, Restatement of the Law of Torts, §262). A force or instrument of harm having been launched with potentialities of danger manifest to the eye of prudence, the one who launches it is under a duty to keep it within bounds (*Moch*). Even so, the question is still open whether the potentialities of danger that will charge with liability are confined to harm to the person, or include injury to property. In either view, however, what is released or set in motion is a physical force. We are now asked to say that a like liability attaches to the circulation of a thought or a release of the explosive power resident in words.

Three cases in this court are said by the plaintiff to have committed us to the doctrine that words, written or oral, if negligently published with the expectation that the reader or listener will transmit them to another, will lay a basis for liability though privity be lacking. These are Glanzer v. Shepard (233 N.Y. 236 (1922)); International Products Co. v. Erie R.R. Co. [, 155 N.E. 662 (N.Y. 1927)], and Doyle v. Chatham & Phenix Nat. Bank [, 171 N.E. 574 (N.Y. 1930)].

In Glanzer v. Shepard the seller of beans requested the defendants, public weighers, to make return of the weight and furnish the buyer with a copy. This the defendants did. Their return, which was made out in duplicate, one copy to the seller and the other to the buyer, recites that it was made by order of the former for the use of the latter. The buyer paid the seller on the faith of the certificate which turned out to be erroneous. We held that the weighers were liable at the suit of the buyer for the moneys overpaid. Here was something more than the rendition of a service in the expectation that the one who ordered the certificate would use it thereafter in the operations of his business as occasion might require. Here was a case where the transmission of the certificate to another was not merely one possibility among many, but the "end and aim of the transaction," as certain and immediate and deliberately willed as if a husband were to order a gown to be delivered to his wife, or a telegraph company, contracting with the sender of a message, were to telegraph it wrongly to the damage of the person expected to receive it. The intimacy of the resulting nexus is attested by the fact that after stating the case in terms of legal duty, we went on to point out that viewing it as a phase or extension of Lawrence v. Fox, or Seaver v. Ransom, we could reach the same result by stating it in terms of contract. The bond was so close as to approach that of privity, if not completely one with it. Not so in the case at hand. No one would be likely to urge that there was a contractual relation, or even one approaching it, at the root of any duty that was owing from the defendants now before us to the indeterminate class of persons who, presently or in the future, might deal with the Stern company in reliance on the audit. In a word, the service rendered by the defendant in Glanzer v. Shepard was primarily for the information of a third person, in effect, if not in name, a party to the contract, and only incidentally for that of the formal promisee. In the case at hand, the service was primarily for the benefit of the Stern company, a convenient instrumentality for use in the development of the business, and only incidentally or collaterally for the use of those to whom Stern and his associates might exhibit it thereafter. Foresight of these possibilities may charge with liability for fraud. The conclusion does not follow that it will charge with liability for negligence.

[A discussion of International Products Co. v. Erie R.R. and Doyle v. Chatham & Phenix National Bank is omitted.]

From the foregoing analysis the conclusion is, we think, inevitable that nothing in our previous decisions commits us to a holding of liability for negligence in the circumstances of the case at hand, and that such liability, if recognized, will be an extension of the principle of those decisions to different conditions, even if more or less analogous. The question then is whether such an extension shall be made.

The extension, if made, will so expand the field of liability for negligent speech as to make it nearly, if not quite, coterminous with that of liability for fraud. Again and again, in decisions of this court, the bounds of this latter liability have been set up, with futility the fate of every endeavor to dislodge them. Scienter has been declared to be an indispensable element except where the representation has been put forward as true of one's own knowledge, or in circumstances where the expression of opinion was a dishonorable pretense. . . . Even an opinion, especially an opinion by an expert, may be found to be fraudulent if the grounds supporting it are so flimsy as to lead to the conclusion that there was no genuine belief back of it. Further than that this court has never gone. Directors of corporations have been acquitted of liability for deceit though they have been lax in investigation and negligent in speech. This has not meant, to be sure, that negligence may not be evidence from which a trier of the facts may draw an inference of fraud (Derry v. Peek, [L.R.] 14 A.C. 337) but merely that if that inference is rejected, or, in the light of all the circumstances, is found to be unreasonable, negligence alone is not a substitute for fraud. . . . A change [from fraud to negligence] so revolutionary, if expedient, must be wrought by legislation. . . .

Liability for negligence if adjudged in this case will extend to many callings other than an auditor's. Lawyers who certify their opinion as to the validity of municipal or corporate bonds with knowledge that the opinion will be brought to the notice of the public, will become liable to the investors, if they have overlooked a statute or a decision, to the same extent as if the controversy were one between client and adviser. Title companies insuring titles to a tract of land, with knowledge that at an approaching auction the fact that they have insured will be stated to the bidders, will become liable to purchasers who may wish the benefit of a policy without payment of a premium. These illustrations may seem to be extreme, but they go little, if any, farther than we are invited to go now. Negligence, moreover, will have one standard when viewed in relation to the employer, and another and at times a stricter standard when viewed in relation to the public. Explanations that might seem plausible, omissions that might be reasonable, if the duty is confined to the employer, conducting a business that presumably at least is not a fraud upon his creditors, might wear another aspect if an independent duty to be suspicious even of one's principal is owing to investors. "Every one making a promise having the quality of a contract will be under a duty to the promisee by virtue of the promise, but under another duty, apart from contract, to an indefinite number of potential beneficiaries when performance has begun. The assumption of one relation will mean the involuntary assumption of a series of new relations, inescapably hooked together." (*Moch.*) "The law does not spread its protection so far." (Robins Dry Dock & Repair Co. v. Flint, 275 U.S. 303 (1927)).

Our holding does not emancipate accountants from the consequences of fraud. It does not relieve them if their audit has been so negligent as to justify a finding that they had no genuine belief in its adequacy, for this again is fraud. It does no more than say that if less than this is proved, if there has been neither reckless misstatement nor insincere profession of an opinion, but only honest blunder, the ensuing liability for negligence is one that is bounded by the contract, and is to be enforced between the parties by whom the contract has been made. We doubt whether the average business man receiving a certificate without paying for it and receiving it merely as one among a multitude of possible investors, would look for anything more.

(2) The second cause of action is yet to be considered.

The defendants certified as a fact, true to their own knowledge, that the balance sheet was in accordance with the books of account. If their statement was false, they are not to be exonerated because they believed it to be true. We think the triers of the facts might hold it to be false.

[The court reviewed the evidence on the second cause of action and noted that accountants are to be judged by a strict standard of construction "when certifying to an agreement between the audit and the entries" as the defendants did here. The court also concluded that the defendants could not protect themselves against a charge that they did not detect the fictitious invoices "by invoking a practice known as that of testing and sampling," on the ground that it was "plainly insufficient" to determine whether there were in fact any accounts at all. The court concluded that the defendants could not escape liability because they had "delegated the performance of this work to agents of their own selection."

Plaintiff's first cause of action was dismissed; a new trial was granted on plaintiff's second cause of action.]

NOTES

1. *Liability for negligent misrepresentation. Ultramares* is still the leading American common law decision on liability for negligent misrepresentation. Does its invocation of the privity limitation make more sense here than it does in the products liability cases? The waterworks cases? If the defendants had been told to mail a copy of their certified statement directly to the plaintiff for use in its lending operations, could the plaintiff have recovered in negligence? Does *Ultramares* imply that only those who pay for the preparation of the report can sue for its negligent preparation? Could the plaintiff recover under a third party beneficiary theory? Could the accountant limit liability for negligence by contract? For fraud?

Note that the Restatement (Second) of Torts §552 limits liability for negligent misrepresentation to, at most, individuals who are members "of a limited group of persons for whose benefit and guidance" the information is supplied, provided that there is reliance on that information in that transaction, or "in a substantially similar transaction." The Restatement position has been adopted in numerous recent cases, including Burbach v. Radon Analytical Labs, Inc., 652 N.W.2d 135 (Iowa 2002), where a homebuyer was allowed to sue the defendant firm whose negligent inspection failed to pick up key structural defects in construction even though the two parties were not in privity. The defendant did not know who might use the report, but given the nature of the inspection, it knew that far from an "indeterminate class," only a single buyer would rely the report.

In New York, *Ultramares* was extensively reexamined in White v. Guarente, 372 N.E.2d 315, 318-319 (N.Y. 1977). There the court held that the plaintiff, a limited partnership specializing in trading and hedging marketable securities, stated a cause of action in negligence against the defendant Arthur Andersen & Co. The partnership had retained the accounting firm to audit the activities of its general partners who had improperly withdrawn their own funds from the agreement. Andersen negligently missed this withdrawal. Unlike the situation in *Ultramares*, the suit did not expose Andersen to liability to "the extensive and indeterminable investing public-at-large" but "rather to a known group possessed of vested rights, marked by a definable limit and made up of certain components." Andersen "must have been aware that a limited partner would necessarily rely on or make use of the audit and tax returns of the partnership, or at least constituents of them, in order to properly prepare his or her own tax returns." Were the limited partners in privity with the defendants, since the partnership hired the defendants to do the audit? See also Credit Alliance Corp. v. Arthur Andersen & Co., 483 N.E.2d 110 (N.Y. 1985), which reiterated that liability for negligence under *Ultramares* depended on whether the defendants supplied the report for a particular purpose to "a known party or parties" of whom the defendants were aware.

2. *From privity to foreseeability and back. Ultramares* received a chillier reception in Rosenblum v. Adler, 461 A.2d 138, 145, 149, 153 (N.J. 1983). There the defendant accounting firm of Touche Ross & Co. was charged with negligent misrepresentation because it failed to ferret out the fraud that Giant Stores Corporation had perpetrated against the plaintiffs, who, under a merger agreement, accepted worthless Giant stock in exchange for shares of their own private corporations. The trial judge dismissed the negligence count against Touche Ross & Co., but the New Jersey Supreme Court remanded for trial. The court first noted the tension between Cardozo's opinions in *MacPherson* and *Ultramares*, and then insisted that privity should no more be a barrier in misrepresentation cases than in physical injury cases. Relying on §552 of the Restatement, the court concluded: "Generally, within the outer limits fixed by the court as a matter of law, the reasonably foreseeable consequences of the negligent act define the duty and should be actionable."

The court concluded that the "auditor's function has expanded from that of a watchdog for management to an independent evaluator of the adequacy and fairness of financial statements issued by management to stockholders, creditors, and others," and continued:

> When the independent auditor furnishes an opinion with no limitation in the certificate as to whom the company may disseminate the financial statements, he has a duty to all those whom that auditor should reasonably foresee as recipients from the company of the statements for its proper business purposes, provided that the recipients rely on the statements pursuant to those business purposes. The principle that we have adopted applies by its terms only to those foreseeable users who receive the audited statements from the business entity for a proper business purpose to influence a business decision of the user, the audit having been made for that business entity. Thus, for example, an institutional investor or portfolio manager who does not obtain audited statements from the company would not come within the stated principle. Nor would stockholders who purchased the stock after a negligent audit be covered in the absence of demonstrating the necessary conditions precedent. Those and similar cases beyond the stated rule are not before us and we express no opinion with respect to such situations.

These expansionist tendencies of accountants' liability were in turn checked, at least in part, in Bily v. Arthur Young & Co., 834 P.2d 745, 767 (Cal. 1992), which rejected the "foreseeability" test of *Rosenblum* on the ground that it could impose "a potential liability far out of proportion to its fault," and held that sophisticated investors could have purchased, if they chose, protection from the auditor by contract. Fearing the contraction of needed auditing services, the court followed §552 and restricted potential liability to a narrow class of persons, who, although not clients, "are specifically intended beneficiaries of the audit report who are known to the auditor and for whose benefit it renders the audit report." In NYCAL Corp. v. KPMG Peat Marwick, LLB, 688 N.E.2d 1368, 1373 (Mass. 1998), the court followed *Bily* and the Restatement in granting a summary judgment to the defendant auditor against a plaintiff who had unbeknownst to the defendant purchased a controlling 35 percent block of shares in the audited firm, which went bankrupt shortly after the purchase. The court rejected the argument that following the Restatement rule "will be rewarding an accountant's efforts to 'remain blissfully unaware' of the report's proposed distribution and uses. . . . [T]he Restatement standard will not excuse an accountant's 'wilful ignorance' of information of which the account would have been aware had the accountant not consciously disregarded that information."

In Walpert, Smullian & Blumenthal, P.A. v. Katz, 762 A.2d 582, 597 (Md. 2000), the court noted that three lines of authority had grown up in the accountant's liability area. First

> [a] significant number follow the *Ultramares* formulation, under which a third party will be denied relief for an auditor's negligence in the absence of a relationship with the auditor that constitutes privity or that is equivalent to privity. The majority of jurisdictions, however, following the Restatement approach: liability is imposed on suppliers of commercial information to third parties who are actually foreseen as the users of the information for a particular purpose. The third view, followed by a few jurisdictions, allows third parties to recover for auditor negligence when their reliance on the audit report was reasonably foreseeable by the auditor. *Rosenblum*

The court then followed *Ultramares* and *Credit Alliance*, and allowed the case to go forward because the plaintiffs had retained the defendants and had attended meetings with the defendant for the specific purpose of deciding whether to make loans to the defunct Magnetics Corporation, whose books the defendant had audited.

3. *Causation in negligent misrepresentation cases.* The element of causation is as critical in cases of negligent misrepresentations as it is for cases of fraudulent misrepresentation. Indeed, the area exhibits many of the complexities found in physical harm cases. In Oregon Steel Mills, Inc. v.

Coopers & Lybrand, LLP, 83 P.3d 322, 330 (Or. 2004), the defendant accountants had negligently and incorrectly prepared consolidated financial statements that delayed the public offering of plaintiff's shares by two months, from April to June 1996, when the shares sold for $2.50 less per share than they would have on the earlier date. Balmer, J., gave the defendant summary judgment on the issue of causation. He noted first that these losses in market value were distinguishable from the reputational losses that might have impaired the plaintiff to raise additional funds in capital markets. Instead, he held that these losses from the occurrence of unrelated market forces did not count as "a reasonably foreseeable result of defendant's wrongful conduct," given the independent intervention of market forces. The analysis here in fact parallels that for cases of delay in the delivery of nonperishable goods or the receipt of a building permit because of a negligent application. In all these cases, it is in a sense foreseeable that the value of plaintiff's project could go either up or down. But in the absence of special circumstances (such as the sale of perishable goods), the only systematic loss is the *interest* on the amount receivable attributable to the delay. Stated otherwise, in some cases the delay will work to the *advantage* of the plaintiff by allowing for a later sale in a rising markets. So long as securities markets are efficiently priced, the defendant is overpenalized if forced to pay for the downturns in value if the plaintiff could pocket any (foreseeable) gains from any interim upturn in value. The interest payment leaves the plaintiff indifferent with respect to time, assuming that the additional costs of completing the new issue are borne by the negligent defendant. For the comparable role of coincidence in physical injury cases, see Berry v. Sugar Notch Borough, *supra* at page 502.

4. *Contracting out of liability for negligent misrepresentation.* Should negligent misrepresentation cases be treated as raising tort issues? In Hedley, Byrne & Co. Ltd. v. Heller & Partners Ltd., [1964] App. Cas. 465, 526 [H.L. 1963], Hedley, Byrne was a firm of advertising agents that had extended over £15,000 of credit to a firm called Easipower. It made this loan only after obtaining a credit report on Easipower from Heller, who allegedly negligently overstated Easipower's creditworthiness. Lord Devlin concluded that in principle it makes no difference "whether financial loss is caused through physical injury or whether it is caused directly."

> If irrespective of contract, a doctor negligently advises a patient that he can safely pursue his occupation and he cannot and the patient's health suffers and he loses his livelihood, the patient has a remedy. But if the doctor negligently advises him that he cannot safely pursue his occupation when in fact he can and he loses his livelihood, there is said to be no remedy. Unless, of course, the patient was a private patient and the doctor accepted half a guinea for his trouble: then the patient can recover all. I am bound to say, my Lords, that I think this to be nonsense. . . . It arises, if it is the law, simply

out of a refusal to make sense. The line is not drawn on any intelligible principle. It just happens to be the line which those who have been driven from the extreme assertion that negligent statements in the absence of contractual or fiduciary duty give no cause of action have in the course of their retreat so far reached.

Lord Devlin nonetheless ruled for the defendant on the strength of its disclaimer. "A man cannot be said voluntarily to be undertaking a responsibility if at the very moment when he is said to be accepting it he declares that in fact he is not."

Once disclaimers are regarded as effective, what presumption should be established about negligence liability in their absence? Professor Goldberg, Accountable Accountants: Is Third-Party Liability Necessary?, 17 J. Legal Stud. 295, 300-301 (1988), defended *Ultramares* on the ground that the default rule should be one of no liability:

> If it turned out that it was appropriate that accountants should compensate third parties for their negligence, it would not be very difficult to have them assume the liability by contract rather than by having it imposed by tort. Third parties could receive explicit assurance in the form of a warranty, guarantee, bond, or a similar device. Even without explicit liability, the negligent accounting firm would suffer the consequences of poor performance in the form of a decline in the value of its "brand name." Since it is probably true that accountants are not very good guarantors, I would guess that accountants would rarely agree to compensate third parties. But it is crucial to recognize that it is unnecessary for courts or legislatures to guess. It is sufficient for them to allow the parties to resolve the problem by contract.

For a defense of the expanded liability of accountants, see Weiner, Common Law Liability of the Certified Public Accountant for Negligent Misrepresentation, 20 San Diego L. Rev. 233 (1983). See also Bishop, Negligent Misrepresentation Through Economists' Eyes, 96 Law Q. Rev. 360 (1980).

5. *Modern securities law and the indeterminate class.* The specter of *Ultramares* haunts modern securities law where vast potential liability for material nondisclosures as well as misstatements is a daily fact of life. Which people therefore under the securities law are entitled to sue for their financial losses? Section 10(b) of the Securities Exchange Act, *supra* at 1202, Note 4, proscribes fraud "in connection with the purchase or sale of securities." In Blue Chip Stamps v. Manor Drug Stores, 421 U.S. 723, 747-748 (1975), the plaintiffs alleged that they did not purchase shares of the defendant's stock because the defendants had made false and misleading negative statements about its value. The Supreme Court held that only actual purchasers and sellers of stocks could sue under the section. The Court feared that the proposed rule would admit an enormous class of

potential plaintiffs into court, place heavy strains on the system of discovery, and require the defendants to litigate against plaintiffs whose claims were wholly hypothetical. In explicit reliance on *Ultramares,* the Court concluded as follows: "[W]hile much of the development of the law of deceit has been the elimination of artificial barriers to recovery on just claims, we are not the first court to express concern that the inexorable broadening of the class of plaintiff who may sue in this area of the law will ultimately result in more harm than good." Does this passage answer Lord Devlin's contention that there is no sensible distinction between financial loss and physical injury cases? If both *Ultramares* and Goodwin v. Agassiz are sound law, is there any reason for a special regime of securities law?

16

ECONOMIC HARMS

SECTION A. INTRODUCTION

This chapter addresses when and how tort law protects economic interests from interference by the actions of others. The protection of these economic interests is not a wholly new theme, for the broader issues have already been touched upon previously in a number of specific contexts. For example, the plaintiff's economic loss flowing from property damage or bodily injury is ordinarily recoverable in tort no matter whether the underlying claim involves negligence, strict liability, or some intentional wrong. Economic interests receive still more explicit protection when the plaintiff seeks a remedy for defamation for trade disparagement, covered in Chapter 13, interference with the right of publicity, a matter already covered in Chapter 14, or for the pecuniary losses attributable to misrepresentation, the subject of Chapter 15.

This chapter extends that analysis by considering three separate instances of economic harms to strangers. Section B examines the extent to which the law protects contractual relationships by supplying a contracting party not only contractual remedies against the promisor, but also tort remedies against a third party who has induced, or threatens to induce, a breach of contract. Section C considers the protection afforded, not to existing contracts, but to advantageous relationships with third parties that the plaintiff hopes to create or maintain. The distinction between the first and second classes is evident enough for in the first, the plaintiff is normally entitled to some relief under an existing agreement against the other party to the contract, while in the second, the disappointed party has no contractual remedy against anybody. Section D offers a glimpse at the legal protection of valuable information at common law, with some discussion of the overlap between the common law rules and the statutory regimes that today regulate patents, copyrights, tradenames, and trademarks. This entire area of intellectual property continues to enjoy exponential legal growth.

In dealing with these issues, two great fears have led courts to narrow the scope of liability. First, as with emotional distress and negligent misrepresentation, courts fear that generalized protection of economic interests against any diminution in value will spawn endless lawsuits and create countless administrative nightmares. The second fear is that "unfair competition," if incautiously expanded, will destroy ordinary business competition and the social benefits it provides. Yet, by the same token, a complete withdrawal of legal protection to market actors could invite antisocial conduct that undermines the incentive to create and market new products by conferring exclusive rights on inventors of patents and authors of copyrightable works. With tangible property, a clear prohibition against trespass is generally sufficient to protect the fruits of individual labor. But with intellectual property, that simple device is not available so that more complex legal rules are required. As in so many other areas, the central task for judges is to balance these conflicting impulses. The complexity of the area, however, is so great that common law remedies often prove insufficient, so some brief note must be made of the statutory schemes from the labor and antitrust statutes, to patent, copyright, and tradename and trademark protection.

SECTION B.   INDUCEMENT OF BREACH OF CONTRACT

The Statute of Labourers (1351)
3 Ed. III 1351

... Because a great part of the people and especially of the, workmen and servants has now died in that pestilence, some, seeing the straights of the masters and the scarcity of servants, are not willing to serve unless they receive excessive wages, and others, rather than through labour to gain their living, prefer to beg in idleness: We ... have seen fit to ordain: that every man and woman of our kingdom of England, of whatever condition, whether bond or free, who is able bodied and below the age of sixty years, not living from trade nor carrying on a fixed craft, nor having of his own the means of living, or land of his own with regard to the cultivation of which he might occupy himself, and not serving another, if he, considering his station, be sought after to serve in a suitable service, he shall be bound to serve him who has seen fit so to seek after him; and he shall take only the wages liveries, meed or salary which, in the places where he sought to serve, were accustomed to be paid in the twentieth year of our reign of England, or the five or six common years next preceding. Provided, that in thus retaining their service, the lords are preferred before others of their bondsmen or their land tenants . . .

And if a reaper or mower, or other workman or servant, of whatever standing or condition he be, who is retained in the service of any one, do depart from the said service before the end of the term agreed, without permission or reasonable cause, he shall undergo the penalty of imprisonment, and let no one, under the same penalty, presume to receive or retain such a one in his service.

Lumley v. Gye
118 Eng. Rep. 749 (K.B. 1853)

The 1st count of the declaration stated that plaintiff was lessee and manager of the Queen's Theatre, for performing operas for gain to him; and that he had contracted and agreed with Johanna Wagner to perform in the theatre for a certain time, with a condition, amongst others, that she should not sing nor use her talents elsewhere during the term without plaintiff's consent in writing: Yet defendant, knowing the premises, and maliciously intending to injure plaintiff as lessee and manager of the theatre, whilst the agreement with Wagner was in force, and before the expiration of the term, enticed and procured Wagner to refuse to perform: by means of which enticement and procurement of defendant, Wagner wrongfully refused to perform, and did not perform during the term.

Count 2, for enticing and procuring Johanna Wagner to continue to refuse to perform during the term, after the order of Vice Chancellor Parker, affirmed by Lord St. Leonards, restraining her from performing at a theatre of defendants.

Count 3. That Johanna Wagner had been and was hired by plaintiff to sing and perform at his theatre for a certain time, as the dramatic artiste of plaintiff, for reward to her, and had become and was such dramatic artiste of plaintiff at his theatre: Yet defendant, well knowing &c., maliciously enticed and procured her, then being such dramatic artiste, to depart from the said employment.

In each count special damage was alleged.

CROMPTON, J. . . . It was said, in support of the demurrer, that it did not appear in the declaration that the relation of master and servant ever subsisted between the plaintiff and Miss Wagner; that Miss Wagner was not averred, especially in the two first counts, to have entered upon the service of the plaintiff; and that the engagement of a theatrical performer, even if the performer has entered upon the duties, is not of such a nature as to make the performer a servant, within the rule of law which gives an action to the master for the wrongful enticing away of his servant. And it was laid down broadly, as a general proposition of law, that no action will lie for procuring a person to break a contract, although such procuring is with a malicious intention and causes great and immediate injury. And the law as to enticing servants was said to be contrary to the general rule and principle of law, and to be anomalous, and probably to have had its origin from the state of society when serfdom existed, and to be founded upon, or upon the equity of, the Statute of Labourers[, 25 Ed. 3 (1349)]. It was said that it would be dangerous to hold that an action was maintainable for persuading a third party to break a contract, unless some boundary or limits could be pointed out; and that the remedy for enticing away servants was confined to cases where the relation of master and servant, in a strict sense, subsisted between the parties; and that, in all other cases of contract, the only remedy was against the party breaking the contract.

Whatever may have been the origin or foundation of the law as to enticing of servants, and whether it be, as contended by the plaintiff, an instance and branch of a wider rule, or whether it be, as contended by the defendant, an anomaly and an exception from the general rule of law on such subjects, it must now be considered clear law that a person who wrongfully and maliciously, or, which is the same thing, with notice, interrupts the relation subsisting between master and servant by procuring the servant to depart from the master's service, or by harbouring and keeping him as servant after he has quitted it and during the time stipulated for as the period of service, whereby the master is injured, commits a wrongful act for which he is responsible at law. I think that the rule applies wherever the wrongful interruption operates to prevent the service during the time for which the parties have contracted that the service shall continue: and I think that the relation of master and servant subsists, sufficiently for the purpose of such action, during the time for which there is in existence a binding contract of hiring and service between the parties; and I think that it is a fanciful and technical and unjust distinction to say that the not having actually entered into the service, or that the service not actually continuing, can make any difference. The wrong and injury are surely the same, whether the wrong doer entices away the gardener, who has hired himself for a year, the night before he is to go to his work, or after he has planted the first cabbage on the first morning of his service; and I should be sorry to support a distinction so unjust, and so repugnant to common sense, unless bound to do so by some rule or authority of law plainly shewing that such distinction exists. The proposition of the defendant, that there must be a service actually subsisting, seems to be inconsistent with the authorities that shew these actions to be maintainable for receiving or harbouring servants after they have left the actual service of the master.....

[Crompton, J., then reviewed earlier cases.]

. . . It appears to me that Miss Wagner had contracted to do work for the plaintiff within the meaning of this rule; and I think that, where a party has contracted to give his personal services for a certain time to another, the parties are in the relation of employer and employed, or master and servant, within the meaning of this rule. And I see no reason for narrowing such a rule; but I should rather, if necessary, apply such a remedy to a case "new in its instance, but" "not new in the reason and principle of it," that is, to a case where the wrong and damage are strictly analogous to the wrong and damage in a well recognised class of cases. In deciding this case on the narrower ground, I wish by no means to be considered as deciding that the larger ground taken by Mr. Cowling is not tenable, or as saying that in no case except that of master and servant is an action maintainable for *maliciously* inducing another to break a contract to the injury of the person with whom such contract has been made. It does not appear to me to be a sound answer, to say that the act in such cases is the act of the party who breaks the contract; for that reason would apply in the acknowledged case of master and servant. Nor is it an answer, to say that there is a remedy against the contractor, and that the party relies on the contract; for, besides that reason also applying to the case of master and servant, the action on the contract and the action against the malicious wrong-doer may be for a different matter; and the damages occasioned by such malicious injury might be calculated on a very different principle from the amount of the debt which might be the only sum recoverable on the contract. Suppose a trader, *with a malicious intent to ruin a rival trader,* goes to a banker or other party who owes money to his rival, and begs him not to pay the money which he owes him, and by that means ruins or greatly prejudices the party: I am by no means prepared to say that an action could not be maintained, and that damages, beyond the amount of the debt if the injury were great, or much less than such amount if the injury were less serious, might not be recovered. . . . In this class of cases it must be assumed that it is the malicious act of the defendant, and that malicious act only, which causes the servant or contractor not to perform the work or contract which he would otherwise have done. The servant or contractor may be utterly unable to pay anything like the amount of the damage sustained entirely from the wrongful act of the defendant: and it would seem unjust, and contrary to the general principles of law, if such wrongdoer were not responsible for the damage caused by his wrongful and malicious act. . . .

Without however deciding any such more general question, I think that we are justified in applying the principle of action for enticing away servants to a case where the defendant *maliciously procures* a party, who is under a valid contract to give her exclusive personal services to the plaintiff for a specified period, to refuse to give such services *during the period for which she had so contracted,* whereby the plaintiff was injured.

I think, therefore, that our judgment should be for the plaintiff.

[The concurring opinions of Erle and Wightman, JJ., are omitted.]

COLERIDGE, J. . . . . In order to maintain this action, one of two propositions must be maintained; either that an action will lie against any one by whose persuasions one party to a contract is induced to break it to the damage of the other party, or that the action, for seducing a servant from the master or persuading one who has contracted for service from entering into the employ, is of so wide application as to embrace the case of one in the position and profession of Johanna Wagner. After much consideration and enquiry I am of opinion that neither of these propositions is true; and they are both of them so important, and, if established by judicial decision, will lead to consequences so general, that, though I regret the necessity, I must not abstain from entering into remarks of some length in support of my view of the law.

It may simplify what I have to say, if I first state what are the conclusions which I seek to establish. They are these: that in respect of breach of contract the general rule of our law is to confine its remedies by action to the contracting parties, and to damages directly and proximately consequential on the act of him who is sued; that, as between master and servant, there is an admitted exception, that this exception dates from the Statute of Labourers, 23 Edw. III, and both on principle and according to authority is limited by it. If I am right in these positions, the conclusion will be for the defendant, because enough appears on this record to show, as to the first, that he, and, as to the second, that Johanna Wagner, is not within the limits so drawn.

First then, that the remedy for breach of contract is by the general rule of our law confined to the contracting parties. . . . There would be such a manifest absurdity in attempting to trace up the act of a free agent breaking a contract to all the advisers who may have influenced his mind, more or less honestly, more or less powerfully, and to make them responsible civilly for the consequences of what after all is his own act, and for the whole of the hurtful consequences of which the law makes him directly and fully responsible, that I believe it will never be contended for seriously. . . . [W]hen you apply the term of effectual persuasion to the breach of a contract, it has obviously a different meaning [from cases where a master orders a trespass by a servant]; the persuader has not broken and could not break the contract, for he had never entered into any; he cannot be sued upon the contract; and yet it is the breach of the contract only that is the cause of damage. Neither can it be said that in breaking the contract the contractor is the agent of him who procures him to do so; it is still his own act; he is principal in so doing, and is the only principal. This answer may seem technical; but it really goes to the root of the matter. It shows that the procurer has not done the hurtful act; what he has done is too remote from the damage to make him answerable for it. [After discussing certain precedents, Judge Coleridge continued:] None of this reasoning applies to the case of a breach of contract: if it does, I should be glad to know how any treatise on the law of contract could be complete without a chapter on this head, or how it happens that we have no decisions upon it. Certainly no subject could well be more fruitful or important; important contracts are more commonly broken with than without persuaders or procurers, and these often responsible persons when the principals may not be so. I am aware that with respect to an action on the case the argument primae impressionis is sometimes of no weight. If the circumstances under which the action would be brought have not before arisen, or are of rare occurrence, it will be of none, or only of inconsiderable weight; but, if the circumstances have been common, if there has been frequently occasion for the action, I apprehend it is important to find that the action has yet never been tried. Now we find a plentiful supply both of text and decision in the case of seduction of servants: and what inference does this lead to, contrasted with the silence of the books and the absence of decisions on the case of breach of ordinary contracts? . . . To draw a line between advice, persuasion, enticement and procurement is practically impossible in a court of justice; who shall say how much of a free agent's resolution flows from the interference of other minds, or the independent resolution of his own? This is a matter for the casuist rather than the jurist; still less is it for the juryman. Again, why draw the line between bad and good faith? If advice given mala fide, and loss sustained, entitle me to damages, why, though the advice be given honestly, but under wrong information, with a loss sustained, am I not entitled to them. According to all legal analogies, the bona fides of him who, by a conscious wilful act, directly injures me will not relieve him from the obligation to compensate me in damages for my loss. Again, where several persons happen to persuade to the same effect, and in the result the party persuaded acts upon the advice, how is it to be determined against whom the action may be brought, whether they are to be sued jointly or severally, in what proportions damages are to be recovered? . . .

I conclude then that this action cannot be maintained because: 1st. Merely to induce or procure a free contracting party to break his covenant, whether done maliciously or not, to the damage of another, for the reasons I have stated, is not actionable; 2d. That the law with regard to seduction of servants from their master's employ, in breach of their contract, is an exception, the origin of which is known, and that that exception does not reach the case of a theatrical performer. . . .

Judgment for plaintiff.

NOTES

1. Protection of contractual interests under Lumley v. Gye. Note that the original Statute of Labourers sought to protect government mandated contracts from interference with third parties. Is it a more, or less, suitable means for the protection of voluntary arrangements, and, if so, of which sort? Note Lumley v. Gye involved a personal services contract with a party of unique operatic skills, a far cry from the reapers and mowers of the statute. Also, note that typically there is little reason to protect ordinary contracts at competitive wages from third party interference, because of the ease of hiring a replacement for the lost worker whom few will have an incentive to lure away in any event. Nonetheless, the protection afforded in *Lumley* is critical to certain contractual arrangements where an employee does possess distinctive attributes or information. In Bowen v. Hall, 6 Q.B.D. 333 (1881), Lumley v. Gye was applied to the contract of an employee brickmaker (albeit one who had knowledge of a secret glazing process) who was induced to breach a definite five-year contract of employment with the plaintiff. The court held that malice was the gist of the tort and noted that although "mere persuasion" was not actionable, "if the persuasion be used for the indirect purpose of injuring the plaintiff, or of benefiting the defendant at the expense of the plaintiff, it is a malicious act." How does this definition of malice differ from the "notice" referred to by Crompton, J., in Lumley v. Gye? Shortly thereafter, in Temperton v. Russell, [1893] 1 Q.B. 715, inducement of breach of contract was held to reach interference with an ordinary contract for the sale of goods, here in the context of a labor dispute. On the early history and expansion of the action, see Note, Tortious Interference with Contractual Relations in the Nineteenth Century: The Transformation of Property, Contract, and Tort, 93 Harv. L. Rev. 1510 (1980).

Perhaps the most controversial historical application of the tort of inducement of breach of contract has stemmed from its use as a weapon of business in labor disputes. The leading case is Hitchman Coal & Coke Co. v. Mitchell, 245 U.S. 229 (1917). The defendants were employees of the Mineworkers Union who had induced the miners at the plaintiff's mine to stay on the job after they had agreed to join the union on some future request. The miners were held in breach of their "yellow-dog" contract between the employer and the workers whereby the miners, working under a contract at will, agreed not to join a union while remaining in the plaintiff's employ. *Hitchman* has been repudiated in the labor context, first in 1932 by the Norris-LaGuardia Act, 29 U.S.C. §§101-115 (2007), which prohibited the enforcement of yellow-dog contracts in federal courts, 29 U.S.C. §103, and thereafter in 1935 by the National Labor Relations Act, 29 U.S.C. §§151-169 (2007), which made it an "unfair labor practice" to discriminate against employees because of their participation in union activities, 29 U.S.C. §158(a)(3). For an early defense of the statute, see Magruder, A Half Century of Legal Influence upon the Development of Collective Bargaining, 50 Harv. L. Rev. 1071 (1937); for a defense of the common law regime, see Epstein, A Common Law for Labor Relations: A Critique of the New Deal Labor Legislation, 92 Yale L.J. 1357, 1370-1375 (1983).

2. Contracts covered by the tort. In *Lumley* the plaintiff's contract afforded him an undeniable cause of action against Wagner. Should the defendant's inducement be actionable when there is some infirmity in the underlying contract? The action in general will not lie when the underlying contract is void, as with gambling contracts in violation of public policy. Yet the tort action is available for inducing nonperformance of contracts with lesser infirmities. Thus, ample authority allows the inducement action even if the contract between the plaintiff and the third party is voidable (say, because a child is underage) or unenforceable (say, because of the statute of limitations or the statute of frauds). See RST §766. "[S]ince men usually honor their promises no matter what flaws a lawyer can find, the offender should not be heard to say that the contract he meddled with could not have been enforced." Harris v. Perl, 197 A.2d 359, 363 (N.J. 1964).

It has also been said that the defendant's conduct is actionable even if the contract between the plaintiff and the defendant is terminable at the will of either party. See, e.g., Walker v. Cronin, 107 Mass. 555 (1871). That general statement is clearly true to the extent that one of the parties is induced to breach some other covenant contained in the underlying contract: In *Walker*, the employee refused to return tools and materials to the employer upon leaving employment terminable at will. But it is highly unlikely that the doctrine applies with equal force when the employee's conduct is *not* in breach of contract, as when he simply leaves the plaintiff for higher wages elsewhere. Nor can at-will employees sue for interference with contract when displaced by new workers who sign on for lower wages.

In modern times, the key use of the tort is intended to enjoin competition by workers who have gone to work for new firms in violation of a covenant not to compete with their former employer. These contracts themselves are scrutinized for potentially anticompetitive effects. But when properly used to protect customer lists, an action lies against the new employer who takes advantage of the situation: "a new employer need not actively induce an employee to quit her job. Nor must a new employer even have knowledge of the covenant in the employee's previous contract, when it hires her, in order to incur liability for tortious interference with that covenant. Rather, the central question is whether, upon learning of the restrictive covenant that binds its new employee, the new employer nevertheless engages the employee to work for him in an activity that would mean violation of the contract not to compete." Fowler v. Printers II, Inc., 598 A.2d 794, 804 (Md. App. 1991). Note that the inducement of breach of contract case does not require that the defendant use illegal means to disrupt plaintiff's contractual relationships with its employees. See CRST Van Expedited, Inc. v. Werner Enterprises, Inc., 479 F.3d 1099 (9th Cir. 2007). In industries like computer software development, where labor turnover is high, does it work to the long-term advantage of all firms to allow workers to switch jobs freely save in exceptional circumstances? For evidence that it might, see Gilson,

The Legal Infrastructure of High Technology Industrial Districts: Silicon Valley, Route 128, and Covenants Not to Compete, 74 N.Y.U. L. R. 575, 578 (1999), who suggests that the economic success of Silicon Valley stems in part from the "employee-knowledge spillover" between firms that California's prohibition against covenants not to compete helps to create.

Nonetheless, in specialized situations inducing the termination of an at-will arrangement could create liability. In Smith v. Ford Motor Co., 221 S.E.2d 282, 296 (N.C. 1976), the defendant Ford pressured one of its dealerships to fire Smith (its president) because of his activities in the Ford Dealer Alliance. The court held that the conduct was actionable because it was motivated by "malice," that is, by dissatisfaction with his role in the dealers organization, and not his ordinary job performance. Lake, J., allowed the plaintiff's action notwithstanding the contract at will. "If the reason for such action be the employee's personal participation in an association not approved by the actor, the burden is upon the actor, when sued for damages for so procuring the termination of the employment relation to show that the participation by the employee in such association afforded reasonable basis for the belief that a legitimate business interest of the actor would thereby be damaged or imperiled."

3. *Basis of liability for inducement of breach of contract.* Today the Restatement (Second) of Torts §766 provides that "[o]ne who intentionally and improperly interferes with the performance of a contract" is subject to tortious liability provided "the actor must have knowledge of the contract with which he is interfering." RST §766, comment *i*. Even then, notice of the existing relationship, while necessary, may not be sufficient to constitute the tort.

On any view, liability for inducement thus stands on a different footing than liability for ordinary physical damage to person and property. One explanation for the difference is offered in Epstein, Inducement of Breach of Contract as a Problem of Ostensible Ownership, 16 J. Legal Stud. 1, 24 (1987), which argues that the notice system tracks the rules used when a bailee sells the bailed goods to a third party without the permission of the owner. The buyer with knowledge of the bailor's interest is treated as a purchaser in bad faith from whom the true owner can recover the goods. Yet that claim of the true owner is often denied when the bailee looks like the "ostensible owner" to the rest of the world, because the third party is now a purchaser in good faith. "The tort of inducement of breach of contract is designed to protect contracts for the sale of labor by preventing others from subsequently acquiring that labor for themselves, once they know it has been committed to another. It is a restriction against double-dealing." Accordingly, the plaintiff may only maintain the action for inducement of breach of contract against one who *knows* of the existence of the contract, as Lumley v. Gye provides. With personal service contracts, moreover, actual notice is typically required, because the recordation systems in use for land and certain valuable chattels (airplanes, cars) are not available. When celebrities are involved, therefore, the best protection may be to publicly announce the signing of a contract in order to place the world on notice of the existence of the contract, without, however, revealing any confidential terms.

An alternative view holds that *inducement* of breach of contract requires "the conjunction of notice, persuasion by the offer of better terms, and receipt of benefits by Inducer." BeVier, Reconsidering Inducement, 76 Va. L. Rev. 877, 885 n. 25 (1990). How often will breaches take place if the inducer does not offer better terms, or at least better long-term prospects? What if the defendant induces breach for the benefit of a third party?

4. Privileged inducements. As with other torts, the party that induces a breach of contract may well have some privilege for committing a prima facie wrong. The Second Restatement gets at this notion by restricting liability for those actions which are done "improperly" based on a balance of motives and interests of the two parties. RST §767, comment *b*. Thus, interference has been held privileged when done in order to further public morals. For example, in Brimelow v. Casson [1924], 1 Ch. 302, the privilege was upheld when the plaintiff was alleged to have employed chorus girls on such unfavorable terms that they had to resort to prostitution to earn enough money to live.

One privilege of great practical importance generally allows the officer or lawyer of a firm to advise the firm to breach an existing contract. The officer or lawyer is not treated as an independent third party acting for economic advantage, but as acting pursuant to a "confidential arrangement" between the parties. See, e.g., Imperial Ice Co. v. Rossier, 112 P.2d 631 (Cal. 1941). The privilege, however, is not absolute: "When acting as an agent within the scope of the qualified privilege, there can be no tortious interference because only two parties exist; the corporation and the contracting party. However, when an officer or director acts beyond the scope of their qualified privilege, they are no longer acting as agents of the corporation and can be personally liable for their acts." Jones v. Lake Park Care Center, Inc., 569 N.W. 2d 369, 377 (Iowa 1997). *Jones* applied this principle against the husband and wife couple who were the sole shareholders of a small day care center. Does any dismissal after bad blood fall within this exception?

5. Inducement of breach of contract: the theory of efficient breach. One notable attack on the doctrine of Lumley v. Gye rests on the principle that the tort of inducement of breach of contract may be misplaced because breach of contract itself may create social wealth by increasing overall consumer satisfaction. See Perlman, Interference with Contract and Other Economic Expectancies: A Clash of Tort and Contract Doctrine, 49 U. Chi. L. Rev. 61 (1982).

Perlman's argument hearkens back to Holmes's famous aphorism: "The only universal consequence of a legally binding promise is that the law makes the promisor pay damages if the promised event does not come to pass." Holmes, The Common Law 301 (1881). In modern terms, the breach of contract is said to be "efficient" whenever it allows the promisor to shift his resources to a higher-valued use. The logic runs as follows: The innocent party is left well off by an award of damages equal to the benefits provided under the contract; the promisor is left better off, having purchased his freedom; therefore the net social welfare is therefore increased. The theory of "efficient breach" thus holds that a promisor should always be allowed to extricate himself unilaterally from a bargain if he is prepared to pay the proper social price, which is only expectation damages. Accordingly, inducement of breach of contract should not be made tortious lest it undermine the incentives of contractual parties not to breach contracts when efficient to do so. Perlman concludes, therefore, that the action should be allowed only where the defendant has used unlawful and independently tortious means, chiefly force or fraud, to induce the breach.

The soundness of the argument depends at least in part on the ability of the expectation damages to leave a promisee indifferent between performance and breach. But if the contract damages do not reflect the full range of objective and subjective losses, the plaintiff's recovery, net of litigation costs, could well leave the innocent promisee worse off. See Epstein, *supra* at 1250, Note 3, at 37-40; Friedmann, The Efficient Breach Fallacy, 18 J. Legal Stud. 1 (1989), arguing in part that the costs of untangling expectation damages may well exceed the costs needed to negotiate a release from the original contract.

Note, too, that expectation damages are not universally regarded as the gold standard of contract remedies. Specific performance is generally allowed in real estate transactions (and other cases involving "unique" goods) and, even with personal service contracts, a promisee may enjoin the promisor from undertaking employment inconsistent with previous contractual obligations. See McChesney, Tortious Interference with Contract Versus "Efficient" Breach: Theory and Empirical Evidence, 28 J. Legal Stud. 131, 185 (1999), for an exhaustive examination of the case law, concluding that "most of the legal rules relevant to inducement are consistent with the property-based model of interference," and not with the efficient breach theory. Early support for that conclusion comes from Lumley v. Wagner, 42 Eng. Rep. 687, 693 (Ch. 1852), the companion case to Lumley v. Gye, in which Lumley enjoined Wagner from singing elsewhere in a manner inconsistent with the efficient breach theory.

> Wherever this Court has not proper jurisdiction to enforce specific performance, it operates to bind men's consciences, as far as they can be bound, to a true and literal performance of their agreements; and it will not

suffer them to depart from their contracts at their pleasure, leaving the party with whom they have contracted to the mere chance of any damages which a jury may give. . . . The effect, too, of the injunction in restraining J. Wagner from singing elsewhere may, in the event of an action being brought against her by the Plaintiff, prevent any such amount of vindictive damages being given against her as a jury might probably be inclined to give if she carried her talents and exercised them at the rival theatre: the injunction may also, as I have said, tend to the fulfilment of her engagement; though, in continuing the injunction, I disclaim doing indirectly what I cannot do directly.

Why no decree ordering Wagner to sing?

SECTION C. INTERFERENCE WITH PROSPECTIVE ADVANTAGE

Tarleton v. M'Gawley
170 Eng. Rep. 153 (K.B. 1793)

This was a special action on the case. The declaration stated that the plaintiffs were possessed and owners of a certain ship called the *Tarleton*, which at the time of committing the grievance was lying at Calabar on the coast of Africa, under the command of Fairweather. That the ship had been fitted out at Liverpool with goods proper for trading with the natives of that coast for slaves and other goods. That also before the [sic] committing the grievance Fairweather had sent a smaller vessel called the *Bannister* with a crew on board, under the command of one Thomas Smith, and loaded with goods proper for trading with the natives, to another part of the said coast called Cameroon, to trade with the natives there. That while the last-mentioned ship was lying off Cameroon, a canoe with some natives on board came to the same for the purpose of establishing a trade, and went back to the shore, of which defendant had notice. And that he well knowing the premises, but contriving and maliciously intending to hinder and deter the natives from trading with the said Thomas Smith, for the benefit of the plaintiffs, with force and arms, fired from a certain ship called the *Othello*, of which he was master and commander, a certain cannon loaded with gunpowder and shot at the said canoe, and killed one of the natives on board the same. Whereby the natives of the said coast were deterred and hindered from trading with the said T. Smith for the benefit, &c. and plaintiffs lost their trade.

The plaintiffs called Thomas Smith, who proved the facts stated in the declaration; and further, that the defendant had declared the natives owed him a debt, and that he would not suffer any ship to trade with them until that was paid; in pursuance of which declaration he committed the act complained of by the plaintiffs. On his cross-examination he admitted that by the custom of that coast no Europeans can trade until a certain duty has been paid to the king of the country for his licence, and that no such duty had been paid, or licence obtained by the captain of the plaintiff's vessel.

Law, for the defendant, contended that the plaintiffs being engaged in a trade which by the law of that country was illicit, could not support an action for an interruption of such illicit commerce, and compared this case to an action brought for interrupting a plaintiff in his endeavours to smuggle goods into this country, or alarming the owner of a house which the plaintiff was about to break into. He also objected that this act of the defendant amounted to a felony, and therefore could not be made the ground of a civil action, but he did not lay much stress on this objection.

LORD KENYON. This action is brought by the plaintiffs to recover a satisfaction for a civil injury which they have sustained. The injury complained of is, that by the improper conduct of the defendant the natives were prevented from trading with the plaintiffs. The whole of the case is stated on the record, and if the parties desire it, the opinion of the Court may hereafter be taken whether it will support an action. I am of opinion it will. This case has been likened to cases which it does not at all resemble. It has been said that a person engaged in a trade violating the law of the country cannot support an action against another for hindering him in that illegal traffick. That I entirely accede to, but it does not apply to this case. This is a foreign law; the act of trading is not itself immoral, and a jus positivum is not binding on foreigners. The king of the country and not the defendant should have executed that law. Had this been an accidental thing, no action could have been maintained, but it is proved that the defendant had expressed an intention not to permit any to trade, until a debt due from the natives to himself was satisfied. If there was any Court in that country to which he could have applied for justice he might have done so, but he had no right to take the law into his own hands.

The plaintiffs had a verdict, and the parties agreed to refer the damages to arbitration.

Note. — In the beginning of the cause the plaintiffs' counsel proposed asking the witnesses whether some of the negroes did not assign their fear of the defendant as a reason for not trading with the plaintiffs, but Lord Kenyon said that no declaration of the negroes could be received in evidence.

NOTES

1. *Prospective advantage versus inducement of breach of contract.* The protection afforded the plaintiff in *Tarleton* is both narrower and broader than that granted in Lumley v. Gye. It is narrower in that prospective advantage

is protected only against interference by means that are unlawful in themselves, in this case the use of force against the natives. But it is broader in that it protects not only the promisee who may have claims against the promisor under an existing contract, but also the promisee who may have no action even though a contract exists (as in contracts terminable at will). The action also protects a party who was never able to form a contract in the first place. Why allow the plaintiff a separate action when the customers are protected by a wide array of tort actions? In evaluating the plaintiff's case in *Tarleton,* should it make a difference whether the customers suffer physical injury or only the loss of a bargain? Note that one frequent justification for the result in *Tarleton* is that the trader's suit helps vindicate the economic interests of potential customers who might be reluctant to incur heavy litigation costs to recover for small economic losses, especially if their interests are numerous and diffuse.

2. *Unlawful means and prospective advantage.* While the facts in *Tarleton* are both novel and dramatic, its underlying principle has a long common law lineage. In Keeble v. Hickeringill, 103 Eng. Rep. 1127, 1128 (Q.B. 1706) (reported K.B. 1809), plaintiff used decoy ducks to attract wild fowl to his meadow for the purpose of capturing and selling them. Defendant, who operated a rival duck decoy of his own in the neighborhood, repeatedly discharged guns nearby, driving away the ducks. In affirming a verdict for plaintiff, Holt, C.J., said:

> [I]f Mr. Hickeringill had set up another decoy on his own ground near the plaintiff, no action would lie because he had as much liberty to make and use a decoy as the plaintiff. . . . One schoolmaster sets up a new school to the damage of an antient school, and thereby the scholars are allured from the old school to come to his new. (The action was held there not to lie.) But suppose Mr. Hickeringill should lie in the way with his guns, and fright the boys from going to school, and their parents would not let them go thither; sure the schoolmaster might have an action for the loss of his scholars.

Holt's brief remarks about the "antient school" contain this bellwether principle of the law: The maxim "prior in time is higher in right" used to establish title to land and chattels has no application to competitive injury. The incumbent may enjoy a "first mover" advantage, but gets no legal protection against the subsequent entrant so long as he does not resort to illegal means. Indeed, one reason why interference with trade proved crucial in *Keeble* was that the plaintiff did not gain possession of the ducks solely because they alighted on his pond in the absence of any showing that they had been wounded or trapped. The theory of trade interference worked, moreover, solely because defendant was the plaintiff's "direct competitor." What result if the defendant shot his guns to kill and capture the ducks, knowing he might frighten them away? A modern animal rights activist determined to protect all wildlife from needless slaughter?

What other means unlawful in themselves are sufficient to support the plaintiff's action? In Evenson v. Spaulding, 150 F. 517, 522 (9th Cir. 1907), the plaintiffs were Iowa manufacturers of high-class buggies and wagons who sold their product in the state of Washington through salesmen and agents. The defendants were employees of an association of Washington buggy manufacturers; they dogged the plaintiffs' salesmen whenever they tried to sell their wagons and buggies to local customers, usually on a public highway. The court recognized that the defendants had the right to compete with the plaintiffs for sales to local customers, but held that the defendants' conduct exceeded the permissible limits of competition with its own "policy of molestation," here "by breaking in on conversations, making false representations as to the nature of the appellees' goods . . . and other offensive acts."

The question of unlawful means also arose in Korea Supply Co v. Lockheed Martin Corp., 63 P.3d 937, 951 (Cal. 2003). The plaintiffs were the brokers for an unsuccessful bidder for a lucrative defense contract for the Republic of Korea. Moreno, J., rejected the two defenses that Lockheed Martin raised against the action. First, he held that, although interference with prospective advantage was an intentional tort, it did not require the plaintiff to prove that the defendant in the bidding process adopted its unlawful means with the "specific intention" to injure the plaintiff. It was enough "that the interference is certain or substantially certain to occur as a result of his action." See RST §766B, comment *d*. Stated otherwise, so long as the defendant knew that its actions would prejudice rival bidders, it did not matter that it did not know which of them would have made the winning bid. If the bidders are not ranked, then who should have standing to sue?

In addition, Moreno, J., affirmed the traditional rule that interference with prospective advantage required proof of unlawful means not needed in inducement of breach of contract cases. He then noted that the unlawful means did not necessarily require the use of either force or fraud. That requirement was "clearly satisfied" when the defendant's agent "engaged in bribery and offered sexual favors to key Korean officials in order to obtain the contract from the Republic of Korea. Under the Foreign Corrupt Practices Act[, 15 U.S.C. §78dd-1(a)(1)(A), (B)], it is unlawful to pay or offer money or anything of value to a foreign official for the purposes of influencing any act or decision of the foreign official. . . ." Would these actions still be unlawful if they only violated Korean but not American law?

People Express Airlines, Inc. v. Consolidated Rail Corp.
495 A.2d 107 (N.J. 1985)

HANDLER, J. This appeal presents a question that has not previously been directly considered: whether a defendant's negligent conduct that interferes with a plaintiff's business resulting in purely economic losses, unaccompanied by property damage or personal injury, is compensable in tort. The appeal poses this issue in the context of the defendants' alleged negligence that caused a dangerous chemical to escape from a railway tank car, resulting in the evacuation from the surrounding area of persons whose safety and health were threatened. The plaintiff, a commercial airline, was forced to evacuate its premises and suffered an interruption of its business operations with resultant economic losses.

I

On July 22, 1981, a fire began in the Port Newark freight yard of defendant Consolidated Rail Corporation (Conrail) when ethylene oxide manufactured by defendant BASF Wyandotte Company (BASF) escaped from a tank car, punctured during a "coupling" operation with another rail car, and ignited. The tank car was owned by defendant Union Tank Car Company (Union Car) and was leased to defendant BASF.

The plaintiff asserted at oral argument that at least some of the defendants were aware from prior experiences that ethylene oxide is a highly volatile substance; further, that emergency response plans in case of an accident had been prepared. When the fire occurred that gave rise to this lawsuit, some of the defendants' consultants helped determine how much of the surrounding area to evacuate. The municipal authorities then evacuated the area within a one-mile radius surrounding the fire to lessen the risk to persons within the area should the burning tank car explode. The evacuation area included the adjacent North Terminal building of Newark International Airport, where plaintiff People Express Airlines' (People Express) business operations are based. Although the feared explosion never occurred, People Express employees were prohibited from using the North Terminal for twelve hours.

The plaintiff contends that it suffered business-interruption losses as a result of the evacuation. These losses consist of cancelled scheduled flights and lost reservations because employees were unable to answer the telephones to accept bookings; also, certain fixed operating expenses allocable to the evacuation time period were incurred and paid despite the fact that plaintiff's offices were closed. No physical damage to airline property and no personal injury occurred as a result of the fire.

According to People Express' original complaint, each defendant acted negligently and these acts of negligence proximately caused the plaintiff's harm. An amended complaint alleged additional counts of nuisance and strict liability based on the defendants' undertaking an abnormally dangerous activity, as well as defective manufacture or design of the tank car, causes of action with which we are not concerned here. . . .

II

The single characteristic that distinguishes parties in negligence suits whose claims for economic losses have been regularly denied by American and English courts from those who have recovered economic losses is, with respect to the successful claimants, the fortuitous occurrence of physical harm or property damage, however slight. It is well-accepted that a defendant who negligently injures a plaintiff or his property may be liable for all proximately caused harm, including economic losses. Nevertheless, a virtually per se rule barring recovery for economic loss unless the negligent conduct also caused physical harm has evolved throughout this century, based, in part, on Robins Dry Dock & Repair Co. v. Flint, 275 U.S. 303 (1927) and Cattle v. Stockton Waterworks Co., 10 Q.B. 453 (1875). This has occurred although neither case created a rule absolutely disallowing recovery in such circumstances. See, e.g., Stevenson v. East Ohio Gas Co., 73 N.E.2d 200 (Ohio Ct. App. 1946) (employee who was prohibited from working at his plant, which was closed due to conflagration begun by negligent rupture of stored liquified natural gas at nearby utility, could not recover lost wages); Byrd v. English, 43 S.E. 419 (Ga. 1903) (plaintiff who owned printing plant could not recover lost profits when defendant negligently damaged utility's electrical conduits that supplied power to the plant); see also Restatement (Second) of Torts §766C (1979) (positing rule of nonrecovery for purely economic losses absent physical harm). But see In re Kinsman Transit Co., 388 F.2d 821, 824 (2d Cir. 1968) (after rejecting an inflexible rule of nonrecovery, court applied traditional proximate cause analysis to claim for purely economic losses).

The reasons that have been advanced to explain the divergent results for litigants seeking economic losses are varied. Some courts have viewed the general rule against recovery as necessary to limit damages to reasonably foreseeable consequences of negligent conduct. This concern in a given case is often manifested as an issue of causation and has led to the requirement of physical harm as an element of proximate cause. In this context, the physical harm requirement functions as part of the definition of the causal relationship between the defendant's negligent act and the plaintiff's economic damages; it acts as a convenient clamp on otherwise boundless liability. The physical harm rule also reflects certain deep-seated concerns that underlie courts' denial of recovery for purely economic losses occasioned by a defendant's negligence. These concerns include the fear of fraudulent claims, mass litigation, and limitless liability, or liability out of proportion to the defendant's fault. . . .

The troublesome concern reflected in cases denying recovery for negligently-caused economic loss is the alleged potential for infinite liability, or liability out of all proportion to the defendant's fault. This objection is also not confined to negligently-caused economic injury. The same objection has been asserted and, ultimately, rejected by this Court and others in allowing recovery for other forms of negligent torts, see H. Rosenblum, Inc. v. Adler, 461 A.2d 138 (N.J. 1983), and in the creation of the doctrine of strict liability for defective products, see Feldman v. Lederle Laboratories, 479 A.2d 374 (N.J. 1984); Henningsen v. Bloomfield Motors, Inc., 161 A.2d 69 (N.J. 1960), and ultrahazardous activities, see Dep't of Envtl. Protection v. Ventron Corp., 468 A.2d 150 (N.J. 1983). The answer to the allegation of unchecked liability is not the judicial obstruction of a fairly grounded claim for redress. Rather, it must be a more sedulous application of traditional concepts of duty and proximate causation to the facts of each case.

It is understandable that courts, fearing that if even one deserving plaintiff suffering purely economic loss were allowed to recover, all such plaintiffs could recover, have anchored their rulings to the physical harm requirement. While the rationale is understandable, it supports only a limitation on, not a denial of, liability. The physical harm requirement capriciously showers compensation along the path of physical destruction, regardless of the status or circumstances of individual claimants. Purely economic losses are borne by innocent victims, who may not be able to absorb their losses. In the end, the challenge is to fashion a rule that limits liability but permits adjudication of meritorious claims. The asserted inability to fix crystalline formulae for recovery on the differing facts of future cases simply does not justify the wholesale rejection of recovery in all cases.

Further, judicial reluctance to allow recovery for purely economic losses is discordant with contemporary tort doctrine [with its twin objectives of legal redress for victims and deterrence of future harms by others].

A

Judicial discomfiture with the rule of nonrecovery for purely economic loss throughout the last several decades has led to numerous exceptions in the general rule. Although the rationalizations for these exceptions differ among courts and cases, two common threads run throughout the exceptions. The first is that the element of foreseeability emerges as a more appropriate analytical standard to determine the question of liability than a per se prohibitory rule. The second is that the extent to which the defendant knew or should have known the particular consequences of his negligence, including the economic loss of a particularly foreseeable plaintiff, is dispositive of the issues of duty and fault.

One group of exceptions is based on the "special relationship" between the tortfeasor and the individual or business deprived of economic expectations. [The Court then refers to liability for negligent misrepresentation under *Rosenblum*.]

Courts have found it fair and just in all of these exceptional cases to impose liability on defendants who, by virtue of their special activities, professional training or other unique preparation for their work, had particular knowledge or reason to know that others, such as the intended beneficiaries of wills or the purchasers of stock who were expected to rely on the company's financial statement in the prospectus (*Rosenblum*), would be economically harmed by negligent conduct. In this group of cases, even though the particular plaintiff was not always foreseeable, the particular class of plaintiffs was foreseeable as was the particular type of injury.

A very solid exception allowing recovery for economic losses has also been created in cases akin to private actions for public nuisance. Where a plaintiff's business is based in part upon the exercise of a public right, the plaintiff has been able to recover purely economic losses caused by a defendant's negligence. See, e.g., Louisiana ex rel. Guste v. M/V Testbank, 752 F.2d 1019 (5th Cir. 1985) (en banc) (defendants responsible for ship collision held liable to all commercial fishermen, shrimpers, crabbers and oystermen for resulting pollution of Mississippi River); Union Oil Co. v. Oppen, 501 F.2d 558 (9th Cir. 1974) (fishermen making known commercial use of public waters may recover economic losses due to defendant's oil spill) . . .

These exceptions expose the hopeless artificiality of the per se rule against recovery for purely economic losses. When the plaintiffs are reasonably foreseeable, the injury is directly and proximately caused by defendant's negligence, and liability can be limited fairly, courts have endeavored to create exceptions to allow recovery. The scope and number of exceptions, while independently justified on various grounds, have nonetheless created lasting doubt as to the wisdom of the per se rule of nonrecovery for purely economic losses. Indeed, it has been fashionable for commentators to state that the rule has been giving way for nearly fifty years, although the cases have not always kept pace with the hypothesis. . . .

We hold therefore that a defendant owes a duty of care to take reasonable measures to avoid the risk of causing economic damages, aside from physical injury, to particular plaintiffs or plaintiffs comprising an identifiable class with respect to whom defendant knows or has reason to know are likely to suffer such damages from its conduct. A defendant failing to adhere to this duty of care may be found liable for such economic damages proximately caused by its breach of duty.

We stress that an identifiable class of plaintiffs is not simply a foreseeable class of plaintiffs. For example, members of the general public, or invitees such as sales and service persons at a particular plaintiff's business premises, or persons travelling on a highway near the scene of a negligently-caused accident, such as the one at bar, who are delayed in the conduct of their affairs and suffer varied economic losses, are certainly a foreseeable class of plaintiffs. Yet their presence within the area would be fortuitous, and the particular type of economic injury that could be suffered by such persons would be hopelessly unpredictable and not realistically foreseeable. Thus, the class itself would not be sufficiently ascertainable. An identifiable class of plaintiffs must be particularly foreseeable in terms of the type of persons or entities comprising the class, the certainty or predictability of their presence, the approximate numbers of those in the class, as well as the type of economic expectations disrupted.

B

Liability depends not only on the breach of a standard of care but also on a proximate causal relationship between the breach of the duty of care and resultant losses. The standard of particular foreseeability may be successfully employed to determine whether the economic injury was proximately caused, i.e., whether the particular harm that occurred is compensable, just as it informs the question whether a duty exists. . . .

We conclude therefore that a defendant who has breached his duty of care to avoid the risk of economic injury to particularly foreseeable plaintiffs may be held liable for actual economic losses that are proximately caused by its breach of duty. In this context, those economic losses are recoverable as damages when they are the natural and probable consequence of a defendant's negligence in the sense that they are reasonably to be anticipated in view of defendant's capacity to have foreseen that the particular plaintiff or identifiable class of plaintiffs is demonstrably within the risk created by defendant's negligence.

III

We are satisfied that our holding today is fully applicable to the facts that we have considered on this appeal. Plaintiff has set forth a cause of action under our decision, and it is entitled to have the matter proceed to a plenary trial. Among the facts that persuade us that a cause of action has been established is the close proximity of the North Terminal and People Express Airlines to the Conrail freight yard; the obvious nature of the plaintiff's operations and particular foreseeability of economic losses resulting from an accident and evacuation; the defendants' actual or constructive knowledge of the volatile properties of ethylene oxide; and the existence of an emergency response plan prepared by some of the defendants (alluded to in the course of oral argument), which apparently called for the nearby area to be evacuated to avoid the risk of harm in case of an explosion. We do not mean to suggest by our recitation of these facts that actual knowledge of the eventual economic losses is necessary to the cause of action; rather, particular foreseeability will suffice. The plaintiff still faces a difficult task in proving damages, particularly lost profits, to the degree of certainty required in other negligence cases. The trial court's examination of these proofs must be exacting to ensure that damages recovered are those reasonably to have been anticipated in view of the defendants' capacity to have foreseen that this particular plaintiff was within the risk created by their negligence.

We appreciate that there will arise many similar cases that cannot be resolved by our decision today. The cause of action we recognize, however, is one that most appropriately should be allowed to evolve on a case-by-case basis in the context of actual adjudications. We perceive no reason, however, why our decision today should be applied only prospectively. Our holdings are well grounded in traditional tort principles and flow from well-established exceptional cases that are philosophically compatible with this decision.

Accordingly, the judgment of the Appellate Division is modified, and, as modified, affirmed. The case is remanded for proceedings consistent with this opinion.

NOTES

1. *Tort recovery for economic loss.* As *People Express* indicates, the common law judges historically have been reluctant to allow any recovery for pure economic losses attributable only to the defendant's negligence. Most notably, in Byrd v. English, 43 S.E. 419, 420 (Ga. 1903), the defendant's negligent excavation severed the power lines, owned by the electric company, that supplied the power that led to the plaintiff's plant. The plaintiff's cause of action was denied on grounds reminiscent of *Winterbottom v. Wright, supra* at 728:

> According to this petition, the damage done by them was to the property of the Georgia Electric Light Company, which was under contract to furnish to the plaintiff electric power, and the resulting damage done to the plaintiff was that it was rendered impossible for that company to comply with its contract. If the plaintiff can recover of these defendants upon this cause of action, then a customer of his, who was injured by the delay occasioned by the stopping of his work, could also recover from them; and one who had been damaged through his delay could in turn hold them liable; and so on without limit to the number of persons who might recover on account of the injury done to the property of the company owning the conduits. To state such a proposition is to demonstrate its absurdity. The plaintiff is suing on account of an alleged tort by reason of which he was deprived of a supply of electric power with which to operate his printing establishment. What was his right to that power supply? Solely the right given him by virtue of his contract with the Georgia Electric Light Company, and with that contract the

defendants are not even remotely connected. If, under the terms of his contract, he is precluded from recovering from the electric light company, that is a matter between themselves for which the defendants certainly can not be held responsible. They are, of course, liable to the company for any wrong that may have been done it, and the damages recoverable on that account might well be held to include any sums which the company was compelled to pay in damages to its customers; but the customers themselves can not go against the defendants to recover on their own account for the injury done the company.

Earlier, in Cattle v. Stockton Waterworks Co., 10 Q.B. 453, 457 (1875), the defendant waterworks company had negligently constructed and maintained its pipes on the land of one Knight. The plaintiff had been hired for a fixed reward to build a tunnel on Knight's land and incurred increased costs when the water from the defendant's leaky pipes flooded his operations. Blackburn, J., conceded that Knight could have recovered damage for the increased cost of the completion if he had constructed the tunnel himself, but he denied that this plaintiff could recover for those same costs. He argued that if the action were allowed "we should establish an authority for saying that, in such a case as that of *Fletcher v. Rylands* the defendant would be liable, not only to an action by the owner of the drowned mine, and by such of his workmen as had their tools or clothes destroyed, but also to an action by every workman and person employed in the mine, who in consequence of its stoppage made less wages than he otherwise would have done." He then distinguished Lumley v. Gye, noting that it was limited to "malicious" actions by the defendant. Does the distinction hold if "malice" in *Lumley* is coterminous with "notice"?

A narrow view of recovery for economic loss was also taken in Robins Dry Dock & Repair Co. v. Flint, 275 U.S. 303, 308-309 (1927). The plaintiffs hired a boat on a time charter with the third-party owner. The terms of the time charter called for the boat to be docked for maintenance and repair once every six months, with payments of money on the charter suspended until the boat was returned to service. While the boat was in the defendant's docks, the defendant negligently damaged the propeller, thereby causing the plaintiffs to lose the use of the boat for a two-week period while the necessary repairs were made. The defendant undertook repair of the boat in ignorance of the time charter or its terms. The accident took place in August 1917, shortly after the United States entered World War I, so the time charter gave the plaintiff highly favorable rates. In an earlier action arising out of the same incident, the plaintiff was not allowed to recover the lost value of the charter from the boatowner on a contract theory: the owner had discharged its obligation by selecting a competent independent contractor for the repairs, The Bjornefjord, 271 F. 682 (2d Cir. 1921). In the instant action the Second Circuit awarded recovery to the plaintiff in tort,

Flint v. Robins Dry Dock & Repair Co., 13 F.2d 3, 5 (2d Cir. 1926), with
Mack, J., arguing as follows:

> Clearly, the result reached involves no injustice to respondent. Its liability for
> its tortious act is for the actual damage done to the combined interests in the
> ship. The measure of the total recovery is the market value of the loss of the
> use. If there had been no charter, the entire loss would have been sustained
> by the owner; therefore he could have recovered that amount himself. The
> wrongdoer has no interest in and should not benefit because of the con-
> tractual obligations of the shipowner to the charterer, or the absence of any
> liability of the owner to the charterer for respondent's negligence. This
> nonliability of the owner is neither a test nor a measure of the wrongdoer's
> liability, for, though the owner be not directly liable to the charterer, he may
> nevertheless be liable over to him as a trustee for so much of the recovery
> from the wrongdoer as exceeds his own personal loss.

Justice Holmes, writing for a unanimous Supreme Court, reversed the
Second Circuit and dismissed the plaintiff-respondent's cause of action:

> The question is whether the respondents have an interest protected by the
> law against unintended injuries inflicted upon the vessel by third persons
> who know nothing of the charter. If they have, it must be worked out through
> their contract relations with the owners, not on the postulate that they have a
> right *in rem* against the ship.
>   Of course the contract of the petitioner with the owners imposed no
> immediate obligation upon the petitioner to third persons, as we already
> have said, and whether the petitioner performed it promptly or with
> negligent delay was the business of the owners and of nobody else. But as
> there was a tortious damage to a chattel it is sought to connect the claim of
> the respondents with that in some way. The damage was material to them
> only as it caused the delay in making the repairs, and that delay would be a
> wrong to no one except for the petitioner's contract with the owners. The
> injury to the propeller was no wrong to the respondents but only to those to
> whom it belonged. But suppose that the respondent's loss flowed directly
> from that source. Their loss arose only through their contract with the
> owners — and while intentionally to bring about a breach of contract may
> give rise to a cause of action, no authority need be cited to show that, as a
> general rule, at least, a tort to the person or property of one man does not
> make the tortfeasor liable to another merely because the injured person was
> under a contract with that other, unknown to the doer of the wrong. The law
> does not spread its protection so far.

Can Judge Mack's position be sustained if the contract between the
charterer and the owner precludes recovery of lost profits attributable to
the negligence of the owner? Can Justice Holmes's position be sustained if

that contract allows expectation damages? For an argument that Holmes's rule is defensible so long as the charterparty arrangement is ignored, whether the rentals move up or down, see Goldberg, Recovery for Pure Economic Loss in Tort: Another Look at *Robins Dry Dock v. Flint,* 20 J. Legal Stud. 249 (1991). In essence, the losses suffered in those cases when charter prices move up are offset by the windfall that is gained when the charterer is released from a losing contract by the wrongful act of a third party. The Holmes position remains impregnable today. See Nautilus Marine, Inc. v. Niemela, 170 F.3d 1195, 1197 (9th Cir. 1999), in which the court rebuffed plaintiff's effort to escape *Robins* by pleading the defendant's recklessness. "The line between recklessness and negligence is sufficiently indistinct that extensive litigation would be likely to ensue before *Robins Dry Dock* could be applied in any case."

With *Robins*, contrast J'Aire Corp. v. Gregory, 598 P.2d 60, 64 (Cal. 1979), in which the plaintiff restaurant could not open for business because the defendant contractor failed to complete work on the heating and air conditioning system on premises owned by a third party and leased in part to plaintiff. The question before the court was "whether a contractor who undertakes construction work pursuant to a contract with the owner of premises may be held liable in tort for business losses suffered by a lessee when the contractor negligently fails to complete the project with due diligence." The court answered the question in the affirmative for much the same reasons adopted in *People Express*.

> [T]his court finds that respondent [defendant] had a duty to complete construction in a manner that would have avoided unnecessary injury to appellant's business, even though the construction contract was with the owner of a building rather than with appellant, the tenant. It is settled that a contractor owes a duty to avoid injury to the person or property of third parties. As appellant points out, injury to a tenant's business can often result in greater hardship than damage to a tenant's person or property. Where the risk of harm is foreseeable, as it was in the present case, the injury to the plaintiff's economic interests should not go uncompensated merely because it was unaccompanied by any injury to his person or property.

Should the tenant in *J'Aire* be limited to its action against its landlord? After *J'Aire*, should construction companies insert clauses in their standard contracts that either require landlords to obtain waivers from actual or prospective tenants against the construction company or that call on the landlord to indemnify the construction company for its expenses or losses? Note, however, that strategy is not open in cases such as *People Express*, in which the plaintiff and defendant are total strangers. If the release of dangerous chemicals is a strict liability action, why require proof of negligence for recovery of economic loss in *People Express*? And why adopt more stringent tests of foresight? Are results in any of these cases defensible under *People Express*?

2. An economic analysis of economic losses. Finding a theoretical justification for disallowing recovery for pure economic loss at common law has not been easy. The defendant is by hypothesis negligent; the plaintiff's harm is typically foreseeable, even if the precise identity of the plaintiff is not; rarely do any intervening acts or events sever the causal connection; and typically there are no affirmative defenses based on plaintiff's misconduct. Why then the denial?

Apart from the obvious administrative concerns, the law and economics literature has offered two explanations for the dominant legal rule. Bishop, Economic Loss in Tort, 2 Oxford J. Legal Stud. 1 (1982), suggests that the economic losses to the plaintiffs do not represent social losses because whatever business is lost by the plaintiff is picked up by some rival firm whose "excess capacity" can meet the increased demand. That argument is vulnerable on two separate grounds. First, some social loss always remains because the substitute performance is more costly than that originally contemplated—otherwise, the plaintiff would not have obtained the business in the first place. Second, the unprotected plaintiff will take excessive pre-cautions to avoid losses that are far more costly than the substitute precautions open to the negligent defendant.

An alternative explanation, suggested in Rizzo, A Theory of Economic Loss in the Law of Torts, 11 J. Legal Stud. 281 (1982), is that the denial of the plaintiff's right is made in order to reduce the number of potential suits by "channelling" tort liability through a small class of plaintiffs, typically those who have suffered physical injury. The property owner who recovers losses can reimburse the contractors and others for their increased costs of completion under contract, as may have been intimated, for example, in both Cattle v. Stockton Waterworks, *supra*, and Robins Dry Dock v. Flint, *supra*. Note that the particular foresight rule in *People Express* bears a close similarity to the special damage rule found in the law of public nuisance, *supra* Chapter 9E? The point here is that those few persons who suffer substantial economic loss may recover, like the airline in *People Express*, while the multitude of other individuals whose losses are indirect, like its customers, cannot. Just such parsimonious logic has been adopted in cases of antitrust industry, Illinois Brick Co. v. Illinois, 431 U.S. 720 (1977), which blocks suits by "indirect purchasers" whose sole remedy, if any, lie against their immediate seller. Note that the limitation to parties in the first ring of economic injury (the airline) has two desirable features. It reduces the number of parties to the suit, and increases the expected damages by each, so as to make the system more manageable. Should the use of class actions allow suits by injured parties outside the first ring?

SECTION D. UNFAIR COMPETITION

Mogul Steamship Co. v. McGregor, Gow & Co.
23 Q.B.D. 598 (1889), affirmed [1892] A.C. 25

BOWEN, L.J. We are presented in this case with an apparent conflict or antinomy between two rights that are equally regarded by the law—the right of the plaintiffs to be protected in the legitimate exercise of their trade, and the right of the defendants to carry on their business as seems best to them, provided they commit no wrong to others. The plaintiffs complain that the defendants have crossed the line which the common law permits; and inasmuch as, for the purposes of the present case, we are to assume some possible damage to the plaintiffs, the real question to be decided is whether, on such an assumption, the defendants in the conduct of their commercial affairs have done anything that is unjustifiable in law. The defendants are a number of shipowners who formed themselves into a league or conference for the purpose of ultimately keeping in their own hands the control of the tea carriage from certain Chinese ports, and for the purpose of driving the plaintiffs and other competitors from the field. In order to succeed in this object, and to discourage the plaintiffs' vessels from resorting to those ports, the defendants during the "tea harvest" of 1885 combined to offer to the local shippers very low freights, with a view of generally reducing or "smashing" rates, and thus rendering it unprofitable for the plaintiffs to send their ships thither. They offered, moreover, a rebate of 5 per cent. to all local shippers and agents who would deal exclusively with vessels belonging to the Conference, and any agent who broke the condition was to forfeit the entire rebate on all shipments made on behalf of any and every one of his principals during the whole year—a forfeiture of rebate or allowance which was denominated as "penal" by the plaintiffs' counsel. It must, however, be taken as established that the rebate was one which the defendants need never have allowed at all to their customers. It must also be taken that the defendants had no personal ill-will to the plaintiffs, nor any desire to harm them except such as is involved in the wish and intention to discourage by such measures the plaintiffs from sending rival vessels to such ports. . . . It is to be observed with regard to all these acts of which complaint is made that they were acts that in themselves could not be said to be illegal unless made so by the object with which, or the combination in the course of which, they were done; and that in reality what is complained of is the pursuing of trade competition to a length which the plaintiffs consider oppressive and prejudicial to themselves. We were invited by the plaintiffs' counsel to accept the position from which their argument started—that an action will lie if a man maliciously and wrongfully conducts himself so as to injure another in that other's trade. Obscurity resides in the language used to state this proposition. The terms "maliciously," "wrongfully," and "injure" are words all of which have accurate meanings, well known to the law, but which also have a popular and less precise signification, into which it is necessary to see that the argument does not imperceptibly slide. An intent to "injure" in strictness means more than an intent to harm. It connotes an intent to do wrongful harm. "Maliciously," in like manner, means and implies an intention to do an act which is wrongful, to the detriment of another. The term "wrongful" imports in its turn the infringement of some right. The ambiguous proposition to which we were invited by the plaintiffs' counsel still, therefore, leaves unsolved the question of what, as between the plaintiffs and defendants, are the rights of trade. For the purpose of clearness, I desire, as far as possible, to avoid terms in their popular use so slippery, and to translate them into less fallacious language wherever possible.

. . . Now, intentionally to do that which is calculated in the ordinary course of events to damage, and which does, in fact, damage another in that other person's property or trade, is actionable if done without just cause or excuse. Such intentional action when done without just cause or excuse is what the law calls a malicious wrong. . . .

. . . The acts of the defendants which are complained of here were intentional and were also calculated, no doubt, to do the plaintiffs damage in their trade. But in order to see whether they were wrongful we have still to discuss the question whether they were done without any just cause or excuse. Such just cause or excuse the defendants on their side assert to be found in their own positive right (subject to certain limitations) to carry on their own trade freely in the mode and manner that best suits them, and which they think best calculated to secure their own advantage.

What, then, are the limitations which the law imposes on a trader in the conduct of his business as between himself and other traders? There seem to be no burdens or restrictions in law upon a trader which arise merely from the fact that he is a trader, and which are not equally laid on all other subjects of the Crown. His right to trade freely is a right which the law recognises and encourages, but it is one which places him at no special disadvantage as compared with others. No man, whether trader or not, can, however, justify damaging another in his commercial business by fraud or misrepresentation. Intimidation, obstruction, and molestation are forbidden; so is the intentional procurement of a violation of individual rights, contractual or other, assuming always that there is no just cause for it. The intentional driving away of customers by shew of violence: Tarleton v. M'Gawley; the obstruction of actors on stage by preconcerted hissing: Clifford v. Brandon[, 170 Eng. Rep. 1183 (N.P. 1809)]; the disturbance of wild fowl in decoys by the firing of guns: Keeble v. Hickeringill[, 103 Eng. Rep. 1127 (Q.B. 1706)]; the impeding or threatening servants or workmen: Garret v. Taylor[, 79 Eng. Rep. 485 (K.B. 1620)]; the inducing persons under personal contracts to break their contracts: Bowen v. Hall; Lumley v. Gye; all are instances of such forbidden acts. But the defendants have been guilty of none of these acts. They have done nothing more against the plaintiffs than pursue to the bitter end a war of competition waged in the interest of their own trade. To the argument that a competition so pursued ceases to have a just cause or excuse when there is ill-will or a personal intention to harm, it is sufficient to reply (as I have already pointed out) that there was here no personal intention to do any other or greater harm to the plaintiffs than such as was necessarily involved in the desire to attract to the defendants' ships the entire tea freights of the ports, a portion of which would otherwise have fallen to the plaintiffs' share. I can find no authority for the doctrine that such a commercial motive deprives of "just cause or excuse" acts done in the course of trade which would but for such a motive be justifiable. So to hold would be to convert into an illegal motive the instinct of self-advancement and self-protection, which is the very incentive to all trade. To say that a man is to trade freely, but that he is to stop short at any act which is calculated to harm other tradesmen, and which is designed to attract business to his own shop, would be a strange and impossible counsel of perfection. But we were told that competition ceases to be the lawful exercise of trade, and so to be a lawful excuse for what will harm another, if carried to a length which is not fair or reasonable. The offering of reduced rates by the defendants in the present case is said to have been "unfair." This seems to assume that, apart from fraud, intimidation, molestation, or obstruction, of some other personal right in rem or in personam, there is some natural standard of "fairness" or "reasonableness" (to be determined by the internal consciousness of judges and juries) beyond which competition ought not in law to go. There seems to be no authority, and I think, with submission, that there is no sufficient reason for such a proposition. It would impose a novel fetter upon trade. The defendants, we are told by the plaintiffs' counsel, might lawfully lower rates provided they did not lower them beyond a "fair freight," whatever that may mean. But where is it established that there is any such restriction upon commerce? And what is to be the definition of a "fair freight"? It is said that it ought to be a normal rate of freight, such as is reasonably remunerative to the shipowner. But over what period of time is the average of this reasonable remunerativeness to be calculated? All commercial men with capital are acquainted with the ordinary expedient of sowing one year a crop of apparently unfruitful prices, in order by driving competition away to reap a fuller harvest of profit in the future; and until the present argument at the bar it may be doubted whether shipowners or merchants were ever deemed to be bound by law to conform to some imaginary "normal" standard of freights or prices, or that Law Courts had a right to say to them in respect of their competitive tariffs, "Thus far shalt thou go and no further." To attempt to limit English competition in this way would probably be as hopeless an endeavour as the experiment of King Canute. . . .

It is urged, however, on the part of the plaintiffs, that even if the acts complained of would not be wrongful had they been committed by a single individual, they become actionable when they are the result of concerted action among several. In other words, the plaintiffs, it is contended, have been injured by an illegal conspiracy. Of the general proposition, that certain kinds of conduct not criminal in any one individual may become criminal if done by combination among several, there can be no doubt. The distinction is based on sound reason, for a combination may make oppressive or dangerous that which if it proceeded only from a single person would be otherwise, and the very fact of the combination may shew that the object is simply to do harm, and not to exercise one's own just rights. In the application of this undoubted principle it is necessary to be very careful not to press the doctrine of illegal conspiracy beyond that which is necessary for the protection of individuals or of the public; and it may be observed in passing that as a rule it is the damage wrongfully done, and not the conspiracy, that is the gist of actions on the case for conspiracy. But what is the definition of an illegal combination? It is an agreement by one or more to do an unlawful act, or to do a lawful act by unlawful means; and the question to be solved is whether there has been any such agreement here. Have the defendants combined to do an unlawful act? Have they combined to do a lawful act by unlawful means? A moment's consideration will be sufficient to shew that this new inquiry only drives us back to the circle of definitions and legal propositions which I have already traversed in the previous part of this judgment. The unlawful act agreed to, if any, between the defendants must have been the intentional doing of some act to the detriment of the plaintiffs' business without just cause or excuse. Whether there was any such justification or excuse for the defendants is the old question over again, which, so far as regards an individual trader, has been already solved. The only differentia that can exist must arise, if at all, out of the fact that the acts done are the joint acts of several capitalists, and not of one capitalist only. The next point is whether the means adopted were unlawful. The means adopted were competition carried to a bitter end. Whether such means were unlawful is in like manner nothing but the old discussion which I have gone through, and which is now revived under a second head of inquiry, except so far as a combination of capitalists differentiates the case of acts jointly done by them from similar acts done by a single man of capital. But I find it impossible myself to acquiesce in the view that the English law places any such restriction on the combination of capital as would be involved in the recognition of such a distinction. If so, one rich capitalist may innocently carry competition to a length which would become unlawful in the case of a syndicate with a joint capital no larger than his own, and one individual merchant may lawfully do that which a firm or a partnership may not. What limits, on such a theory, would be imposed by law on the competitive action of a joint-stock company limited, is a problem which might well puzzle a casuist. The truth is, that the combination of capital for purposes of trade and competition is a very different thing from such a combination of several persons against one, with a view to harm him, as falls under the head of an indictable conspiracy. There is no just cause or excuse in the latter class of cases. There is such a just cause or excuse in the former. . . . Would it be an indictable conspiracy to agree to drink up all the water from a common spring in a time of drought; to buy up by preconcerted action all the provisions in a market or district in times of scarcity; to combine to purchase all the shares of a company against a coming settling-day; or to agree to give away articles of trade gratis in order to withdraw custom from a trader? May two itinerant match-vendors combine to sell matches below their value in order by competition to drive a third match-vendor from the street? . . .

In the result, I agree with Lord Coleridge, C.J., and differ, with regret, from the Master of the Rolls. The substance of my view is this, that competition, however severe and egotistical, if unattended by circumstances of dishonesty, intimidation, molestation, or such illegalities as I have above referred to, gives rise to no cause of action at common law. I myself should deem it to be a misfortune if we were to attempt to prescribe to the business world how honest and peaceable trade was to be carried on in a case where no such illegal elements as I have mentioned exist, or were to adopt some standard of judicial "reasonableness," or of "normal" prices, or "fair freights," to which commercial adventurers, otherwise innocent, were bound to conform.

In my opinion, accordingly, this appeal ought to be dismissed with costs.

[Fry, L.J., issued an opinion concurring in the judgment of Bowen, L.J. Lord Esher, M.R., dissenting:]

It follows that the act of the defendants in lowering their freights far beyond a lowering for any purpose of trade — that is to say, so low that if they continued it they themselves could not carry on trade — was not an act done in the exercise of their own free right of trade, but was an act done evidently for the purpose of interfering with, i.e. with intent to interfere with, the plaintiffs' right to a free course of trade, and was therefore a wrongful act as against the plaintiffs' right; and as injury ensued to the plaintiffs, they had also in respect of such act a right of action against the defendants. The plaintiffs, in respect of that act, would have had a right of action if it had been done by one defendant only; they have it still more clearly when that act was done by several defendants combined for that purpose. For these reasons I come to the conclusion that the plaintiffs were entitled to judgment. The damages, if that be the correct conclusion as to the right of action, are to be ascertained. They are, in my opinion, the difference between the freight of 25s., which the plaintiffs were forced to accept, and the freight they would have obtained without other interference than a legal fair competition in 1885, and damages at large for being prevented from endeavouring to earn freight from Hankow to England in subsequent years, after taking into account the probability of using their ships in some other trade. I am of opinion that the appeal should be allowed.

NOTES

1. *Predatory pricing.* *Mogul* is one of the first cases in which the defendants have been sued for entering into a scheme of predatory pricing, i.e., a practice of selling below cost in the short run in the hope of obtaining monopoly gains later, after driving the competition from the market. In dealing with the legality of the practice, Bowen, L.J., did not concentrate on the social losses that predation might generate, or on the market power, if any, commanded by the defendants, which increased with the group membership. Instead, he was content to show that the defendant's practices did not involve the use of forbidden means: fraud, misrepresentation, intimidation, obstruction, and molestation headed his list. For discussion, see Epstein, Intentional Harms, 4 J. Legal Stud. 391, 431 (1975).

The modern view of predation does not dispute the illegality of force and fraud. But it asks the further question of whether predation constitutes an activity that is likely to cause social losses, even when restricted to downward price movements; and, if so, whether a court is capable of distinguishing between the predation and ordinary competition. The modern law and economics literature has generally defended the no-liability outcome in *Mogul* on the ground that predation is not an effective way for any firm or group to gain market power. The classic article on the subject is McGee, Predatory Price Cutting: The Standard Oil (N.J.) Case, 1 J.L. & Econ. 137 (1958), in which the author first concluded that mergers and acquisitions, but not predation, vaulted Standard Oil to its dominant market position. McGee then expressed doubt that predation could ever lead to monopoly. Historically, the defendants' combination in *Mogul* broke up even before the legal issues were resolved on appeal, and no successful effort of wide-scale predation has yet been uncovered.

Notwithstanding the paucity of empirical evidence on the point, some writers have advocated, roughly speaking, a definition of predation that renders it illegal to sell a product below its marginal cost of production, a test adumbrated in Esher, M.R.'s, dissent, when he defines the unfair price as one at which the defendants could not "continue" to sell their wares. See Areeda and Turner, Predatory Pricing and Related Practices under Section 2 of the Sherman Act, 88 Harv. L. Rev. 697 (1975). The major critique of this position is that no firm can hope to recoup in the long run the losses that it must incur in the short run to flood the market with low-cost products, so that consistent with *Mogul*, "[t]he antitrust offense of predation should be forgotten." See Easterbrook, Predatory Strategies and Counterstrategies, 48 U. Chi. L. Rev. 263 (1981). That position carried the day in Matsushita Electric Industrial Co., Ltd. v. Zenith Radio Corp. 475 U.S. 574 (1986), when the Supreme Court upheld a grant of summary judgment for the defendant Japanese television manufacturers charged with a conspiracy to drive their American competitors out of business, imposing a very high burden of proof on the plaintiffs given the inherent implausibility of their predation claim. More recently, the Supreme Court extended its views on predatory pricing to the converse situation of predatory-bidding. In Weyerhaeuser v. Ross-Simmons HardWood Lumber Co., 127 S. Ct. 1069, 1073, 1077 (2007), a unanimous Supreme Court rejected Ross-Simmons's antitrust claim that Weyerhaeuser had engaged in unfair trade practices by using "its dominant position in the alder sawlog market to drive up the prices for alder sawlogs to levels that severely reduced or eliminated the profit margins of Weyerhaeuser's alder sawmill competition." Applying the same tough attitude it took toward predatory pricing in *Matshushita*, the Court reasoned that excessive intervention could easily deter beneficial competition, given the many procompetitive reasons for high bids, including the desire to build up future inventories. In addition, Thomas, J., noted "[a] predatory-bidding scheme requires a buyer of inputs to suffer losses today on the chance that it will reap supracompetitive profits in the future." Accordingly, the Court limited these claims to a narrow class of cases where the buyer had to show first that the defendant's high bids "led to below-cost pricing of the predator's outputs," and second, that "the defendant has a dangerous probability of recouping the losses incurred in bidding up input prices through the exercise of monopsony [i.e. buyer-side monopoly] power." For exhaustive discussion of these issues, see Symposium: Buyer Power and Antitrust: Anticompetitive Overbuying by Power Buyers, 72 Antitrust L. J. (Issue 2, 2005).

2. *The English trilogy.* *Mogul* is the first of three major cases decided around 1900 that attempted to define the limits of fair competition at common law. The other two cases were Allen v. Flood, [1898] A.C. 1, and Quinn v. Leathem, [1901] A.C. 495, both of which involved labor, not trade, disputes. In Allen v. Flood, the defendant Allen represented the ironworkers union; the plaintiff Flood and his coworkers were members of the shipwrights union. Both members of both unions worked for the Glengall Iron Co. under contracts at will. Allen told Glengall that the ironworkers would walk off the job unless the shipwrights were dismissed. To keep the service of the ironworkers, Glengall dismissed the plaintiffs, who promptly sued. The holding in the House of Lords states the central proposition of the case in abstract form: "An act lawful in itself is not converted by a malicious or a bad motive into an unlawful act so as to make

the doer of the act liable to a civil action." The House of Lords dismissed the plaintiff's claim. An excerpt from Lord Herschell's lengthy opinion charts the move from this abstract proposition to the law of trade disputes:

> In Temperton v. Russell [[1893] 1 Q.B. 715, [*supra* at 1248], the further step was taken by the majority of the Court . . . of asserting that it was immaterial that the act induced was not the breach of a contract, but only the not entering into a contract, provided that the motive of desiring to injure the plaintiff, or to benefit the defendant at the expense of the plaintiff, was present. It seems to have been regarded as only a small step from the one decision to the other, and it was said that there seemed to be no good reason why, if an action lay for maliciously inducing a breach of contract, it should not equally lie for maliciously inducing a person not to enter into a contract. So far from thinking it a small step from the one decision to the other, I think there is a chasm between them. The reason for a distinction between the two cases appears to me to be this: that in the one case the act procured was the violation of a legal right, for which the person doing the act which injured the plaintiff could be sued as well as the person who procured it; whilst in the other case no legal right was violated by the person who did the act from which the plaintiff suffered: he would not be liable to be sued in respect of the act done, whilst the person who induced him to do the act would be liable to an action. . . .

In Quinn v. Leathem, [1901] A.C. 495, the last case in the trilogy, the plaintiff Leathem was a wholesale meat slaughterer. The defendant union demanded that he replace his current workers with union members paid at union wages. The union refused to accept plaintiff's offer to pay his own workers union scale; it was, however, prepared to admit the fired workers as union members, but without any seniority. When the plaintiff refused to comply with the union's demands, the union (in what today is called a secondary boycott) warned the plaintiff's best customer, his brother-in-law Munce, that his own workers would be called off the job unless Munce stopped buying his meat from the plaintiff. Munce yielded, and the plaintiff sued the union. The House of Lords upheld his claim. As stated in the headnote: "A combination of two or more, without justification or excuse, to injure a man in his trade by inducing his customers or servants to break their contracts with him or not to deal with him or continue in his employment is, if it results in damage to him, actionable." Lord Shand distinguished *Quinn* from *Allen* in a single sentence. "In Allen v. Flood the purpose of the defendant was by the acts complained of to promote his own trade interest, which it was held he was entitled to do, although injurious to his competitors, whereas in the present case, while it was clear there was a combination, the purpose of the defendants was to injure the plaintiff in his trade as distinguished from the intention of legitimately advancing their own interests." Is a union's interest to secure work for its own members a permissible justification under *Mogul*? For criticism of *Quinn*, see C. Gregory, Labor and the Law ch. 2 (2d rev. ed. 1958). For a defense of *Quinn* and an attack on *Allen*, see Petro, unions and the Southern Courts: Part III — The Conspiracy and Tort Foundations of the Labor Injunction, 60 N.C. L. Rev. 544, 558-567 (1982). Does the Union in *Allen* or *Flynn* stand a good chance to recoup its losses if forced to go out on strike to make good their respective threats?

In England the Trade Disputes Act, 1906, 6 Ed. VII ch. 47 removed these questions of trade union power from the common law. The key provisions of the Act: (a) made trade unions, as distinguished from their members, completely immune from liability in tort; (b) made the actions of individual persons done pursuant to agreement or combination actionable only to the extent that they would have been actionable if done without any such agreement or combination; and (c) abolished in the context of labor disputes the torts of inducement of breach of contract, interference with trade generally, and interference "with the right of some other person to dispose of his capital or his labour as he wills." For critical commentary see Rowley, Toward a Political Economy of British Labor Law, 51 U. Chi. L. Rev. 1135 (1984).

Both *Allen* and *Quinn* proved highly influential in the United States. For an approach congruent with *Quinn*, see Plant v. Wood, 57 N.E. 1011 (Mass. 1900), in which the classic Holmes dissent relies on Allen v. Flood. Note that the American labor law has supplanted many of the common law rules. Unlike the British system, however, it has replaced them with a system of collective bargaining that is in turn subject to extensive administrative and judicial control, which includes detailed regulations of secondary boycotts. See National Labor Relations Act, as amended 29 U.S.C. §§151-169 (2007).

3. Malice in the trade cases. The leading American authority on the place of malice in unfair competition cases is Tuttle v. Buck, 119 N.W. 946, 948 (Minn. 1909). The plaintiff was a barber by trade and the defendant a banker. The plaintiff claimed that the defendant, acting out of sheer malice, sought to drive him out of the barbering business. Defendant hired two barbers, gave them rent-free use of a barber shop, and by "threats of his personal displeasure sought to persuade members of the general public not to frequent the plaintiff's business." The trial judge upheld the complaint on demurrer and the decision was affirmed on appeal. Elliott, J., writing for the court, held that the wholly malicious conduct of the defendant, if proved, overstepped the proper bounds of fair competition — only to express thereafter his personal doubts about the sufficiency of the plaintiff's factual allegations: "There is no allegation that the defendant was intentionally running the business at a financial loss to himself, or that after driving the plaintiff out of business the defendant closed up or intended to close up his shop. From all that appears from the complaint he may have opened the barber shop, energetically sought business from his acquaintances and the customers of the plaintiff, and as a result of his enterprise and command of capital obtained it, with the result that the plaintiff, from want of capital, acquaintance, or enterprise, was unable to stand the competition and was thus driven out of business."

How long will any economic entity survive or prosper if motivated solely by malice instead of self-interest? See generally Ames, How Far an Act May Be a Tort Because of the Wrongful Motive of the Actor, 18 Harv. L. Rev. 411 (1905).

International News Service v. Associated Press
248 U.S. 215 (1918)

PITNEY, J. [The plaintiff Associated Press served some 900 newspapers throughout the United States in the gathering and distributing of news, which its member papers then sold to the public. Its annual budget was about $3,500,000. The defendant International News Service performed the same service for some 400 newspapers for about $2,000,000 per annum.]

The parties are in the keenest competition between themselves in the distribution of news throughout the United States; and so, as a rule, are the newspapers that they serve, in their several districts. . . .

The bill was filed to restrain the pirating of complainant's news by defendant in three ways: First, by bribing employees of newspapers published by complainant's members to furnish Associated Press news to defendant before publication, for transmission by telegraph and telephone to defendant's clients for publication by them; Second, by inducing Associated Press members to violate its by-laws and permit defendant to obtain news before publication; and Third, by copying news from bulletin boards and from early editions of complainant's newspapers and selling this, either bodily or after rewriting it, to defendant's customers.

The District Court, upon consideration of the bill and answer, with voluminous affidavits on both sides, granted a preliminary injunction under the first and second heads; but refused at that stage to restrain the systematic practice admittedly pursued by defendant, of taking news bodily from the bulletin boards and early editions of complainant's newspapers and selling it as its own. The court expressed itself as satisfied that this practice amounted to unfair trade, but as the legal question was one of first impression; it considered that the allowance of an injunction should await the outcome of an appeal. 240 F. 983, 996 (S.D.N.Y 1917). Both parties having appealed, the Circuit Court of Appeals sustained the injunction order so far as it went, and upon complainant's appeal modified it and remanded the cause with directions to issue an injunction also against any bodily taking of the words or substance of complainant's news until its commercial value as news had passed away. 245 F. 244, 253 (2d Cir. 1917). The present writ of certiorari was then allowed.

The only matter that has been argued before us is whether defendant may lawfully be restrained from appropriating news taken from bulletins issued by complainant or any of its members, or from newspapers published by them, for the purpose of selling it to defendant's clients. Complainant asserts that defendant's admitted course of conduct in this regard both violates complainant's property right in the news and constitutes unfair competition in business. And notwithstanding the case has proceeded only to the stage of preliminary injunction, we have deemed it proper to consider the underlying questions, since they go to the very merits of the action and are presented upon facts that are not in dispute. As presented in argument, these questions are: 1. Whether there is any property in news; 2. Whether, if there be property in news collected for the purpose of being published, it survives the instant of its publication in the first newspaper to which it is communicated by the news-gatherer; and 3. Whether defendant's admitted course of conduct in appropriating for commercial use matter taken from bulletins or early editions of Associated Press publications constitutes unfair competition in trade.

The federal jurisdiction was invoked because of diversity of citizenship, not upon the ground that the suit arose under the copyright or other laws of the United States. Complainant's news matter is not copyrighted. . . .

But the news element — the information respecting current events contained in the literary production — is not the creation of the writer, but is a report of matters that ordinarily are *publici juris*; it is the history of the day. It is not to be supposed that the framers of the Constitution, when they empowered Congress "to promote the progress of science and useful arts, by securing for limited times to authors and inventors the exclusive right to their respective writings and discoveries" (Const., Art. I, §8, par. 8), intended to confer upon one who might happen to be the first to report a historic event the exclusive right for any period to spread the knowledge of it.

We need spend no time, however, upon the general question of property in news matter at common law, or the application of the copyright act, since it seems to us the case must turn upon the question of unfair competition in business. And, in our opinion, this does not depend upon any general right of property analogous to the common-law right of the proprietor of an unpublished work to prevent its publication without his consent; nor is it foreclosed by showing that the benefits of the copyright act have been waived. We are dealing here not with restrictions upon publication but with the very facilities and processes of publication. The peculiar value of news is in the spreading of it while it is fresh; and it is evident that a valuable property interest in the news, as news, cannot be maintained by keeping it secret. Besides, except for matters improperly disclosed, or published in breach of trust or confidence, or in violation of law, none of which is involved in this branch of the case, the news of current events may be regarded as common property. What we are concerned with is the business of making it known to the world, in which both parties to the present suit are engaged. That business consists in maintaining a prompt, sure, steady, and reliable service designed to place the daily events of the world at the breakfast table of the millions at a price that, while of trifling moment to each reader, is sufficient in the aggregate to afford compensation for the cost of gathering and distributing it, with the added profit so necessary as an incentive to effective action in the commercial world. The service thus performed for newspaper readers is not only innocent but extremely useful in itself, and indubitably constitutes a legitimate business. The parties are competitors in this field; and, on fundamental principles, applicable here as elsewhere, when the rights or privileges of the one are liable to conflict with those of the other, each party is under a duty so to conduct its own business as not unnecessarily or unfairly to injure that of the other.

Obviously, the question of what is unfair competition in business must be determined with particular reference to the character and circumstances of the business. The question here is not so much the rights of either party as against the public but their rights as between themselves. And although we may and do assume that neither party has any remaining property interest as against the public in uncopyrighted news matter after the moment of its first publication, it by no means follows that there is no remaining property interest in it as between themselves. For, to both of them alike, news matter, however little susceptible of ownership or dominion in the absolute sense, is stock in trade, to be gathered at the cost of enterprise, organization, skill, labor, and money, and to be distributed and sold to those who will pay money for it, as for any other merchandise. Regarding the news, therefore, as but the material out of which both parties are seeking to make profits at the same time and in the same field, we hardly can fail to recognize that for this purpose, and as between them, it must be regarded as quasi property, irrespective of the rights of either as against the public. . . .

The peculiar features of the case arise from the fact that, while novelty and freshness form so important an element in the success of the business, the very processes of distribution and publication necessarily occupy a good deal of time. Complainant's service, as well as defendant's, is a daily service to daily newspapers; most of the foreign news reaches this country at the Atlantic seaboard, principally at the City of New York, and because of this, and of time differentials due to the earth's rotation, the distribution of news matter throughout the country is principally from east to west; and, since in speed the telegraph and telephone easily outstrip the rotation of the earth, it is a simple matter for defendant to take complainant's news from bulletins or early editions of complainant's members in the eastern cities and at the mere cost of telegraphic transmission cause it to be published in western papers issued at least as early as those served by complainant. Besides this, and irrespective of time differentials, irregularities in telegraphic transmission on different lines, and the normal consumption of time in printing and distributing the newspaper, result in permitting pirated news to be placed in the hands of defendant's readers sometimes simultaneously with the service of competing Associated Press papers, occasionally even earlier.

Defendant insists that when, with the sanction and approval of complainant, and as the result of the use of its news for the very purpose for which it is distributed, a portion of complainant's members communicate it to the general public by posting it upon bulletin boards so that all may read, or by issuing it to newspapers and distributing it indiscriminately, complainant no longer has the right to control the use to be made of it; that when it thus reaches the light of day it becomes the common possession of all to whom it is accessible; and that any purchaser of a newspaper has the right to communicate the intelligence which it contains to anybody and for any purpose, even for the purpose of selling it for profit to newspapers published for profit in competition with complainant's members.

The fault in the reasoning lies in applying as a test the right of the complainant as against the public, instead of considering the rights of complainant and defendant, competitors in business, as between themselves. The right of the purchaser of a single newspaper to spread knowledge of its contents gratuitously, for any legitimate purpose not unreasonably interfering with complainant's right to make merchandise of it, may be admitted; but to transmit that news for commercial use, in competition with complainant — which is what defendant has done and seeks to justify — is a very different matter. In doing this defendant, by its very act, admits that it is taking material that has been acquired by complainant as the result of organization and the expenditure of labor, skill, and money, and which is salable by complainant for money, and that defendant in appropriating it and selling it as its own is endeavoring to reap where it has not sown, and by disposing of it to newspapers that are competitors of complainant's members is appropriating to itself the harvest of those who have sown. Stripped of all disguises, the process amounts to an unauthorized interference with the normal operation of complainant's legitimate business precisely at the point where the profit is to be reaped, in order to divert a material portion of the profit from those who have earned it to those who have not; with special advantage to defendant in the competition because of the fact that it is not burdened with any part of the expense of gathering the news. The transaction speaks for itself, and a court of equity ought not to hesitate long in characterizing it as unfair competition in business.

. . . It is no answer to say that complainant spends its money for that which is too fugitive or evanescent to be the subject of property. That might, and for the purposes of the discussion we are assuming that it would, furnish an answer in a common-law controversy. But in a court of equity, where the question is one of unfair competition, if that which complainant has acquired fairly at substantial cost may be sold fairly at substantial profit, a competitor who is misappropriating it for the purpose of disposing of it to his own profit and to the disadvantage of complainant cannot be heard to say that it is too fugitive or evanescent to be regarded as property. It has all the attributes of property necessary for determining that a misappropriation of it by a competitor is unfair competition because contrary to good conscience.

The contention that the news is abandoned to the public for all purposes when published in the first newspaper is untenable. Abandonment is a question of intent, and the entire organization of the Associated Press negatives such a purpose. The cost of the service would be prohibitive if the reward were to be so limited. No single newspaper, no small group of newspapers, could sustain the expenditure....

It is to be observed that the view we adopt does not result in giving to complainant the right to monopolize either the gathering or the distribution of the news, or, without complying with the copyright act, to prevent the reproduction of its news articles; but only postpones participation by complainant's competitor in the processes of distribution and reproduction of news that it has not gathered, and only to the extent necessary to prevent that competitor from reaping the fruits of complainant's efforts and expenditure, to the partial exclusion of complainant, and in violation of the principle that underlies the maxim sic utere tuo, etc.

It is said that the elements of unfair competition are lacking because there is no attempt by defendant to palm off its goods as those of the complainant, characteristic of the most familiar, if not the most typical, cases of unfair competition. But we cannot concede that the right to equitable relief is confined to that class of cases. In the present case the fraud upon complainant's rights is more direct and obvious. Regarding news matter as the mere material from which these two competing parties are endeavoring to make money, and treating it, therefore, as quasi property for the purposes of their business because they are both selling it as such, defendant's conduct differs from the ordinary case of unfair competition in trade principally in this that, instead of selling its own goods as those of complainant, it substitutes misappropriation in the place of misrepresentation, and sells complainant's goods as its own.

[The Court then brought its opinion to a close by considering: (1) whether plaintiff is barred in equity because it has "unclean hands," since it utilizes "tips" obtained from defendant's service, and concluded that this practice "is not shown to be such as to constitute an unconscientious or inequitable attitude . . . so as to fix upon complainant the taint of unclean hands"; (2) whether the injunction was too broad, and decided that although it may be subject to some criticism it should be left to the trial court to modify it if necessary at a later stage in the case.]

The decree of the Circuit Court of Appeals will be affirmed.

[Justice Holmes, in an opinion in which Justice McKenna concurred, would have limited relief to requiring defendant to give express credit to plaintiff for the news it took.]

BRANDEIS, J., dissenting. . . . News is a report of recent occurrences. . . . The general rule of law is, that the noblest of human productions — knowledge, truths ascertained, conceptions, and ideas — become, after voluntary communication to others, free as the air to common use. Upon these incorporeal productions the attribute of property is continued after such communication only in certain classes of cases where public policy has seemed to demand it. These exceptions are confined to productions which, in some degree, involve creation, invention, or discovery. But by no means all such are endowed with this attribute of property. The creations which are recognized as property by the common law are literary, dramatic, musical, and other artistic creations; and these have also protection under the copyright statutes. The inventions and discoveries upon which this attribute of property is conferred only by statute, are the few comprised within the patent law. . . .

Plaintiff further contended that defendant's practice constitutes unfair competition, because there is "appropriation without cost to itself of values created by" the plaintiff; and it is upon this ground that the decision of this court appears to be based. To appropriate and use for profit, knowledge and ideas produced by other men, without making compensation or even acknowledgment, may be inconsistent with a finer sense of propriety; but, with the exceptions indicated above, the law has heretofore sanctioned the practice. Thus it was held that one may ordinarily make and sell anything in any form, may copy with exactness that which another has produced, or may otherwise use his ideas without his consent and without the payment of compensation, and yet not inflict a legal injury; and that ordinarily one is at perfect liberty to find out, if he can by lawful means, trade secrets of another, however valuable, and then use the knowledge so acquired gainfully, although it cost the original owner much in effort and in money to collect or produce.

Such taking and gainful use of a product of another which, for reasons of public policy, the law has refused to endow with the attributes of property, does not become unlawful because the product happens to have been taken from a rival and is used in competition with him. The unfairness in competition which hitherto has been recognized by the law as a basis for relief, lay in the manner or means of conducting the business; and the manner or means held legally unfair, involves either fraud or force or the doing of acts otherwise prohibited by law. In the "passing off" cases (the typical and most common case of unfair competition), the wrong consists in fraudulently representing by word or act that defendant's goods are those of plaintiff. In the other cases, the diversion of trade was effected through physical or moral coercion, or by inducing breaches of contract or of trust or by enticing away employees. In some others, called cases of simulated competition, relief was granted because defendant's purpose was unlawful; namely, not competition but deliberate and wanton destruction of plaintiff's business. . . .

Nor is the use made by the International News Service of the information taken from papers or bulletins of Associated Press members legally objectionable by reason of the purpose for which it was employed. The acts here complained of were not done for the purpose of injuring the business of the Associated Press. Their purpose was not even to divert its trade, or to put it at a disadvantage by lessening defendant's necessary expenses. The purpose was merely to supply subscribers of the International News Service promptly with all available news. . . .

[Justice Brandeis then argued that the complexity of the problem called for legislative and administrative solutions. He also pointed out, as an illustration of how the public interest might be affected, that British and French governments refused to give INS access to the war news from the front because of the pro-German sympathies of its Hearst papers.]

Courts are ill-equipped to make the investigations which should precede a determination of the limitations which should be set upon any property right in news or of the circumstances under which news gathered by a private agency should be deemed affected with a public interest. Courts would be powerless to prescribe the detailed regulations essential to full enjoyment of the rights conferred or to introduce the machinery required for enforcement of such regulations. Considerations such as these should lead us to decline to establish a new rule of law in the effort to redress a newly-disclosed wrong, although the propriety of some remedy appears to be clear.

NOTE

The Limits of INS. Will the catalogue of tort actions ever be closed if common law decisions can create novel property interests whenever one person tries to take advantage of the labor of another? Would the court have allowed the action if the INS had only serviced papers that were not in direct competition with papers serviced by the Associated Press? Would Brandeis, J., have remained in dissent if the Hearst papers had been allowed access to the front by the British authorities?

The lower courts have been cautious in responding to *INS*. Learned Hand in particular was a staunch believer in limiting its reach. In Cheney Bros. v. Doris Silk Corp., 35 F.2d 279, 280 (2d Cir. 1929), the plaintiff was a silk manufacturer "which puts out each season many new patterns, designed to attract purchasers by their novelty and beauty." The expected life of any new pattern was generally about eight or nine months, and about 80 percent of the patterns marketed typically proved to have no consumer appeal. Design patents were costly to obtain, and copyright protection was then generally unavailable as a matter of law. The plaintiff sought to enjoin the defendant who copied one of plaintiff's popular patterns and undersold the plaintiff. Hand, J., appealed to legislative deference in denying the plaintiff any relief under the supposed "general doctrine" of *INS*:

> [W]e think that no more was covered than situations substantially similar to those then at bar [in *INS*]. The difficulties of understanding it otherwise are insuperable. We are to suppose that the court meant to create a sort of common-law patent or copyright for reasons of justice. Either would flagrantly conflict with the scheme which Congress has for more than a century devised to cover the subject-matter.
>
> Qua patent, we should at least have to decide, as tabula rasa, whether the design or machine was new and required invention; further, we must ignore the Patent Office whose action has always been a condition upon the creation of this kind of property. Qua copyright, although it would be simpler to decide upon the merits, we should equally be obliged to dispense with the conditions imposed upon the creation of the right. Nor, if we went so far, should we know whether the property so recognized should be limited to the periods prescribed in the statutes, or should extend as long as the author's grievance. It appears to us incredible that the Supreme Court should have had in mind any such consequences. To exclude others from the enjoyment of a chattel is one thing; to prevent any imitation of it, to set up a monopoly in the plan of its structure, gives the author a power over his fellows vastly greater, a power which the Constitution allows only Congress to create.

However, *INS* showed renewed vitality in a dispute over the creation and use of the Dow Jones Averages for financial futures. In Board of Trade of City of Chicago v. Dow Jones & Co., Inc., 456 N.E.2d 84, 90 (Ill. 1983), Dow Jones was allowed to enjoin the use of its index as the basis for a futures contract traded over the Chicago Board of Trade's exchanges:

> To hold that defendant has a proprietary interest in its indexes and averages which vests it with the exclusive right to license their use for trading in stock index futures contracts would not preclude plaintiff and others from marketing stock index futures contracts. The extent of the defendant's monopoly would be limited, for as defendant points out, there are an infinite number of stock market indexes which could be devised.

Should it matter that, before acting unilaterally, the Board of Trade had offered Dow Jones between $1 and $2 million per year for the use of its index? On the relationship between *INS* and the *Dow Jones* case, see Baird,

Common Law Intellectual Property and the Legacy of *International News Service v. Associated Press,* 50 U. Chi. L. Rev. 411 (1983); for a qualified defense of *INS,* see Epstein, International News Service v. Associated Press: Custom and Law As Sources of Property Rights in News, 78 Va. L. Rev. 87 (1992); Baird, The Story of INS v. AP, in Intellectual Property Stories (Ginsburg & Dreyfuss ed., 2006). How ought *INS* be read today?

The National Basketball Association v. Motorola, Inc.
105 F.3d 841 (2d Cir. 1997)

WINTER, J.

Motorola, Inc. and Sports Team Analysis and Tracking Systems ("STATS") appeal from a permanent injunction entered by Judge Preska. The injunction concerns a handheld pager sold by Motorola and marketed under the name "SportsTrax," which displays updated information of professional basketball games in progress. The injunction prohibits appellants, absent authorization from the National Basketball Association and NBA Properties, Inc. (collectively the "NBA"), from transmitting scores or other data about NBA games in progress via the pagers, STATS's site on America On-Line's computer dial-up service, or "any equivalent means."

The crux of the dispute concerns the extent to which a state law "hot-news" misappropriation claim based on International News Service v. Associated Press, 248 U.S. 215 (1918) ("INS"), survives preemption by the federal Copyright Act and whether the NBA's claim fits within the surviving INS-type claims. We hold that a narrow "hot-news" exception does survive preemption. However, we also hold that appellants' transmission of "real-time" NBA game scores and information tabulated from television and radio broadcasts of games in progress does not constitute a misappropriation of "hot news" that is the property of the NBA.

I. BACKGROUND

The facts are largely undisputed. Motorola manufactures and markets the SportsTrax paging device while STATS [through reporters who listen to or watch the games] supplies the game information that is transmitted to the pagers. The product became available to the public in January 1996, at a retail price of about $200. SportsTrax's pager has an inch-and-a-half by inch-and-a-half screen and operates in four basic modes: "current," "statistics," "final scores" and "demonstration." It is the "current" mode that gives rise to the present dispute. In that mode, SportsTrax displays the following information on NBA games in progress: (i) the teams playing; (ii) score changes; (iii) the team in possession of the ball; (iv) whether the team is in the free-throw bonus; (v) the quarter of the game; and (vi) time remaining in the quarter. The information is updated every two to three minutes, with more frequent updates near the end of the first half and the end of the game. There is a lag of approximately two or three minutes between events in the game itself and when the information appears on the pager screen. . . .

II. THE STATE LAW MISAPPROPRIATION CLAIM

A. SUMMARY OF RULING

[Winter, J. first traces the early evolution of the broadcast of baseball and other events, and notes that before 1976 the "general understanding" was that live broadcasts were not copyrightable and that much doubt remained "whether a recorded broadcast or videotype of such an event was copyrightable."]

. . . In 1976, however, Congress passed legislation expressly affording copyright protection to simultaneously-recorded broadcasts of live performances such as sports events. See 17 U.S.C. §101. Such protection was not extended to the underlying events.

The 1976 amendments also contained provisions preempting state law claims that enforced rights "equivalent" to exclusive copyright protections when the work to which the state claim was being applied fell within the area of copyright protection. Based on legislative history of the 1976 amendments, it is generally agreed that a "hot-news" INS-like claim survives preemption. However, much of New York misappropriation law after INS goes well beyond "hot-news" claims and is preempted.

We hold that the surviving "hot-news" INS-like claim is limited to cases where: (i) a plaintiff generates or gathers information at a cost; (ii) the information is time-sensitive; (iii) a defendant's use of the information constitutes free-riding on the plaintiff's efforts; (iv) the defendant is in direct competition with a product or service offered by the plaintiffs and (v) the ability of other parties to free-ride on the efforts of the plaintiff or others would so reduce the incentive to produce the product or service that its existence or quality would be substantially threatened.[8] We conclude that SportsTrax does not meet that test.

---

8. Some authorities have labeled this element as requiring direct competition between the defendant and the plaintiff in a primary market. [See] Restatement (Third) of Unfair Competition, §38 cmt. c, at 412-13; see also National Football League v. Delaware, 435 F. Supp. 1372 (D. Del. 1977). In that case, the NFL sued Delaware over the state's lottery game which was based on NFL games. In dismissing the wrongful misappropriation claims, the court stated:

C. THE STATE-LAW MISAPPROPRIATION CLAIM

The theory of the New York misappropriation cases relied upon by the district court is considerably broader than that of INS. However, we believe that [any] broad misappropriation doctrine based on amorphous concepts such as "commercial immorality" or society's "ethics" is preempted. Such concepts are virtually synonymous for wrongful copying and are in no meaningful fashion distinguishable from infringement of a copyright. The broad misappropriation doctrine relied upon by the district court is, therefore, the equivalent of exclusive rights in copyright law. . . .

In light of [more recent] cases . . . that emphasize the narrowness of state misappropriation claims that survive preemption, most of the broadcast cases relied upon by the NBA are simply not good law. Those cases were decided at a time when simultaneously-recorded broadcasts were not protected under the Copyright Act and when the state law claims they fashioned were not subject to federal preemption. For example, *Metropolitan Opera* [Assn. v. Wagner-Nichols Recorder Corp., 101 N.Y.S. 2d 483 (N.Y. Sup. Ct. 1950), *aff'd*, 107 N.Y.S.2d 795 (1st Dept. 1951)] involved the unauthorized copying, marketing, and sale of opera radio broadcasts. As another example, in Mutual Broadcasting System v. Muzak Corp., 30 N.Y.S.2d 419 (Sup. Ct. 1941), the defendant simultaneously retransmitted the plaintiff's baseball radio broadcasts onto telephone lines. . . .

Our conclusion, therefore, is that only a narrow "hot-news" misappropriation claim survives preemption for actions concerning material within the realm of copyright.

[The Court then restates the five elements set out above, *supra* at 1285.]

INS is not about ethics; it is about the protection of property rights in time-sensitive information so that the information will be made available to the public by profit-seeking entrepreneurs. If services like AP were not assured of property rights in the news they pay to collect, they would cease to collect it. The ability of their competitors to appropriate their product at only nominal cost and thereby to disseminate a competing product at a lower price would destroy the incentive to collect news in the first place. The newspaper-reading public would suffer because no one would have an incentive to collect "hot news."

We therefore find the extra elements — those in addition to the elements of copyright infringement — that allow a "hot-news" claim to survive

---

While courts have recognized that one has a right to one's own harvest, this proposition has not been construed to preclude others from profiting from demands for collateral services generated by the success of one's business venture.

The court also noted, "It is true that Delaware is thus making profits it would not make but for the existence of the NFL, but I find this difficult to distinguish from the multitude of charter bus companies who generate profit from servicing those of plaintiffs' fans who want to go to the stadium or, indeed, the sidewalk popcorn salesman who services the crowd as it surges towards the gate."

preemption are: (i) the time-sensitive value of factual information, (ii) the free-riding by a defendant, and (iii) the threat to the very existence of the product or service provided by the plaintiff.

2. The Legality of SportsTrax

We conclude that Motorola and STATS have not engaged in unlawful misappropriation under the "hot-news" test set out above. To be sure, some of the elements of a "hot-news" INS claim are met. The information transmitted to SportsTrax is not precisely contemporaneous, but it is nevertheless time-sensitive. Also, the NBA does provide, or will shortly do so, information like that available through SportsTrax. It now offers a service called "Gamestats" that provides official play-by-play game sheets and half-time and final box scores within each arena. It also provides such information to the media in each arena. In the future, the NBA plans to enhance Gamestats so that it will be networked between the various arenas and will support a pager product analogous to SportsTrax. SportsTrax will of course directly compete with an enhanced Gamestats.

However, there are critical elements missing in the NBA's attempt to assert a "hot-news" INS-type claim. As framed by the NBA, their claim compresses and confuses three different informational products. The first product is generating the information by playing the games; the second product is transmitting live, full descriptions of those games; and the third product is collecting and retransmitting strictly factual information about the games. The first and second products are the NBA's primary business: producing basketball games for live attendance and licensing copyrighted broadcasts of those games. The collection and retransmission of strictly factual material about the games is a different product: e.g., box-scores in newspapers, summaries of statistics on television sports news, and real-time facts to be transmitted to pagers. In our view, the NBA has failed to show any competitive effect whatsoever from SportsTrax on the first and second products and a lack [of] any free-riding by SportsTrax on the third.

With regard to the NBA's primary products — producing basketball games with live attendance and licensing copyrighted broadcasts of those games — there is no evidence that anyone regards SportsTrax or the AOL site as a substitute for attending NBA games or watching them on television. In fact, Motorola markets SportsTrax as being designed "for those times when you cannot be at the arena, watch the game on TV, or listen to the radio . . . ."

The NBA argues that the pager market is also relevant to a "hot-news" INS-type claim and that SportsTrax's future competition with Gamestats satisfies any missing element. We agree that there is a separate market for the real-time transmission of factual information to pagers or similar devices, such as STATS's AOL site. However, we disagree that SportsTrax is in any sense free-riding off Gamestats.

An indispensable element of an INS "hot-news" claim is free-riding by a defendant on a plaintiff's product, enabling the defendant to produce a directly competitive product for less money because it has lower costs. SportsTrax is not such a product. The use of pagers to transmit real-time information about NBA games requires: (i) the collecting of facts about the games; (ii) the transmission of these facts on a network; (iii) the assembling of them by the particular service; and (iv) the transmission of them to pagers or an on-line computer site. Appellants are in no way free-riding on Gamestats. Motorola and STATS expend their own resources to collect purely factual information generated in NBA games to transmit to Sports-Trax pagers. They have their own network and assemble and transmit data themselves.

. . . SportsTrax and Gamestats are each bearing their own costs of collecting factual information on NBA games, and, if one produces a product that is cheaper or otherwise superior to the other, that producer will prevail in the marketplace. This is obviously not the situation against which *INS* was intended to prevent: the potential lack of any such product or service because of the anticipation of free-riding.

[Injunction denied.]

Ely-Norris Safe Co. v. Mosler Safe Co.
7 F.2d 603 (2d Cir. 1925)

Suit in equity by the Ely-Norris Safe Company against the Mosler Safe Company. From decree of dismissal, plaintiff appeals. Reversed.

The jurisdiction of the District Court depended upon diverse citizenship, and the suit was for unfair competition. The bill alleged that the plaintiff manufactured and sold safes under certain letters patent, which had as their distinctive feature an explosion chamber, designed for protection against burglars. Before the acts complained of, no one but the plaintiff had ever made or sold safes with such chambers, and, except for the defendant's infringement, the plaintiff has remained the only manufacturer and seller of such safes. By reason of the plaintiff's efforts the public has come to recognize the value of the explosion chamber and to wish to purchase safes containing them. Besides infringing the patent, the defendant has manufactured and sold safes without a chamber, but with a metal band around the door, in the same place where the plaintiff put the chamber, and has falsely told its customers that this band was employed to cover and close an explosion chamber. Customers have been thus led to buy safes upon the faith of the representation, who in fact wished to buy safes with explosion chambers, and would have done so, but for the deceit.

The bill prayed an injunction against selling safes with such metal bands, and against representing that any of its safes contained an explosion chamber. From the plaintiff's answers to interrogatories it appeared that all the defendant's safes bore the defendant's name and address, and were sold as its own. Furthermore, that the defendant never gave a customer reason to suppose that any safe sold by it was made by the plaintiff. . . .

HAND, J. (after stating the facts as above.) American Washboard Co. v. Saginaw Mfg. Co., 103 F. 281 (6th Cir. [1900]), was . . . a case in substance like that at bar, because there the plaintiff alleged that it had acquired the entire output of sheet aluminum suitable for washboards. It necessarily followed that the plaintiff had a practical monopoly of this metal for the articles in question, and from this it was a fair inference that any customer of the defendant, who was deceived into buying as an aluminum washboard one which was not such, was a presumptive customer of the plaintiff, who had therefore lost a bargain. This was held, however, not to constitute a private wrong, and so the bill was dismissed. . . .

We must concede, therefore, that on the cases as they stand the law is with the defendant, and the especially high authority of the court which decided American Washboard Co. v. Saginaw Mfg. Co., supra, makes us hesitate to differ from their conclusion. Yet there is no part of the law which is more plastic than unfair competition, and what was not reckoned an actionable wrong 25 years ago may have become such today. We find it impossible to deny the strength of the plaintiff's case on the allegations of its bill. As we view it, the question is, as it always is in such cases, one of fact. While a competitor may, generally speaking, take away all the customers of another that he can, there are means which he must not use. One of these is deceit. The false use of another's name as maker or source of his own goods is deceit, of which the false use of geographical or descriptive terms is only one example. But we conceive that in the end the questions which arise are always two: Has the plaintiff in fact lost customers? And has he lost them by means which the law forbids? The false use of the plaintiff's name is only an instance in which each element is clearly shown.

In the case at bar the means are as plainly unlawful as in the usual case of palming off. It is as unlawful to lie about the quality of one's wares as about their maker; it equally subjects the seller to action by the buyer. . . . The reason, as we think, why such deceits have not been regarded as actionable by a competitor, depends only upon his inability to show any injury for which there is a known remedy. In an open market it is generally impossible to prove that a customer, whom the defendant has secured by falsely describing his goods, would have bought of the plaintiff, if the defendant had been truthful. Without that, the plaintiff, though aggrieved in company with other honest traders, cannot show any ascertainable loss. He may not recover at law, and the equitable remedy is concurrent. The law does not allow him to sue as a vicarious avenger of the defendant's customers.

But, if it be true that the plaintiff has a monopoly of the kind of wares concerned, and if to secure a customer the defendant must represent his own as of that kind, it is a fair inference that the customer wants those and those only. Had he not supposed that the defendant could supply him, presumably he would have gone to the plaintiff, who alone could. At least, if the plaintiff can prove that in fact he would, he shows a direct loss, measured by his profits on the putative sale. If a tradesman falsely foists on a customer a substitute for what the plaintiff alone can supply, it can scarcely be that the plaintiff is without remedy, if he can show that the customer would certainly have come to him, had the truth been told.

Yet that is in substance the situation which this bill presents. It says that the plaintiff alone could lawfully make such safes, and that the defendant has sold others to customers who asked for the patented kind. It can make no difference that the defendant sold them as its own. The sale by hypothesis depended upon the structure of the safes, not on their maker. To be satisfied, the customer must in fact have gone to the plaintiff, or the defendant must have infringed. Had he infringed, the plaintiff could have recovered his profit on the sale; had the customer gone to him, he would have made that profit. Any possibilities that the customers might not have gone to the plaintiff, had they been told the truth, are foreclosed by the allegation that the plaintiff in fact lost the sales. . . .

Decree reversed.

Mosler Safe Co. v. Ely-Norris Safe Co.
273 U.S. 132 (1926)

HOLMES, J. [after summarizing the facts set out in the decision below.] At the hearing below all attention seems to have been concentrated on the question passed upon and the forcibly stated reasons that induced this Court of Appeals to differ from that for the Sixth Circuit. But, upon a closer scrutiny of the bill than seems to have been invited before, it does not present that broad and interesting issue. The bill alleges that the plaintiff has a patent for an explosion chamber as described and claimed in said Letters Patent; that it has the exclusive right to make and sell safes containing such an explosion chamber; that no other safes containing such an explosion chamber could be got in the United States before the defendant, as it is alleged, infringed the plaintiff's patent, for which alleged infringement a suit is pending. It then is alleged that the defendant is making and selling safes with a metal band around the door at substantially the same location as the explosion chamber of plaintiff's safes, and has represented to the public that the said metal band was employed to cover or close an explosion chamber by reason of which the public has been led to purchase defendant's said safes as and for safes containing an explosion chamber, such as is manufactured and sold by the plaintiff herein. It is alleged further that sometimes the defendant's safes have no explosion chamber under the band but are bought by those who want safes with a chamber and so the defendant has deprived the plaintiff of sales, competed unfairly and damaged the plaintiff's reputation. The plaintiff relies upon its patent suit for relief in respect of the sales of safes alleged to infringe its rights. It complains here only of false representations as to safes that do not infringe but that are sold as having explosion chambers although in fact they do not.

It is consistent with every allegation in the bill and the defendant in argument asserted it to be a fact, that there are other safes with explosion chambers beside that for which the plaintiff has a patent. The defendant is charged only with representing that its safes had an explosion chamber, which, so far as appears, it had a perfect right to do if the representation was true. If on the other hand the representation was false as it is alleged sometimes to have been, there is nothing to show that customers had they known the facts would have gone to the plaintiff rather than to other competitors in the market, or to lay a foundation for the claim for a loss of sales. The bill is so framed as to seem to invite the decision that was obtained from the Circuit Court of Appeals, but when scrutinized is seen to have so limited its statements as to exclude the right to complain.

Decree reversed.

NOTES

1. *Passing off.* Would the existence of plaintiff's monopoly on all explosion chambers justify its demand for an injunction? Damages? Both? How might damages be calculated if allowed? What result if all plaintiffs who made safes with explosion chambers joined together in suit?

In one sense, the plaintiff's case for passing off builds on the elements of ordinary misrepresentation already developed in Chapter 15, and recognized in the context of unfair competition as early as *Mogul*. Initially, the passing off action builds from the admitted proposition that a disappointed buyer has an action against the seller who has passed off its own goods as the superior product of a rival. Yet in practice that suit may prove too costly for any individual purchaser to mount to recover its trifling losses attributable to the defendant's misrepresentation. Nor would that suit, even if successful, vindicate the interests of the rival in its product's reputation and good will. In passing off cases, therefore, the *competitor* not the purchaser is the plaintiff. The claim is that the defendant has falsely represented that its own product is better than it really is, by pretending that his product is the plaintiff's, or by claiming that his product has desirable attributes associated with the plaintiff's product that it, in fact, lacks. The substantive underpinnings of passing off are clear enough: The defendant's misrepresentation induces third parties to desert the plaintiff. The measure of damages is the profits from lost sales, which depend critically on the fraction of defendant's buyers (often less than 100 percent) that would have migrated to the plaintiff's wares if the passing off had not happened.

2. *Product disparagement.* Clearly distinct from passing off are claims for product disparagement. With disparagement the defendant asserts that the plaintiff's product is worse than it really is, so as to induce consumers to purchase other products, including the defendant's. See Tex Smith, The Harmonica Man v. Godfrey, *supra* at 1063. Disparagement is really a form of product defamation, although many courts treat it as a distinct tort not governed by the myriad of defamation rules such as those concerning innuendo or special damages. As the court noted in Dairy Stores, Inc. v. Sentinel Publishing Co., 516 A.2d 220, 224 (N.J. 1986):

> Although the two causes sometimes overlap, actions for defamation and product disparagement stem from different branches of tort law. A defamation action, which encompasses libel and slander, affords a remedy for damage to one's reputation. By comparison an action for product disparagement is an offshoot of the cause of action for interference with contractual relations, such as sales to a prospective buyer. The two causes may merge when a disparaging statement about a product reflects on the reputation of the business that made, distributed or sold it. If, for example, a statement about the poor quality of a product implies that the seller is fraudulent, then the statement may be actionable under both theories.

For more on product disparagement, see Restatement (Third) Unfair Competition §2.

3. *The Lanham Act.* There is a close kinship between actions for unfair competition and those for violation of the Lanham Act, 15 U.S.C. §§1051-1141 (2007), the trademark statute. Its general intention is expressed in §1127: "The intent of this Act is to regulate commerce within the control of Congress by making actionable the deceptive and misleading use of marks in such commerce . . . [and] to protect persons engaged in such commerce against unfair competition. . . ." The statute provides protection for both common law and statutory trademarks. The section also protects a diverse collection of marks, symbols, design elements, and characters that the public, or some relevant portion thereof, directly associates with the plaintiff or its product. The Restatement (Third) Unfair Competition, §2, comment *b,* notes how the Act undid the restrictive rule in *Ely-Norris:*

> As originally enacted, §43(a) of the Act, 15 U.S.C. §1125(a), recognized a right of action against "a false designation of origin, or any false description or representation" used in connection with any goods or services in favor of "any person who believes that he is or is likely to be damaged." Some early interpretations confined §43(a) to misrepresentations relating to source; other interpretations viewed it as a codification of existing common law liability under the "single source" doctrine. Subsequent decisions, however,

established the section's general applicability to deceptive advertising and rejected the attempt to engraft the common law limitations onto the statutory tort. The 1988 revision of §43(a) confirmed its application to both misrepresentations of source and other deceptive representations made in connection with the marketing of goods and services.

Note that *Ely-Norris*'s requirement that the plaintiff establish actual harm has survived in federal trademark litigation. In Mosley v. Secret Catalogue, Inc., 537 U.S. 418 (2003), Stevens, J., held that under the Federal Trademark Dilution Act, 15 U.S.C. §1125(c), a plaintiff could only recover on proof of actual economic harm. The "mere likelihood" of harm was insufficient.

4. *Trademark and tradename litigation: direct competitors.* A veritable explosion of cases constantly tests the outer limits of trademark and tradename protection. The classic suits seek to enjoin direct competitors. In Warner Bros., Inc. v. Gay Toys, Inc., 658 F.2d 76 (2d Cir. 1981), the court allowed Warner Bros. to enjoin Gay Toys from the marketing of its "Dixie Racer," a 1969 Dodge Charger complete with a bright orange color, Confederate flag decal, numbers on the door, and the various symbols of the "General Lee," all based on the then popular television series, *The Dukes of Hazzard*. As commonly happens, the defendant had sought unsuccessfully to obtain a license from the plaintiff to market Dukes of Hazzard cars. Thereafter, it had modified the features of an existing car to bear greater resemblance to the Dukes of Hazzard car, from which it still differed in certain respects. Notwithstanding those residual differences, the plaintiff obtained a preliminary injunction against the defendant by marshaling a wide array of evidence to show that ordinary customers confused defendant's car with the original Dukes of Hazzard line: the defendant's Dixie Racer had sales far in excess of its other cars in the same line; dealers sold the defendant's car as "The Dukes of Hazzard Car"; and, as consumer surveys had determined, 80 percent of the children asked thought the Dixie Racer was the Dukes of Hazzard car. What evidence might be introduced to rebut the charge of trademark violation? Could the case have been treated as one of unfair competition at common law?

The question of automotive confusion arises with real as well as toy cars. In Esercizio v. Roberts, 944 F.2d 1235 (6th Cir. 1991), the defendant Roberts made kits and cars that duplicated the distinctive Ferrari exterior on its limited production models. Ferrari's "trade dress" claim with regard to its "unique and distinctive exterior shape" was upheld by the court, which noted that the Ferrari exterior had obtained a powerful "secondary meaning" in the eyes of consumers. The plaintiff established confusion from the similarity of the two marks, from the actual confusion reported by consumers, and from defendant's conscious decision to copy the plaintiff's design for its own commercial advantage. Note the trademark protection was available in perpetuity even though the plaintiff had acquired a design patent for its exterior. Why the difference? See Epstein, Intellectual Property: Old Boundaries and New Frontiers, 76 Ind. L.J. 803, 825-827 (2001).

5. *Trademark and tradename litigation: other applications.* Although most trademark litigation takes place between direct competitors, trademark protection need not be so limited. In MGM-Pathé Communications v. Pink Panther Patrol, 774 F. Supp. 869, 875 (S.D.N.Y. 1991), the plaintiff owned the registered trademark THE PINK PANTHER, which applies to the popular series of films about its bumbling detective hero. It also lent its trademark to producers of a wide range of consumer and children's goods. The defendant was a gay rights defense organization that used the PINK PANTHER name in connection with an upside down pink triangle (used by the Nazis to mark homosexuals) as its symbol. Even though the defendant group sold no goods in competition with the plaintiffs, the court enjoined its use of the PINK PANTHER trademark on the ground that ordinary individuals could mistakenly assume that the owners of the trademark sponsored or otherwise supported the activities of the patrol. It "is indeed entirely likely that a large percentage of the population of the United States might see and hear both plaintiff's and defendants' names during a single evening of nationwide television broadcasting, if a telecast of an MGM film should be followed by a newscast including reference to the Patrol's activities."

But tradename protection (and common law misappropriation) claims were both denied in New Kids on the Block v. New America Publishing, Inc., 971 F.2d 302, 308 (9th Cir. 1992). Two newspapers, USA Today and The Star, ran popularity polls on (900) phone lines, asking callers to say which of the (five) New Kids was the hottest (or coolest). Kozinski, J., held that defendant's use of their tradename was a privileged *nominative* use because there was no other conceivable way in which any newspaper could otherwise refer to the group in order to get their readers' opinions about it. "It is no more reasonably possible, however, to refer to the New Kids as an entity than it is to refer to the Chicago Bulls, Volkswagens or the Boston Marathon without using the trademark." The use of the name was therefore adjudged fair because "[b]oth *The Star* and *USA Today* reference the New Kids only to the extent necessary to identify them as the subject of the polls; they do not use the New Kids' distinctive logo or anything else that isn't needed to make the announcements intelligible to readers. Finally, nothing in the announcement suggests joint sponsorship or endorsement by the New Kids." Should it make a difference that the New Kids have their own (900) numbers for their fans to use? See generally Heald, Federal Intellectual Property Law and the Economics of Preemption, 76 Iowa L. Rev. 959 (1991).

Finally, in Ty, Inc. v. Perryman, 306 F.3d 509 (7th Cir. 2002), the plaintiff firm held the trademark to Beanie Babies under which it sold its beanbag stuffed animals. The defendant, Perryman bought and sold secondhand stuffed beanbag animals at bargainbeanies.com. Posner, C.J., held that the plaintiff did not have any action for trademark infringement or dilution against this derivative use of the name. He first stressed that the key function of trademarks is to reduce the search costs for individuals, who can now rely on the brand as "a concise and unequivocal identifier" instead of having to resort to individual product inspections. That said, he concluded that a second-hand "market is unlikely to operate efficiently if sellers who specialize in serving it cannot use 'Beanies' to identify their business. Perryman's principal merchandise is Beanie Babies, so that to forbid it to use 'Beanies' in its business name and advertising (Web or otherwise) is like forbidding a used car dealer who specializes in selling Chevrolets to mention the name in his advertising. . . . " Should the result here differ if Ty could show that the frequent use of the term "beanie" by unauthorized resellers converts the term from a protected trademark into a generic description?

6. *Patents.* Inventions have long received explicit statutory protection, which defines patentable subject matter "any new and useful process, machine, manufacture, or composition of matter, or any new and useful improvement thereof." Other requirements are originality, novelty, and nonobviousness. See generally 35 U.S.C. §§100-105 (2007). Procedurally, a patent application must be filed within one year of its public use or publication, and it must contain "a written description of the invention, and of the manner and process of making and using it, in such full, clear, concise, and exact terms as to enable any person skilled in the art to which it pertains . . . to make and use the same," concluding "with one or more claims particularly pointing out and distinctly claiming the subject matter which the applicant regards as his invention." 35 U.S.C. §112 (2007). Why are the procedural elements for the perfection of a patent so critical to the operation of the system?

On the economic function of the patent system, see Kitch, The Nature and Function of the Patent System, 20 J.L. & Econ. 265 (1977), which claims that the system has two functions: prospect and reward. The reward function acts as a spur to invention by conferring an exclusive monopoly. The prospect function (on analogy to the rule in mining law that allows the party who discovers a vein of ore to have the first crack at its exploitation) helps insure that certain "prospects"—here new inventions—will be efficiently and sensibly developed by giving exclusive rights in the period between the time an invention is first patented and the time it is first commercially exploited. This function is of special importance with drugs that cannot be marketed until they receive regulatory approval. The prospect theory has been criticized for downplaying the risk that the holder of a broad patent will seek to exploit it not through development, but by blocking the use of the invention by other parties. A broad patent therefore has the undesirable effect of forcing people to "invent around" patented devices. What is the relationship between a law of patents and a law of trade secrets? Why are both needed? For criticism of the prospect theory, see Lemley, Ex Ante Versus Ex Post Justifications For Intellectual Property, 71 U. Chi. Law. Rev. 129 (2004).

7. *Federal preemption of state unfair competition laws: unpatentable designs.* Both *INS* and *Mosler Safe* were decided as a matter of general federal common law under the then-applicable doctrine of Swift v. Tyson, 41 U.S. 1 (1842). The further *federal* common law development of the doctrine has been blocked by Erie R.R. v. Tompkins, 304 U.S. 64 (1938), which held that federal judges could not fashion a "general" federal common law under their general diversity jurisdiction. *Erie* has not, however, eliminated the traditional tension over whether courts or legislatures should decide what protection is appropriate in unfair competition cases. To the contrary, as *NBA* notes, state law unfair competition claims only survive when federal copyright, patent, and trademark statutes do not preempt their use. Here the fundamental text is Art. I, §8, cl. 8 of the United States Constitution, which gives Congress the power "[t]o promote the Progress of Science and useful Arts, by securing for limited times to Authors and Inventors the exclusive Right to their respec-tive Writings and Discoveries."

One early foray into the preemption question was Sears, Roebuck & Co. v. Stiffel Co., 376 U.S. 225, 231-232 (1964). Sears, Roebuck marketed pole lamps that were substantially identical to those sold by Stiffel Corporation. Stiffel's design patent claim for injunctive relief was rejected by the trial judge "for want of invention." The trial judge, however, accepted Stiffel's unfair competition claim when Sears sold lamps identical to Stiffel's even though there was no "palming off" or confusion as to source. The Supreme Court reversed, noting that patents, as a form of monopoly, only issue when the stringent conditions set out in the federal statute are satisfied. "To allow a State by use of its law of unfair competition to prevent the copying of an article which represents too slight an advance to be patented would be to permit the State to block off from the public something which federal law has said belongs to the public. The result would be that while federal law grants only 14 or 17 years' protection [now 20, ed.] to genuine inventions, States could allow perpetual protection to articles too lacking in novelty to merit any patent at all under federal constitutional standards."

Sears was applied in Bonito Boats, Inc. v. Thunder Craft Boats, Inc., 489 U.S. 141, 159-160 (1989), to strike down a state statute, Fla. Stat. §559.94 (1987), outlawing the use of the "plug molding" process. This process allowed one competitor to use the hull of a rival producer as the "plug" to create a mold which it then used to make identical hulls for its own use. No passing off or confusion was involved, but the plug mold technique allowed a later competitor to produce a hull at lower cost than the initial entrant. In Interpart Corp. v. Italia, 777 F.2d 678, 685 (Fed. Cir. 1985), the federal circuit held that the plug mold statute was not preempted because it only restricted the use of a single method to reproduce a hull shape, without precluding "copying the product by hand, by using sophisticated machinery, or by any method other than the direct molding process." The Supreme Court disagreed and limited protection for the hull design to that available under the federal patent statutes.

> The Florida scheme offers [its] protection for an unlimited number of years to all boat hulls and their component parts, without regard to their ornamental or technological merit. Protection is available for subject matter for which patent protection has been denied or has expired, as well as for designs which have been freely revealed to the consuming public by their creators.
> ... We think it clear that such protection conflicts with the federal policy "that all ideas in general circulation be dedicated to the common good unless they are protected by a valid patent."

8. Trade secrets. Current law also gives extensive protection to trade secrets, defined in Restatement of Torts §757, comment *b* (1939) as:

> any formula, pattern, device or compilation of information which is used in one's business, and which gives him an opportunity to obtain an advantage over competitors who do not know or use it. It may be a formula for a chemical compound, a process of manufacturing, treating or preserving materials, a pattern for a machine or other device, or a list of customers.

The Restatement (Third) Unfair Competition, §39 (1995), now provides:

> A trade secret is any information that can be used in the operation of a business or other enterprise and that is sufficiently valuable and secret to afford an actual or potential economic advantage over others.

Trade secrets often protect certain types of unpatentable materials (e.g., industrial "know-how"). Sometimes firms treat as trade secrets materials of doubtful patentability, or even matters that are clearly patentable, if they believe, as is often the case with "process" patents, that the disclosure of information through patenting will allow others to make undetectable but unauthorized use of their process.

After *Sears,* it was an open question whether patent law preempted state trade secret law. The Court resolved that doubt in favor of extended trade secret protection in Kewanee Oil Co. v. Bicron Corp., 416 U.S. 470, 483, 484 (1974), both for nonpatentable and patentable trade secrets. On the former, Burger, C.J., wrote: "Abolition of trade secret protection would, therefore, not result in increased disclosure to the public of discoveries in the area of nonpatentable subject matter. Also, it is hard to see how the public would be benefited by disclosure of customer lists or advertising campaigns; in fact, keeping such items secret encourages businesses to initiate new and individualized plans of operation, and constructive competition results." The Court approved of trade secret protection for arguably patentable material. "Certainly the patent policy of encouraging invention is not disturbed by the existence of another form of incentive to invention. In this respect the two systems are not and never would be in conflict. Similarly, the policy that matter once in the public domain must remain in the public domain is not incompatible with the existence of trade secret protection. By definition a trade secret has not been placed in the public domain." Finally, the Court extended trade secret protection to cases of clear patentability, because its denial might encourage private parties to adopt complex and costly security devices that could hamper innovation or, in the alternative, be driven to apply for a patent that they otherwise would not seek.

On the general question of preemption, see Goldstein, *Kewanee Oil Co. v. Bicron Corp.*: Notes on a Closing Circle, 1974 Sup. Ct. Rev. 81 (1974).

9. Copyrights. For the current legal position on preemption under the copyright laws, see The Copyright Act of 1976, 17 U.S.C. §301 (2007), governing works created as of January 1, 1978. It first preempts state law with respect to "works of authorship that are fixed in a tangible medium of expression" only to later provide that "[n]othing in this title annuls or limits any rights or remedies under the common law or statutes of any State with respect to (1) subject matter that does not come within the subject matter of copyright . . . including works of authorship not fixed in any tangible medium of expression, or . . . (3) activities violating legal or equitable rights that are not equivalent to any of the exclusive rights within the general scope of copyright." In ProCD, Inc. v Zeidenberg, 86 F.3d 1447, 1454 (7th Cir. 1996), the defendant Zeidenberg used a data base supplied by ProCD for commercial purposes in violation of his agreement with the plaintiff ProCD. Easterbrook, J., denied that Zeidenberg's otherwise valid contract action was preempted by the copyright act.

> Rights "equivalent to any of the exclusive rights within the general scope of copyright" are rights established by law — rights that restrict the options of persons who are strangers to the author. Copyright law forbids duplication, public performance, and so on, unless the person wishing to copy or perform the work gets permission; silence means a ban on copying. A copyright is a right against the world. Contracts, by contrast, generally affect only their parties; strangers may do as they please, so contracts do not create "exclusive rights."

For different views on this preemption argument, compare Lemley, Intellectual Property and Shrinkwrap Licenses, 68 S. Cal. L. Rev. 1239, 1255-1259 (1995), with Epstein, *ProCD v. Zeidenberg:* Do Doctrine and Function Mix, Contract Stories 94, 113-121 (D. Baird, ed., 2006). On the copyright law generally, see Landes and Posner, An Economic Analysis of Copyright Law, 18 J. Legal Stud. 325 (1989).

17

TORT IMMUNITIES

SECTION A.   INTRODUCTION

Our examination of basic tort doctrines has covered the full range of physical and intangible interests. To complete our picture of the tort system, we must examine when the distinctive status of the defendant provides an advantage — i.e., an immunity — in tort litigation not because of what he has done, but because of who he is. Sometimes the defendant receives absolute immunity from suit. Other times the defendant receives partial (or, as is often said, "qualified") immunity so that a higher threshold — usually some form of wilful or malicious conduct, but invariably higher than ordinary negligence — must be crossed before the plaintiff can successfully sue.

These immunity rules exhibit a remarkable diversity in both their origin and structure. Some immunities were created at common law, some by statute, and some under the Constitution. The attitude toward these immunities seems to be in constant flux. Many personal immunities, such as those that bar suits between spouses, between children and parents, or against charities, have been narrowed or abandoned. In contrast, governmental and official immunities seem to have expanded somewhat in recent years although their ultimate shape remains in flux. Section B addresses domestic or intrafamily immunity and covers suits between parent and child and between husband and wife. Section C turns to charitable immunity; Section D addresses municipal immunity; and Section E discusses sovereign immunity, with special reference to the liability of the United States under the Federal Tort Claims Act. Finally, Section F deals with official immunity, primarily under federal law.

SECTION B.   DOMESTIC OR INTRAFAMILY IMMUNITIES

1. *Parent and Child*

a. Suits Between Parent and Child

The rule that a minor child may not maintain a tort action against her father or mother apparently originated in the decision of the Mississippi Supreme Court in Hewlett v. George, 9 So. 885, 887 (Miss. 1891). The case arose when a mother committed her minor daughter to an asylum after she had engaged in loose and immoral practices in Chicago. The suit recognized that emancipated children could sue their parents as if they were strangers, but in the most general terms drew the line at suits between members of the nuclear family.

> [S]o long as the parent is under obligation to care for, guide and control, and the child is under reciprocal obligation to aid and comfort and obey, no such action as this can be maintained. The peace of society, and of the families composing society, and a sound public policy, designed to subserve the repose of families and the best interests of society, forbid to the minor child a right to appear in court in the assertion of a claim to civil redress for personal injuries suffered at the hands of the parent. The state, through its criminal laws, will give the minor child protection from parental violence and wrongdoing, and this is all the child can be heard to demand.

Most American courts followed *Hewlett* until Dunlap v. Dunlap, 150 A. 905, 912-913 (N.H. 1930), which breached the law insofar as it allowed a child to reach an insurance policy taken out by his father in his capacity as his son's employer on the ground that the insurance policy operated like "a trust fund of $10,000 to be applied solely to the liquidation of his liability to his son" for in both types of cases "the parties' interest and the family interest become for and not against a recovery." Subsequently Briere v. Briere, 224 A.2d 588, 590, 591 (N.H. 1966), abrogated the doctrine, after examining the "main reasons" the defendant urged in support of the parent-child immunity:

> (1) [T]he preservation of parental authority and family harmony; (2) depletion of the family exchequer; and (3) the danger of fraud and collusion. Analyzing these reasons in reverse order, we must agree that there is danger of fraud and collusion. However, this is true of suits between husband and wife, which we allow, between near relatives, and between host and guest, often intimate friends, all of which stand on the same footing as actions between strangers. Our court system, with its attorneys and juries, is experienced and reasonably well fitted to ferret out the chicanery which might exist in such

cases. In short, we are unwilling to espouse the doctrine that the mere opportunity for fraud and collusion should be an insuperable barrier to an honest and meritorious action by a minor.

The court next argued that the depletion of the family exchequer was a reason of "no substantial weight," as the parent always has the power to cover the risk with insurance. It then turned to the impact of suit on parental authority:

> Parental authority does not appear to be in any real jeopardy in the circumstances before us. In fact, it is difficult, if not impossible, to perceive how such authority and family peace can be jeopardized more in an ordinary tort action for negligence by an unemancipated minor against a parent than by an action in contract or to protect property rights or for an assault — all of which are permitted in this state. To allow such a distinction as now exists between tort and other forms of action is indeed not only to perpetuate confusion and irreconcilable decisions, but to entrench a policy from which changing times have drained most of such vitality as it may have once possessed.

There is general agreement today that any blanket form of parental immunity is indefensible. There is some question, however, as to what should be done once that blanket immunity is removed. In Goller v. White, 122 N.W.2d 193, 198 (Wis. 1963), a case for negligent supervision, the court wrote:

> After a careful review of the arguments for and against the parental-immunity rule in negligence cases, we are of the opinion that it ought to be abrogated except in these two situations; (1) Where the alleged negligent act involves an exercise of parental authority over the child; and (2) where the alleged negligent act involves an exercise of ordinary parental discretion with respect to the provision of food, clothing, housing, medical and dental services, and other care. Accordingly, the rule is abolished in personal-injury actions subject to these noted exceptions.

Goller in turn was explicitly rejected in Gibson v. Gibson, 479 P.2d 648, 653 (Cal. 1971), where the court reasoned:

> In short, although a parent has the prerogative and the duty to exercise authority over his minor child, this prerogative must be exercised within reasonable limits. The standard to be applied is the traditional one of reasonableness, but viewed in light of the parental role. Thus, we think the proper test of a parent's conduct is this: what would an ordinarily prudent *parent* have done in similar circumstances?
>
> We choose this approach over the *Goller*-type formula for several reasons. First, we think that the *Goller* view will inevitably result in the drawing of

arbitrary distinctions about when particular parental conduct falls within or without the immunity guidelines. Second, we find intolerable the notion that if a parent can succeed in bringing himself within the "safety" of parental immunity, he may act negligently with impunity.

As a third approach, the New York Court of Appeals simply abolished the defense of intrafamilial immunity without setting the appropriate scope of liability for parental negligence. See Gelbman v. Gelbman, 245 N.E.2d 192 (N.Y. 1969). That approach was also taken in the Restatement (Second) of Torts, which in §895G provides:

> (1) A parent or child is not immune from tort liability to the other solely by reason of that relationship.
> (2) Repudiation of a general tort immunity does not establish liability for an act or omission that, because of the parent-child relationship, is otherwise privileged or is not tortious.

The abrogation of tort immunity also has proved attractive in ordinary business contexts. Thus, in Dzenutis v. Dzenutis, 512 A.2d 130, 135 (Conn. 1986), the court concluded that "because of the general prevalence of liability insurance in the business activity setting, it is appropriate for us to recognize that in most instances family harmony will not be jeopardized by allowing suits between parents and children arising out of business activities conducted away from the home. . . ." Many states have provided for this result by statute. See, e.g., N.C. Gen. Stat. §1-539.21 (2001), which provides that the parent-child relationship does not bar any action "for wrongful death, personal injury or property damage arising out of operation of a motor vehicle owned or operated by the parent or child." Many insurance companies have less confidence than either courts or legislatures in their ability to prevent fraud on a case-by-case basis, and thus include policy language that creates a "family member exclusion," which has withstood the public policy challenge to it. See, e.g., Shelter General Insurance Co. v. Lincoln, 590 N.W.2d 726 (Iowa 1999). The scope of this immunity is, moreover, limited only to the parent. In Riordan v. Corp. of the Presiding Bishop of the Church of Jesus Christ of Latter-Day Saints, 242 F. Supp. 2d 635, 640 (D. Mo. 2003), the federal court forecast that a Missouri state court "would hold that the child of an employee can maintain a cause of action against his parent's employer under the doctrine of respondeat superior even though the parent is immune from being sued by his or her child."

In ordinary family settings, the approach in *Gibson* and the Restatement has gained some ground. See, e.g., Broadbent v. Broadbent, 907 P.2d 43 (Ariz. 1995), holding that it was a jury question whether a mother acted as a reasonable and prudent parent when she left her two-and-one-half-year-old son unattended by the side of a pool. Modern cases often deal with questions that arise in the context of the fractured or indeed dysfunctional family. In Henderson v. Woolley, 644 A.2d 1303 (Conn. 1994), the court refused to extend the doctrine of parental immunity to cover cases of sexual abuse. But later in Ascuitto v. Farricielli, 711 A.2d 708, 713 (Conn. 1998), it held that the doctrine of parental immunity applied to the noncustodial parent of a divorced couple as "consistent with the policy of encouraging divorced parents to assume responsibility for their children." The court in Chenault v. Huie, 989 S.W.2d 474 (Tex. App. 1999), was influenced by the parental immunity doctrine when it refused to create a duty of care in a pregnant woman, a crack addict, toward her unborn infant out of fear that "every woman would be obligated to maintain her body in the best possible reproductive condition so long as it was reasonably foreseeable she might bear a child at some point in the future." It therefore held that the only protection for the child was found in the criminal law. Back to *Hewlett*?

For a recent tally on parental immunity, see Herzfeld v. Herzfeld, 781 So.2d 1070 (Fla. 2001), which reports that 7 jurisdictions have never adopted or recognized the doctrine; 11 states have abrogated it completely, and two-thirds of the states have carved out exceptions to the basic rule.

For the classic statement in defense of the *Dunlap* rule, see McCurdy, Torts Between Persons in Domestic Relation, 43 Harv. L. Rev. 1030 (1930), an article published just days before *Dunlap* was handed down.

b. Third-Party Actions

Parental immunity has created conceptual confusion in connection with third-party actions, especially after the liberalized rules of comparative negligence and contribution already canvassed in *American Motorcycle, supra* at 409. The central dilemma is this: If the parent cannot be subject to direct suit by the child, should a third party, if sued by the child, be allowed to sue the parent for contribution? In Holodook v. Spencer, 324 N.E.2d 338, 343 (N.Y. 1974), the New York Court of Appeals denied contribution where the claim against the parent was only for negligent supervision. "If the instant negligent supervision claims were allowed, it would be the rare parent who could not conceivably be called to account in the courts for his conduct toward his child, either by the child directly or by virtue of the procedures allowed by *Dole*," *supra* at 415, for contribution. *Holodook* in turn yielded to Nolechek v. Gesuale, 385 N.E.2d 1268, 1273 (N.Y. 1978), in which a minor was killed when he rode his motorcycle into a steel cable that defendants had suspended close to a public road. The defendants sought contribution and indemnity on the ground that the parents had negligently entrusted their son with a dangerous instrumentality, i.e., the motorcycle, even though he was blind in one eye and had not obtained an operator's license for the cycle. The court justified its distinction between negligent supervision and negligent entrustment of a dangerous instrumentality on the ground that negligent supervision "in general, creates no direct, unreasonable hazard to third parties," while negligent entrustment surely does on the ground that a "dangerous instrument in the hands of an infant child may foreseeably cause various types of harm: personal injury, property damage, or, as in this case, exposure to tort liability." Is the distinction maintainable? Why not impute the negligence of the parent to the child under the comparative negligence regime? Note that under this regime, the conflict of interest between parent and child is eliminated because the parent can now bring the child's suit without fear of being exposed to a third party claim for contribution or indemnity.

2. *Husband and Wife*

The immunity between husband and wife had its origins at common law in the rule that the husband and wife were one person in law and hence could not be on opposite sides of any lawsuit for either personal injury or property damage. In some states the rule was so powerful that it barred actions for torts that occurred during the marriage even after the divorce or separation. See Phillips v. Barnet, 1 Q.B.D. 436 (1876).

The erosion of the strict common law position came in stages. The passage of the Married Women's Acts of the nineteenth century allowed suits between spouses for loss or damage to property: conversion, trespass to chattels, waste, and damage to real property. See Minier v. Minier, 4 Lans. 421 (N.Y. 1870). But states found fresh and independent reasons of policy for preserving the immunity for personal injury actions. Such suits were regarded as a threat to the harmony of the marriage relationship or were said to facilitate fraud against insurance companies. Some courts barred suits between husband and wife for wrongs that took place before the marriage, Greenberg v. Owens, 157 A.2d 689 (N.J. 1960), even when the action was commenced before it. See also Spector v. Weisman, 40 F.2d 792 (D.C. Cir. 1930). Likewise, the immunity has been extended to cases in which separation, divorce, or death has ended the marriage relationship before the onset of the suit. See, e.g., Gates v. Gates, 587 S.E.2d 32, 34 (Ga. 2003), which held that the plaintiff wife could not maintain an action after the couple divorced for a motorcycle accident that occurred before marriage: "[T]he law of interspousal tort immunity is still the same as it was under the common law, that is, that marriage extinguishes antenuptial rights of action between the husband and the wife, and after marriage the wife cannot maintain an action against her husband based on a tortious injury to her person, though committed prior to coverture. . . ." The court further held that any change in a well-established law required legislative change.

In recent years, the immunity has further eroded. The Restatement (Second) of Torts §895F (1979) takes the view that the immunity should be abolished, and, by 1997, 45 states and the District of Columbia had completely eliminated the immunity. The remaining five states (Georgia, Massachusetts, Nevada (no interspousal immunity), Rhode Island (abrogated—§15-4-17), and Vermont (no interspousal immunity)) have overturned the doctrine in some critical areas, including intentional torts or automobile accidents. These changes were usually accomplished by judicial decision, and occasionally by statute, see, e.g., Va. Code Ann. §8.01-220.1 (West 2007).

The subject still raises some troublesome cases of "outrageous" misconduct such as Lusby v. Lusby, 390 A.2 77 (Md. 1977), where a husband ran his wife off the road with a rifle, raped her, and allowed others to do the same. Subsequently in Bozman v. Bozman, 830 A.2d 450 (Md. 2003), the Maryland court abrogated the doctrine of sovereign immunity in its entirety, by allowing a husband to sue his wife for malicious prosecution when she had charged him with stalking, harassment, and multiple violations of a protective order. See generally Tobias, Interspousal Tort Immunity in America, 23 Ga. L. Rev. 359 (1989). In the context of automobile accidents, insurance companies have responded with the family exclusion clauses referred to above. These clauses are usually upheld, but they have occasionally been struck down. See, e.g., Meyer v. State Farm Mutual Auto Insurance Co., 689 P.2d 585 (Colo. 1984), a decision later overturned by statute, Colo. Rev. Stat. §10-4-418(2)(b) (1999). See also State Farm Mutual Auto Insurance Co. v. Nationwide Mutual Insurance Co., 516 A.2d 586 (Md. 1986), which held that the exclusion clause was invalid only for the compulsory minimum coverage, but could be included in any additional coverage offered. Why the distinction?

SECTION C. CHARITABLE IMMUNITY

The common law immunity for charitable institutions has also been in retreat. This immunity appears to have originated in the English case of The Feoffees of Heriot's Hospital v. Ross, 8 Eng. Rep. 1508 (H.L.E. 1846). There the court thought tort payments would constitute an improper diversion of trust funds from their original purpose, in defiance of the wishes of its grantor. *Heriot's Hospital* was overruled in England about 20 years later in Mersey Docks Trustees v. Gibbs, [1866] L.R. 1 H.L. 93, but this immunity was given new life in this country by Massachusetts in McDonald v. Massachusetts General Hospital, 120 Mass. 432, 436 (1876), and Maryland in Perry v. House of Refuge, 63 Md. 20 (1885). In *McDonald*, the plaintiff's action for medical malpractice was rebuffed. "The liability of the defendant corporation can extend no further than this: if there has been no neglect on the part of those who administer the trust and control its management, and if due care has been used by them in the selection of their inferior agents, even if injury has occurred by the negligence of such agents, it cannot be made responsible. The funds intrusted to it are not to be diminished by such casualties. . . . "

Generally speaking, this immunity was not applied to tort suits, such as actions for nuisance, brought by strangers against charitable institutions, but to those who by conduct "impliedly waived their rights to recovery." The orthodox view was stated in Powers v. Massachusetts Homoeopathic Hospital, 109 F. 294, 304 (1st Cir. 1901), as follows:

> If, in their dealings with their property appropriate to charity, they [members of the hospital board] create a nuisance by themselves or their servants, if they dig pitfalls in their grounds and the like, there are strong reasons for holding them liable to outsiders, like any other individual or corporation. The purity of their aims may not justify their torts; but, if a suffering man avails himself of their charity, he takes the risks of malpractice, if their charitable agents have been carefully selected.

Thereafter the erosion continued apace, culminating in President and Directors of Georgetown College v. Hughes, 130 F.2d 810 (D.C. Cir. 1942), the leading judicial decision limiting charitable immunity.

Modern cases and statutes tend to observe to the earlier distinctions. In Cowan v. Hospice Support Care, Inc., 603 S.E.2d 916, 919 (Va. 2004), the plaintiff's elderly mother had been placed in a non-medical hospice support facility where she broke her leg when an aide sought to lift her from the bed. The break was not immediately noticed and several days later she died from the complications of a belated surgery. Keenan, J., barred the action against the *organization* for ordinary negligence on familiar grounds: "As a practical matter, a charity's performance of its mission may be thwarted by litigation directed at the charity's failure to perform its activities in accordance with standards of ordinary care. For this reason, our Commonwealth's public policy in favor of promoting the activities of charitable organizations has been employed to shield charities from liability for their acts of simple negligence. . . . While this immunity shields a charity from claims made by its beneficiaries, the immunity does not extend to protect the charity from claims made by persons who have no beneficial relationship to the charity but are merely invitees or strangers."

Even those states that retain partial immunity do not extend it to businesses run by charitable institutions, to cases in which there is negligence in the selection of the charity's servants, or to nuisance cases. See New Jersey's Charitable Immunity Act, N.J.S.A. 2A:53A-7a, which protects any nonprofit association "organized exclusively for religious, charitable or educational purposes," from suits by any "beneficiary, to whatever degree." For a convenient summary of the current rules, see 5 Harper, James & Gray, Torts (3d ed.) §29.17.

SECTION D.   MUNICIPAL CORPORATIONS

1.   At Common Law

Municipal immunity apparently had its origin in the English decision of Russell v. The Men of Devon, 100 Eng. Rep. (K.B. 1788), which denied a tort action against the members of an unincorporated town out of fear that the liabilities could eventually devolve to individual inhabitants who were ill-equipped to meet them. In the United States this immunity evolved to cover incorporated towns, to which this rationale did not apply. This tort immunity for municipal corporations survived well into the twentieth century for reasons that tracked those put forth for charitable immunity. The immunity of municipal corporations helped prevent the diversion of public assets towards private gain; since municipalities received no profits from discharging their public duties, so too they should be insulated from economic loss. To this day, there is a deep split in the case law with some courts holding the purchase of liability insurance amounts to the extent of coverage as a waiver of municipal immunity, see Evans v. Housing Authority of Raleigh, 602 S.E.2d 668 (N.C 2004), and others not, see Powell v. Clay County Board of Supervisors, 924 So. 2d 523 (Miss. 2006). Should the question be decided under the standard law of third-party beneficiary contracts?

To these familiar arguments, three distinctive justifications have long been added. First, unlike the states of which they were mere subdivisions, municipal corporations were not full and complete legal persons and therefore could not be held vicariously responsible for the wrongdoings of their servants. Second, municipal bodies could not be treated as fully voluntary actors since they were under public duties to provide a wide range of local services. Third, removing tort immunity would embroil the municipalities in endless wrangling and litigation that would impede their effective discharge of essential governmental functions. For a critical appraisal of these arguments, see RST §895C, comment *c*, and 5 Harper, James & Gray, Torts (3d ed.) §29.3.

Early on the basic immunity rule was subject to one important qualification. Beginning with Bailey v. City of New York, 3 Hill 531 (N.Y. 1842), almost all American jurisdictions extended municipal immunity only to "governmental" activities. For its "proprietary" functions, municipalities were treated like private corporations engaged in private business.

The governmental-proprietary distinction has been subjected to sustained scholarly criticism. See, e.g., Wells and Hellerstein, the Governmental-Proprietary Distinction in Constitutional Law, 66 Va. L. Rev. 1073 (1980). In Fuller and Casner, Municipal Tort Liability in Operation, 54 Harv. L. Rev. 437, 442-443 (1941), the authors said:

> After an enormous amount of litigation on what is a proprietary function or a governmental function, these may now be classified within broad limits: activities of fire prevention, police, education, and general government are governmental; municipal railways, airports, gas, water, and light systems are proprietary; activities involving streets, sidewalks, playgrounds, bridges, viaducts, and sewers are governmental in some jurisdictions and proprietary in others. Criteria for determination of these classes of functions are neither certain nor carefully followed by the courts. . . . Borderline cases cause unending trouble, especially when the complex interrelationships of the municipal functions make it difficult to charge a tort to any particular activity. There is also difficulty in obtaining agreement about what facts shall be sufficient as a basis for proprietary liability. . . .
>
> Thus the governmental-proprietary rule often produces legalistic distinctions that have only remote relationship to the fundamental considerations of municipal tort responsibility. It does not seem good policy to permit the chance that a school building may or may not be producing a rental income at the time to determine whether a victim may recover for his fall into a dark and unguarded basement stairway or elevator shaft. Instances like those found in Chicago could be multiplied. There the city is liable for negligently driven vehicles of the library, water, and garbage disposal departments, but not for those concerned with health or police. Jurisdiction over streets by the city of Chicago opens the way to recovery for injuries from street defects, but the immunity rule applies when the Chicago Park District happens to have jurisdiction.

The problems noted by Fuller and Casner persist to this day in those jurisdictions that rely on the governmental-proprietary split. For example, in Gretkowski v. City of Burlington, 50 F. Supp. 2d 292, 296 (D. Ver. 1998), the plaintiff claimed that she was injured while walking on a bicycle path that had been negligently maintained by the City of Burlington, which pleaded the common law doctrine of municipal immunity in its defense. The court noted that earlier Vermont cases had held that maintenance of streets and roads was a governmental function, but the maintenance of sewers and a ski rope tow was not. It concluded the battle of analogies by holding that "[t]he operation of the Bikepath most closely resembles the operation of a park, which the Vermont courts have stated is a governmental function."

More recently in Considine v. City of Waterbury, 905 A.2d 70, 82 (Conn. 2006), the plaintiff fell into a glass window of a restaurant that leased space from a municipal golf course owned and operated by the city. In allowing the action to go forward, the Connecticut Supreme Court held that it fell under Conn. Gen. Stat. §52-557n(a)(B) (2007), which permits suits for negligence "in the performance of functions from which the political subdivision derives a special corporate profit or pecuniary benefit." Vertefeuille, J., affirmed the decision below after letting out howls of protest that the distinction was "illusory, elusive, arbitrary, unworkable, and a quagmire." That distinction, of course, is only one of many found in the Connecticut statute. Yet so long as some preservation of municipal immunity is required, what language better draws the line?

2. By Statute

Illinois offers notable effort to codify the rules for municipal liability. Its 1965 statute creates an elaborate framework that provides local governments extensive immunity from tort liability. Some significant sections of the total enactment are reprinted below.

745 Illinois Compiled Statutes Annotated
(West 1993 & Supp. 2006)

10/2-102.   PUNITIVE OR EXEMPLARY DAMAGES

Notwithstanding any other provision of law, a local public entity is not liable to pay punitive or exemplary damages in any action brought directly or indirectly against it by the injured party or a third party. In addition, no public official is liable to pay punitive or exemplary damages in any action arising out of an act or omission made by the public official while serving in an official executive, legislative, quasi-legislative or quasi-judicial capacity, brought directly or indirectly against him by the injured party or a third party.

10/2-103.   ADOPTION OR FAILURE TO ADOPT ENACTMENT — FAILURE TO
              ENFORCE LAW

A local public entity is not liable for an injury caused by adopting or failing to adopt an enactment or by failing to enforce any law.

10/2-104.   ISSUANCE, DENIAL, SUSPENSION OR REVOCATION OF
              PERMIT, ETC.

A local public entity is not liable for an injury caused by the issuance, denial, suspension or revocation of, or by the failure or refusal to issue, deny, suspend or revoke, any permit, license, certificate, approval, order or similar authorization where the entity or its employee is authorized by enactment to determine whether or not such authorization should be issued, denied, suspended or revoked.

10/2-105. INSPECTION OF PROPERTY — FAILURE TO MAKE OR NEGLIGENT INSPECTION

A local public entity is not liable for injury caused by its failure to make an inspection, or by reason of making an inadequate or negligent inspection, of any property, other than its own, to determine whether the property complies with or violates any enactment or contains or constitutes a hazard to health or safety.

10/2-106. ORAL PROMISE OR MISREPRESENTATION

A local public entity is not liable for an injury caused by an oral promise or misrepresentation of its employee, whether or not such promise or misrepresentation is negligent or intentional.

10/2-107. LIBEL — SLANDER — PROVISION OF INFORMATION

A local public entity is not liable for injury caused by any action of its employees that is libelous or slanderous or for the provision of information either orally, in writing, by computer or any other electronic transmission, or in a book or other form of library material.

10/2-108. PUBLIC WELFARE GOODS OR MONEY — GRANTING OR FAILURE TO GRANT

A local public entity is not liable for any injury caused by the granting, or failure to grant, public welfare goods or monies.

10/2-109. ACTS OR OMISSIONS

A local public entity is not liable for an injury resulting from an act or omission of its employee where the employee is not liable.

10/2-111. EXISTING DEFENSES

Nothing contained herein shall operate to deprive any public entity of any defense heretofore existing and not described herein.

10/2-201.   DETERMINATION OF POLICY OR EXERCISE OF DISCRETION

Except as otherwise provided by Statute, a public employee serving in a position involving the determination of policy or the exercise of discretion is not liable for an injury resulting from his act or omission in determining policy when acting in the exercise of such discretion even though abused.

10/2-202.   EXECUTION OR ENFORCEMENT OF LAW

A public employee is not liable for his act or omission in the execution or enforcement of any law unless such act or omission constitutes willful and wanton conduct.

In addition to the above immunities for public employees the statute also confers parallel immunities on public entities under 10/2-109. Whatever the liability, moreover, the Illinois statute authorizes the public entity to purchase liability insurance on its own behalf. 745 Ill. Comp. Stat. Ann. 10/9-103 (West 1993 & Supp. 2006).

The above list of statutory immunities, although long, has proved stable over time. It has, however, generated reams of litigation in borderline areas. For example, the statute does not exclude municipal liability in ordinary automobile actions. Other statutory provisions set out detailed rules of liability where the local government operates and maintains property. Here, as a general matter, the "public entity has the duty to exercise ordinary care to maintain its property in a reasonably safe condition" and then only when it has had adequate notice of the dangerous condition to allow it "to have taken measures to remedy or protect" against the dangerous condition. 745 Ill. Comp. Stat. 10/3-102(a). The statute also elaborates the responsibility of local governments to maintain public streets, signs (10/3-104) and recreational areas (10/3-106), and for supervising activities on its property (10/3-108) and waterways (10/3-110). Still other provisions explicitly preserve the assumption of risk defense for various "hazardous recreational activity," as regards both participants and spectators (10/3-109). The code contains entire articles devoted to police and correctional activities (Article IV), fire protection and rescue services (Article V), and medical, hospital, and public health activities (Article VI).

3. Under the Constitution

The law of local governmental immunity is further complicated by the vast body of constitutional tort law that addresses the scope of both municipal and official liability under 42 U.S.C. §1983, which provides in part as follows:

> Every person who, under color of any statute, ordinance, regulation, custom, or usage, of any State or Territory or the District of Columbia, subjects, or causes to be subjected, any citizen of the United States or other person within the jurisdiction thereof to the deprivation of any rights, privileges, or immunities secured by the Constitution and laws, shall be liable to the party injured in an action at law, suit in equity, or other proper proceeding for redress.

The provision raises many questions about the liability of municipal governments, state governments, public officials, and private parties.

Municipal governments. The critical case is Monell v. Department of Social Services of the City of New York, 436 U.S. 658, 694 (1978), which treated a municipal corporation as a "person" for the purposes of §1983. *Monell* then addressed the potential liability of local governments for constitutional torts committed by their employees, initially by rejecting the common law rules of vicarious liability. "Instead, it is when execution of a government's policy or custom, whether made by its lawmakers or by those whose edicts or acts may fairly be said to represent official policy, inflicts the injury that the government as an entity is responsible under §1983." In Canton v. Harris, 489 U.S. 378, 388 (1989), the Court explored the scope of the policy or custom rule under §1983 when the local police department was sued for its "failure to train" its officials in the proper mode of giving medical care to suspects in custody. The Court refused to apply either ordinary negligence theories or general doctrines of vicarious liability. Instead, it adhered to its original view that policy and custom controlled, and concluded "that the inadequacy of police training may serve as the basis for §1983 liability only where the failure to train amounts to deliberate indifference to the rights of persons with whom the police come into contact." For a comprehensive analysis rejecting *Monell*'s "policy and custom" position in favor of the common law approach, see Kramer and Sykes, Municipal Liability under §1983: A Legal and Economic Analysis, 1987 Sup. Ct. Rev. 249.

State governments. Whatever the correct reading of *Monell*, §1983 does not extend to hold the state itself liable for the conduct of its officials acting under color of state law. In Will v. Michigan Department of State Police, 491 U.S. 58, 64 (1989), the Supreme Court held by a five-to-four vote that states were not persons under that section. At a textual level, the Court followed the general rule that "in common usage, the term 'person' does not include the sovereign," and "statutes employing the [word] are ordinarily construed to exclude it." At a structural level, it held that any major redefinition in federal/state relations should be introduced in "unmistakably clear" language, not found in this statute. Should Congress amend §1983 to reverse *Will*?

Public officials. In Brosseau v. Haugen, 543 U.S. 194, 198 (2004), officer Brosseau shot Haugen after he disobeyed her command to remain put, resisted arrest, and attempted to flee, all offenses for which he was convicted. He sought to maintain a private §1983 action under the Fourth Amendment guarantee against unreasonable searches and seizures for her excessive use of force. The Supreme Court held that she was entitled to a qualified immunity from suit even if her use of force were excessive. "Qualified immunity shields an officer from suit when she makes a decision that, even if constitutionally deficient, reasonably misapprehends the law governing the circumstances she confronted."

Private parties. In Wyatt v. Cole, 504 U.S. 158, 164 (1992), the Court, speaking through O'Connor, J., held that private parties were not entitled to any immunity, absolute or qualified, under §1983. The Court held that none of the reasons for creating a qualified immunity for public officials under Harlow v. Fitzgerald, 457 U.S. 396 (1982), *infra* at 1346, carried over to ordinary private persons who availed themselves of the state replevin powers. "[E]xtending *Harlow* qualified immunity to private parties would have no bearing on whether public officials are able to act forcefully and decisively in their jobs or on whether qualified applicants enter public service." The Court left for another day the possibility that a private defendant could raise the weaker, subjective good faith defense that showed an absence of malice and/or the presence of probable cause for the seizure.

In Richardson v. McKnight, 521 U.S. 399, 404 (1997), a sharply divided court refused to cut back on *Wyatt*, when it denied qualified immunity to prison guards who were employees of private not-for-profit organizations. Breyer, J., found no "'firmly rooted' tradition of immunity applicable to privately employed prison guards," and refused to create the immunity on the ground that these guards discharged the same functions as prison guards who worked for the state. Scalia, J., dissented on the ground that the functional approach should dominate the immunity questions in the absence of a clear historical record. He also thought that the provision of qualified immunity against suit was needed to insure that private prison guards had the necessary "incentive for discipline" in their work.

Finally, in Brentwood Academy v. Tennessee Secondary School Athletic Association, 531 U.S. 288, 298, 307 (2001), the Court asked whether §1983 liability attached to private bodies acting under color of state law. The plaintiff school sued the defendant organization and its executive director under §1983 for violating their rights under the First and Fourteenth Amendment by wrongly charging the academy with recruiting violations. A sharply divided Supreme Court held the Association was a person engaged in state action under §1983 when 84 percent of its members were public high schools. Speaking for the majority, Justice Souter wrote: "The nominally private character of the Association is overborne by the pervasive entwinement of public institutions and public officials in its composition and workings, and there is no substantial reason to claim unfairness in applying constitutional standards to it." Justice Thomas's dissent stressed the separation of the defendant's operation from ordinary state control: "The State of Tennessee did not create the TSSAA. The State does not fund the TSSAA and does not pay its employees. In fact, only 4% of the TSSAA's revenue comes from the dues paid by member schools; the bulk of its operating budget is derived from gate receipts at tournaments it sponsors. The State does not permit the TSSAA to use state-owned facilities for a discounted fee, and it does not exempt the TSSAA from state taxation."

SECTION E. SOVEREIGN IMMUNITY

The ability of private citizens to sue the sovereign is the subject of a long and complex history. One of the entrenched principles of English common law — embodied in the ancient maxim "the king can do no wrong" — was that no private citizen could sue the sovereign in his own court without his consent. That principle worked itself into the fabric of American law through the early decision of Chief Justice Marshall in Cohens v. Virginia, 19 U.S. 264 (1821), and received its classic expression by Justice Holmes in Kawananakoa v. Polyblank, 205 U.S. 349 (1907): "A sovereign is exempt from suit, not because of any formal conception or obsolete theory, but on the logical and practical ground that there can be no legal right as against the authority that makes the law on which the right depends." Until 1946, the right to sue the United States was hedged about with various limitations and depended on the consent of the United States in individual cases. In 1946, however, Congress passed the Federal Tort Claims Act, 28 U.S.C. §§2671-2680 (2000). This statute authorized damages actions against the federal government to those suffering harm from what, except for the traditional immunity, would be the tortious conduct of its employees. But this waiver was neither unqualified nor universal submission for, as with municipal liability, Congress created a complex structure with many statutory exceptions, all of which have been subjected to a constant stream of litigation.

Federal Torts Claims Act
28 U.S.C. §§2671-2680 (2007)

§2674.   LIABILITY OF UNITED STATES

The United States shall be liable, respecting the provisions of this title relating to tort claims, in the same manner and to the same extent as a private individual under like circumstances, but shall not be liable for interest prior to judgment or for punitive damages. . . .

§2680.   EXCEPTIONS

The provisions of this chapter and section 1346(b) of this title shall not apply to —
(a) Any claim based upon an act or omission of an employee of the Government, exercising due care, in the execution of a statute or regulation, whether or not such statute or regulation be valid, or based upon the exercise or performance or the failure to exercise or perform a discretionary function or duty on the part of a federal agency or an employee of the Government, whether or not the discretion involved be abused.
(b) Any claim arising out of the loss, miscarriage, or negligent transmission of letters or postal matter. . . .
(h) Any claim arising out of assault, battery, false imprisonment, false arrest, malicious prosecution, abuse of process, libel, slander, misrepresentation, deceit, or interference with contract rights: *Provided,* That, with regard to acts or omissions of investigative or law enforcement officers of the United States Government, the provisions of this chapter and section 1346(b) of this title [28 U.S.C.] shall apply to any claim arising, on or after the date of the enactment of this proviso, out of assault, battery, false imprisonment, false arrest, abuse of process, or malicious prosecution. For the purpose of this subsection, "investigative or law enforcement officer" means any officer of the United States who is empowered by law to execute searches, to seize evidence, or to make arrests for violations of Federal law.
(i) Any claim for damages caused by the fiscal operations of the Treasury or by the regulation of the monetary system.
(j) Any claim arising out of the combatant activities of the military or naval forces, or the Coast Guard, during time of war.

The basic statutory scheme first requires that the plaintiff resort to state law to establish a basic prima facie case. If that case is made out, then the action shifts to whether the government can raise any of the defenses under the statute. The Supreme Court has addressed both issues.

United States v. Olsen
546 U.S. 43 (2005)

JUSTICE BREYER delivered the opinion of the Court.

The Federal Tort Claims Act (FTCA or Act) authorizes private tort actions against the United States "under circumstances where the United States, if a private person, would be liable to the claimant in accordance with the law of the place where the act or omission occurred." 28 U.S.C. §1346(b)(1). We here interpret these words to mean what they say, namely, that the United States waives sovereign immunity "under circumstances" where local law would make a "*private person*" liable in tort. (Emphasis added.) And we reverse a line of Ninth Circuit precedent permitting courts in certain circumstances to base a waiver simply upon a finding that local law would make a "state or municipal entit[y]" liable. See, e.g., Hines v. United States, 60 F.3d 1442, 1448 (1995). . . .

I

In this case, two injured mine workers (and a spouse) have sued the United States claiming that the negligence of federal mine inspectors helped bring about a serious accident at an Arizona mine. The Federal District Court dismissed the lawsuit in part upon the ground that their allegations were insufficient to show that Arizona law would impose liability upon a private person in similar circumstances. The Ninth Circuit, in a brief *per curiam* opinion, reversed this determination. It reasoned from two premises. First, where "unique governmental functions" are at issue, the Act waives sovereign immunity if "a state or municipal entity would be [subject to liability] under the law . . . where the activity occurred." Second, federal mine inspections being regulatory in nature are such "unique governmental functions," since "there is no private-sector analogue for mine inspections." The Circuit then held that Arizona law would make "state or municipal entities" liable in the circumstances alleged; hence the FTCA waives the United States' sovereign immunity. Olsen v. United States, 362 F.3d 1240 (9th Cir. 2004).

II

We disagree with both of the Ninth Circuit's legal premises.

A

The first premise is too broad, for it reads into the Act something that is not there. The Act says that it waives sovereign immunity "under circumstances where the United States, if a *private person*," not "the United States, if a state or municipal entity," would be liable. 28 U.S.C. §1346(b)(1) (emphasis added). Our cases have consistently adhered to this "private person" standard. In Indian Towing Co. v. United States, 350 U.S. 61, 64, (1955), this Court rejected the Government's contention that there was "no liability for negligent performance of 'uniquely governmental functions.'" It held that the Act requires a court to look to the state-law liability of private entities, not to that of public entities, when assessing the Government's liability under the FTCA "in the performance of activities which private persons do not perform." In Rayonier Inc. v. United States, 352 U.S. 315, (1957), the Court rejected a claim that the scope of FTCA liability for "uniquely governmental" functions depends on whether state law "imposes liability on municipal or other local governments for the negligence of their agents acting in" similar circumstances. And even though both these cases involved Government efforts to *escape* liability by pointing to the *absence* of municipal entity liability, we are unaware of any reason for treating differently a plaintiff's effort to *base* liability solely upon the fact that a State would impose liability upon a municipal (or other state governmental) entity. Indeed, we have found nothing in the Act's context, history, or objectives or in the opinions of this Court suggesting a waiver of sovereign immunity solely upon that basis.

B

The Ninth Circuit's second premise rests upon a reading of the Act that is too narrow. The Act makes the United States liable "in the same manner and to the same extent as a private individual under *like circumstances*." 28 U.S.C. §2674 (emphasis added). As this Court said in *Indian Towing*, the words "like circumstances" do not restrict a court's inquiry to the *same circumstances*, but require it to look further afield. . . . The Court there considered a claim that the Coast Guard, responsible for operating a lighthouse, had failed "to check" the light's "battery and sun relay system," had failed "to make a proper examination" of outside "connections," had "fail[ed] to check the light" on a regular basis, and had failed to "repair the light or give warning that the light was not operating." Indian Towing, 350 U.S., at 62. These allegations, the Court held, were analogous to allegations of negligence by a private person "who undertakes to warn the public of danger and thereby induces reliance." It is "hornbook tort law," the Court added, that such a person "must perform his 'good Samaritan' task in a careful manner."

The Government in effect concedes that similar "good Samaritan" analogies exist for the conduct at issue here. It says that "there are private persons in 'like circumstances'" to federal mine inspectors, namely "private persons who conduct safety inspections." And other Courts of Appeals have found ready private person analogies for Government tasks of this kind in FTCA cases. *E.g.*, Dorking Genetics v. United States, 76 F.3d 1261 (2nd Cir. 1996) (inspection of cattle). . . . These cases all properly apply the logic of *Indian Towing*. Private individuals, who do not operate lighthouses, nonetheless may create a relationship with third parties that is similar to the relationship between a lighthouse operator and a ship dependent on the lighthouse's beacon. The Ninth Circuit should have looked for a similar analogy in this case.

III

Despite the Government's concession that a private person analogy exists in this case, the parties disagree about precisely which Arizona tort law doctrine applies here. We remand the case so that the lower courts can decide this matter in the first instance. The judgment of the Ninth Circuit is vacated, and the case is remanded for proceedings consistent with this opinion.

It is so ordered.

NOTE

Finding the proper analogy. Is it appropriate to appeal to good Samaritan actions when a government agency is under a statutory duty to act? In Pate v. Oakwood Mobile Homes, 374 F.3d 1081, 1086 (11th Cir. 2004), the plaintiff was injured when he fell at his employer's mobile-home manufacturing facility that OSHA inspectors had cited as dangerous. The employer failed to rectify the condition within the statutory time, but OSHA had not followed up with any enforcement action. Barkett, J., rejected the plaintiff's claim against the United States, drawing a sharp distinction between those cases where the government acts as an inspector, and those with "acting in its capacity as a contracting-party and a landowner," where its own responsibility would be unambiguous. In its inspector role, however, she held that the applicable rule was from the RST §324A, which provides:

> One who undertakes, gratuitously or for consideration, to render services to another which he should recognize as necessary for the protection of a third person or his things, is subject to liability to the third person for physical harm resulting from his failure to exercise reasonable care to protect his undertaking if (a) his failure to exercise reasonable care increases the risk of such harm, or (b) he has undertaken to perform a duty owed by the other to the third person, or (c) the harm is suffered because of reliance of the other or the third person upon the undertaking.

She then held that Pate's claim under (c) failed for "insufficient evidence" in the absence of any showing that "Pate's employers relied on OSHA in their failure to abate the hazard," in the face of the abatement order. She further held that even if such reliance had been established, it would count for naught because the basic statute "places ultimate responsibility on the employer in ensuring compliance with safety regulations, not OSHA."

Berkovitz v. United States
486 U.S. 531 (1988)

JUSTICE MARSHALL delivered the opinion of the Court.

The question in this case is whether the discretionary function exception of the Federal Tort Claims Act (FTCA or Act) bars a suit based on the Government's licensing of an oral polio vaccine and on its subsequent approval of the release of a specific lot of that vaccine to the public.

I

On May 10, 1979, Kevan Berkovitz, then a 2-month-old infant, ingested a dose of Orimune, an oral polio vaccine manufactured by Lederle Laboratories. Within one month, he contracted a severe case of polio. The disease left Berkovitz almost completely paralyzed and unable to breathe without the assistance of a respirator. The Communicable Disease Center, an agency of the Federal Government, determined that Berkovitz had contracted polio from the vaccine.

Berkovitz, joined by his parents as guardians, subsequently filed suit against the United States in Federal District Court. [A suit against Lederle was settled prior to the filing of this case.] The complaint alleged that the United States was liable for his injuries under the FTCA because the Division of Biologic Standards (DBS), then a part of the National Institutes of Health, had acted wrongfully in licensing Lederle Laboratories to produce Orimune and because the Bureau of Biologics of the Food and Drug Administration (FDA) had acted wrongfully in approving release to the public of the particular lot of vaccine containing Berkovitz's dose. According to petitioners, these actions violated federal law and policy regarding the inspection and approval of polio vaccines.

[The District Court concluded] that neither the licensing of Orimune nor the release of a specific lot of that vaccine to the public was a "discretionary function" within the meaning of the FTCA. . . .

A divided panel of the Court of Appeals reversed. 822 F.2d 1322 (CA3 1987). . . .

II

[The Court then set out the statutory provisions and continued.]

This exception, as we stated in our most recent opinion on the subject, "marks the boundary between Congress' willingness to impose tort liability upon the United States and its desire to protect certain governmental activities from exposure to suit by private individuals." United States v. Varig Airlines, 467 U.S. 797, 808 [(1984)].

The determination of whether the discretionary function exception bars a suit against the Government is guided by several established principles. This Court stated in *Varig* that "it is the nature of the conduct, rather than the status of the actor, that governs whether the discretionary function exception applies in a given case." Id., at 813. In examining the nature of the challenged conduct, a court must first consider whether the action is a matter of choice for the acting employee. This inquiry is mandated by the language of the exception; conduct cannot be discretionary unless it involves an element of judgment or choice. See Dalehite v. United States, 346 U.S. 15, 34 (1953) (stating that the exception protects "the discretion of the executive or the administrator to act according to one's judgment of the best course"). Thus, the discretionary function exception will not apply when a federal statute, regulation, or policy specifically prescribes a course of action for an employee to follow. In this event, the employee has no rightful option but to adhere to the directive. And if the employee's conduct cannot appropriately be the product of judgment or choice, then there is no discretion in the conduct for the discretionary function exception to protect.

Moreover, assuming the challenged conduct involves an element of judgment, a court must determine whether that judgment is of the kind that the discretionary function exception was designed to shield. The basis for the discretionary function exception was Congress' desire to "prevent judicial 'second-guessing' of legislative and administrative decisions grounded in social, economic, and political policy through the medium of an action in tort." *Varig.* The exception, properly construed, therefore protects only governmental actions and decisions based on considerations of public policy. See *Dalehite*: ("Where there is room for policy judgment and decision there is discretion"). In sum, the discretionary function exception insulates the Government from liability if the action challenged in the case involves the permissible exercise of policy judgment.

This Court's decision in *Varig Airlines* illustrates these propositions. The two cases resolved in that decision were tort suits by the victims of airplane accidents who alleged that the Federal Aviation Administration (FAA) had acted negligently in certifying certain airplanes for operation. The Court characterized the suits as challenging the FAA's decision to certify the airplanes without first inspecting them and held that this decision was a discretionary act for which the Government was immune from liability. In reaching this result, the Court carefully reviewed the statutory and regulatory scheme governing the inspection and certification of airplanes. Congress had given the Secretary of Transportation broad authority to establish and implement a program for enforcing compliance with airplane safety standards. In the exercise of that authority, the FAA, as the Secretary's designee, had devised a system of "spot-checking" airplanes for compliance. This Court first held that the establishment of that system was a discretionary function within the meaning of the FTCA because it represented a policy determination as to how best to "accommodat[e] the goal of air transportation safety and the reality of finite agency resources." The Court then stated that the discretionary function exception also protected "the acts of FAA employees in executing the 'spot-check' program" because under this program the employees "were specifically empowered to make policy judgments regarding the degree of confidence that might reasonably be placed in a given manufacturer, the need to maximize compliance with FAA regulations, and the efficient allocation of agency resources." Thus, the Court held the challenged acts protected from liability because they were within the range of choice accorded by federal policy and law and were the results of policy determinations.

In restating and clarifying the scope of the discretionary function exception, we intend specifically to reject the Government's argument, pressed both in this Court and the Court of Appeals, that the exception precludes liability for any and all acts arising out of the regulatory programs of federal agencies. That argument is rebutted first by the language of the exception, which protects "discretionary" functions, rather than "regulatory" functions. The significance of Congress' choice of language is supported by the legislative history. . . . The discretionary function exception applies only to conduct that involves the permissible exercise of policy judgment. The question in this case is whether the governmental activities challenged by petitioners are of this discretionary nature.

III

Petitioners' suit raises two broad claims. First, petitioners assert that the DBS violated a federal statute and accompanying regulations in issuing a license to Lederle Laboratories to produce Orimune. Second, petitioners argue that the Bureau of Biologics of the FDA violated federal regulations and policy in approving the release of the particular lot of Orimune that contained Kevan Berkovitz's dose. We examine each of these broad claims by reviewing the applicable regulatory scheme and petitioners' specific allegations of agency wrongdoing. . . .

A

Under federal law, a manufacturer must receive a product license prior to marketing a brand of live oral polio vaccine....

[The Court then sets out in great detail the regulations governing the issue of licenses. The manufacturer must first select a proper seed strain of virus and develop separate monopools, which are then combined into consumer-level products. These monopools are extensively tested, and the manufacturer must submit both a sample of the finished product and the data from the tests performed. These are evaluated under the public health act "to insure continued safety, purity and potency" of the vaccine. The Court held that the discretionary function exception did not bar a cause of action that charged that "DBS issued a product license without first receiving data that the manufacturer must submit showing how the product, at the various stages of the manufacturing process, matched up against regulatory safety standards" because the DBS has "no discretion to issue a license without first receiving the required test data." The Court then held that the discretionary function exception did not protect the government if it licensed Orimune "either without determining whether the vaccine complied with regulatory standards or after determining that the vaccine failed to comply." It then held that if the DBS made an "incorrect determination" under applicable standards then liability "turns on whether the manner and method of determining compliance with the safety standards at issue involves agency judgment of the kind protected by the discretionary function exception...." [The Court remanded that question to the District Court conditional on petitioners deciding to pursue this claim.]

B

The regulatory scheme governing release of vaccine lots is distinct from that governing the issuance of licenses. The former set of regulations places an obligation on manufacturers to examine all vaccine lots prior to distribution to ensure that they comply with regulatory standards. These regulations, however, do not impose a corresponding duty on the Bureau of Biologics. Although the regulations empower the Bureau to examine any vaccine lot and prevent the distribution of a noncomplying lot, they do not require the Bureau to take such action in all cases. The regulations generally allow the Bureau to determine the appropriate manner in which to regulate the release of vaccine lots, rather than mandating certain kinds of agency action. The regulatory scheme governing the release of vaccine lots is substantially similar in this respect to the scheme discussed in United States v. Varig Airlines.

Given this regulatory context, the discretionary function exception bars any claims that challenge the Bureau's formulation of policy as to the appropriate way in which to regulate the release of vaccine lots. . . .

The discretionary function exception, however, does not apply if the acts complained of do not involve the permissible exercise of policy discretion. Thus, if the Bureau's policy leaves no room for an official to exercise policy judgment in performing a given act, or if the act simply does not involve the exercise of such judgment, the discretionary function exception does not bar a claim that the act was negligent or wrongful. . . .

Viewed in light of these principles, petitioners' claim regarding the release of the vaccine lot from which Kevan Berkovitz received his dose survives the Government's motion to dismiss [because he alleged that, in violation of this strict policy that precluded independent policy judgment, "employees of the Bureau knowingly approved the release of a lot that did not comply with safety standards."

Reversed and remanded.]

NOTES

1. *Government regulation and administration under the FTCA. Berkovitz* and *Varig* increase the play in the joints by rejecting the government's categorical stance that all regulatory activities fall within the discretionary function exception. Instead, both cases require the lower courts to examine on a case-by-case basis the details of complex regulatory schemes and the administrative practices they spawn. The Supreme Court adhered to this basic position in United States v. Gaubert, 499 U.S. 315, 324 (1991), by allowing the discretionary function exception to protect the Federal Home Loan Bank Board (FHLBB) from charges of negligent supervision of a bank that it ran on a day-to-day basis. Plaintiff was the key shareholder and officer of the bank who had been forced to step down from his management position and to post a personal $25,000,000 guarantee against future bank failures. His action against the FHLBB for the loss in value of his stock and for his liability on the guarantee failed, as the Court summarized the interaction between statutory authority and administrative discretion by noting that "if a regulation allows the employee discretion, the very existence of the regulation creates a strong presumption that a discretionary act authorized by the regulation involves consideration of the same policies which led to the promulgation of the regulations."

2. *The discretionary function exception in lower courts.* The lower courts have struggled with defining the discretionary function exception in a wide range of cases.

a. Design and warning. In Lindgren v. United States, 665 F.2d 978 (9th Cir. 1982), the plaintiff, who was seriously injured while waterskiing on the

Colorado River, alleged that the government was negligent, first in artificially lowering the level of the river and second in failing to warn the plaintiff of the changes in the water level. The court affirmed the trial judge's ruling that any decision to raise or lower water levels fell within the discretionary function exception of the FTCA, but refused to conclude that this exception necessarily protected the government's failure to warn of the change in water level. Although the court thought it was too onerous to ask the government to issue a warning each time it changed the water level, it instructed the trial judge on remand to decide whether it was "not as administratively burdensome" to post a "one-time" warning to users that the water level in the river could change without notice.

With *Lindgren,* contrast Gotha v. United States, 115 F.3d 176, 181 (3d Cir. 1997), in which plaintiff slipped and fell on a steep pathway leading to a Navy facility. The district court applied the discretionary function exception on the ground that "a complex set of policy imperatives" lay behind the Navy's decision. On appeal Weis, J., took a different view. "This case is not about a national security concern, but rather a mundane, administrative, garden-variety, housekeeping problem that is about as far removed from the policies applicable to the Navy's position as it is possible to get." If the government had won in *Gotha,* when would it lose?

b. Inspections and screenings. In C.R.S. v. United States, 11 F.3d 791, 799 (8th Cir. 1993), the father-plaintiff contracted AIDS from a transfusion while in the National Guard, and later transmitted the disease to his wife and one of his children. The court held that both the 1983 screening procedures adopted by the Military Blood Program Office and its 1985 decision not to notify the plaintiff that he was at risk from the transfusion were protected by the discretionary function exception. Even though lower level officials performed the tasks, the statutory scheme, fairly read, did not subject them to any specific mandatory duty. Accordingly, they exercised a discretionary function under the Act.

Similarly, in Irving v. United States, 162 F.3d 154, 169 (1st Cir. 1998), Selya, J., uneasily held, nearly 20 years after the accident occurred, that the discretionary function exception barred allegations of a negligent OSHA inspection.

> This case has disturbing aspects. The government's inspectors appear to have been negligent and the plaintiff suffered grievous harm. Arrayed in opposition, however, is the core policy that underlies the discretionary function exception: an abiding concern about exposing the government to far-flung liability for action (or inaction) in situations in which it has reserved to its own officials the decision about whether or not to act. Even if the decision may seem wrong in retrospect, or if its implementation is negligent, such decisionmaking by its nature typically requires a balancing of interests (e.g., how to deploy scarce government resources in the accomplishment of

worthwhile — but expensive — public needs.) Congress reasonably struck this balance by requiring that, ordinarily, liability will not inhere absent an authoritative decision that a specific act should become a government responsibility.

Should the FTCA be modified to include a specific exception for negligent inspections patterned on the 10/2-105 of the Illinois Act?

3. Misrepresentation. A second important exception to the basic waiver of sovereign immunity under the Federal Tort Claims Act applies to cases of "misrepresentation." One possible application of the section is to cases in which individual plaintiffs rely on government statements to their financial detriment. In United States v. Neustadt, 366 U.S. 696 (1961), the Supreme Court barred the plaintiff's cause of action alleging that he had relied on an appraisal made by a Federal Housing Administration official in purchasing his home for more than it was worth. *Neustadt* was sharply limited (if formally distinguished) in Block v. Neal, 460 U.S. 289, 297-298 (1983). There the misrepresentation exception did not protect a government employee of the Farmers Home Administration, who "undertook to supervise construction" of plaintiff's house, an undertaking that was held to be "distinct from any duty to use due care in communicating information to respondent." Is the separation of the two duties consistent with *Neustadt*'s conclusion that the negligent misrepresentation exception applied when the government had breached its "duty to use due care in obtaining and communicating information upon which [the plaintiff] may reasonably be expected to rely in the conduct of his economic affairs"? The Court in *Block* stressed that the government's interpretation "would encourage the Government to shield itself completely from tort liability by adding misrepresentations to whatever otherwise actionable torts it commits."

More recently, Trentadue v. United States, 397 F.3d 840, 855 (10th Cir. 2005), noted *supra* at 98, refused to apply the misrepresentation exception in a suit for extreme and outrageous conduct, brought by the family members of the decedent who complained of callous treatment when, without warning of its condition, they received the body of the decedent that had been marred with severe lacerations and bruises. The government had urged that the misrepresentation exception applied because infliction of emotional distress necessarily entails a false communication of the state of the body. Tymkovich, J., emphatically rejected the claim: "Plaintiffs' emotional distress arises from the government's callous treatment of the family in the aftermath of Trentadue's death, including its shipping of Trentadue's battered remains to unsuspecting family members. Two essential components of negligent misrepresentation — reliance and pecuniary loss — are not present on the record before us."

4. Assault and battery. In Sheridan v. United States, 487 U.S. 392, 403 (1988), an obviously intoxicated off-duty serviceman fired several rifle shots that injured the plaintiffs, who were riding in their automobiles. Both sides agreed that the assault and battery exception protected the government for the wrongs committed by the serviceman. However, the Court refused to apply this exception to the plaintiffs' further claim that three naval corpsmen were negligent when, having discovered the serviceman "lying face down in a drunken stupor" with a loaded weapon, they failed to take him into custody or to alert the appropriate officials that he was on the prowl. "If the Government has a duty to prevent a foreseeably dangerous individual from wandering about unattended, it would be odd to assume that Congress intended a breach of that duty to give rise to liability when the dangerous human instrument was merely negligent but not when he or she was malicious." The liability, therefore, was imposed wholly without regard to whether the drunken serviceman was within or beyond the scope of his employment. See *Bushey, supra* at 429.

5. *Injuries incident to military service.* One vitally important implied exception under the FTCA is for injuries "incident to military service." The exception was first announced in Feres v. United States, 340 U.S. 135 (1950), in which the decedent was killed by a fire in his barracks allegedly started by a defective heating unit. The plaintiff's negligence action was not caught by any of the explicit exceptions to the FTCA, including (j) (relating to combatant activities), but the Supreme Court barred suit under the FTCA for three distinct reasons. First, the statute could not supply the remedy because it would make the obligations of a soldier turn upon the place where he is stationed, when military law requires uniform rules for all personnel. Second, the threat of liability would undermine the discipline that commanding officers had over their troops. Finally, the presence of a comprehensive system of veteran's benefits precluded the development of tort liability. What is the strength of these rationales, when the government is sued for the failure to provide safe equipment for its barracks? Why is a uniform federal law more important in military matters than for other forms of regulation or administrative control? Why does exception (j) not provide the full measure of government immunity in this area?

Whatever its soundness, *Feres* was extended in Stencel Aero Engineering Corp. v. United States, 431 U.S. 666 (1977), in which the Court held that a manufacturer sued by a national guard officer on a products liability theory could not maintain an action for indemnity or contribution against the United States. *Feres* was further extended in United States v. Johnson, 481 U.S. 681, 691, 700 (1987), to bar a wrongful death action brought on behalf of a Coast Guard helicopter pilot killed during a rescue mission, allegedly due to the negligence of FAA air controllers. For the five-justice majority, Justice Powell applied *Feres* even though the government wrongs were committed by civilian and not military personnel, holding that the three reasons given in *Feres* made the veterans benefit system the exclusive source of remedy for all service-related injuries. The Court noted specifically that "military discipline involves not only obedience to orders, but more generally duty and loyalty to one's service and to one's country." Justice Scalia's biting dissent ridiculed the special solicitude shown the military in this context, noting that "the morale of Lieutenant Commander Johnson's comrades-in-arms will not likely be boosted by news that his widow and children will receive only a fraction of the amount they might have recovered had he been piloting a commercial helicopter at the time of his death. . . . *Feres* was wrongly decided and heartily deserves the 'widespread, almost universal criticism' it has received."

6. *Medical injuries under* Feres. Lower courts have struggled to apply *Feres* to medical injuries that originate in military service, but manifest themselves thereafter. Under the so-called genesis test, neither the serviceman nor his dependents can recover for injuries whose origins are in active military service, which includes claims for birth defects that allegedly arose out of negligent exposure to toxic pesticides, or from negligent vaccination, incident to the 1991 Persian Gulf War. "[B]ecause such non-servicemen's suits would require courts to engage in exactly the same intrusion into military decisions as would servicemen's suits, such as by requiring military personnel to testify against their commanding officers, they would pose almost as many problems—judicially and militarily—as would a serviceman's suit over the same issue" Minns v. United States, 155 F.3d 445, 449 (4th Cir. 1998). See generally Note: Making Intramilitary Tort Law More Civil: A Proposed Reform of the *Feres* Doctrine, 95 Yale L.J. 992 (1986).

SECTION F. OFFICIAL IMMUNITY

Clinton v. Jones
520 U.S. 681 (1997)

JUSTICE STEVENS delivered the opinion of the Court.

This case raises a constitutional and a prudential question concerning the Office of the President of the United States. Respondent, a private citizen, seeks to recover damages from the current occupant of that office based on actions allegedly taken before his term began. The President submits that in all but the most exceptional cases the Constitution requires federal courts to defer such litigation until his term ends and that, in any event, respect for the office warrants such a stay. Despite the force of the arguments supporting the President's submissions, we conclude that they must be rejected.

I

[The complaint pertained to events that took place on the afternoon of May 8, 1991, at an official conference in Little Rock. Plaintiff was a state employee who alleged Clinton made to her "abhorrent" sexual advances, which she "vehemently" rejected. She further claimed that after the incident, she was treated by her coworkers in a "hostile and rude manner," and that after Clinton became President he defamed her personally to a reporter, by implying that she had accepted his advances and vicariously by having various people speaking on his behalf brand her as a "liar." The plaintiff brought state law claims for defamation and intentional infliction of emotional distress, seeking both actual and punitive damages. Stevens, J. treated the charge as stating a state law cause of action, and noted that, with the possible exception of the charge, "the alleged misconduct of the petitioner was unrelated to any of his official duties as President of the United States, and, indeed, occurred before he was elected to that office. . . ."]

IV

Petitioner's principal submission — that "in all but the most exceptional cases," the Constitution affords the President temporary immunity from civil damages litigation arising out of events that occurred before he took office — cannot be sustained on the basis of precedent.

Only three sitting Presidents have been defendants in civil litigation involving their actions prior to taking office. Complaints against Theodore Roosevelt and Harry Truman had been dismissed before they took office; the dismissals were affirmed after their respective inaugurations. Two companion cases arising out of an automobile accident were filed against John F. Kennedy in 1960 during the Presidential campaign. After taking office, he unsuccessfully argued that his status as Commander in Chief gave him a right to a stay under the Soldiers' and Sailors' Civil Relief Act of 1940, 50 U.S.C. App. §§501-525. The motion for a stay was denied by the District Court, and the matter was settled out of court. Thus, none of those cases sheds any light on the constitutional issue before us.

The principal rationale for affording certain public servants immunity from suits for money damages arising out of their official acts is inapplicable to unofficial conduct. In cases involving prosecutors, legislators, and judges we have repeatedly explained that the immunity serves the public interest in enabling such officials to perform their designated functions effectively without fear that a particular decision may give rise to personal liability. . . .

That rationale provided the principal basis for our holding that a former President of the United States was "entitled to absolute immunity from damages liability predicated on his official acts." Nixon v. Fitzgerald, 457 U.S. at 749. Our central concern was to avoid rendering the President "unduly cautious in the discharge of his official duties."

This reasoning provides no support for an immunity for *unofficial* conduct. As we explained in *Fitzgerald*, "the sphere of protected action must be related closely to the immunity's justifying purposes." Because of the President's broad responsibilities, we recognized in that case an immunity from damages claims arising out of official acts extending to the "outer perimeter of his authority." But we have never suggested that the President, or any other official, has an immunity that extends beyond the scope of any action taken in an official capacity.

Moreover, when defining the scope of an immunity for acts clearly taken *within* an official capacity, we have applied a functional approach. "Frequently our decisions have held that an official's absolute immunity should extend only to acts in performance of particular functions of his office." Hence, for example, a judge's absolute immunity does not extend to actions performed in a purely administrative capacity. As our opinions have made clear, immunities are grounded in "the nature of the function performed, not the identity of the actor who performed it." Petitioner's effort to construct an immunity from suit for unofficial acts grounded purely in the identity of his office is unsupported by precedent.

V

[Stevens, J., then argues that the historical record affords no reason to extend the scope of Presidential immunity.]

VI

Petitioner's strongest argument supporting his immunity claim is based on the text and structure of the Constitution. He does not contend that the occupant of the Office of the President is "above the law," in the sense that his conduct is entirely immune from judicial scrutiny. The President argues merely for a postponement of the judicial proceedings that will determine whether he violated any law. His argument is grounded in the character of the office that was created by Article II of the Constitution, and relies on separation-of-powers principles that have structured our constitutional arrangement since the founding.

As a starting premise, petitioner contends that he occupies a unique office with powers and responsibilities so vast and important that the public interest demands that he devote his undivided time and attention to his public duties. He submits that—given the nature of the office—the doctrine of separation of powers places limits on the authority of the Federal Judiciary to interfere with the Executive Branch that would be transgressed by allowing this action to proceed.

We have no dispute with the initial premise of the argument. . . .

It does not follow, however, that separation-of-powers principles would be violated by allowing this action to proceed. The doctrine of separation of powers is concerned with the allocation of official power among the three co-equal branches of our Government. . . . Thus, for example, the Congress may not exercise the judicial power to revise final judgments, or the executive power to manage an airport. Similarly, the President may not exercise the legislative power to authorize the seizure of private property for public use. And, the judicial power to decide cases and controversies does not include the provision of purely advisory opinions to the Executive, or permit the federal courts to resolve nonjusticiable questions.

Of course the lines between the powers of the three branches are not always neatly defined. But in this case there is no suggestion that the Federal Judiciary is being asked to perform any function that might in some way be described as "executive." Respondent is merely asking the courts to exercise their core Article III jurisdiction to decide cases and controversies. . . .

Rather than arguing that the decision of the case will produce either an aggrandizement of judicial power or a narrowing of executive power, petitioner contends that—as a byproduct of an otherwise traditional exercise of judicial power—burdens will be placed on the President that will hamper the performance of his official duties. . . .

Petitioner's predictive judgment finds little support in either history or the relatively narrow compass of the issues raised in this particular case. As we have already noted, in the more than 200-year history of the Republic, only three sitting Presidents have been subjected to suits for their private actions. If the past is any indicator, it seems unlikely that a deluge of such litigation will ever engulf the Presidency. As for the case at hand, if properly managed by the District Court, it appears to us highly unlikely to occupy any substantial amount of petitioner's time.

Of greater significance, petitioner errs by presuming that interactions between the Judicial Branch and the Executive, even quite burdensome interactions, necessarily rise to the level of constitutionally forbidden impairment of the Executive's ability to perform its constitutionally mandated functions. . . . The fact that a federal court's exercise of its traditional Article III jurisdiction may significantly burden the time and attention of the Chief Executive is not sufficient to establish a violation of the Constitution. Two long-settled propositions, first announced by Chief Justice Marshall, support that conclusion.

[The first proposition is that "when the President takes official action, the Court has the authority to determine whether he has acted within the law."

The second proposition is that "the President is subject to judicial process in appropriate circumstances."]

In sum, "[i]t is settled law that the separation-of-powers doctrine does not bar every exercise of jurisdiction over the President of the United States." *Fitzgerald*, 457 U.S. at 753-754, [and it] does not require federal courts to stay all private actions against the President until he leaves office.

[Jurist:]
[The concurring opinion of Justice Breyer is omitted.]

VII

The Court of Appeals described the District Court's discretionary decision to stay the trial as the "functional equivalent" of a grant of temporary immunity. Concluding that petitioner was not constitutionally entitled to such an immunity, the court held that it was error to grant the stay. Although we ultimately conclude that the stay should not have been granted, we think the issue is more difficult than the opinion of the Court of Appeals suggests. Strictly speaking the stay was not the functional equivalent of the constitutional immunity that petitioner claimed, because the District Court ordered discovery to proceed. Moreover, a stay of either the trial or discovery might be justified by considerations that do not require the recognition of any constitutional immunity. The District Court has broad discretion to stay proceedings as an incident to its power to control its own docket. Although we have rejected the argument that the potential burdens on the President violate separation-of-powers principles, those burdens are appropriate matters for the District Court to evaluate in its management of the case. The high respect that is owed to the office of the Chief Executive, though not justifying a rule of categorical immunity, is a matter that should inform the conduct of the entire proceeding, including the timing and scope of discovery.

Nevertheless, we are persuaded that it was an abuse of discretion for the District Court to defer the trial until after the President leaves office. Such a lengthy and categorical stay takes no account whatever of the respondent's interest in bringing the case to trial. The complaint was filed within the statutory limitations period — albeit near the end of that period — and delaying trial would increase the danger of prejudice resulting from the loss of evidence, including the inability of witnesses to recall specific facts, or the possible death of a party.

The decision to postpone the trial was, furthermore, premature. The proponent of a stay bears the burden of establishing its need. In this case, at the stage at which the District Court made its ruling, there was no way to assess whether a stay of trial after the completion of discovery would be warranted. Other than the fact that a trial may consume some of the President's time and attention, there is nothing in the record to enable a judge to assess the potential harm that may ensue from scheduling the trial promptly after discovery is concluded. We think the District Court may have given undue weight to the concern that a trial might generate unrelated civil actions that could conceivably hamper the President in conducting the duties of his office. If and when that should occur, the court's discretion would permit it to manage those actions in such fashion (including deferral of trial) that interference with the President's duties would not occur. But no such impingement upon the President's conduct of his office was shown here.

[Affirmed.]

[The concurring opinion of Justice Breyer is omitted.]

NOTES

1. *Presidential immunity*. After *Clinton* was handed down, the president was ordered to testify at a deposition during which he was asked about his possible involvement with a former White House intern, Monica Lewinsky. The rest is history. For a contemporary account, see Baker, Linda Tripp Briefed Jones Team on Tapes: Meeting Occurred Before Clinton Deposition, Washington Post, Feb. 14, 1998, at A1.

Doctrinally, *Clinton* clearly distinguished the Court's earlier decision in Nixon v. Fitzgerald, 457 U.S. 731 (1982), in which former President Richard Nixon claimed absolute immunity after he left office. Fitzgerald brought a suit in connection with his whistleblowing activities as a management analyst with the Department of the Air Force that embarrassed the Nixon administration. In sustaining the president's claim for immunity, largely on separation of powers grounds. Powell, J., observed:

> [The constitutional] grant of authority establishes the President as the chief constitutional officer of the Executive Branch, entrusted with supervisory and policy responsibilities of utmost discretion and sensitivity. These include the enforcement of federal law — it is the President who is charged constitutionally to "take Care that the Laws be faithfully executed"; the conduct of foreign affairs — a realm in which this Court has recognized that "[i]t would be intolerable that courts, with the relevant information, should review and perhaps nullify actions of the Executive taken on information properly held secret"; and management of the Executive Branch — a task for which "imperative reasons requir[e] an unrestricted power [in the President] to remove the most important of his subordinates in their most important duties."

Do any of these rationales point to extending the immunity to sitting presidents for acts done prior to taking office?

2. *Absolute versus qualified immunity for government officials*. The use of absolute immunity has generally been regarded as an unfortunate necessity that sacrifices justice in individual cases for some larger social good. Learned Hand, J., forcefully defended that uneasy result in Gregoire v.

Biddle, 177 F.2d 579, 581 (2d Cir. 1949), an action for false arrest brought against the United States attorney general by a Frenchman who had been detained as a German alien during World War II, even after the Enemy Alien Hearing Board had ruled he was French:

> It does indeed go without saying that an official, who is in fact guilty of using his powers to vent his spleen upon others, or for any other personal motive not connected with the public good, should not escape liability for the injuries he may so cause; and, if it were possible in practice to confine such complaints to the guilty, it would be monstrous to deny recovery. The justification for doing so is that it is impossible to know whether the claim is well founded until the case has been tried, and that to subject all officials, the innocent as well as the guilty, to the burden of trial and to the inevitable danger of its outcome, would dampen the ardor of all but the most resolute, or the most irresponsible, in the unflinching discharge of their duties.. . . . In this instance it has been thought in the end better to leave unredressed the wrongs done by dishonest officers than to subject those who try to do their duty to the constant dread of retaliation.

Absolute immunity has generally been conferred on state and local legislators, see Tenney v. Brandhove, 341 U.S. 367 (1951), which was construed to cover all activities, including introducing and voting on legislation targeting the elimination of the particular office held by the plaintiff. So long as the action is not strictly "ministerial," the motive is irrelevant. See Bogan v. Scott-Harris, 523 U.S. 44 (1998). That absolute privilege also extends to "judges, prosecutors, witnesses, and other persons acting 'under color of law' who perform official functions in the judicial process," including a police officer sued for damages for alleged perjured testimony that led to the plaintiff's false conviction. Briscoe v. LaHue, 460 U.S. 325 (1983).

Nonetheless, only a qualified immunity was extended to other public officials in Butz v. Economou, 438 U.S. 478 (1978), where the Court held that cabinet officials, when sued for allegedly instituting an investigation against plaintiff in retaliation for his criticism of the Department of Agriculture, were only entitled to a qualified immunity. Accordingly, the defendant had to demonstrate his subjective good faith in order to win on summary judgment. In Harlow v. Fitzgerald, 457 U.S. 800, 812-813, 816-817 (1982), the companion case to *Nixon*, involving suits against the president' senior aides, Powell, J., held that "[i]n order to establish entitlement to absolute immunity a Presidential aide first must show that the responsibilities of his office embraced a function so sensitive as to require a total shield from liability." Powell, J., then held that such immunity might be called forth in national security cases, but not for the ordinary advice-giving function involved in the case before him. He backed off the subjective good faith element in *Butz* to hold:

> In the context of *Butz*'s attempted balancing of competing values, it now is clear that substantial costs attend the litigation of the subjective good faith of government officials. Not only are there the general costs of subjecting officials to the risks of trial — distraction of officials from their governmental duties, inhibition of discretionary action, and deterrence of able people from public service. There are special costs to "subjective" inquiries of this kind. Immunity generally is available only to officials performing discretionary functions. In contrast with the thought processes accompanying "ministerial" tasks, the judgments surrounding discretionary action almost inevitably are influenced by the decisionmaker's experiences, values, and emotions. These variables explain in part why questions of subjective intent so rarely can be decided by summary judgment. Yet they also frame a background in which there often is no clear end to the relevant evidence. Judicial inquiry into subjective motivation therefore may entail broad-ranging discovery and the deposing of numerous persons, including an official's professional colleagues. Inquiries of this kind can be peculiarly disruptive of effective government.

In Mitchell v. Forsyth, 472 U.S. 511 (1985), an action for invasion of privacy by a warrantless wiretap of a radical political group, the Court held that the Attorney General, like cabinet officers, was only entitled to a qualified immunity even when engaged in national security affairs. The Court adhered to the standard announced in *Harlow* that the "Attorney General will be entitled to immunity so long as his actions do not violate 'clearly established statutory or constitutional rights of which a reasonable person would have known,'" and pointedly concluded that in some cases the Attorney General "should" be made to hesitate before invading individual constitutional rights.

3. Official immunity for common law torts. The attitude toward official immunity for common law torts has also switched over the years. In Barr v. Matteo, 360 U.S. 564 (1959), a defamation suit, the Court extended an absolute immunity to high government officials acting within the "outer perimeter" of their official duties. That decision was effectively undermined in *Butz* and *Harlow*. In Westfall v. Erwin, 484 U.S. 292, 293, 300 (1988), the Court further held that federal employees could claim absolute immunity from state law tort actions only for conduct that was both "within the scope of their official duties and . . . discretionary in nature." *Westfall* thus made it still harder for federal employees at all levels to obtain summary judgment. The Court in *Westfall* invited Congress to legislate on this question, noting that "Congress is in the best position to provide guidance for the complex and often highly empirical inquiry into whether absolute immunity is warranted in a particular context." Congress promptly responded with the Federal Employees Liability Reform Act of 1988, or the Westfall Act, 28 U.S.C. §2679(b)(1). The House Report to the Act accepted the Department of Justice's position that *Westfall* could materially undermine the ability of many federal agencies to adequately perform their programmatic responsibilities. H.R. Rep. No. 100-694, Federal Employees Liability Reform and Tort Compensation Act of 1988 (Pub. L. No. 100-694), Cong. Rec. 5945, 5947. The Report further noted that the Act was intended to restore the absolute immunity available under *Barr. Id.* at 5946, 5947. Accordingly, the Act makes an action for money damages against the United States the *exclusive* remedy for harms arising from the "negligent or wrongful act or omission" of a federal employee "acting within the scope of his office or employment." 28 U.S.C. §2679(b)(1). The Court has held that the Westfall Act bars common law actions against an employee even when the discretionary function exception under the FTCA insulates the United States from liability for the employee's conduct. See United States v. Smith, 499 U.S. 160 (1991). Should the Supreme Court reinstate absolute immunity for federal officials for constitutional torts?

4. *The theory of official immunity.* Government and official immunity could in principle cover everything from the mundane automobile accidents to the highest and most sensitive decisions of state. The range of the doctrine is revealed in the variety of tort claims against which it is interposed: defamation, invasion of privacy, and false arrest—not to mention the intentional torts of breaking and entering property, and assault and battery, committed during routine arrests and searches. What is the best substantive approach to these divisive issues?

The threshold challenge in all official immunity cases asks why any government official should escape the ordinary rigors of the tort law, especially under a government "not of men, but of laws." The usual answer appeals, if not to necessity, then at least to utility. Government could not function properly if its officials were routinely exposed to tort liability for discharging their public duties. To be sure, all private parties face the possibility of suit, but public officials, unlike private individuals, do not have the option of simply refusing to act; rather, they are bound to perform their duties. Police officers must arrest, prosecutors must prosecute, and judges must try cases. Regulators must issue regulations and legions of government officials must pass on thousands of applications for licenses, grants, assistance payments, and the like. Officials making hundreds of decisions a year would face an intolerable situation if even a tiny fraction resulted in suit. The ablest people could be deterred from taking public employment or from acting in a forceful fashion.

The same concerns can be translated into economic terms. The nub of the argument lies in the implicit asymmetry in the incentives imposed on public officials left wholly unprotected by any immunity doctrine. A public employee must shoulder the enormous costs of liability for an arguably incorrect decision, even if fully vindicated. Even full payment of legal fees does not remove the inescapable personal burdens of litigation. But that same employee will not share in the enormous gains to the public at large from sound decisions. Why, therefore, should any public official take all the risks for none of the gain? On the underlying problem of agency costs, see Jensen and Meckling, Theory of the Firm: Managerial Behavior, Agency Costs, and Ownership Structure, 3 J. Fin. Econ. 305 (1976).

One way to restore the possible balance would be to pay public officials enormous wages to compensate for the risk of potential tort liability. Yet who determines what salary is needed to offset potential liabilities, administrative costs, and personal wear and tear. In addition, the purchase of private tort insurance could easily encourage disgruntled persons to sue. At best, however, a perfect system of employee compensation could never eliminate the very heavy social costs from disrupting public services. Bulking up compensation to offset liability does not solve the basic problem. The other way to restore the needed symmetry between official rewards and official burdens is to release the public official from liability, in whole or in part. Once again the system is brought into balance since the official in question, who cannot capture the full gain, now escapes bearing the full loss, albeit at the cost of individual redress for government wrongs. At this point, however, the risk of underdeterrence necessarily requires some direct administrative control of government personnel.

On the general question of official immunity, see Symposium, Civil Liability of Government Officials, 42 Law & Contemp. Probs. 1 (1978); Cass, Damage Suits Against Public Officers, 129 U. Pa. L. Rev. 1110 (1981).

TABLE OF CASES

TABLE OF RESTATEMENT SECTIONS

RESTATEMENT (THIRD) OF TORTS — PRODUCTS LIABILITY

RESTATEMENT (THIRD) OF TORTS — UNFAIR COMPETITION

TABLE OF SECONDARY AUTHORITIES

INDEX